THE GREAT WAR ILLUSTRATED
1917

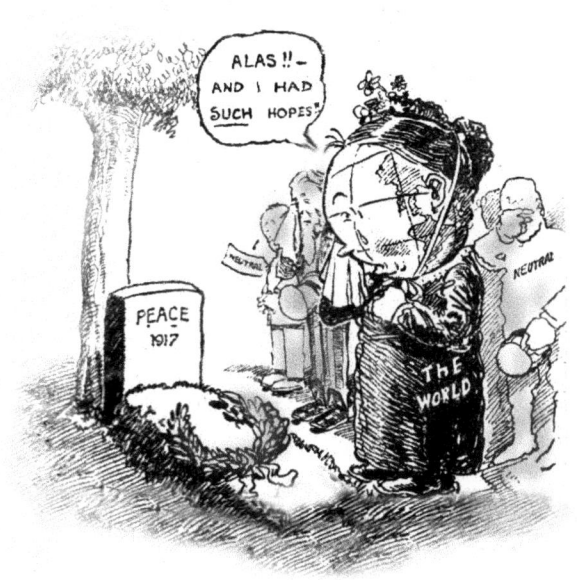

THE GREAT WAR ILLUSTRATED 1917

A selection of 1,000 images illustrating events at Arras; the Nivelle offensive; the battles of Messines Ridge, Passchendaele and Cambrai; the capture of Jerusalem; the air war and unrestricted submarine campaign.

William Langford & Jack Holroyd

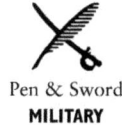

Pen & Sword
MILITARY

Dedicated to the One True Sovereign
*who was disregarded by the nations when, in 1914, men elected to fight
among themselves on behalf of their own sovereignties*

First published in Great Britain in 2017 and republished in this format in 2023 by
PEN & SWORD MILITARY
an imprint of
Pen & Sword Books Ltd
Yorkshire – Philadelphia

Copyright © William Langford & Jack Holroyd 2017, 2023

ISBN 978 1 39902 450 1

The right of William Langford & Jack Holroyd to be identified as Authors of this
Work has been asserted by them in accordance with the
Copyright, Designs and Patents Act 1988.

A CIP catalogue record for this book is available from the British Library

*All rights reserved. No part of this book may be reproduced or transmitted
in any form or by any means, electronic or mechanical including photocopying,
recording or by any information storage and retrieval system,
without permission from the Publisher in writing.*

Designed by Factionpress
Printed and bound in the UK by CPI Group (UK) Ltd, Croydon, CR0 4YY.

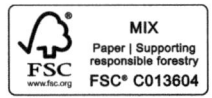

Pen & Sword Books Limited incorporates the imprints of After the Battle, Atlas,
Archaeology, Aviation, Discovery, Family History, Fiction, History, Maritime, Military,
Military Classics, Politics, Select, Transport, True Crime, Air World, Frontline Publishing,
Leo Cooper, Remember When, Seaforth Publishing, The Praetorian Press, Wharncliffe
Local History, Wharncliffe Transport, Wharncliffe True Crime and White Owl.

For a complete list of Pen & Sword titles please contact

PEN & SWORD BOOKS LIMITED
47 Church Street, Barnsley, South Yorkshire, S70 2AS, England
E-mail: enquiries@pen-and-sword.co.uk
Website: www.pen-and-sword.co.uk
or
PEN AND SWORD BOOKS
1950 Lawrence Road, Havertown, PA 19083, USA
E-mail: uspen-and-sword@casematepublishers.com
Website: www.penandswordbooks.com

Contents

	Foreword by Nigel Cave	6
	Introduction	8
Chapter One	**The German Retreat – *Der Betrieb 'Alberich'***	9
Chapter Two	**Arras – Vimy Ridge**	41
Chapter Three	**Bloody April – The Red Baron – *Air War, Fighters***	177
Chapter Four	**The Nivelle Failure – French Army Revolt**	253
Chapter Five	**Unrestricted Submarine Warfare**	317
Chapter Six	**America Joins the Fray – Russia Leaves**	359
Chapter Seven	**Capture of The Wytschaete–Messines Ridge**	417
Chapter Eight	**Third Battle of Ypres – Passchendaele**	441
Chapter Nine	**The Battle of Cambrai**	461
Chapter Ten	**Highlight of 1917 – the Capture of Jerusalem**	469
	The Great War Illustrated in Focus	475
	Index	507

Foreword

by Nigel Cave

The Great War Illustrated 1917

In 1916 the war had been changed from the one of annihilation, the destruction of the enemy's ability to resist by decisive, quick blows, to one of attrition, the grinding down of the enemy's ability to continue the fight. Both sides recognised that by the summer of 1916 this was the reality of the fighting on the Western Front.

This new strategic situation was first shown at Verdun in 1916, partly in its original concept by Falkenhayn and then by the seemingly unrelenting series of attacks at vast cost in human lives over the course of the year from the offensive's start in February. It was followed by the infantryman's nightmare of the Somme – a much shorter battle but far more expensive in losses of men.

By the end of that battle it had become clear that the most plentiful resource, manpower, was being used up at an alarming rate. The Germans took the first initiative by shortening their line through the withdrawal to the Hindenburg Line, freeing up a substantial number of divisions. New infantry tactics were widely adopted and the machinery of war – machine guns, mortars, guns, vehicles, communications – became increasingly plentiful and sophisticated.

The allies attempted to break the deadlock by a series of offensives – the ill-fated Nivelle Offensive, Arras, Messines, Third Ypres (Passchendaele) and Cambrai. In the last of these the increasing sophistication of the offensive was illustrated by the mass use of tanks, a complex, imaginative artillery fire plan and developments in air power. But there was no breakthrough; far from it, for the German army showed not only that it was capable of fighting a brilliant defensive battle but could effectively adopt new offensive tactics, as shown by the counter offensive at Cambrai. The armies in the field were very tired and morale was low amongst all the armies as winter ended the campaigning season.

The Great War was also an economic war. The British blockade had led to the 'turnip' winter in 1916/17 in Germany. After some hesitation, the Germans returned to a policy of unrestricted submarine warfare, which threatened Britain's very existence until new tactics (convoys) and equipment (for example depth charges and primitive aircraft carriers) relieved the pressure; indeed, it was the submarine threat that provided the background to Haig's thinking for an offensive in Flanders in the summer.

Two key events were to have a long term significance far greater than the war itself. In February there was a revolution in Russia; at first the country maintained its military efforts, but the October Revolution and the arrival of Lenin saw Russia seeking to get out of the war as soon as possible and an armistice was signed. Almost as momentous was the arrival of the United States on the scene in April. Although her military capability was limited (something which continued to some degree right to the end of the war), the potential was enormous; and it certainly provided the Germans with a clear idea that the war had to be ended by 1919, by which time the American armies would provide overwhelming force and be well trained in the conduct of modern, industrial warfare. The greater significance, perhaps, was the projection of American power far from her shores; apart from a hiatus in the twenties and thirties, this was to be the new world reality.

Elsewhere there was an allied disaster in Italy in November at Caporetto (and the clearest sign yet of the implementation of new tactics, producing a return to open warfare); the Ottoman Empire showed signs of crumbling around the edges (best illustrated by the fall of Jerusalem at the end of the year); even the front in Salonika began to stir from its long slumber. The Austro-Hungarian Empire was under new leadership, with the accession of Emperor and King Charles I in November; a deeply committed Catholic, he was keen to come to a just peace.

Although it might not have felt like it to the soldier in the trenches, the signs were all there to suggest that 1918 had the potential to be the most decisive year of this horrendous war.

Nigel Cave

The Taylor Picture Library

A rich source of illustrations available to authors and graphic designers today, depicting all aspects of the historic mayhem of the Great War, are to be found in the printed volumes that were published throughout the 1914-1918 period and after. Some of these appeared firstly in weekly instalments as magazines with the option of having them bound. Others began life as bound books and nearly always in sets. Famous writers of the day contributed articles and, where photographs of certain battles were unobtainable, gifted illustrators and graphic artists were commissioned and used their imaginations to depict certain events, such as the winning of a Victoria Cross, or some dreadful atrocity perpetrated by the 'cowardly hun'.

As with press release photographs of the day, likewise, some captions for pictures in books should be viewed with some caution, as propaganda hype drove the writers to maintain and fuel continuing support from among the English speaking peoples for, what had been sold from the outset of hostilities to be, a worldwide crusade against evil empires.

Beginning in the nineteen eighties the Director at Pen and Sword Books, Charles Hewitt, started acquiring sets of First World War books which included: twenty volumes of *The Times History of the War* and a complete set of *The Great War* by H. W. Wilson and J. A. Hammerton. These were added to the Peter Taylor collection of printed books. This has meant that hundreds of thousands of pictures are now available for re-use, thanks to the scanning and picture correcting technology developed in recent years.

This new four volume set (a fifth covering events in 1918 is planned) of *The Great War Illustrated* volumes 1914 to 1917, researched by Roni Wilkinson, constitutes a catalogue of images that have been revived electronically and brought up to reproduction standard.

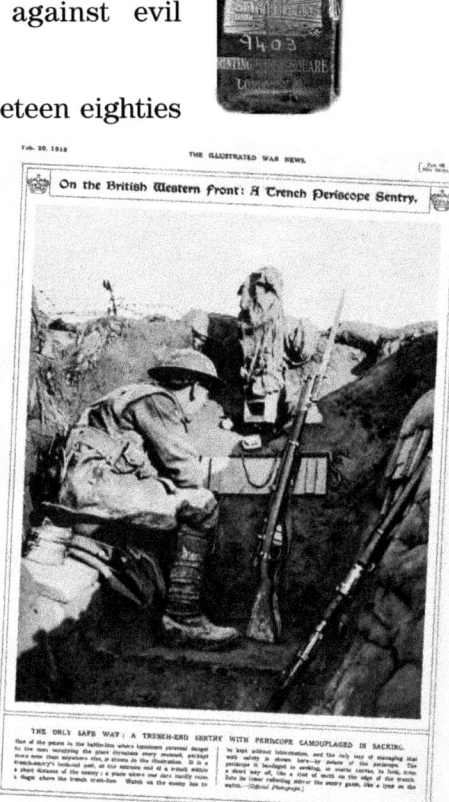

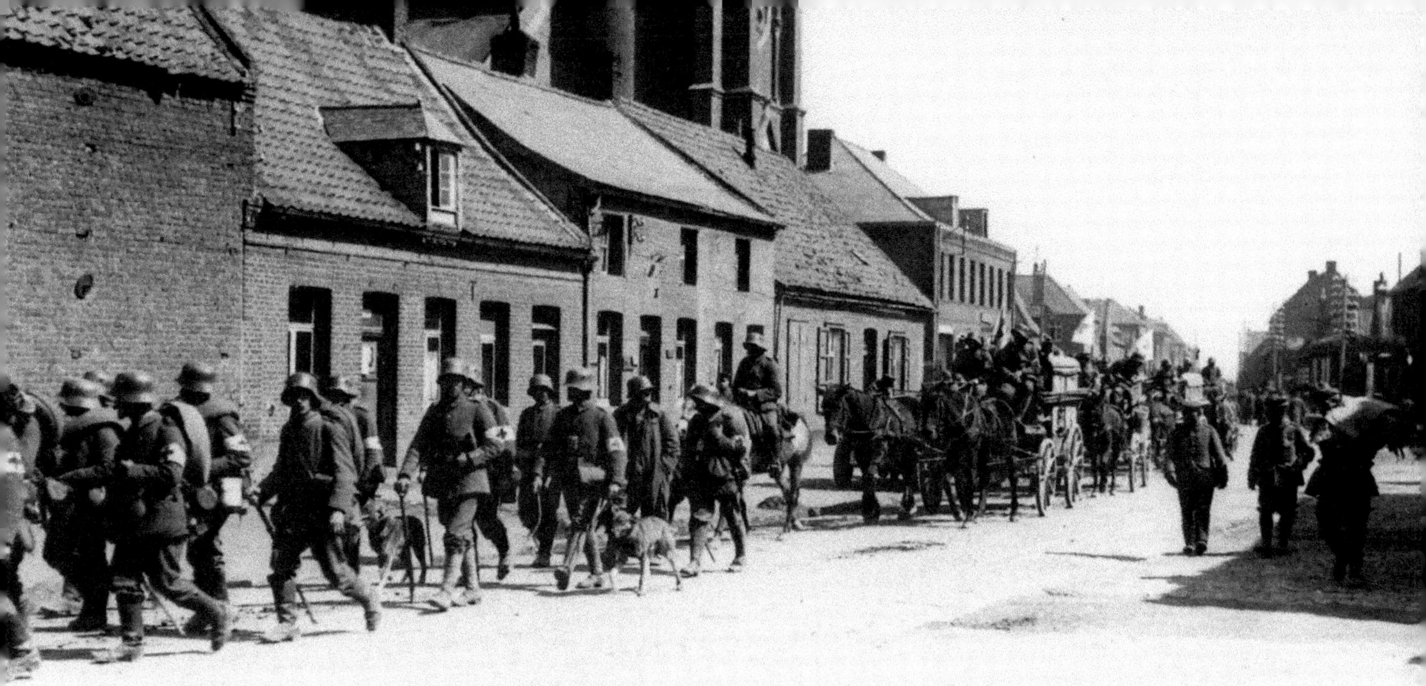

Chapter One: The German Retreat – *Der Betrieb 'Alberich'*

17GW002 German troops withdrawing through the streets of Péronne during the fall back to the prepared postions of the Hindenburg Line.

17GW001 British and French troops in reserve lines at Le Verguier, France, during the German Retreat to the Hindenburg Line, April 1917.

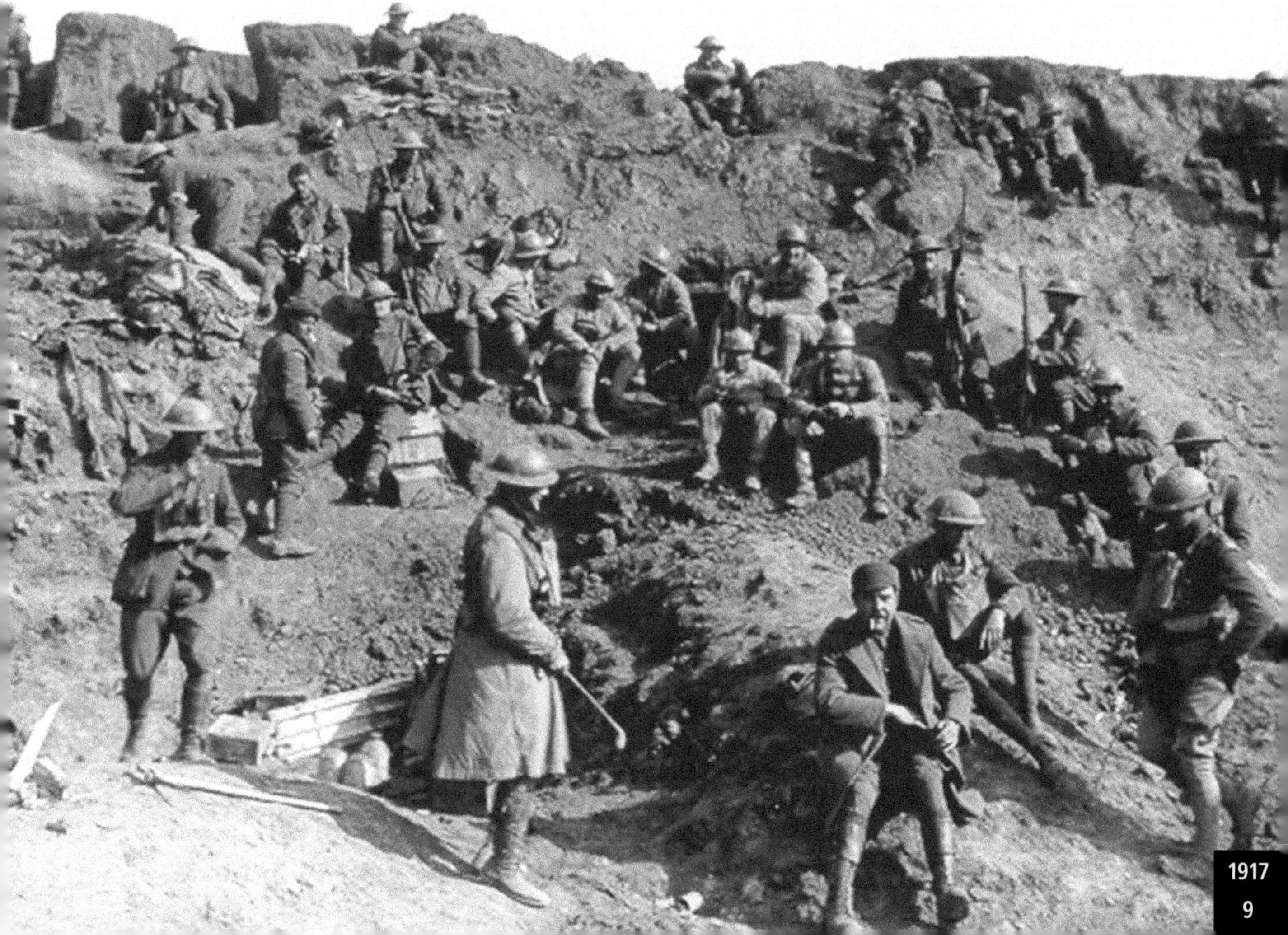

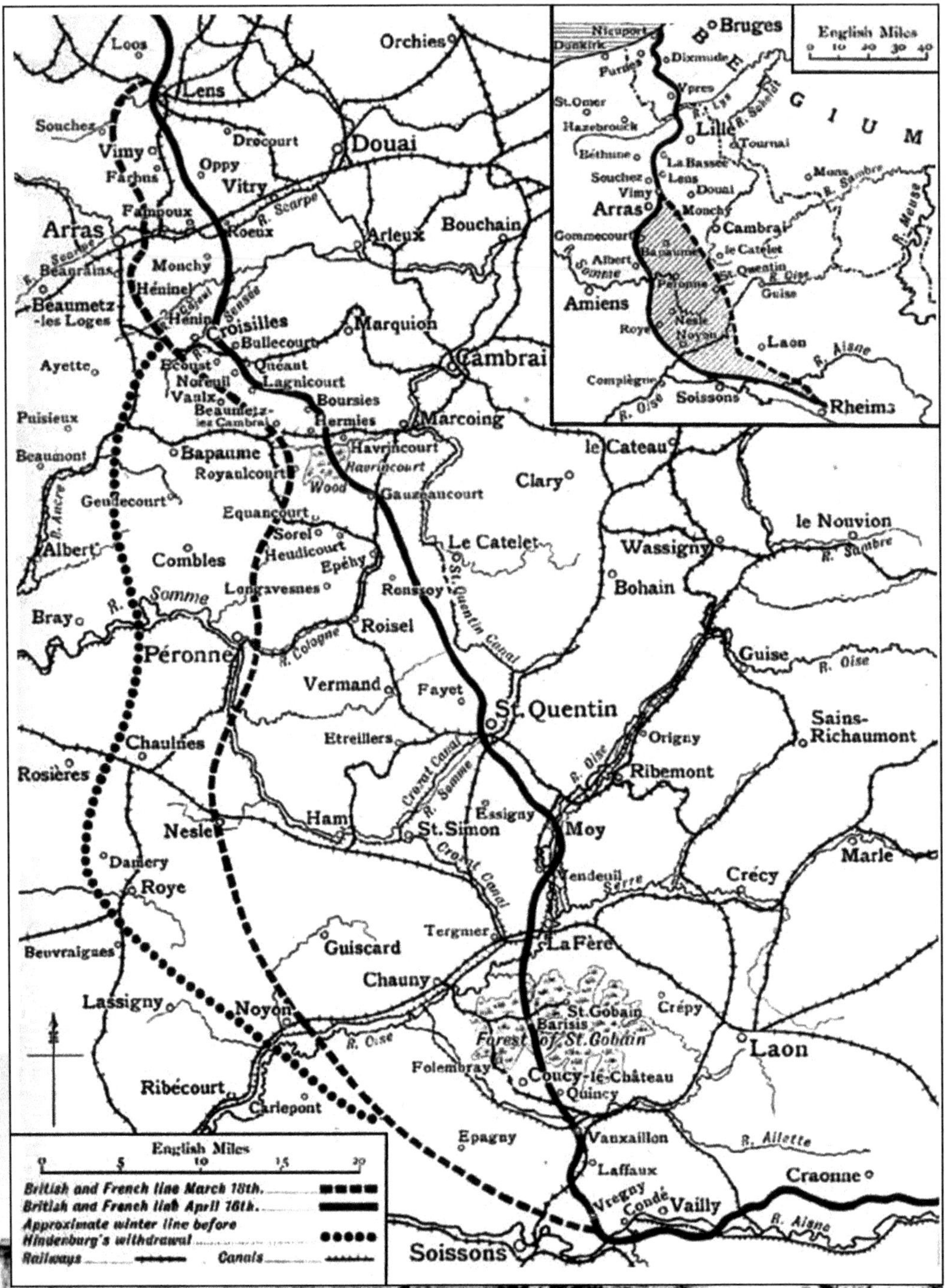

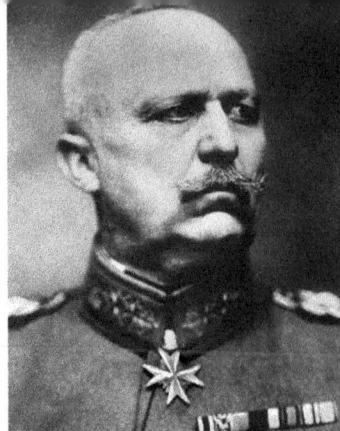

17GW008 Erich Friedrich Wilhelm Ludendorff commented:

'The shortening of our front made it stronger and safer. The enemy's plans were countered. The lines of attack they had chosen were no longer suitable and the ground we had abandoned left them no resources. If they wanted to use it they had to repair everything and very heavy work was necessary in order to prepare an attack. We could, accordingly, thin out the troops and withdraw divisions. The result that had been sought by Operation Alberich and the occupation of the Siegfried position was fully obtained.'

At the outset of 1917 the Allies, overestimating German losses of the Somme and Verdun fighting, believed that just one more major offensive would be enough to break through the German lines and drive them out of France and Belgium. At the request of the American President Wilson, the Germans informally made clear their peace terms in January 1917, which were rejected by the allies. The French General Nivelle was determined to launch another major offensive at Champagne in the spring of 1917, but the German withdrawal to the Hindenburg Line disrupted these plans.

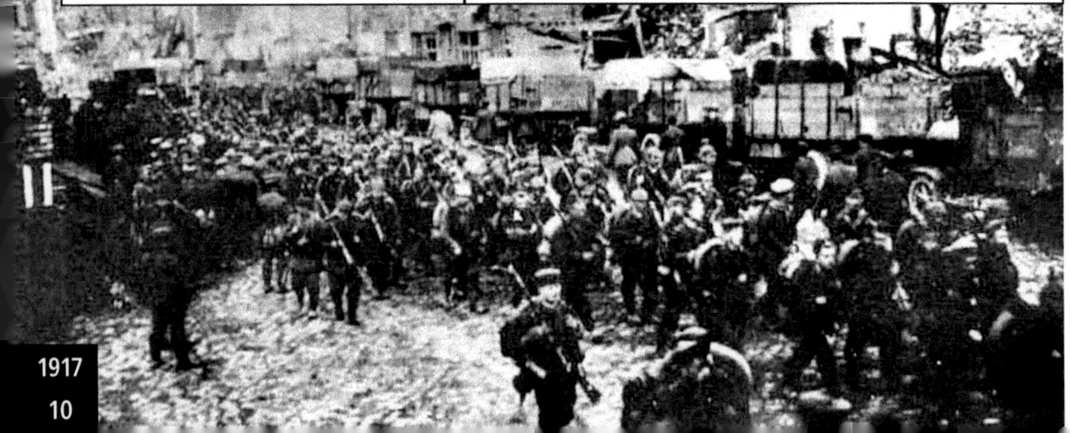

17GW002 German troops withdrawing through the streets of Péronne during the fall back to the prepared postions the Germans called the Siegfried Line and the Allies the Hindenburg Line.

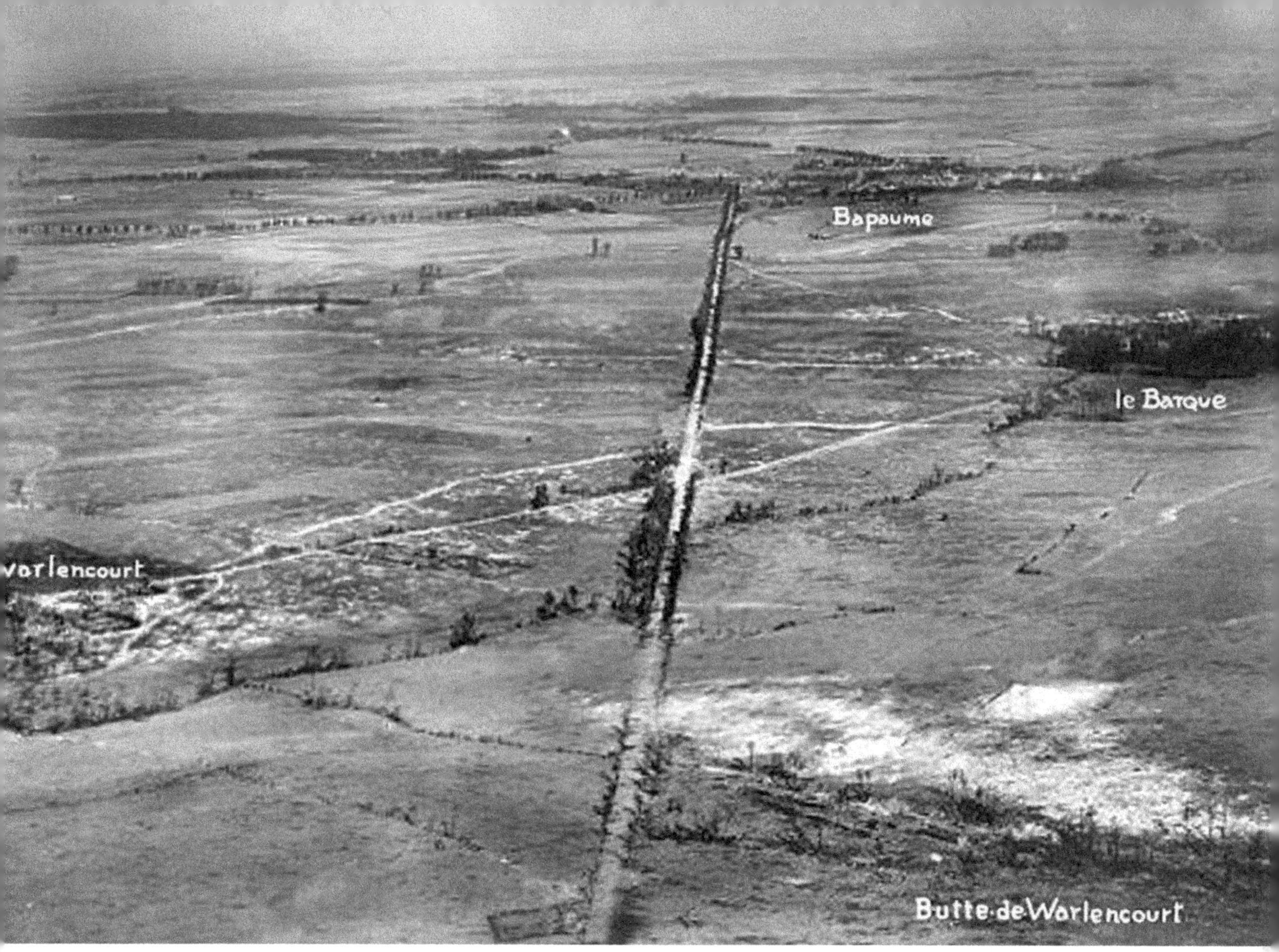

17GW013 The Butte de Warlencourt, which marked the limit of the British advance during the Battle of the Somme and from where the German withdrawal began on 24 February 1917. The Albert–Bapaume road runs from bottom to top; the British front line can be seen at the bottom right of the picture in front of the mound (Butte). As the Germans pulled back towards Bapaume their rear guard was engaged by elements of the 2nd Australian Division and fighting took place at Le Barque and elsewhere on this sector. After three weeks' fighting the withdrawal carried on from Bapaume to the prepared positions of the Hindenburg Line.

17GW014 The Butte de Warlencourt was an ancient burial mound off the Albert–Bapaume road, north-east of Le Sars in the Somme département of northern France. Some of the fiercest fighting took place on and around the Butte which was riddled with tunnels and dugouts and heavily defended by mortars, machine guns and belts of barbed wire the Butte commanded the road to Bapaume and although the British managed to get onto the Butte, they were always removed by counter attacks. On the German withdrawal, February 1917, the British 151 Brigade finally occupied it.

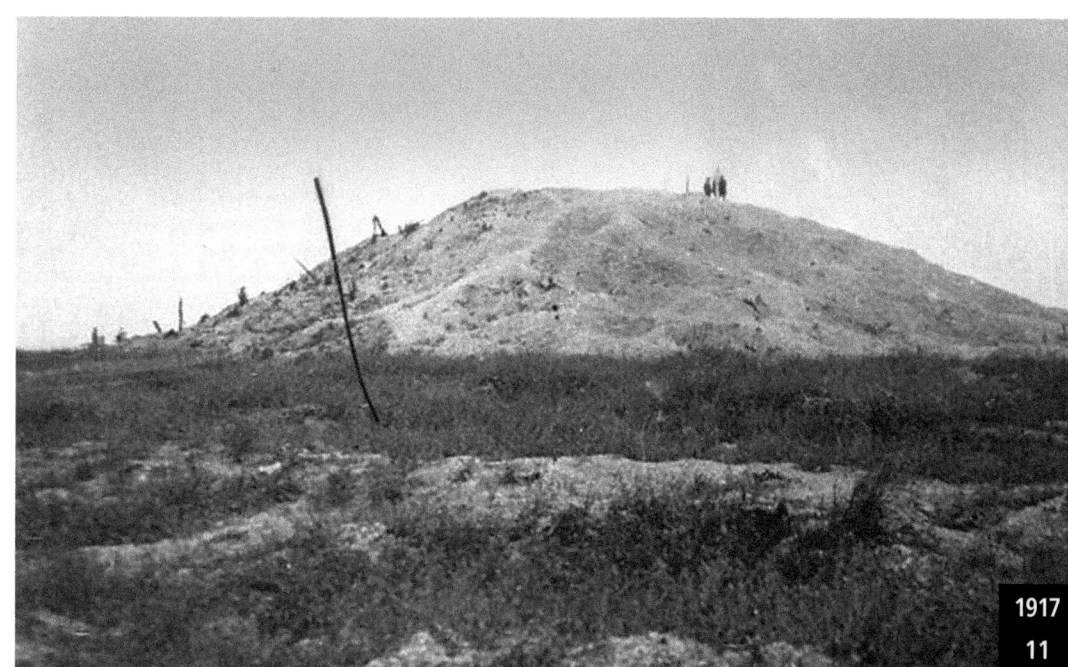

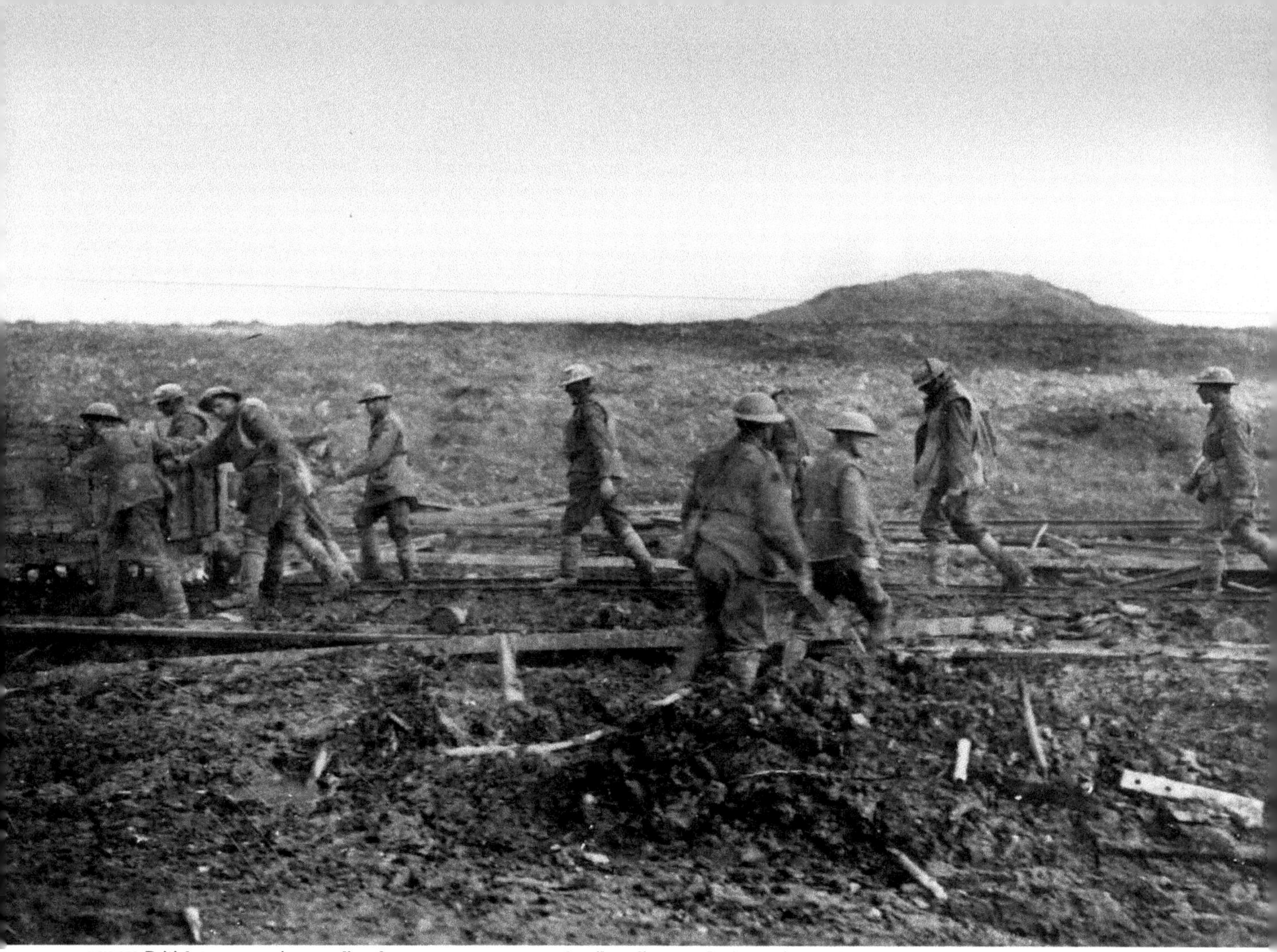

17GW053 British troops moving supplies along a narrow gauge trench railway line near Le Sars, with the Butte de Warlencourt on the horizon.

17GW055 A British officer takes cover during a German barrage near Le Sars.

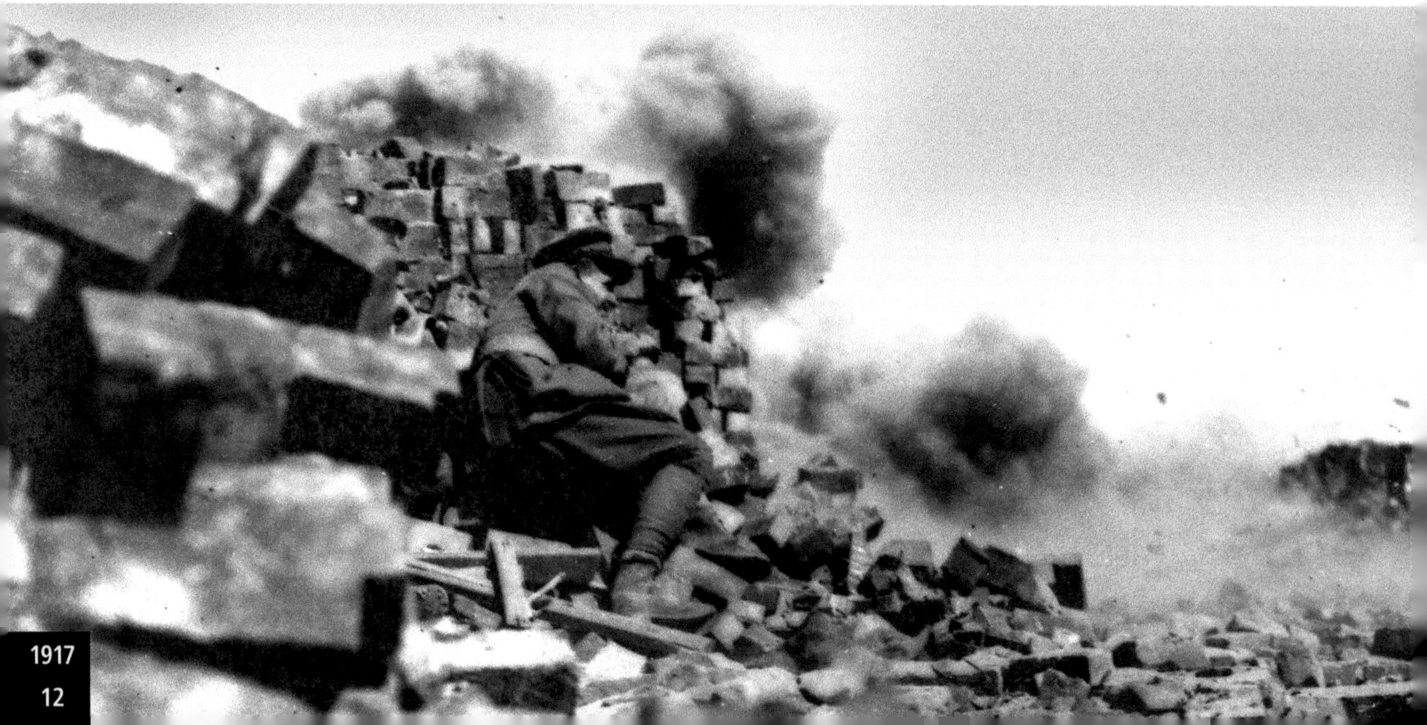

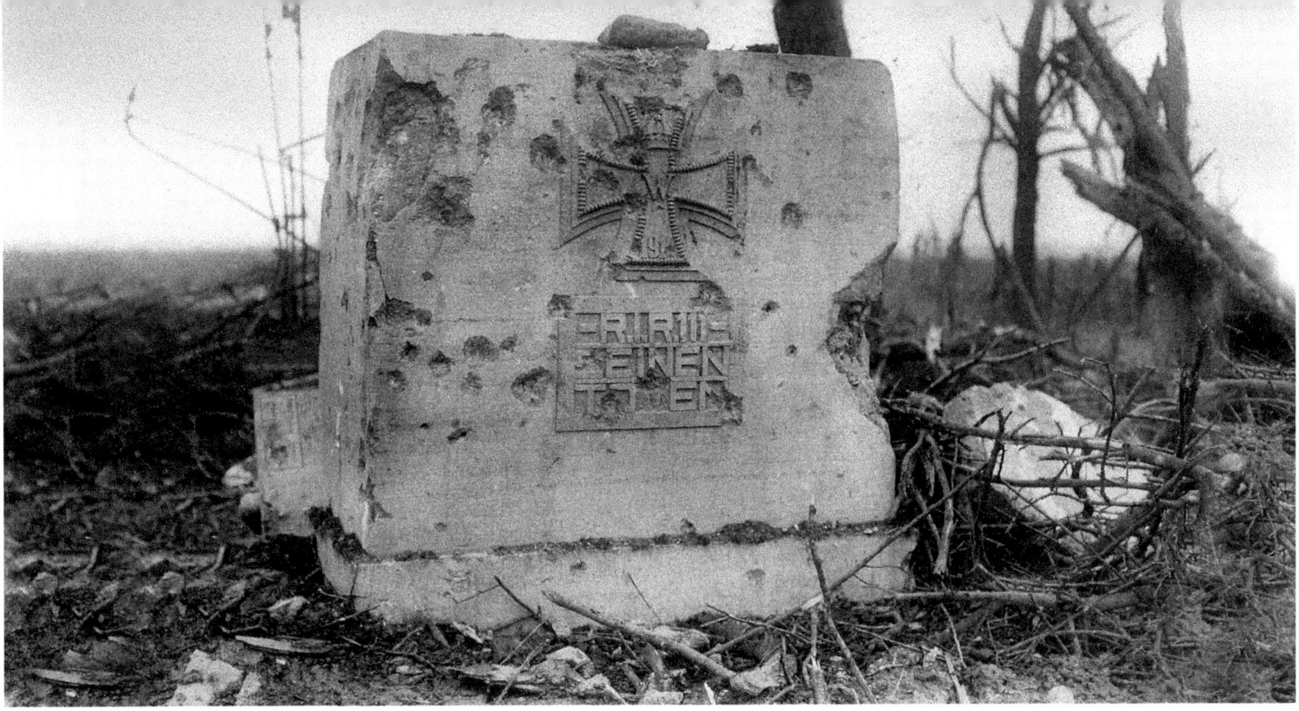

17GW057 The base of a memorial in a German cemetery at Le Sars; it is still there today.

17GW056 Allied advances were delayed as roads had to be rebuilt and more pack animals and carts were organised. The Germans systematically destroyed the territory across which they withdrew. Support artillery and transport to carry supplies were needed for attacks on the villages where the German rearguard was putting up fierce resistance. Each day of delay gained time for the Germans to develop the Hindenburg Line defences.

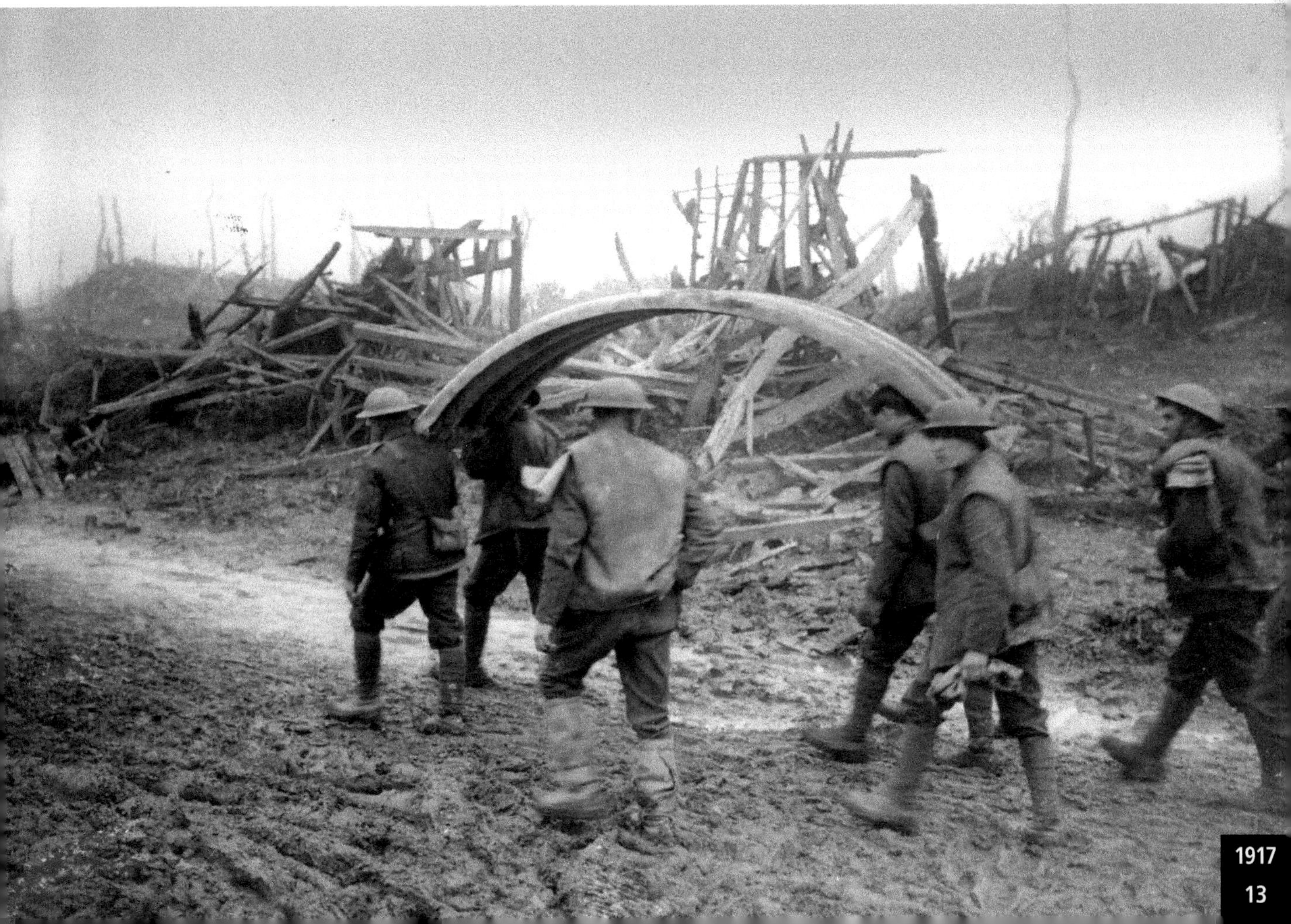

1917
13

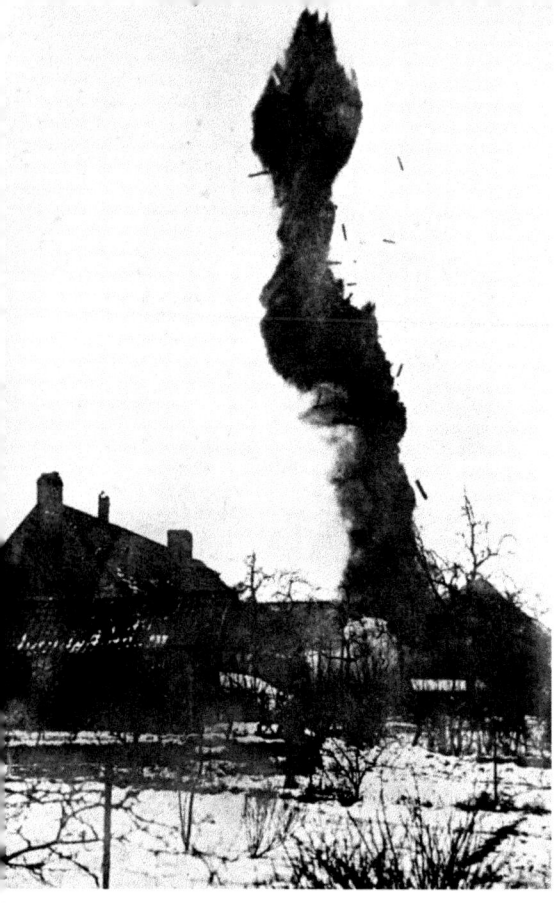

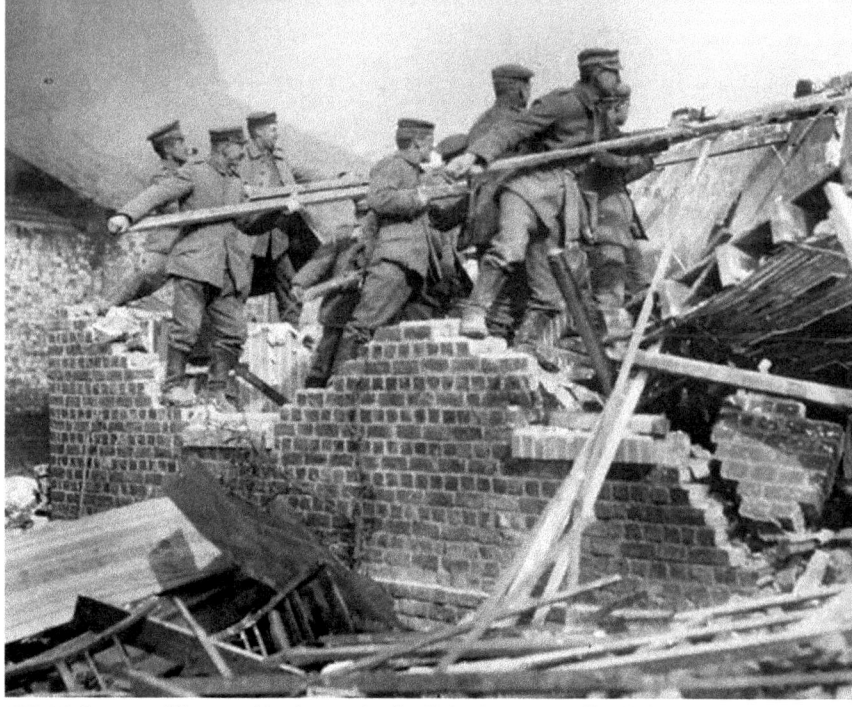

17GW018 German soldiers wrecking houses, leaving little of use to the allies, before withdrawing to the Hindenburg Line.

17GW015 German engineers demolishing houses in Bapaume to prevent the British from using them for billeting.

17GW016 Officers outside a command shelter.

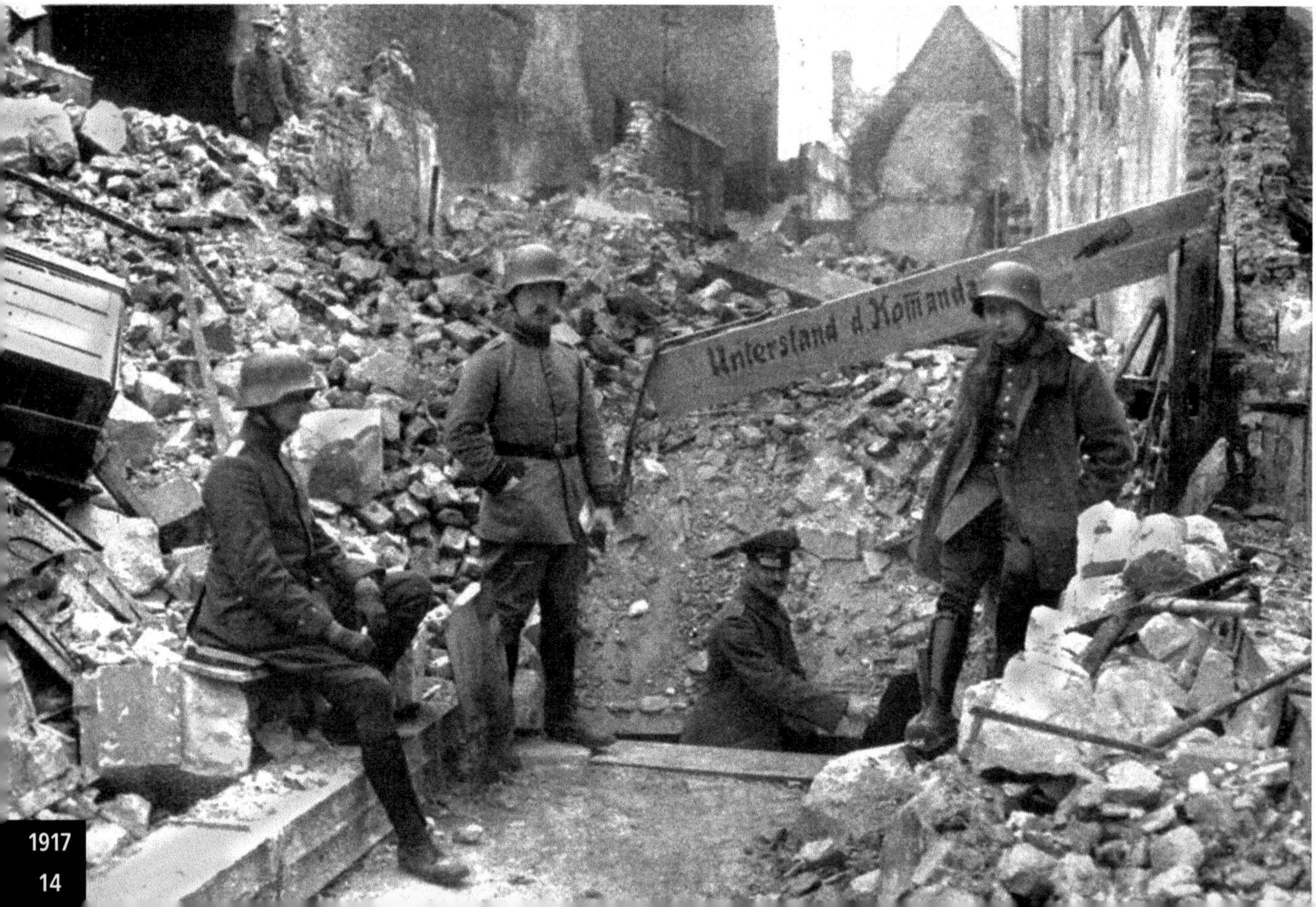

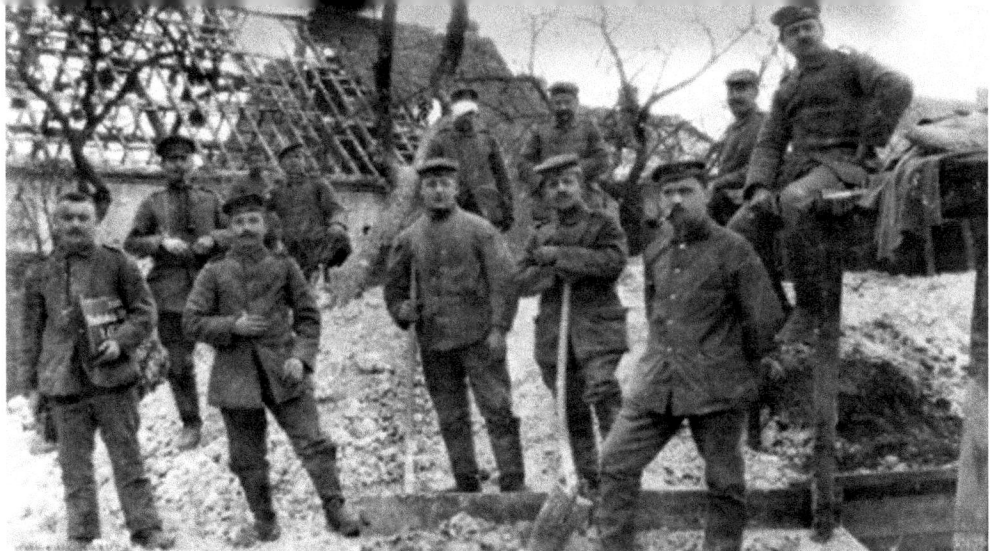

17GW021 German pioneers preparing defences of the Siegfried Line, (or Hindenburg Line, so named by the allies).

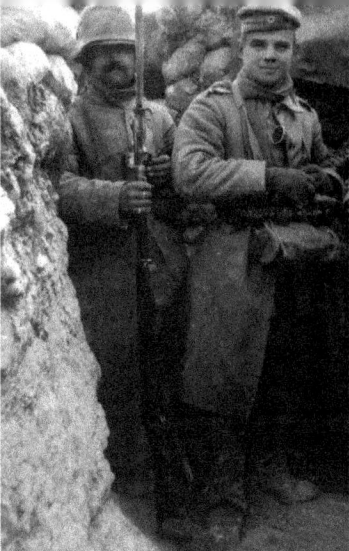

17GW022 Troops manning the Hindenburg Line.

17GW023 Some of the mischief carried out at Péronne by the retreating Germans: this section of road has been blocked by felled trees. Note that the three trees left standing have been partly cut through.

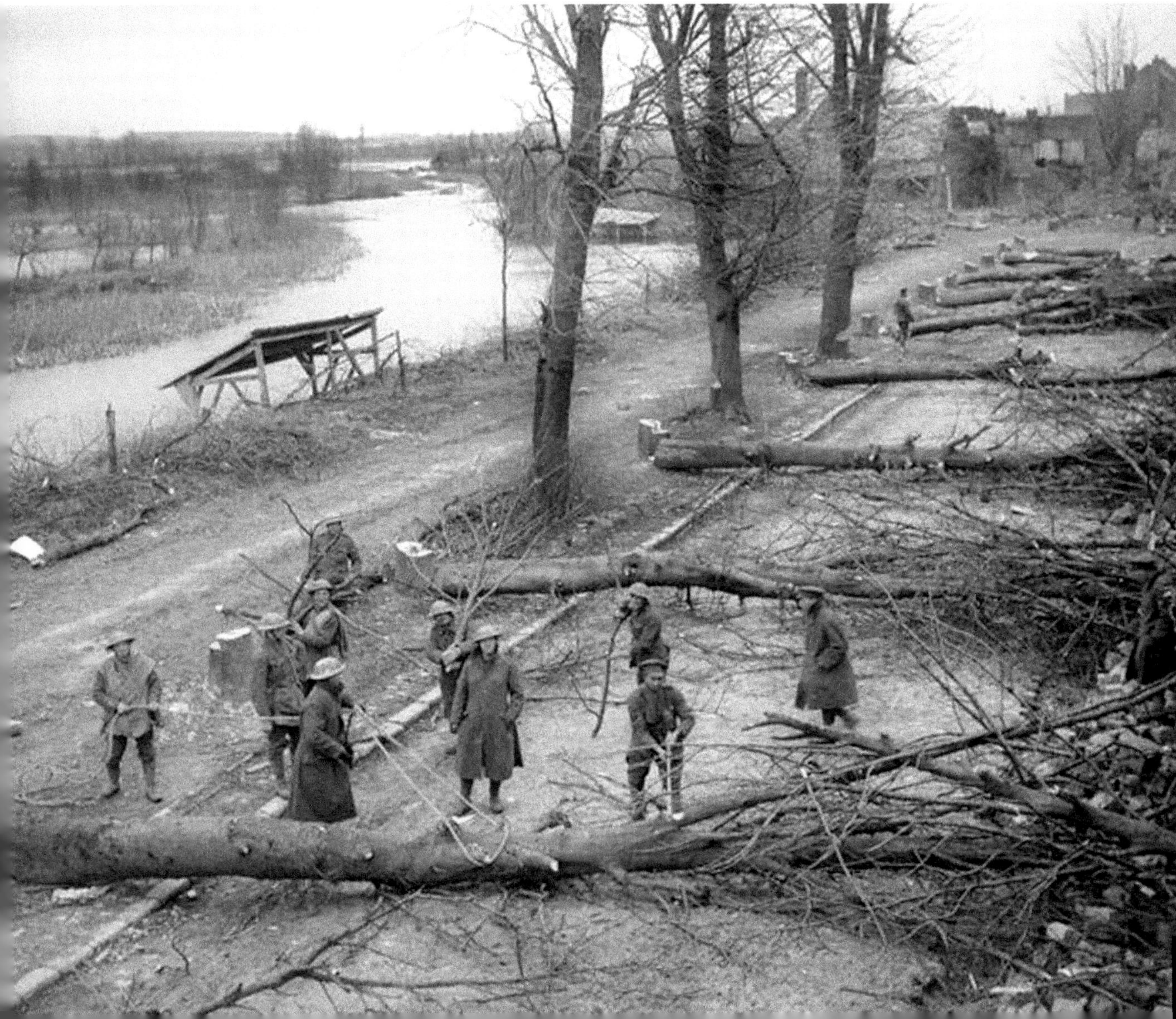

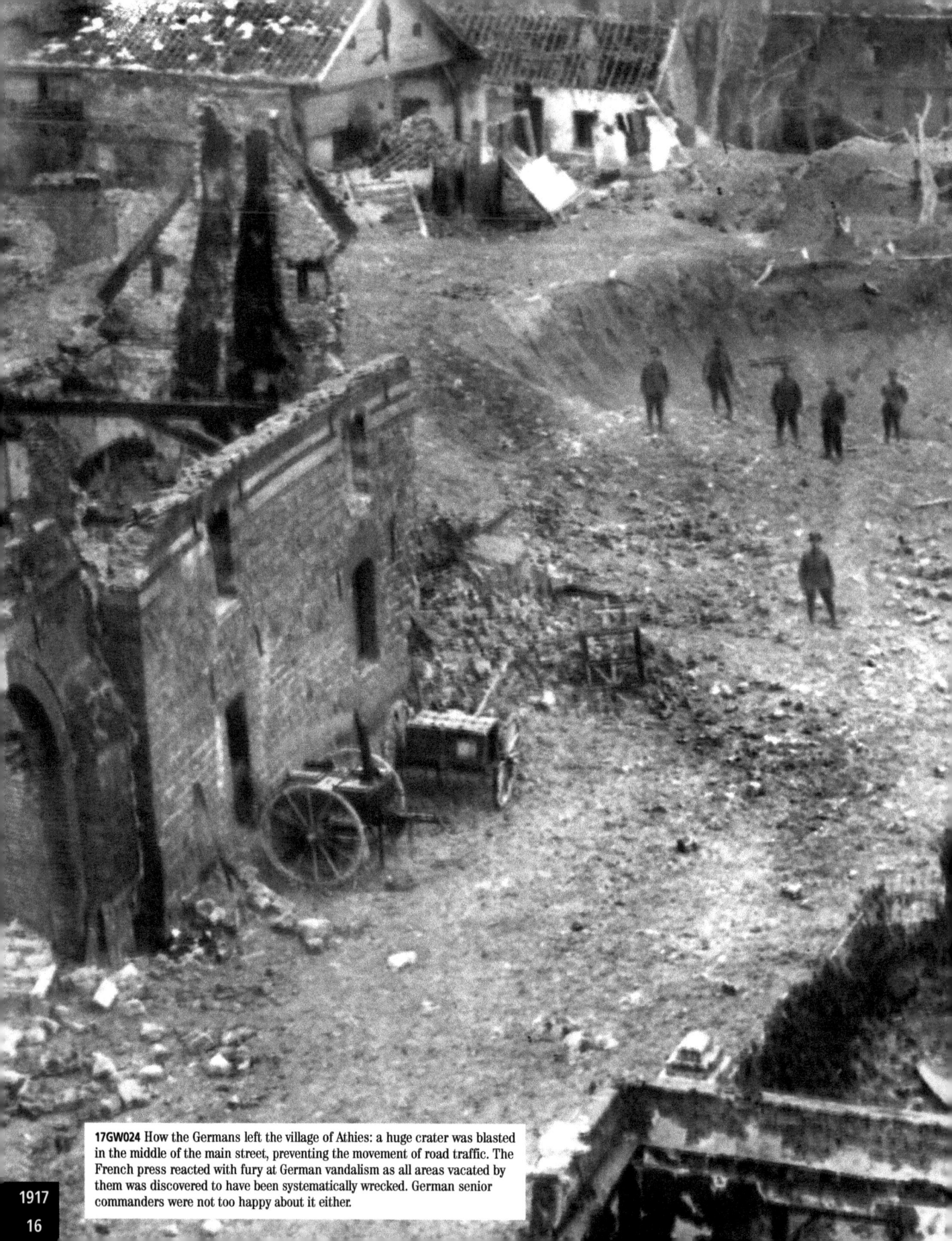

17GW024 How the Germans left the village of Athies: a huge crater was blasted in the middle of the main street, preventing the movement of road traffic. The French press reacted with fury at German vandalism as all areas vacated by them was discovered to have been systematically wrecked. German senior commanders were not too happy about it either.

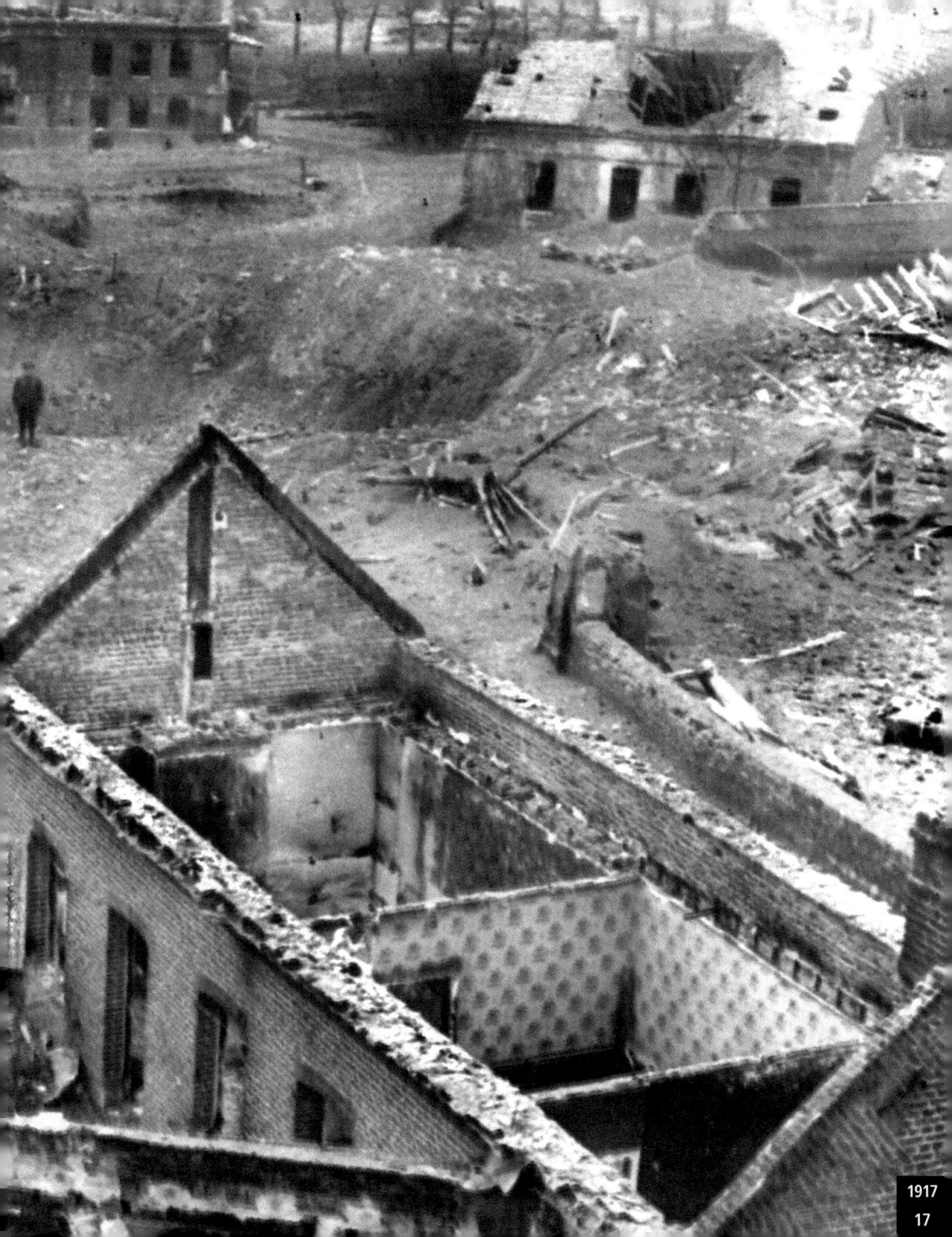

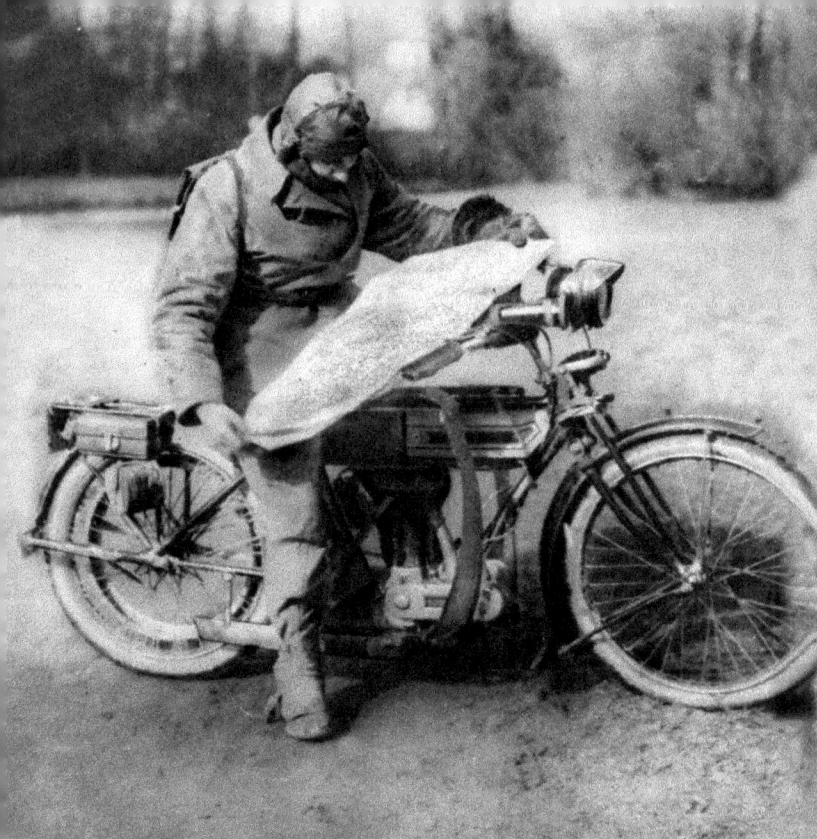

17GW025 A British despatch rider checks his map against the unfamiliar 'liberated' territory.
17GW029 A British officer points out the way forward.

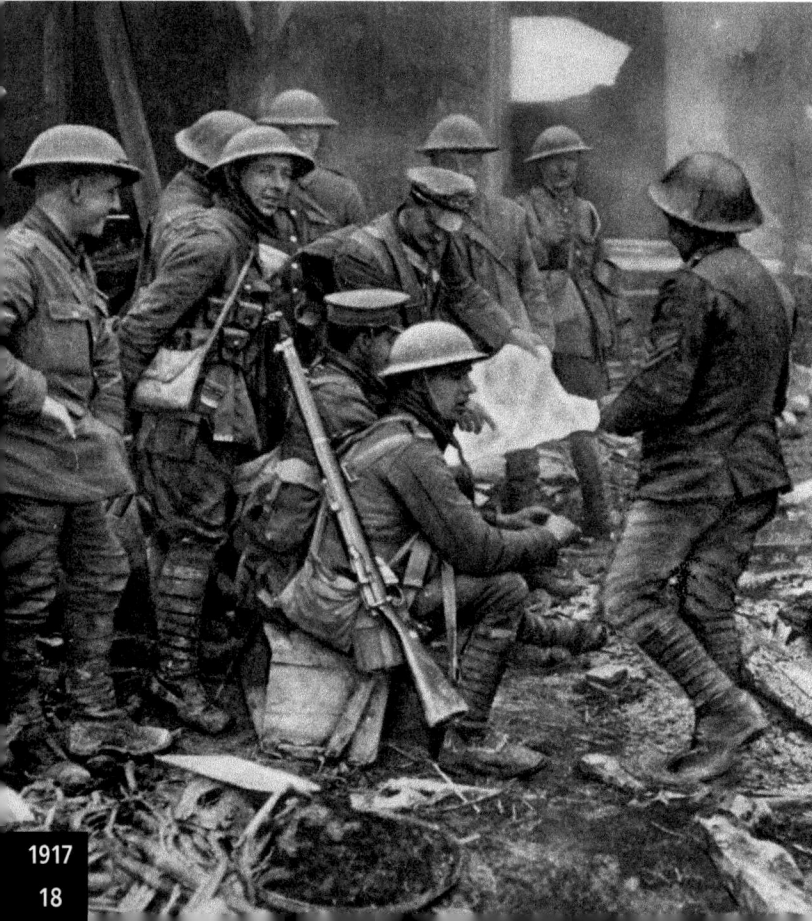

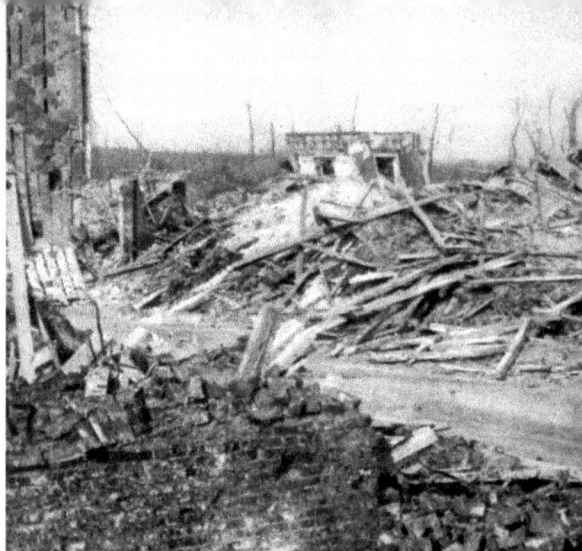

17GW026 The village of Puisieux at the northern end of the Somme front and where a rear guard action was fought by the Germans.

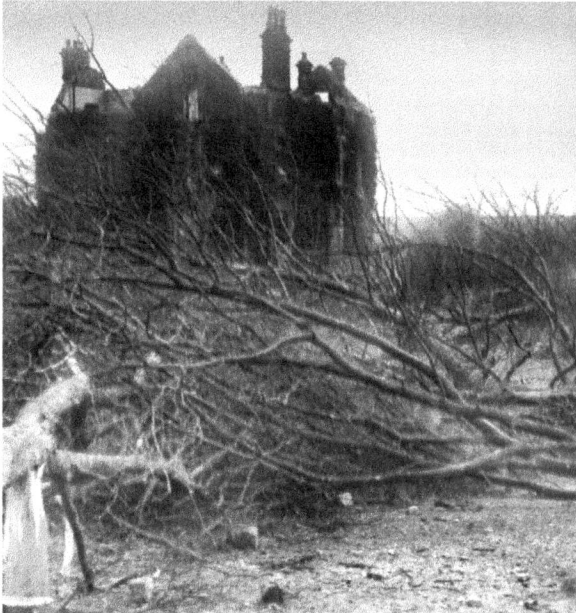

17GW032 Destruction of the fruit trees (contrary to the Hague convention).

17GW031 British troops passing the church at Athies; everything over a ten mile deep area and all along the front was systematically ruined by the Germans.

17GW030 Cyclists following up the withdrawing Germans.

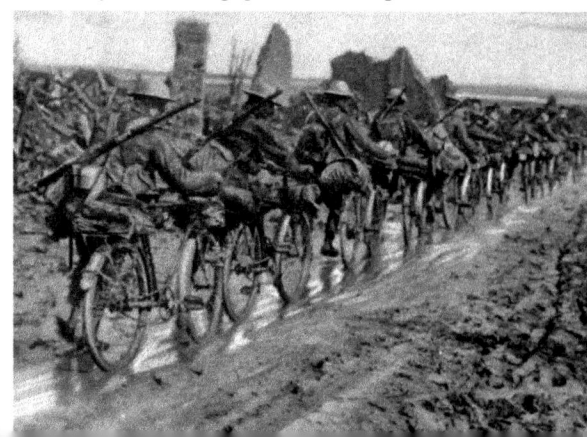

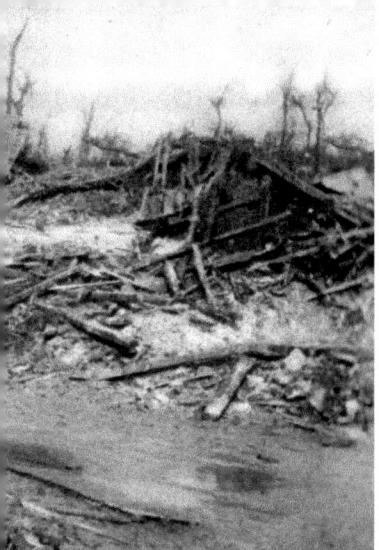
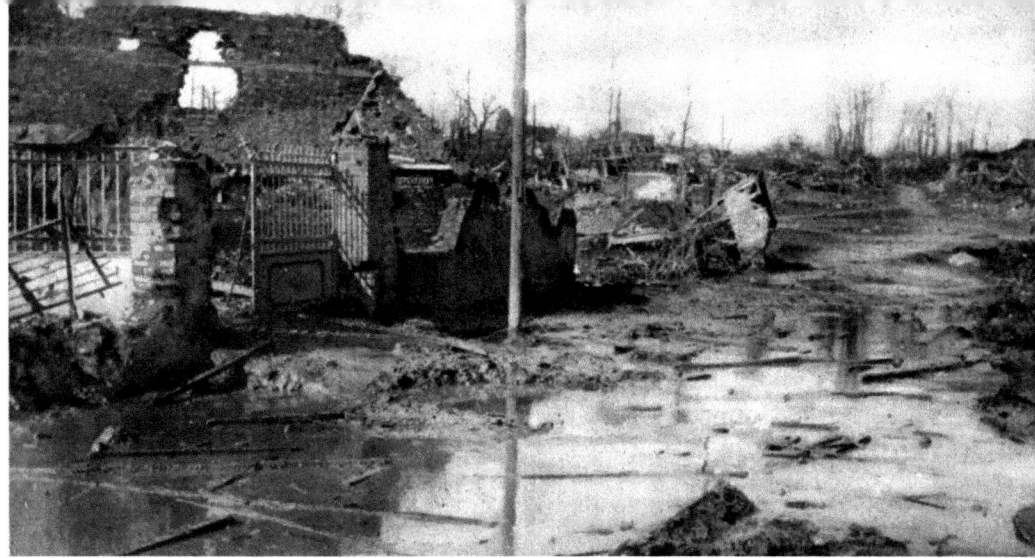

17GW027 A farm at Puisieux destroyed in the fighting as the Germans withdrew to their prepared positions.

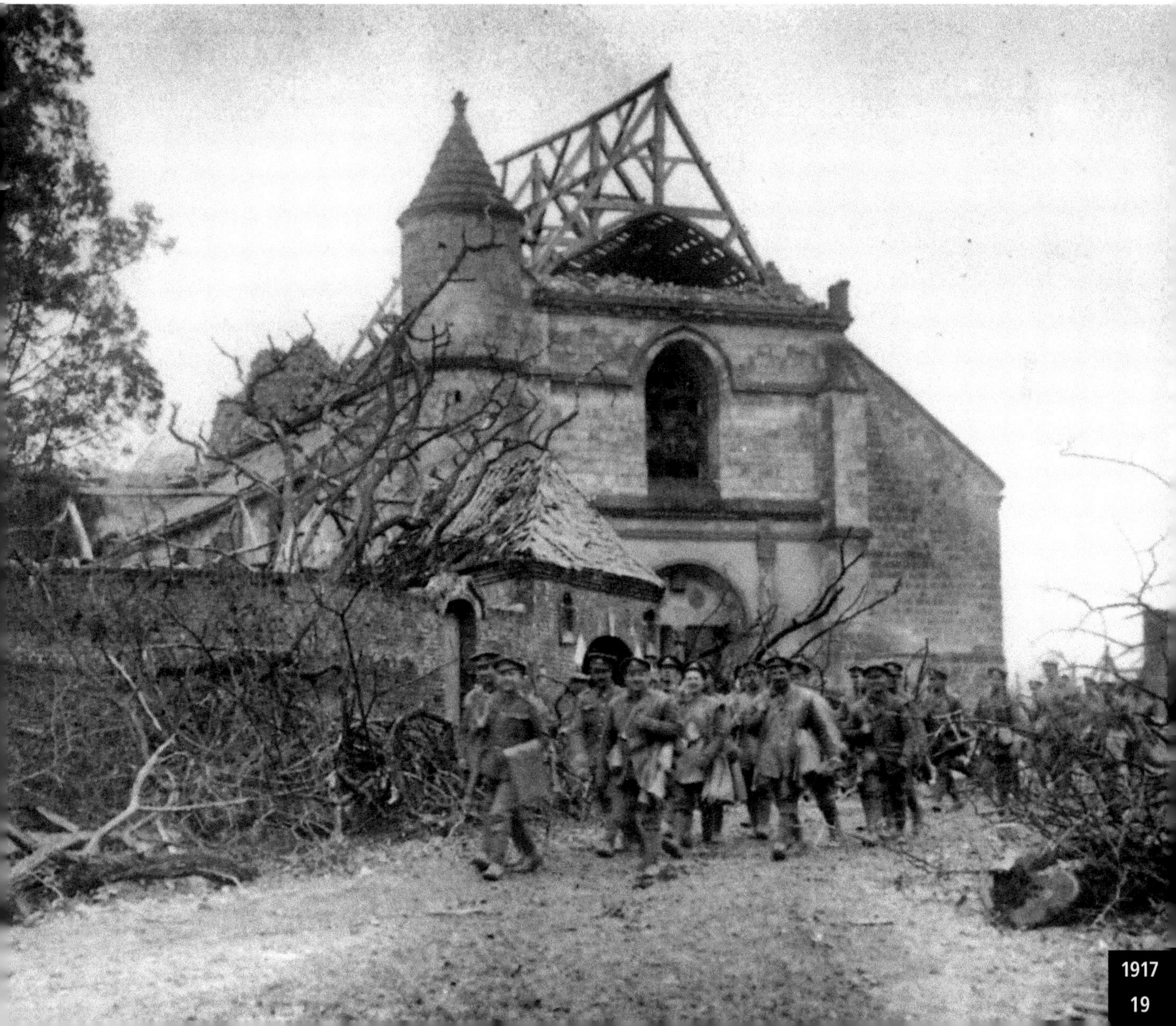

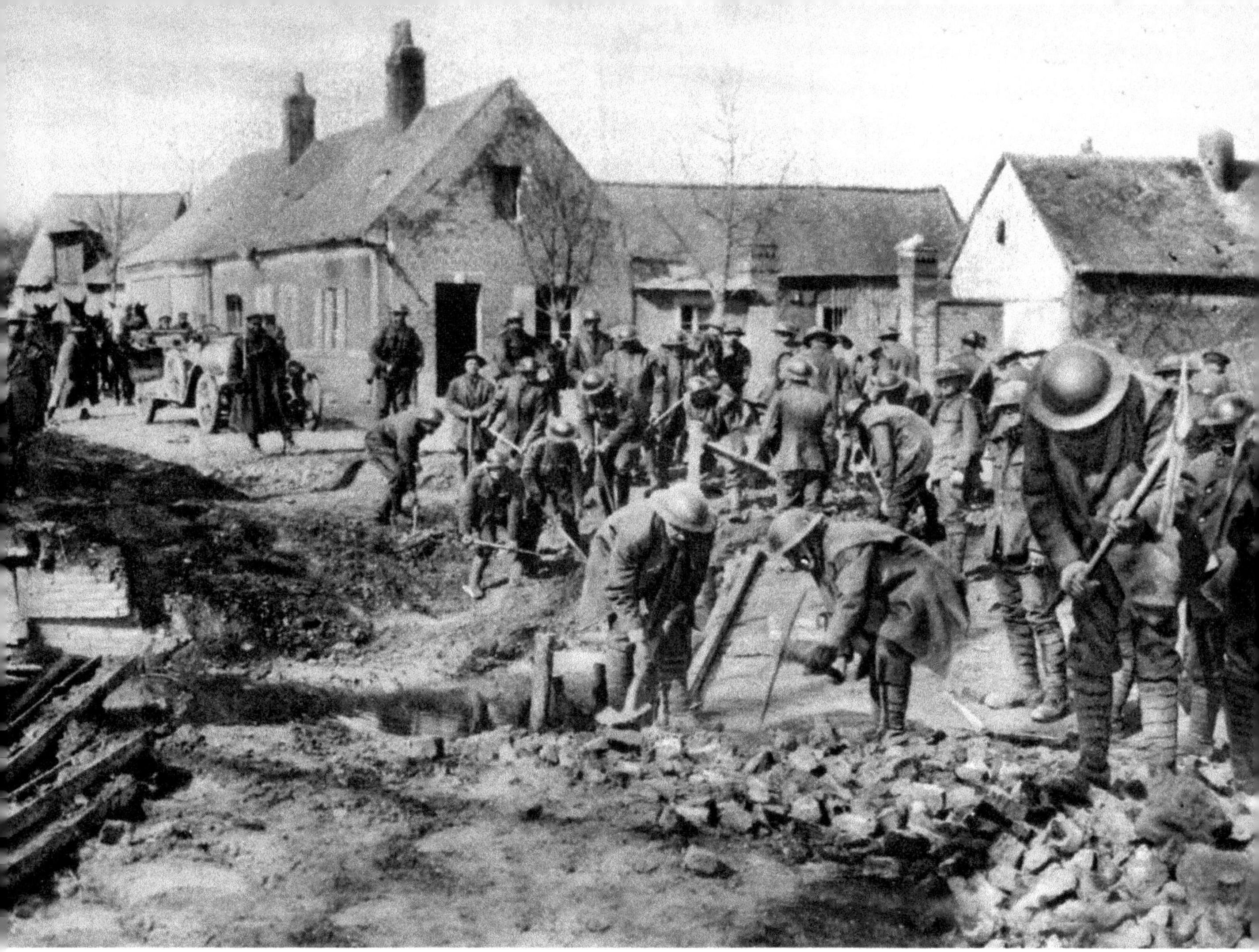

17GW033, 17GW034, 17GW035. Australian engineers and pioneers clearing rubble, filling in craters and bridging waterways where the Germans had systematically destroyed the infrastructure of the countryside they had vacated.

17GW020. British Tommies reversing a former German trench so as to have the fire step on the other side, thus the parados became the parapet.

17GW036. British supply wagons, unable to use the severly damaged roads, attempting to use the open fields alongside them.

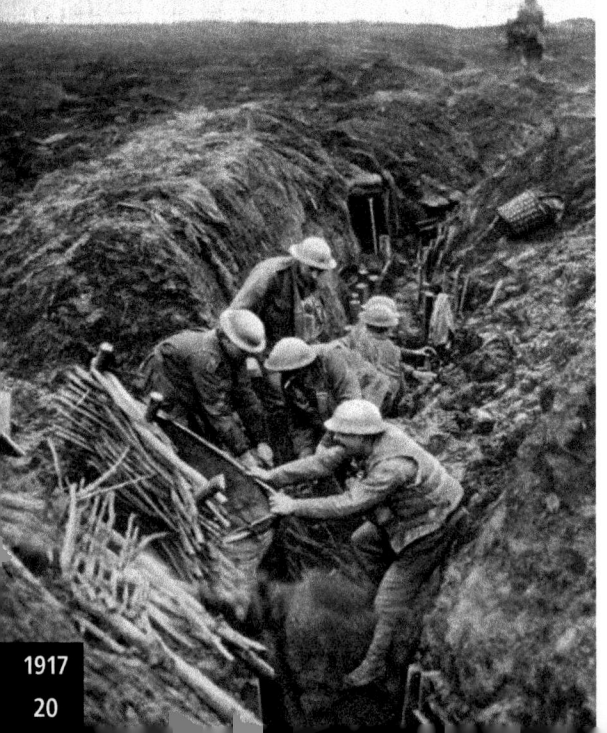

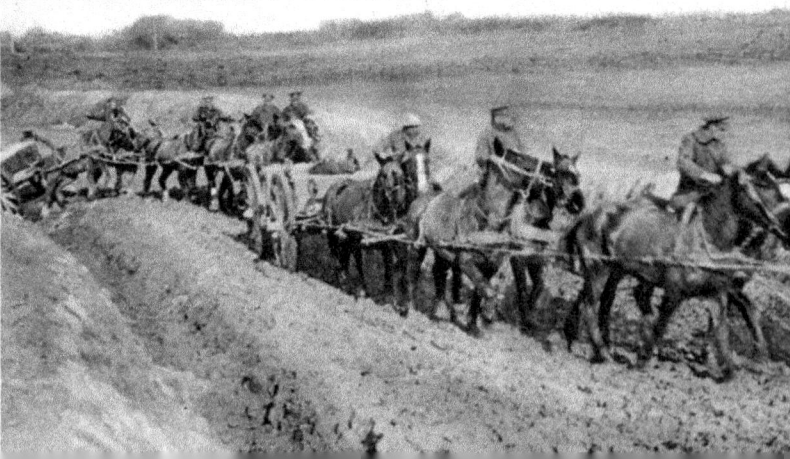

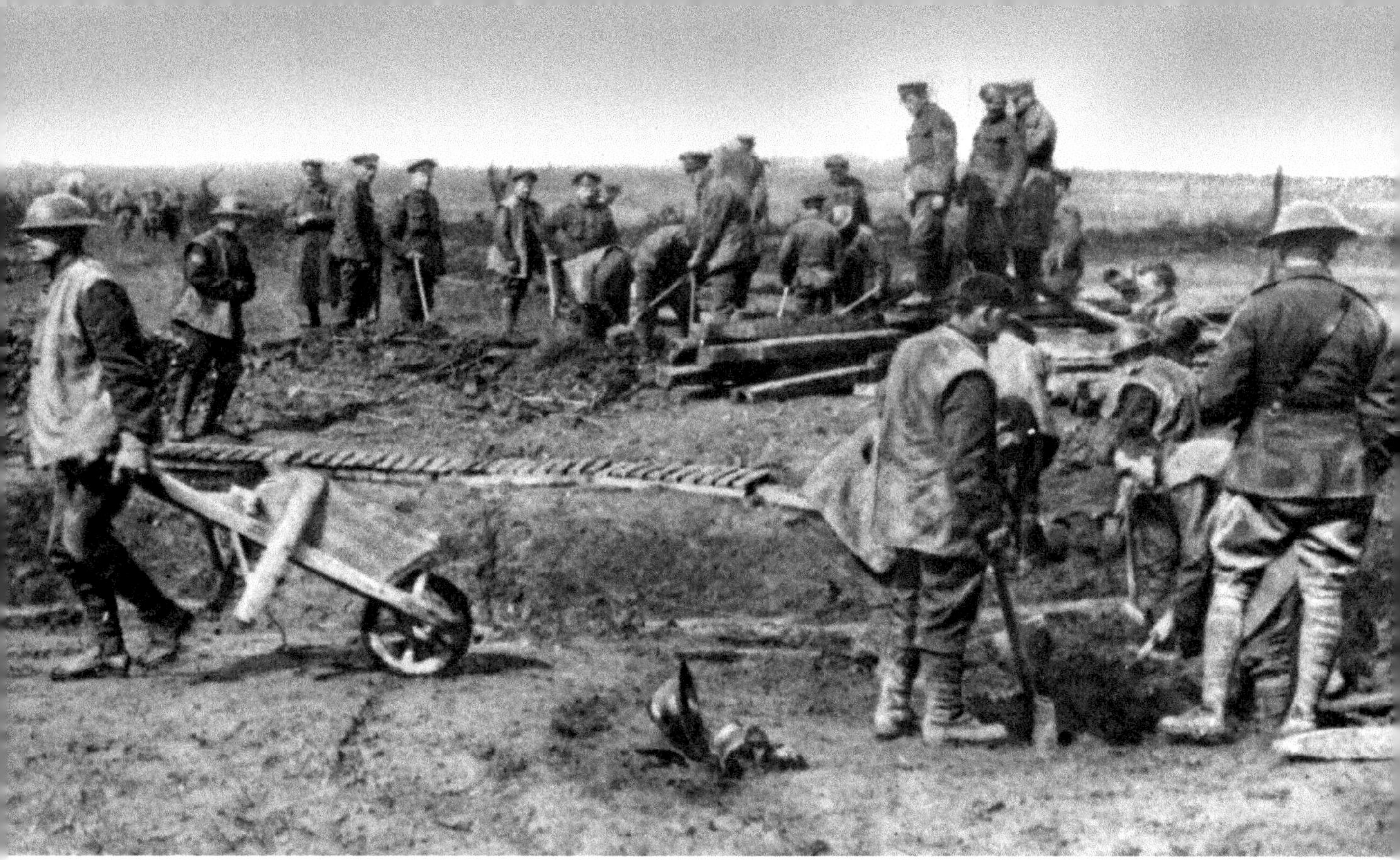

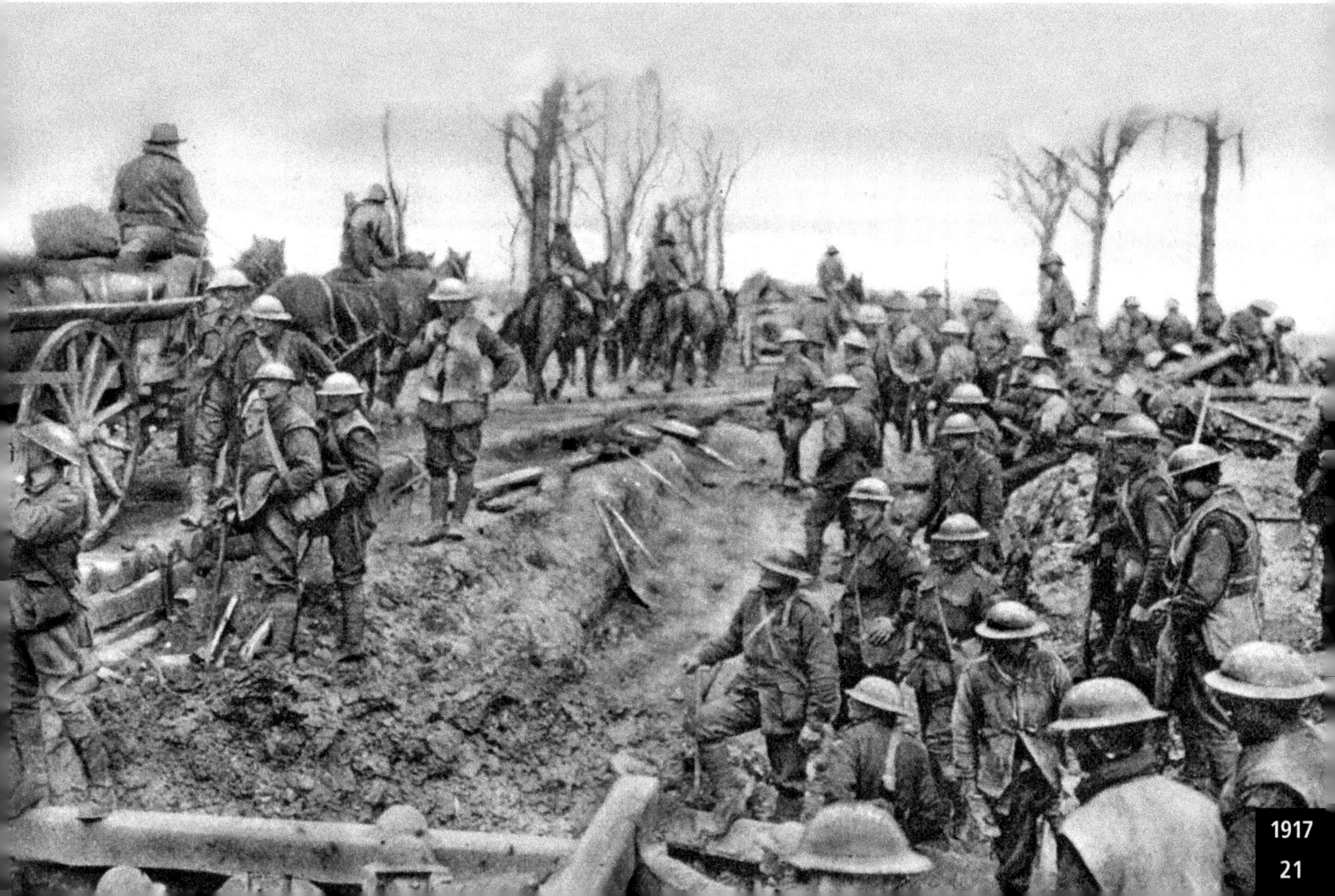

1917

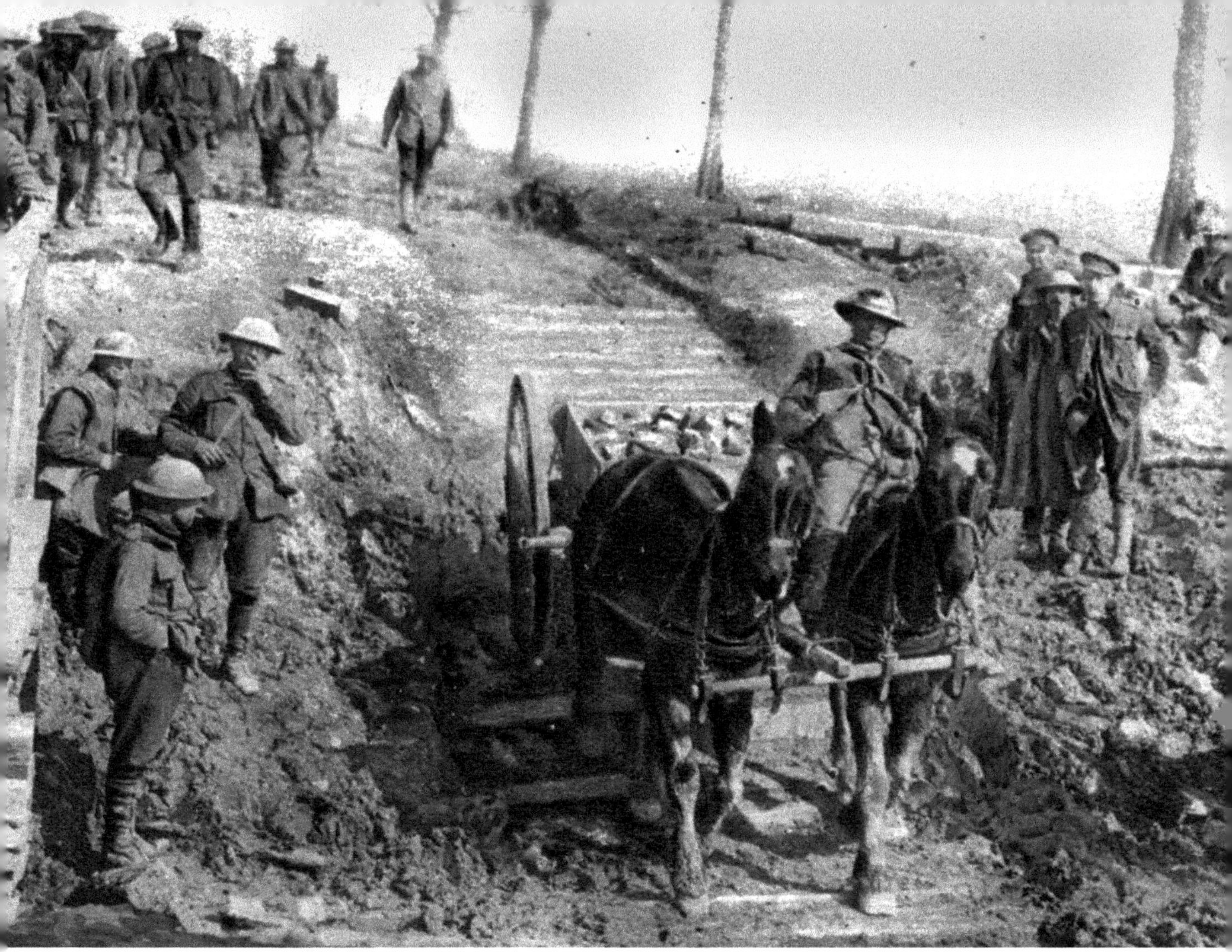

17GW038 Australians, having completed repairs to a damaged road, try out the corduroy (made up of logs) surface with a cart full of rubble.

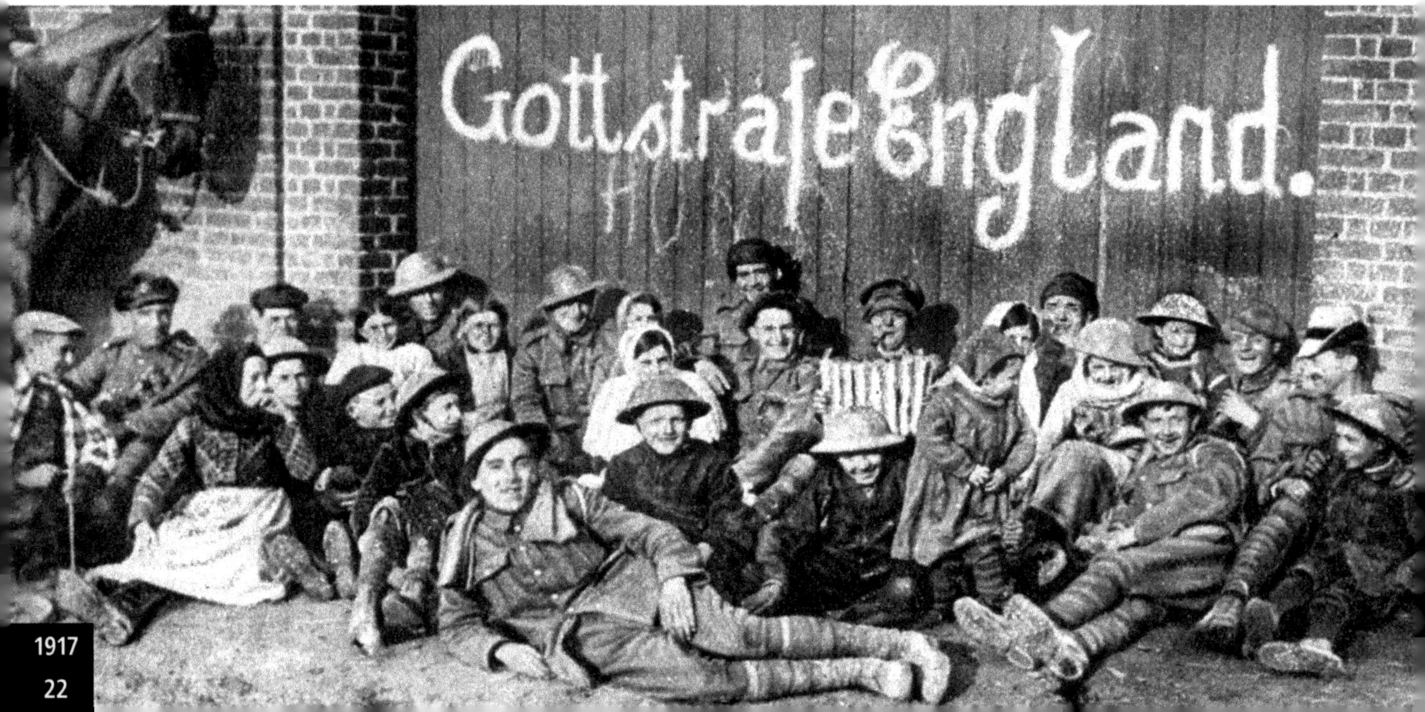

Gott strafe England.

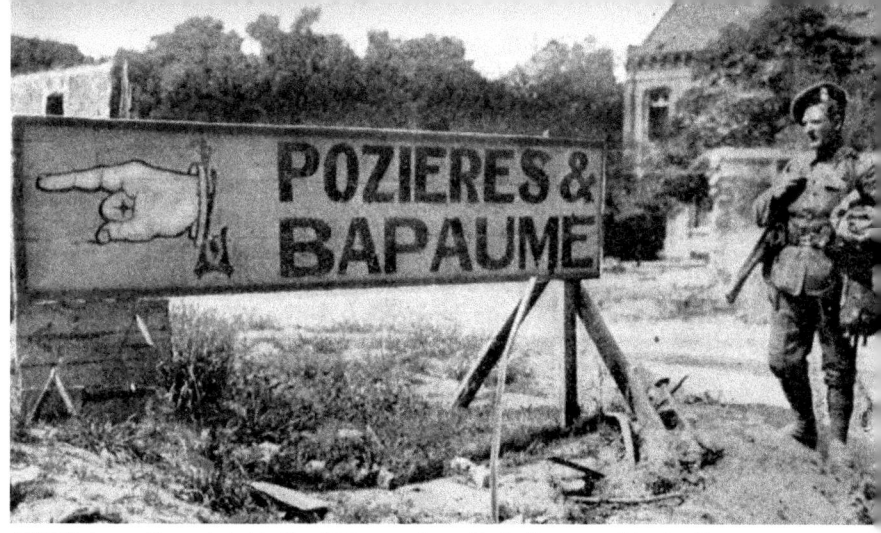

17GW039 A recently erected sign directing men and supplies in the appropriate direction.

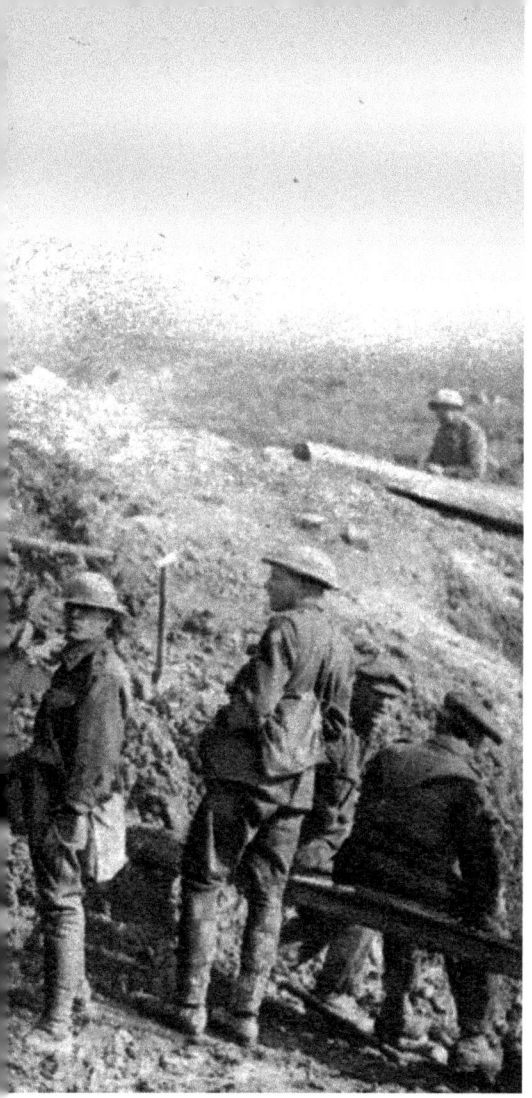

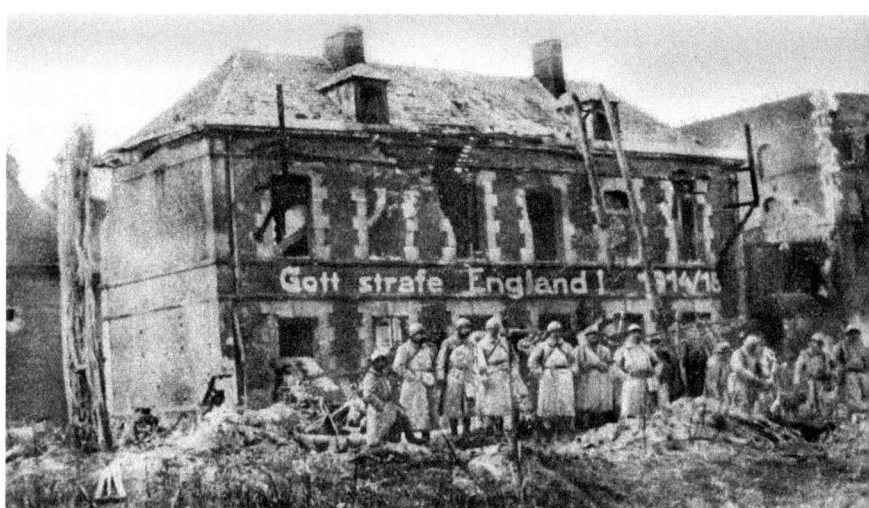

17GW041, 17GW042, 17GW040 Slogans were daubed over some of the buildings in towns evacuated by the Germans: *'Gott strafe England'* which translates as 'God punish England'; French village children and Tommies enjoying departure of the 'Hun'. *'Nicht ärgern, nur wundern!'* on this building – 'Don't be angry, just be amazed!' a quote from Goethe.

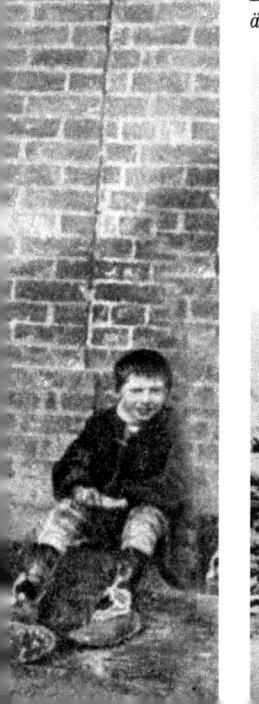

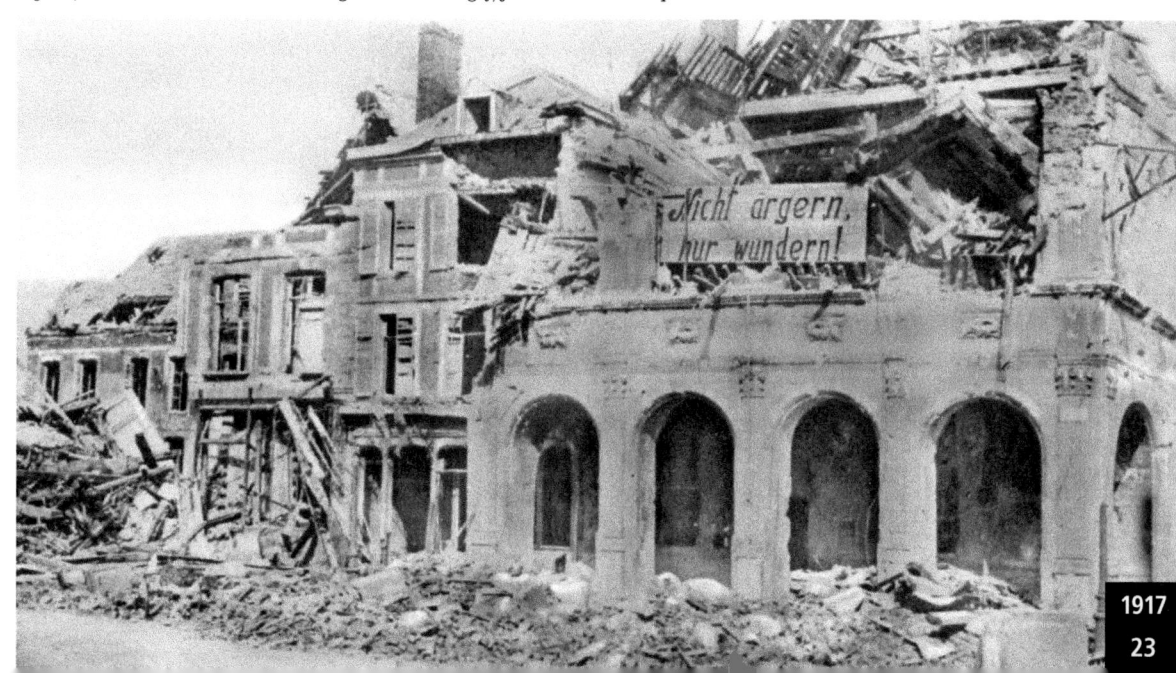

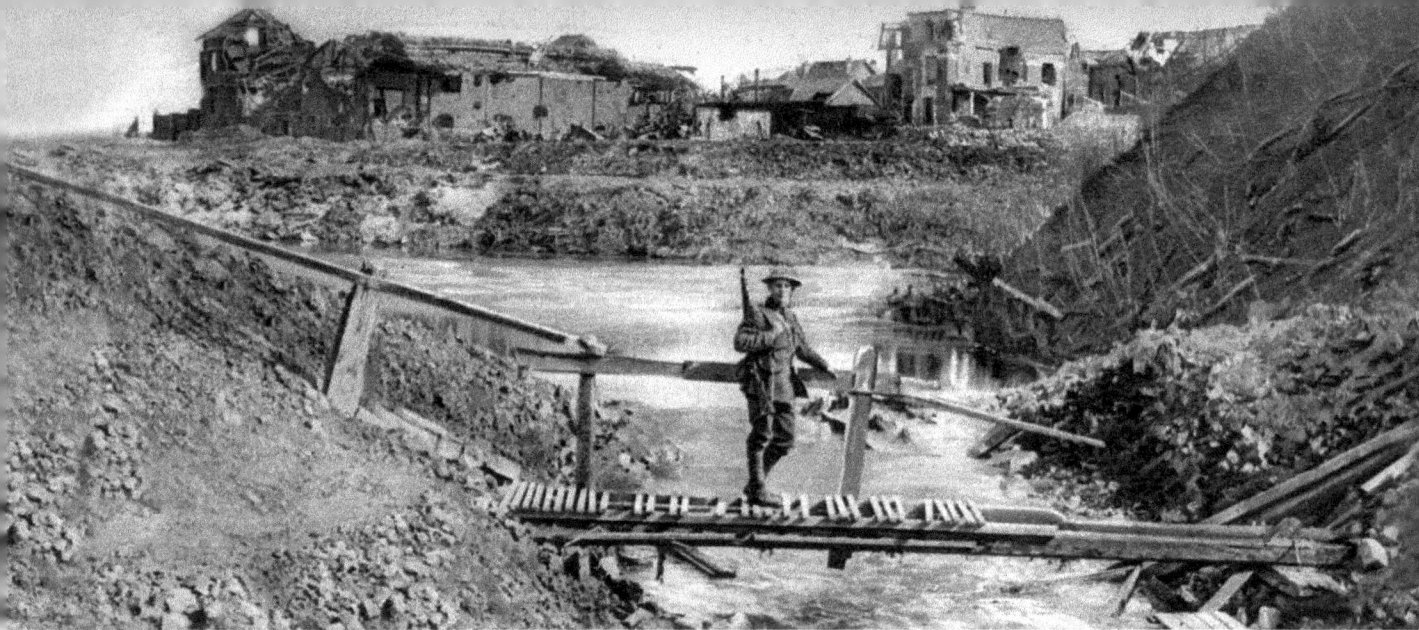

17GW046 Havoc on the approaches to the town of Péronne, which was occupied by the British on 18 March, after the German withdrawal.
17GW045 A British advance guard in the streets of Péronne.

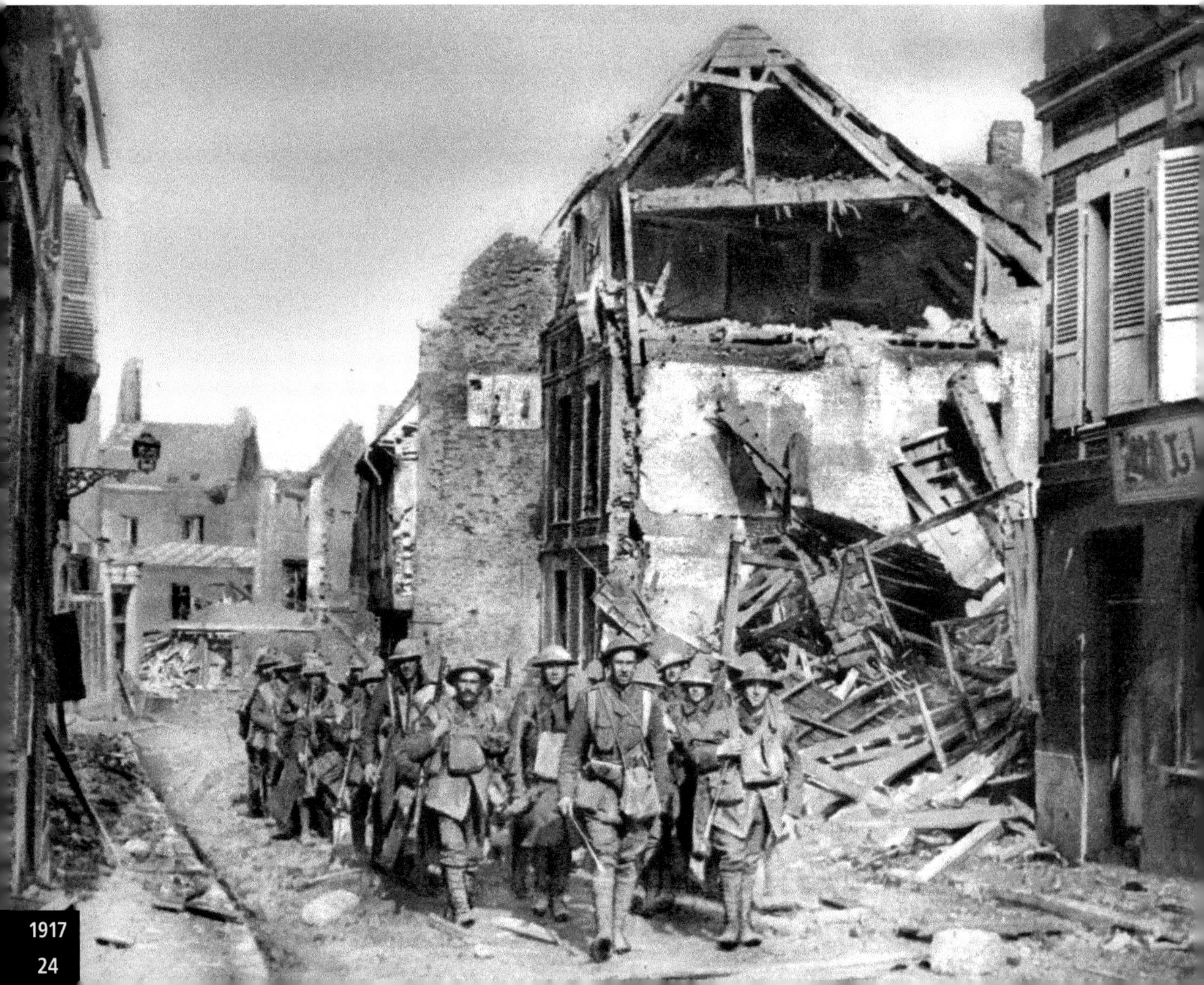

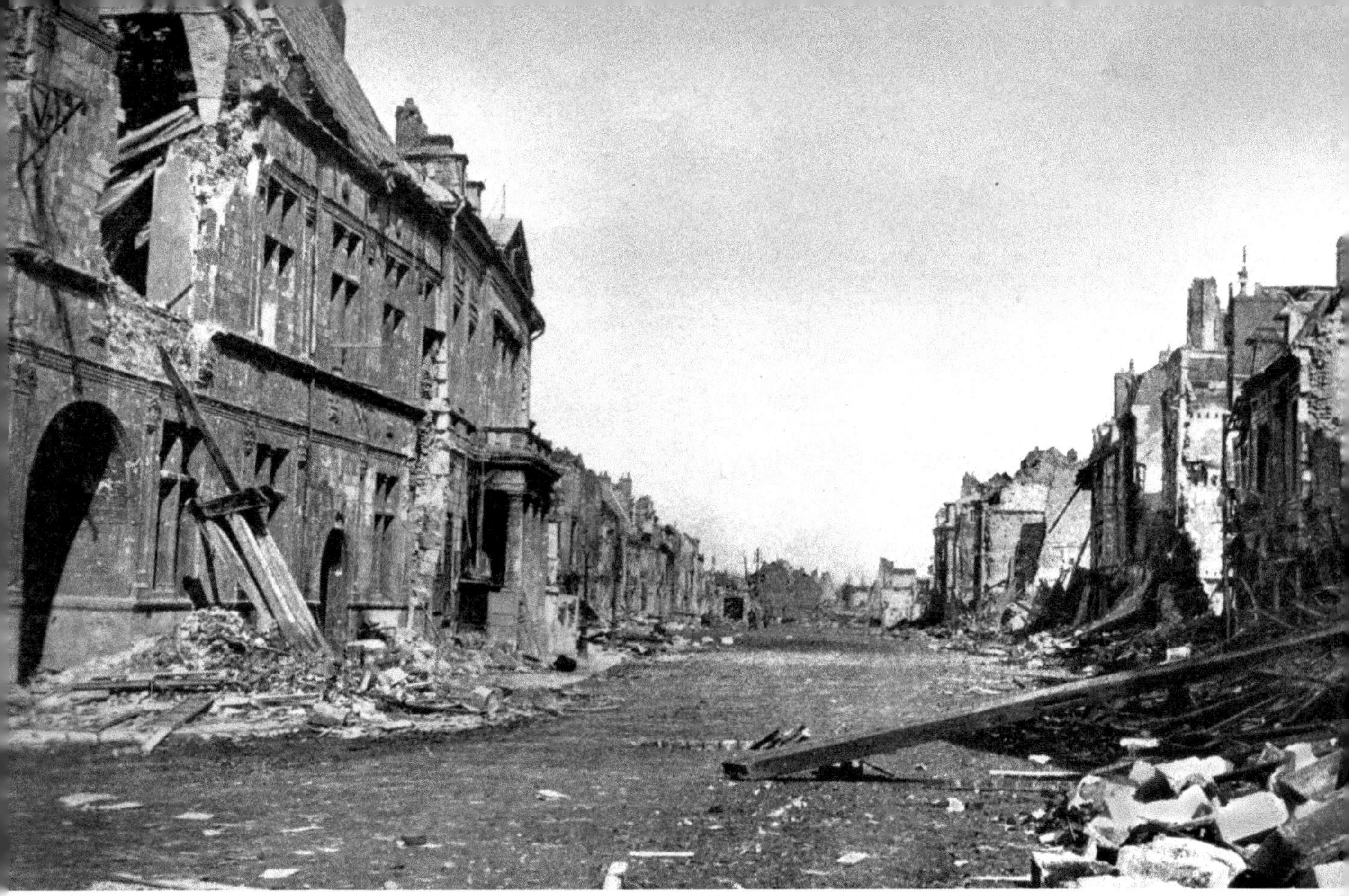

17GW047, 17GW048. The streets of Péronne – the scenes of utter devastation that greeted the British.

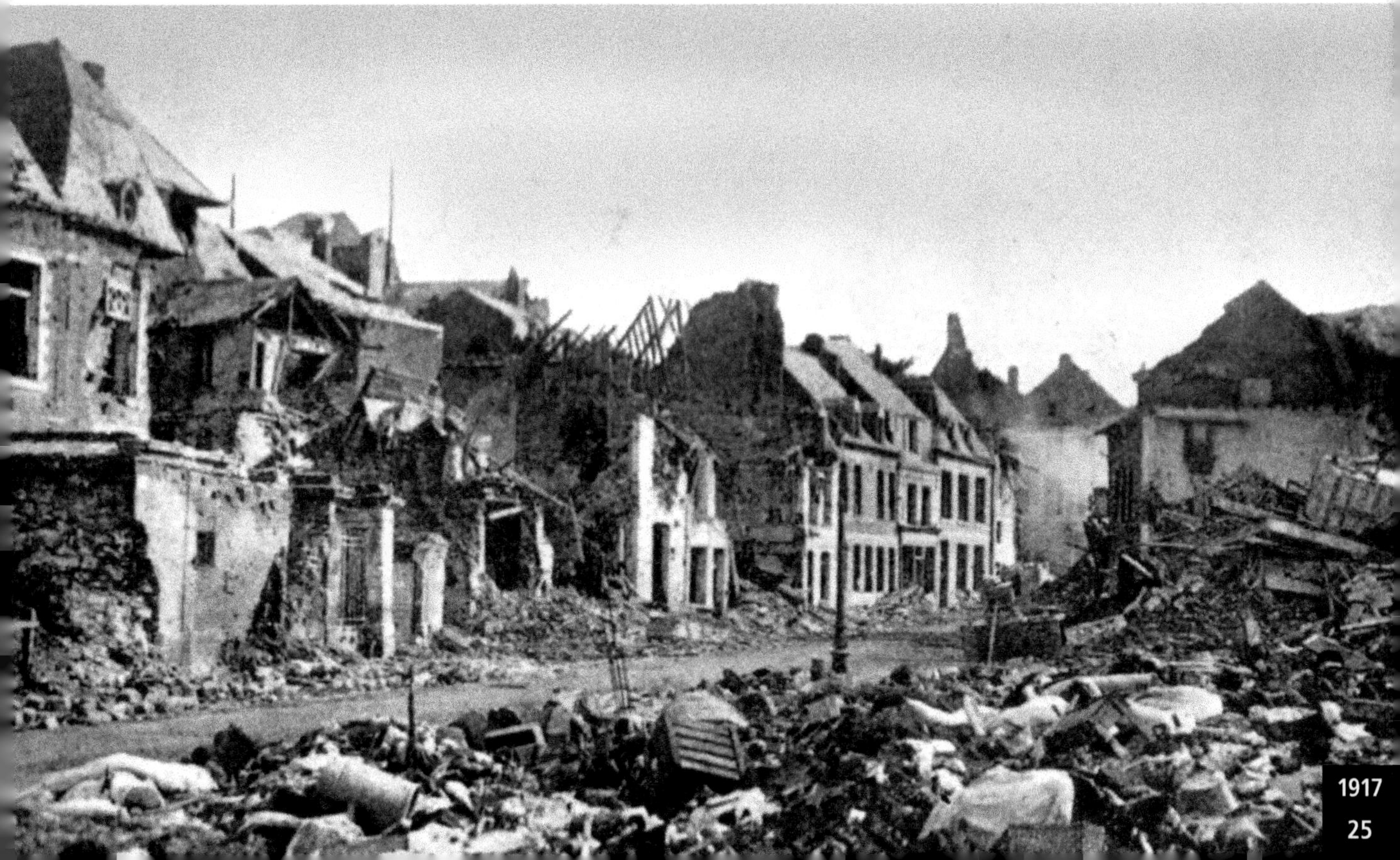

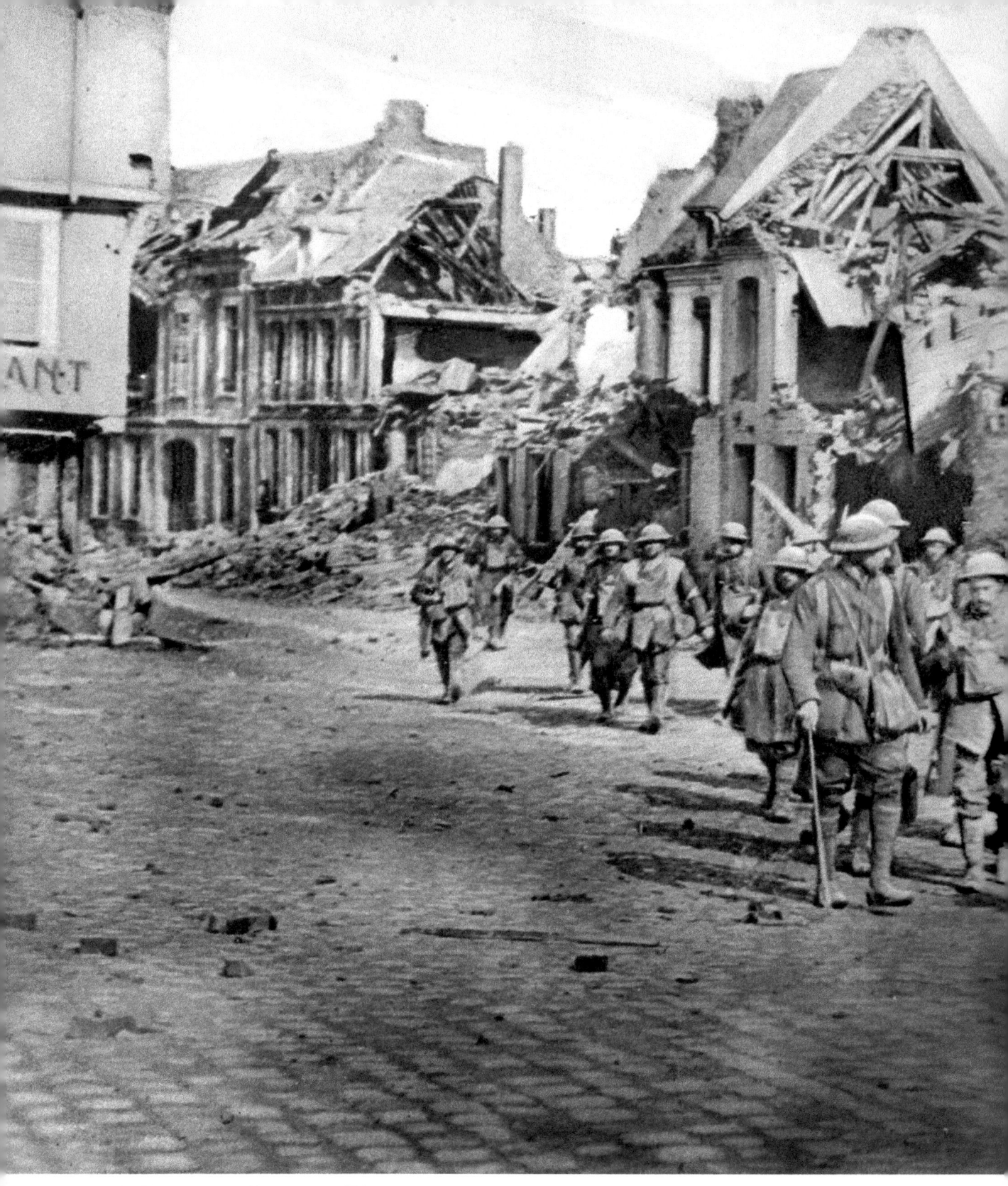
17GW050 A British advance guard in the streets of Péronne.

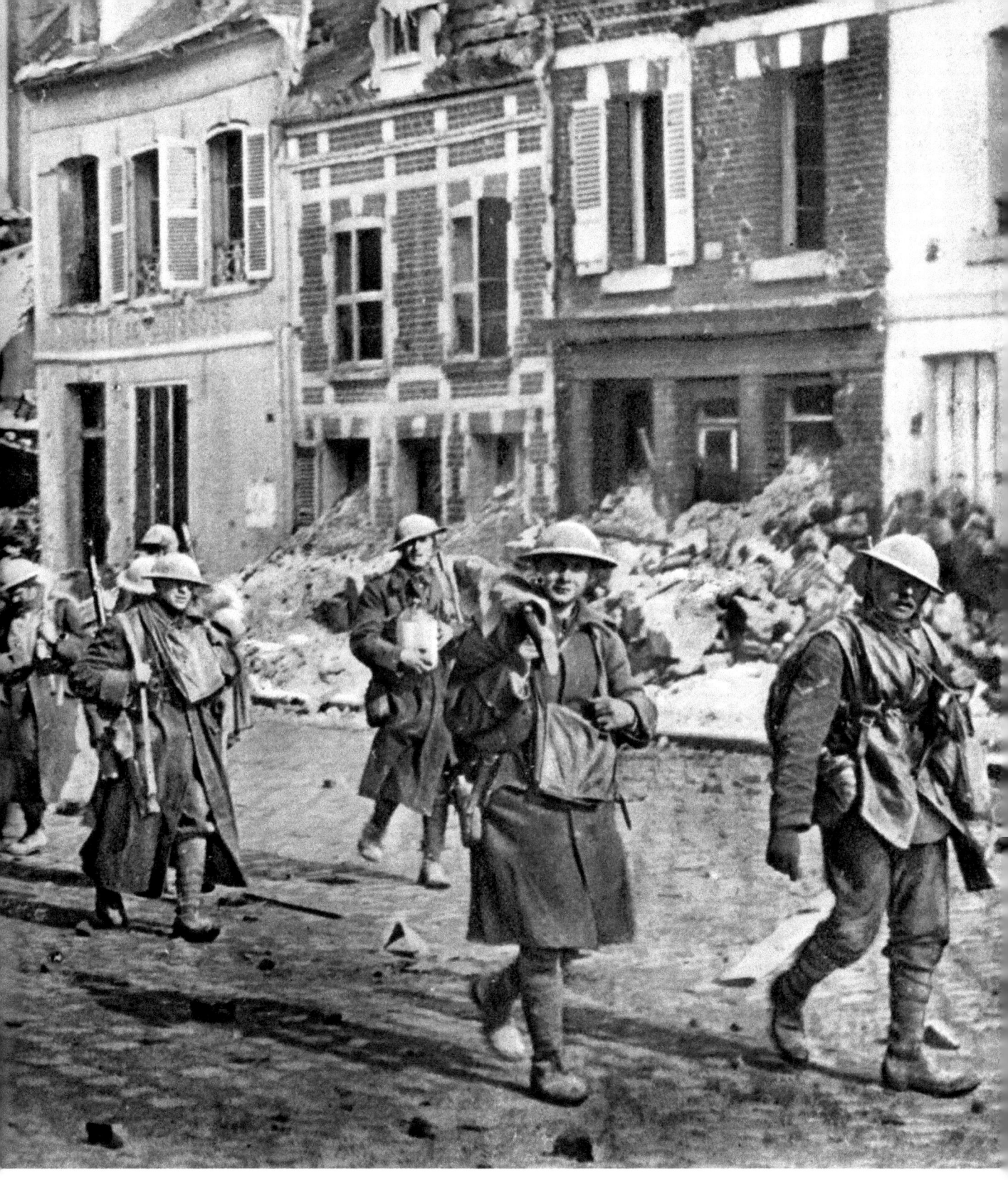

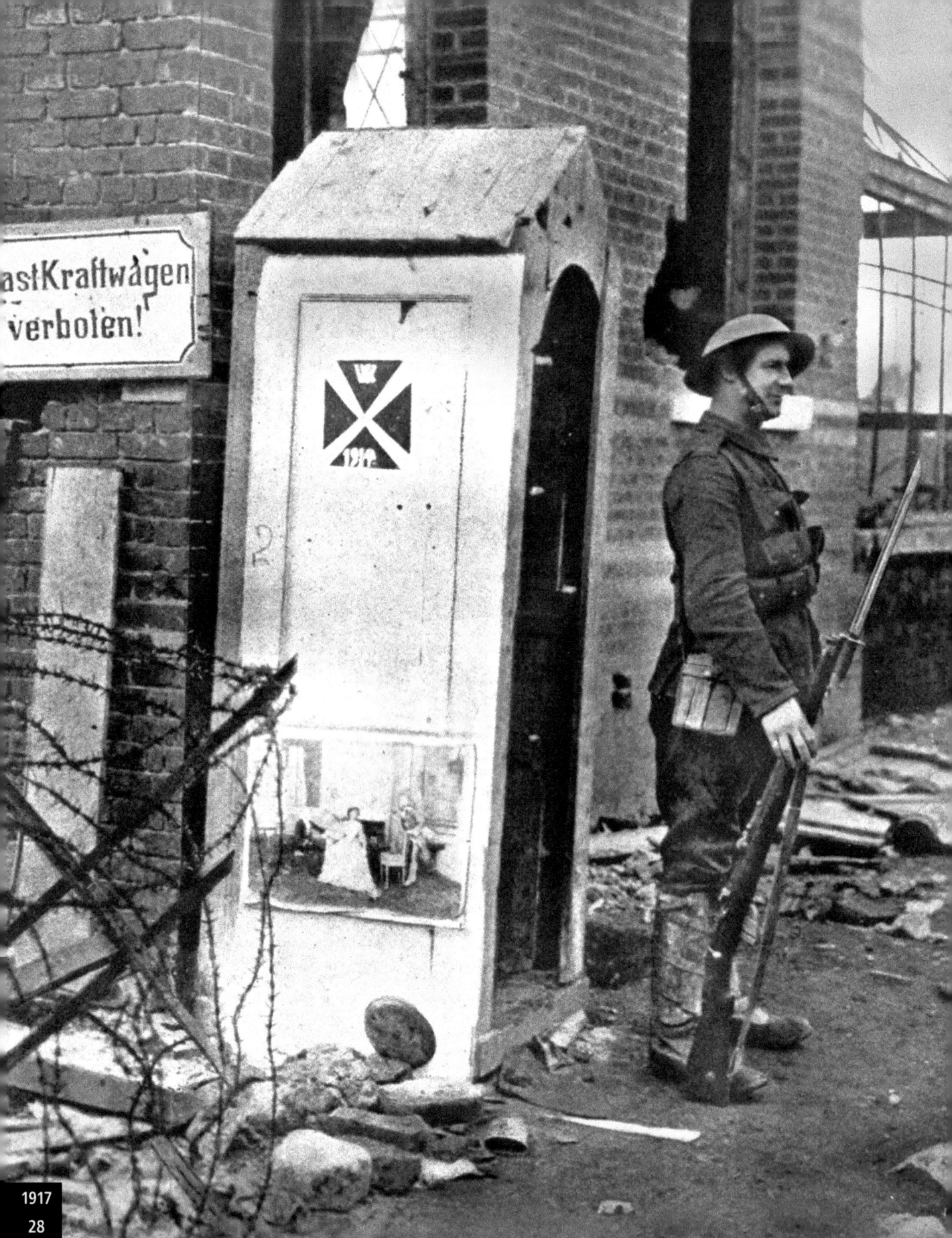

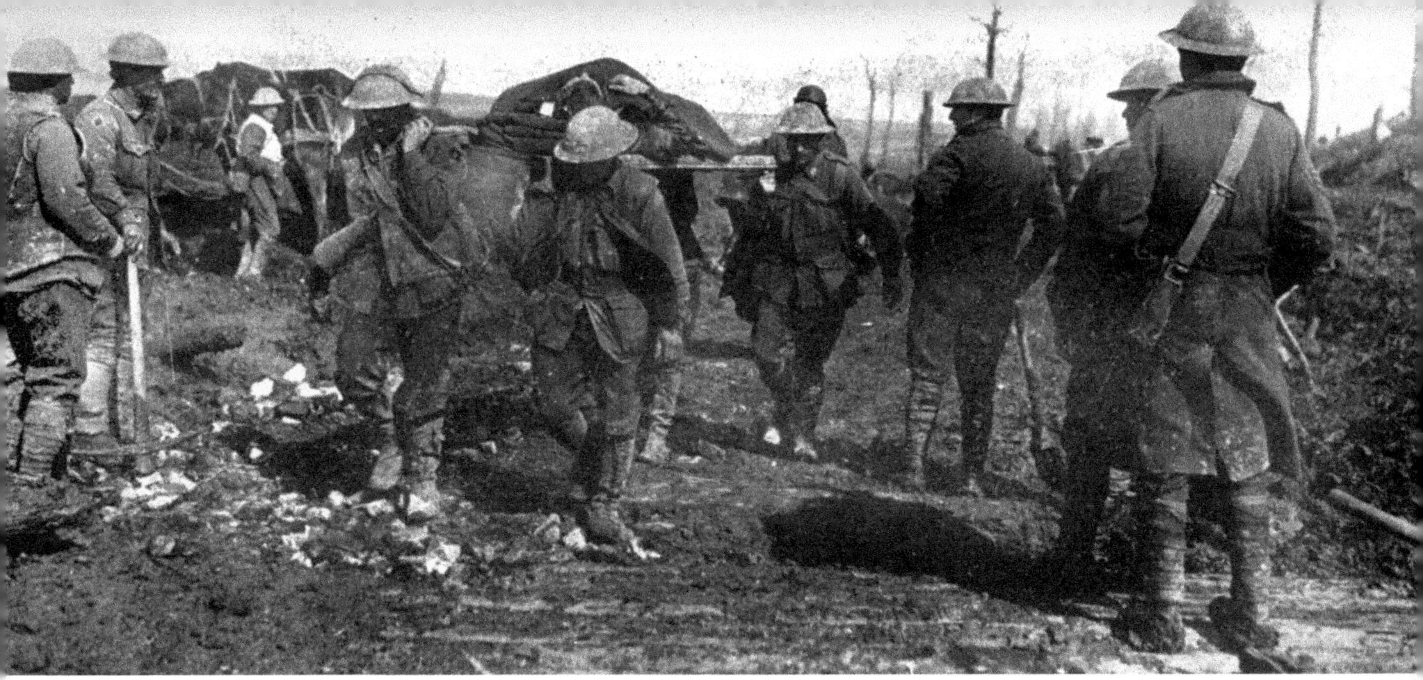

17GW052 An injured Royal Flying Corps pilot is being stretchered back to an aid post near Le Sars. Australian troops of the 2nd Pioneer Battalion halt in their work of repairing the Bapaume road as the party passes by.

17GW049 Under new management – a German sentry box in Bapaume put to good use by the British.

17GW060 An Australian work detail of 8 Brigade resting on the outskirts of Bapaume shortly after the town had been evacuated by the Germans. The men are wearing waterproof waders over their trousers.

17GW058 Australians of 8 Brigade moving through the smoking streets of Bapaume with extreme caution, on 17 March, the Germans having just left. Buildings have been demolished by controlled explosions and anything that may have proved useful to the allies had been destroyed or spoiled.

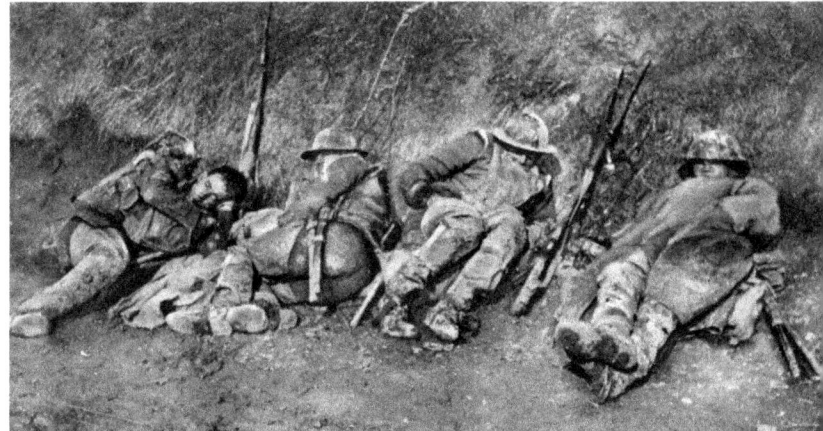

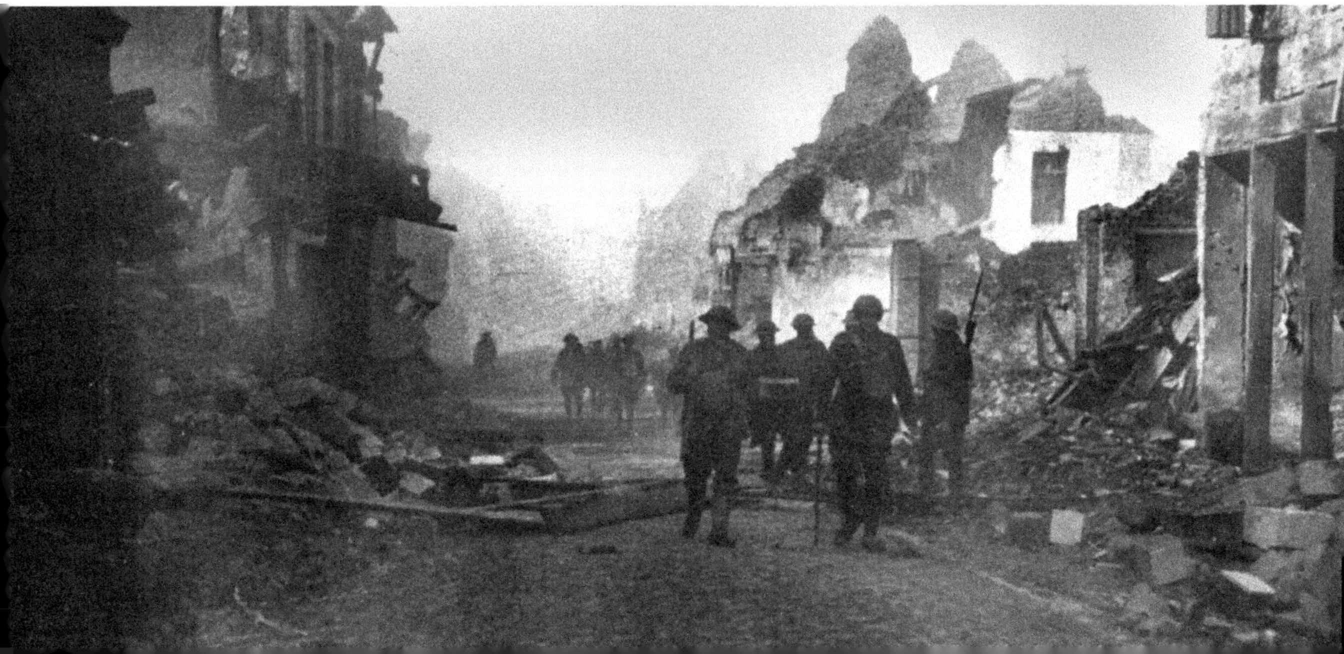

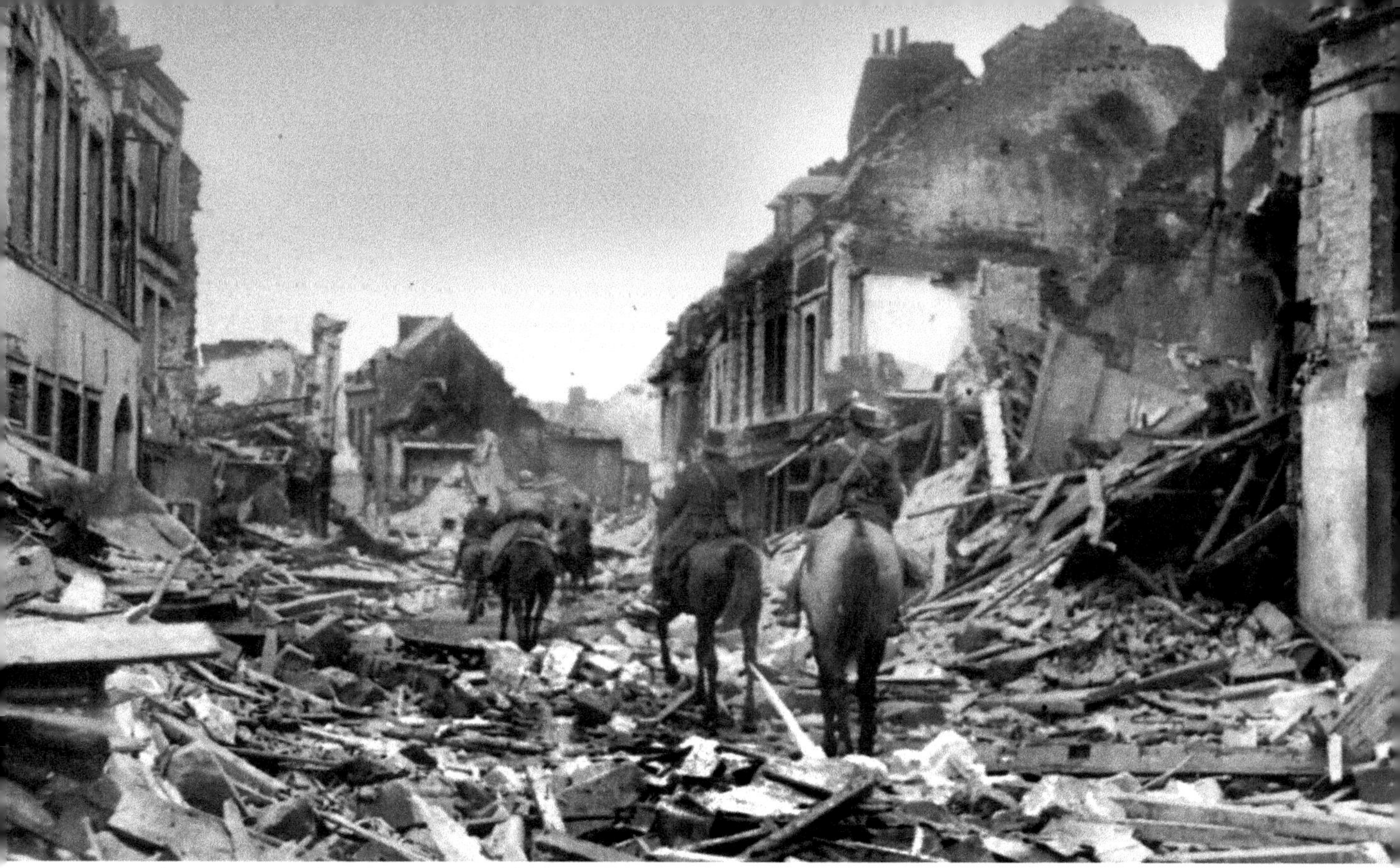

17GW012 A mounted patrol of the 2nd Australian Division in Bapaume, 19 March 1917. The town had been in allied hands for two days and the streets had been made near impassable by the retreating Germans. Booby traps had been left everywhere.

17GW061 Cheerful victors at a street barricade in Bapaume. These Australians of the 30th Battalian were among the first into the still-burning streets. Note the officer with his Webley service revolver drawn; also the soldier wearing a souvenir *pickelhaube*.

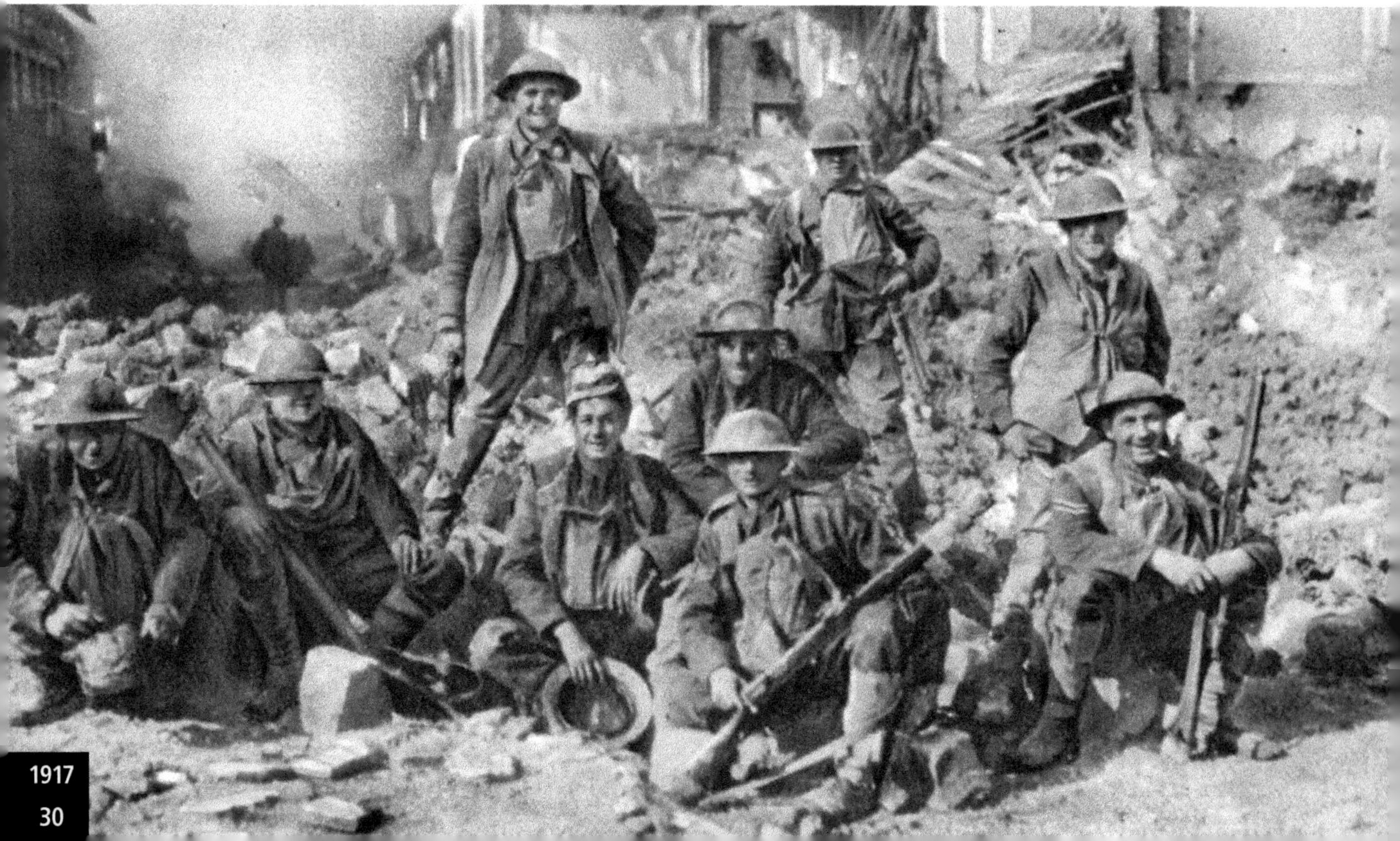

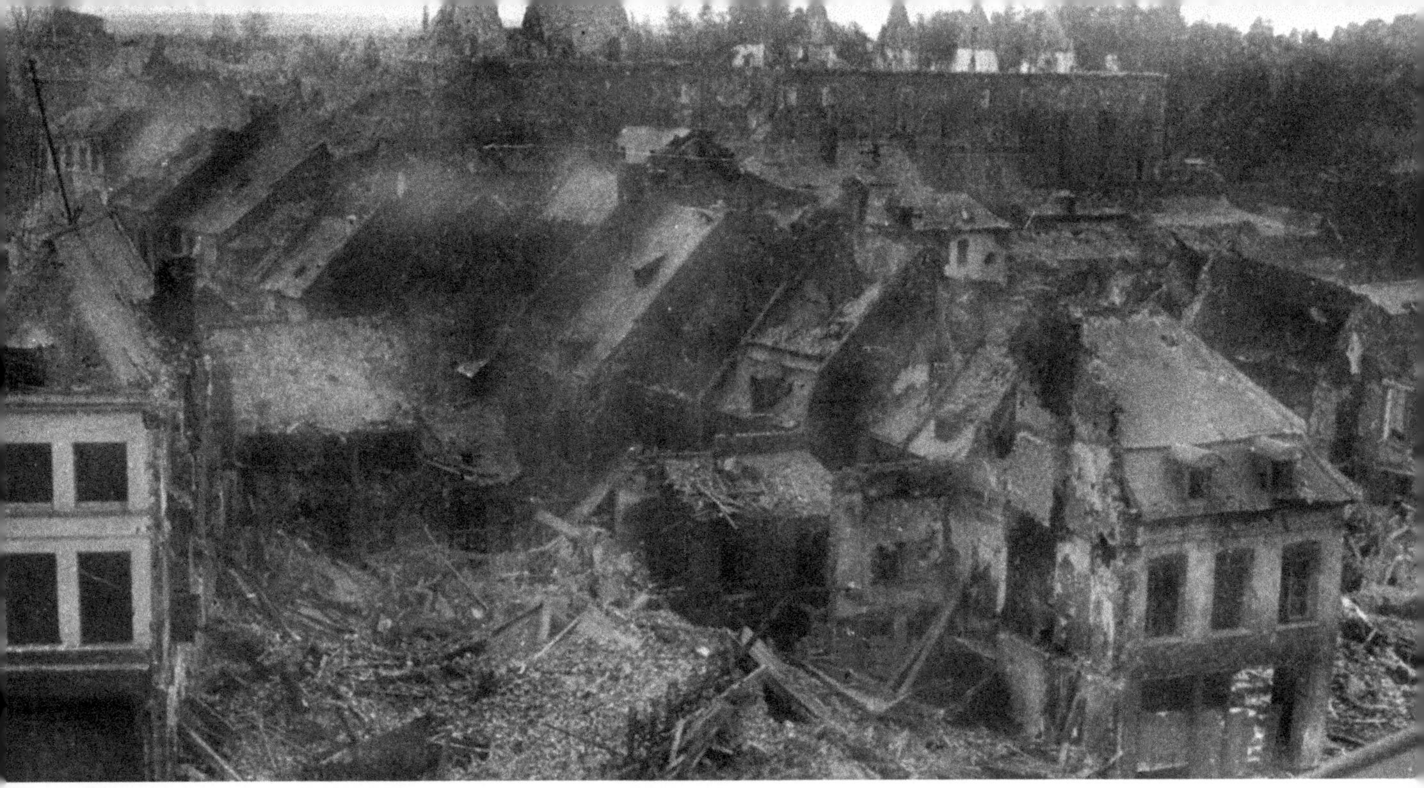

17GW059, 17GW063. Bapaume seen from the tower of the Mairie (town hall) before the booby trap bomb exploded.

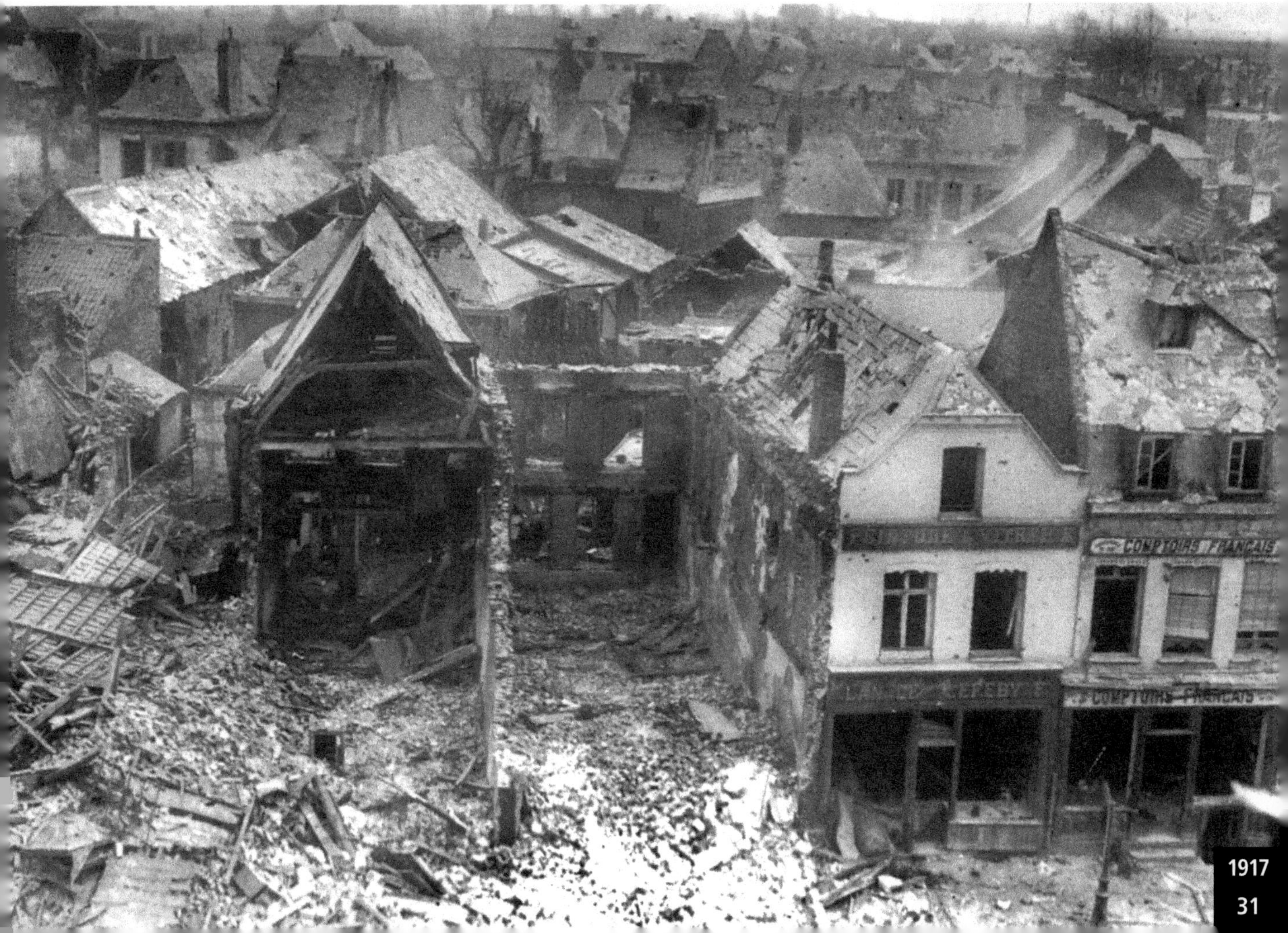

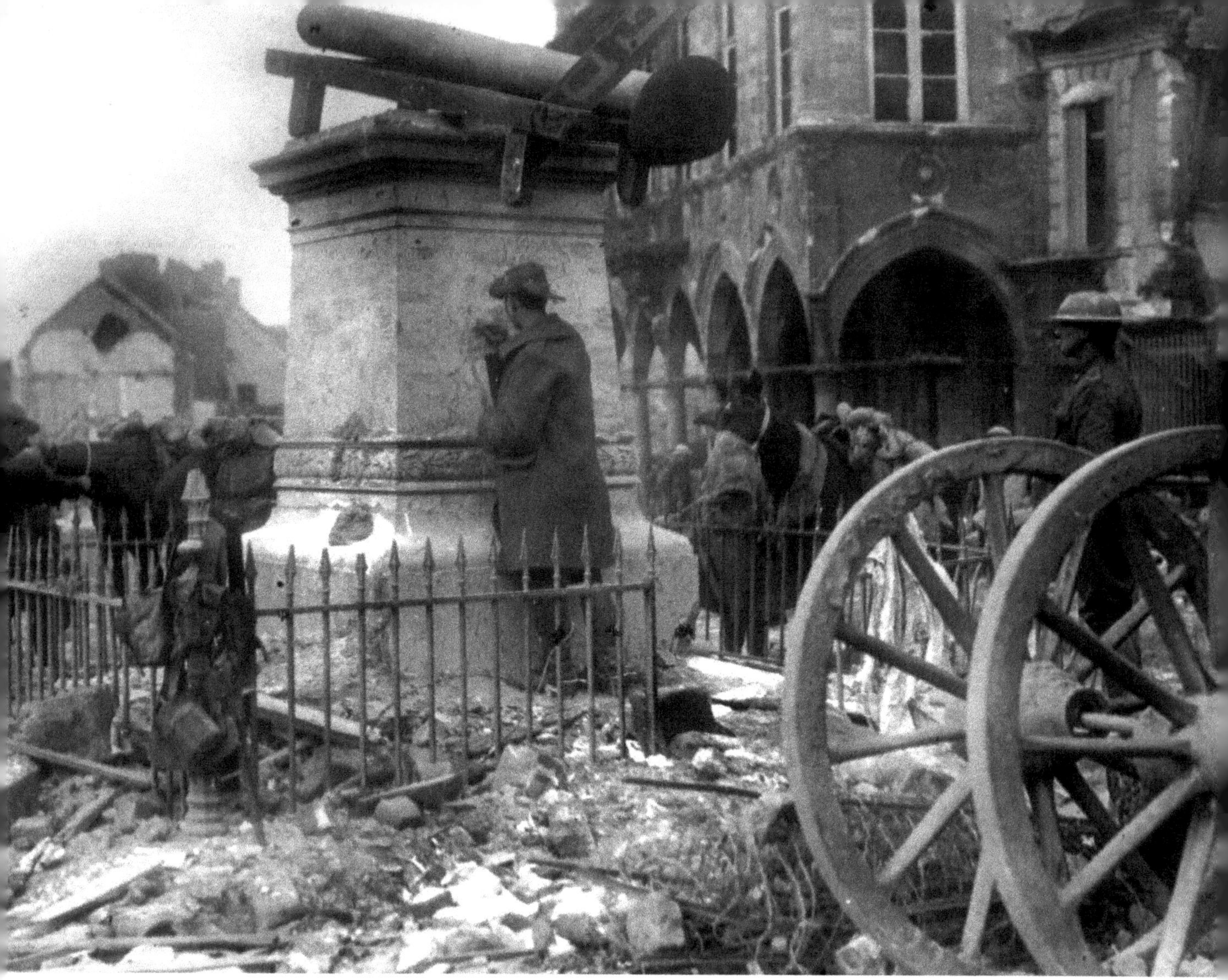

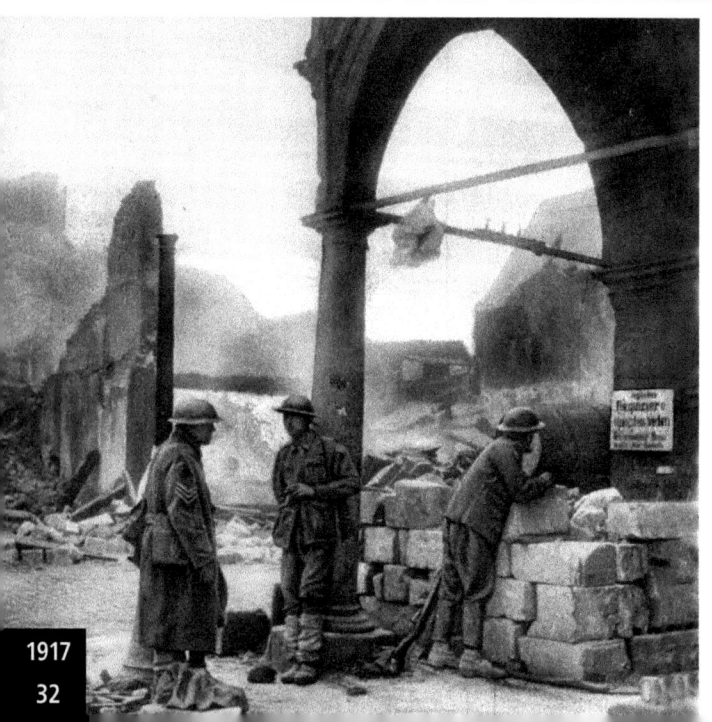

17GW019, 17GW017, 17GW065. Men of the Australian 2nd Division outside the Mairie (town hall) in Bapaume. The town was occupied by the Australians on 17 March 1917, following the German withdrawal to the Hindenburg Line. The Australian soldier above is scratching his name on a pedestal and doubtless many others followed to make their mark. They found the town hall, surprisingly, intact and proceeded to use the building to receive officers and civilians who came to inspect the damage caused by the fighting. At the time there was an explosive device with a delayed action fuse concealed in the building. A week later, 25 March, the timed mine blew the building to pieces, killing thirty people. The dead included local French politicians Raoul Briquet and Albert Tailliandier, who were organizing financial support for the inhabitants of the region.

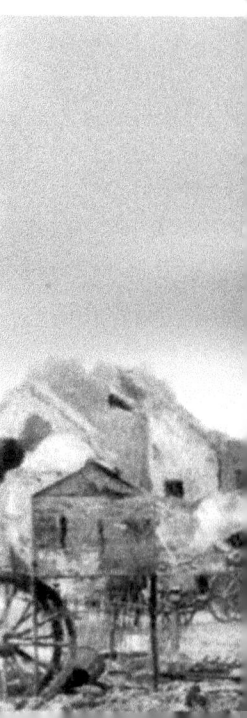

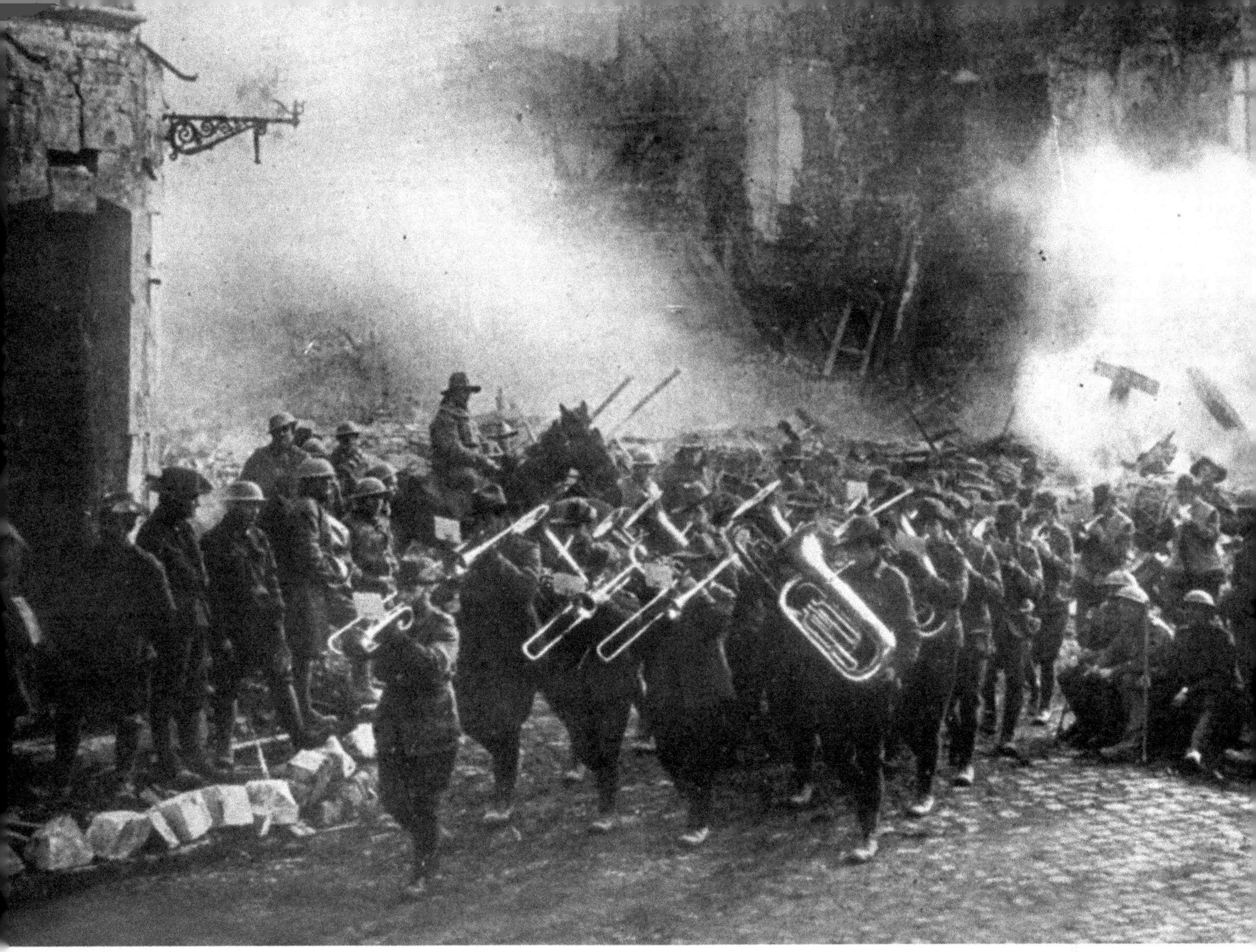

17GW062 The band of 5 Brigade playing in the Place Faidherbe, 19 March, as destroyed buildings were still burning.

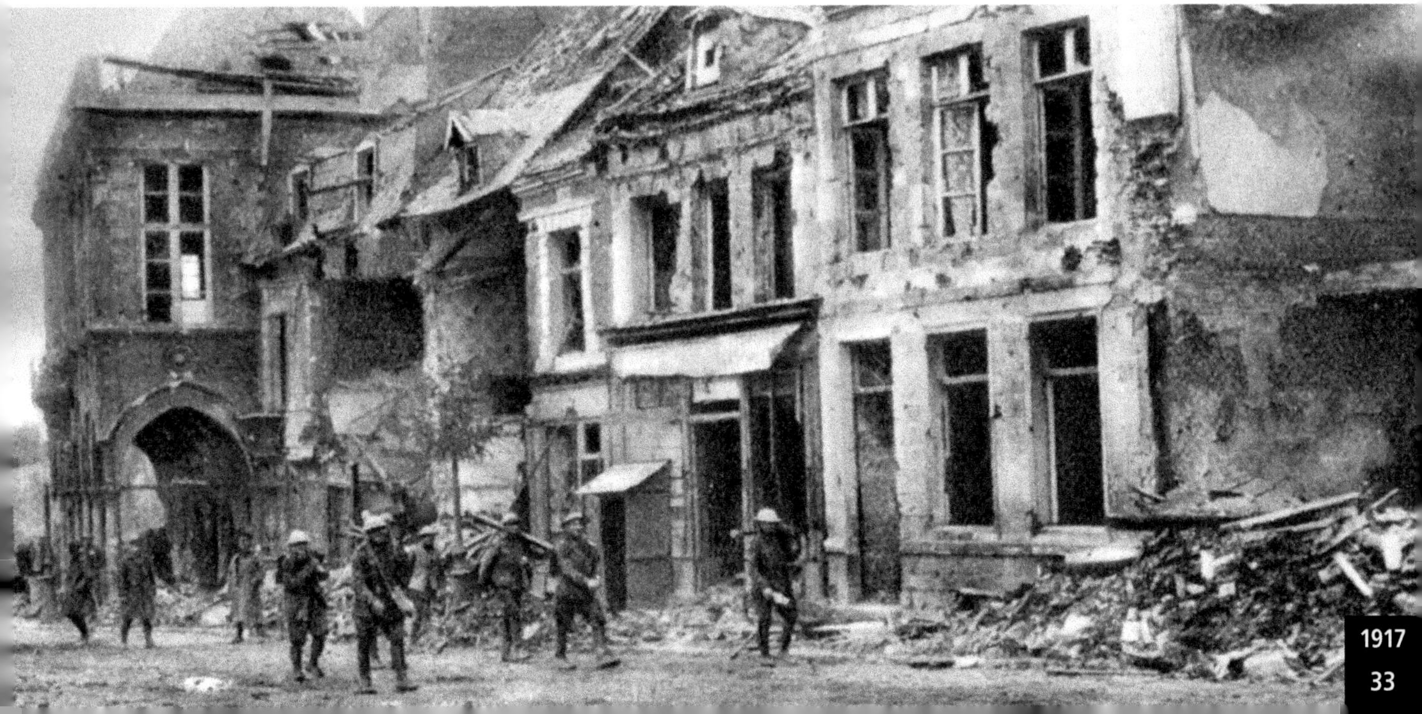

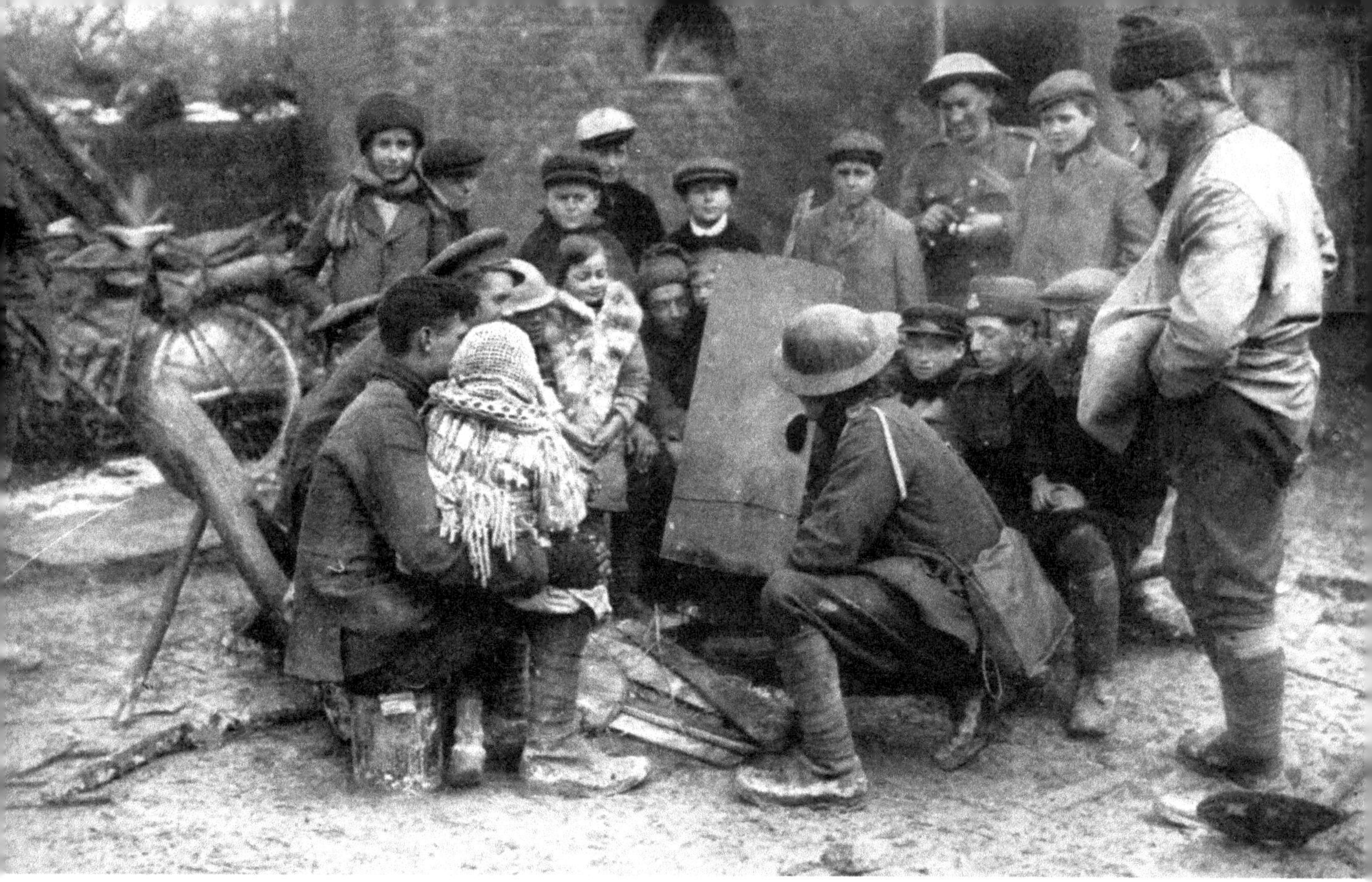

17GW064 French village children being amused by British troops round the makings of a camp fire in a street.

17GW011 A water detail of British and French soldiers around a well. Many water sources had been deliberately contaminated.

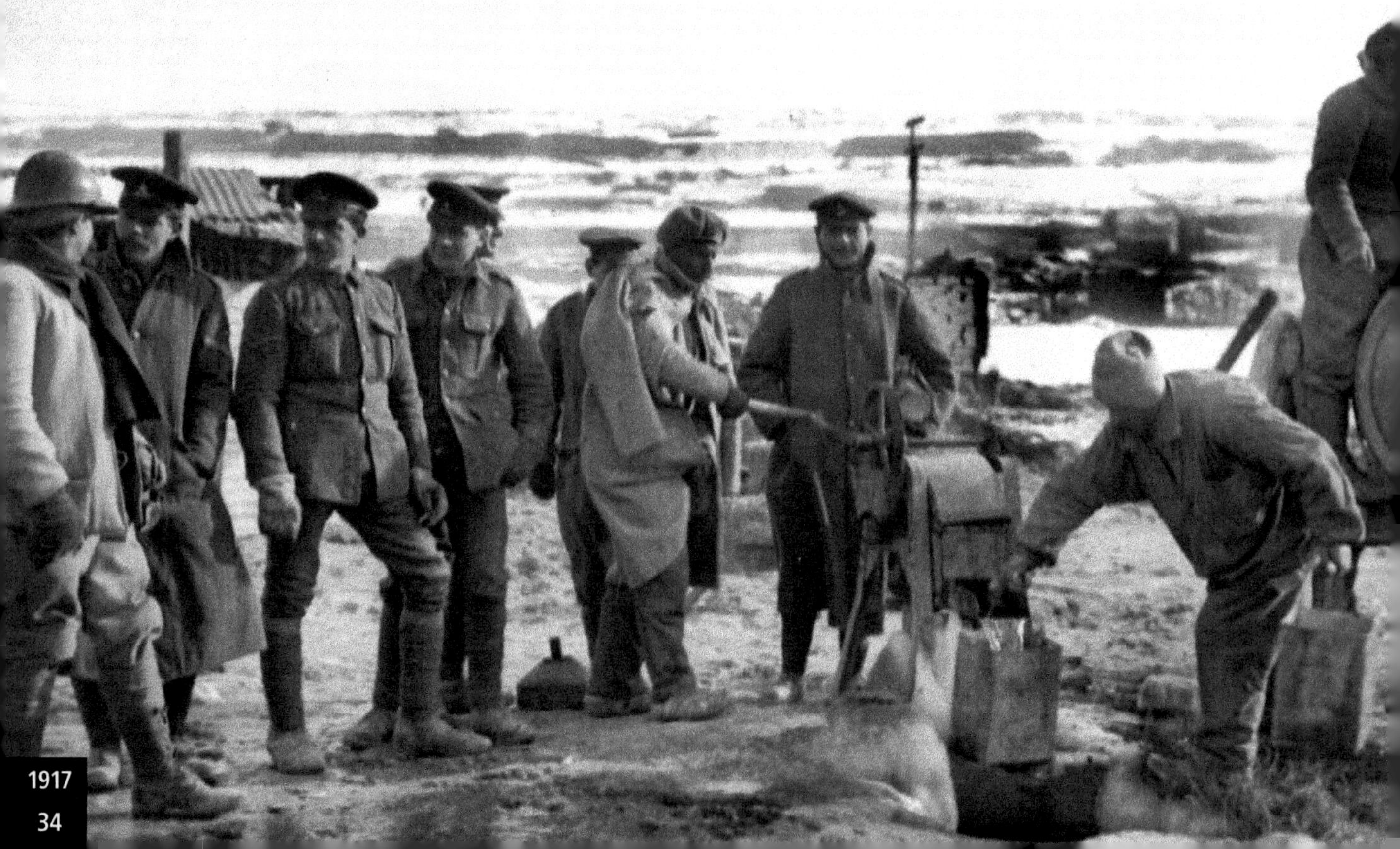

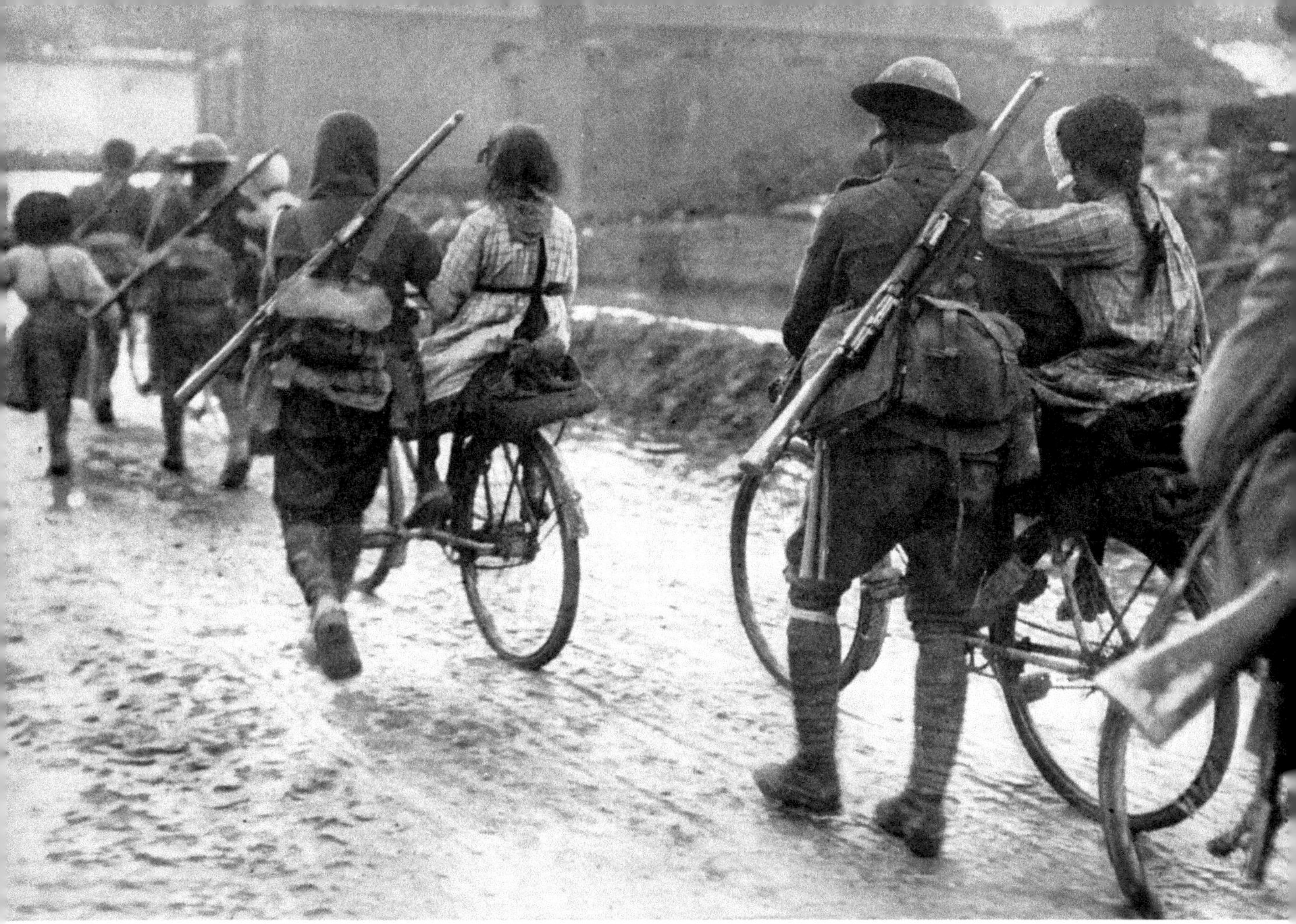

17GW066, 17GW067. French children enjoying bike rides provided by members of the Cyclist Corps.

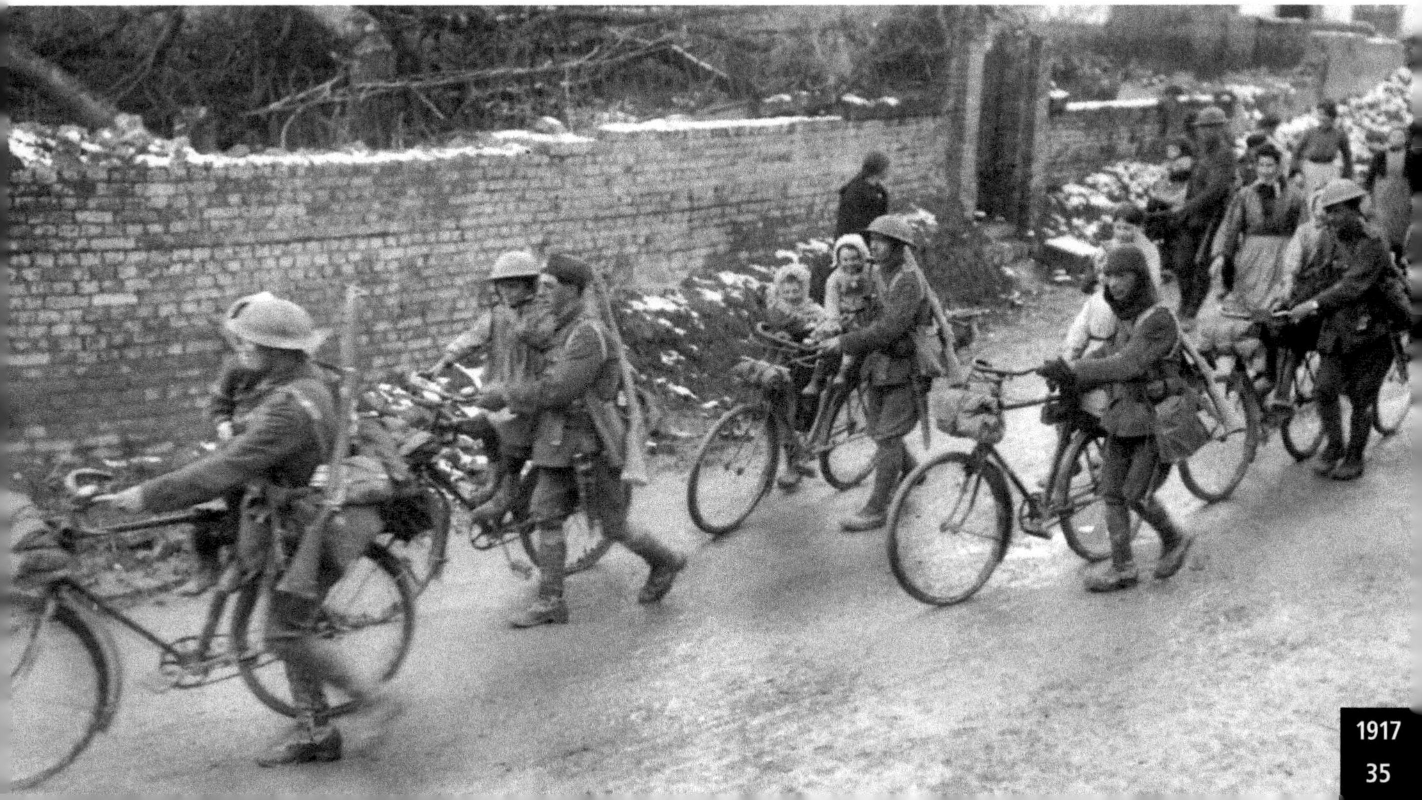

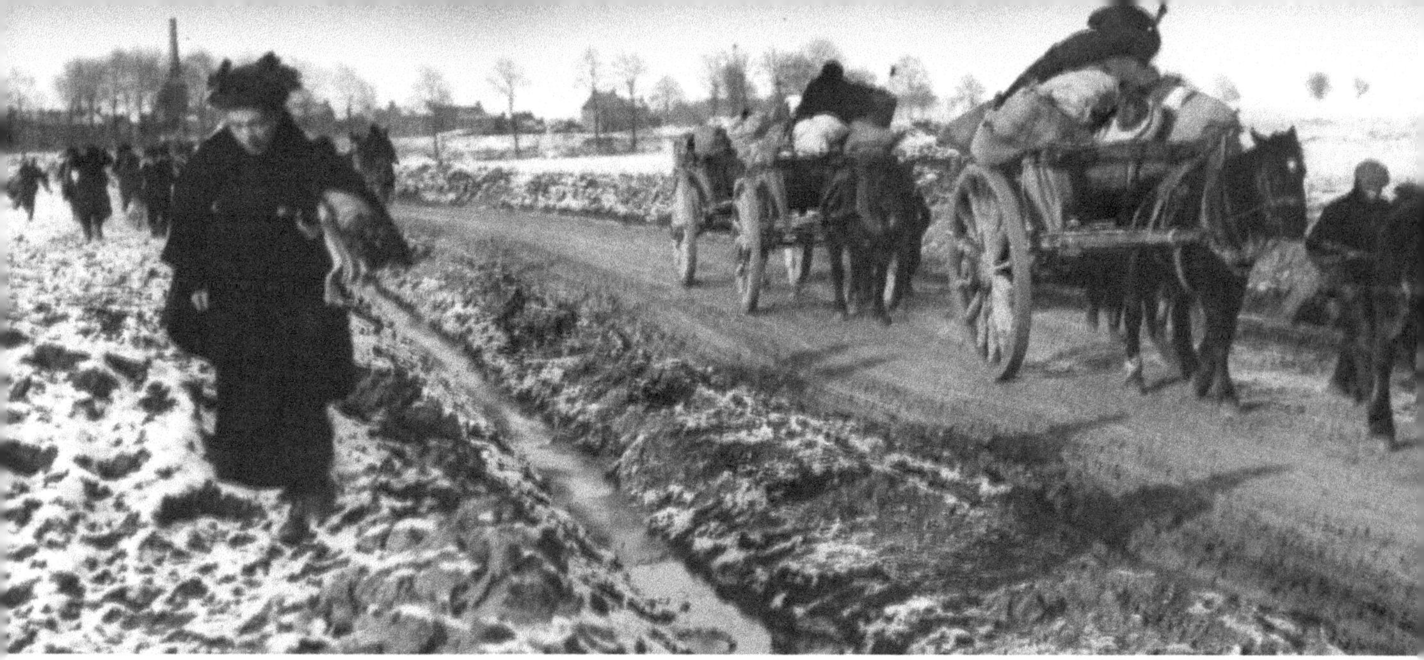

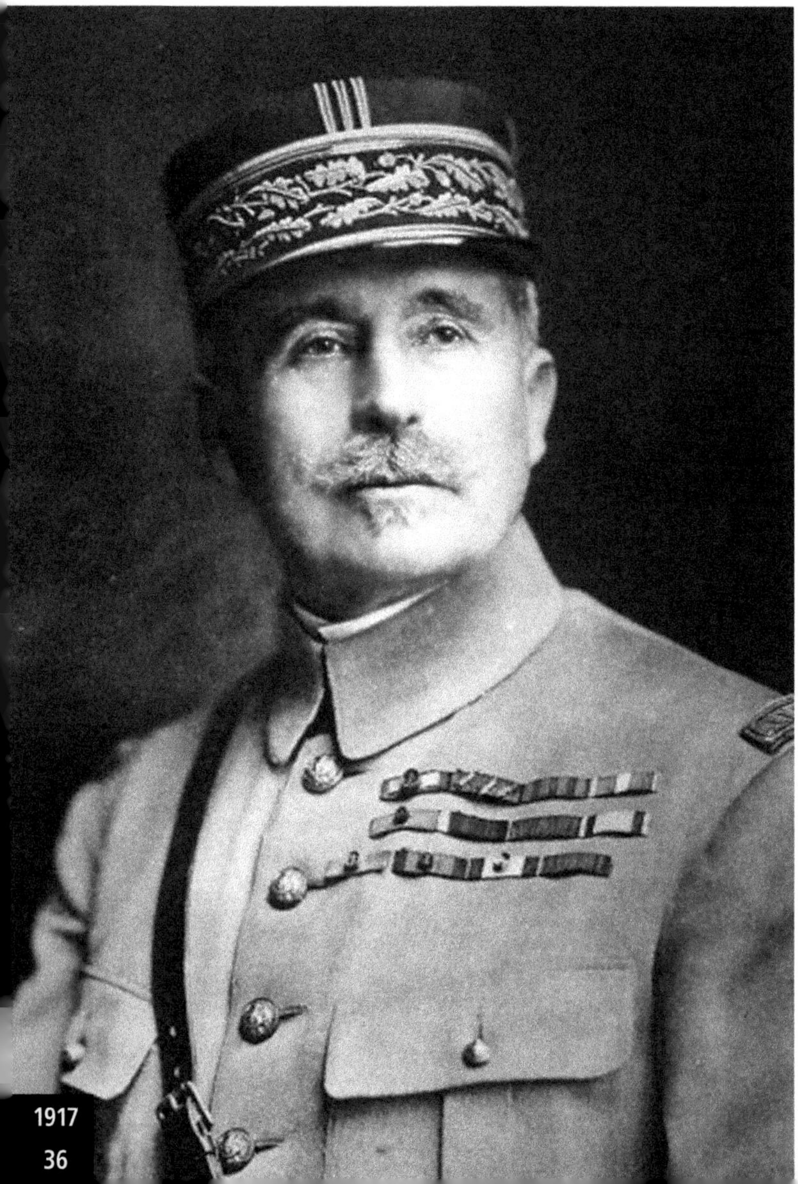

17GW070 The area the Germans had withdrawn from had been turned into a wasteland and the active male civilians moved east for forced labour. Those who remained, old men, women and children, were left with a few days' supply of food.

17GW069 French civilians gather around a British army's official photographer's car for a distribution of food.

17GW069 Women and children left in the village of Nesle chat to French and British troops.

17GW072 In December 1916 General Robert Nivelle, following several successful months in command at Verdun, became the commander in chief of the French armies on the Western Front, succeeding Joffre. Fluent in English (his mother was British) and a convincing speaker, he persuaded reluctant French politicians (and dazzled Lloyd George) to engage in a huge spring offensive, centred on the Chemin des Dames, to the east of Rheims. The British attack at Arras was designed to commit the Germans to that area, whilst the French offensive was launched a week or so later. Once that began, Haig could halt – or at least limit – his attack. Nivelle promised great things; and it was the failure to live up to these that caused his downfall and shook (but never broke) the French army's morale. The relative failure of Nivelle's offensive was a contributory factor to the British attack continuing far longer than originally intended. The timing of the German withdrawal came as a considerable surprise; its importance to the French attack was the number of divisions (and associated artillery) that this straightening of the line freed up for the use of the Germans – who, in any case, had a pretty shrewd idea what was being planned for them.

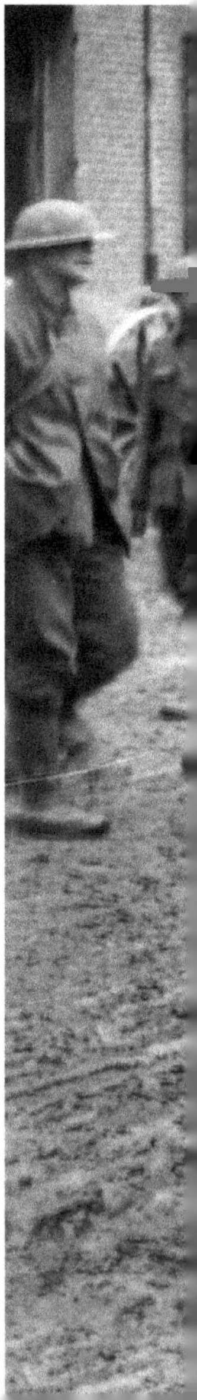

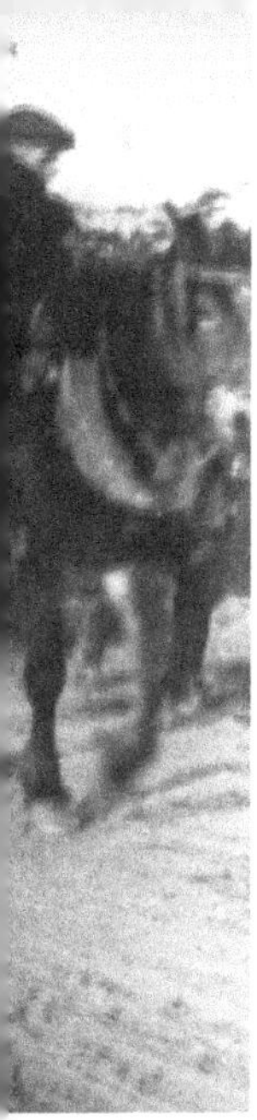

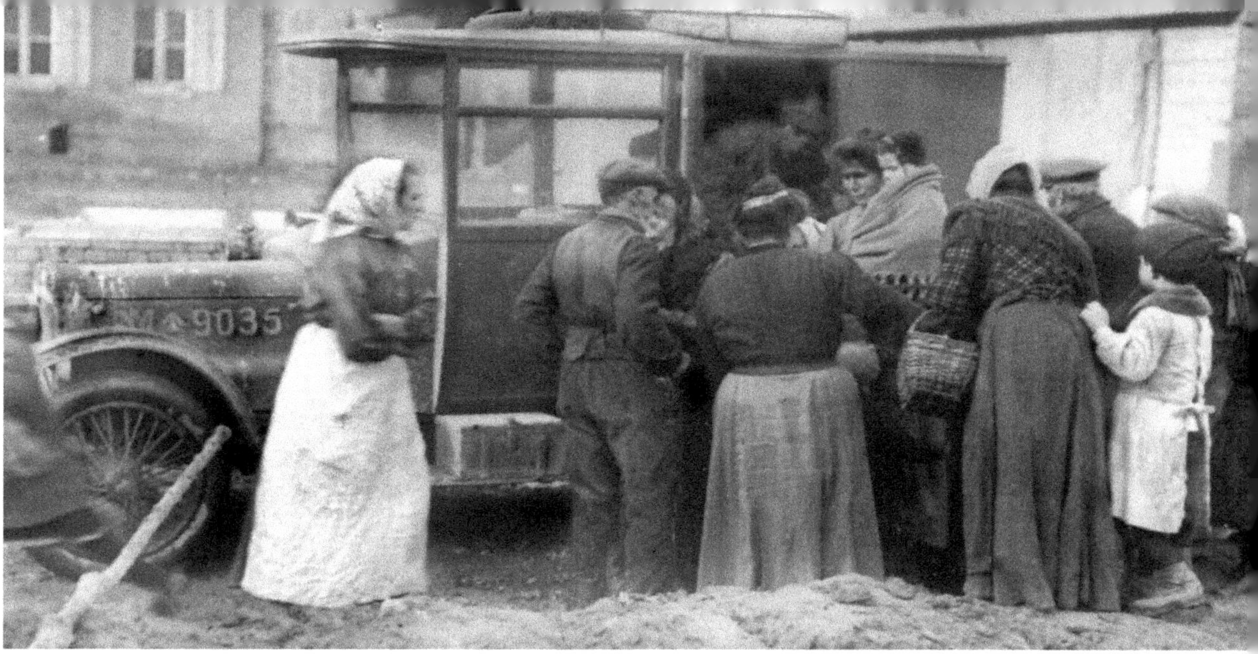

1917

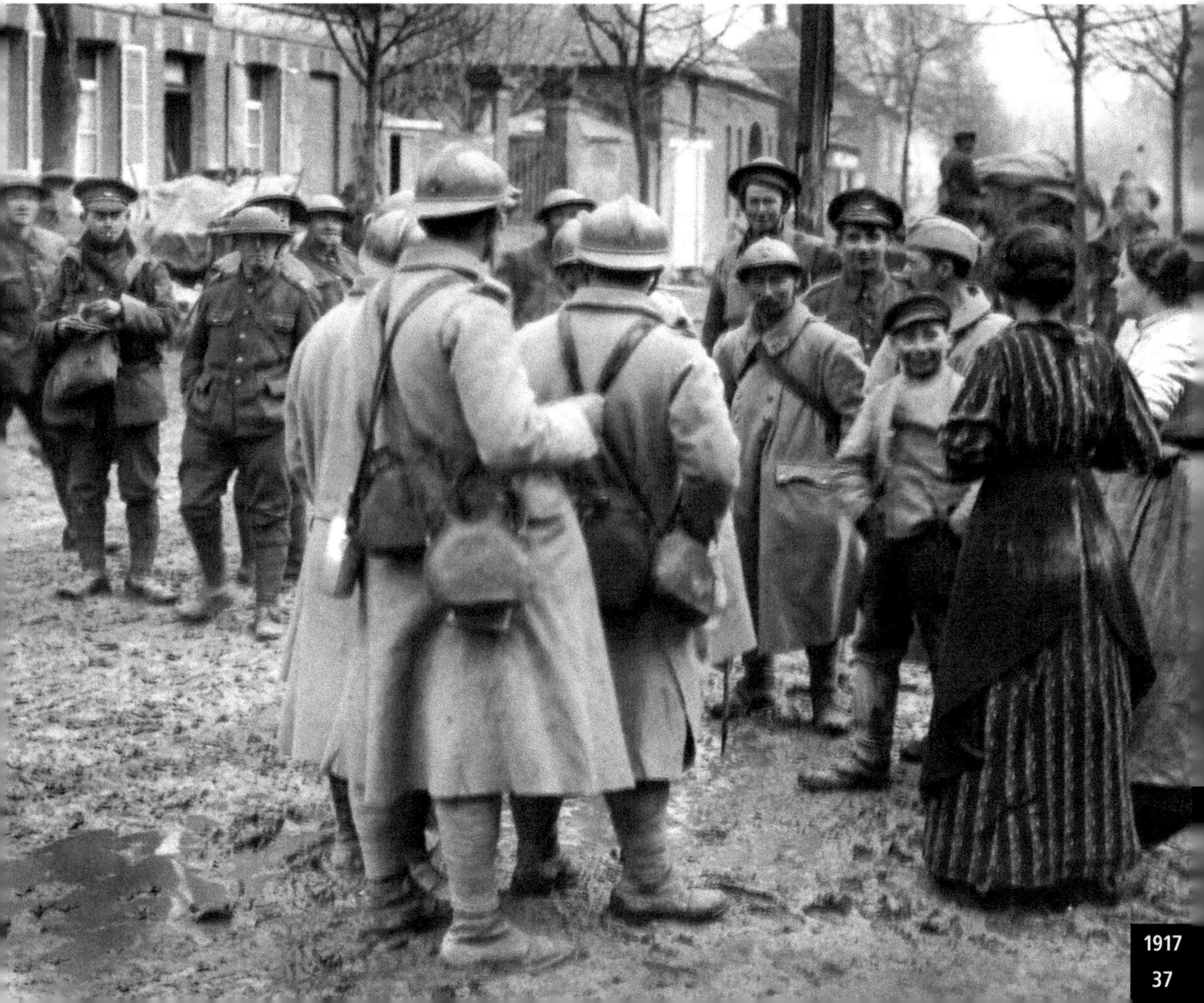

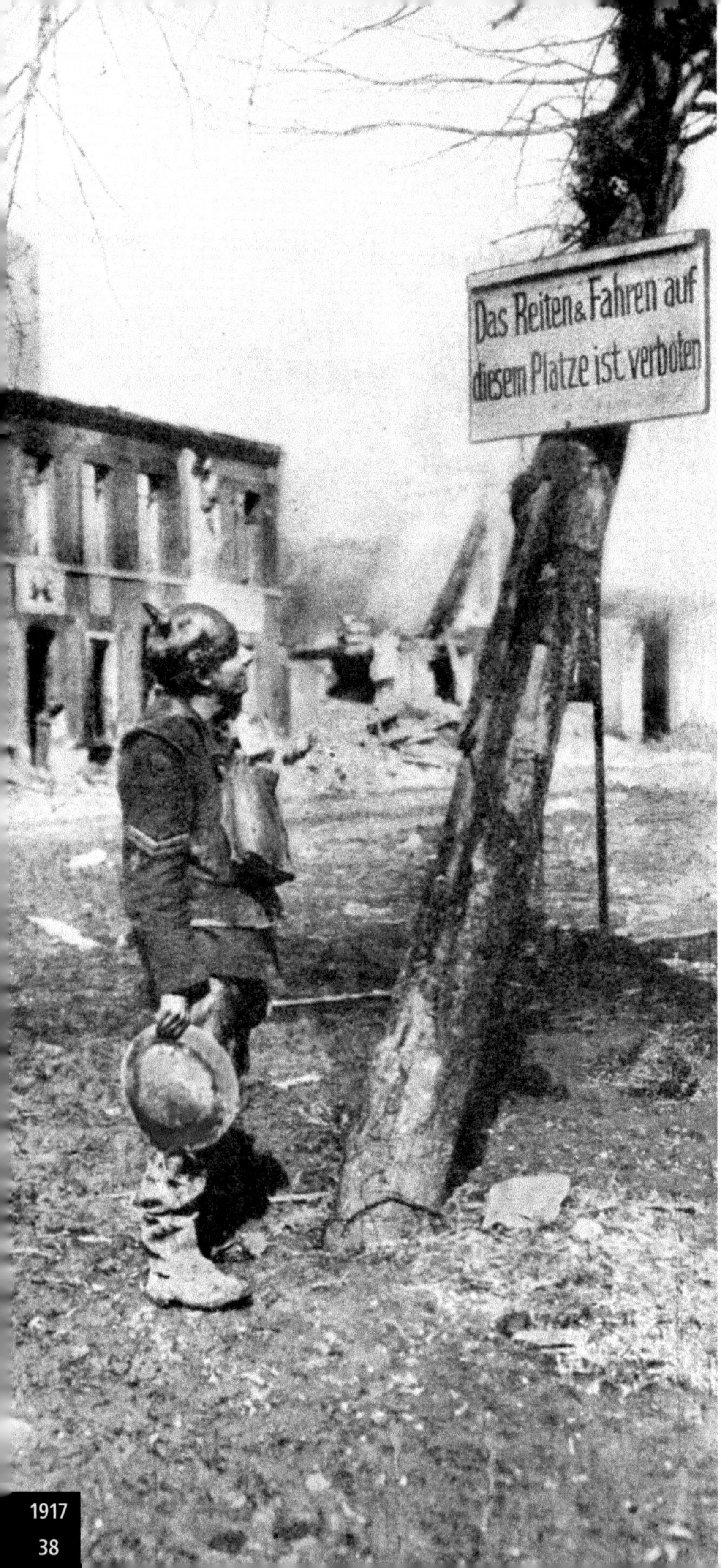

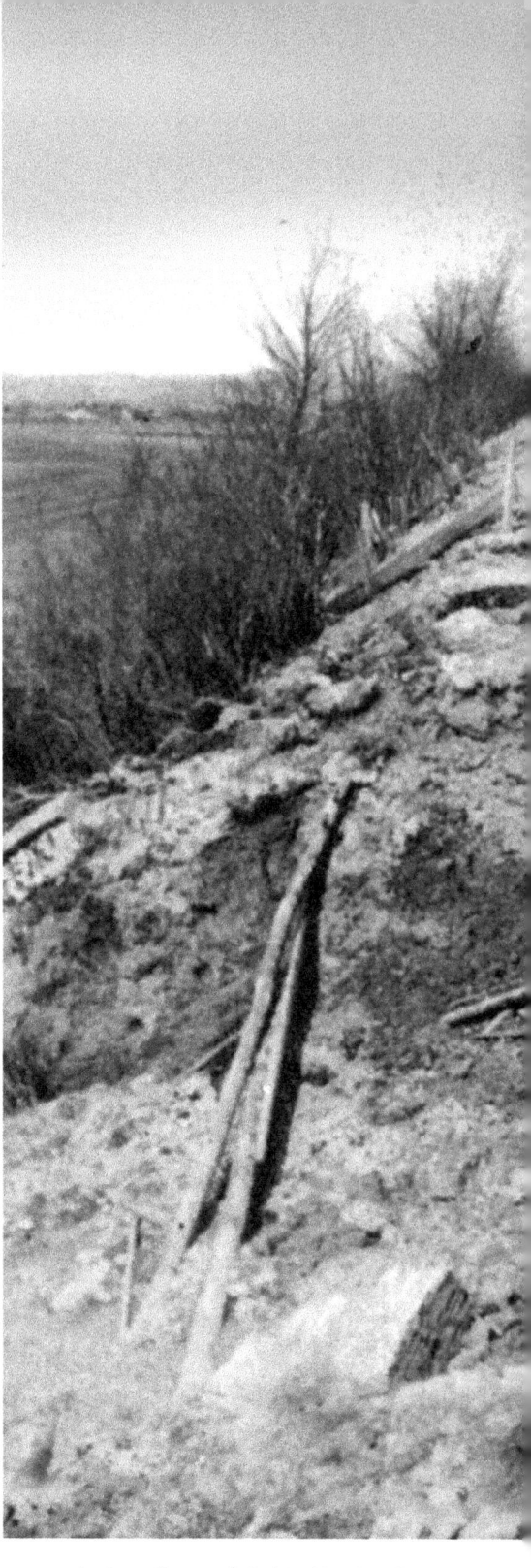

17GW068 An Australian corporal of the 30th Battalion reads one of the many signs left by the retreating Germans: *Das Reiten & Fahren auf diesen Platze ist verboten* – Riding and driving on this ground is forbidden.

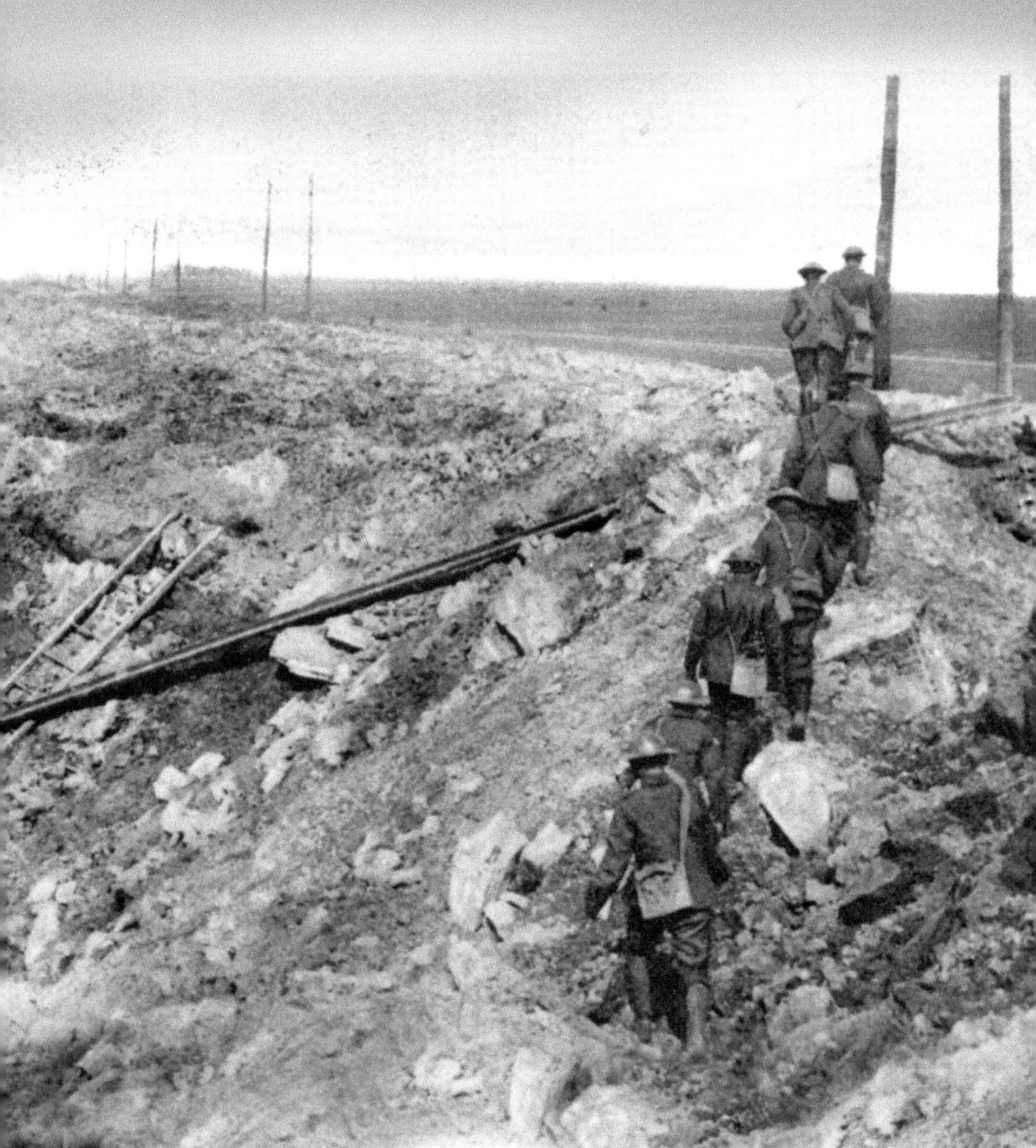

17GW073 British troops make their way up to a totally wrecked railway viaduct and embankment. In addition to burning villages and towns, cutting down fruit trees, poisoning wells and blowing up crossroads, entire lengths of railway were rendered unusable: the railway tracks were twisted out of shape on fires made of railway sleepers; even the hardcore foundation was taken up. In the instance above, the line of telegraph poles has been left (likely at the request of the German artillery spotters manning the Hindenburg Line on the horizon).

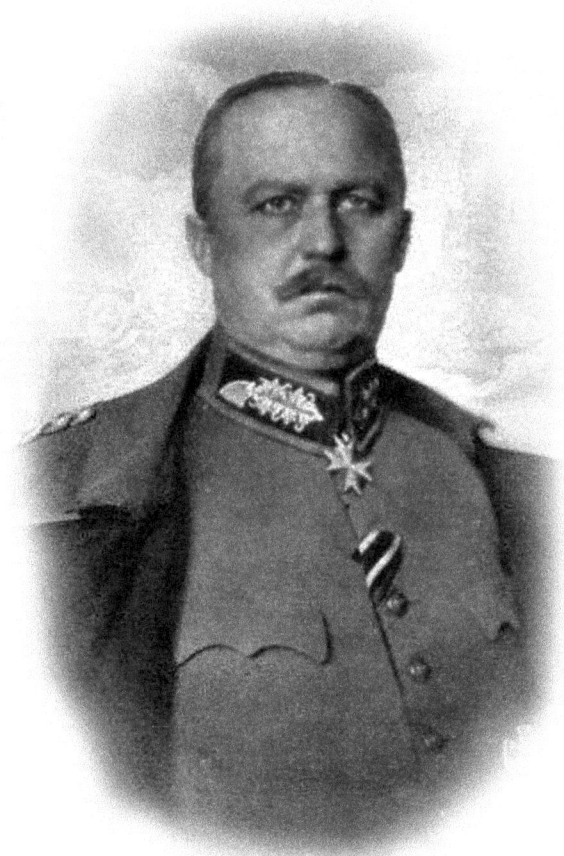

General der Infanterie Erich Friedrich Wilhelm Ludendorff on Operation *'Alberich'*:
The main point was to avoid a battle.
We also had to salvage all equipment that was not built into the ground and the raw materials necessary to warfare, to destroy communication lines, villages and wells, in order to prevent a massive and quick occupation of the terrain by the enemy.
The order was issued that springs were not to be poisoned.
(But wells were by throwing dead animals down them.)

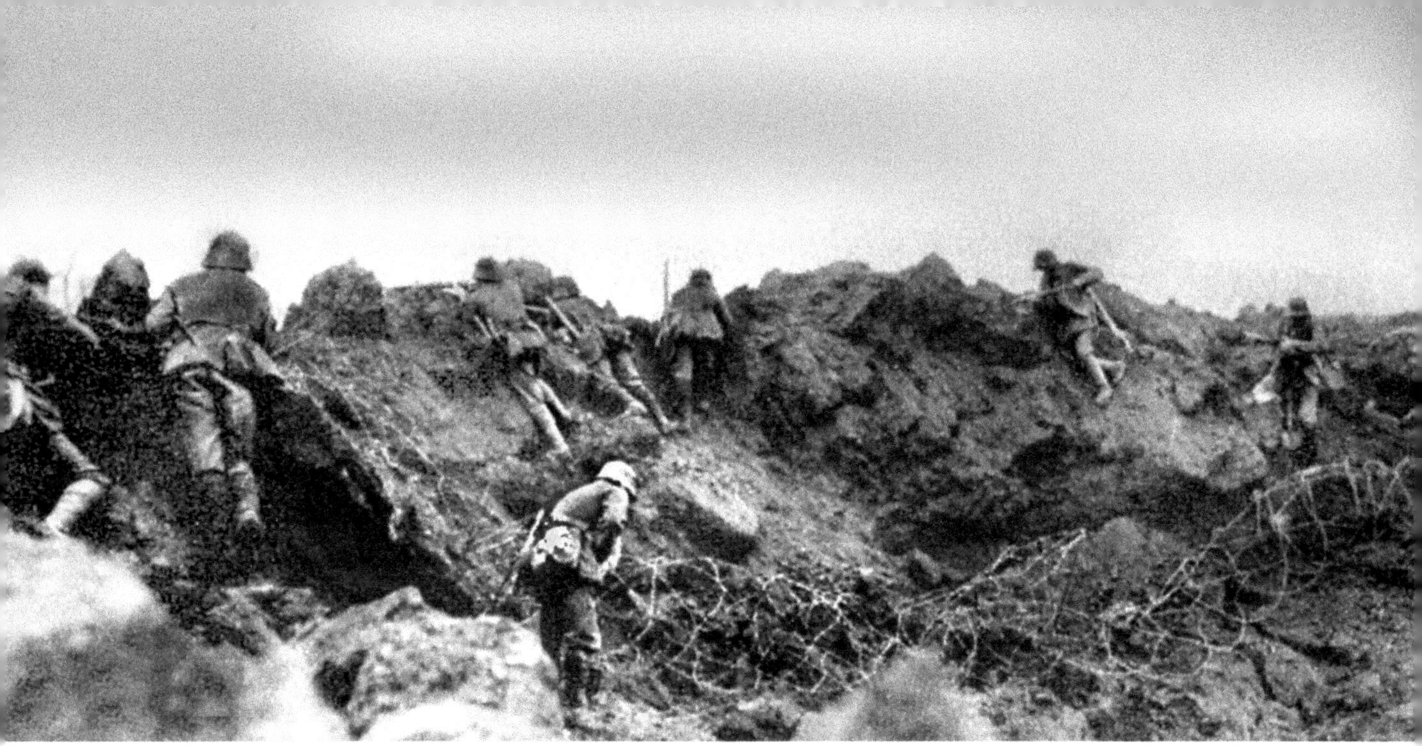

Chapter Two: Arras – Vimy Ridge

17GW075 German *Sturmtruppen* consolidating for defence a recently blown mine crater near Arras.

17GW074 A pipe band of a Scottish regiment playing through the ruined streets of Arras, April 1917.

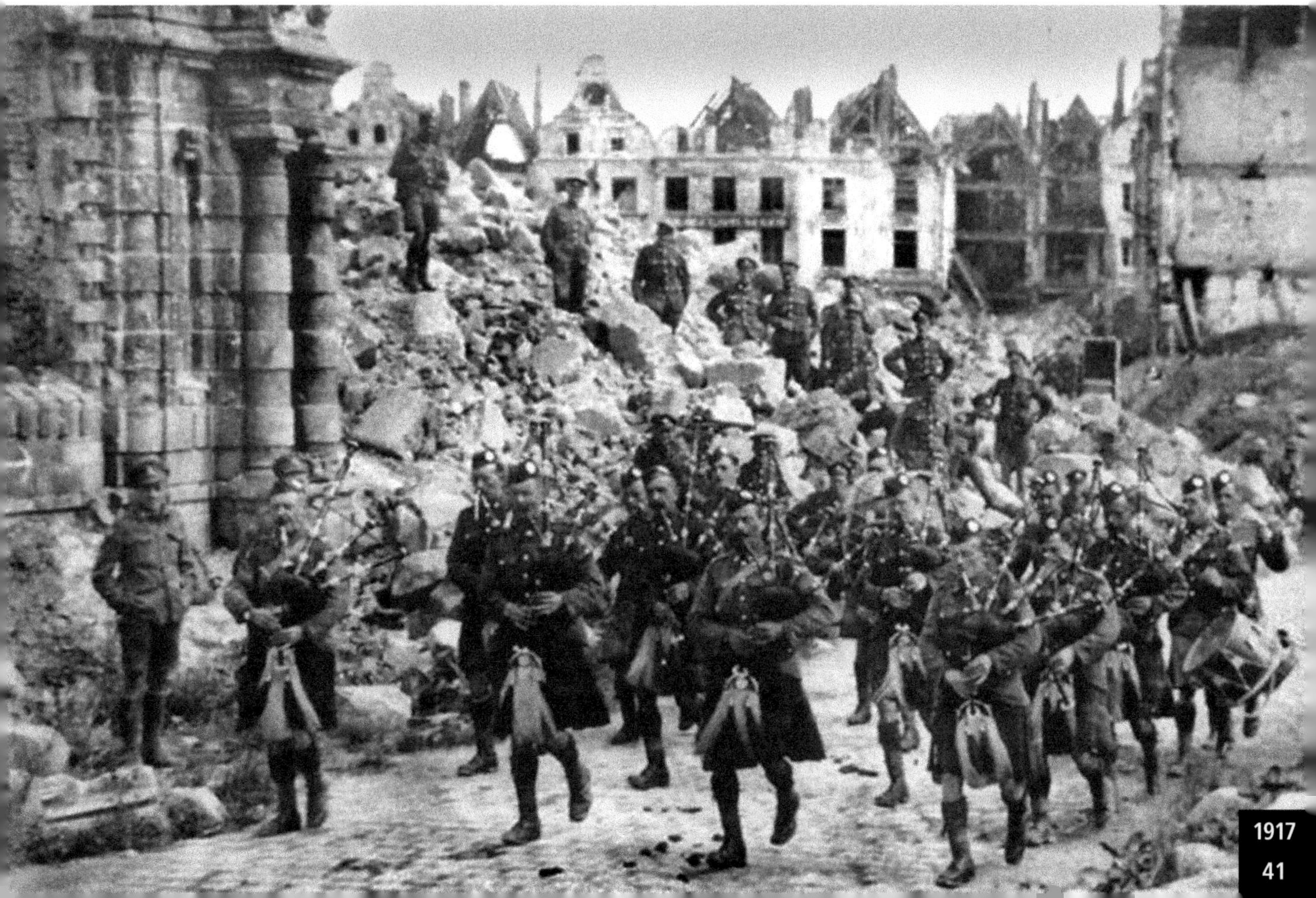

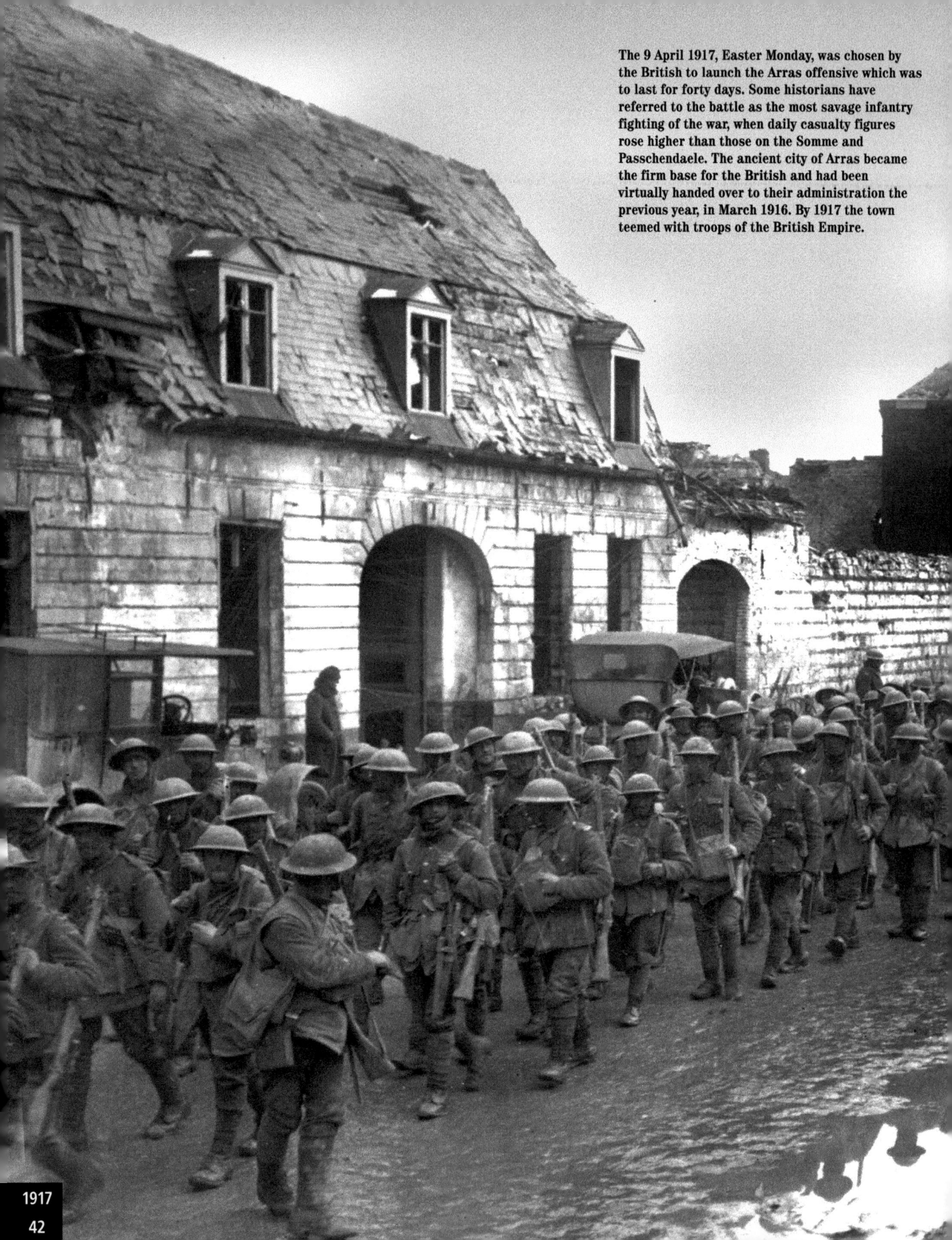

The 9 April 1917, Easter Monday, was chosen by the British to launch the Arras offensive which was to last for forty days. Some historians have referred to the battle as the most savage infantry fighting of the war, when daily casualty figures rose higher than those on the Somme and Passchendaele. The ancient city of Arras became the firm base for the British and had been virtually handed over to their administration the previous year, in March 1916. By 1917 the town teemed with troops of the British Empire.

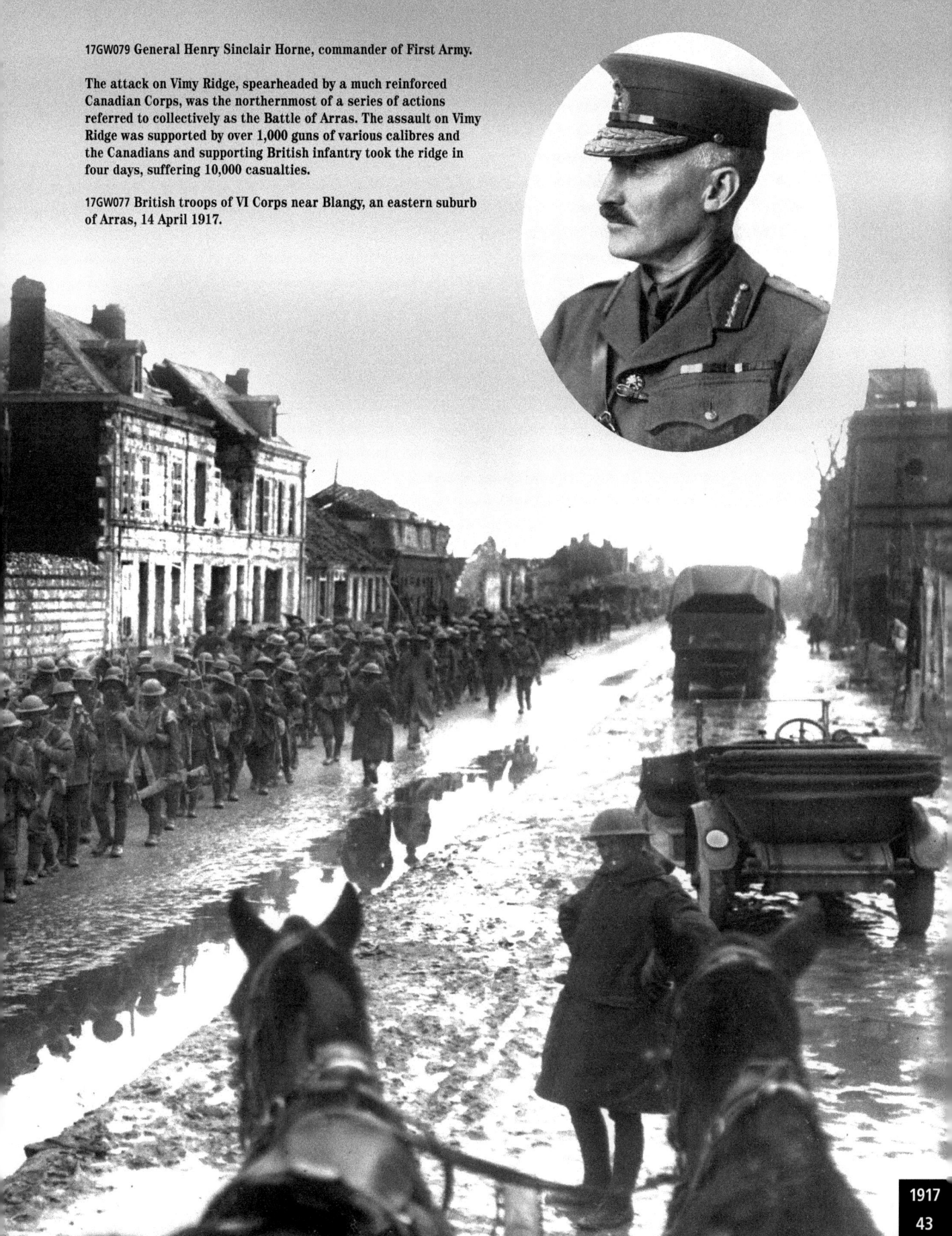

17GW079 General Henry Sinclair Horne, commander of First Army.

The attack on Vimy Ridge, spearheaded by a much reinforced Canadian Corps, was the northernmost of a series of actions referred to collectively as the Battle of Arras. The assault on Vimy Ridge was supported by over 1,000 guns of various calibres and the Canadians and supporting British infantry took the ridge in four days, suffering 10,000 casualties.

17GW077 British troops of VI Corps near Blangy, an eastern suburb of Arras, 14 April 1917.

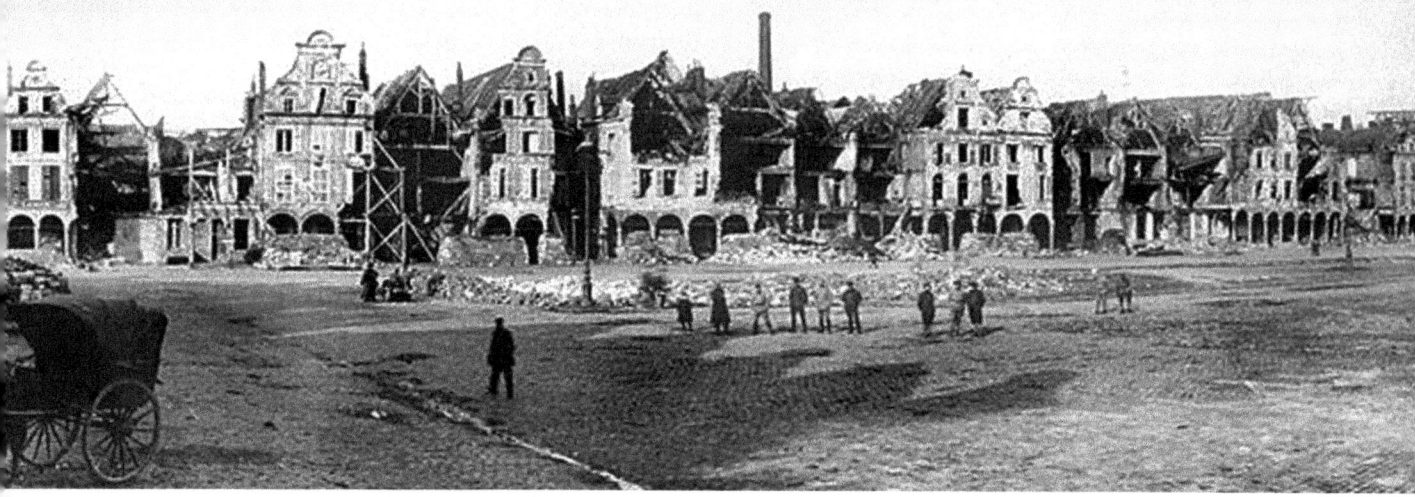

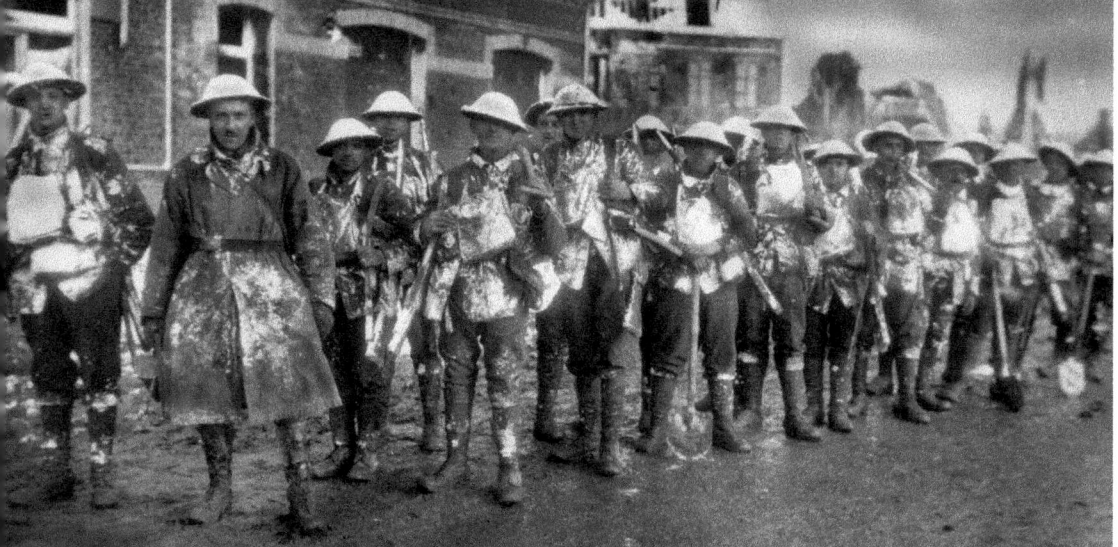

17GW225 The Grand Place, Arras, at the time when the British took over this sector of the Western Front.

17GW227 Soldiers forming a working party in the city of Arras, 10 April 1917. The British offensive east of the town has just begun.

17GW229 A French youngster, who has acquired a British steel helmet, selling newspapers – the *Daily Mail* or the *Daily Mirror* – to British troops at Arras.

17GW228 A British supply convoy entering Arras through the Baudimont Gate.

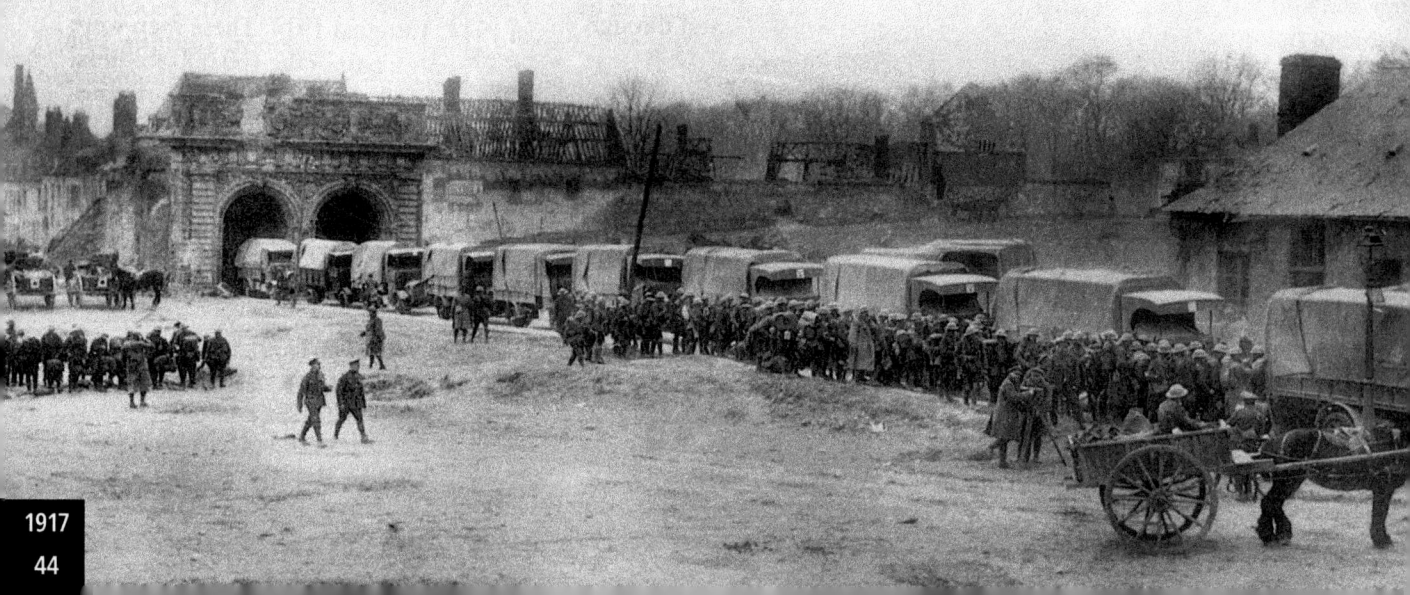

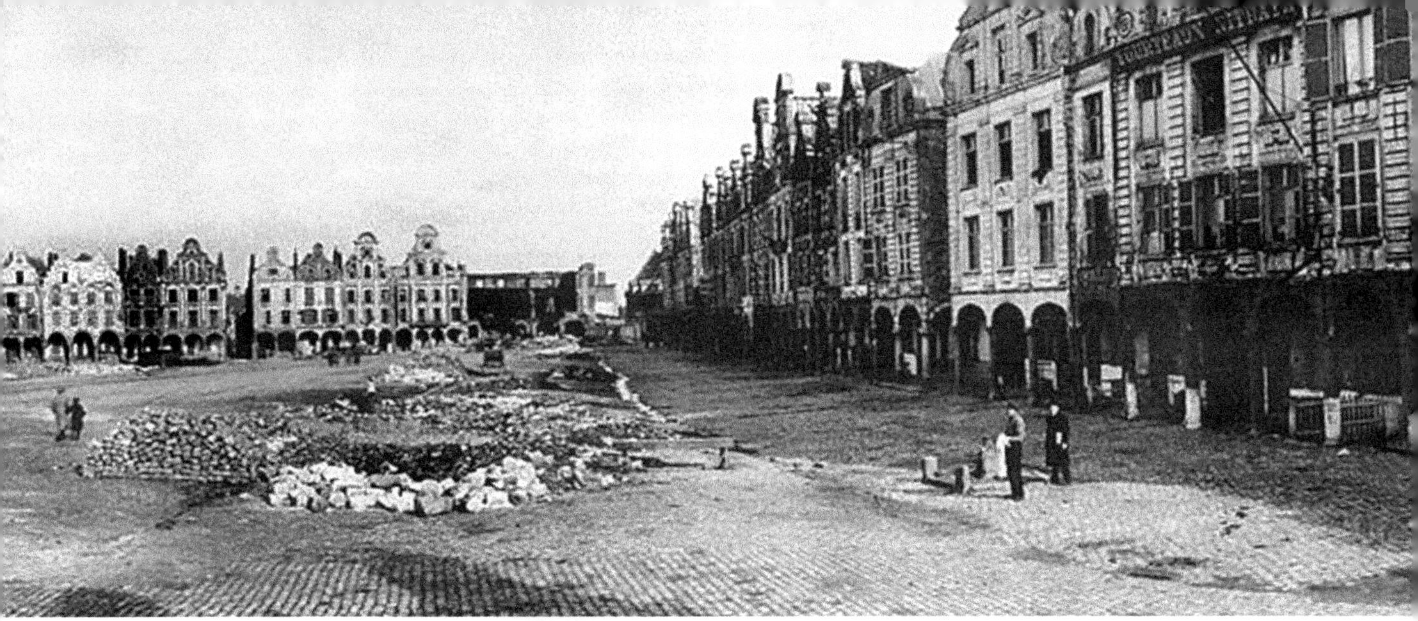

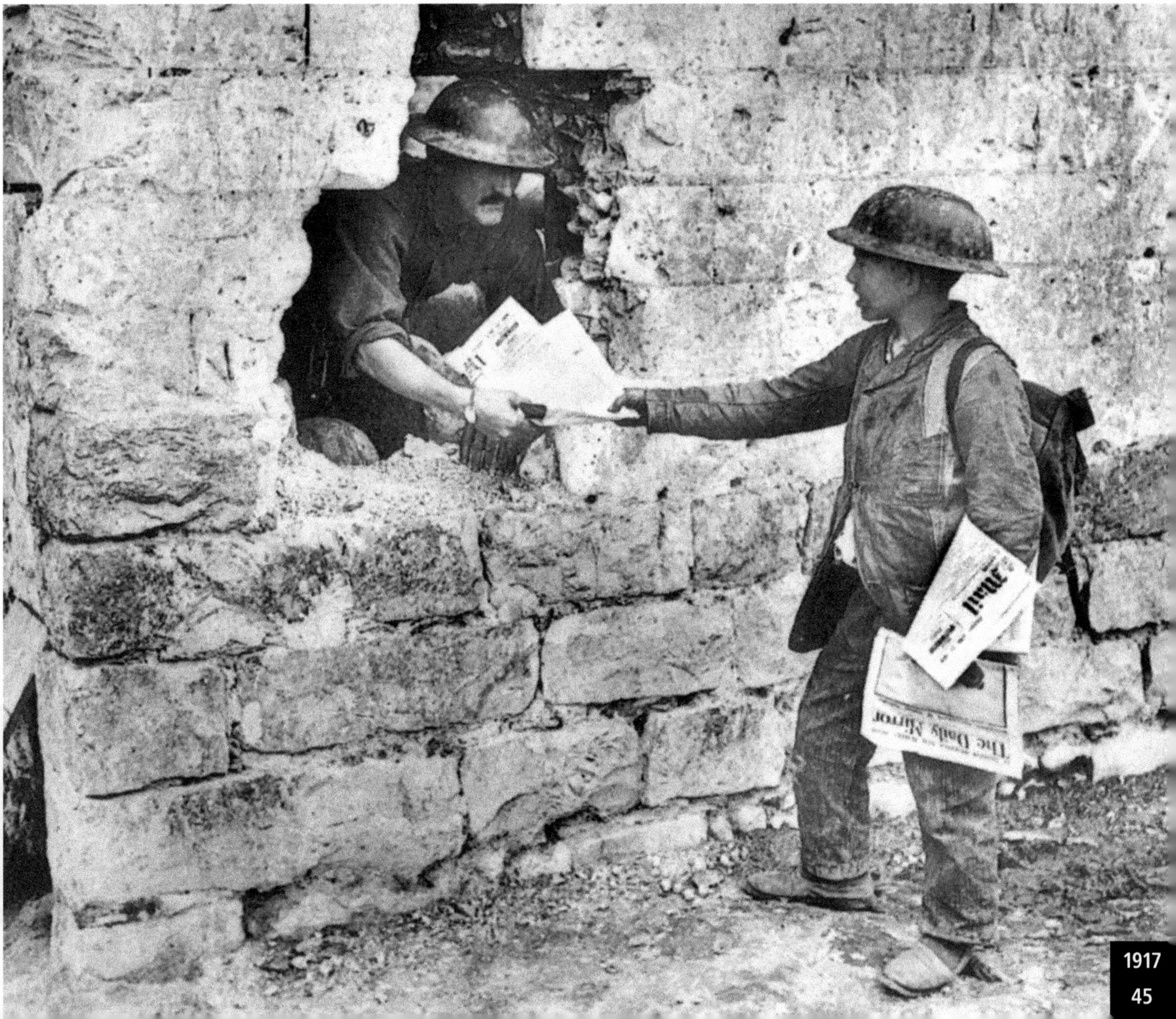

1917
45

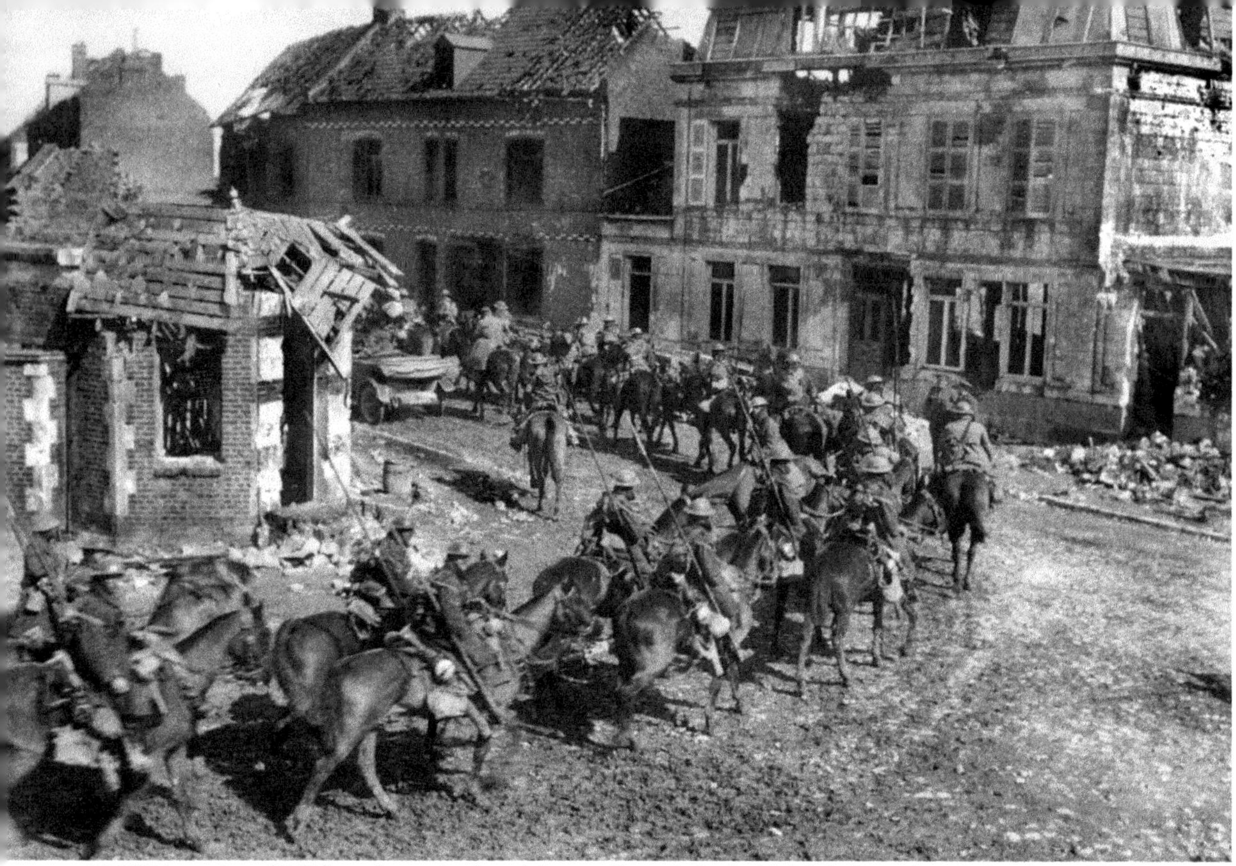

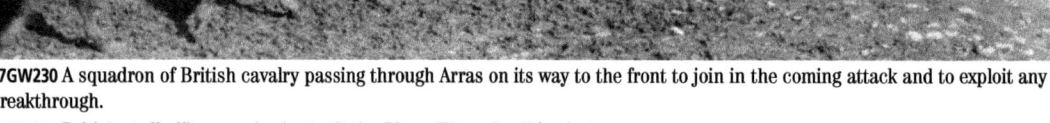

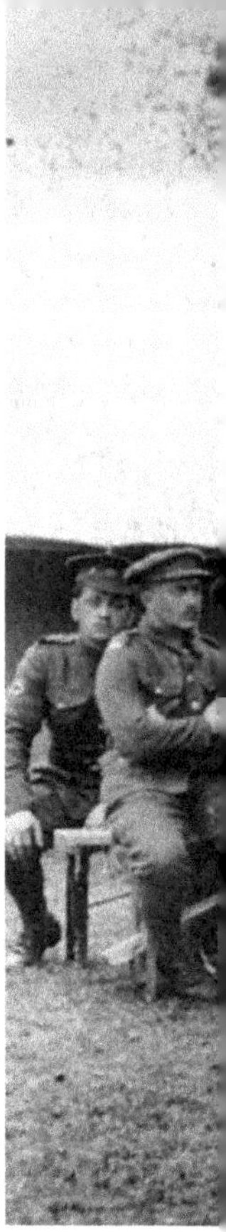

17GW230 A squadron of British cavalry passing through Arras on its way to the front to join in the coming attack and to exploit any breakthrough.

17GW232 British staff officers arrive in the Petite Place (Place des Héros), Arras.

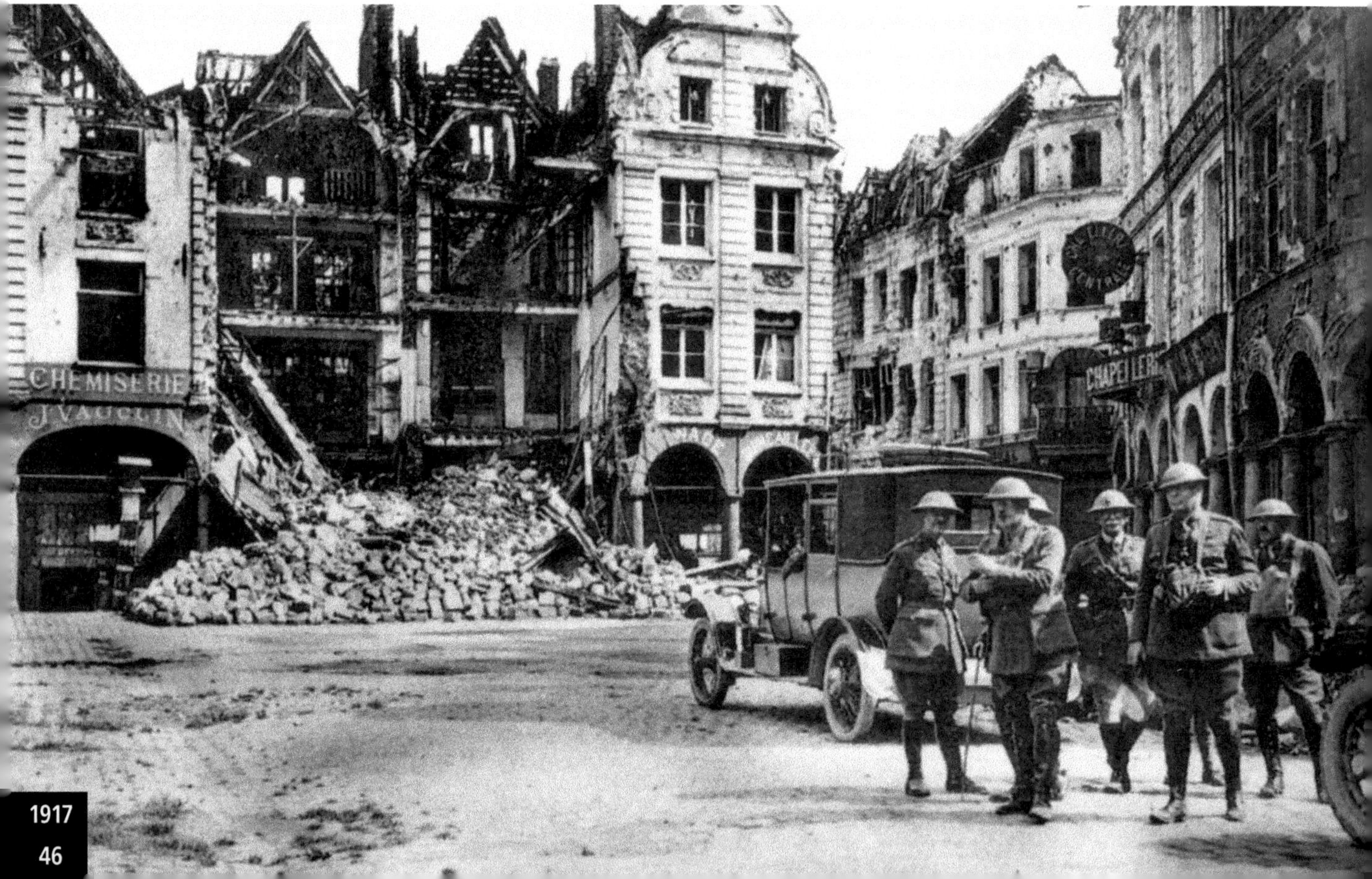

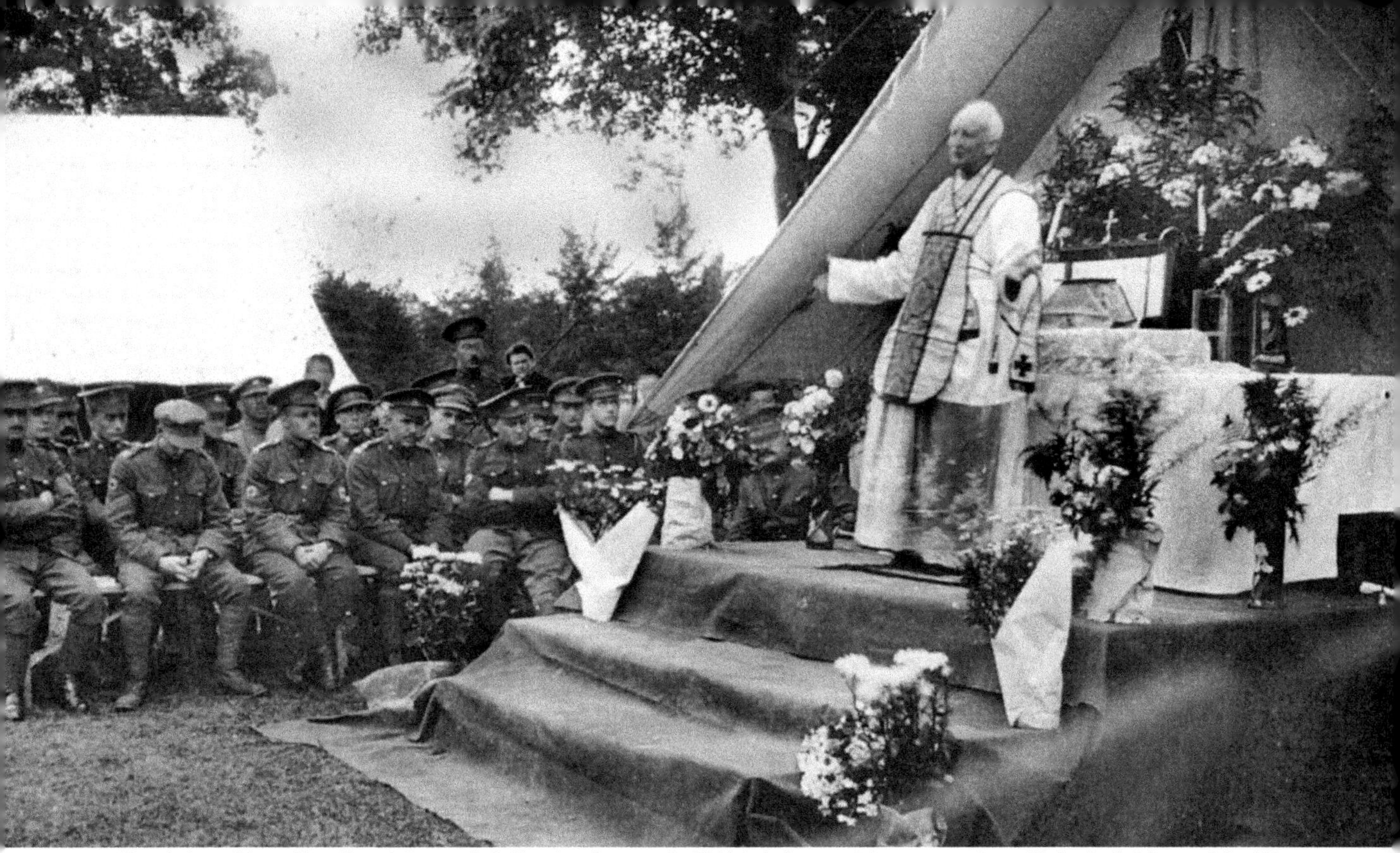

17GW231 Mass being celebrated by a French Roman Catholic priest for men of a Field Ambulance unit in a camp at Arras. Obviously God favoured the Allies and could be petitioned for victories – so it was reasoned.

17GW233 A troop of Rolls Royce built armoured cars in the streets of Arras. However, they would prove of little value on the Western Front until open warfare returned in the summer of 1918.

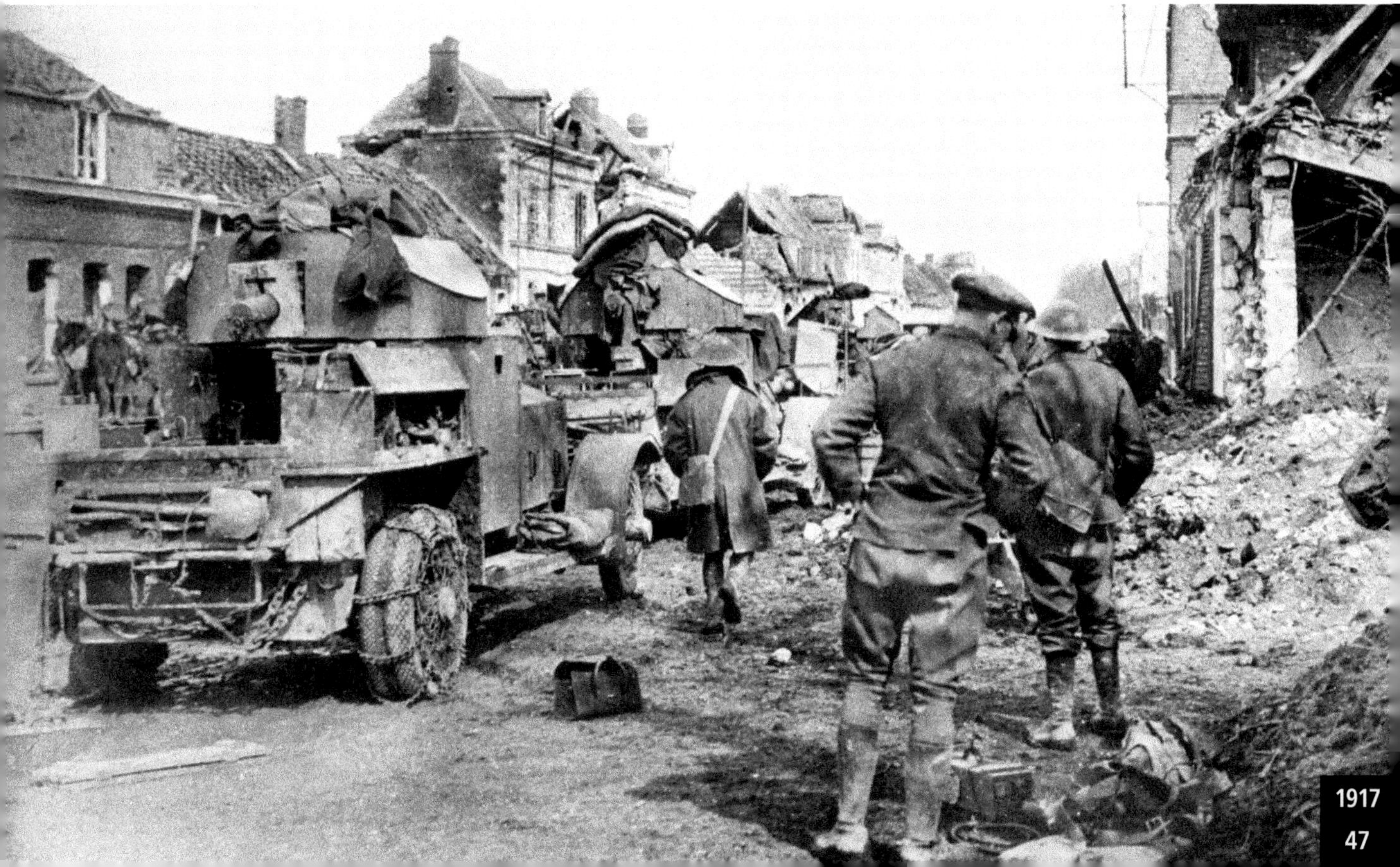

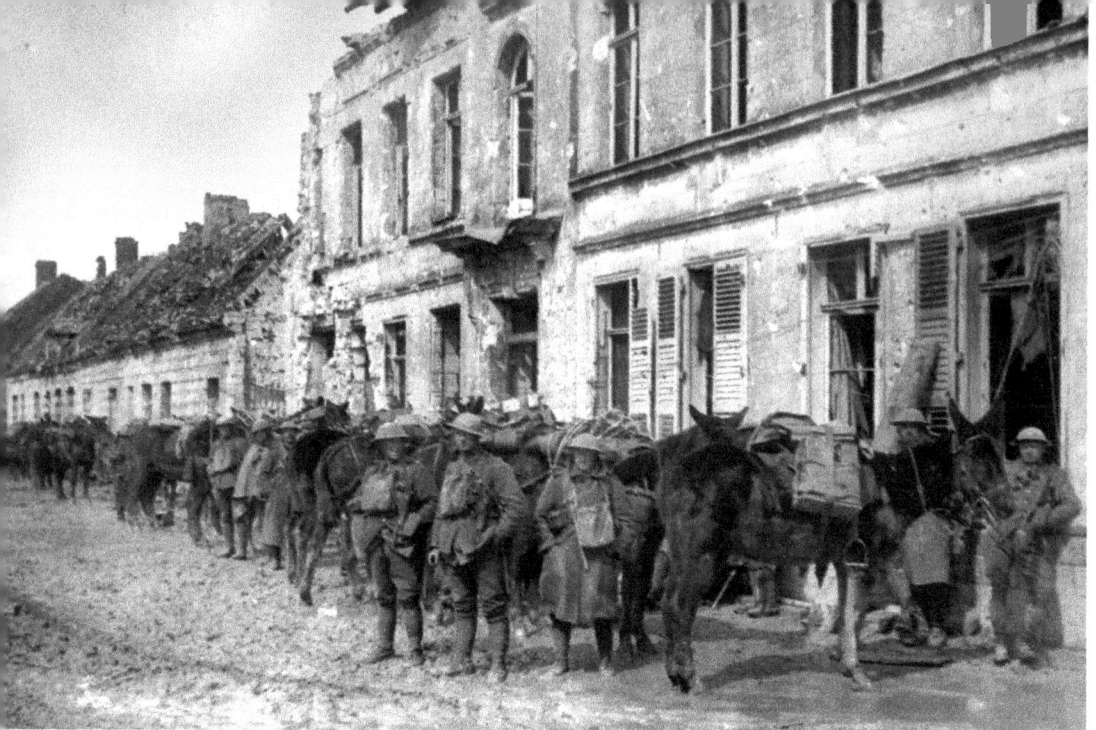
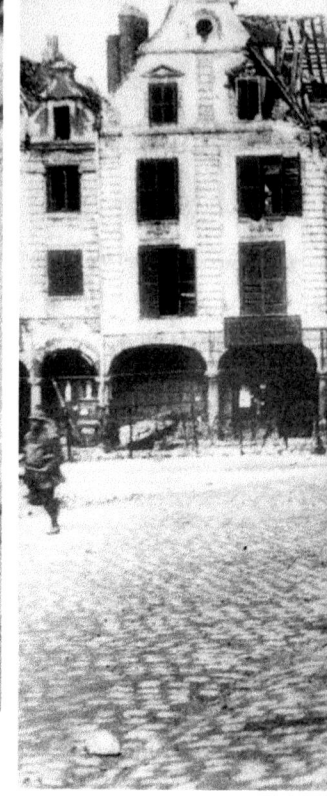

17GW248 Pack mules in a street in Arras.

17GW254 A German shell has exploded in the Grand Place, Arras, and British soldiers are fleeing the danger running into the Petite Place. The town was in the range of the German guns and was shelled regularly and systematically.

17GW245 The Baudimont Gate, Arras, with a British supply convoy passing through on the way to the front.

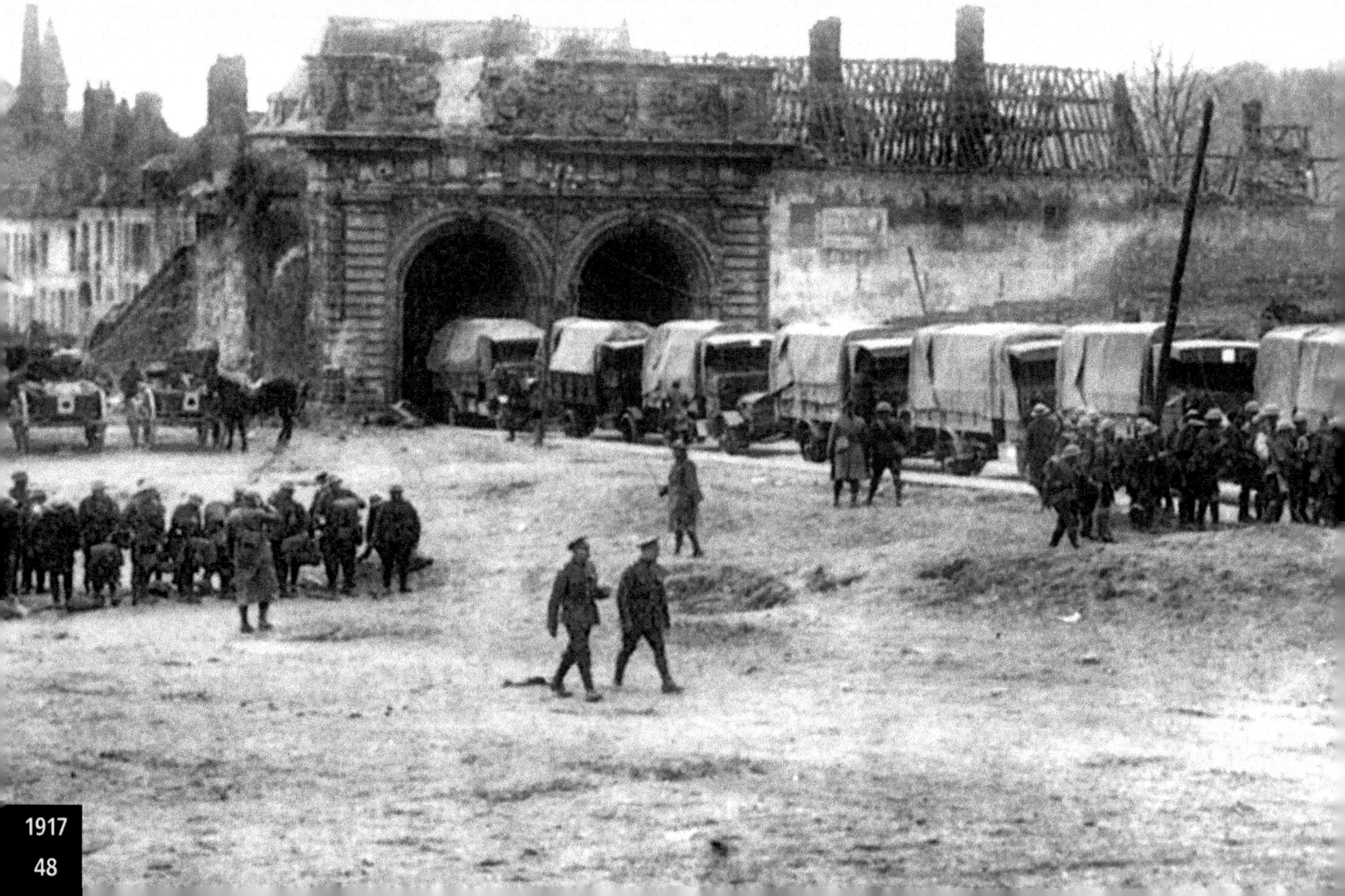

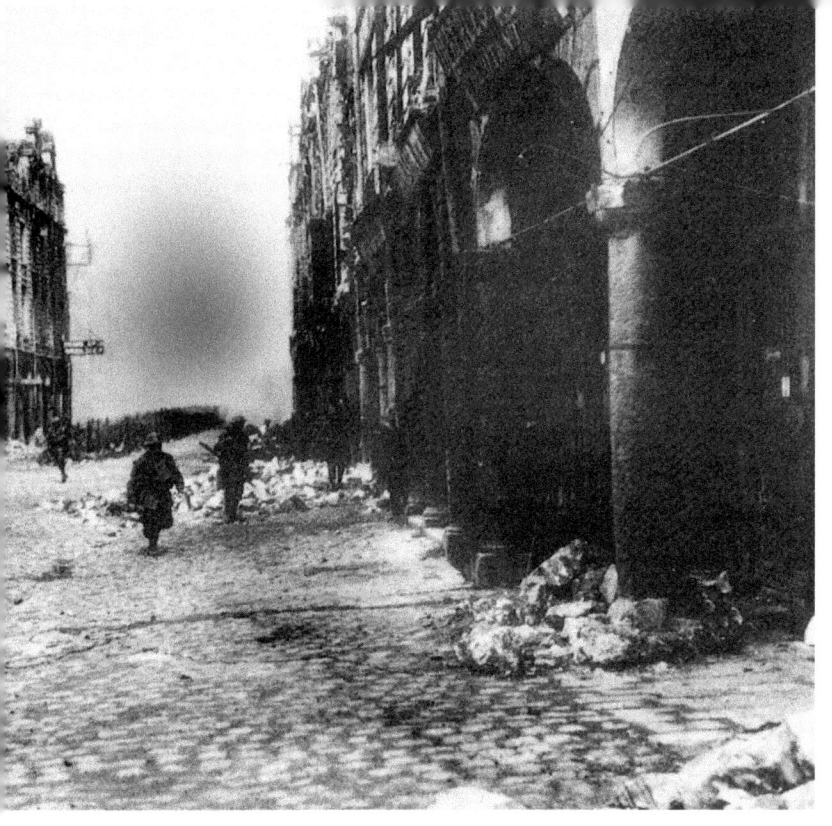
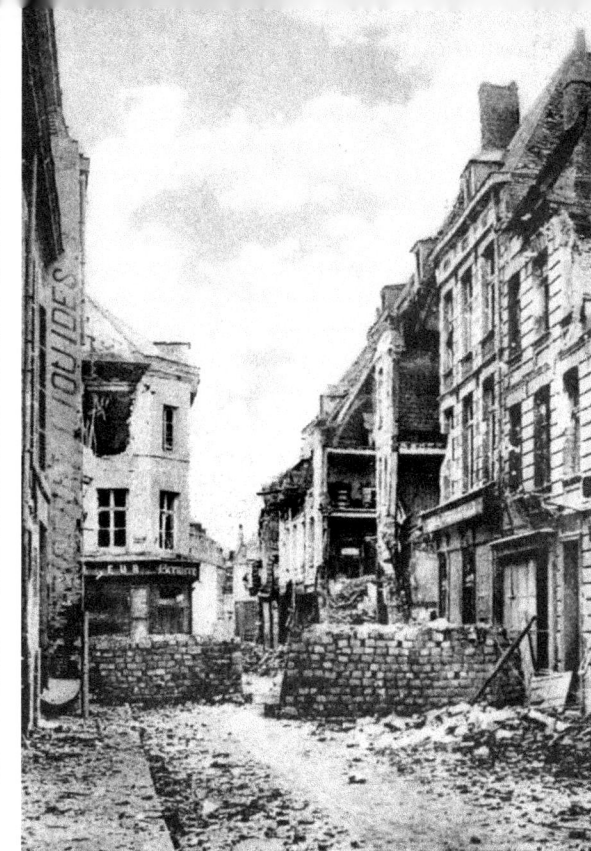

17GW244 The rue Pasteur, Arras. Barricades and barbed wire entanglements were errected as a precaution in the event of a German breakthrough.

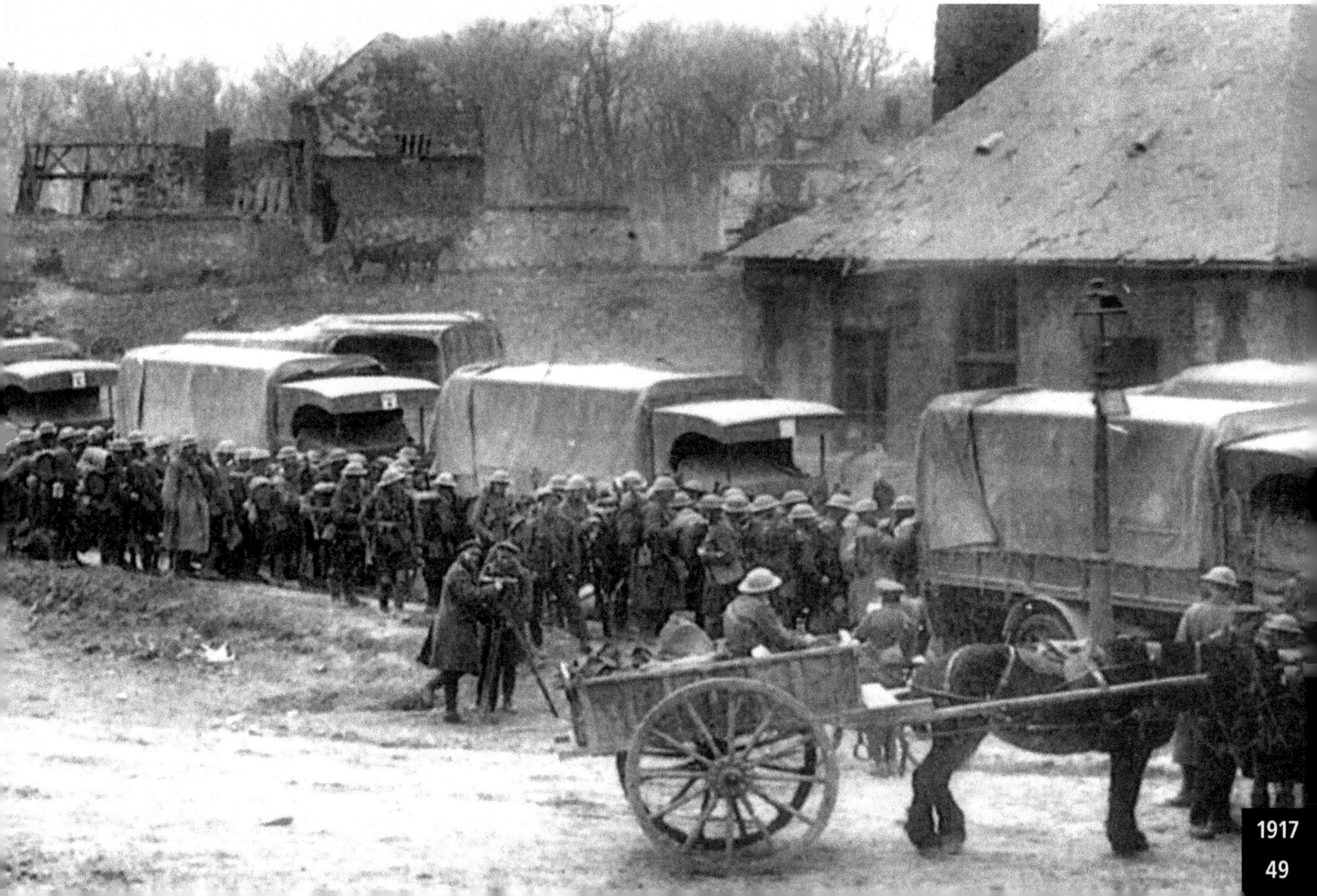

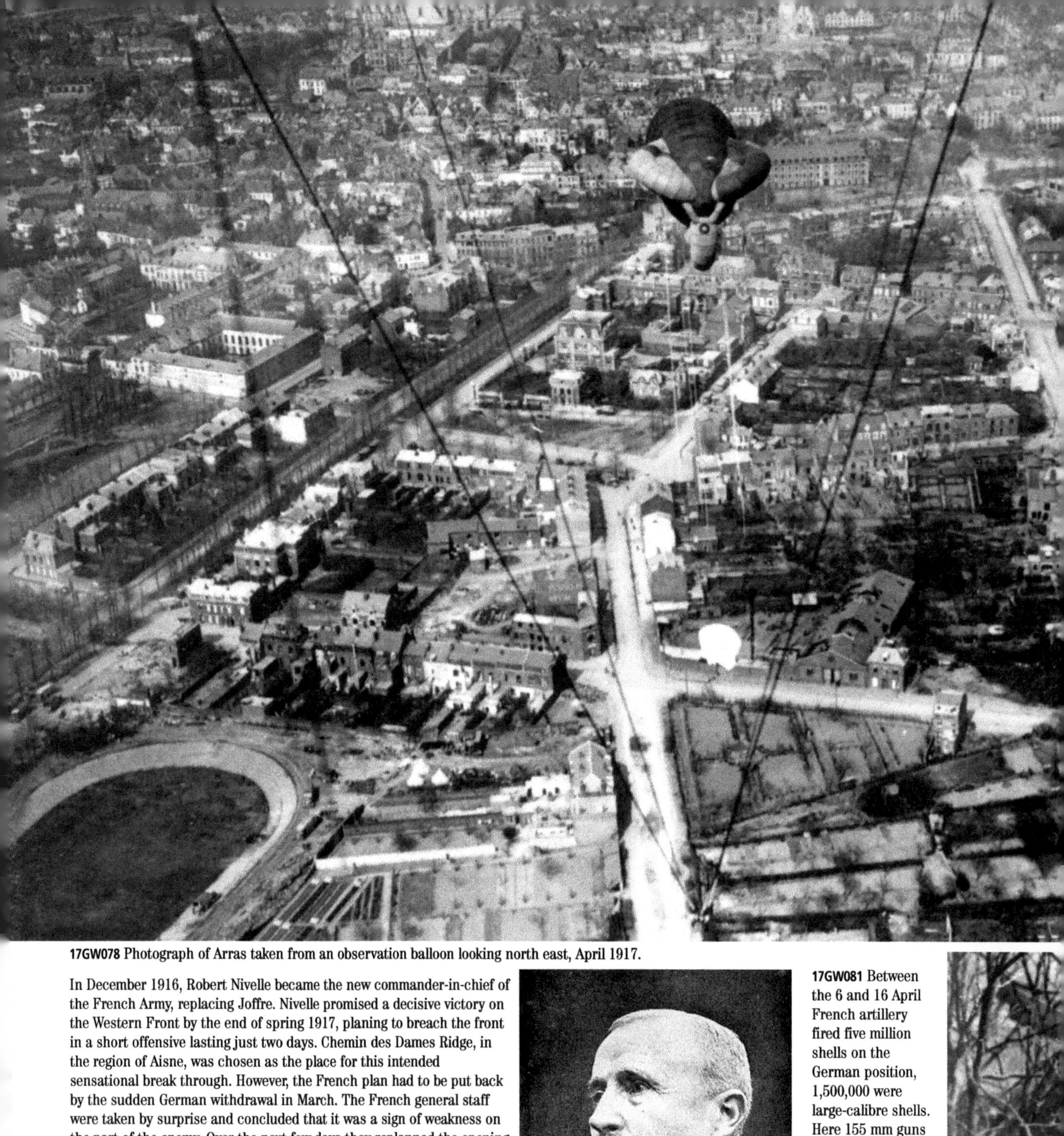

17GW078 Photograph of Arras taken from an observation balloon looking north east, April 1917.

In December 1916, Robert Nivelle became the new commander-in-chief of the French Army, replacing Joffre. Nivelle promised a decisive victory on the Western Front by the end of spring 1917, planing to breach the front in a short offensive lasting just two days. Chemin des Dames Ridge, in the region of Aisne, was chosen as the place for this intended sensational break through. However, the French plan had to be put back by the sudden German withdrawal in March. The French general staff were taken by surprise and concluded that it was a sign of weakness on the part of the enemy. Over the next few days they replanned the opening stages of their offensive but failed to discover the real strength of the Hindenburg Line defences.

Two diversionary attacks were carried out in the days leading up to the French main offensive, the first on 9 April by the British and Canadians in the Arras-Vimy sector and the second by the French at Saint-Quentin.

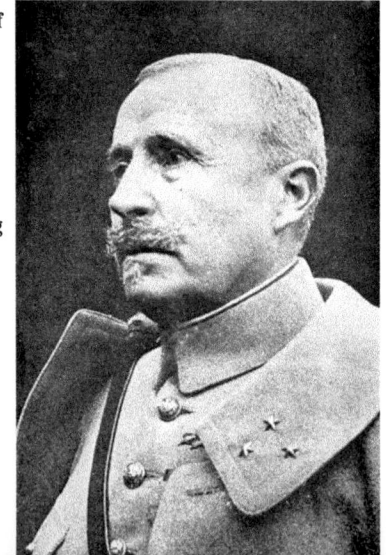

17GW080 Robert Georges Nivelle, artillery officer, who promised a great victory but instead failed spectacularly and shook the French army into multiple acts of disobedience.

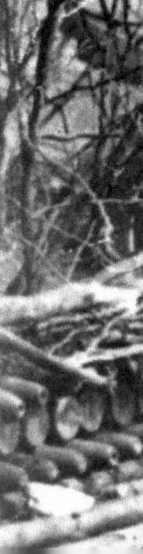

17GW081 Between the 6 and 16 April French artillery fired five million shells on the German position, 1,500,000 were large-calibre shells. Here 155 mm guns are in action near Cormicy. The bombardment lasted for two weeks.

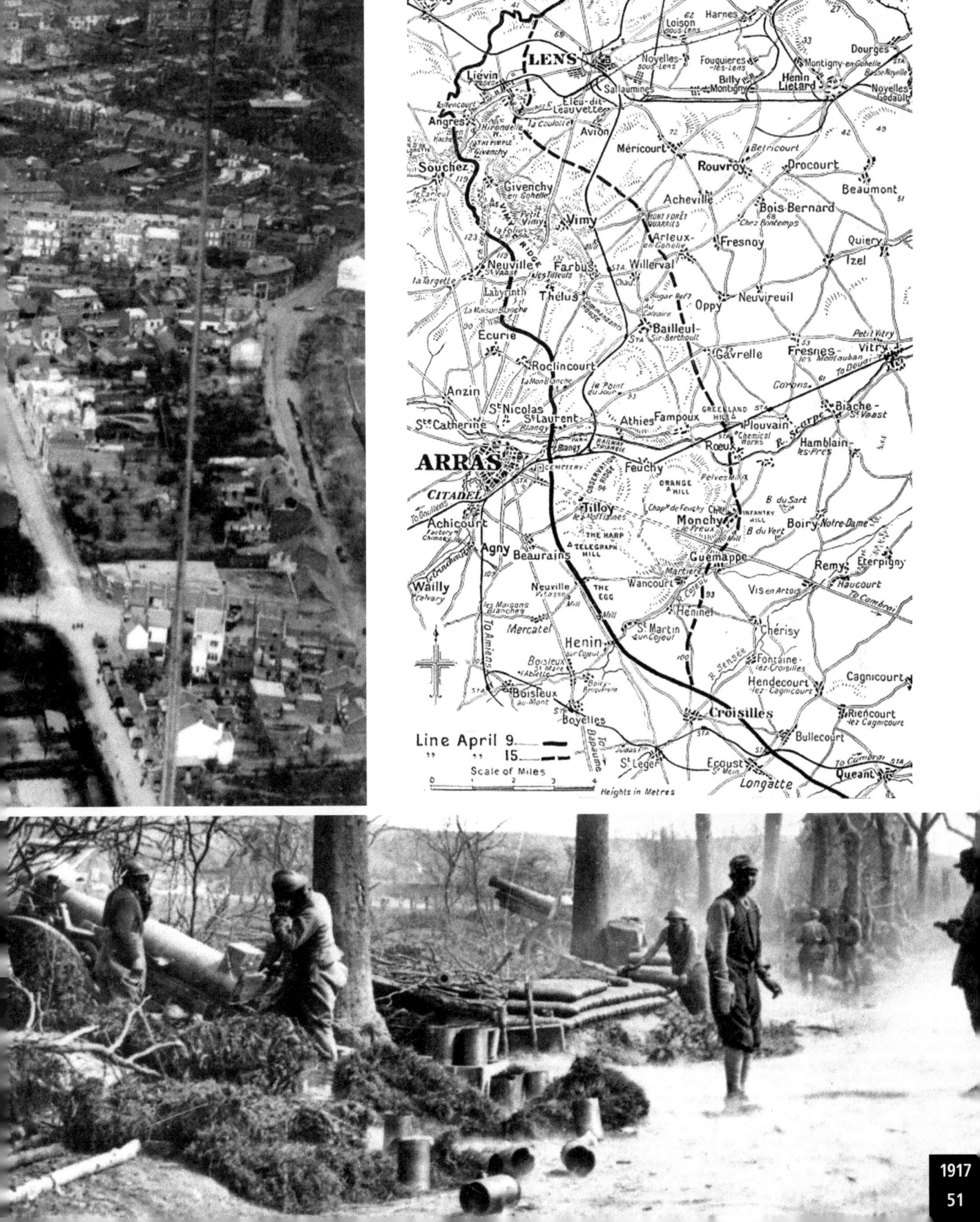

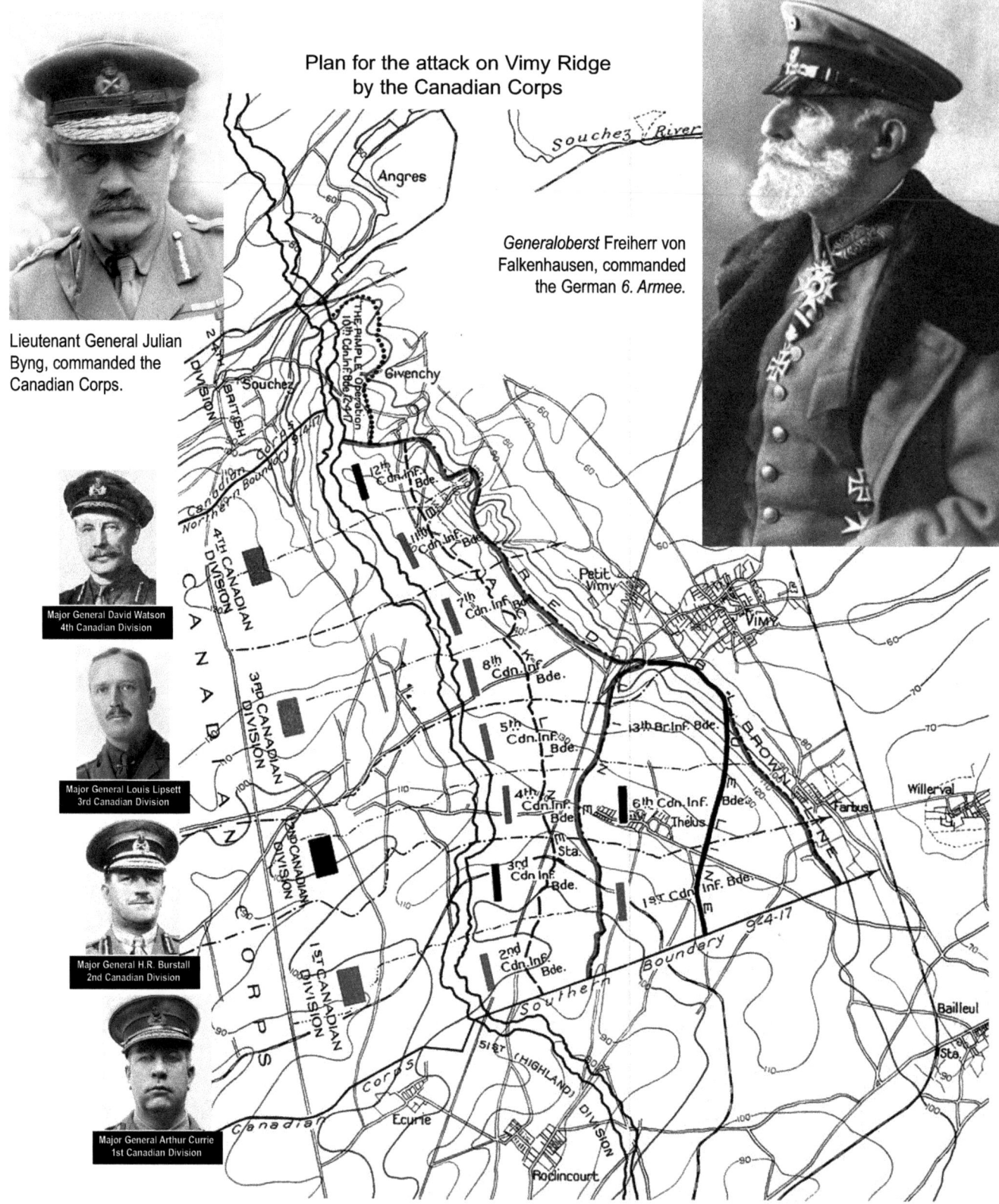

Plan for the attack on Vimy Ridge by the Canadian Corps

Lieutenant General Julian Byng, commanded the Canadian Corps.

Generaloberst Freiherr von Falkenhausen, commanded the German *6. Armee*.

Major General David Watson
4th Canadian Division

Major General Louis Lipsett
3rd Canadian Division

Major General H.R. Burstall
2nd Canadian Division

Major General Arthur Currie
1st Canadian Division

The Canadian Corps, of four divisions, was to attack three divisions of the German Sixth Army (*6. Armee*). The attack, which took place from 9 to 12 April 1917, was part of the opening phase of the Battle of Arras, a diversionary attack for the French Nivelle Offensive. The objective of the Canadian Corps, supplemented by the 5th (British) Division and other British formations and units, was to capture the German-held high ground at the northernmost end of the Arras Offensive.

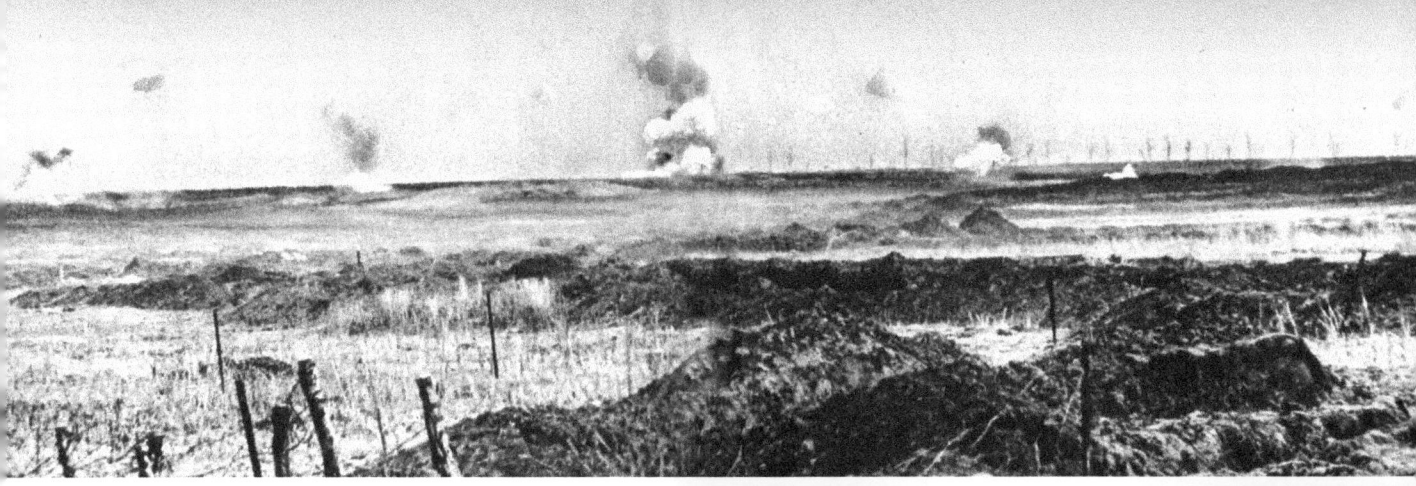

17GW107 The original heading for this picture reads: 'On Easter Monday morning – the German Front on Vimy Ridge undergoing bombardment' and caption: 'The enemy's trenches while the tornado of British shells was bursting on them.'

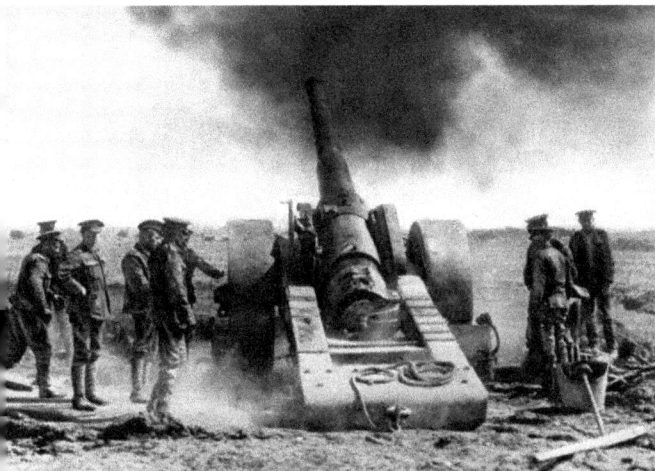
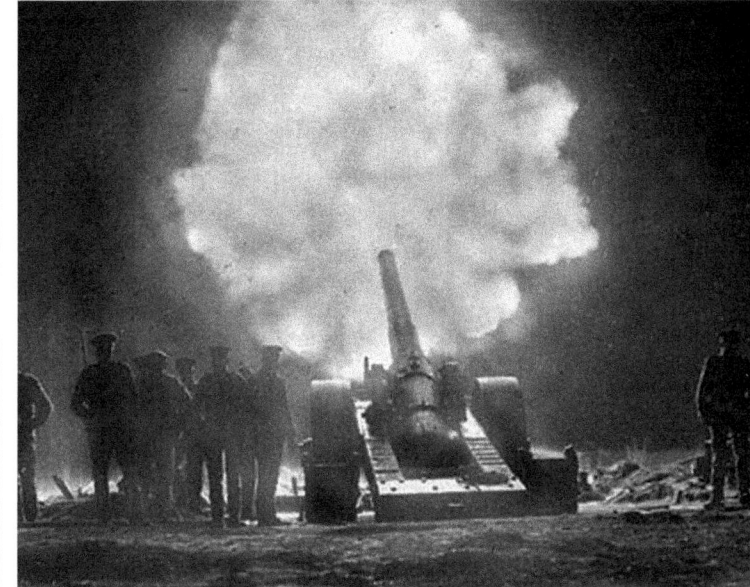

17GW103, 17GW104, 17GW106. British Royal Artillery naval guns bombarding the German positions day and night prior to the start of the Battle of Arras, Easter Monday, April 1917.

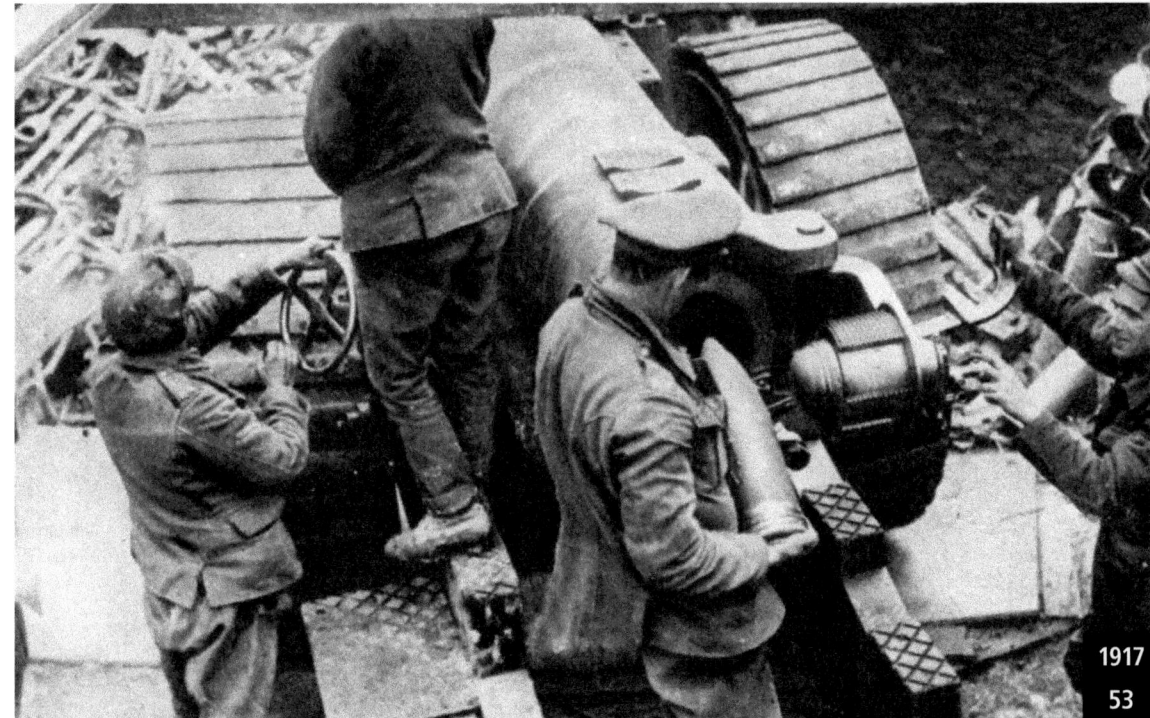

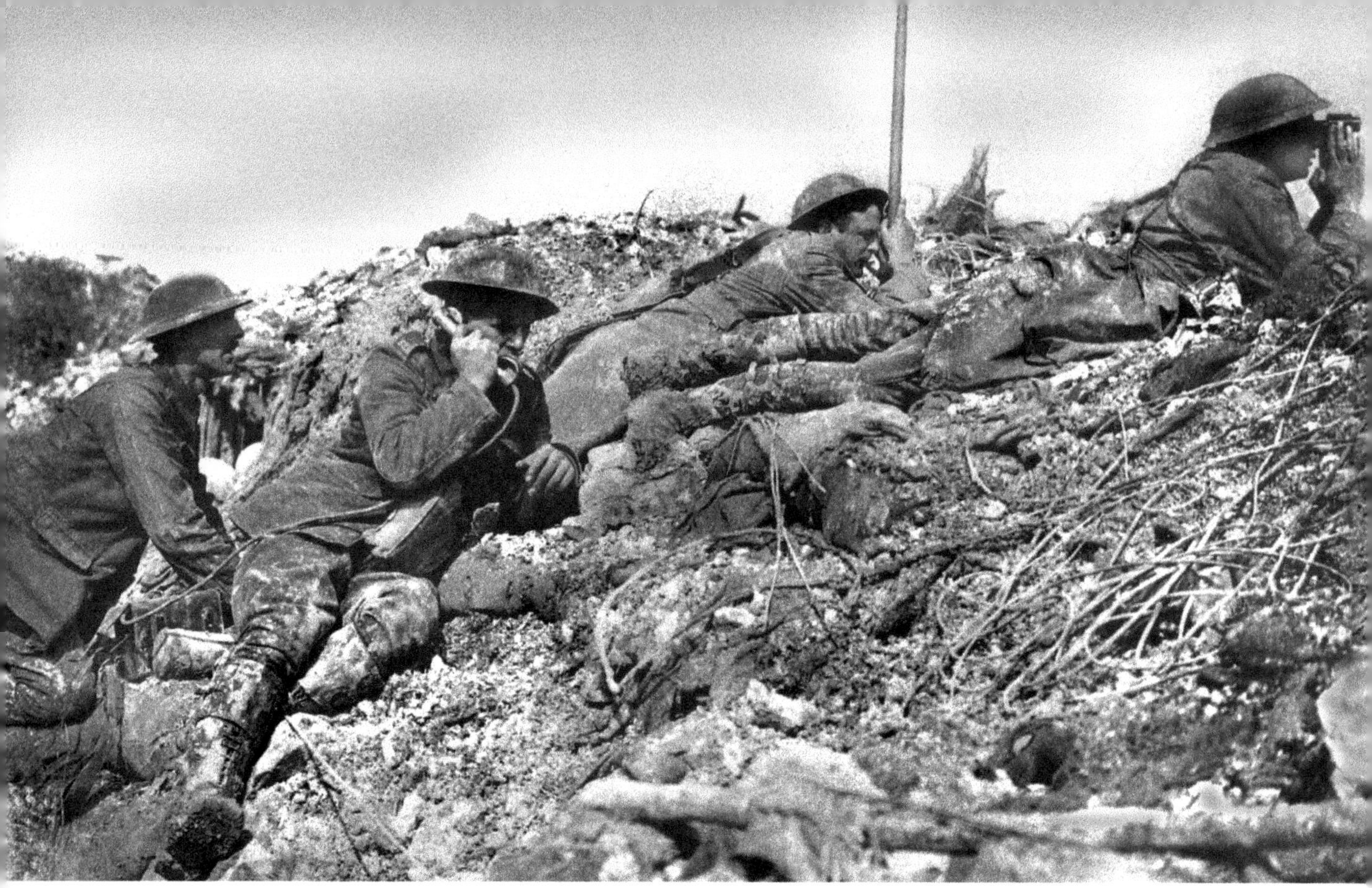

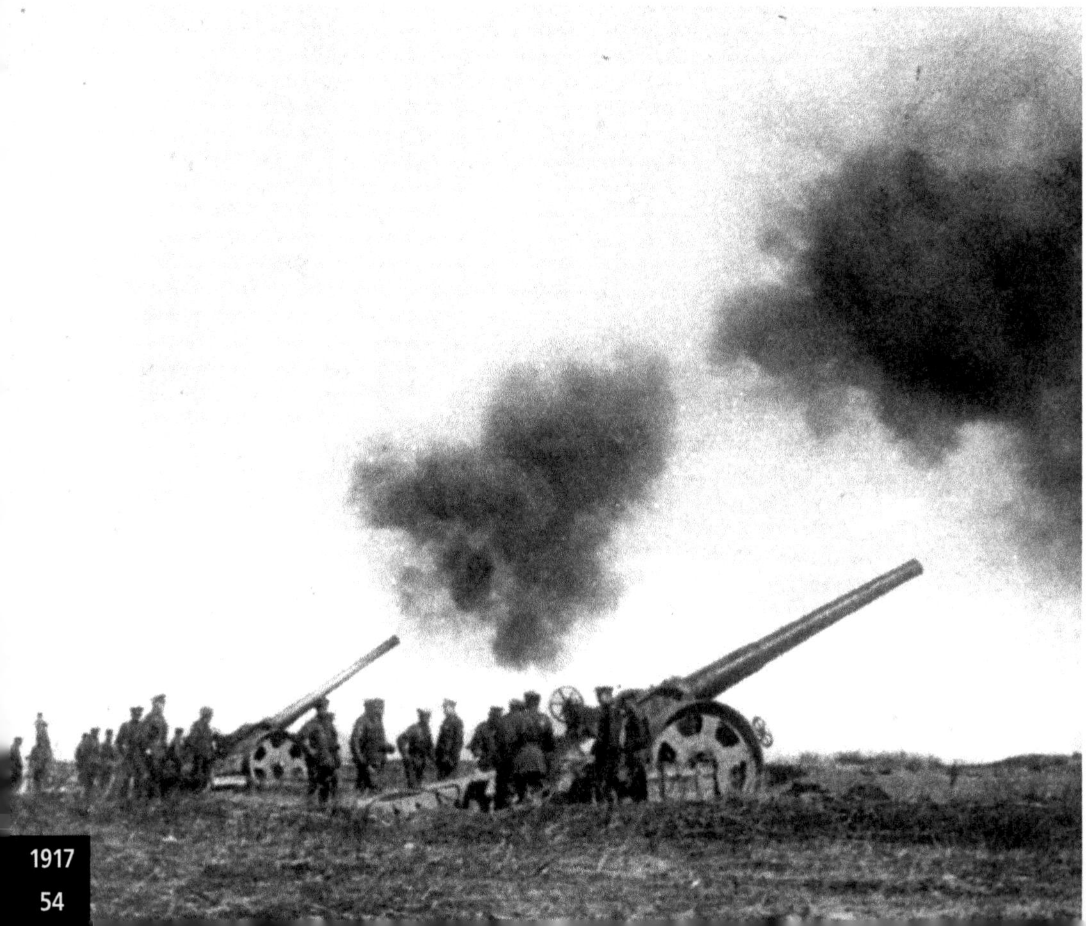

17GW109, 17GW104. The rim of 'Cuthbert' mine crater, two miles northeast of Arras, Artillery Forward Observation Officers of the 12th Division relaying gun corrections to the artillery. Naval guns mounted on gun carriages firing on the German positions.

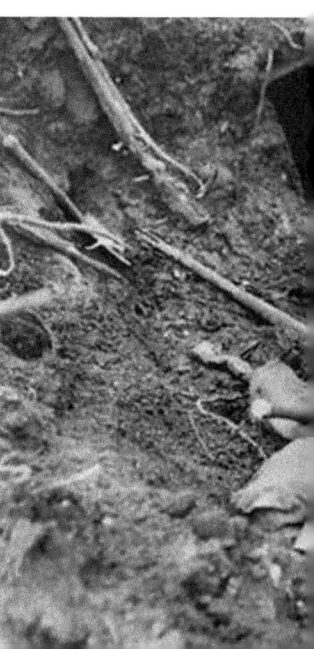

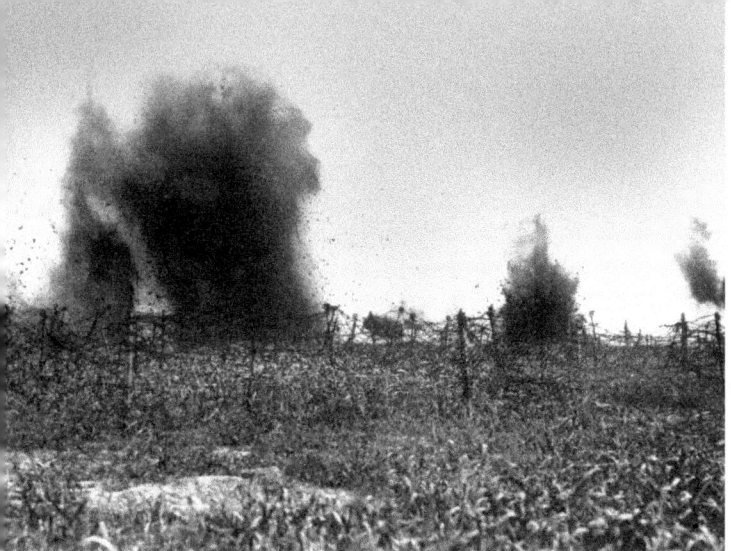
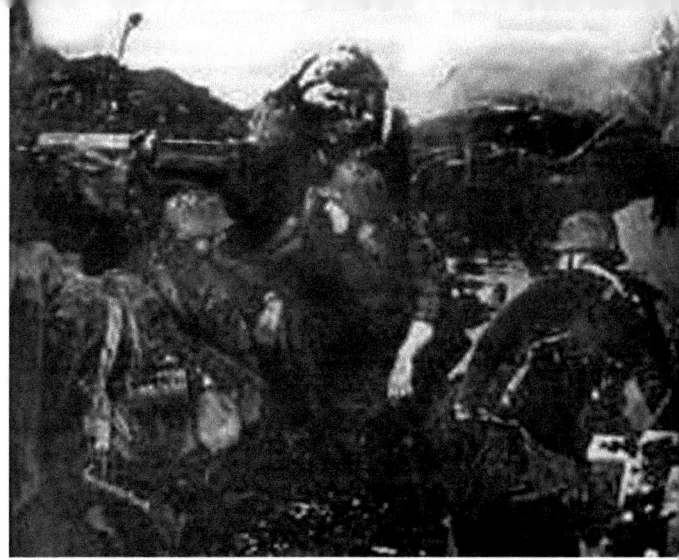

17GW110 British shells bursting among the German barbed wire entanglements in preparation for an infantry attack.

17GW111, 17GW115, 17GW114, 17GW117, 17GW116. The effect on a British bombardment on German positions.

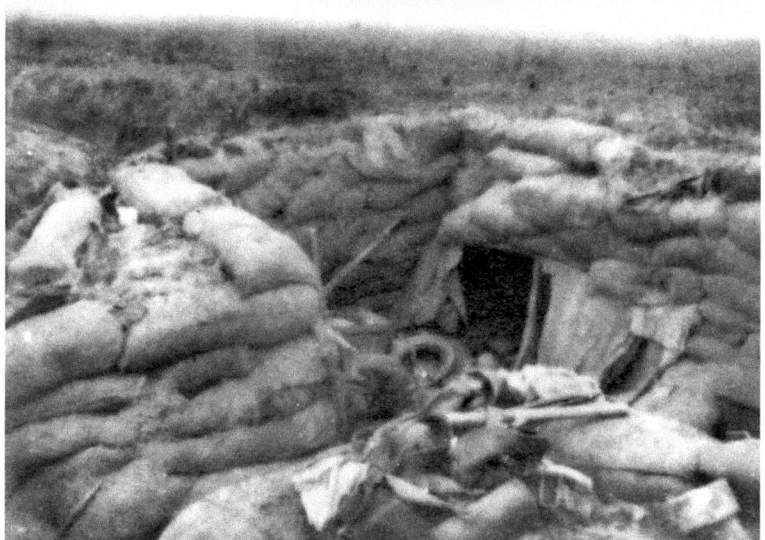
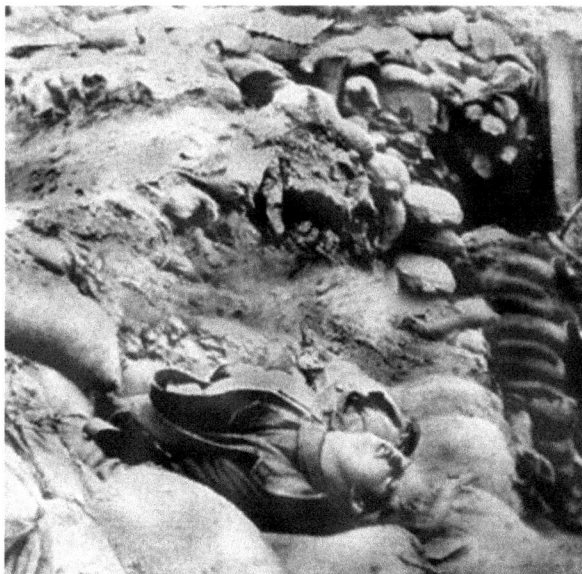
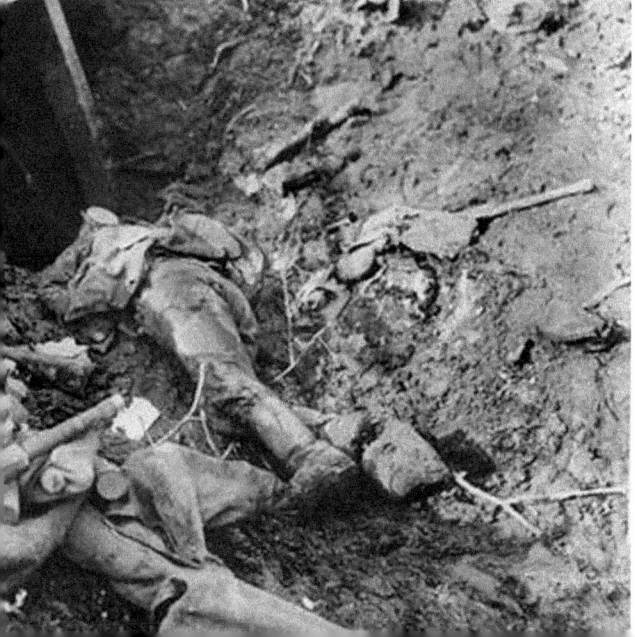
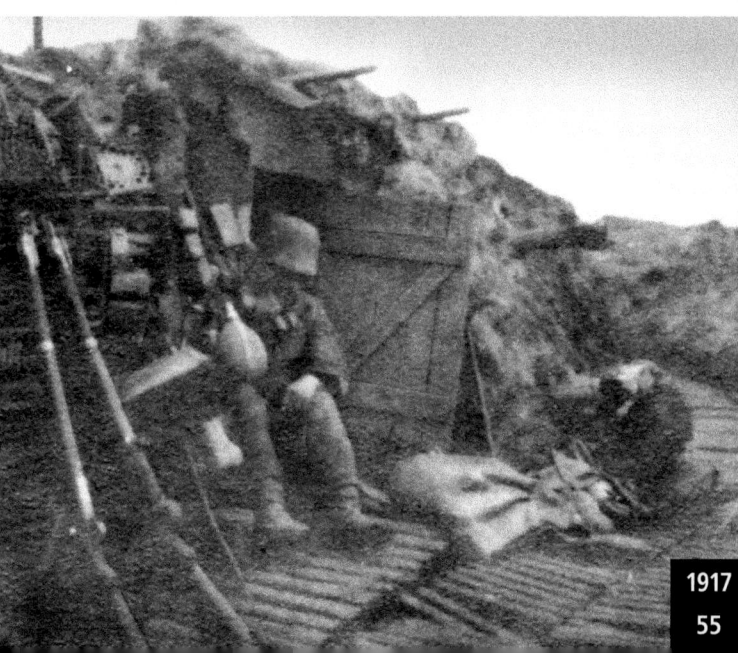

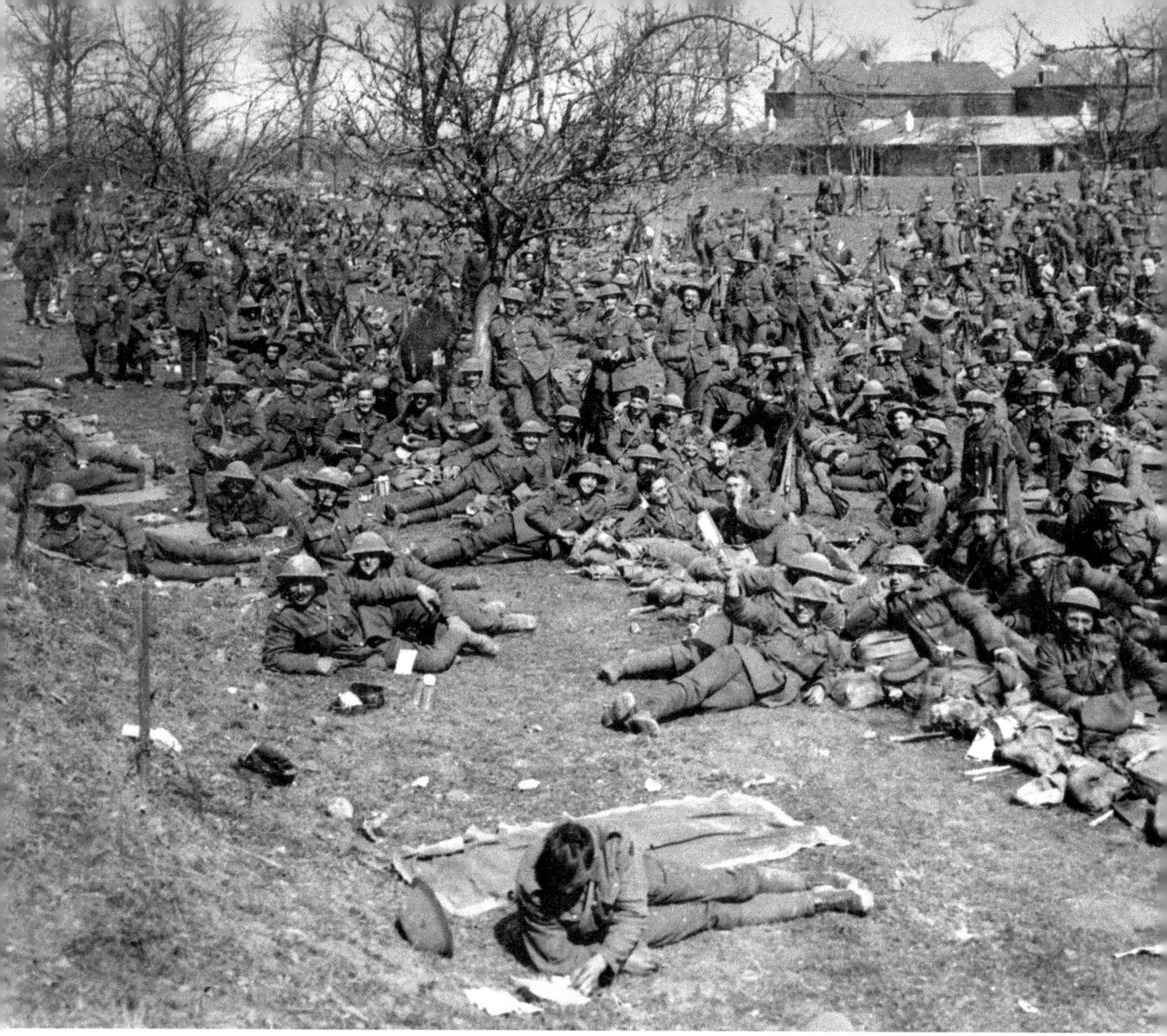

17GW082 Men of the 10th Battalion Royal Fusiliers enjoying the spring sunshine at Wagnonlieu 8 April 1917. Two days later all changed: On 10 April the battalion took part in the capture of Monchy-le-Preux on the Arras–Cambrai road. The fighting took place in a snow storm and casualties were heavy. The battalion lost twelve officers and 240 other ranks.

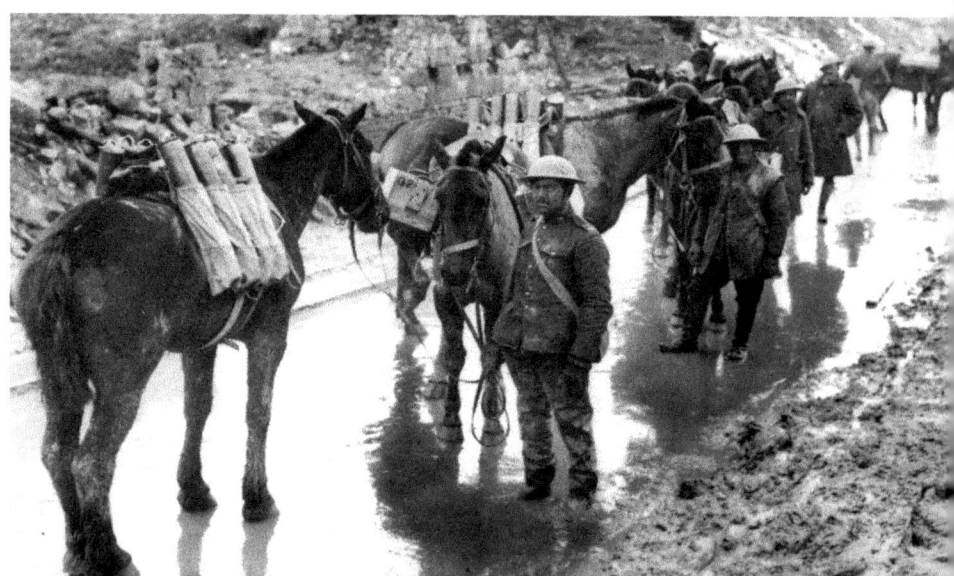

17GW133 Artillery shells for the 20th Canadian Field Battery. The Canadian Corps' field artillery comprised thirty brigades, equipped with 480 18-pounder guns and 138 4.5 inch howitzers. Bombardment of the German positions on Vimy Ridge was to be one of the fiercest to date. For the battle the Canadian artillery was reinforced by many guns from First Army.

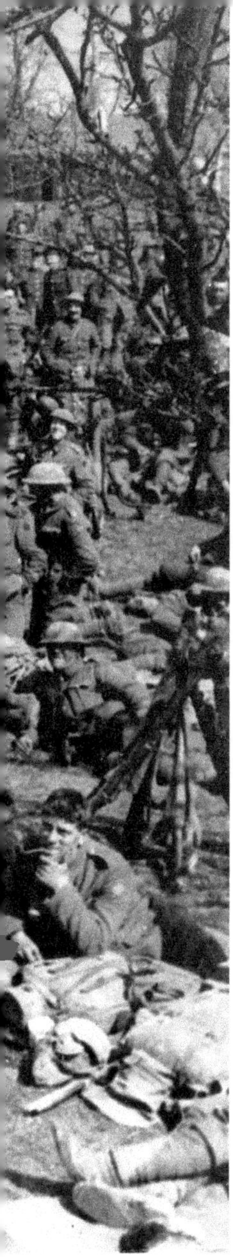

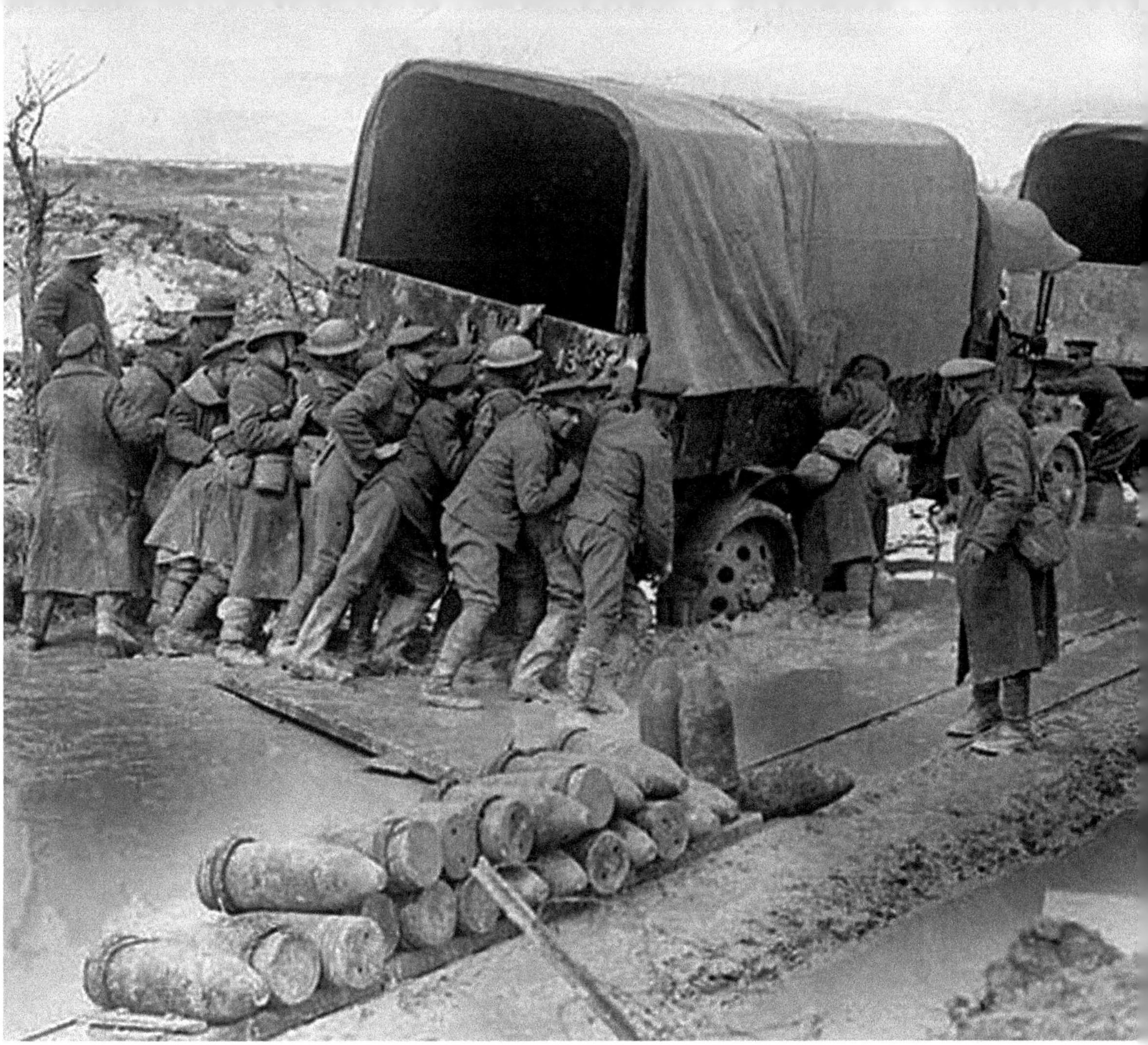

17GW120 Canadians helping to get a bogged down lorry back on the road near Arras, April, 1917.

17GW135 A pigeon is released, bearing a message from an officer.

17GW134 An 18-pounder field gun being man-handled into its firing position.

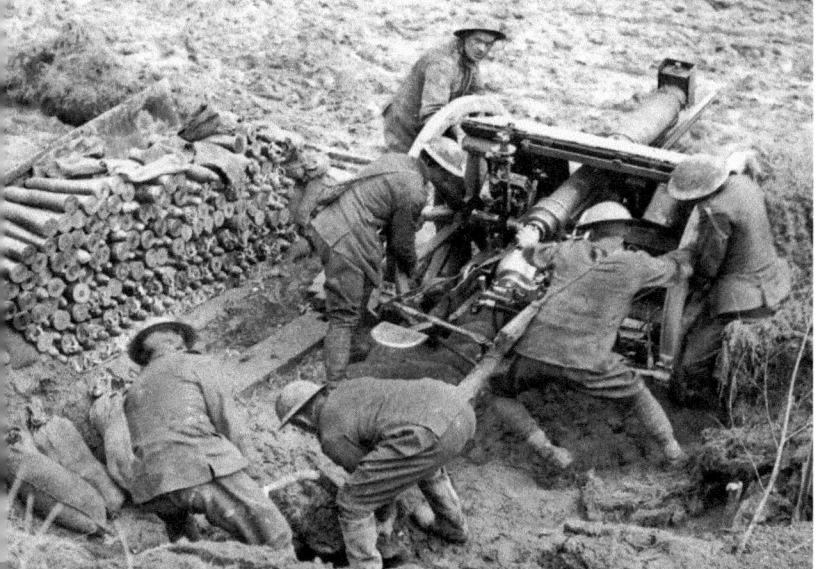

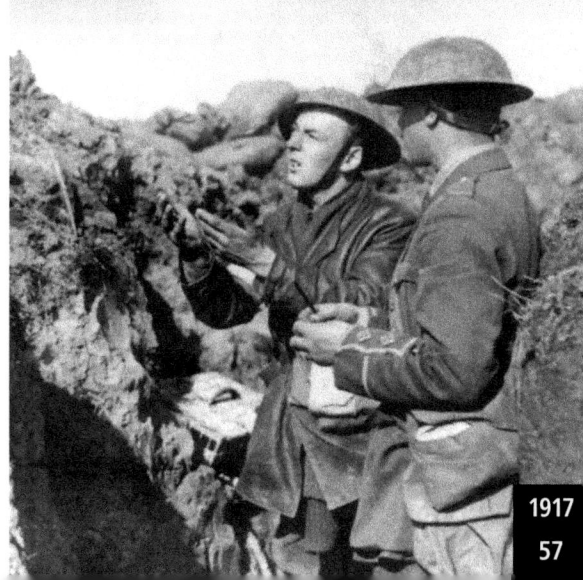

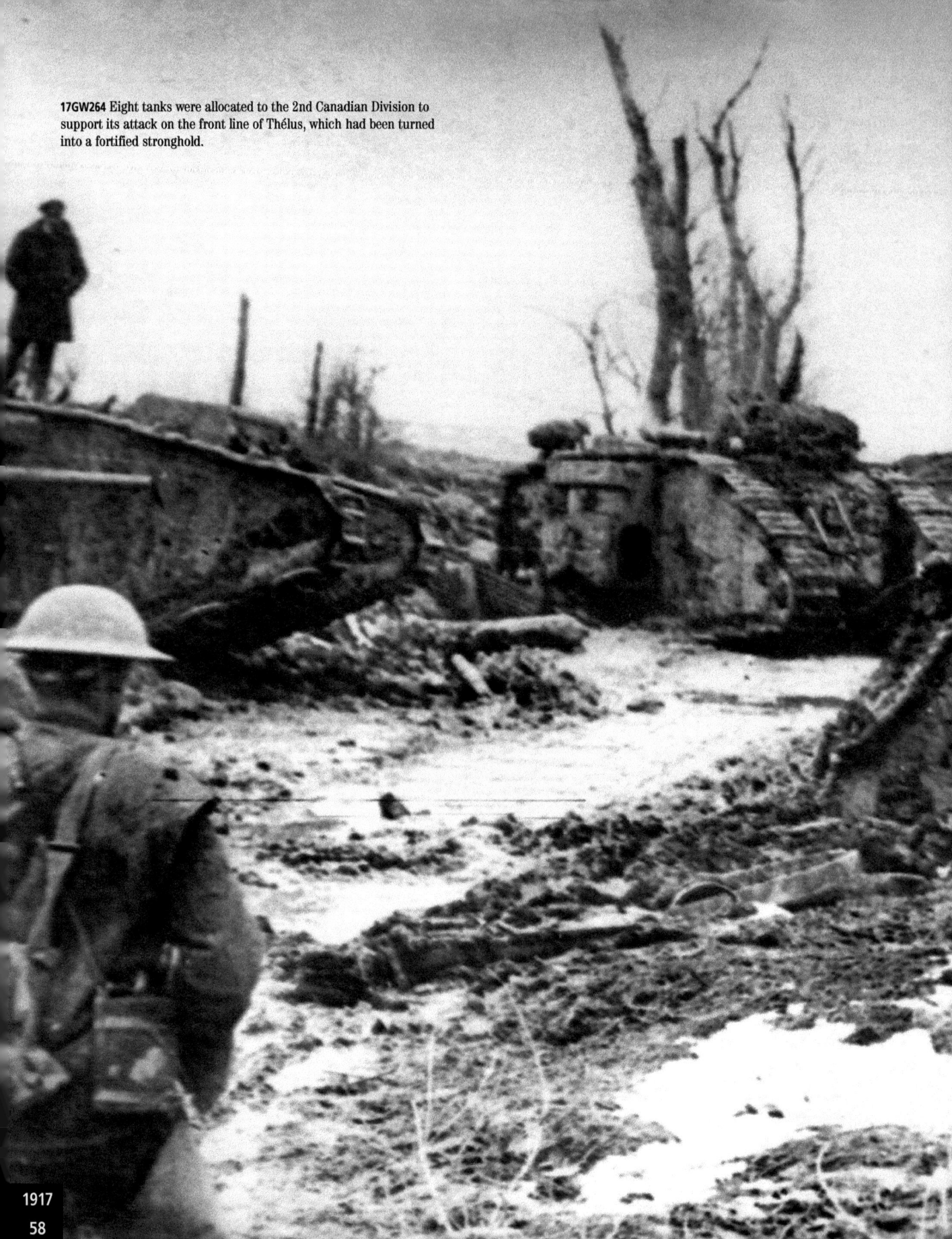

17GW264 Eight tanks were allocated to the 2nd Canadian Division to support its attack on the front line of Thélus, which had been turned into a fortified stronghold.

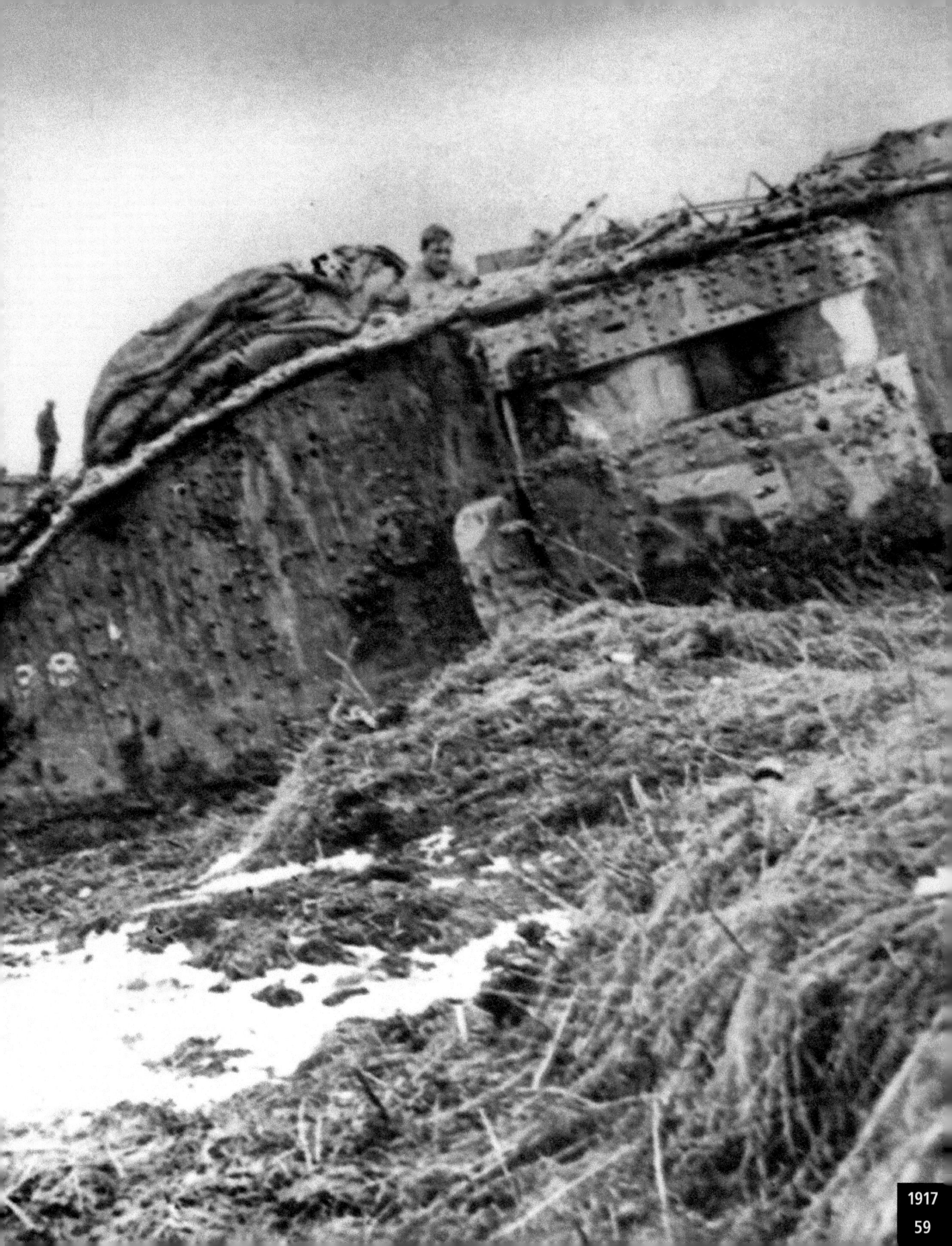

Easter Monday morning, 9 April 1917, the chronicler of the 15th Battalion, (48th Highlanders of Canada), Kim Beattie, recorded the minutes leading up to the attack by the Canadians on Vimy Ridge:

'The infantry of the entire Canadian Army Corps were lying there in the drizzling dark, waiting for the moment when they would make the first concentrated attack as a Corps, the four divisions side by side. It was raining a thin, cold driving rain.

'Five minutes to go... for miles men tensing for the spring as a Hun machine gun coldly chattered over the the prone line of No.4 Company and a lazy star shell went up and over, misted and beautiful, then sizzled out in the evil water of a crater.

'Two minutes; one minute; thirty seconds; men gasped – perhaps a brief prayer. A mighty roar shook the trenches and the stupendous, stunning barrage crashed down before the Highland line. In a flicker of time the dawn was raving. A frantic shower of flares sprayed up through the fog from the German lines.

Now they were up and moving like automatons towards the inferno.'

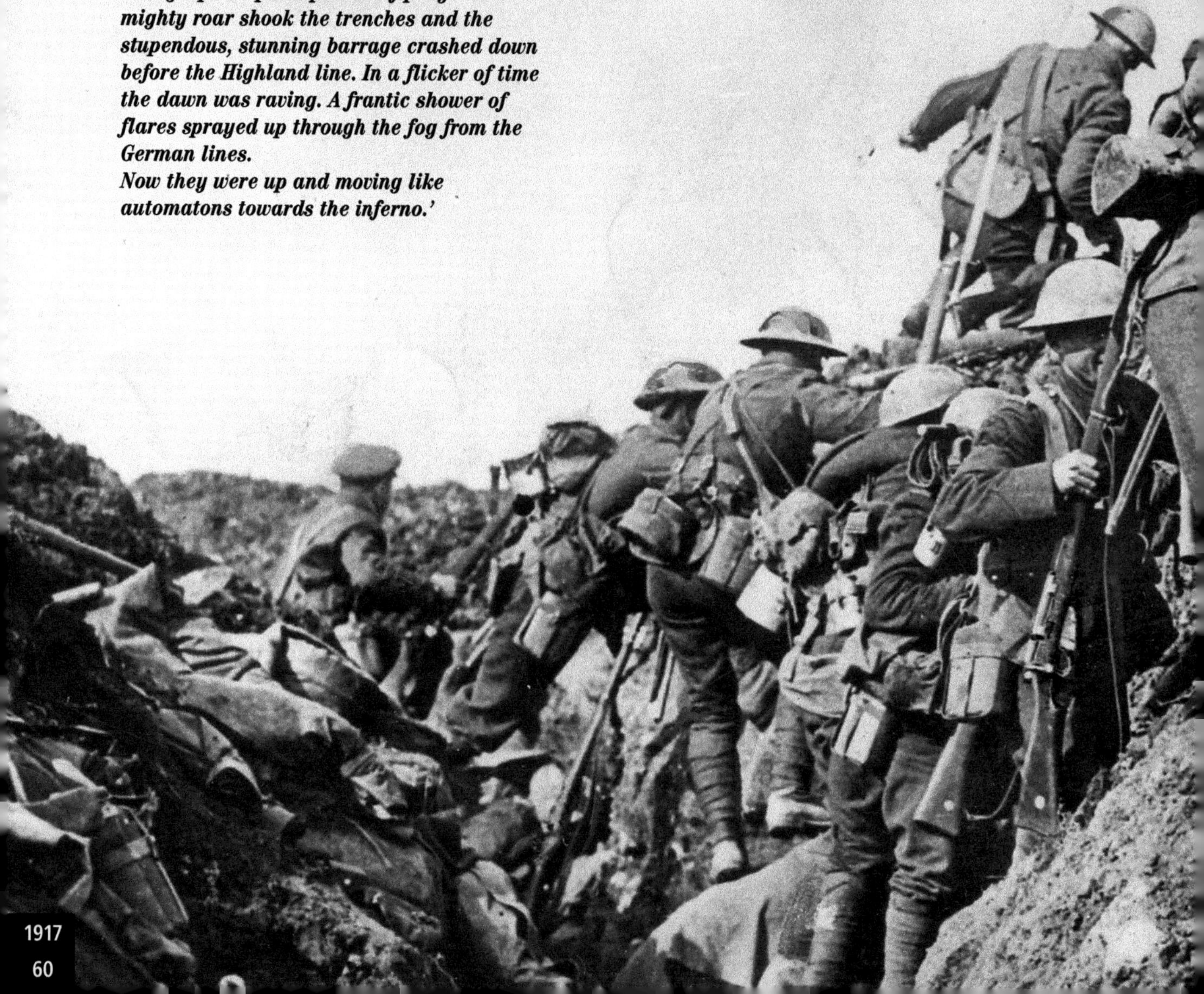

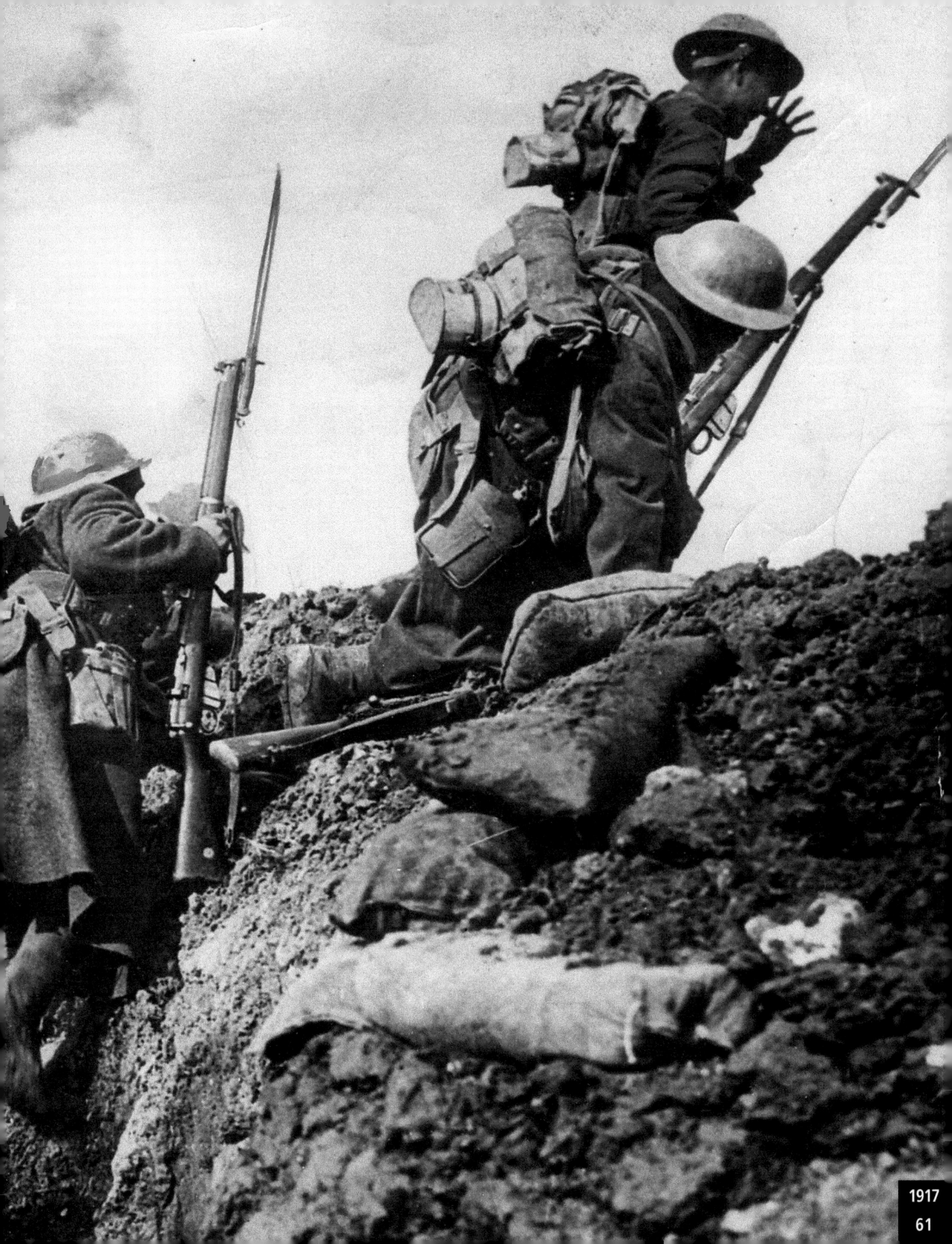

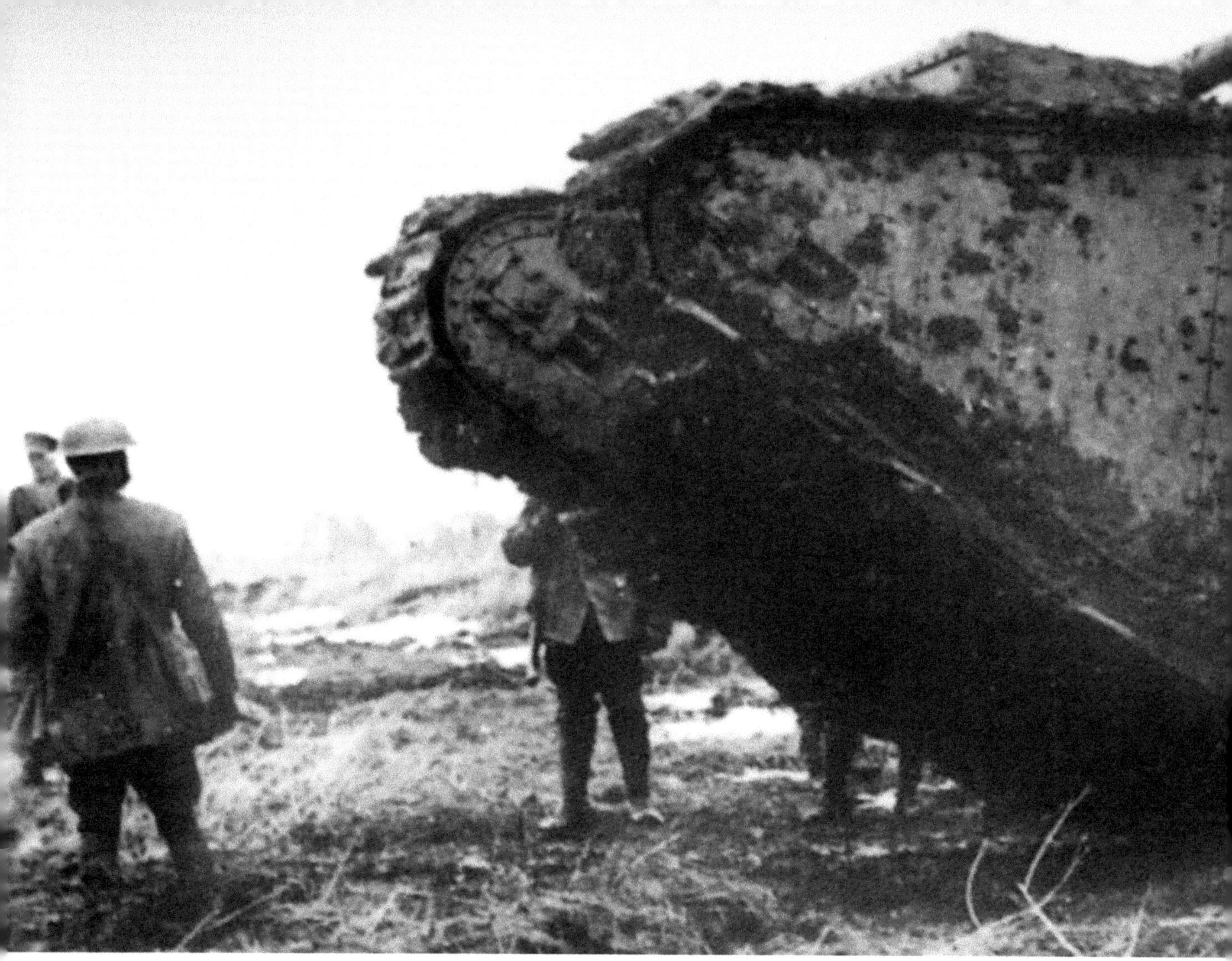

17GW265, 17GW266. The 2nd Division was supported by eight tanks during the attack, some of which are seen here with the 25th Battalion (Nova Scotia Rifles) leading 5 Brigade. They captured 390 prisoners and three machine guns.

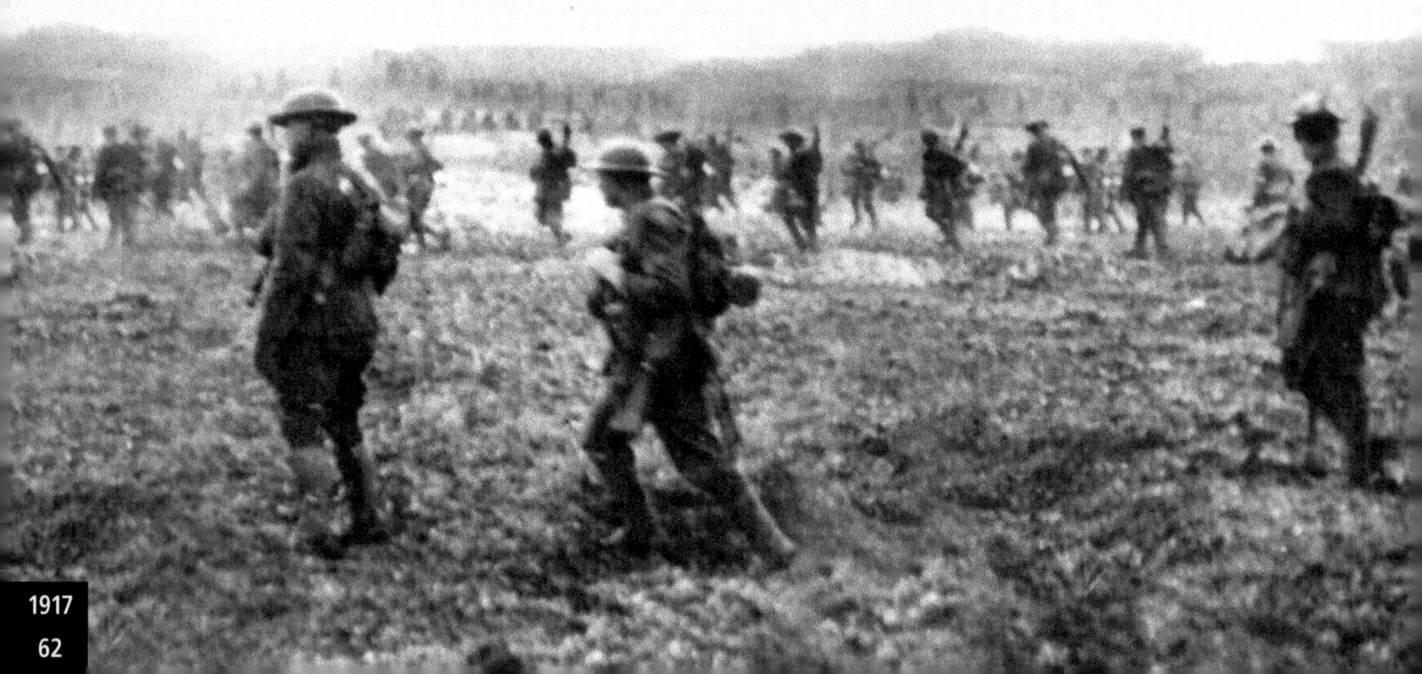

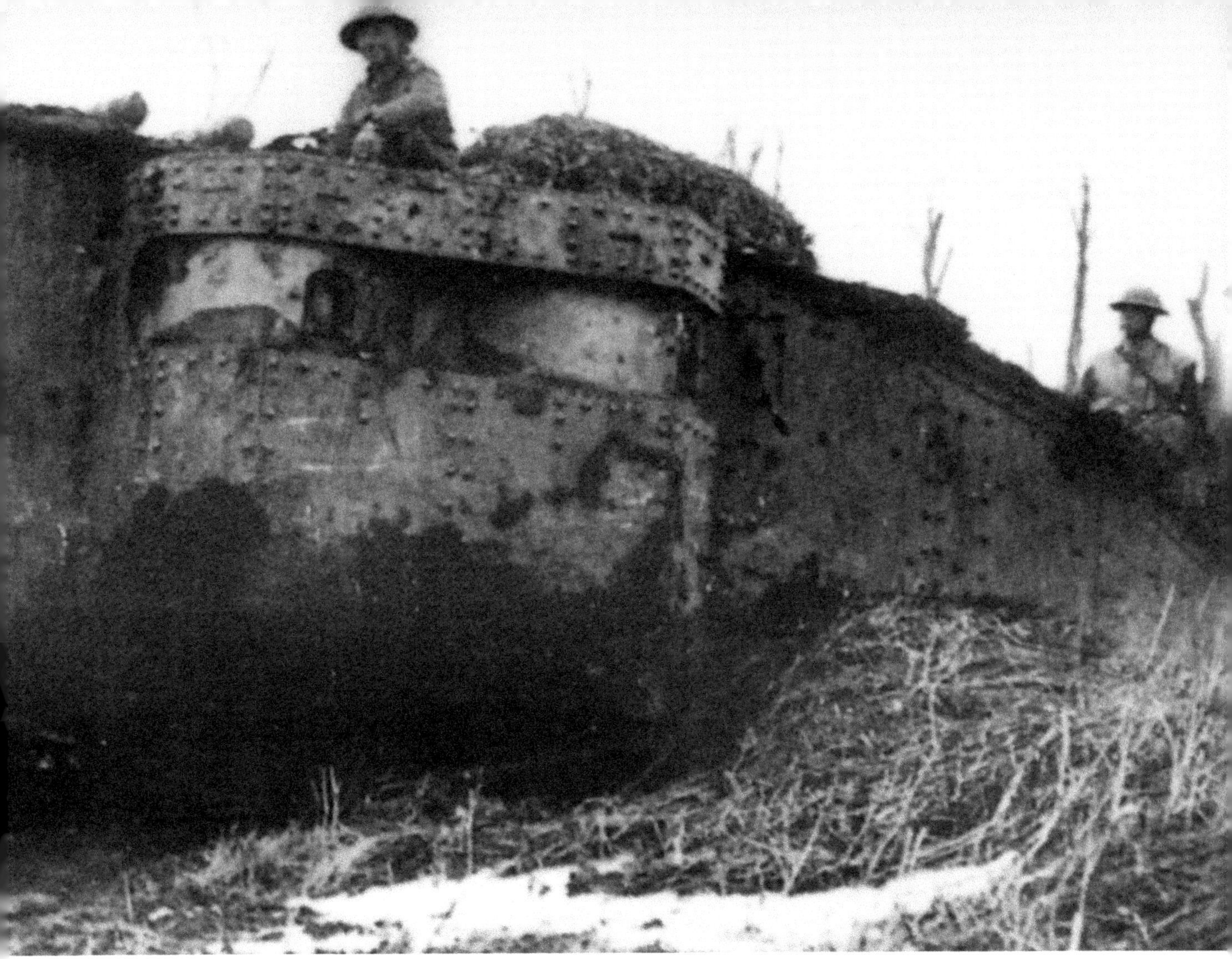

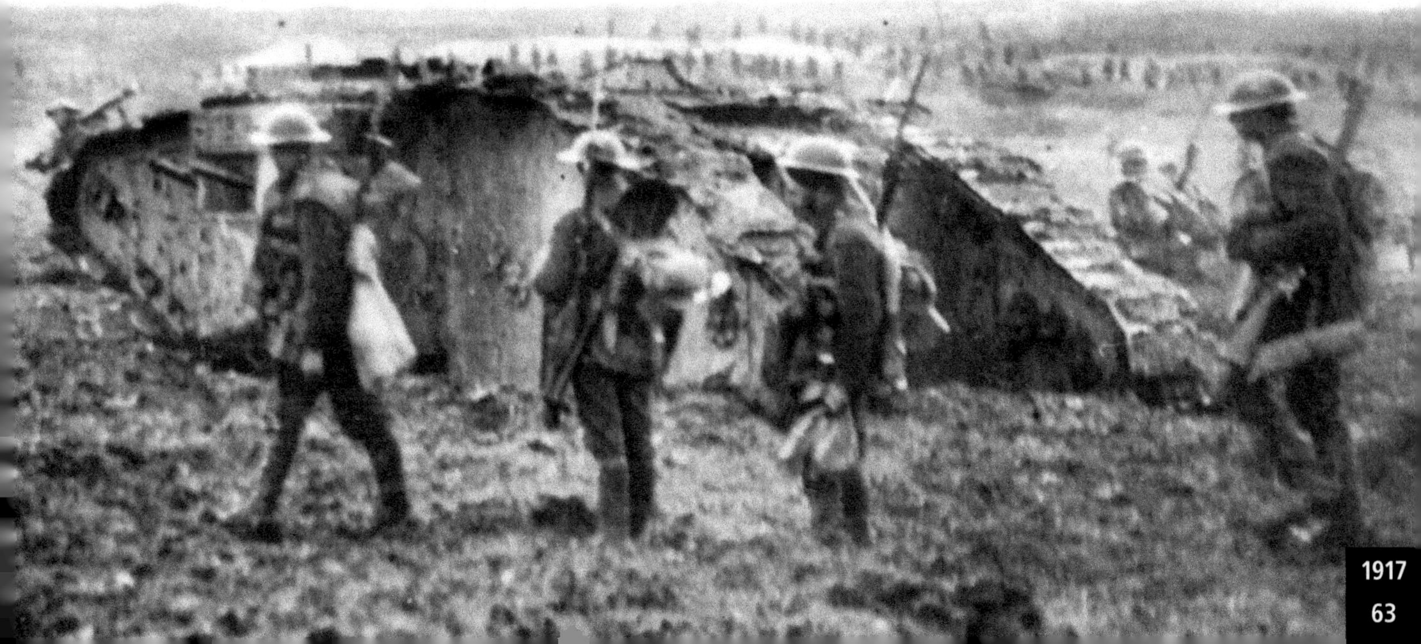

1917

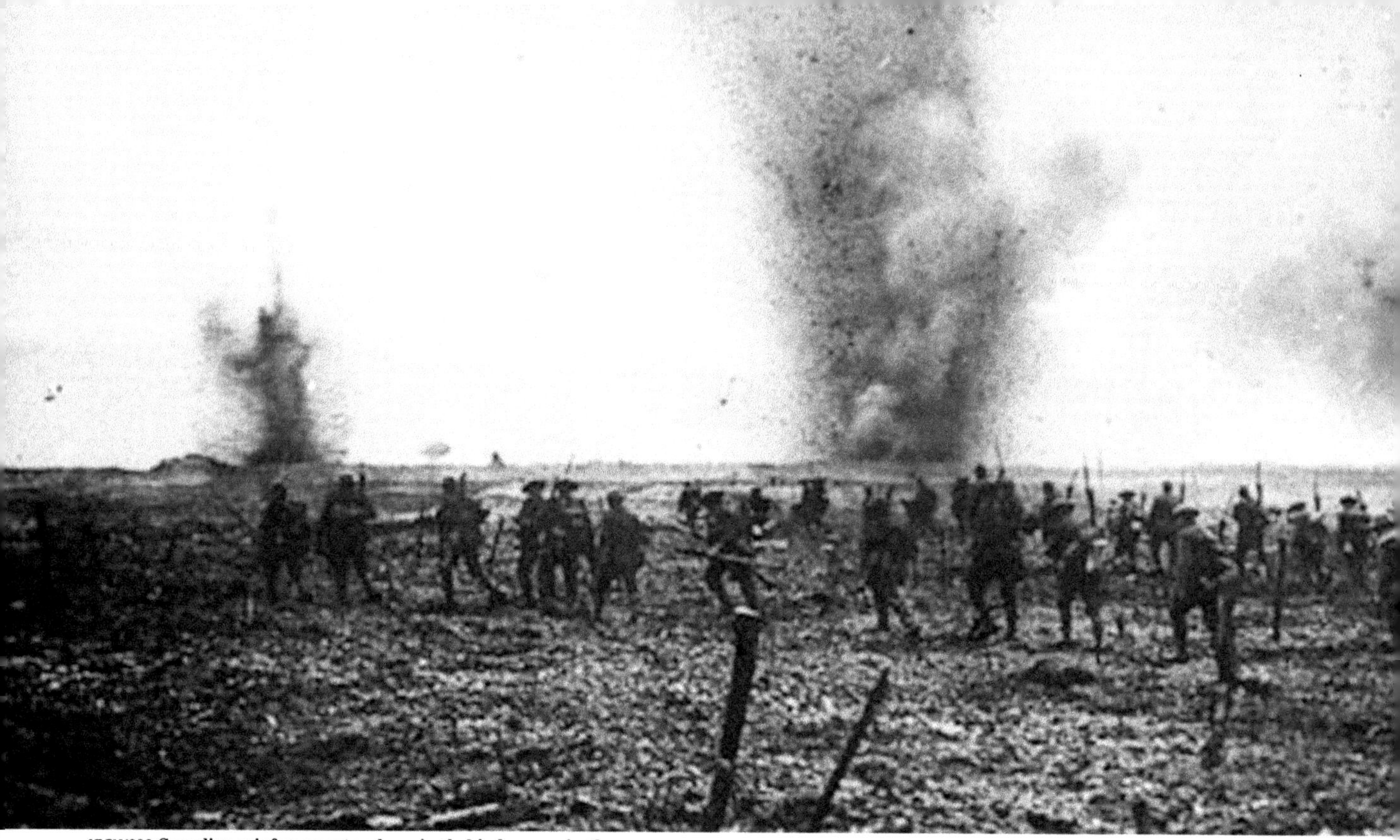

17GW090 Canadian reinforcements advancing behind a barage.

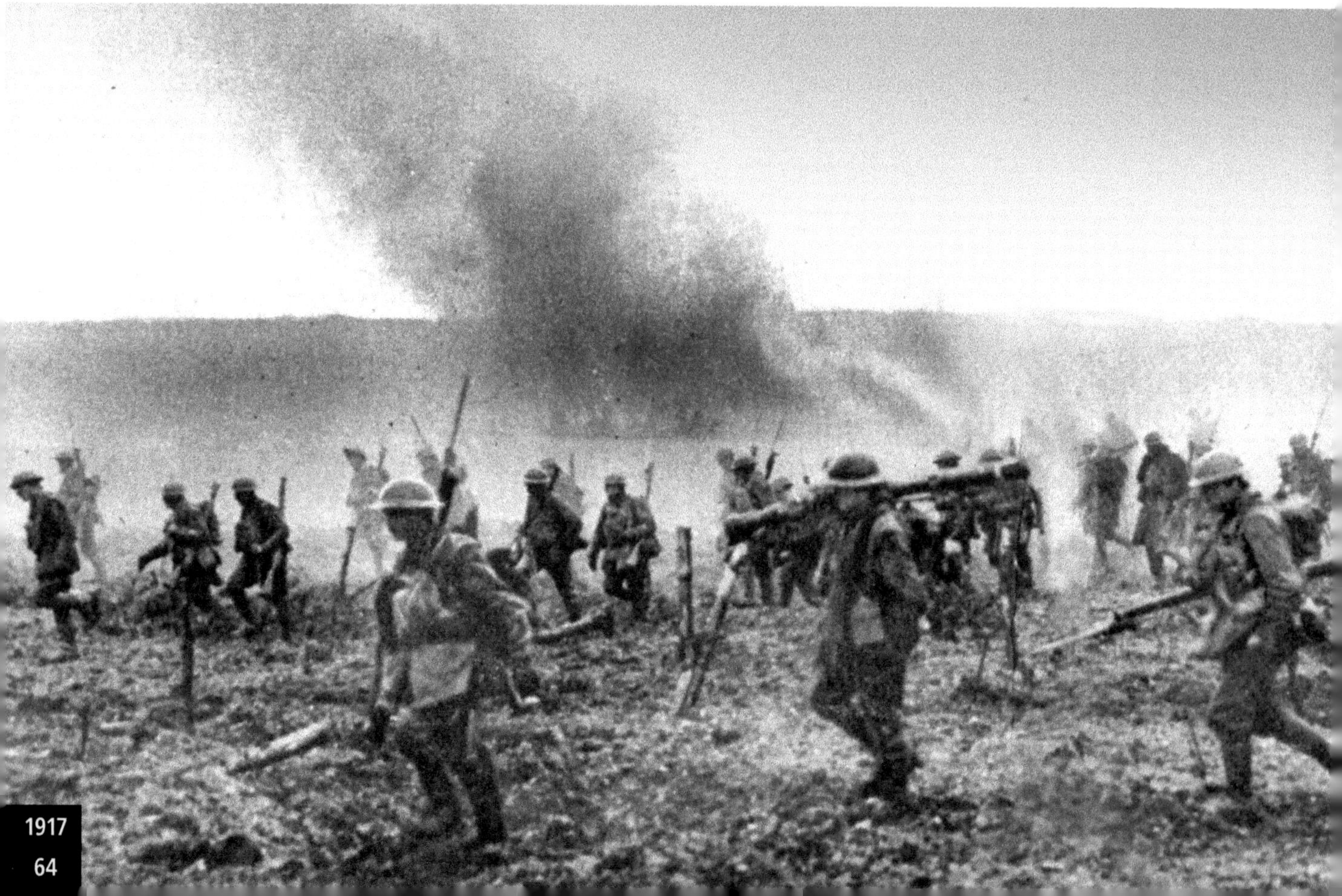

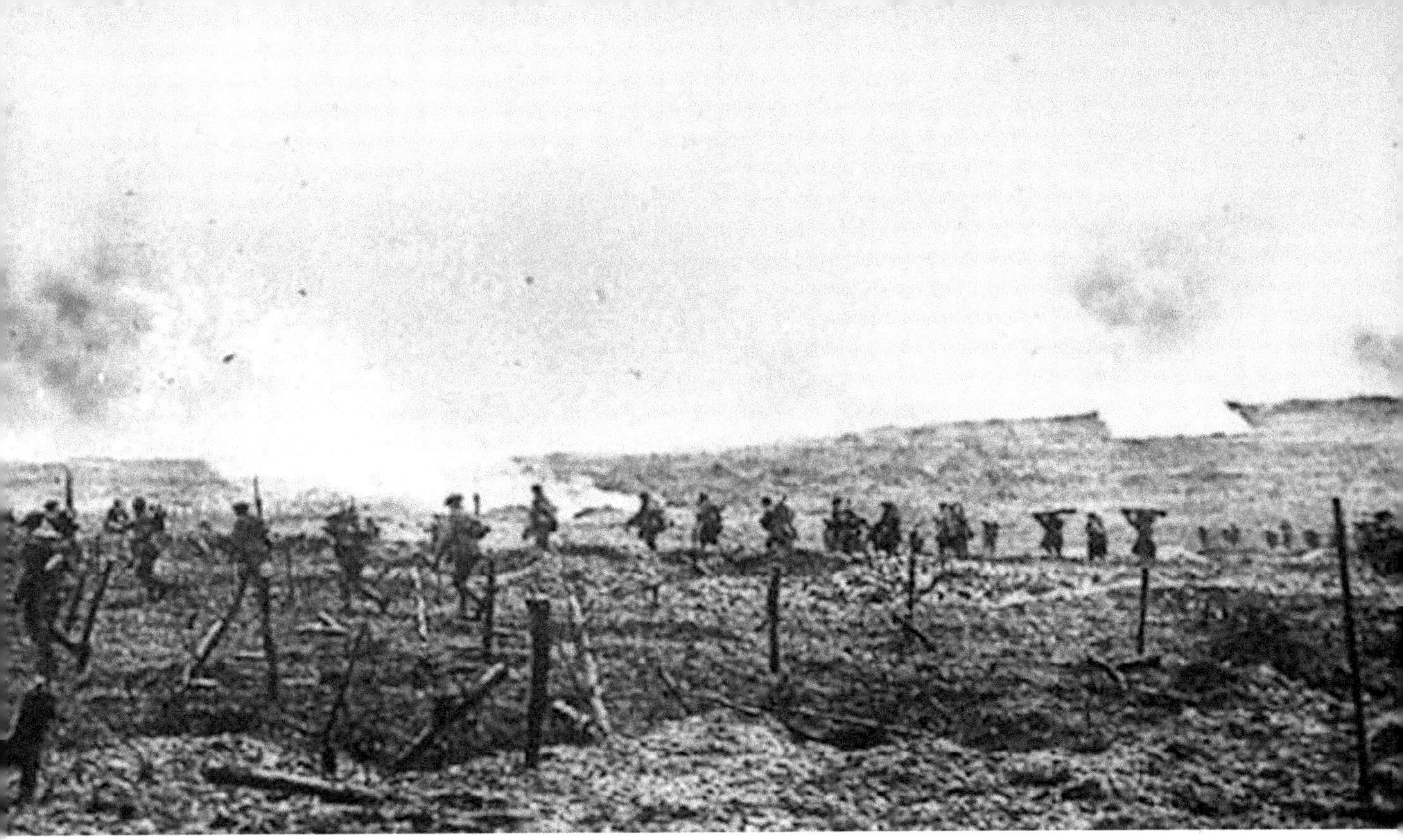

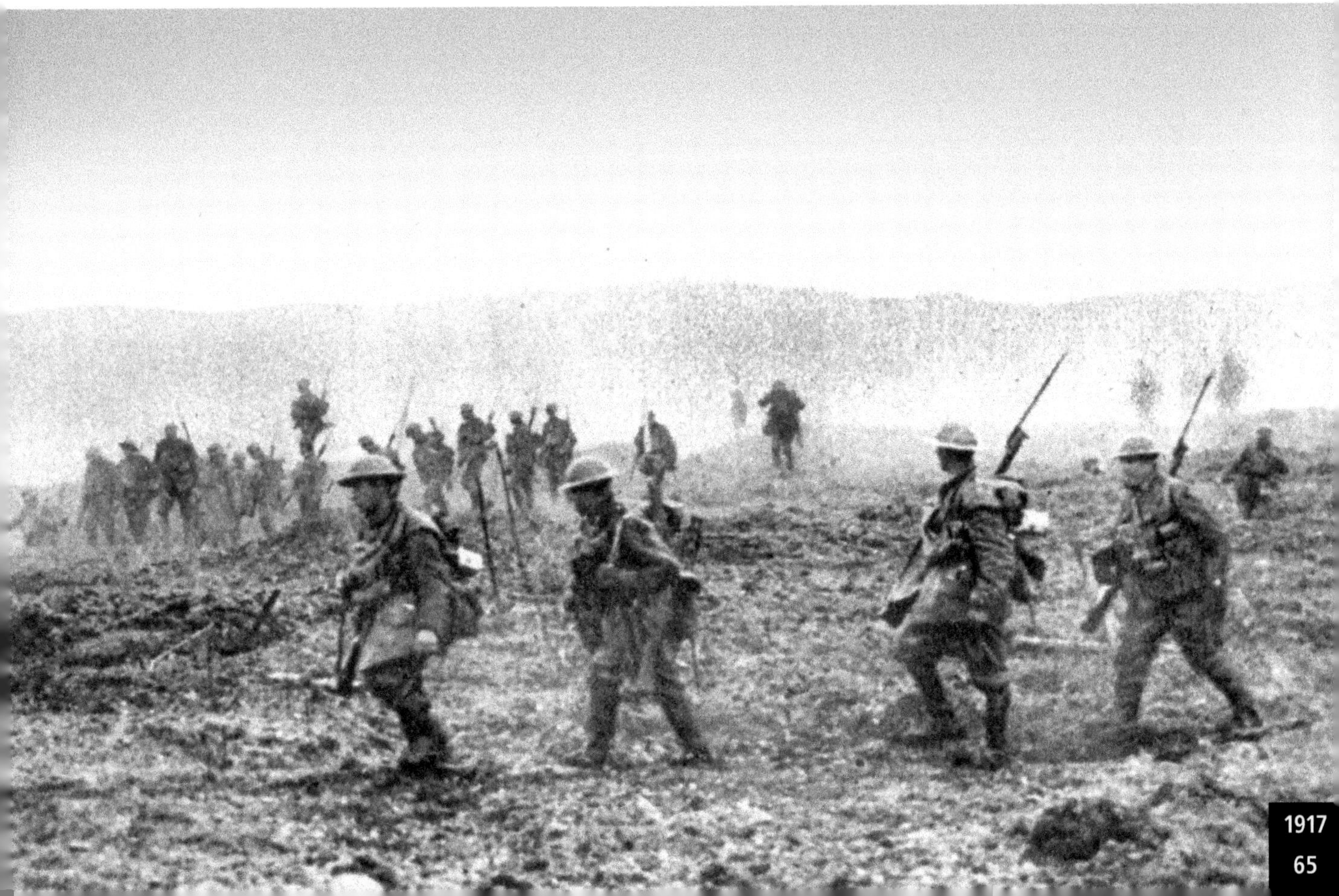

1917

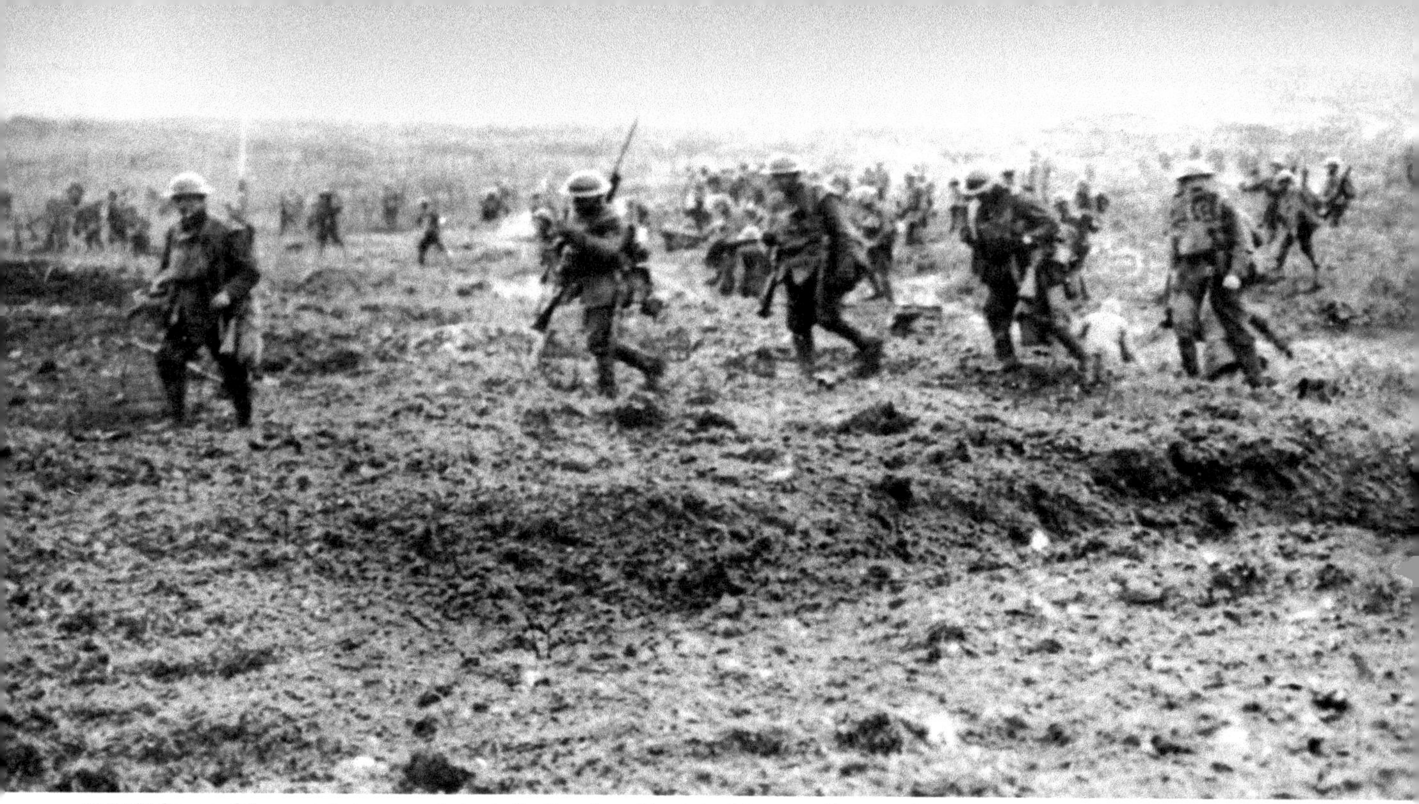

17GW131 Groups of German infantry surrendering to the Canadians. The state of the ground bears testimony to the severe pounding by the British artillery.

17GW121 By 7.00 hrs Easter Monday morning, 9 April 1917, the Canadians had taken much of Vimy Ridge and are seen here consolidating the conquered ground. It took until the 12th to take the northern end, finally falling to a Canadian and two British divisions.

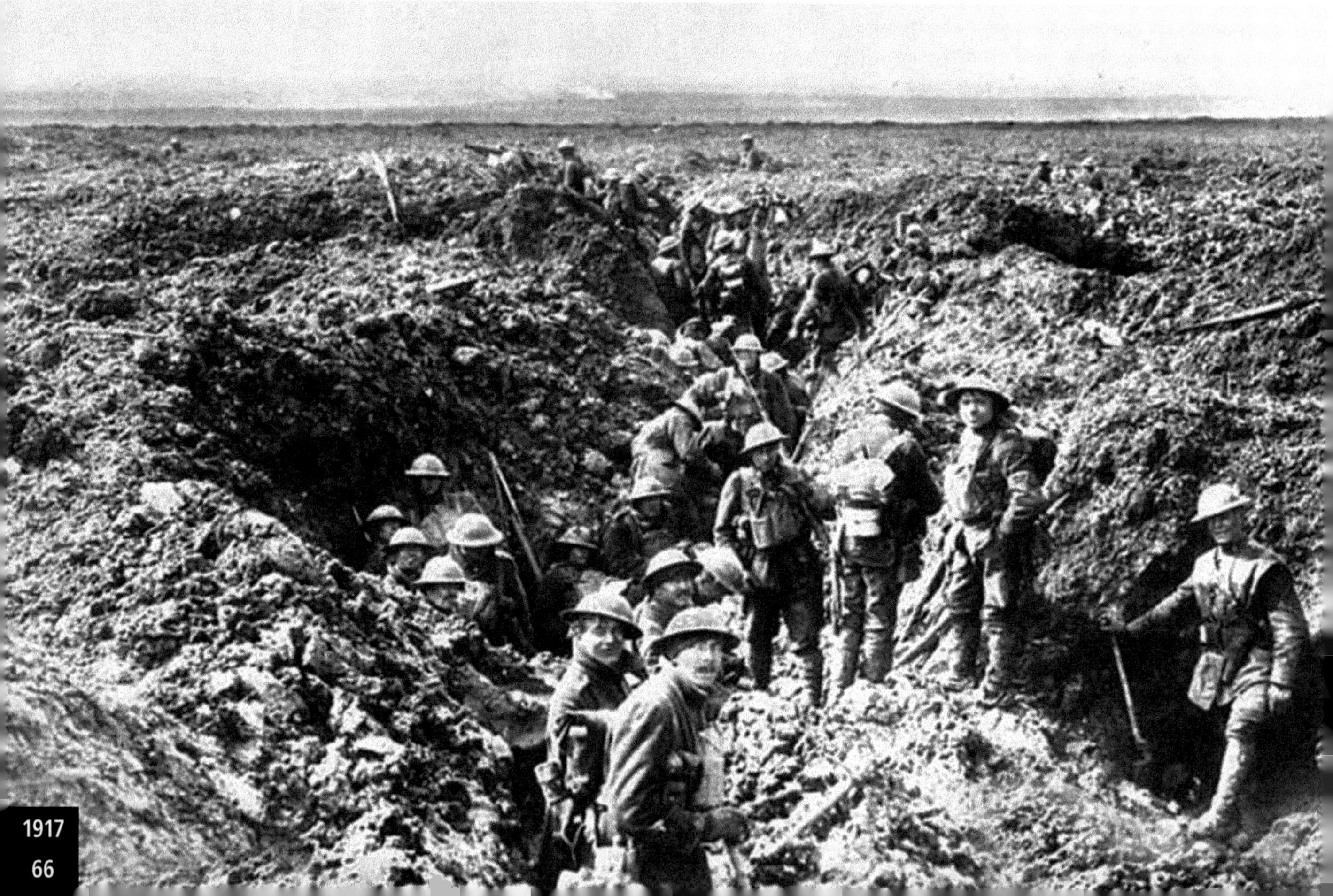

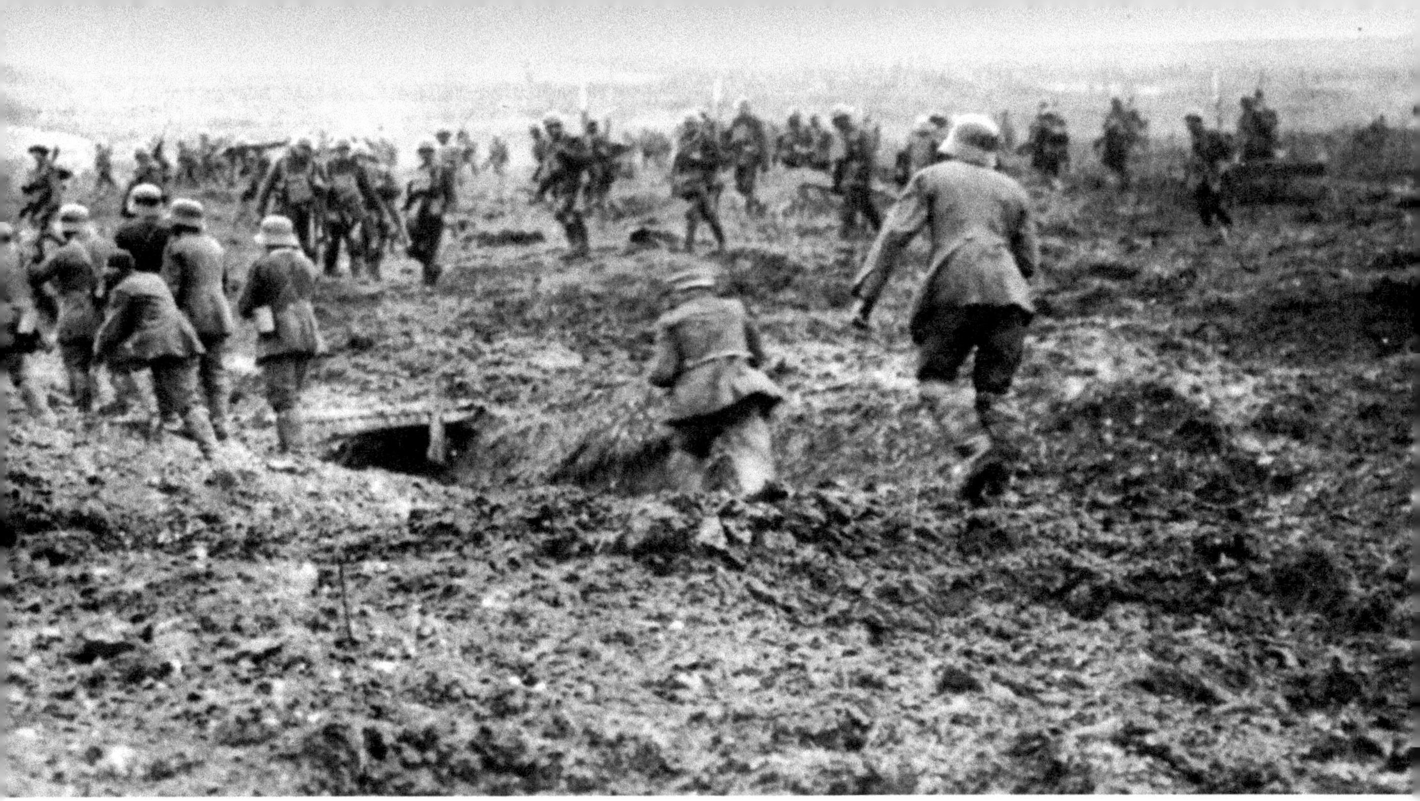

17GW096 Checking a dead German soldier for identification papers, letters, postcards – or anything that might prove of use to Canadian intelligence.

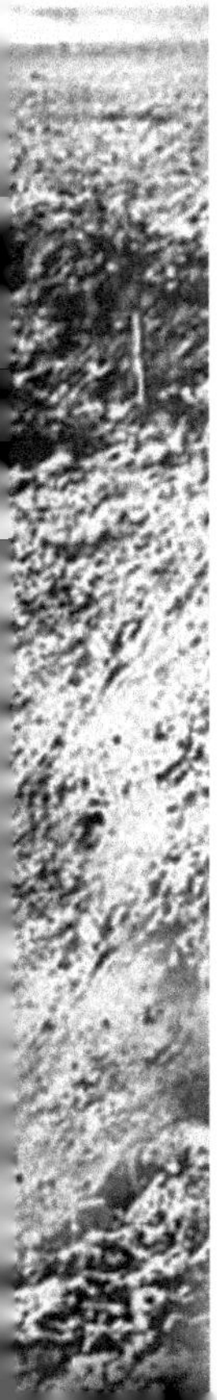

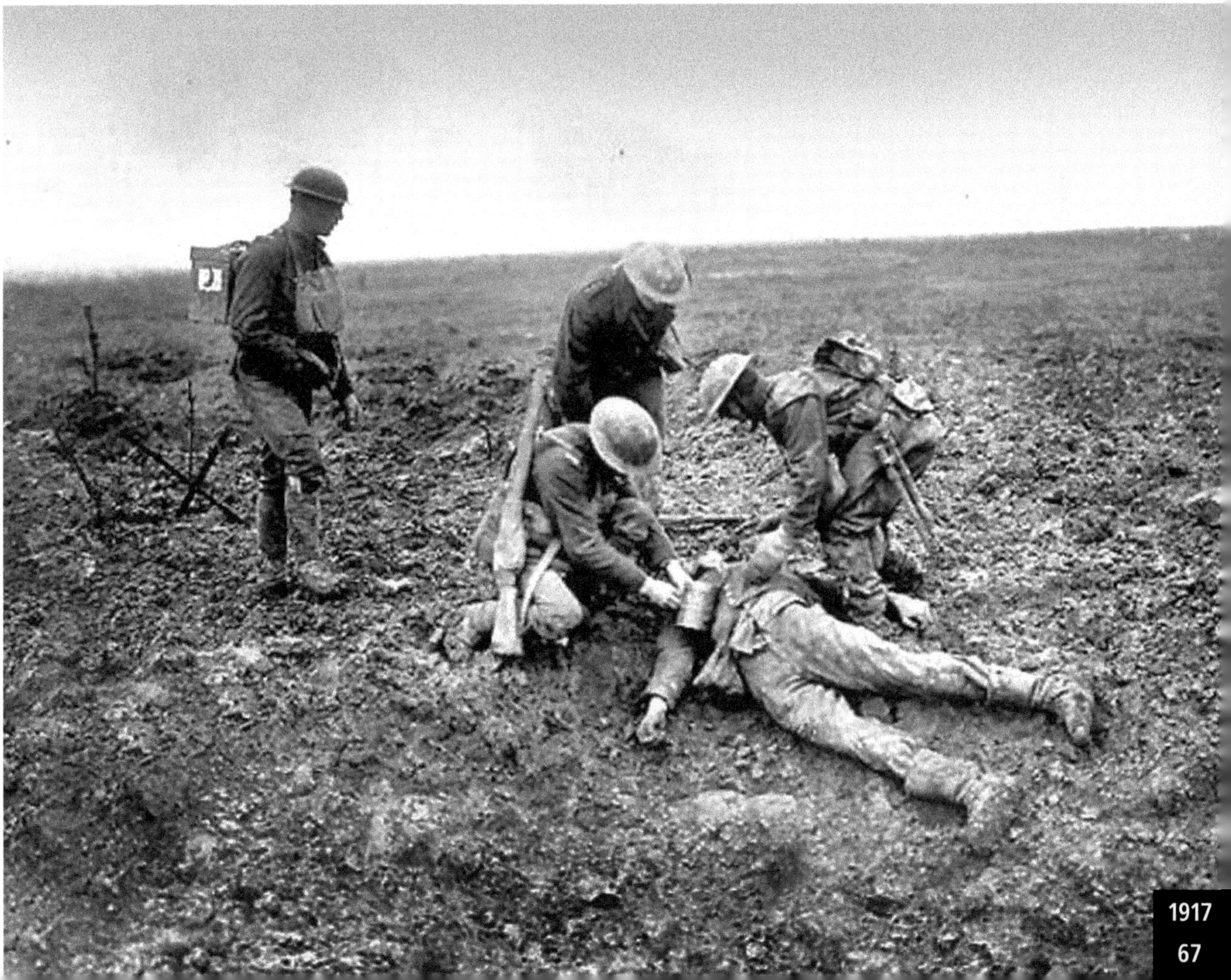

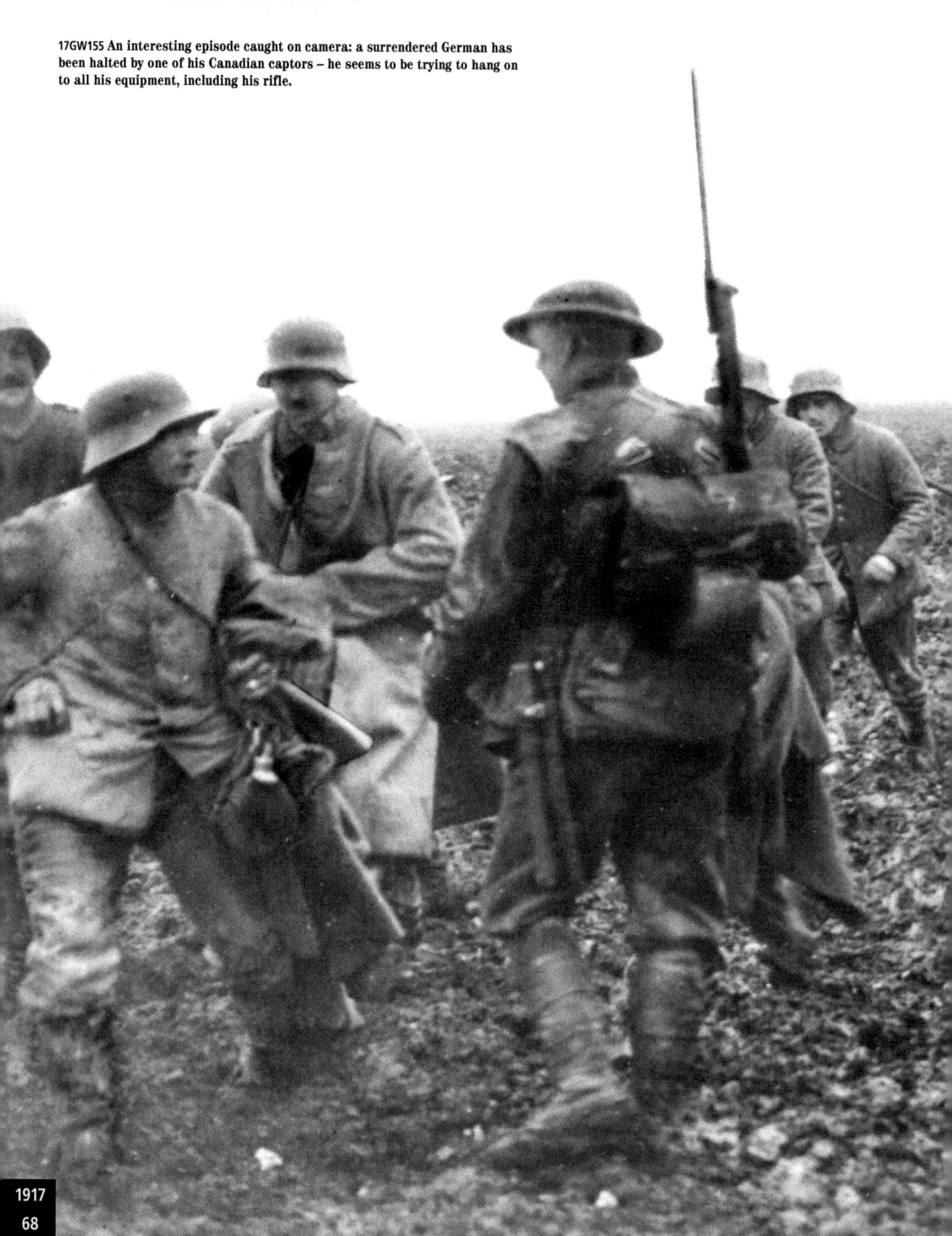
17GW155 An interesting episode caught on camera: a surrendered German has been halted by one of his Canadian captors – he seems to be trying to hang on to all his equipment, including his rifle.

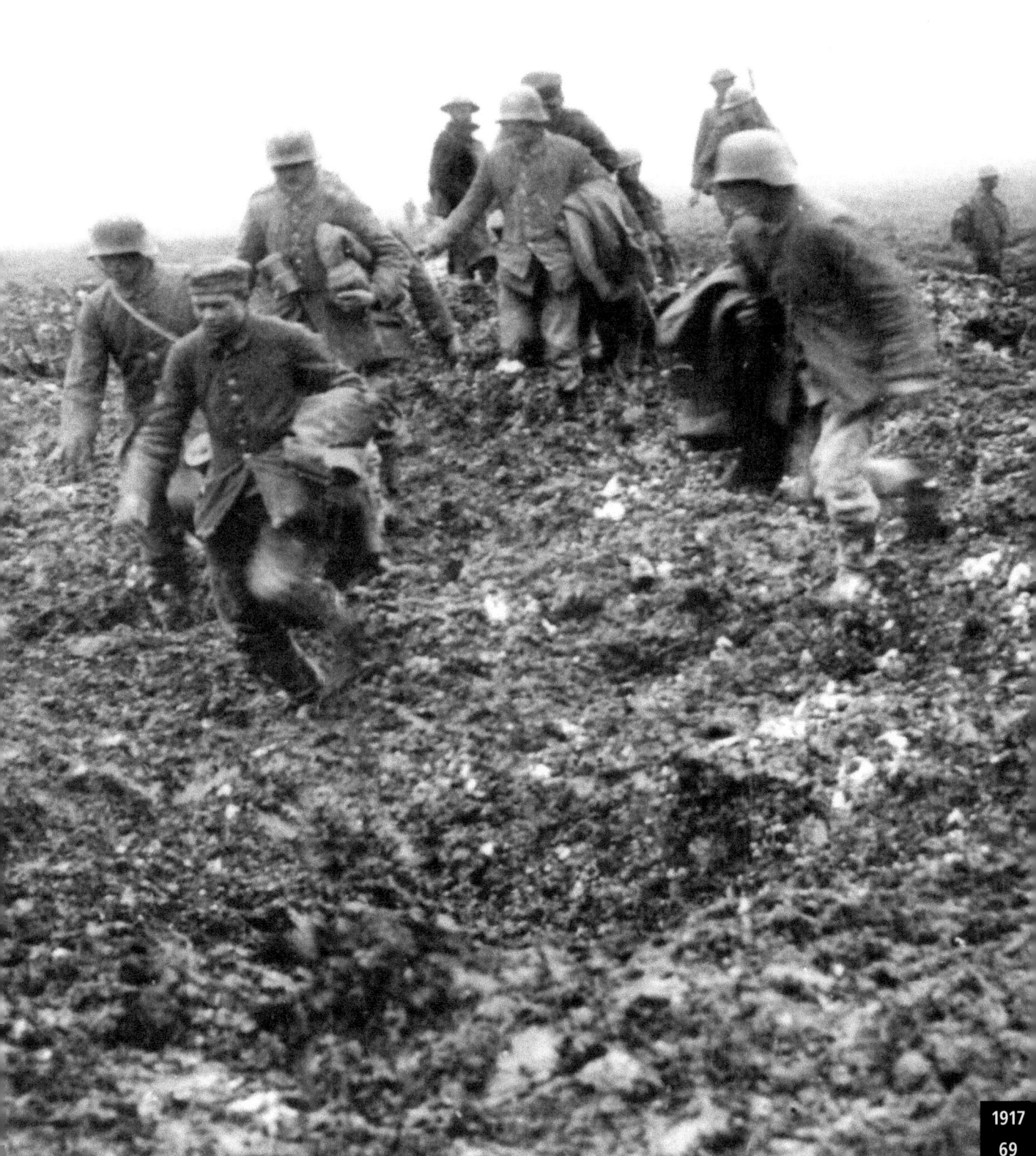

1917
69

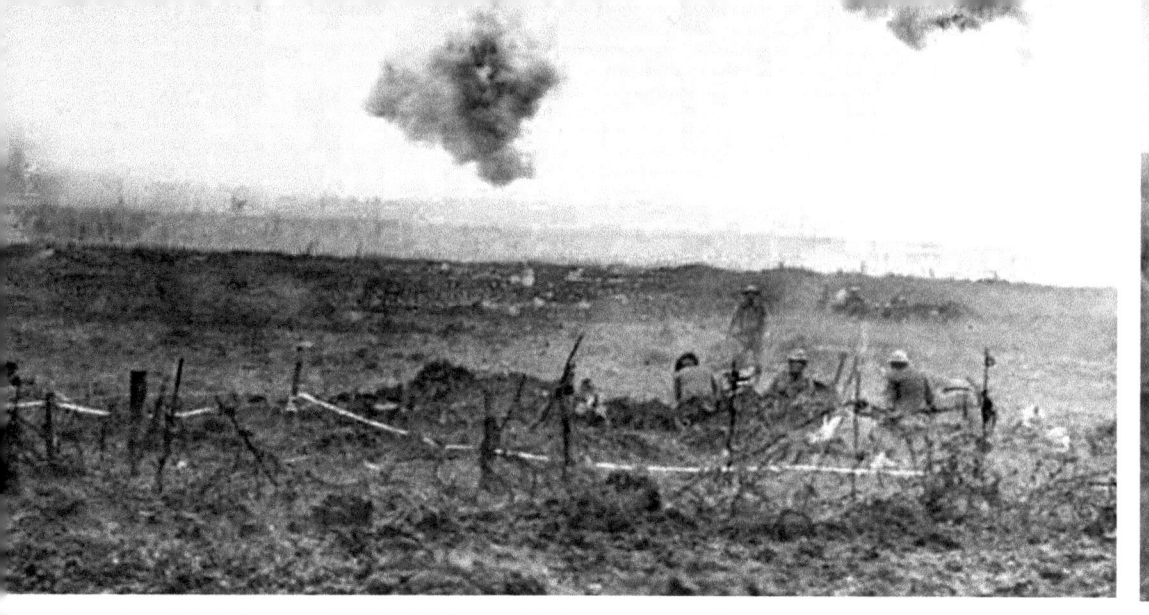
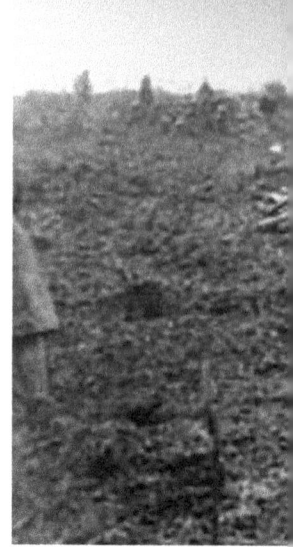

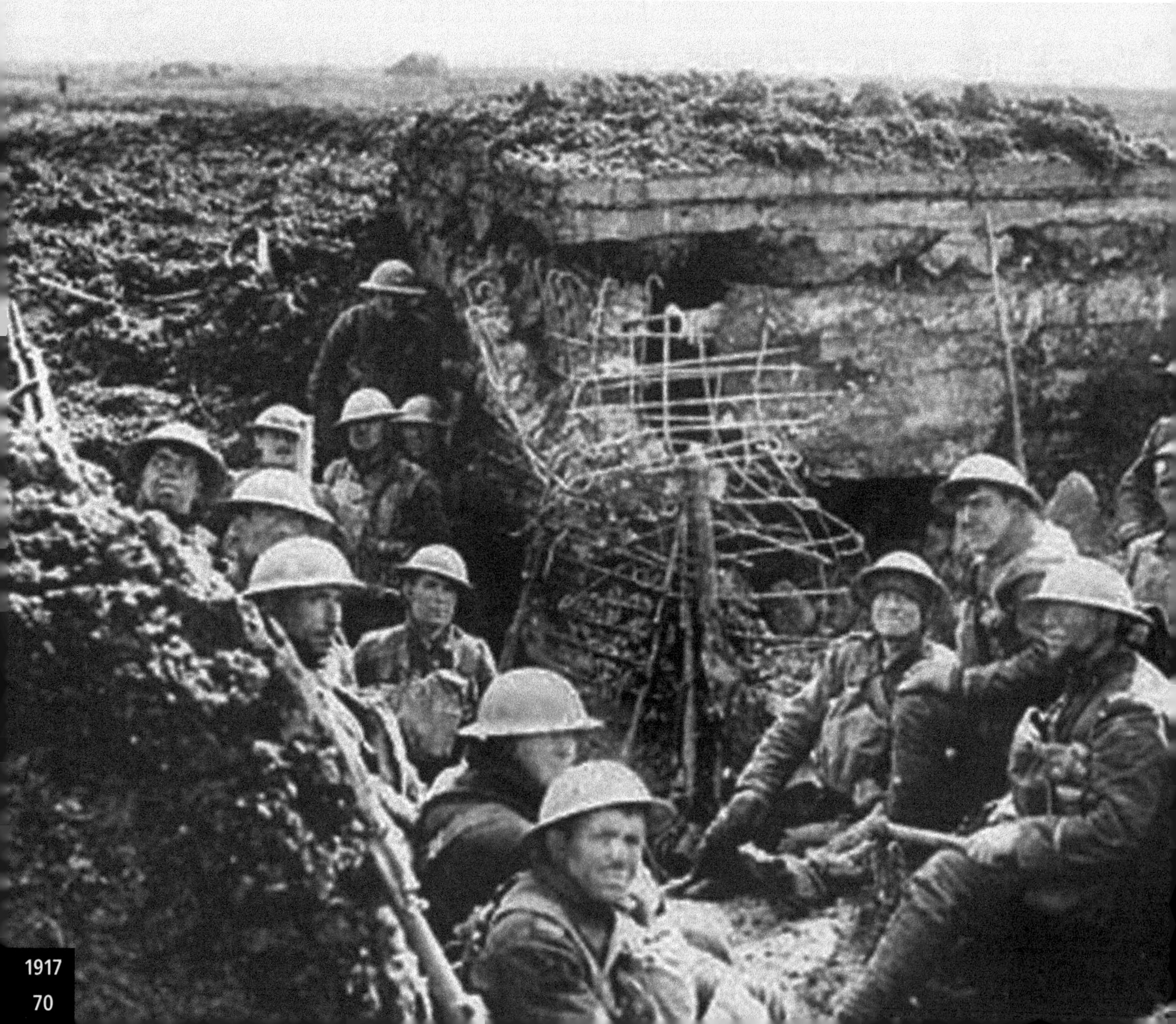

1917

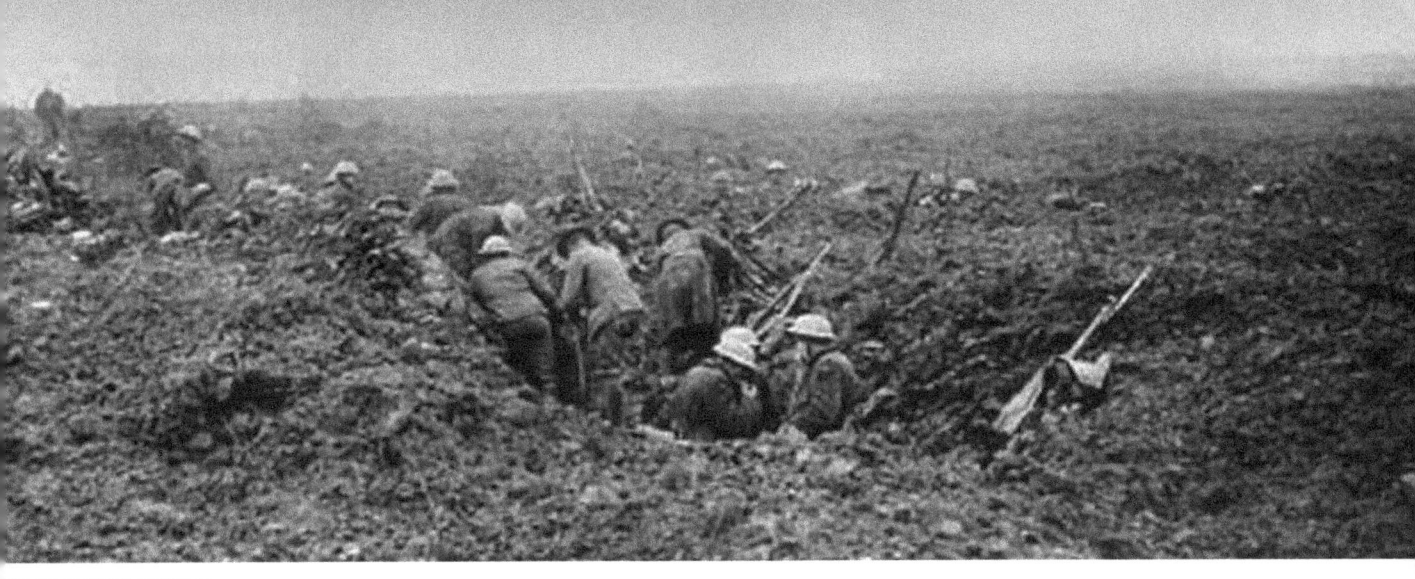

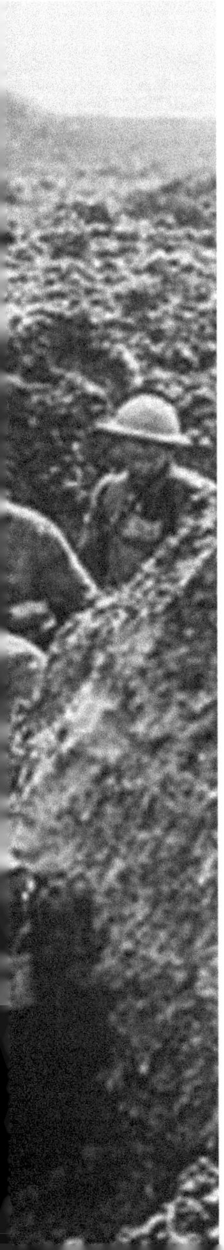

17GW154, 17GW157, 17GW158, 17GW159. Canadian infantry in possession of the German positions east of Vimy Ridge. In the first picture air burst from German guns can be seen exploding over the lost ground. The trenches had been thoroughly smashed by the British artillery and the Canadians had to construct fresh defences. In the picture below identification panels have been laid out to signal the extent of the Canadian advance to allied aircraft. Note the damage to the bunker, which reveals the reinforcement rods used in the construction.

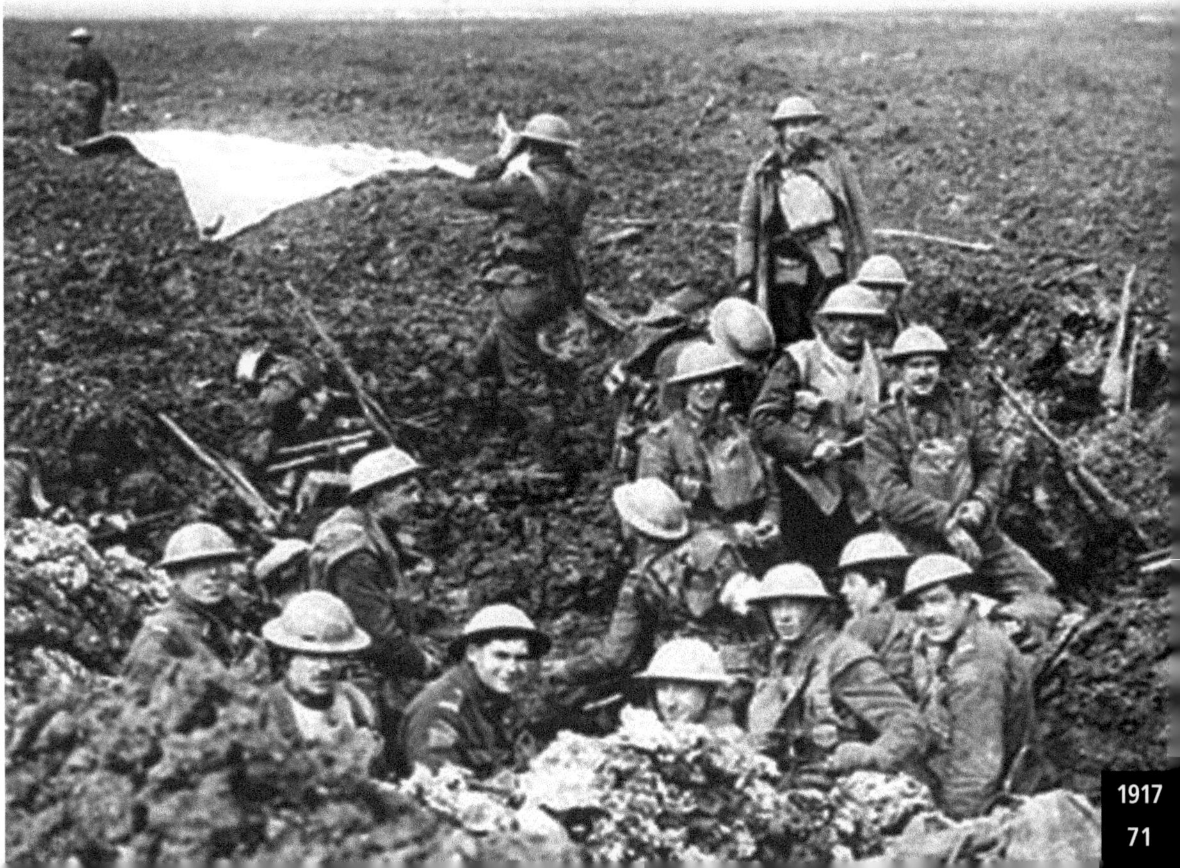

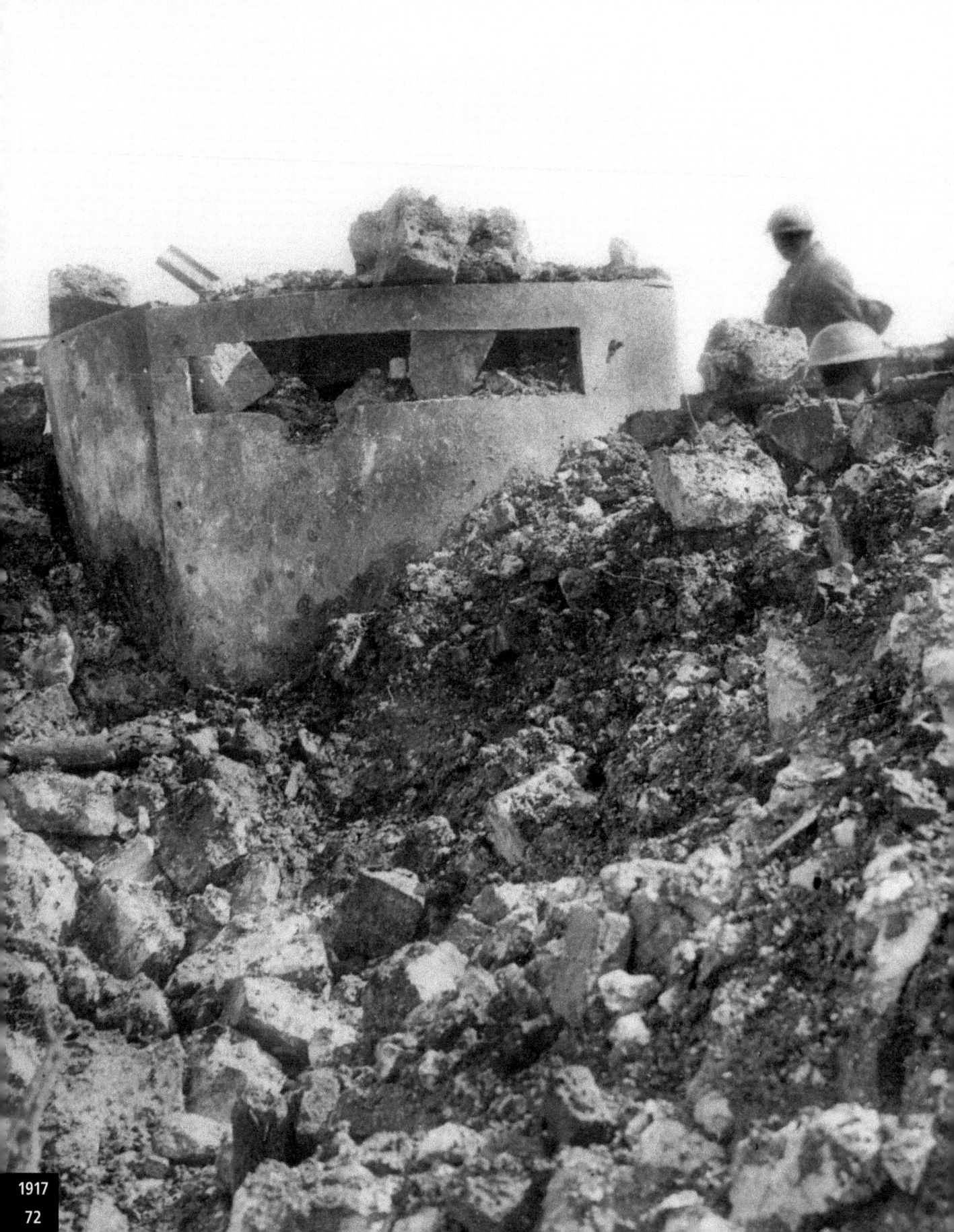

17GW118 A German machine gun emplacement in the village of Thélus. Although the tremendous artillery barage had dislocated the German defence, Maxim machine guns still poured fire on the advancing Canadians. The reason for this was that a number of machine guns were protected from all but a direct hit by being sited in emplacements constructed of concrete and steel plate.

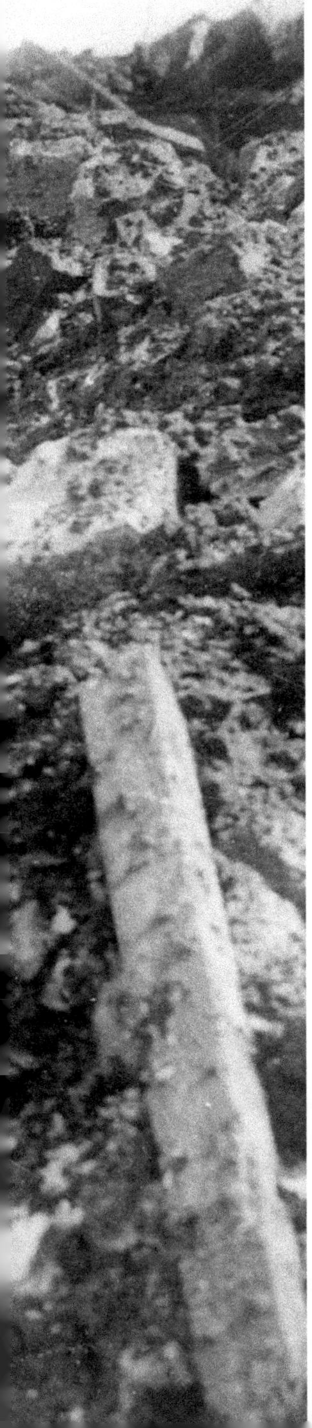

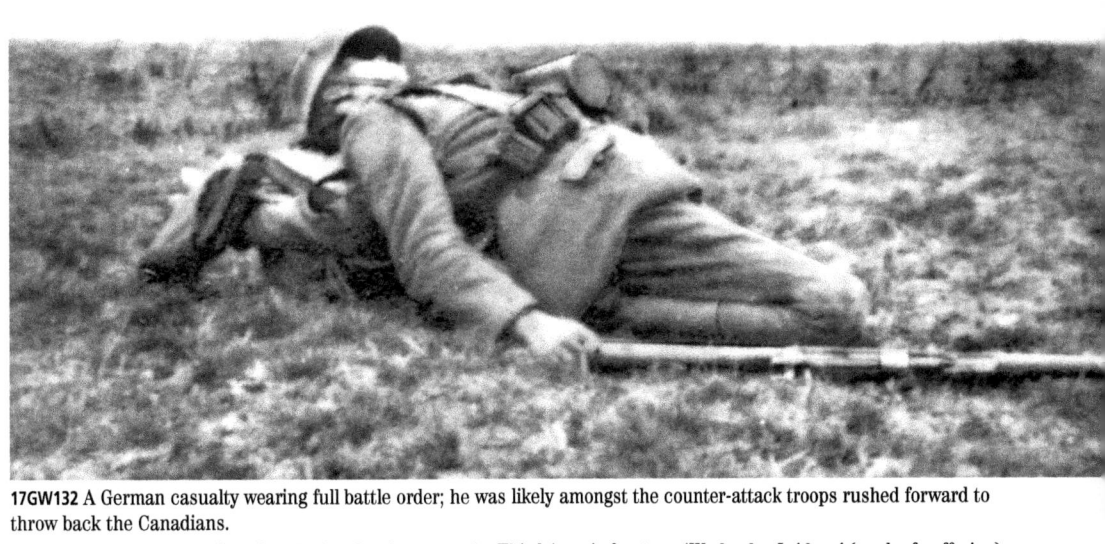

17GW132 A German casualty wearing full battle order; he was likely amongst the counter-attack troops rushed forward to throw back the Canadians.

17GW113 The Germans referred to the bombardment on the Third Army's front as *'Woche des Leidens'* (week of suffering). However, on the First Army front, which included the Canadian Corps, the preliminary barrage lasted two weeks longer.

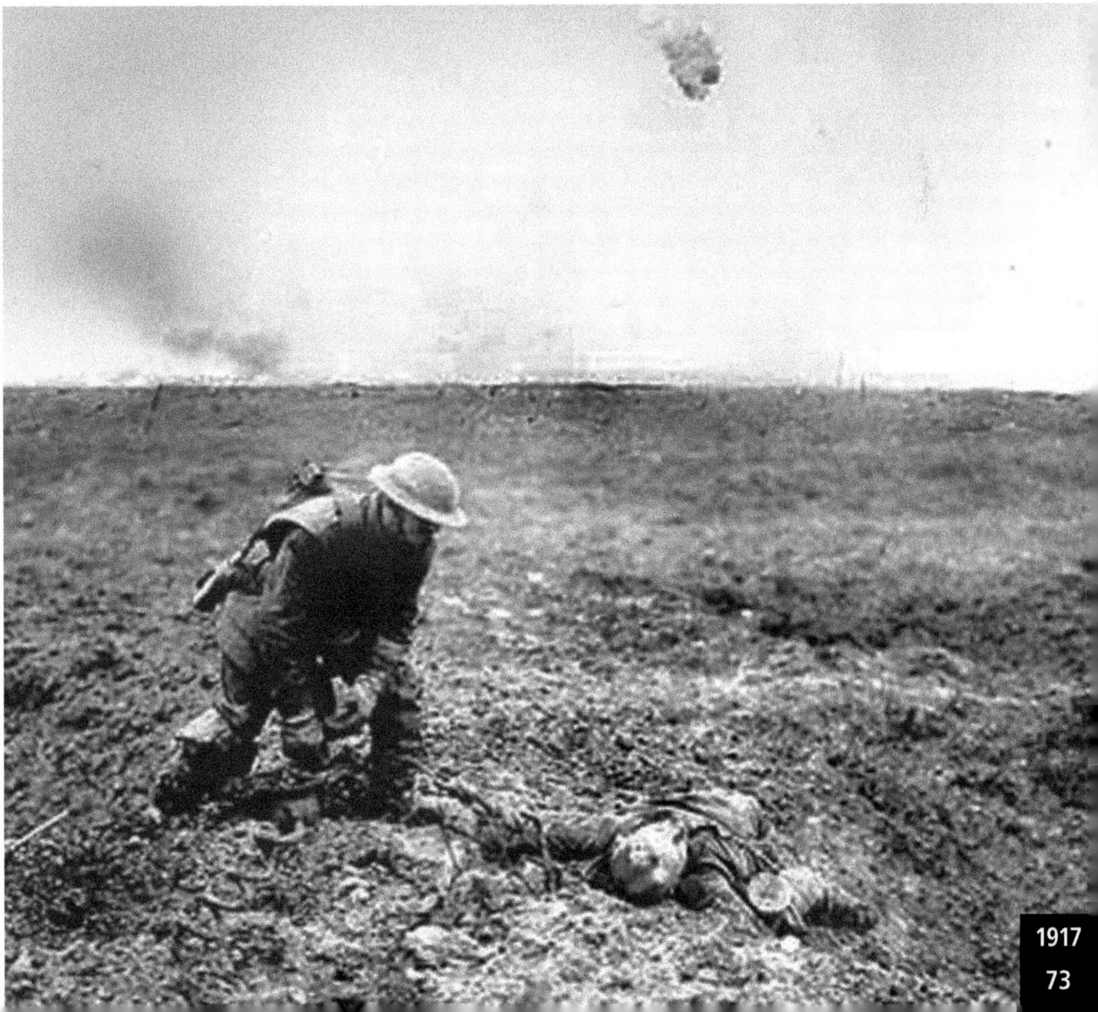

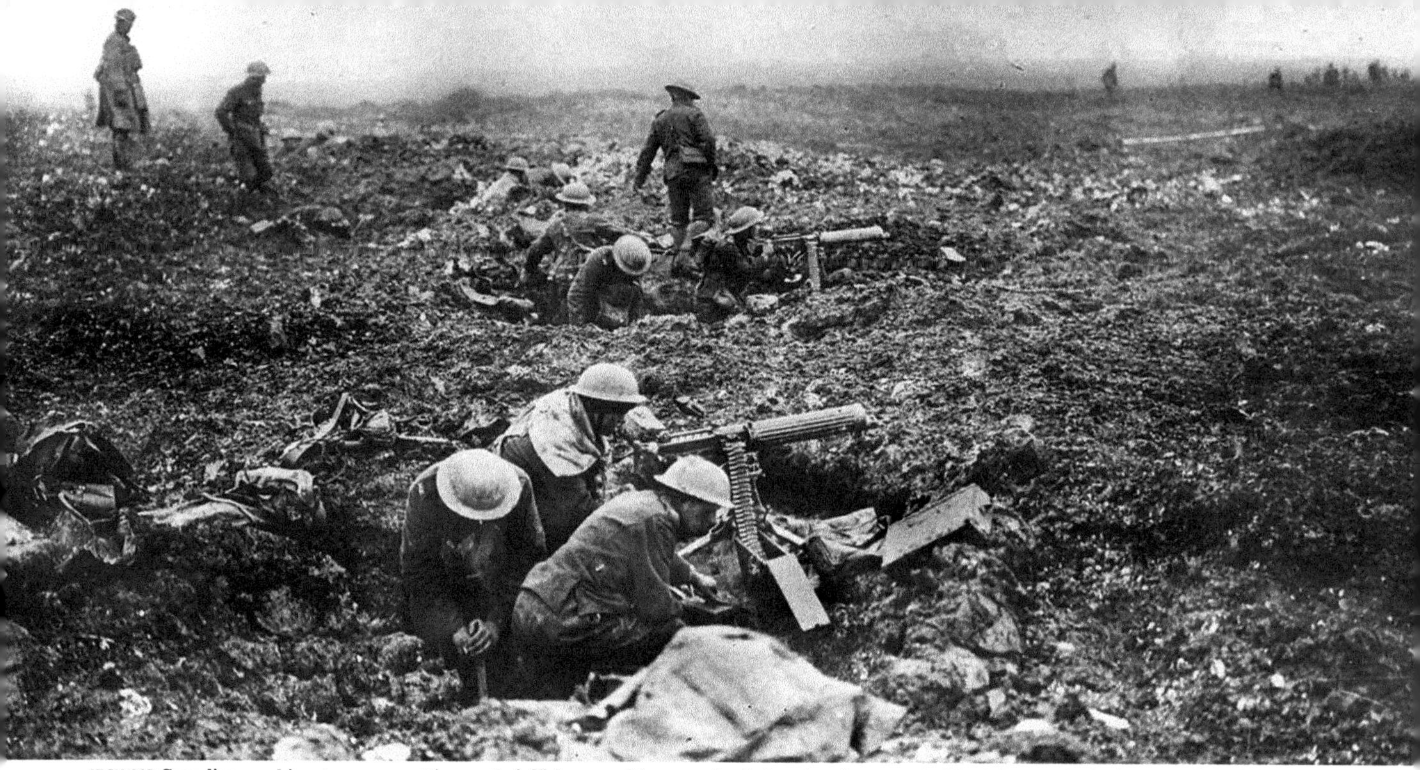

17GW093 Canadian machine gun crews setting up their Vickers machine guns in shell craters in support of the infantry who had captured the Ridge.

17GW136 A concrete constructed German artillery position littered with shell carriers for the 77 mm field gun. The Canadians advance was so rapid that many gunners were taken completely by surprise.

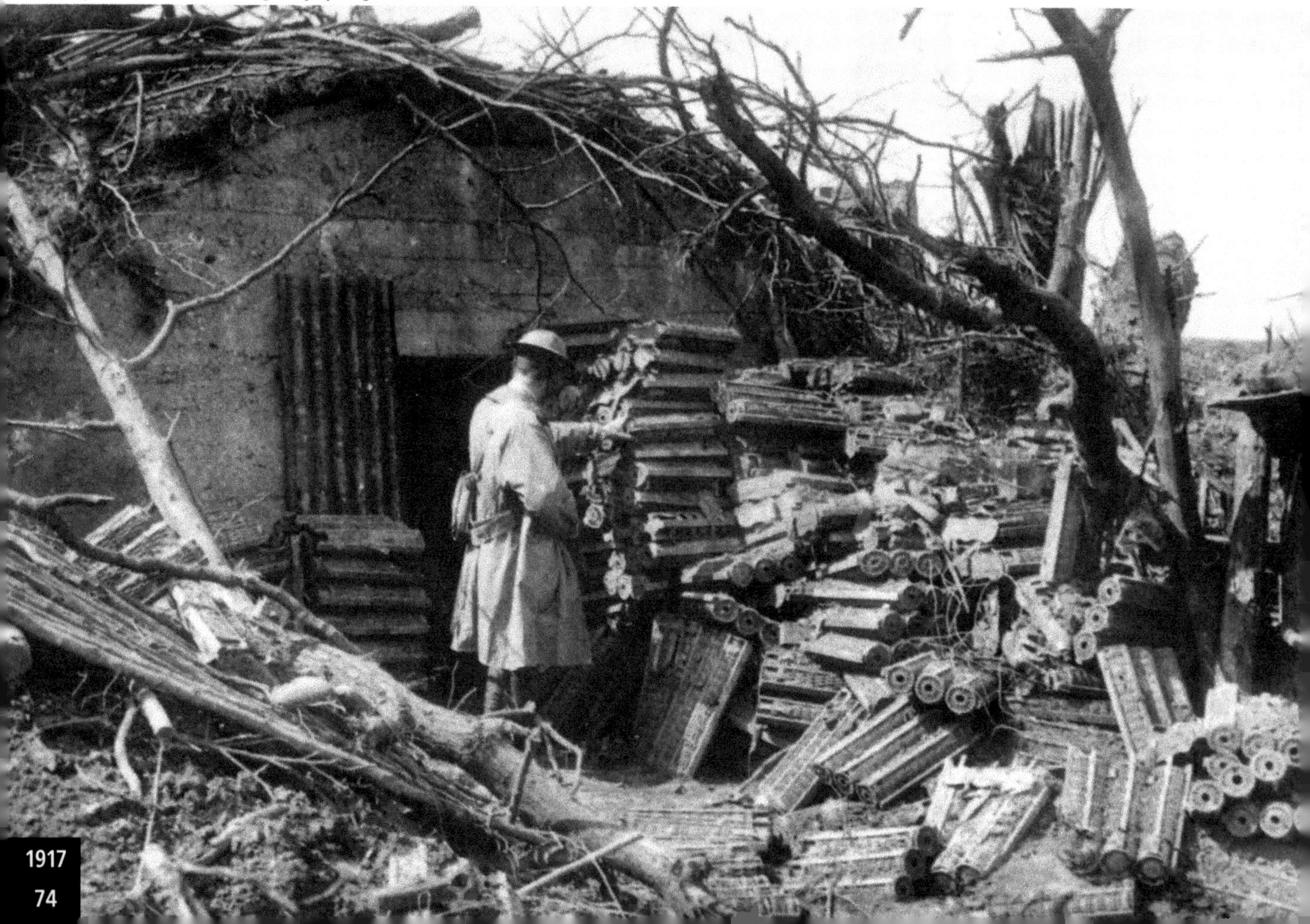

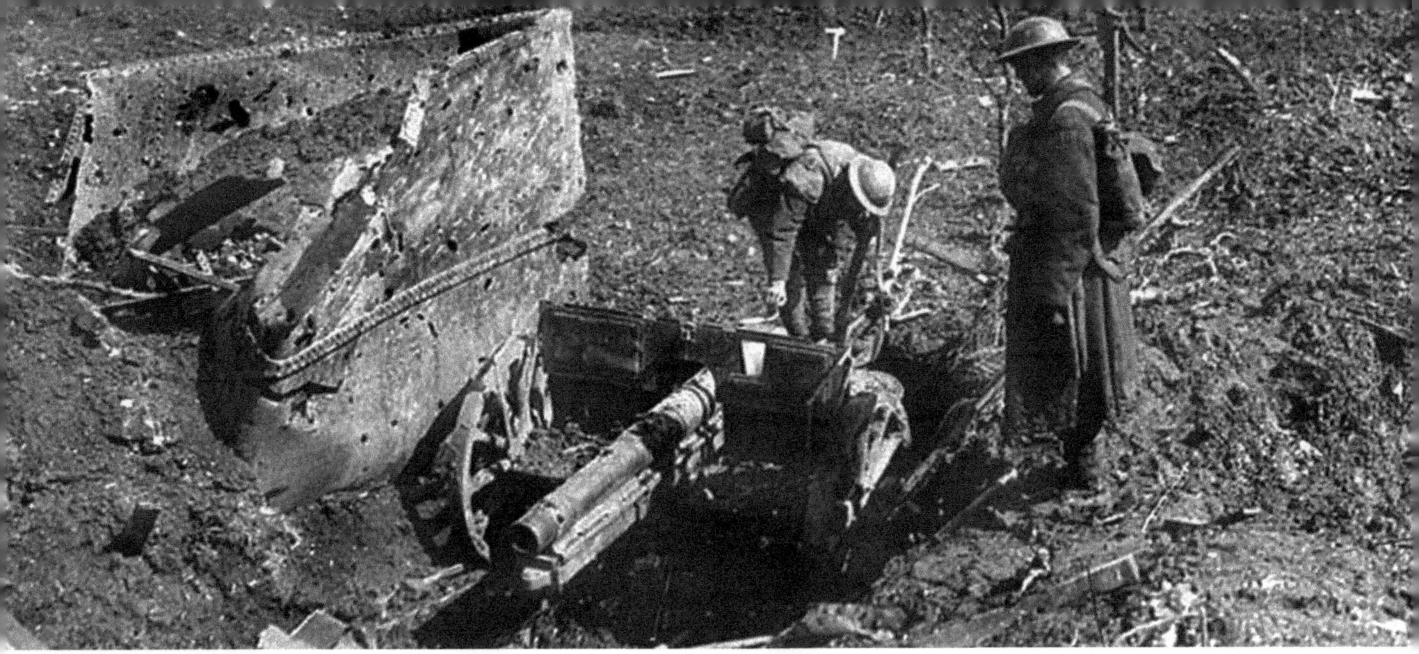

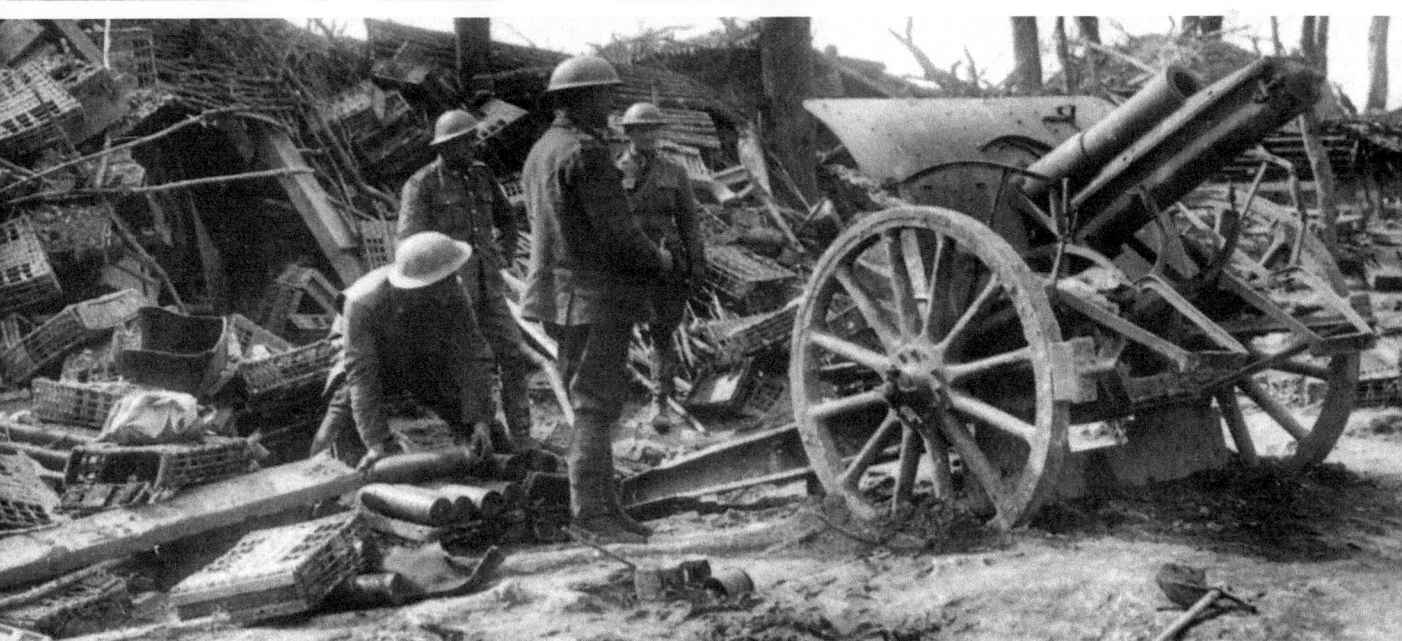

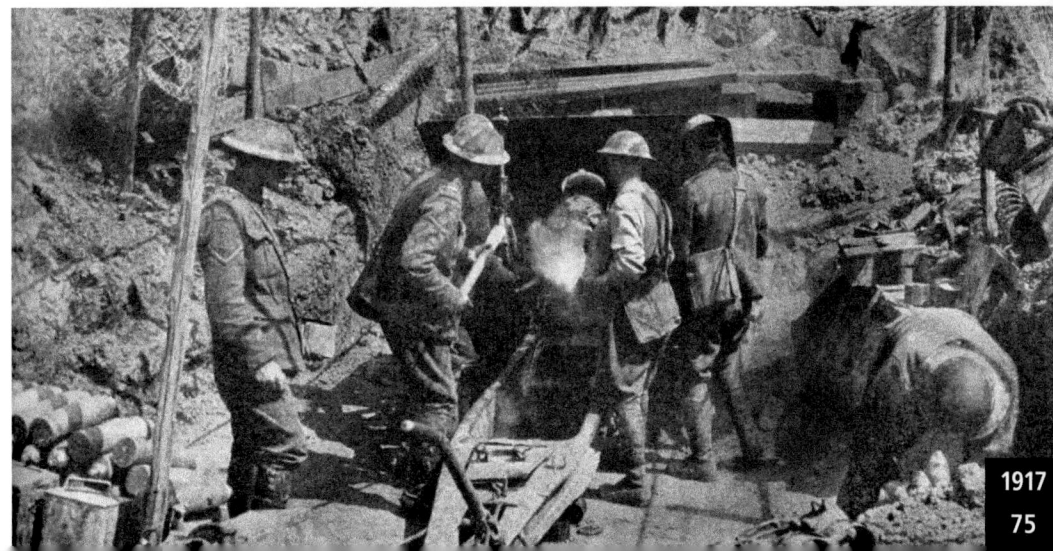

17GW122 A smashed German 77 mm field gun; the bunker appears to have been totally destroyed.

17GW137 A captured howitzer, in good working order, is swung around and shells are fired in the direction of the German rear positions.

17GW138 A captured 77 mm field gun has been turned to bring fire down on its previous owners.

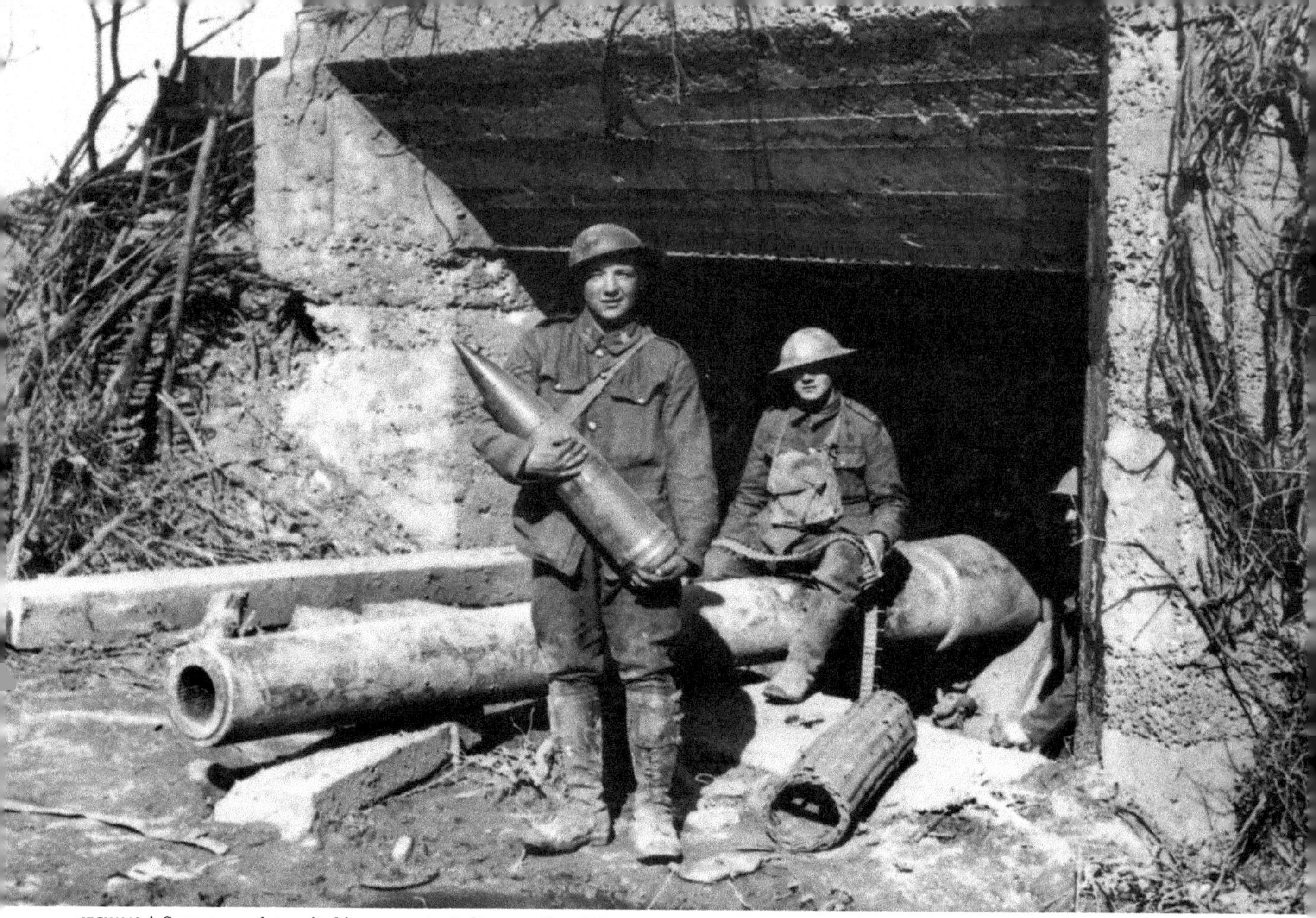

17GW140 A German naval gun sited in a concrete shelter near Vimy Ridge.

17GW142 The Germans were using guns of various calibres. The one being examined here by two Canadian officers appears to be an obsolescent model.

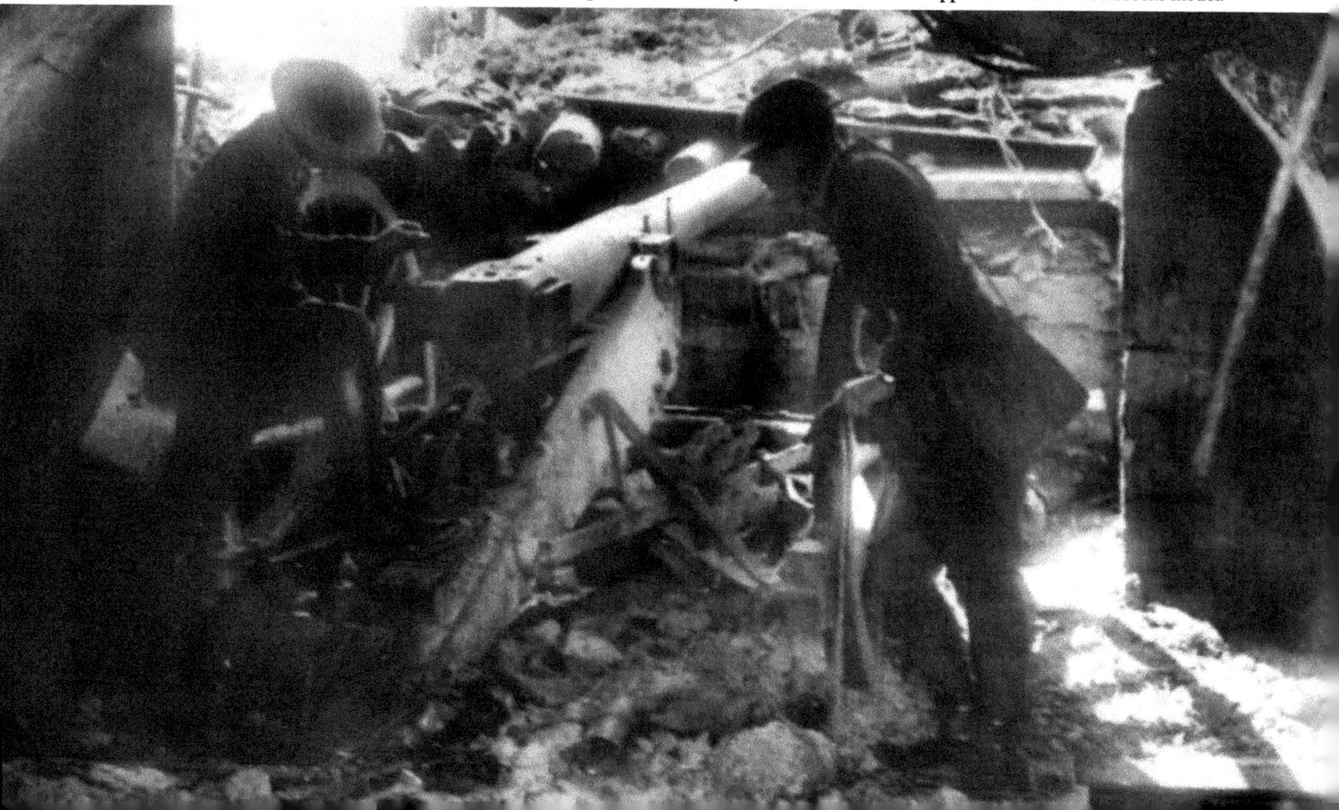

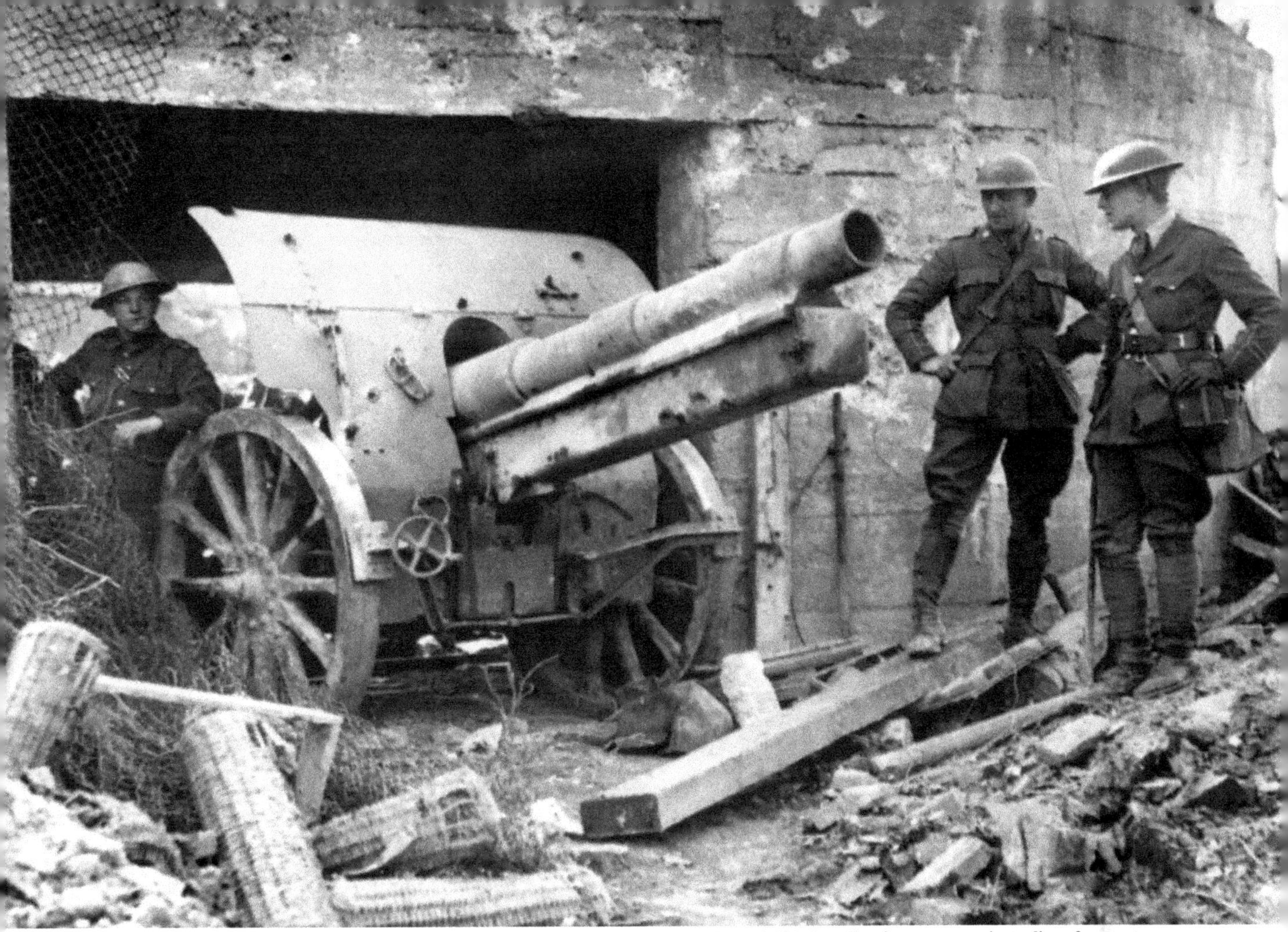

17GW141 A 15 cm howitzer. After the village of Thélus had been captured the Canadians (31st and 28th Battalions) came up against a line of concrete gun emplacements which they eventually captured.

17GW144 A 15 cm howitzer reduced to scrap metal by a direct hit on the front of the shelter.

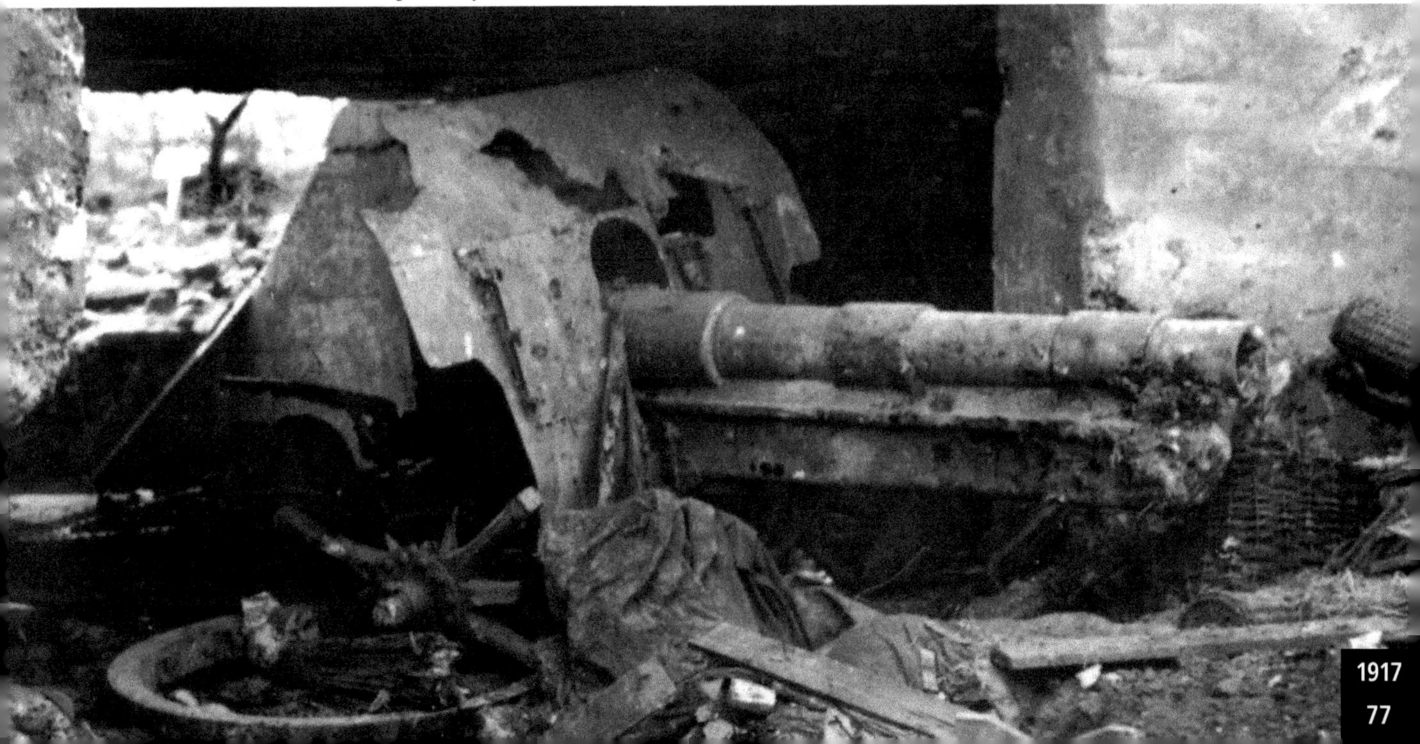

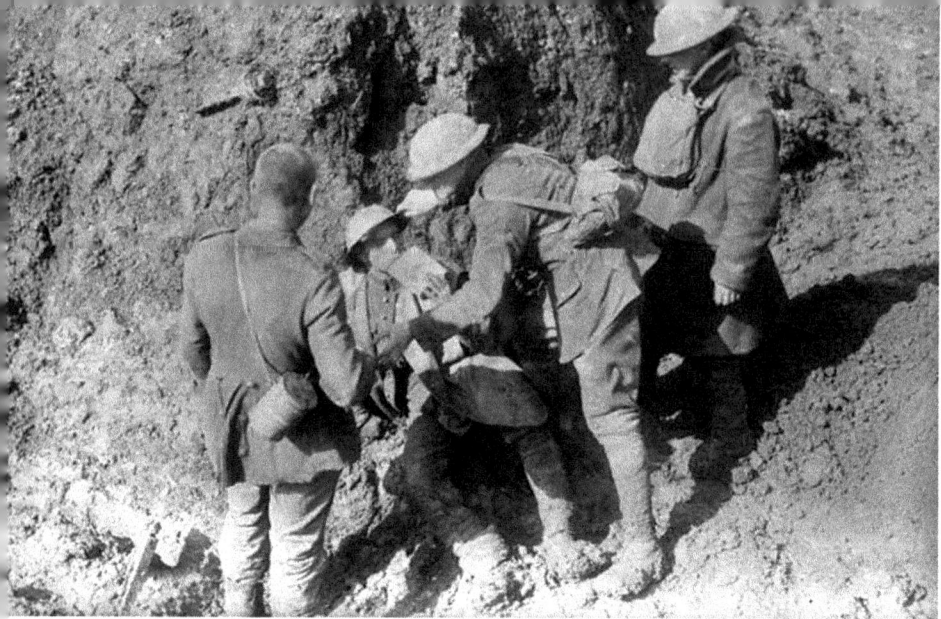
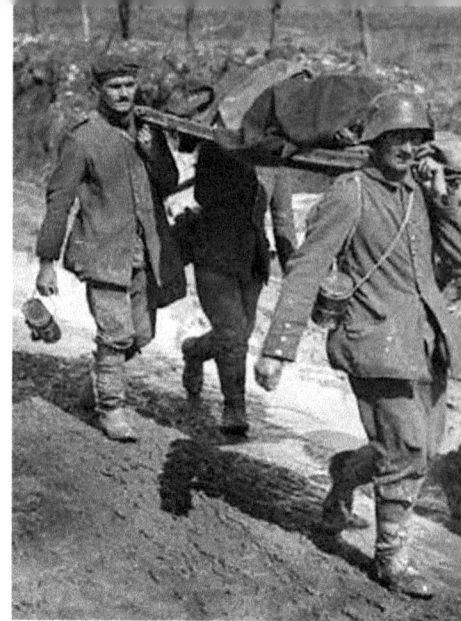

17GW125, 17GW199. A wounded Canadian is being given a drink of water whilst a German prisoner looks on. The fighting over, the German helps the wounded man back to the aid post.

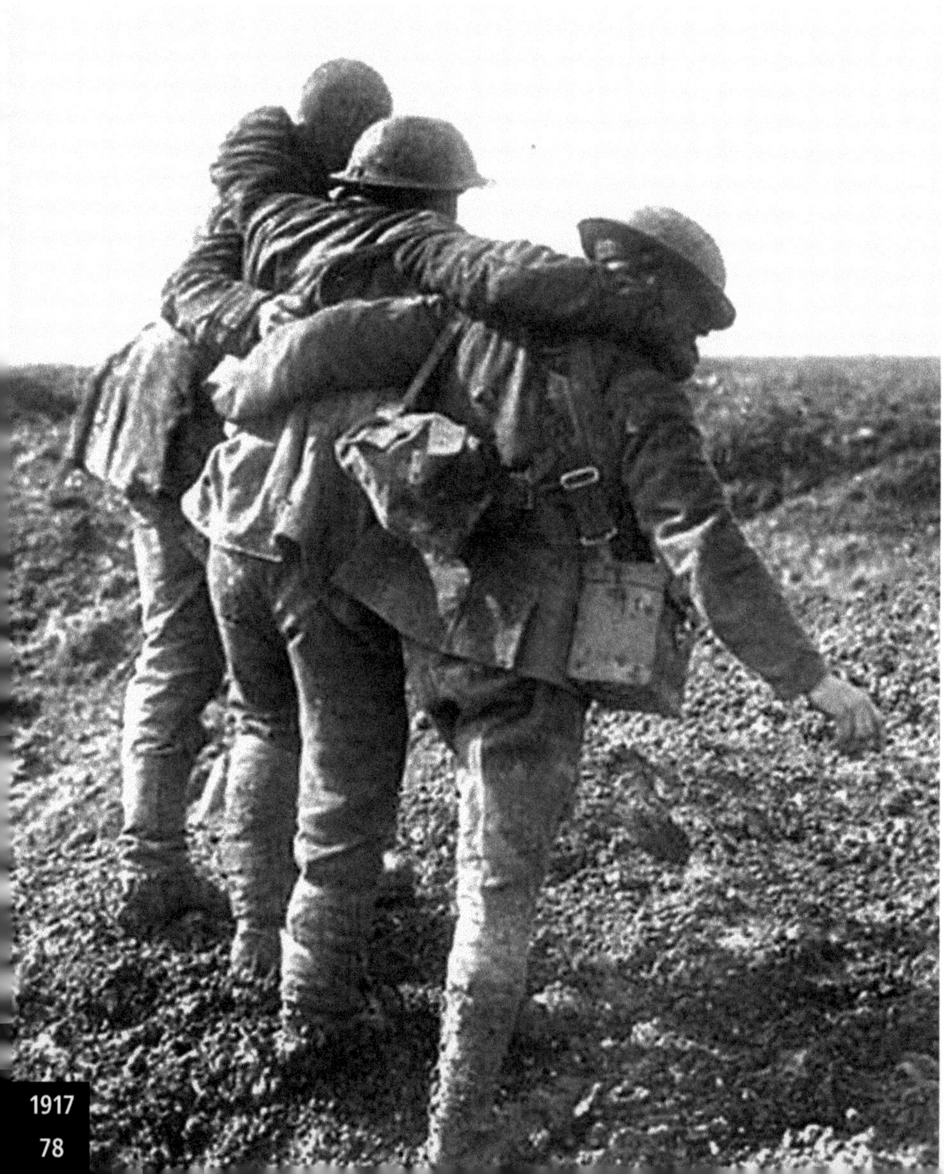

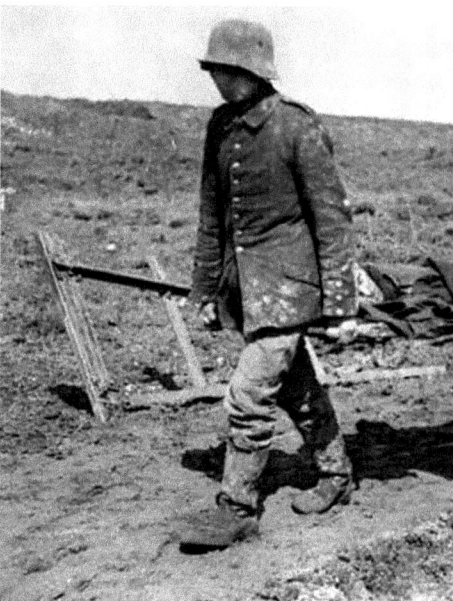
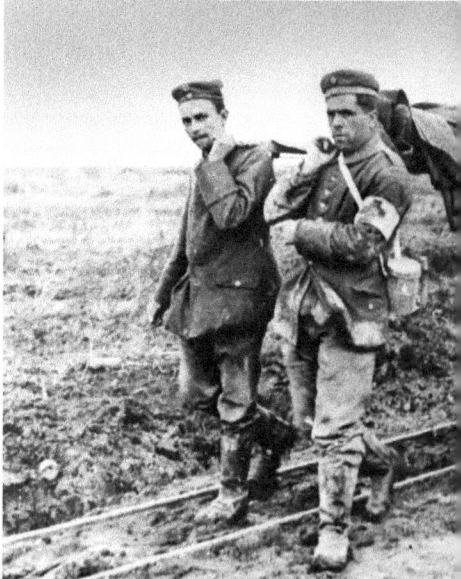

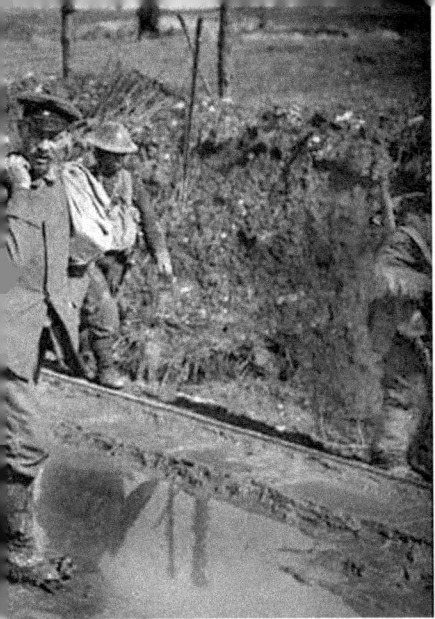
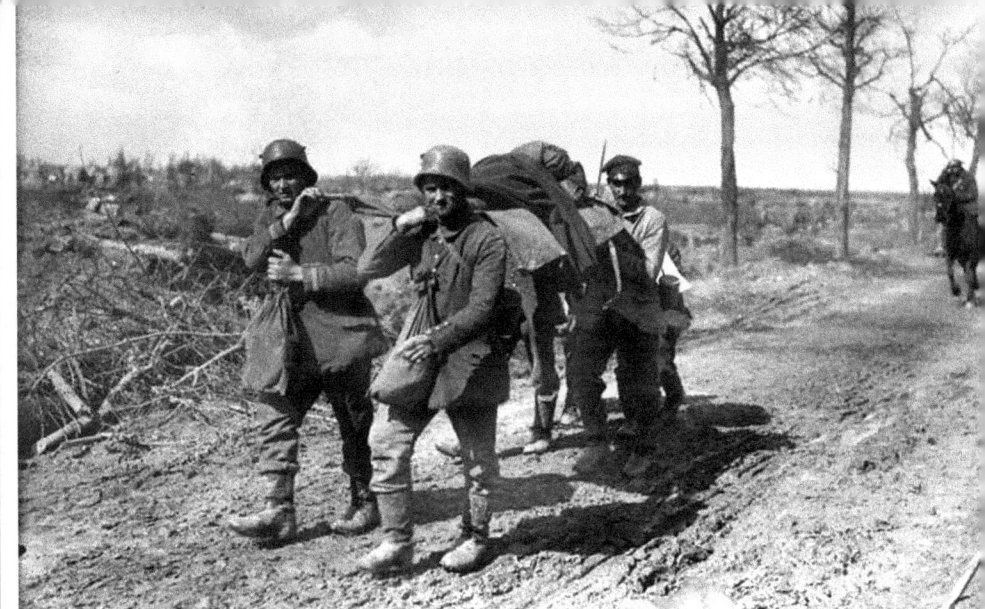

17GW124, 17GW123, 17GW128, 17GW126, 17GW129. Stretcher cases being carried back for treatment. German prisoners are being employed for the job; one prisoner appears to be wearing a British steel helmet.

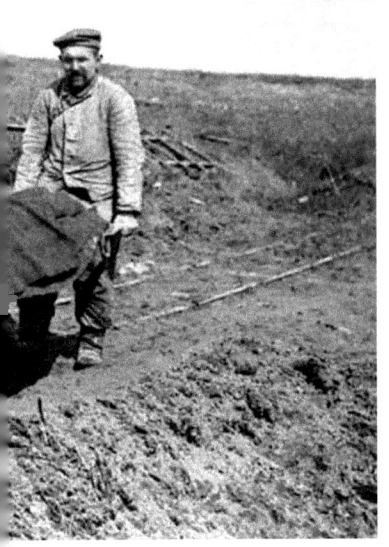
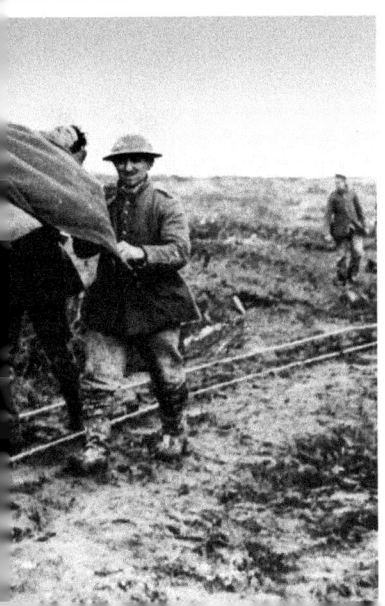

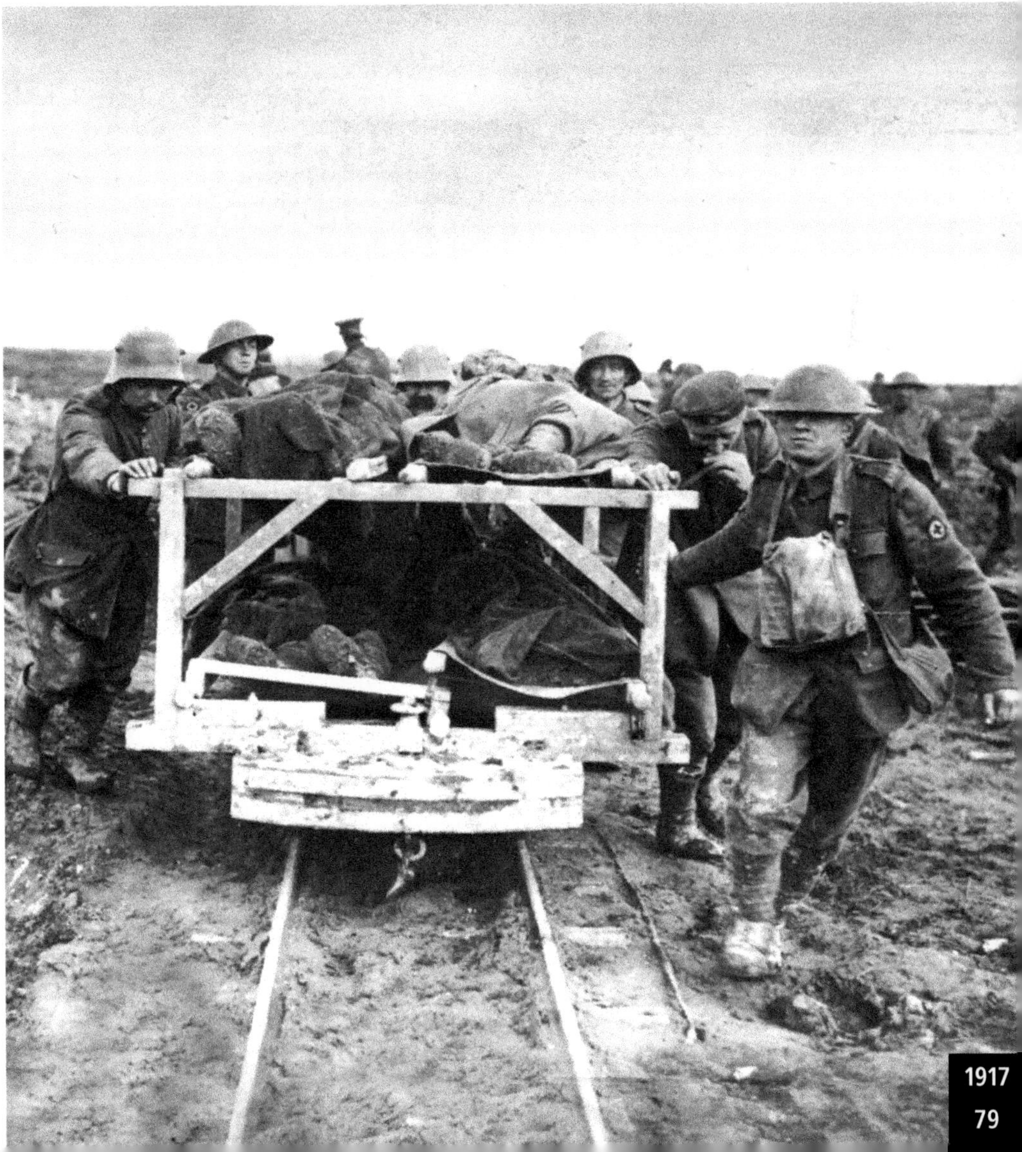

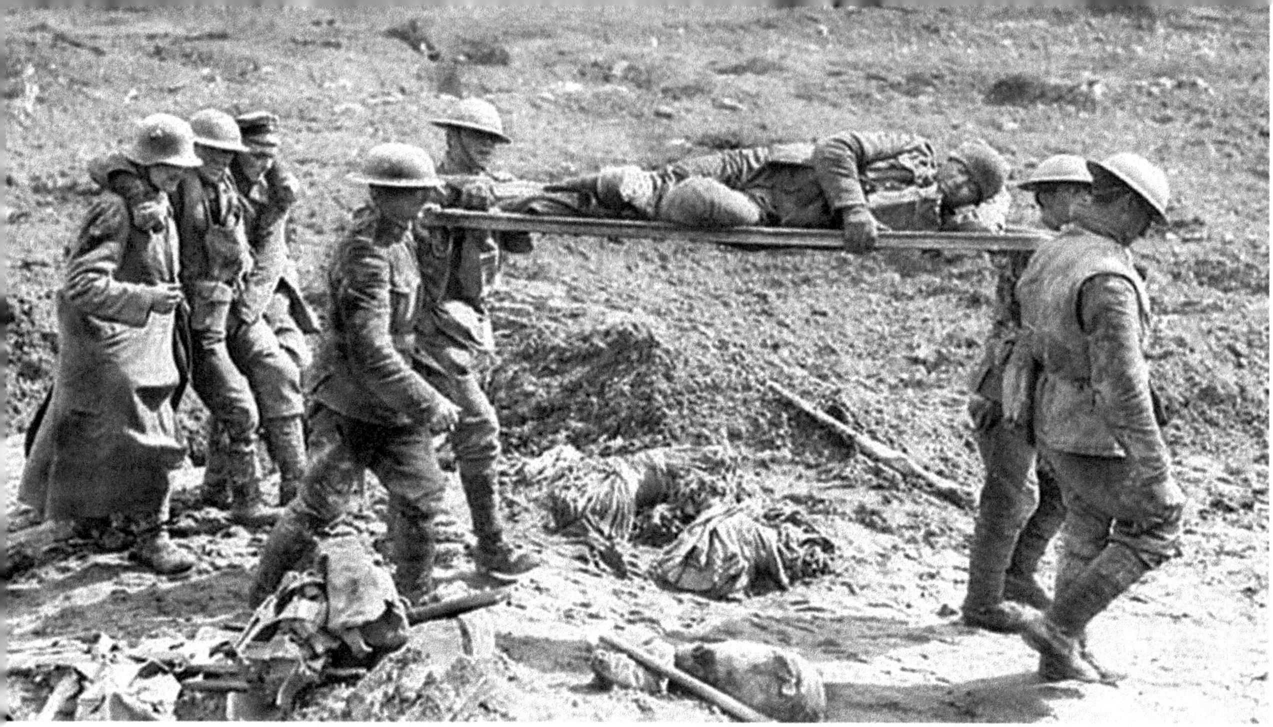

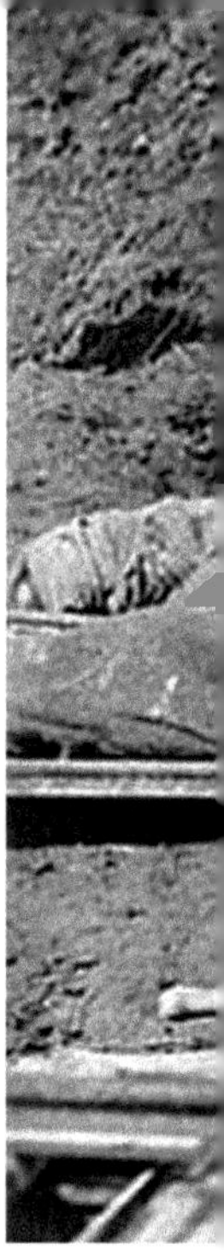

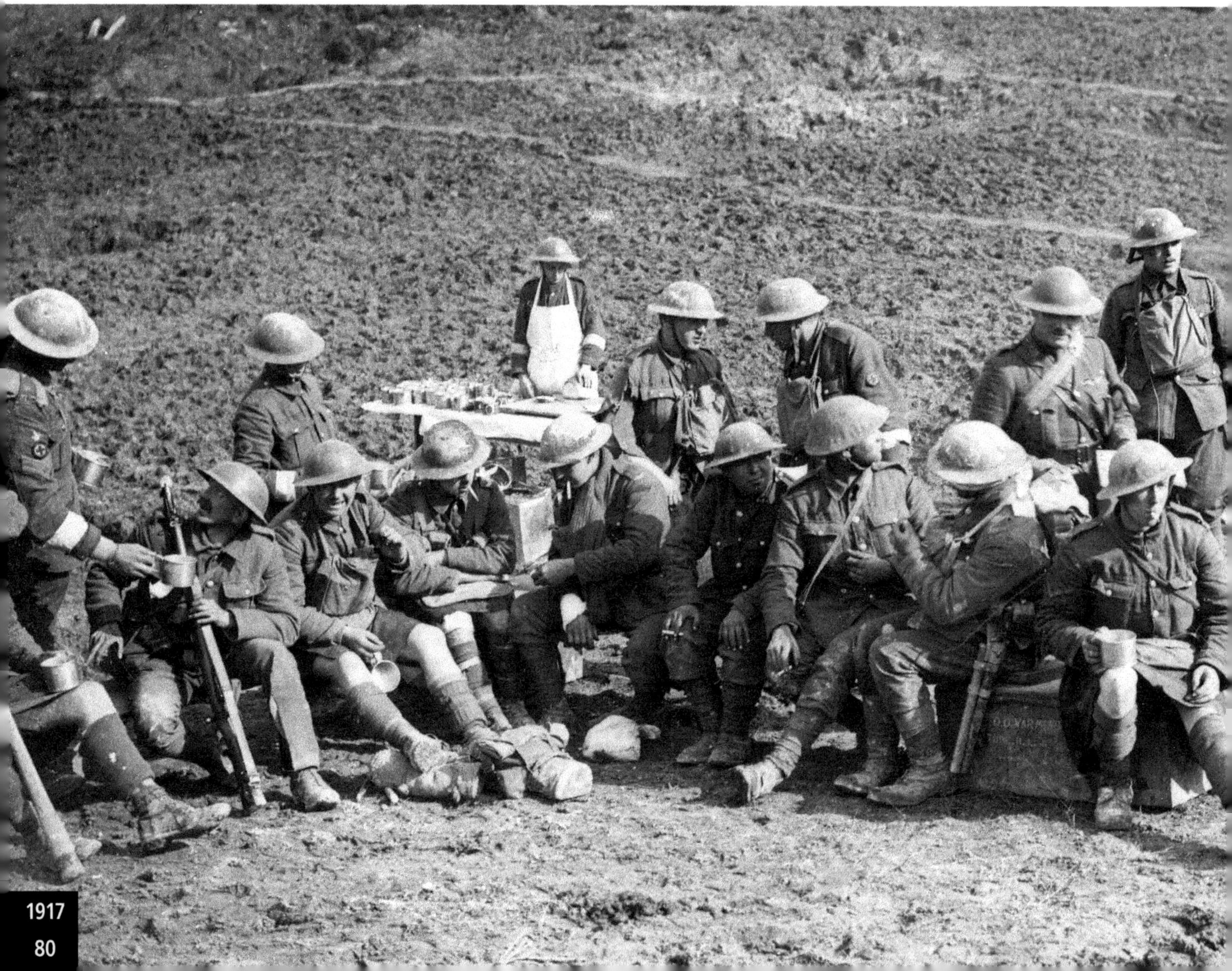

1917

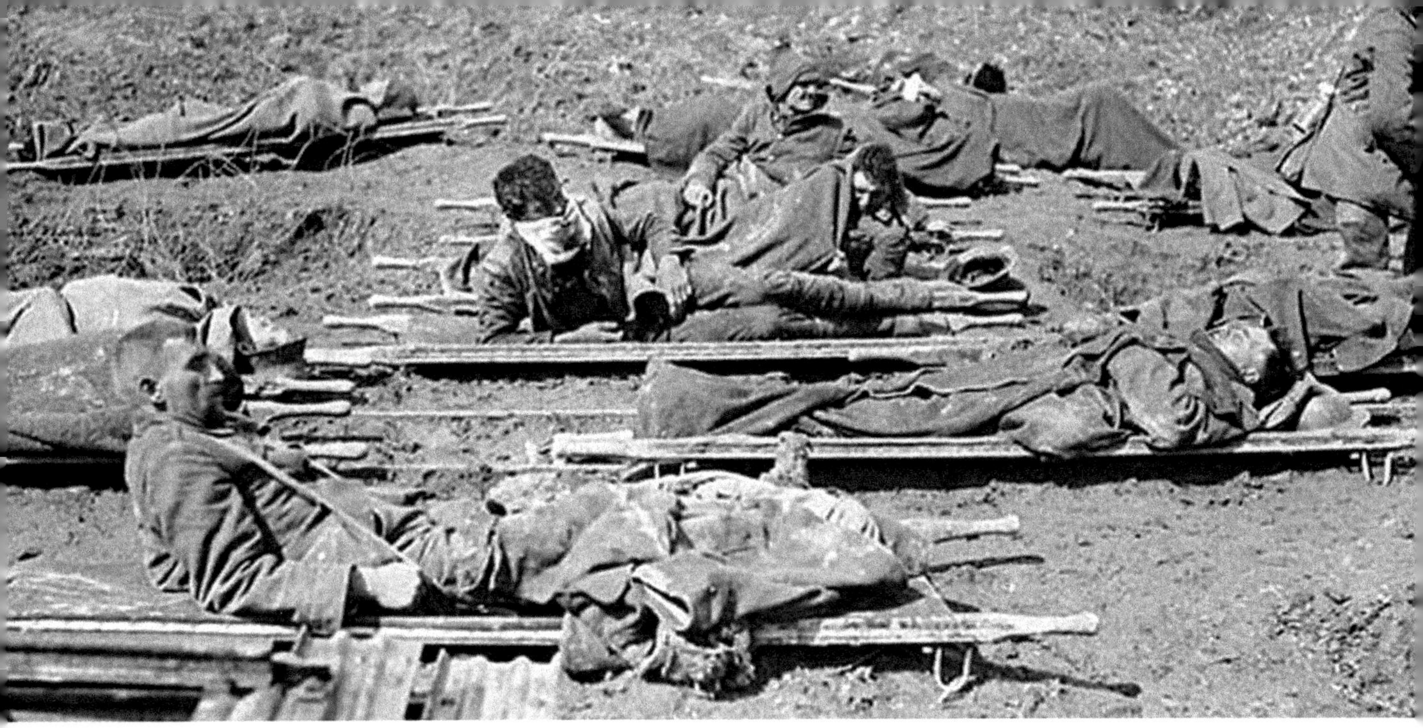

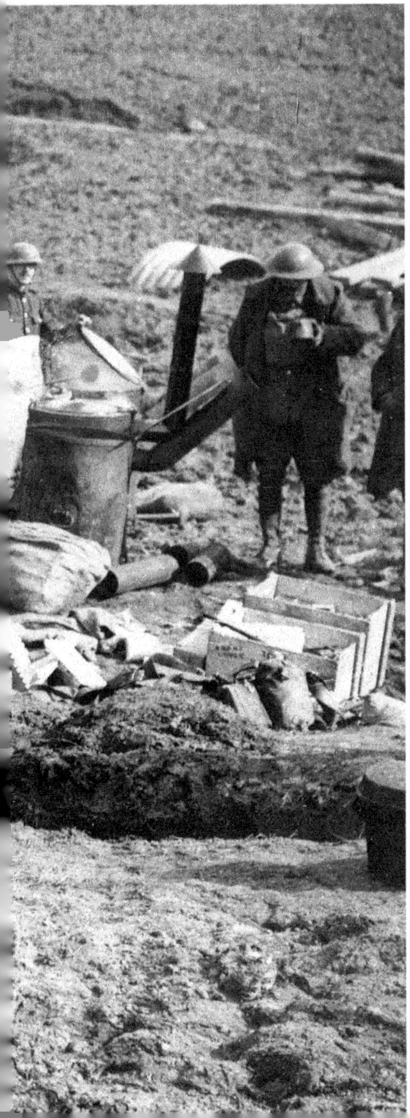

17GW127, 17GW130. Wounded Canadians and Germans being brought into an Advance Dressing Station.

17GW086 Stretcher bearers taking a welcome break, enjoying a drink and something to eat.

17GW139 One of the light railways employed to take stretcher cases to Casualty Clearing Stations.

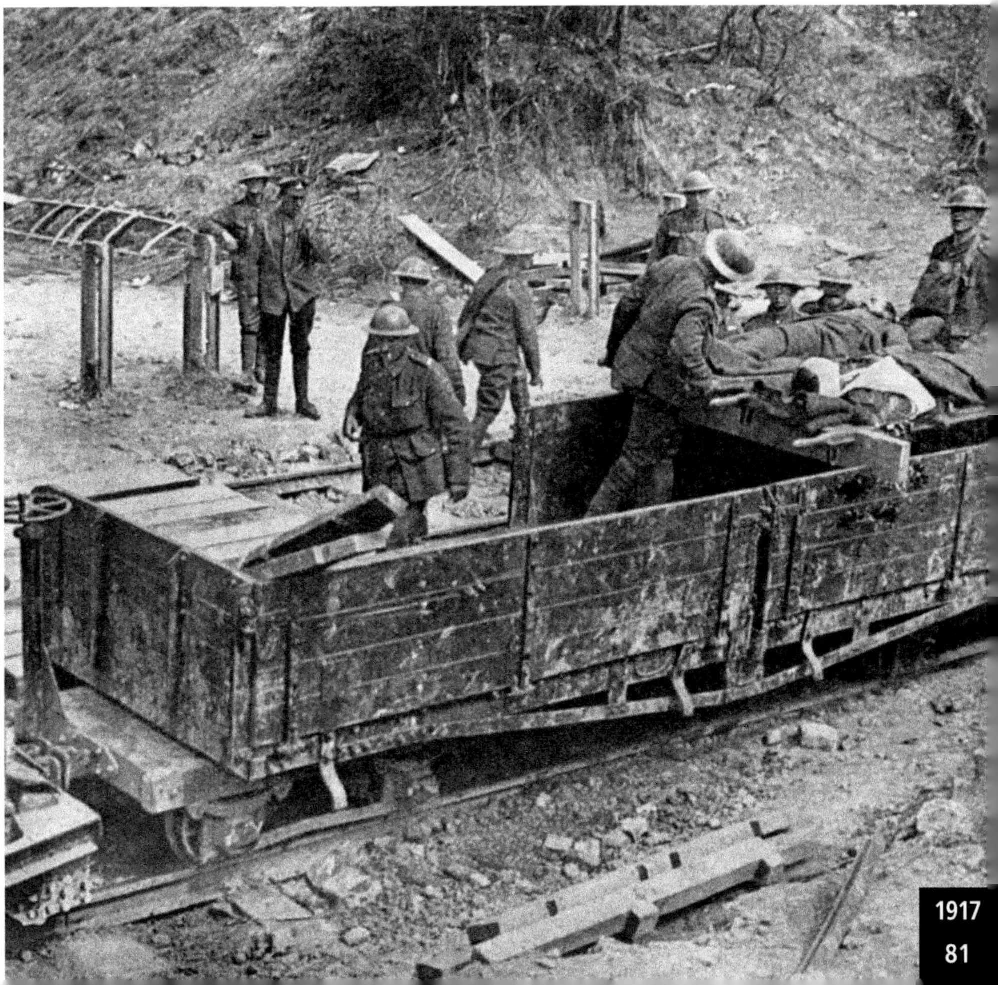

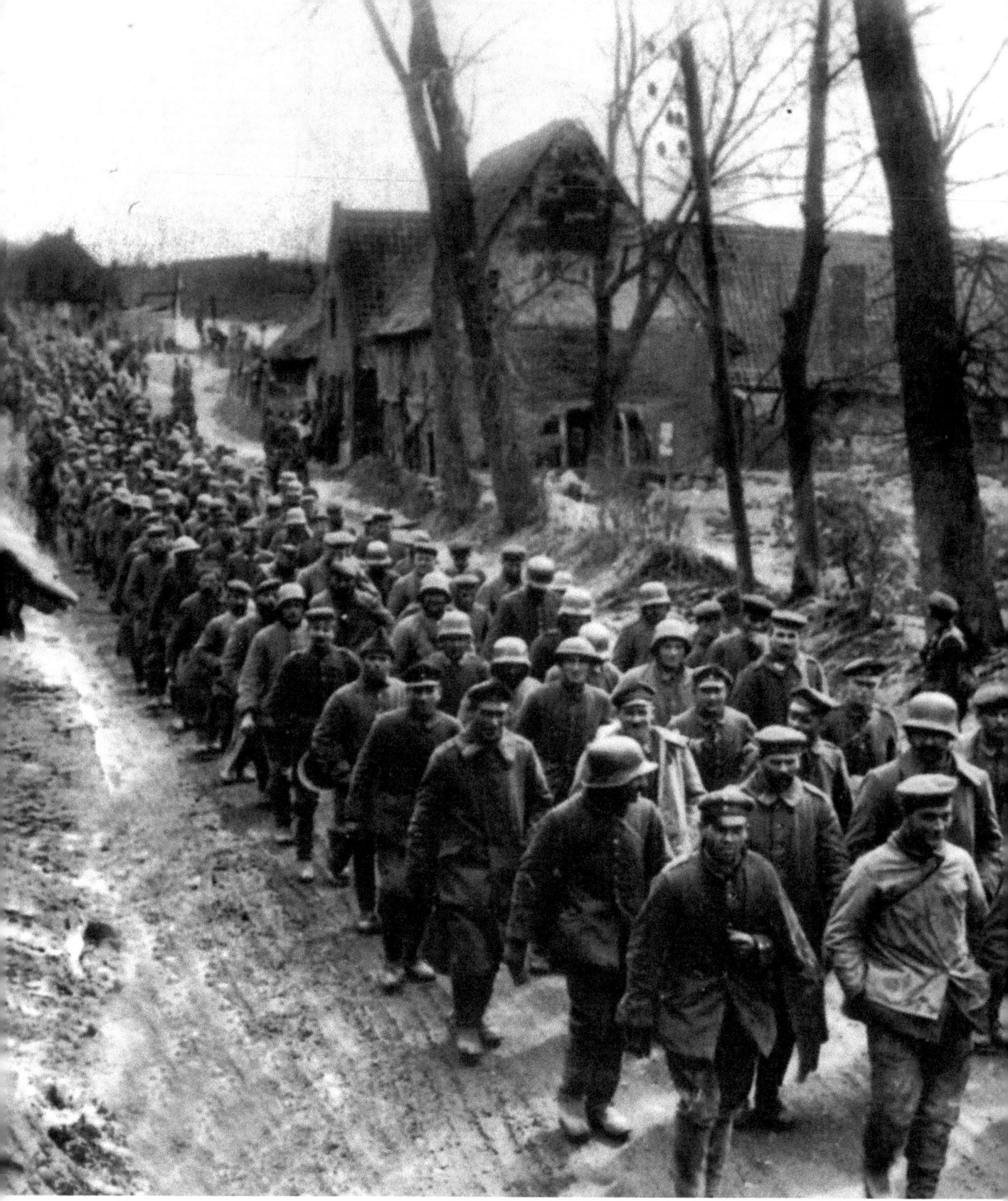

17GW145 A large number of German prisoners marching down a road west of Vimy Ridge.

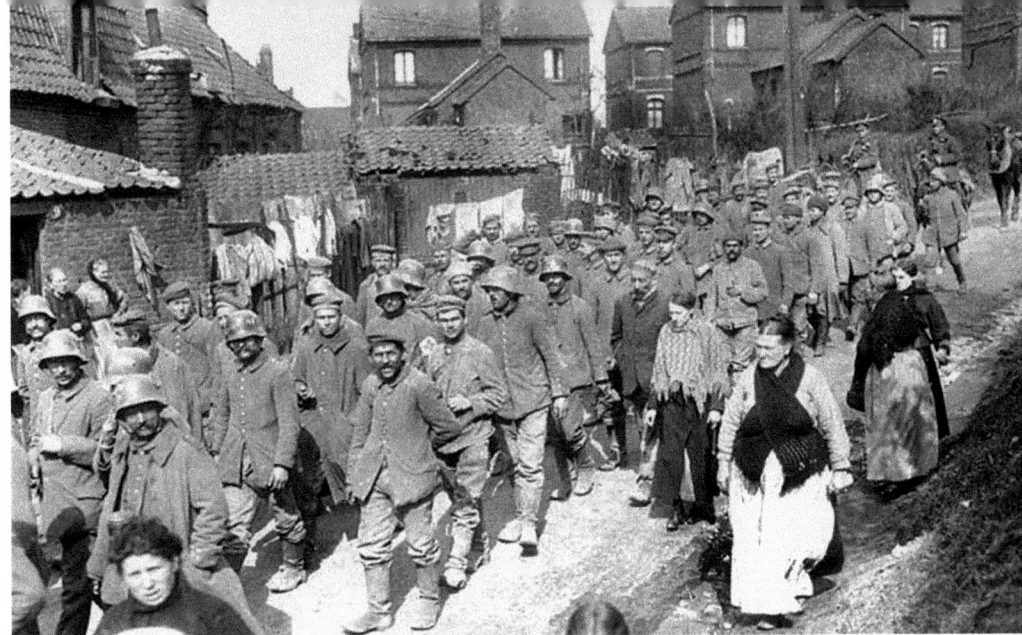

17GW146 German prisoners being escorted through the streets by French women who seem to be enjoying the unusual experience of seeing the invaders vanquished.

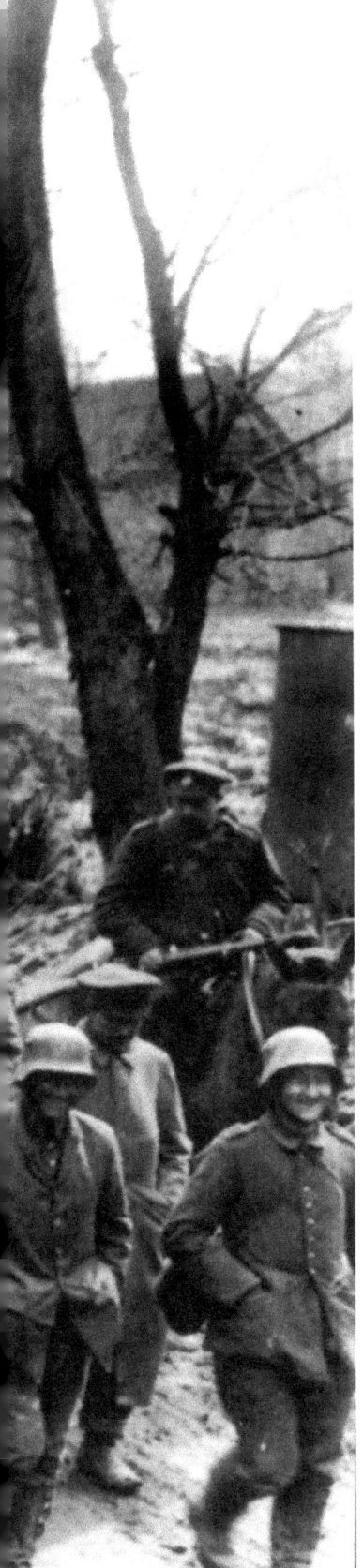

17GW147 German prisoners taken at Vimy Ridge having a bite to eat and drink.

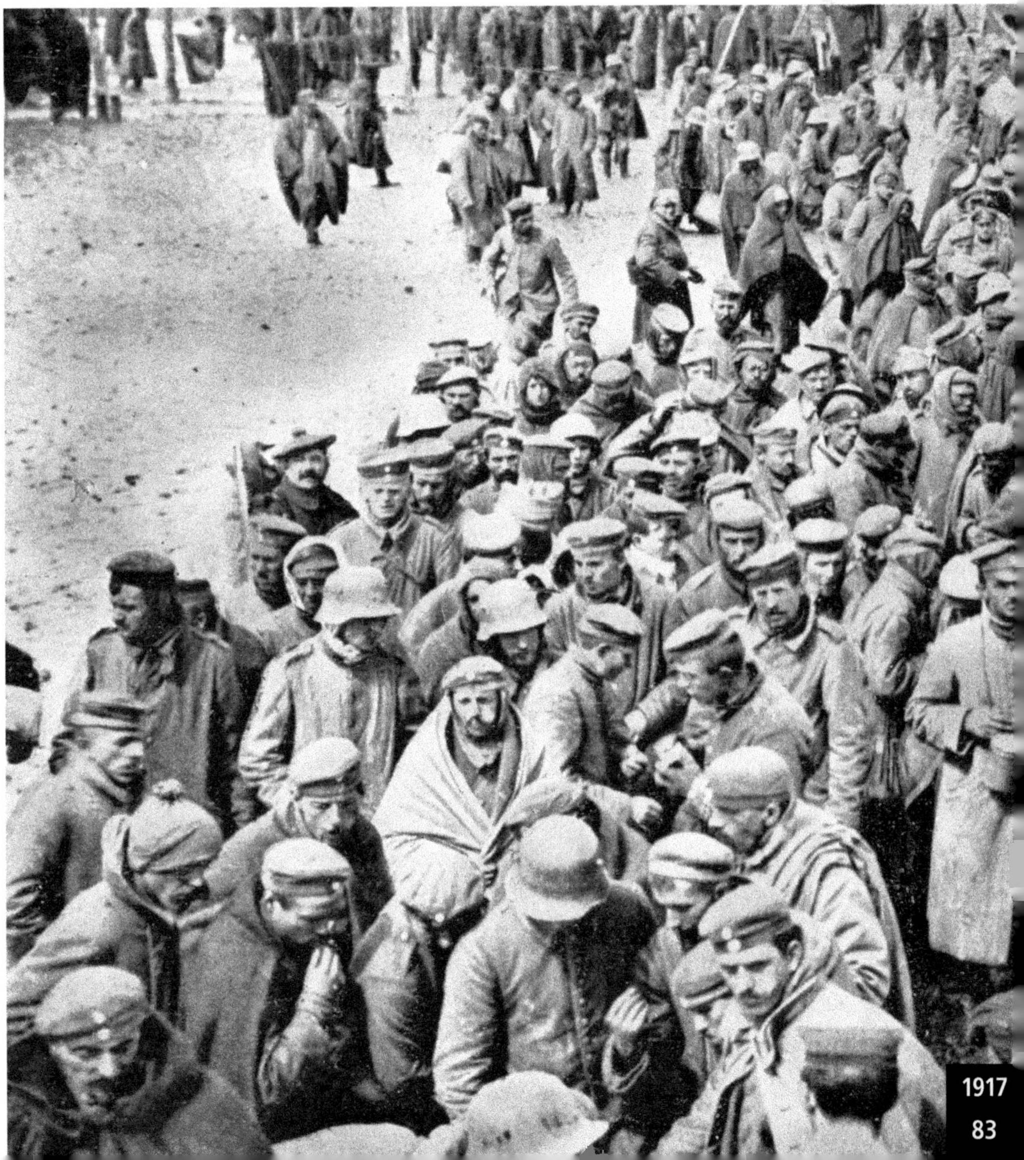

1917

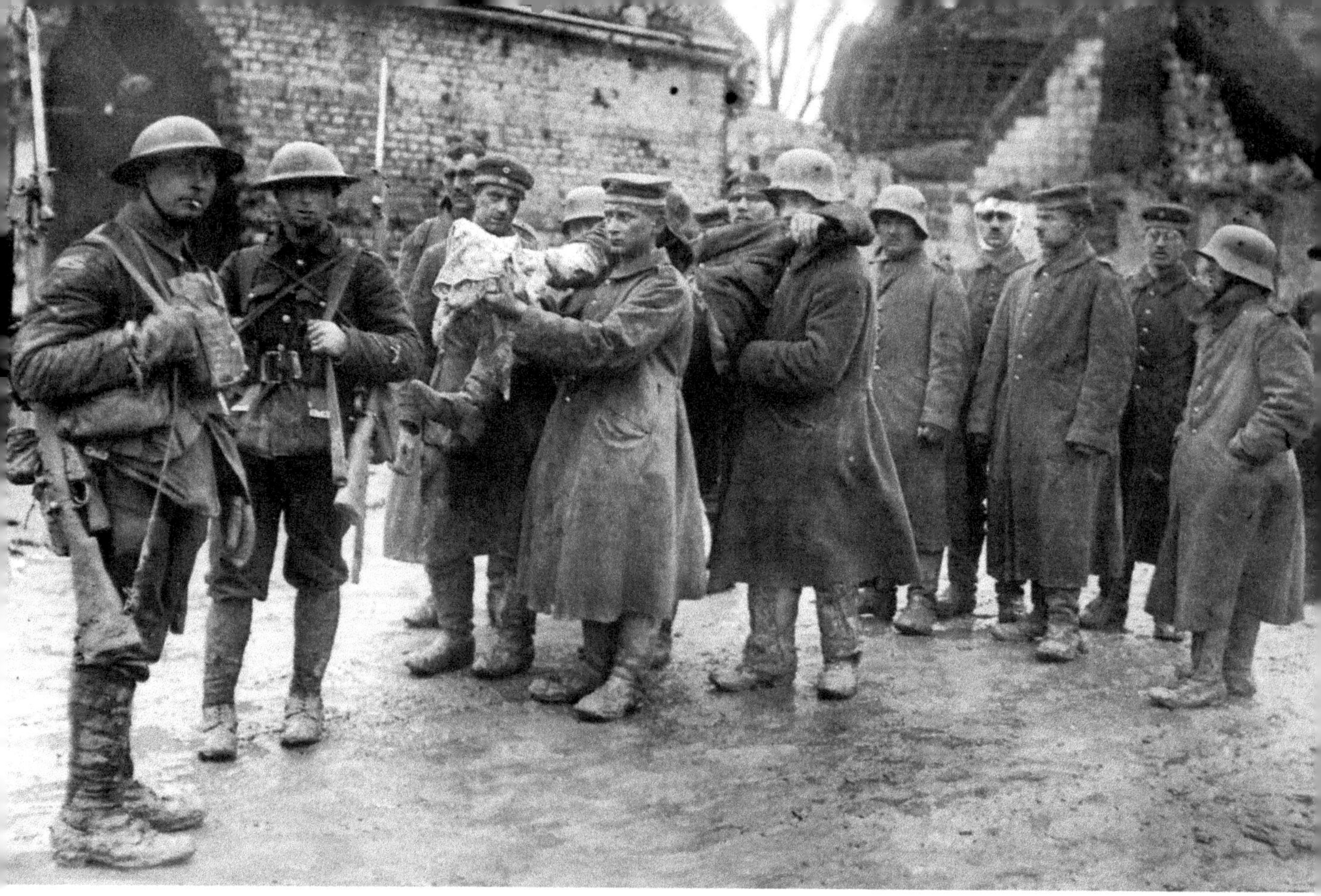

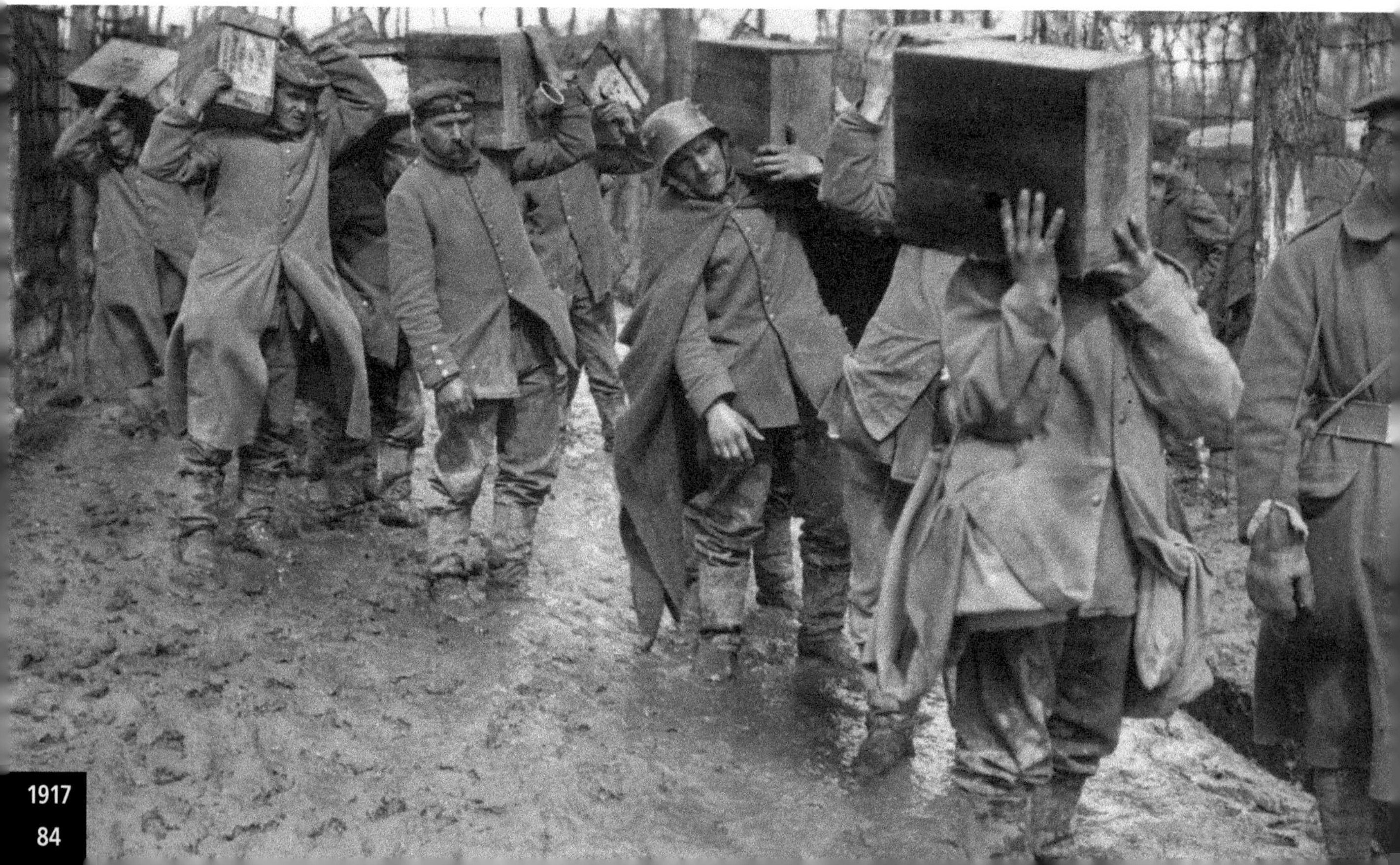

1917

17GW247 German prisoners carrying a wounded comrade in Arras.

17GW252 Prisoners taken at Arras being used to collect boxes of food to feed themselves and their comrades, who are looking on from behind the barbed wire of a prisoner of war cage. Lettering on one of the boxes reads 'Corned Beef'.

17GW251 German prisoners in Arras; note the fraternizing taking place – prisoners no longer presented a threat and fellow feeling for the hardships and dangers mutually shared provided a basis for acts of friendship.

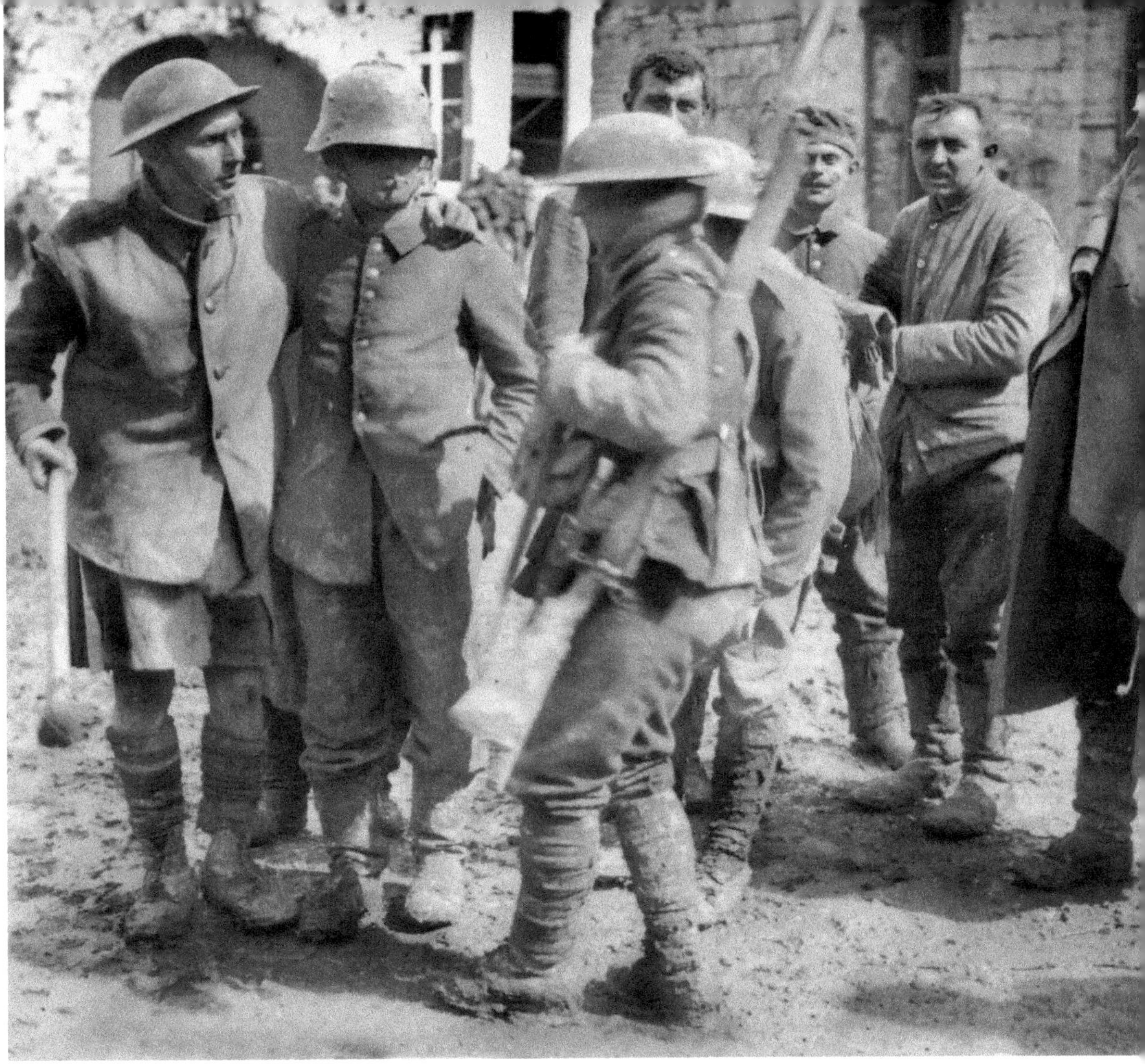

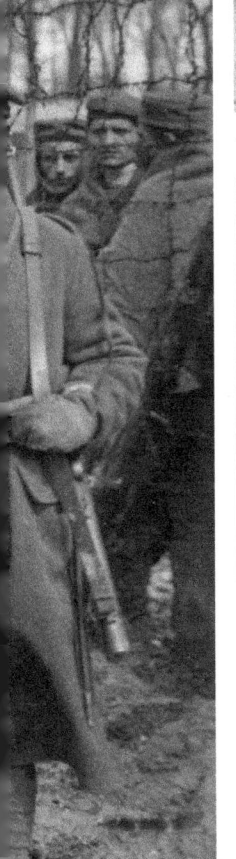

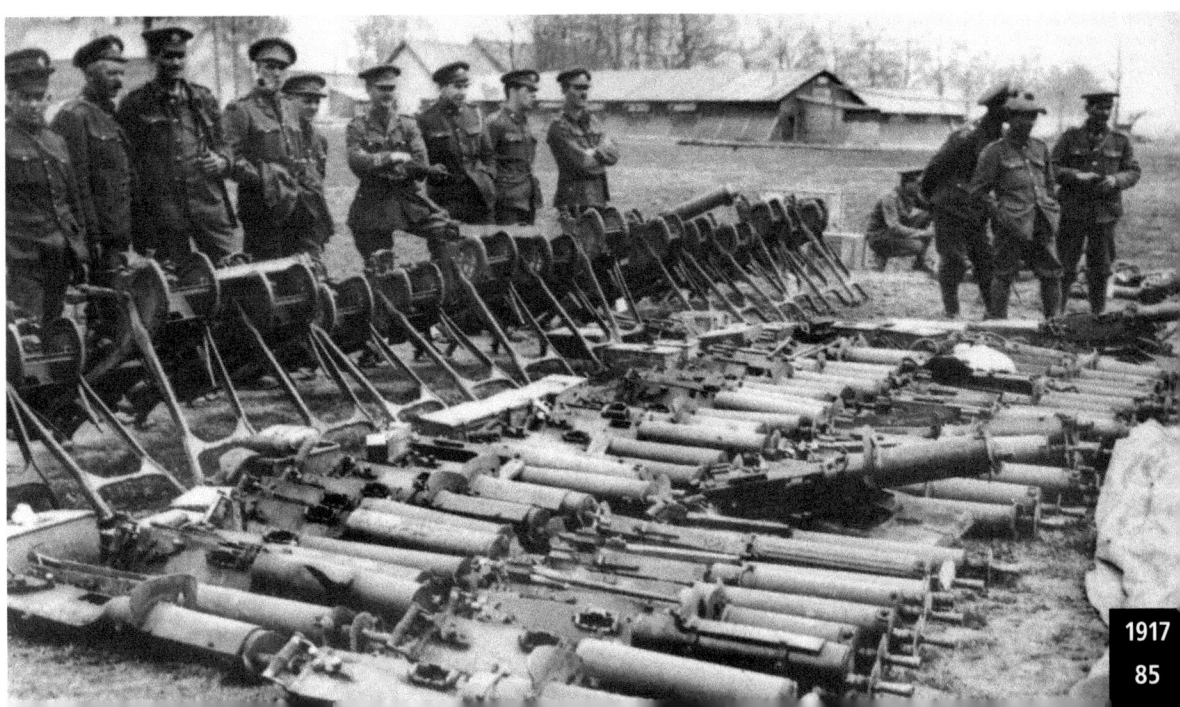

17GW253 German machine guns captured at Vimy.

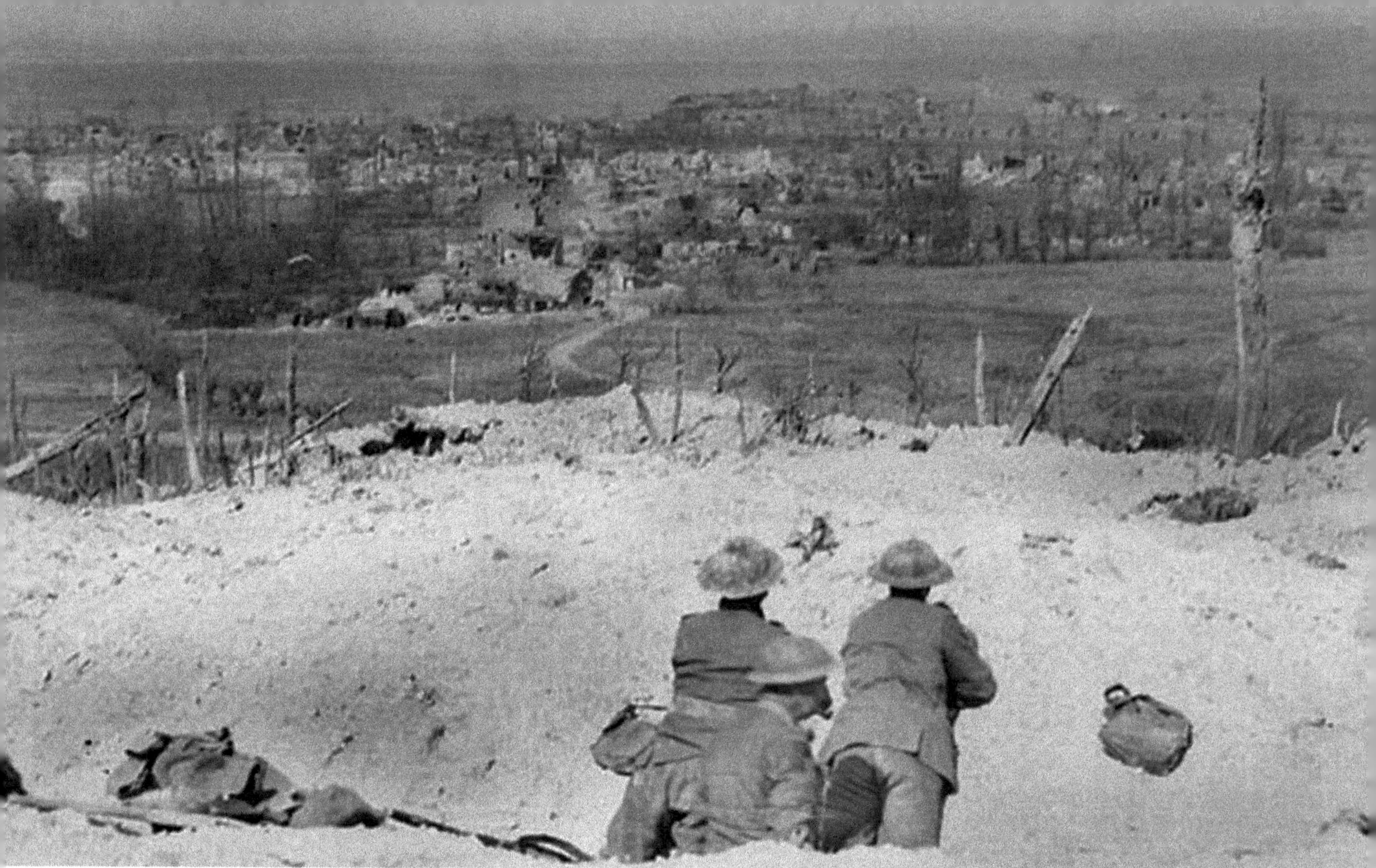

17GW145 Canadians looking down on the village of Vimy.
17GW148 Canadian infantry in dugouts on Vimy ridge enjoying a brew up.

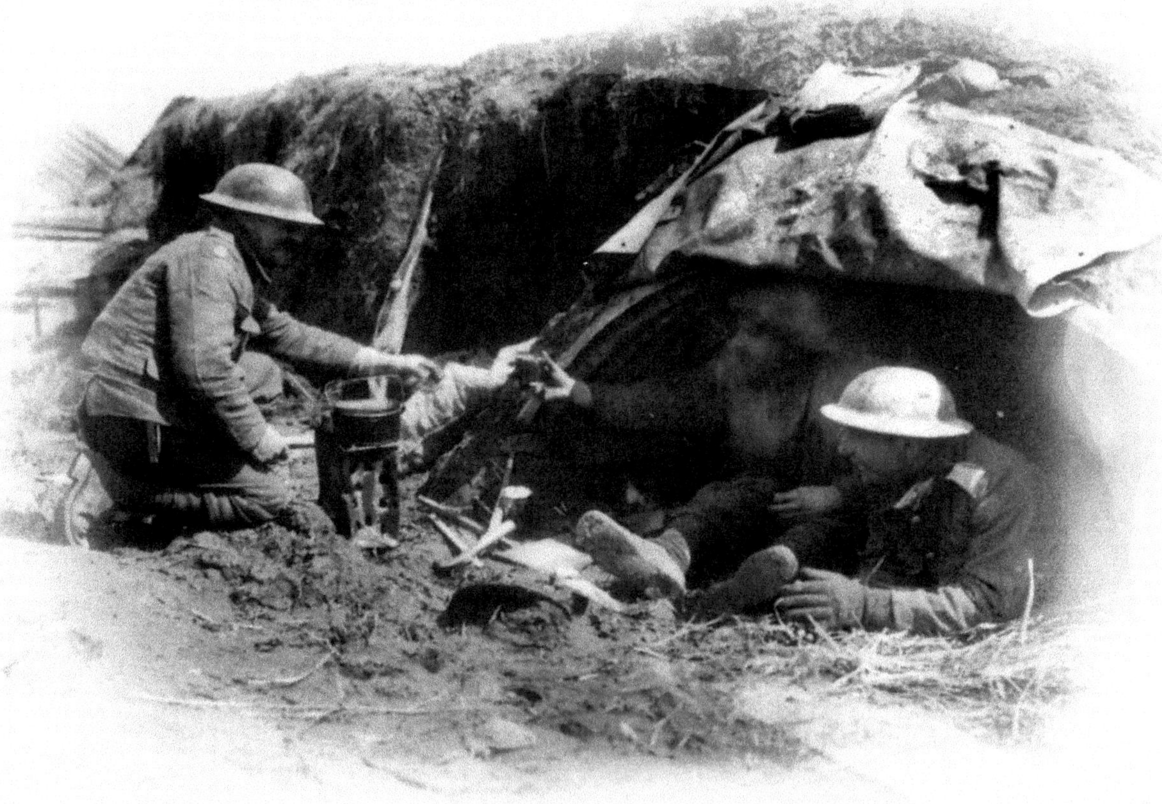

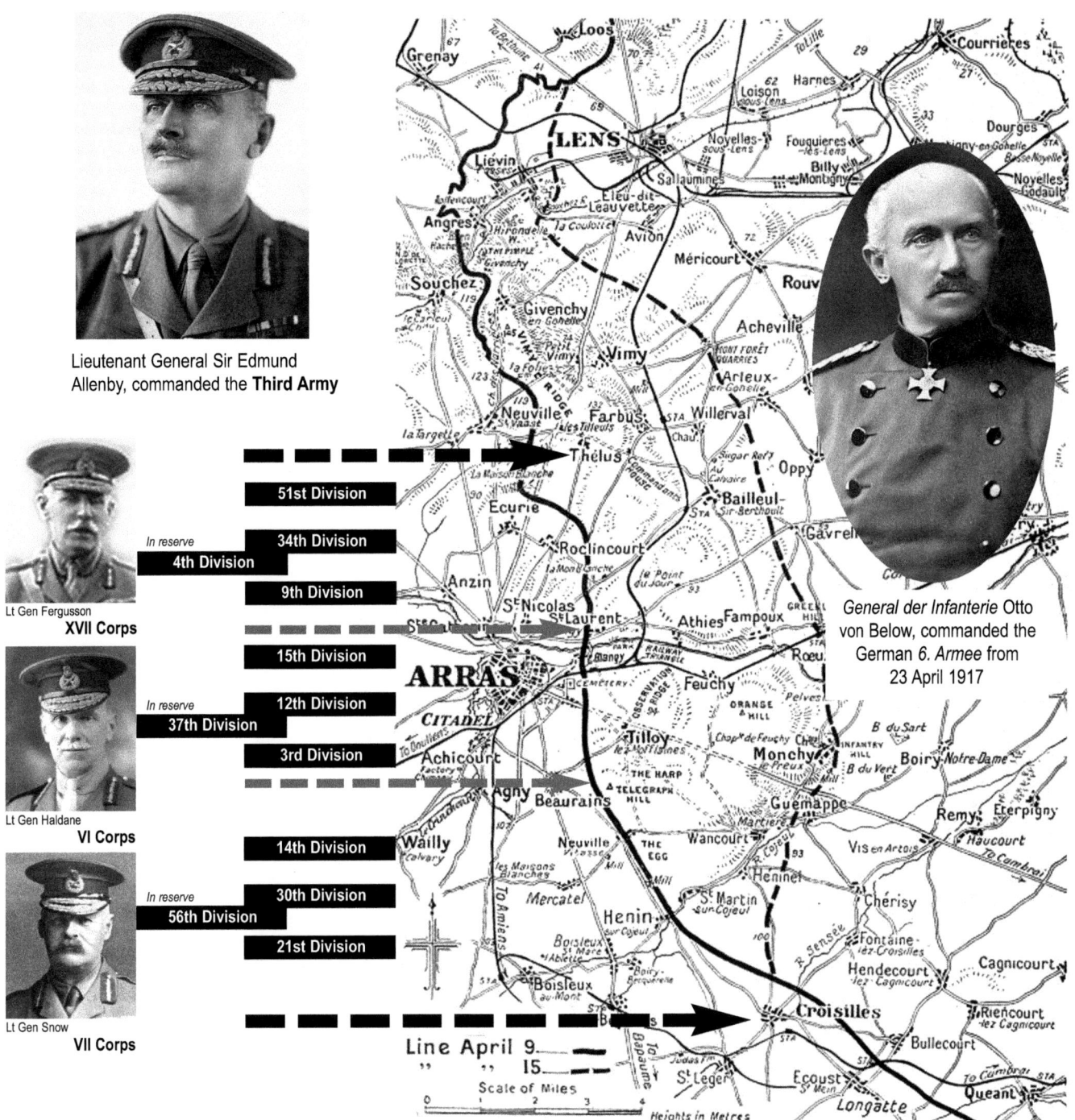

Lieutenant General Sir Edmund Allenby, commanded the **Third Army**

Lt Gen Fergusson
XVII Corps

Lt Gen Haldane
VI Corps

Lt Gen Snow
VII Corps

General der Infanterie Otto von Below, commanded the German *6. Armee* from 23 April 1917

XVII Corps was directed to take an area between the Scarpe River and Farbus Wood on their left. This gave it the major objectives of the village of Fampoux alongside the Scarpe and the southern end of Vimy Ridge.

VI Corps was to attack the area between the village of Tilloy les Mofflaines on the main Arras – Cambrai Road and the Scarpe River to its left.

VII Corps formed the right flank of the Third Army's attack. Their objectives were to advance on a line from Tilloy les Mofflaines south to Croisilles. Acting as the pivot of the attack, it would start its attack later.

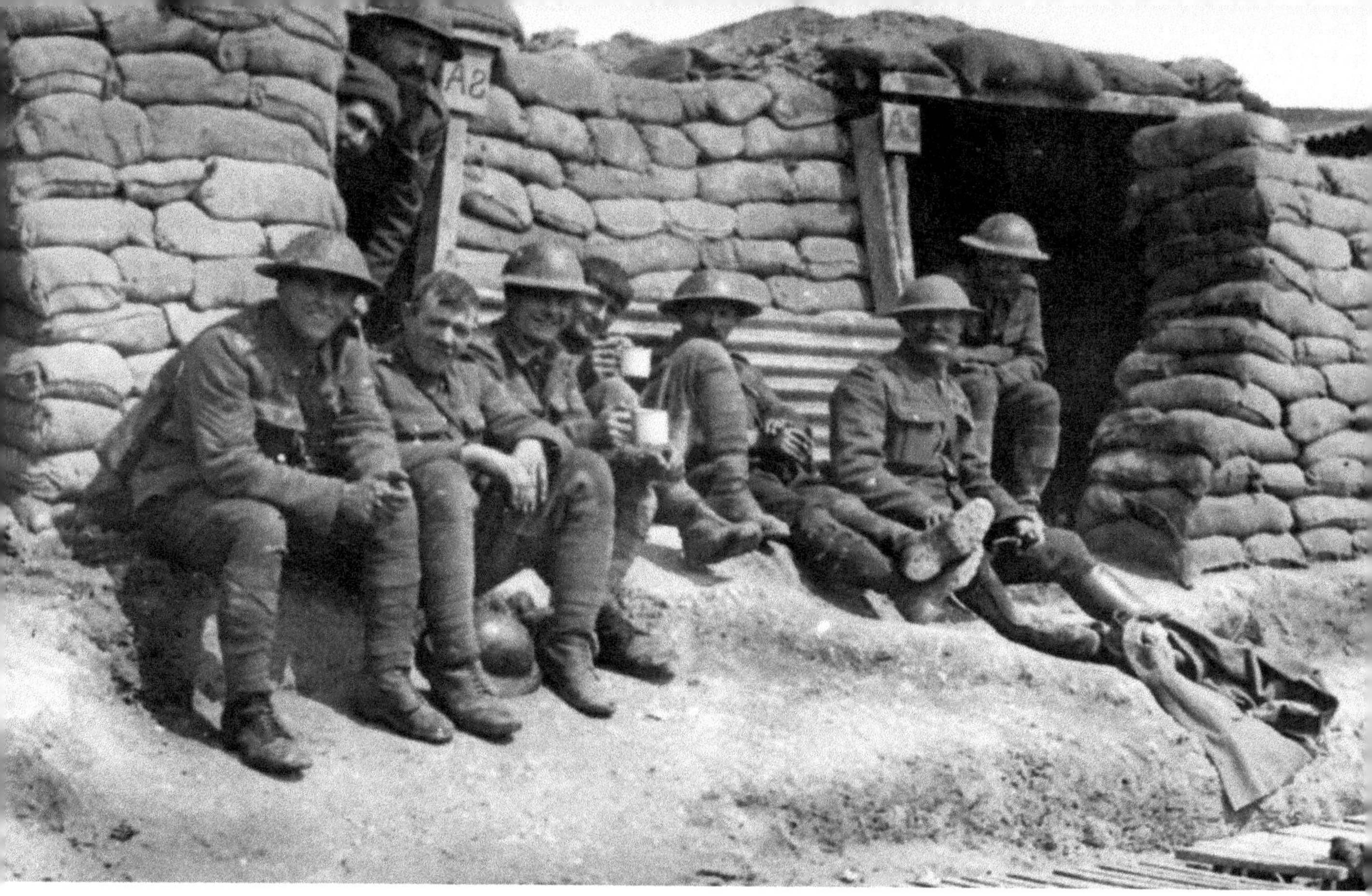

1917

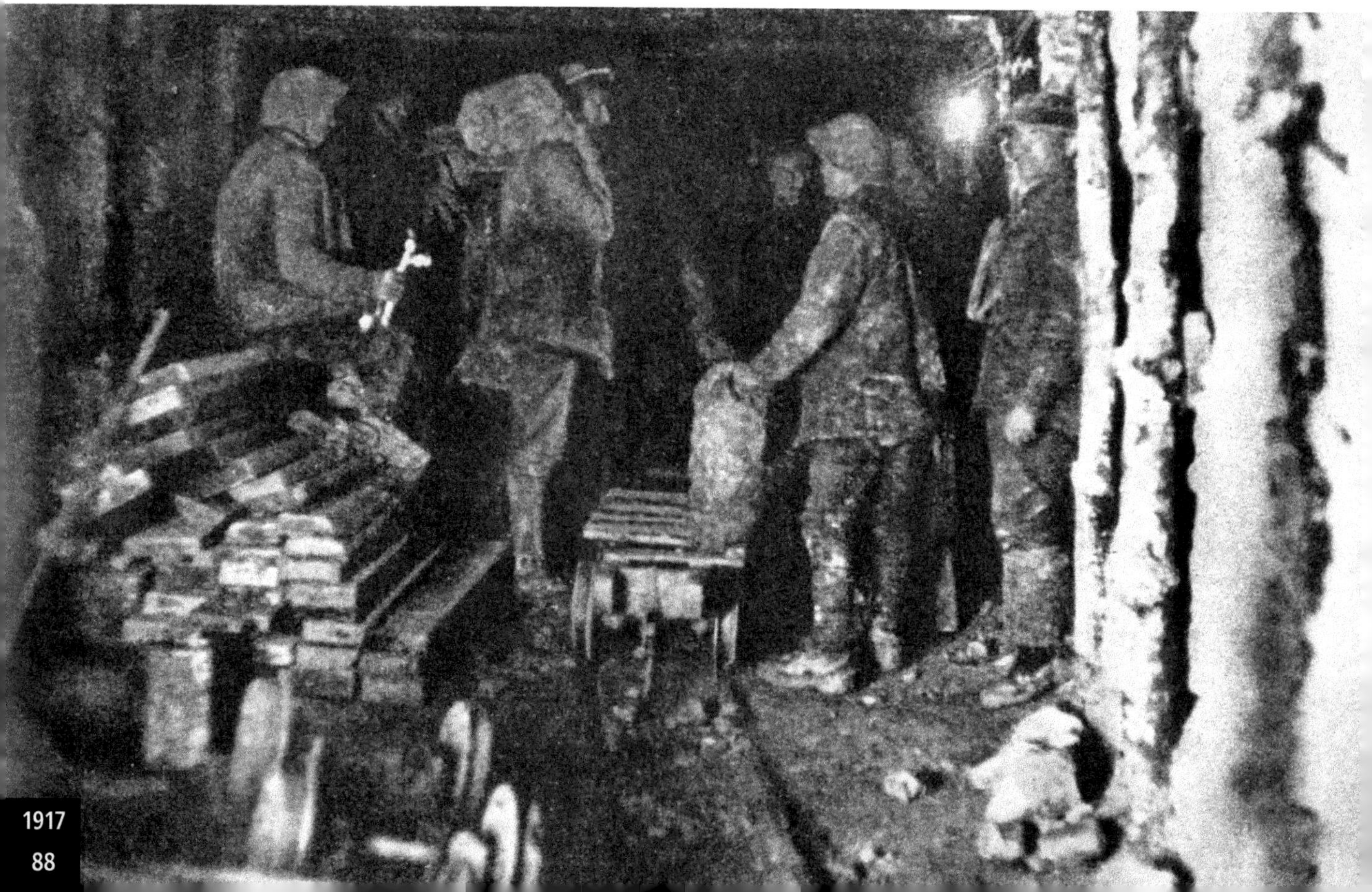

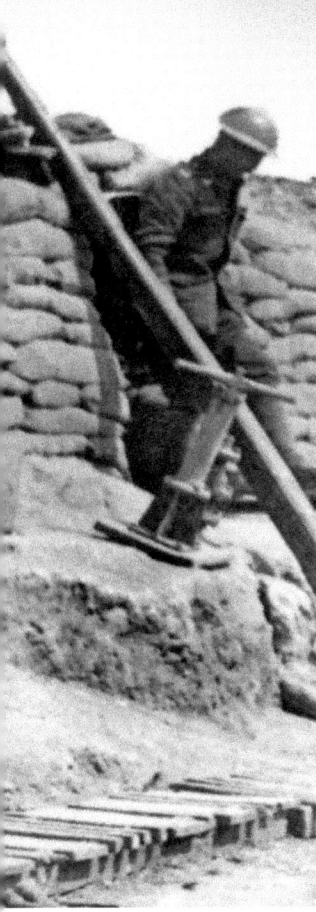

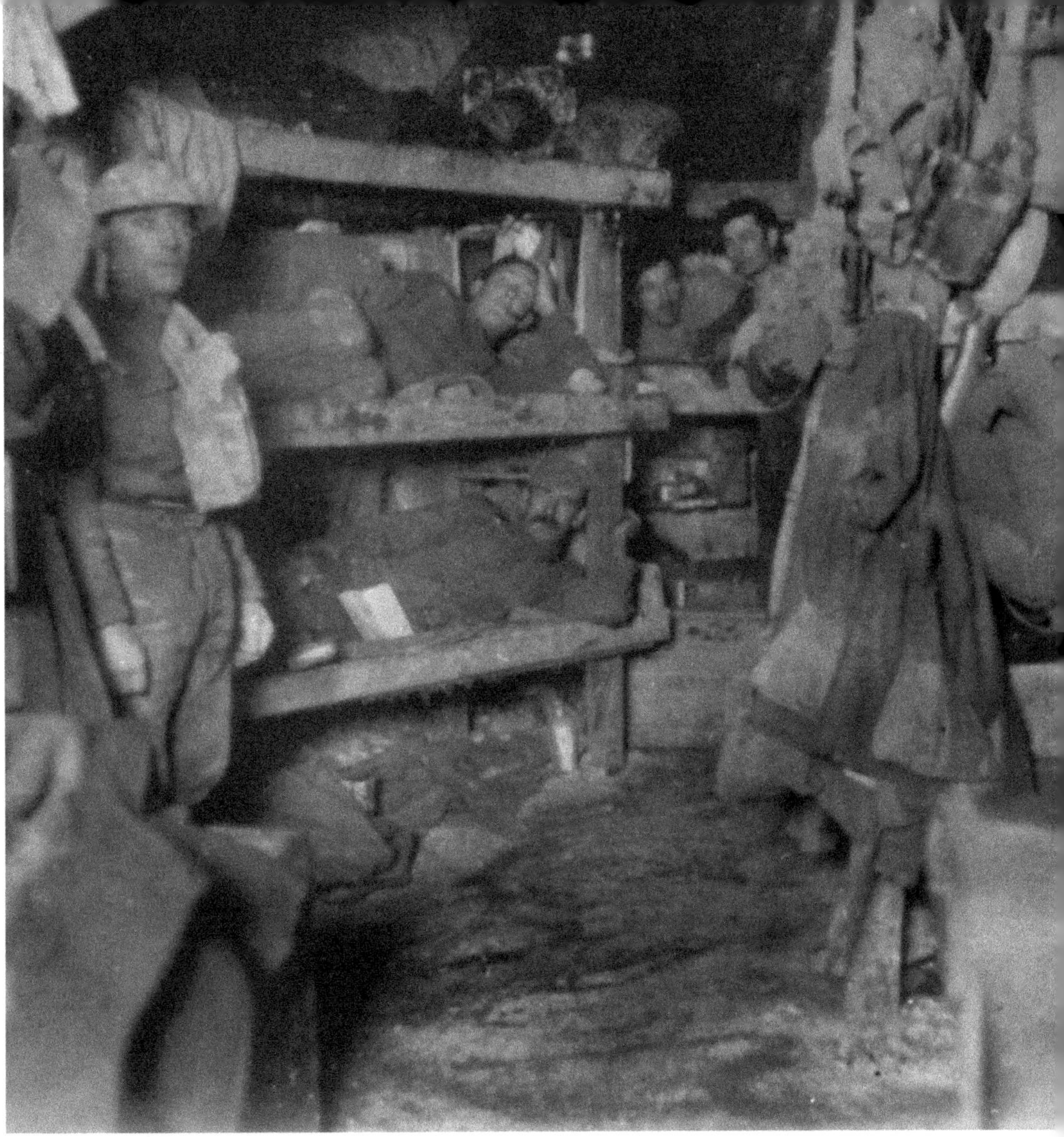

17GW188 NCOs and men of the City of London Regiment before the Battle of Arras.

17GW189, 17GW190. Much of Arras stood on medieval subterranean quarries or 'caves'. These were developed and acted as shelters for thousands of men and their supplies.

One Arras cave could accommodate 4,000 men and Saint Sauveur tunnel some 2,000 soldiers. Here we see a tunnel being extended by sappers.

17GW191 A group of New Zealand tunnelers wearing mine rescue breathing apparatus. They developed an underground city, putting in a light-railway system and electric lighting. They were managers for the complex under Arras. For the battle the New Zealand tunnellers blew holes to the surface so that the attacking troops could get as close as possible to the enemy.

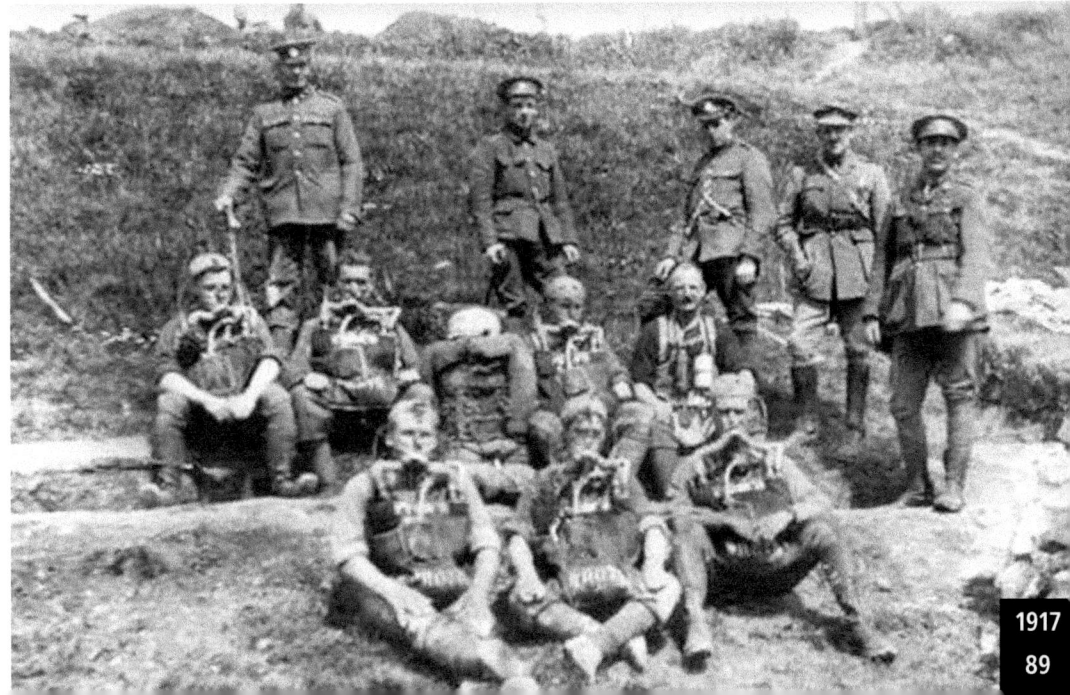

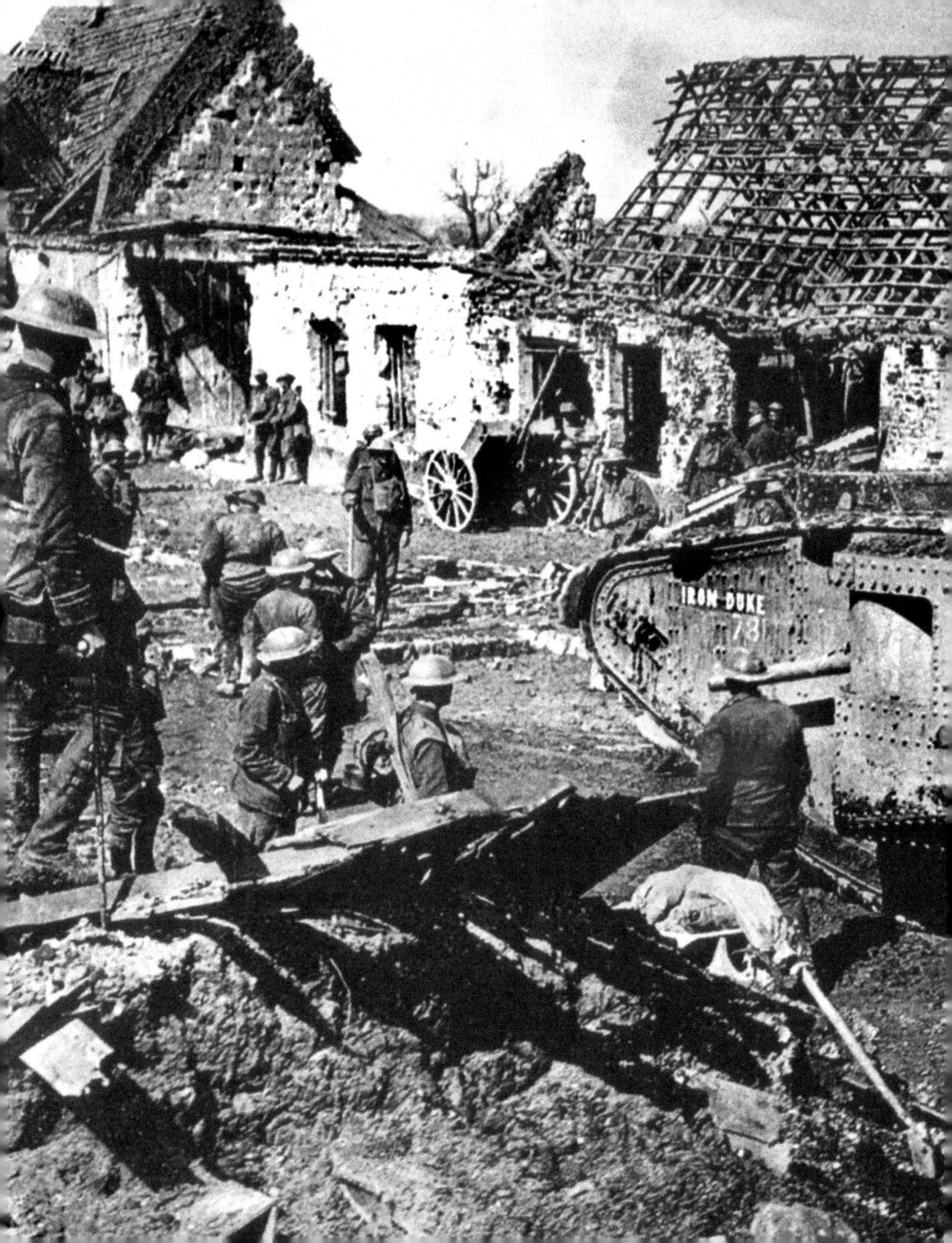

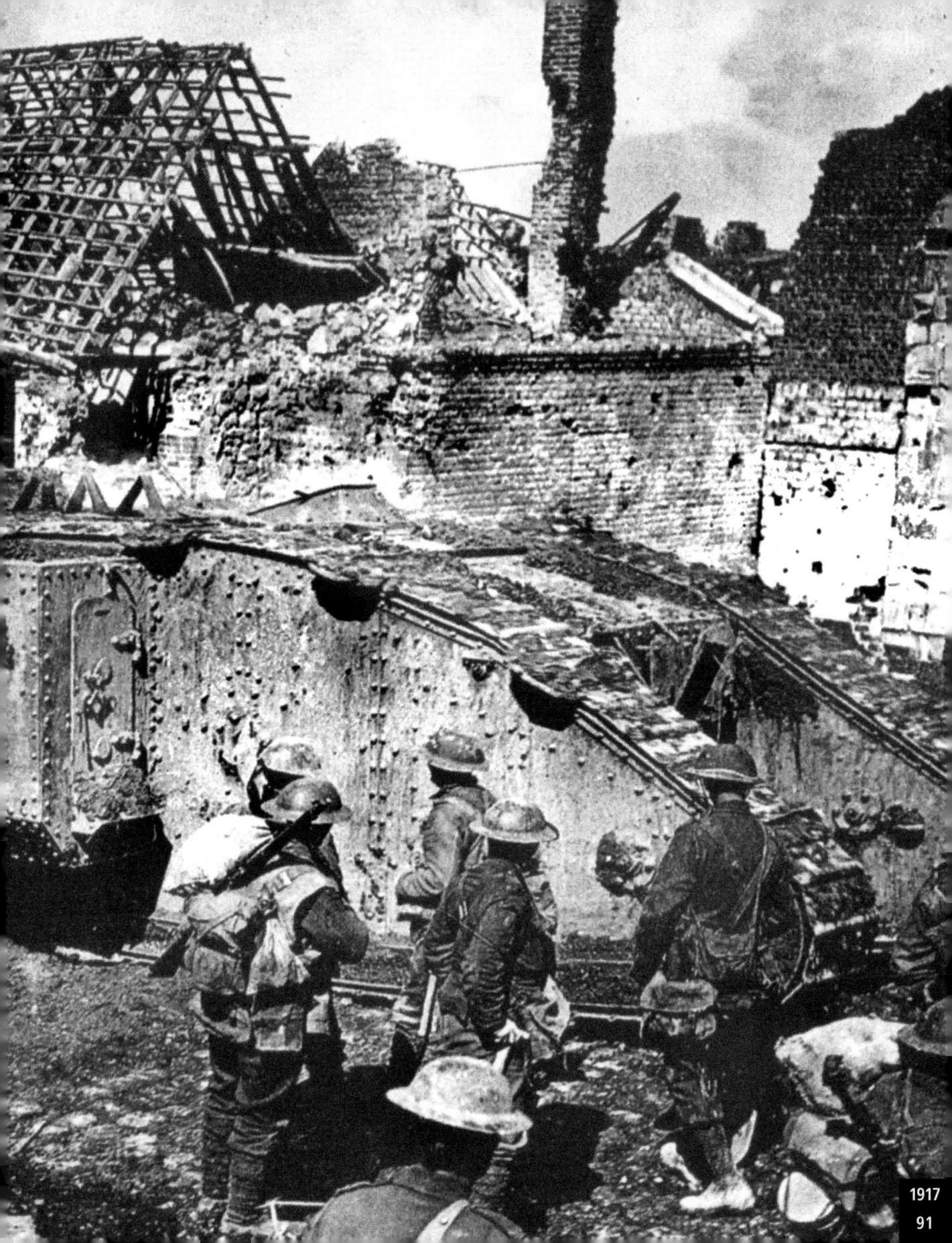

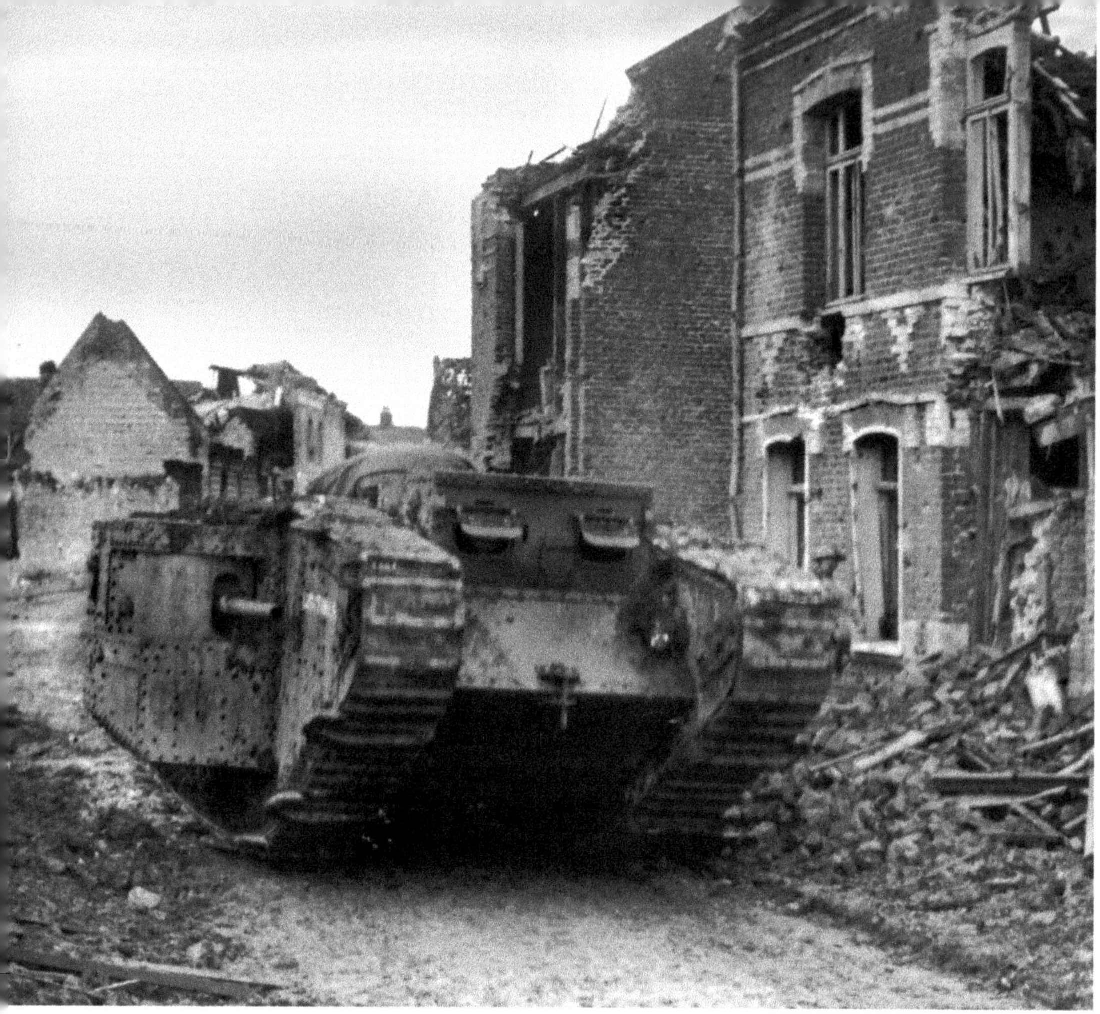

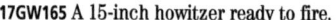

17GW160, 17GW161. Two tanks, *Lusitania* and *Iron Duke* (previous page), of the Third Army's allotment of forty for the Easter Monday attack east of Arras. Eight were assigned to XVII Corps and sixteen to each of the other two corps. They were to be employed against the German second and third lines and strongly held strongpoints

17GW165 A 15-inch howitzer ready to fire.

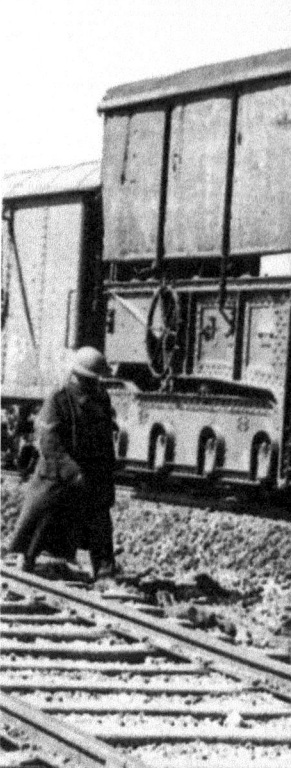

17GW163 A 12-inch railway gun near Arras.

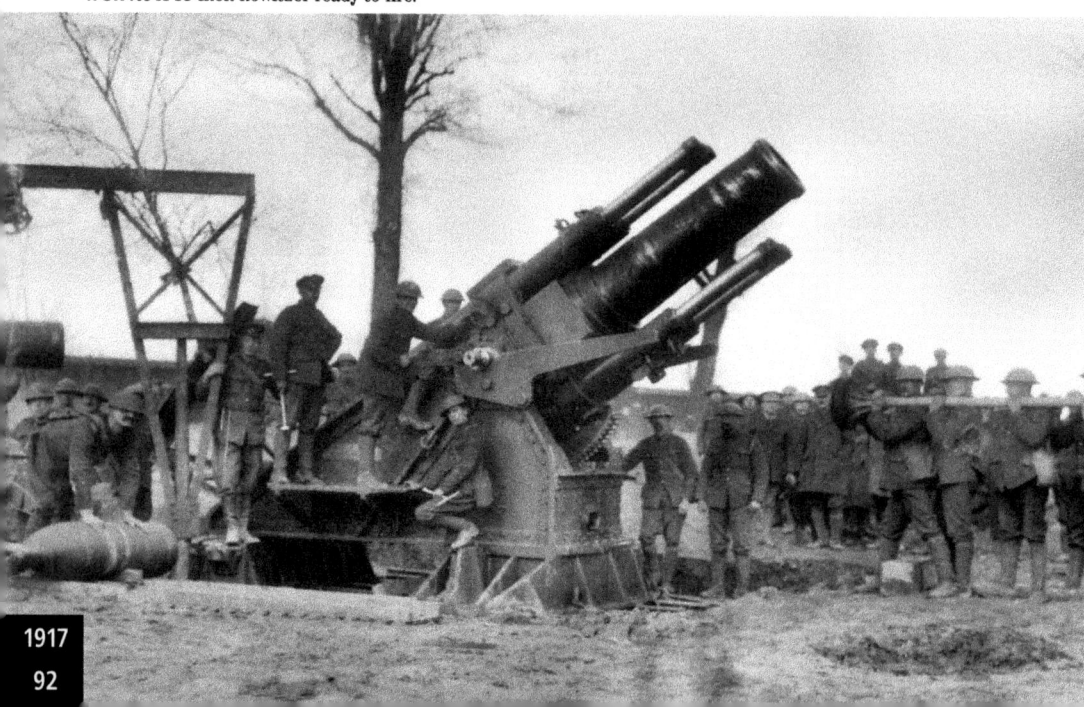

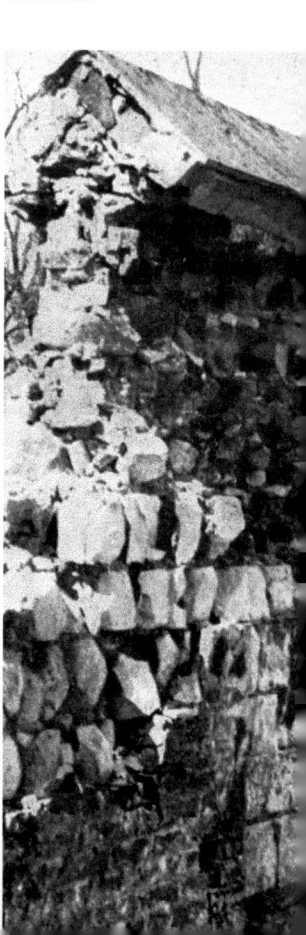

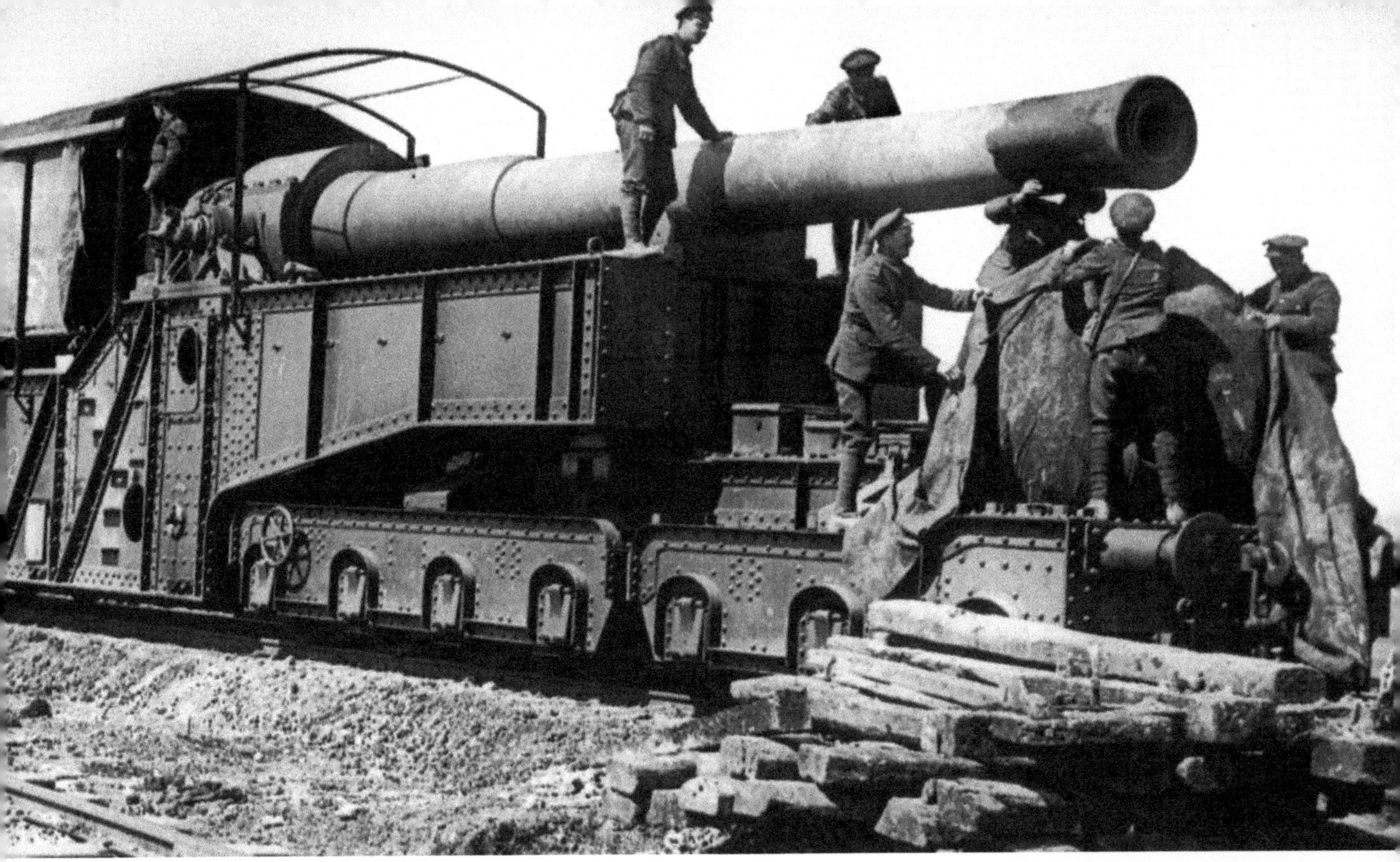

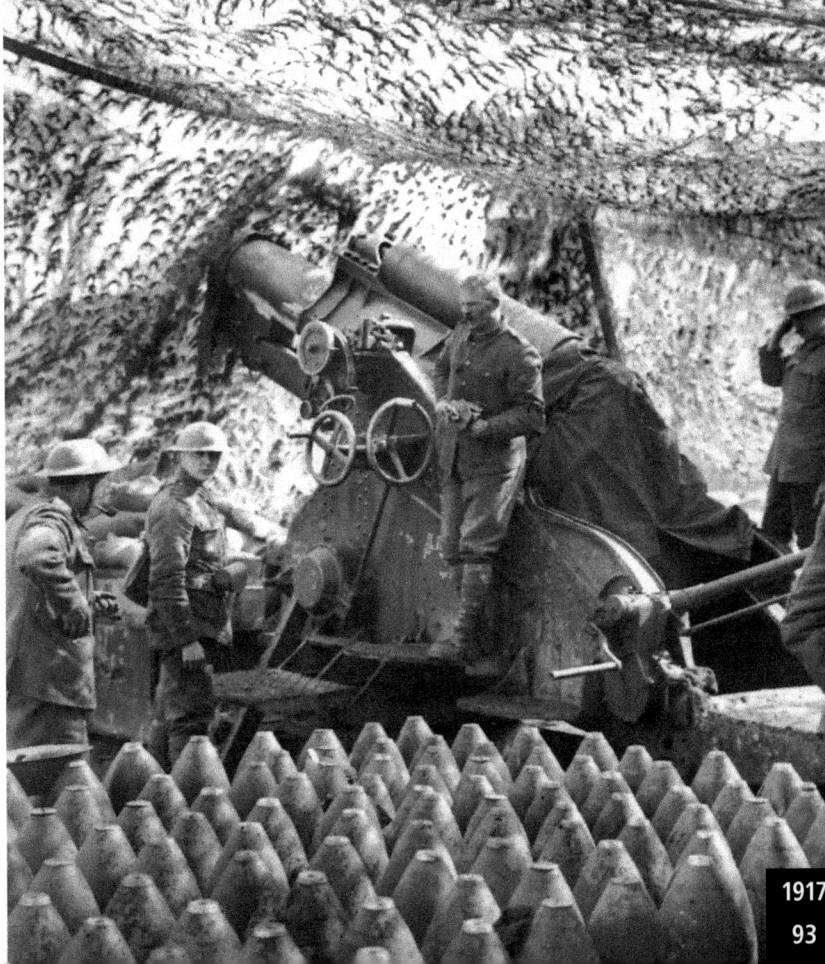

17GW162 A 9.2-inch howitzer of the 91st Battery, Royal Garrison Artillery, Arras 1 April 1917.
17GW164 A 9.2-inch howitzer near Arras.

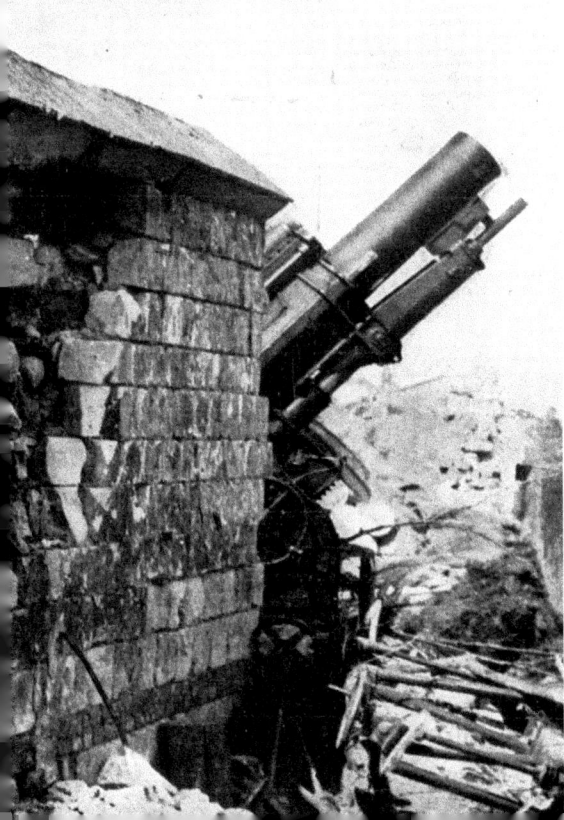

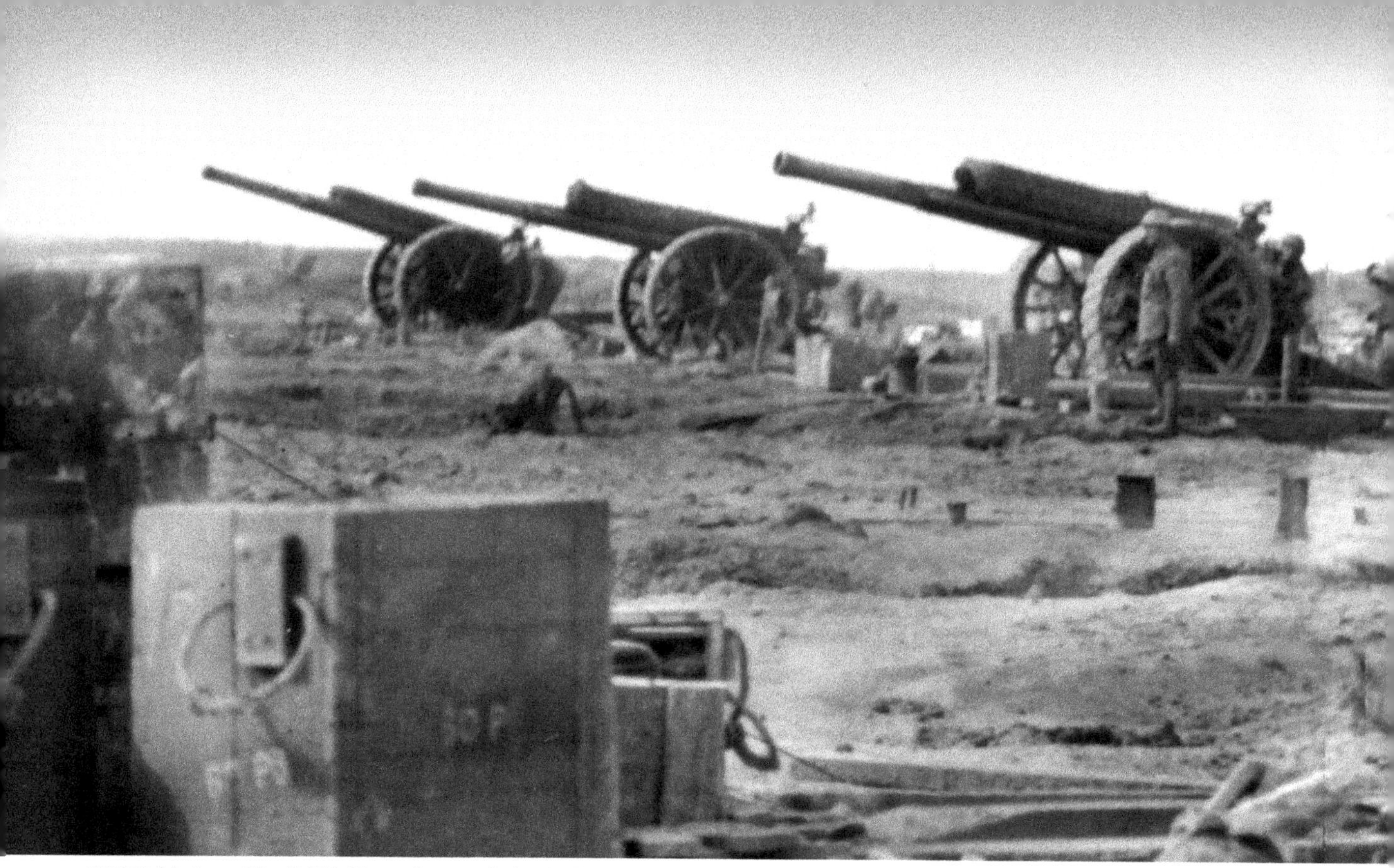

17GW166 A battery of five British 60-pounder guns during the Battle of Arras. The British Third Army, the Canadians at Vimy, along with other formations of the First Army that were to join the offensive later, had 258 guns of this type.

17GW167 Hauling a howitzer into position.

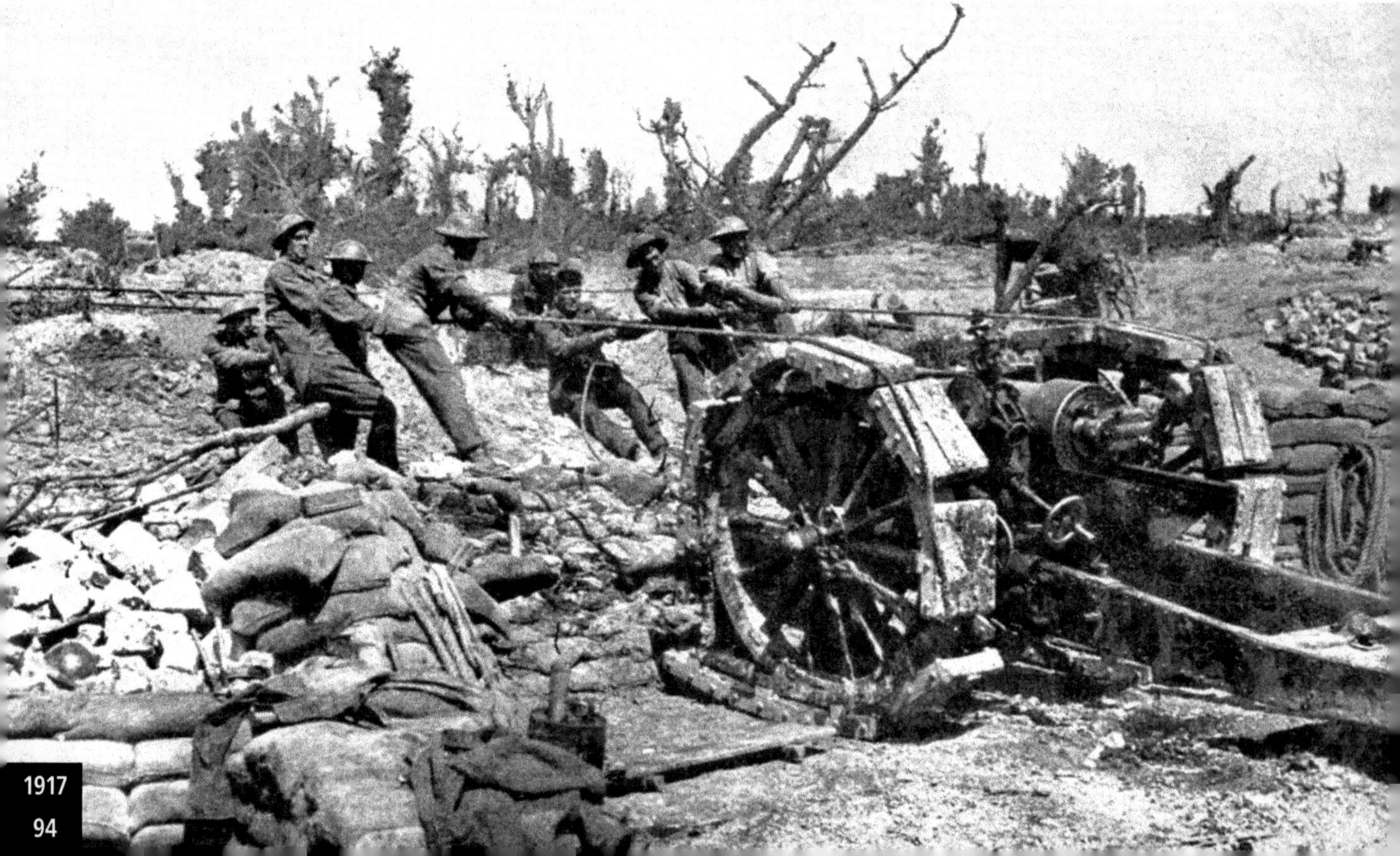

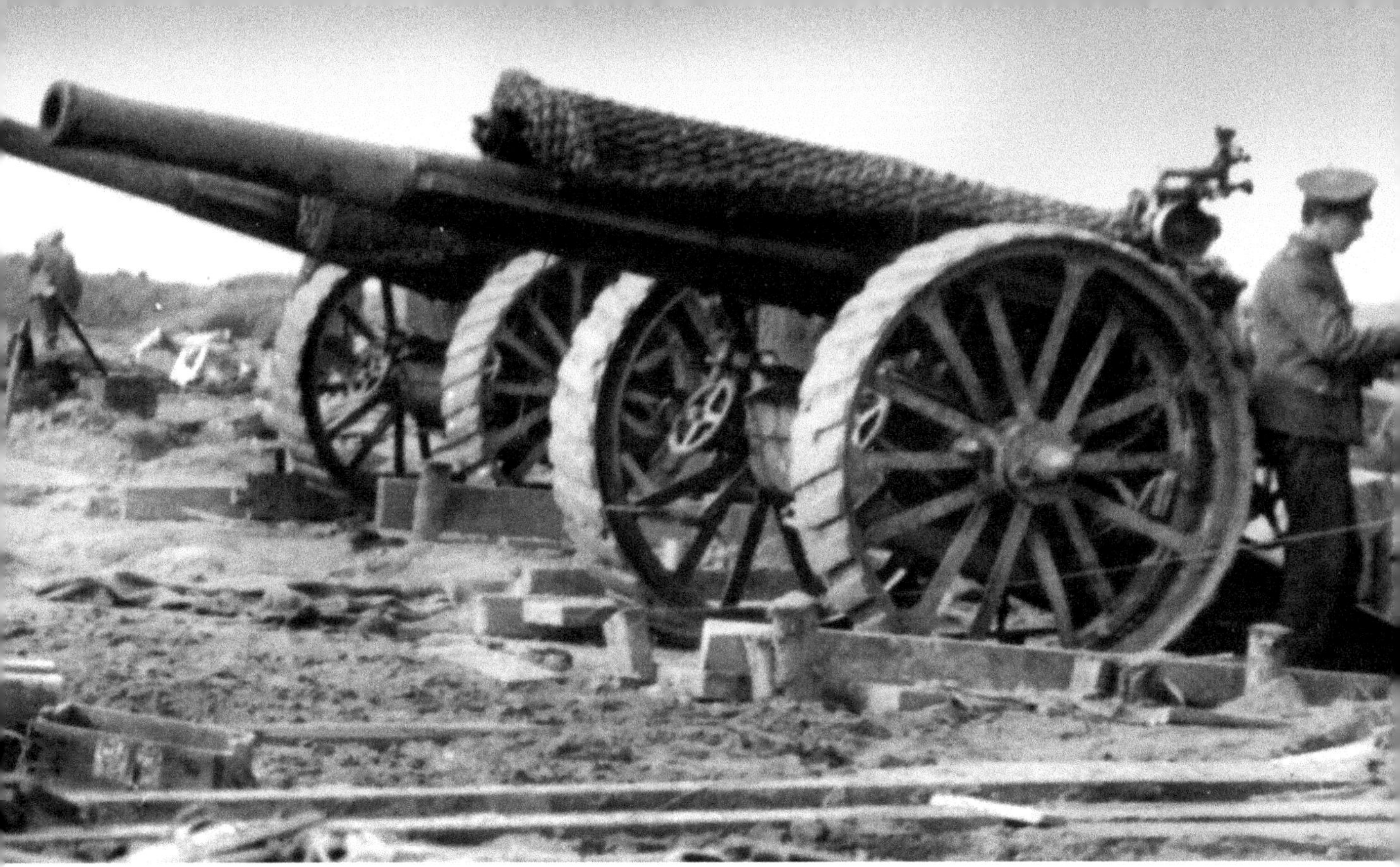

17GW168 Bringing up the ammunition in the vicinty of Arras. The battles of Arras and Messines would consume 5,000,000 shells of all calibres.

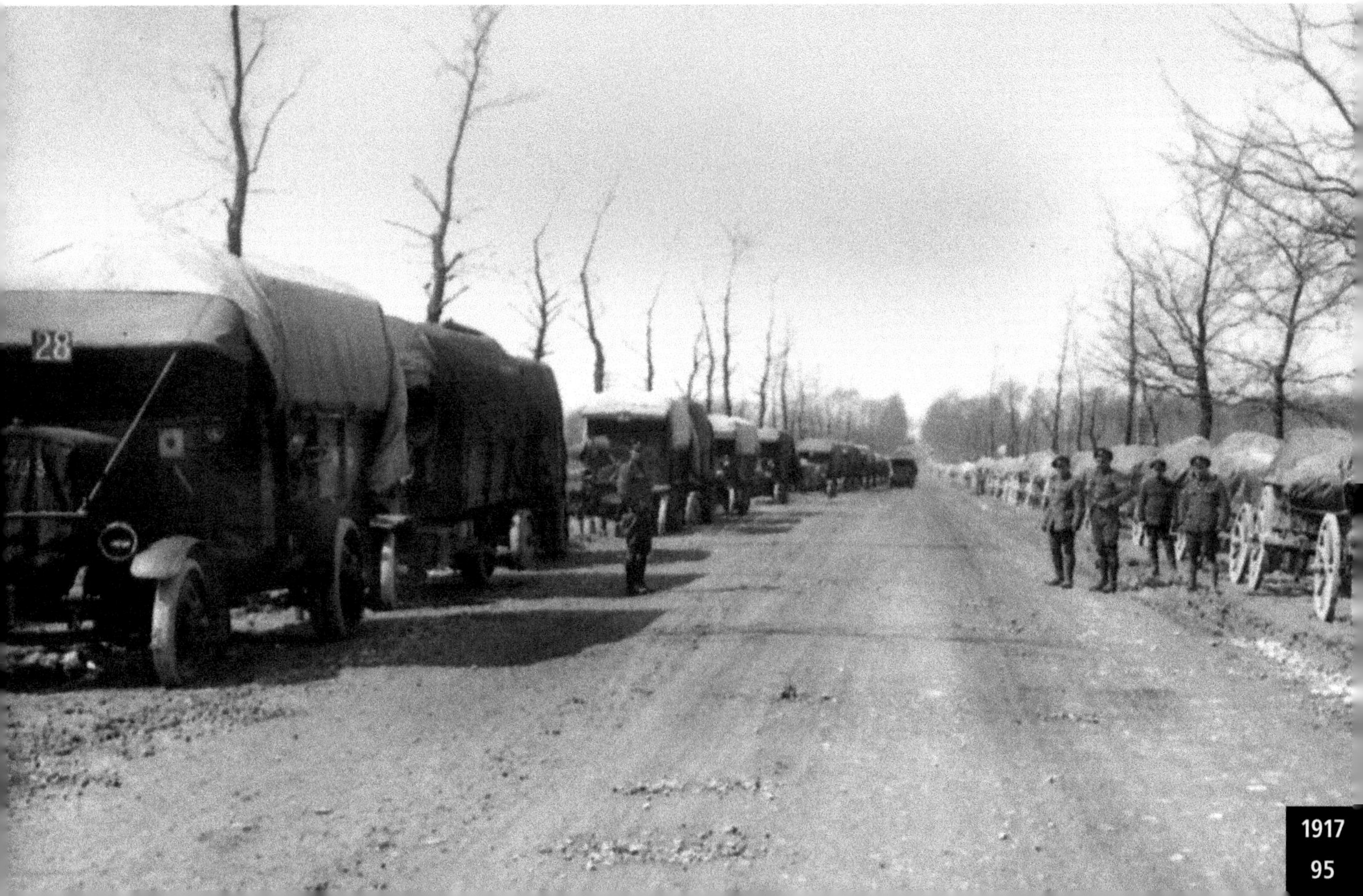

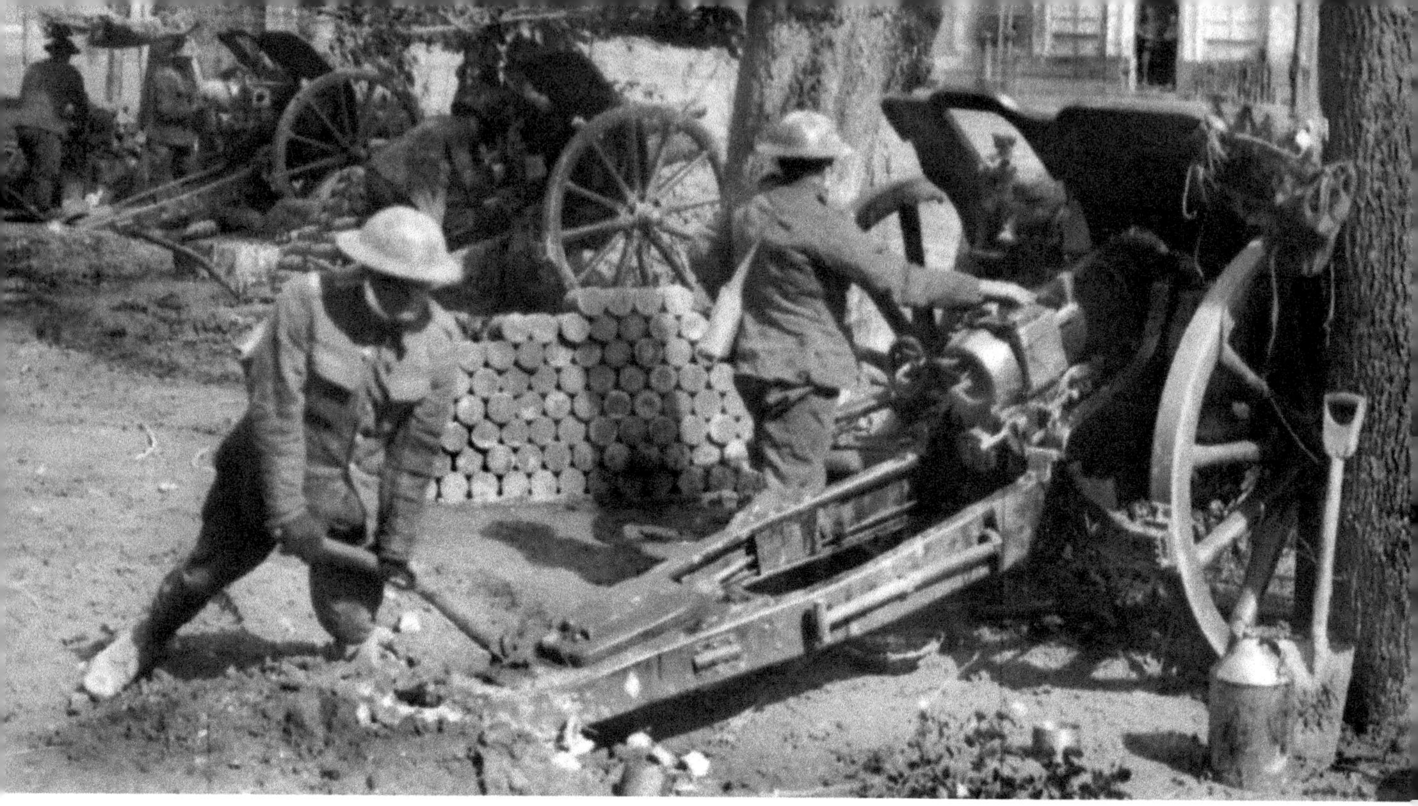

17GW169 A battery of 4.5-inch howitzers in the eastern suberbs of Arras. The Third Army had 276 of these guns employed in smashing up the German wire.

17GW170 A battery of 4.5-inch howitzers in a public park in Arras. During the attack these weapons were tasked with firing on fixed positions in the German Second and Third lines. 18-pounders were to provide the creeping barrage ahead of the advancing infantry.

17GW171 An 18-pounder is being manhandled into a firing position in a graveyard in an Arras suburb. The Third Army had 858 of these guns in action in April 1917. They could fire as many as 300 shells in a twenty-four hour period. Each day the 18-pounders used up almost 255,000 shells. An efficient and constant supply was all part of the planning by the various corps and divisional staffs involved in the big offensive at Arras.

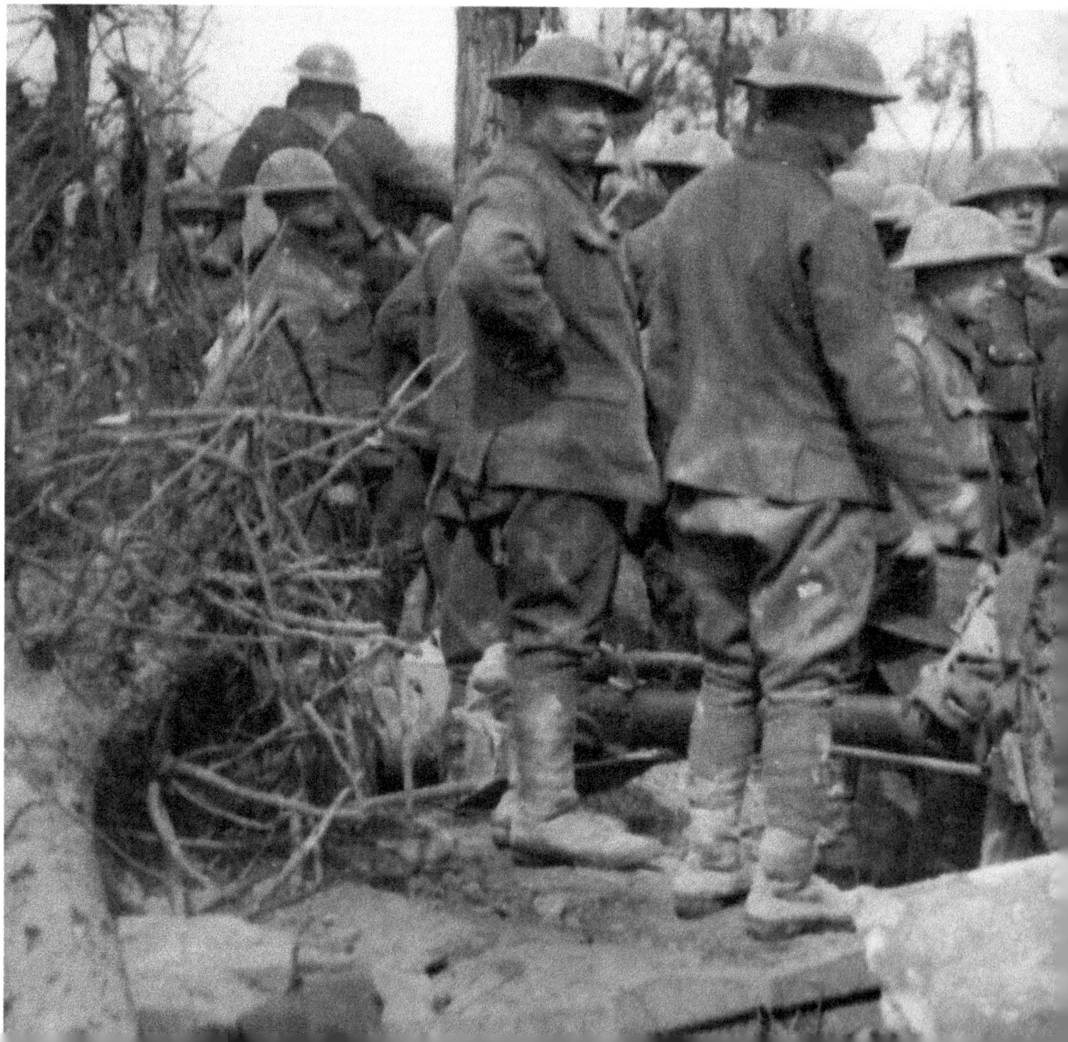

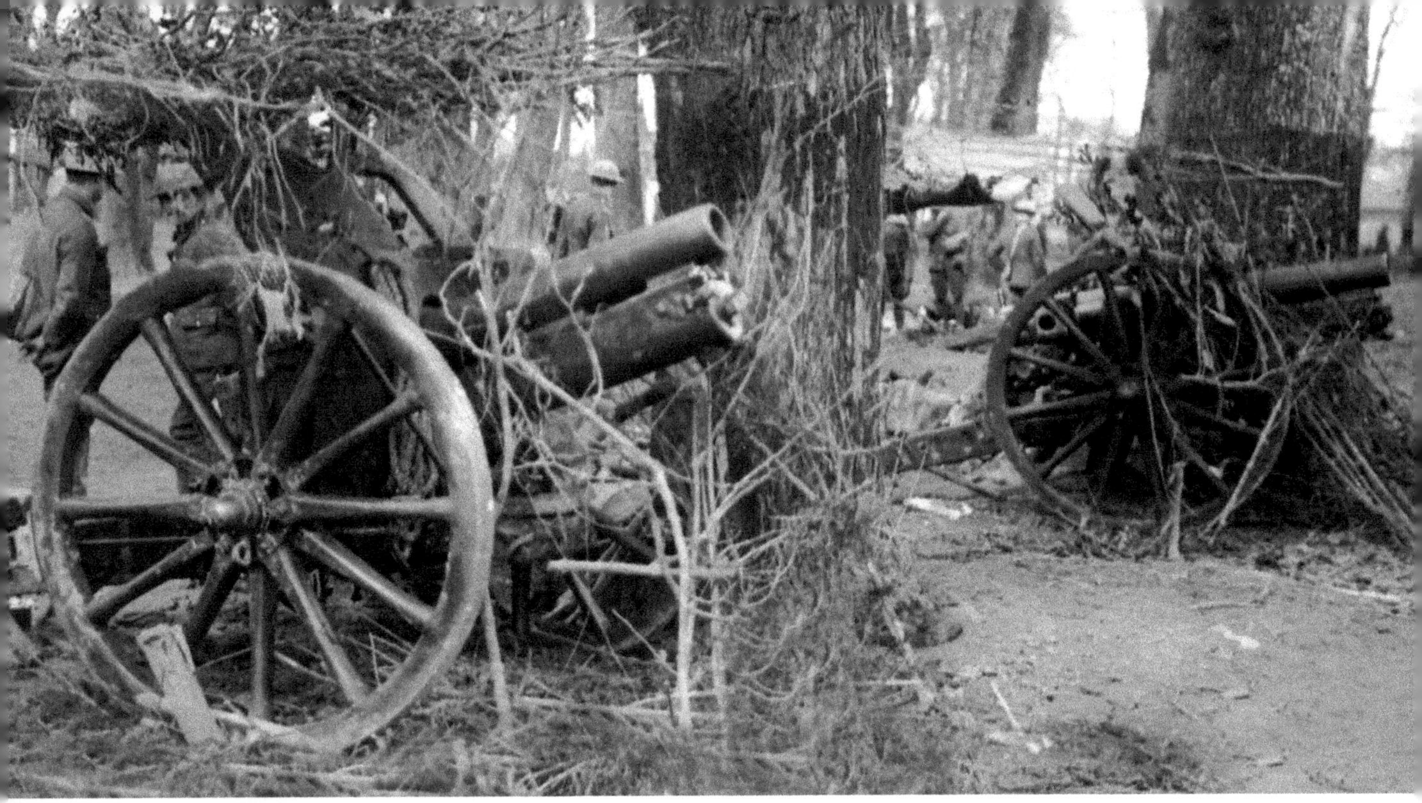

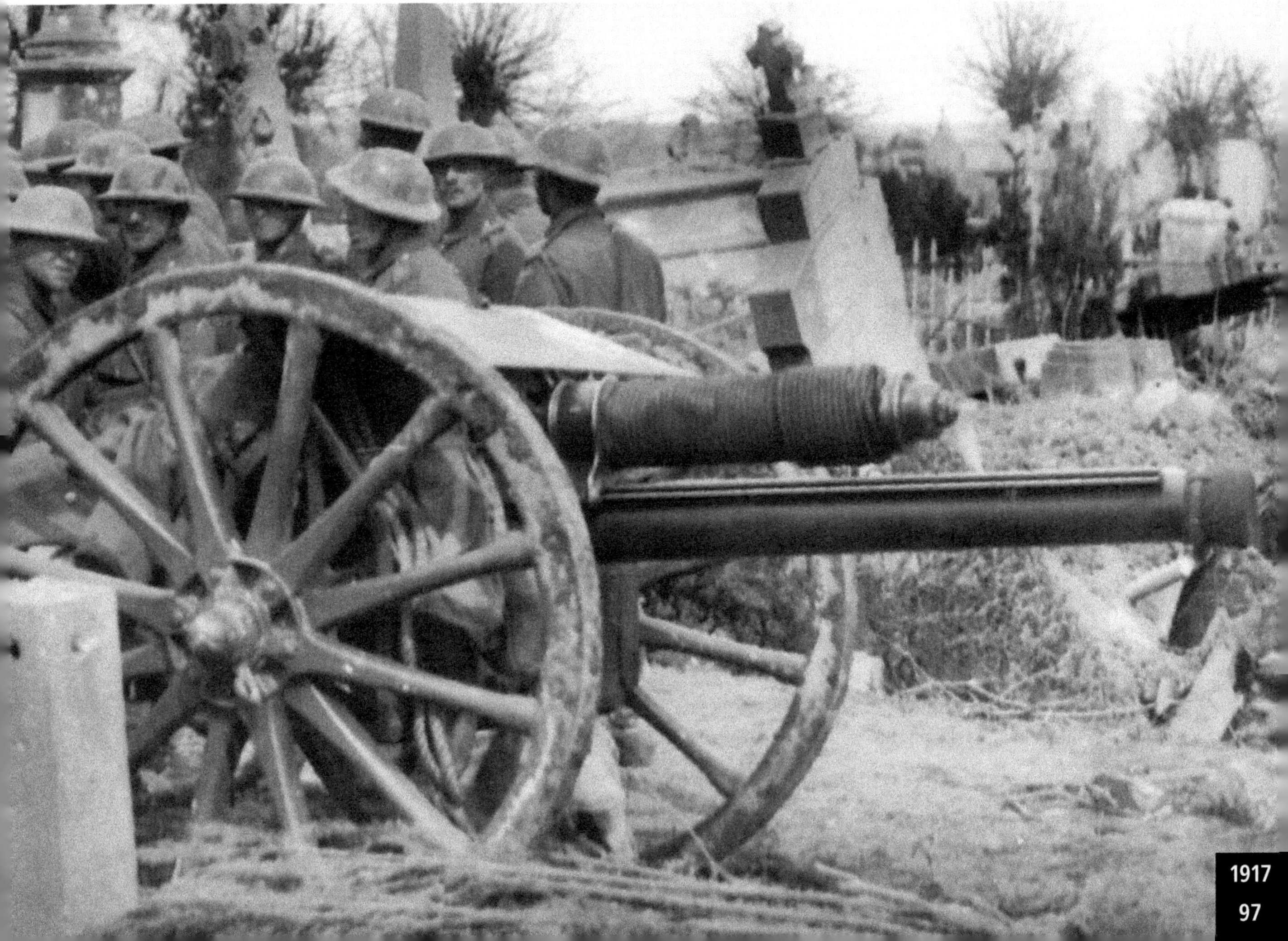

1917

97

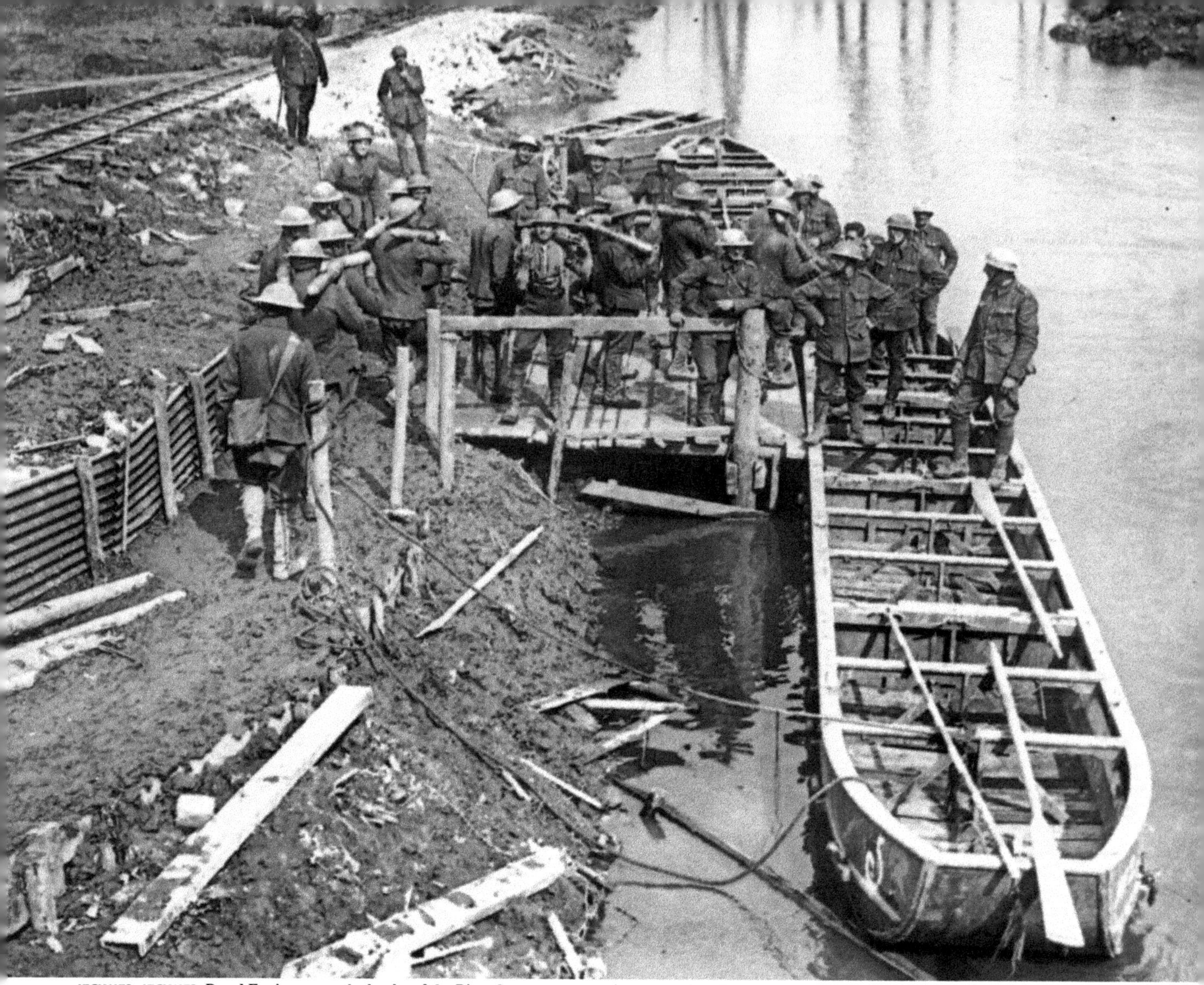

17GW172, 17GW173. Royal Engineers on the banks of the River Scarpe constructing a crossing. The attack would advance parallel to the river which, more or less, on 9 April was the boundary between XVII and VI Corps and Third Army.

17GW182 A two-foot guage trench tramway at the Royal Engineers depot at 'Oxford Circus', on the outskirts of Arras, April 1917.

17GW174 A trench tramway being constructed by Royal Engineers Arras, April 1917.

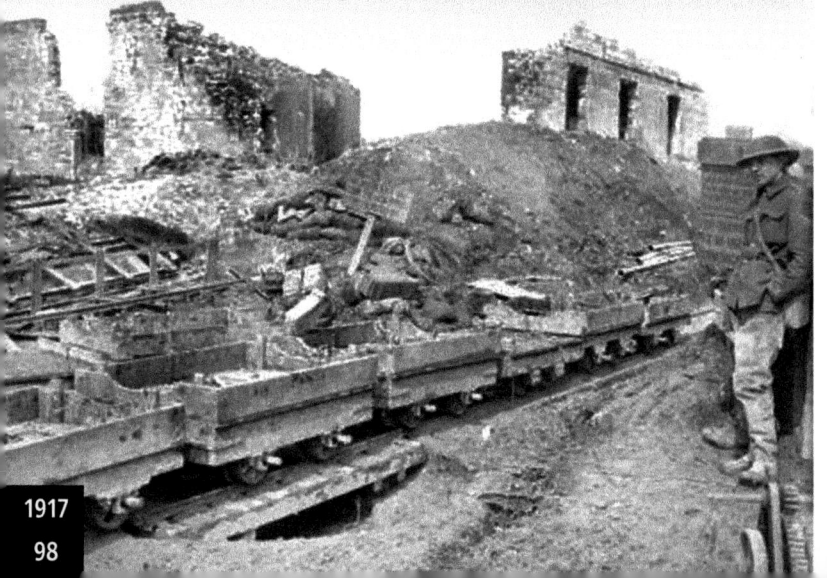

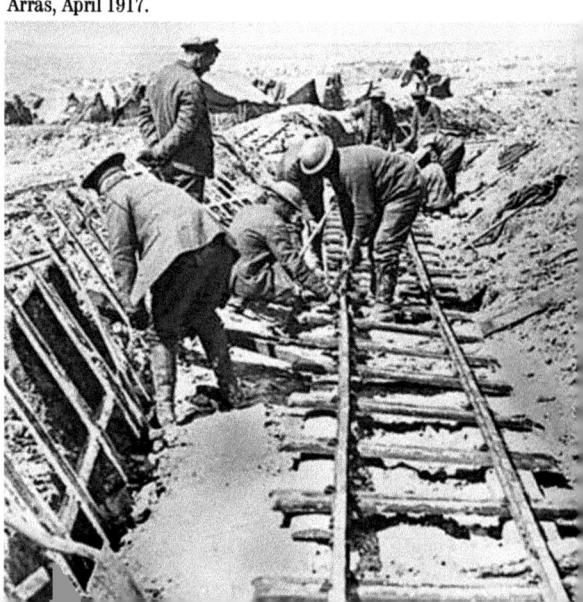

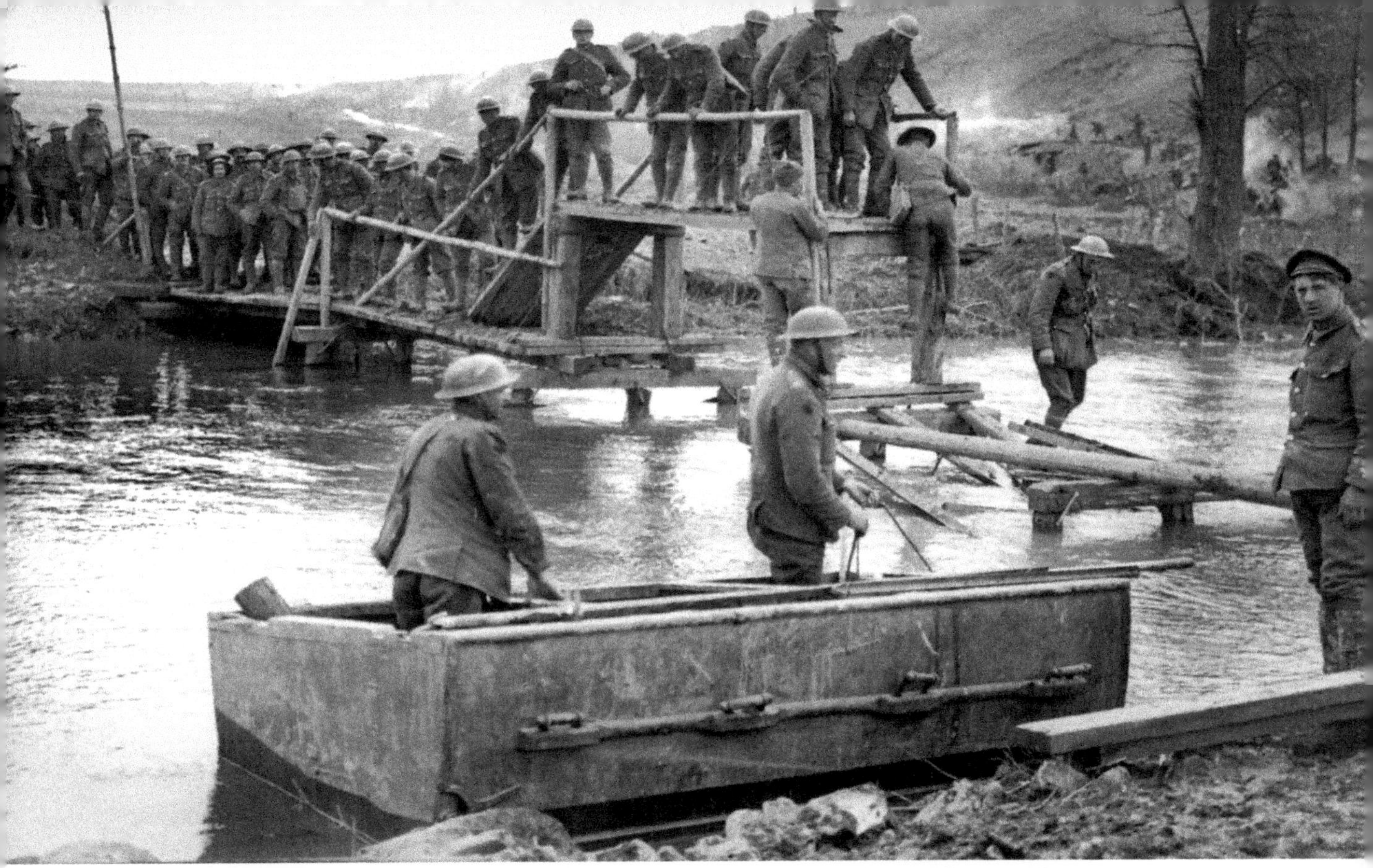

17GW183, 17GW177. Royal Engineers fixing scaling ladders in front line trenches, 8 April 1917, the day before the infantry assault.

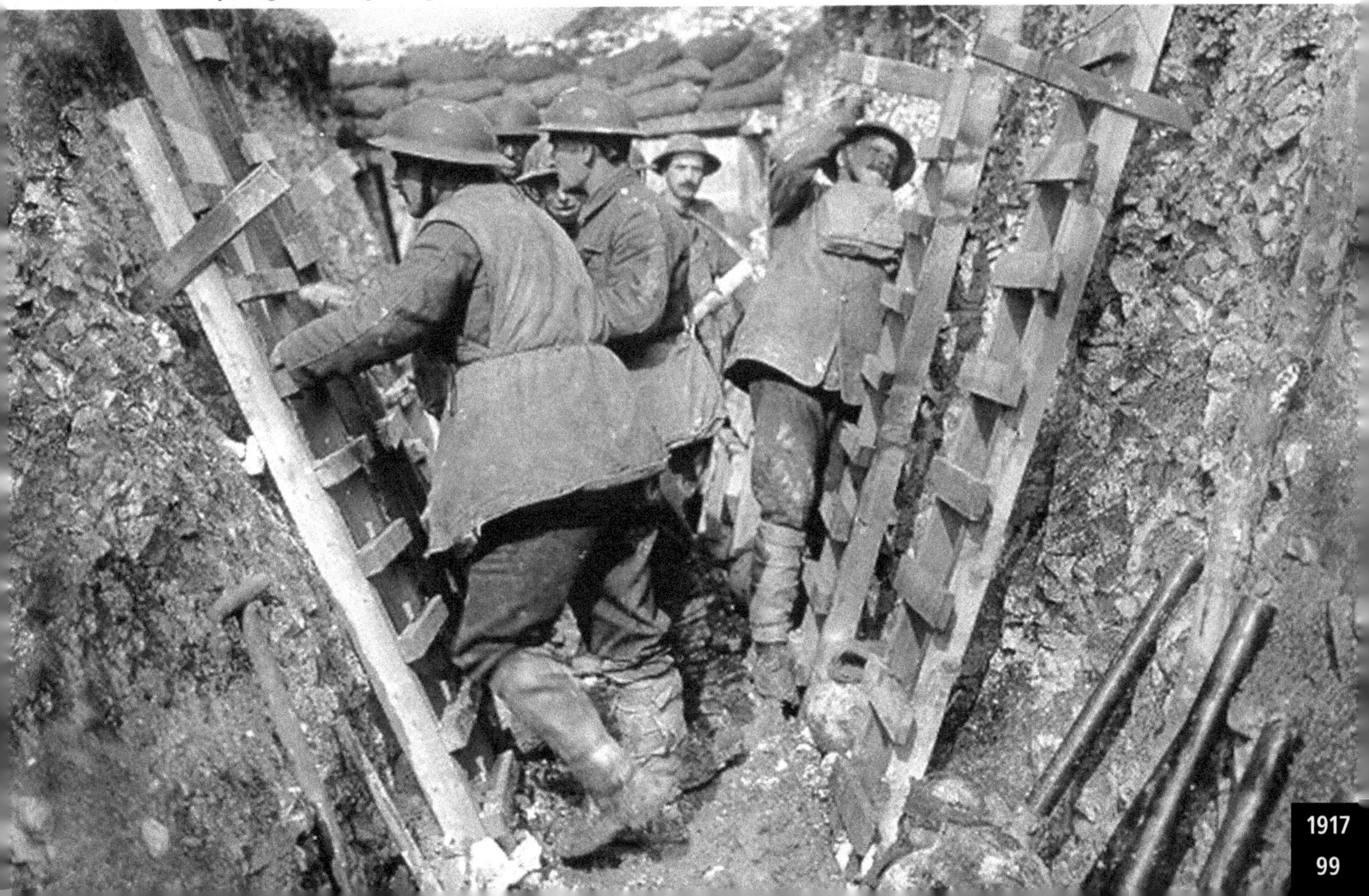

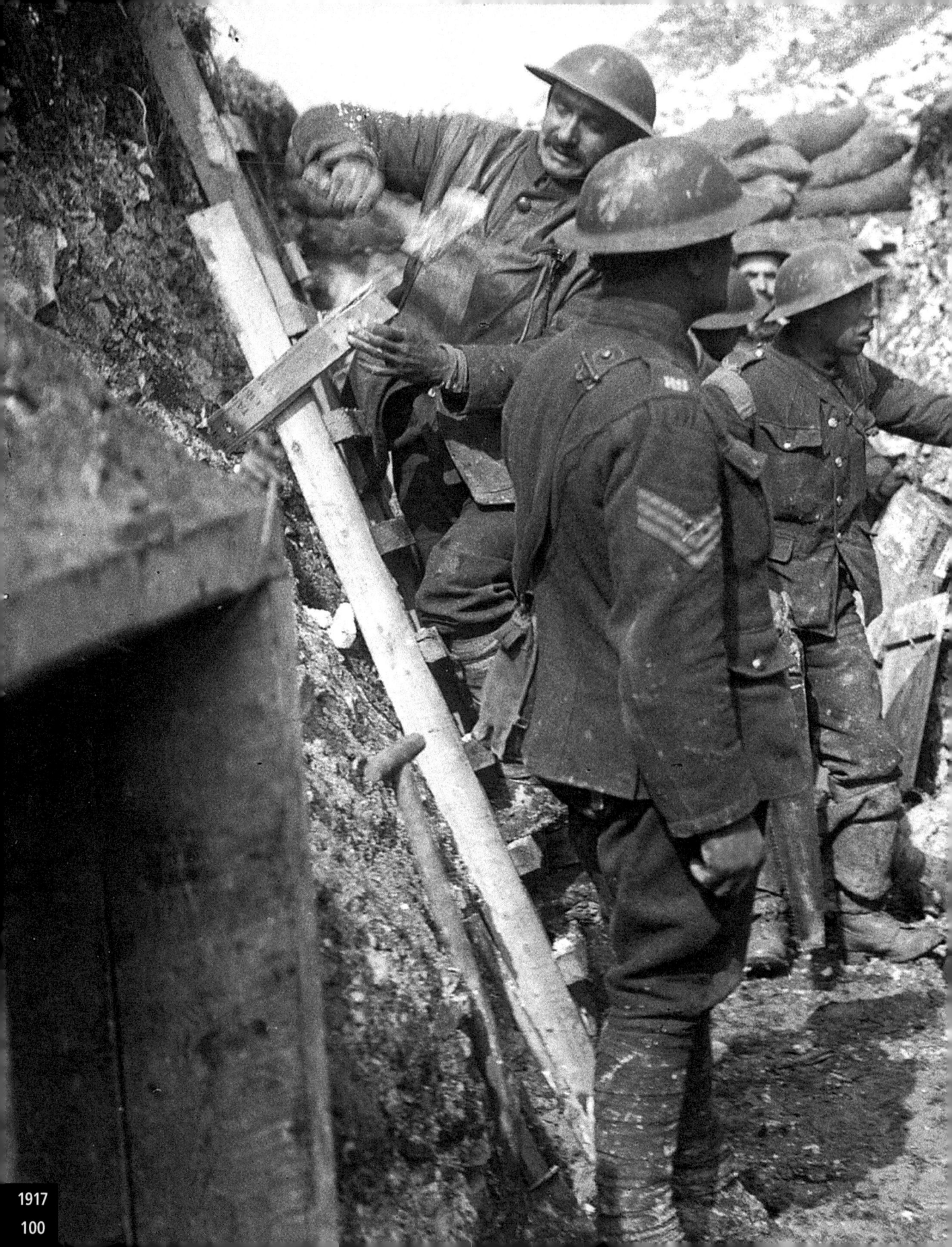

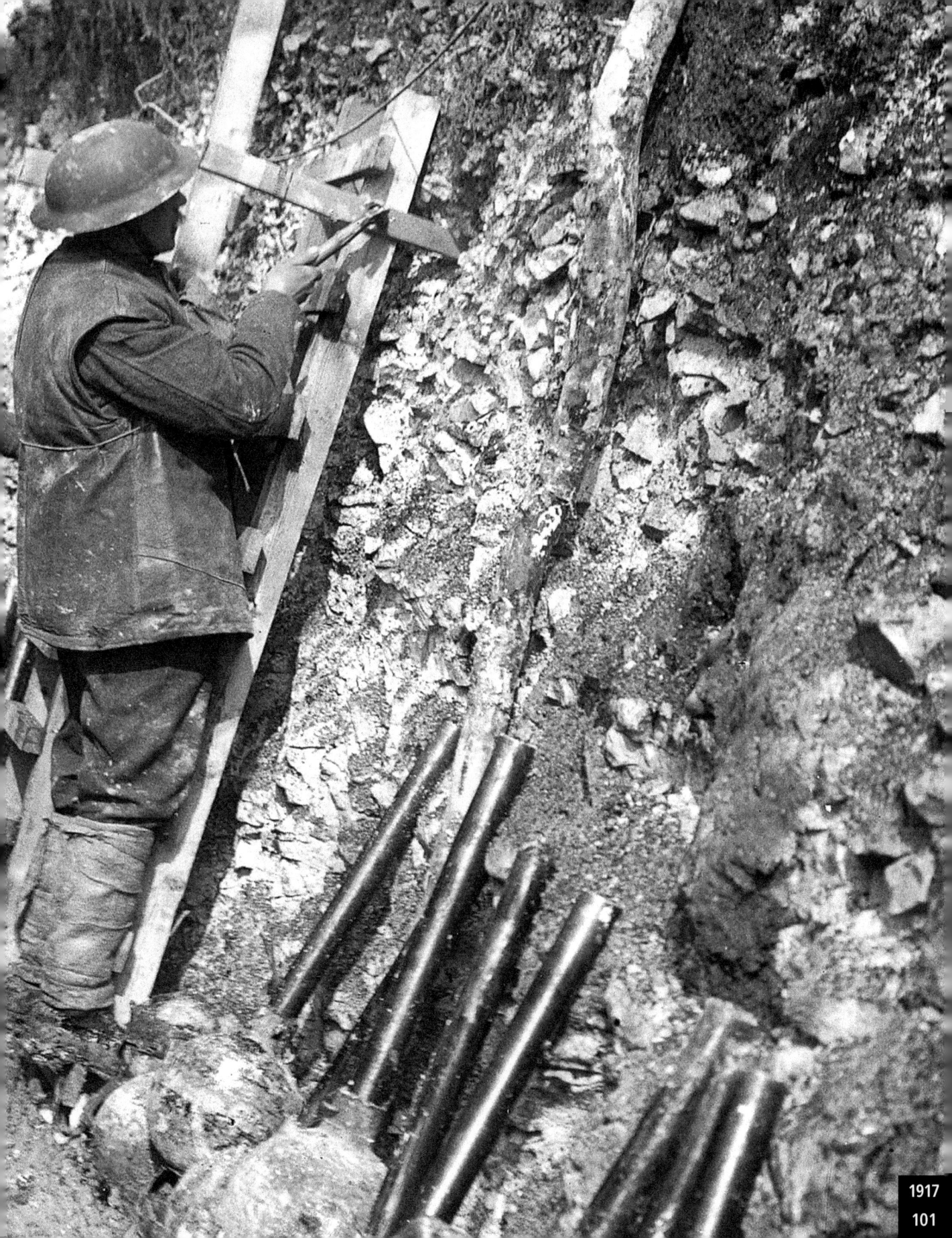

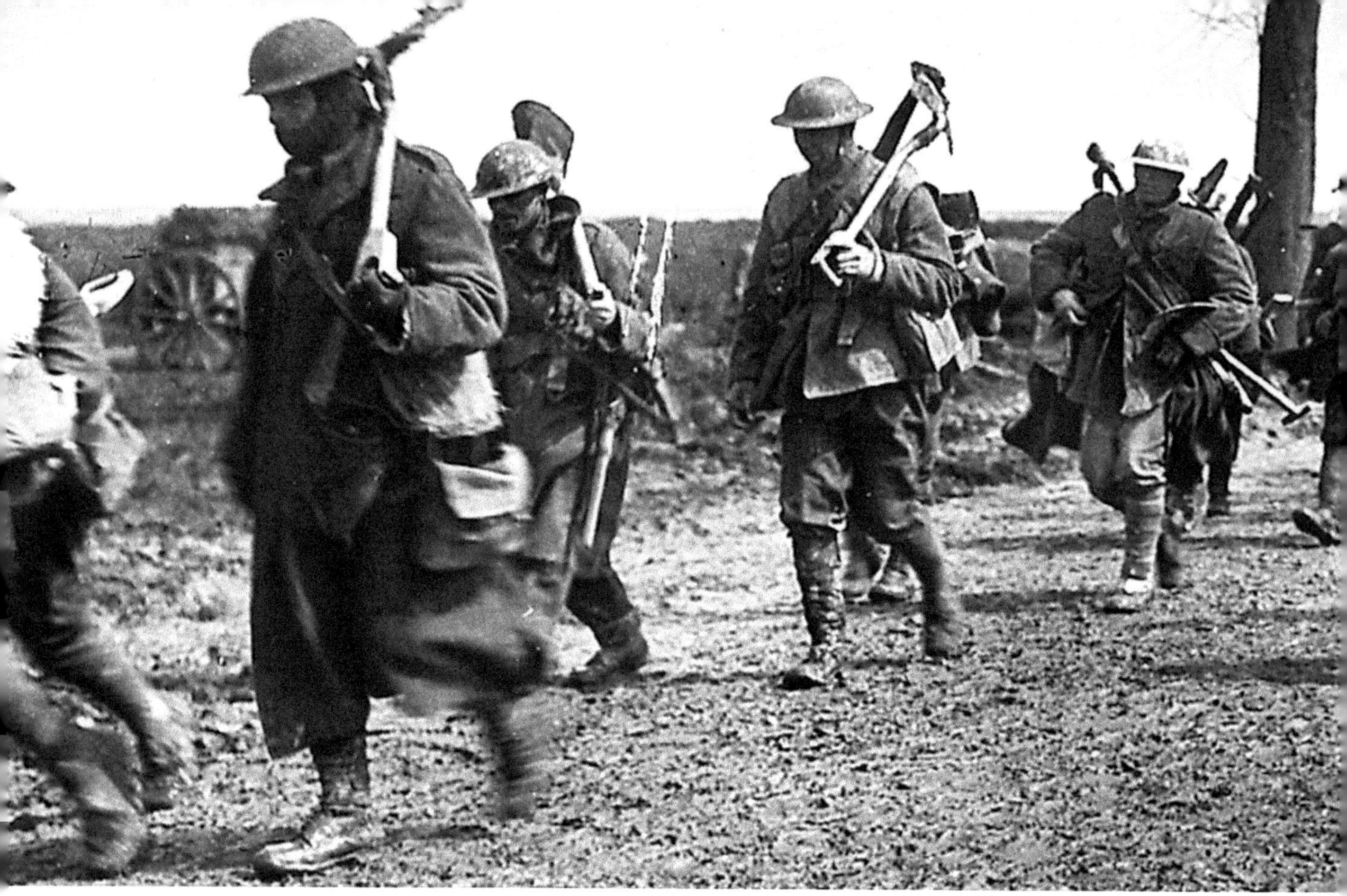

17GW174 Sappers returning from constructing scaling ladders in the forward trenches pass infantry moving up to occupy their positions for the attack.

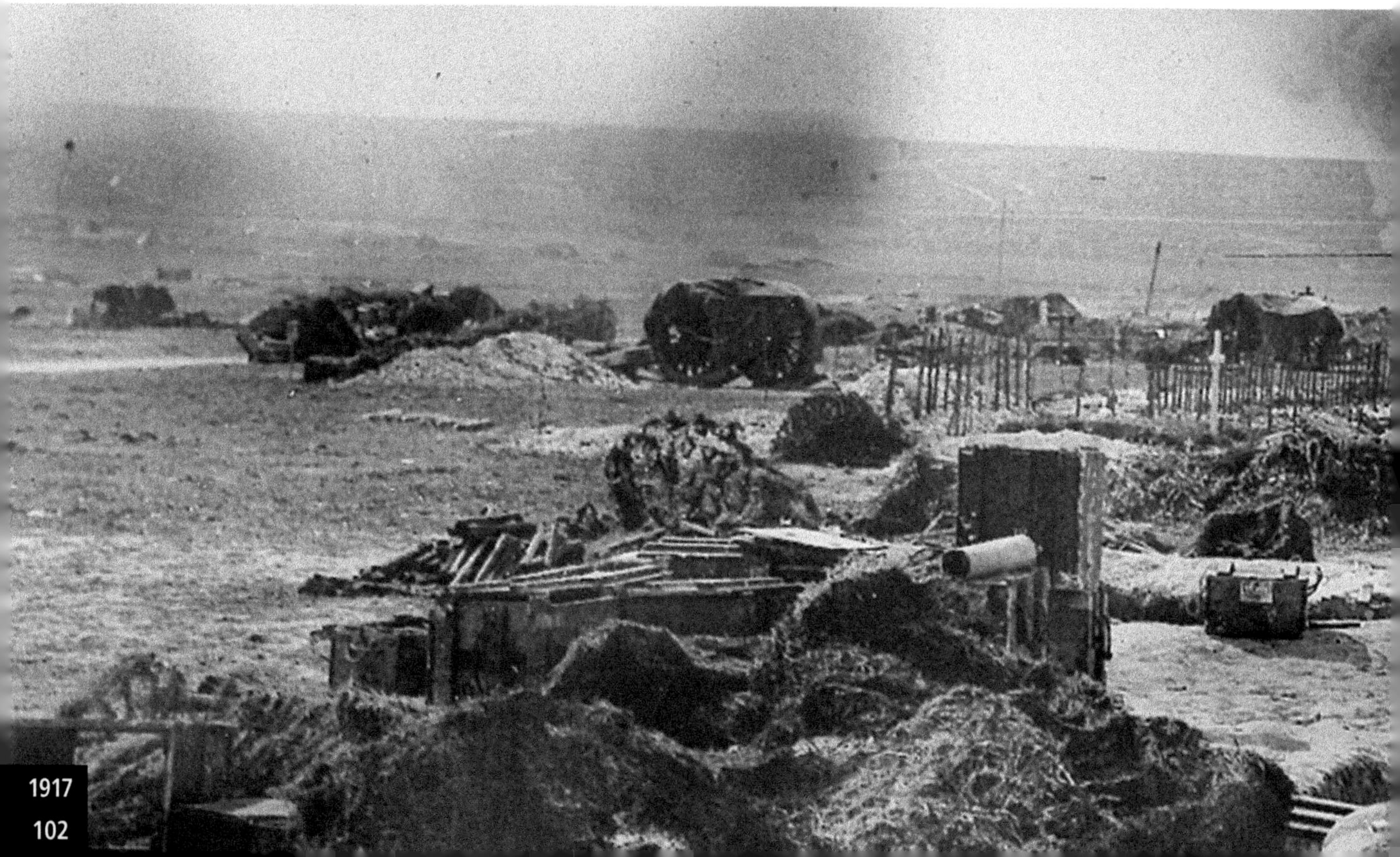

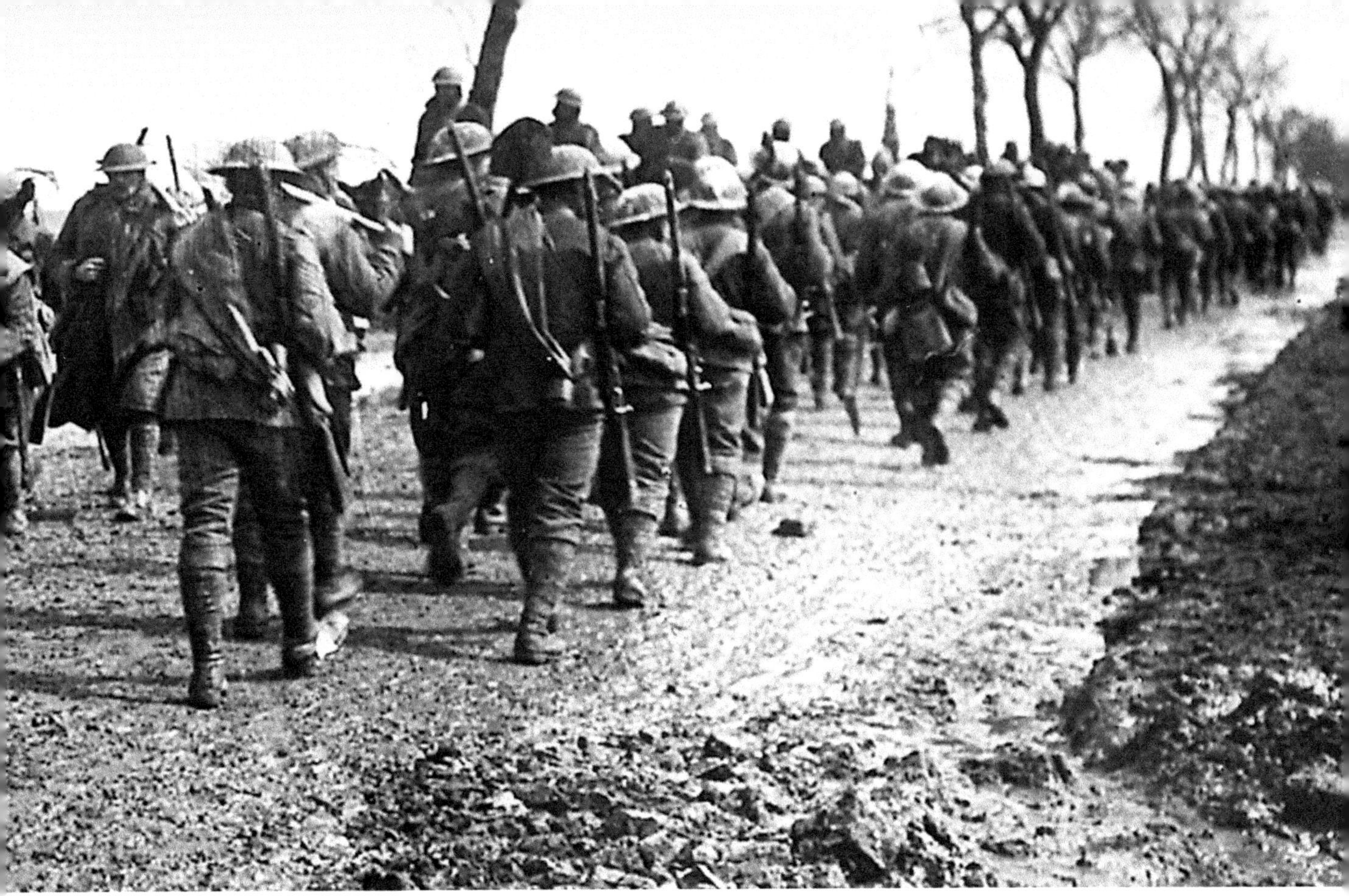

17GW186 British artillery dug in near an old cemetery, with shells bursting nearby. The view is of Orange Hill and beyond towards Monchy-le-Preux.

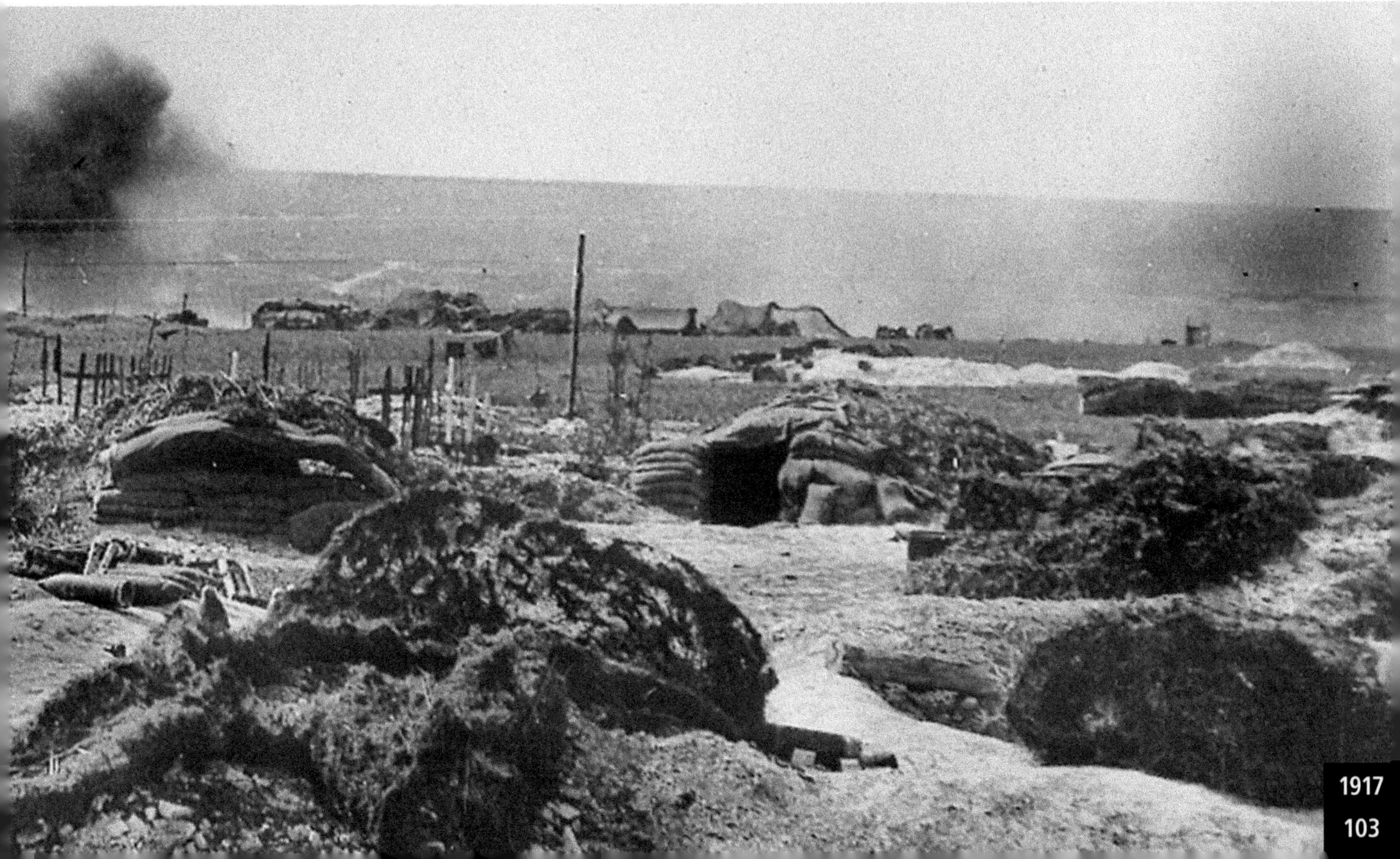

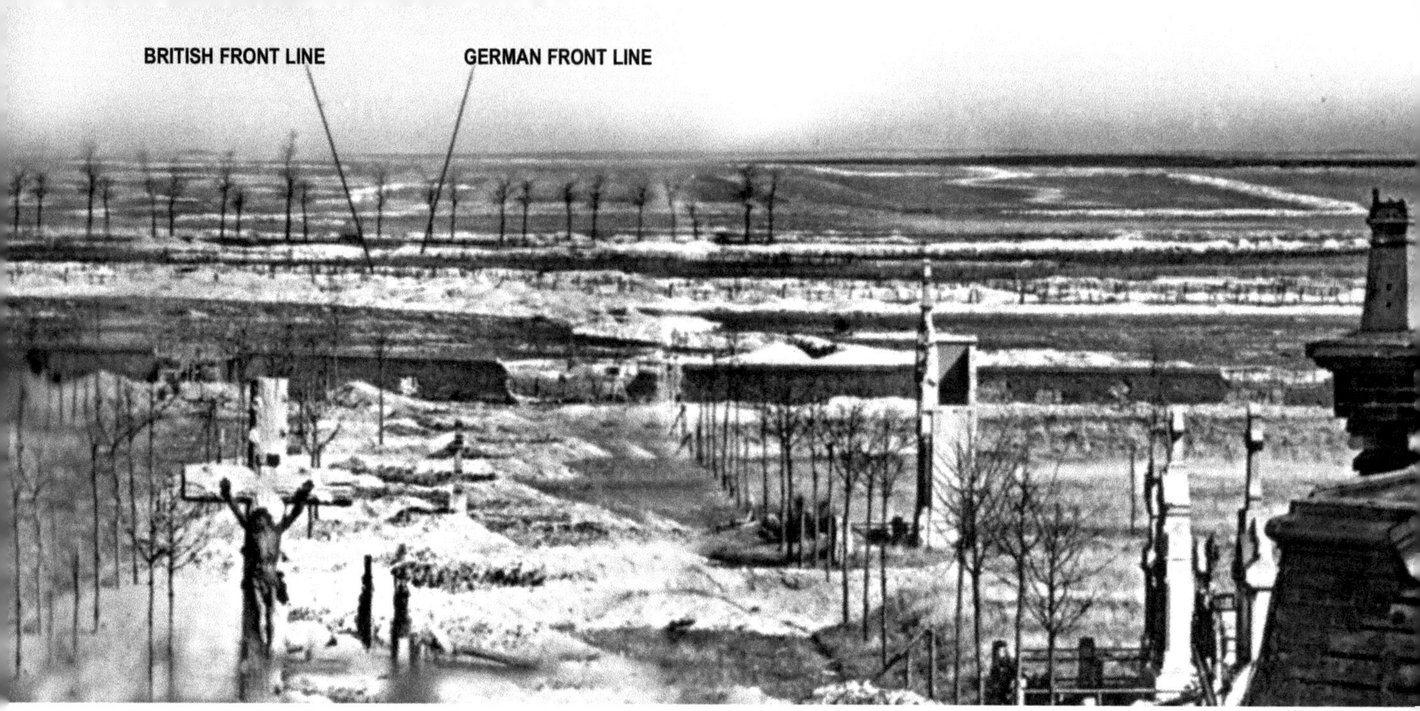

BRITISH FRONT LINE   GERMAN FRONT LINE

17GW187 Looking eastwards across a cemetery over the front lines. The British communication trench zig-zags from in front of the crucifix, through the broken cemetery wall towards the line of trees.

17GW192 The British Expeditionary Force has penetrated the Hindenburg Line: infantry, artillery, tanks and cavalry feature in this image typifying the Arras operation.

17GW193 An artillery column on the banks of the Scarpe, at the village of Athies.

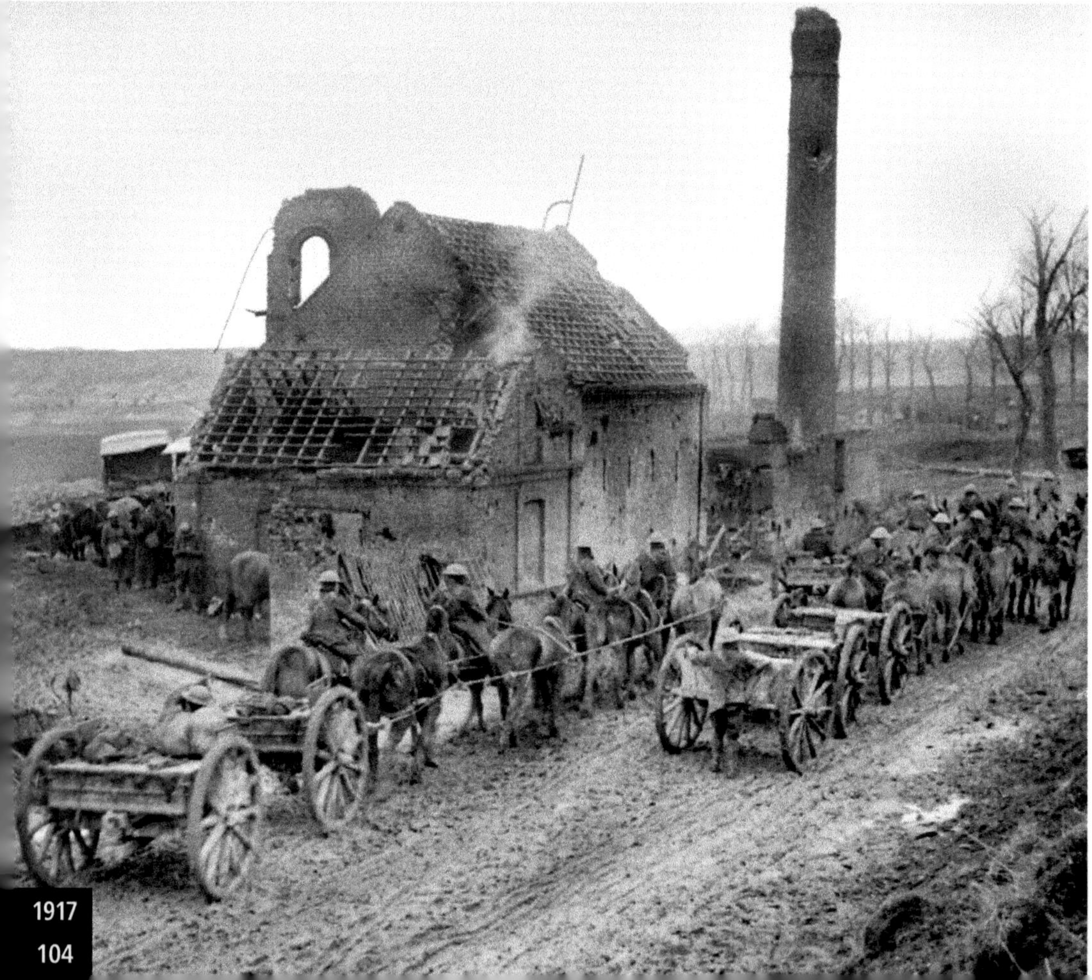

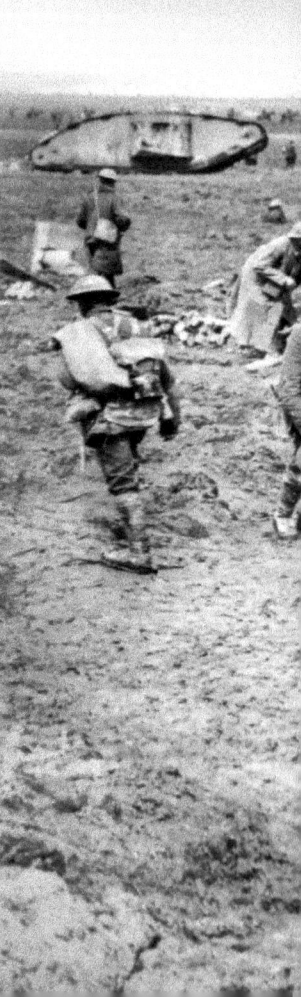

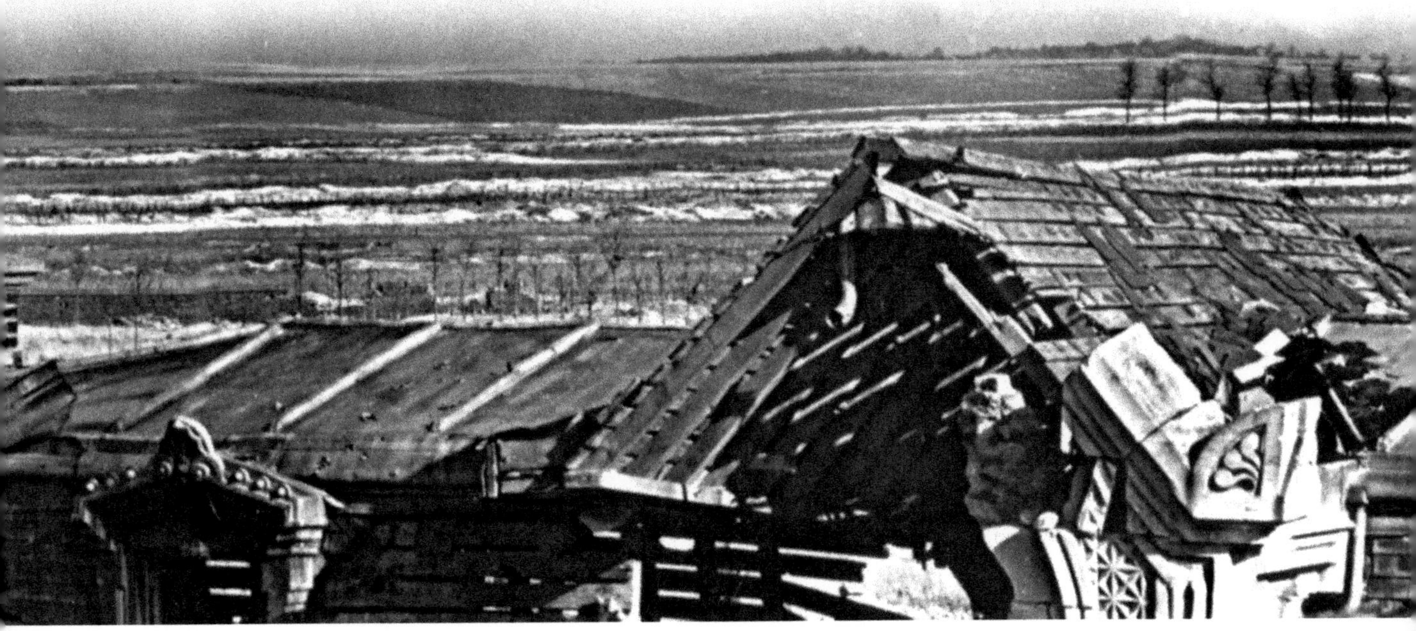

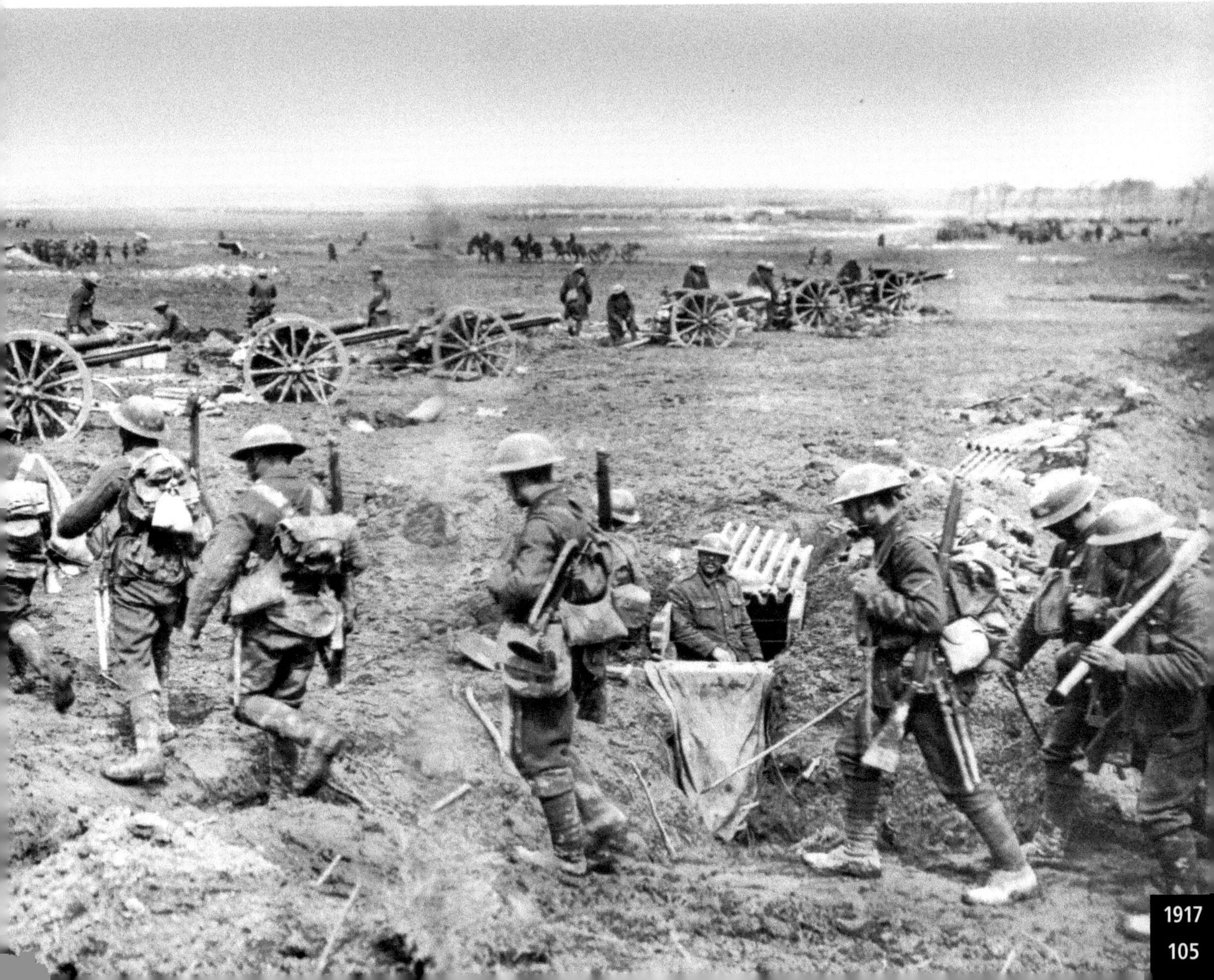

1917

105

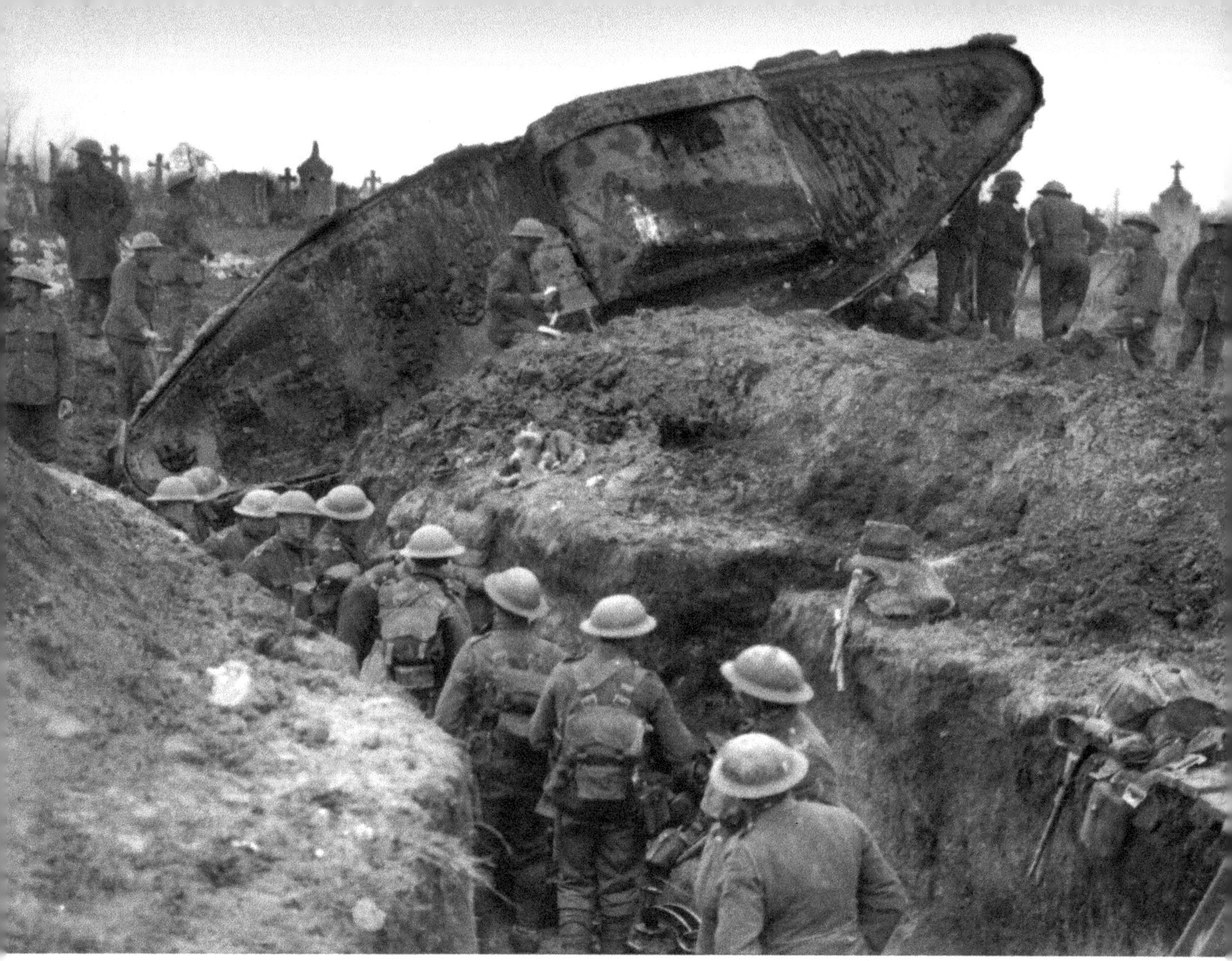

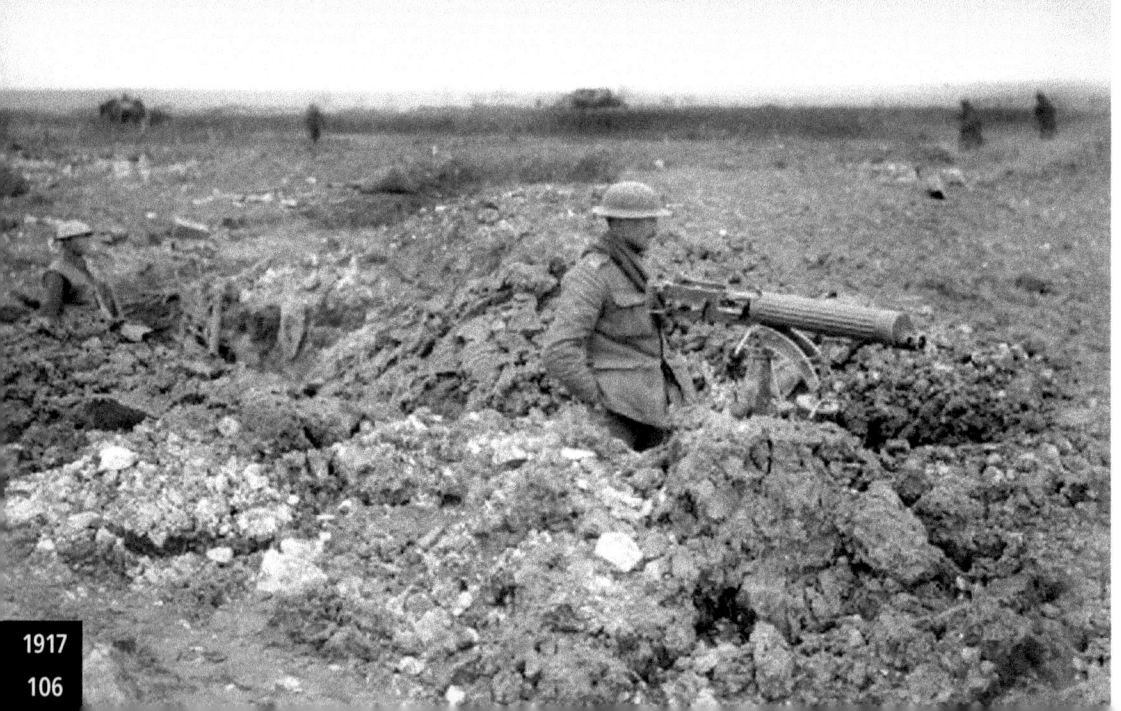

17GW195 In a graveyard near Arras and well within the British lines, this Mark II tank has slid into a communication trench and is being dug out. A machine gun crew await the order to advance.

17GW184 Machine gunners near the village of Feuchy at the opening of the Arras offensive.

17GW194 Another tank, a Male, has become bogged down in captured territory along the Fampoux road, close to the river Scarpe.

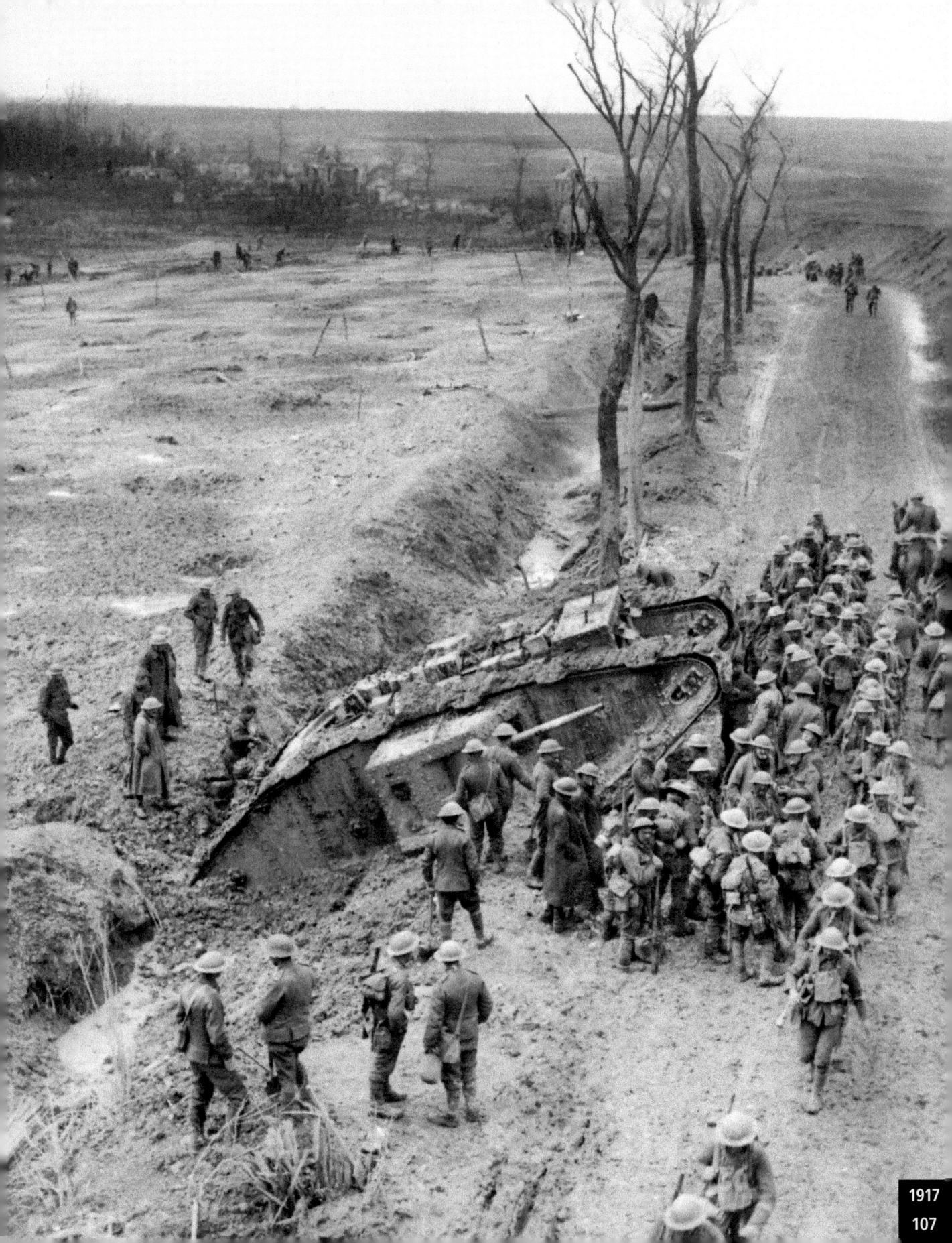

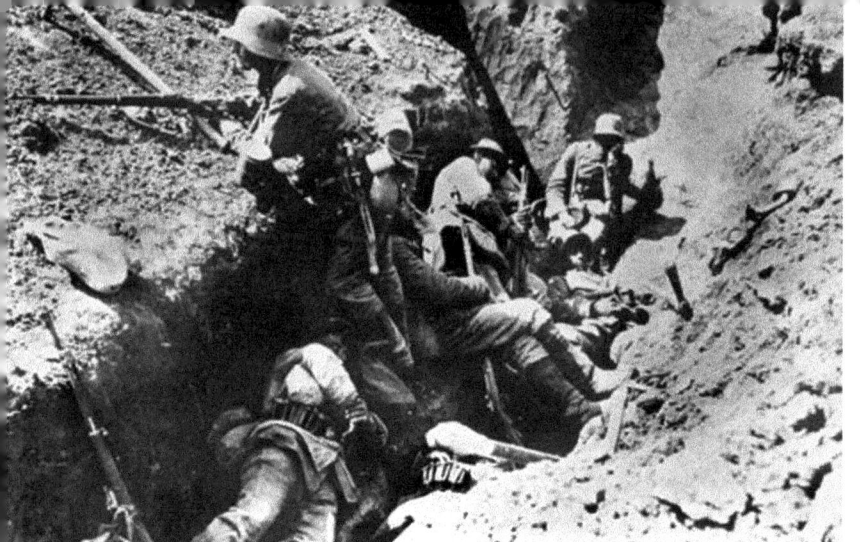
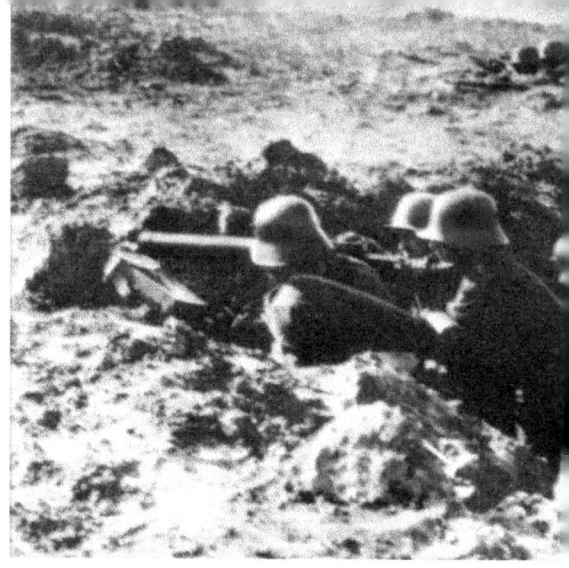

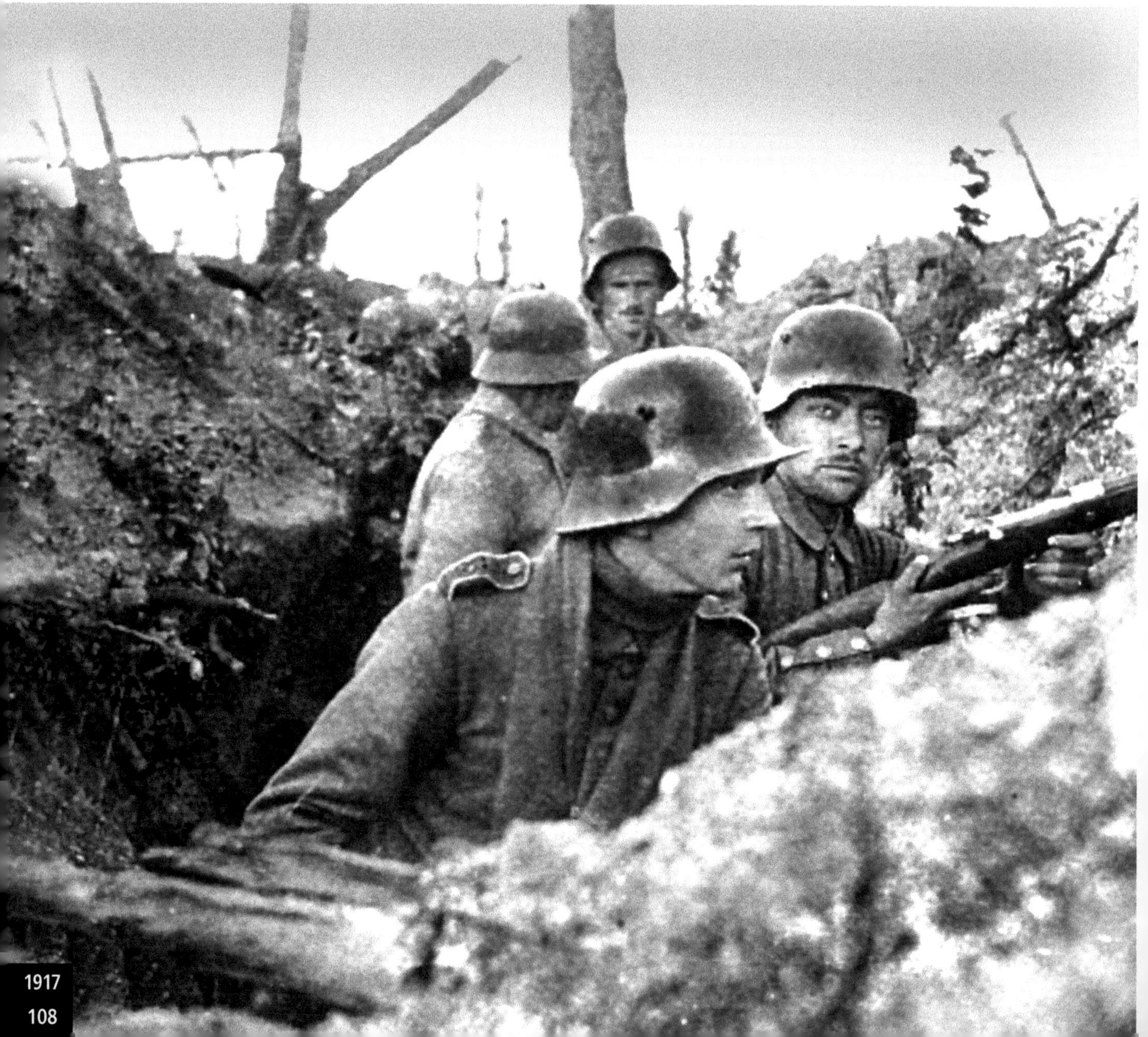

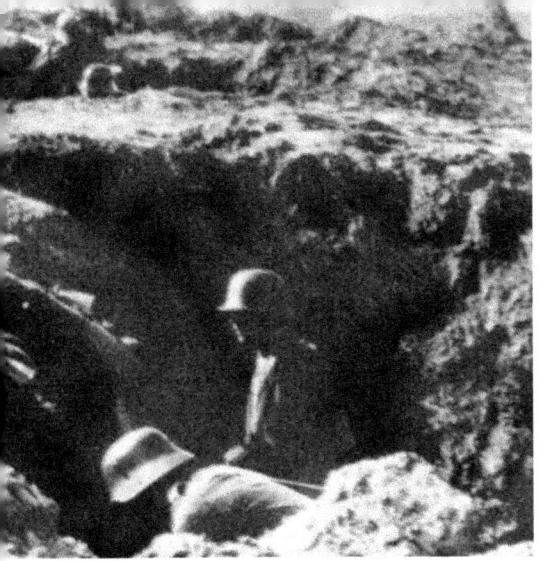
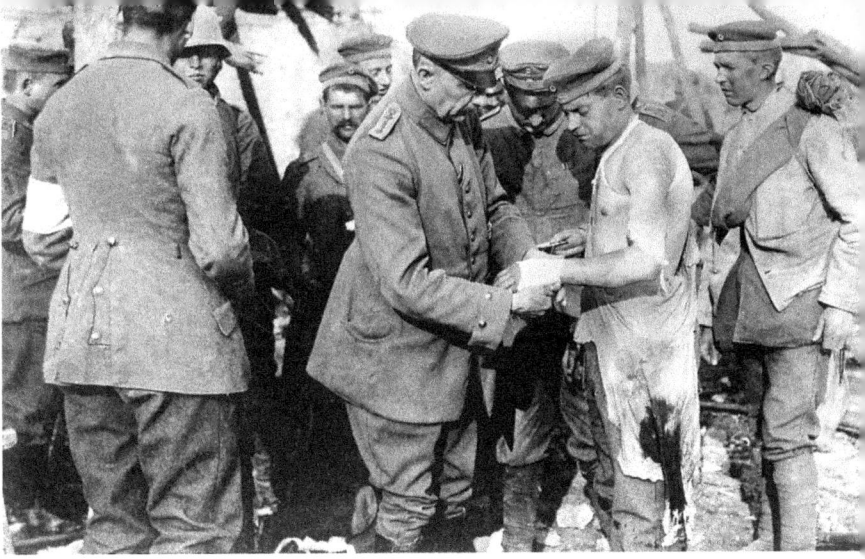

17GW197, 17GW208, 17GW204. German troops fighting at Arras. Their lines had been broken along the length of Vimy Ridge and south of the Scarpe along a twelve mile front.

17GW199 German walking wounded having their injuries attended to during the fighting.

17GW196 Machine gun team operating their *Maschinengewehr* 08, or MG 08, the German Army's standard machine gun.

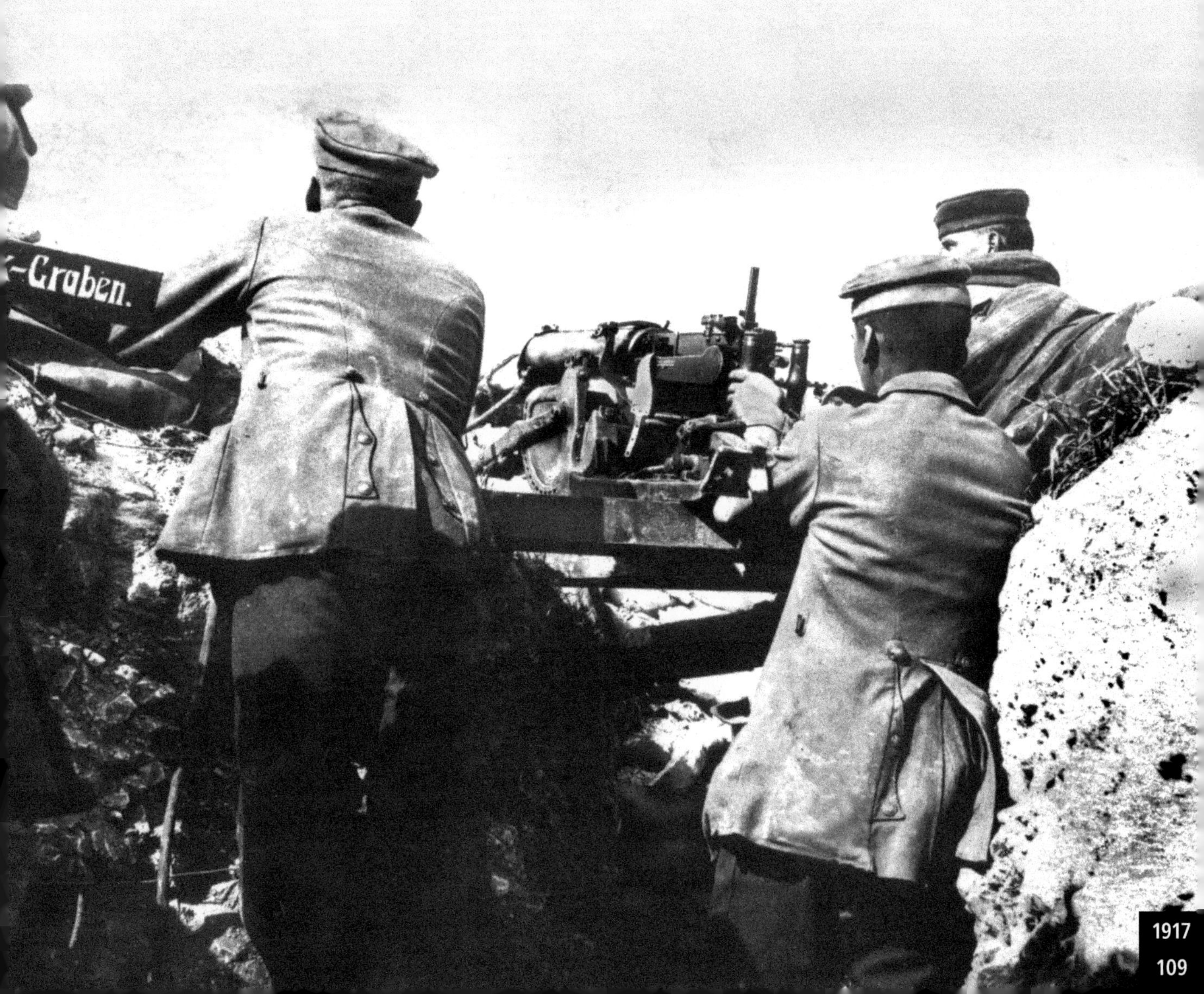

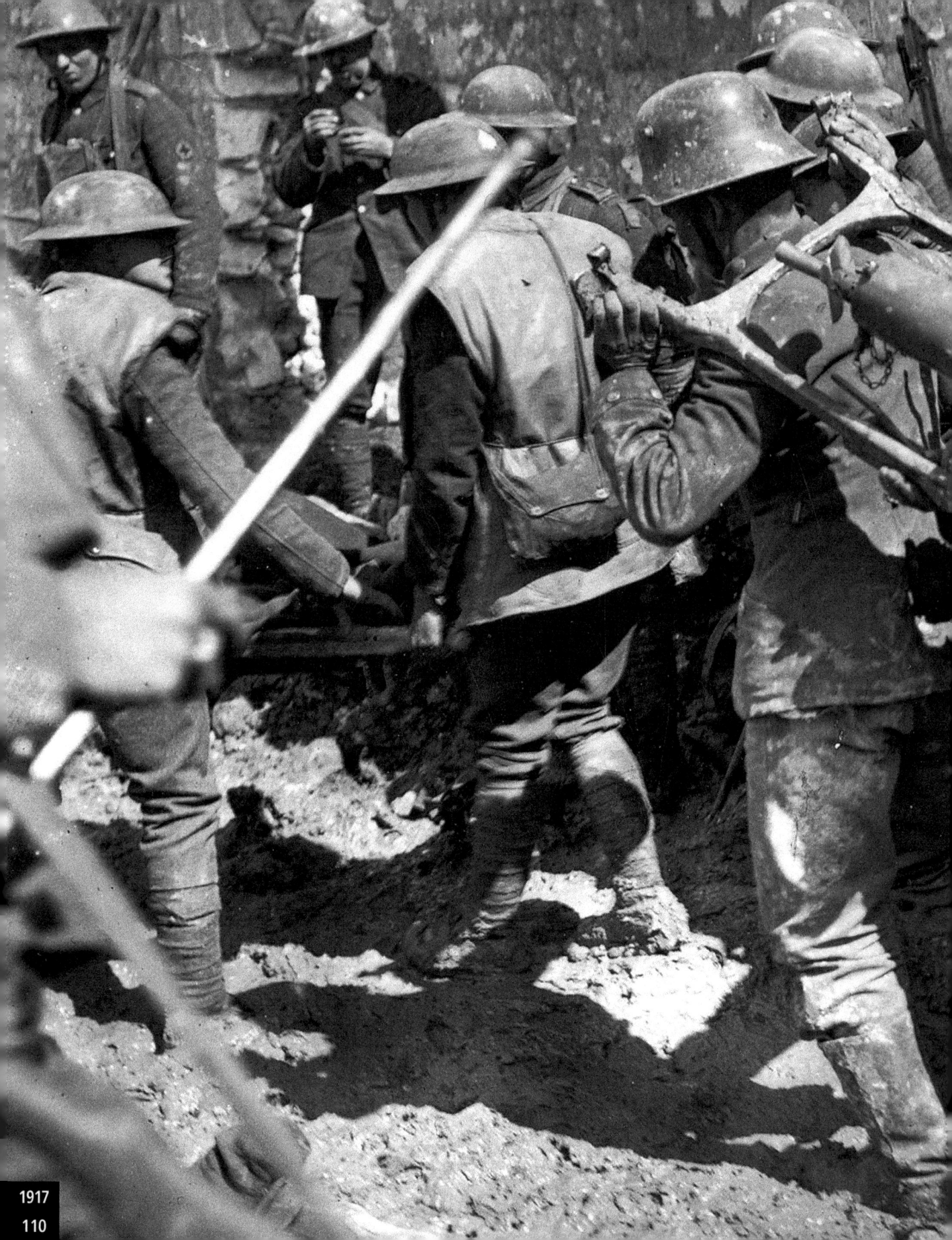

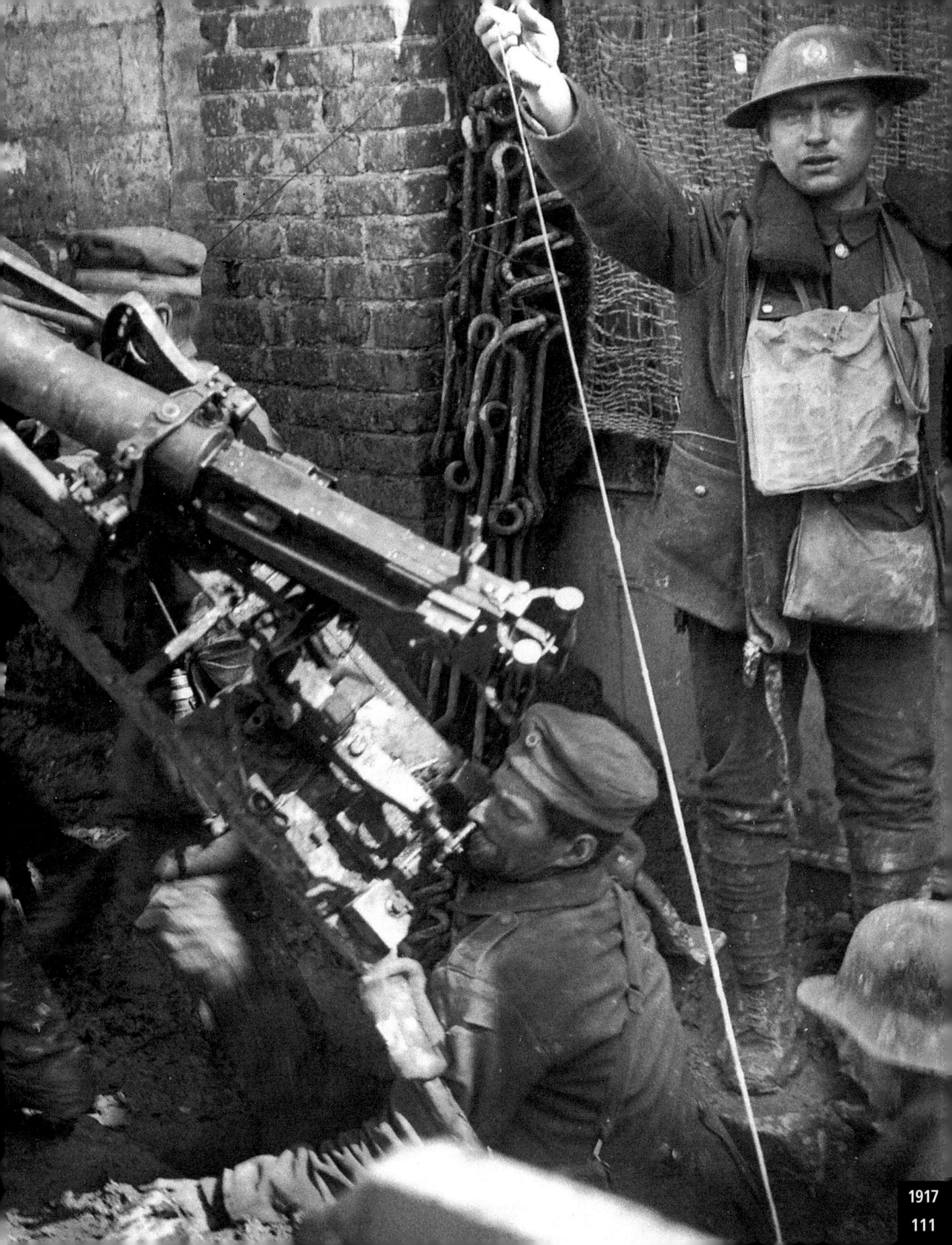

17GW089 German machine gunners captured on the first day of the Arras offensive are made to carry their machine gun out of its cellar position.
17GW209, 17GW207. Wounded Germans being stretchered from their trenches and cared for by their captors.

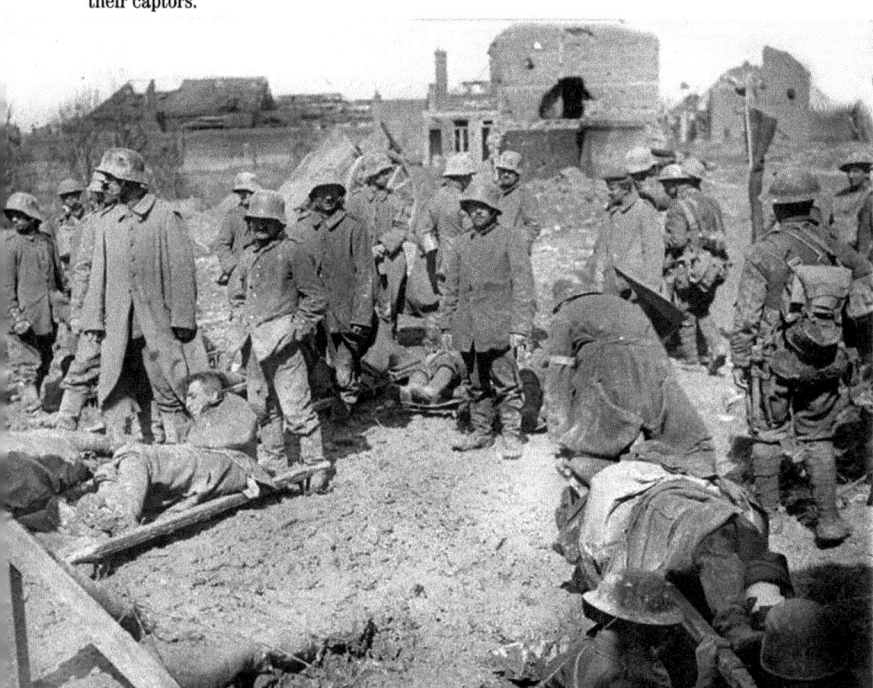
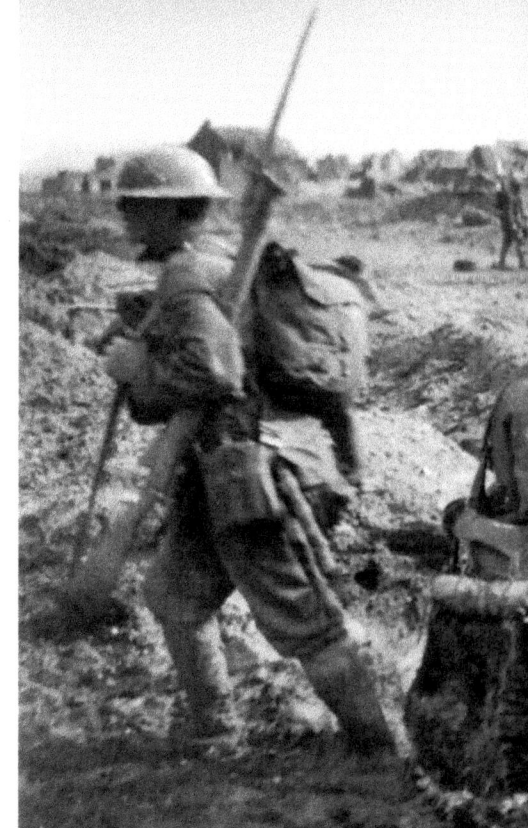

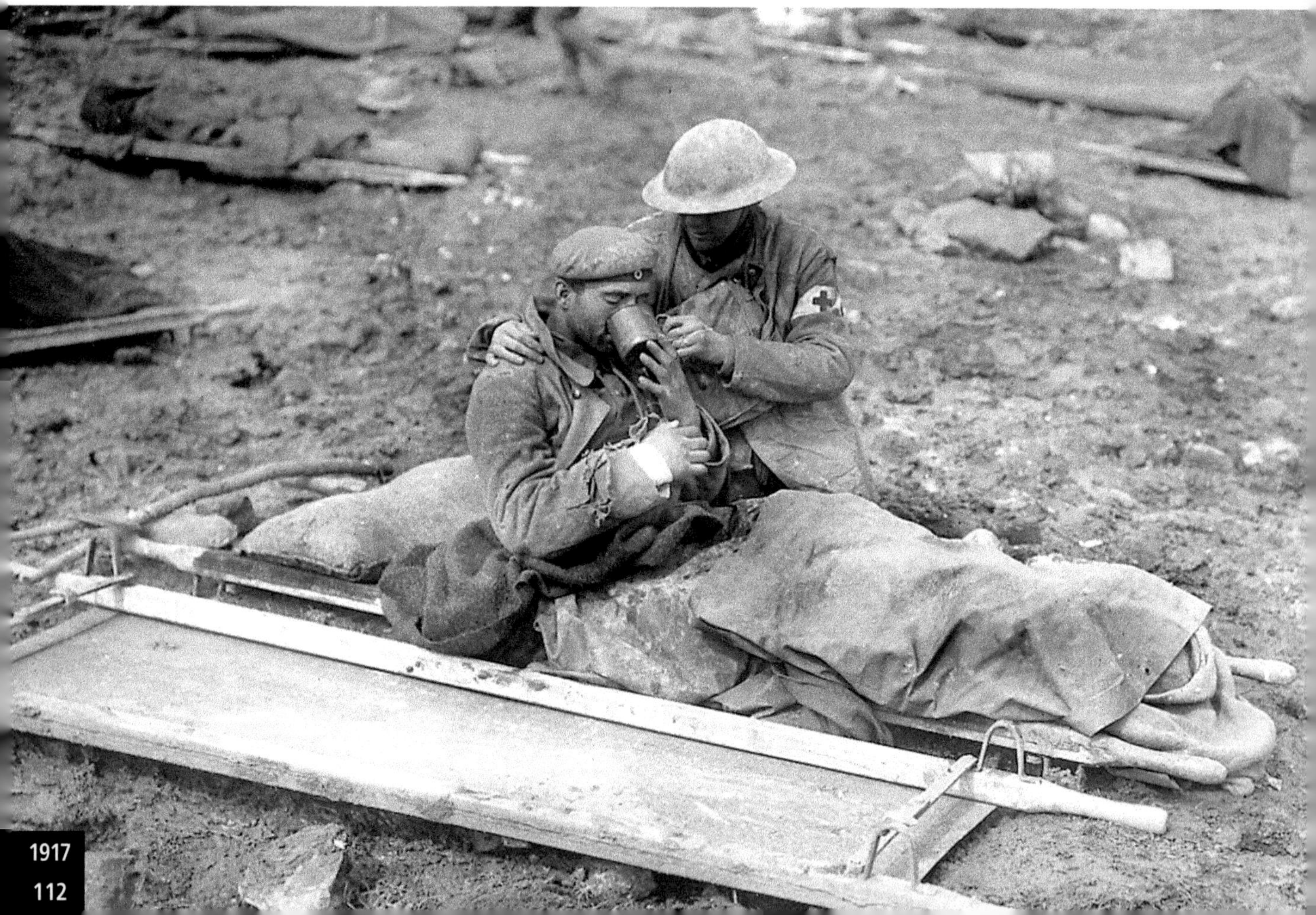

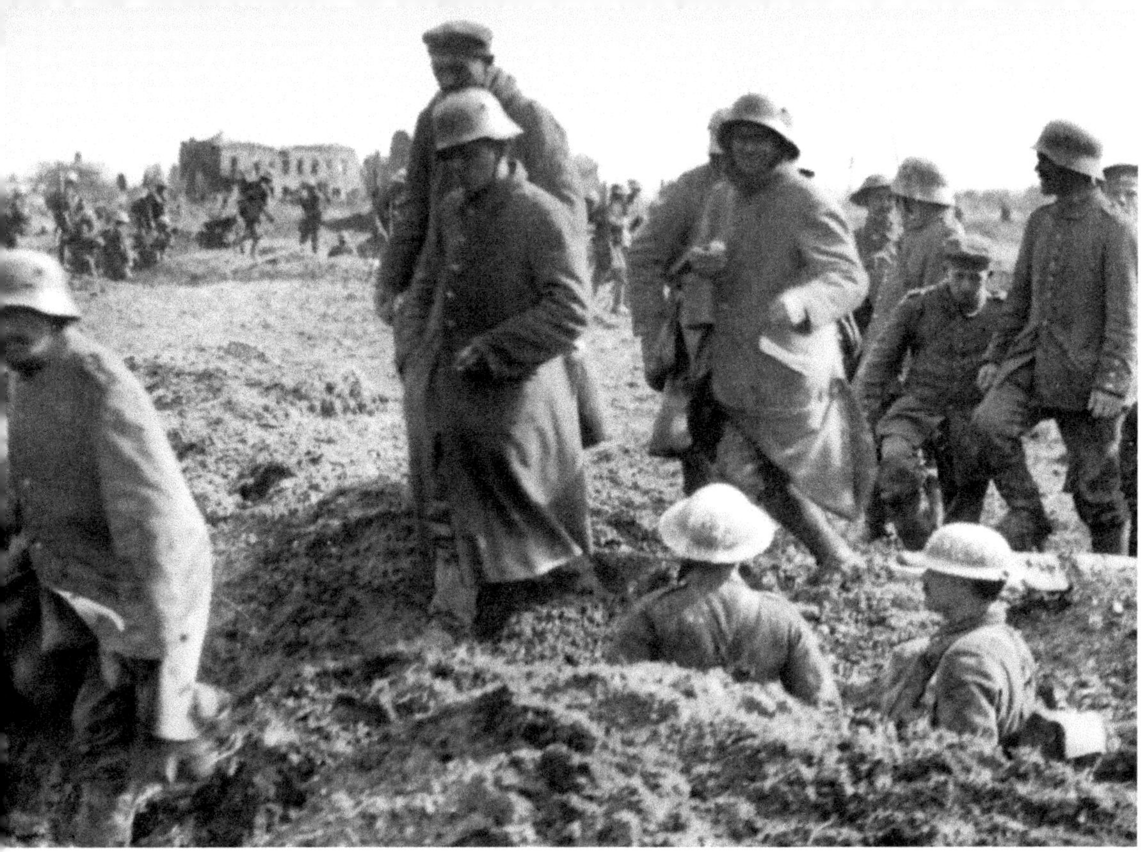

17GW211, 17GW200. The first batch of prisoners taken on the first day of the attack east of Arras. A tank had rolled over the German wire, crushing it flat, allowing the 12th Battalion, London Regiment to get in to the German lines. The 56th (London) Division advanced one and a quarter miles, capturing over 600 prisoners with a loss of 882 men.

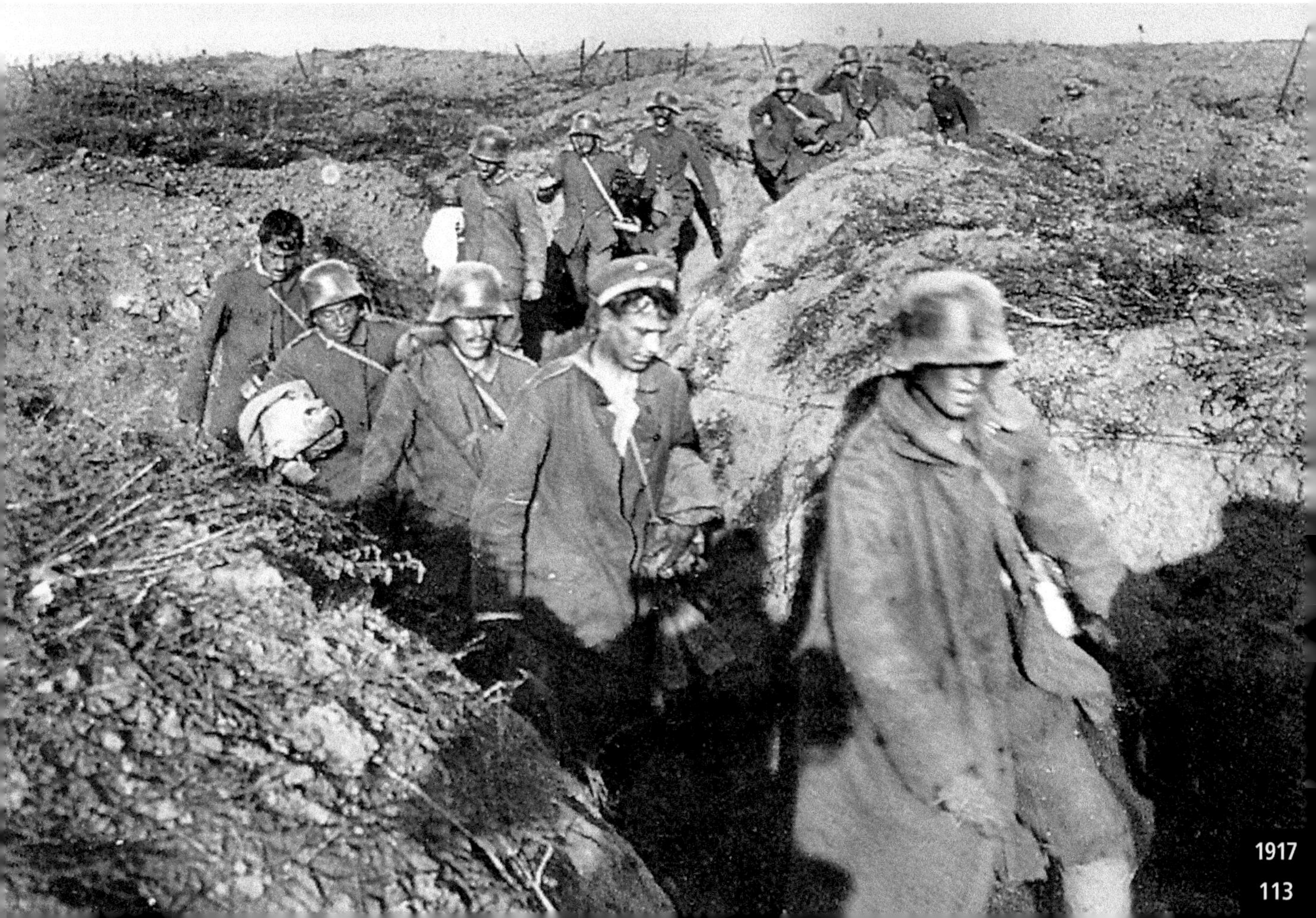

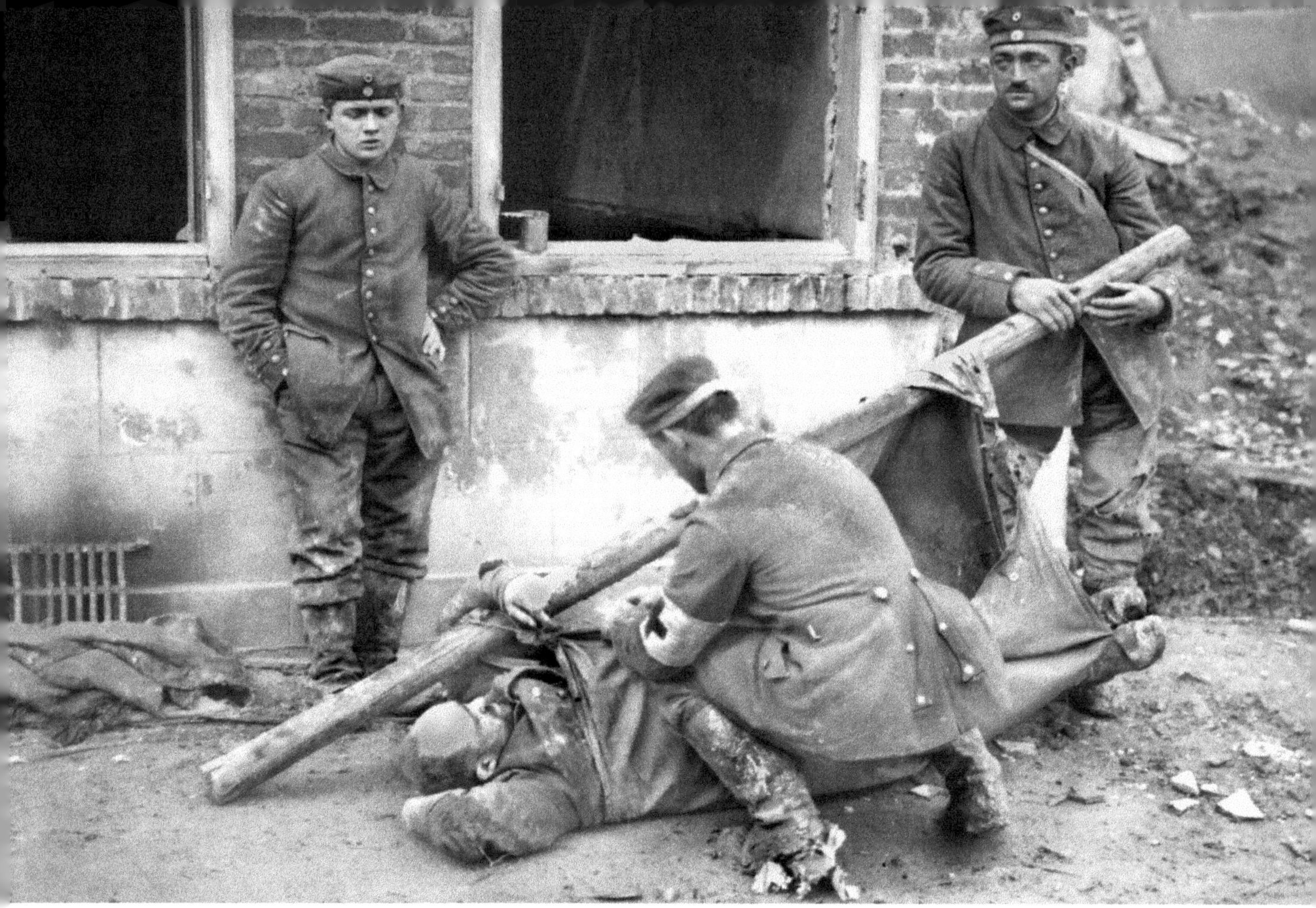

17GW213 German prisoners, stretcher bearers, moving a wounded comrade by means of a make-shift hammock – a pole and canvas contraption.

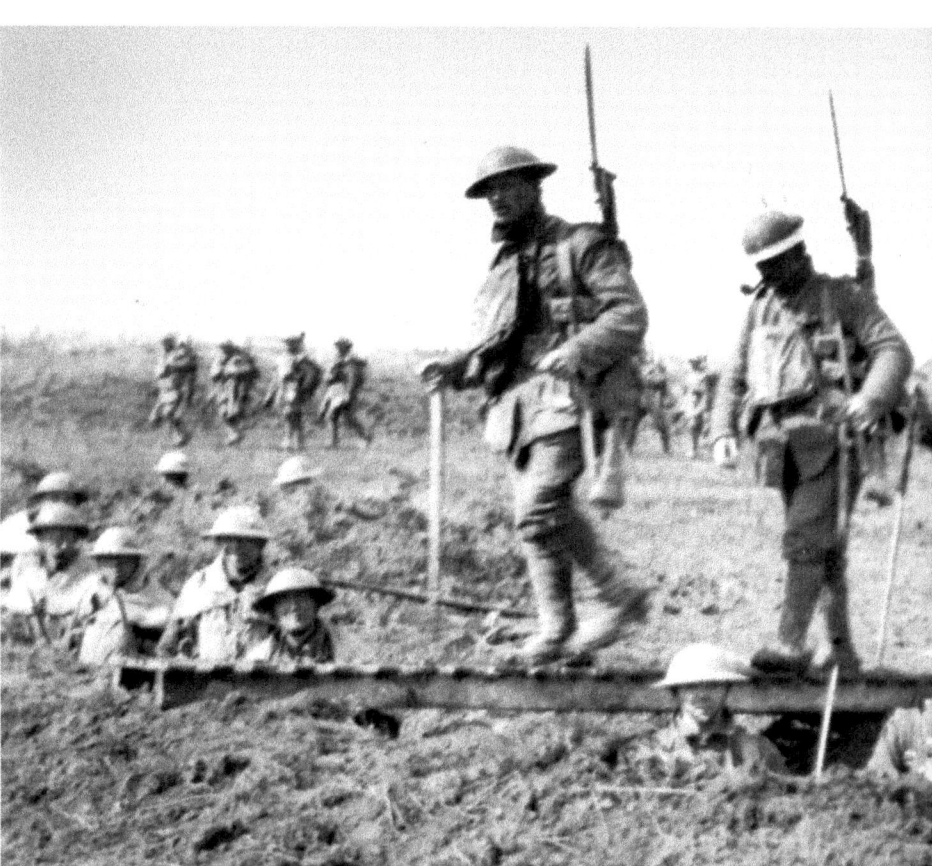

17GW212 Assaulting infantry advancing through smashed barbed wire entanglements, easily flattened by the tank.

17GW210 Support troops, kept in reserve during the initial assault, moving across No Man's Land and on into the captured German positions to occupy the ground taken by the attacking battalions.

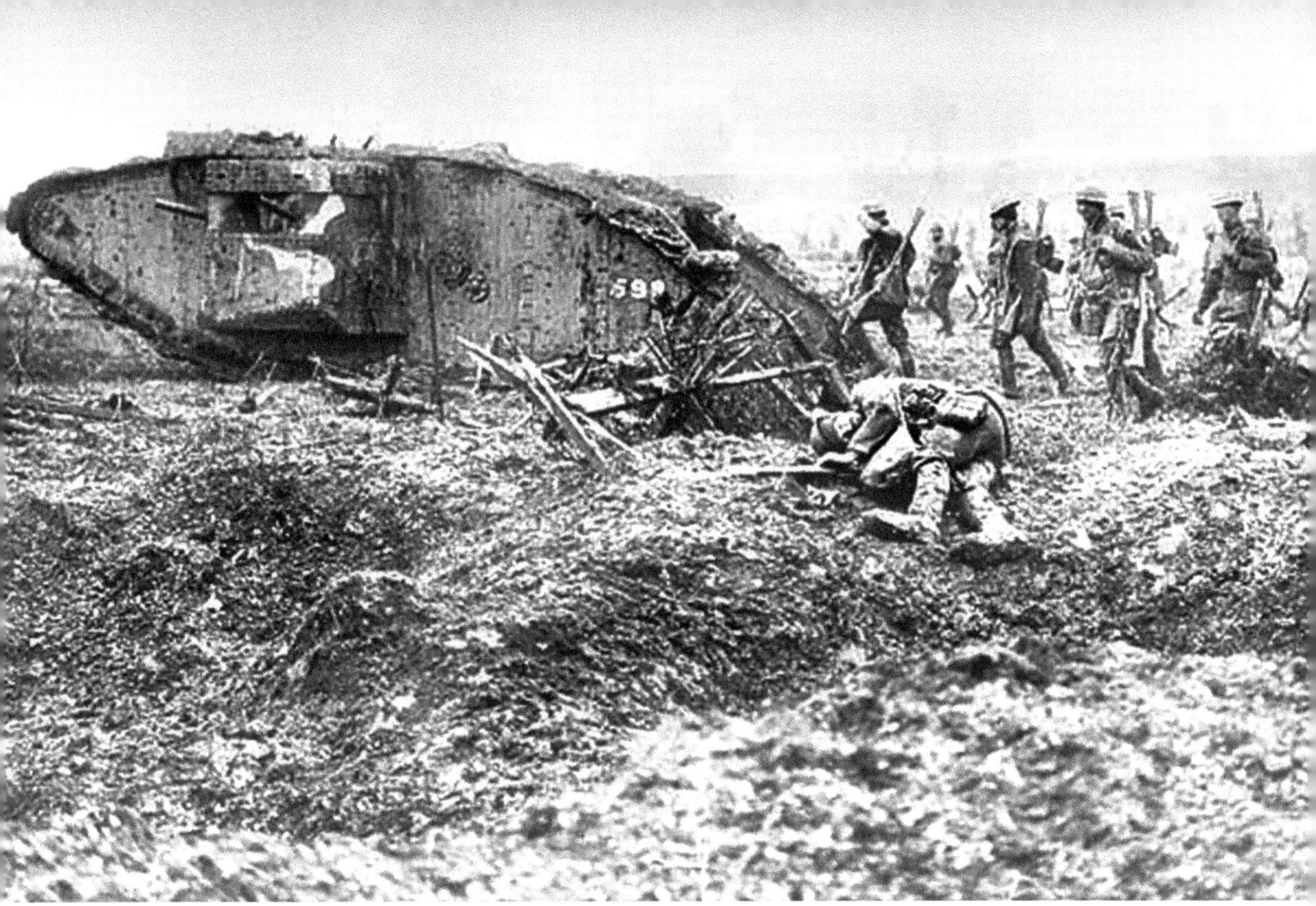

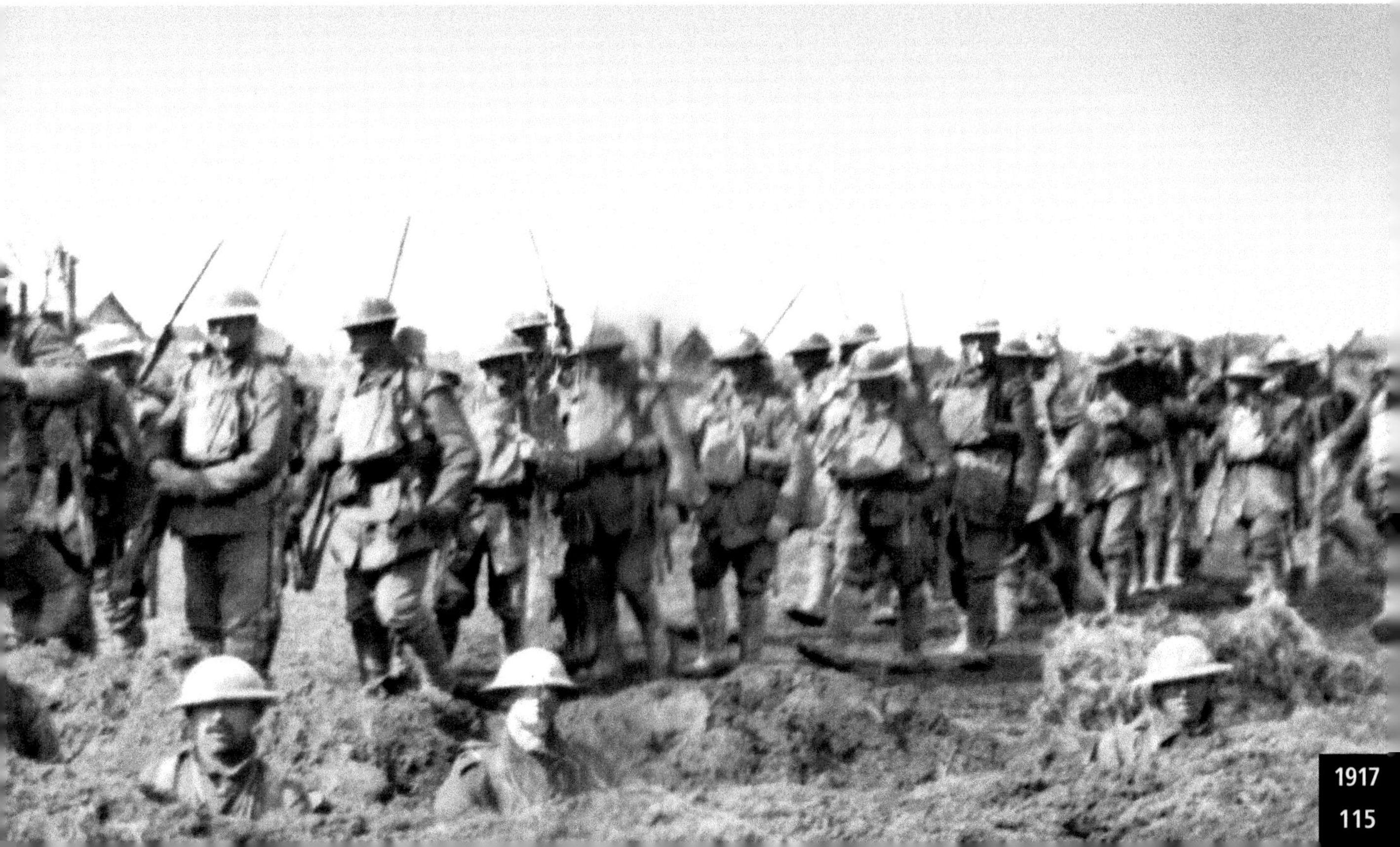

1917

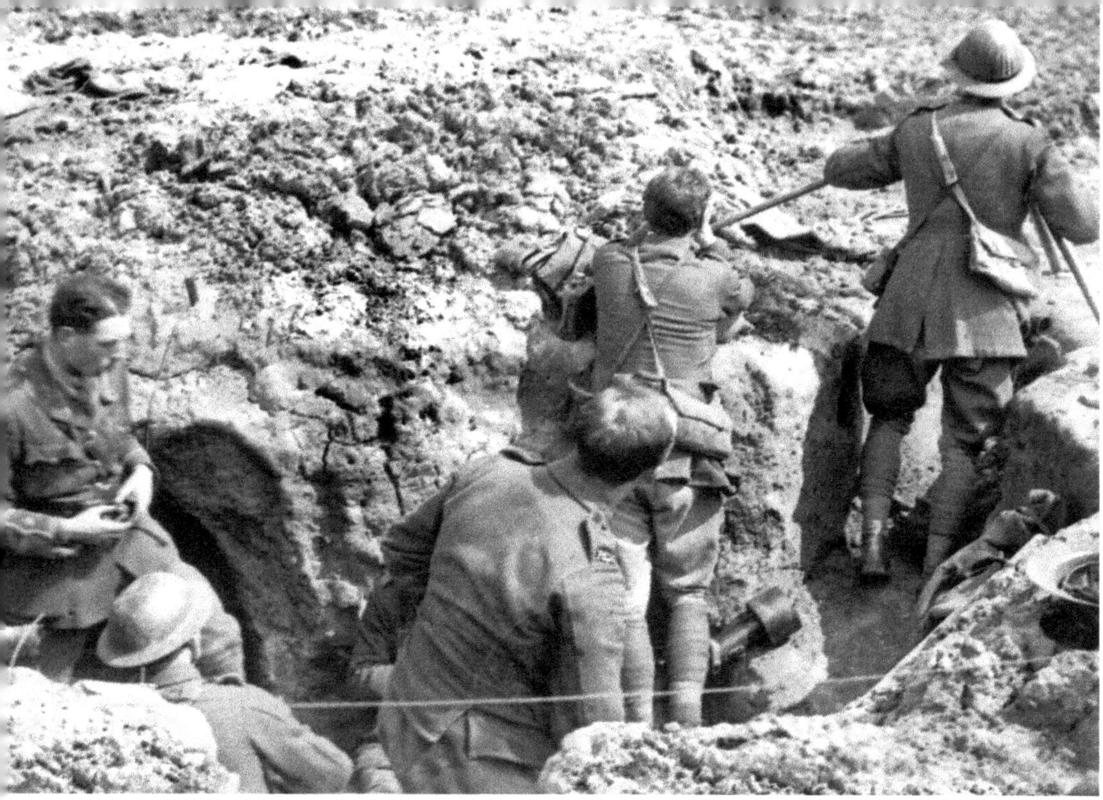

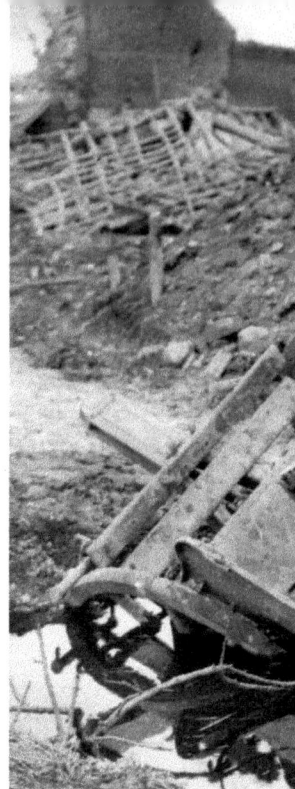

17GW214 Officers of the Royal Garrison Artillery observing the German positions with a Portuguese artillery officer; by May 1917 several units of the Portuguese Expeditionary Corps had arrived in France.

17GW215 A German artillery caisson abandoned in a bomb crater near Feuchy.

17GW216 A Tommy grabs some shut eye among German artillery shells.

17GW217, 17GW218. German 77mm field guns are turned around to face their former owners.

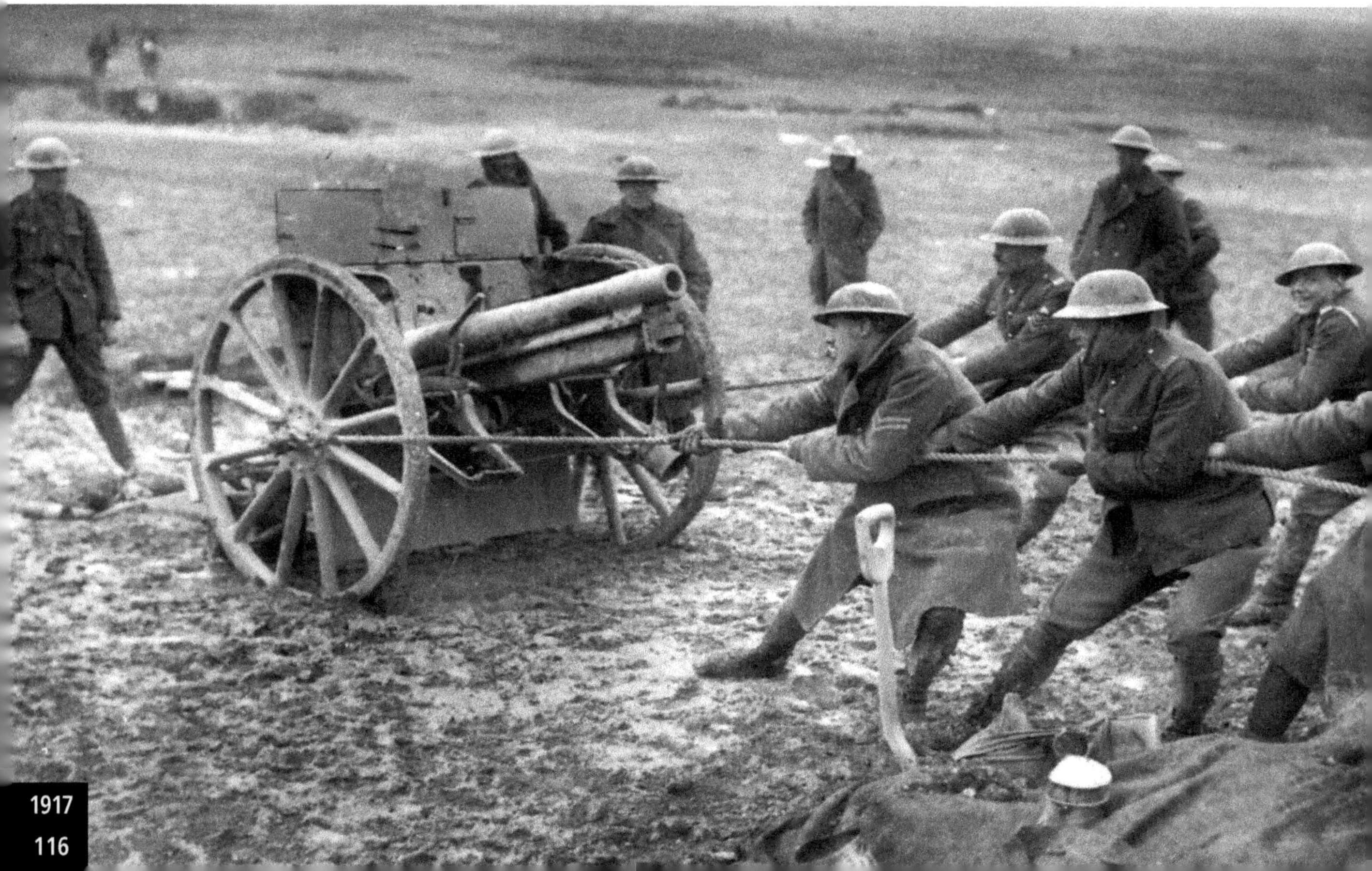

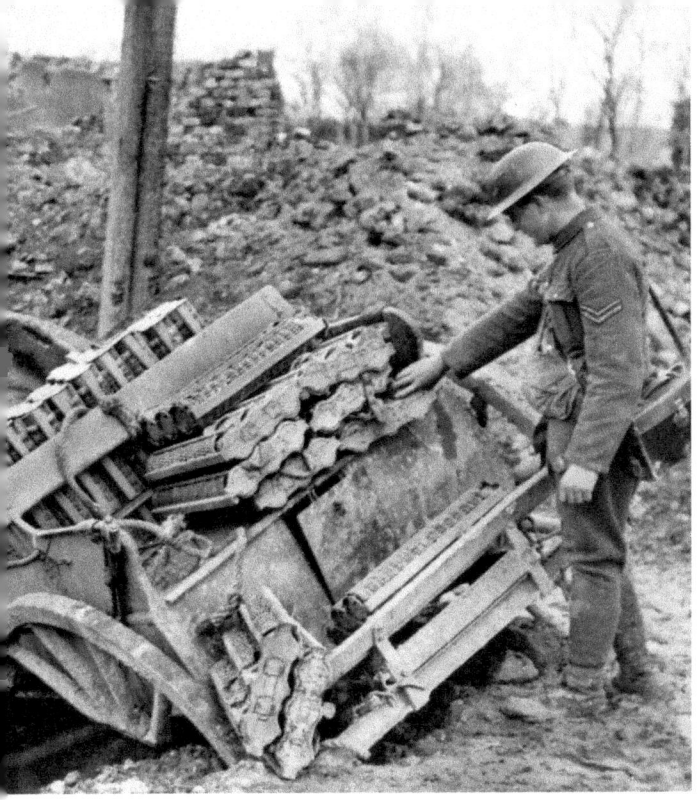
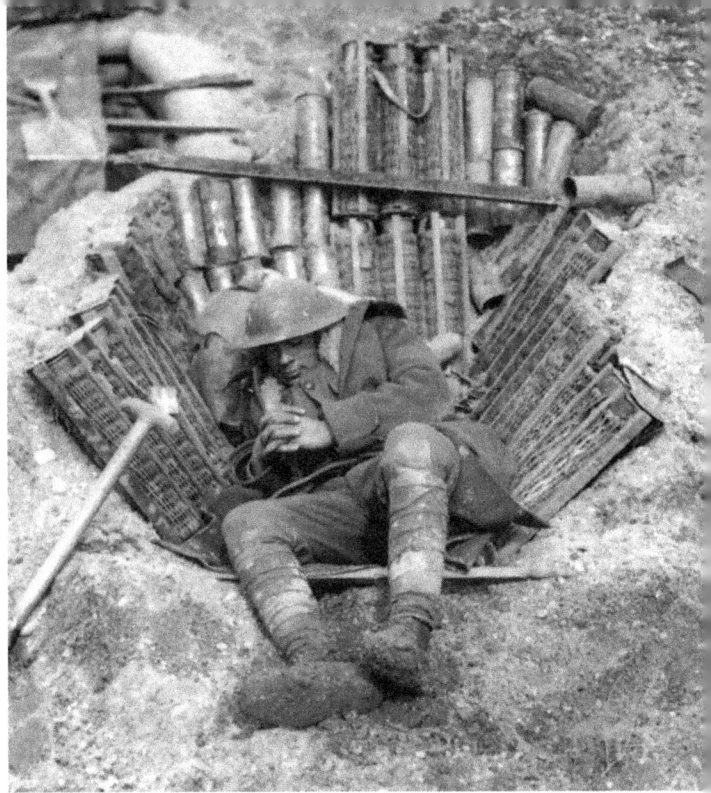
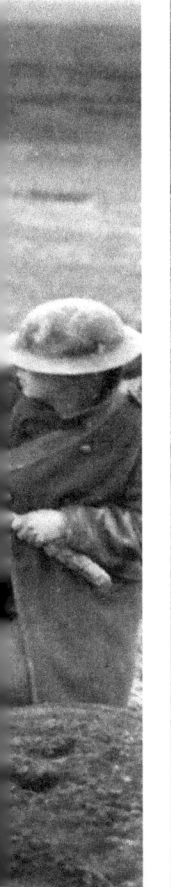

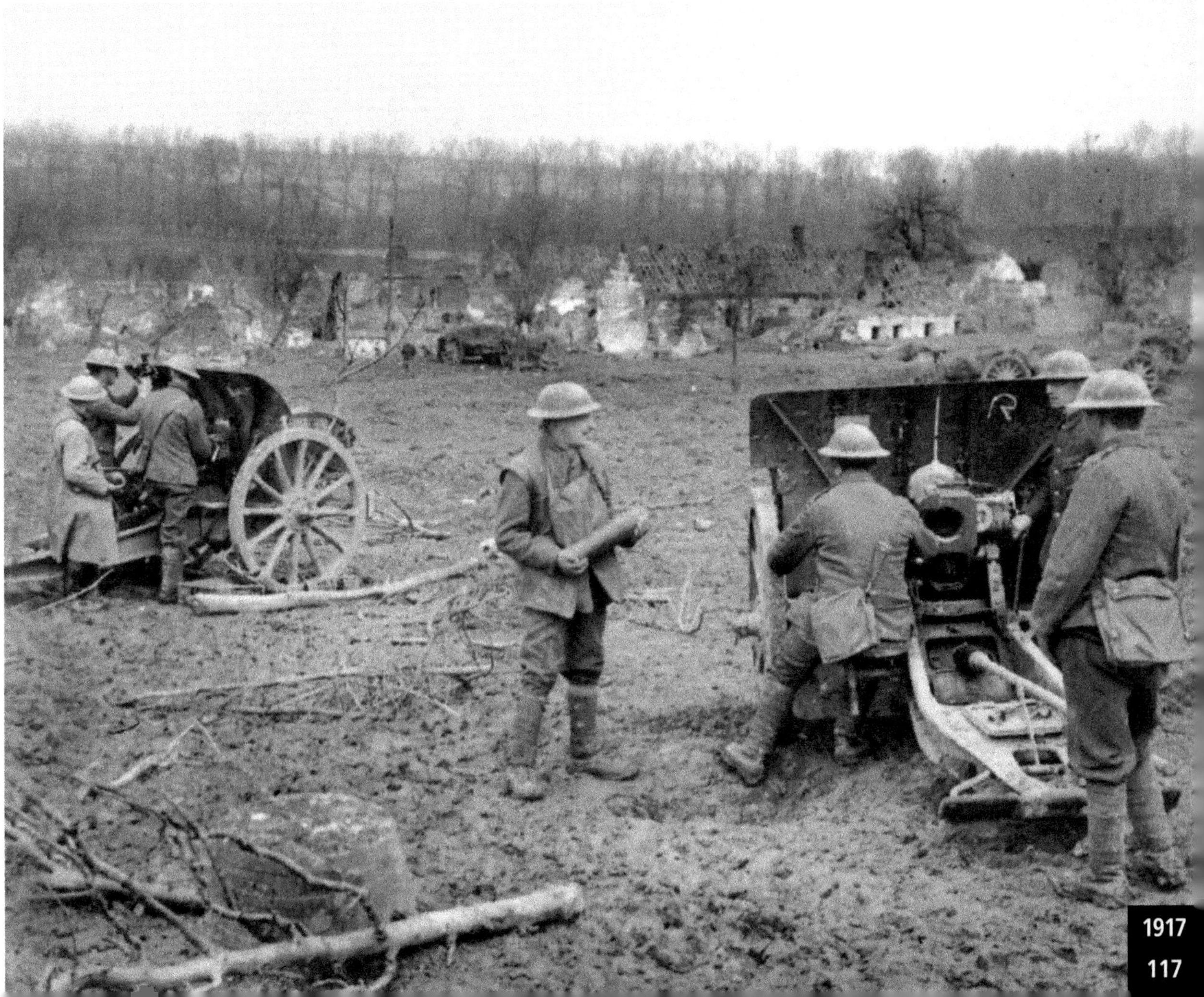

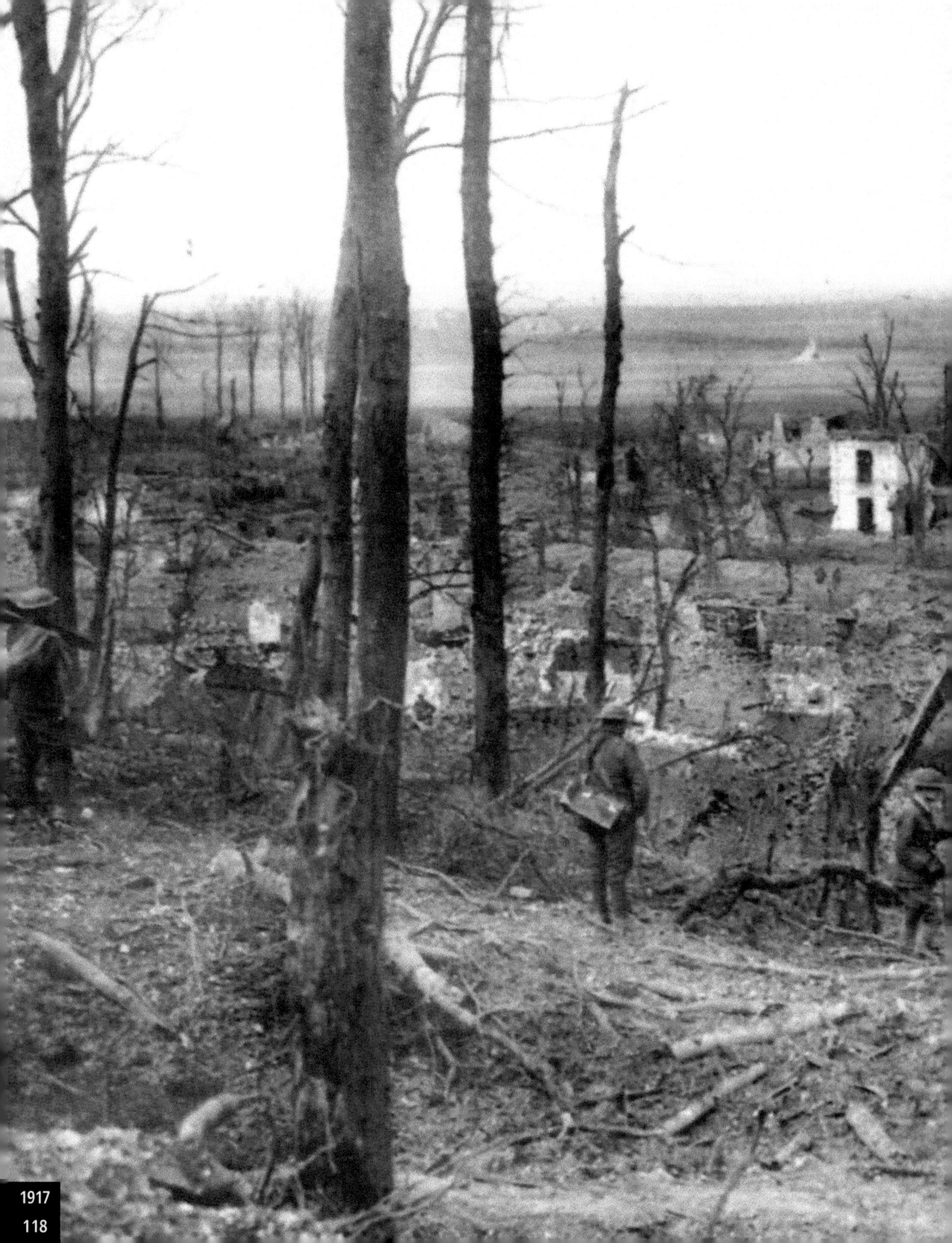

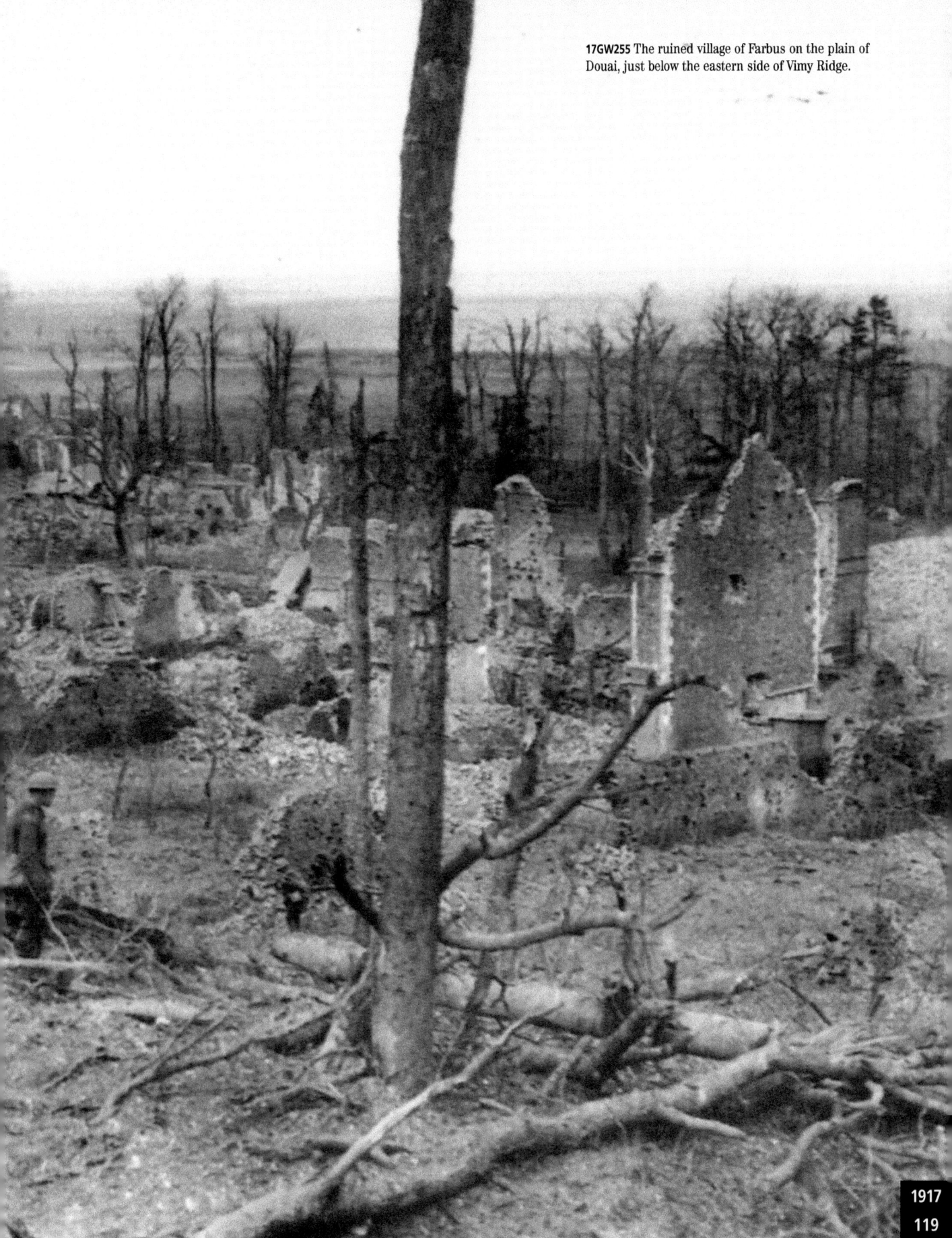

17GW255 The ruined village of Farbus on the plain of Douai, just below the eastern side of Vimy Ridge.

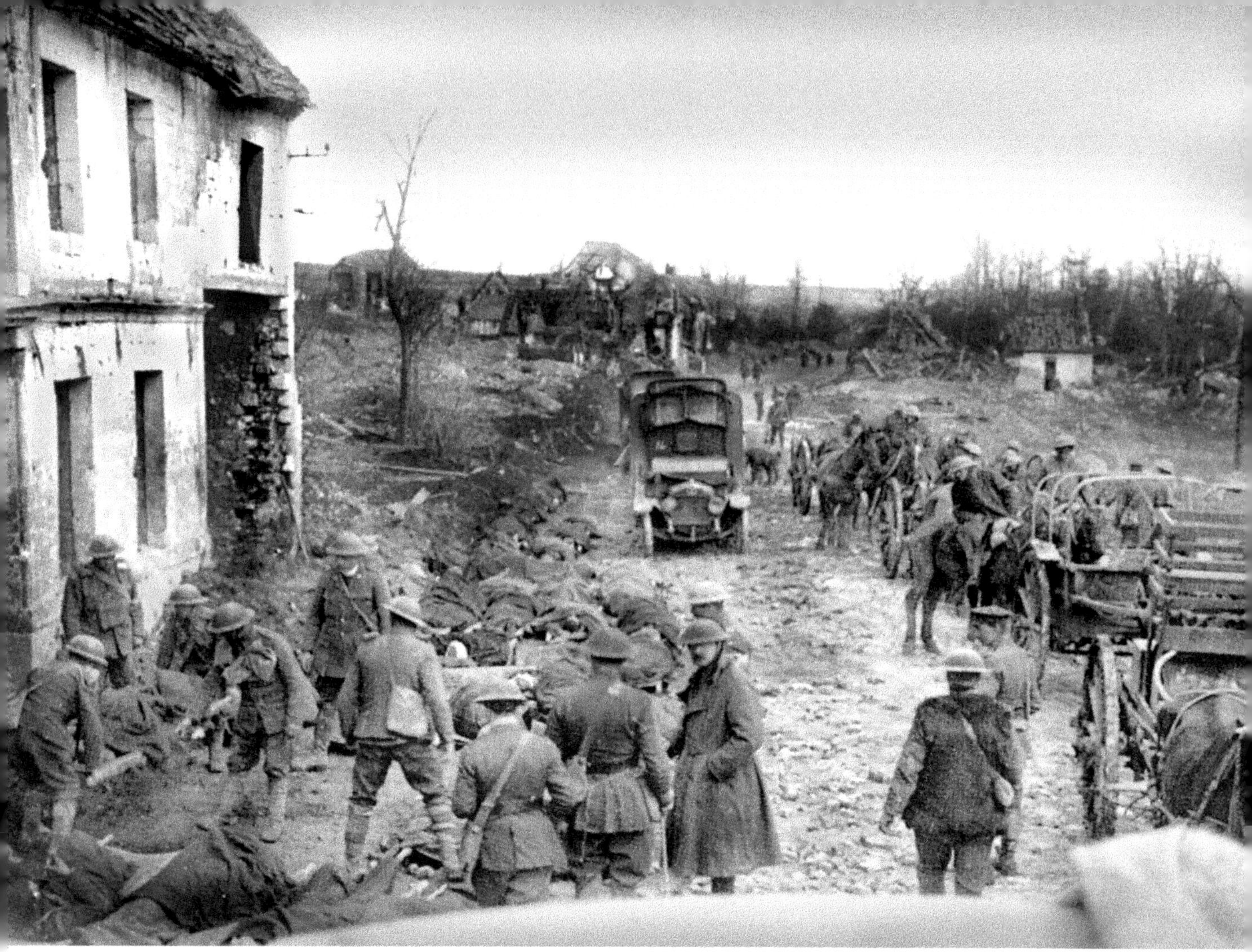

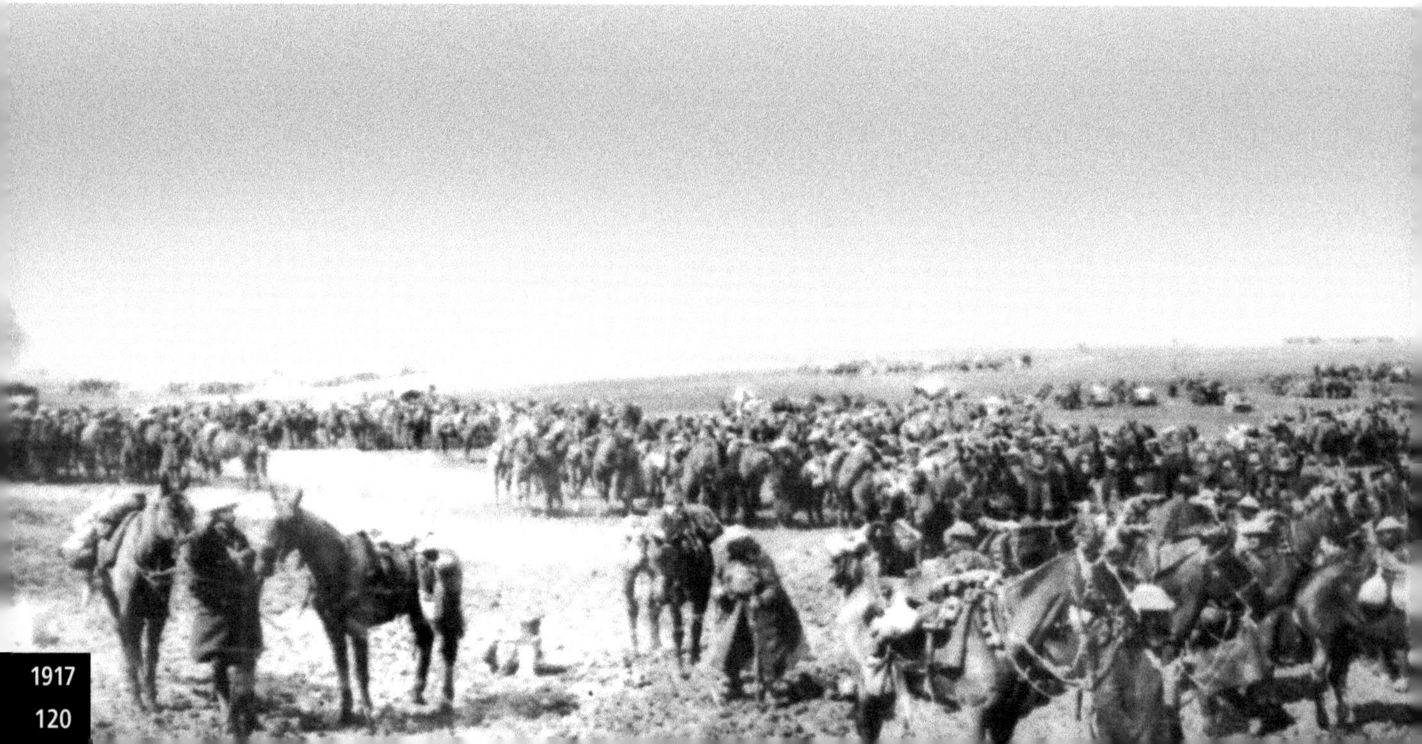

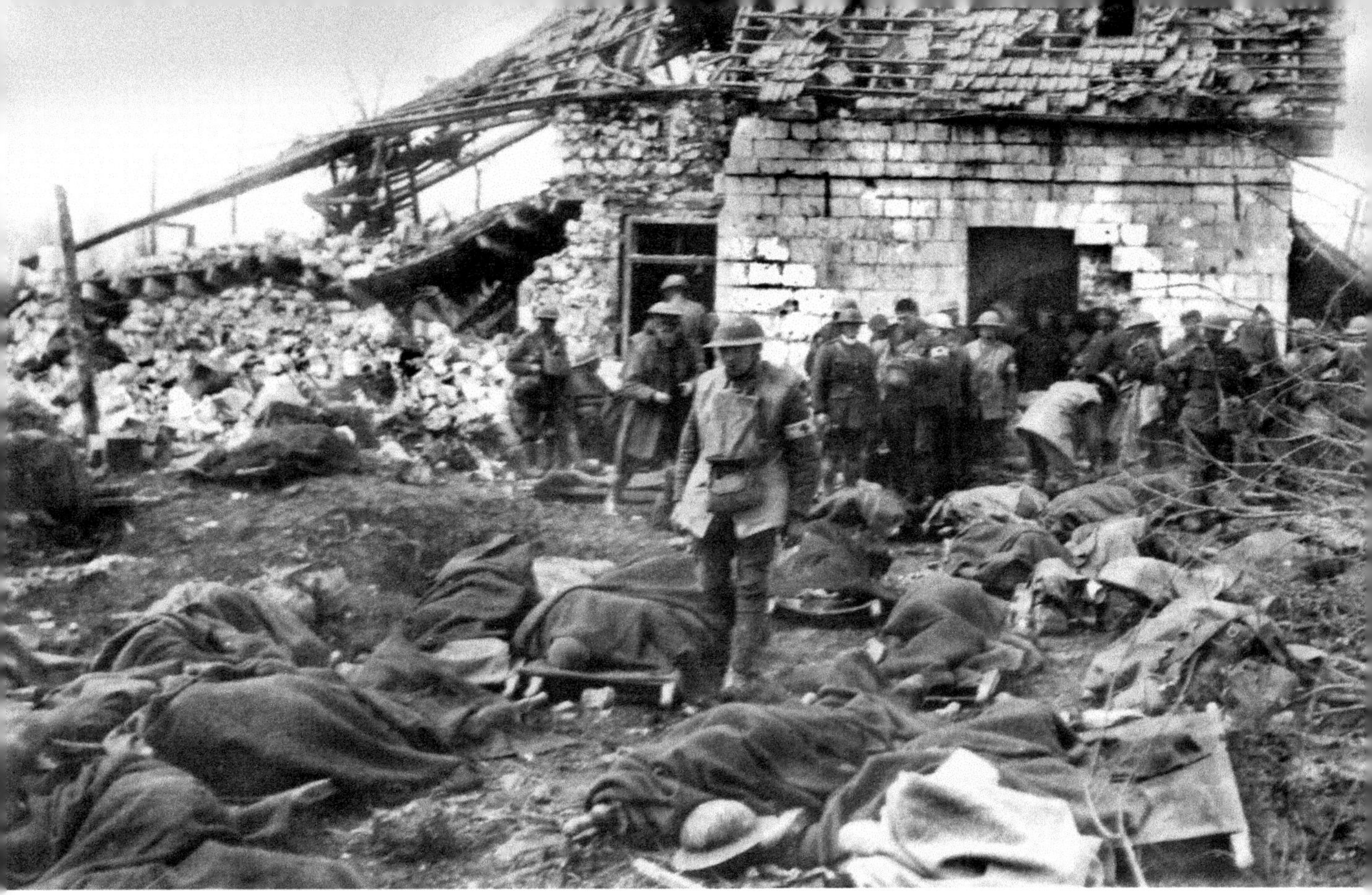

17GW201, 17GW219. An Advanced Dressing Station, or Collecting Post, near Tilloy-lès-Mofflaines, where the more serious cases were treated before being evacuated to one of the Main Dressing Stations. The random placing of the stretchers and covered heads would indicate that this was the area reserved for those who had succumbed to their wounds.

17GW220 The 1st Cavalry Division gathered northwest of Arras prior to the offensive. The infantry was to take the Brown Line on the map, whereupon the division would advance to achieve a breakthrough. Once in open terrain the cavalry was to ride for Boiry-Notre-Dame, between Cambrai and Douai. It was hoped this would confuse the Germans as to which town the mounted drive was aimed at.

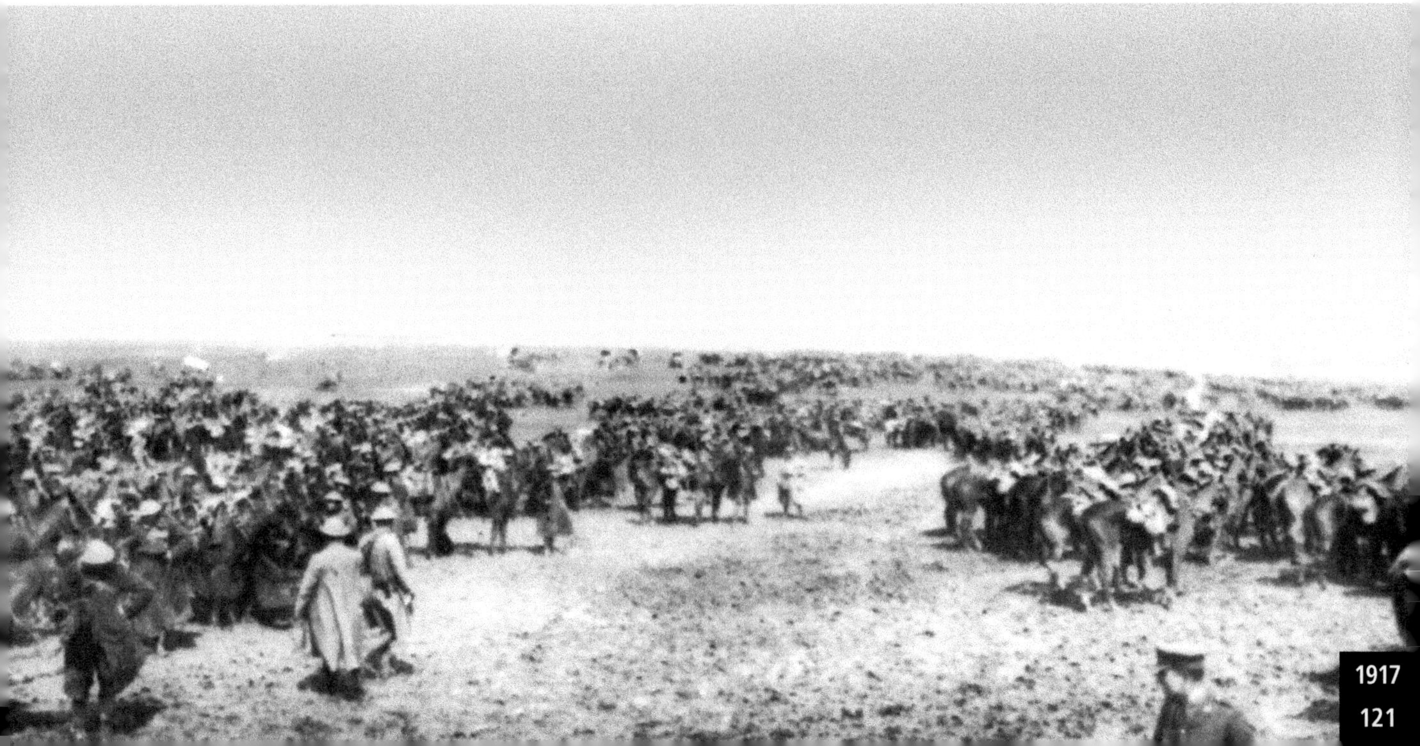

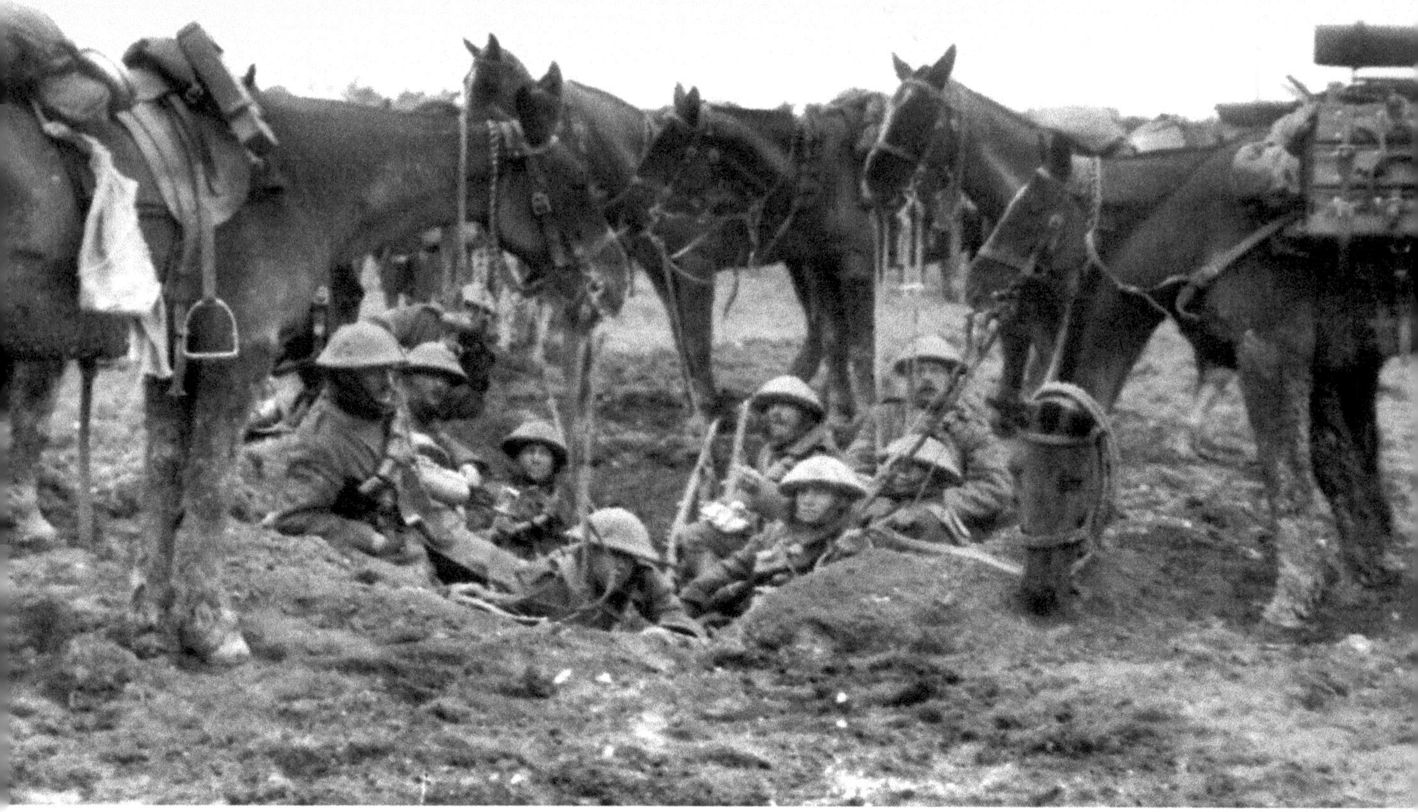

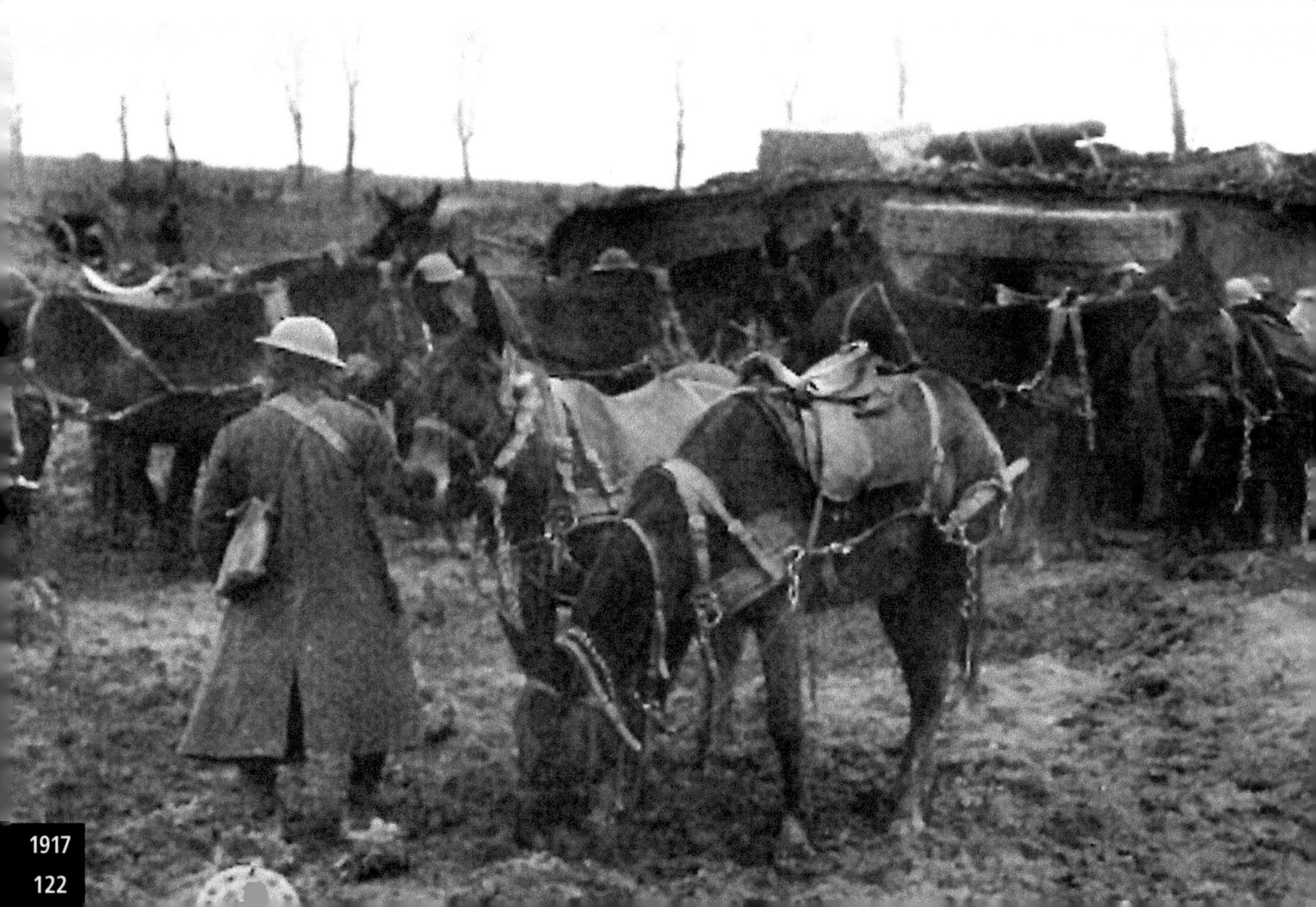

1917
122

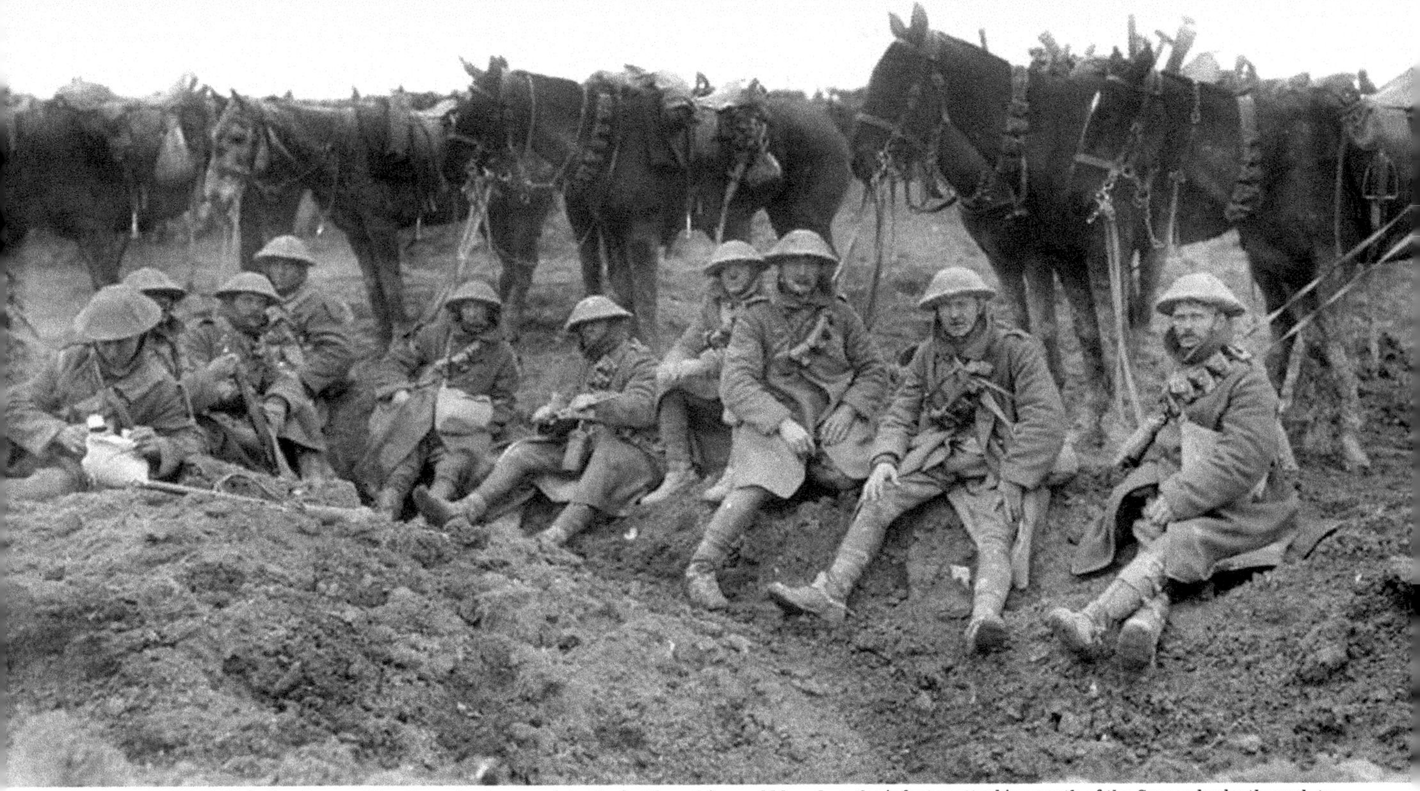

17GW221, 17GW222. British Cavalry awaiting the order to move into the battle – this would be when the infantry attacking south of the Scarpe broke through to the Brown Line.

17GW203 Ancient and modern – a tank surrounded by cavalry horses and transport mules.

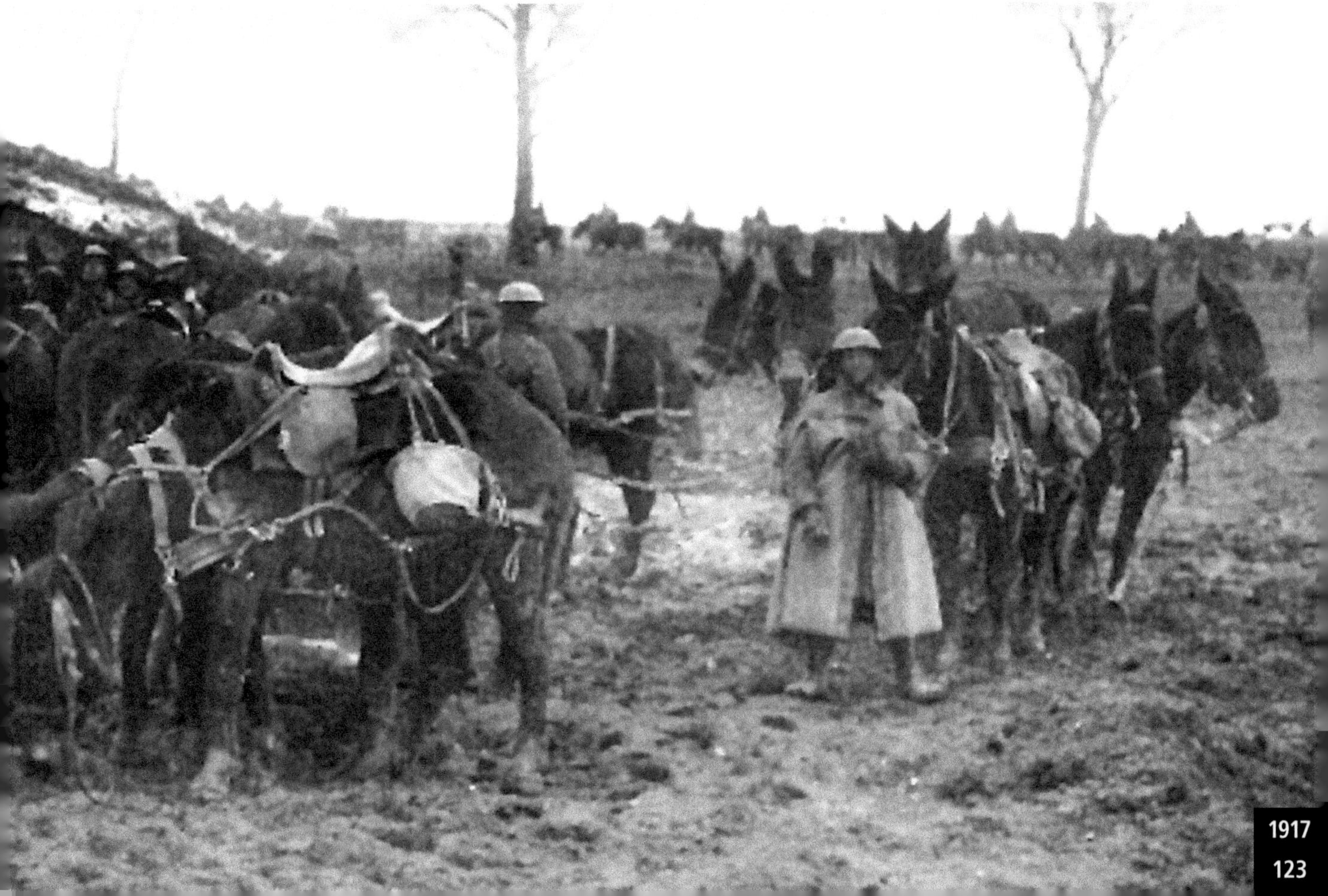

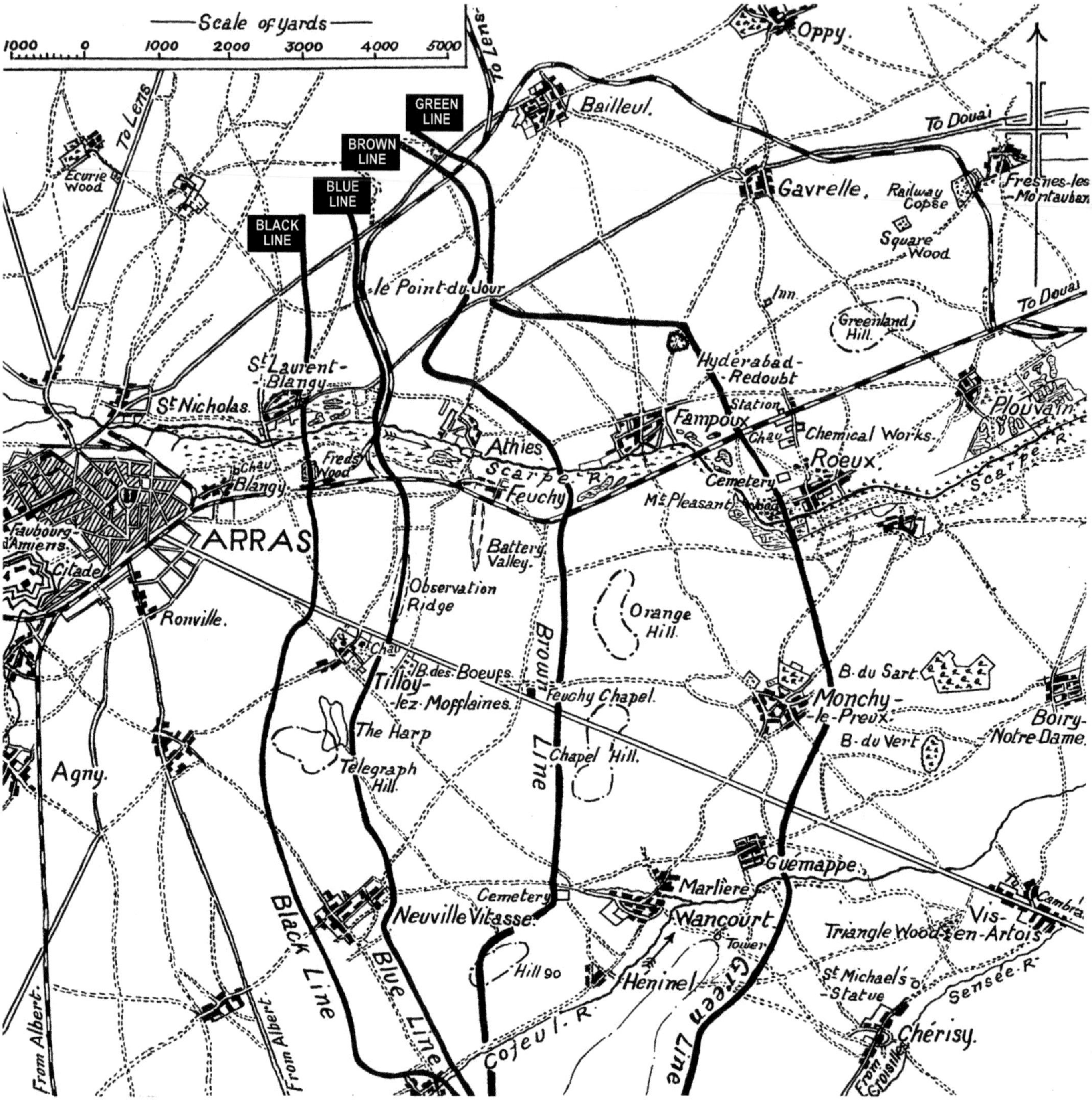

The first day at Arras was a success and gains of three and a half miles was achieved. Monchy-le-Preux was taken two days later when four regiments from 3rd Cavalry Division supported the infantry attack. The 3rd Dragoon Guards reached the Monchy road south of the village where they dismounted and took up firing positions with their machine guns, joining up a line between 111 and 112 Infantry Brigades. The Essex Yeomanry, 10th Hussars and the Royal Horse Guards entered the streets of Monchy from the north.

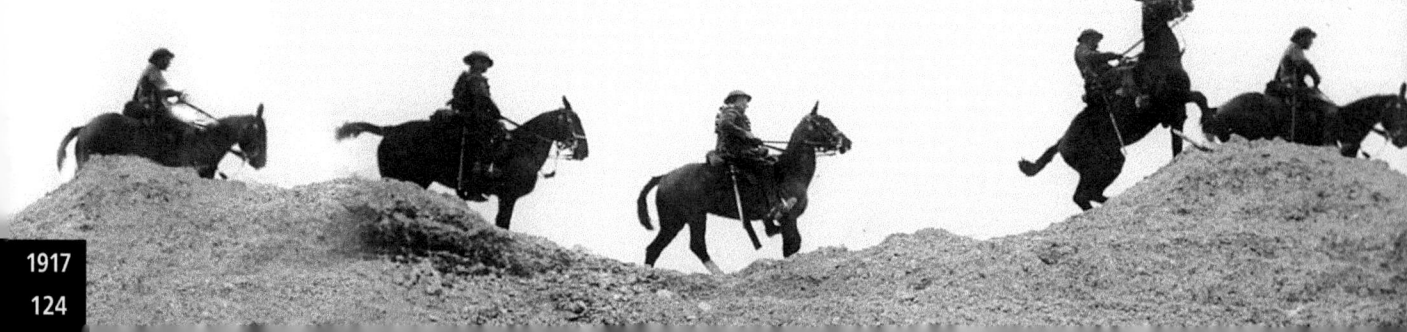

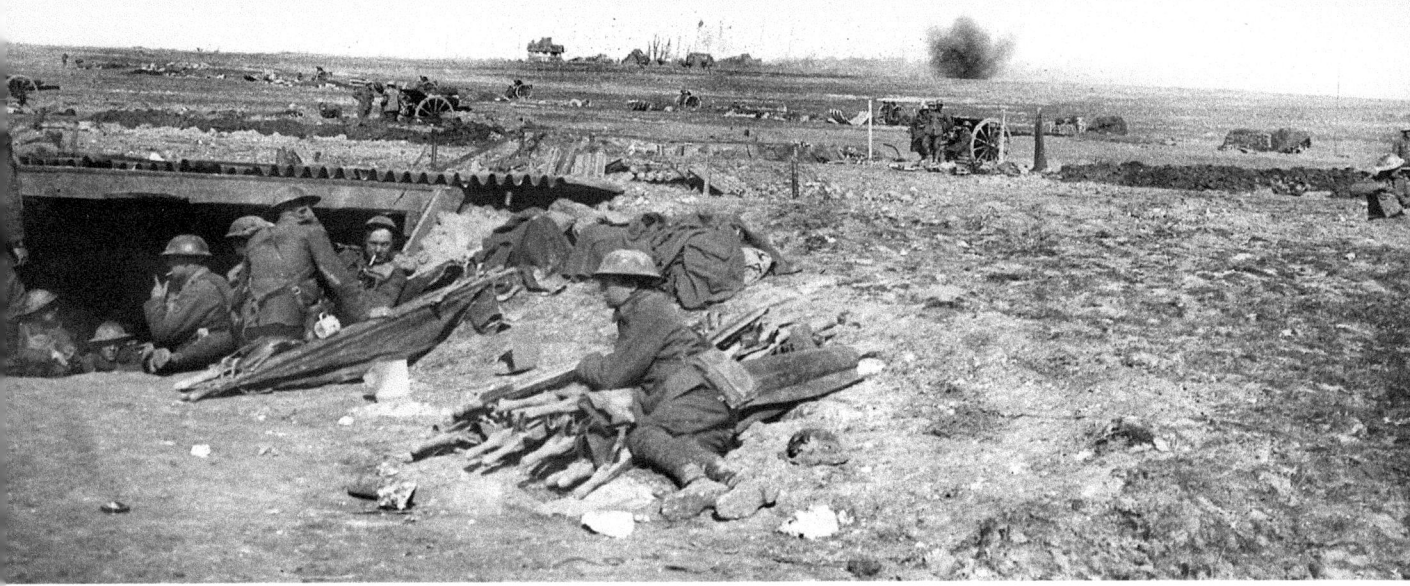

17GW180, 17GW294. Monchy-le-Preux, seen from the western approaches; in the foreground is a Field Dressing Station with stretcher bearers resting up. The prominent building on the skyline is 'Villa Barbara' so named by the Germans. They begin to take note as the German barrage hots up.

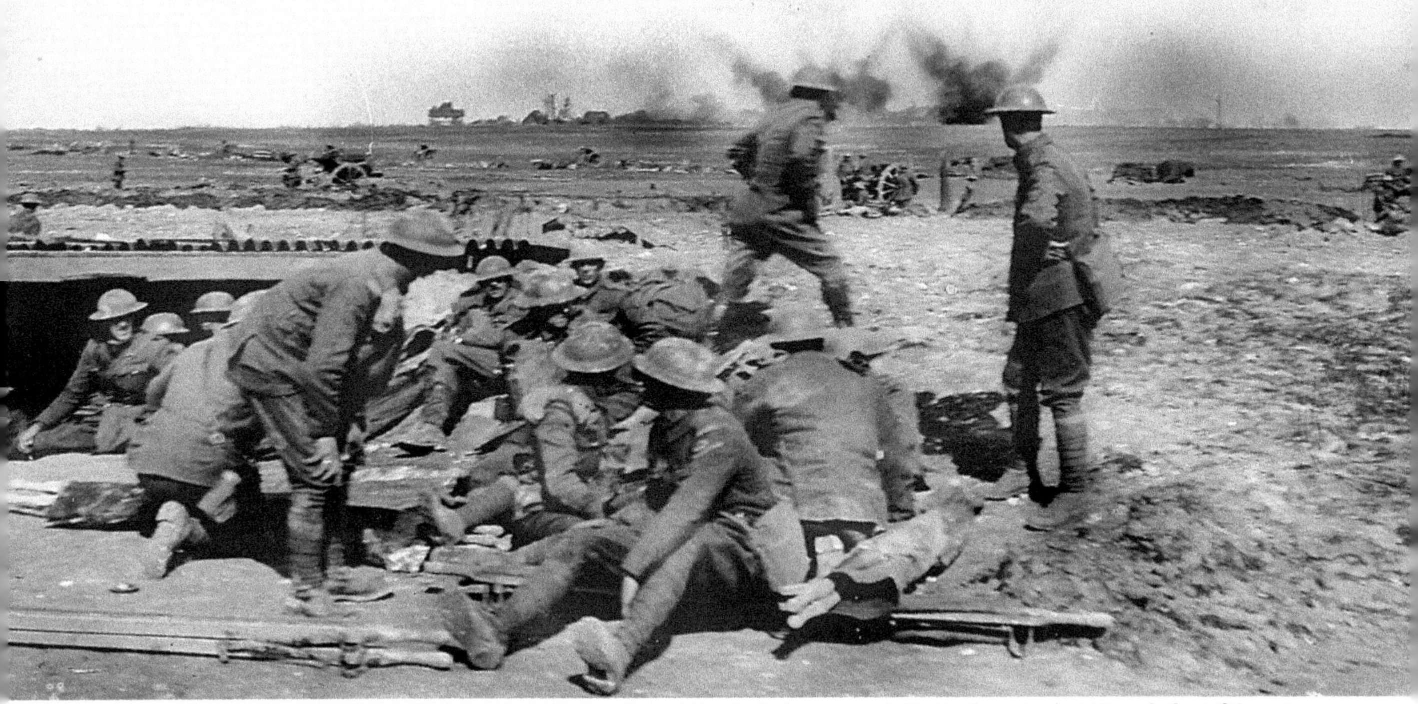

17GW176 Occupying a dominant position on the top of the hill is the village of Monchy-le-Preux, occupied by the Germans since the early days of the war; as viewed from the Arras-Cambrai road.

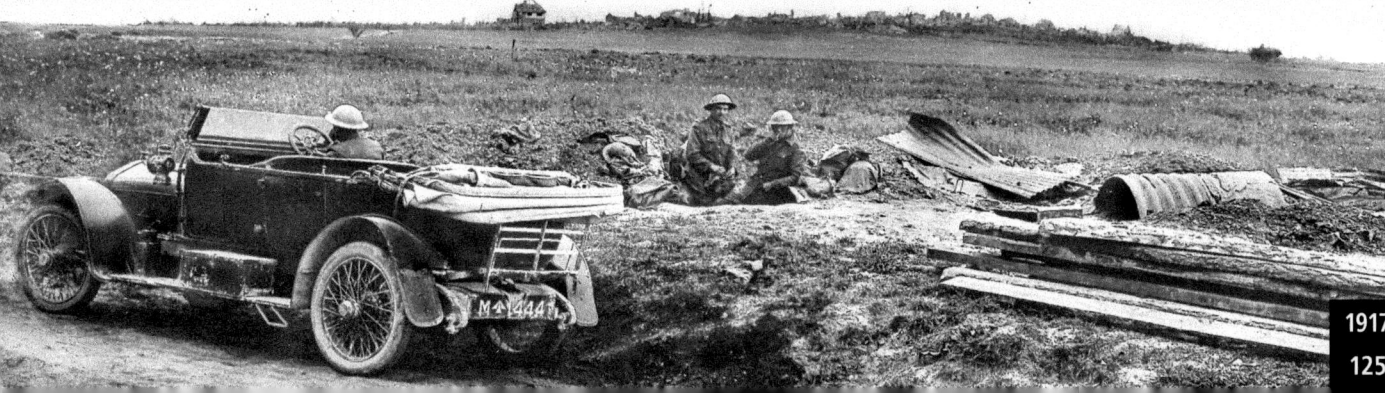

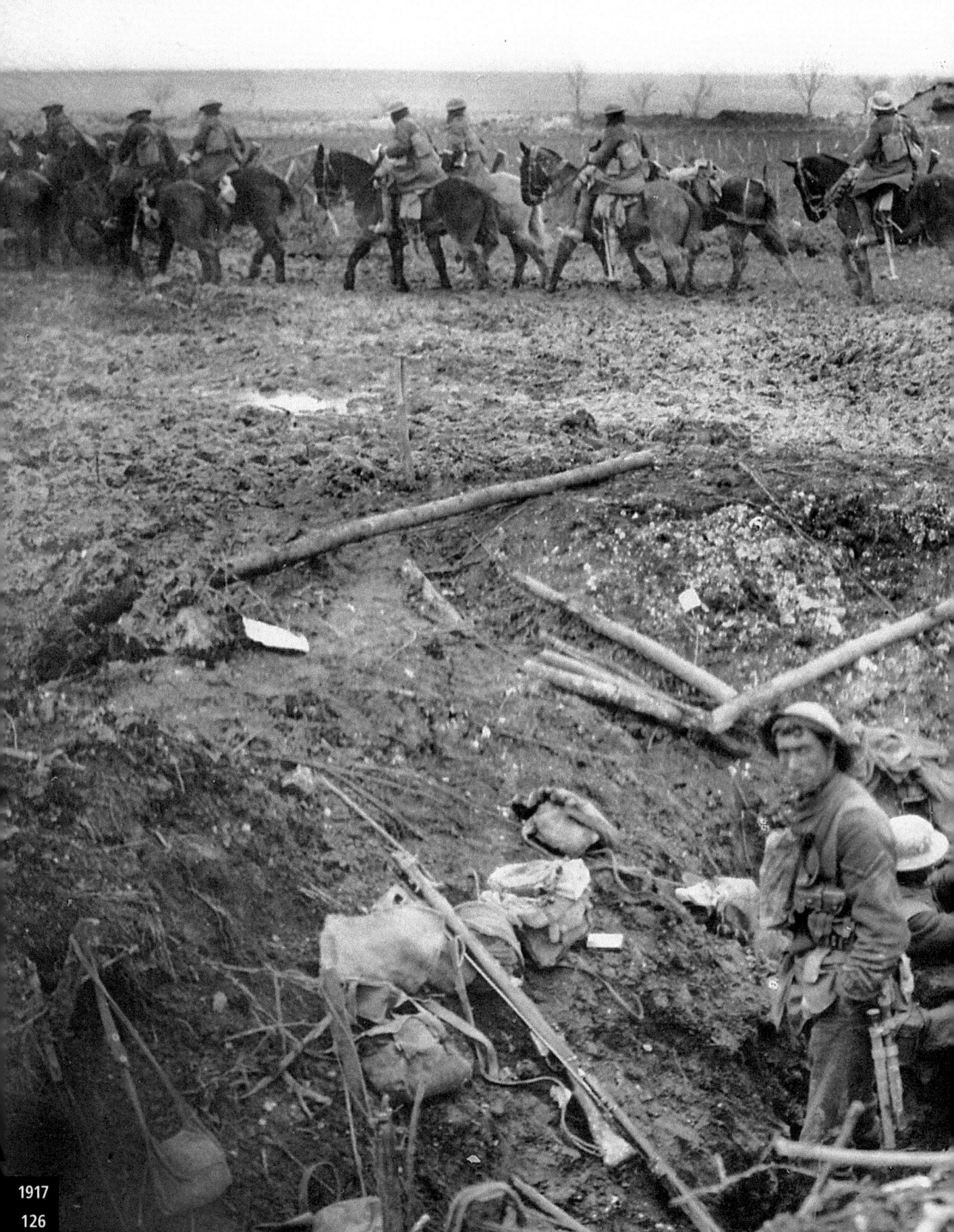

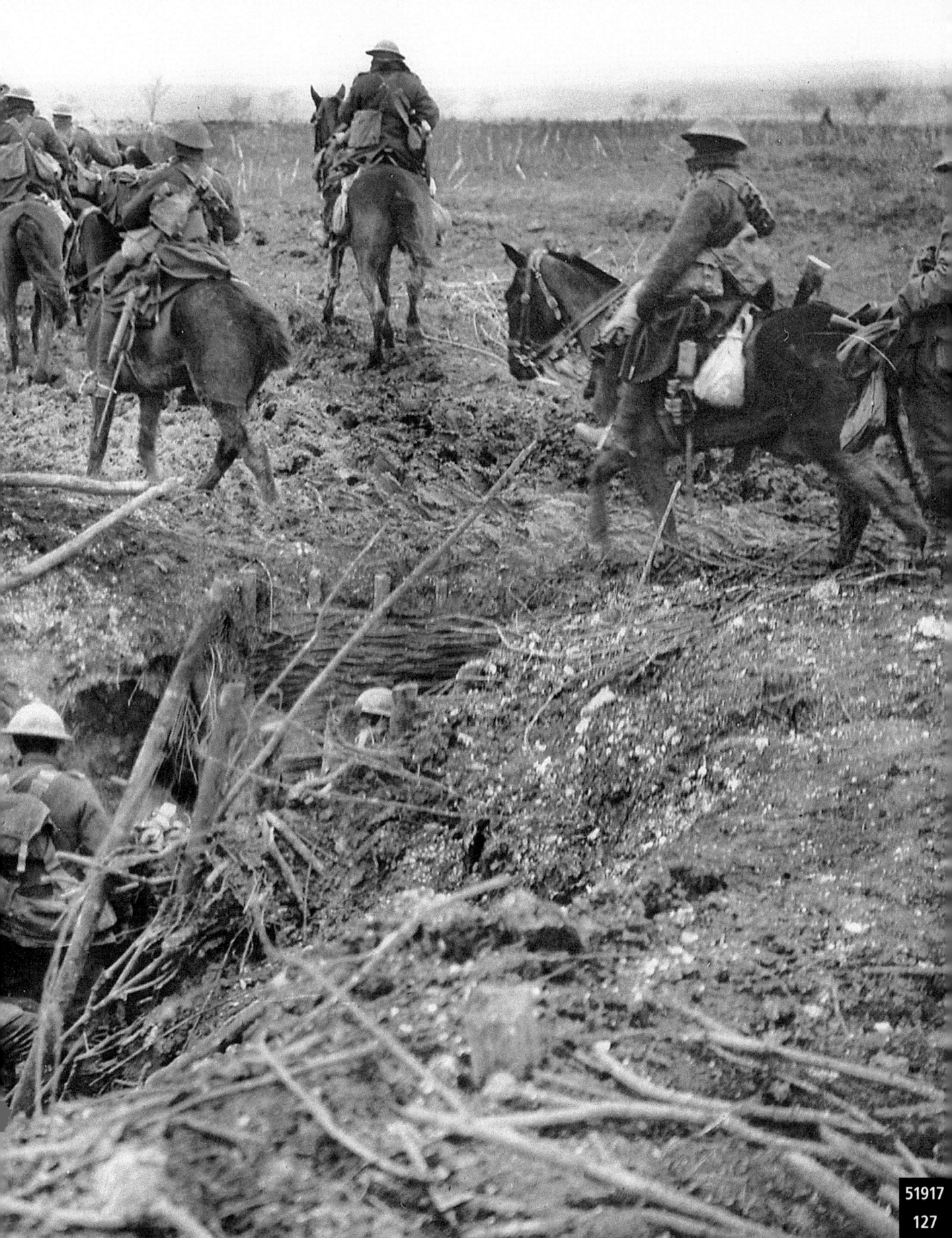

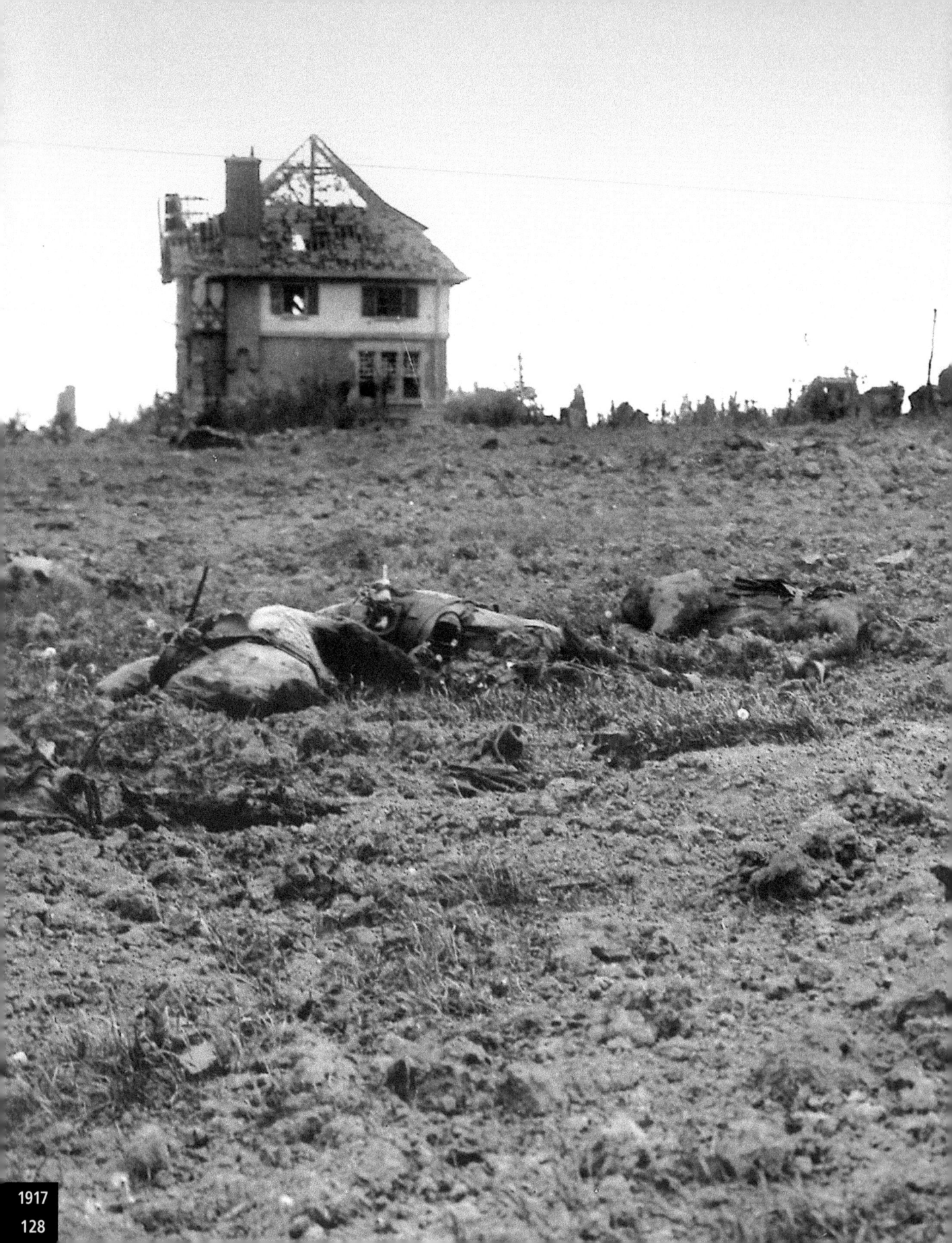

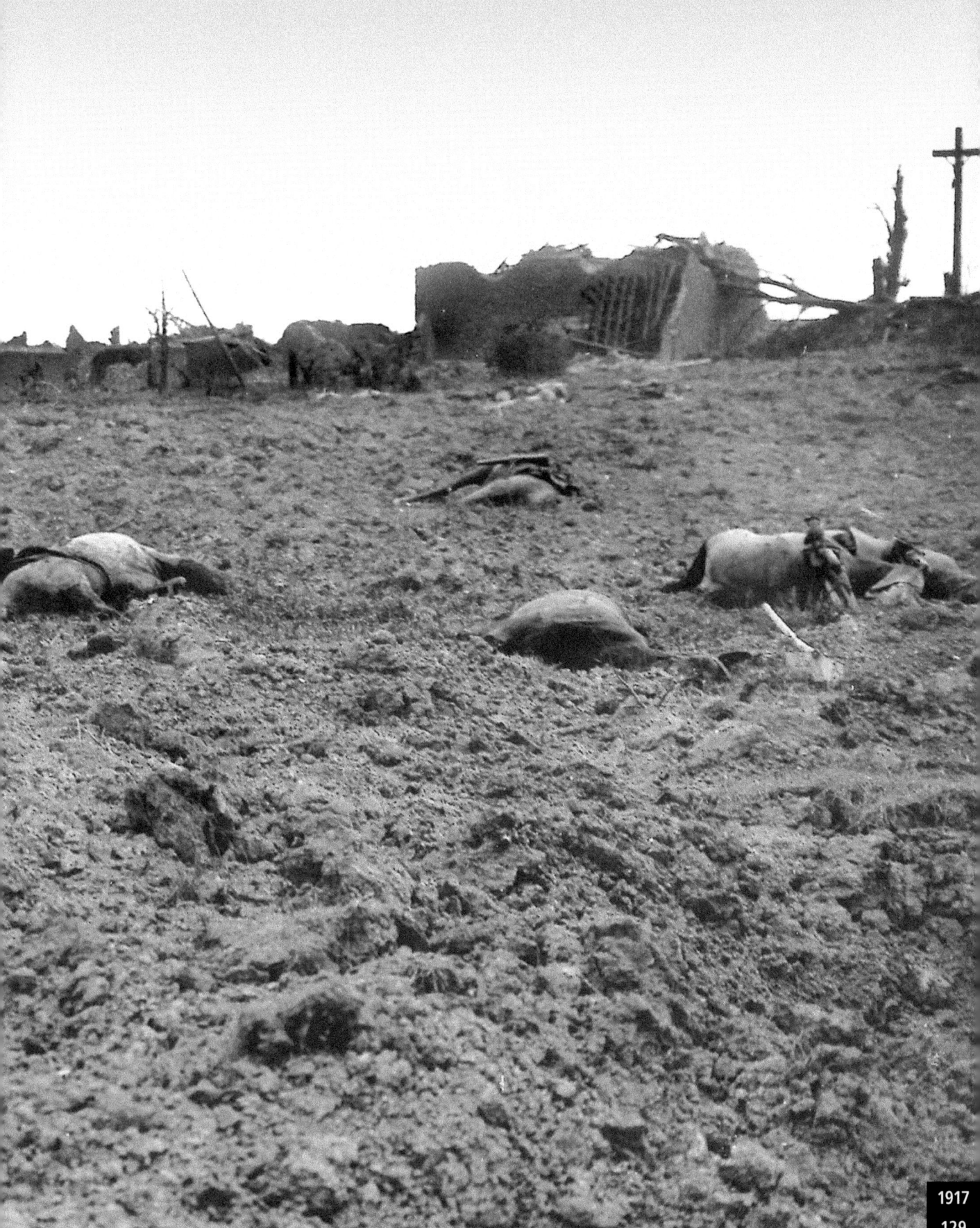

17GW179, 17GW178, 17GW226. The British cavalry at Monchy-le-Preux.

'I started off for Monchy, the runner showing me the way. In five minutes we were at the foot of the village. As we turned the bend of the road to go up the hill, I stopped. The sight that greeted me was so horrible that I almost lost my head. Heaped on top of one another and blocking up the roadway for as far as one could see lay the mutilated bodies of our men and their horses. These bodies torn and gaping had stiffened into fantastic attitudes. All the hollows in the road were filled with blood. This was the cavalry.'

Captain Alan Thomas, 6th Battalion Royal West Kents.

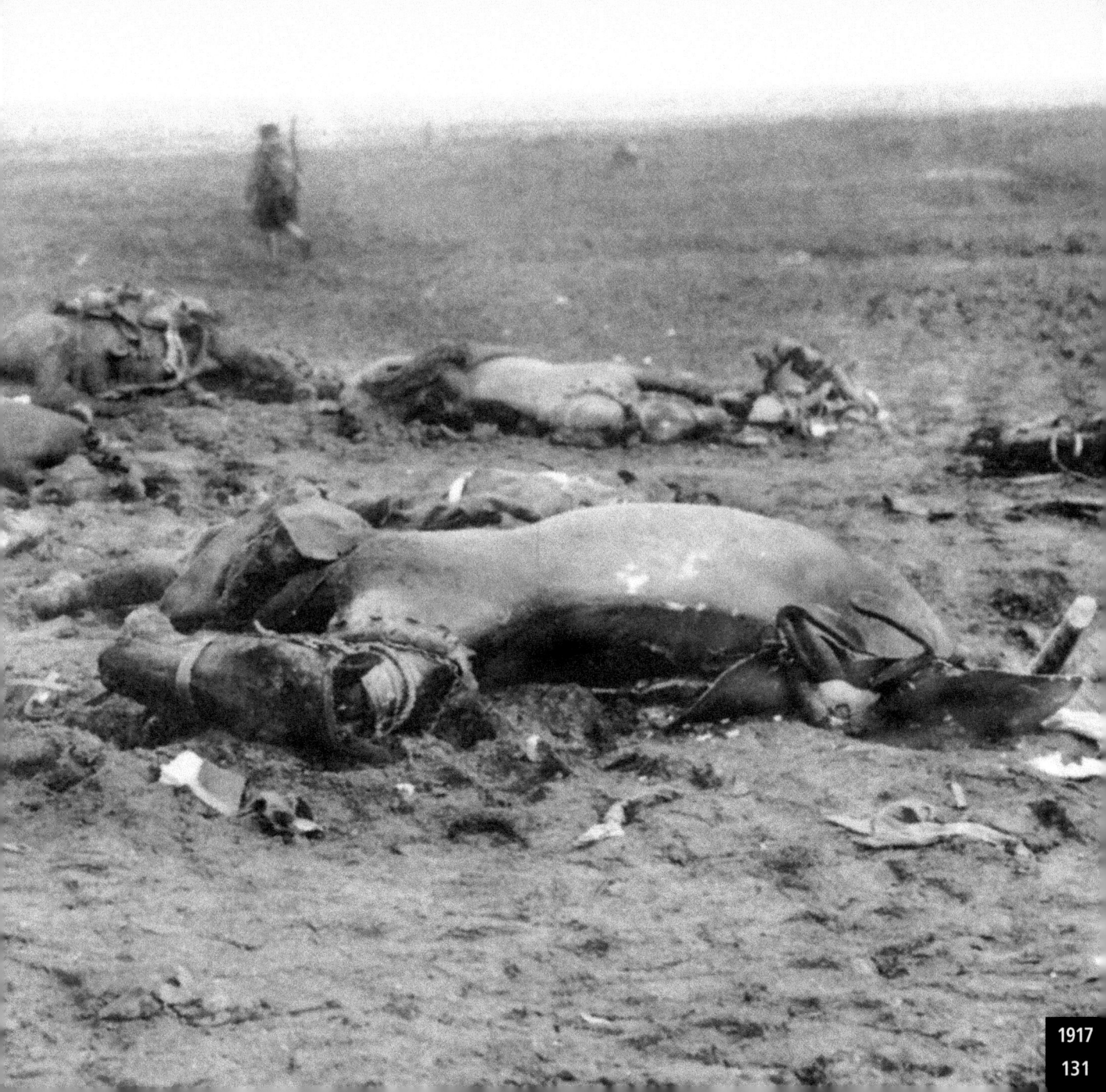

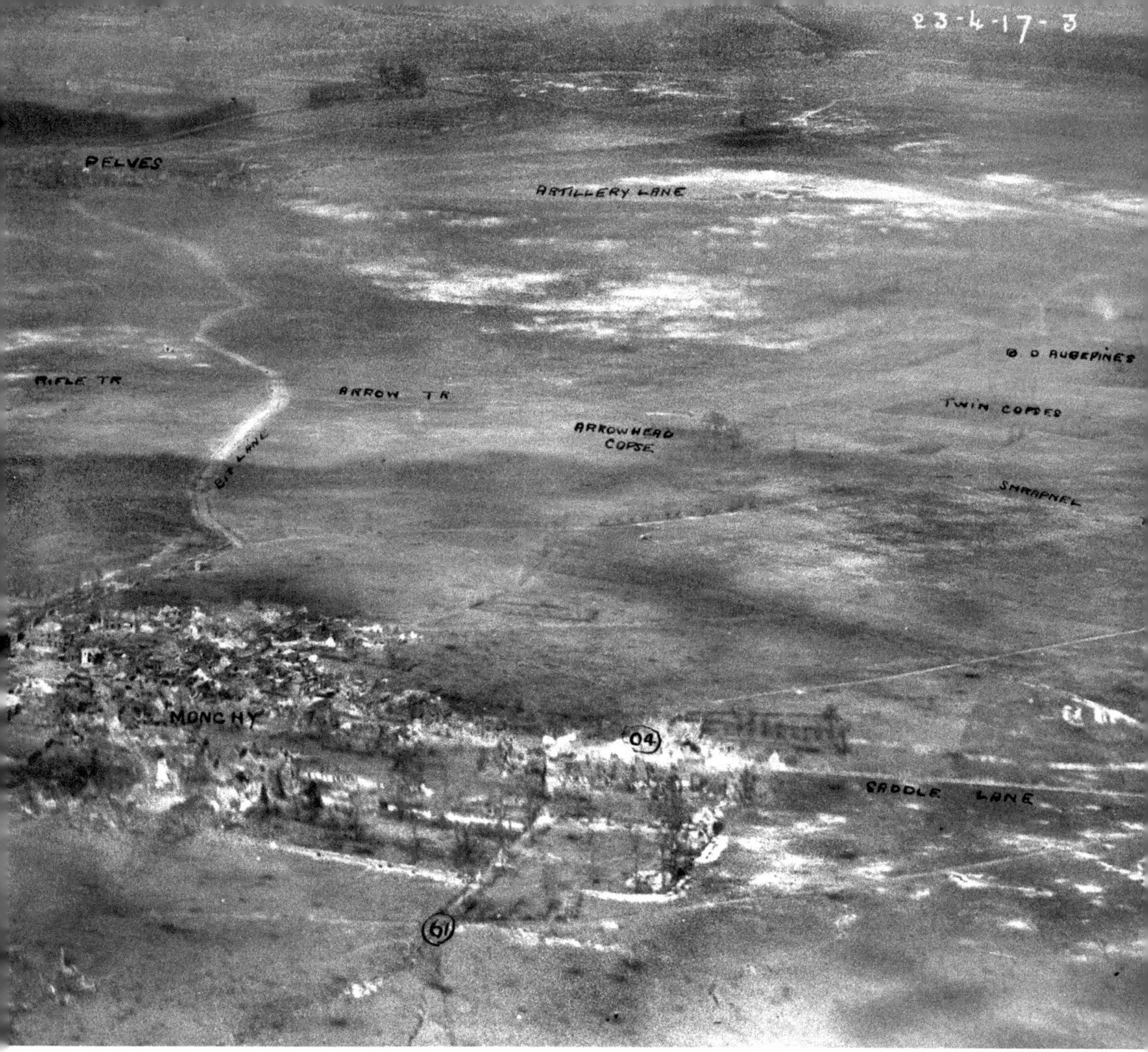

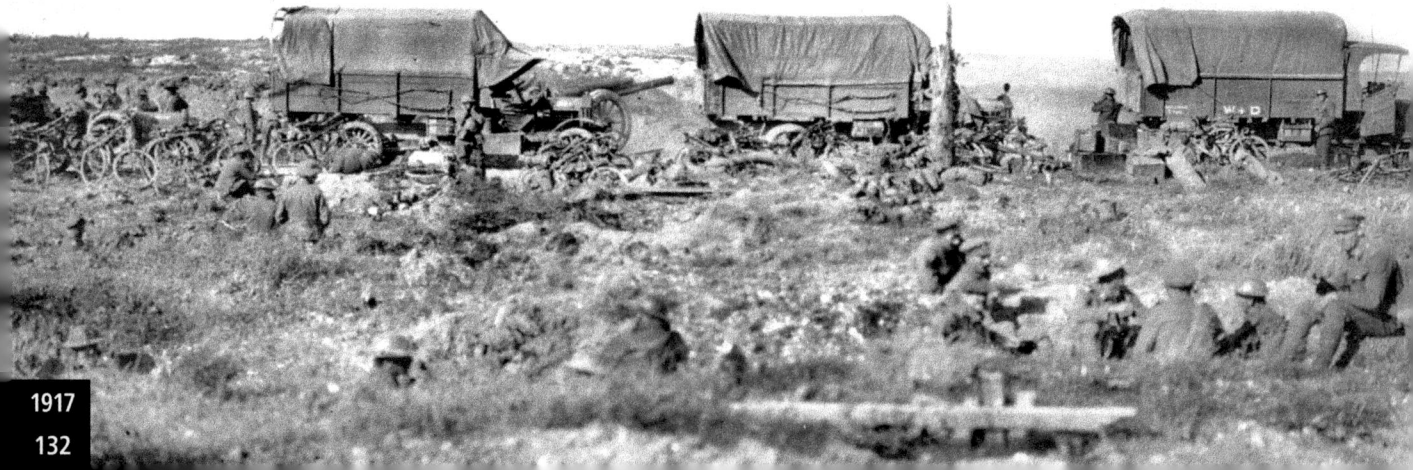

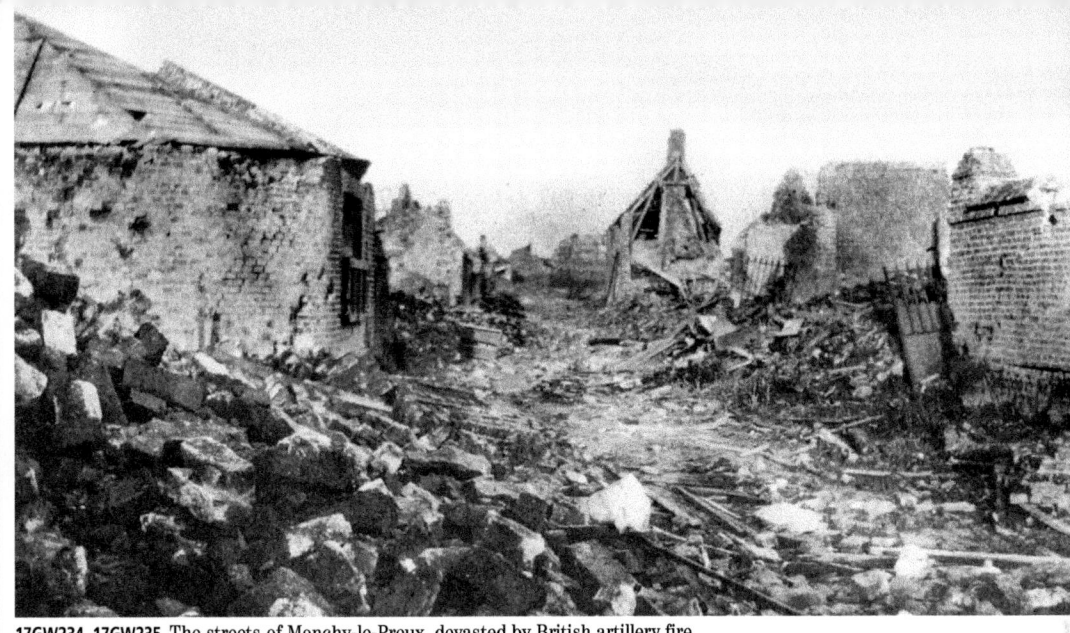

17GW234, 17GW235. The streets of Monchy-le-Preux, devastated by British artillery fire.

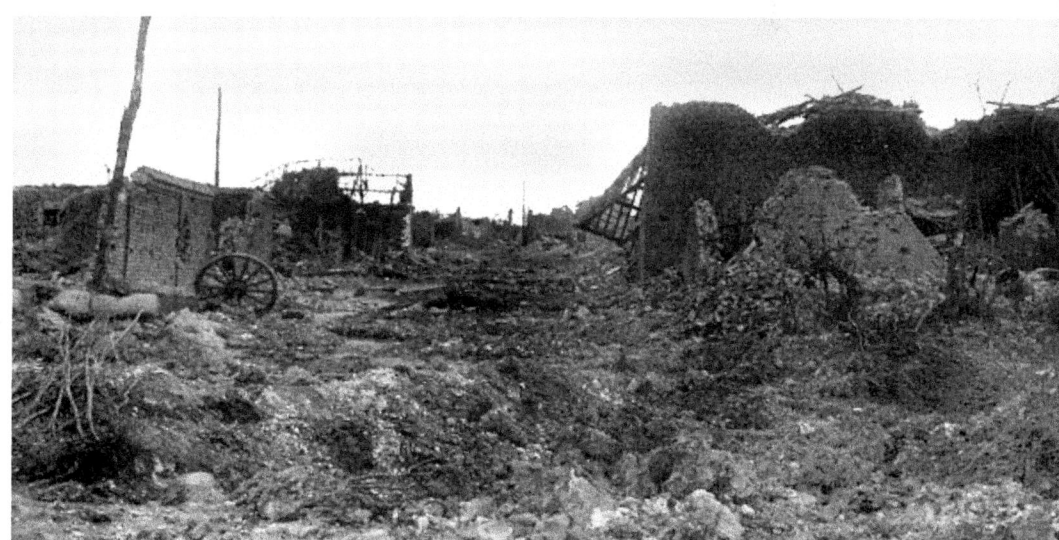

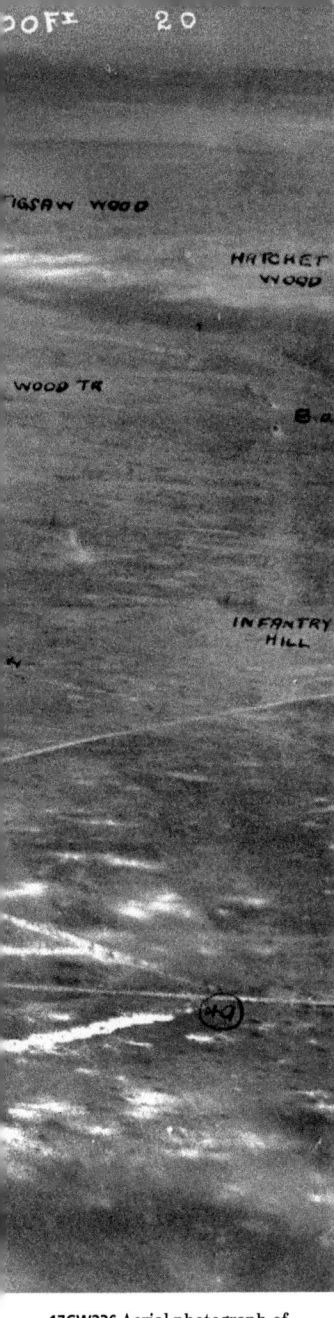

17GW236 Aerial photograph of Monchy taken on 23 April 1917, at the opening of the Second Battle of the Scarpe.

17GW238 A German ammunition wagon abandoned in Monchy, 11 April.

17GW239 An artillery battery halted on the Arras to Cambrai road after the fall of Monchy.

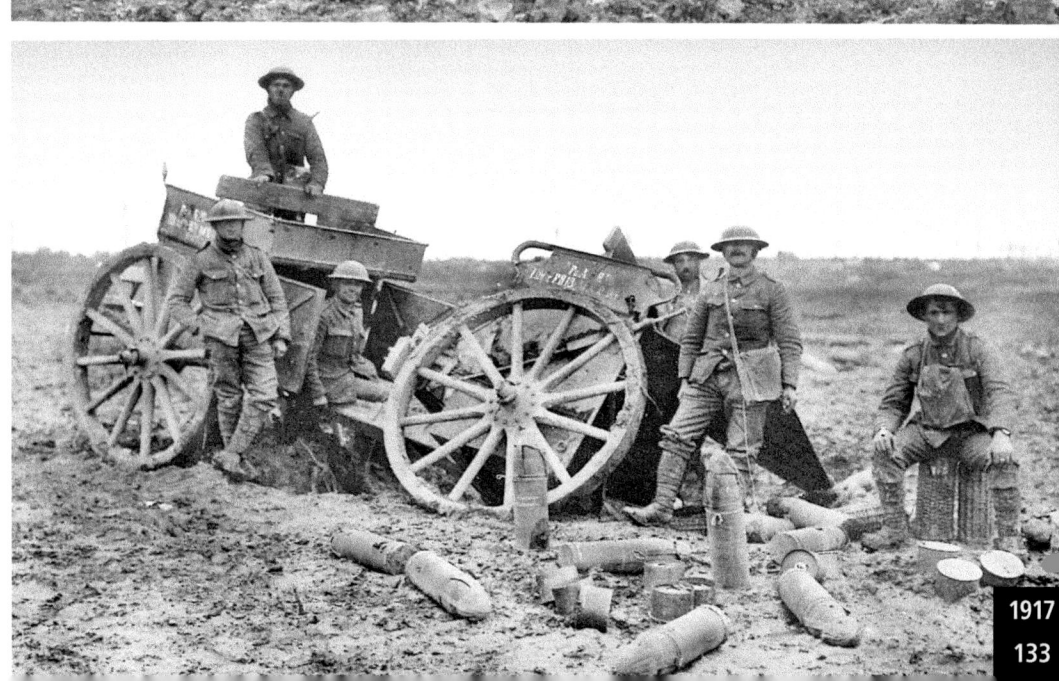

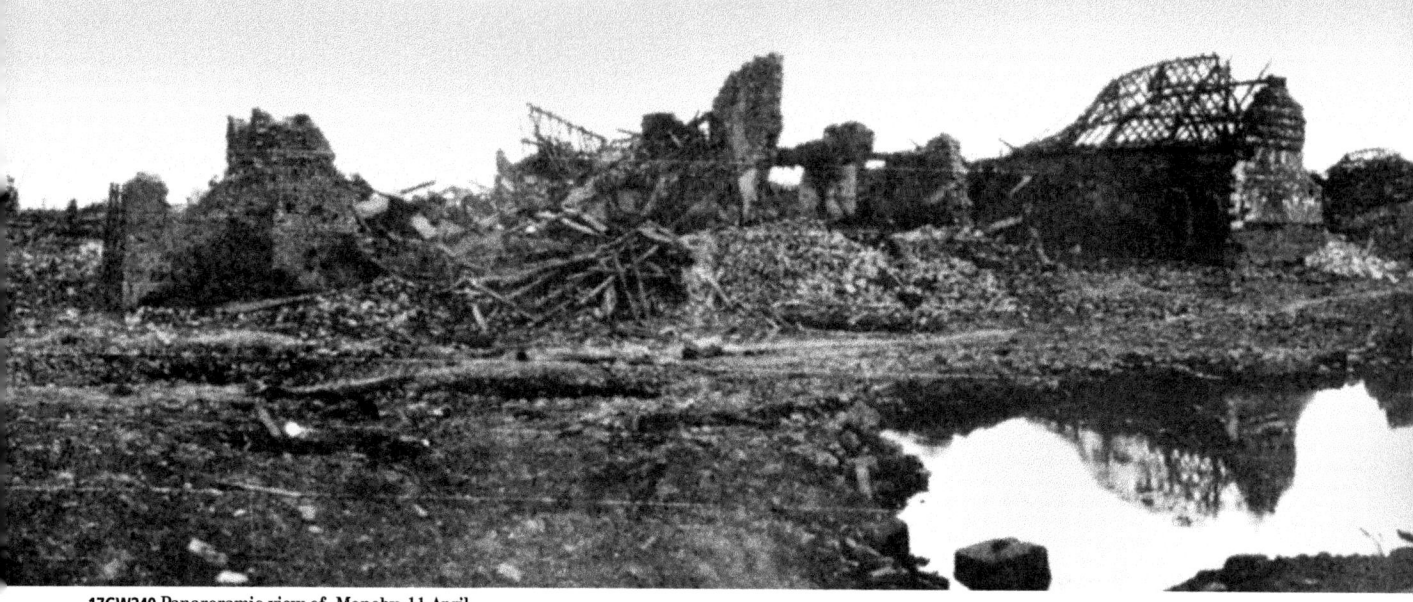

17GW240 Panaroramic view of Monchy, 11 April.

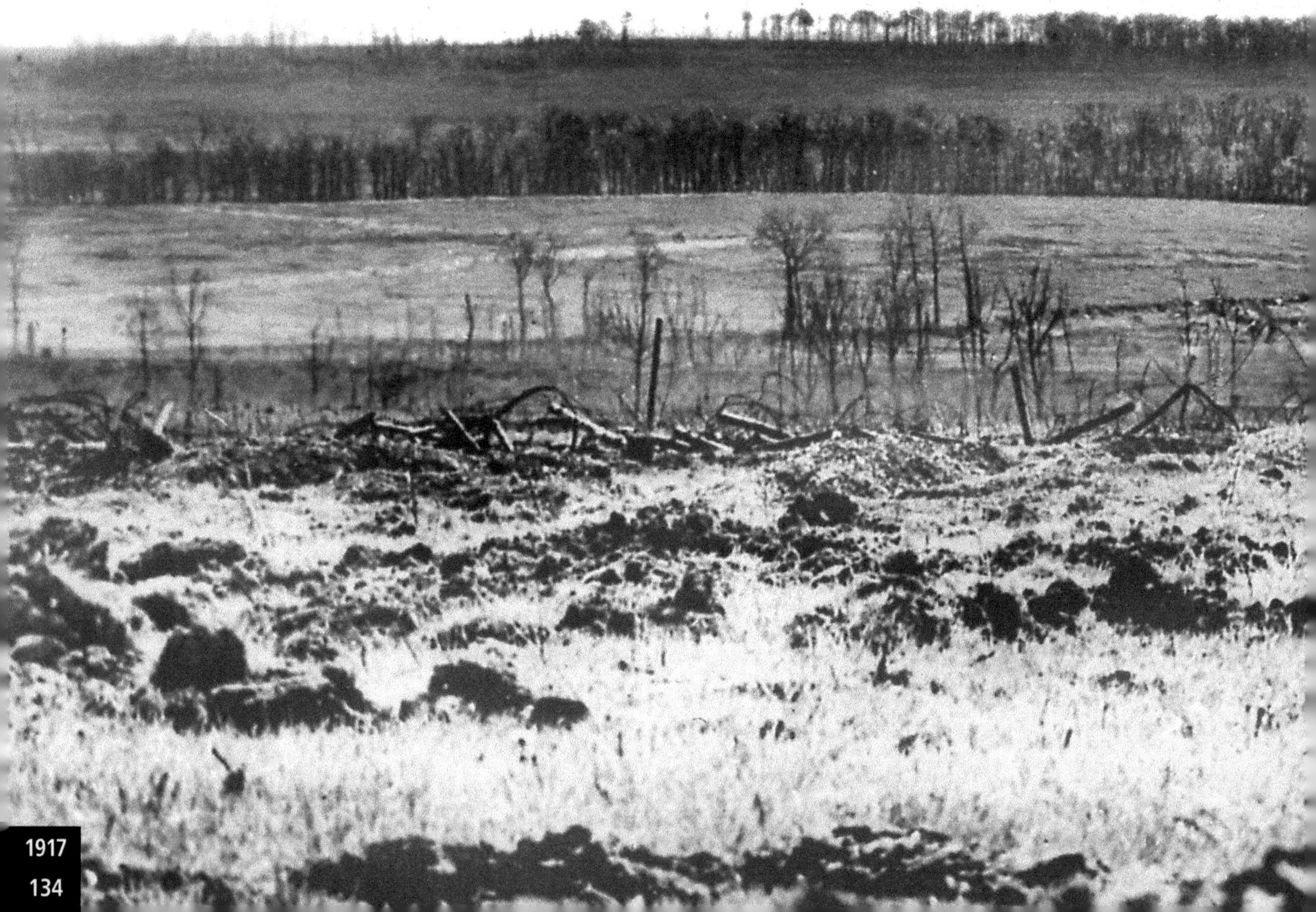

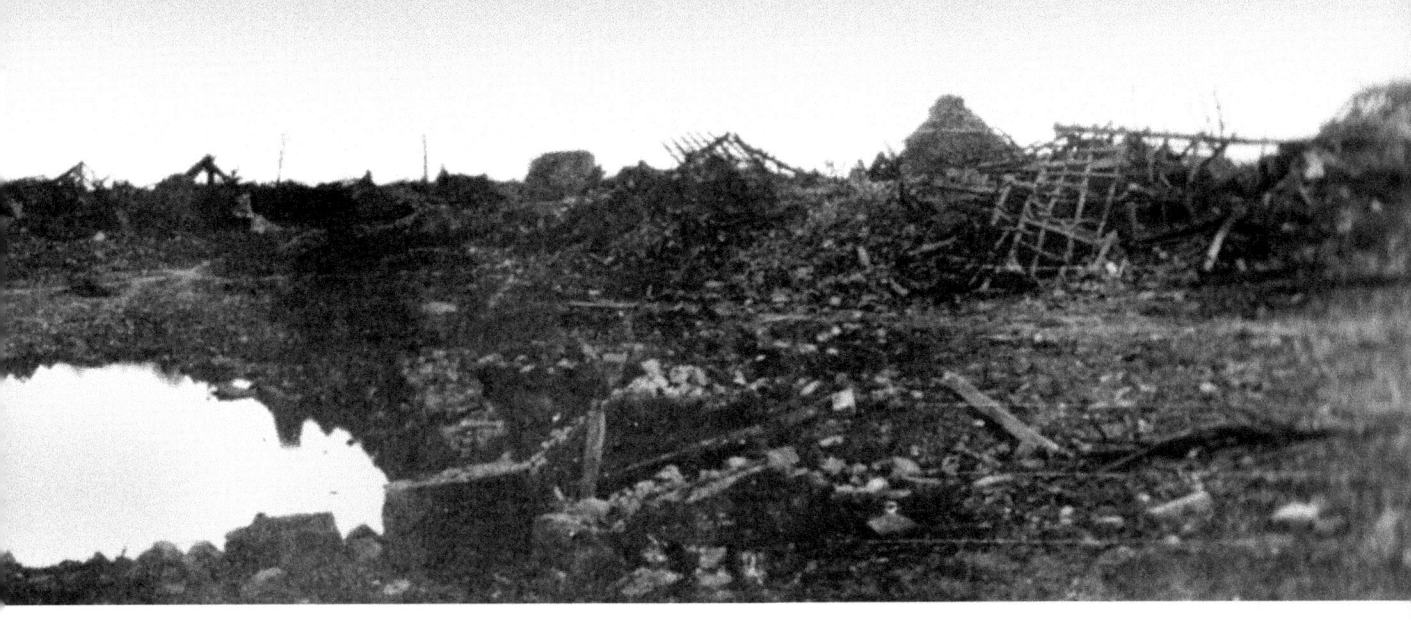

17GW241 View from Monchy looking east towards Bois du Sart (trees on the horizon) and the German positions on the high ground.

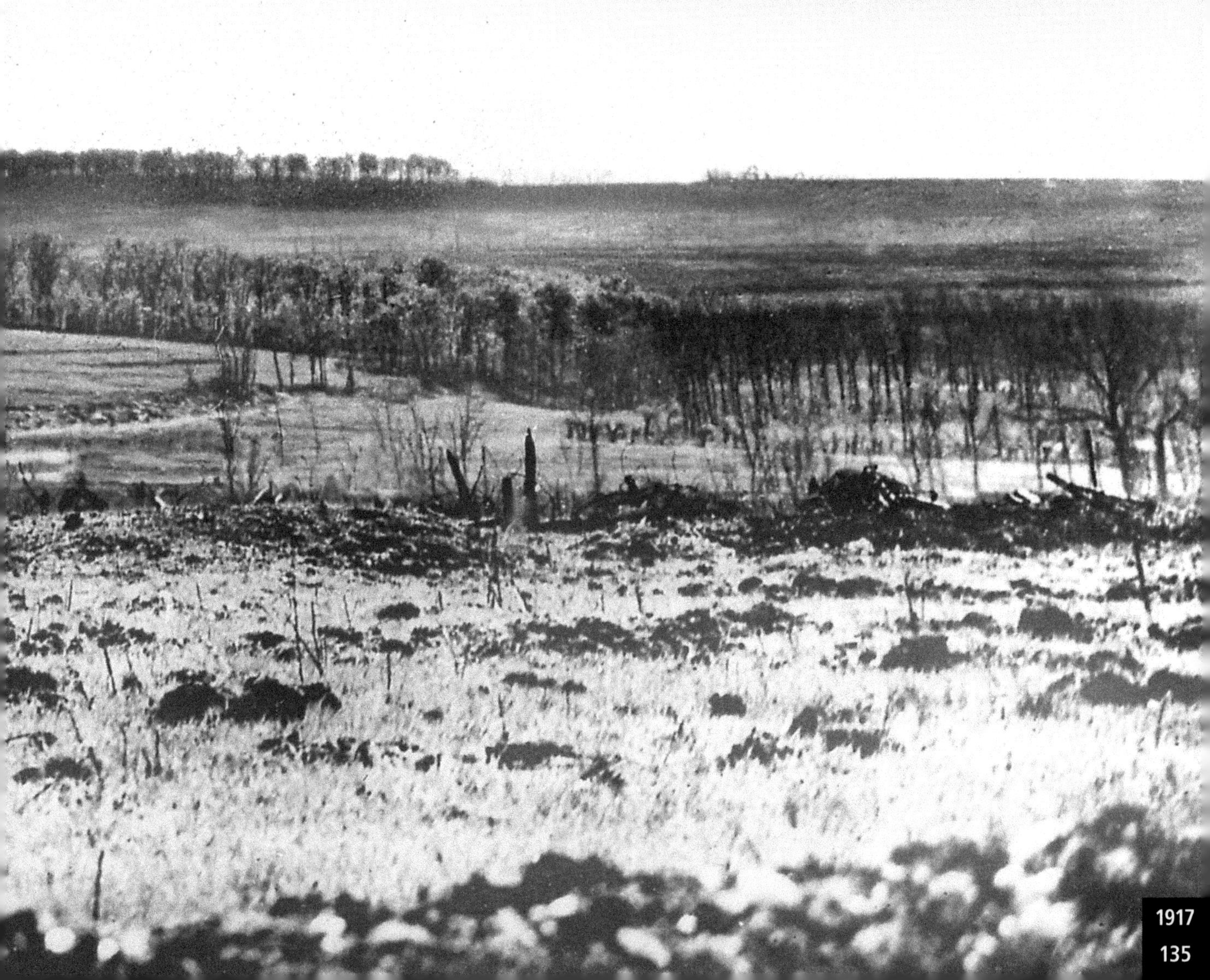

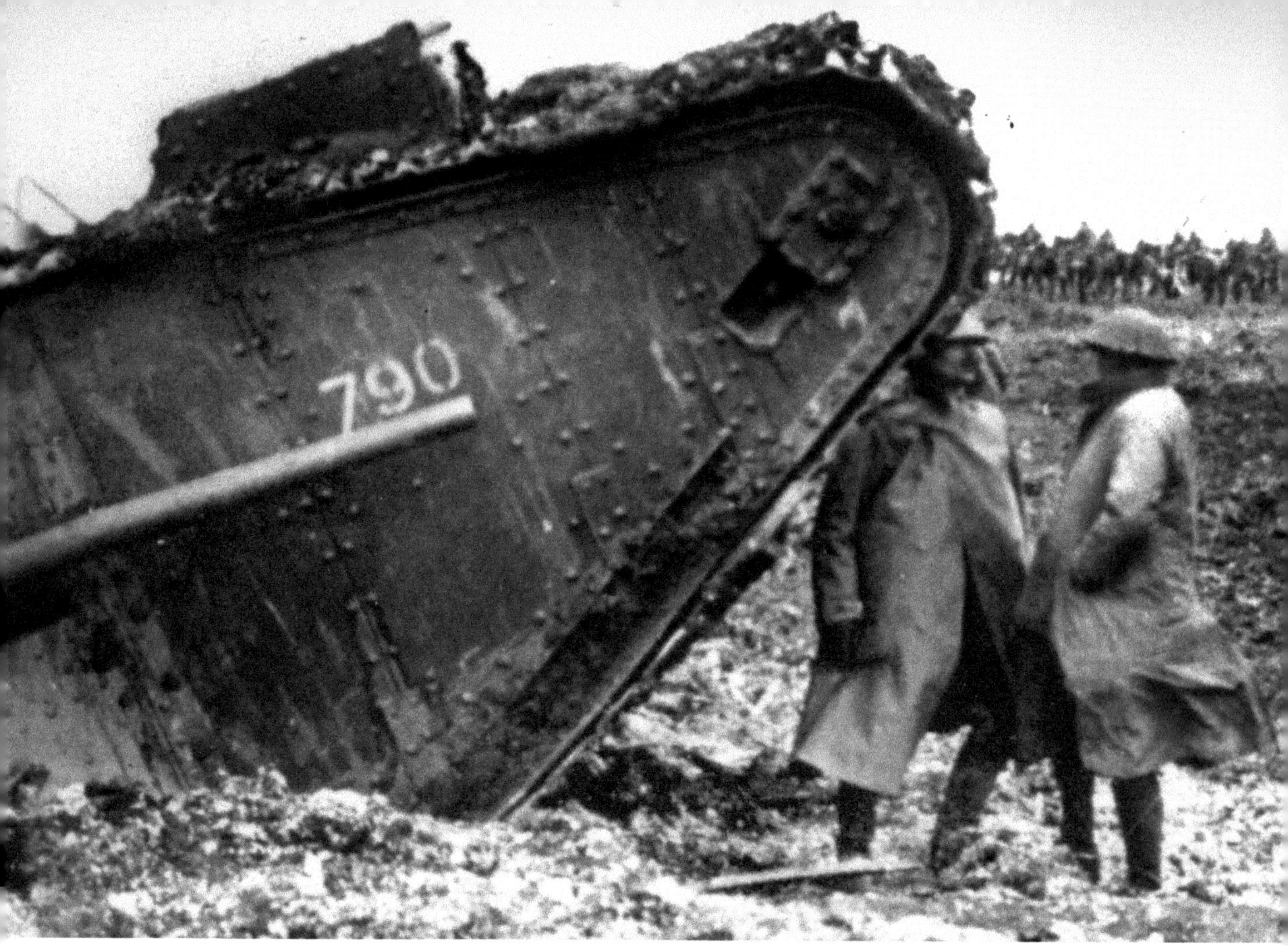

17GW242 The modern cavalry, the tank, is temporarily bogged down while the ancient variety awaits orders to exploit any breakthrough. VI Corps cavalry, the Northamptonshire Yeomanry, penetrated further than Feuchy – that had just been taken by the infantry – and, south of the River Scarpe, at Fampoux, succeeded in capturing six German guns before they joined up with units of XVII Corps advancing north of the Scarpe.

17GW249 A captured 77 mm gun firing at the German lines.

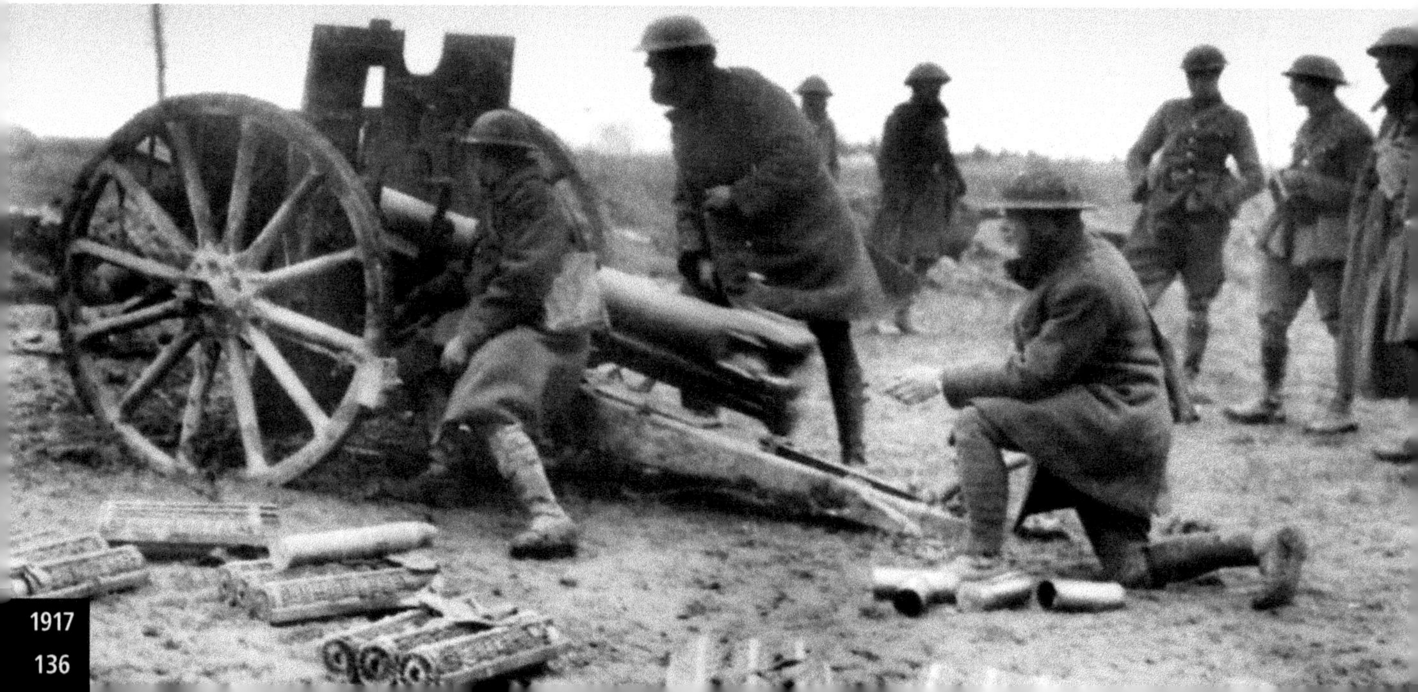

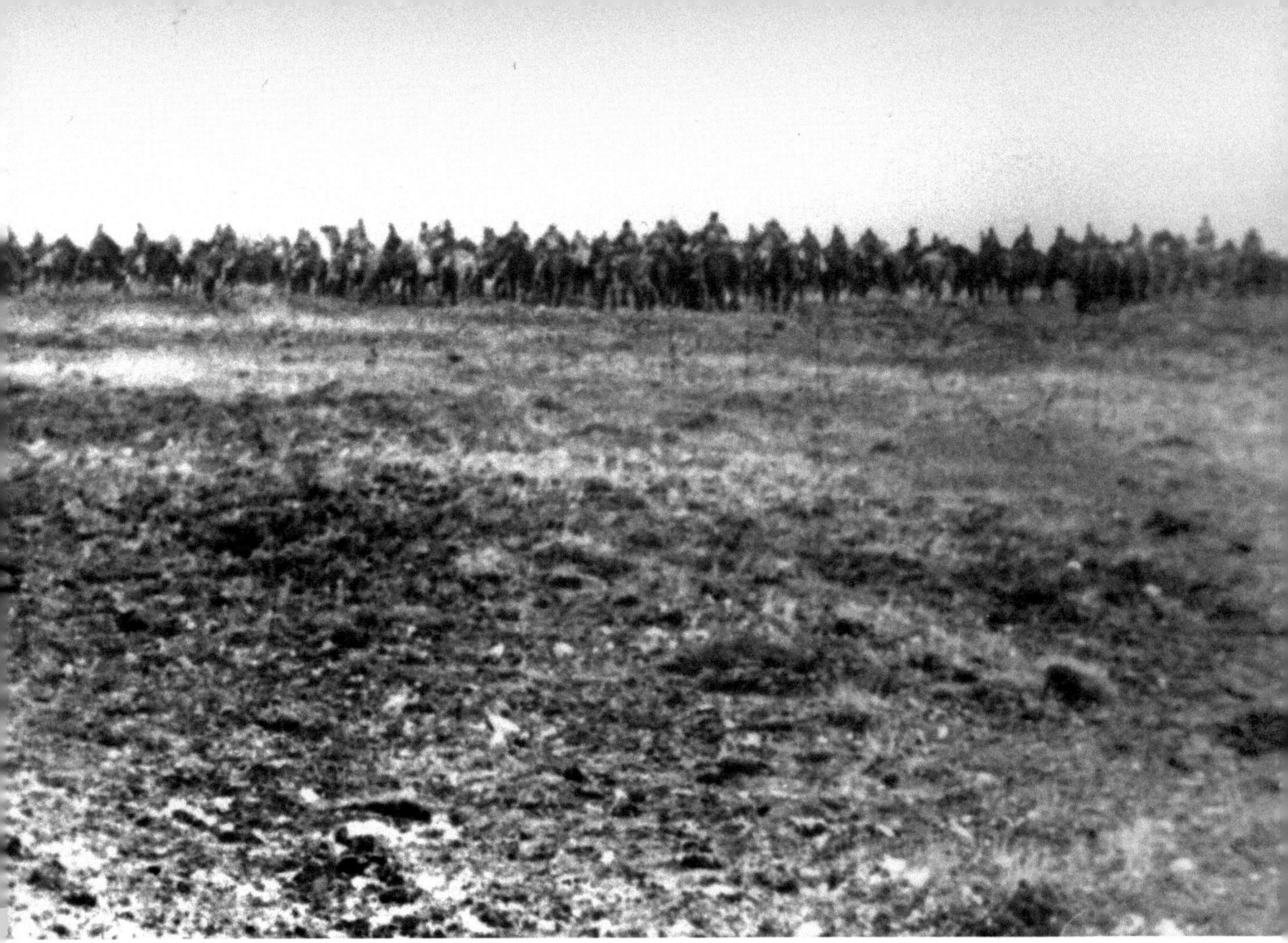

17GW243 A captured howitzer in 'Happy Valley'.

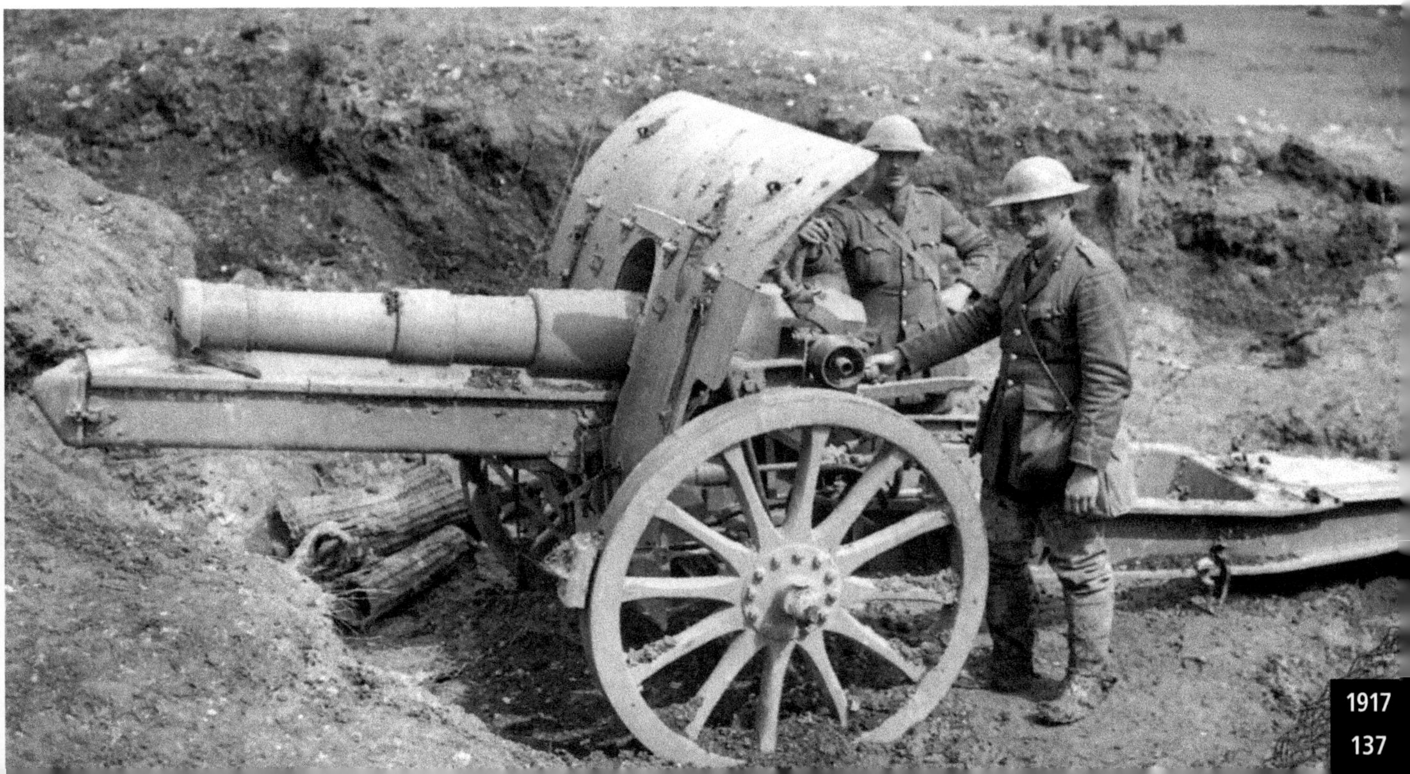

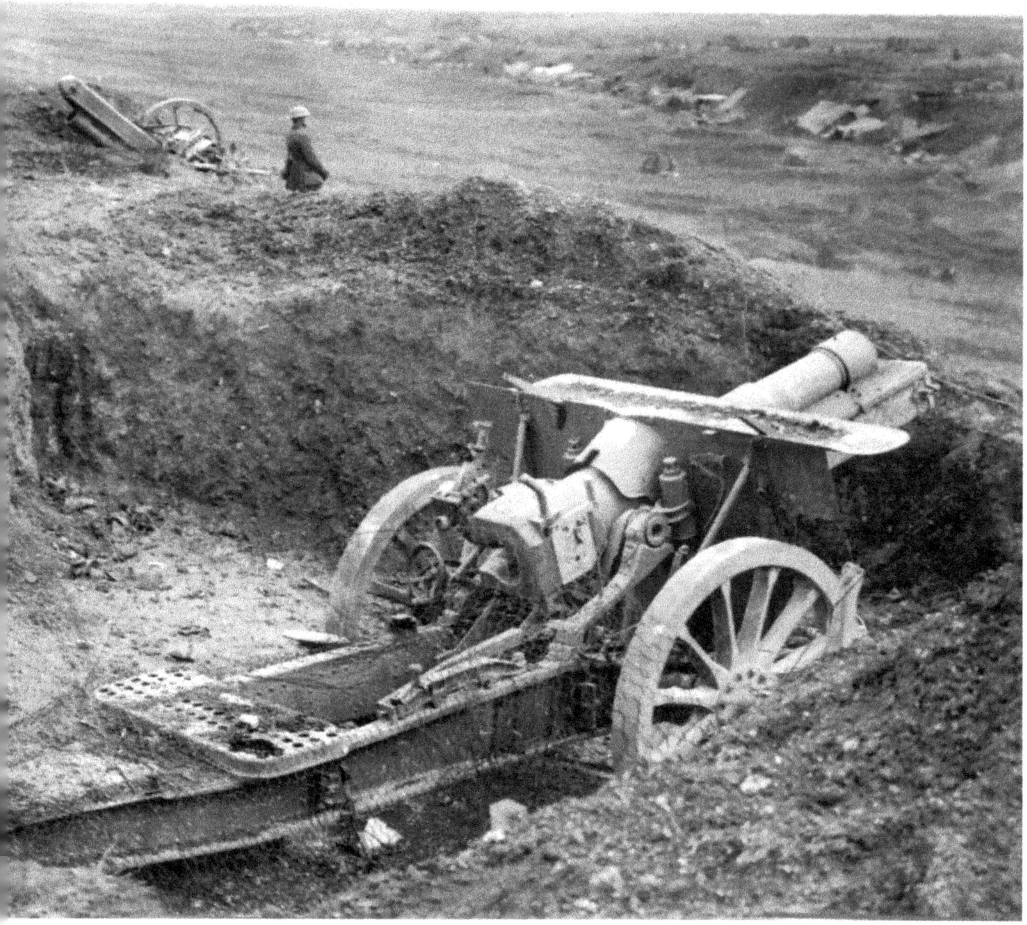

17GW243 A captured howitzer in 'Happy Valley', reversed to face the German positions.

17GW258 British soldiers sheltering in a ruined house, captured in the first day's fighting. The assaulting units and reserves became too exhausted to follow through the successful breakthrough. Cavalry, kept in reserve to exploit successes, was too far back to attack Gavrelle, Oppy and Vitry-en-Artois and its deployment was hampered by snow fall.

17GW257, 17GW258. Men of the Royal Engineers Signal Service, April 1917, during the Battle of Arras, operating Daylight Signalling Lamps. Should the light be inadvertantly pointed towards the enemy it would immediately draw rifle fire. Post war this branch of the Royal Engineers would become the Royal Corps of Signals.

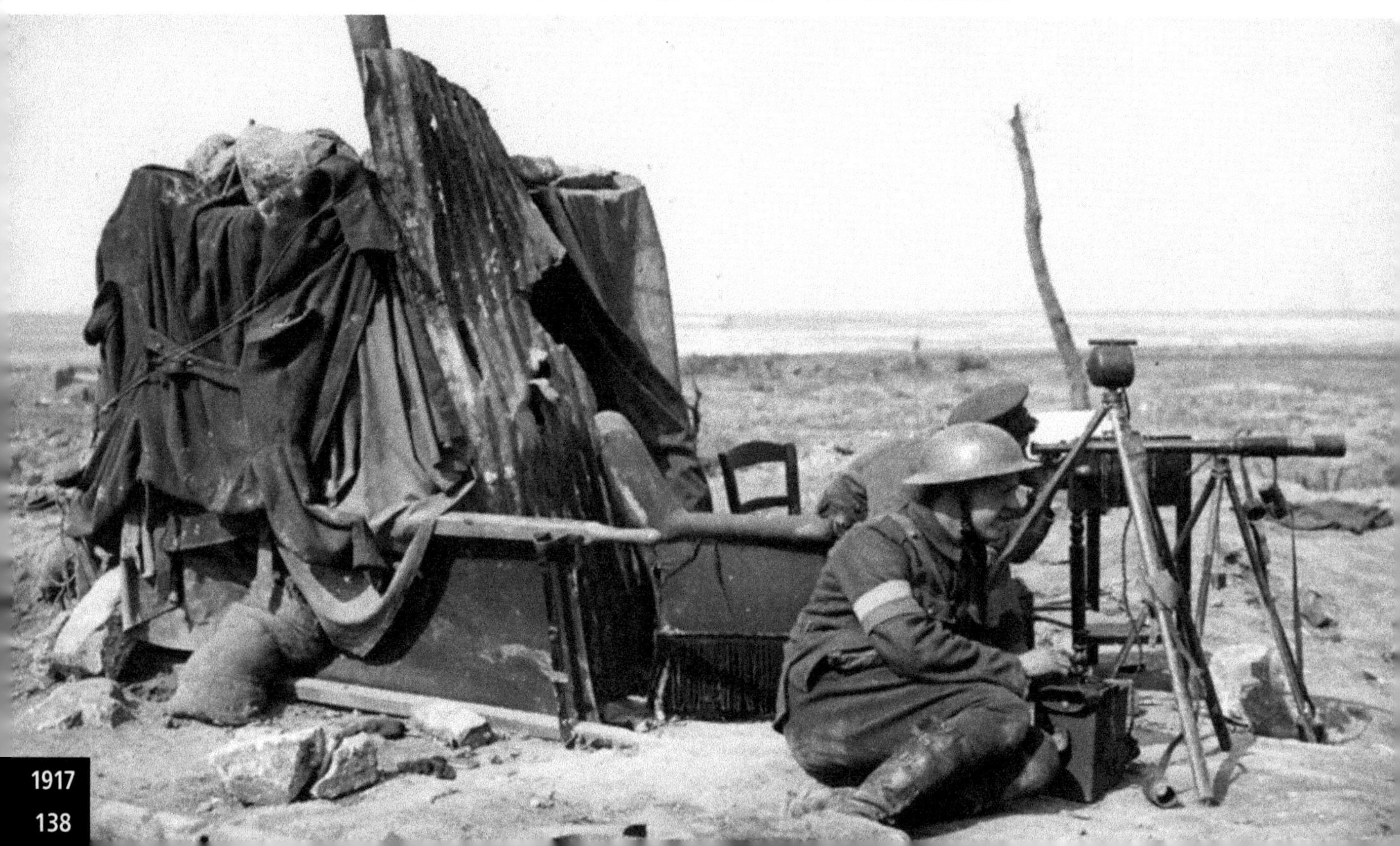

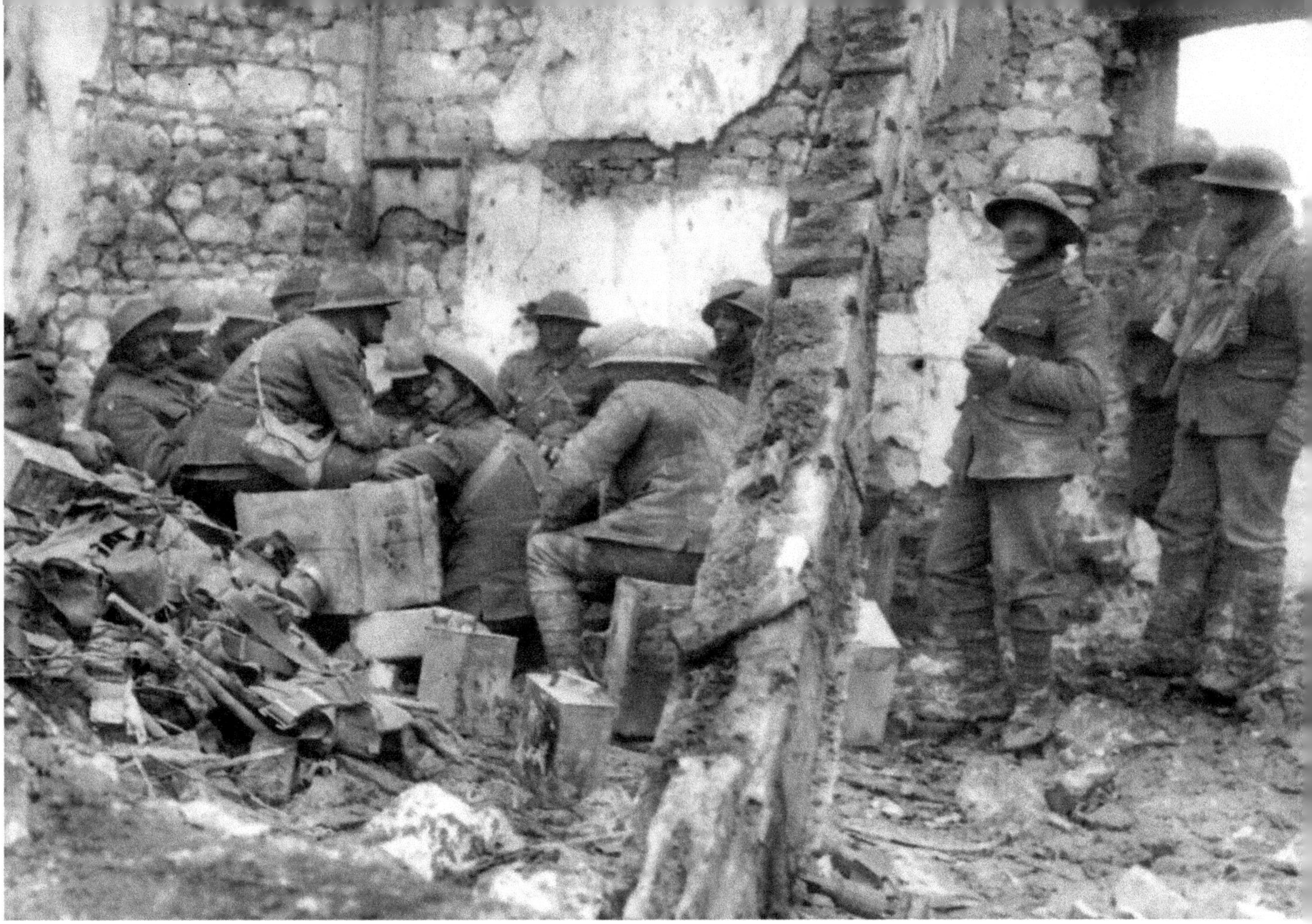

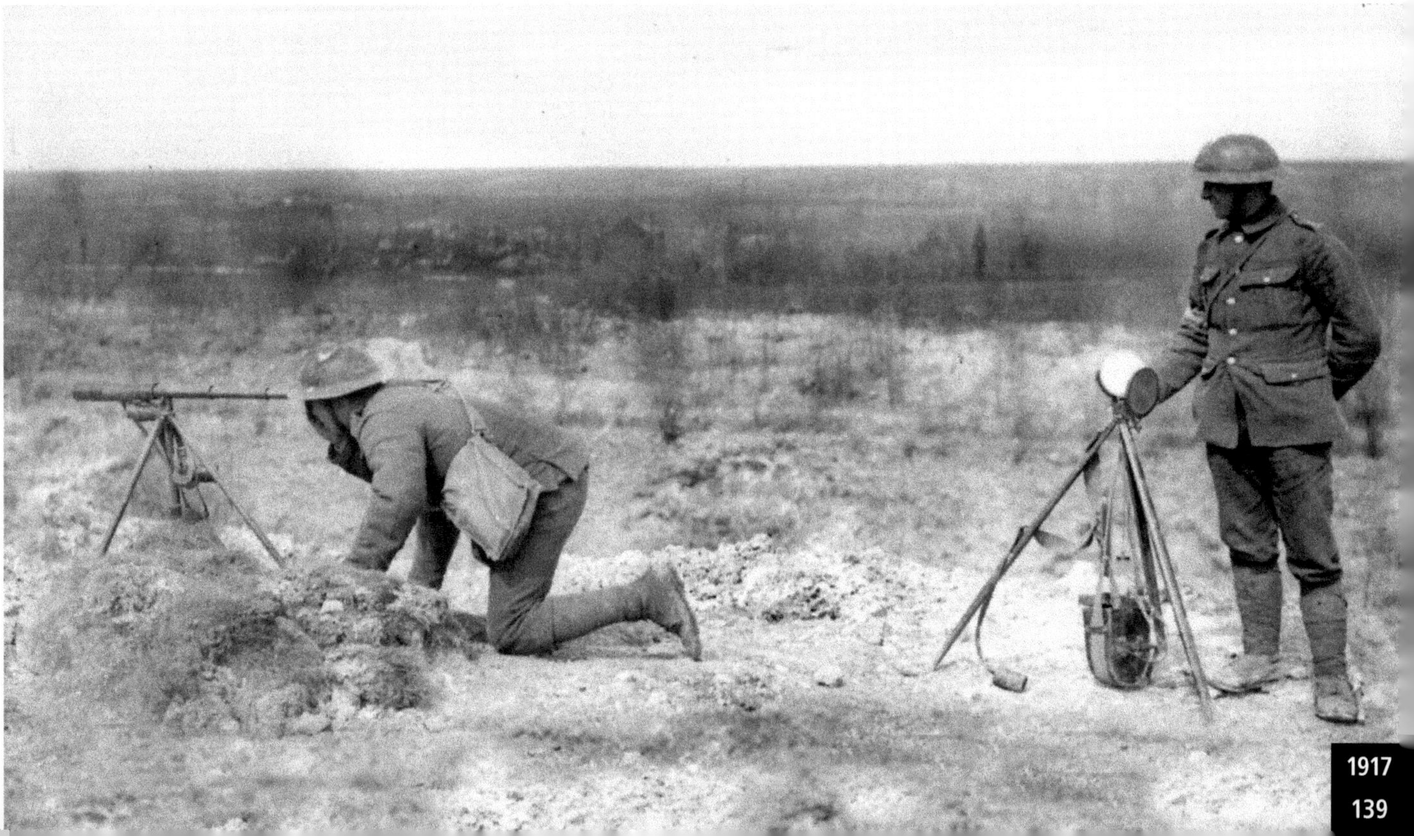

1917

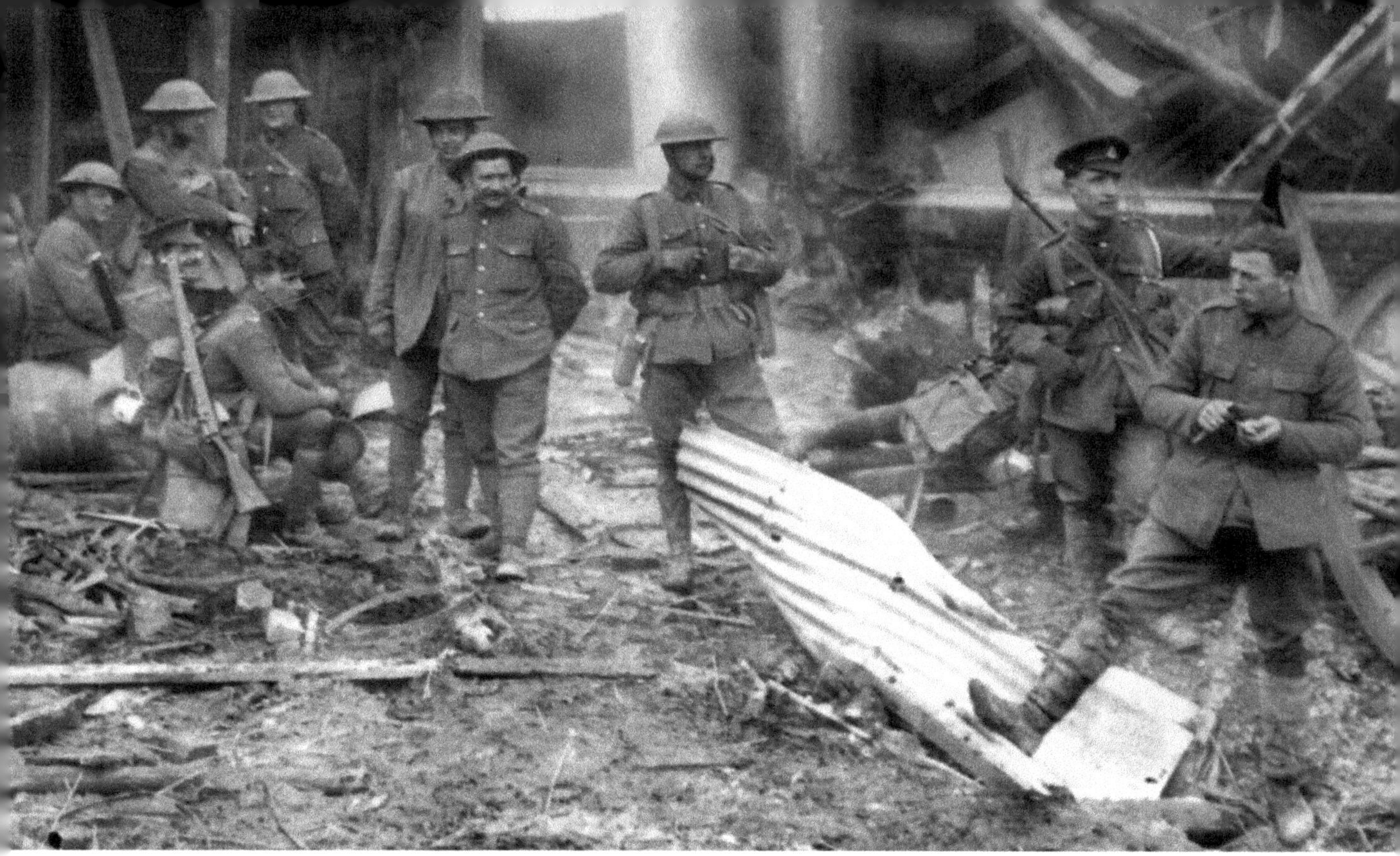

17GW260 British troops north of the River Scarpe resting after their initial gains on the first day of the battle. It had been planned that the follow-up to all gains would be made south of the river.

17GW261 A scene at Feuchy road junction: officers of the King's Royal Rifle Corps receiving their personal items of equipment by supply convoy (under protection of the cavalry. A watchful eye is being kept on the skies which may indicate an unidentified flying machine is approaching.

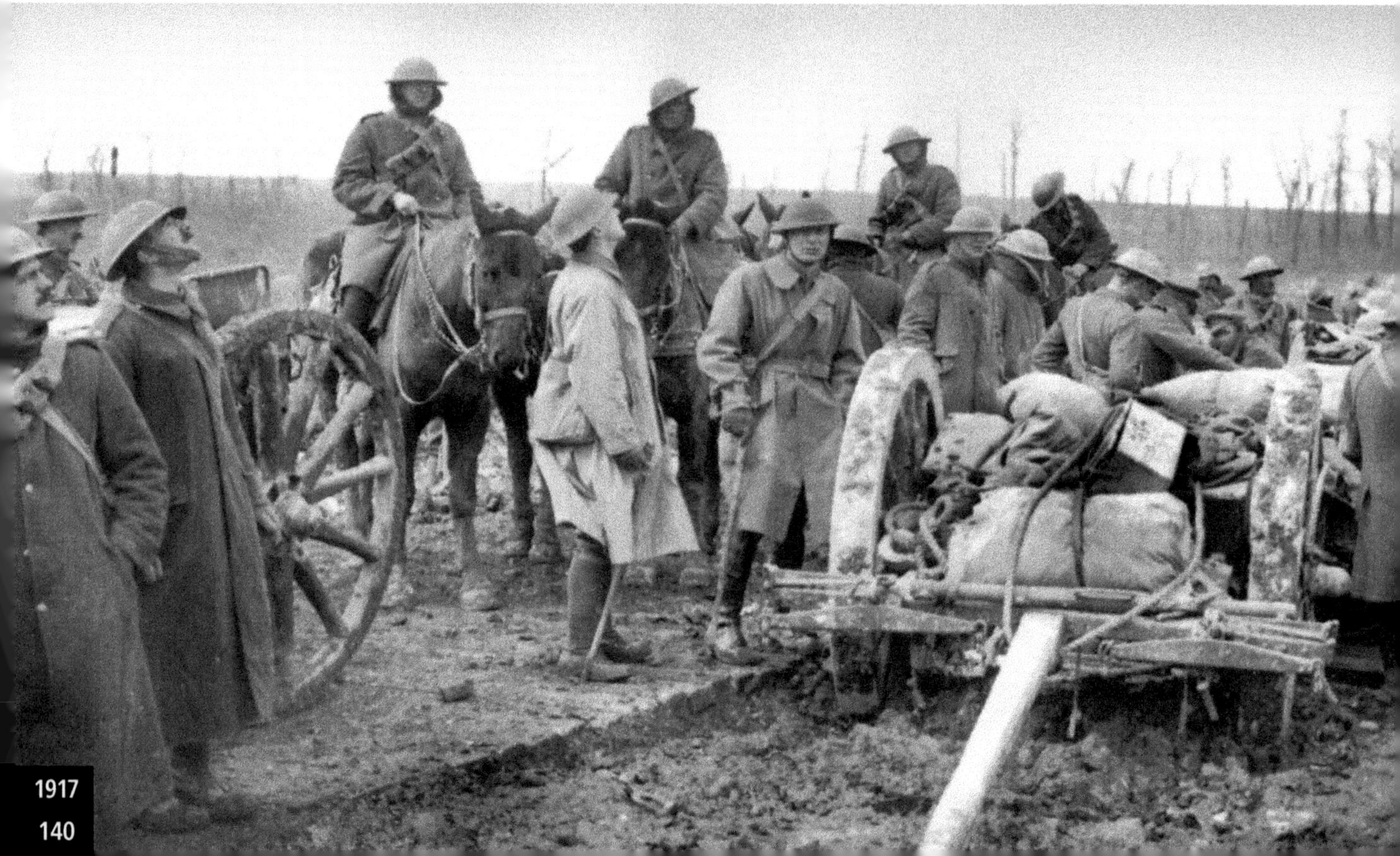

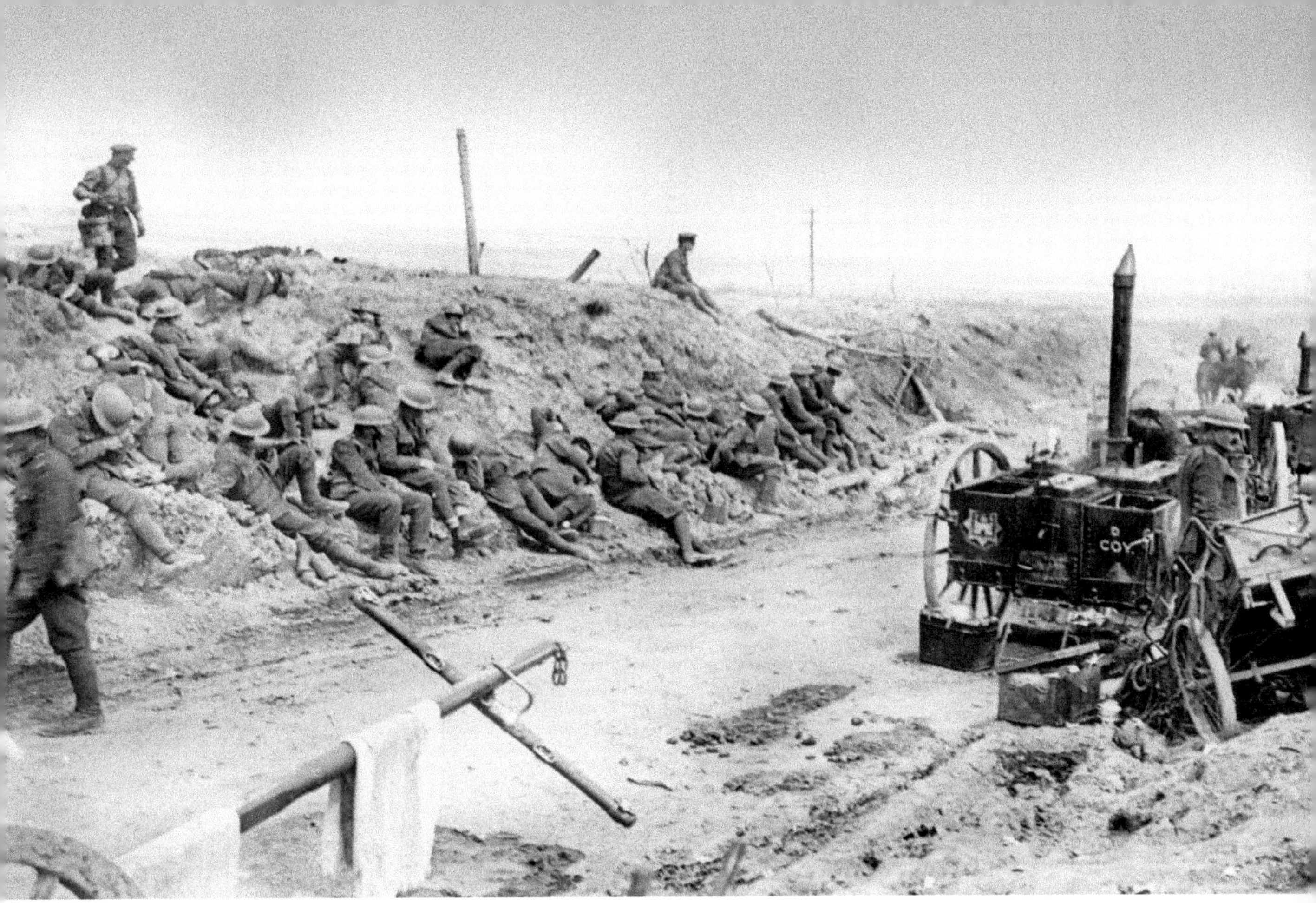

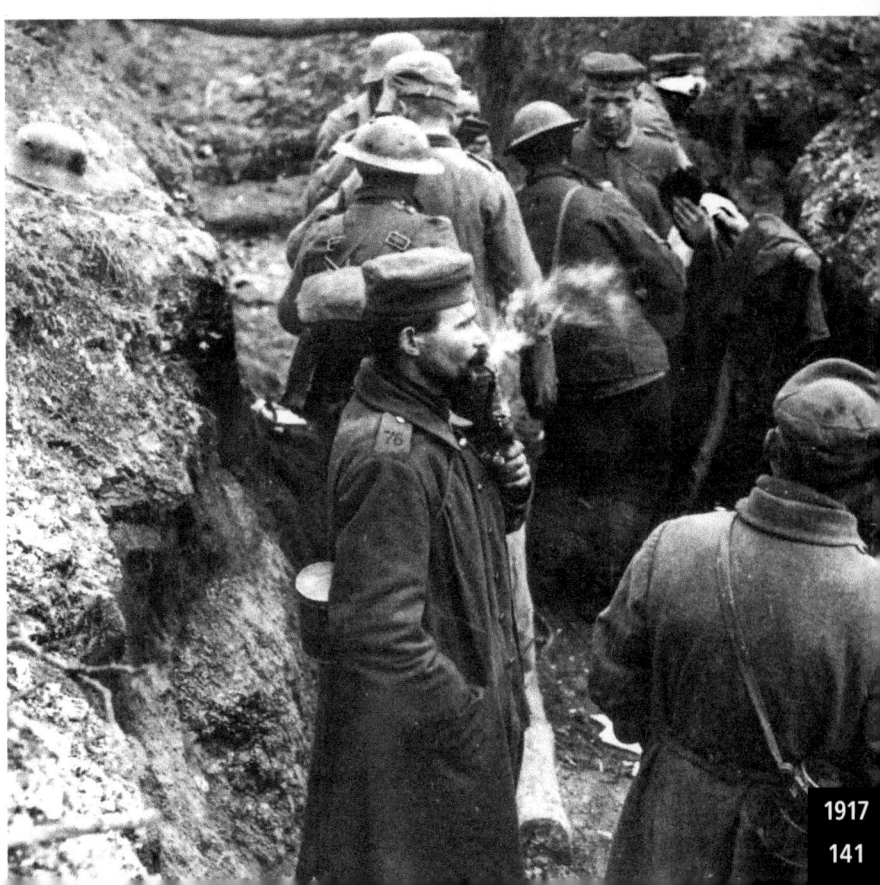

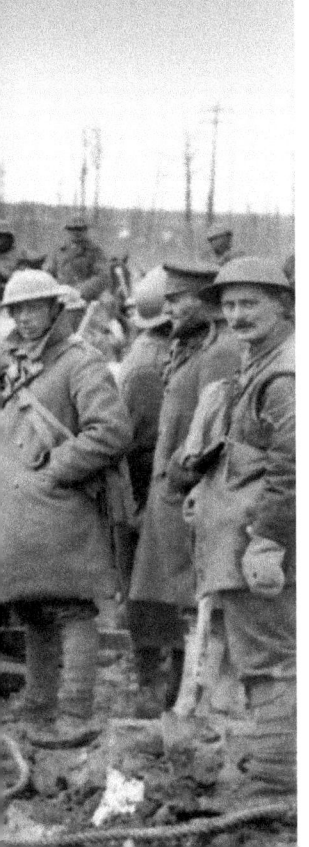

17GW262 A battalion of the East Surrey Regiment at the roadside with their field kitchens in what was, until recently, German-held territory. Failure to follow up the gains was attributed to the poor roads and congestion.

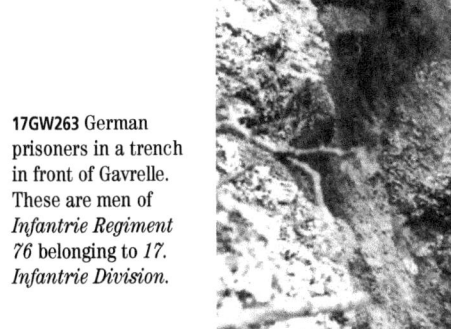

17GW263 German prisoners in a trench in front of Gavrelle. These are men of *Infantrie Regiment 76* belonging to *17. Infantrie Division*.

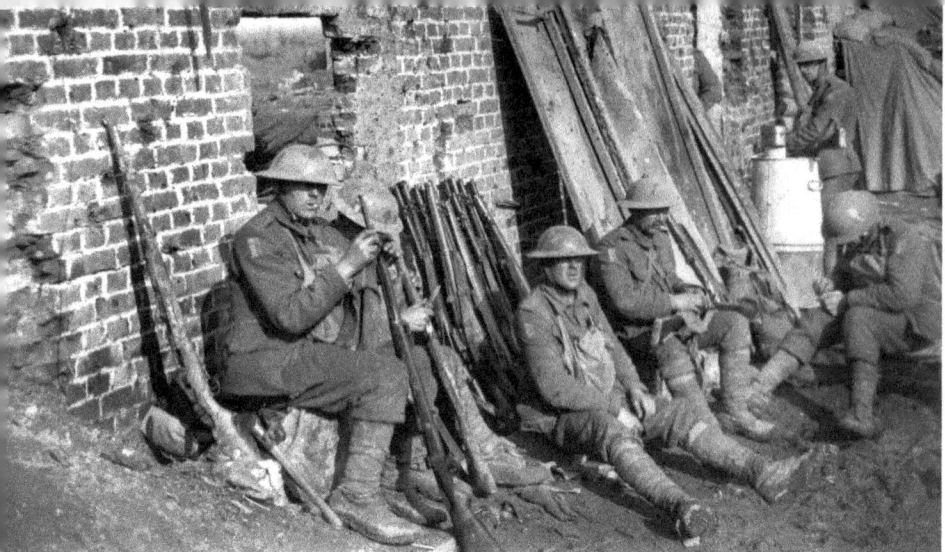

17GW267 Men of the Dorsetshire Regiment; some are cleaning captured German rifles, another appears to be preparing hot food; note the stretchers.

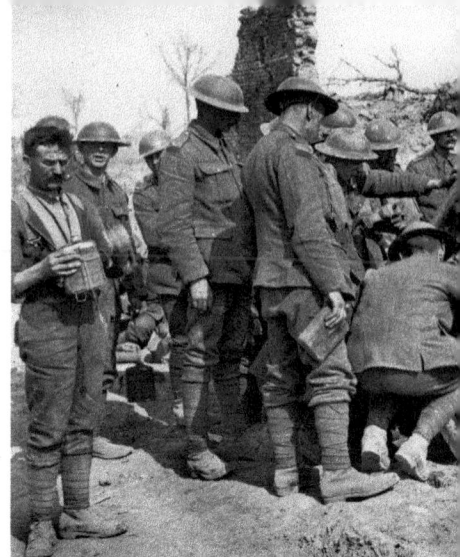

17GW267, 17GW269. Men of the York and Lancaster Regiment at Oppy Wood: a member of a Lewis gun team fitting a magazine. An infantry attack at Gavrelle.

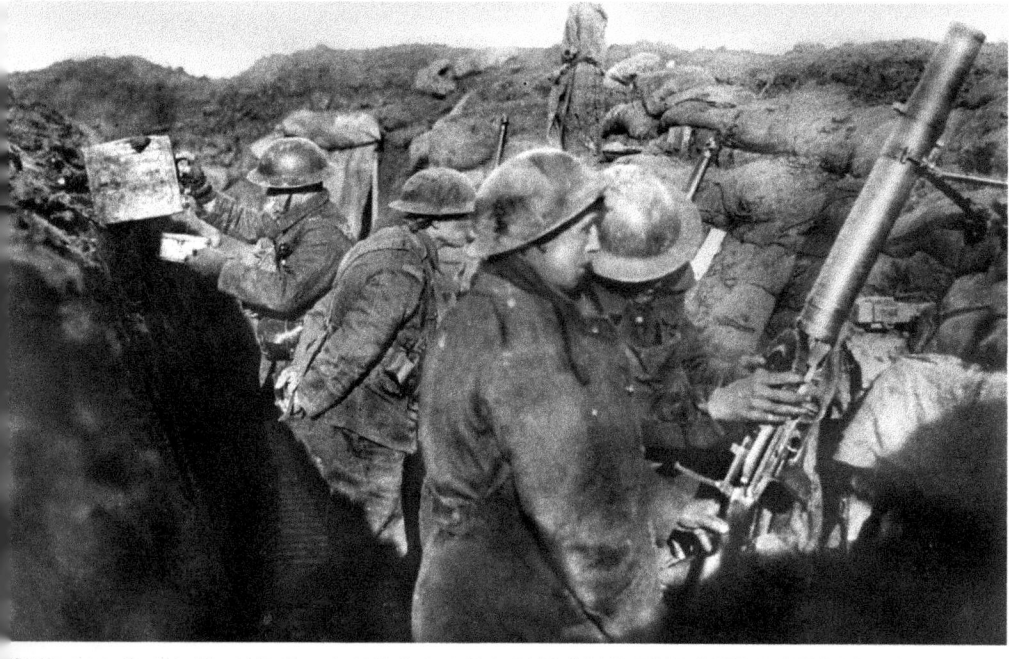

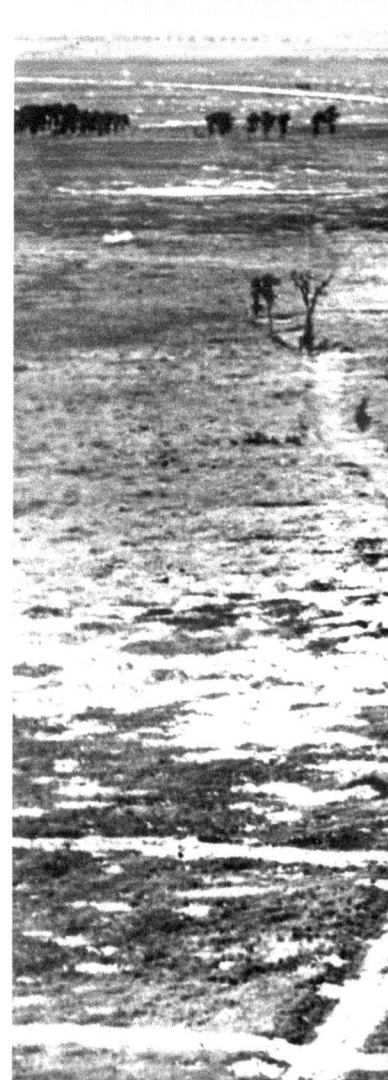

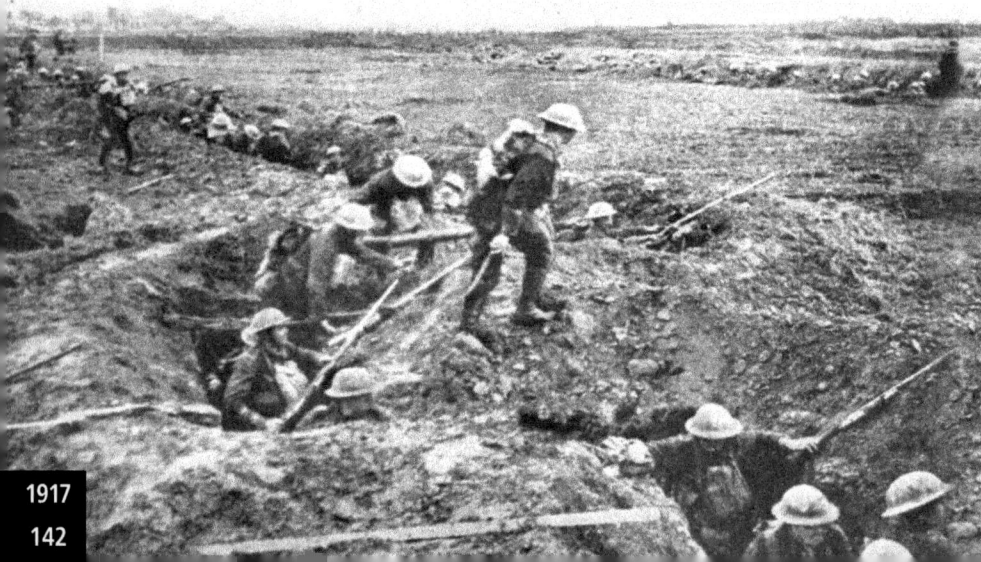

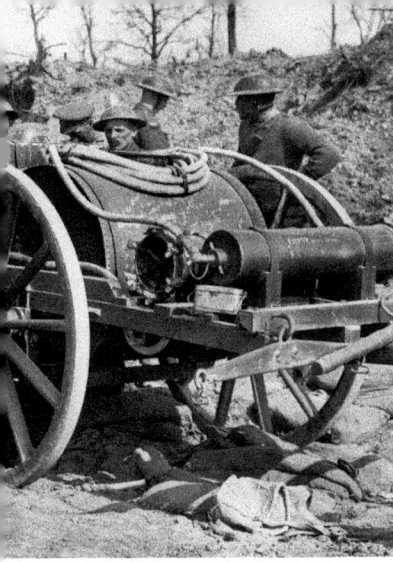 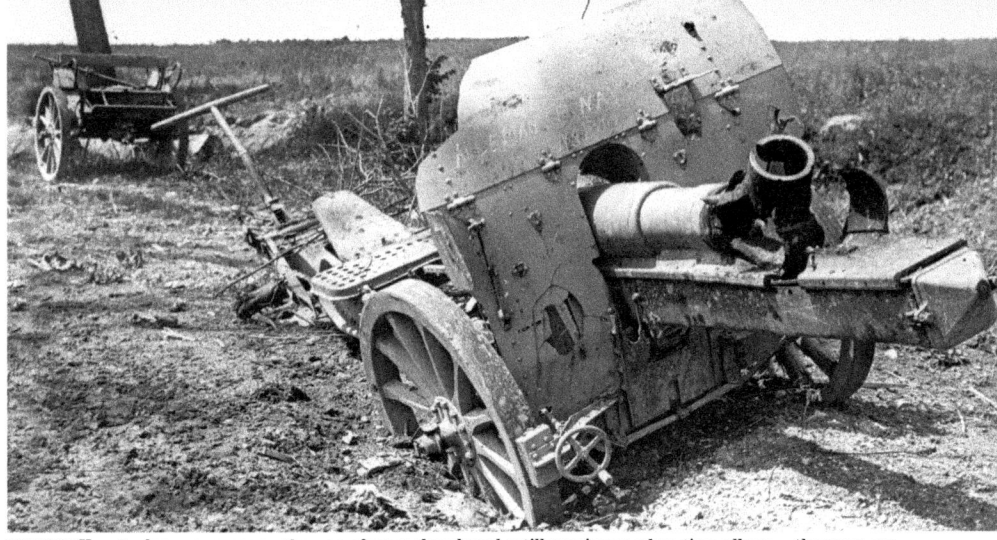

17GW085 Precious fluid: men filling up their water bottles near Wancourt, 29 April 1917.

17GW268 How to deny your enemy the use of your abandoned artillery pieces: when time allows – the guns are 'spiked'. This German 5.9 cm weapon, abandoned at Gavrelle, has had a shell placed in the muzzle by its fleeing crew and another shell in the breech; the gun was then triggered by a very, very long lanyard.

17GW271 A low flying aircraft of the RFC photographs a shell bursting in Oppy Wood – 1917.

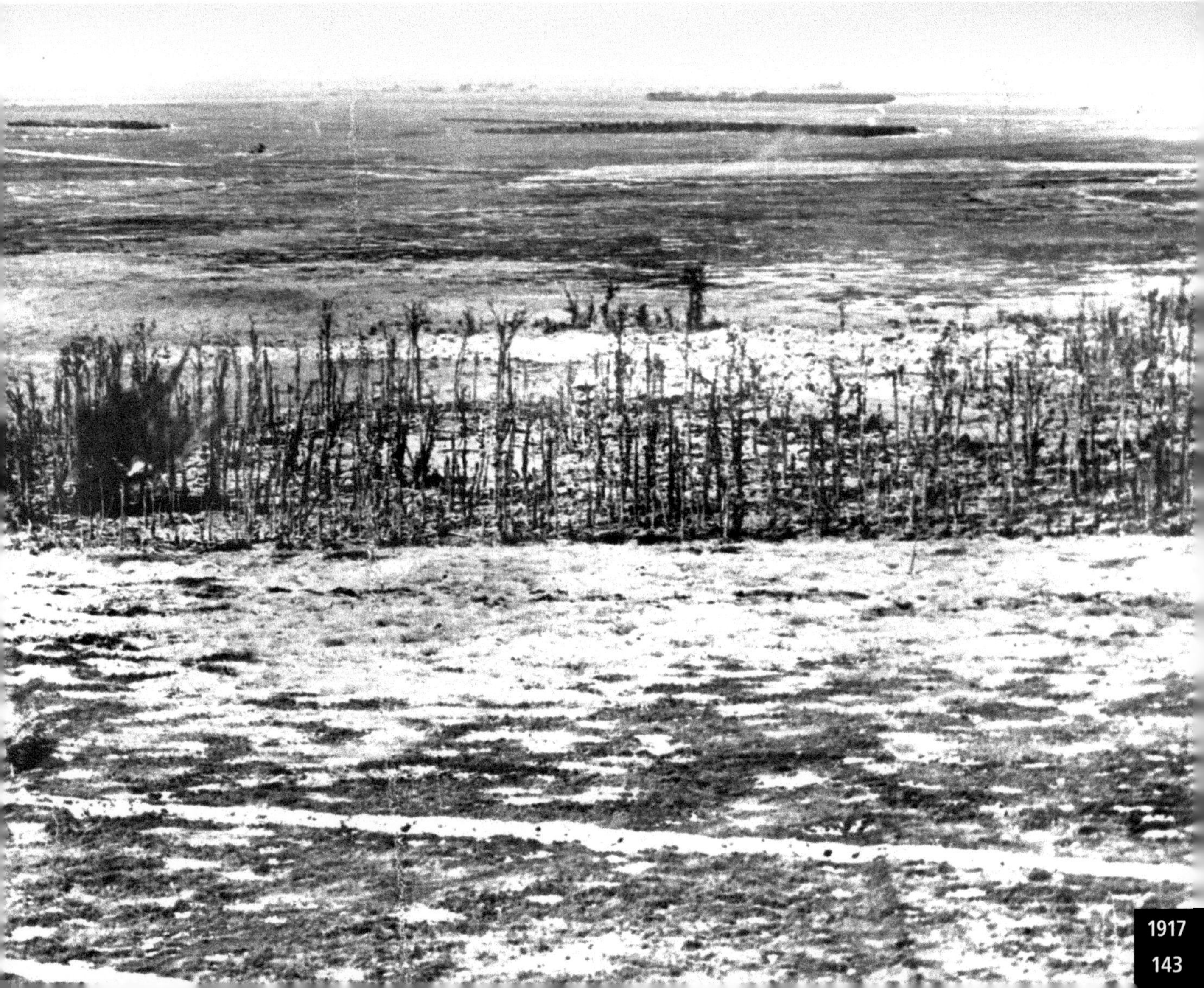

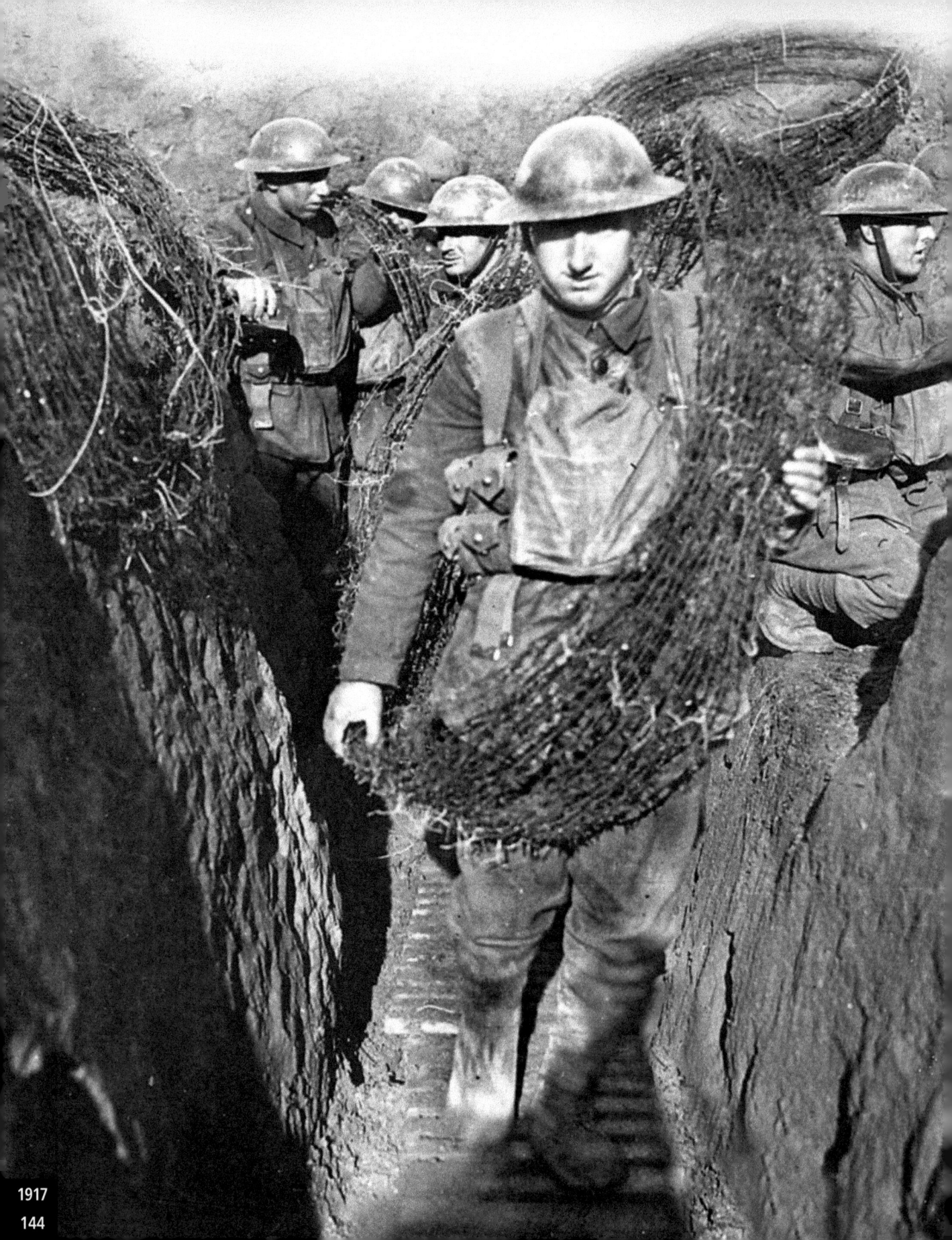

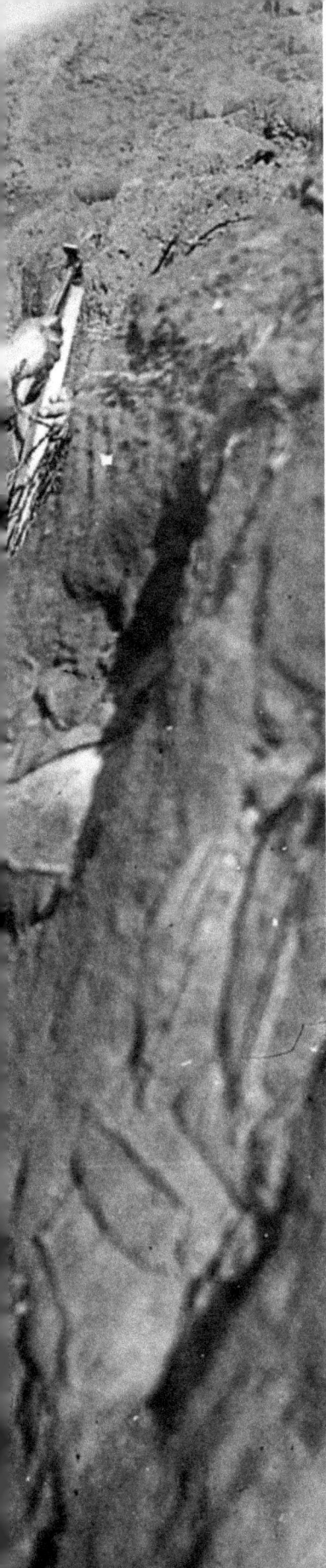

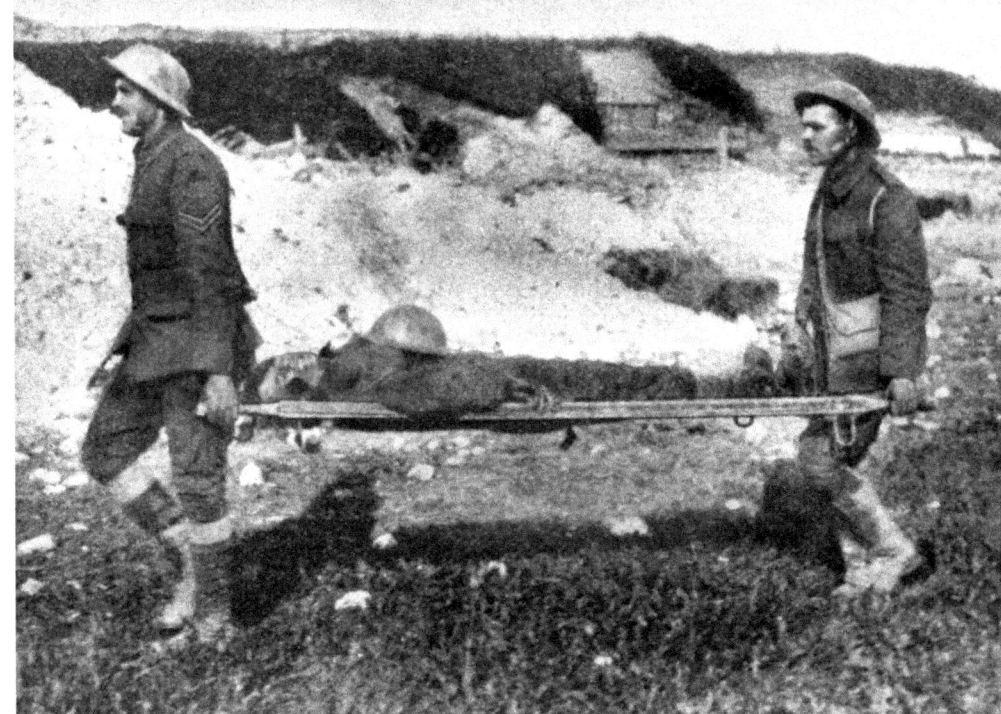

17GW275 Two men of Royal Field Artillery, 29th Division, carrying a comrade to safety during the fighting near Gavrelle.

17GW273 A wiring party of the York and Lancaster Regiment in the trenches near Gavrelle. The men do not appear to be wearing gloves to handle the barbed wire coils.

17GW274 Six smiling faces from the 10th Royal Fusiliers peering from a captured dug-out at Feuchy crossroads. The village had been in German hands for three years. Morale was high among the British as the initial territory gains made at Arras served to eclipse the disasters and disappointments of 1916.

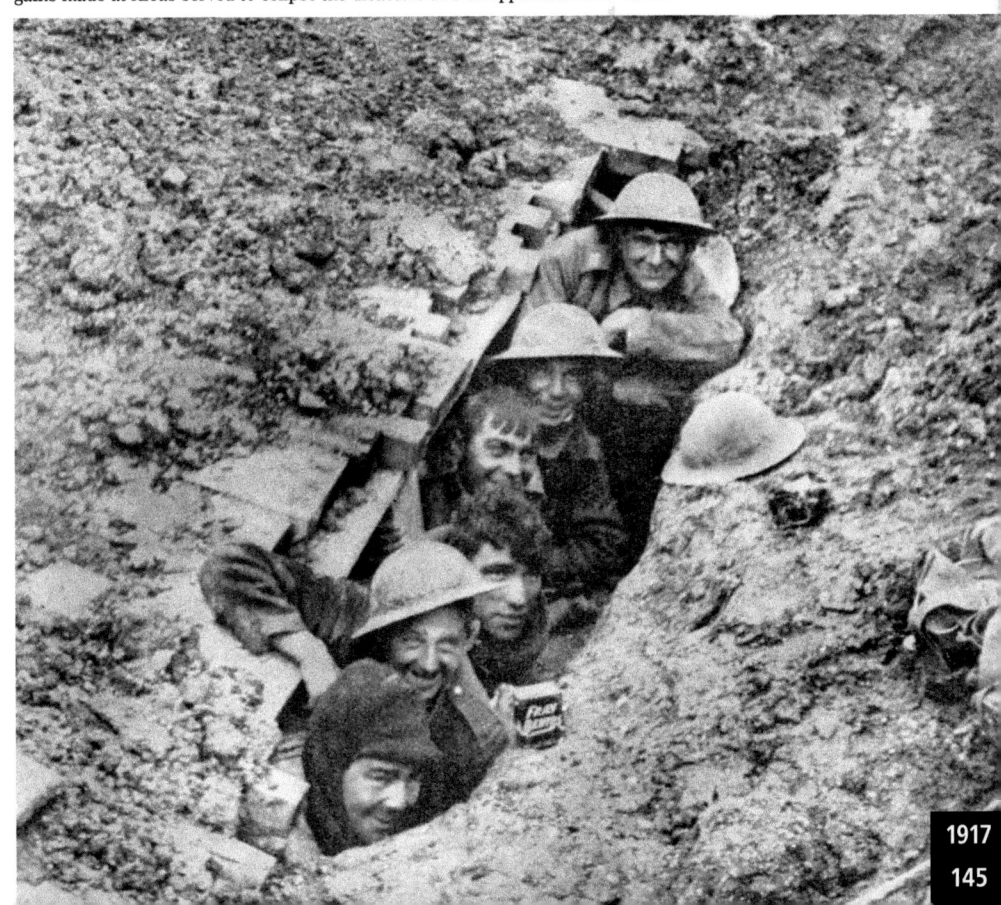

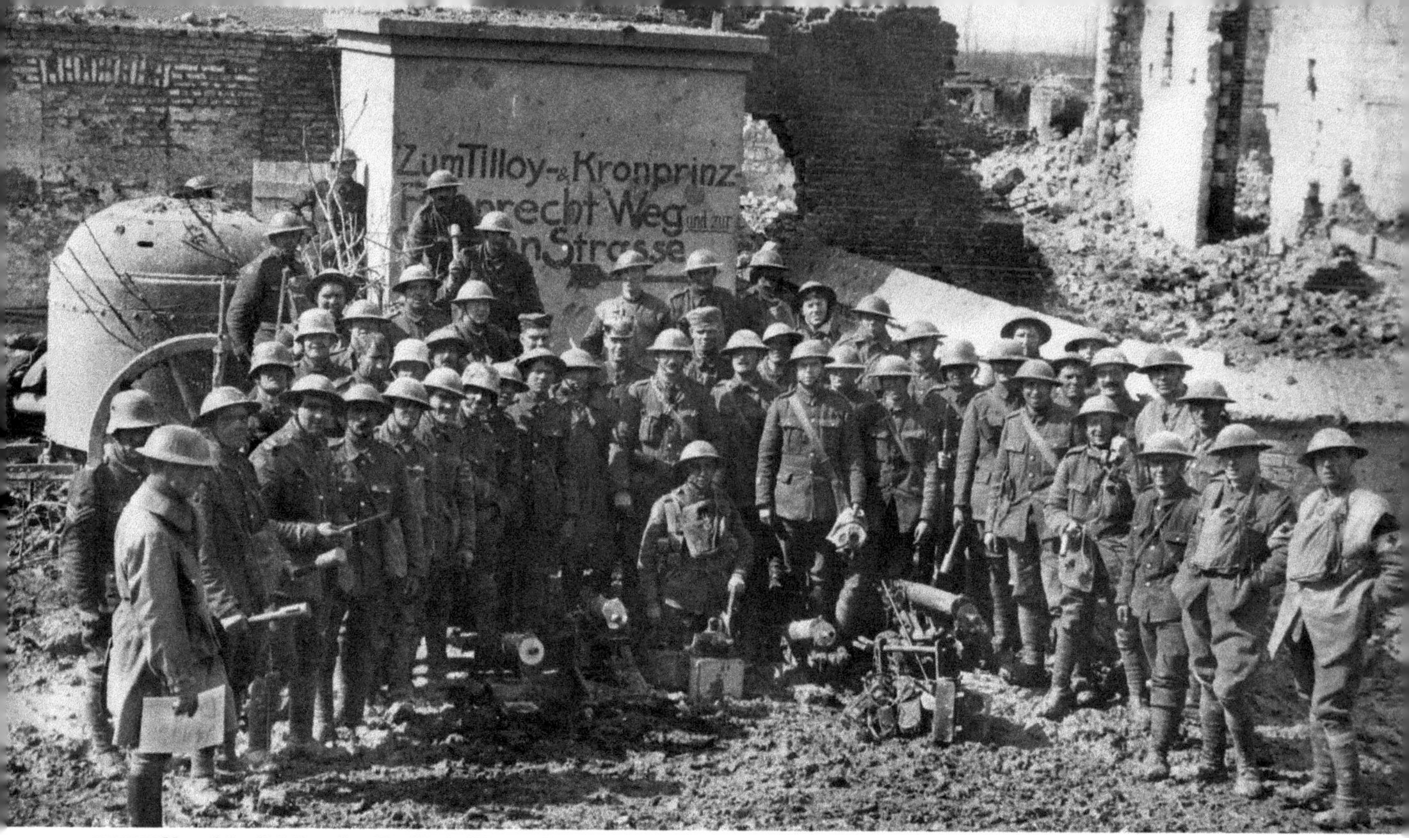

17GW276 Men of the 12th Battalion The King's (Liverpool) Regiment showing many trophies taken during the Arras fighting. Behind them is a German steel, mobile, observation post. The German wording painted on the French memorial, which is serving as a signpost, reads: *For Tilloy- and Crown Prince Rupprecht Way and South Street.*

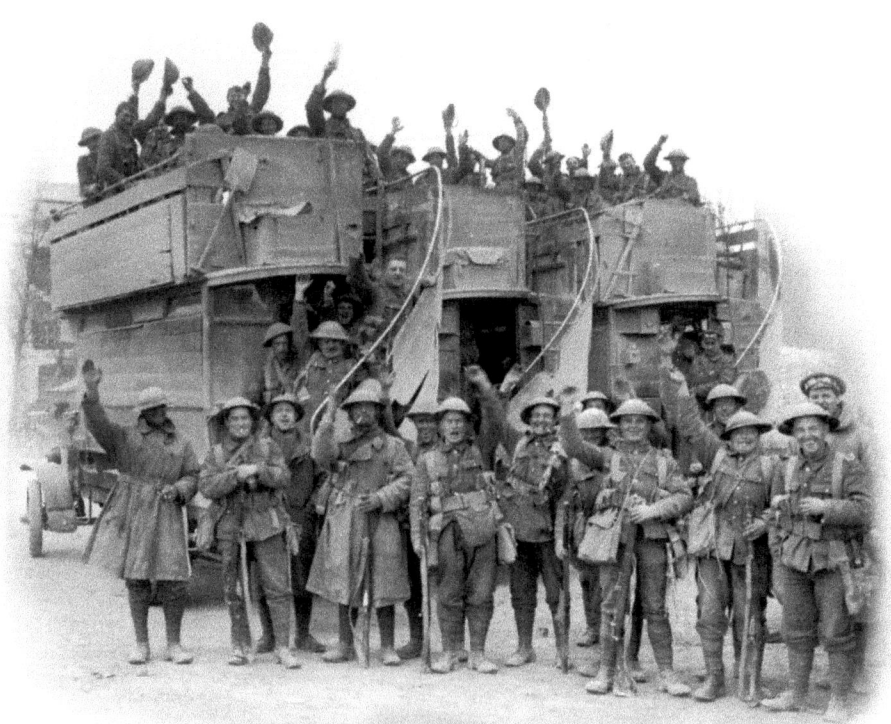

17GW272 British infantry about to board double-decker buses taking them to a rest camp following their successful capture of Monchy-le-Preux, wave cheerfully for the camera.

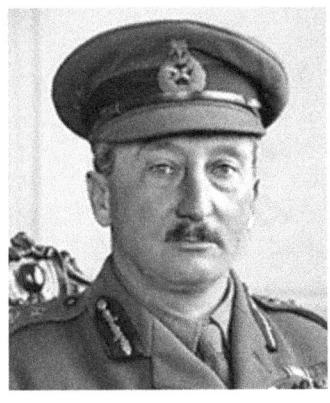

General Sir Hubert Gough commander Fifth Army

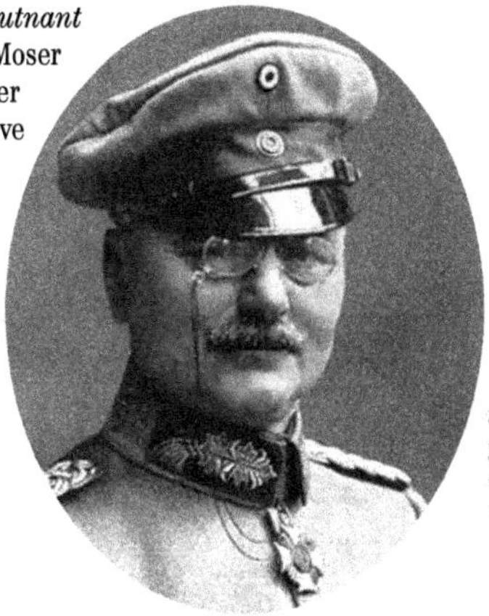

Generalleutnant Otto von Moser commander XIV Reserve Corps

Bullecourt 11 April 1917

South of Arras it was planned that two divisions, the British 62nd Division and the Australian 4th Division, would attack either side of Bullecourt village and drive the Germans out of their fortified positions.

The attack took place on 11 April with eleven tanks supporting the infantry. The 4th Division briefly occupied sections of German trenches but were forced to retreat with heavy losses. The Germans captured two of the tanks.

A spoiling operation, launched by the Germans at Lagnicourt, came four days later. *Generalleutnant* Otto von Moser, commanding *XIV Reserve Corps*, had noted that the 1st Australian Division was holding an extended frontage of 13,000 yards and he acted accordingly. The objective of von Moser's counter attack was to drive back the advanced posts, destroy supplies and guns and then fall back to the Hindenburg defences. Attacking with twenty-three battalions, the Germans penetrated the front line at the junction of the 1st and 2nd Australian divisions and occupied the village of Lagnicourt. Counter-attacks by two Australian battalions restored the front line. The action ended with the Australians suffering 1,010 casualties, against 2,313 German.

Bullecourt 3 to 17 May 1917

After the initial attack had failed to penetrate the German lines, preparations for a second attempt got underway. British artillery began a bombardment of the village. The 2nd Australian Division attacked east of Bullecourt village, intending to drive through the Hindenburg Line to take Hendecourt-lès-Cagnicourt. The British from the 62nd (2nd West Riding) Division attacked Bullecourt. It was eventually taken by the British 7th Division and then held by the 62nd Division. When the offensive was called off on 17 May, few of the objectives had been achieved. The Australians were in possession of much of the German trench system between Bullecourt and Riencourt-lès-Cagnicourt, but had been unable to capture Hendecourt. To the west, British troops had pushed the Germans out of Bullecourt but incurred heavy losses. They had been unable to reach Hendecourt.

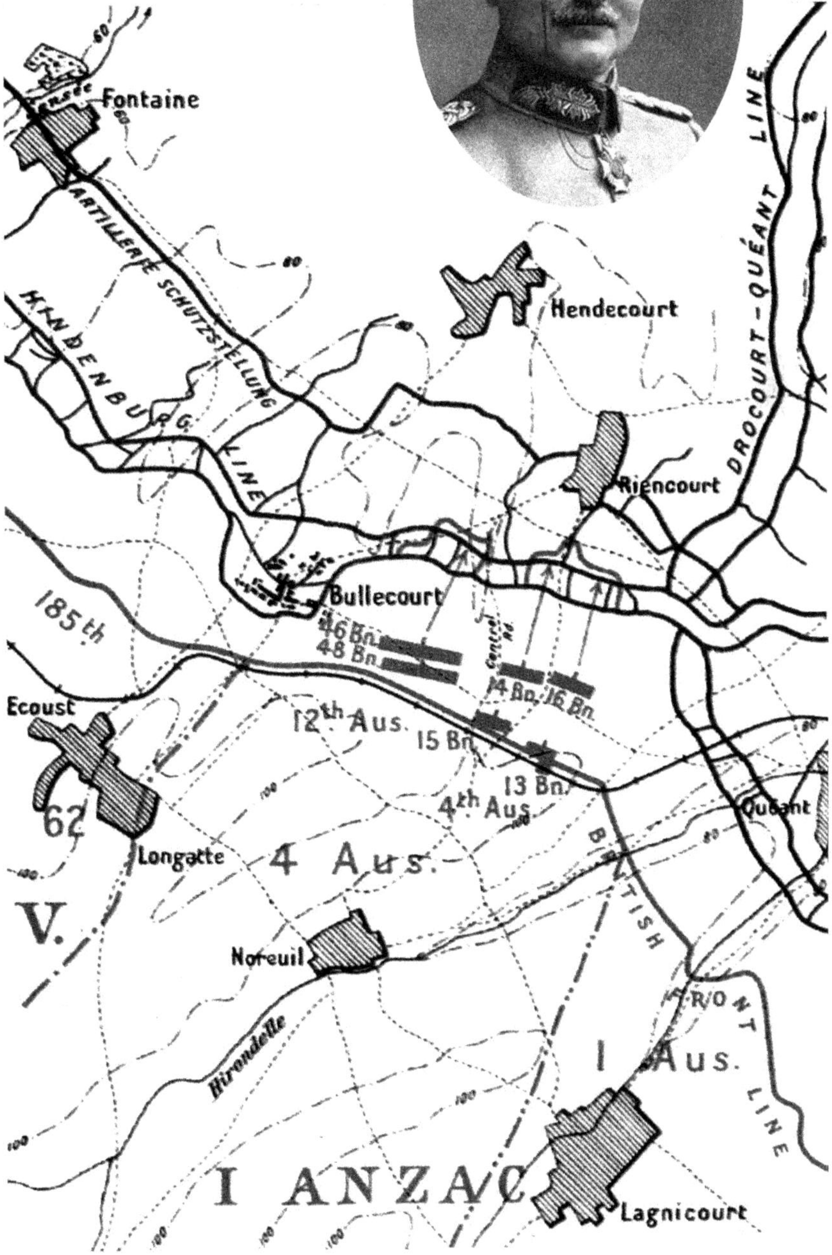

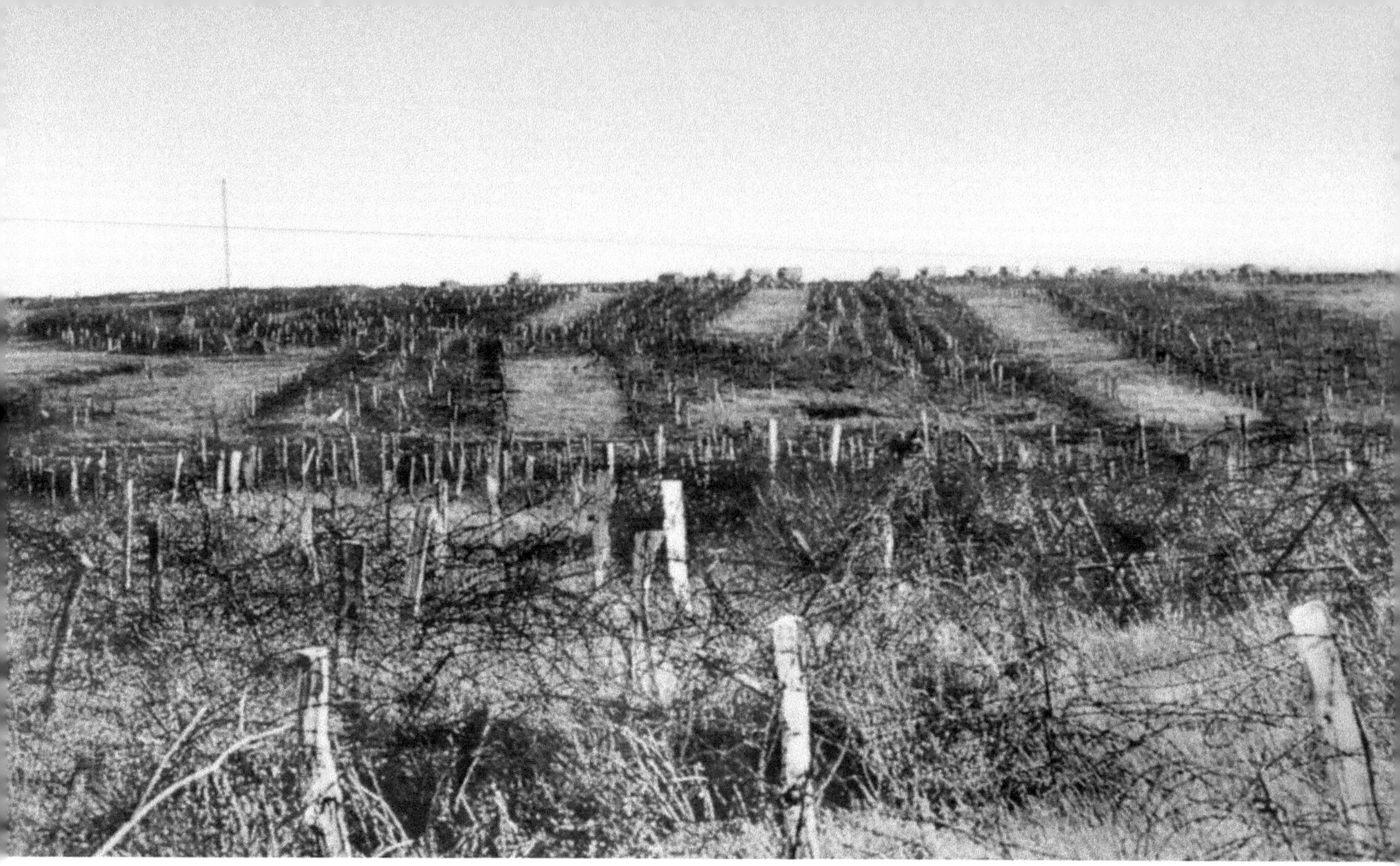

17GW282 Barbed wire entanglements of the Hindenburg Line constructed by the Germans; these were not put down in a haphazard fashion, but were carefully designed to funnel attacking infantry into fire zones, where they could be cut to pieces.

17GW284 British 9.2-inch howitzers resited to support the attacks at Bullecourt, follwing the relative successes north and northeast of Arras.

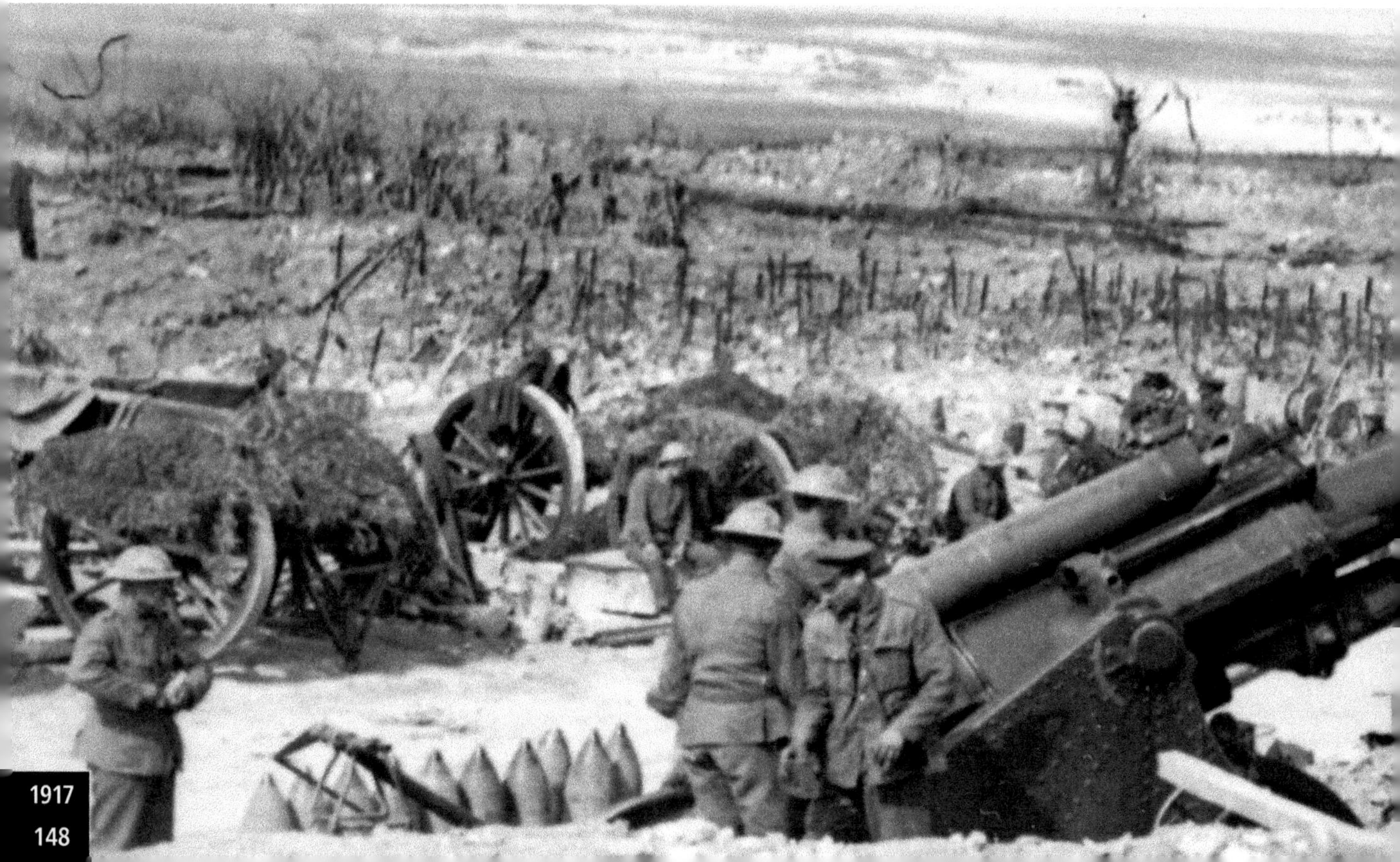

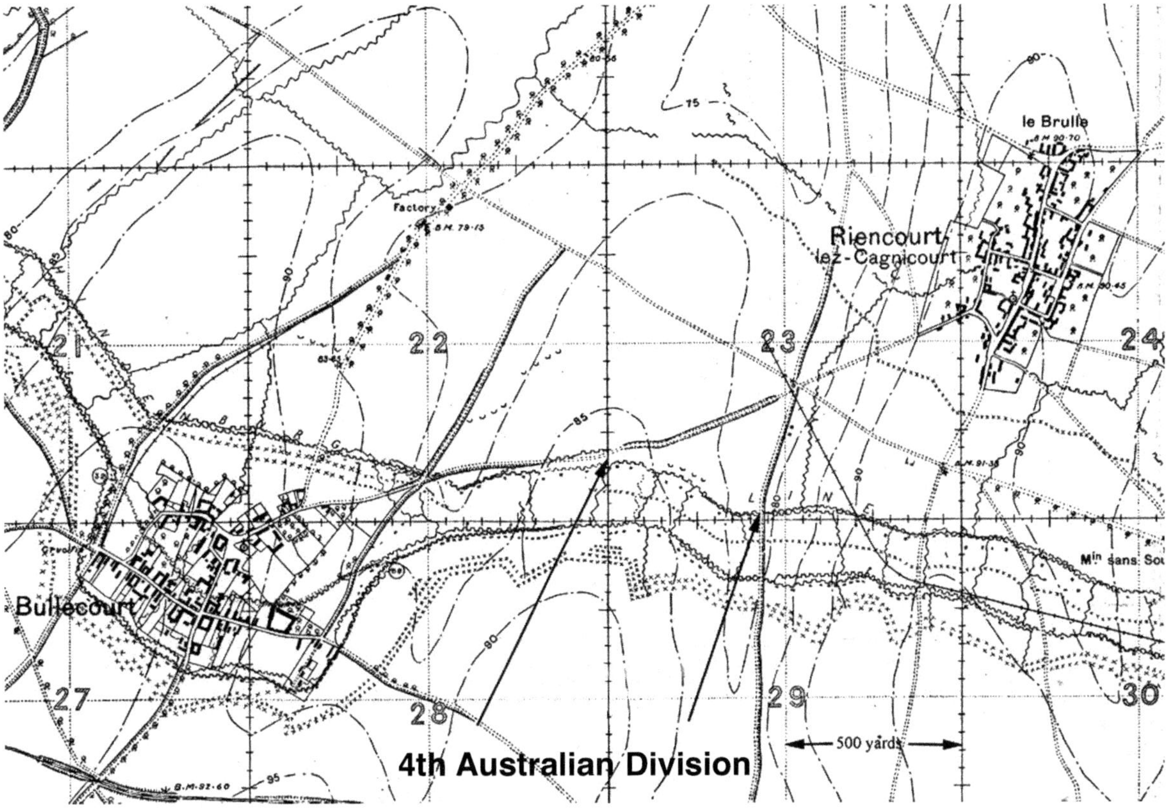

4th Australian Division

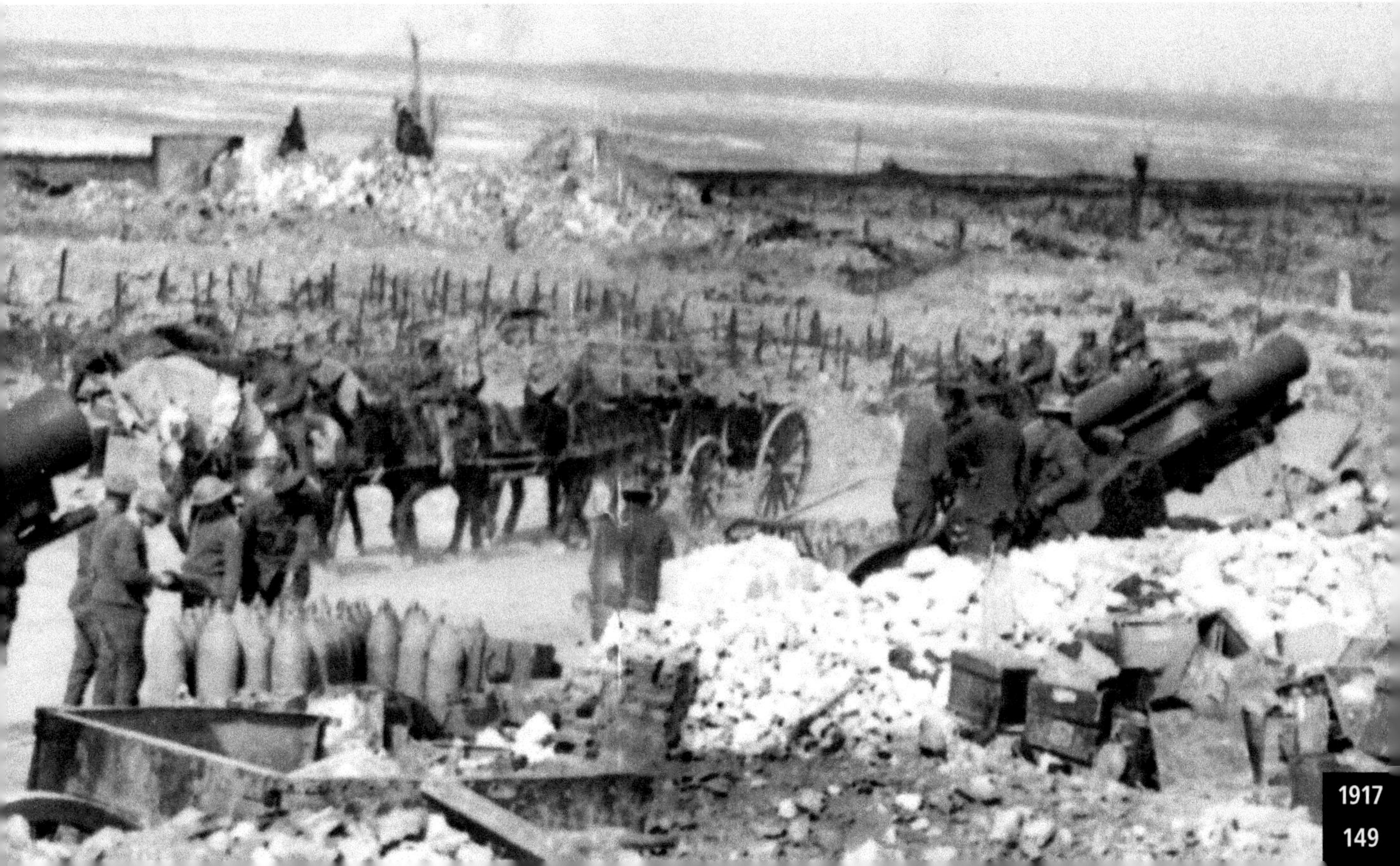

← 500 yards →

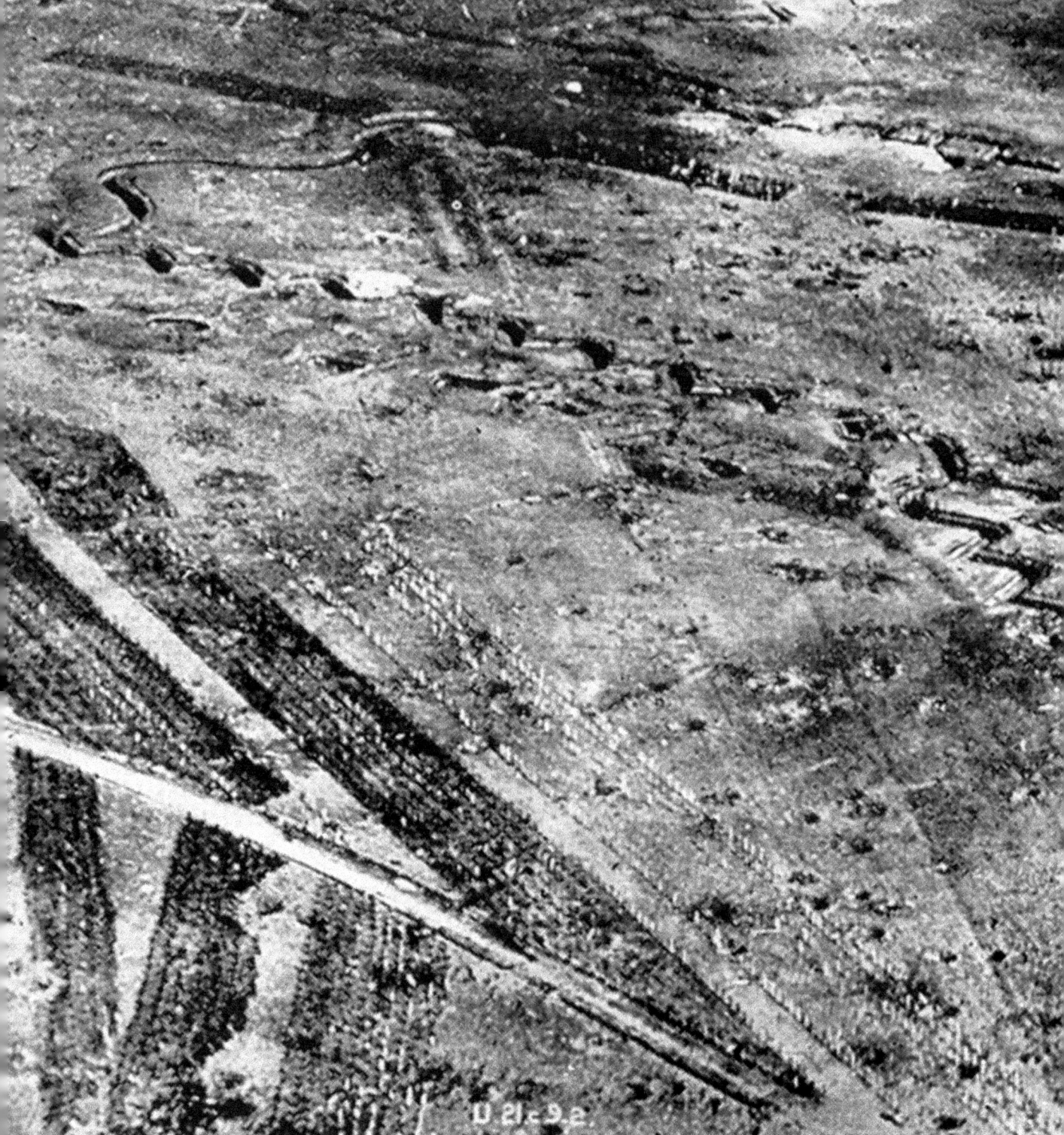
17GW280 A section of the Hindenburg Line in front of Bullecourt.

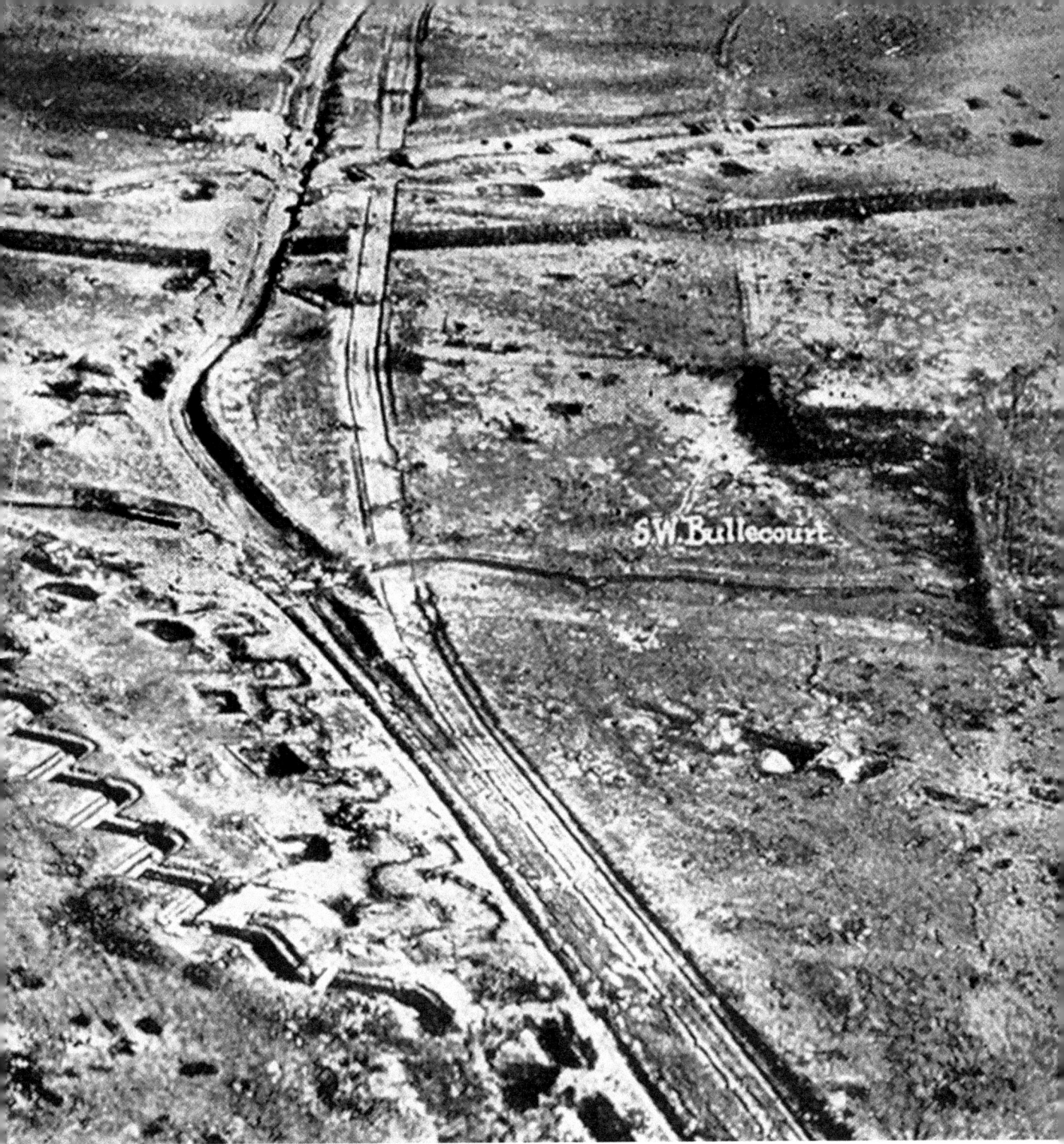

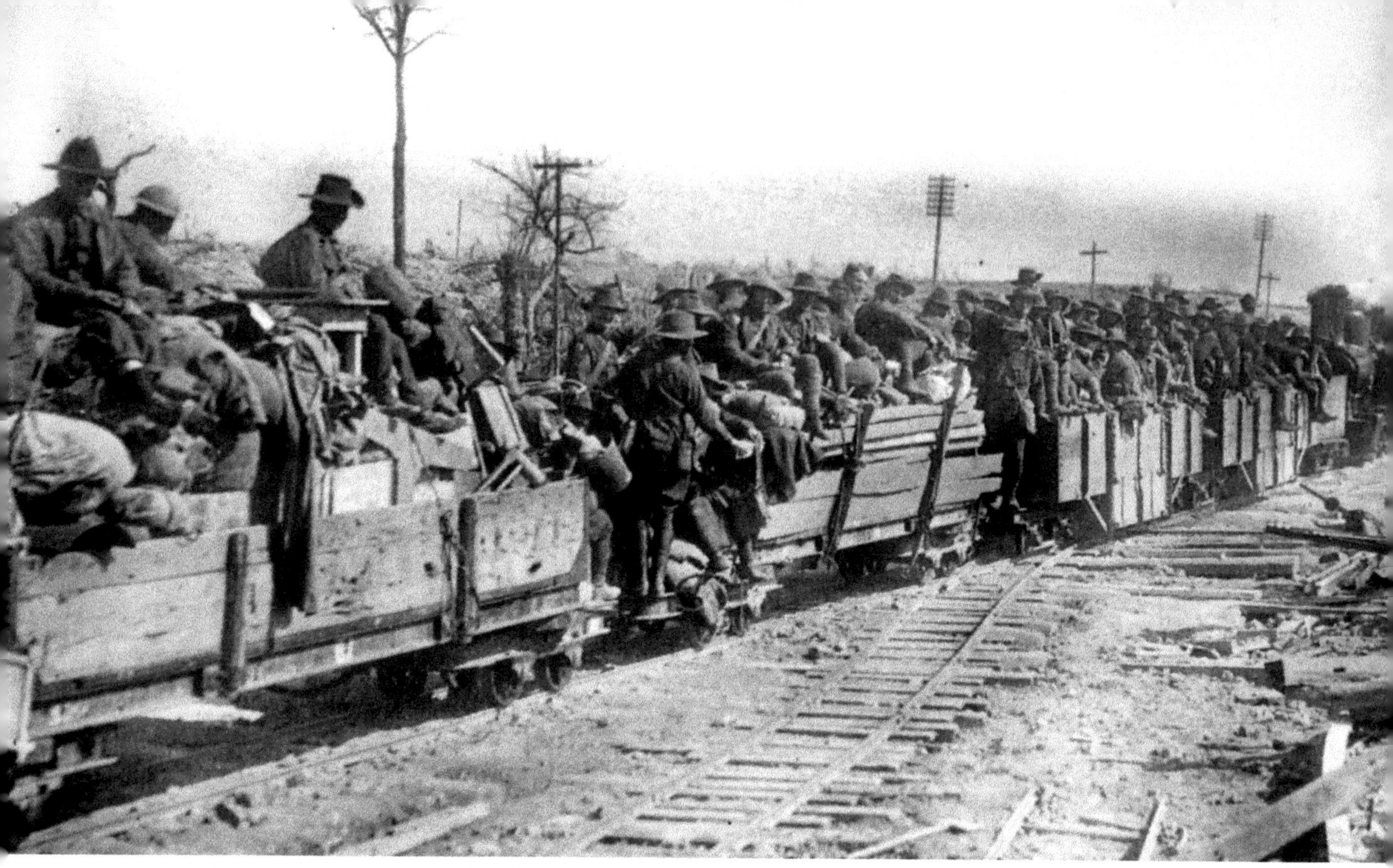

17GW283 Australian infantry moving up with their equipment and trench building stores on a narrow gauge track.

17GW282 Australian gunners bringing up an 18-pounder before the battle.

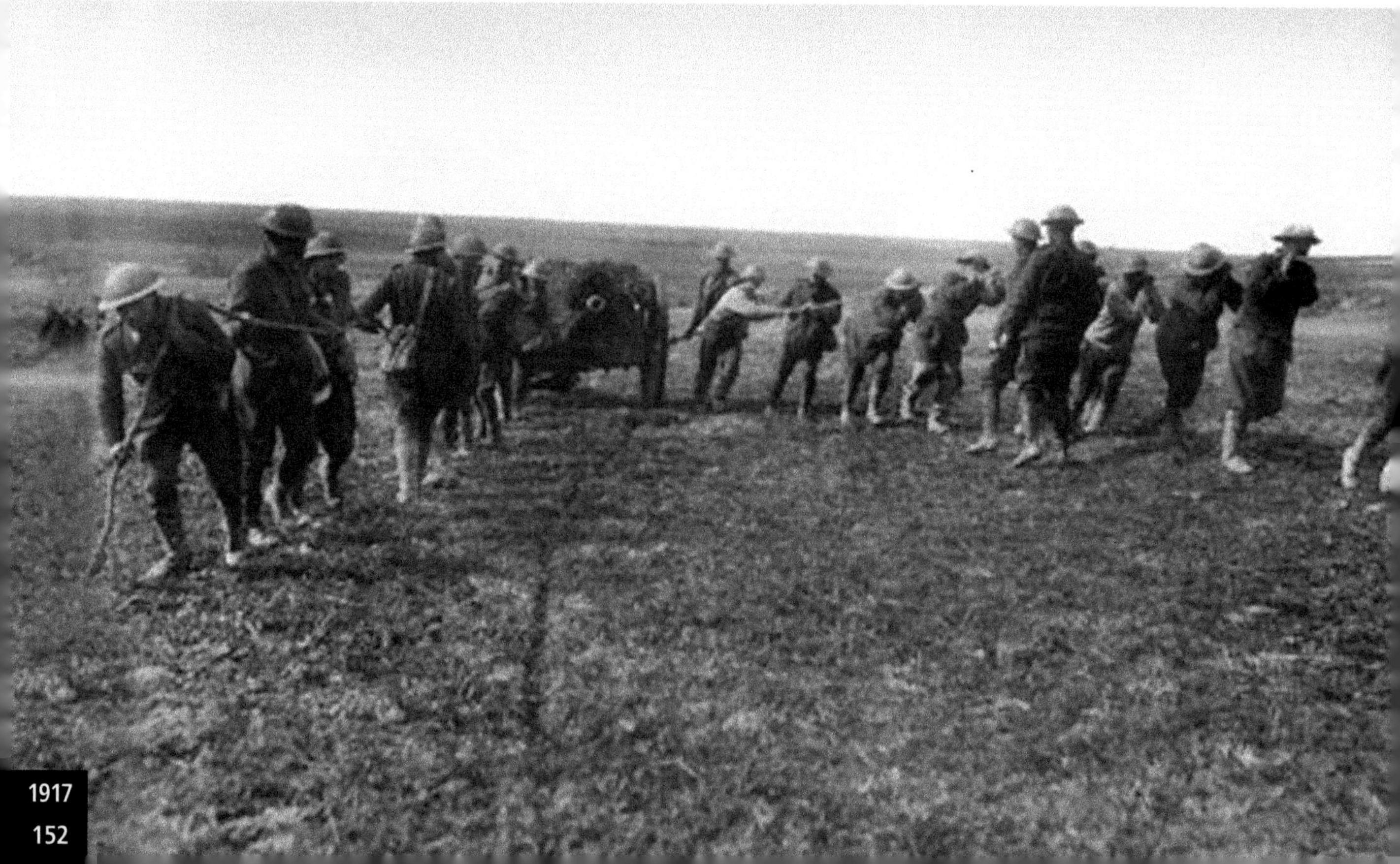

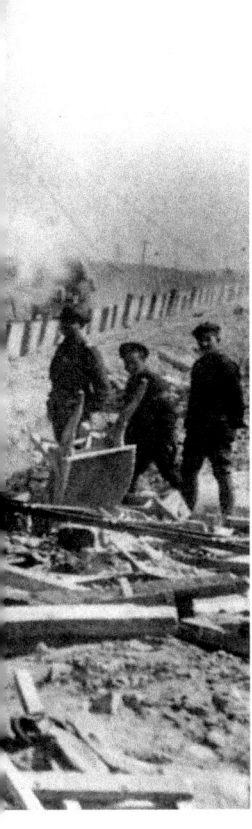
17GW293 Australian infantry on the eve of the attack on Bullecourt.

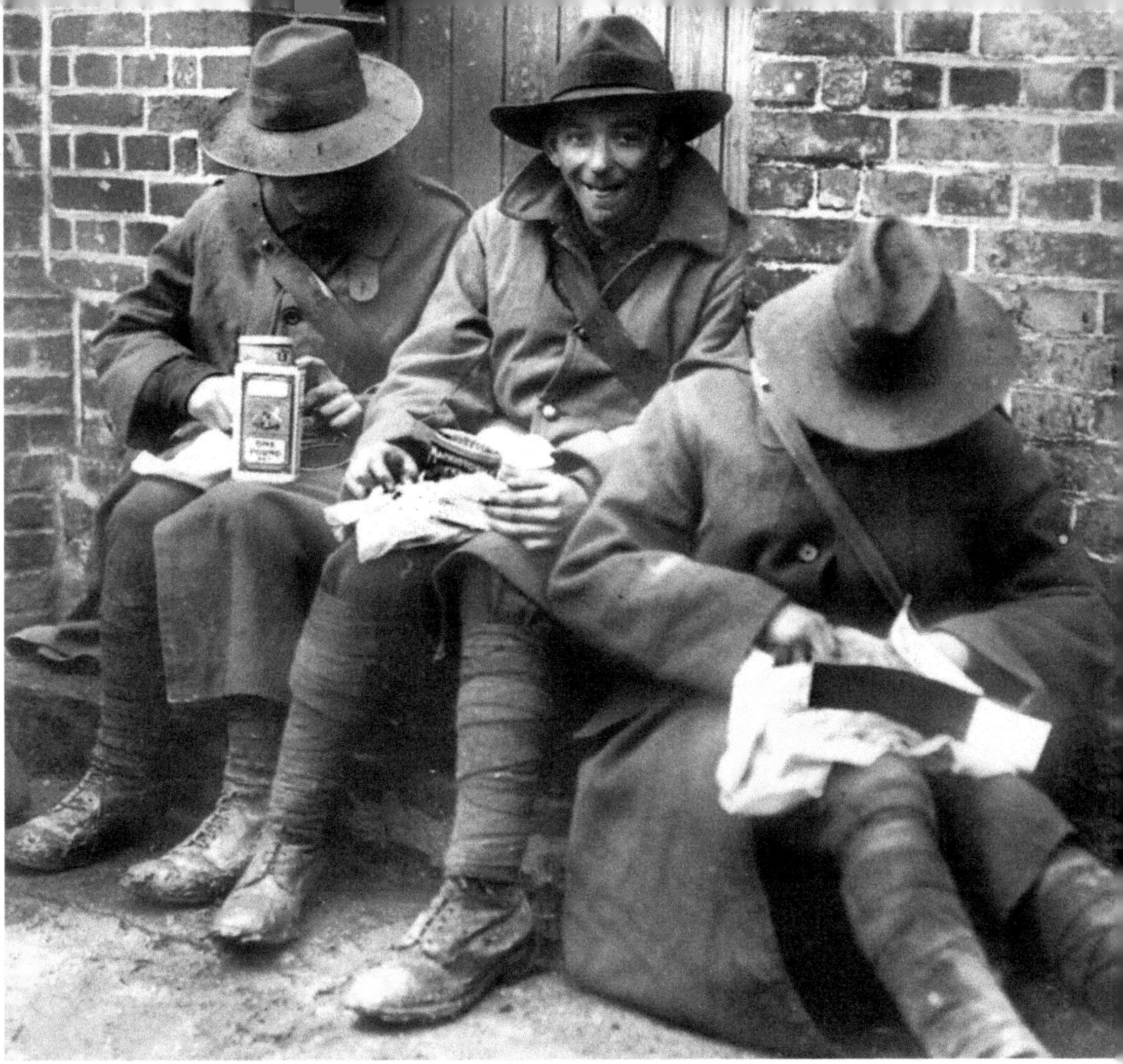

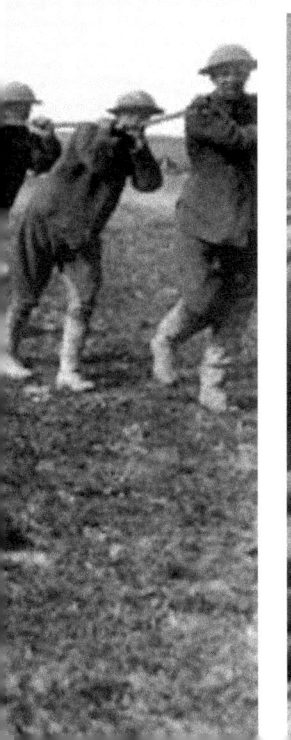

17GW289 An Australian 18-pounder gun crew before the attack on Bullecourt.

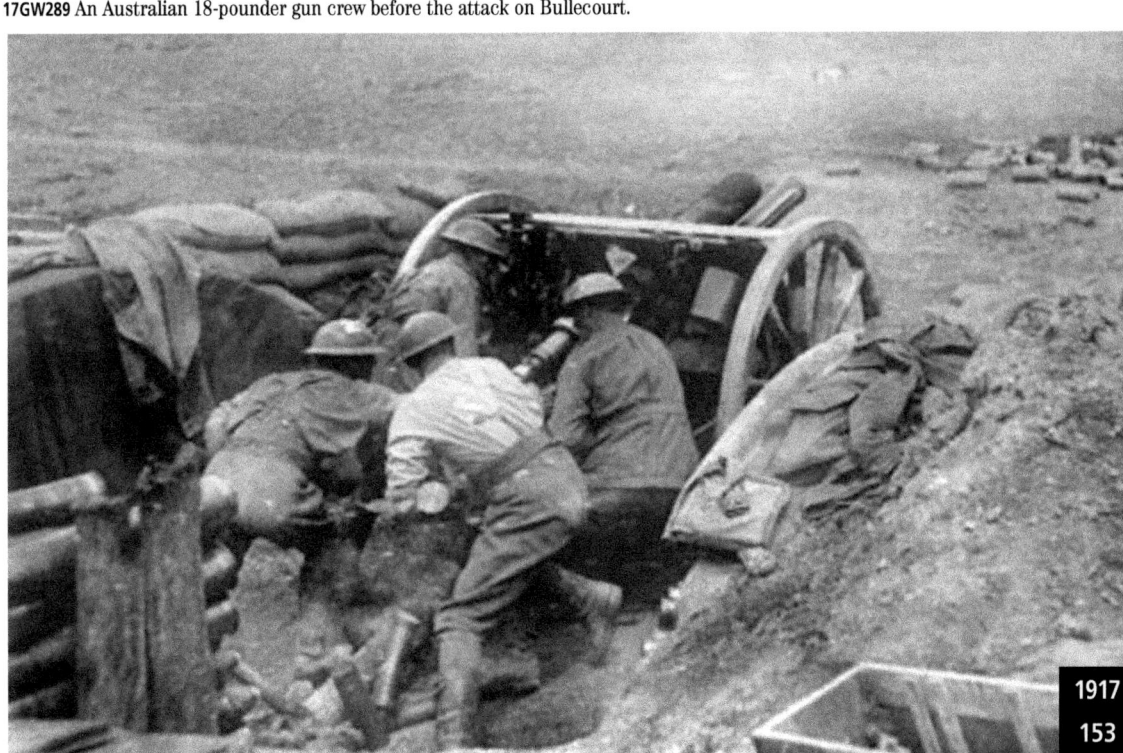

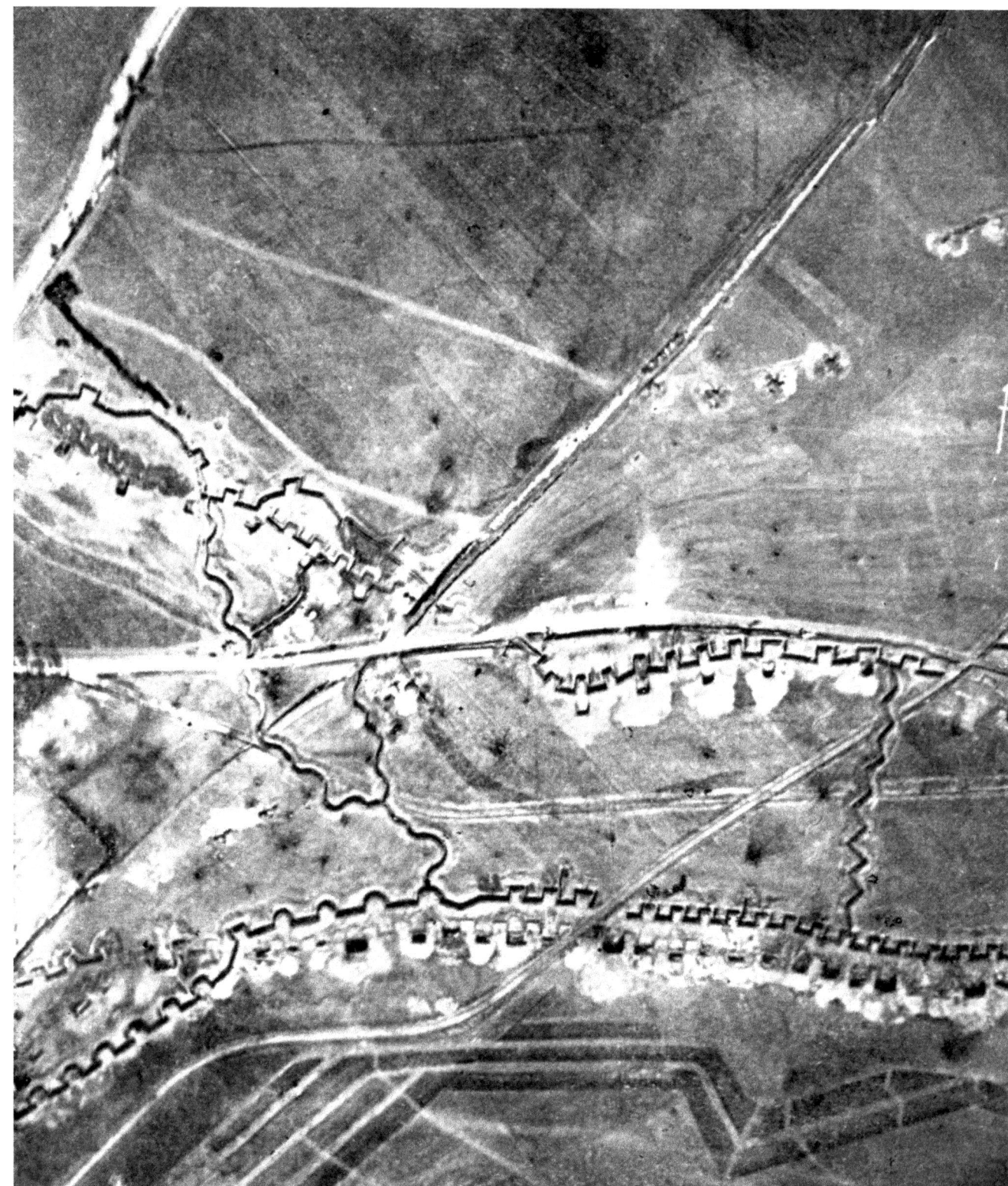

17GW300 Aerial photograph of the Hindenburg Line east of Bullecourt, taken on 3 April 1917. This sector was attacked by 12 Brigade, Australian 4th Division, on 11 April with the support of tanks (for the first time) and no artillery support. The tanks proved unreliable and insufficiently protected against small arms fire. The area shown was captured but resupply and reinforcement was made too difficult by German artillery and heavy machine-gun fire.

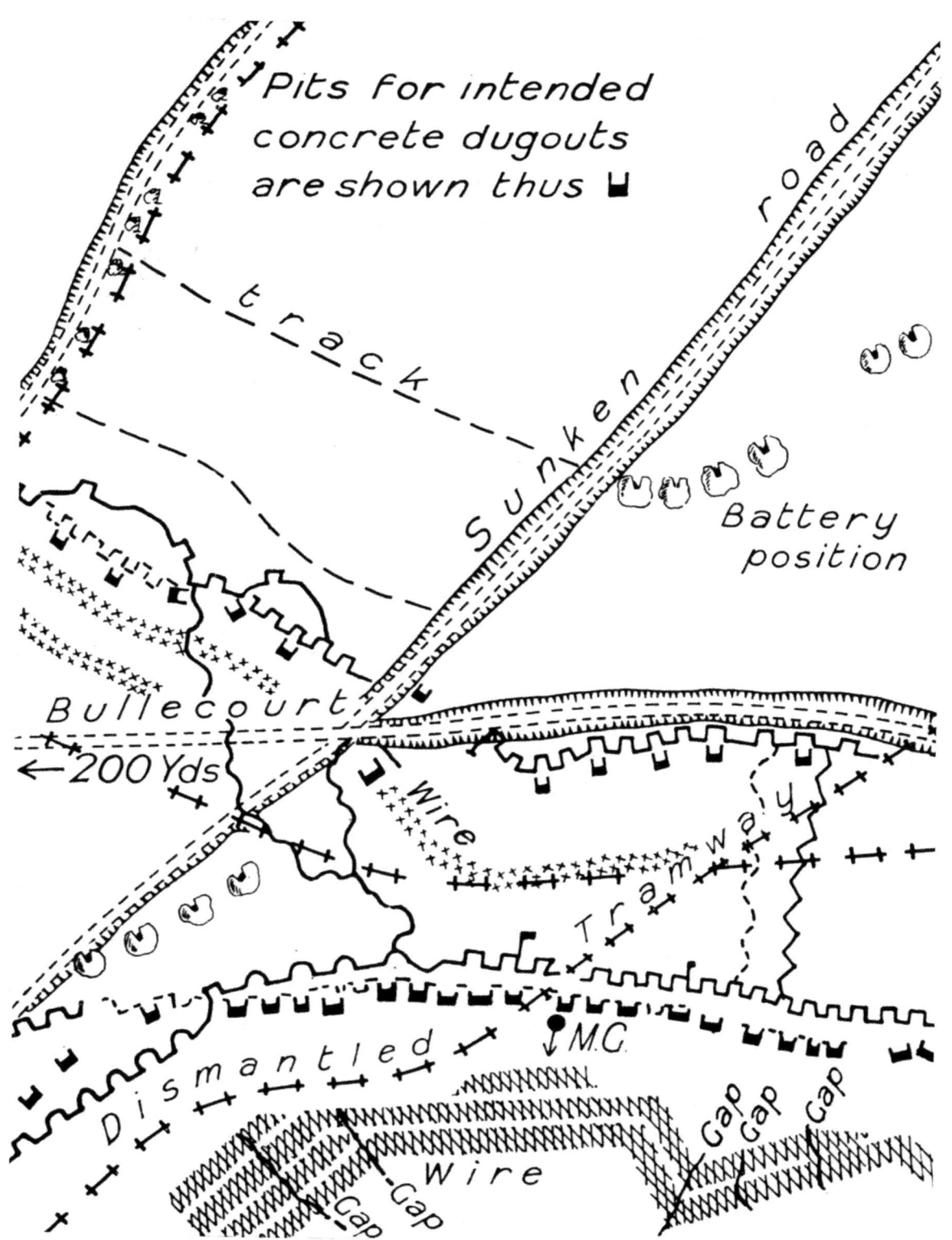

17GW301 Identification and interpretation of the photograph: gaps in the wire have been highlighted, along with one machine gun that was sited to bring down fire on infantry using the gaps.

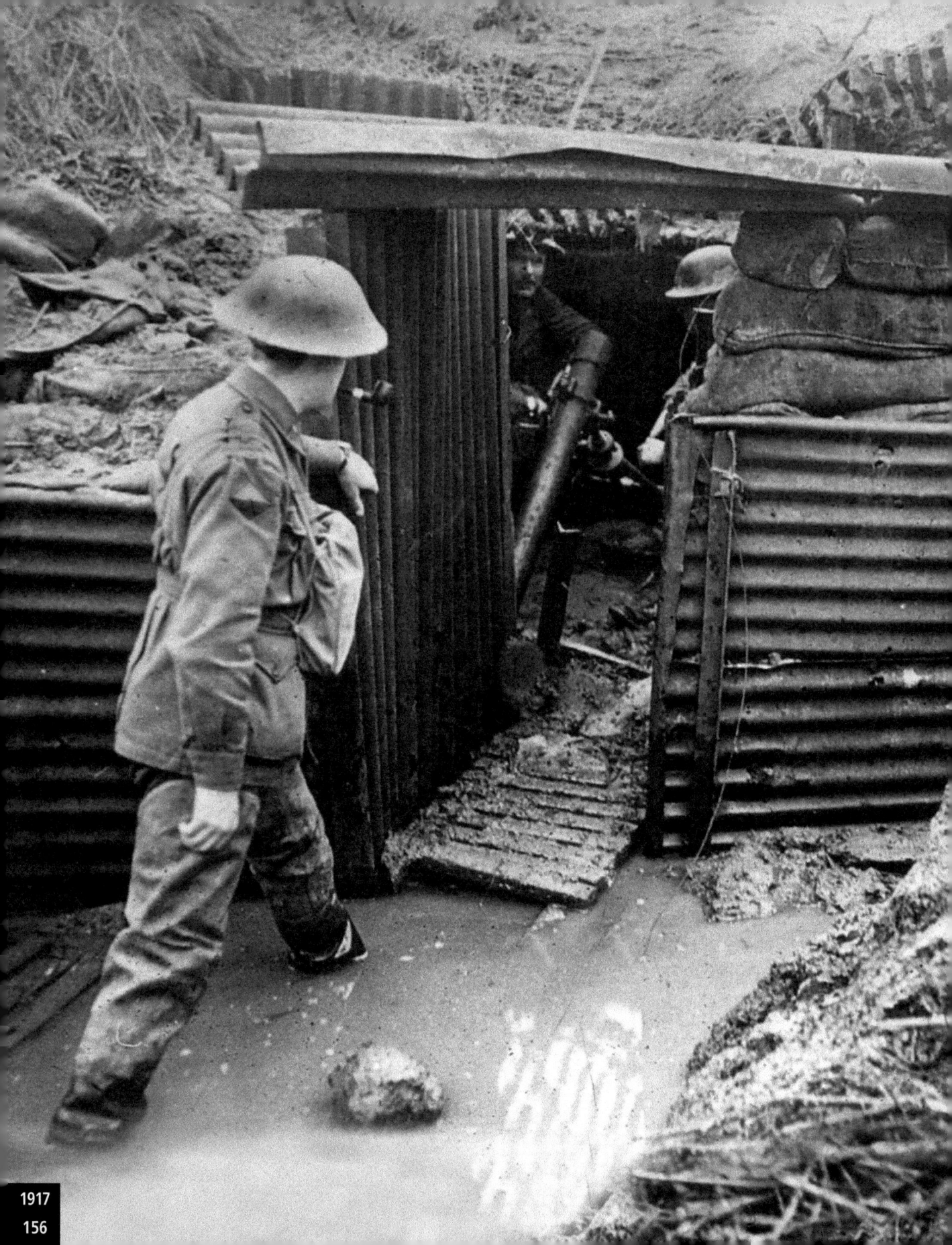

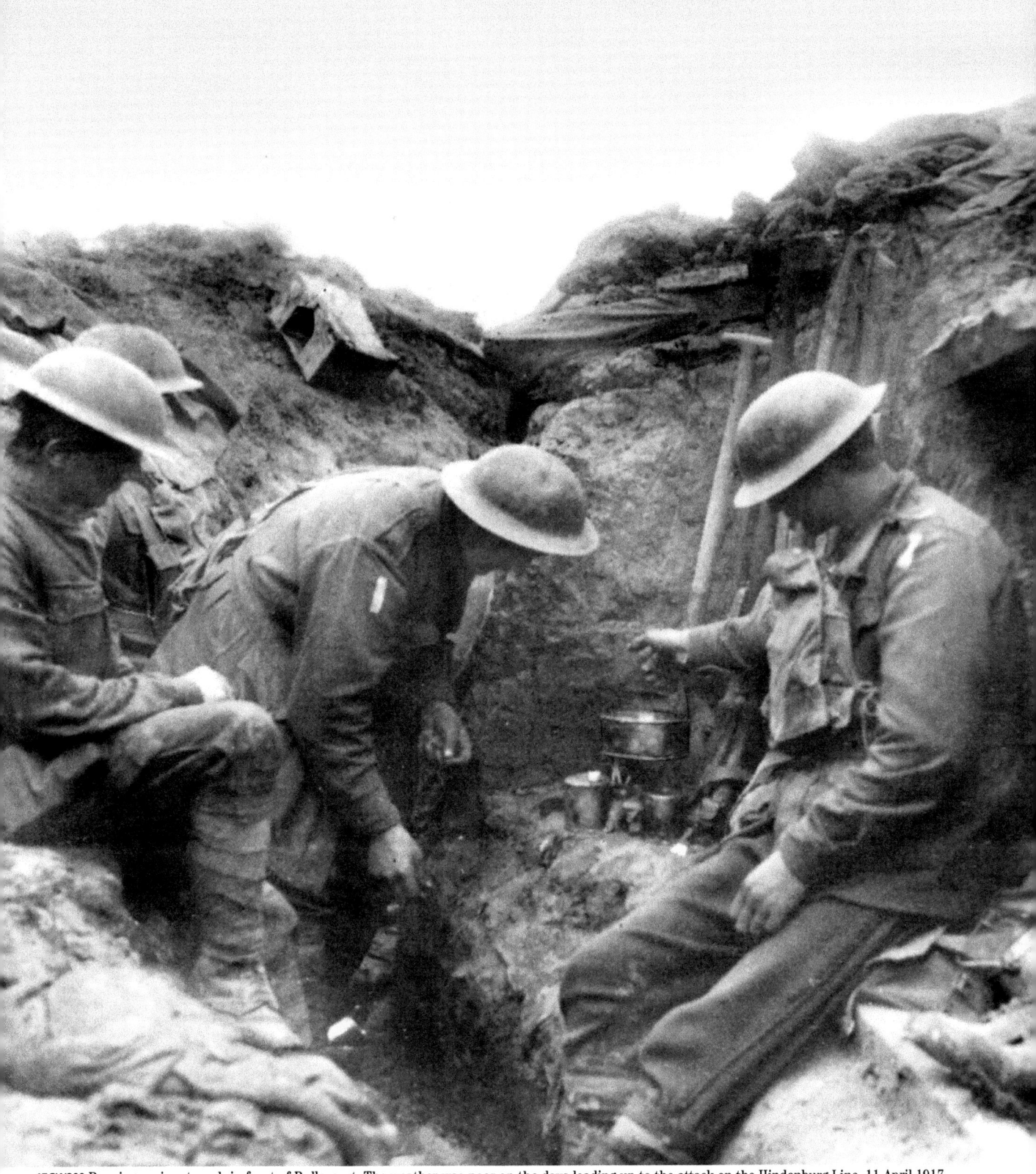

17GW299 Brewing up in a trench in front of Bullecourt. The weather was poor on the days leading up to the attack on the Hindenburg Line, 11 April 1917.

17GW295 An Australian infantry officer checking a mortar position.

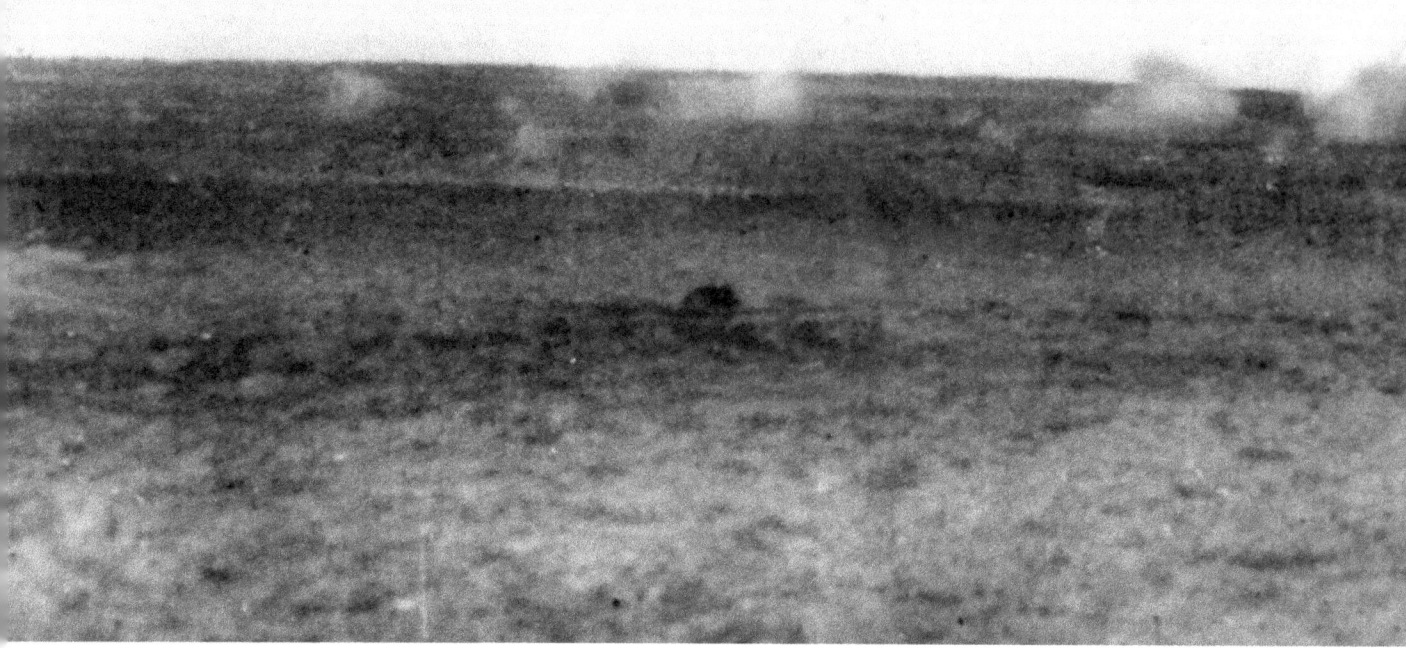

17GW298 German shells bursting in front of their barbed wire. The Australians advanced across this flat area without support from their own artillery and their main objectives were not taken; they did, however, make lodgements in the German first and second lines.

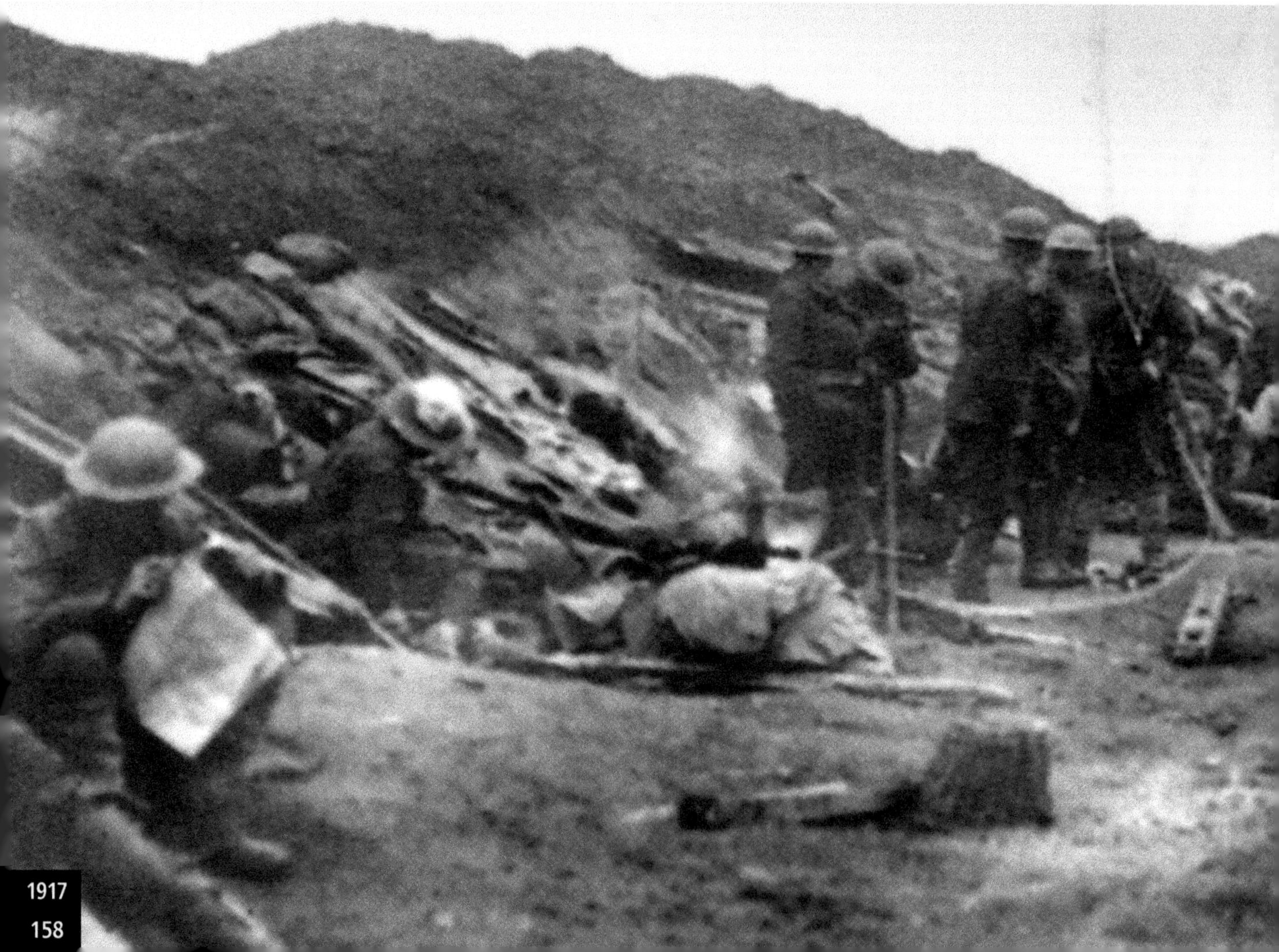

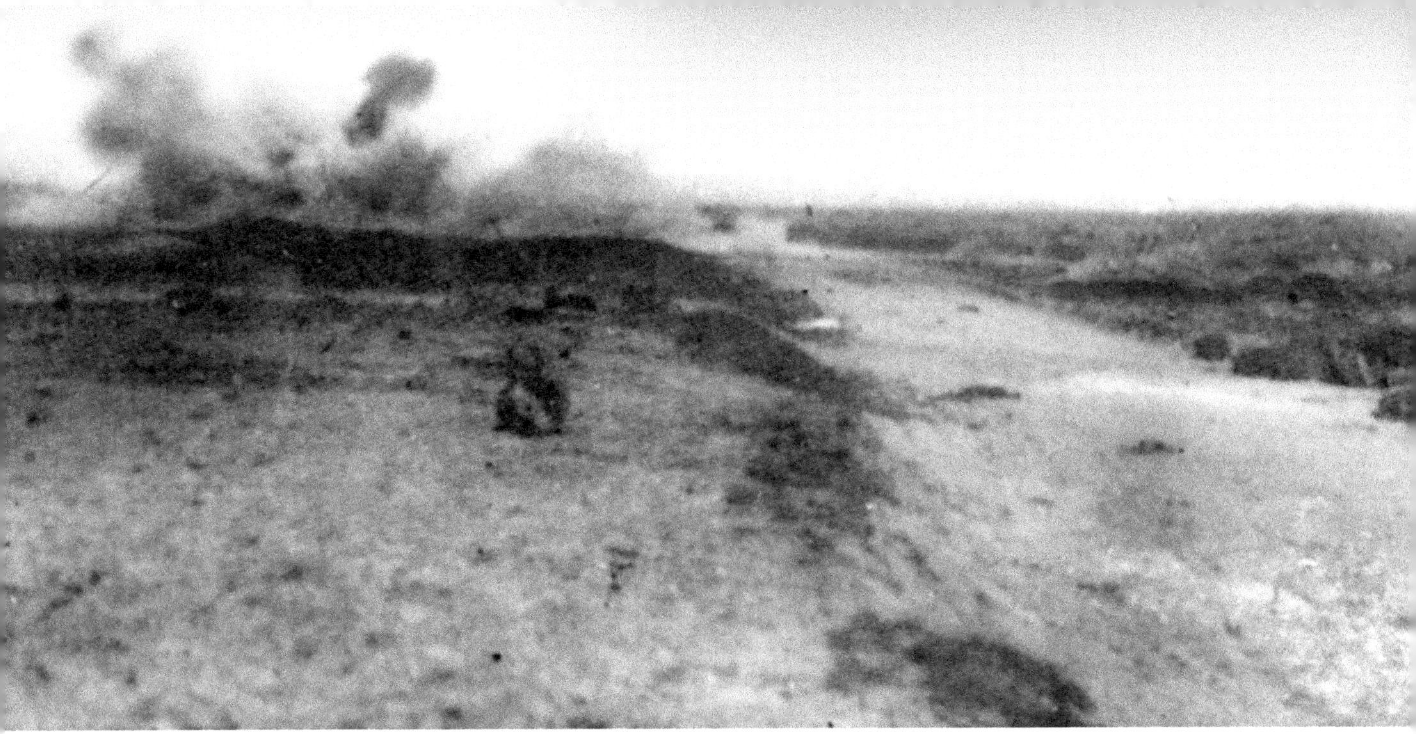

17GW297 Australian infantry in the captured German lines, sheltering in the dismantled tramway.

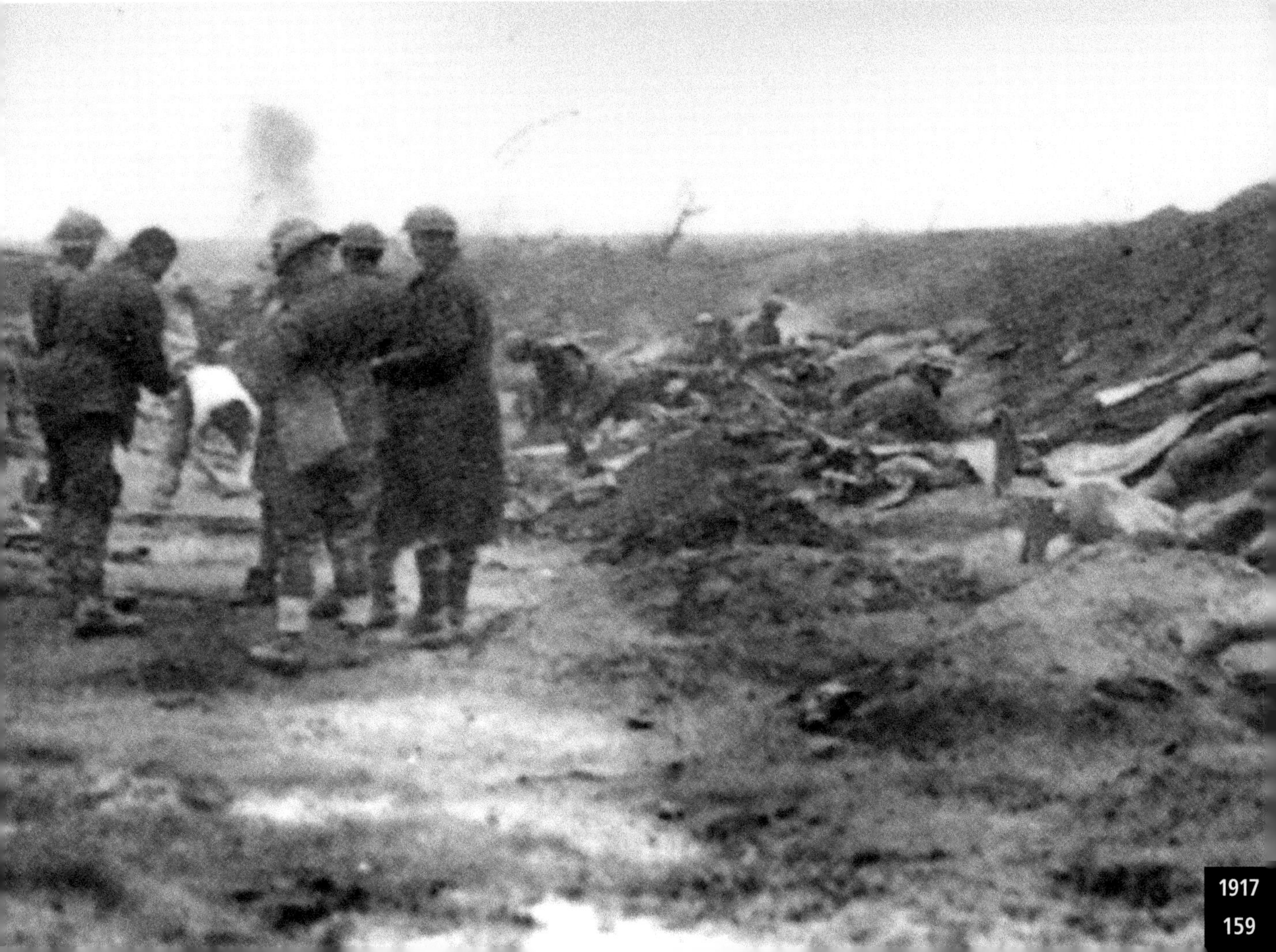

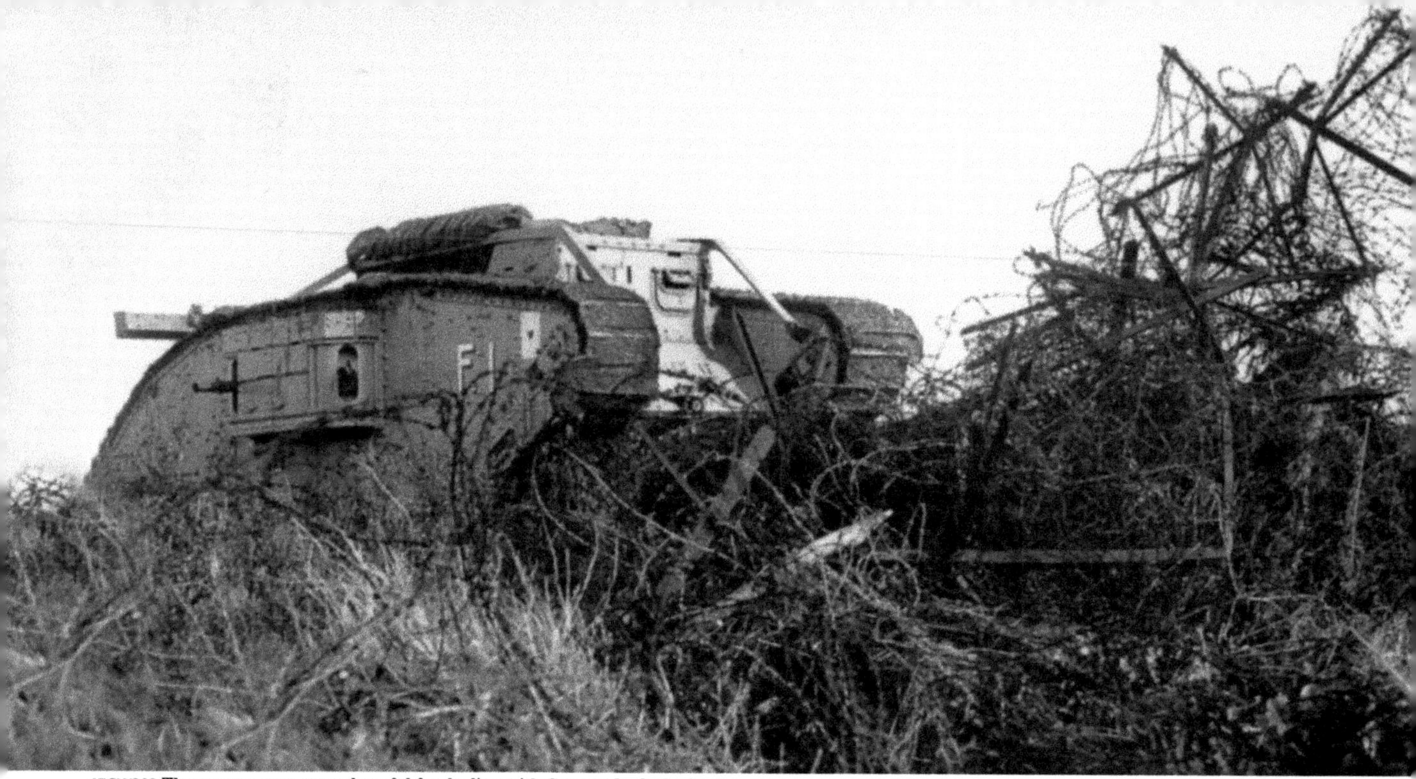

17GW302 The new weapon proved useful for dealing with German barbed wire; however, concentrated fire from machine guns could penetrate the tank's armour. They were slow and mechanically still unreliable.

17GW297 An Australian Stokes mortar team cleaning their bombs in the German line. The mortar itself is covered by a tarpaulin sheet.

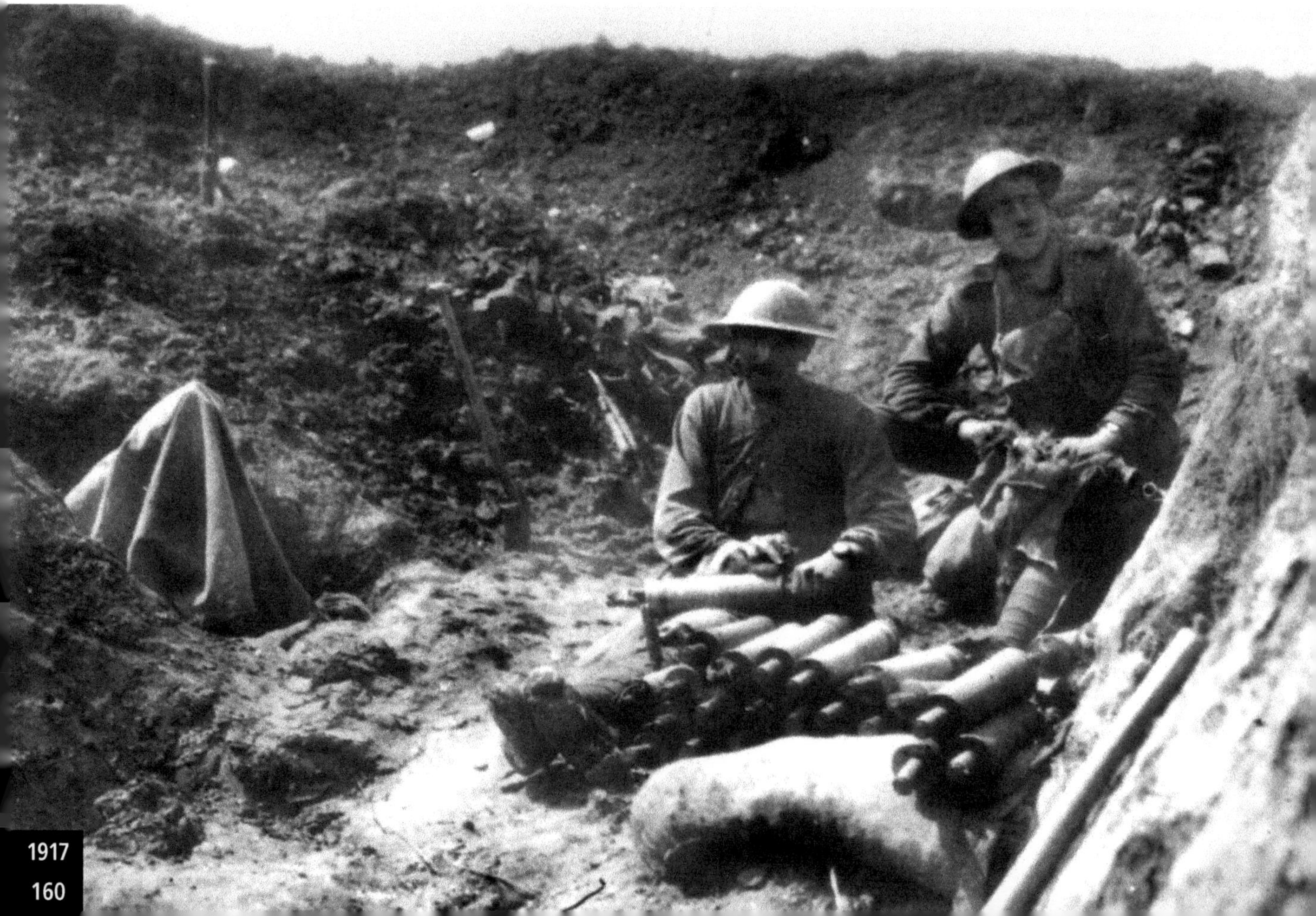

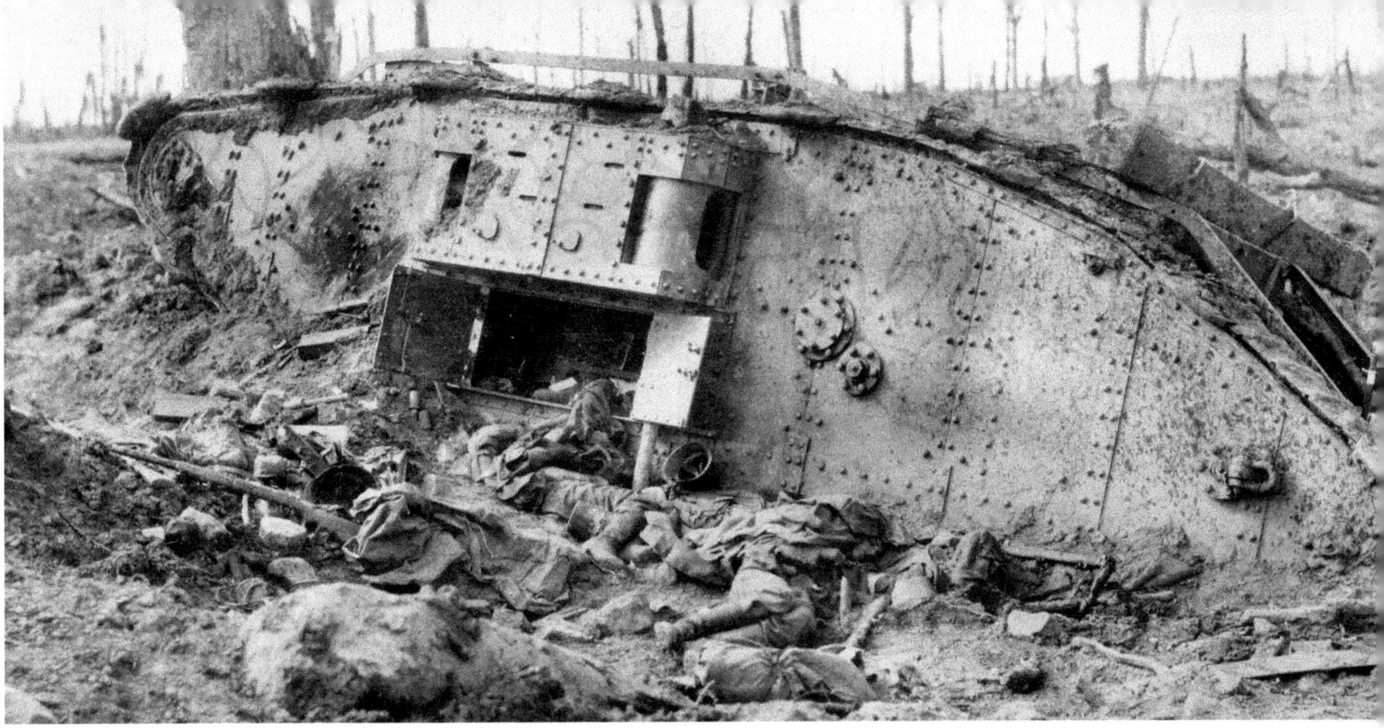

17GW303, 17GW304, 17GW307. Destroyed and captured British tanks east of Bullecourt.

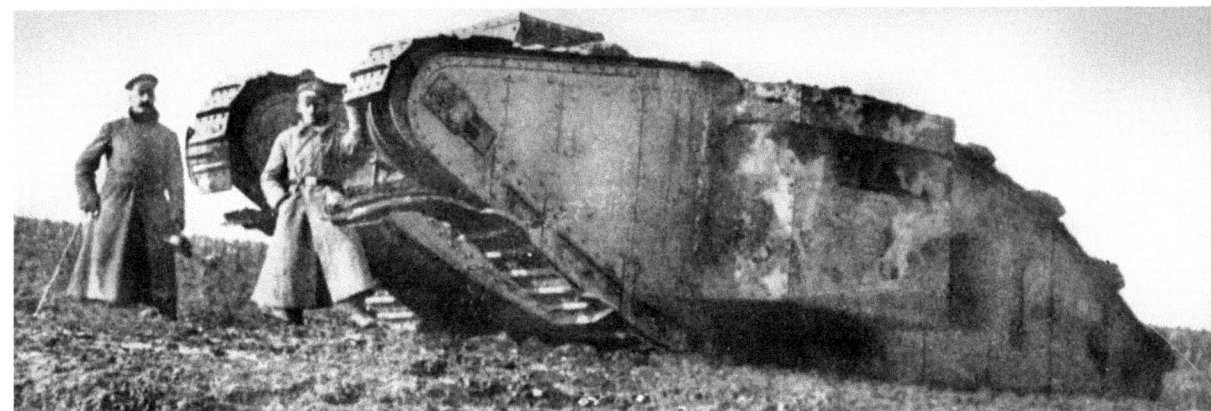

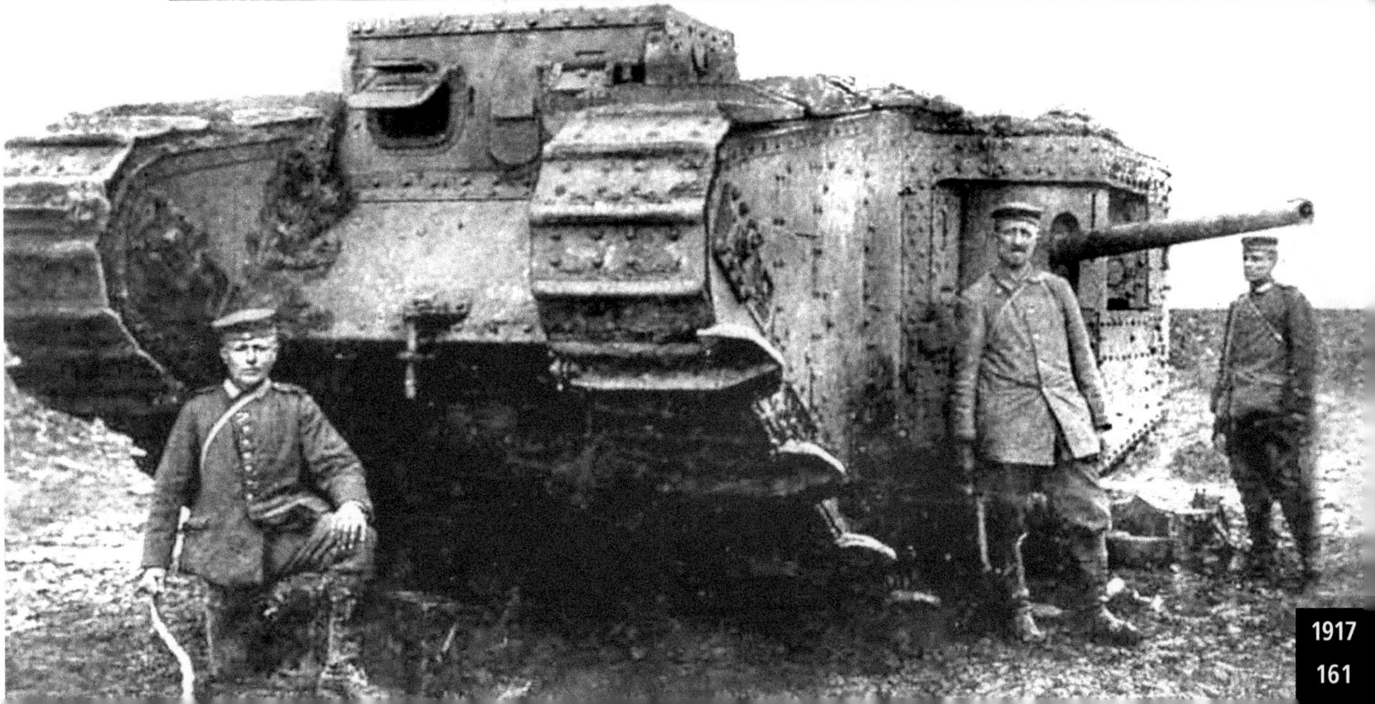

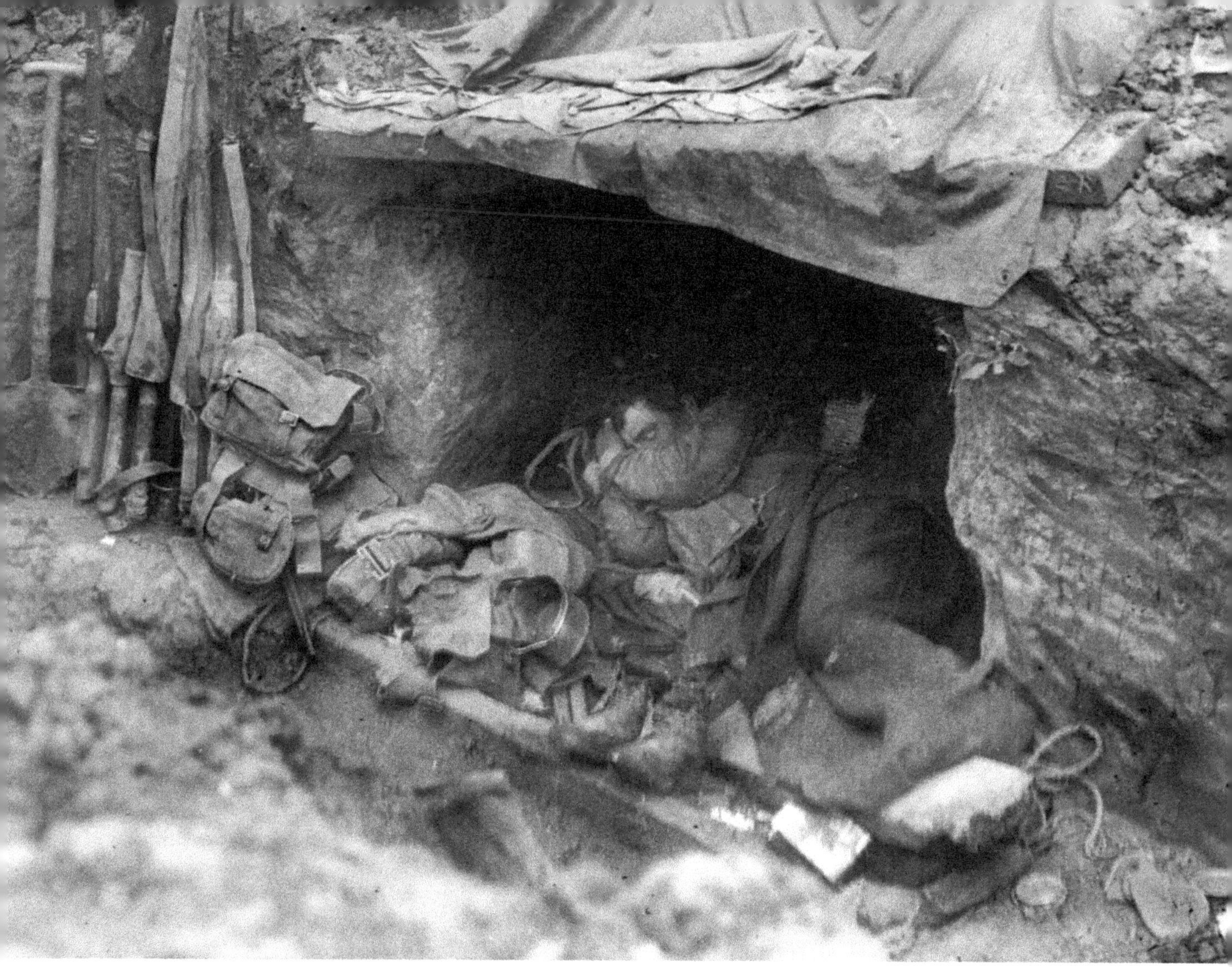

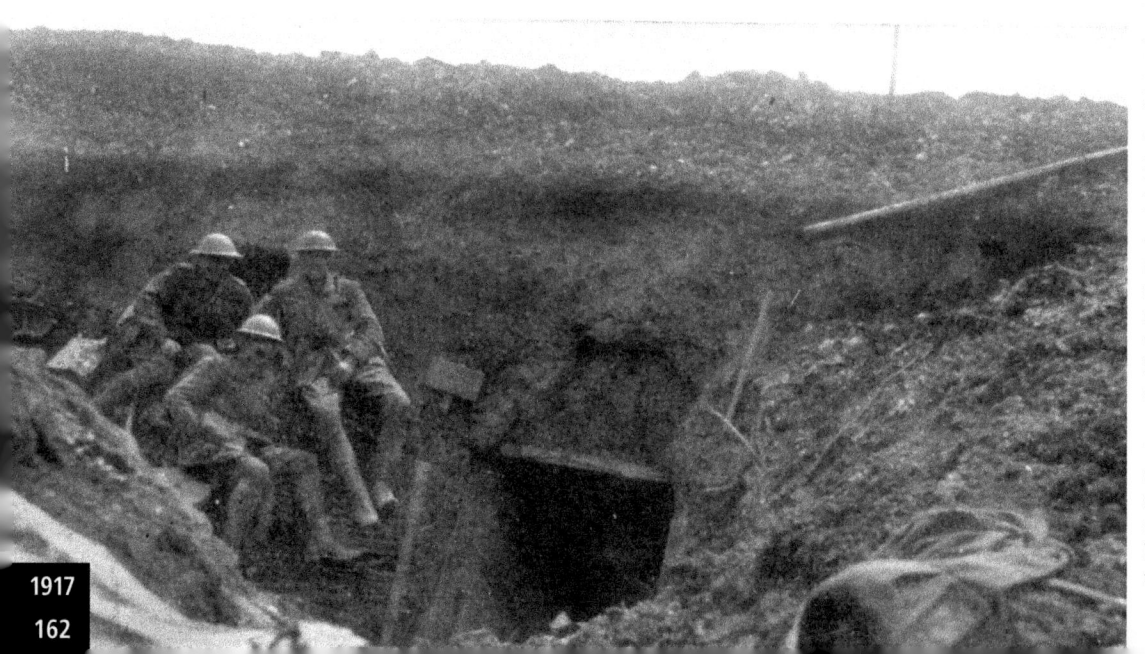

17GW310, 17GW309, 17GW308. An Australian soldier catching some sleep in a first line dugout. Australians in captured German trenches near Bullecourt.
The 48th Battalion became cut off and isolated when its sister battalion, the 46th Battalion, was effectively wiped out. Surrounded, the 48th carried on fighting but steadily running short of ammunition. The order to make a fighting withdrawal was given when they began being shelled by their own artillery.

17GW311 An Australian official photographer stands over the body of a German soldier partially buried in a captured trench.

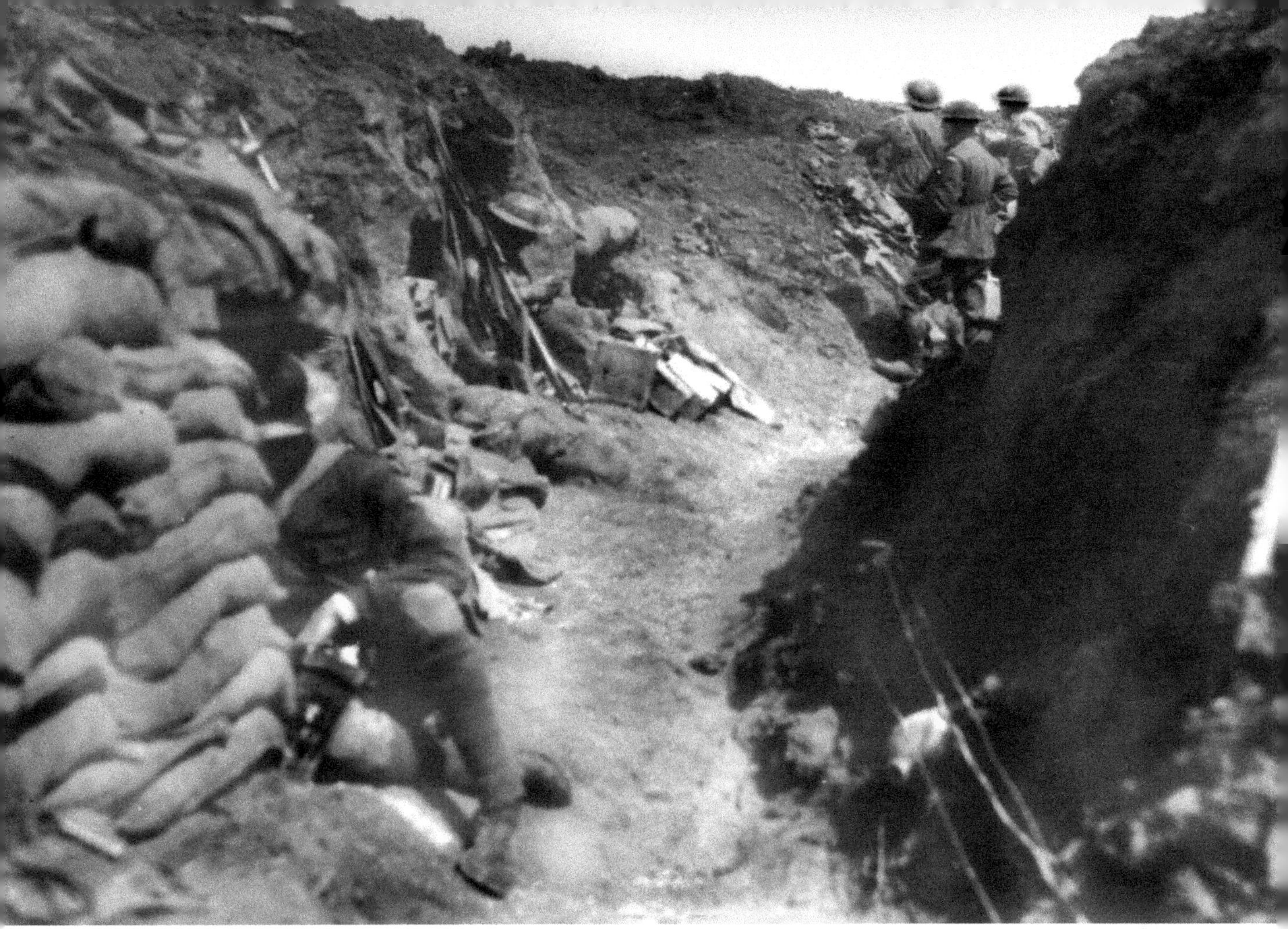

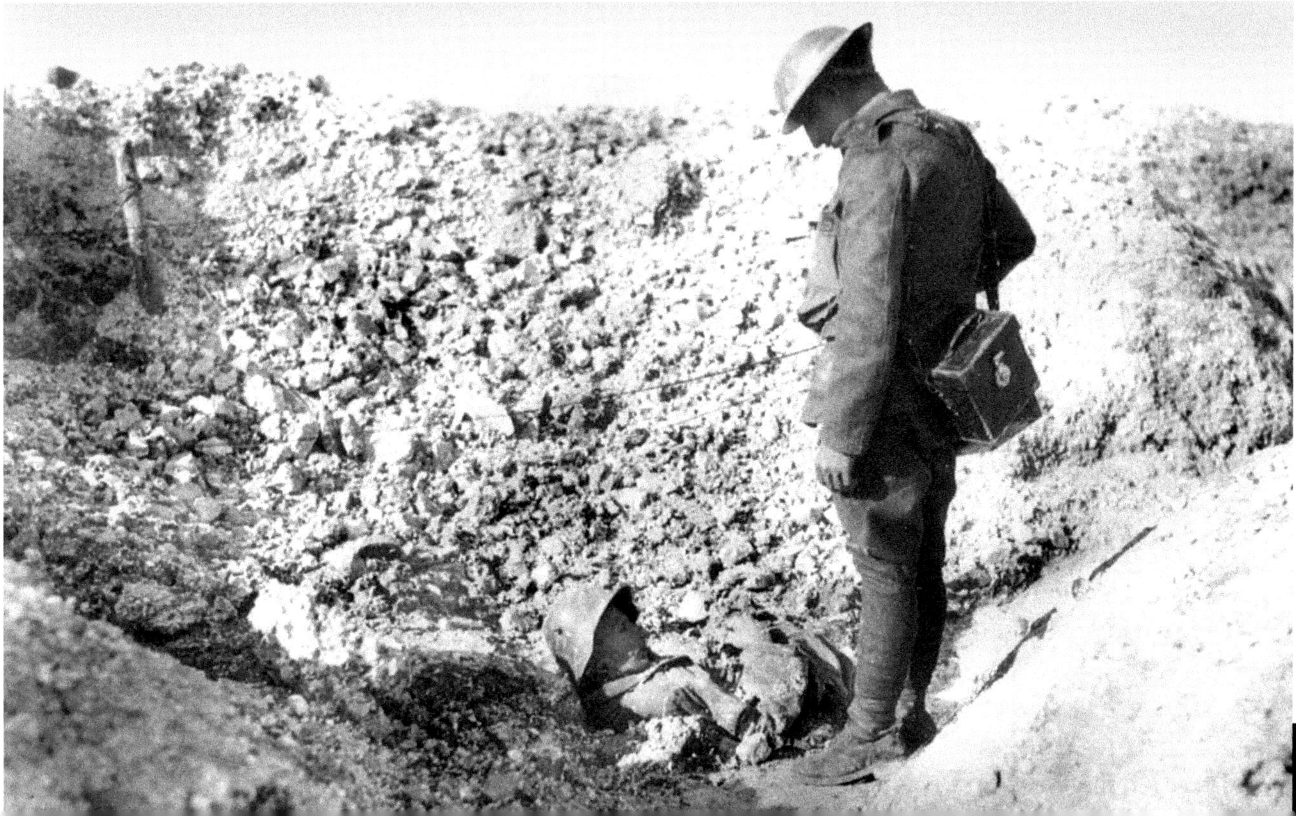

1917

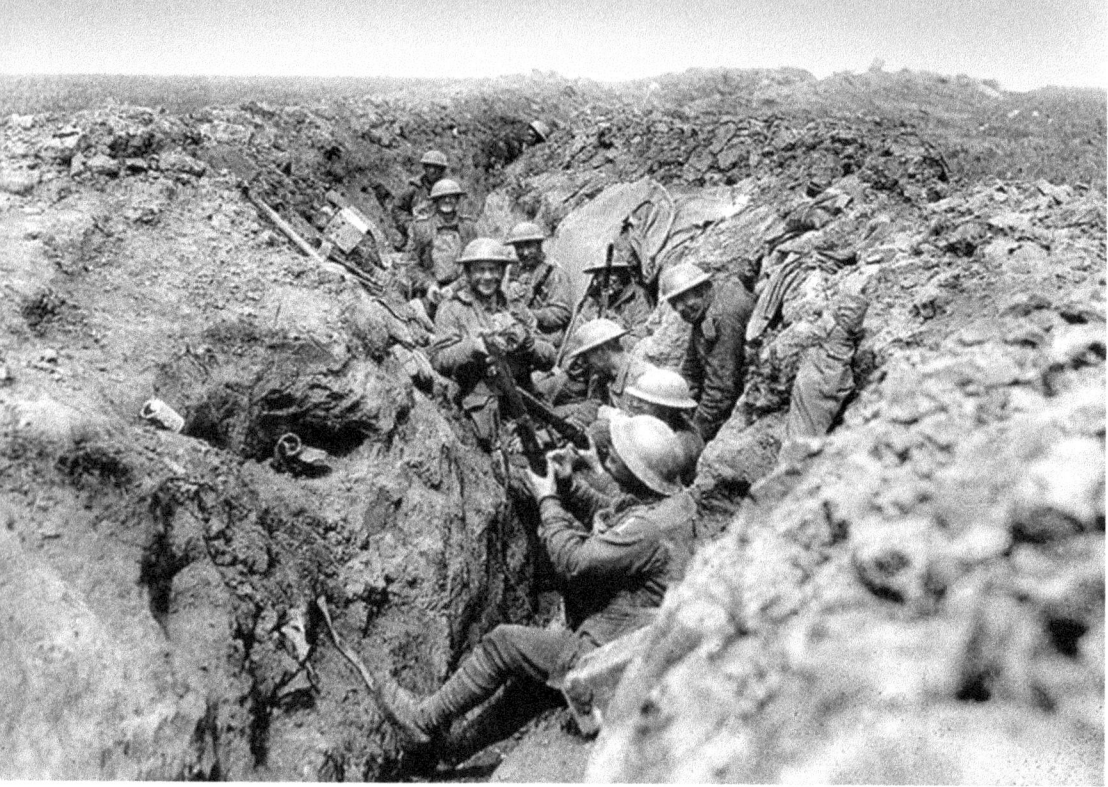
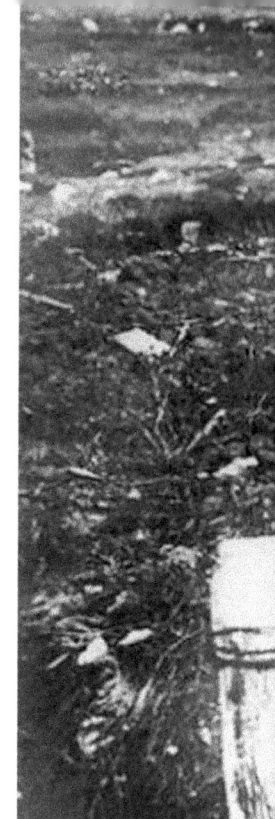

17GW325 Australians making themselves at home in a captured section of the Hindenburg Line.

17GW326 Australians soldiers stretchering a wounded comrade away from the front line at Bullecourt.

17GW327 A German *Maschinengewehr* 08/15, with its crew of four operating it, near Arras.

17GW326 A German regimental aid post (*Truppenverbandplatz*), where wounds were treated and redressed.

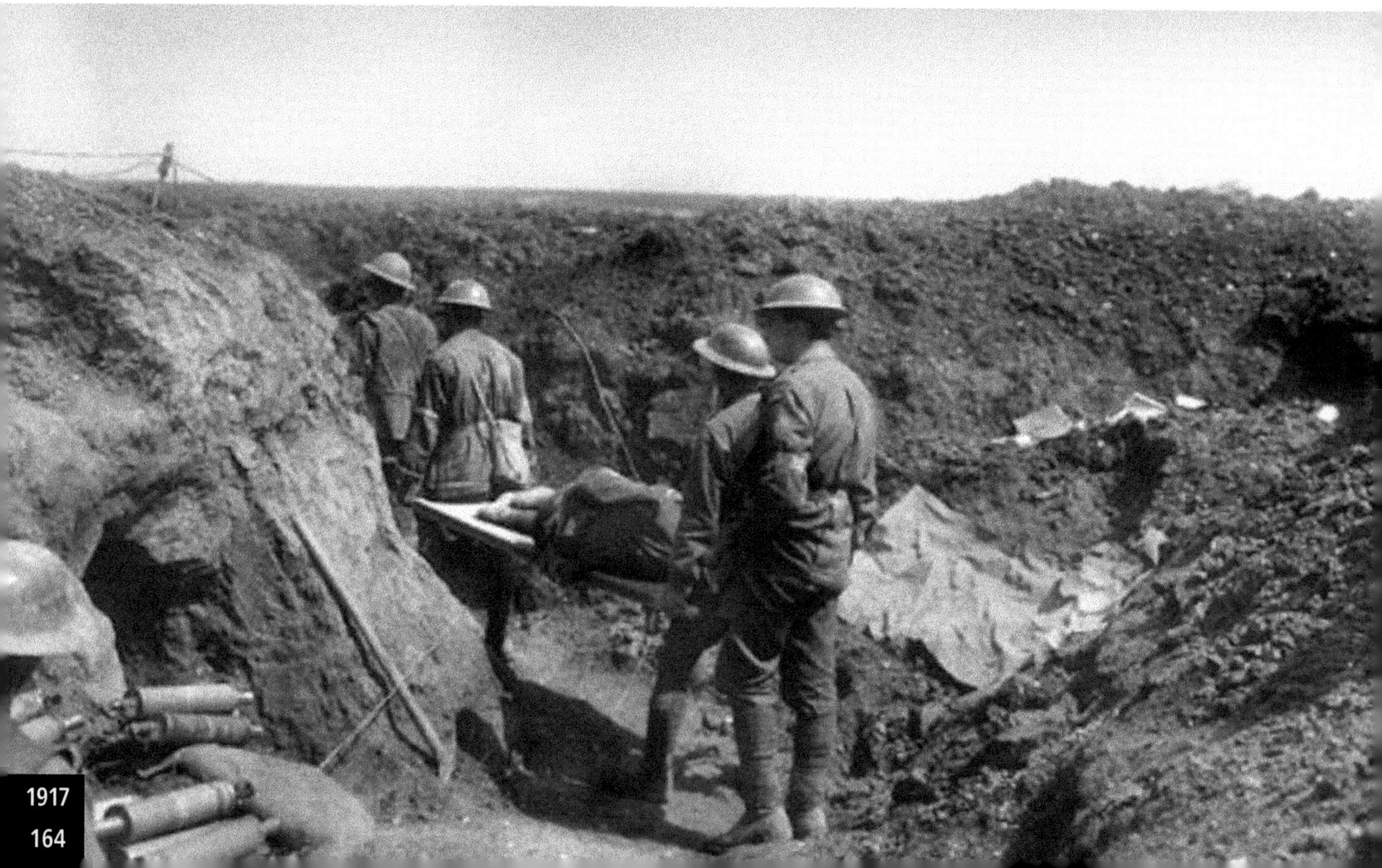

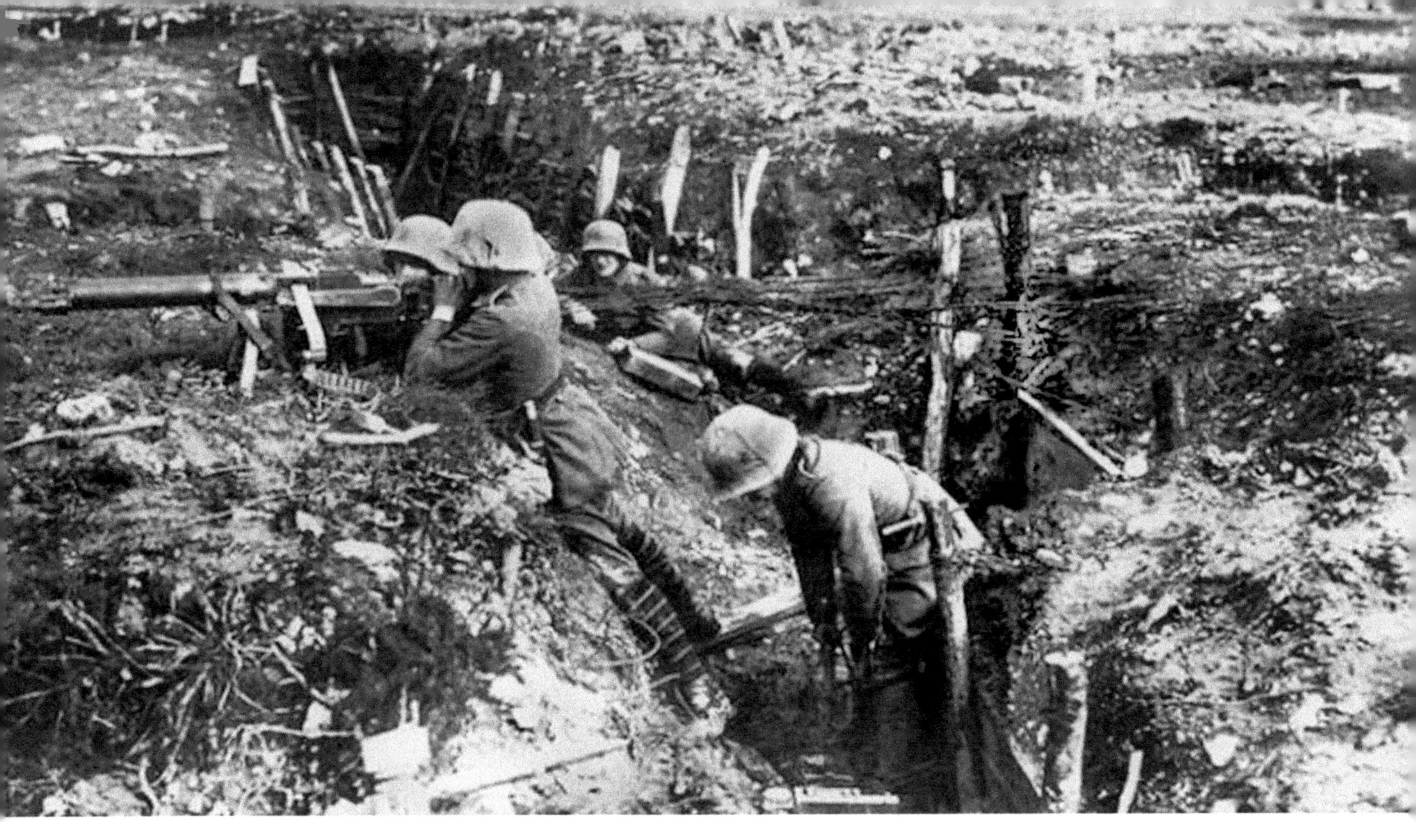

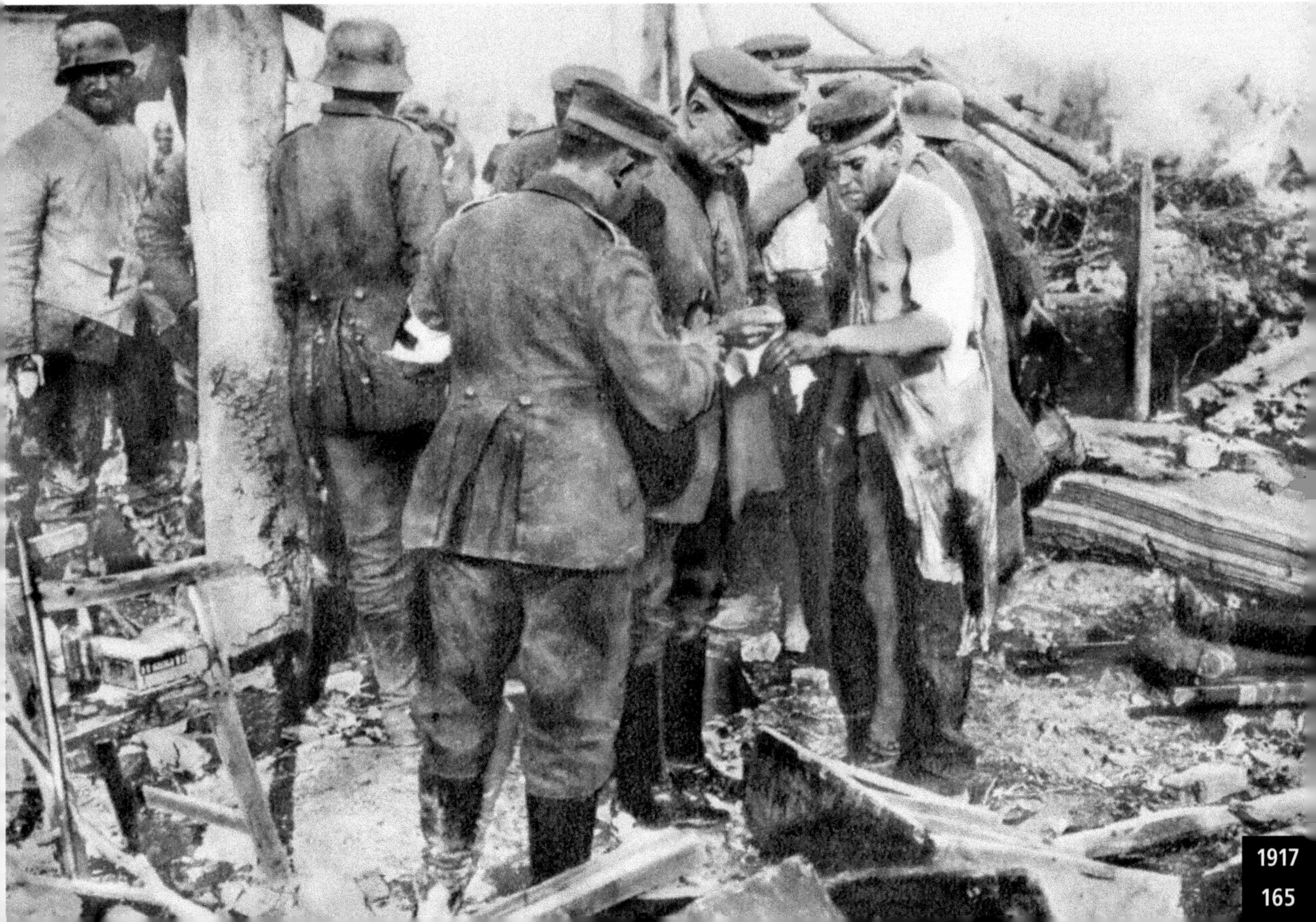

1917
165

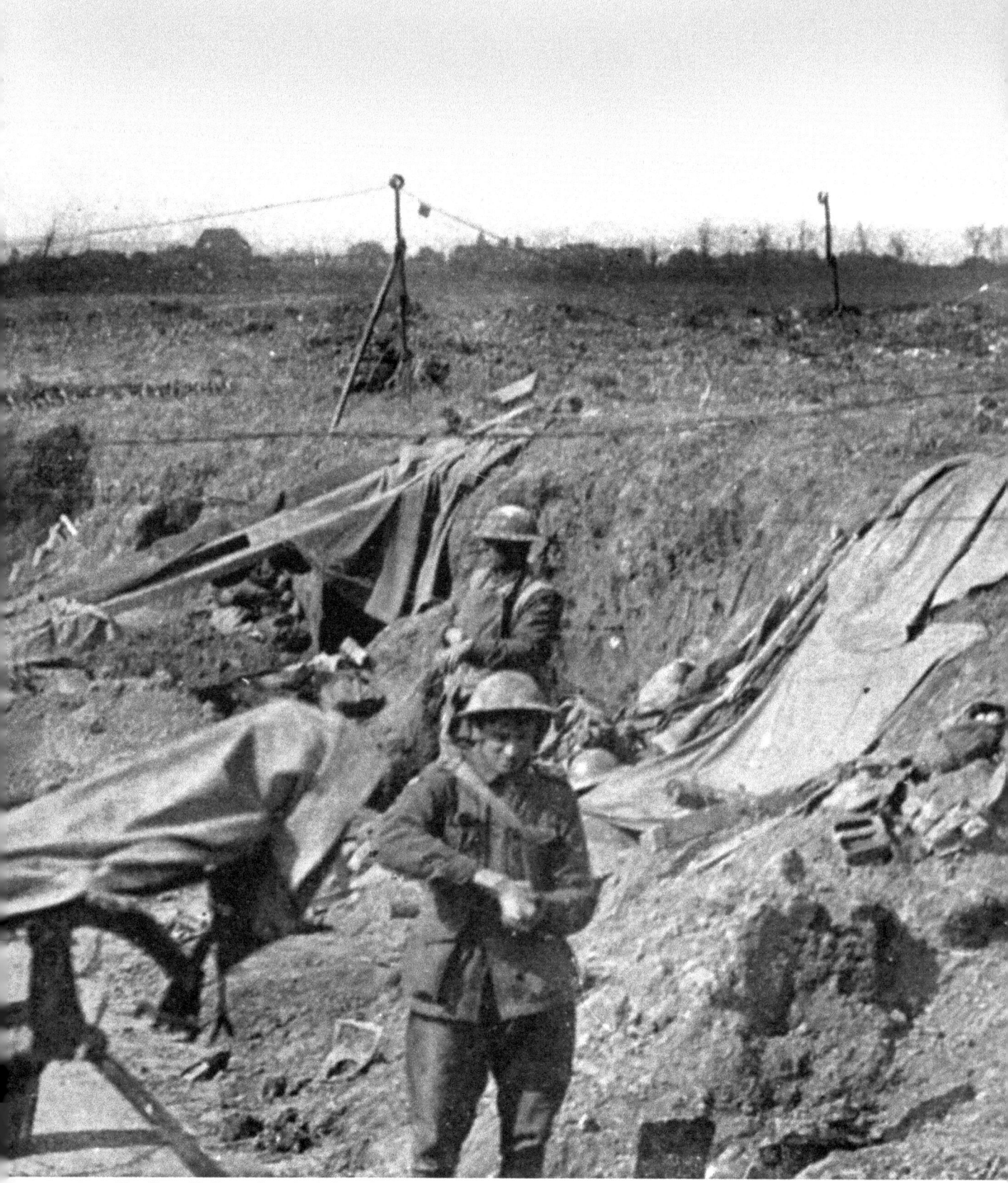

17GW306 The village of Bullecourt is on the skyline; this picture was taken from a sunken road near Noreuil. An officer from the 22nd Australian Machine Gun Company is observing the wire in front of Bullecourt, 23 April 1917.

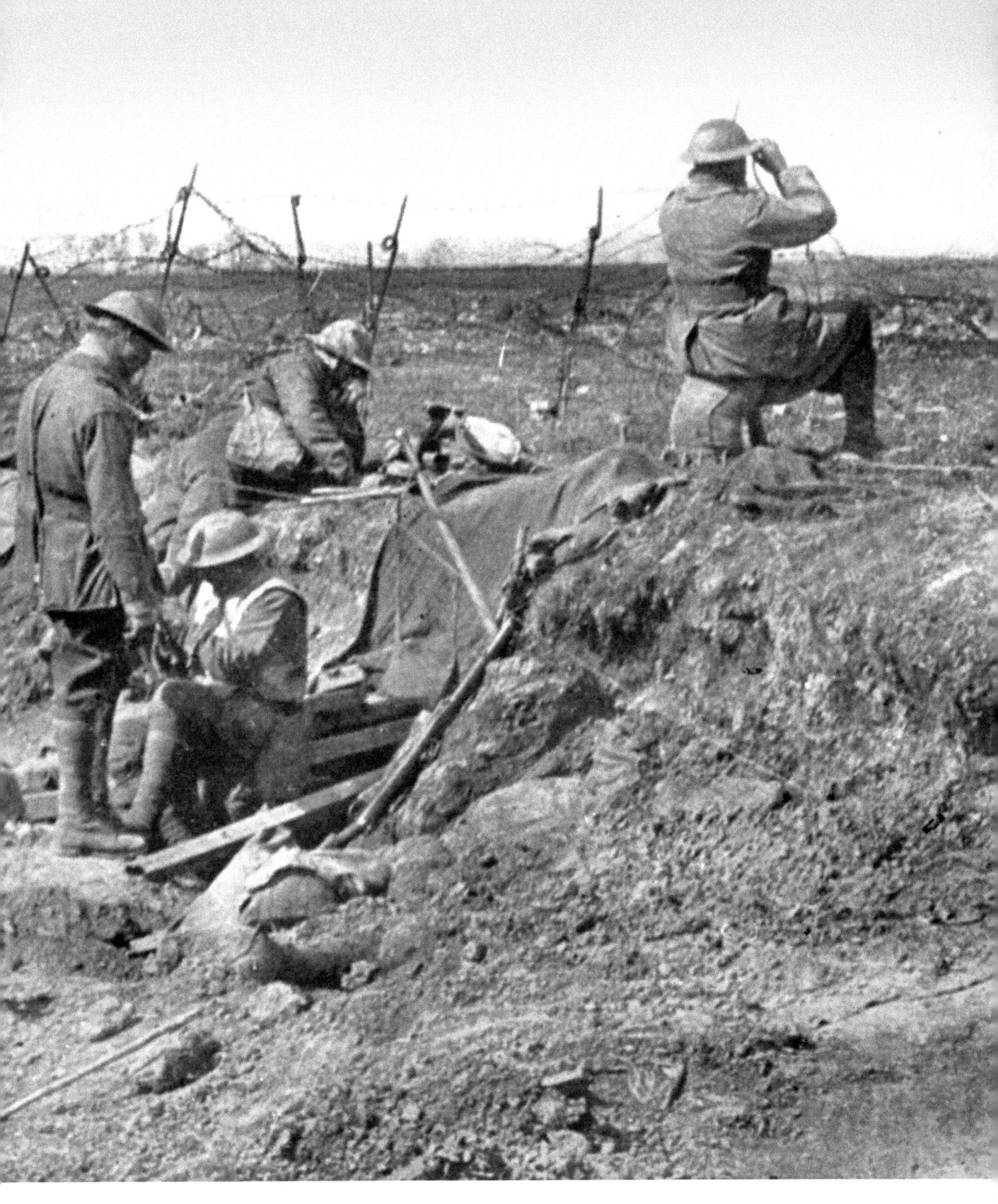

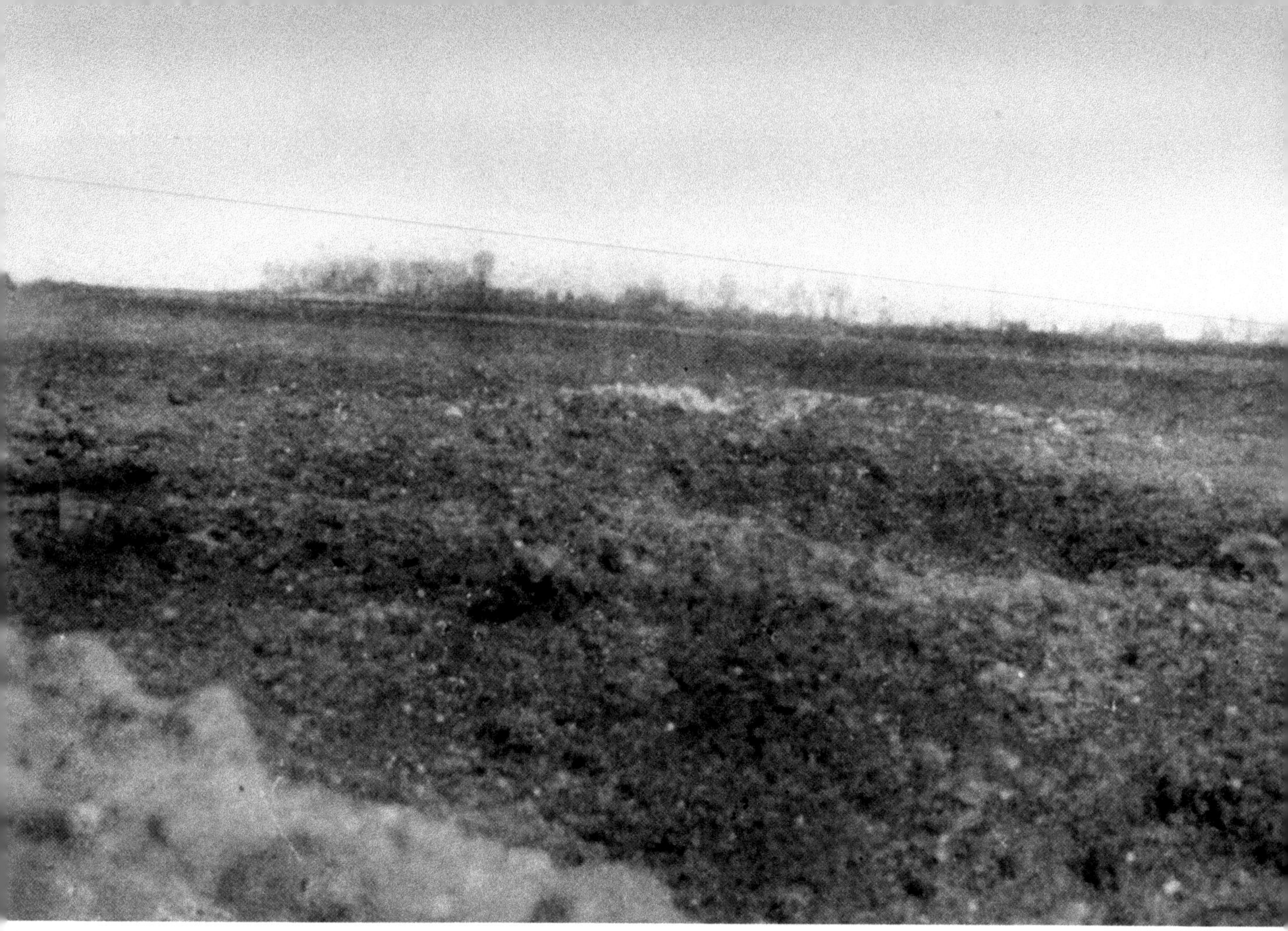

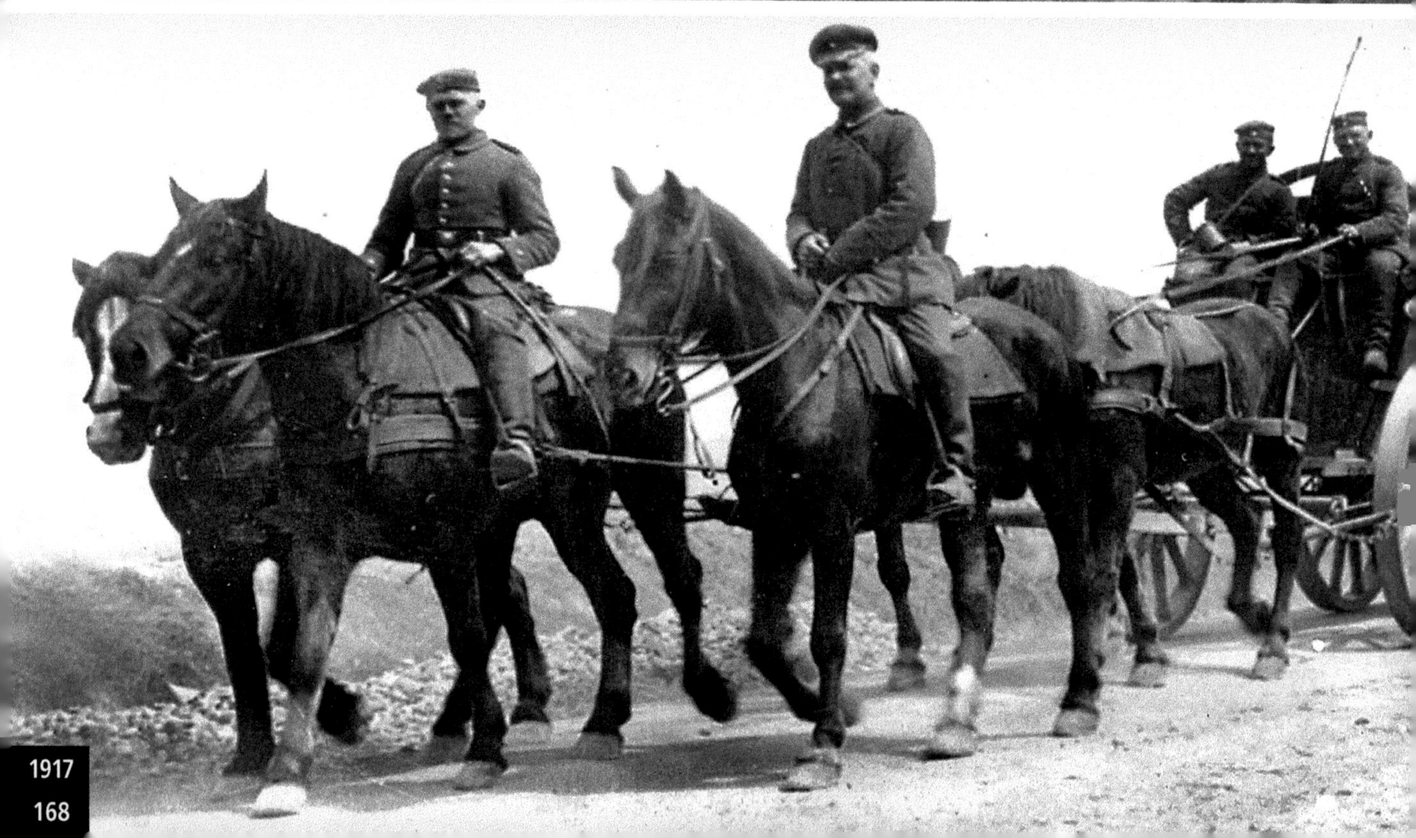

1917

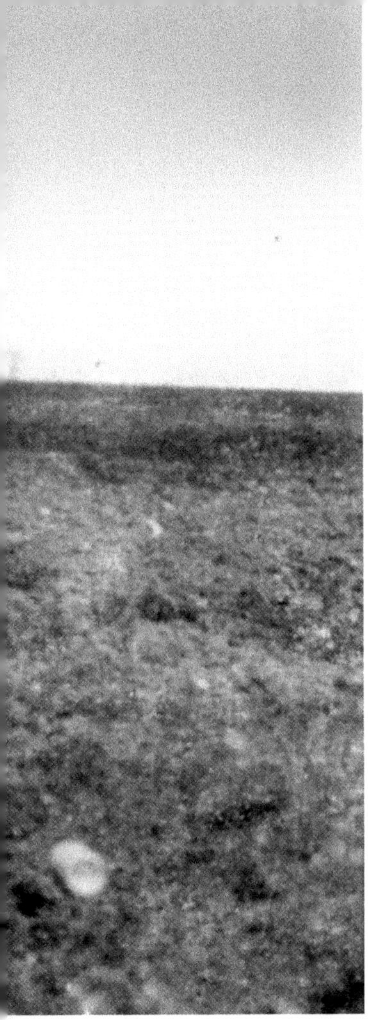

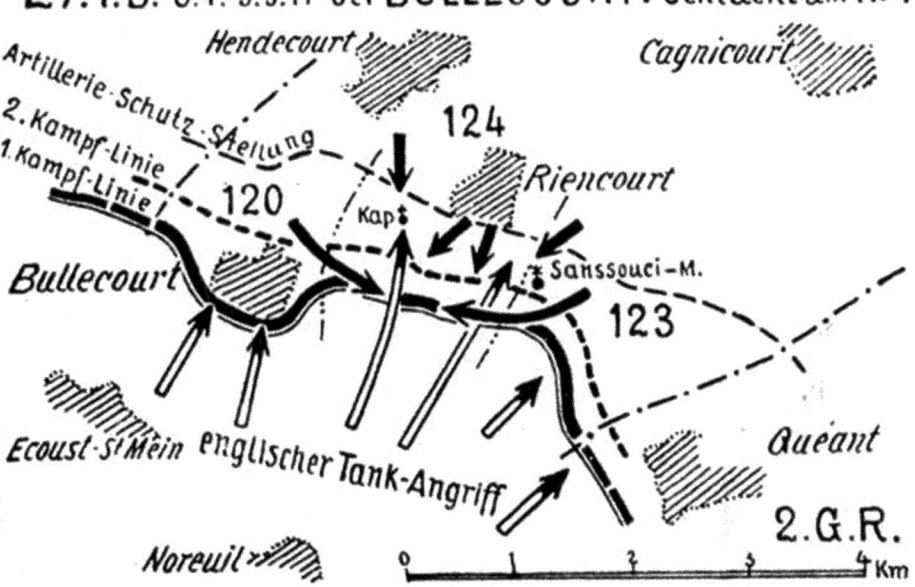

17GW305 Official German map showing the Australian break through into their first and second lines east of Bullecourt, 11 April. Also depicted is the German counter attack.

17GW318 The village of Riencourt-lès-Cagnicourt on the horizon and behind the Hindenburg Line defence system was the main objective of the attack; however, it was found impossible to reach either on 11 April or on 3 May. The photograph was taken on 8 May 1917 from the Australian lodgement within the Hindenburg Line. At the time the trenches were held by the Australian 8th Battalion.

17GW320 Bringing up supplies – this German column is on the Arras-Cambrai road, May 1917.

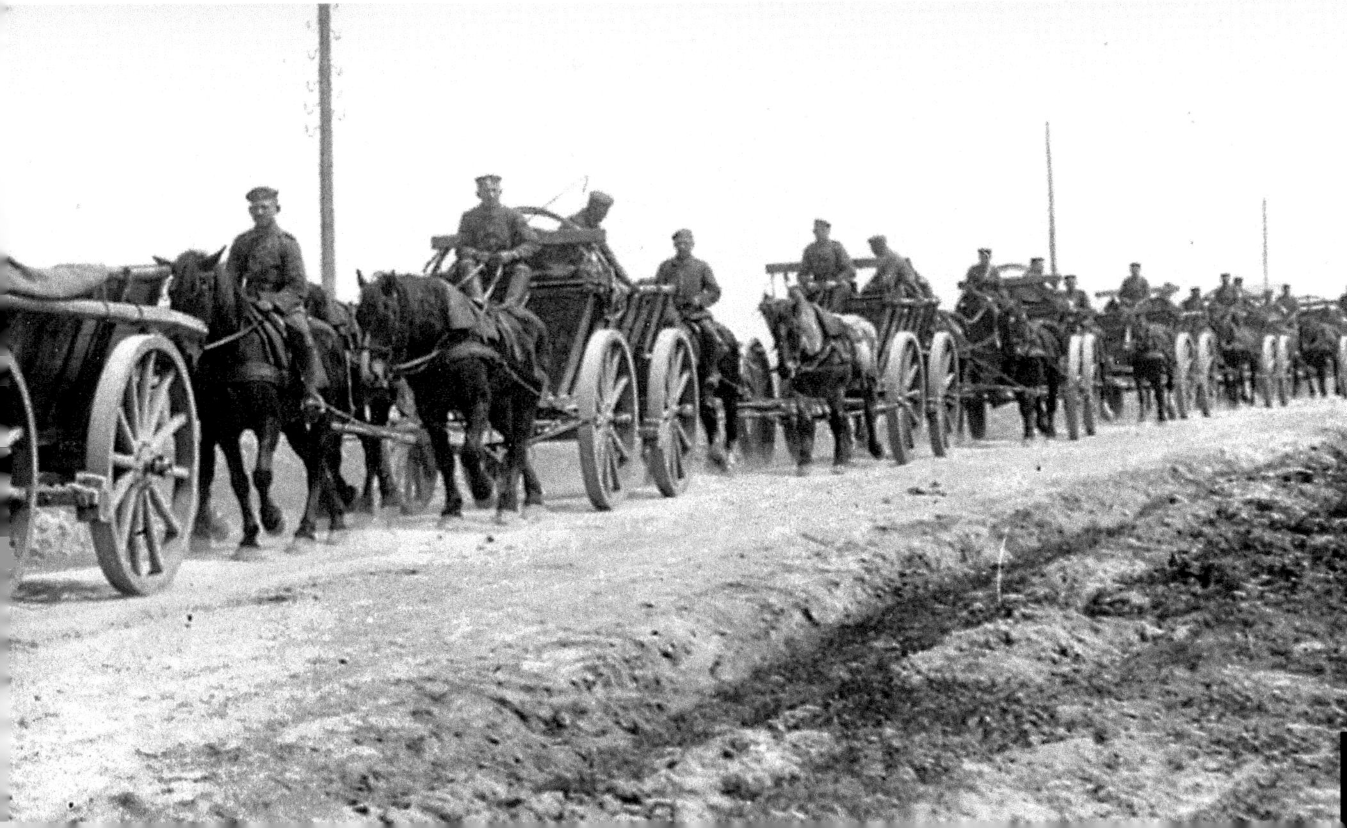

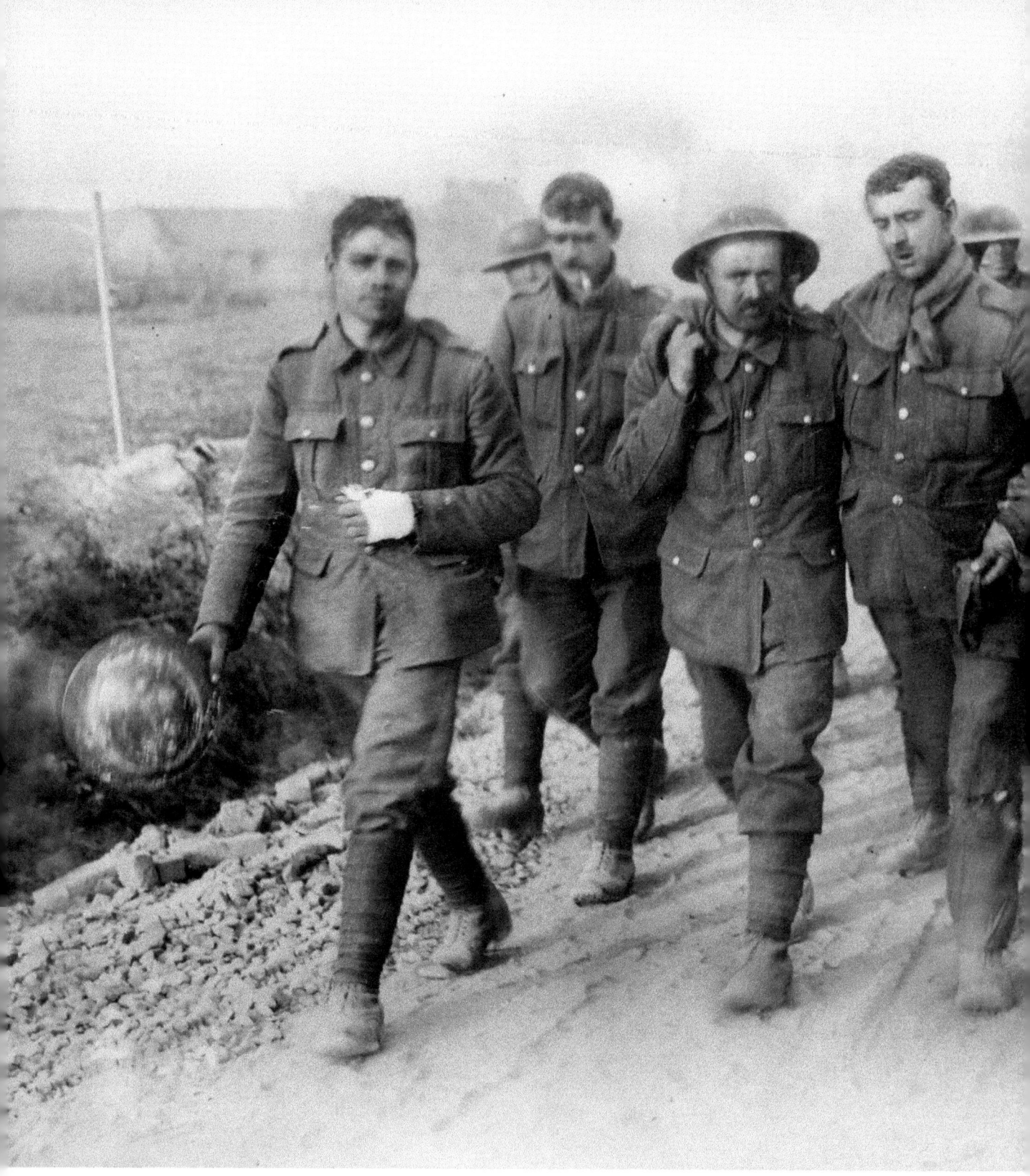
17GW330 British prisoners taken during the fighting in May 1917.

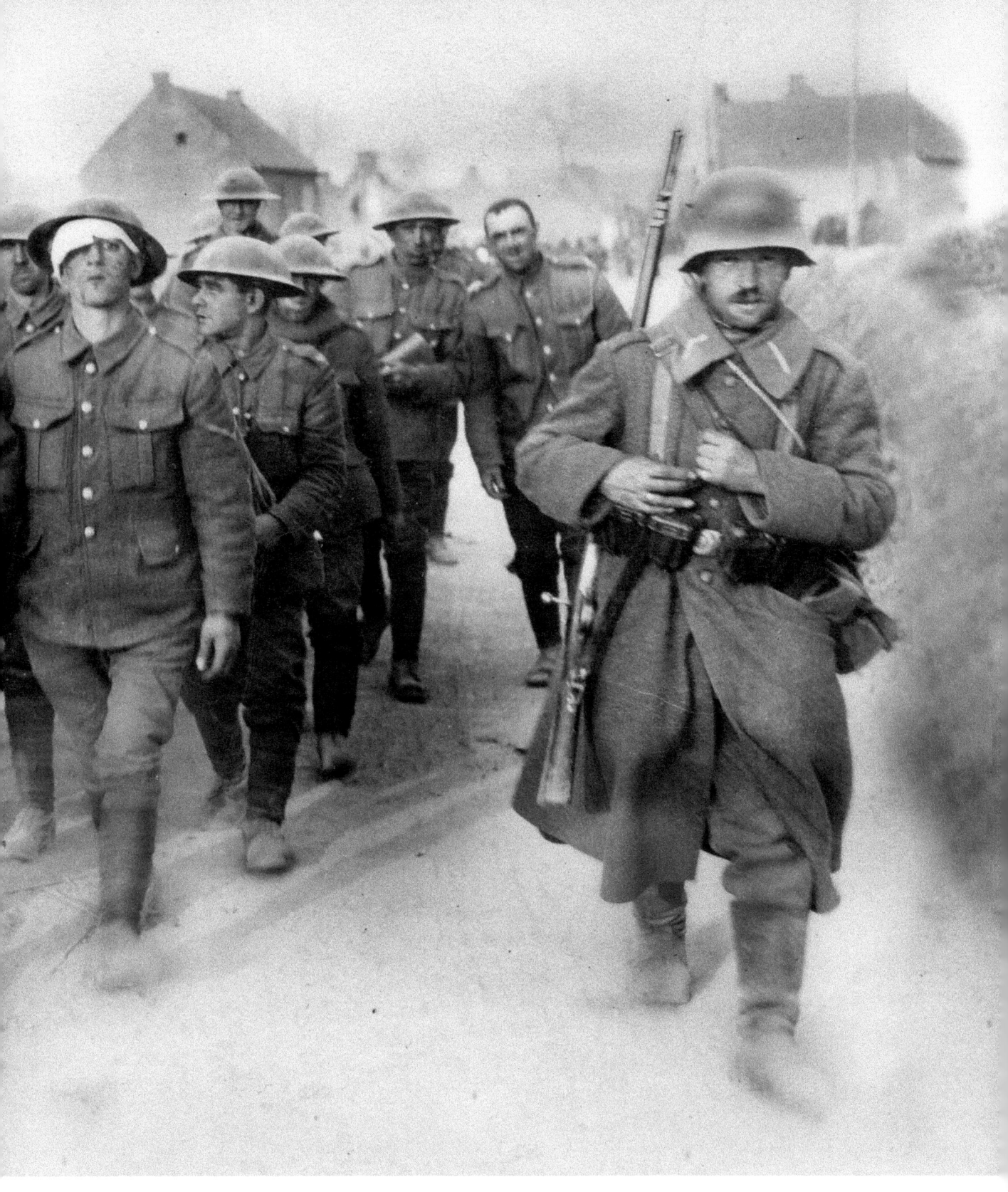

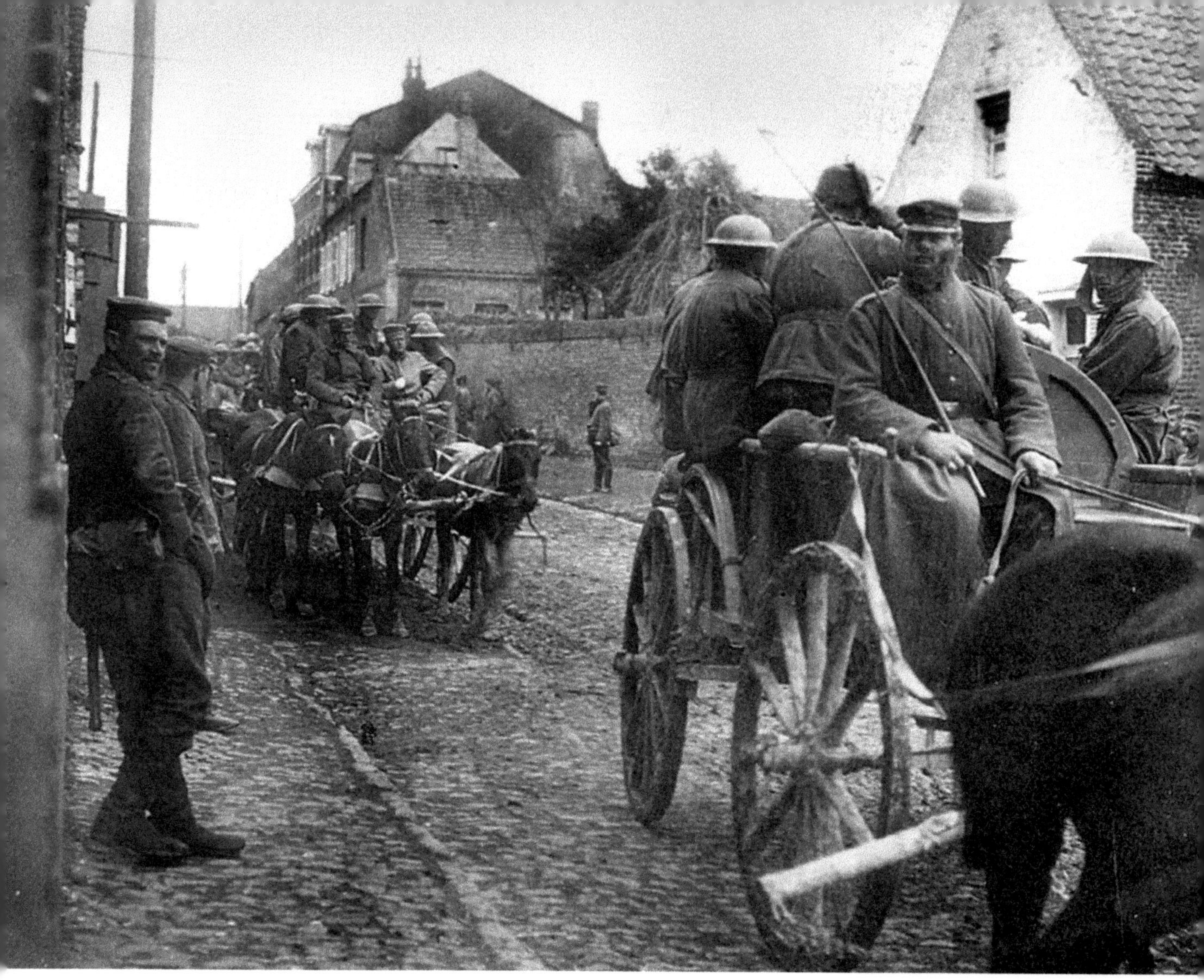

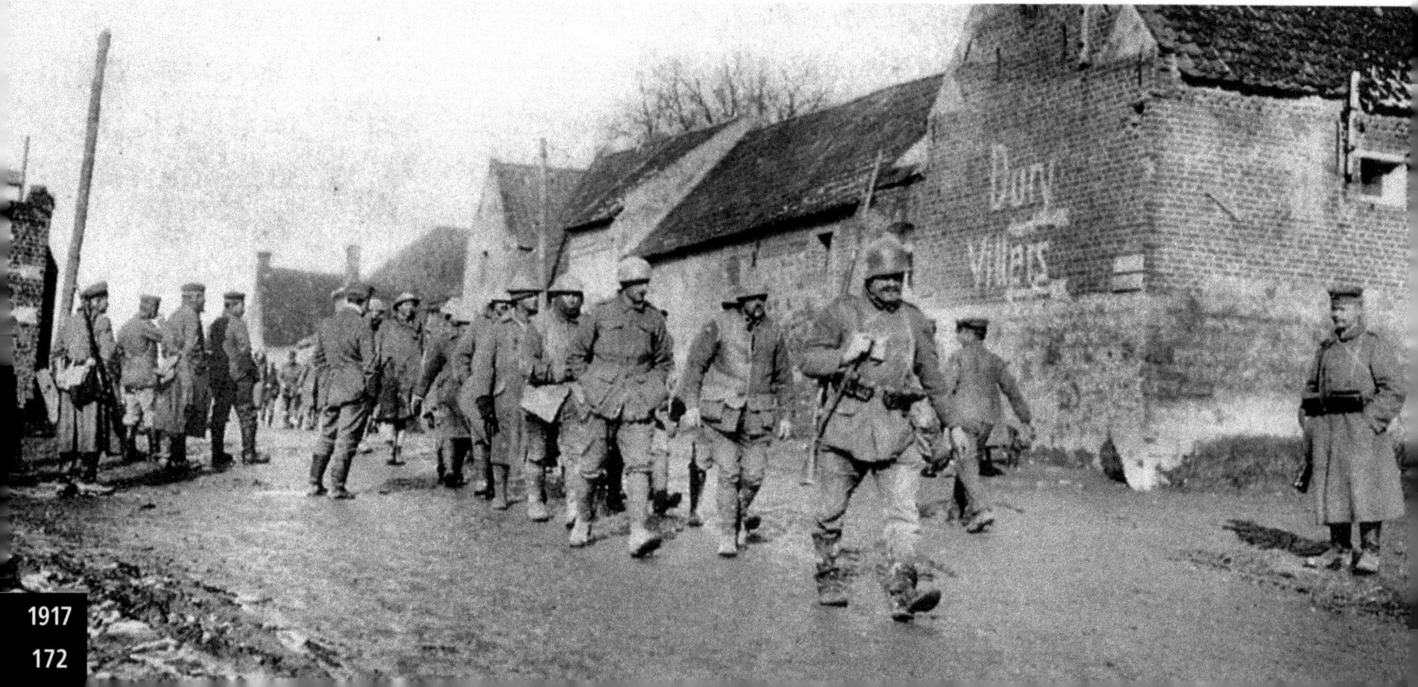

1917

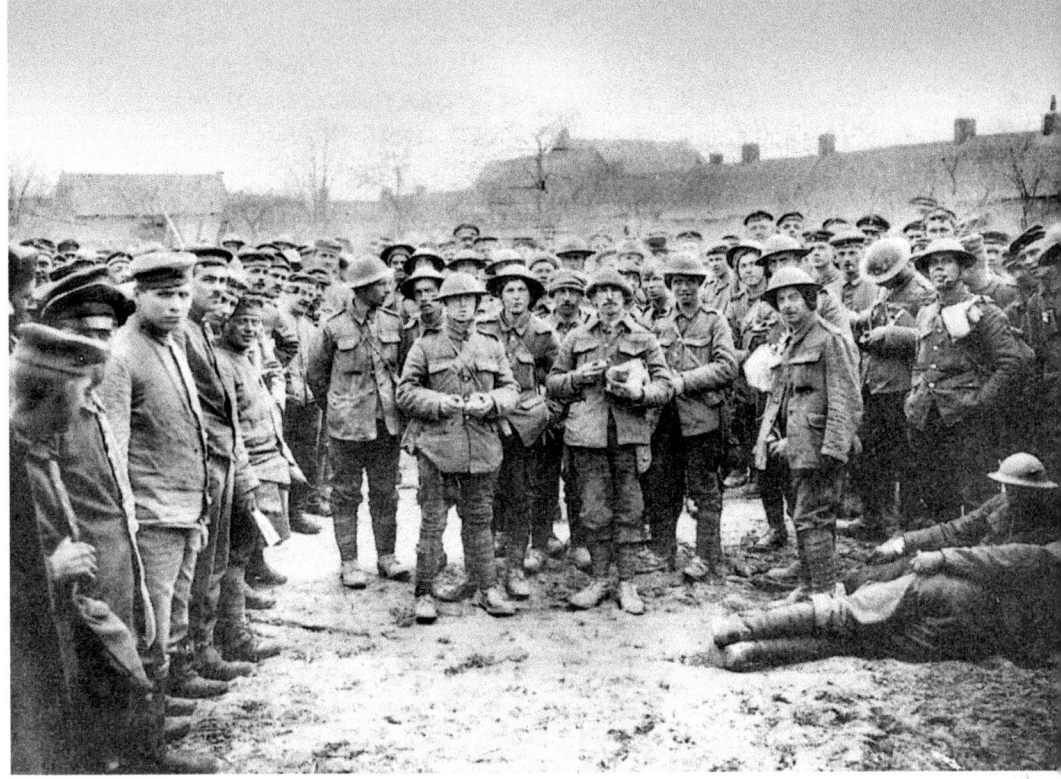

17GW322 British prisoners taken during the Arras offensive.

17GW312 Captured Australians being transported by cart through the village of Saudemont.

17GW313 Captured Australians being marched to the rear.

17GW313 Captured British prisoners resting in an outbuilding on their way to a prisoner of war camp.

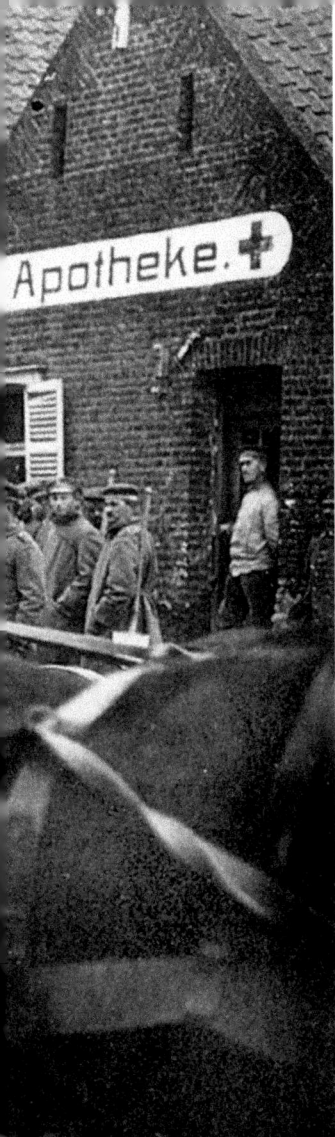

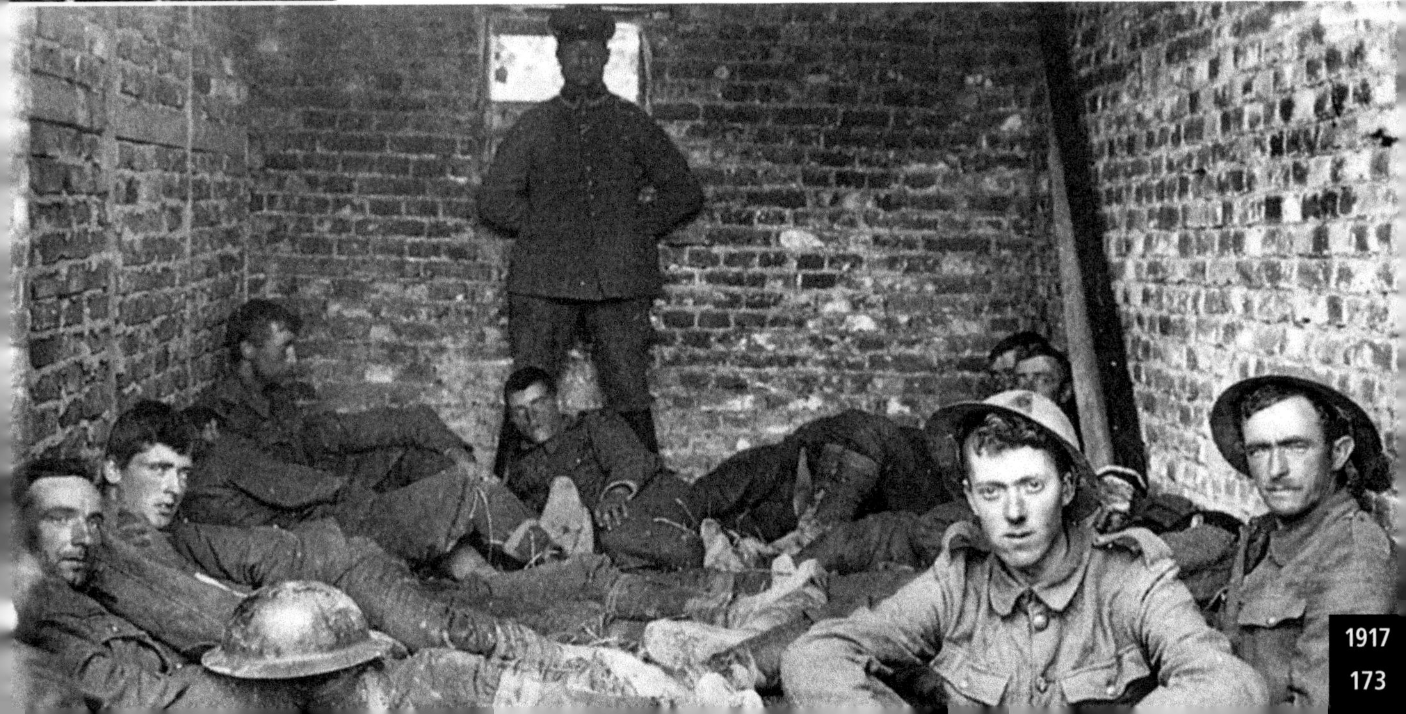

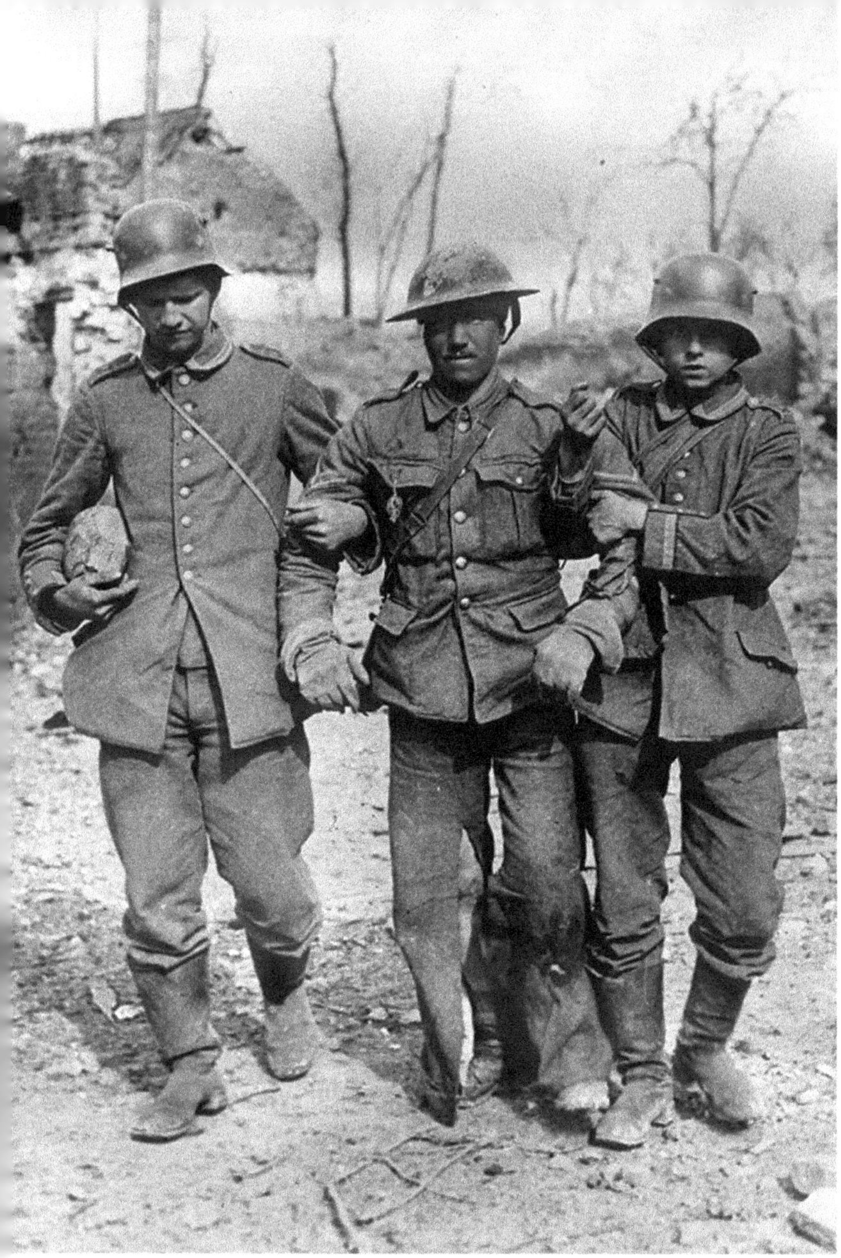

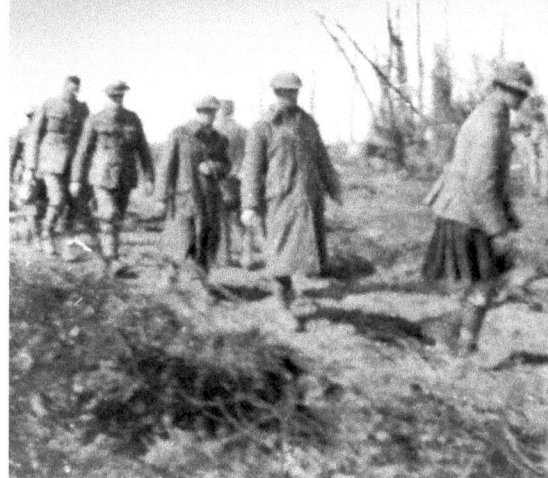

17GW321 British soldiers taken prisoner during the fighting east of Arras.

17GW323 A wounded British corporal being helped by his former enemies. Note the German soldier on his left, who appears to be a youngster in his mid teens.

17GW319 A British soldier of a Scottish regiment killed in the fighting at Arras. The German's have removed the boots from the corpse. In Germany leather for footwear was becoming scarce.

17GW316 An Australian Vickers machine gun crew on the move.

17GW315 The 4th Australian Infantry Division's supply wagons during the May attack. The Australians had fought for two weeks at this part of the Hindedburg Line and lost 292 officers and 7,190 men killed or captured. The British lost some 300 officers and 6,500 men during the Battle of Bullecourt.

17GW317 The railway embankment which ran parallel to the Hindenburg Line south east of Bullecourt. Situated in this embankment was the HQ for the Australian 48th Battalion 11 April. It was used by Brigadier General Gellibrand, 6 Brigade during the second assault launched on 3 May.

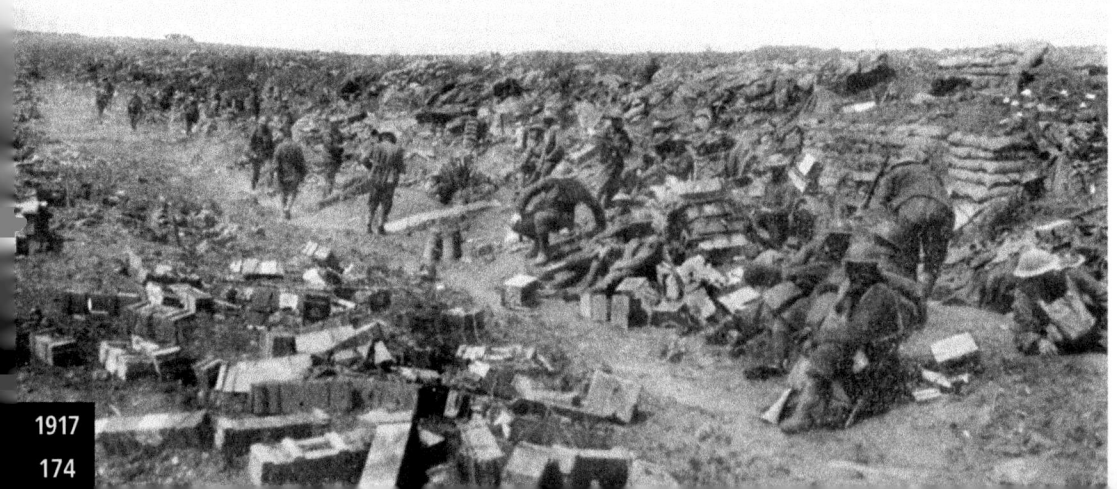

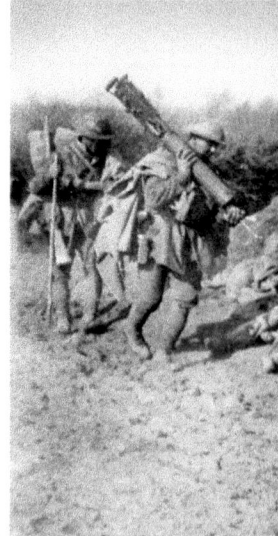

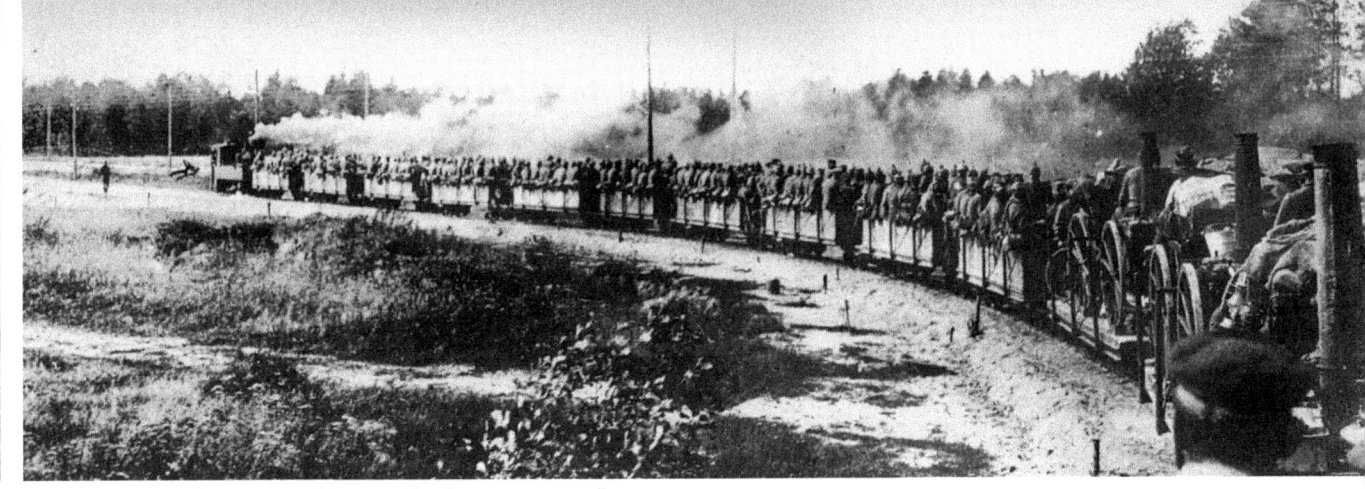
17GW324 German reinforcements arriving near Vimy by narow gauge railway.

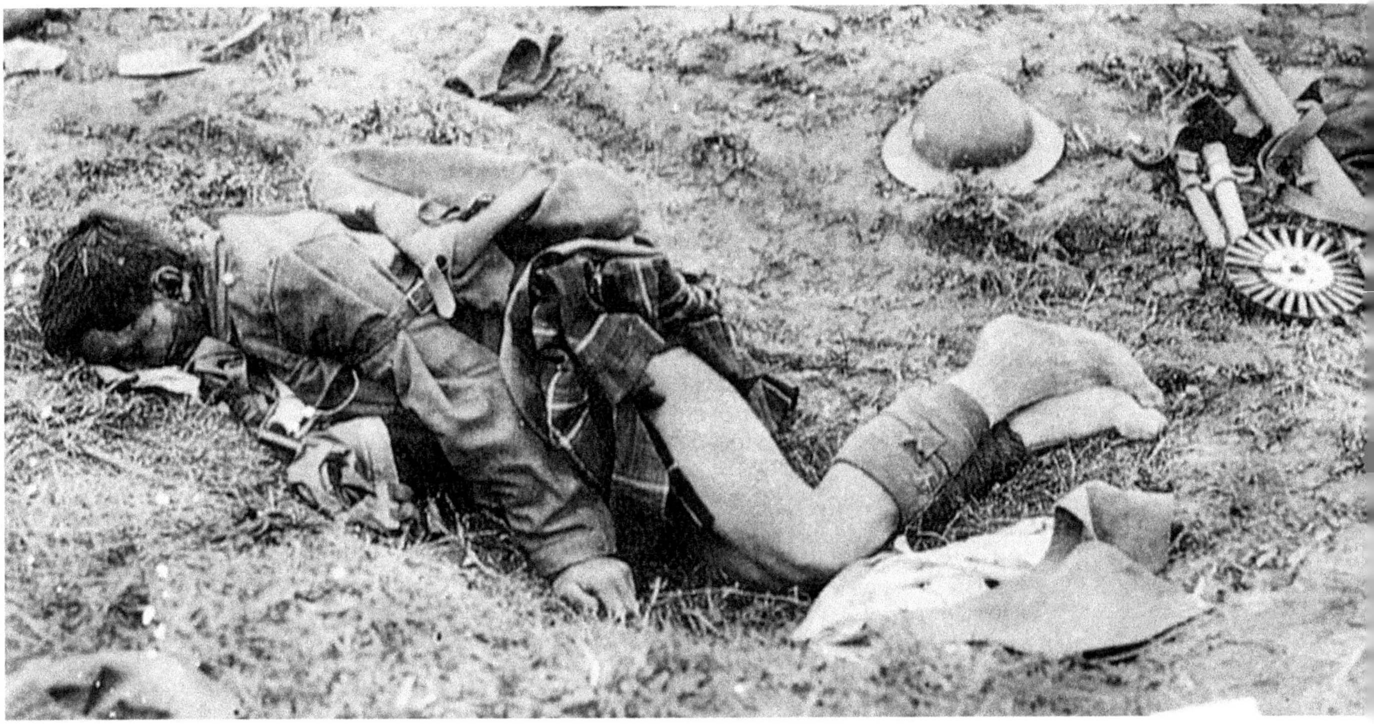

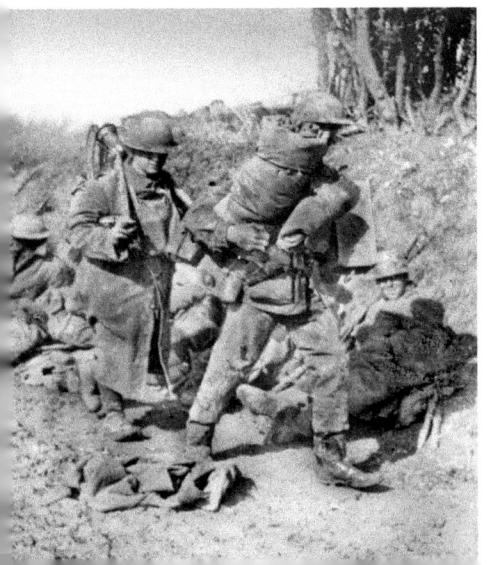

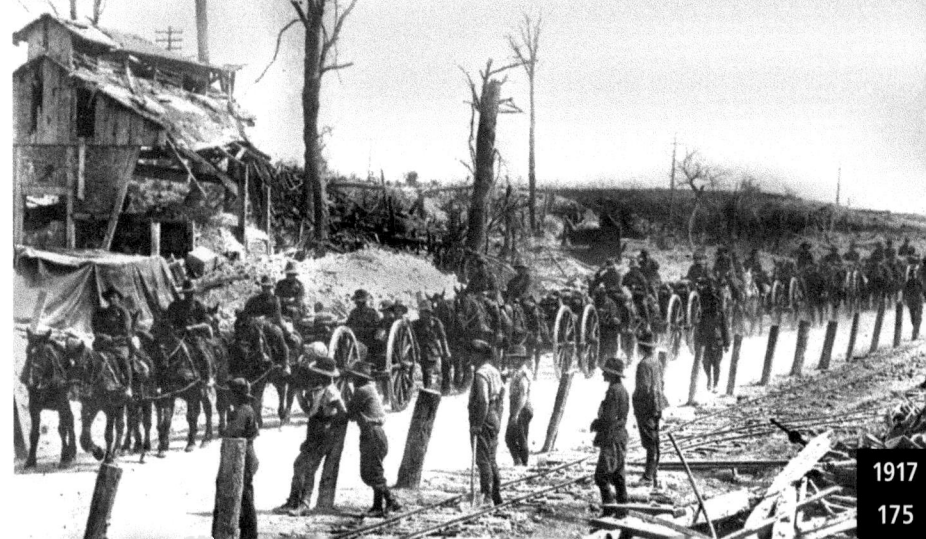

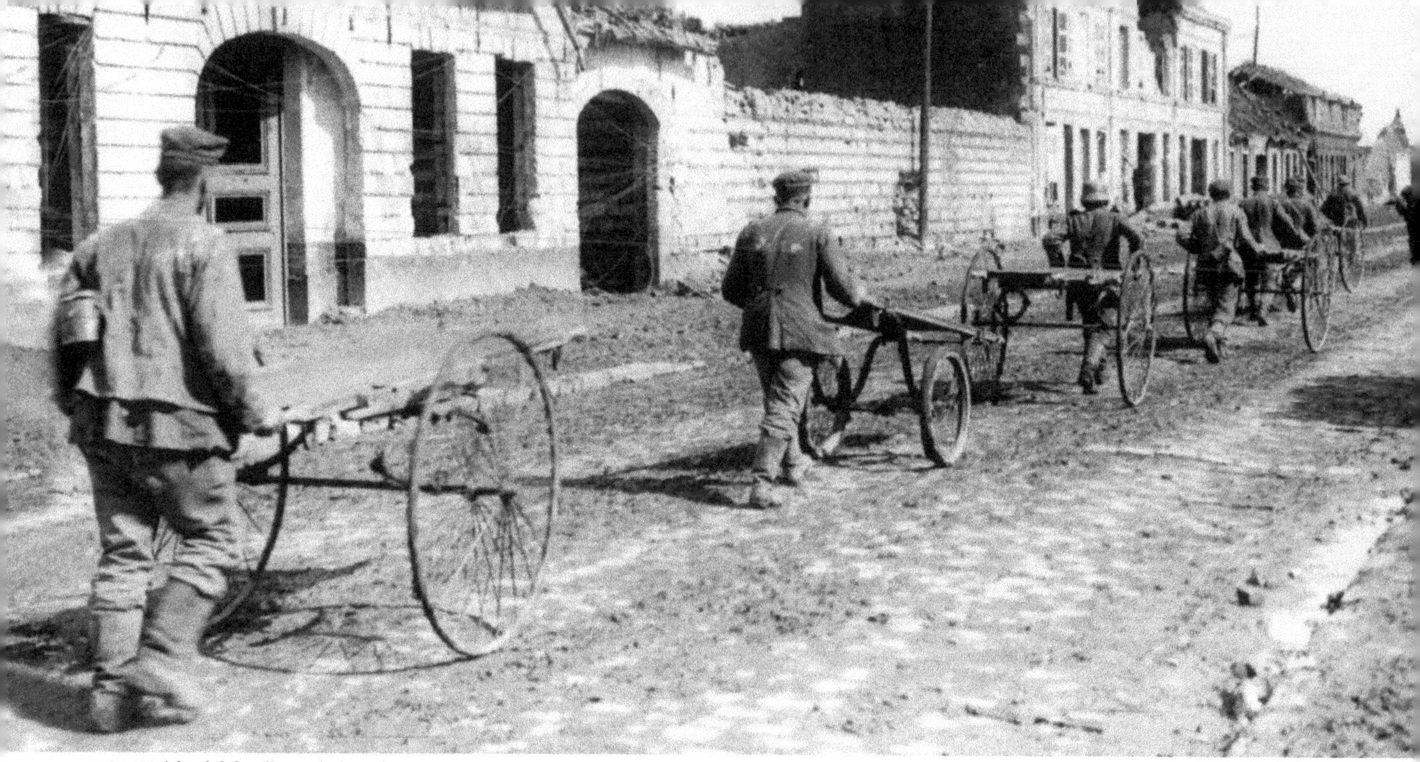

17GW329 A burial detail consisting of German prisoners of war on its way out of Arras to collect corpses for interment in the rapidly growing cemeteries.

As had been intended, the offensive at Arras (which officially ended on 15 May) succeeded in 'fixing' German troops to the Arras sector – and, indeed, drew in reinforcements. However, the Germans had, through their withdrawal to the Hindenburg Line, considerably increased the availability of reserve formations. Some notable successes were achieved in the very early days, but the Germans rapidly recovered their poise and control of the situation. The capture of the whole length of Vimy Ridge, well known to the general public from operations in the area earlier in the war, was a boost for morale. But it was a disappointing battle, overshadowed by the failure of Nivelle to come remotely close to his stated – and promised – objectives. The daily casualty rate (a total of over 120,000) in the BEF, in what was, admittedly, a shorter battle, was substantially higher than that suffered during the Somme the previous year.

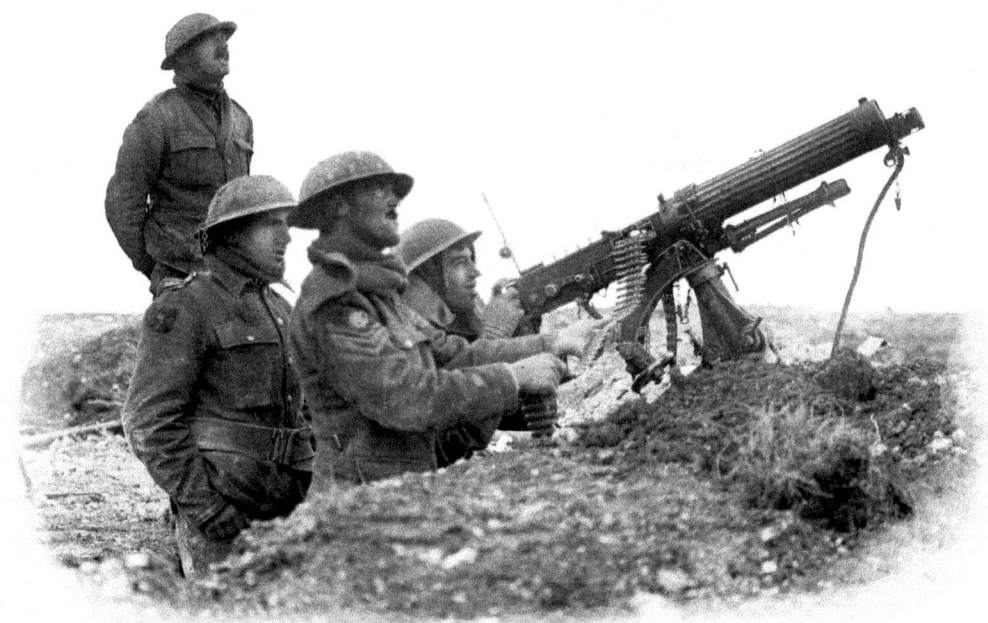

17GW087 A British Vickers machine gun crew takes on an intruder flying over their lines.

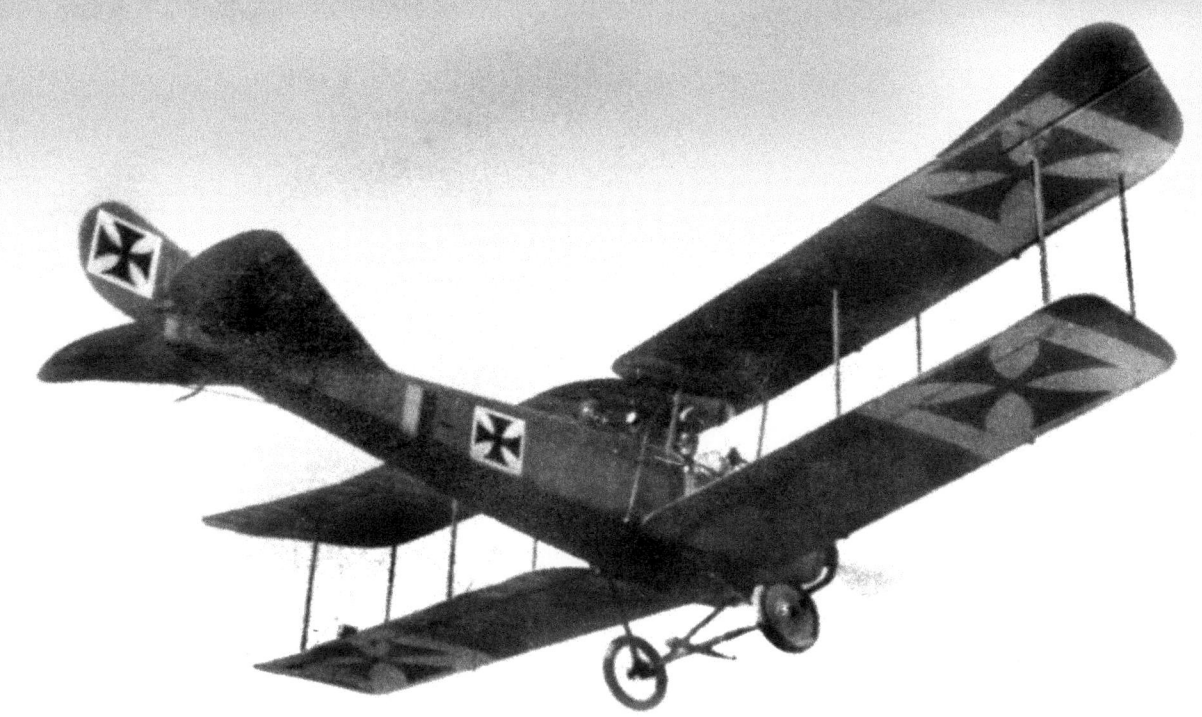

Chapter Three: Bloody April – The Red Baron – *Air War, Fighters*

17GW331 The Albatros CI two-seater, powered by either a 150hp Benz or a 160hp Mercedes engine, equipped many German squadrons throughout 1915.

17GW333 Members of No.1 Squadron pose with their SE.5a fighters at Clairmarais South, St Omer, in July 1918.

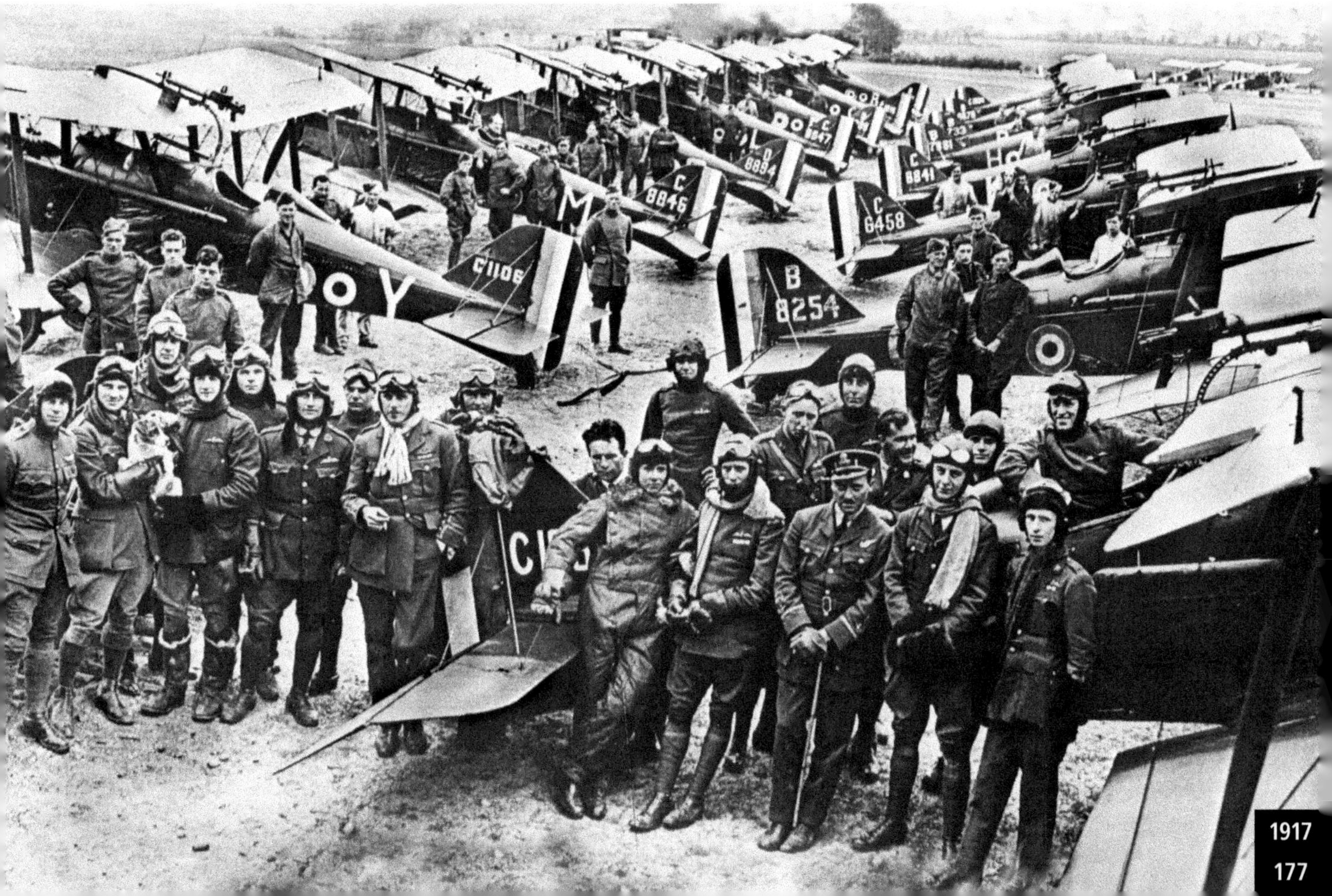

The twentieth century was three years old when, on 17 December, 1903, Orville Wright piloted the first powered flying machine twenty feet above a wind-swept beach in North Carolina. The flight lasted twelve seconds and covered 120 feet. Three more flights were made that day, with Orville's brother Wilbur piloting the longest flight, lasting fifty-nine seconds, over a distance of 852 feet. Heavier than air powered flight had arrived – how would the new wonder be employed? Just over a decade on and the flying machine went to war, contributing a further dimension to the killing game that had been played for thousands of years by the tribes and nations of the world.

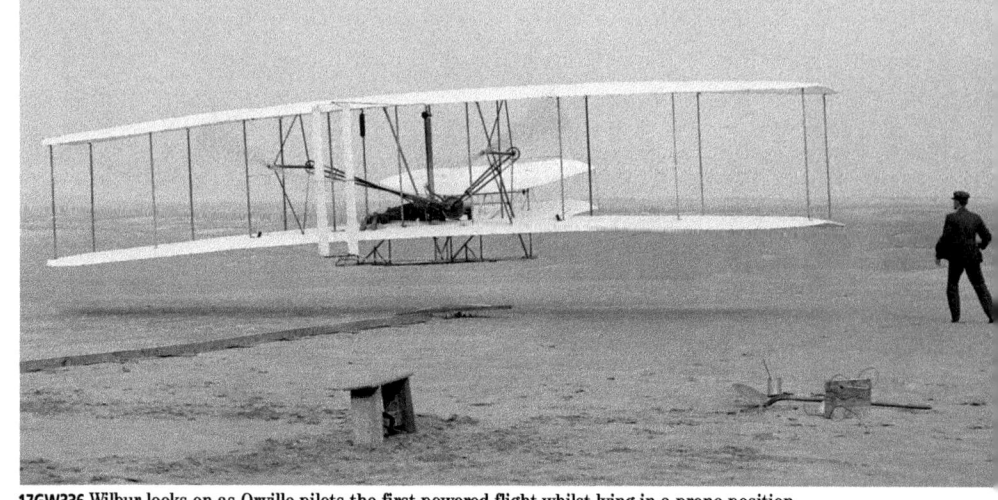

17GW336 Wilbur looks on as Orville pilots the first powered flight whilst lying in a prone position.

17GW337 A national flying competition in Germany in 1910: a German-built Wright biplane passes over a Prussian officer at an airfield near Berlin. The military possibilities for the new fangled flying contraptions were being weighed up.

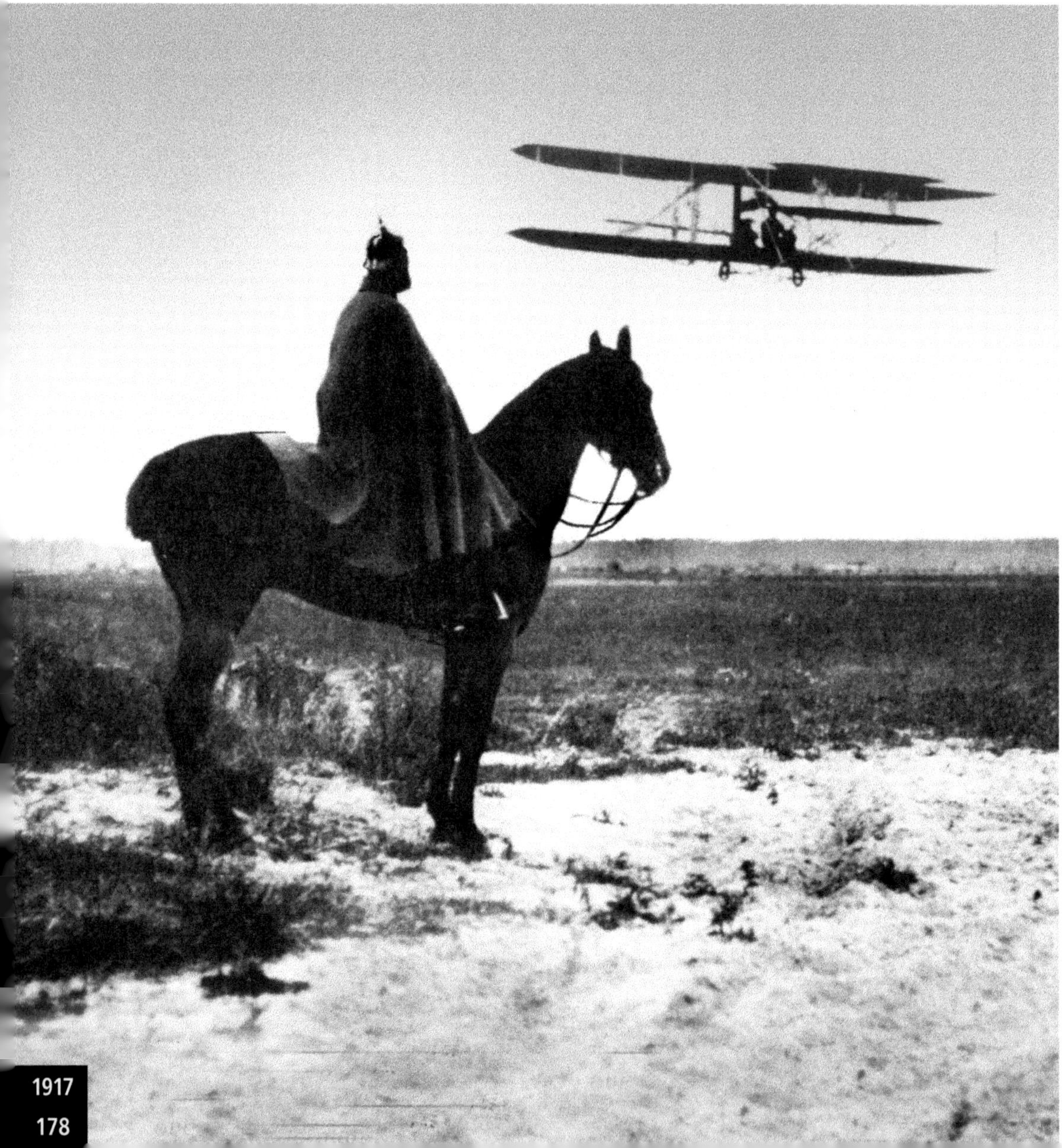

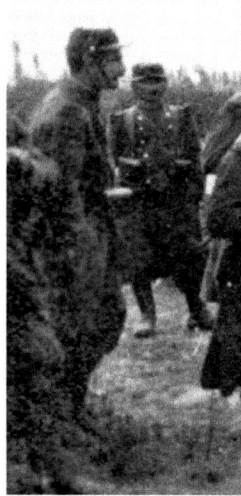

17GW340 By 1911 Austria-Hungary had formed a flying school that boasted five aircraft. Students, who have just qualified, stand before a Taube.

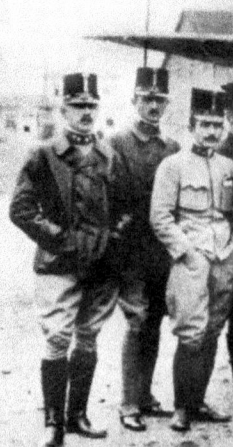

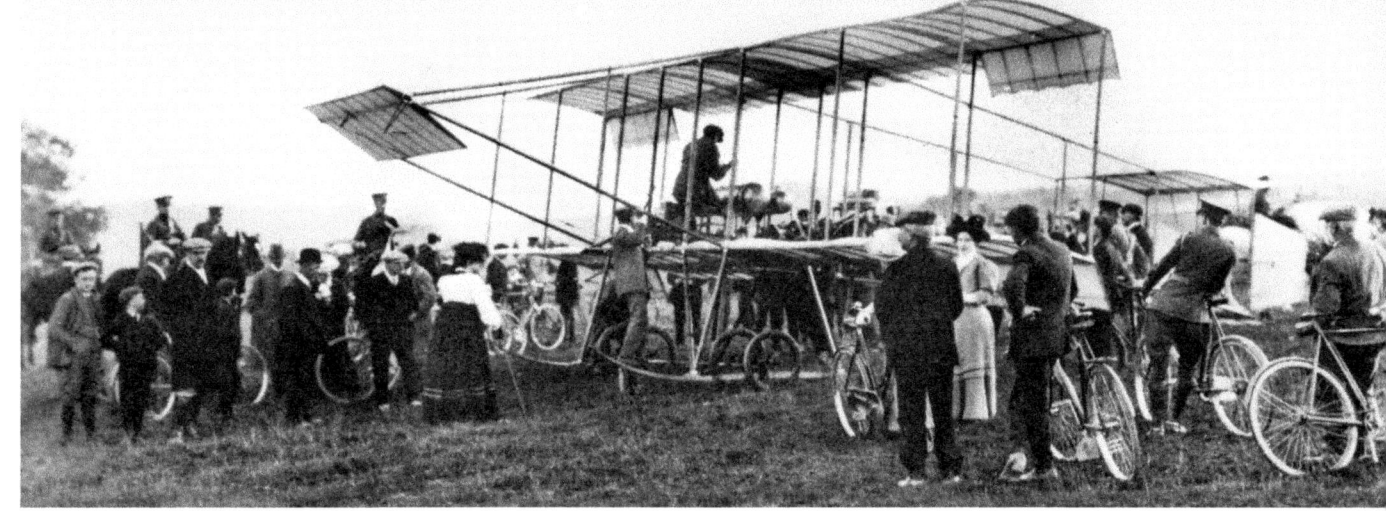

17GW338 Civilian spectators cluster around a Bristol Boxkite at the British Army's manoeuvres in 1910 as the pilot, Captain Dickson, makes ready for a take-off.

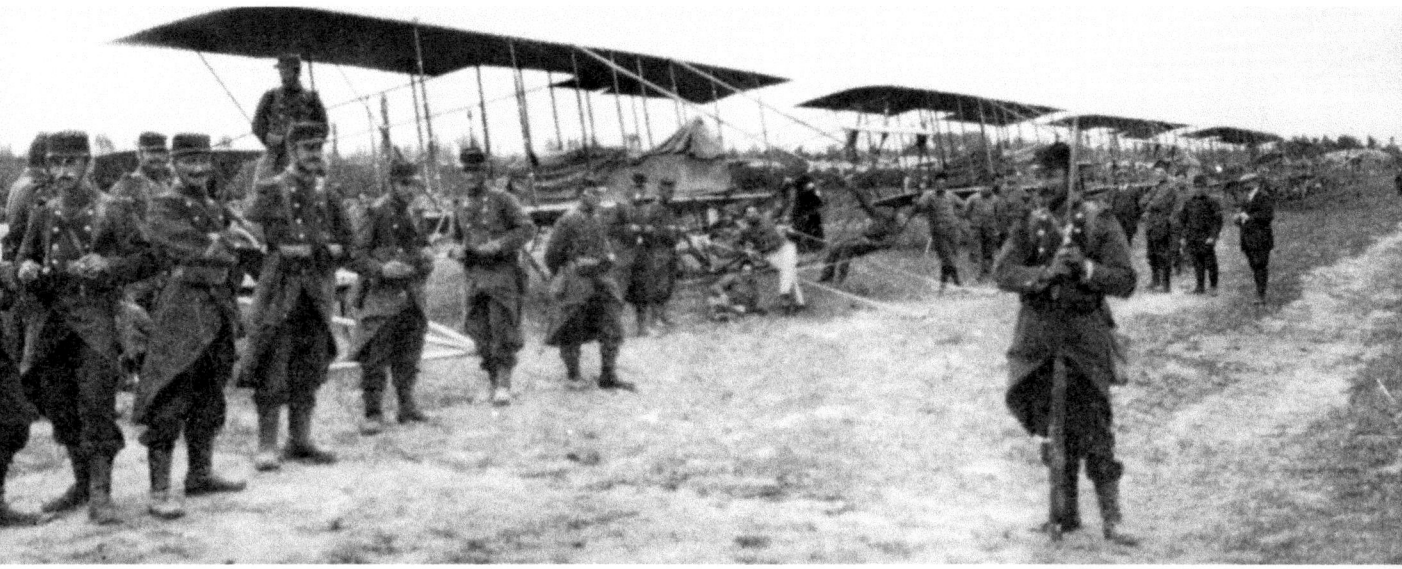

17GW339 French biplanes are lined up during the army manoeuvres in 1912. With two years to go before the Great War, the French had begun forming squadrons (escadrille) and the one pictured is Escadrille MF5, indicating it to be the fifth formed, and was equipped with the Maurice Farman built machines.

17GW334 Hugh Montague Trenchard.
With the outbreak of the First World War, Hugh Trenchard was appointed Officer Commanding the Military Wing of the Royal Flying Corps. Trenchard's duties included providing replacements and raising new squadrons for service on the continent. Trenchard initially set himself a target of 12 squadrons. However, Lord Kitchener set the target at 60.
In October 1914, Kitchener sent for Trenchard and ordered him to provide a battle-worthy squadron immediately. The squadron was needed to support land and naval forces seeking to prevent the German flanking manoeuvres during the Race to the Sea taking place in France. Only 36 hours later, No. 6 Squadron took off for Belgium. Trenchard was promoted to brigadier general and appointed Officer Commanding the RFC in France. In late 1915 Haig was appointed commander of the British Expeditionary Force and, in the following year, with the RFC expanding, Trenchard was promoted to major general.

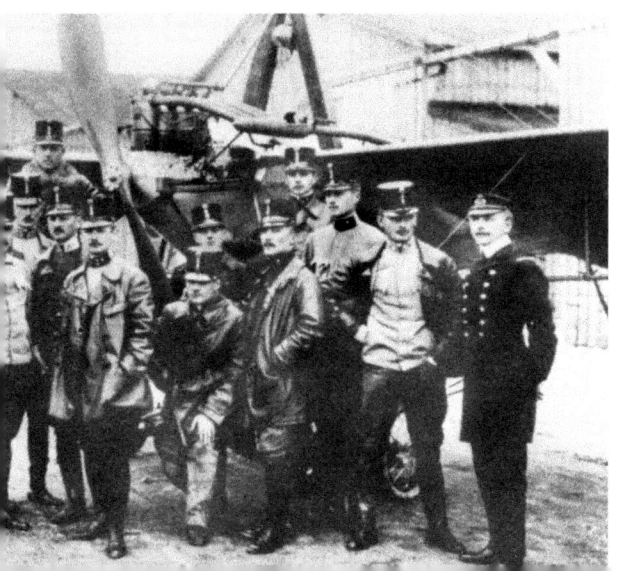

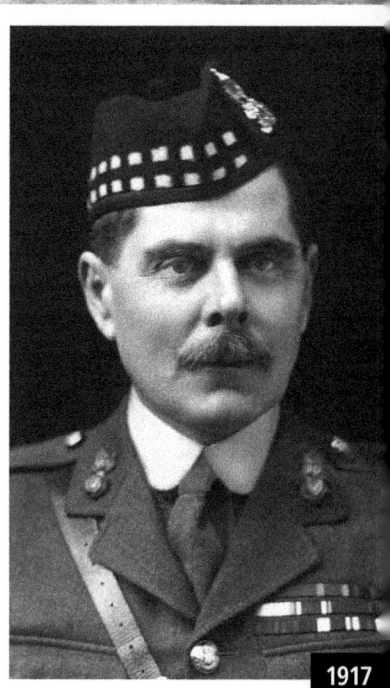

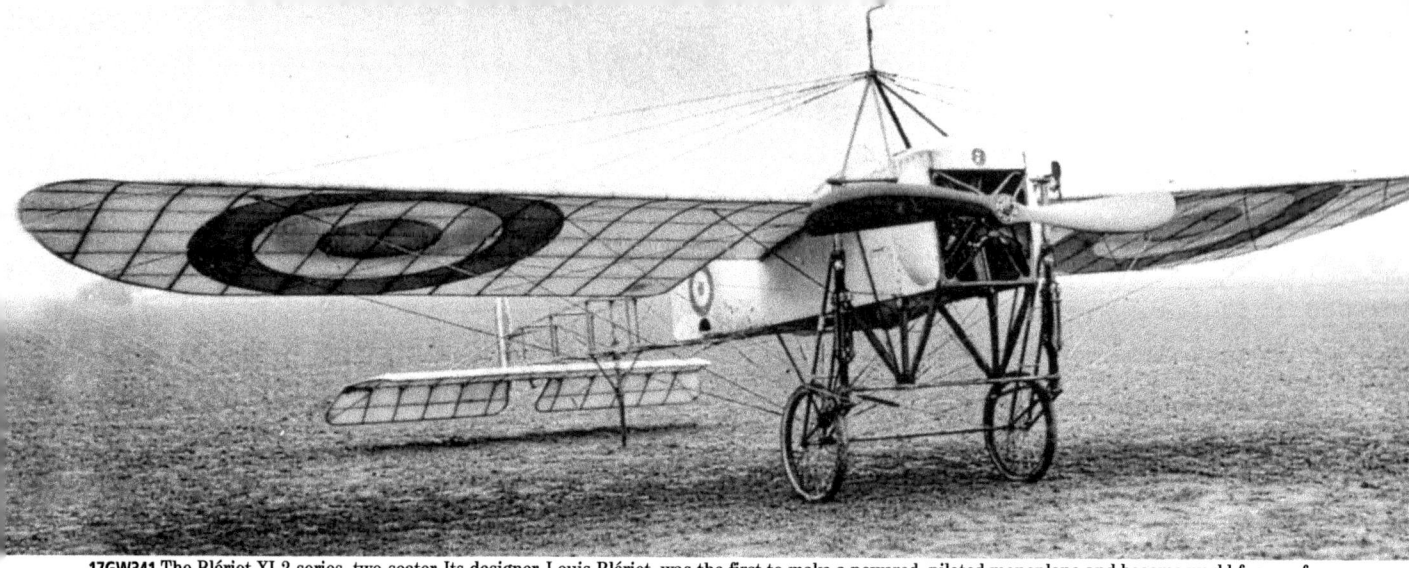

17GW341 The Blériot XI-2 series, two-seater. Its designer, Louis Blériot, was the first to make a powered, piloted monoplane and became world famous for making the first flight across the English Channel in a heavier than air aircraft in 1909.

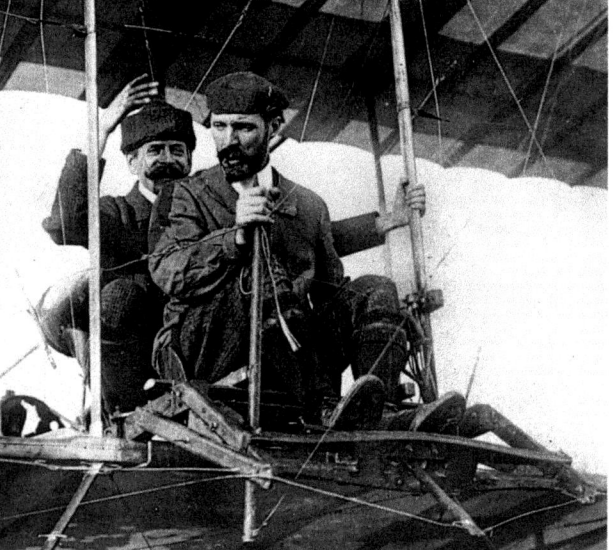

17GW344 *'Tenez serré, Monsieur!'* Henri Farman, one of the great French aircraft designers, orders his passenger to hang on tight as he opens the throttle on this early model flying machine at the Rheims exhibition in 1909.

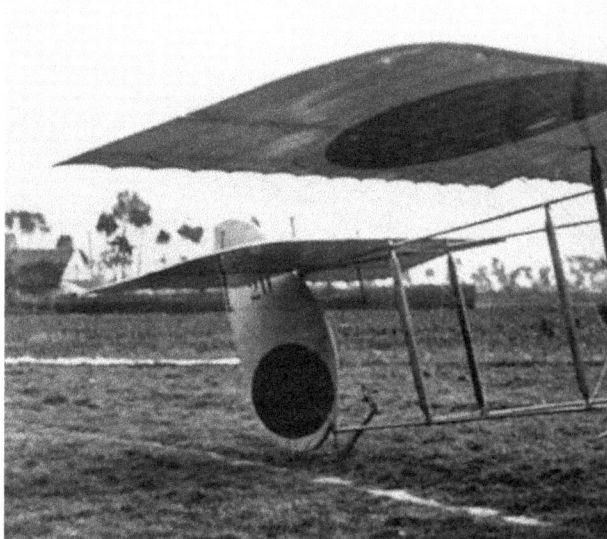

17GW345 The Farman HF20 two-seater observation aircraft and later training machine.

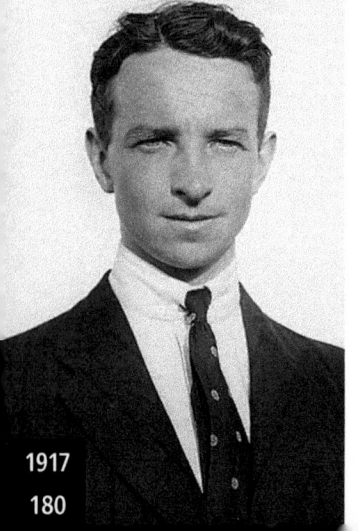

17GW349 Thomas Octave Murdoch Sopwith, British aviation pioneer and designer.

17GW347 The Sopwith Tabloid: in August 1914 four of these machines were transported to France in crates to form an Aircraft Park where aeroplanes could be on hand as replacements for operational machines. Other Tabloids were flown out to the Aircraft Park. At sea level the Tabloid could reach just over 90 mph

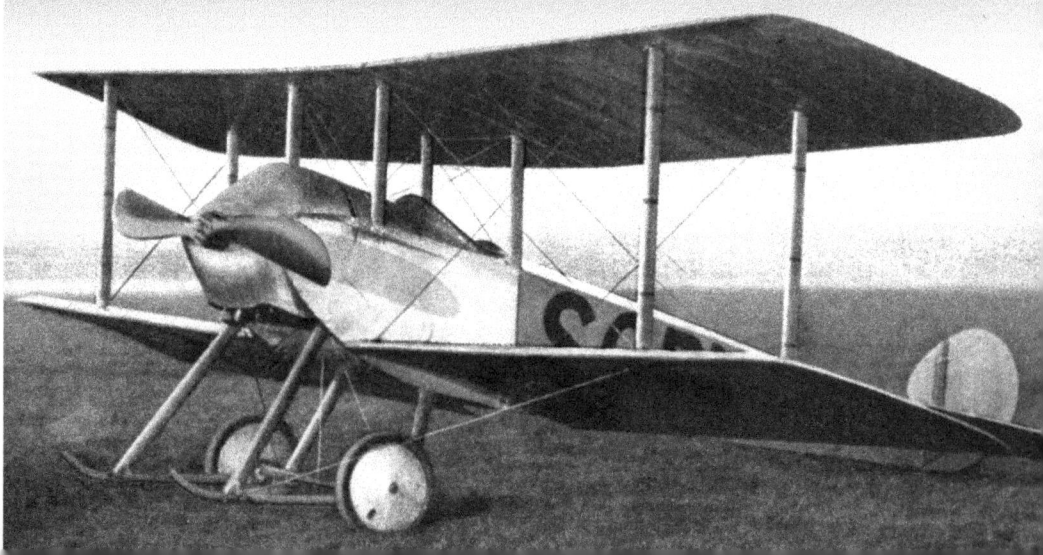

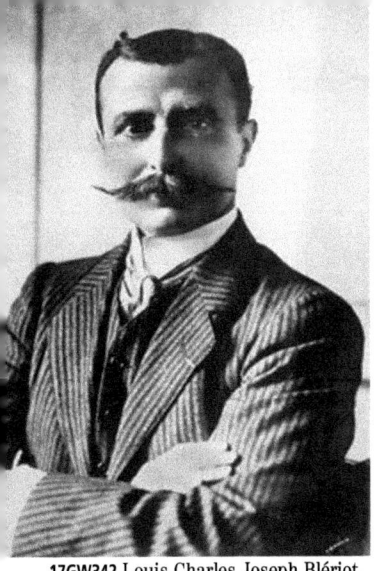
17GW342 Louis Charles Joseph Blériot.

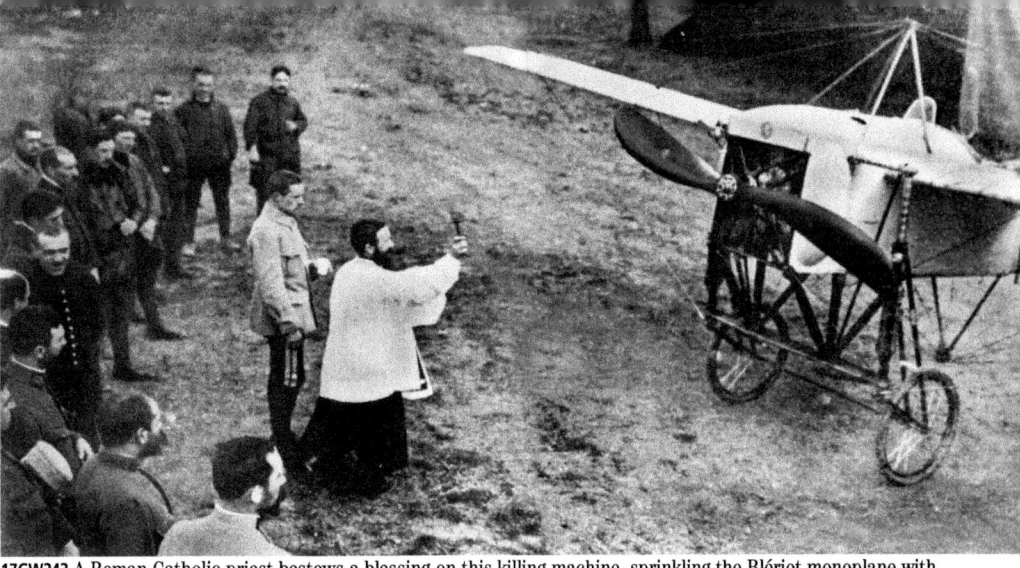
17GW343 A Roman Catholic priest bestows a blessing on this killing machine, sprinkling the Blériot monoplane with holy water. The pilot and other French aviators observe the ceremony.

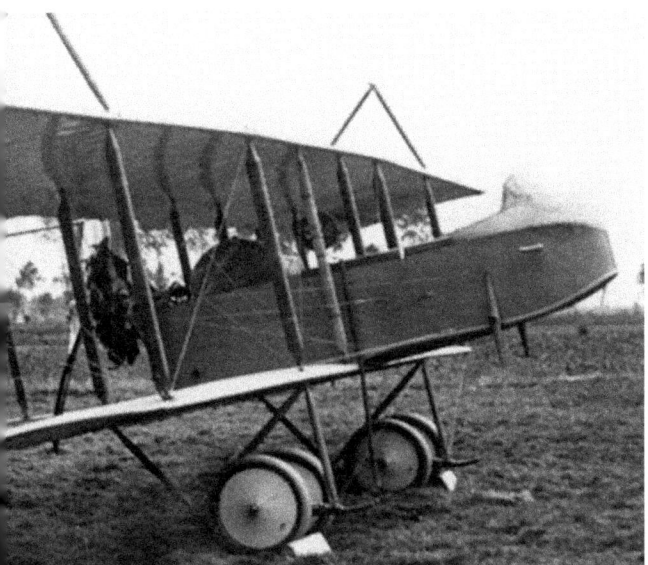
17GW350 The BE2c (B.E. stood for Blériot Experimental); built by the Royal Aircraft Factory was used by the RFC for reconnaissance work.

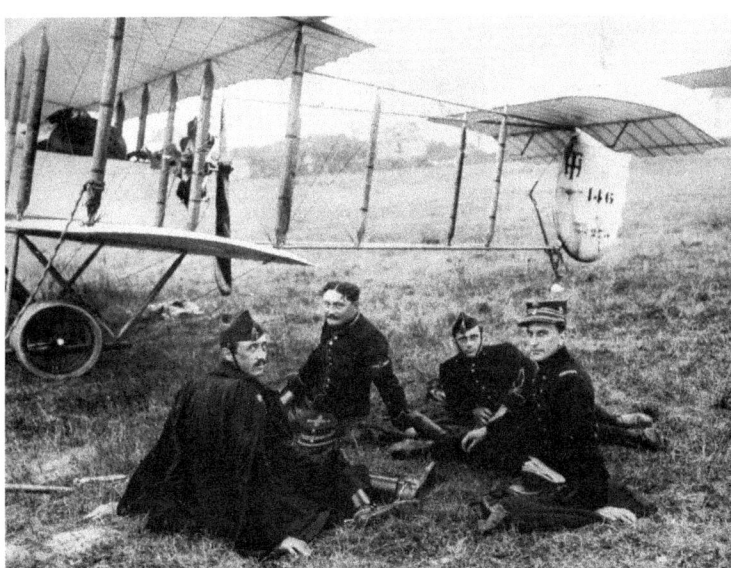
17GW346 Belgian air force pilots with their Farman HF20 weeks after the outbreak of war and the invasion of their country.

When war broke out, the air services of Great Britain, the Royal Naval Air Service and the Royal Flying Corps, owned a mixed collection of unrelated and largely unsuitable aeroplanes. With some urgency they had to be arranged in units most convenient for the arm of the services they had to equip. The aeroplanes of the RFC were frail, slow and unarmed; they were no different from aircraft used for sporting and instructional flying. RFC pilots, trained in the traditions of the Army, looked upon their aeroplanes as the eyes of the Army.

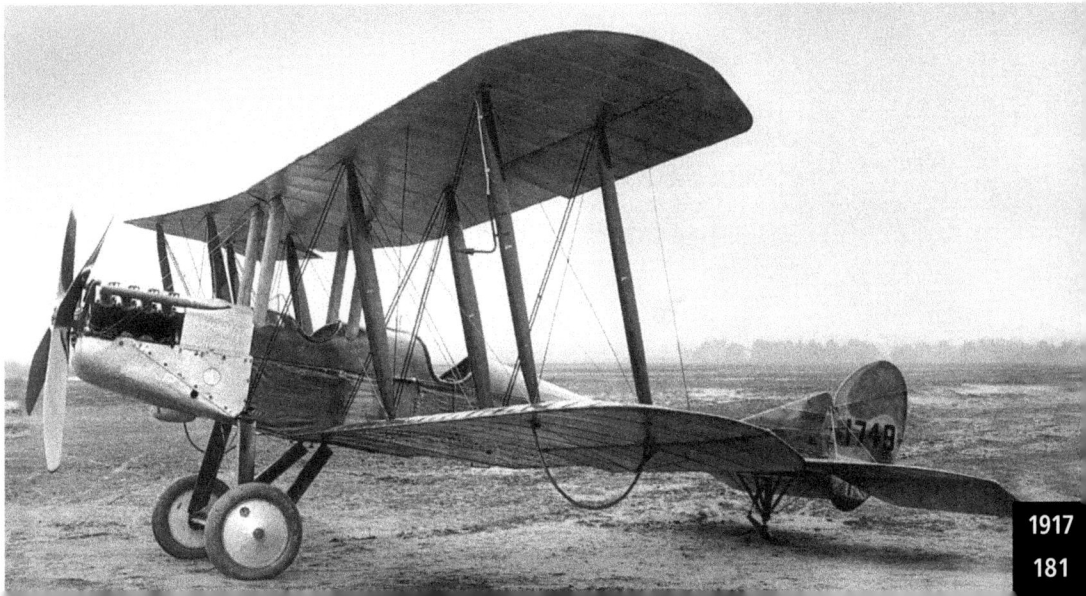

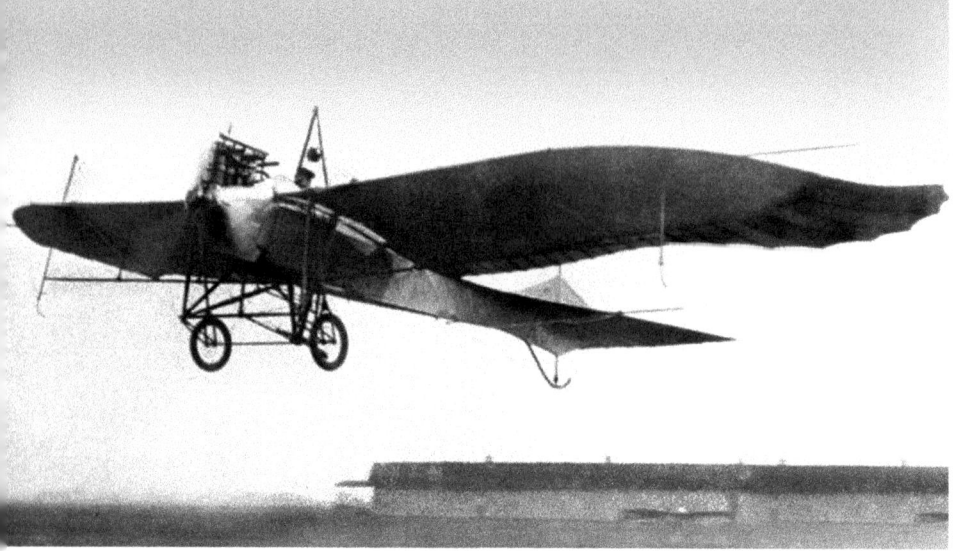

17GW352 The Taube was a popular flying machine prior to the First World War and was used by the air forces of Italy and Austria-Hungary. Even the Royal Flying Corps operated at least one Taube in 1912. Once the war began, it soon proved inferior as a serious warplane and, as a result, was soon replaced by newer and more effective designs. However, its use by the Germans as a scout for its advancing armies in the opening moves of 1914 was effective and its distinctive shape appeared menacing to the retreating allied soldiers.

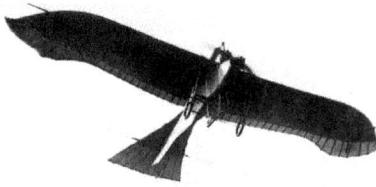

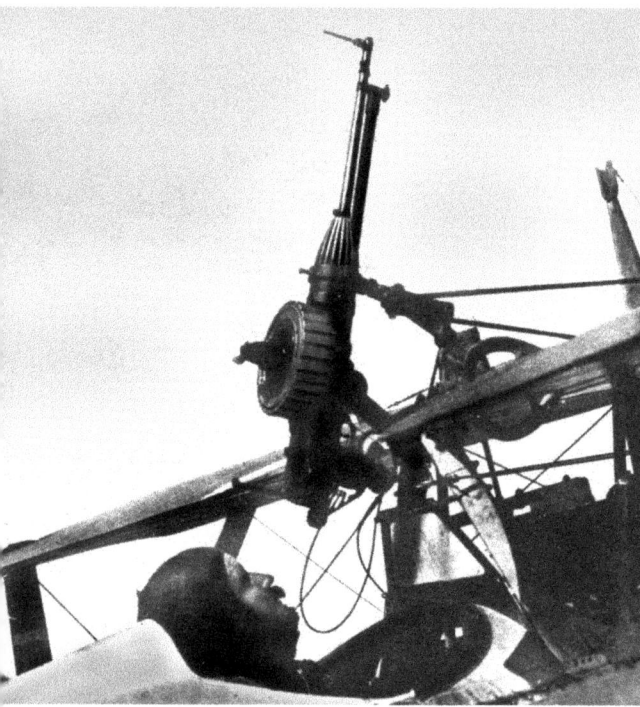

17GW356 A solution arrived at for firing forward and avoiding hitting the aircraft's propeller; here the Lewis gun was mounted on the upper wing, which enabled the pilot to fire in the direction of flight.

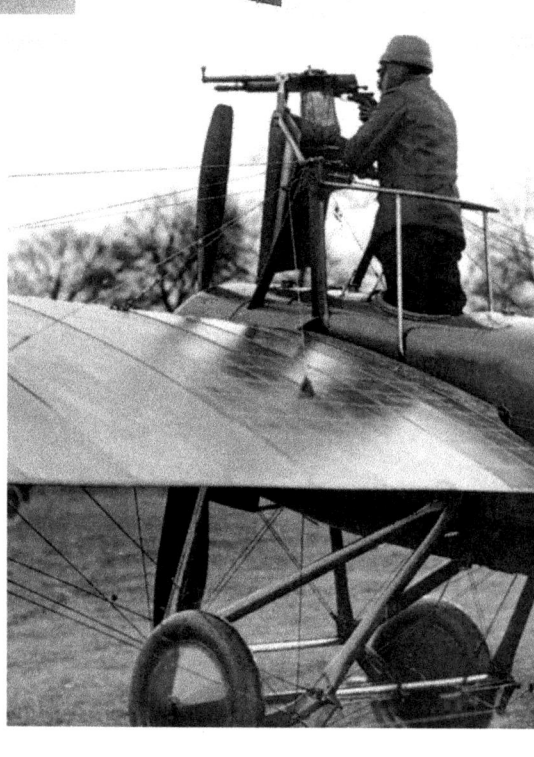

17GW358 The arc of the propellor was avoided on this French two-seater monoplane, with the observer firing a Hotchkiss machine gun from a specially constructed and precarious perch.

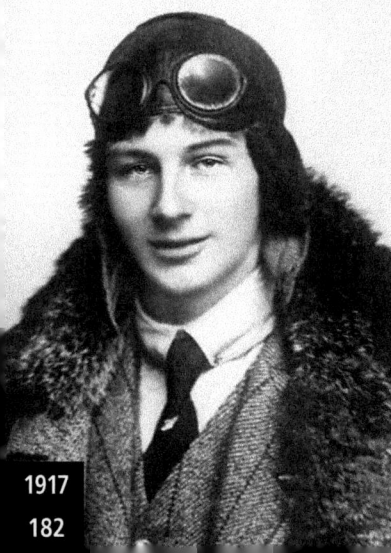

17GW351 Anton Herman Gerard Fokker. 'Anthony' Fokker was a Dutch businessman with his factory near Berlin. When war broke out the German government took control of the factory. Fokker remained as director and alleged designer of many aircraft for the Imperial German Army Air Service (*Luftstreitkräfte*). Fokker is often credited with having invented the synchronization device which enabled First World War aircraft to fire through the spinning propeller. It was incorporated into the famous Fokker Eindecker, its use directly led to a phase of German air superiority known as the 'Fokker Scourge' in 1915.

17GW362 A Fokker Eindecker EI, with its single Spandau machine gun firing through the propeller arc with the aid of an interrupter gear.

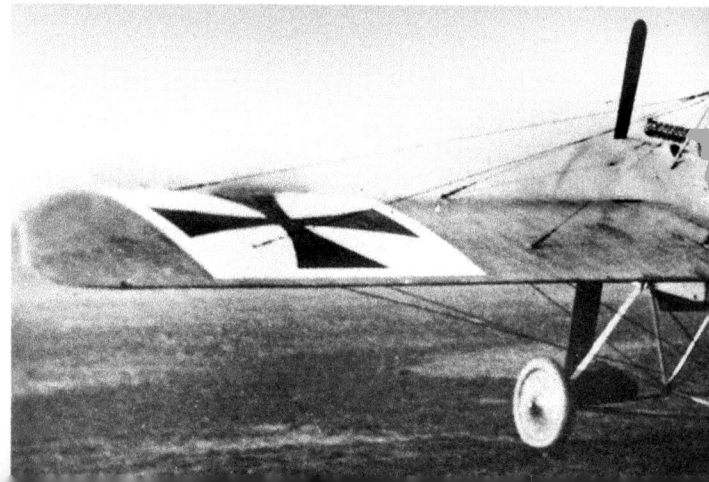

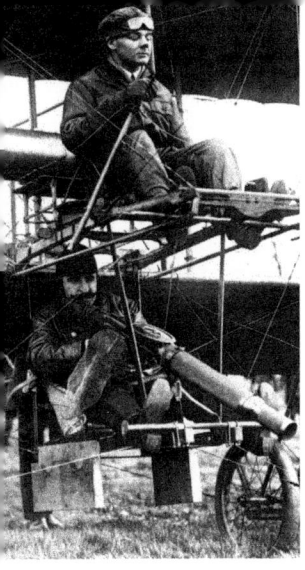

17GW354 In 1914, when opponents met in the skies over Belgium and France, they took shots at each other with pistols or rifles; mounting a machine gun was the answer and various options were tried. Here a Lewis gun is being tried slung underneath the pilot.

17GW355 An early attempt to mount a Lewis gun fired by the pilot. The angle was to the right in order to clear the propellor, which meant the pilot had to fly the plane crab-like in order to hit an enemy aircraft.

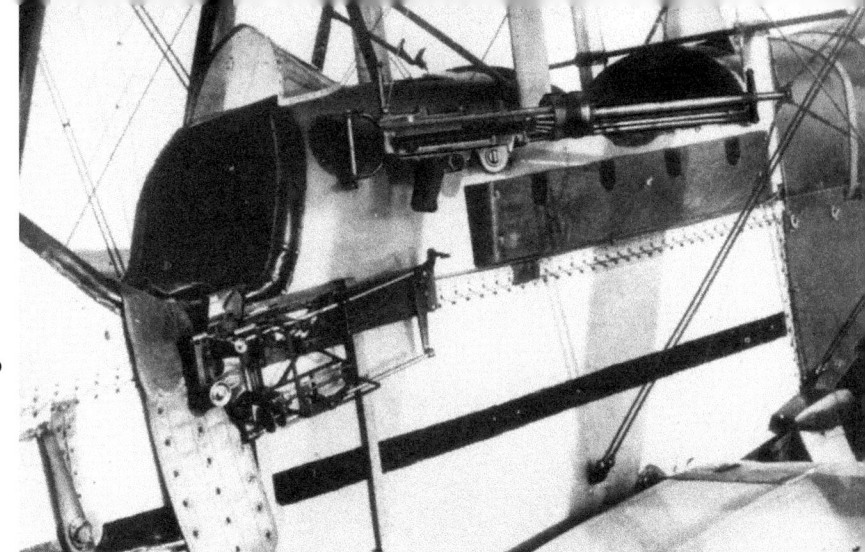

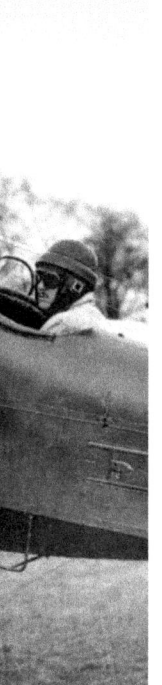

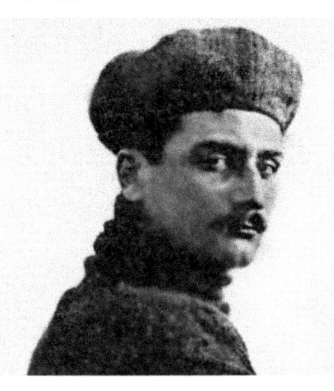

17GW360 Roland Georges Garros was a pre-war aviator who, on the outbreak of war, served with Escadrille MS26. He fitted bullet deflectors to his aircraft propellor blades and achieved the first ever shooting down of an aircraft by a fighter firing through a tractor propeller on 1 April 1915; two more victories over German aircraft were achieved on 15 and 18 April 1915.

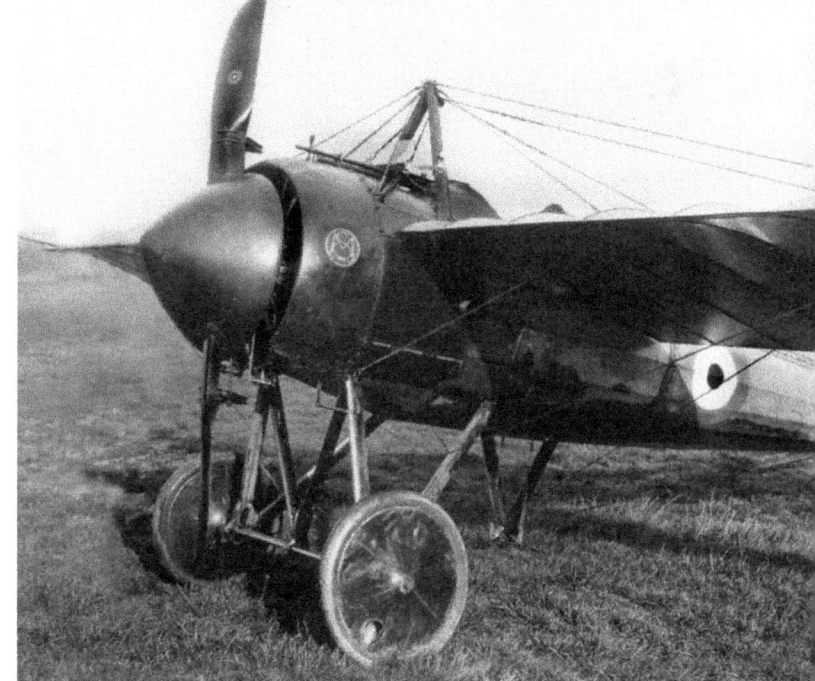

17GW358 French Morane-Saulnier with deflectors fitted to each blade.

17GW361 A good view of an Eindecker EIII – it was was soon to become the favored mount of the German air aces: Ernst Udet is the officer examining the ammunition belt.

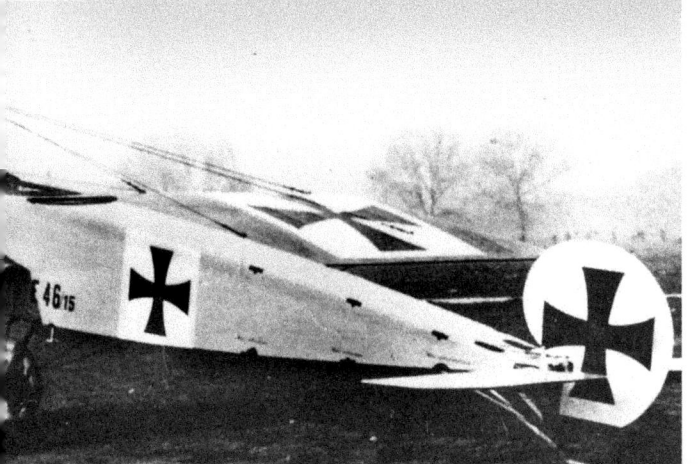

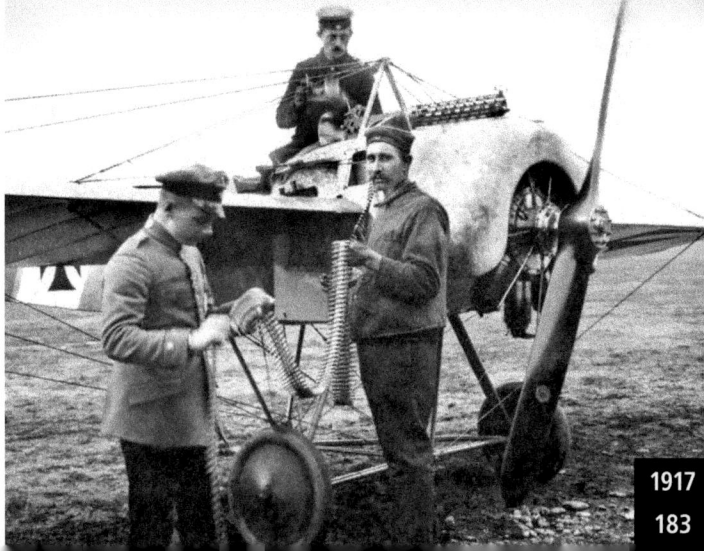

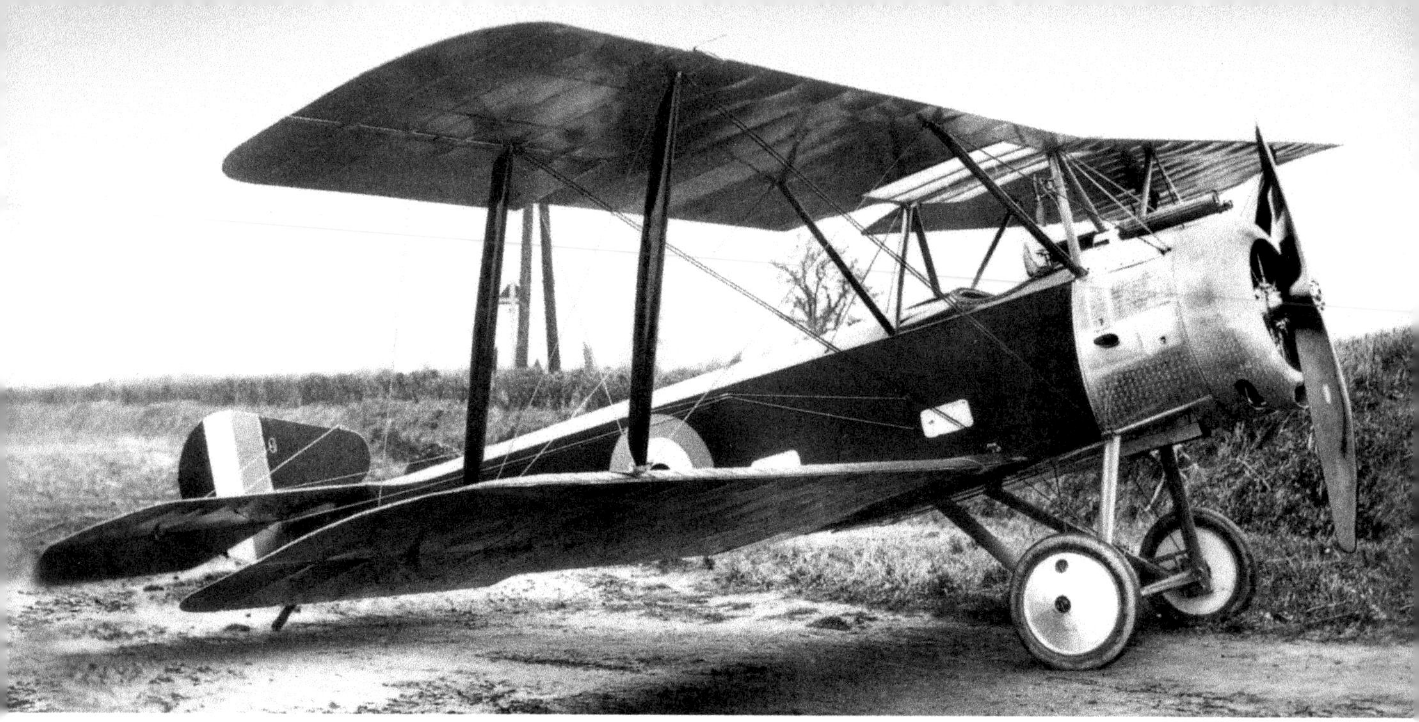

17GW542 The first British aircraft to carry a machine gun synchronised to fire through the spinning propellor was the Sopwith 1½ Strutter. The rate of fire was 300 rounds per minute. The German Albatros, with its twin machine guns, could (theoretically) fire 2,000 rounds per minute. The Strutter was in squadron service for twelve months 1915-1916, mainly by the Royal Naval Air Service.

17GW543 Standard defensive armament for the German two-seater reconnaissance aircraft, the Parabellum MG14, an adaptation of the Maxim gun system intended for use on aircraft and zeppelins.

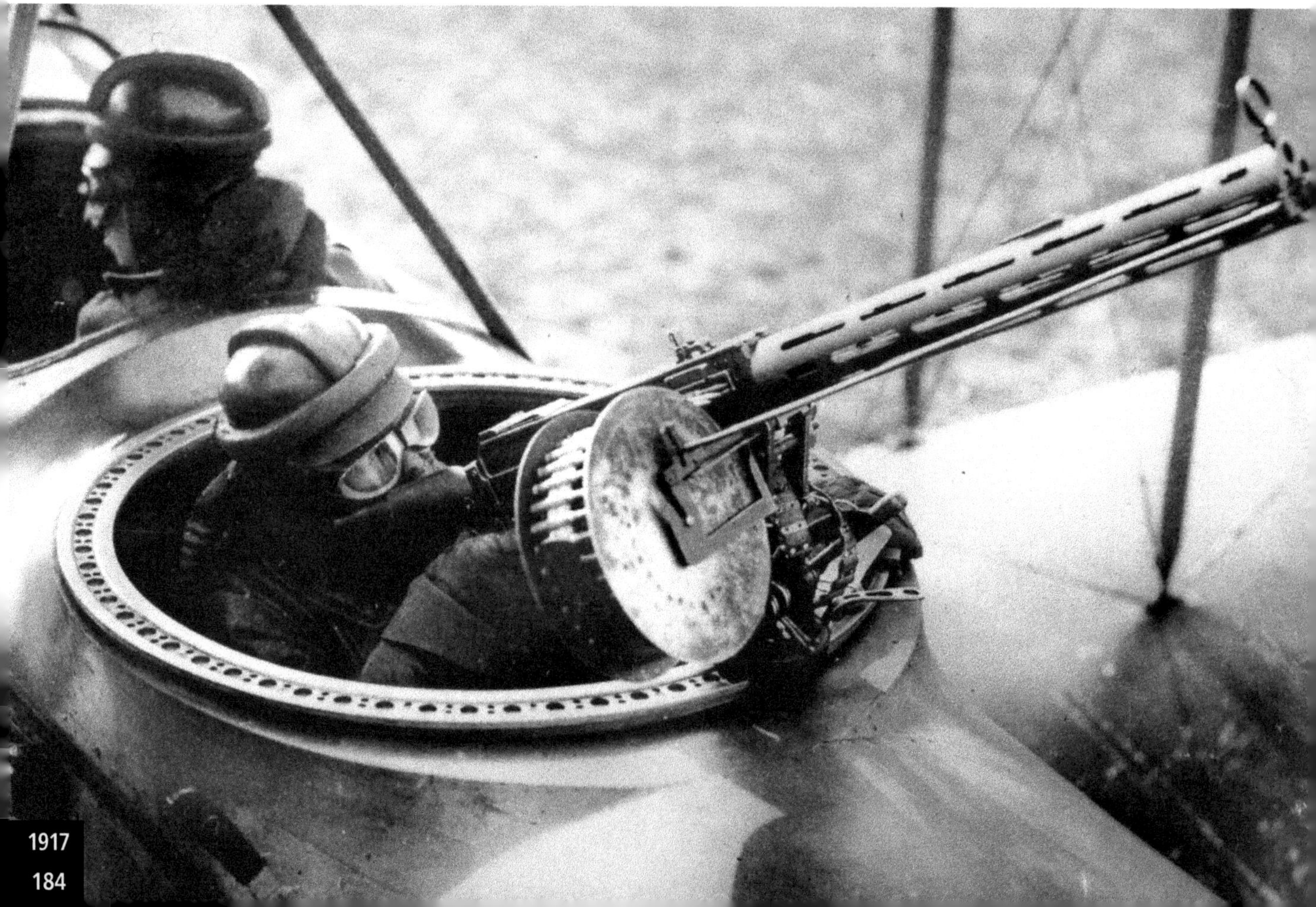

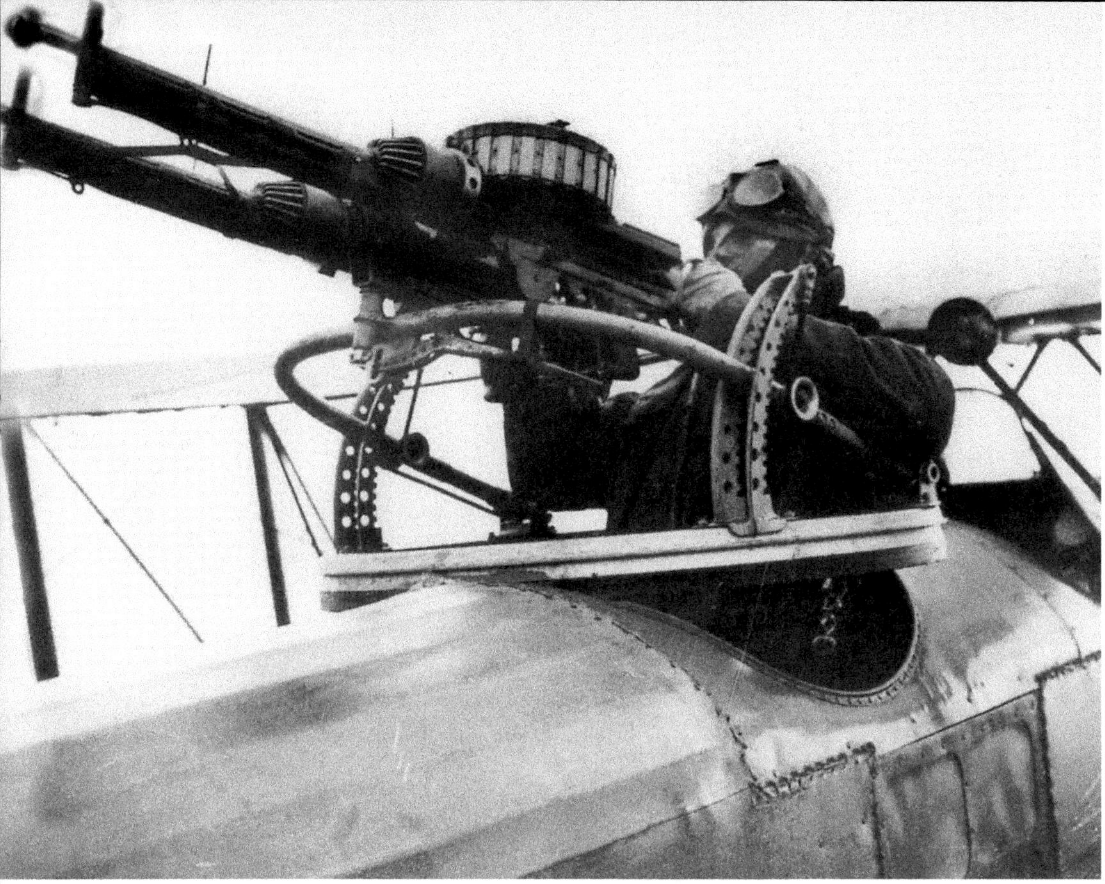

17GW544 The French Breguet 14A2 biplane for reconnaissance and bombing. Pictured in December 1917. The defensive armaments have been given a strong punch with the twin Lewis guns. Its strong construction was able to sustain much damage and had a good overall performance. The Breguet 14 is considered to have been one of the best aircraft of the war.

17GW545 *Leutnant* Gontermann (in goggles) in the cockpit of a RFC FE2D that he had forced down behind the German lines. Gontermann was killed in October 1917, when his score of kills stood at 39.

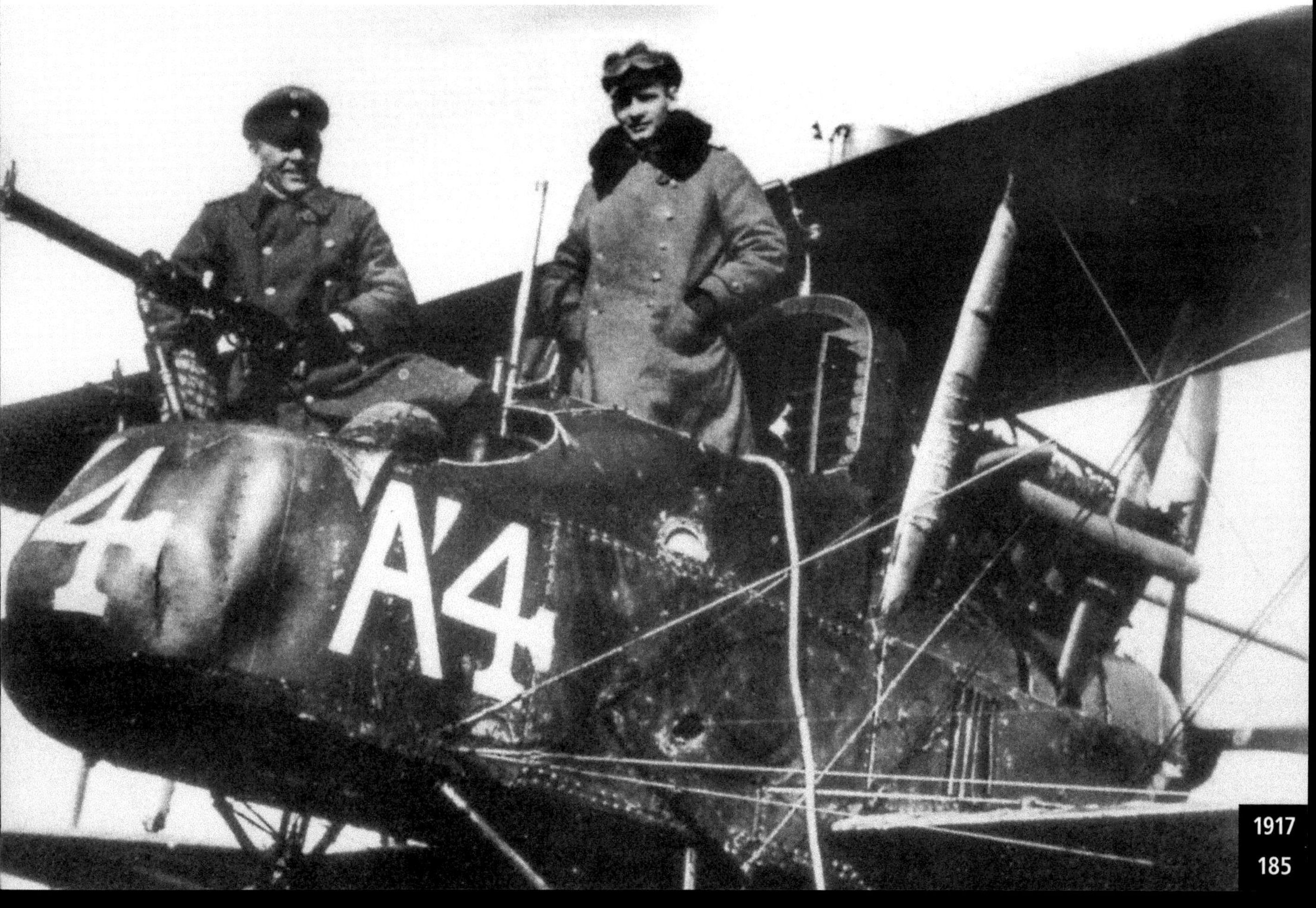

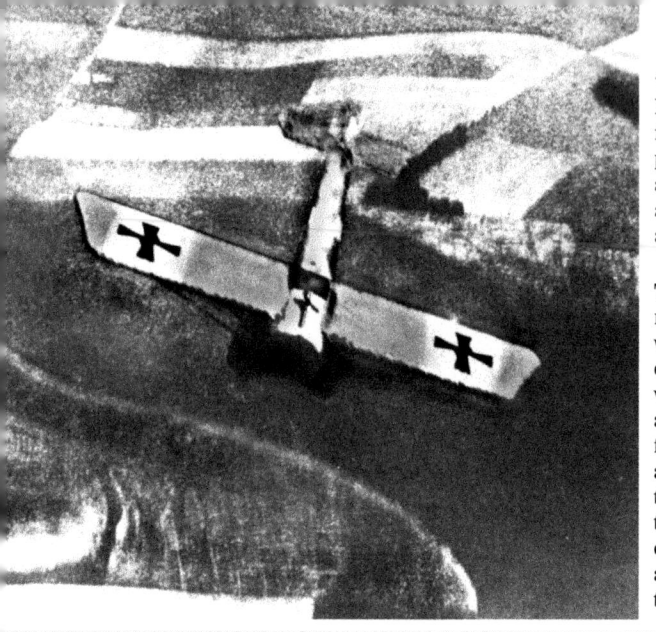

17GW363 A Focker Eindecker coming in for the kill and photographed in the act by the RFC aircraft it is attacking.

The term 'Ace' referred to a pilot who achieved five confirmed 'kills' or victories. Along with aircraft development flying aces began to appear, men who, in the main, conducted themselves in a chivalrous manner and were likened to the knights of old.

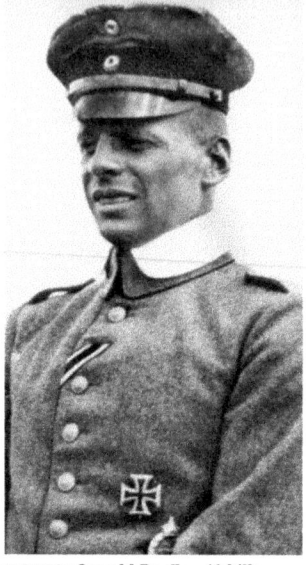

17GW364 Oswald Boelke, 40 kills. Died October 1916.

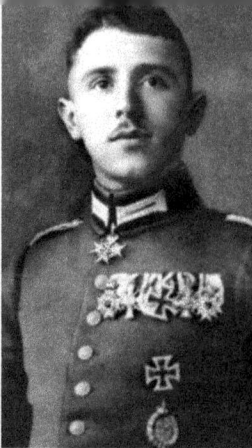

17GW365 Max Immelmann. 15 kills. Died June 1916. First German flying ace. A pioneer in fighter tactics, he originated a manoeuvre that was associated with his name.

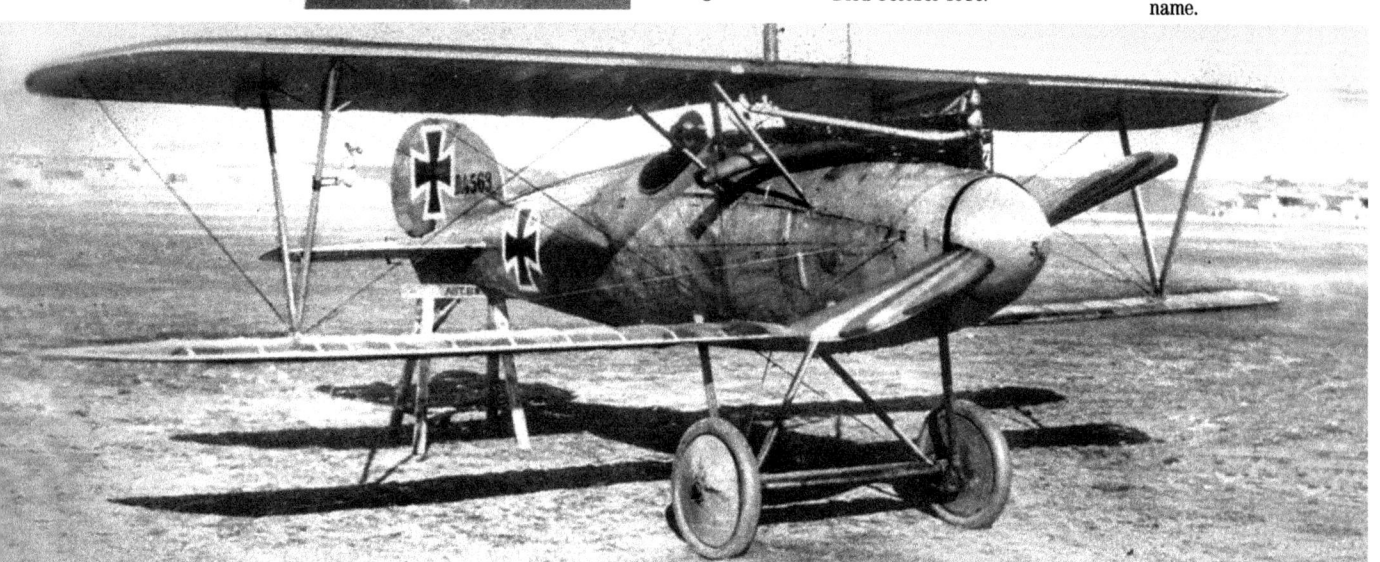

17GW395 The Albatros D.III was used by the *Luftstreitkräfte* and the Austro-Hungarian Air Service (*Luftfahrtruppen*) The D.III was flown by many top German aces. It was the pre-eminent fighter during the period of German aerial dominance known as 'Bloody April' 1917.

17GW393 The LFG Roland CII, usually known as the *Walfisch* (Whale), was an advanced German reconnaissance aircraft. It had a much lower drag than comparable aircraft of its time. British fighter ace, Albert Ball, commented in the autumn of 1916 that the CII was 'the best German machine to date'.

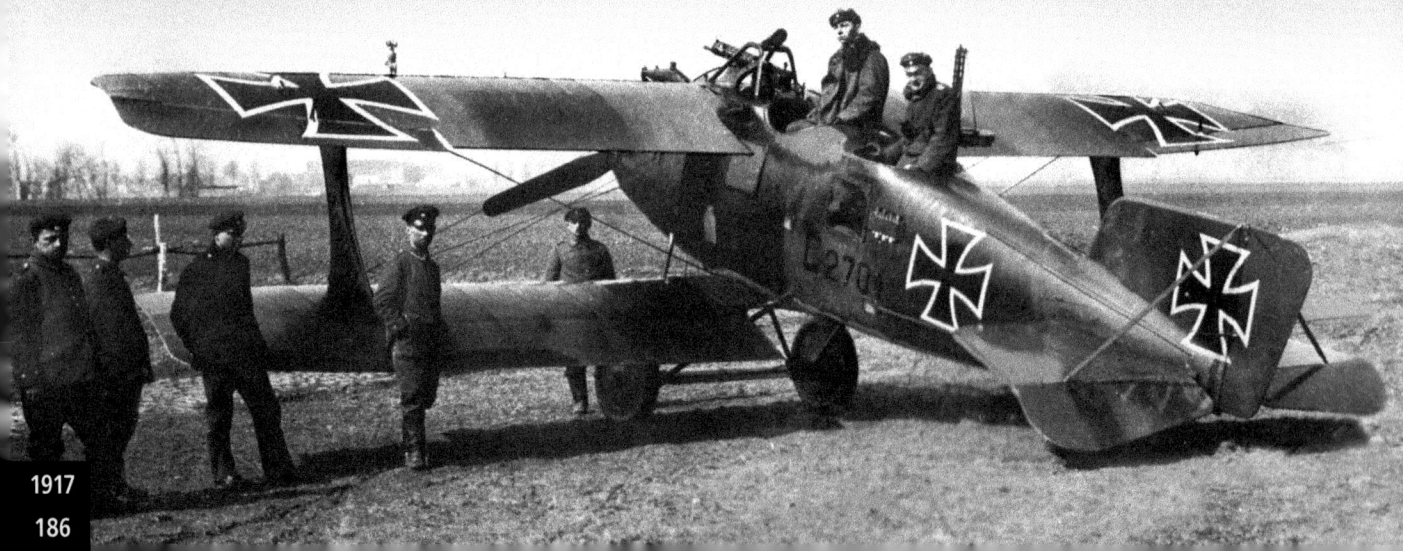

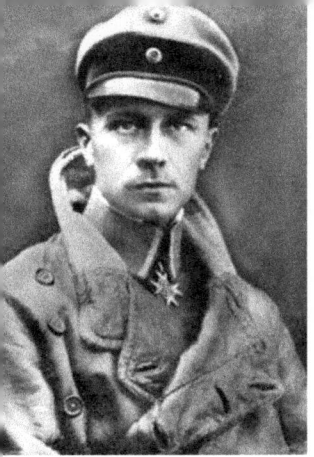 17GW366 Eduard Ritter von Schleich, 35 kills.
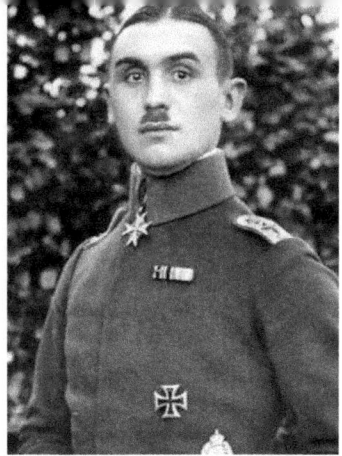 17GW367 Rudolf Berthold, 44 kills.
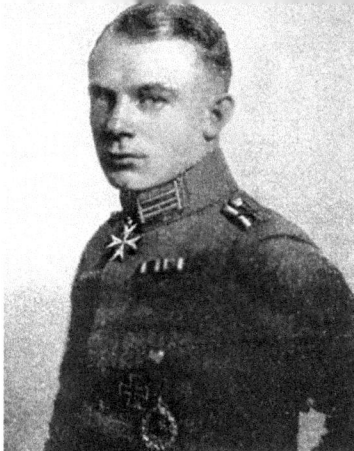 17GW368 Ernst Udet, 62 kills.
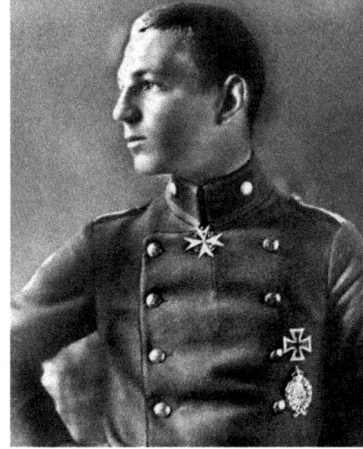 17GW369 Erich Loewenhardt, 53 kills. Died 1918.

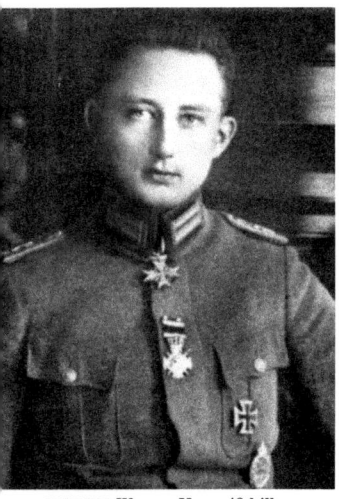 17GW370 Werner Voss, 48 kills. Died 1917.
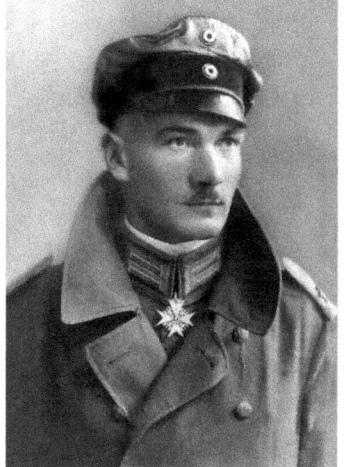 17GW371 Fritz Rumey, 45 kills. Died 1918.
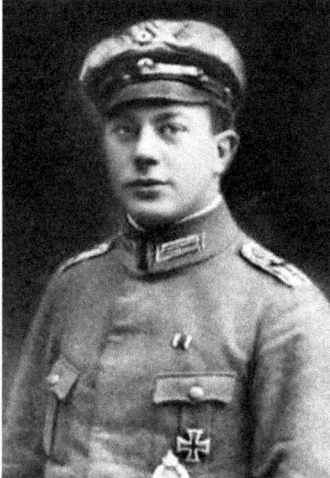 17GW372 Paul Bäumer, 43 kills.
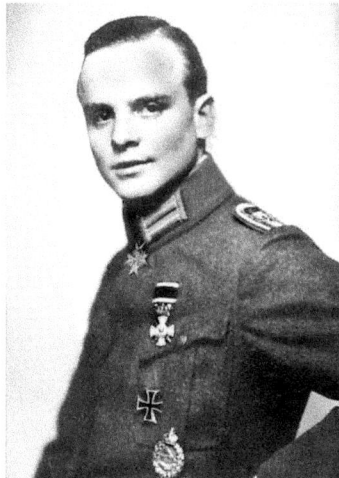 17GW373 Josef Jacobs, 41 kills.

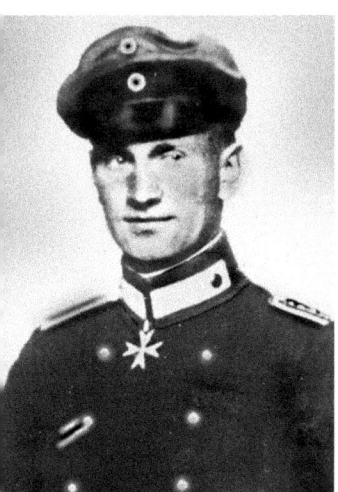 17GW374 Bruno Loerzer, 41 kills.
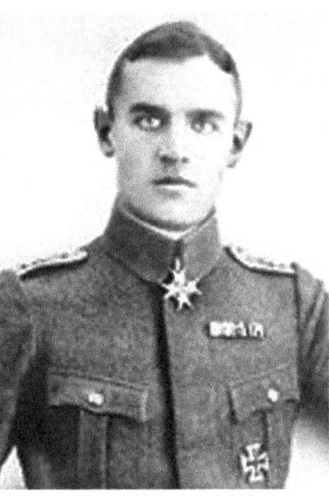 17GW375 Franz Büchner, 40 kills.
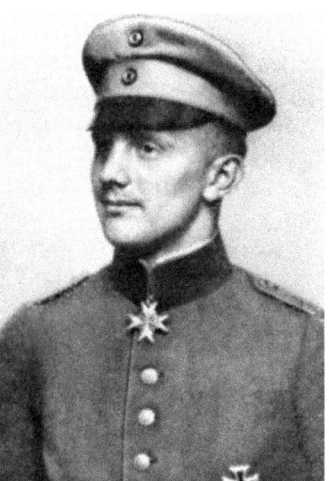 17GW376 Lothar von Richthofen, 40 kills.
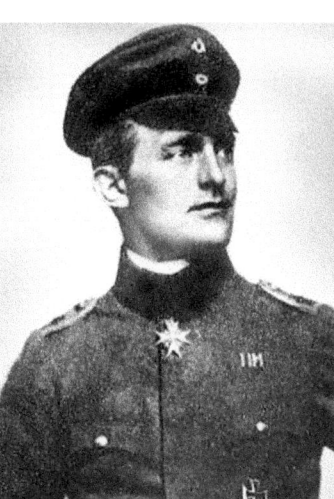 17GW377 Carl Menckhoff, 39 kills.

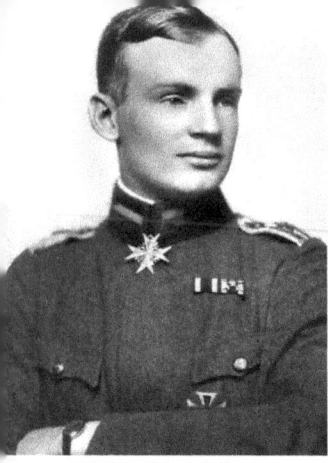 **17GW380** Heinrich Gontermann, 39 kills. Died 1917.

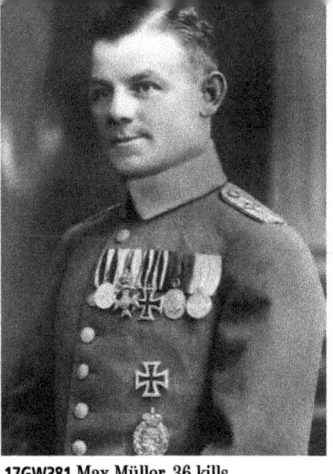 **17GW381** Max Müller, 36 kills. Died 1918.

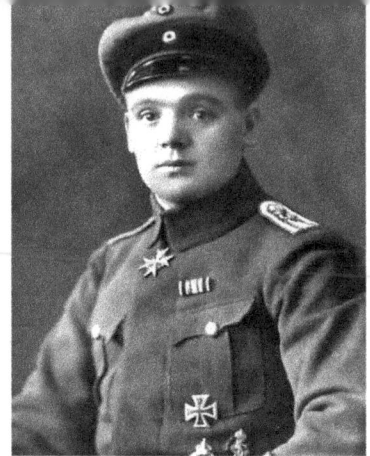 **17GW382** Julius Buckler, 35 kills.

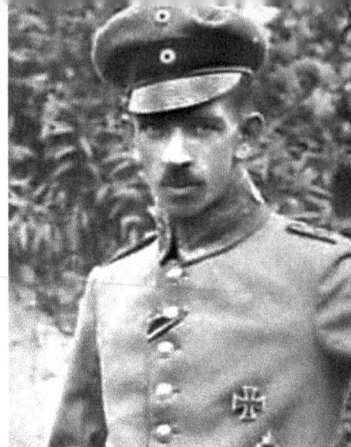 **17GW383** Gustav Döre, 35 kills.

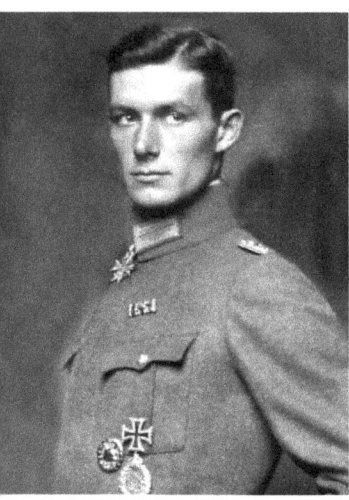 **17GW384** Josef Veltjens, 34 kills.

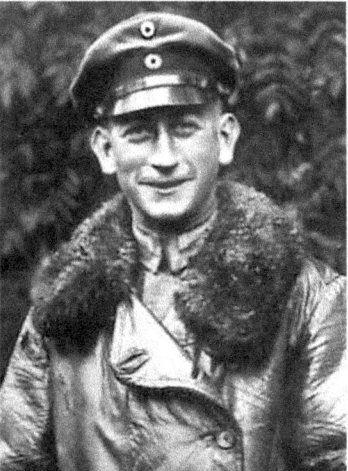 **17GW385** Otto Könnecke, 33 kills.

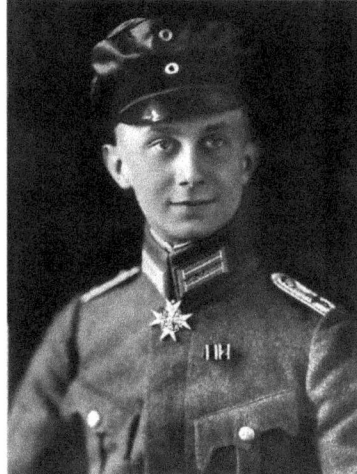 **17GW386** Kurt Wolff, 33 kills. Died 1917.

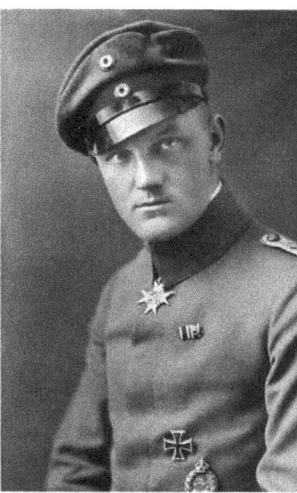 **17GW387** Heinrich Bongartz, 33 kills.

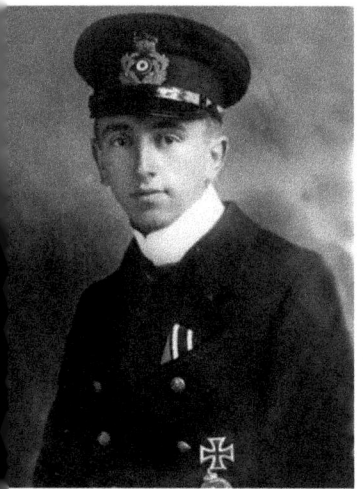 **17GW388** Theo Osterkamp, 32 kills.

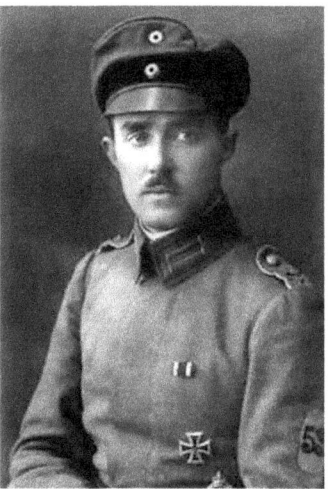 **17GW389** Emil Thuy, 32 kills.

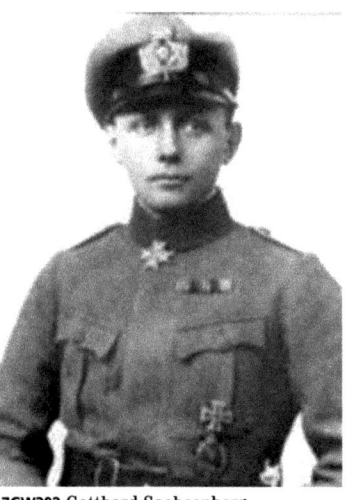 **17GW392** Gotthard Sachsenberg, 31 kills.

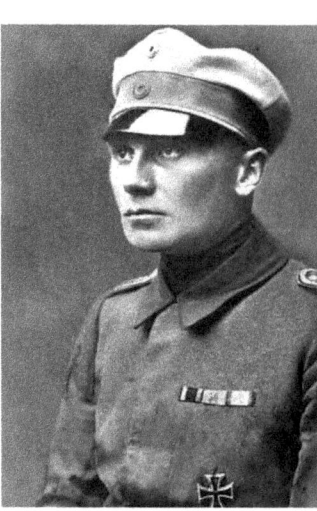 **17GW391** Karl Bolle, 31 kills.

THE GERMAN MILITARY GLORIFIED THEIR AVIATORS, TURNING INIVIDUALS INTO HEROES, PUBLICISING THEIR NUMBER OF KILLS AND HAVING THEIR PORTRAITS PUT ON SALE TO THE PUBLIC.

Dominance of the air over Arras in spring 1917 was essential for reconnaissance and the British sought to achieve this. Trenchard's aircraft, acting in support of ground forces, carried out artillery spotting, photography of trench systems and bombing. Aerial observation was hazardous work, as the aircraft had to fly at slow speeds and low altitude over the German lines. In March 1917 it became even more dangerous with the arrival of the 'Red Baron', Manfred von Richthofen, with his experienced and better equipped *Jagdstaffel – Jasta 11* (Richthofen's Flying Circus). Its deployment led to sudden increased losses of Allied pilots and April 1917 was to become known as Bloody April. Between 4 and 8 April, the RFC lost 75 aircraft and had 105 aircrew casualties on operations; for the whole of the month it lost 245 aircraft.

17GW397 A line up of *Jasta 11* Albatros DIII fighters at Douai in March 1917. The second in line is the red painted machine of The Red Baron, *Rittmeister* Manfred Freiherr von Richthofen. The RFC and *Service d' Aviation* were were about to experience appalling losses in crews and machines.

17GW379 The Red Baron, centre, with his younger brother, Lothar, at his left shoulder; next to him is *Leutnant* Kurt Wolff. Festner (12 kills) and Schaefer (30 kills) are the other two. The original caption: *5 unserer erfolgreichsten Kampfflieger.* (Five of our most successful fighter pilots.) March 1917.

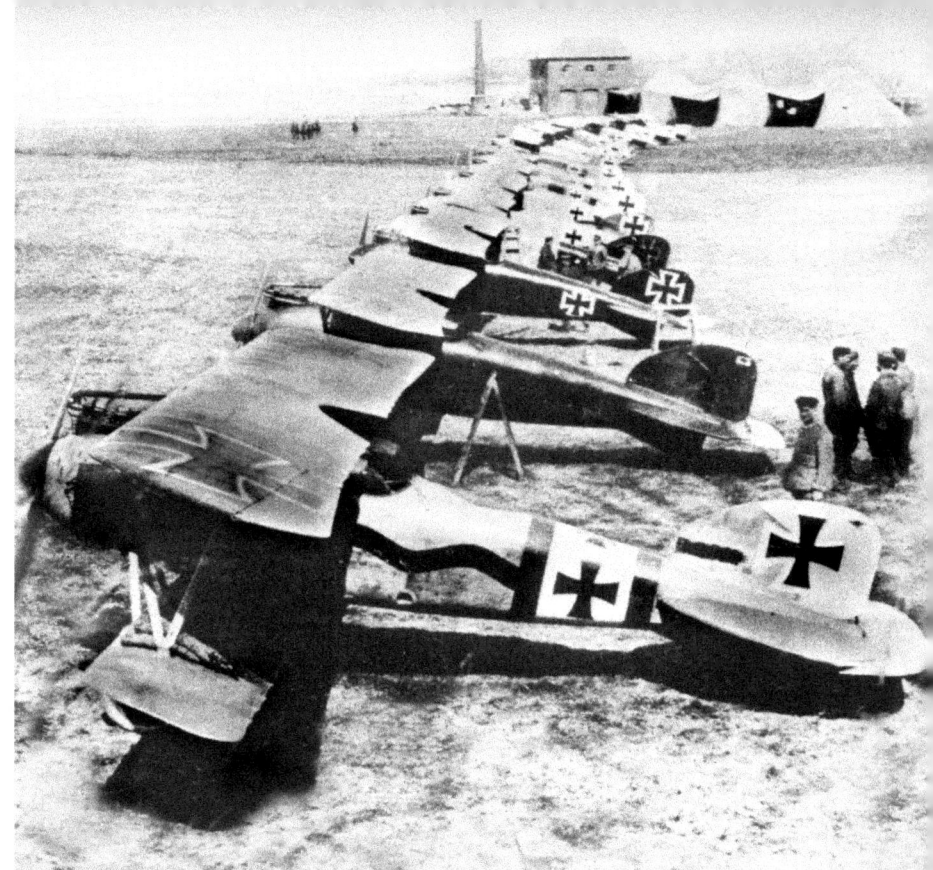

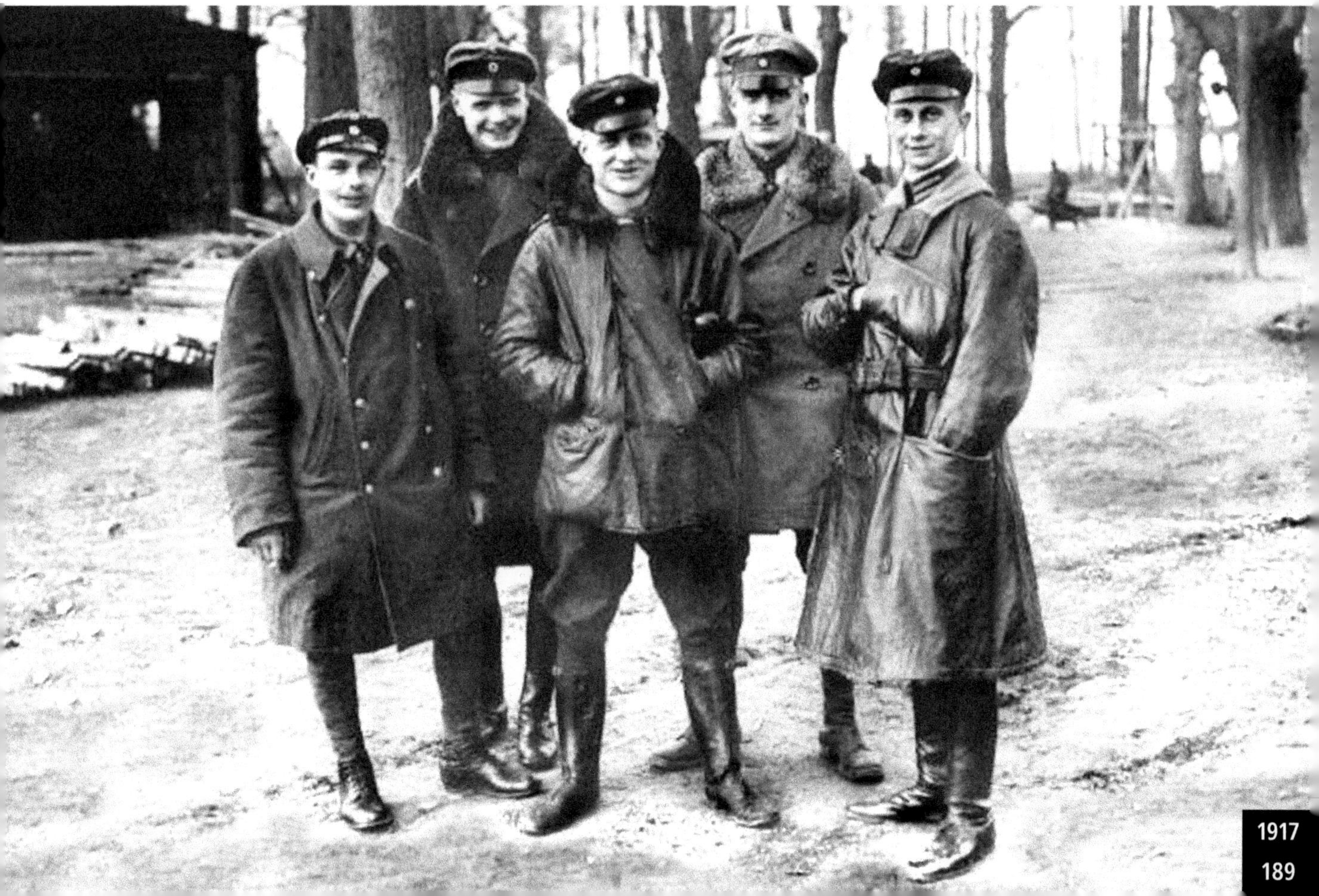

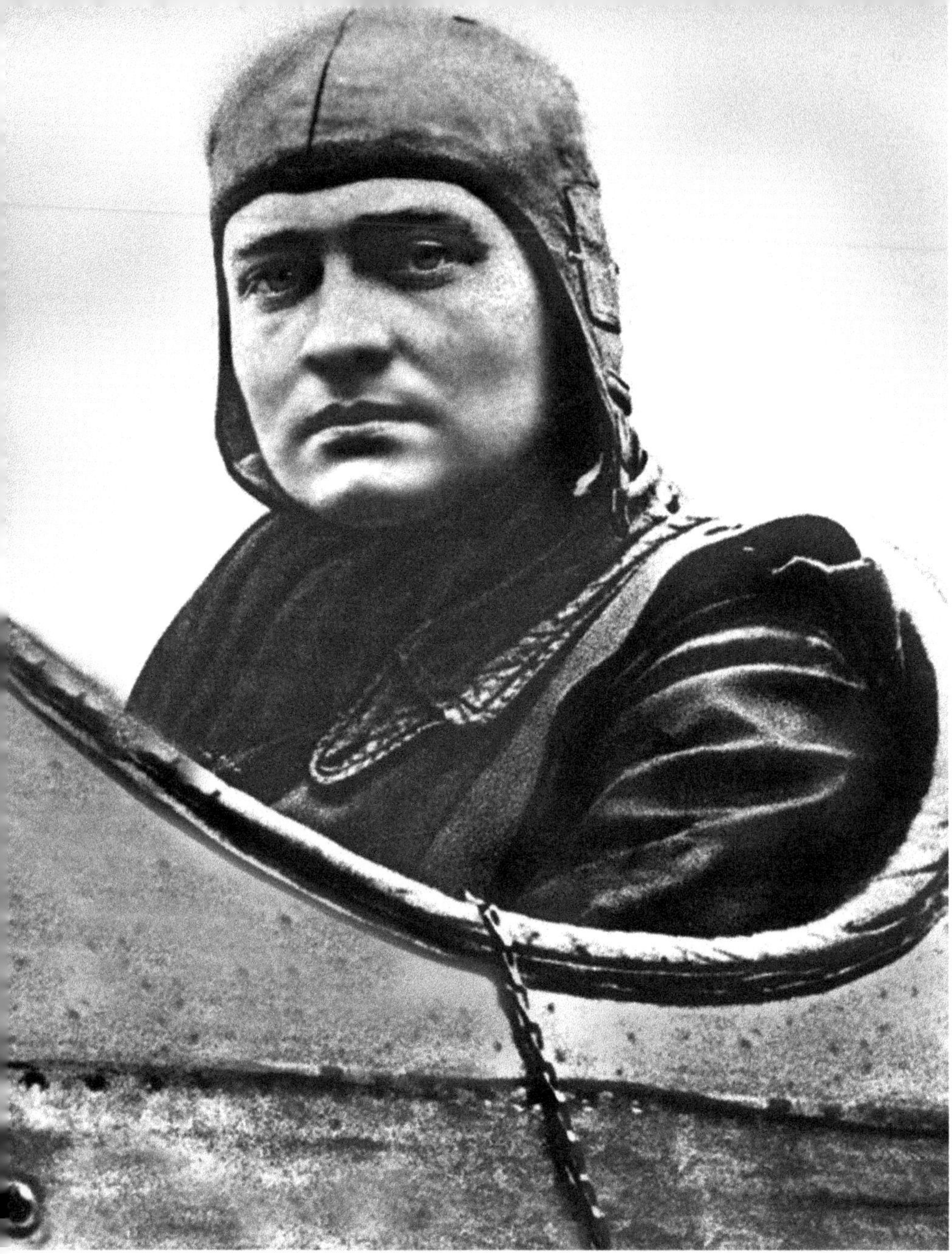

17GW401 Manfred von Richthofen in the cockpit of his red painted Albatros DVa. By the time he was brought down and killed, on 21 April 1918, he had scored 80 kills

Quotes by Richthofen on his enemies – the French and the British – giving an insight into his mindset when it came to single combat, legalized murder and the callous killer role he embraced:

The murder of a man is still murder, even in wartime.

I honoured the fallen enemy by placing a stone on his beautiful grave.

Everything depends on whether we have for opponents those French tricksters or those daring rascals, the English. I prefer the English. Frequently their daring can only be described as stupidity. In their eyes it may be pluck and daring.

The French attacking spirit is like bottled lemonade. It lacks tenacity. The Englishmen, on the other hand, one notices that they are of Germanic blood. Sportsmen easily take to flying, and Englishmen see in flying nothing but a sport.

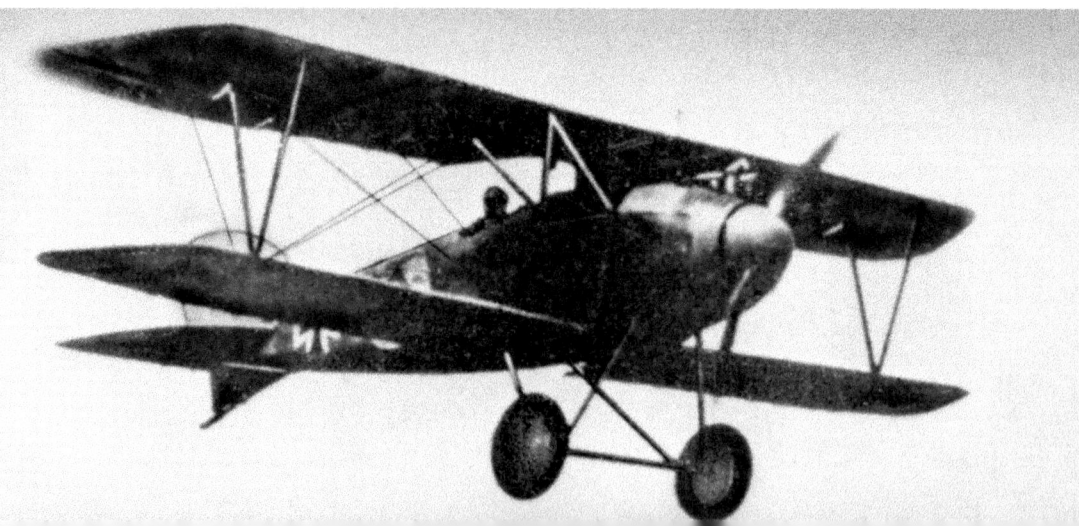

17GW402 A rare picture of an Albatros DIII in flight.

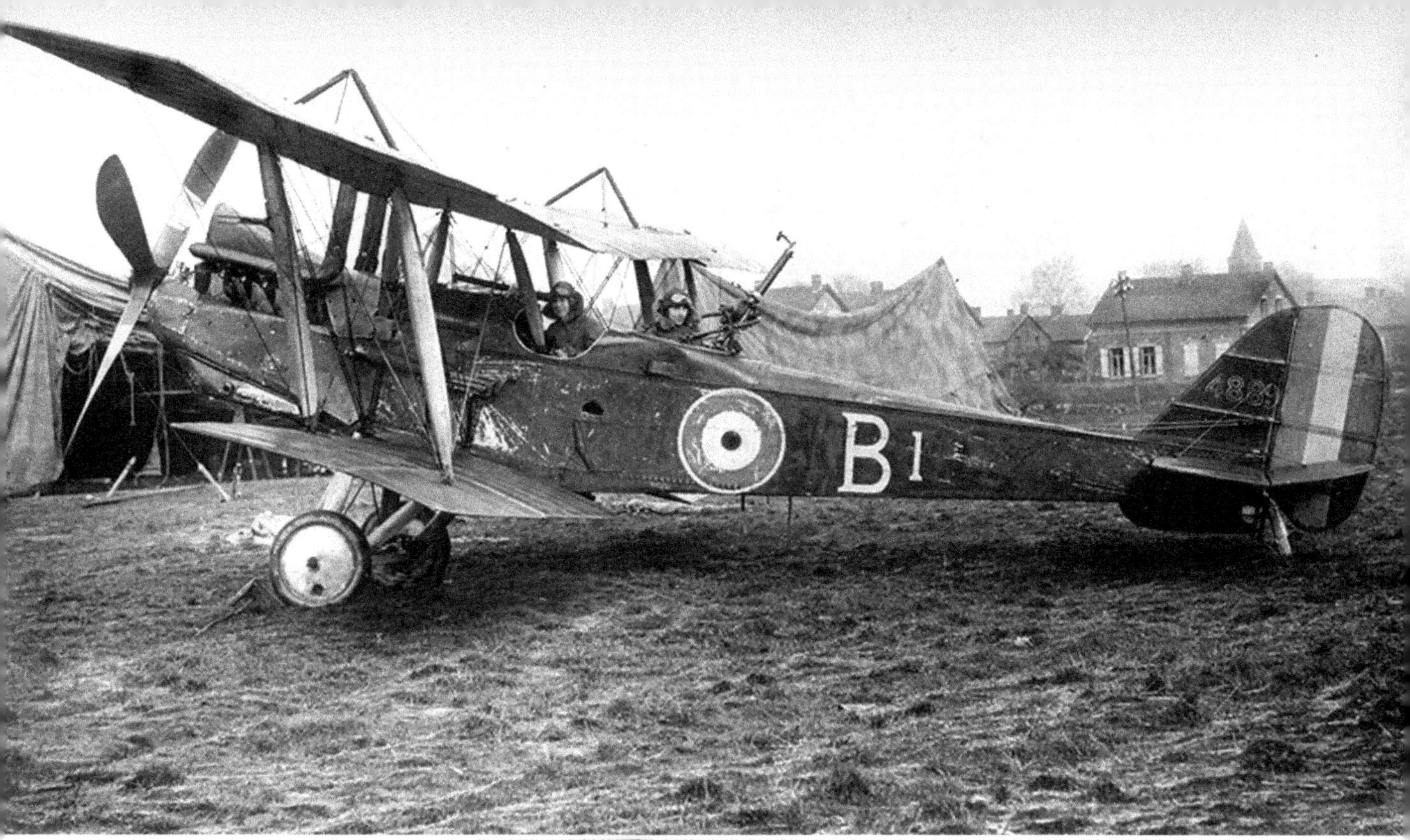

17GW403 British RE.8 two-seater reconnaissance aircraft, popular with the crews for stability in flight, which made it good for observation but it was a problem when taking evasive action from German fighters. Although it had a machine gun for defence it could be successfully attacked from beneath.

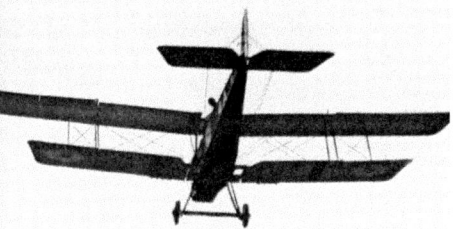

17GW404 A good example of a blind approach from behind and below on a British RE.8 two-seater; the observer is is peering over the fuselage to view the aircraft carrying the photographer flying beneath. He would have been unable to use his Lewis gun at that angle. Richtohofen attacked some RE.8s from this angle.

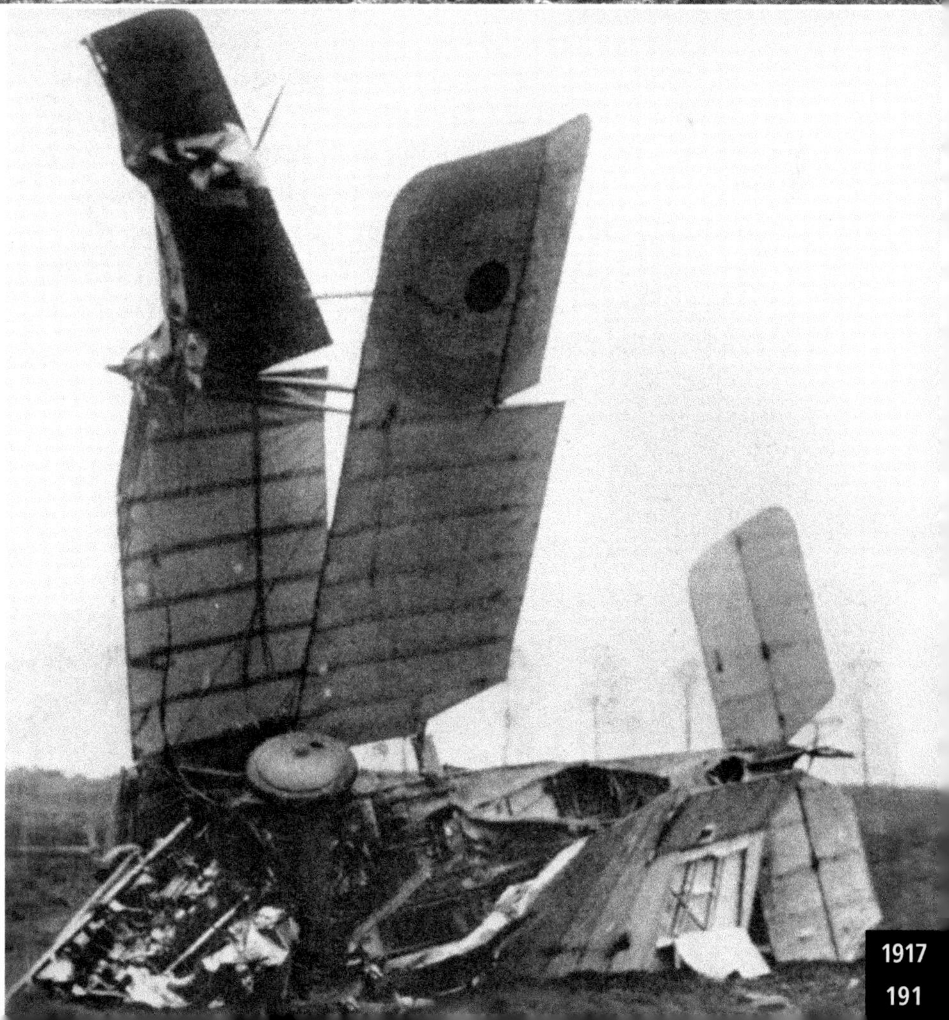

17GW405 During April 1917 Richtohofen's *Jasta 11* brought down six RE.8s in as many minutes. One of them is seen here.

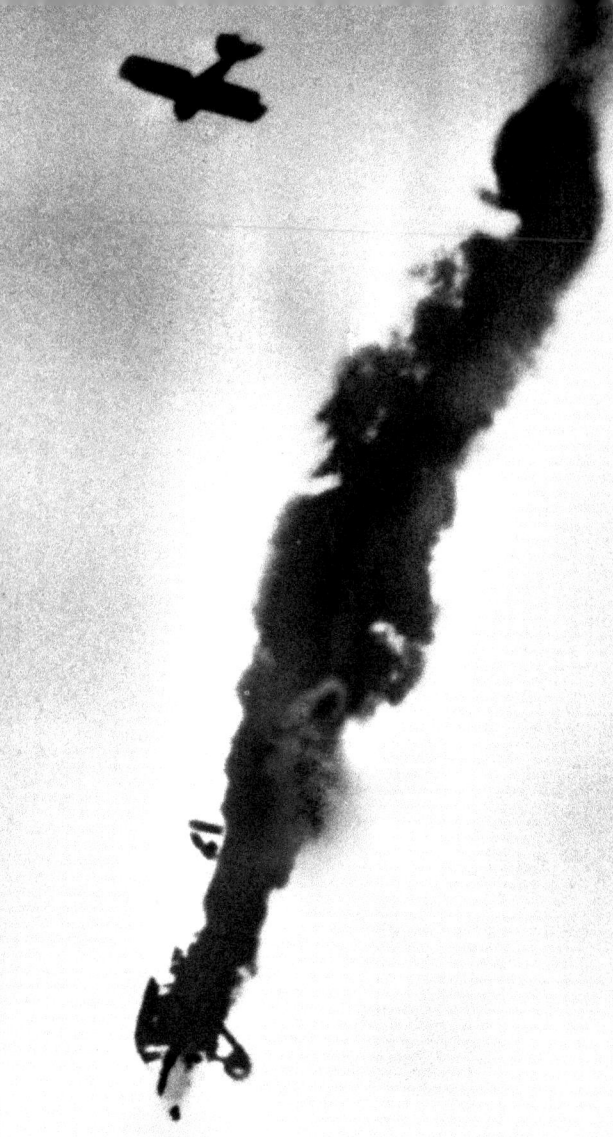

On the Western Front the spirit of both hunter and medieval jouster lived among many German, French and British fighter pilots. They were the twentieth century 'knights of the air' and the newspapers and peoples of the belligerent nations embraced the concept. Heroes were easily identified and individual pilots began building up their scores of 'victories' or 'kills' – the German pilots sought for themselves the award of the *Pour le Mérite* (the Blue Max). Frederick the Great established the order in 1740. The motto was in French, which was the language of the Prussian court in the eighteenth century. The French sought their nation's highest award the *Ordre national de la Légion d'honneur* and the British their Victoria Cross.

17GW410 A German pilot, flying an Albatros fighter, circles to watch the final outcome of his victorious dogfight. The RFC two seater plunges earthward on fire – should the machine begin spinning it would indicate the doomed pilot has lost control – it had become known as the 'death spin'. Parachutes were not carried in British aircraft.

17GW411 Australian stretcher bearers carry the body of a British pilot away from the wreckage of a single seater SE.5A.

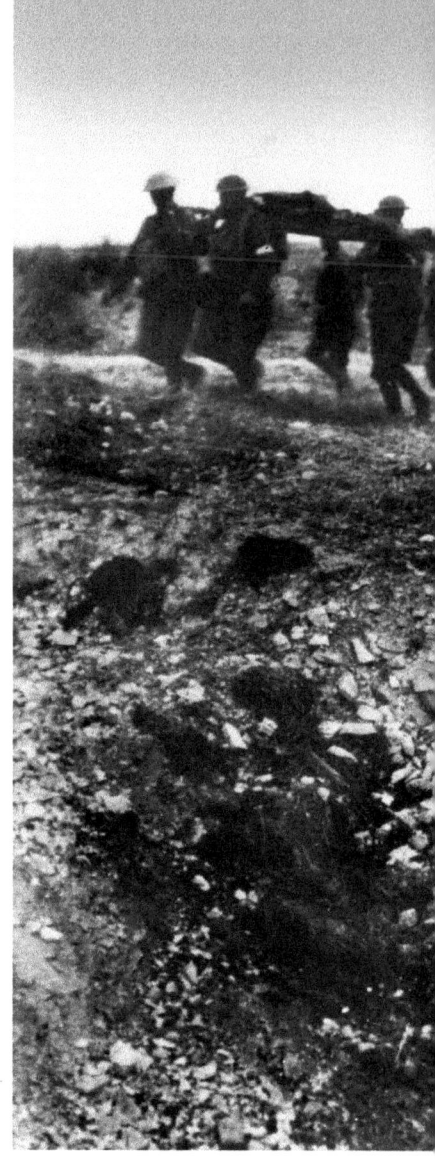

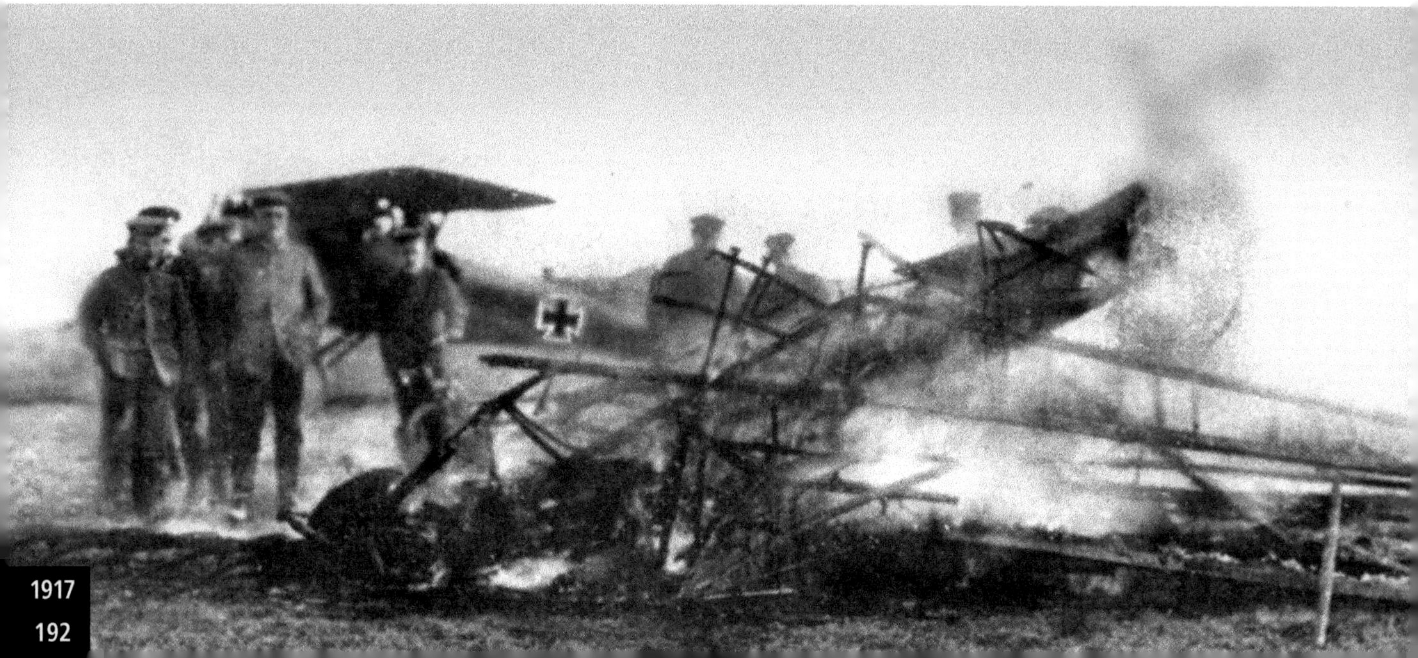

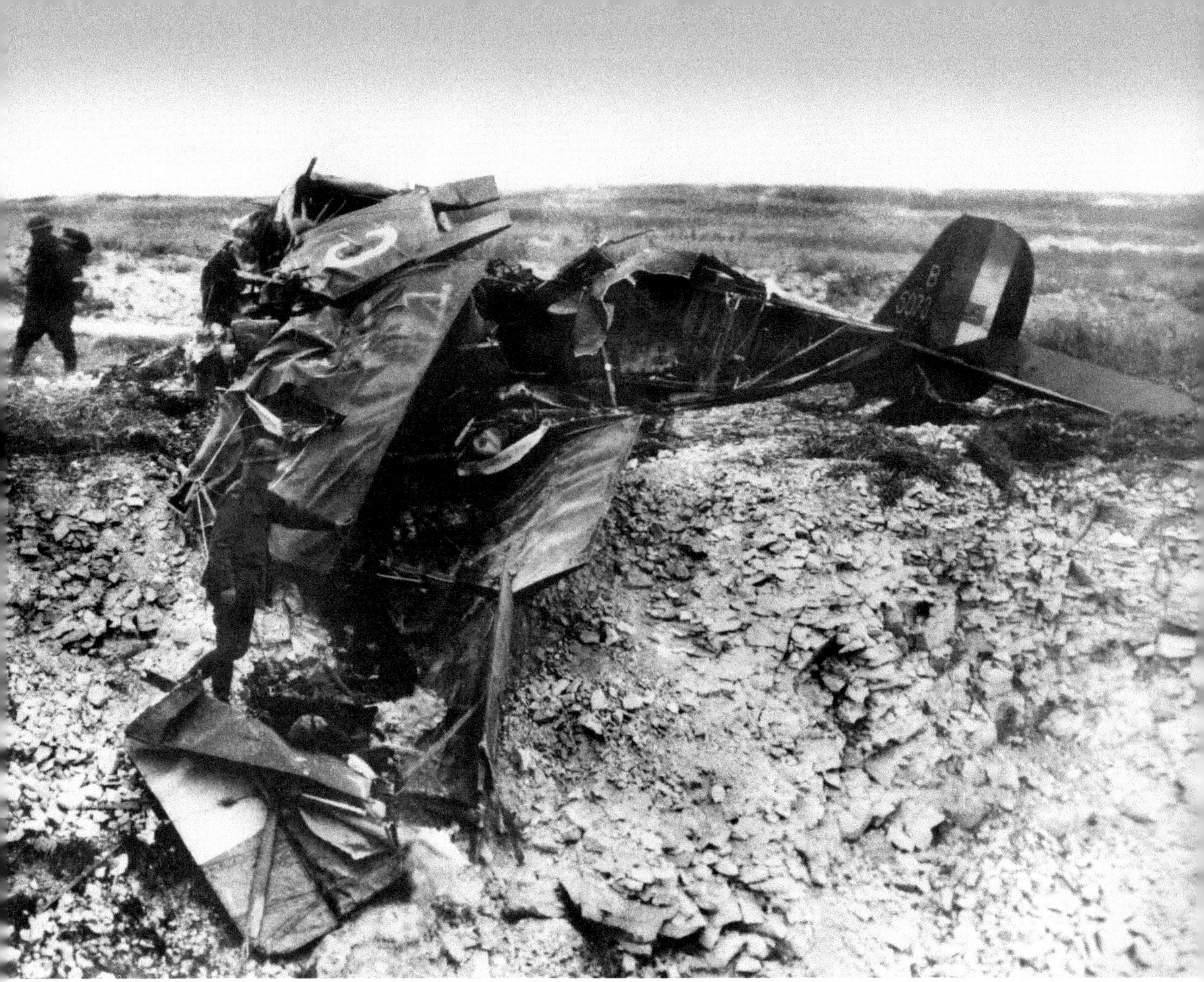

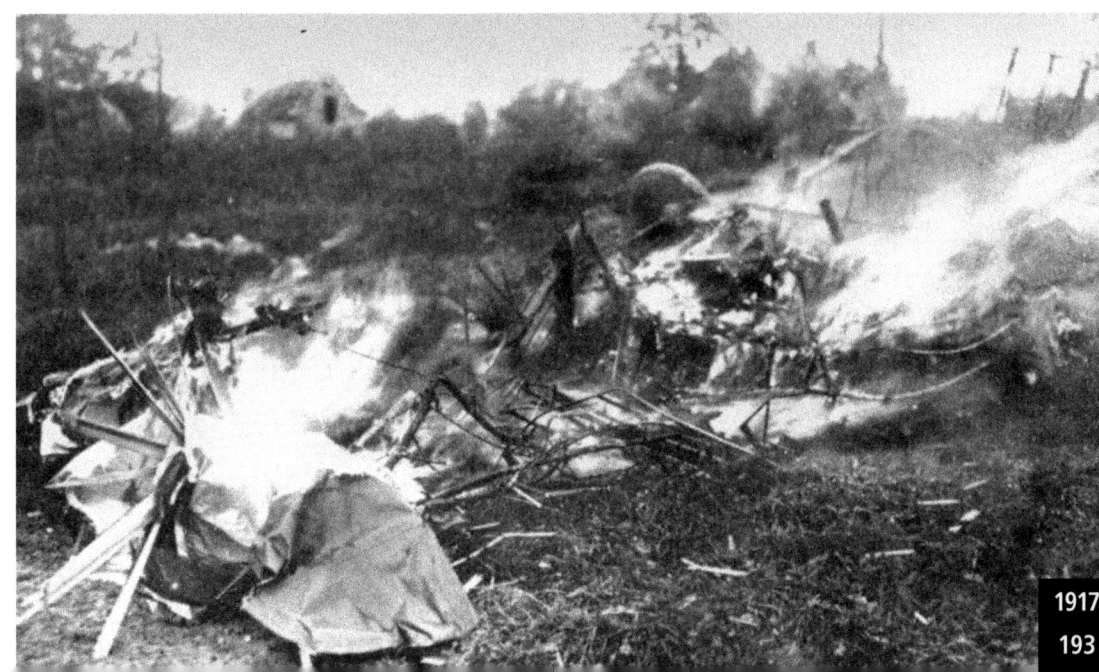

17GW413 An Albatros pilot has landed alongside his victim to view the results of his prowess as a fighter pilot and to collect a souvenir, usually the aircraft's ID number. Richthofen landed alongside his third kill to seek a souvenir from the FE.2b he had sent down in flames. There was little left of the two occupants but after some poking around he found the battered number plate. Both Immelmann and Karl Wolf are know to have followed this practice.

17GW413 Another RFC machine burns, having lost an air duel.

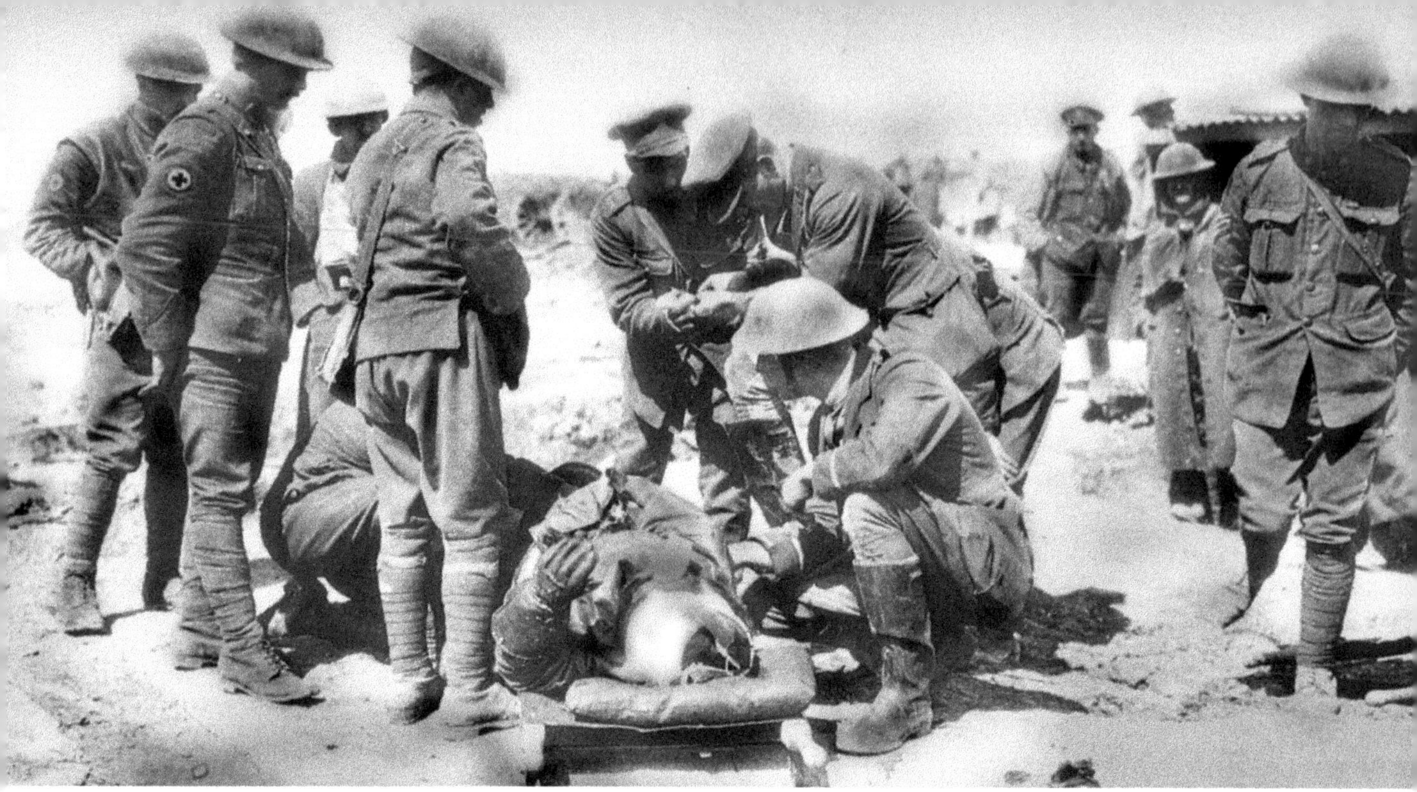

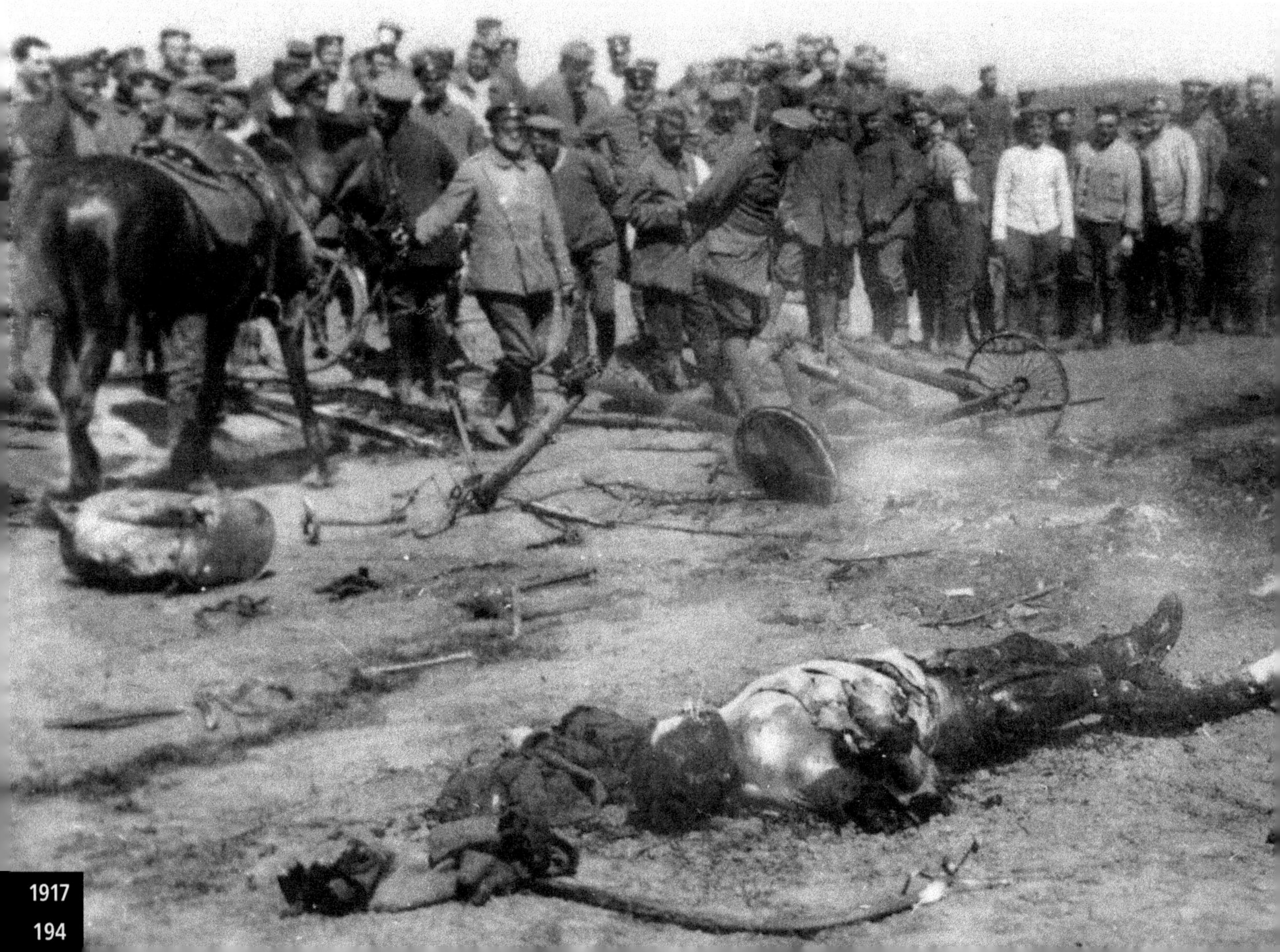

1917
194

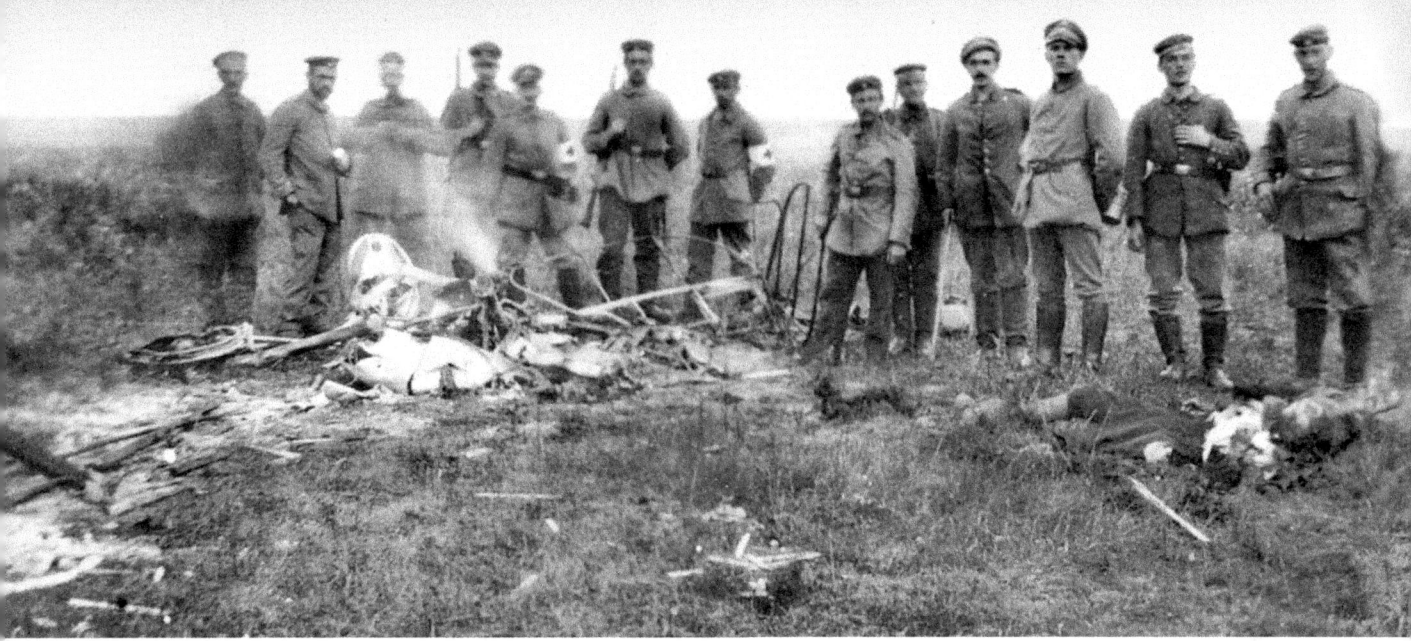

17GW407 An RFC aviator, having come down in the British lines and barely alive, receives first aid from British medical officers and orderlies.
17GW406, 17GW408, 17GW409. British airmen killed in crashes behind the German lines, some meeting their ends in the way dreaded by all aviators: being burned alive as their machines hurtled to the ground. The fuel tank was directly in front of the pilot and the airstream ensured the pilot quickly became engulfed in flames.

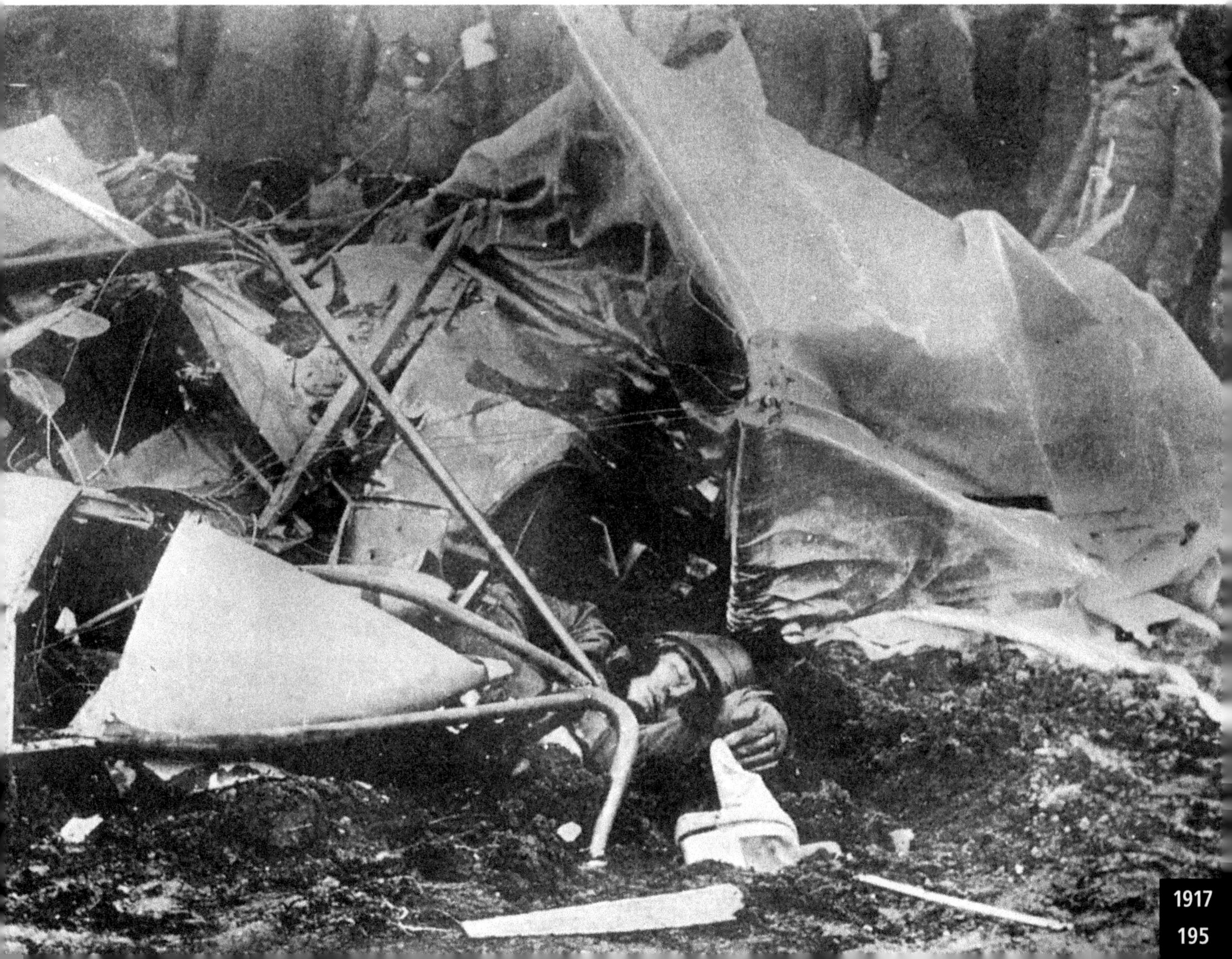

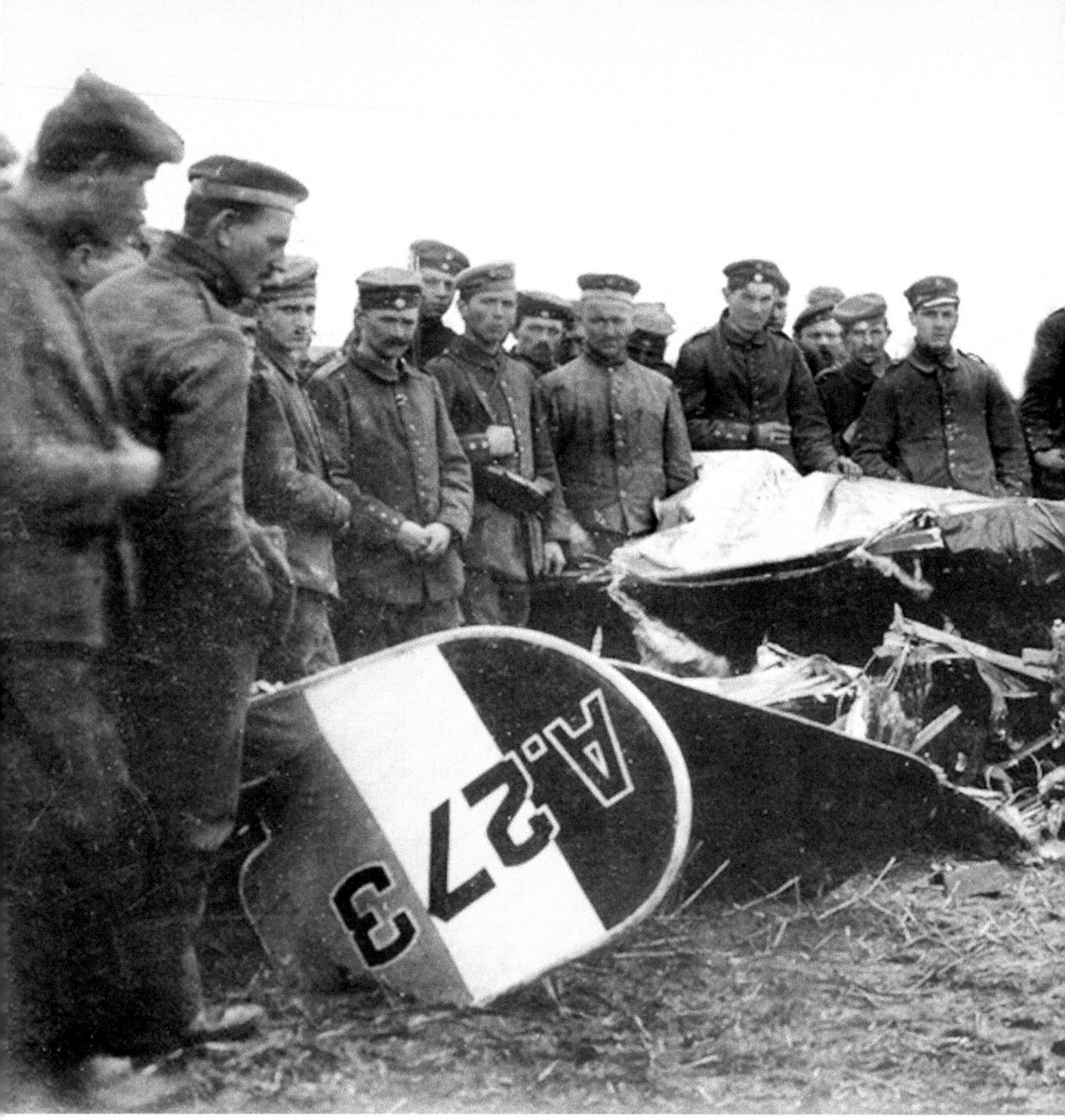

17GW418 The crumpled remains of Lieutenant William P Garnett, 60 Squadron RFC, can be seen lying beside his smashed Nieuport 17.c aircraft, 30 March 1917, in the vicinity of Gavrelle, north west of Arras. He was the fourth victim of Leutnant Karl Wolff, *Jasta 11*.

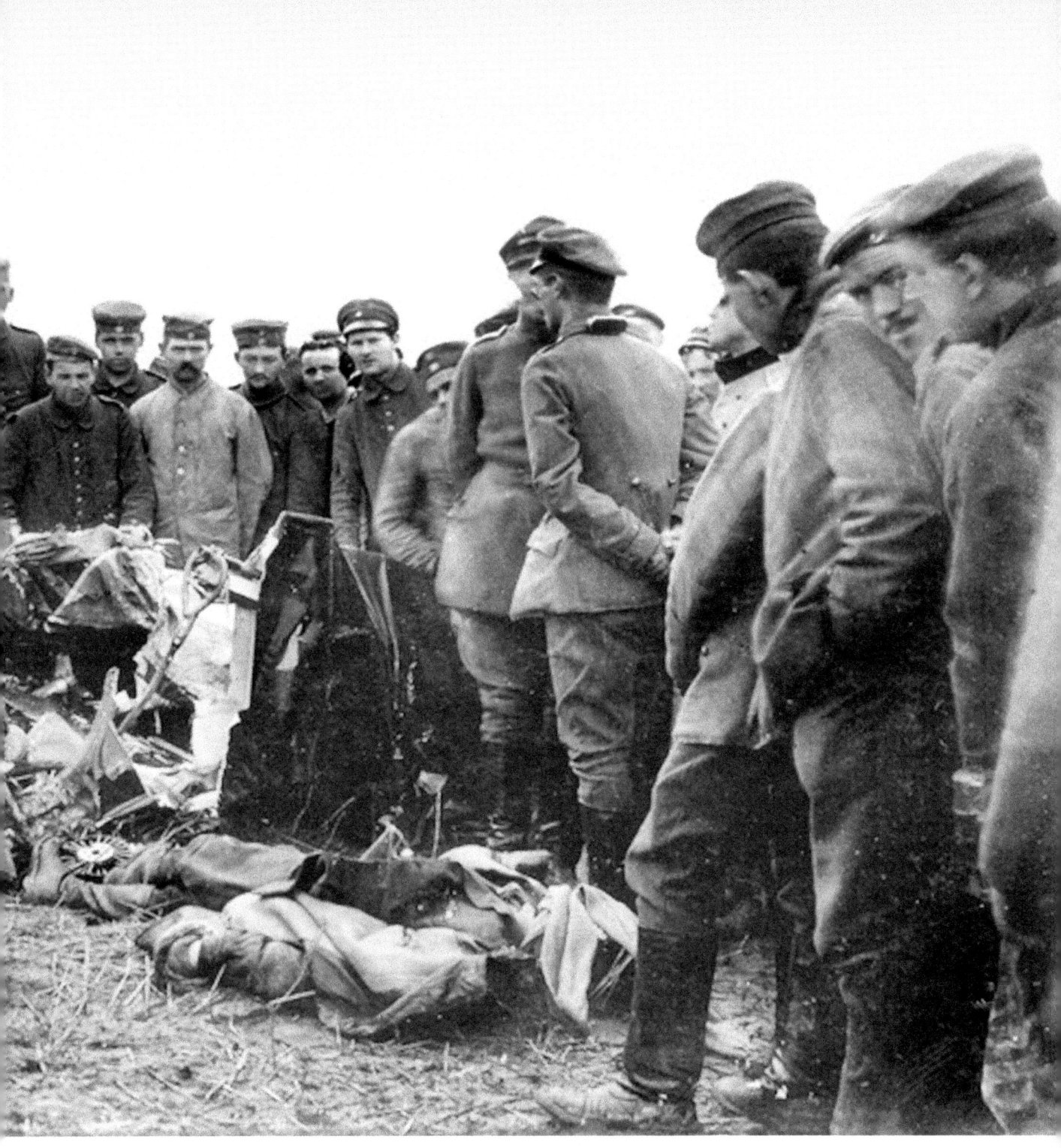

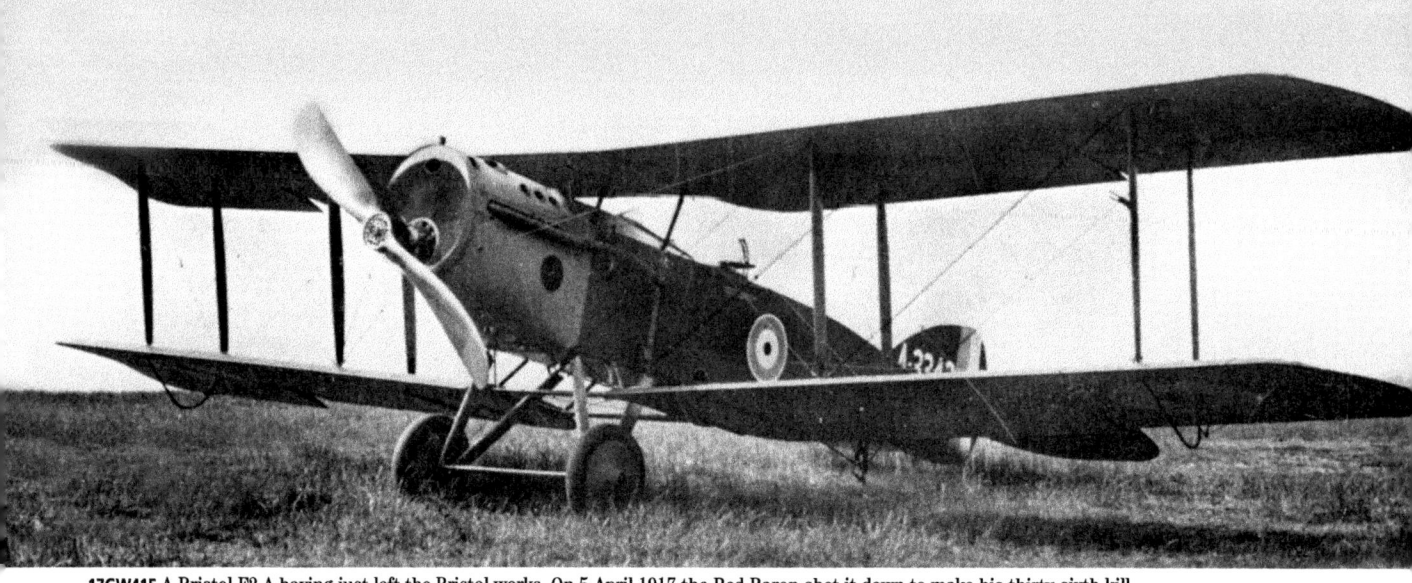

17GW415 A Bristol F2.A having just left the Bristol works. On 5 April 1917 the Red Baron shot it down to make his thirty-sixth kill.

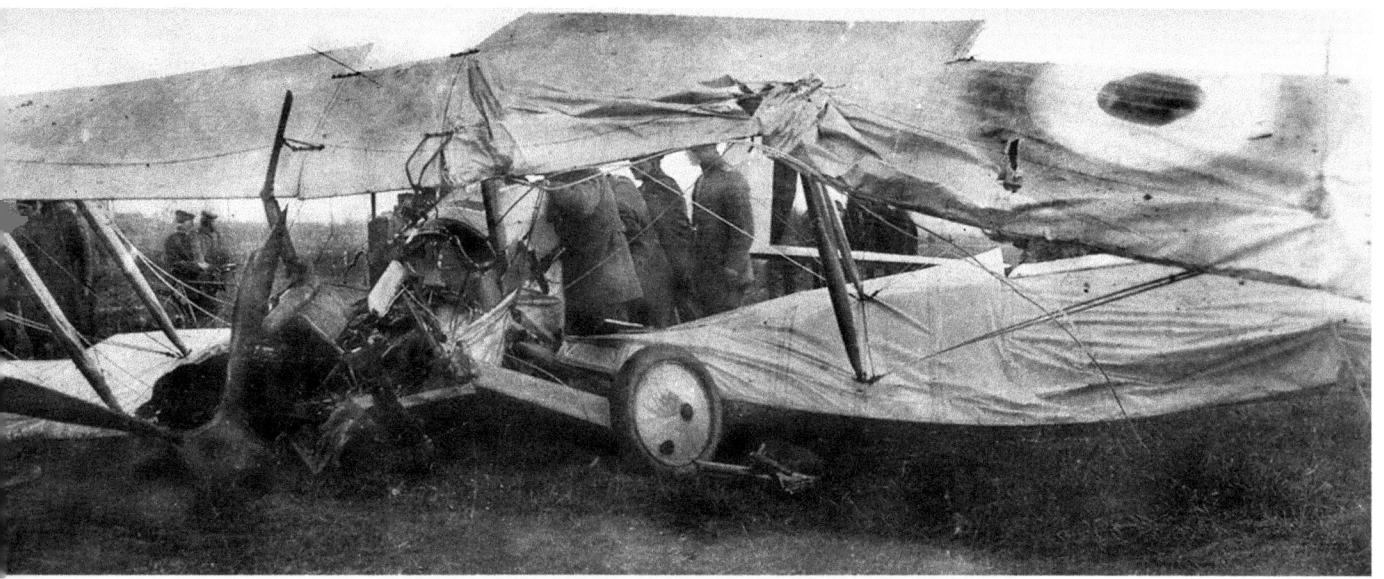

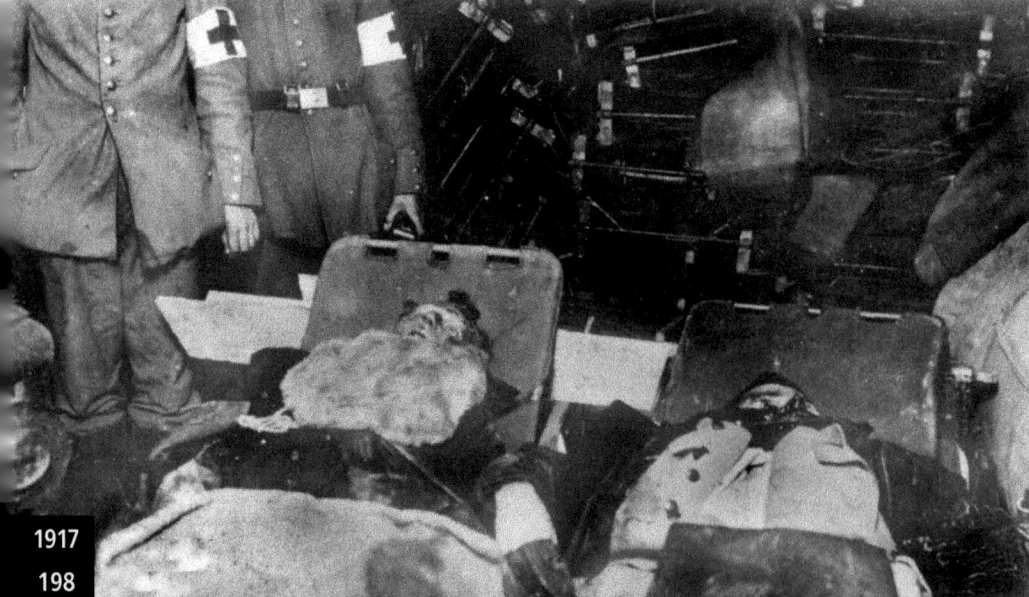

17GW415 A shot down BE.2 with the pilot's cockpit smashed, but the observer's cockpit intact, receives attention from German soldiers who are rendering aid to a crew member.

17GW420 A wrecked Belgian BE.2c belonging to the *6ème Escadrille*, brought down at Koekelare, 8 April 1917.

17GW419 Two seriously injured British airmen brought into a German field hospital.

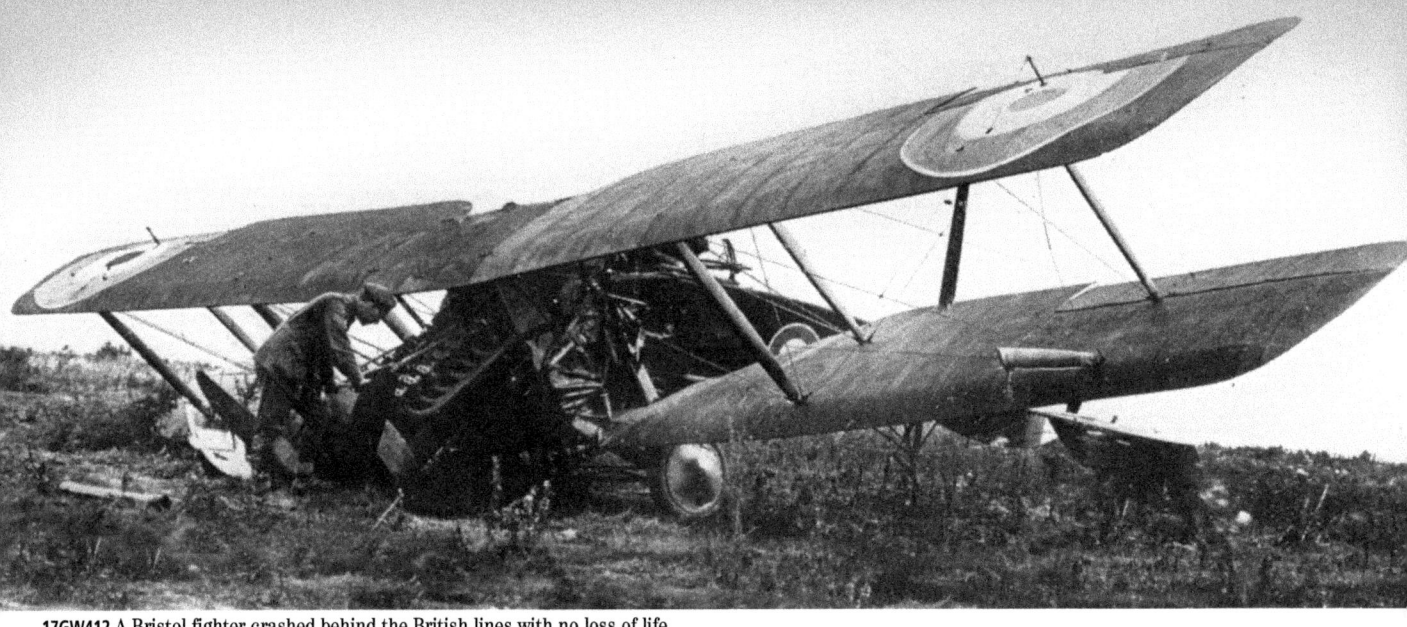

17GW412 A Bristol fighter crashed behind the British lines with no loss of life.

17GW417 An British FE.8 forced down by the German ace, *Leutnant* Kurt Wolff, 9 March 1917, at Annay, on the Lens-Carvin road. The FE.8 was a single-seat fighter operating on the Western Front from summer 1916 to early 1917. Its speed of 80mph and single Lewis gun meant that it was hopelessly outclassed. This machine, on landing, suffered a damaged starboard wheel and flipped over.

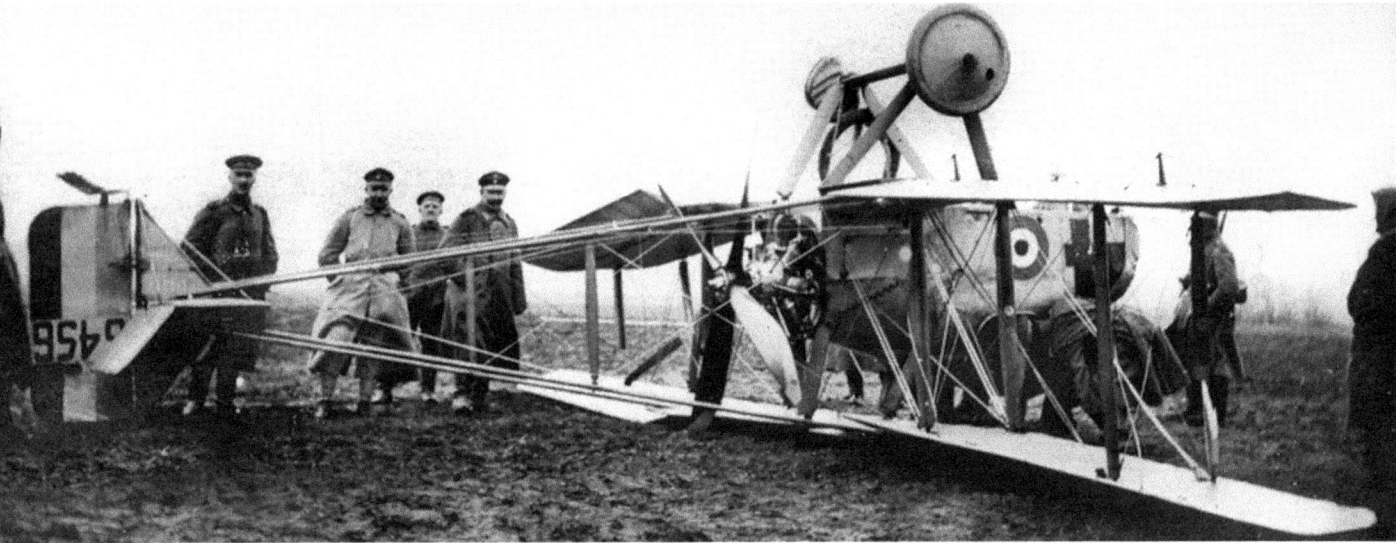

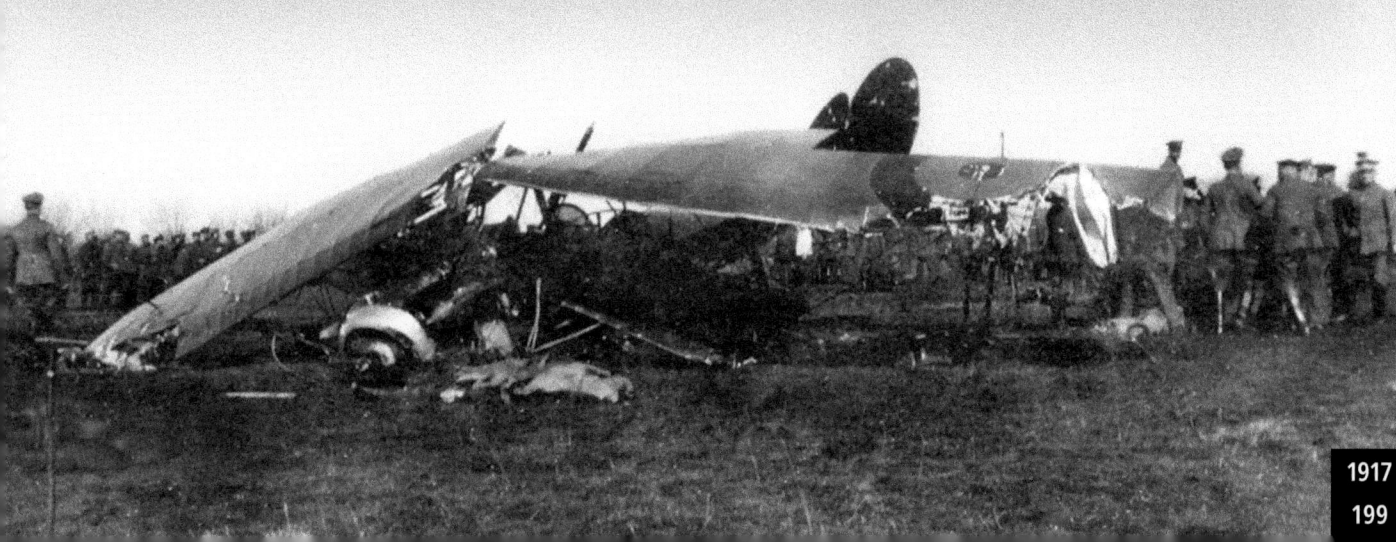

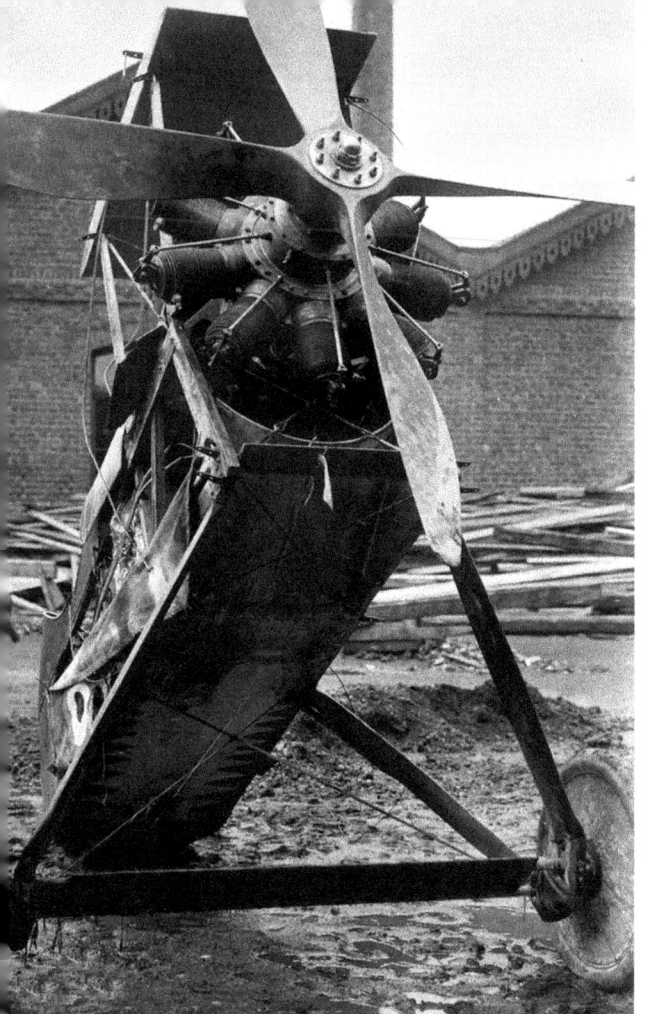

17GW421 Original German caption for this propaganda postcard depicting the remains of a Airco DH.2 in a scrap yard:

Abgeschossener franz Flieger!
(Another downed French aviator!)

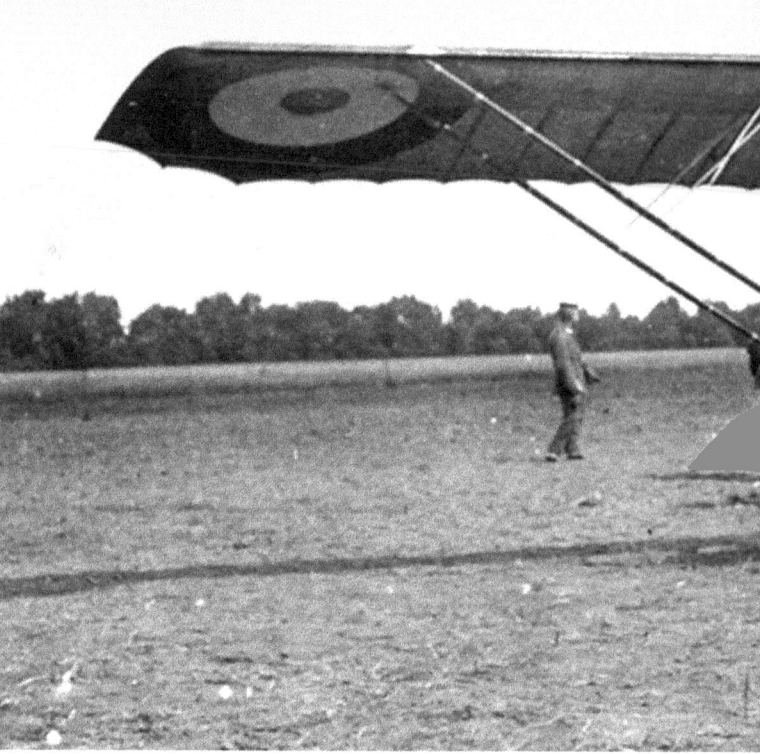

17GW422 A captured intact French Caudron G.3. This type of single-engined French biplane was widely used as a reconnaissance aircraft and flown by the RFC in that role until late 1917.

17GW423 A French Nieuport 23 after a heavy landing behind the German lines. The type was used by the British, French, Italians, Belgians and Russians.

17GW424 The body of a French aviator lies beside this two-seater Breguet 14 belonging to Escadrille Br.127. The emblem of a winged elephant decorates the fuselage.

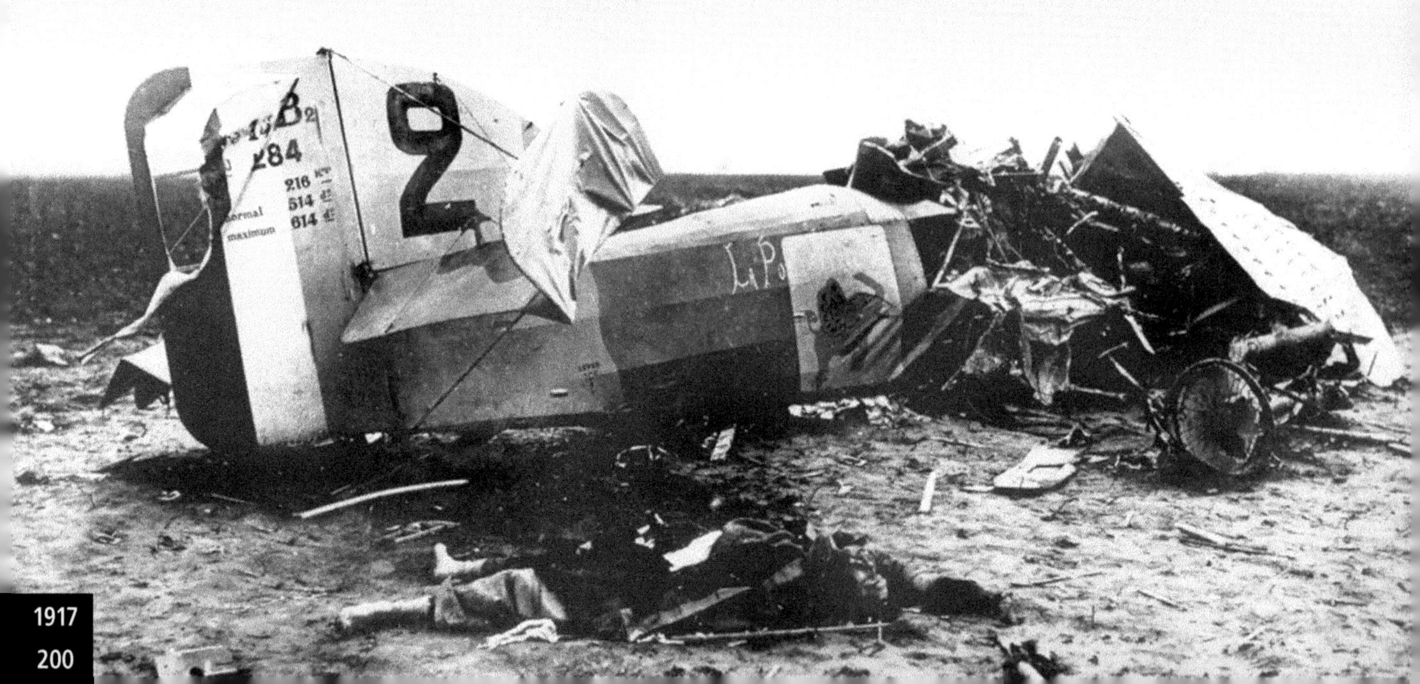

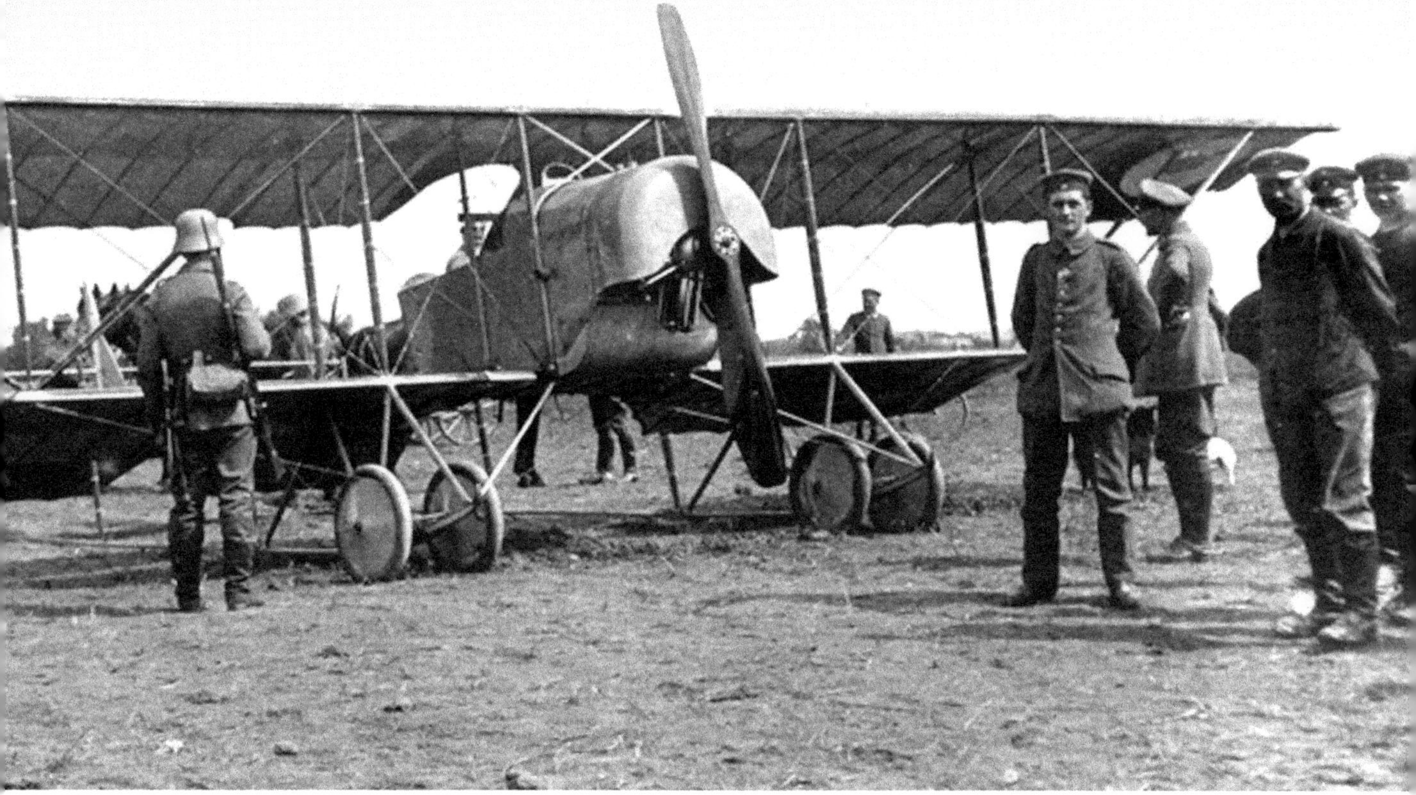

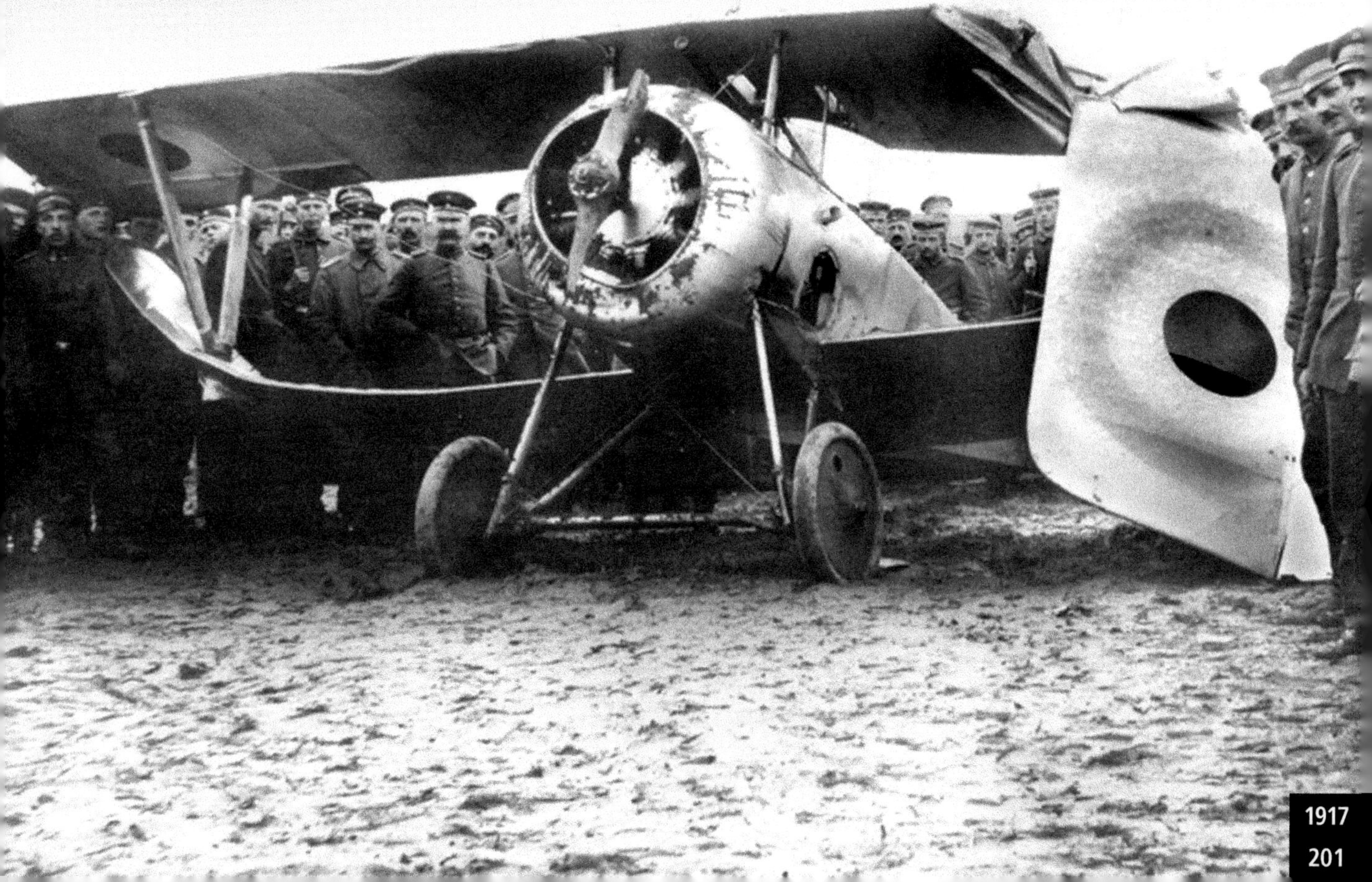

1917

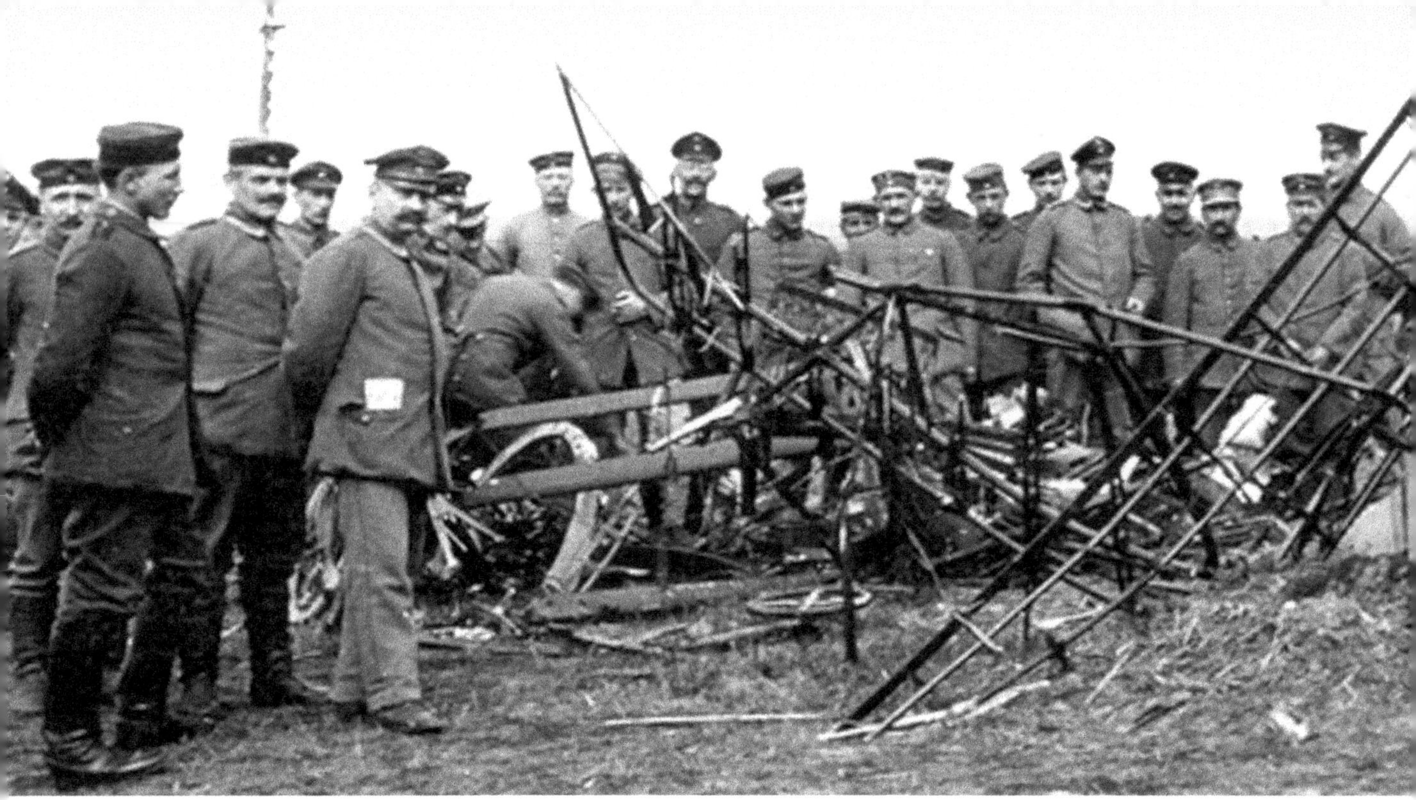

17GW425 Encouragement for family and relatives back in the Fatherland: German troops form a backdrop to a downed and burnt out French pusher biplane.

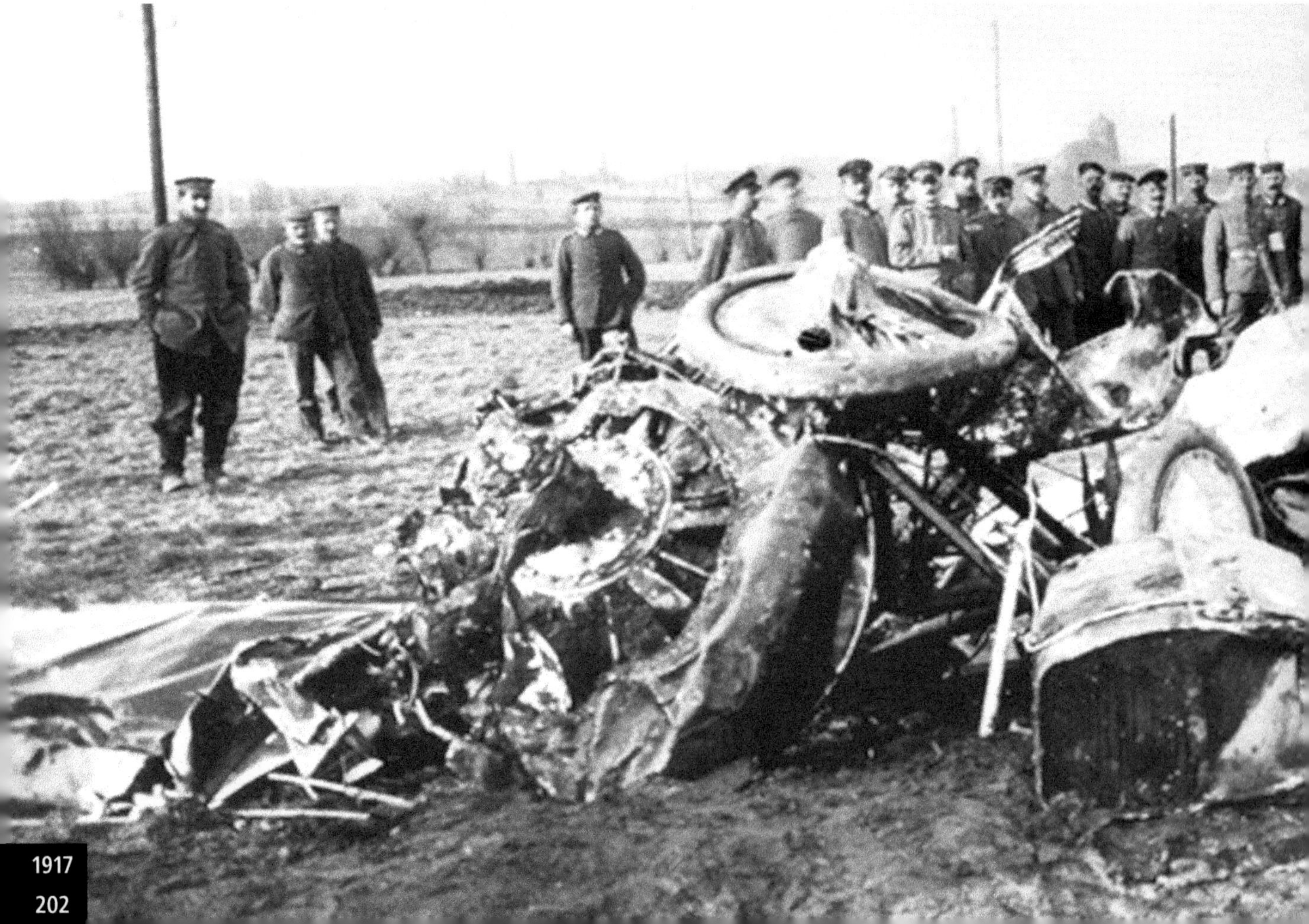

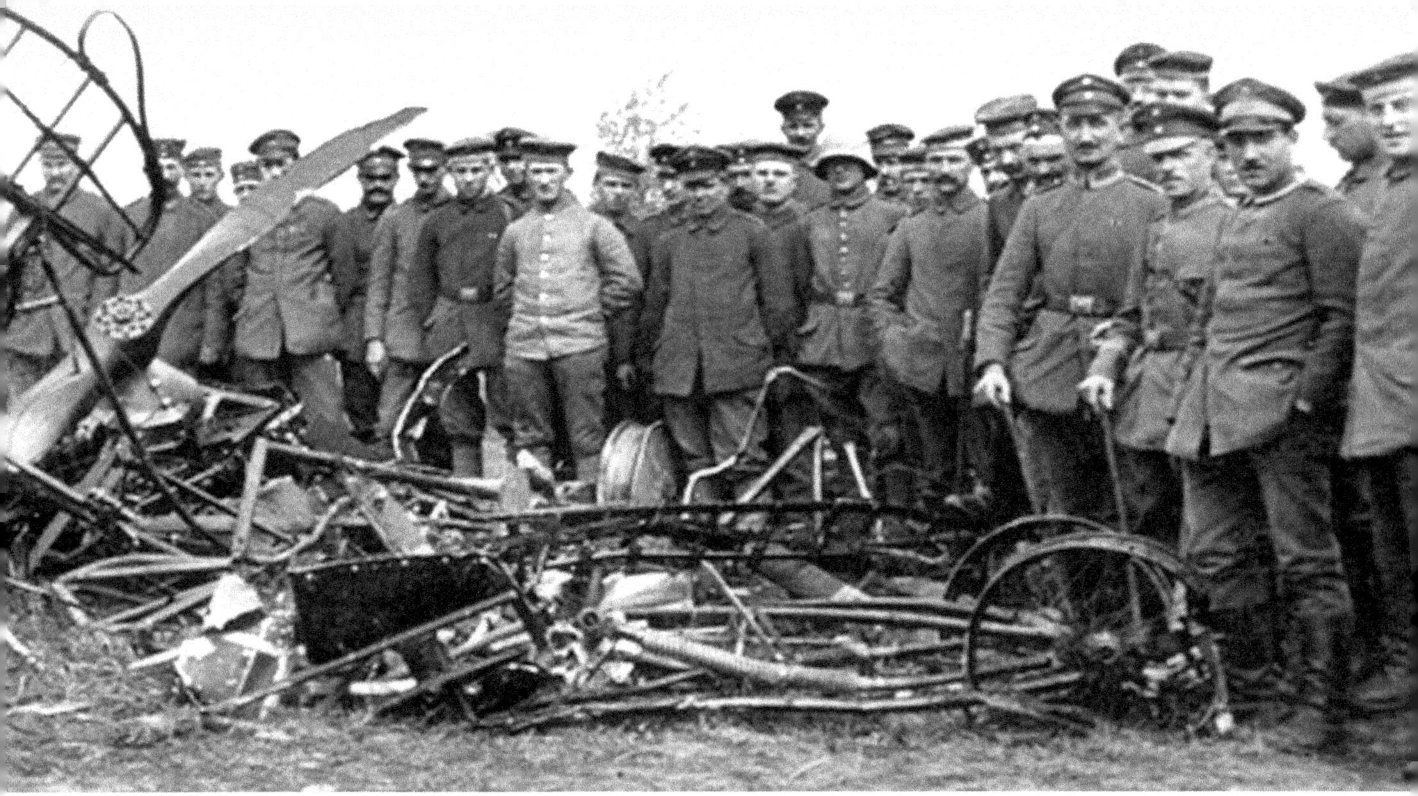

17GW426 With the high Allied losses of aircraft in the spring of 1917, there were plenty of group opportunities for German soldiers to have a morale boosting photograph that could be sent home.

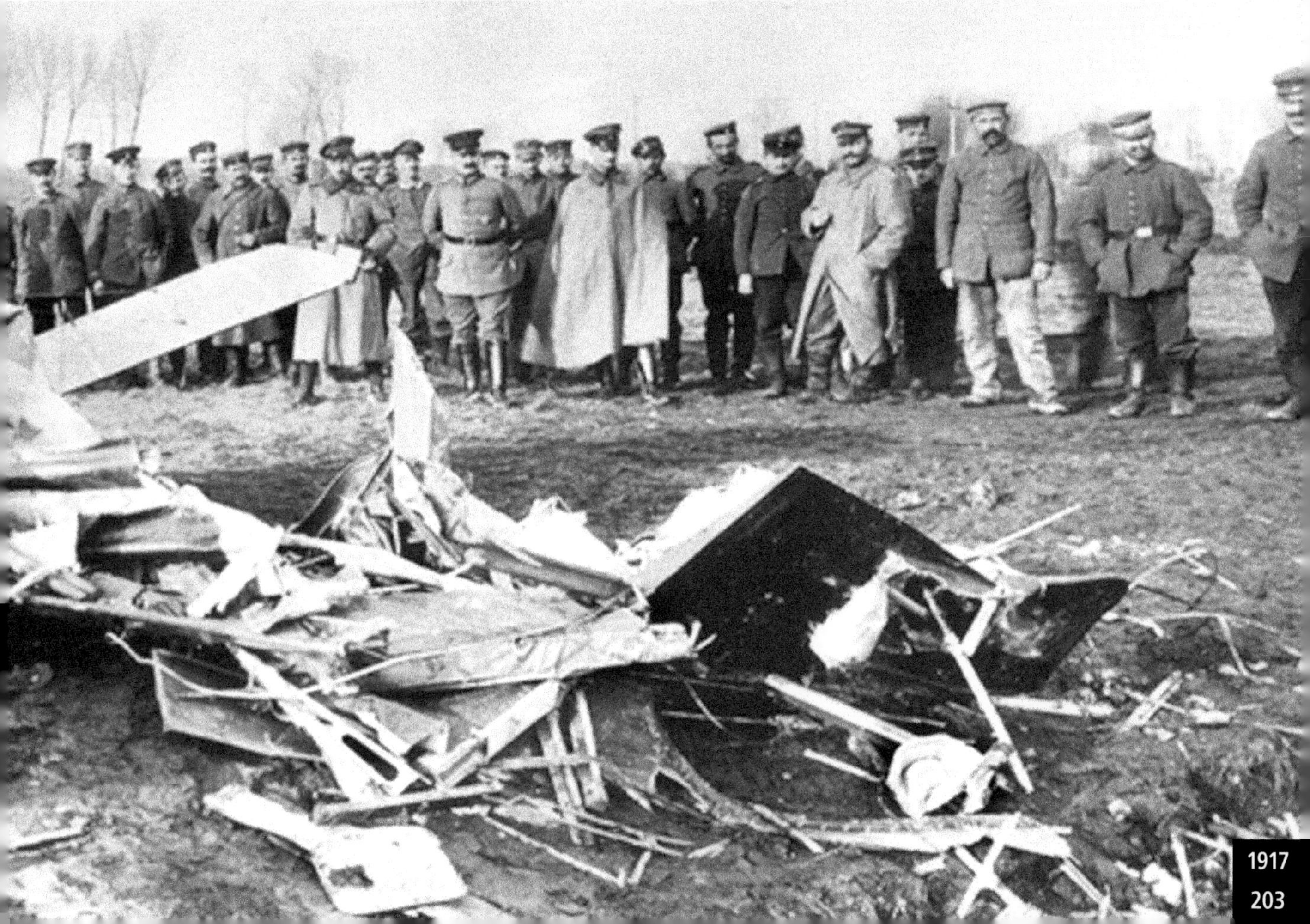

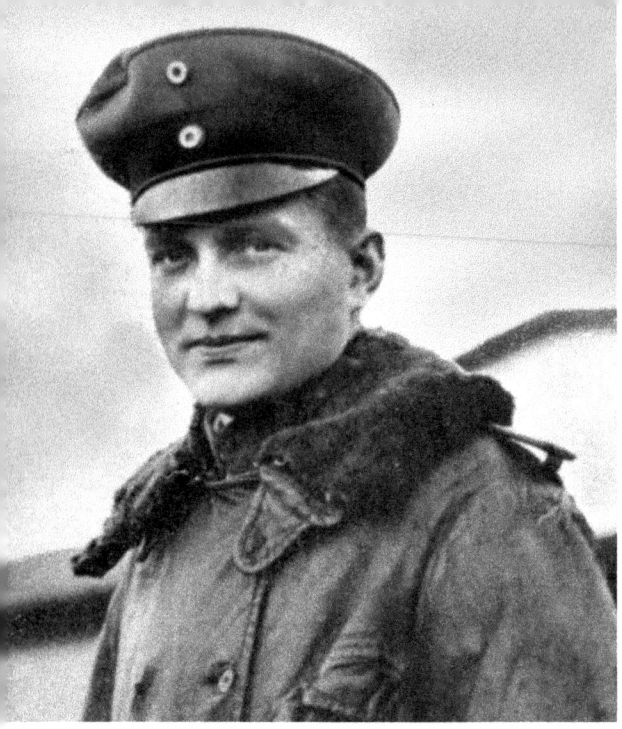

17GW428 *Rittmeister* Manfred Freiherr von Richthofen – a seldom seen photograph of the hero of Germany.

At the time of the Battle of Arras 1917 the month of April became known as 'Bloody April'. Despite the largely successful British air support during the ground assault east of Arras, particularly heavy casualties were suffered by the Royal Flying Corps at the hands of the German *Luftstreitkräfte*. During that month the British lost 245 aircraft, 211 aircrew killed or missing and 108 men became prisoners of war. The *Luftstreitkräfte* recorded the loss of 66 aircraft during the same period.

17GW429 Richthofen on parade with Air Service personnel at the *Kaiser Truppenschau* (Kaiser's inspection) at Coutrai. Under Richthofen's leadership, *Jasta 11* scored 89 victories during 'Bloody April'.

17GW427 Downed Sopwith Pup N6186 near Écourt-St Quentin, May 1917.

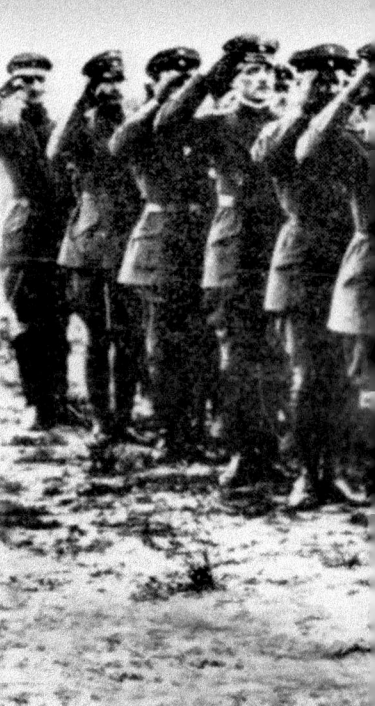

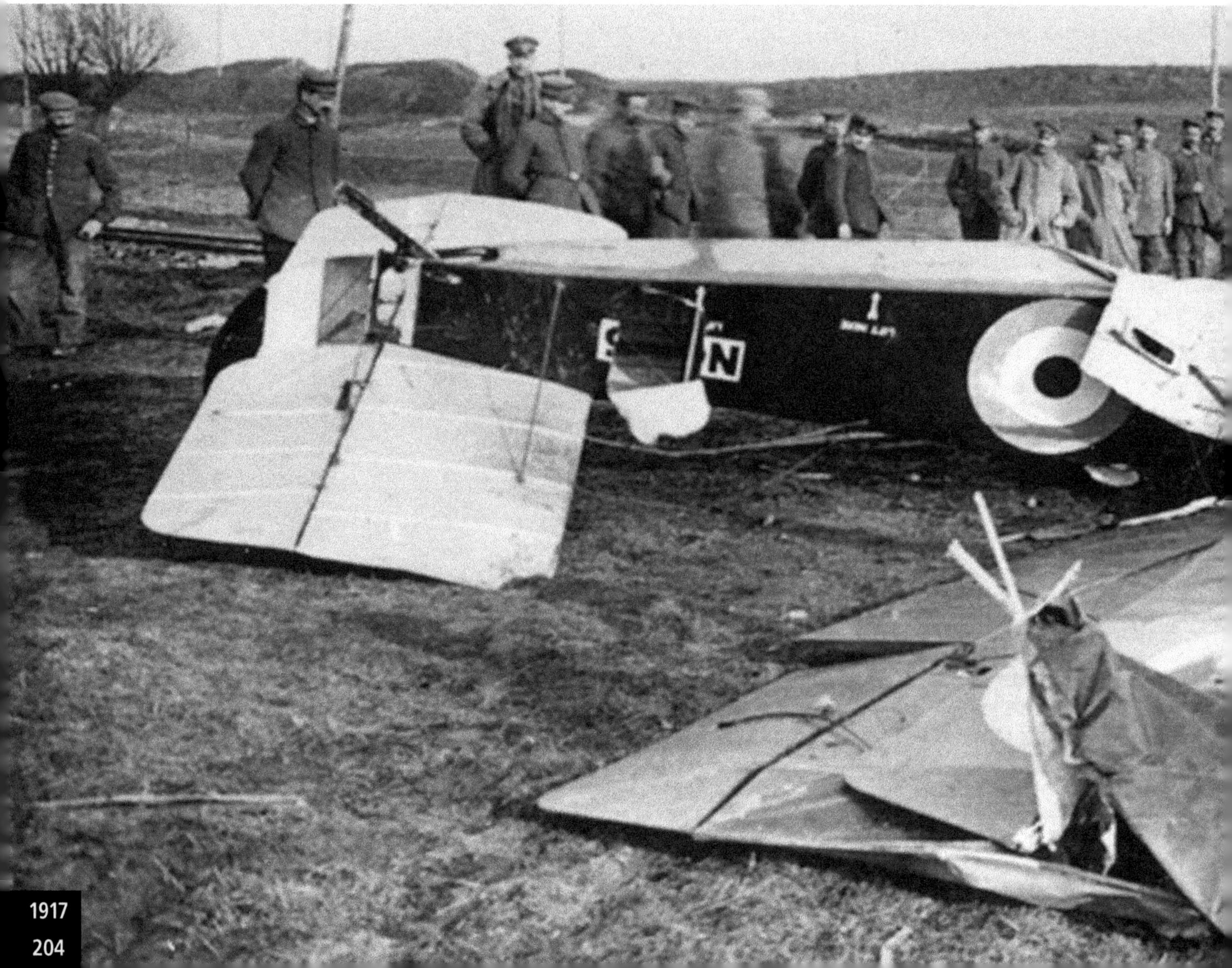

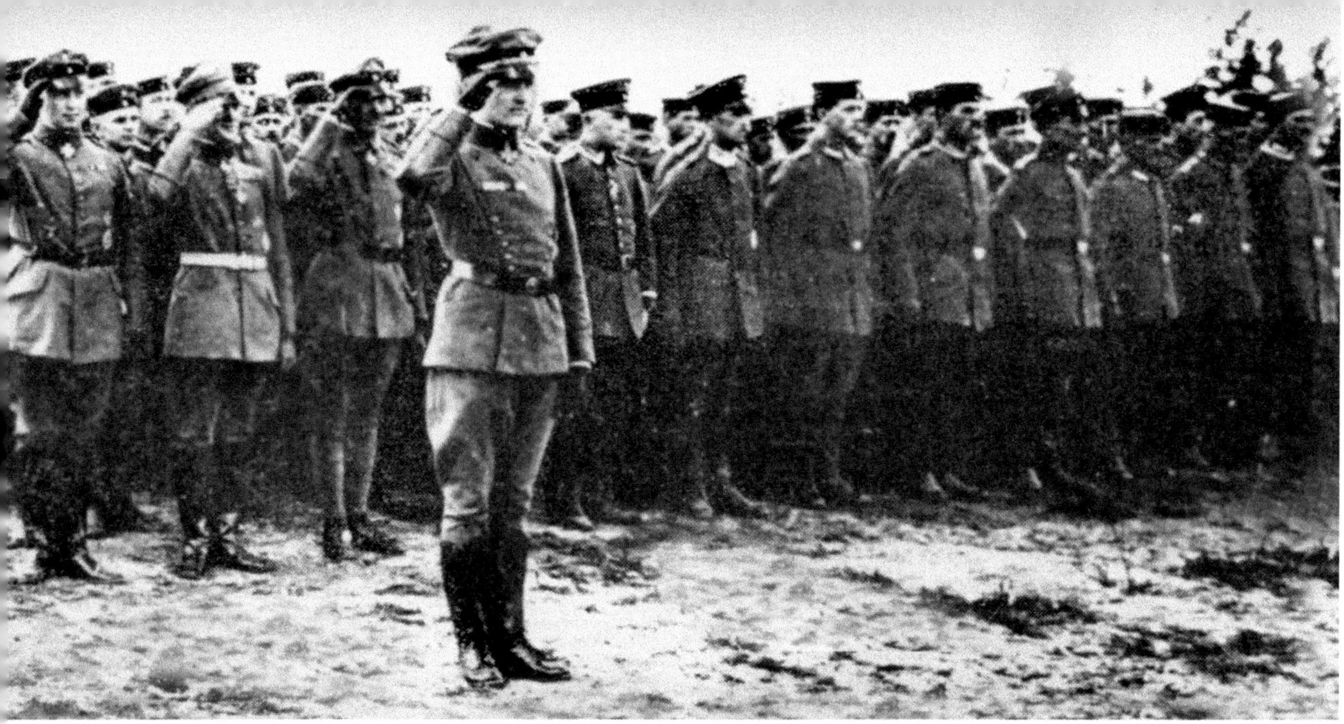

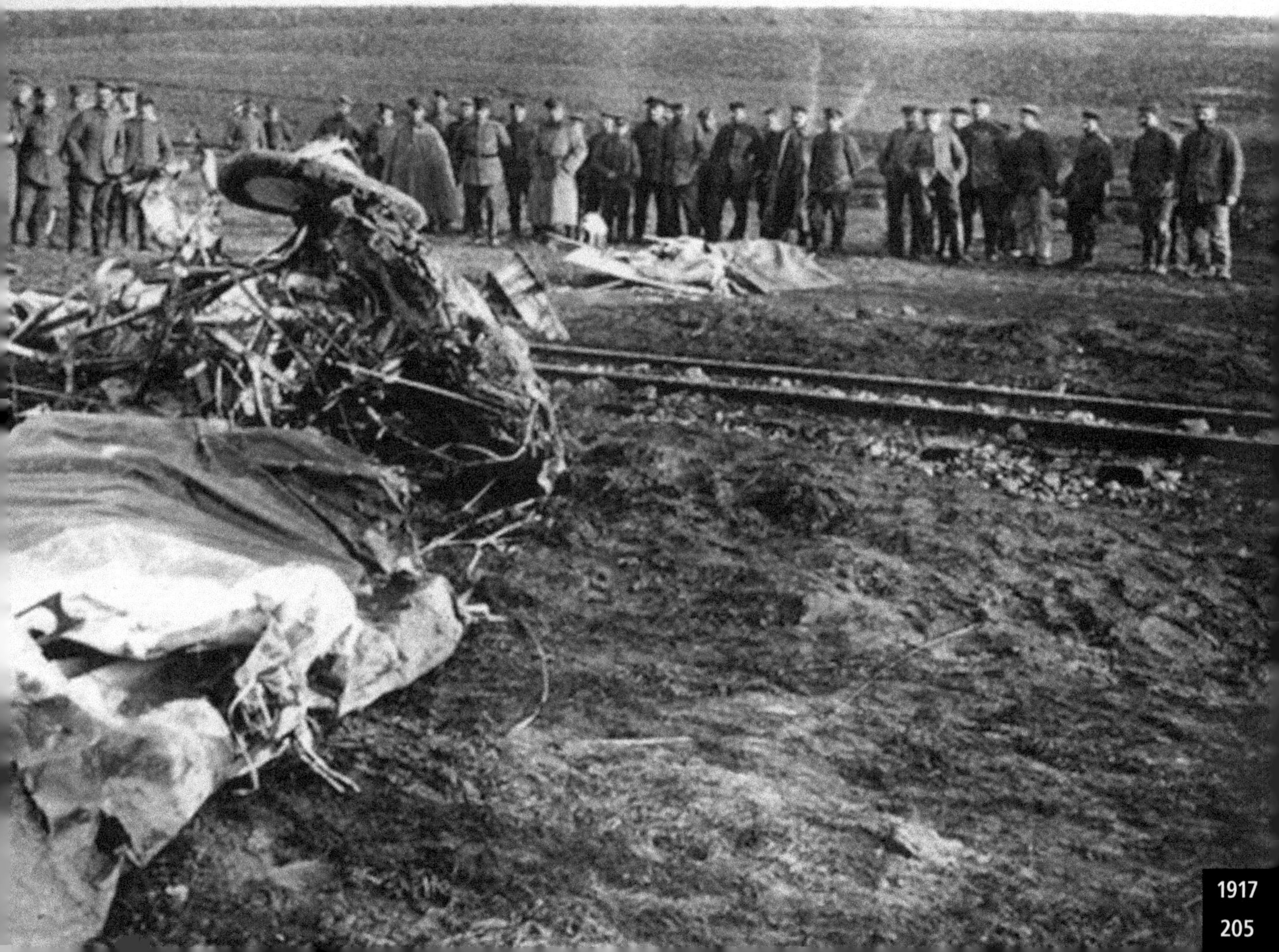

1917

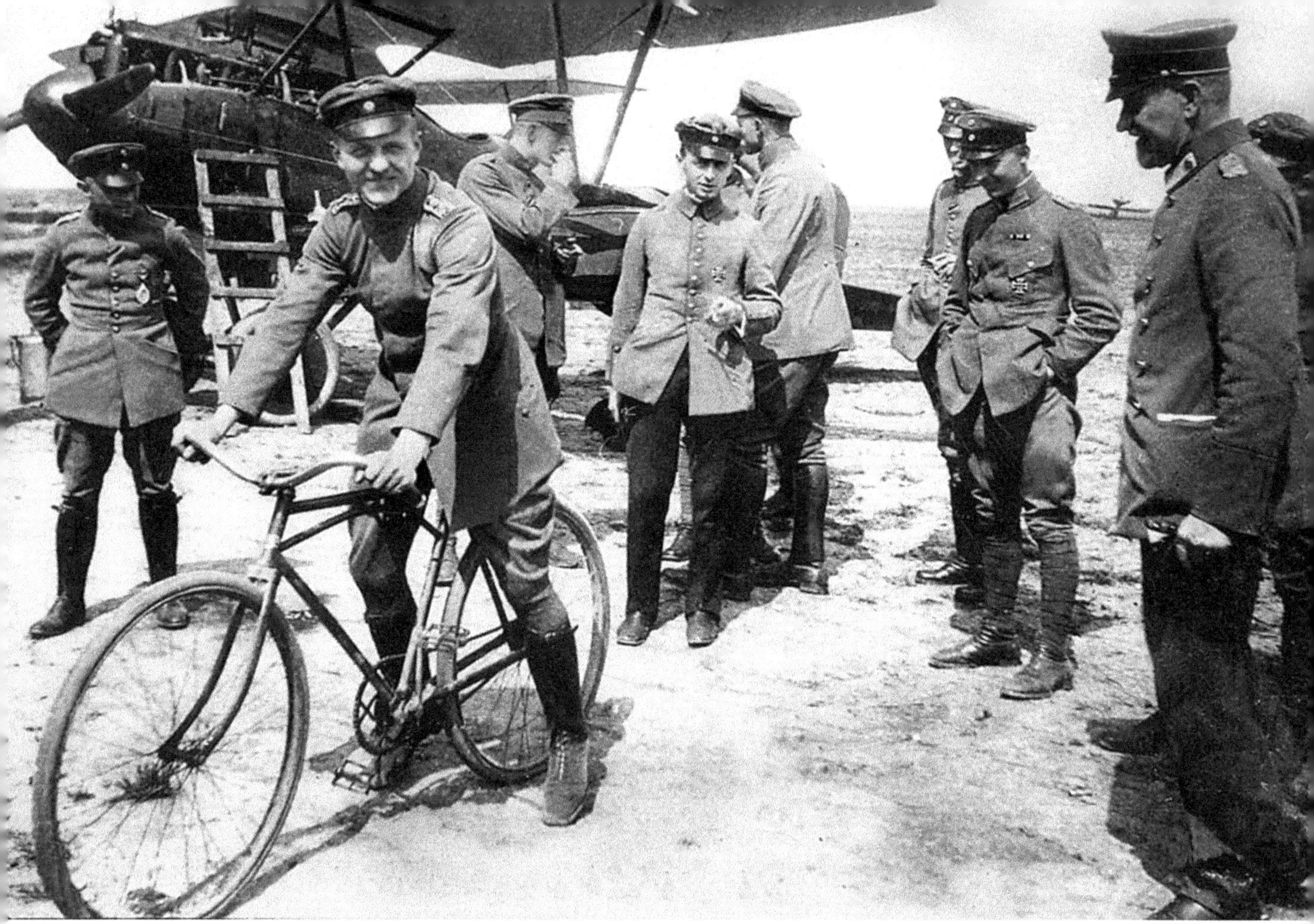

17GW432 Albrecht Freiherr von Richthofen visited his sons, Manfred and Lothar, at Roucourt, where *Jasta 11* was stationed in April 1917. The Red Baron takes to a bicycle for the camera. There appears to be a nosed-over aircraft in the background.

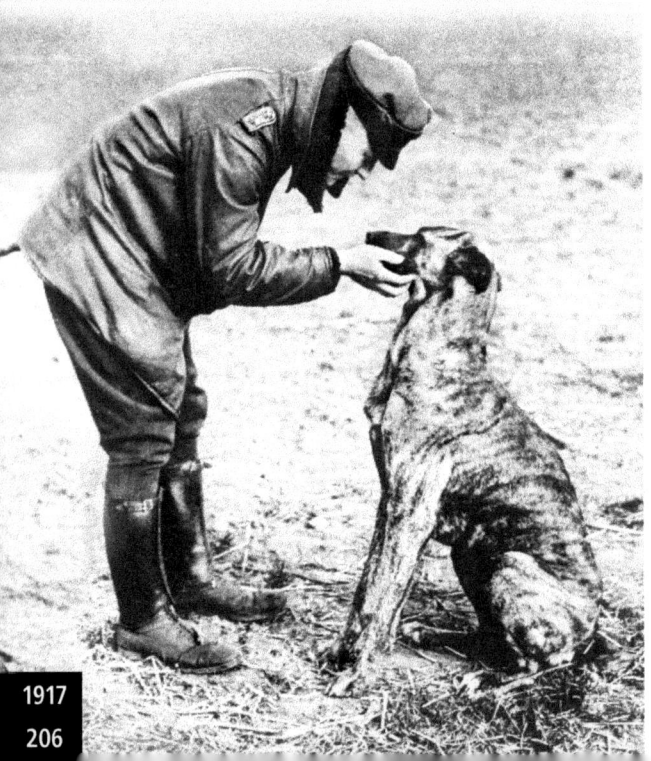

17GW431 The Red Baron with his dog Moritz. *'He likes to accompany the flying machines at the start... frequently a flying-man's dog is killed by the propeller. One day he rushed in front of a flying-machine which had been started up. The propeller caught him... one of his ears was cut off. A long ear and a short ear are a poor match.'*

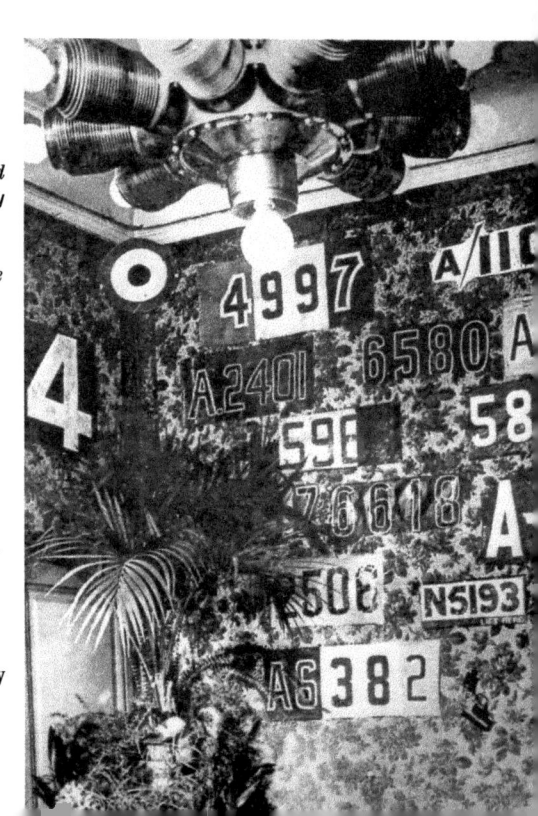

17GW432 The room of von Richthofen with a trophy wall bearing the serial numbers of his victims cut from the wreckage. The chandelier is a rotary engine from one of his kills.

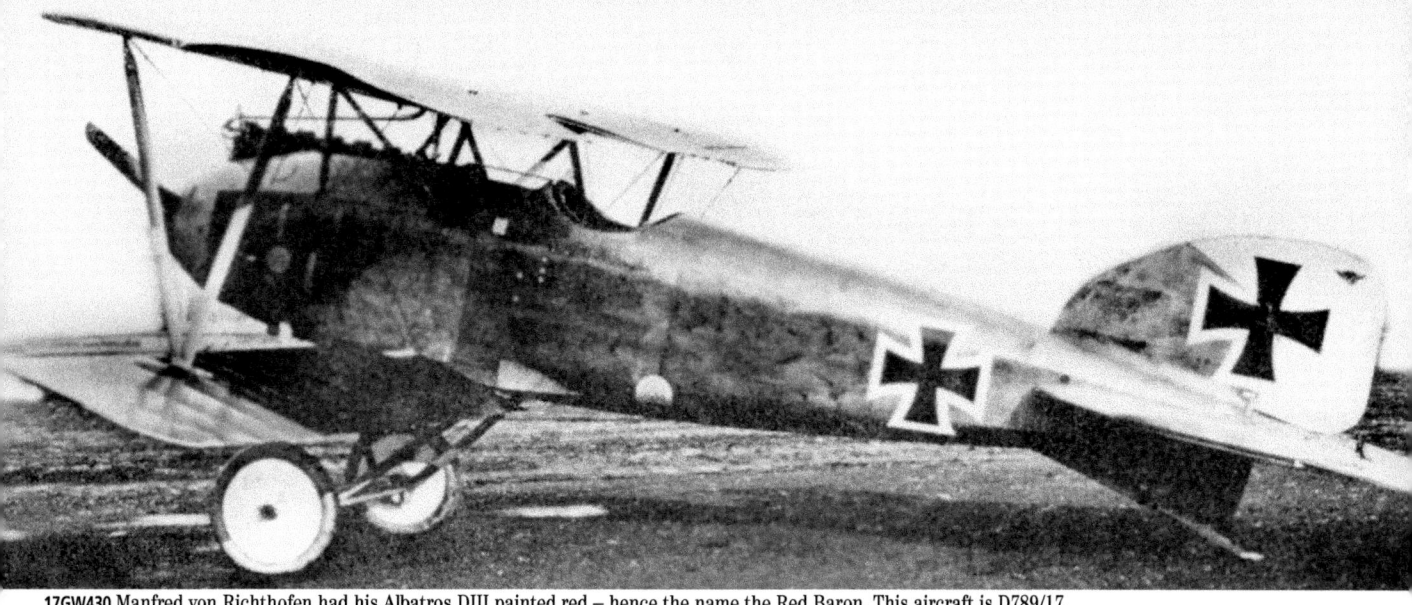

17GW430 Manfred von Richthofen had his Albatros DIII painted red – hence the name the Red Baron. This aircraft is D789/17.

17GW433 Pilots of *Jasta 11* in March 1917: Seated in the cockpit is Manfred von Richthofen; crouched on the wing is Karl Emil Schaefer; (standing left to right), Karl Allmenroeder, Hans Hintsch, Sabastian Festner, Kurt Wolff. Georg Simon and Otto Brauneck; (kneeling) Esser and Constantin Krefft; seated at the front is the Red Baron's younger brother, Lothar von Richthofen.

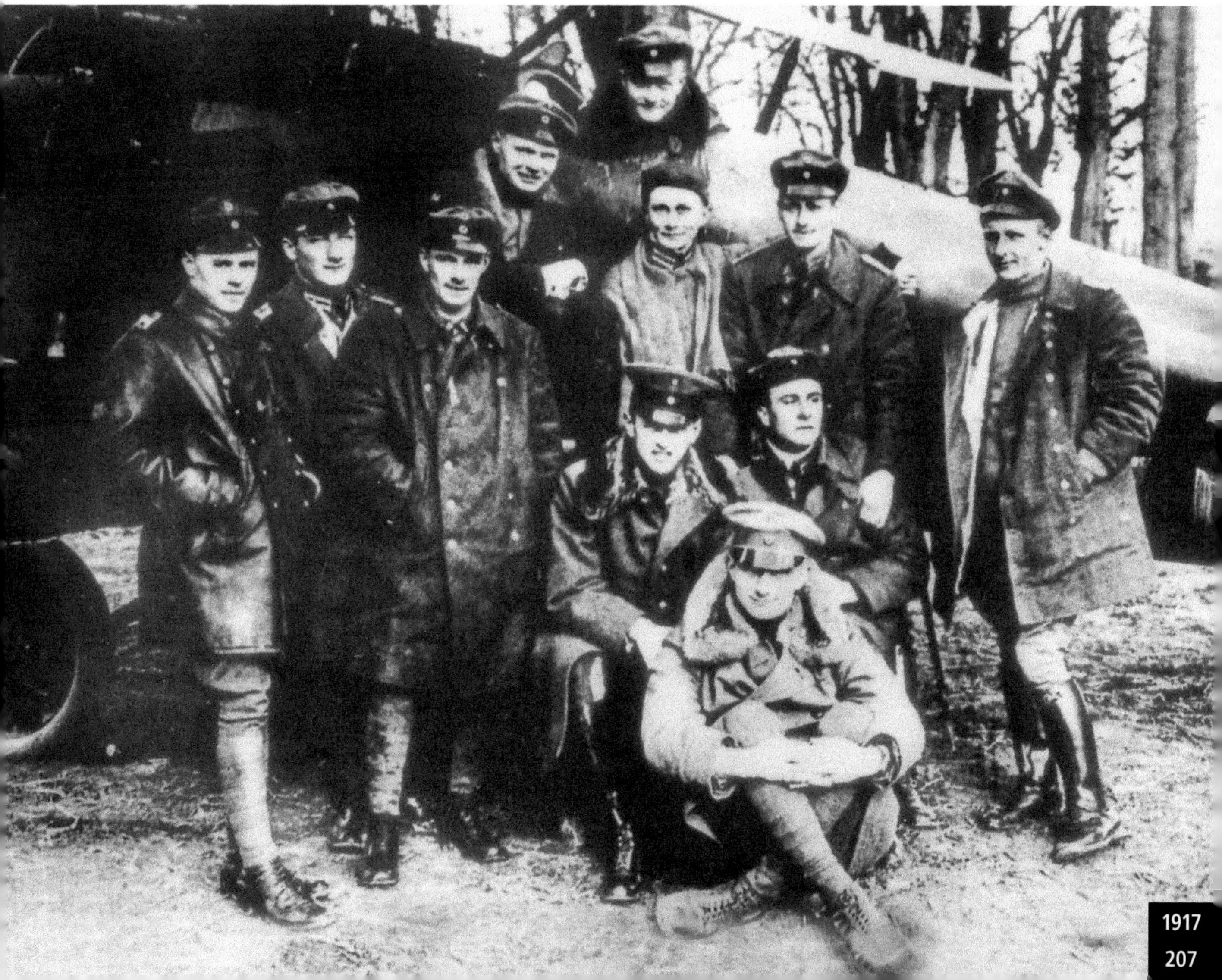

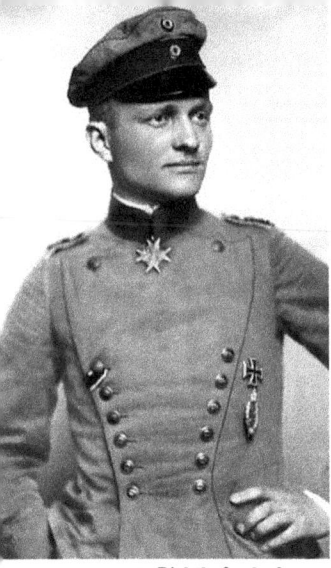

17GW435 Richthofen had begun to consider himself indestructable until he was wounded during a dogfight.

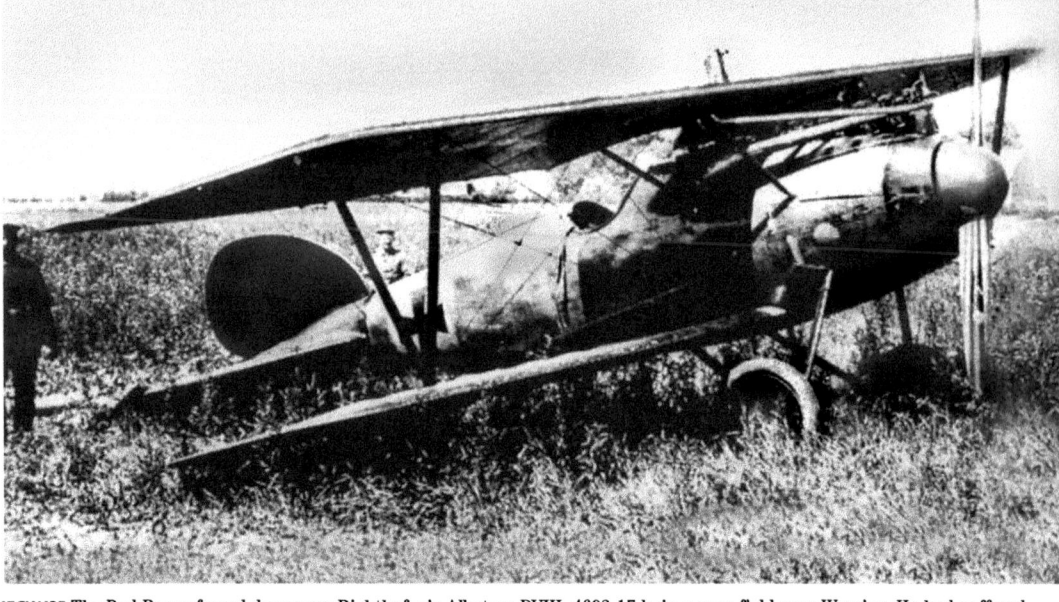

17GW435 The Red Baron forced down: von Richthofen's Albatros DVIII, 4693-17-b, in a corn field near Wervicq. He had suffered a deep scalp wound and had struggled to remain conscious.

On the morning of 6 July 1917, von Richthofen was leading *Jasta 11* to intercept a number of reported British aircraft. They spotted six FE.2ds from 20 Squadron and attacked. The tactic of the outclassed British was to form a defensive circle, where each machine could bring fire to bear. More German machines arrived until forty were ranged against the turning FEs. Four Sopwith triplanes of No.10 Naval Squadron dove in to even the odds a little. The British drove four German aircraft down and one was seen to crash. Two FEs eventually fell to the overwhelming numbers, but the other two managed to edge over the British lines. The observer and gunner of one of the FEs, Second Lieutenant Woodbridge, had kept up a constant fire throughout. He claimed four enemy machines shot down and mentioned in his report seeing another, a red Albatros, spin away – it was the Red Baron.

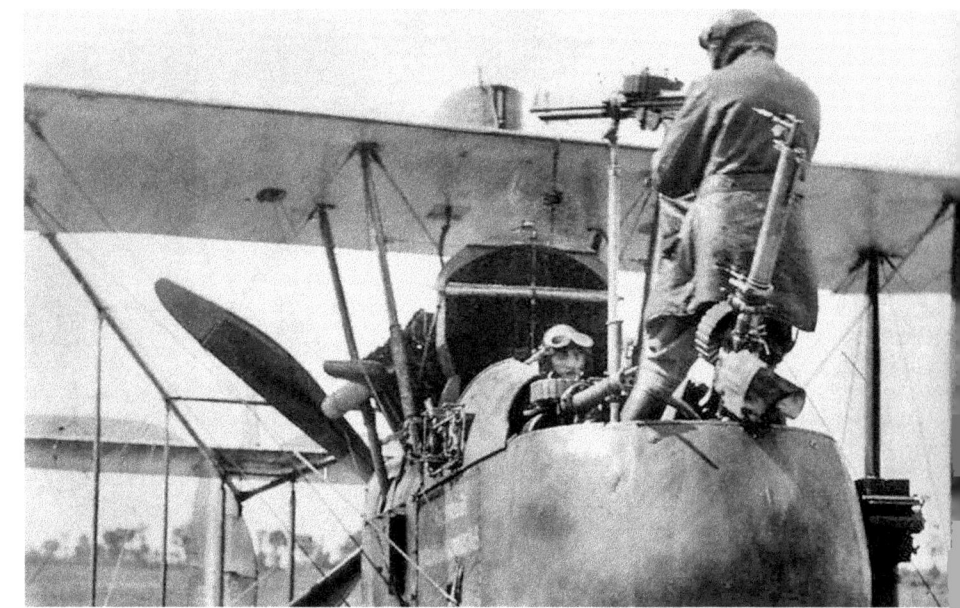

17GW438 The armament carried by the FE.2b. When attacked by enemy machines the RFC pilots would fly in a circle, giving their collective Lewis guns a good field of fire. Defending against a stern attack was risky as is being demonstrated here. It involved the observer standing without a harness.

17GW440 A FE.2b. of No.20 Squadron, RFC. They were equipped with this outdated machine until September 1917. These aircraft were replaced by Bristol F.2b machines and No.20 became a fighter-bomber squadron.

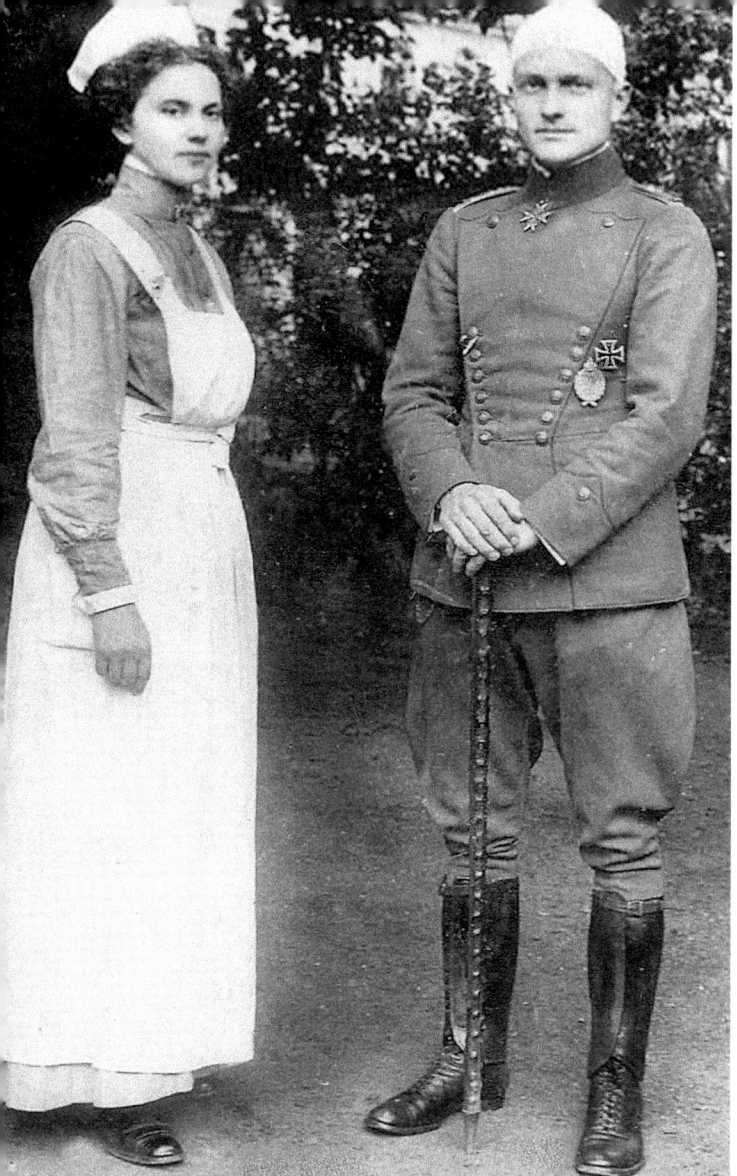

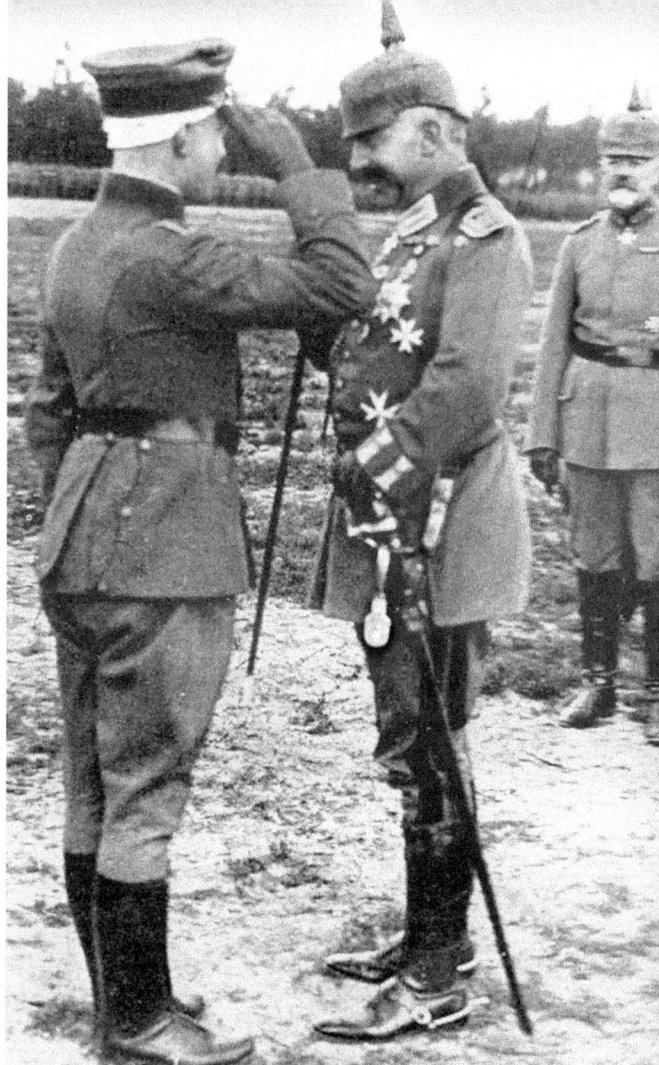

17GW442 Richthofen meets the Kaiser. He salutes his Emperor, who had requested his attendance at a review of troops somewhere in Flanders in August 1917.

17GW441 The Red Baron with his nurse, Fräulein Kätie Otersdorf, in the grounds of St Nicholas's hospital in Courtrai. Richthofen holds a *Geschwaderstock*, a walking stick, which became his badge of office.

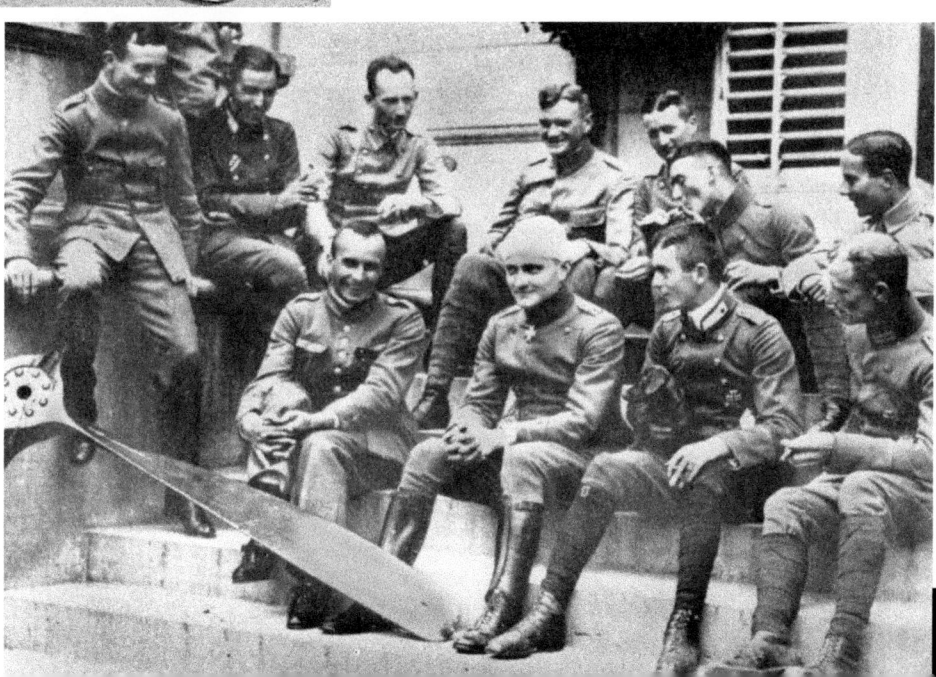

17GW443 Richthofen receives a hospital visit from pilots of his recently formed *Geschwader*. They have brought him a propellor from a downed FE.s, likely as a reminder of how the British almost killed him. They are enjoying a joke together – could they be teasing him about the beautiful nurse assigned to look after him?

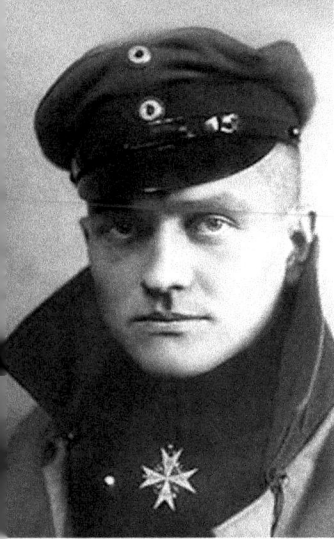

17GW445 Manfred Albrecht Freiherr von Richthofen had become the object of a cult of hero-worship, encouraged by German official propaganda. He had become such a legend that it was feared his death would be a blow to the morale of the German people.

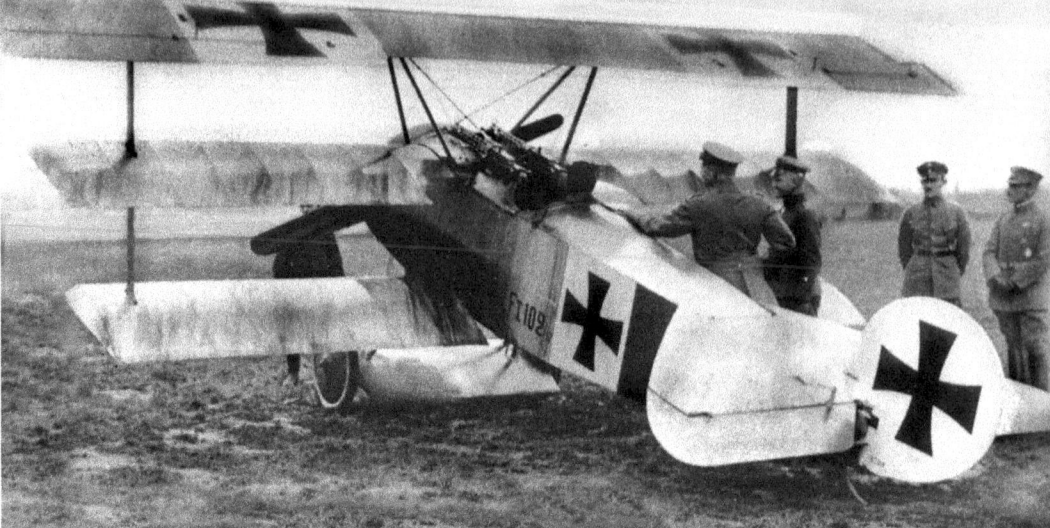

17GW444 On 28 August 1917, the first Fokker Triplane was delivered to Richthofen's *Geschwader*. Werner Voss, leader of *Jasta 10*, flew the machine for the first time. Three days later the Red Baron is seen here explaining the aircraft's performance to *Generalmajor* Karl von Lossberg, Chief of Staff to *4.Armee*.

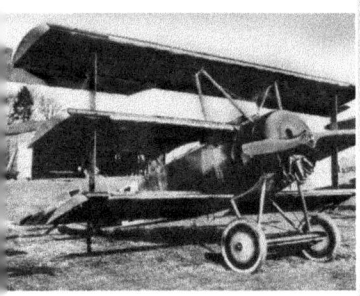

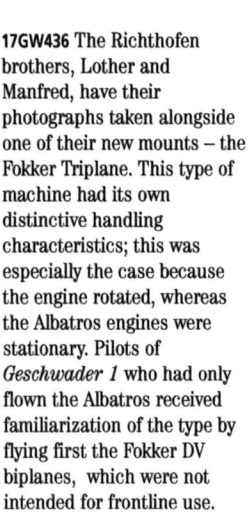

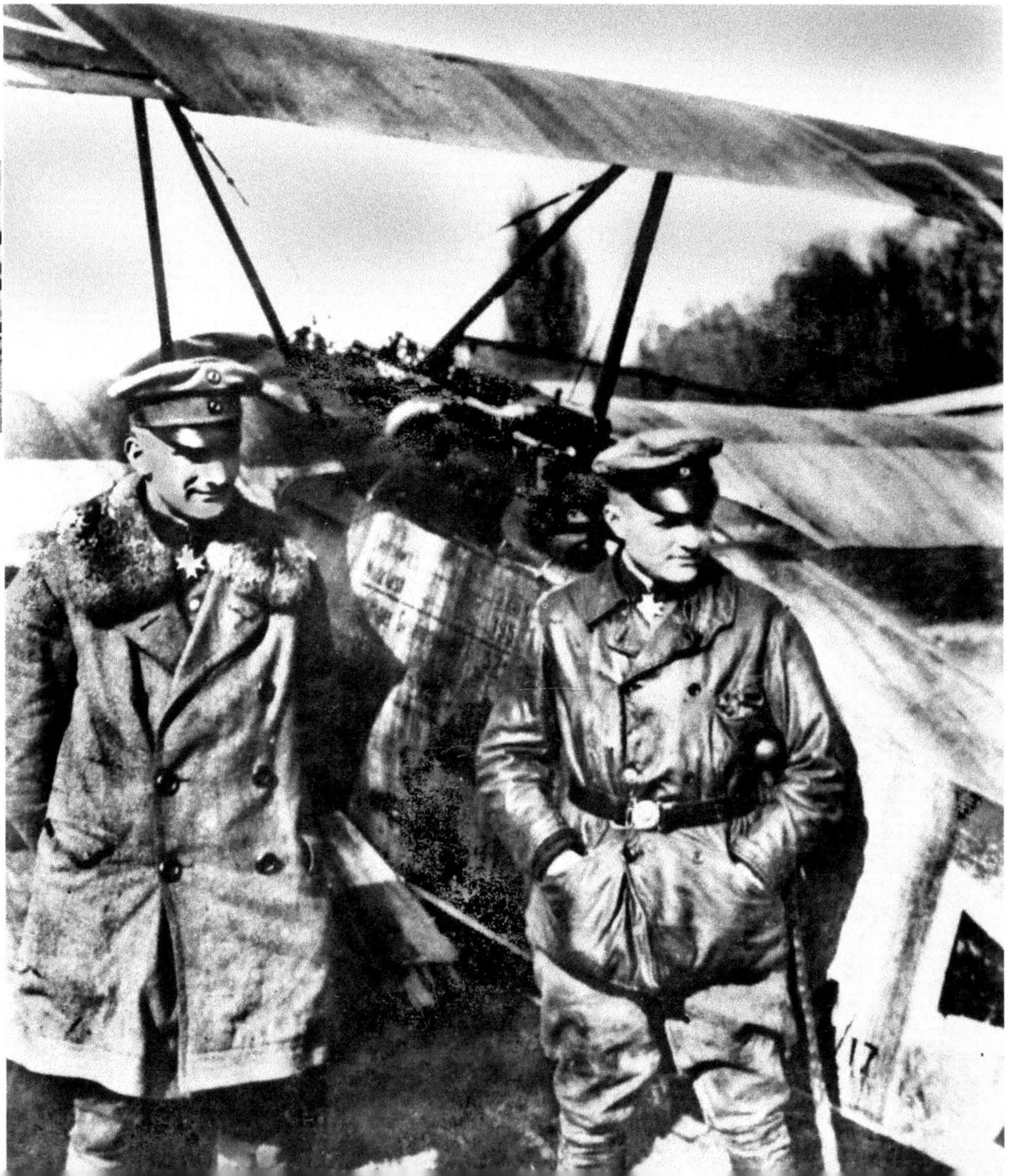

17GW436 The Richthofen brothers, Lother and Manfred, have their photographs taken alongside one of their new mounts – the Fokker Triplane. This type of machine had its own distinctive handling characteristics; this was especially the case because the engine rotated, whereas the Albatros engines were stationary. Pilots of *Geschwader 1* who had only flown the Albatros received familiarization of the type by flying first the Fokker DV biplanes, which were not intended for frontline use.

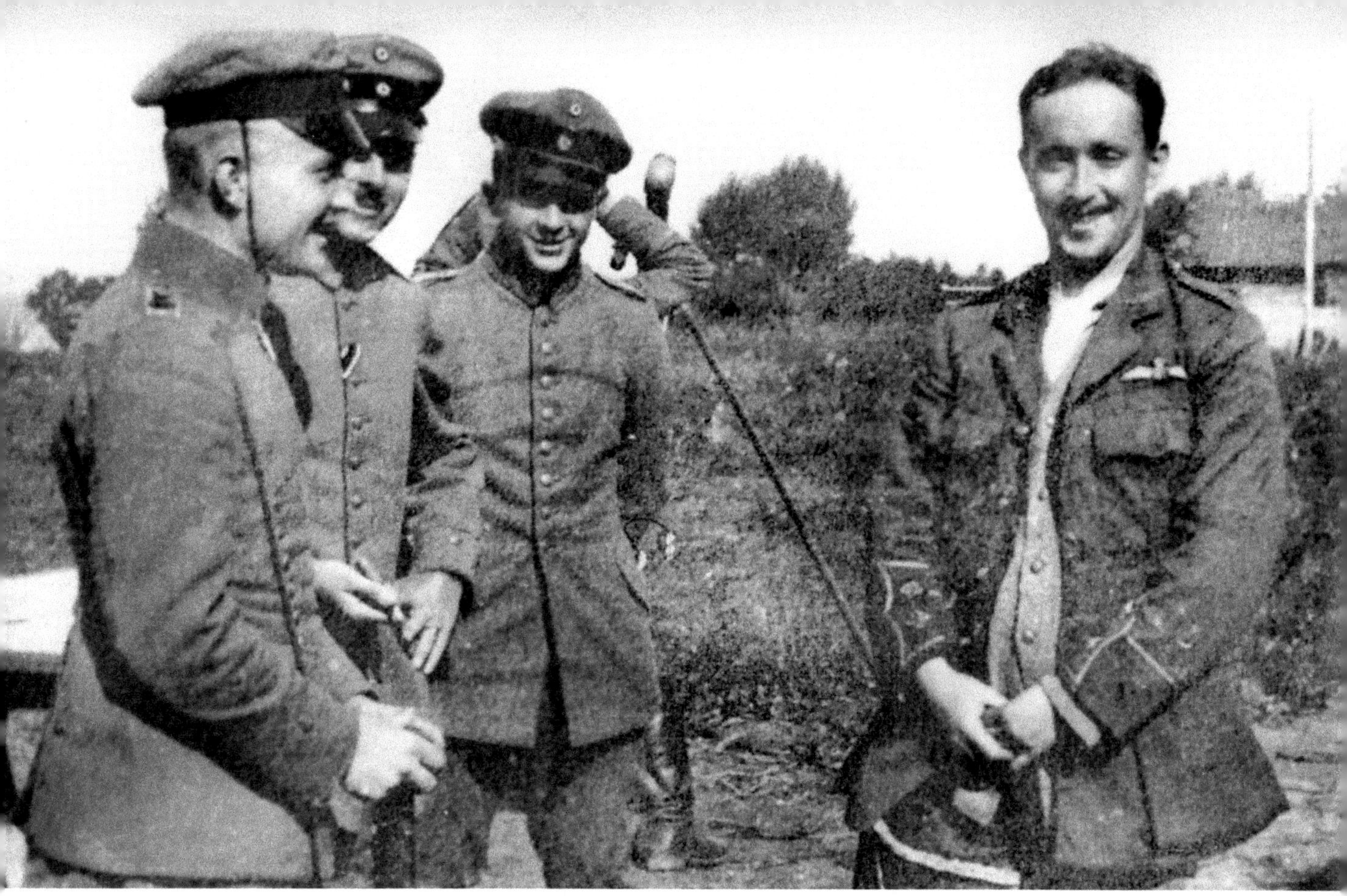

17GW446 Richthofen plays host to his sixty-first 'kill', Lieutenant Algernon F. Bird, No.46 Squadron, RFC. At this time fifty-four crew had been killed in encounters with the Red Baron, Lieutenant Bird was one of twenty-nine who had survived. All four are enjoying a joke together which typifies the perverse chivalry entertained by the 'knights of the air' towards the vanquished enemy.

17GW447 Charred victims of von Richthofen, a pilot and observer, shot out of the sky near Méricourt, France. No chivalrous *bonhomme* for these men and their families.

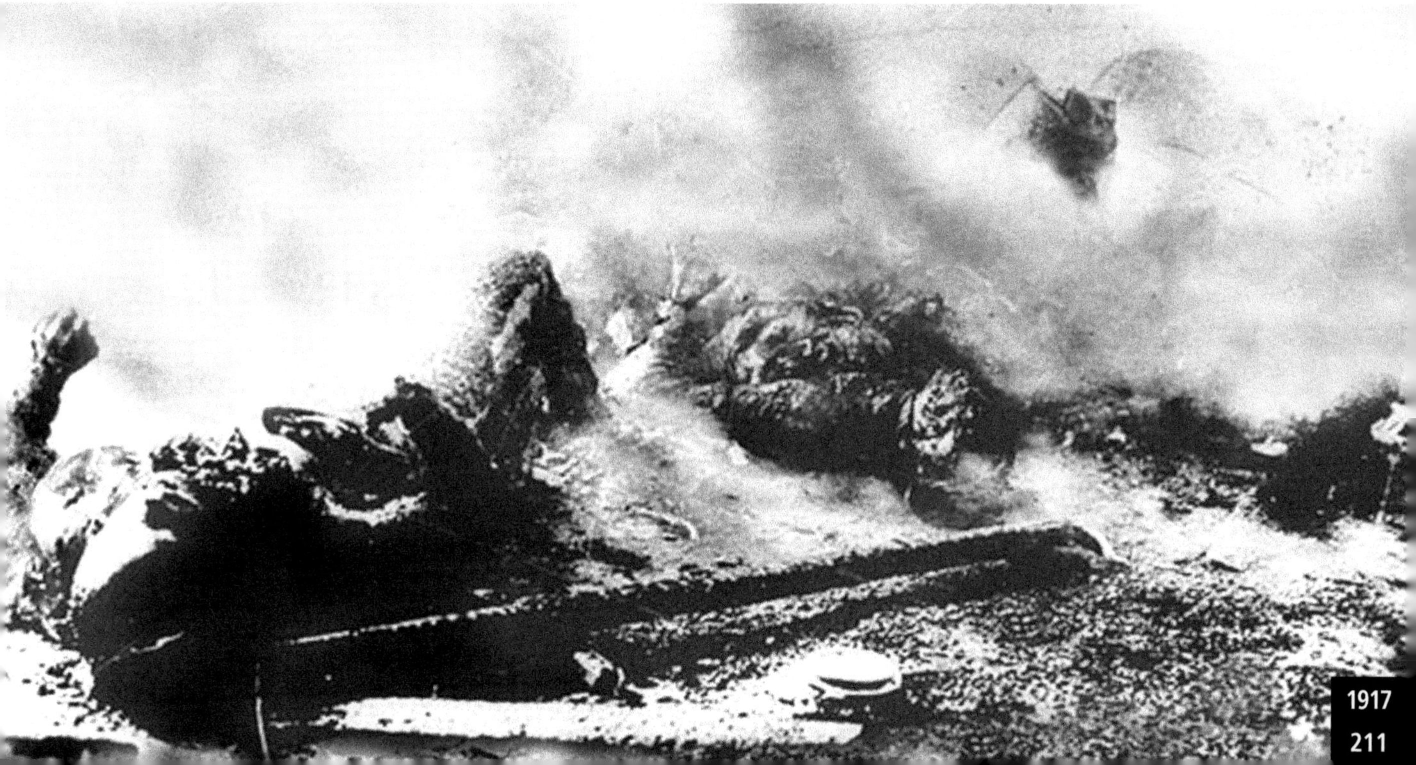

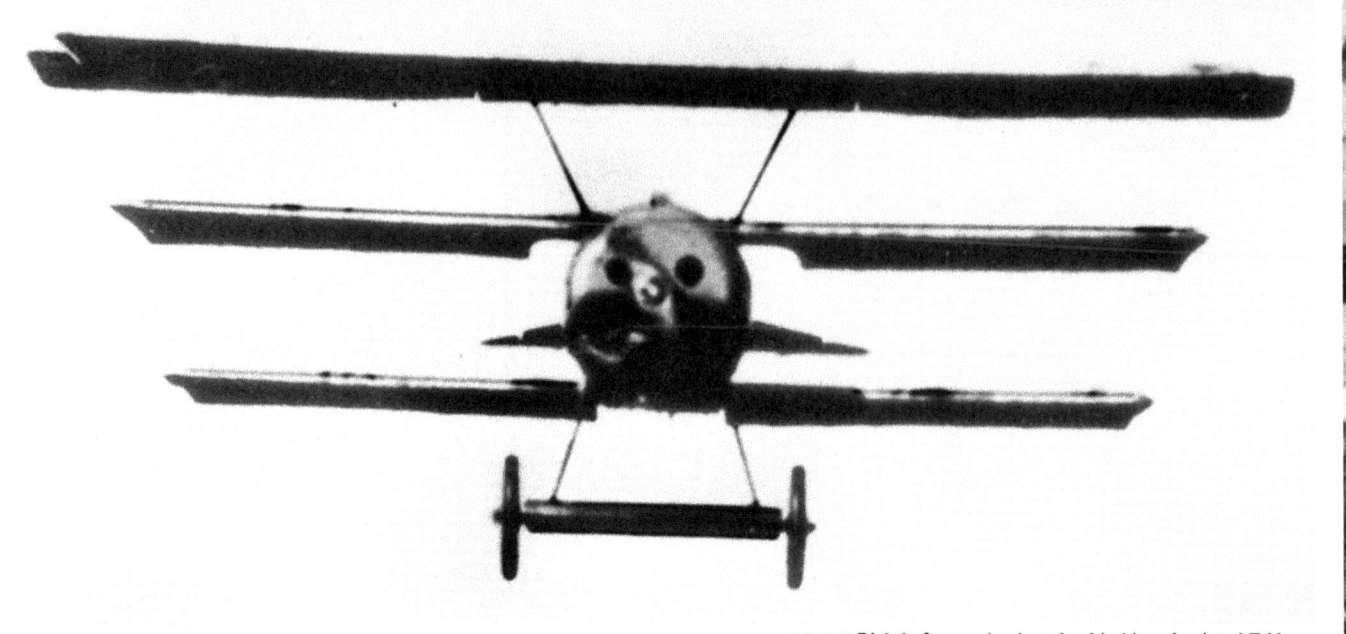

17GW449 Richthofen coming in to land in his red painted Fokker Dr.I Triplane. This would have been the astern approach view of an allied aircraft under attack and the odds for survival would have been very low.

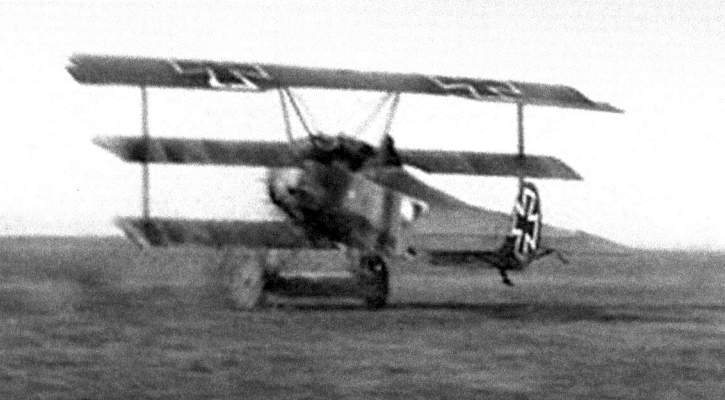

17GW450, 17GW451, 17GW452. Lothar von Richthofen, the Red Baron's younger brother, while attempting to destroy a Bristol F.2b of No.62 Squadron, RFC, on 13 March, 1918, was forced to crash land when the upper wing of his Triplane ripped away during his diving attack. The F.2b would have been his 30th kill. He spent the next four months in hospital.

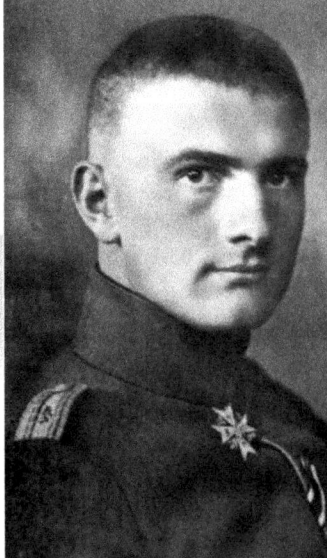

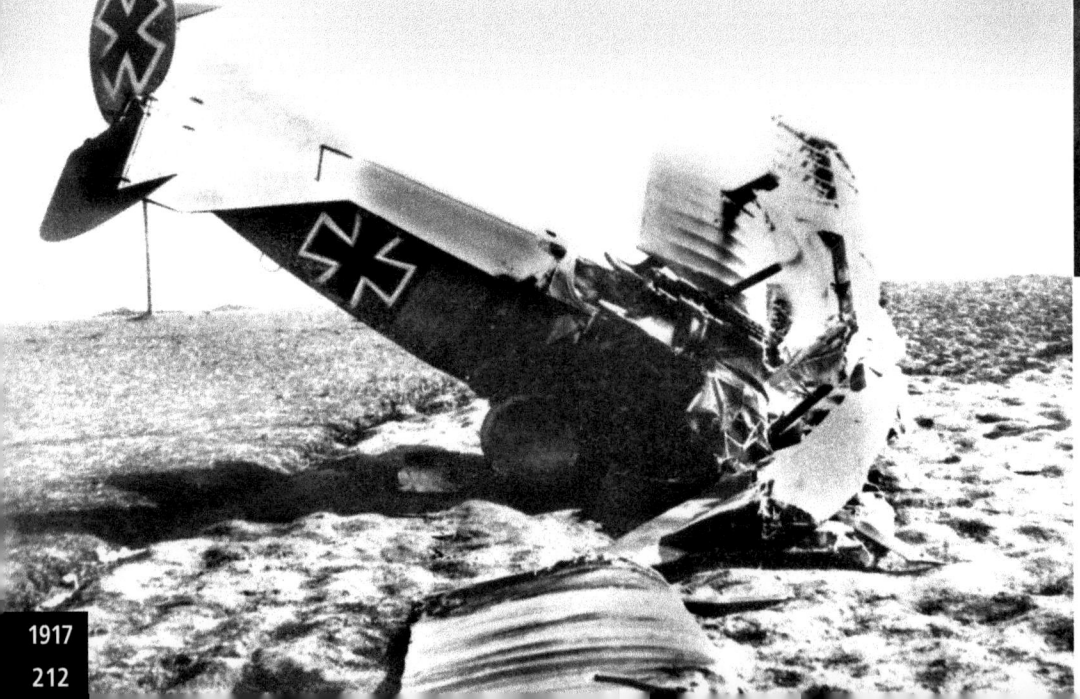

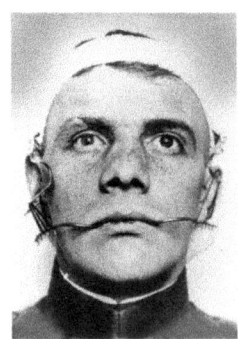

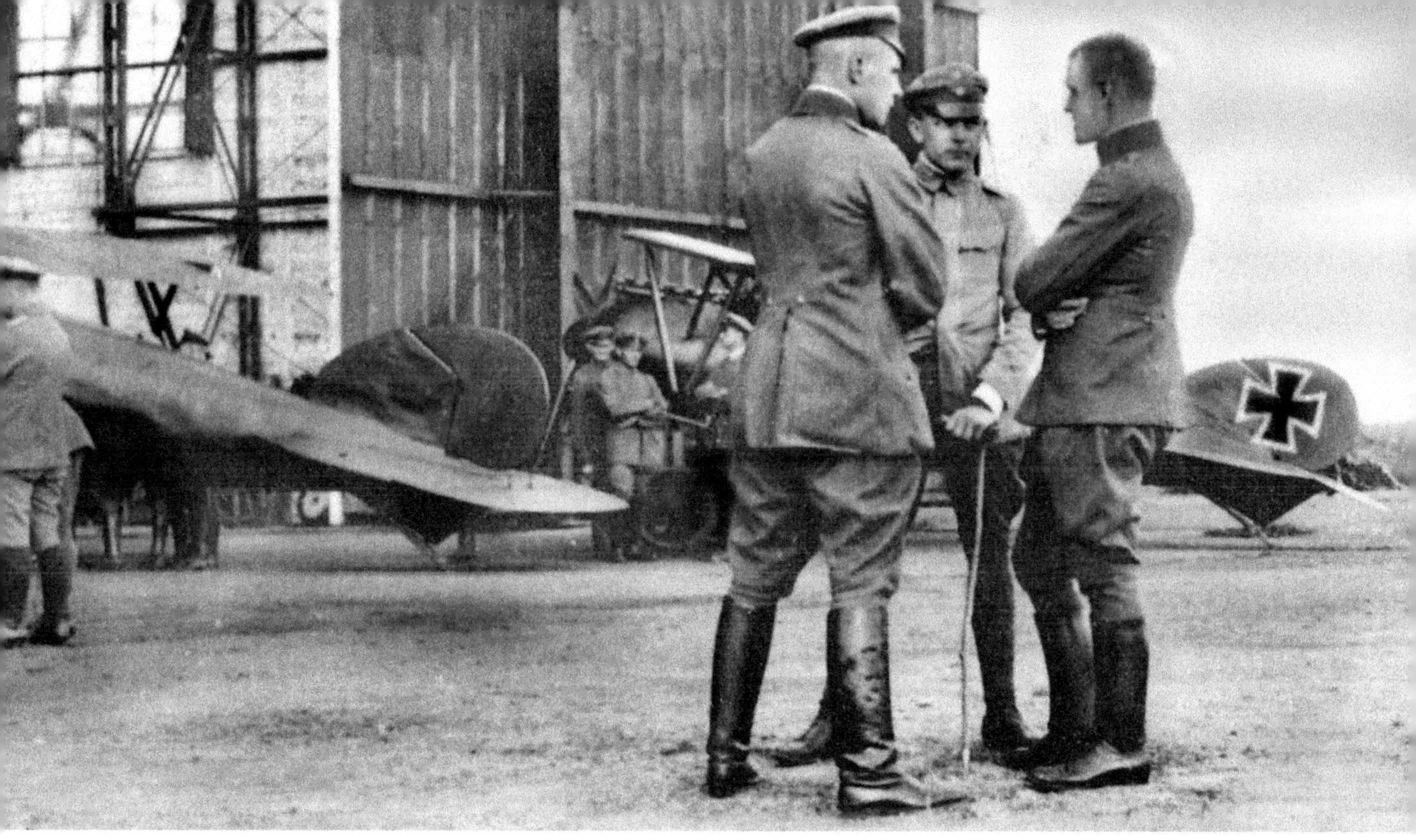

17GW448 The Red Baron, seen here visiting *Kampfgeschwader 3* bomber base at Gontrode, Belgium, where he is conferring with *Hauptmann* Rudolf Kleine, *KG3's* commander (left); the unit's adjutant, *Oberleutnant* Gerlich, is standing centre. Escorting bombers was not to Richthofen's liking as he much preferred the hunting role rather than the defending one. Although equipped with the Triplanes some *JG I* pilots continued to fly the Albatros, as teething troubles were experienced with the new three-winged machines.

17GW454 Richthofen meets the Commanding Officer of the German Air Service, General von Hoeppner, during the planning stages for the German Spring Offensive in 1918.

17GW455 The Red Baron talking to Herr Georg Michaelis, Imperial Chancellor, on the Somme front in 1917.

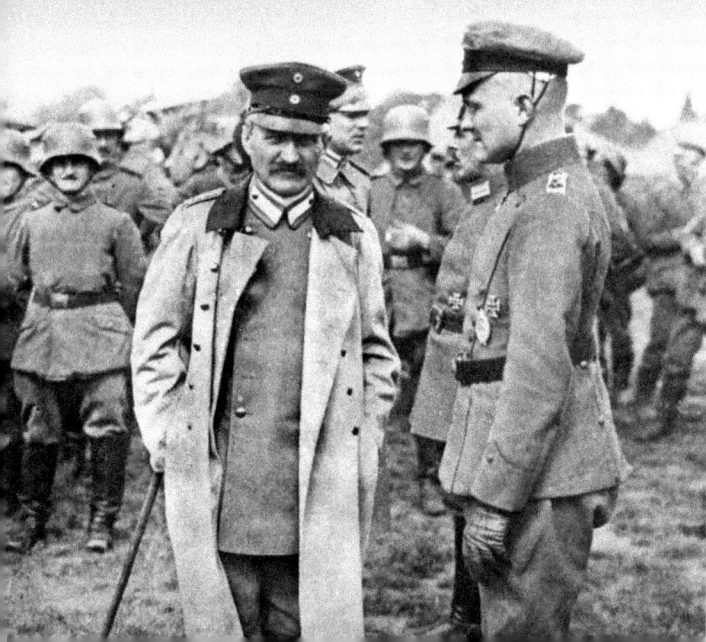

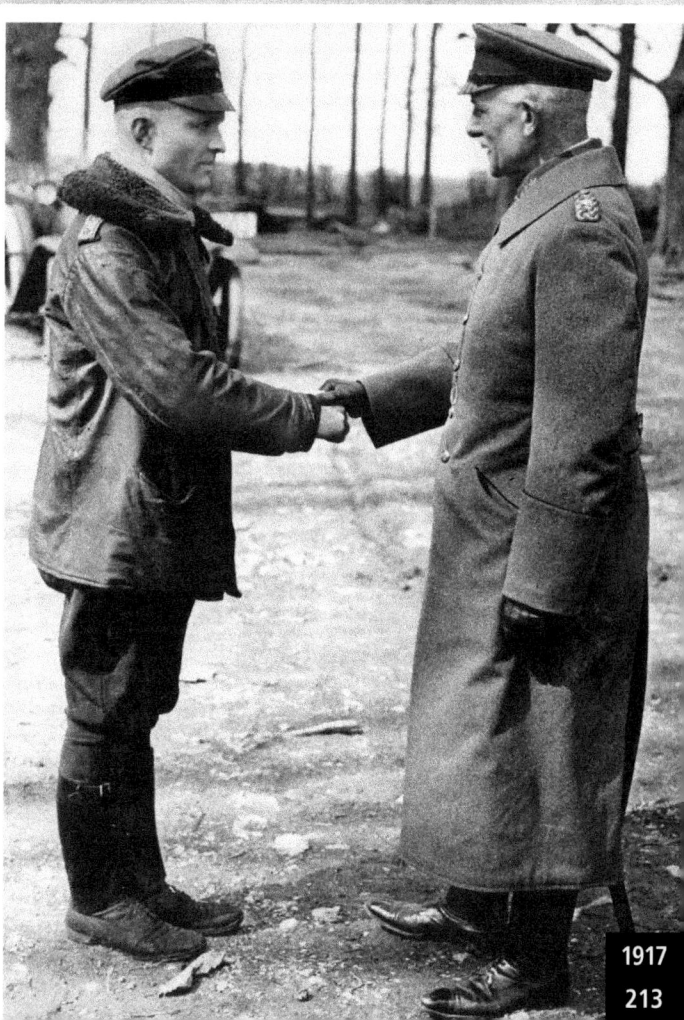

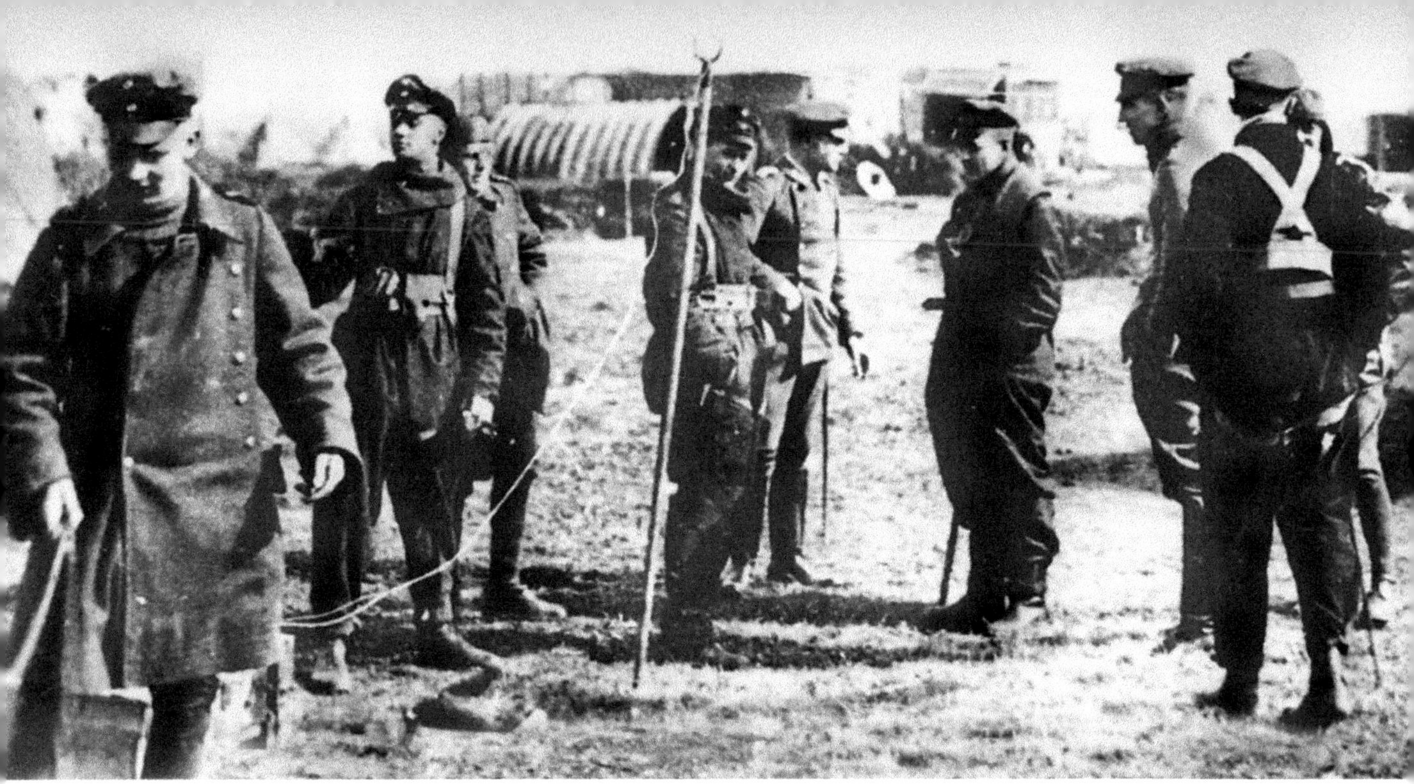

17GW458, 17GW460. Awaiting orders for take-off at Cappy, 21 April 1918.
Ernst Udet made comparisons with the Red Baron's *JG 1* and other *Staffeln* serving on the Western Front: *'Other Staffeln billet themselves in a French chateau or village 20 or 30 kilometres behind the Front. The Richthofen Geschwader is crowded into metal huts that can be dismantled in a few hours then re-assembled. They are seldom more than 20 kilometres behind the most advanced line. Other Staffeln take off two or three times a day, Richthofen and his men go up five times.'* Fokkers of *Jasta 11* being prepared for take-off. Note the changed style of the national symbol from the cross *pattée* to the simplified version. This change in markings assists in ruling out contending photographs of the Red Baron's 'last flight'. On the fatal day his machine bore the new cross.

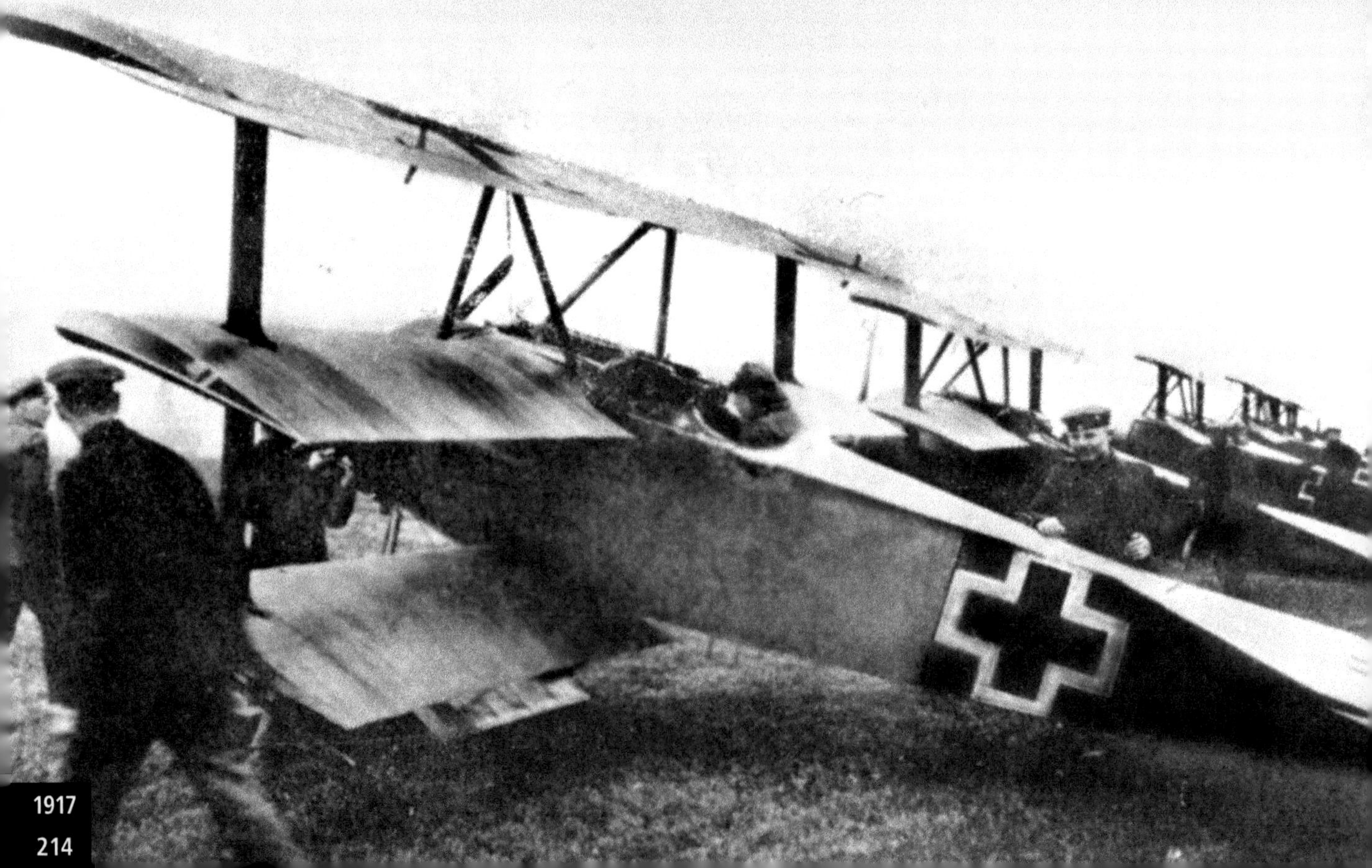

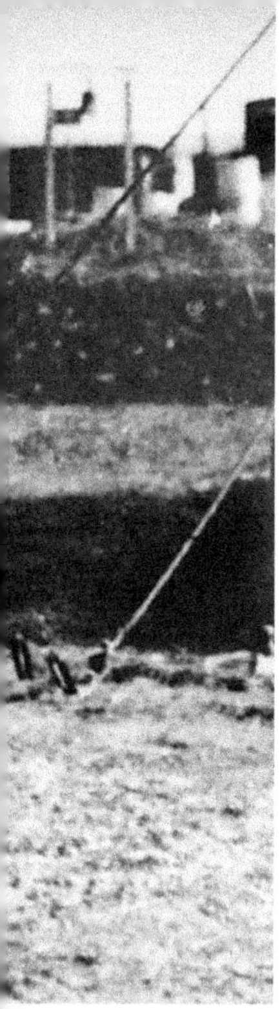

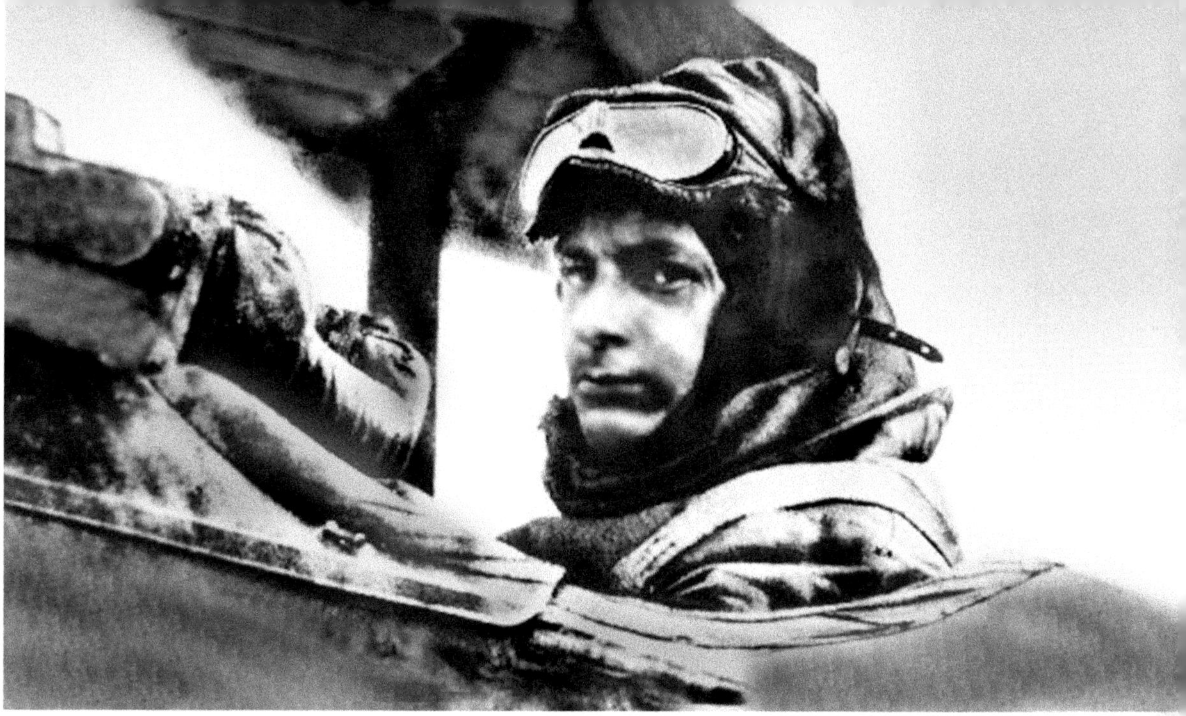

17GW461, 17GW464. Ernst Udet was the second-highest scoring German ace of the war, with 62 kills. He was 22 years old when the war ended. Along with Herman Göring, he helped build the new *Luftwaffe* for Hitler.

17GW465 On 7 July 1918, following the death of Wilhelm Reinhard, successor to von Richthofen, Herman Göring was appointed commander of the famed 'Flying Circus'.

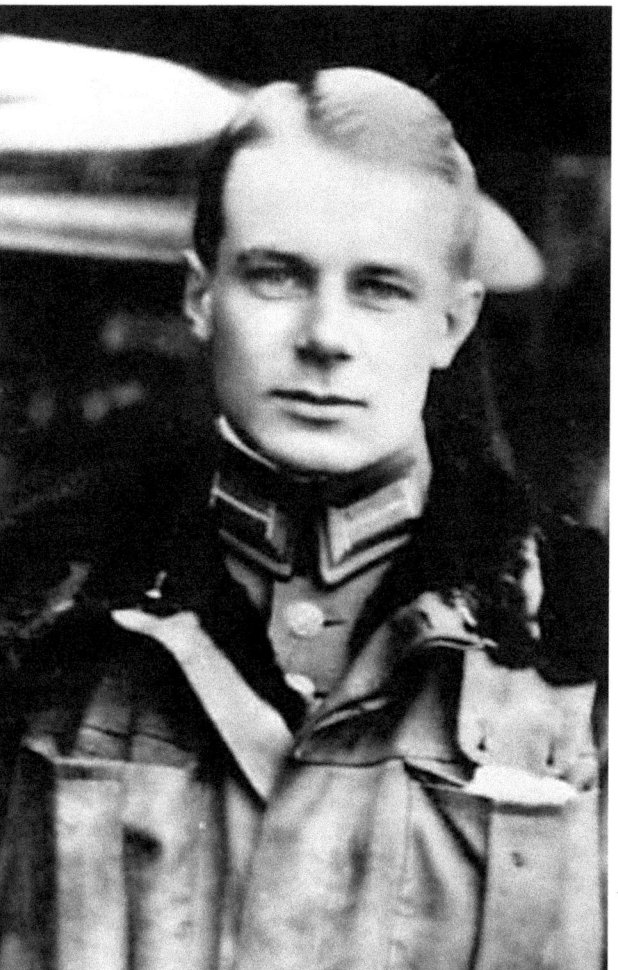

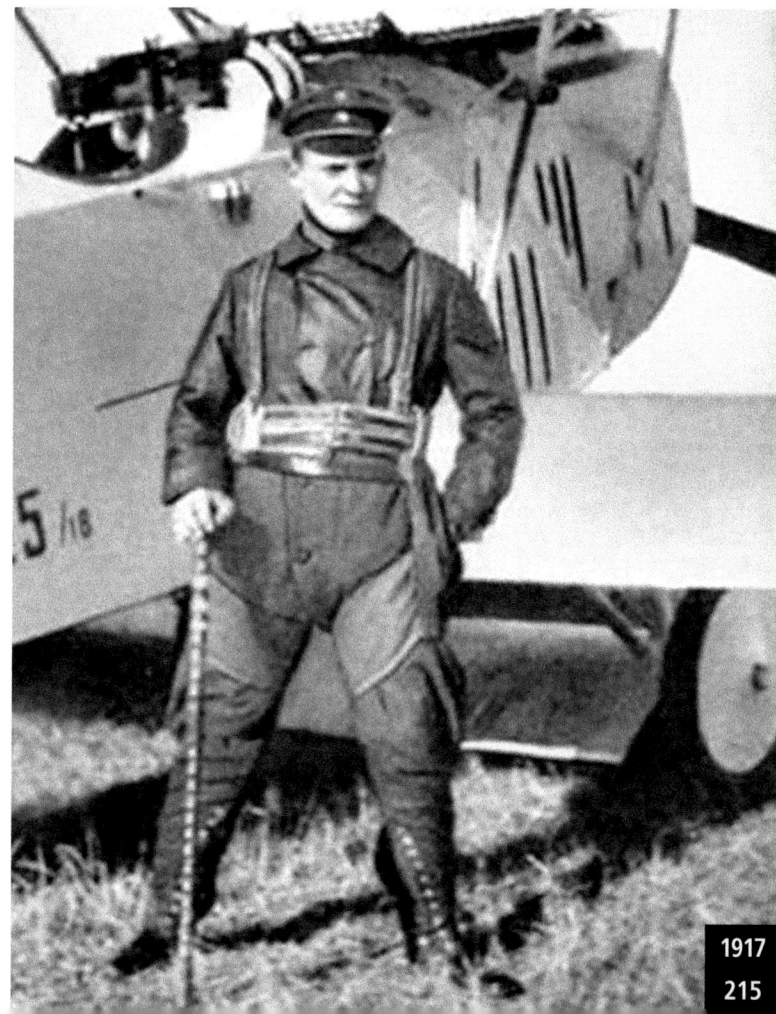

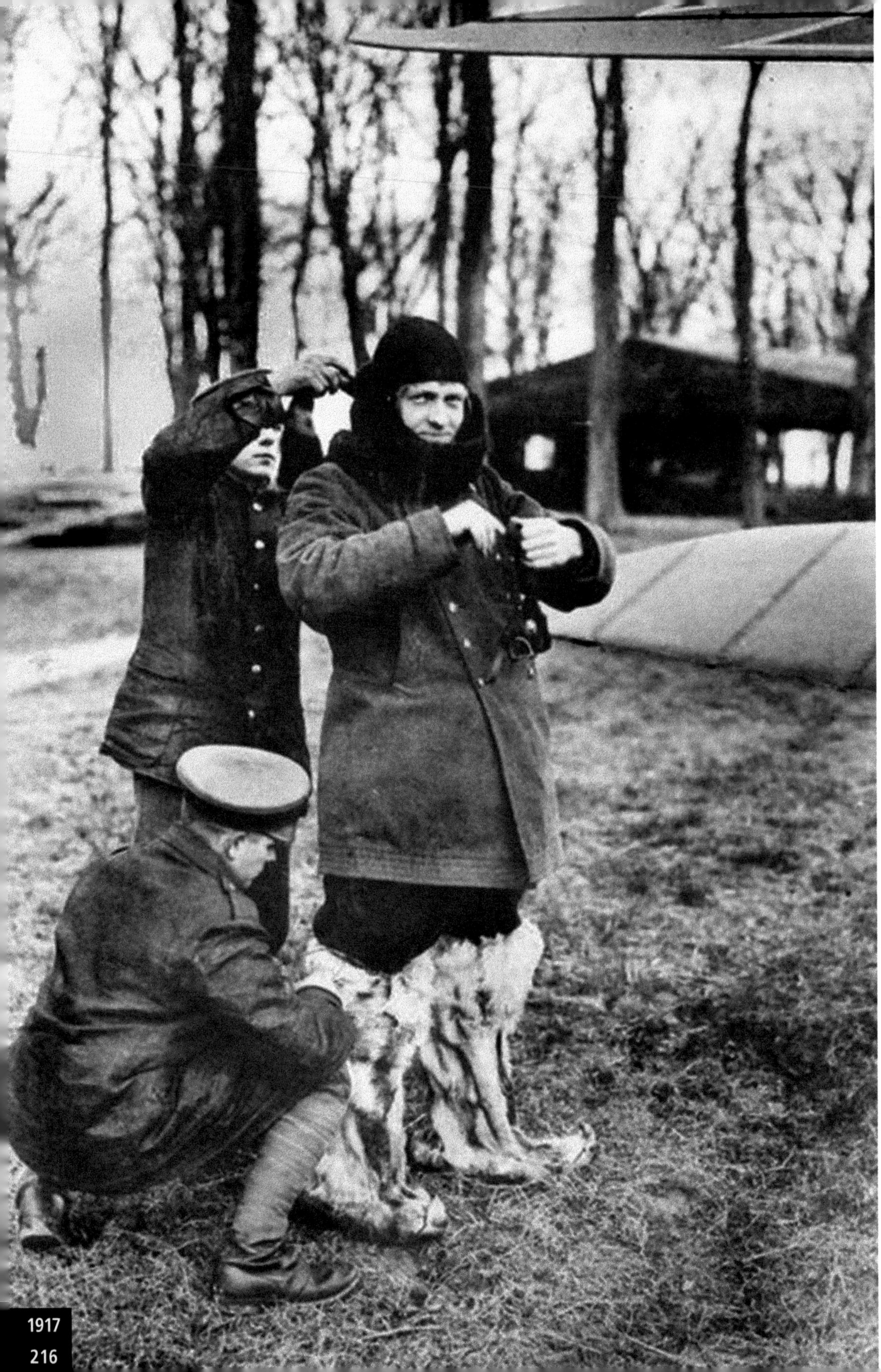

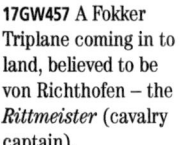

17GW457 A Fokker Triplane coming in to land, believed to be von Richthofen – the *Rittmeister* (cavalry captain).

17GW456 Richthofen being dressed by attendants for a sortie, much in the manner of medieval knights of old. Because of the fur boots this picture is sometimes captioned as being the Red Baron about to take off on his last flight, 21 April 1918; however the aircraft appears to be a biplane rather than a triplane of the type in which he was killed.

17GW462 On the morning of his last flight Sunday, 21 April, some of Richthofen's men tied a wheelchock to the tail of his pet dog, Moritz, as a joke and this photograph shows a wheelchock, rope and dog, so it is sometimes captioned as the final photograph of the famous air ace. Perhaps the old style cross on the Triplane would indicate otherwise.

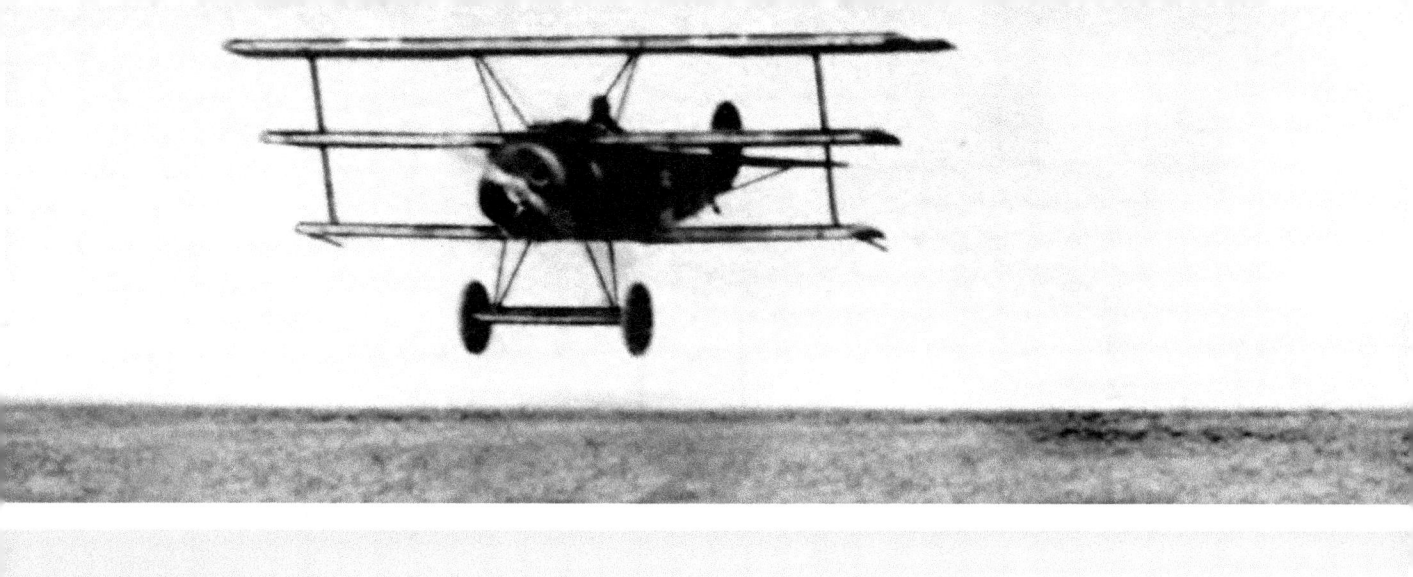

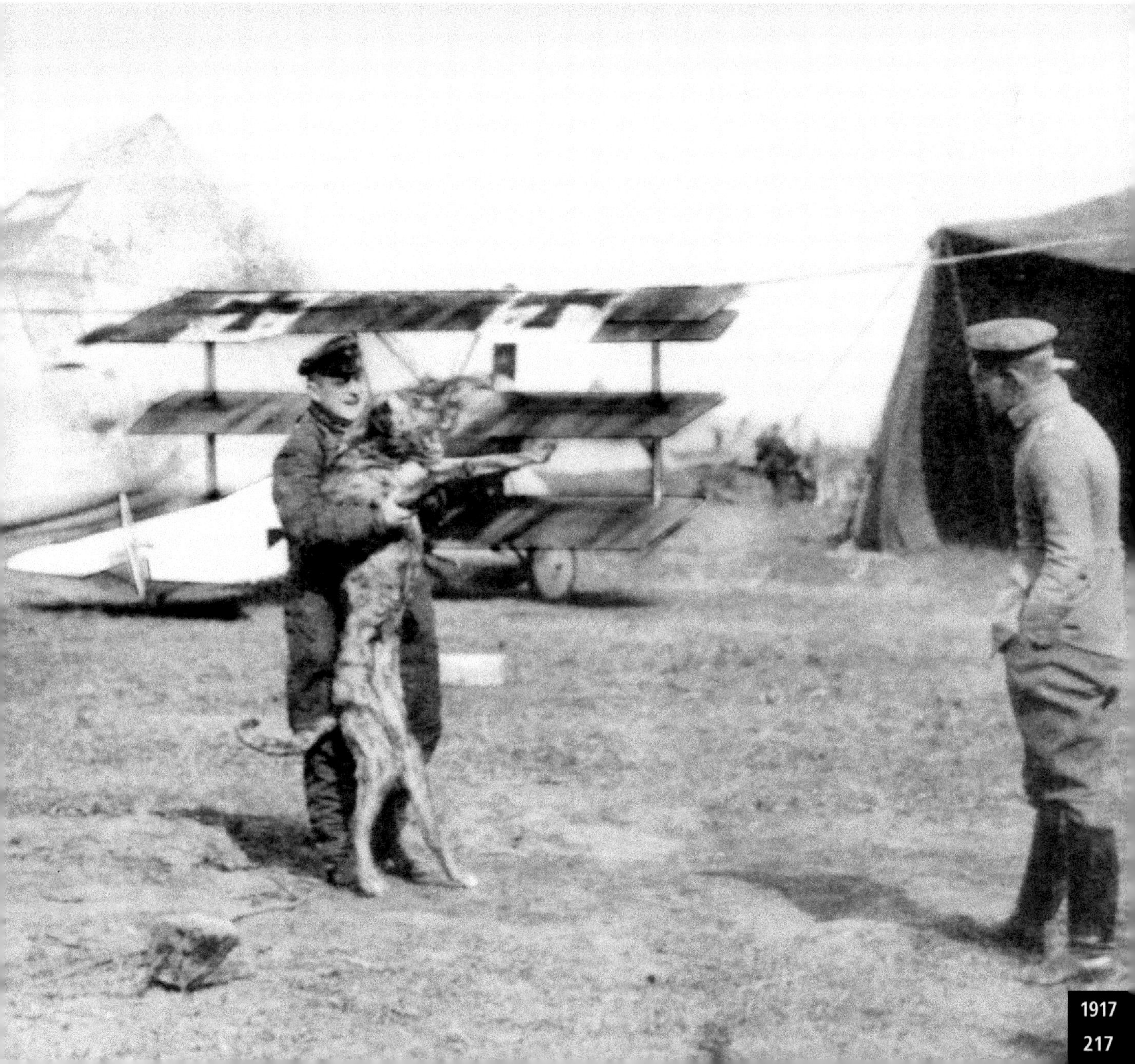

1917
217

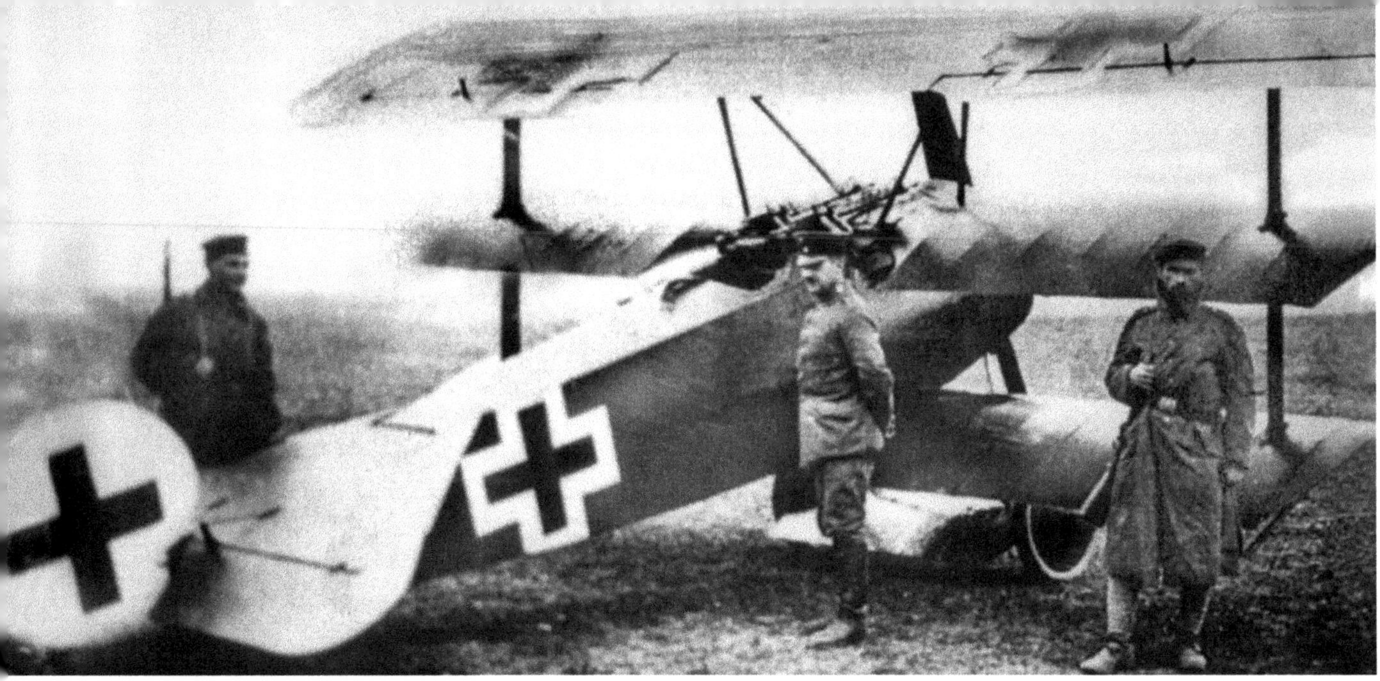

17GW466 The mount of von Richthofen, DR I 425/17, red paint work ; the overpainted crosses places this picture closer to the day he was finally destroyed. On 20 April he had shot down two aircraft, bringing his final score to 80 kills.

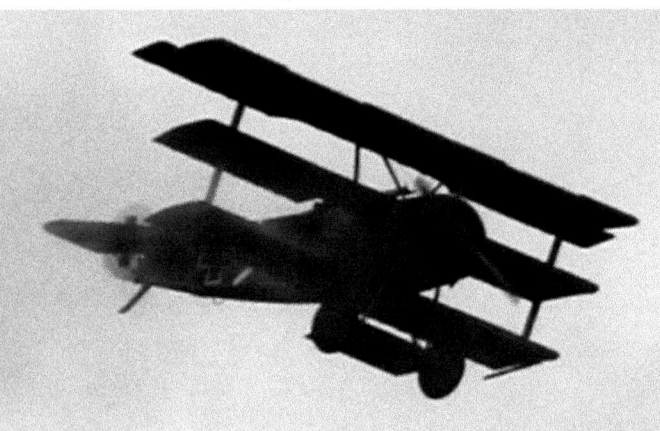

Second Lieutenant Wilfrid R May ('Wop'), a Canadian pilot flying with the newly formed No.209 Squadron (1 April 1918), was on his first combat mission over the area of the River Somme when his squadron of fifteen Sopwith Camels attacked two German reconnaisance machines. Suddenly, they were swooped on by scouts of *JG 1* led by the Red Baron. After some initial manourvering, 'Wop' May was selected as a victim by von Richthofen. The Canadian powered down to tree top level and began weaving as the all-red Triplane attempted to line him up as his 81st kill. Captain A Roy Brown, leader of the squadron, saw the plight of his fellow Canadian and immediately dropped down after the three-strutter; he was an experienced pilot with nine kills to his credit. May later reported: *'I was attacked by a red triplane which chased me over the lines low to the ground. While he was on my tail, Captain Brown attacked and shot it down. I observed it crash into the ground'* Brown in his report considered that he had hit and downed the red scout: *'I dived on a pure red triplane which was firing on Lieutenant May. I got a long burst into him and he went down vertical and was observed to crash by Lieutenant Mellersh and Lieutenant May.'*
Did Brown fatally wound von Richthofen causing him to crash land? The single bullet that killed the German ace came from beneath and not from above.

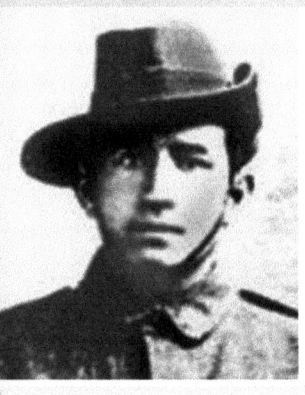

As the three planes raced low over Morlancourt Ridge, in the 4th (Australian) Division's sector, Sergeant Popkin, along with other Australian machine gunners and riflemen, blazed away at the red triplane. The Baron was hit by a .303 calibre bullet which passed diagonally upwards from right to left, tearing through his lungs and heart.
17GW484, 17GW487, 17GW486, Sergeant Cedric Bassett Popkin, 24th Machine Gun Company. Australian operating a Lewis gun in the AA role.

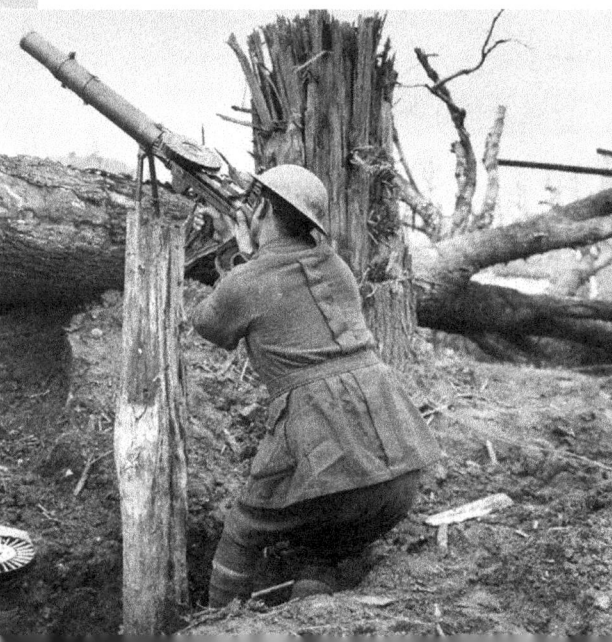

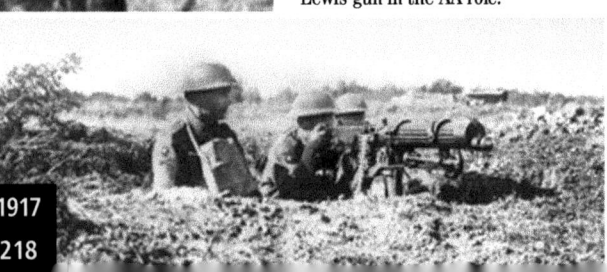

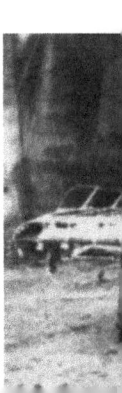

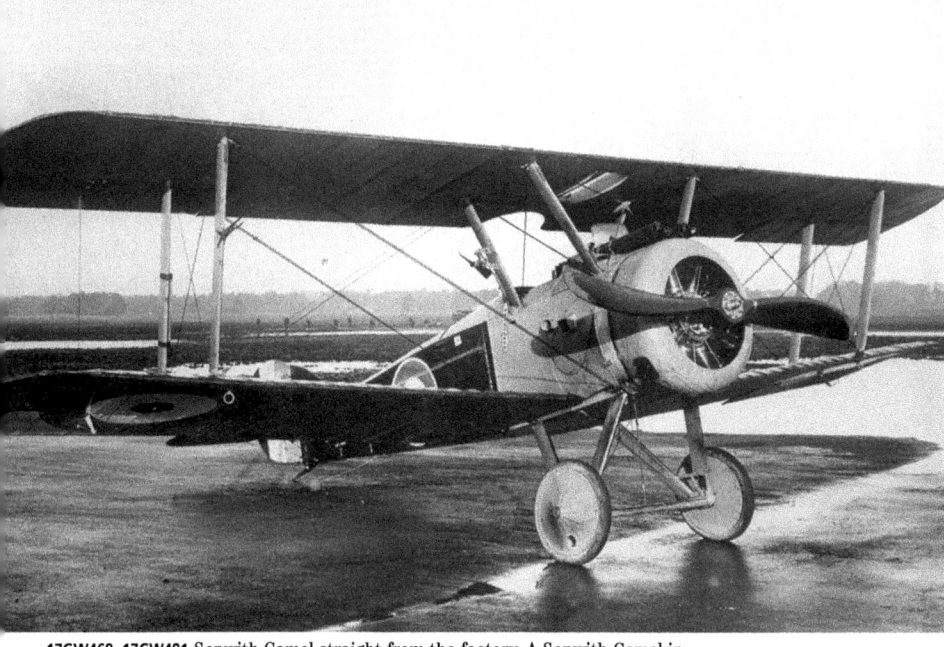
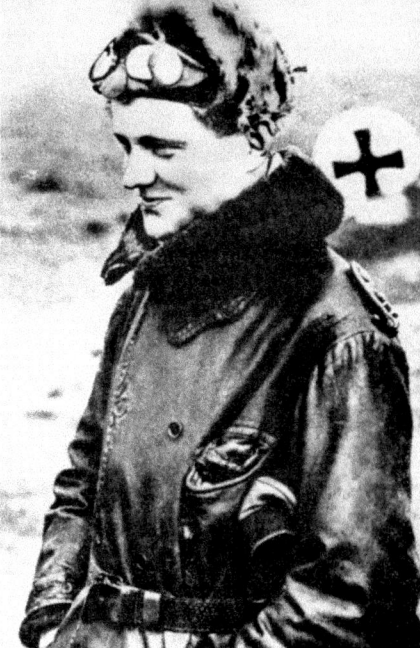

17GW468, 17GW481 Sopwith Camel straight from the factory. A Sopwith Camel in the markings of a No.209 Squadron machine. Each aircraft had its own individual markings and the RAF roundel on the fuselage was dropped by this squadron.

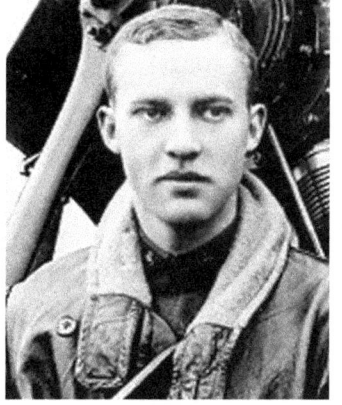 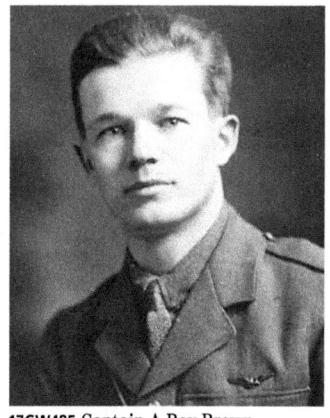 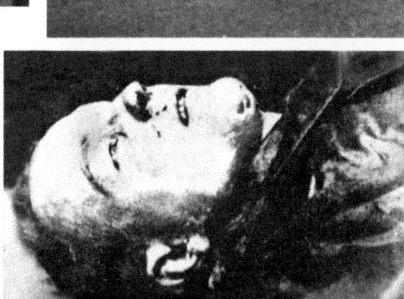

17GW482 Lieutenant Wilfrid May.   **17GW485** Captain A Roy Brown.

The Red Baron made an emergency landing on a ridge by the Bray to Corbie road, north of Vaux-sur-Somme. One witness, Australian Gunner George Ridgway, stated that when he and other soldiers reached the plane Richthofen was still alive but died seconds later. Sergeant Ted Smout, recalled that Richthofen uttered the word *kaputt* before he died.

17GW488, 17GW489, 17GW490. Manfred von Richthofen died at 10.45 am. His body was taken to Poulainville airfield and was examined and photographed. His machine was quickly reduced to a wreck by souvenir hunters. Injuries to his face were caused by him impacting with his machine guns. He had released his harness to work on a malfunctioning gun.

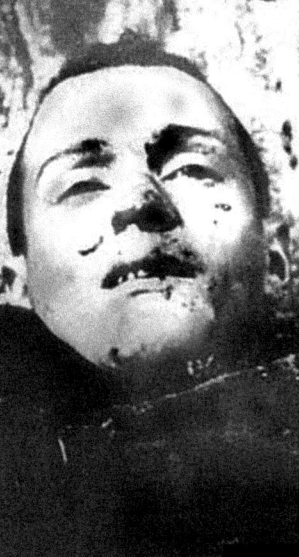
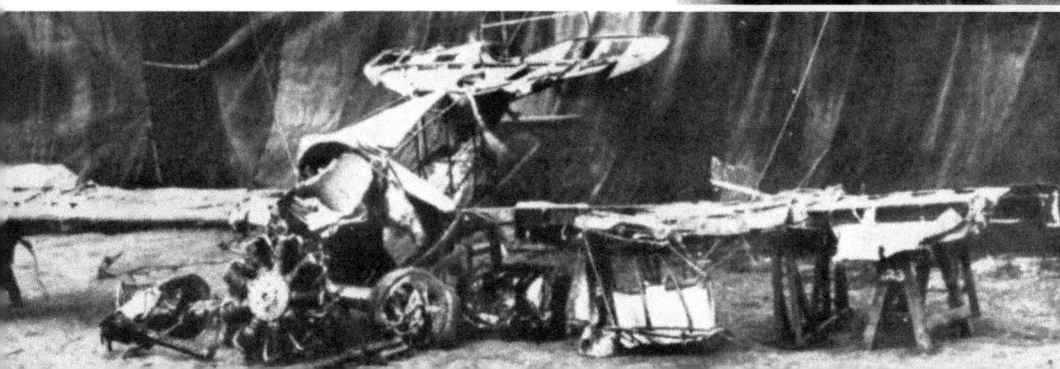

Hawker won his Victoria Cross on 25 July 1915 for his actions when on patrol over Passchendaele; flying a Bristol Scout, he attacked three German aircraft in succession destroying them. The first, after he had emptied a complete drum of bullets from his aircraft's single Lewis machine gun into it, went spinning down out of control. The second was driven to the ground damaged and the third, an Albatros C.I, which he attacked at a height of about 10,000 feet, burst into flames and crashed. Pilot *Oberleutnant* Uebelacker and observer *Hauptmann* Roser were both killed.

On 23 November 1916 Lanoe Hawker took off from the airfield at Bertangles in an Airco DH.2, as a member of A Flight. The flight was led by Captain Andrews. Two German aircraft were spotted over Achiet and Andrews led an attack. Suddenly a great number of German scouts were seen above and Andrews signalled to break off, but saw Hawker diving to continue the attack on what could have been decoys. Andrews and another pilot (Saundby) flew after Hawker to act as cover. After losing contact with the other DH.2s, Hawker began a lengthy dogfight with an Albatros D.II flown by *Leutnant* Manfred von Richthofen of *Jasta II*. The Albatros was faster than the DH.2 and better armed, with a pair of IMG 08 machine guns. Richthofen fired 900 rounds during the running battle. Running low on fuel, Hawker eventually broke away from the combat and attempted to return to Allied lines. The Red Baron's guns jammed fifty yards from the lines, but a bullet from his last burst struck Hawker in the back of his head, killing him instantly. His plane spun from 1,000 ft and he crashed 200 metres east of Luisenhof Farm, south of Bapaume. Hawker had become the eleventh kill of the German ace. Men of the Royal Grenadiers reported burying Hawker 250 yards east of Luisenhof Farm, by the roadside. Later Richthofen claimed Hawker's Lewis gun from the wreck as a trophy and hung it above the door of his quarters.

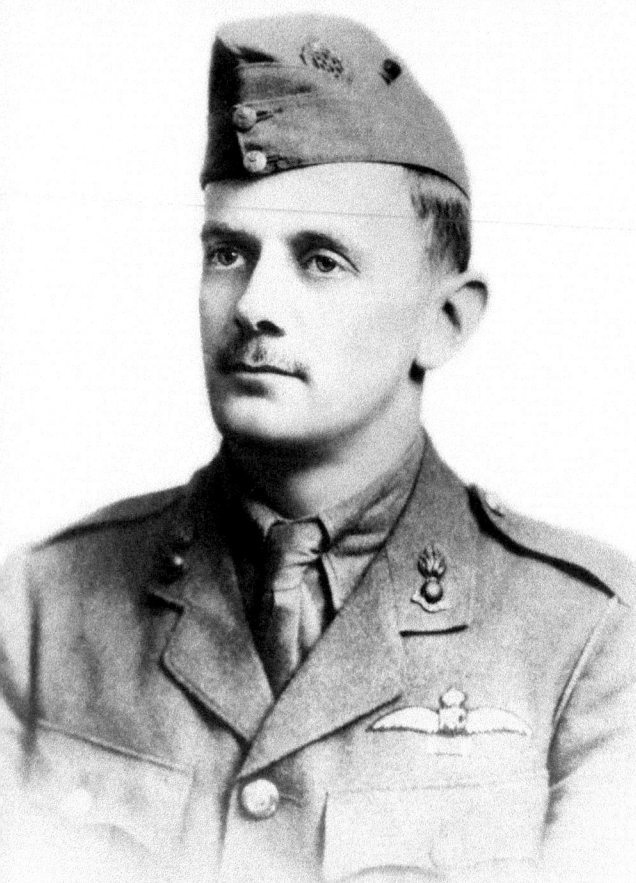

17GW562 Lanoe George Hawker VC, Richthofen's most famous kill.

17GW563 David Greswolde Lewis, Richthofen's final victim.

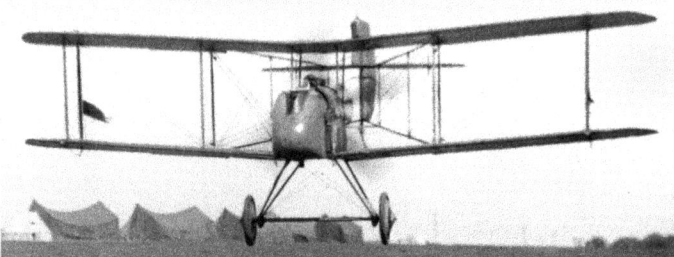

17GW565 Lanoe Hawker VC was flying a DH.2 when Richthofen shot him in the head.

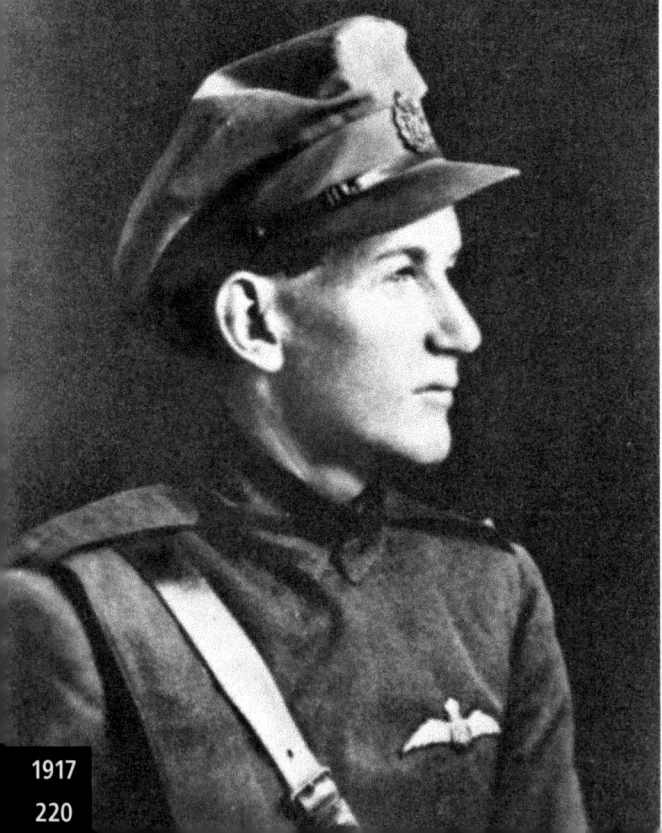

'Tommy' Lewis, became the last of the legendary Baron Von Richthofen's eighty victories. David Lewis took off on 20 April 1918, on an offensive patrol led by Captain Douglas Bell of C Flight. The flight was attacked and Lewis later related events:
'About four miles over the German lines, we met approximately fifteen German triplanes, which endeavoured to attack us from behind, but Bell frustrated this attempt by turning to meet them, so the fight started with the two patrols firing at each other head on. A few seconds after the fight began Major Barker's petrol-tank was hit by an incendiary bullet, which caused the tank to explode and shatter his machine. I was attacking a bright blue machine, which was on a level with me and was just about to finish this adversary off when I heard the rat-tat-tat of machine-guns coming from behind me and saw the splintering of struts just above my head.'
Lewis wheeled round and found himself face to face with *le petit rouge*, the bright red Triplane of Baron von Richthofen. Lewis, flying a Sopwith Camel, twisted and turned in the endeavour to avoid his line of fire, but he was up against too experienced a fighter. Lewis continues, *'only once did I manage to have him at a disadvantage, and then only for a few seconds, but in those few ticks of a clock I shot a number of bullets into his machine and thought I would have the honour of bringing him down, but in a trice the positions were reversed and he had set my emergency petrol-tank alight, and I was hurtling earthward in flames.'*
Lewis goes on to relate how he hit the ground just north-east of Villers-Bretonneux 'at a speed of sixty miles an hour and was thrown clear' of the wreckage. Except for minor burns he was completely unhurt. Lewis's compass, his goggles, the elbow of his coat, and one trouser leg were hit by Richthofen's bullets, but it is truly miraculous how this young Rhodesian beat the odds to survive a duel with death incarnate. Manfred von Richthofen commenced a pass, coming to within one hundred feet of the ground and waved to the downed Rhodesian pilot and a column of German infantry.

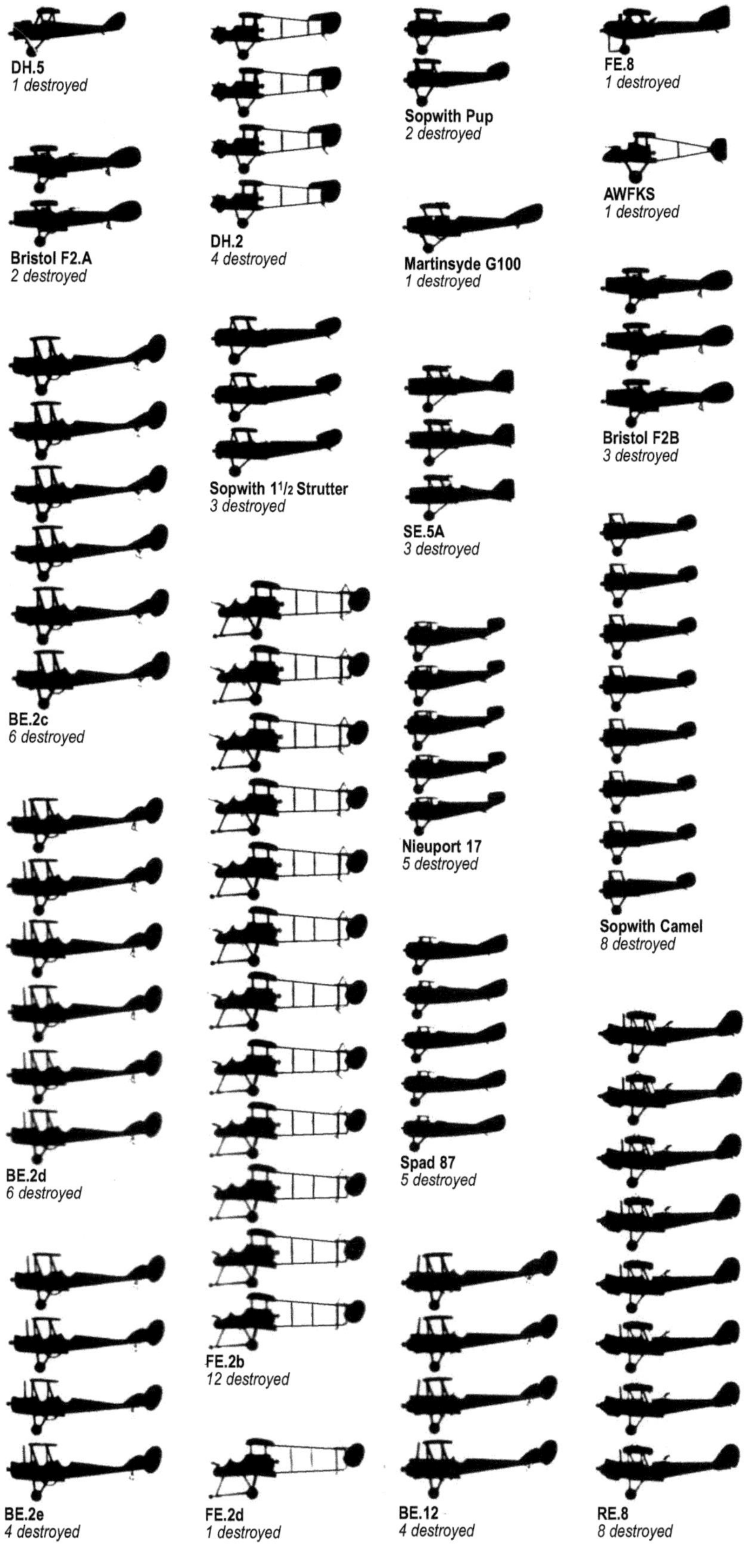

DH.5
1 destroyed

Bristol F2.A
2 destroyed

BE.2c
6 destroyed

BE.2d
6 destroyed

BE.2e
4 destroyed

Sopwith Pup
2 destroyed

Martinsyde G100
1 destroyed

DH.2
4 destroyed

Sopwith 1½ Strutter
3 destroyed

FE.2b
12 destroyed

FE.2d
1 destroyed

SE.5A
3 destroyed

Nieuport 17
5 destroyed

Spad 87
5 destroyed

BE.12
4 destroyed

FE.8
1 destroyed

AWFKS
1 destroyed

Bristol F2B
3 destroyed

Sopwith Camel
8 destroyed

RE.8
8 destroyed

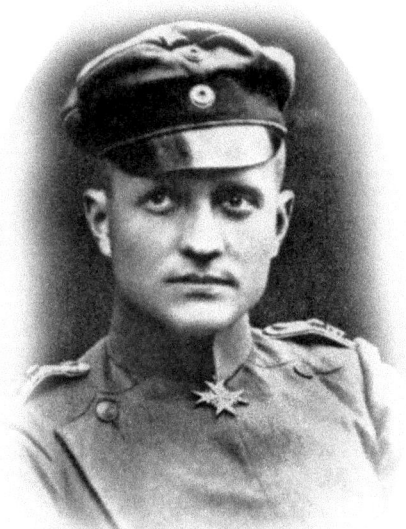

17GW564, 17GW566. The Red Baron's 'glory board' depicting all 80 kills, comprising twenty types. They are all British apart from one Belgian Spad. In common with all fighter aces, the majority of victims were reconnaissance machines rather than fighters. German Government propaganda made much of the feats of Richthofen and his like, creating heroes for the people to to look to. It proved so successful that even his enemies came to be in awe of his prowess, (as witnessed by the funeral with full military honours indulged in by the Australians). Not all were so impressed nor overawed, and a desecration of Richthofen's grave by the local French population occured that night and the grave marker was stolen.

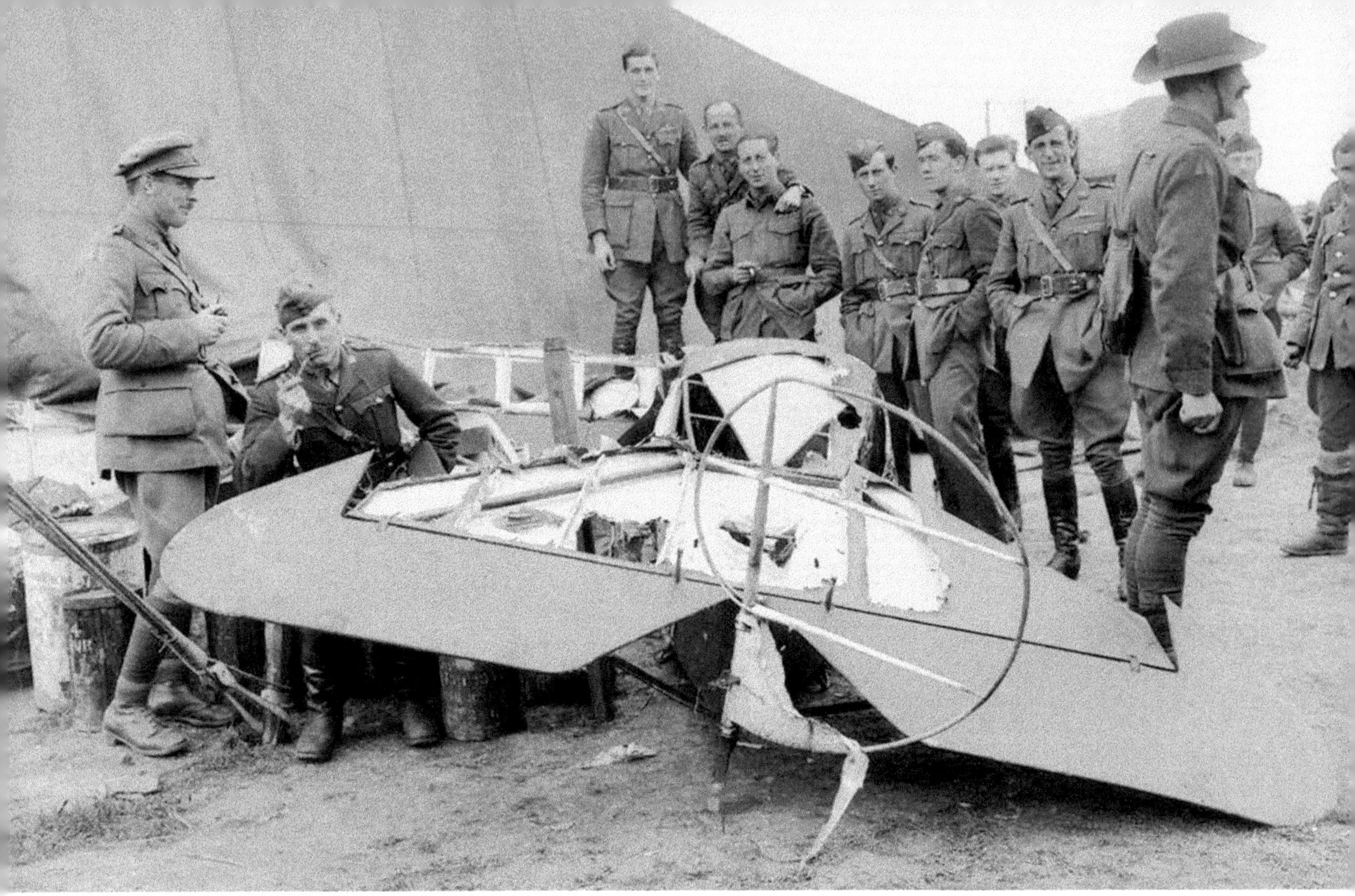

17GW491 Two Spandau IMG 08 were fitted to the cowling of the Fokker Triplane. On the Red Baron's last fight one of the weapons had ceased to function and the other was misfiring because of a split firing pin. Lieutenant May would likely have been shot down had the guns been working. Richthofen had released his harness and was working to free the mechanism when a single bullet fired from below fatally wounded him.

17GW492 Pilots of 3 Squadron AFC based at the airfield at Poulainville stand beside the wreck of Richthofen's machine which is being stripped of bits and pieces as souvenirs.

17GW494 Two machine guns from Richthofen's aircraft. Left to right: Lieutenant N. Mulroney (pilot); Lieutenant O G Witcomb (observer) and Lieutenant F J Mart (observer) examine the Spandau machine guns of the Red Baron. All three are members of 3 Squadron. Australian Flying Corps (AFC)

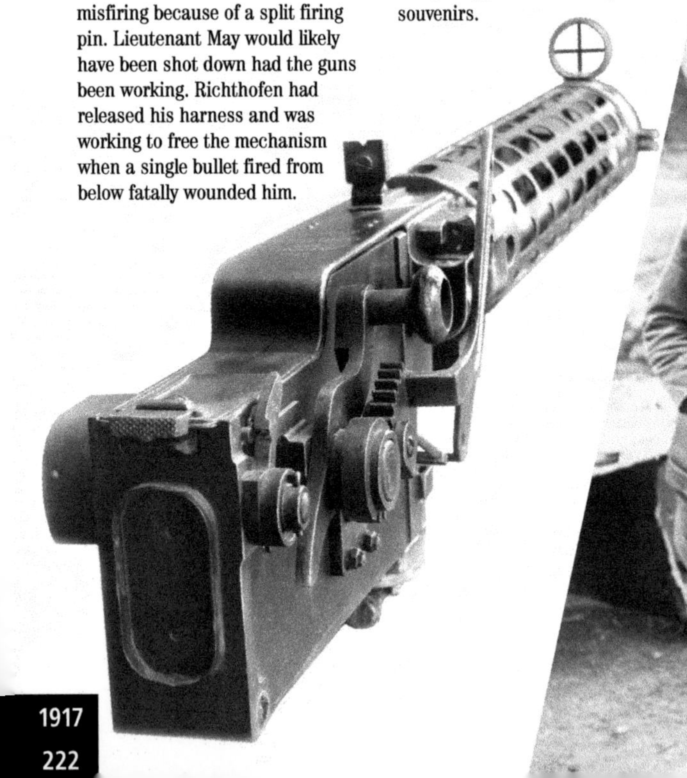

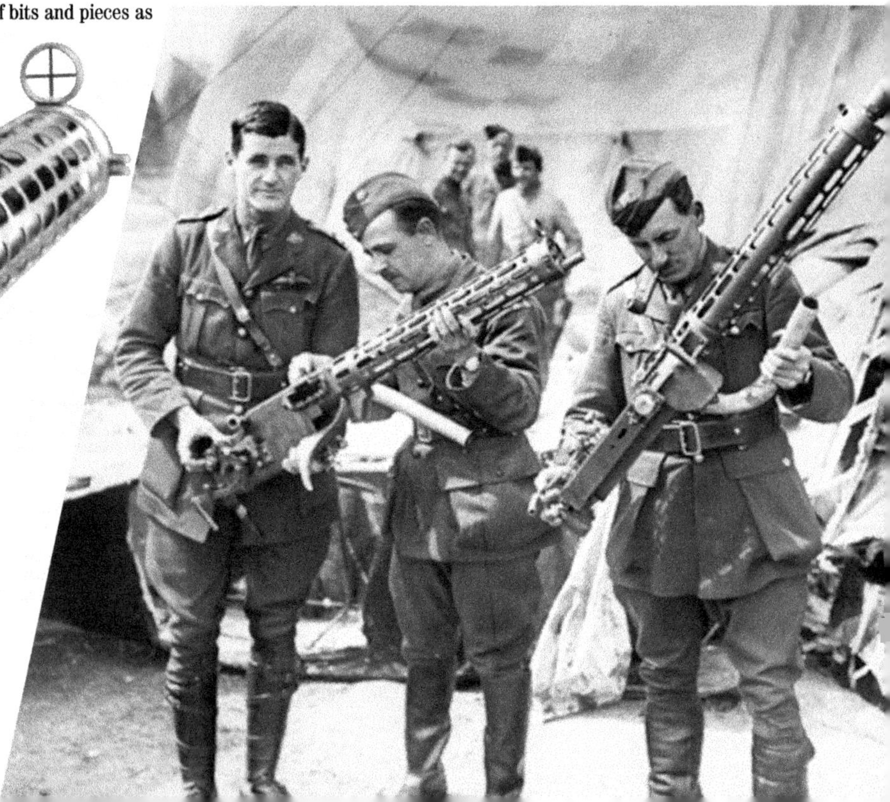

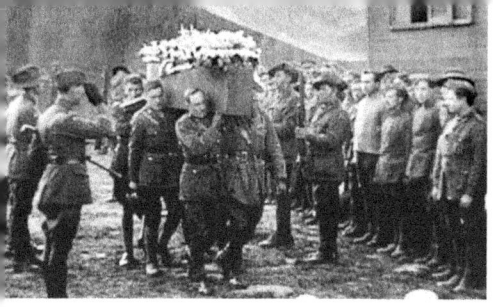

17GW495, 17GW497, 17GW496, 17GW496, 17GW498, 17GW493, 17GW500, 17GW499, 17GW501, 17GW502. Richthofen was buried with full military honours, with much saluting and presenting of arms, on 22 April 1918 at Bertangles. Six Australian pilots served as pall bearers. However, some of the local people did not view the Boche warrior and slayer of their aviators with the same respect and that night the grave was desecrated.

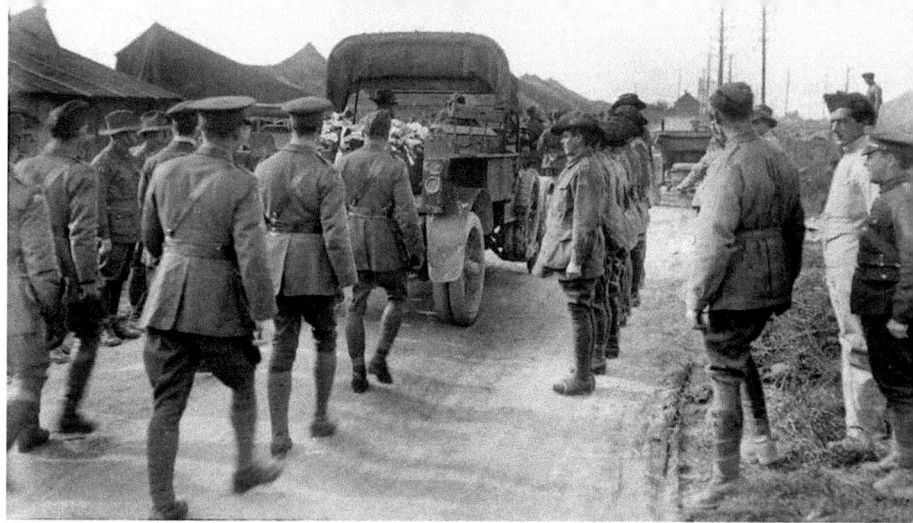

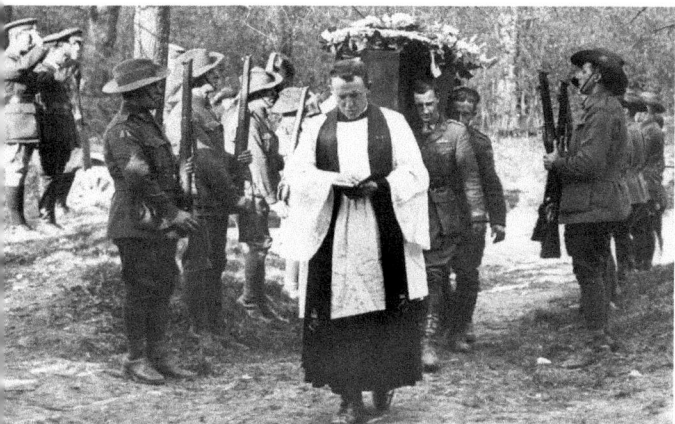

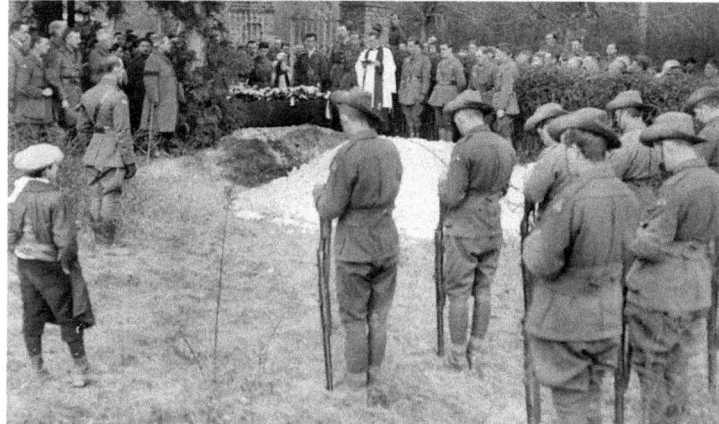

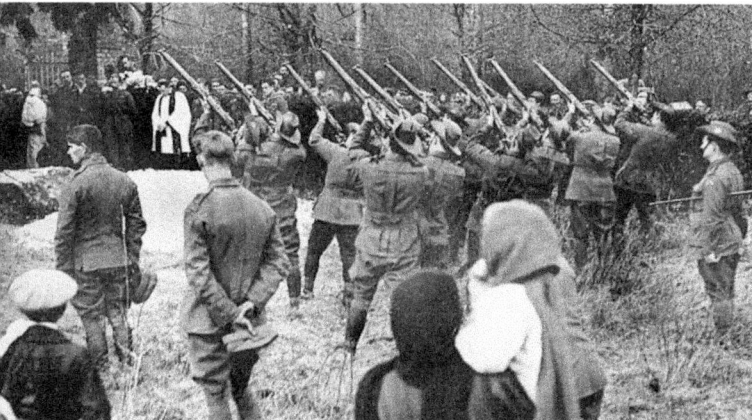

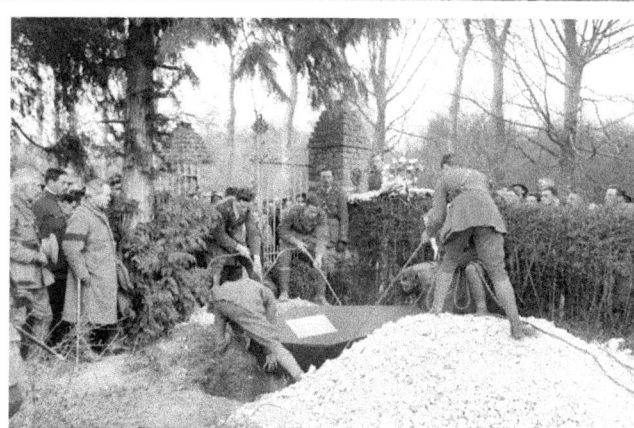

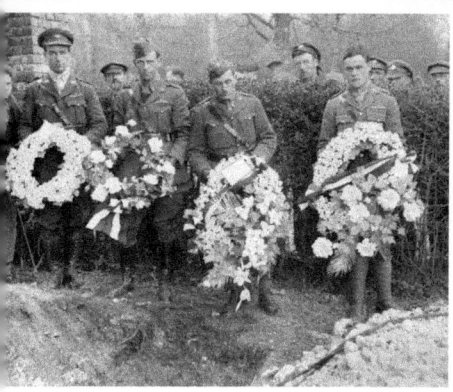

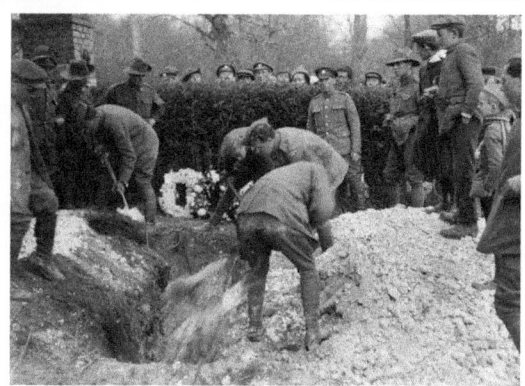

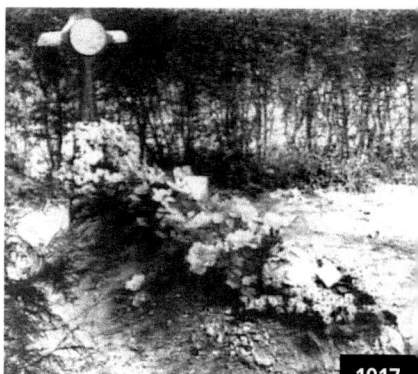

The Royal Flying Corps, unlike Germany which promoted its air heroes such as the Red Baron, had a policy of keeping their pilots' identities firmly under wraps, believing it to be more useful to promote a squadron's team effort, rather than any individual's glory. The effect was that while photos and stories of the Red Baron appeared in newspapers worldwide, in Britain the leading kills scorer, Major 'Mick' Mannock, or the mysterious 'Captain X', as the press referred to him, was virtually unknown until the policy gradually changed.

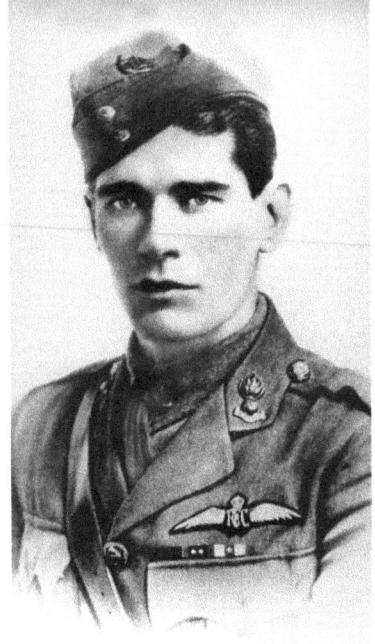

17GW503 Edward Corringham Mick Mannock VC, DSO and 2 Bars, MC and Bar. Mannock was the highest scoring British ace, with 73 kills. He was driven by hatred for the 'Hun' and when officers of his squadron proposed a toast to the memory of 'a chivalrous foe' – the Red Baron – he walked out of the mess, muttering 'I hope he roasted all the way down'.

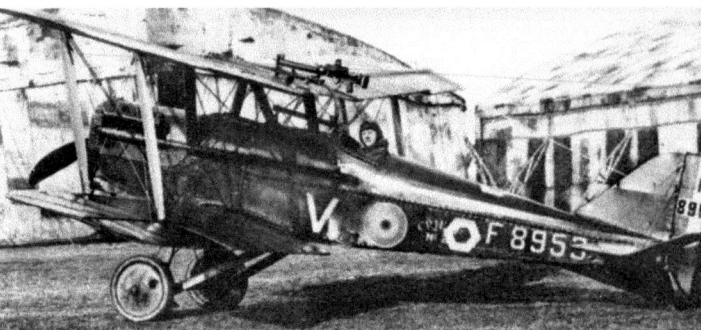

17GW505 Aircraft V of No.85 Squadron commanded by Mannock until his death on 26 July, 1918. Although warning others about flying low into ground fire, that is what he himself did and a shot fired from below set his engine on fire, causing him to crash in flames: the very death he had wished on von Richthofen.

Mannock formulated this set of rules for new pilots.
1. Pilots must dive to attack with zest, and must hold their fire until they get within one hundred yards of their target.
2. Achieve surprise by approaching from the East. (From the German side of the front.)
3. Utilize the sun's glare and clouds to achieve surprise.
4. Pilots must keep physically fit by exercise and the moderate use of stimulants.
5. Pilots must sight their guns and practice as much as possible as targets are normally fleeting.
6. Pilots must practice spotting machines in the air and recognizing them at long range, and treat every aeroplane as an enemy until it is certain it is not.
7. Pilots must learn where the enemy's blind spots are.
8. Scouts must be attacked from above and two-seaters from beneath their tails.
9. Pilots must practice quick turns, as this manoeuvre is more used than any other in a fight.
10. Pilots must practice judging distances in the air as these are very deceptive.
11. Decoys must be guarded against – a single enemy is often a decoy – therefore the air above should be searched before attacking.
12. If the day is sunny, machines should be turned with as little bank as possible, otherwise the sun glistening on the wings will give away their presence.
13. Pilots must keep turning in a dog fight and never fly straight except when firing.
14. Pilots must never, under any circumstances, dive away from an enemy, as he gives his opponent a non-deflection shot – bullets are faster than aeroplanes.
15. Pilots must keep their eye on their watches during patrols, and on the direction and strength of the wind.

17GW504 The Royal Aircraft Factory S.E.5a. The S.E.5, along with the Camel, was instrumental in regaining allied air superiority in mid-1917 and maintaining it for the rest of the war, ensuring there was no repetition of 'Bloody April' 1917, when the RFC suffered heavy losses at the hands of the *Luftstreitkräfte*.

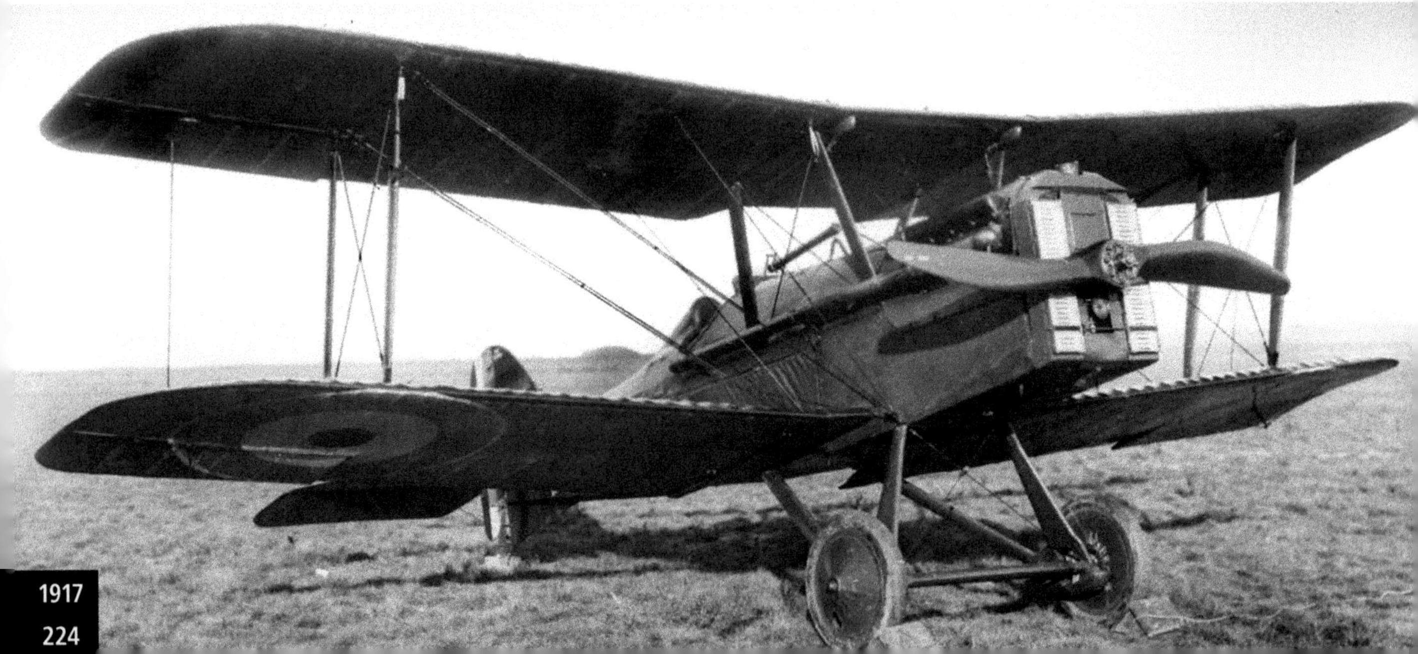

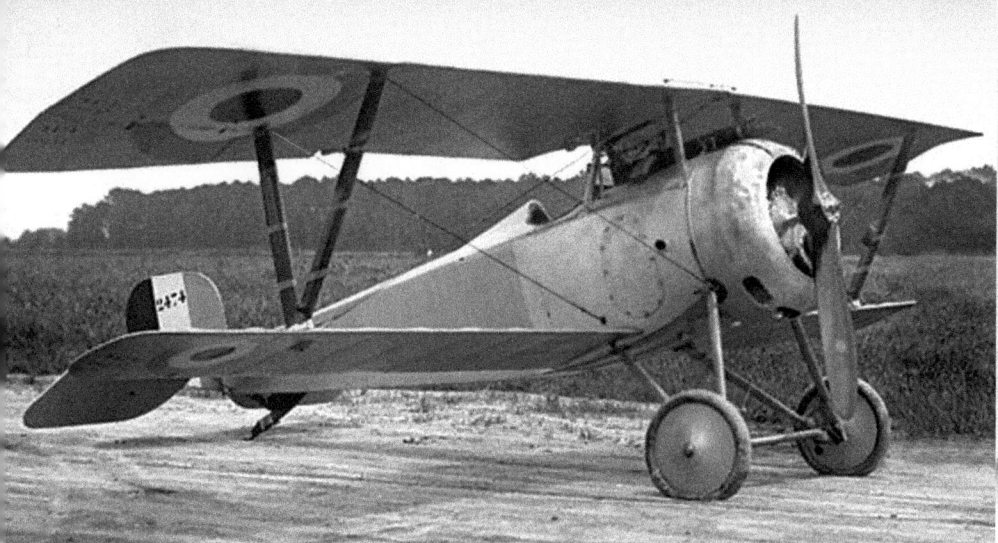
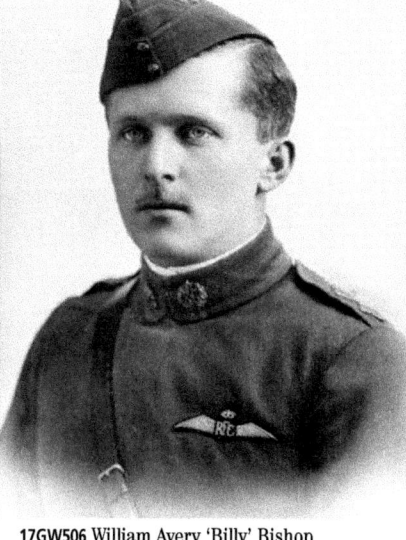

17GW507 The French built Nieuport 17 was ordered by the Royal Flying Corps and Royal Naval Air Service, as it was superior to British fighters available in 1917. British squadrons that used the type were Nos 1, 29, 32, 40 and 60 of the Royal Flying Corps. However, by mid-1917, the Nieuport was losing its superiority to the German Albatros D III.

17GW506 William Avery 'Billy' Bishop VC, DSO and Bar, MC, DFC, Ld'H, CdeG. A Canadian flying ace officially credited with 72 kills.

17GW508, 17GW509. Billy Bishop, with his machine B1566, of No.60 Squadron. He was posted to this squadron in time for the Battle of Arras and his first air combat took place on 25 March 1917, when he shot down an Albatros single-seater. His second kill came six days later with another Albatros. As 'Bloody April' began, with the RFC being shot out of the sky by Richthofen's pilots, Bishop destroyed four enemy machines and an observation balloon. This earned him the Military Cross. During this period of fierce air fighting he frequently put in over seven hours flying time each day. By May his score of kills had risen to twenty, then, on 2 May 1917, he had nine encounters in which he attacked nineteen aircraft in total, shooting down two. For this he was awarded the Disnguished Service Order. One month later he was awarded the Victoria Cross: single-handed he attacked an enemy airfield at dawn just as the machines were being brought out. Three aircraft which took off to attack him he shot down and many aircraft were damaged in his strafing attacks. He then flew his bullet riddled Nieuport safely back to his base at Filescamps Farm. His VC was awarded ('gazetted' – listed in the *London Gazette*) on 11 August 1917. By the middle of the month his score of kills was forty-five and he was promoted to major. As the squadron was re-equipping with SE 5s, he was posted back home to Canada to assist in recruiting.

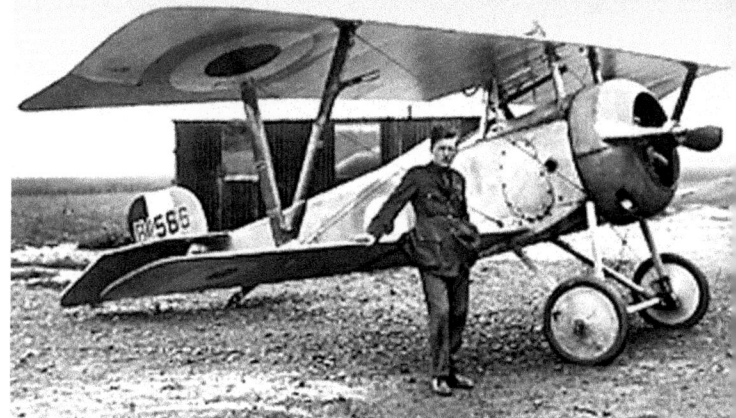

When Bishop returned to Europe in 1918 he was given command of No.85 Squadron and in one period of twelve days shot down twenty-five enemy aircraft.

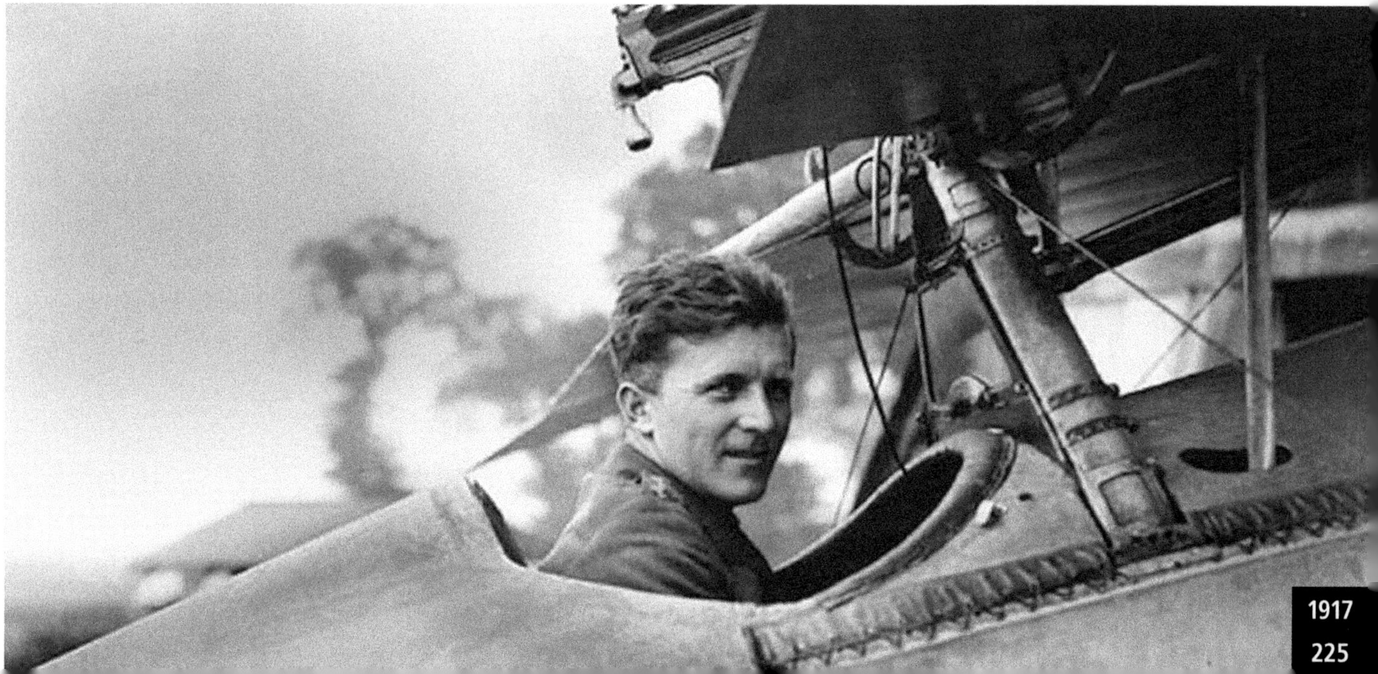

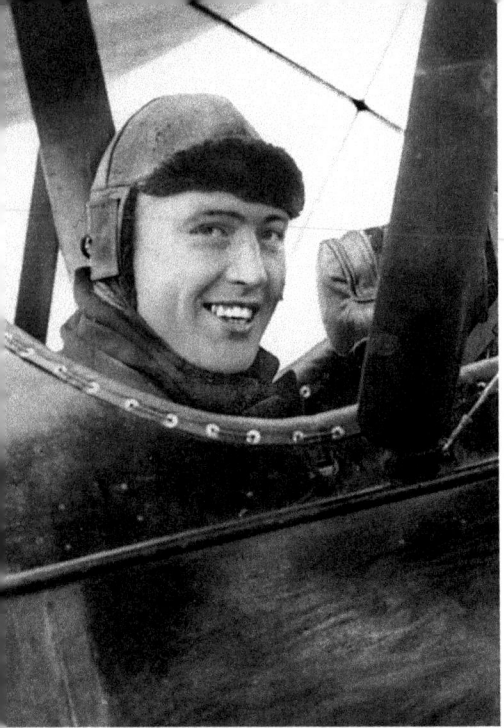

17GW506 Raymond Collishaw, DSO and Bar, OBE, DSC, DFC, CdeG, officially credited with 60 kills.

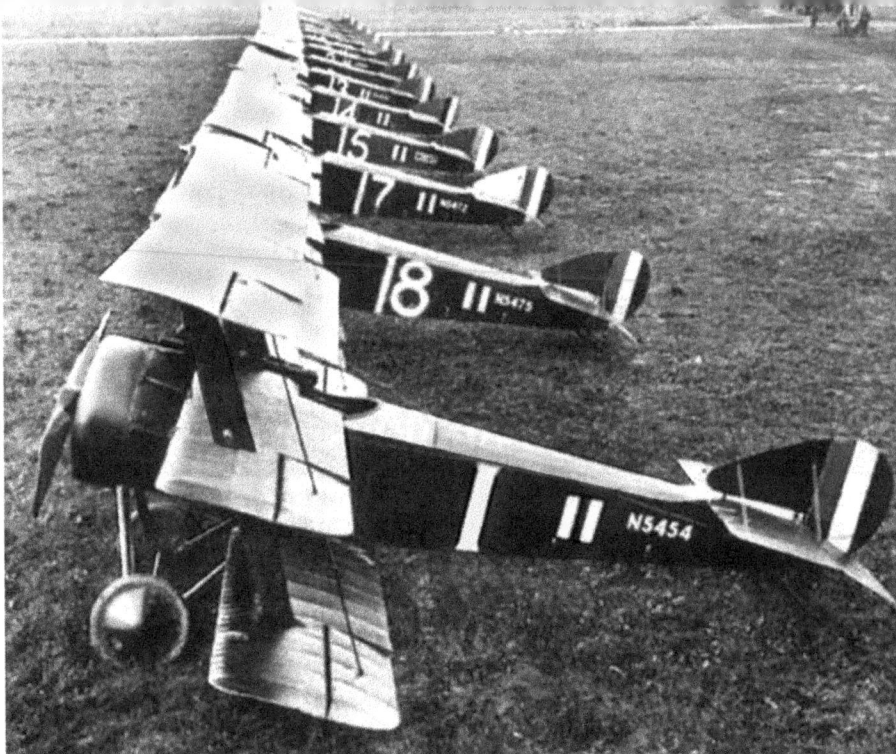

17GW510 Triplanes of No.1 Naval Squadron at Bailleul, France.

By the end of May 1917, the Royal Flying Corps was in need of reinforcements, after Bloody April and Collishaw was posted to No.10 Naval Squadron as a flight commander. Collishaw's B Flight was composed entirely of Canadians. Collishaw's flight painted their Sopwith Triplanes black and called themselves the 'All-Black Flight', which later became known simply as the Black Flight. It was considered to be one of the most successful fighting units of the war. The aircraft of Black Flight had names: Ellis Reid, of Toronto, flew *Black Roger*; J E Sharman, of Winnipeg, flew *Black Death*; Gerry Nash, of Hamilton, called his machine *Black Sheep*; Marcus Alexander, of Toronto, called his plane *Black Prince*. Collishaw, had the name *Black Maria* painted on his machine.

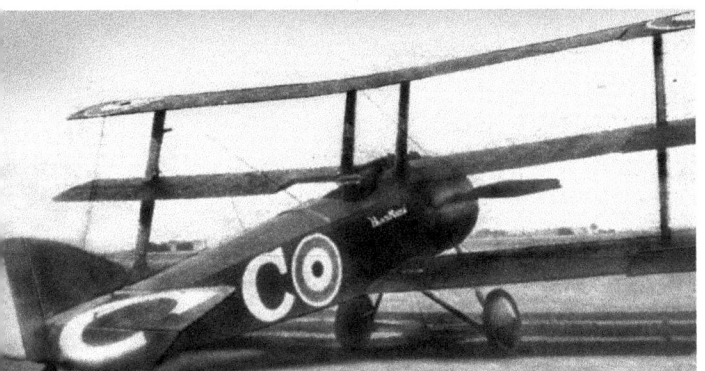

17GW512 Raymond Collishaw's customized aircraft – *Black Maria* in 1917.

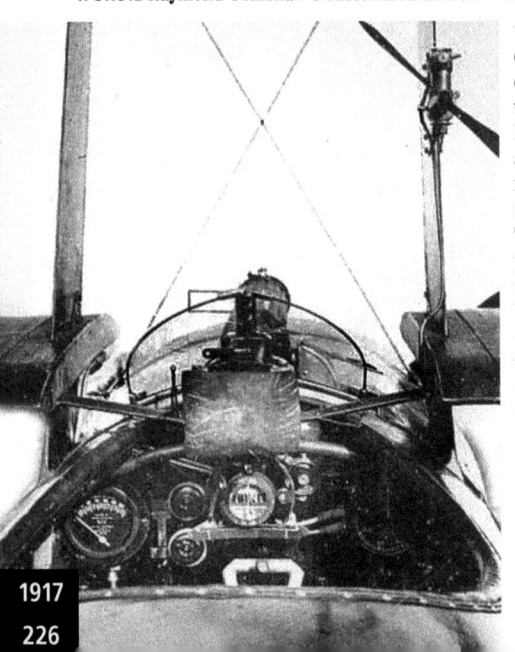

17GW511 The Triplane design, with the split centre wing, afforded the pilot a better view looking forward and all-round vision was much improved by the narrow wings of the Triplane. (Note the padded protection in front of the gun breech.) Unlike the German pilots, who were not prevented from personalizing their machines, the British high command took a dim view of the 'vulgar practice'.

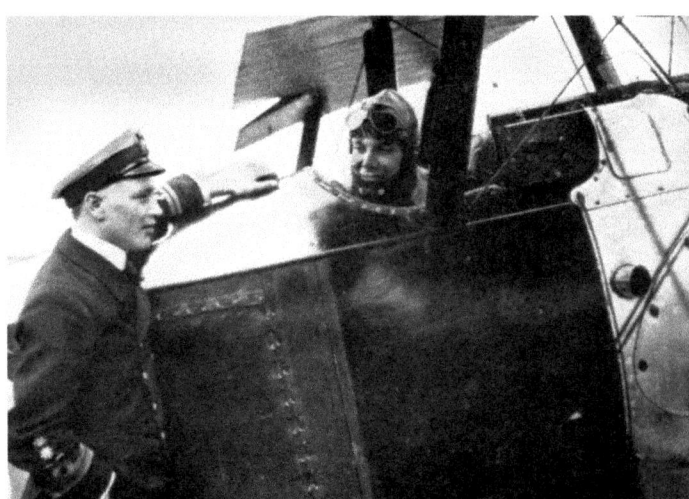

17GW514 Collishaw, in Naval uniform, talking to Captain Whealey (five kills).

During their first two months the All Blacks claimed a record eighty-seven German aircraft destroyed or forced down – which brought Collishaw and the unit little publicity. On the other hand their German opponents knew them well, including the pilots of Richthofen's Flying Circus, who were losing heavily to the Black Flight. Collishaw later claimed that this was because officials in the regular Royal Flying Corps were loath to give credit to naval pilots.

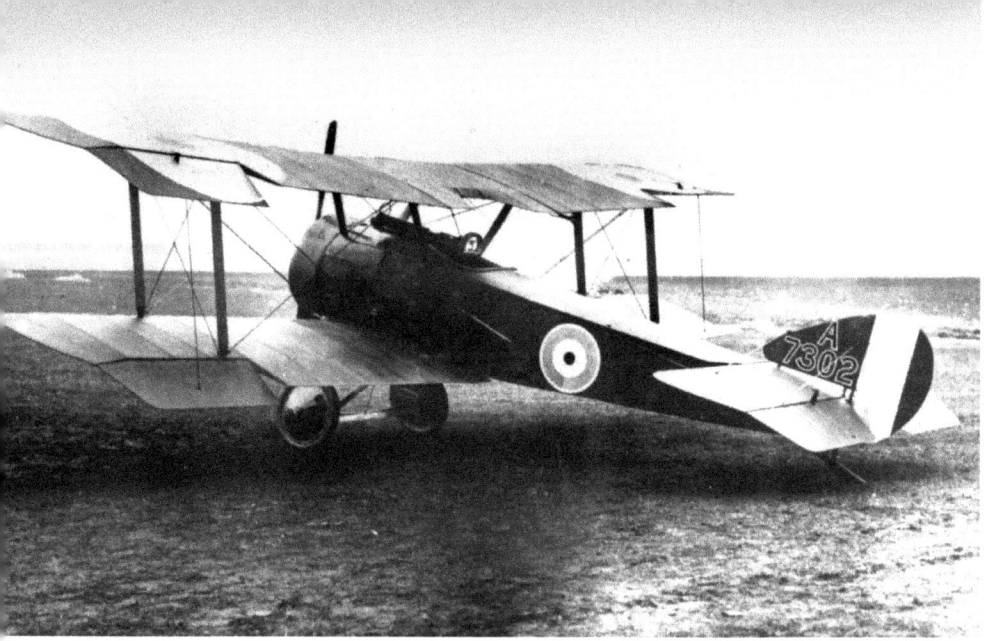

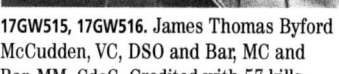

17GW515, 17GW516. James Thomas Byford McCudden, VC, DSO and Bar, MC and Bar, MM, CdeG. Credited with 57 kills.

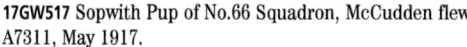

17GW517 Sopwith Pup of No.66 Squadron, McCudden flew A7311, May 1917.

McCudden began his career in the RFC as an air mechanic in 1913. By the time of his death in a flying accident on 9 July 1918, aged twenty-three, he had risen through the ranks to become a major. At the time of his death he had received more decorations for bravery than any other airman of British nationality serving in the First World War. He had fifty-seven aerial victories, placing him seventh on the list of the war's most successful aces. The majority of his successes were achieved with 56 Squadron RFC while flying the SE5a. In December 1917 he was given his own machine, an SE5a (B4891). McCudden achieved nine kills in only six days. On 2 April 1918 Captain James McCudden was awarded the Victoria Cross. The citation in the *London Gazette* read: *'For most conspicuous bravery, exceptional perseverance, keenness, and very high devotion to duty'*. During a routine flight from England to France, 9 July 1918, Major McCudden VC, landed at a small airfield, at Auxi-le-Chateau to ask directions. On taking off again and at a height of about 70 feet, his engine cut out, causing him to dive into the ground and he was killed.

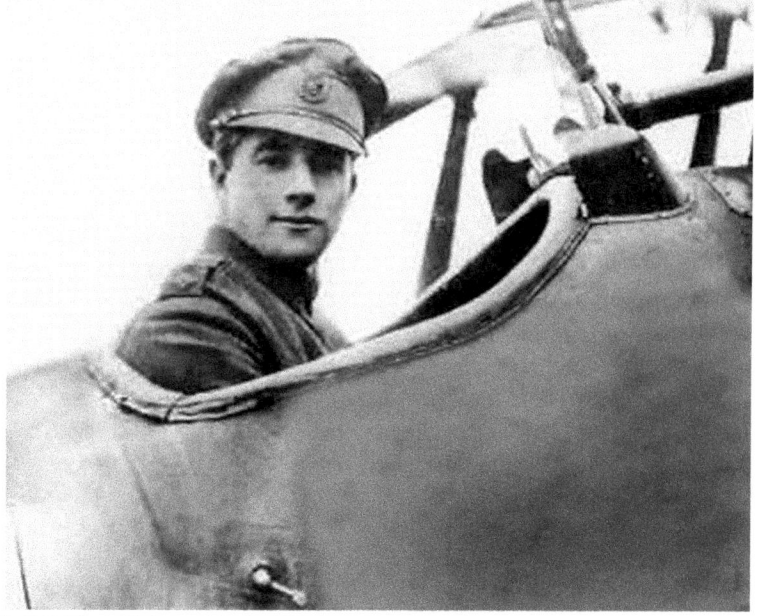

Major McCudden was buried with full military honours in Waverns Military Cemetery. Unfavourable comparisons were made by some of RAF personnel at the time with the enormous fuss made two months earlier, at the funeral given for the enemy ace von Richthofen.

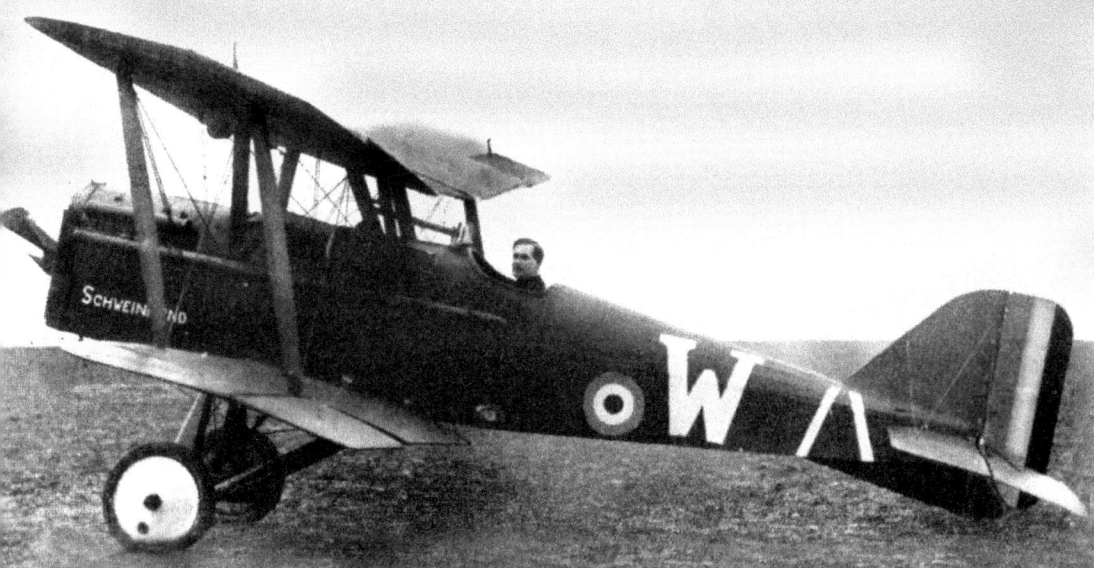

17GW518 When No.56 Squadron arrived in France in 1917 it began making a reputation. The SE5a, *Schweinhund*, was Grinnel-Milne's aircraft.

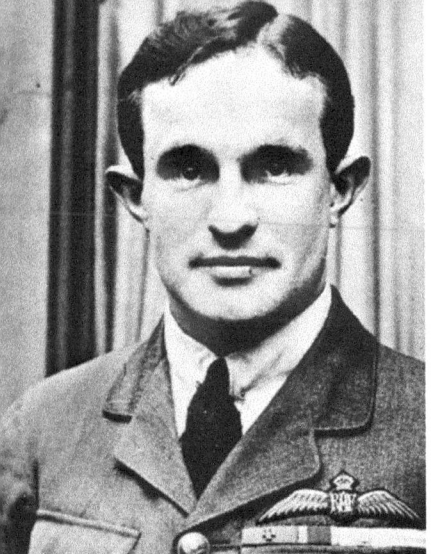

17GW519 Andrew Frederick Weatherby Beauchamp-Proctor VC, DSO, MC & Bar, DFC, 54 kills.

A South African recipient of the Victoria Cross, he was South Africa's leading ace of the First World War. In September 1917, No.84 Squadron went to France flying the SE5a. Operations began in the Ypres sector flying escort to bombers and making operational patrols. Under the command of Major William Sholto Douglas, the unit became one of the most effective scout squadrons during 1918. It would be credited with a victory total of 323 victories and would produce twenty-five aces. Among them Beauchamp-Proctor would be pre-eminent, with almost triple the number of successes of the second leading ace. He was not particularly esteemed as a flier, but was an incredibly accurate shot. His initial confirmed victory came on 3 January 1918, when he sent a German two-seater down out of control. He then claimed four more victories in February, becoming an ace on the final day of the month. March brought four more victories; three of them were scored within five minutes on 17 March. He tallied one kill in April. Among his eleven victories for the month of May were five on 19 May. By the end of the month, his score had risen to twenty-one kills: sixteen fighters and five observation aircraft. On 3 August, he was granted one of the first ever Distinguished Flying Crosses. Towards the end of his servive he chose to to 'blind' the enemy by concentrating on shooting down kite balloons and observation aircraft. On 8 October, he was hit by ground fire and wounded in the arm, ending his front line service.

17GW520 No.84 Squadron's SE5a fighters lined up just before the German offensives in the Spring of 1918.

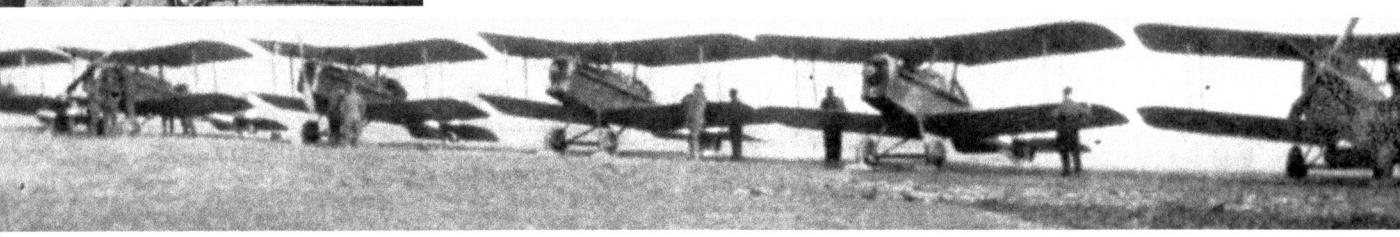

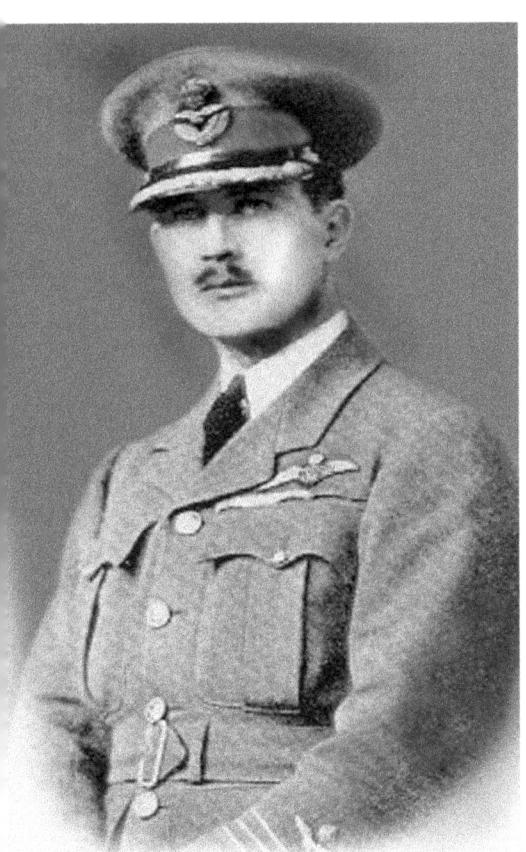

17GW522 Donald Roderick MacLaren DSO, MC and Bar, DFC, was credited with 54 victories and, after the war, helped found the Royal Canadian Air Force. The third most successful Canadian ace of the war – behind Billy Bishop and William Collishaw.

In November, 1917 he crossed to France and reported to 46 Squadron RFC, which was flying temperamental Sopwith Camels. On March 6, 1918 MacLaren had his first aerial combat. with a Hannover CIII. The type was unique in having a biplane tail.

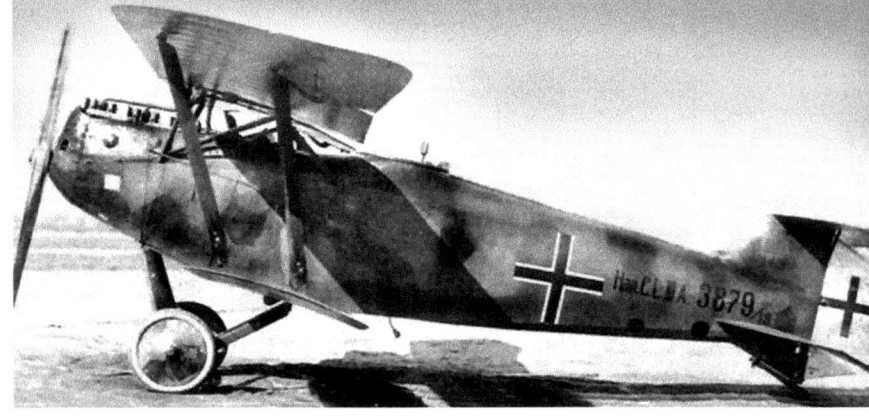

AWARDED THE MILITARY CROSS

For conspicuous gallantry and devotion to duty. On one occasion, when on low bombing work, he bombed a long-range enemy gun 9,000 yards behind the lines, obtaining from a height of 200 feet two direct hits on the gun truck and two on the railway track alongside. When returning to our lines he encountered a hostile two-seater machine, which he shot down and sent it crashing to earth. He then attacked a balloon, which burst into flames, and finally, observing another enemy two-seater plane, he engaged it and eventually succeeded in crashing it to earth. He has set an excellent example of gallantry and skill to his squadron.

His last fight came on 9 October 1918, only a few weeks before the Armistice, with the destruction of a two-seater, leaving him with a total kill of 48 aircraft and 6 balloons.

Billy Barker, a Canadian flyer, became the most decorated serviceman in the history of Canada. He began his service in the RFC as an observer and scored kills as a gunner in the BE.2. He then trained as a pilot. On 25 April 1917, during the Arras Offensive, Barker, flying an RE.8 with observer Lieutenant Goodfellow, spotted over 1,000 German troops sheltering in support trenches. The duo directed artillery fire into the positions, thereby avoiding a counter-attack.

He was transferred to Italy on 7 November 1917, temporarily in command of No.28 Squadron.

17GW527 Major Barker's Sopwith Camel, which was his favourite mount.

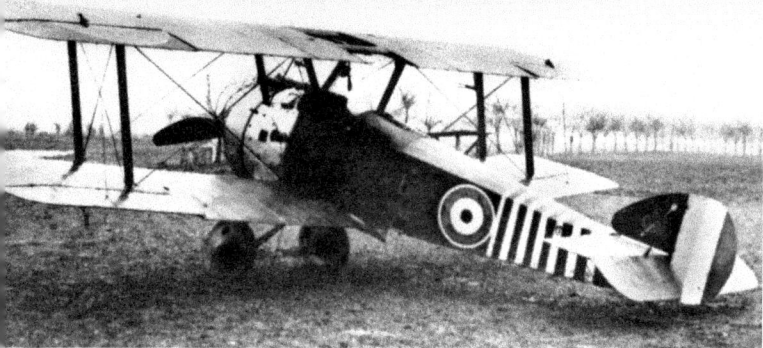

One of his most successful, and also most controversial raids – fictionalized by Ernest Hemingway in the short story *The Snows of Kilimanjaro* – was on 25 December 1917. Catching the Germans off guard, he and his wingman, shot up the airfield of *Fliegerabteilung (A) 204*, setting fire to one hangar and damaging four German aircraft before dropping a placard wishing their opponents a 'Happy Christmas'.

Barker was awarded the Victoria Cross for his actions on Sunday, 27 October 1918 when he attacked a Rumpler two-seater which broke up. He was suddenly bounced by fifteen plus enemy machines and he was wounded three times in the legs, then his left elbow was blown away. He managed to control his Sopwith Snipe and shoot down three more enemy aircraft. The dogfight took place above the lines of the Canadian Corps. Severely wounded and bleeding profusely, Barker force landed inside Allied lines, his life being saved by the men of an RAF Kite Balloon Section. The fuselage of his Snipe aircraft was recovered from the battlefield and is preserved at the Canadian War Museum, Ottawa, Ontario.

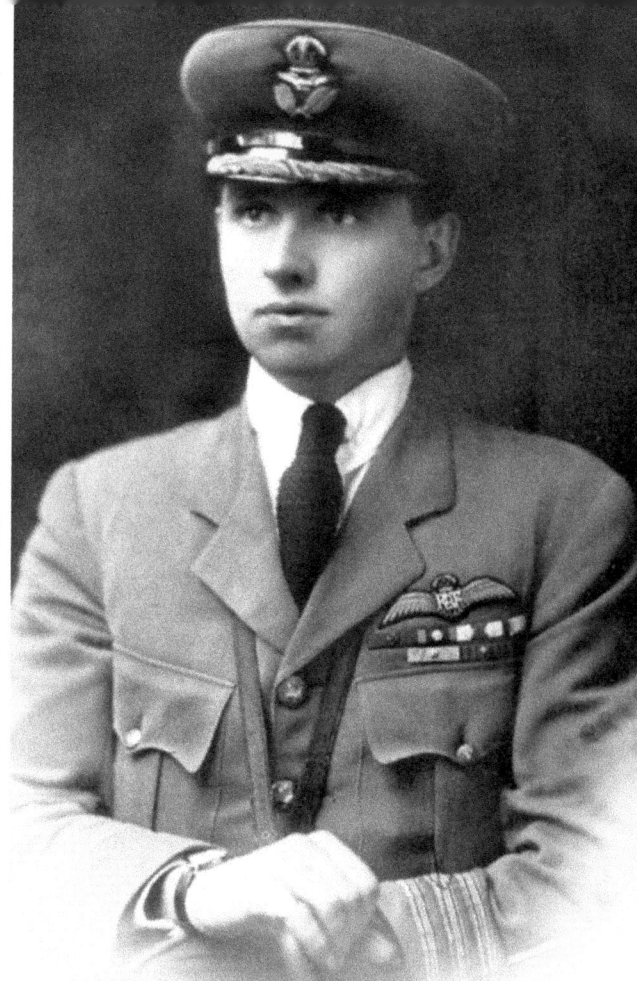

17GW524 William George 'Billy' Barker VC, DSO & Bar, MC & Two Bars. 53 confirmed kills.

17GW528 Sopwith Snipe of No.208 Squadron. It was while flying this type with No.201 Squadron that Barker won his VC.

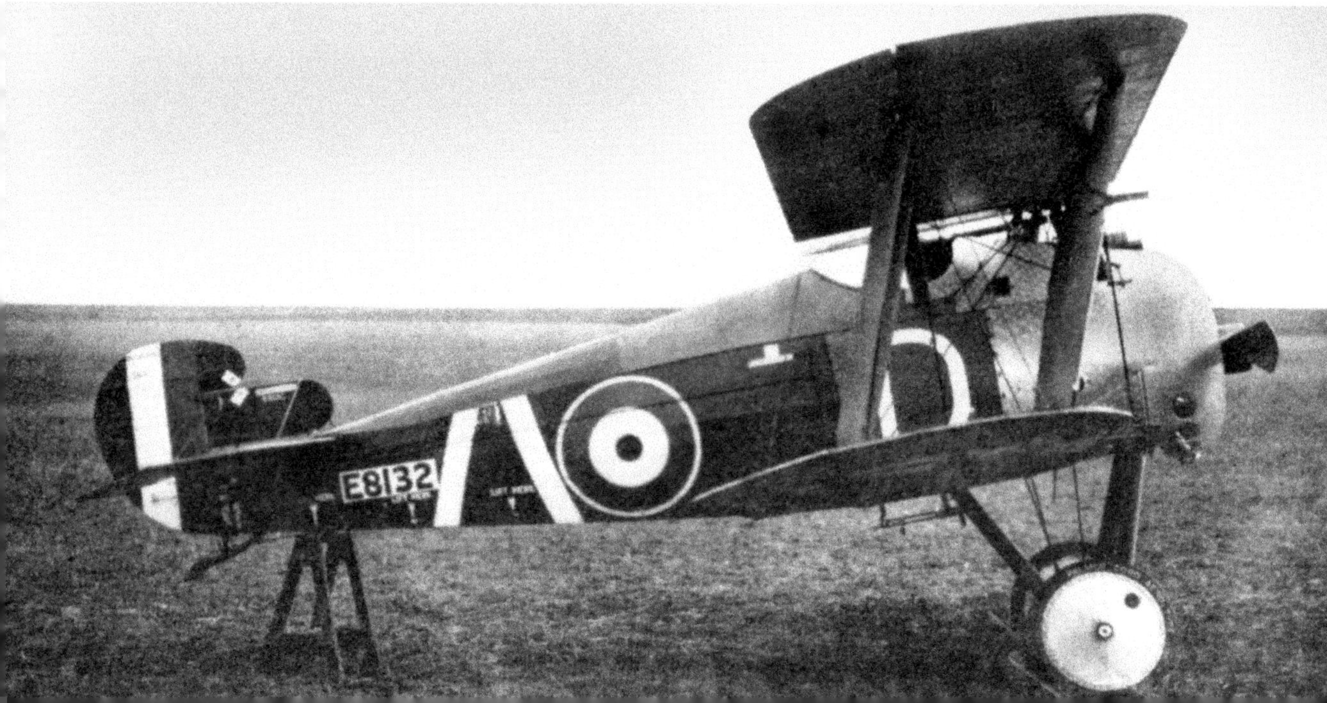

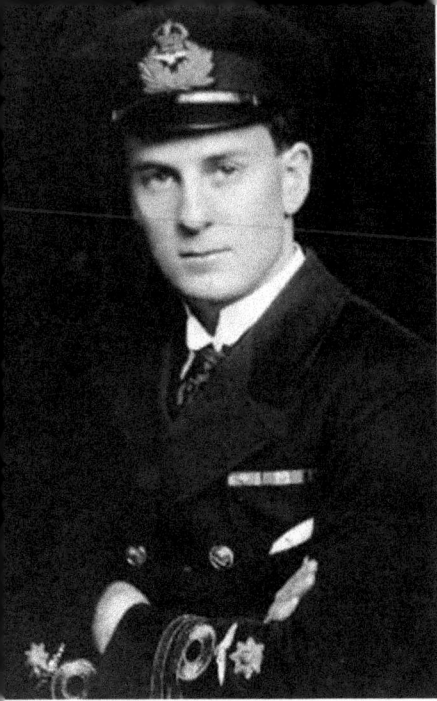

Australian born, Robert Little travelled to England in 1915 and learned to fly at his own expense before joining the Royal Naval Air Service (RNAS). Posted to the Western Front in June 1916, he flew Sopwith Pups, Triplanes and Camels with No. 8 Squadron RNAS, achieving thirty-eight victories within a year and earning the Distinguished Service Order and Bar, the Distinguished Service Cross and Bar, and the French Croix de Guerre. In March 1918 he scored a further nine victories with No.3 Squadron RNAS, which on 1 April became No. 203 Squadron Royal Air Force. He was killed in action on the night of 27 May 1918, aged twenty-two.

On 24 April 1917, the Australian fought a DFW C.V, forcing it to land. Little followed the German aircraft down personally to take its two-man crew prisoner at gunpoint. However, in landing, his Triplane nosed over in a ditch, prompting the surrendering German pilot to comment, 'It looks as if I have brought you down, not you me, doesn't it?'

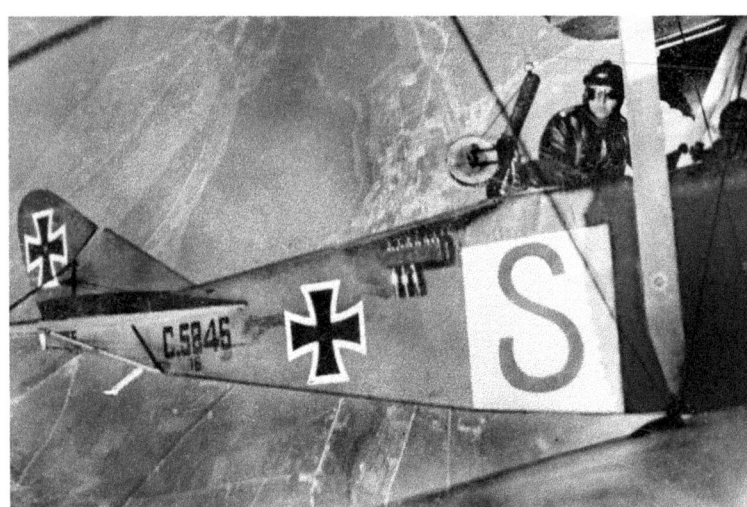

17GW529 Robert Alexander Little, DSO & Bar, DSC & Bar, credited with 47 kills.

17GW530 Banking to port – a DFW C.V.

On 27 May 1918, Captain Little received reports of Gotha bombers in the vicinity, and took off in a Sopwith Camel. As he closed with one of the intruders, his plane was caught in a searchlight beam and he was struck by a bullet that passed through both his thighs. He crash-landed in a field near Nœux and bled to death before he was discovered the following morning by a passing gendarme. It was not established where the bullet came from – it may have been friendly ground fire.

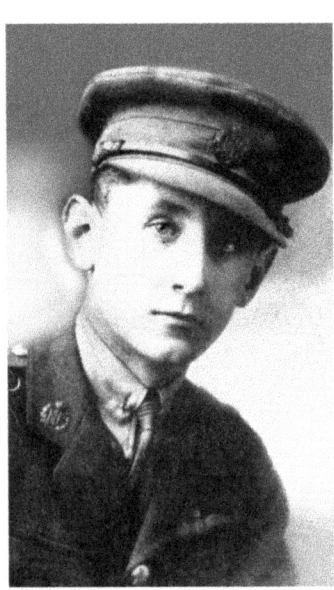

17GW531 Philip Fletcher Fullard CBE, DSO, MC, credited with 46 kills.

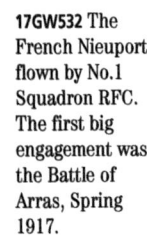

17GW532 The French Nieuports flown by No.1 Squadron RFC. The first big engagement was the Battle of Arras, Spring 1917.

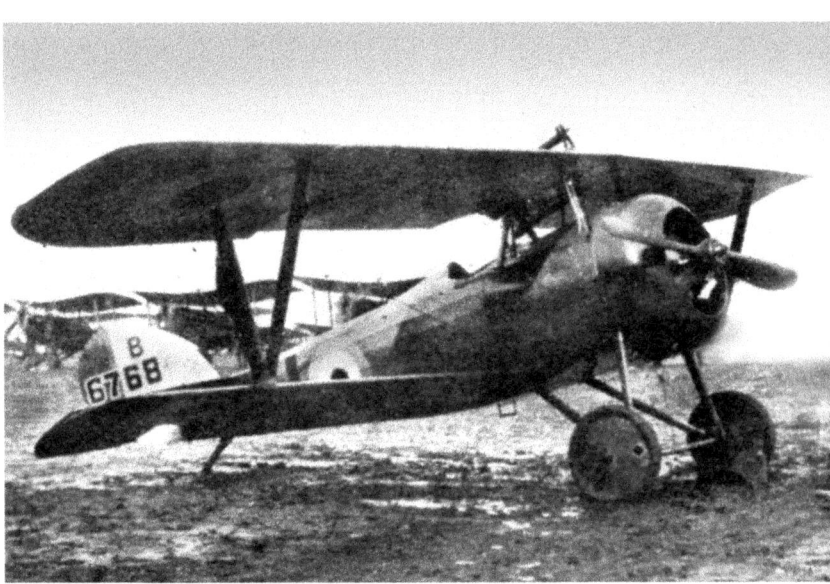

Fullard's first assignment in France was with No.1 Squadron RFC in May 1917. He scored steadily over a six month period, opening up his victories with two downed in May, followed by five in June (making him an 'ace'). He was appointed a flight commander and promoted to captain. In this role he scored more victories, with eight in July and twelve in August. In September he was awarded the Military Cross and in the month of October he scored eleven kills. The following month he brought down two more, one of them the German ace *Leutnant* Hans Hoyer. Two days after his fortieth victory he broke his leg playing football in a match between his squadron and an infantry battalion. During his period in hospital the *Tatler* magazine featured him on the front page of its January edition making the interesting comment: '*It is apparently only by accident that we get the details of some of the heroic exploits which are being performed every hour of the twenty-four by our flying men.* He did not return to duty until near the end of the war, when on 24 September 1918 he was appointed acting major. During his period of active service Fullard once brought down four German aircraft in a single day, and he and another pilot once brought down seven enemy aircraft before breakfast, with Fullard accounting for three. Also, during the three months Fullard served as commander, his flight of six pilots brought down more enemy aircraft than any other in France, without suffering a single casualty.

Captain McElroy, No.40 Squadron RFC, was one Britain's top scoring air aces (and Ireland's highest) of the First World War.
On 26 July 1918, 'McIrish' McElroy received a second Bar to his Military Cross. (He was one of only ten airmen to receive a second Bar.) On the 31st of the month, he reported destroying a Hannover C for his 47th victory. He then set out again. He failed to return from this flight and was posted missing. Later it was learned that he had been killed by ground fire. He was twenty-five years old.

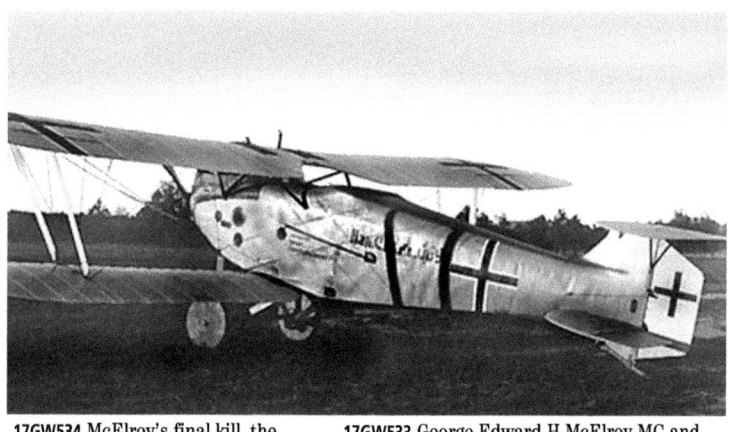

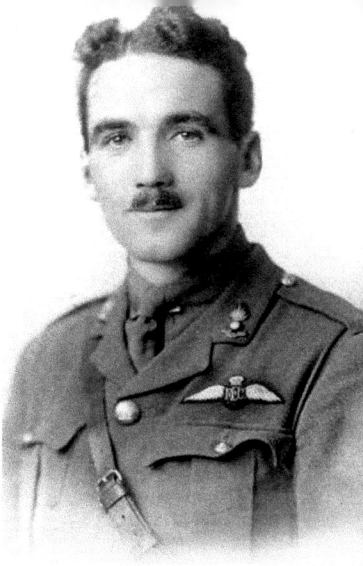

17GW534 McElroy's final kill, the Hannover CL.III, was primarily used as a ground attack machine.

17GW533 George Edward H McElroy MC and Two Bars, DFC and Bar. He was credited with 47 kills.

'I only scrap because it is my duty. Nothing makes me feel more rotten than to see them go down, but you see it is either them *or* me, *so I must do my duty best to make it a case of* them.'

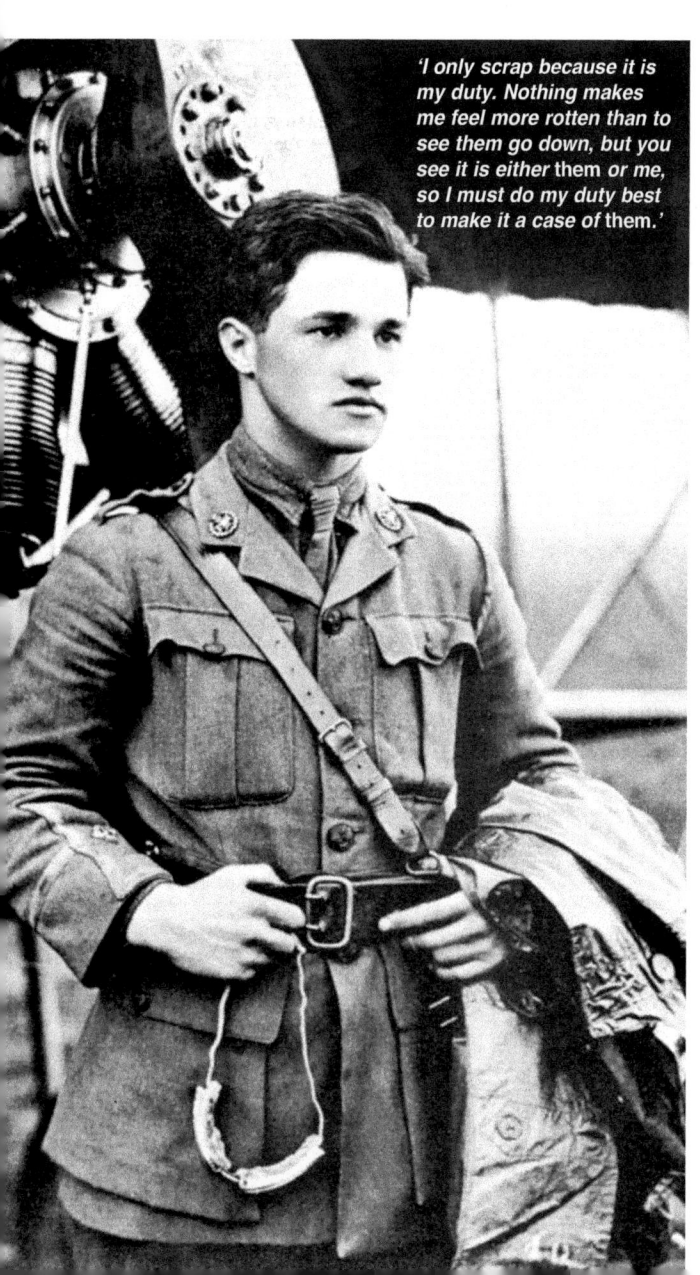

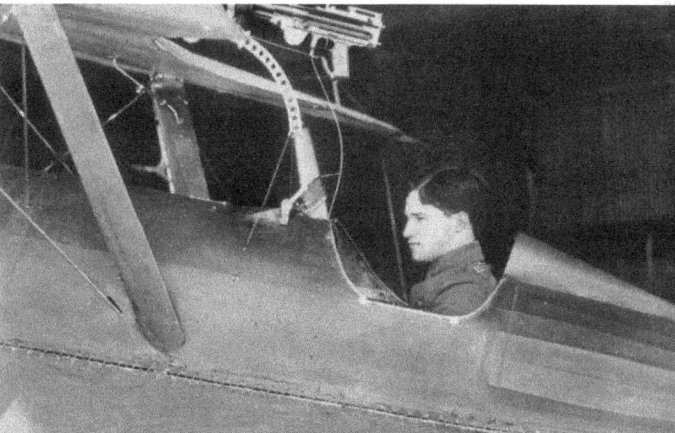

Albert Ball, VC, DSO and Two Bars, MC. At the time of his death on 7 May 1917, he was the United Kingdom's leading flying ace, with 44 kills. He remained its fourth highest scorer behind Edward Mannock, James McCudden, and George McElroy.

Albert Ball joined No.13 Squadron where he flew on reconnaissance operations before being posted in May 1916 to No. 11 Squadron, a fighter unit. From then until his return to England on leave in October, he had scored many aerial victories, earning two Distinguished Service Orders and the Military Cross. He was the first ace to become a British national hero. Ball was posted to No.56 Squadron, which deployed to the Western Front in April 1917. He crashed to his death in a field in France on 7 May, (there were no bullet holes in the aircraft nor his body) sparking a wave of national mourning and posthumous recognition, which included the award of the Victoria Cross for his actions during his final tour of duty. The famous German flying ace Manfred von Richthofen, remarked upon hearing of Ball's death that he was *'by far the best English flying man'*.

In his last letter Ball wrote *'I do get tired of always living to kill, and am really beginning to feel like a murderer. Shall be so pleased when I have finished.'*

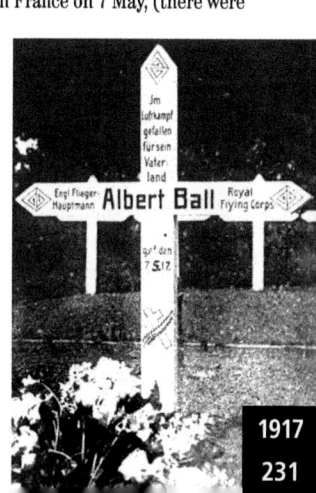

17GW537 German gravemarker in Annoeullin Cemetery.

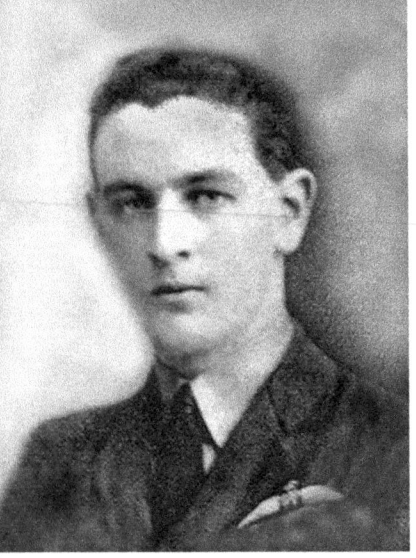

17GW539 John Inglis Gilmour DSO, MC and Two Bars He was the highest scoring Scotsman in the Royal Flying Corps, with 44 kills.

March 1916. He was assigned to No.27 Squadron. They were the only squadron equipped with the Martinsyde G.100, commonly called the 'Elephant'. It received its nickname for being large and ungainly. It was too big and too slow. It was equipped with a Lewis machine gun mounted on the upper wing firing over the propeller, and a second one on the fuselage pointed toward the rear. Despite its shortcomings, Gilmour scored three victories before the Elephants were withdrawn from service.

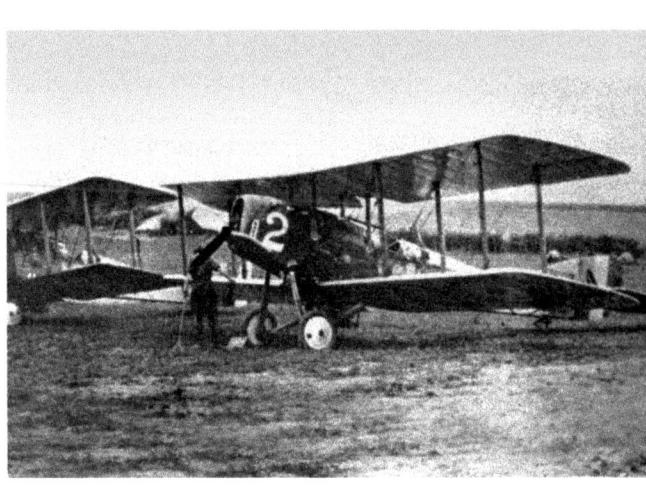

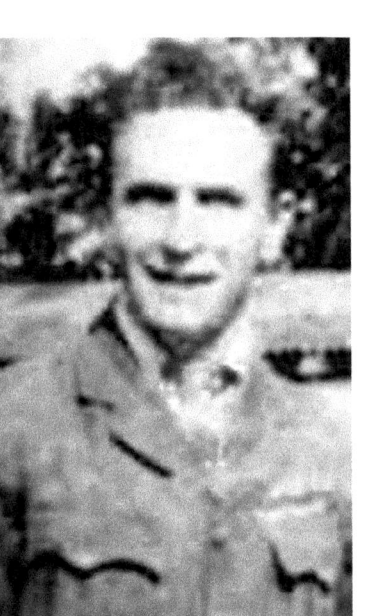

17GW546 James Ira Thomas 'Taffy' Jones DSO, MC, DFC and Bar, MM. He was credited with 40 kills.

In 1913, Jones enlisted in the Territorial Force, though he was soon transferred into the newly established Royal Flying Corps. serving as an air mechanic on ground duties (where he earned the Military Medal) before volunteering for flying duties as an Observer.

He commenced pilot training in August 1917 after being commissioned. He joined No. 74 Squadron. Jones recorded 37 kills in just three months whilst flying the SE.5. In September 1918 Jones was awarded the Military Cross. His citation reads:

For conspicuous gallantry and devotion to duty. This officer, one of an offensive patrol, engaged and shot down in flames a two-seater, which fell to earth. Ten days later, on offensive patrol, he shot down a Hannover two-seater, which crashed. The next day, when patrolling, he pursued, overtook and shot down an Albatross two-seater. During the same flight he met a Halberstadt two-seater and killed the observer, who either jumped or fell overboard, but had to break off as his ammunition was finished. The next day he shot a balloon down in flames. Three days later he got a good burst with both guns on a Pfalz scout, both wings coming off. He has driven two others down out of control.

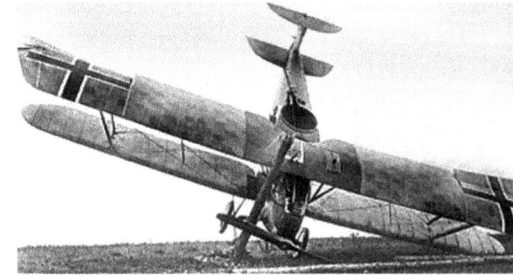

17GW549 Halberstadt two-seater.
17GW550 Pfalz Scout.

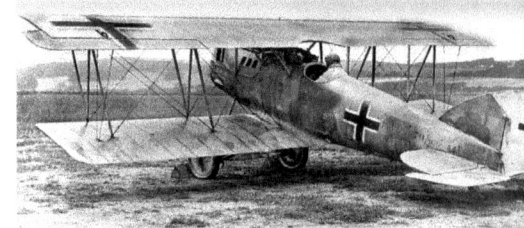

'My habit of attacking Huns dangling from their parachutes led to many arguments in the mess. Some officers, of the Eton and Sandhurst type, thought it was "unsportsmanlike" to do it. Never having been to a public school, I was unhampered by such considerations of form. I just pointed out that there was a bloody war on, and that I intended to avenge my pals.'

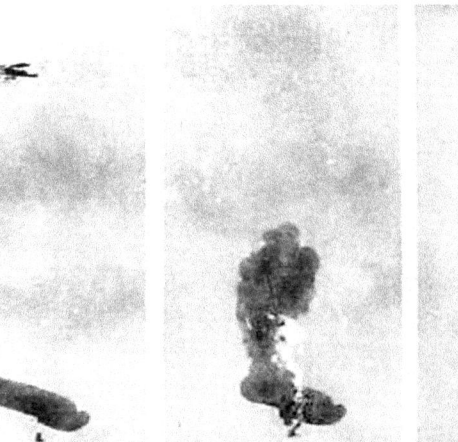
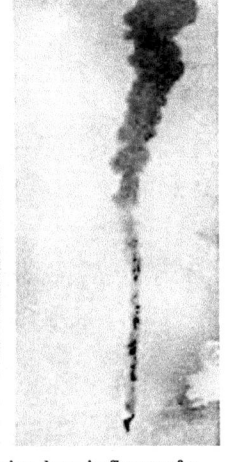
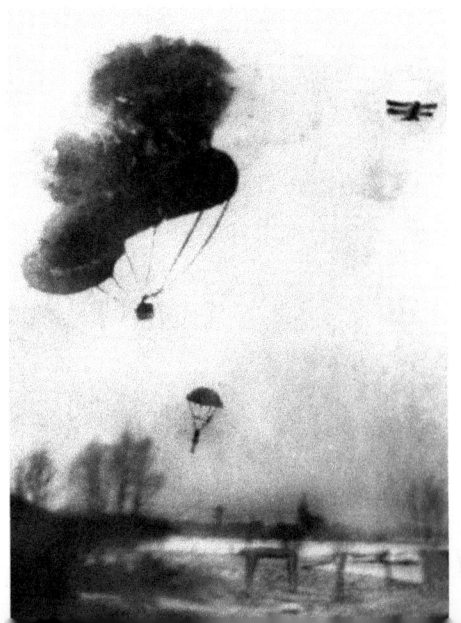

17GW547 A sequence of photographs showing the bringing down in flames of a German Parseval-Sigsfeld observation balloon by dropping a bomb on it.

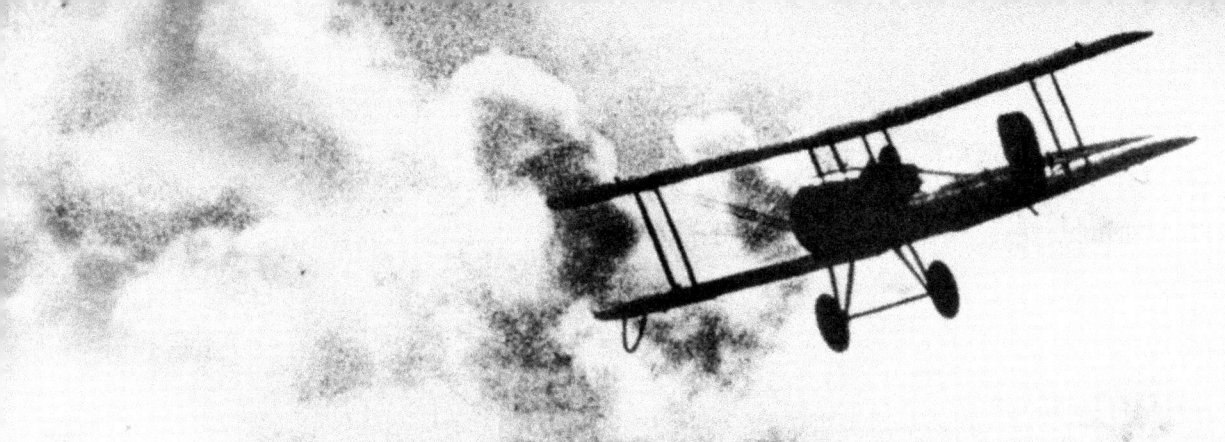

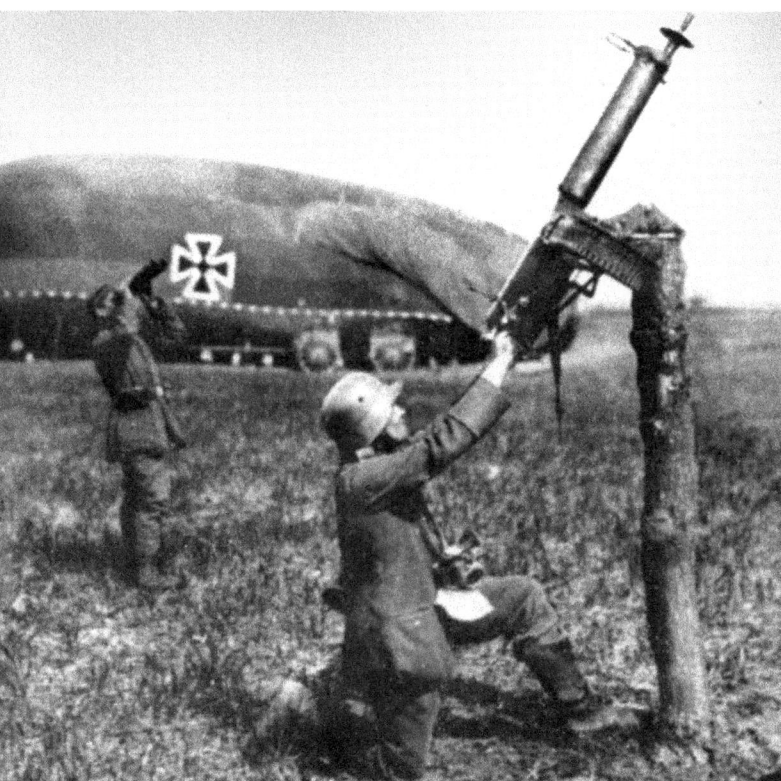

17GW581, 17GW579, 17GW582, 17GW580. Airmen who regularly attacked observation balloons were considered to be a bit mad by other airmen, as it was considered to be near suicidal to attack one. The Germans ringed their *drachen* (dragon) balloons with machine guns and aniti aicraft batteries. The German balloonist artillery observers would escaped to the ground by parachute when the attack was being pushed home. The parachute was not strapped to the back of the user but was contained in a compartment above the basket.

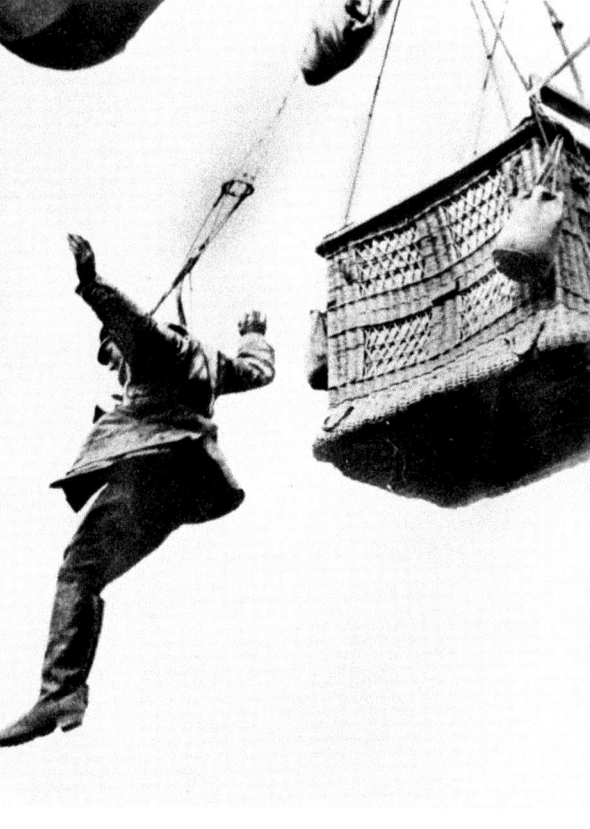

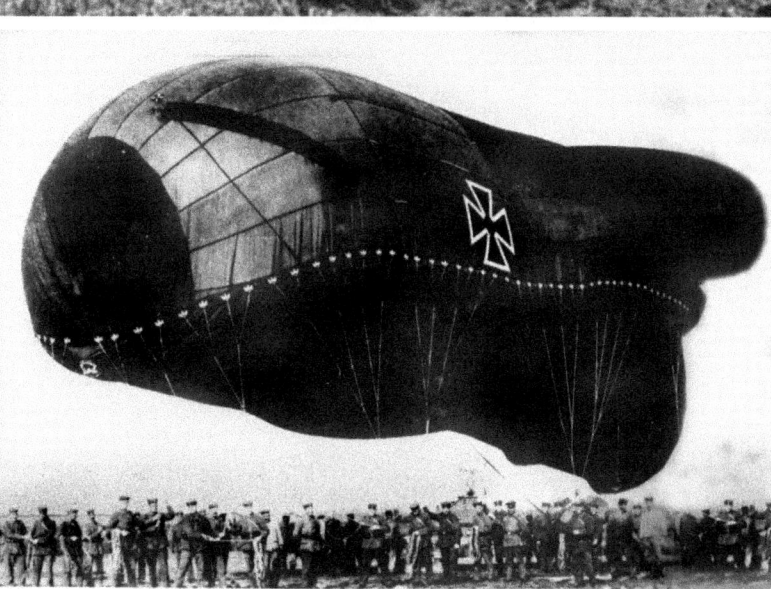

1917
233

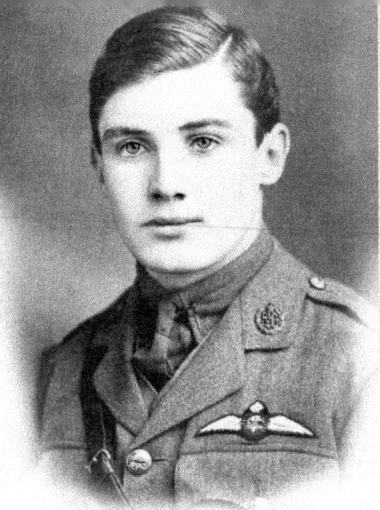

'If only I could have brought him down alive!'

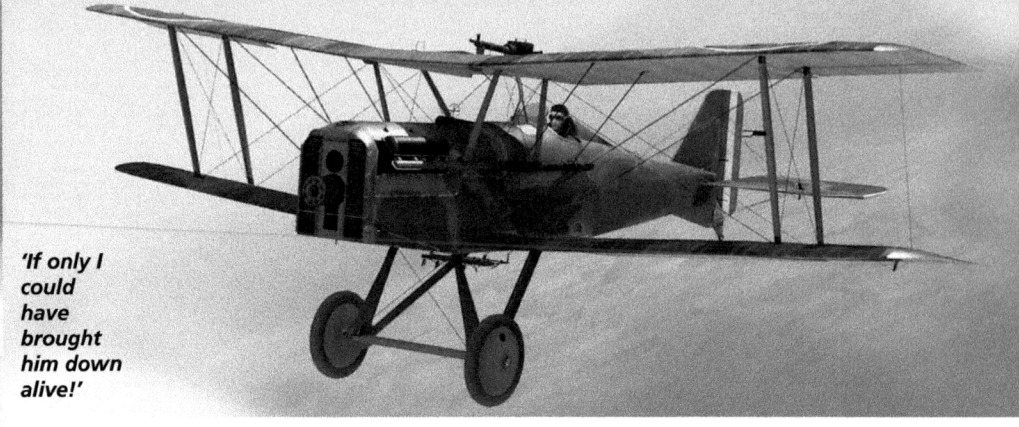

17GW584 Arthur Percival Foley Rhys-Davids, was an ace of No.56 Squadron RFC with 23 kills. In September 1917 he was involved in a dogfight with German ace Werner Voss, commander of *Jasta 10*, of Richthofen's Circus and shot him down. It is often considered to be the most famous air action of the war.

On 23 September, Captain James McCudden led No.56 Squadron on a sortie over the front lines at a height of 9,000 feet. There were a large number of aircraft, both British and German, in the air that evening. McCudden dived on a German reconnaissance machine and shot it down. Regrouping his six machines at 6,000 feet, he spotted another German formation. McCudden indicated that he was about to lead an attack when he noticed ahead an SE.5 spiraling down with a German Triplane on its tail. The SE.5, from No.609 Squadron RFC, was piloted by a Lieutenant Harold A. Hamersley, who was still in control of his shot-up aircraft and was desparately trying to throw the German off. He was running out of air space as the ground rushed up with every second. However, the German stayed on his tail, firing all the way. McCudden and Rhys-Davids went to the rescue, attacking one from either side, and soon the German found himself in the midst of six circling British machines. McCudden explained:

'The German triplane was in the middle of our formation, and its handling was wonderful to behold. The pilot seemed to be firing at us all simultaneously, and although I got behind him a second time I could hardly stay there for a second. His movements were so quick and unpredictable.'

The six pilots of No.56 Squadron, James McCudden, Rhys-Davids, Geoffrey Hilton Bowman, Richard Maybery, Keith Muspratt, and Verschoyle Cronyn were engaged in battle with the German ace Werner Voss – victor of 48 aerial conflicts – who, despite the odds, made no attempt to escape. A burst from the German's twin machine guns ripped along McCudden's upper wing; Muspratt and Cronyn were forced out of the unequal fight with hits to their engines. Another six SE.5s from No.56 Squadron – C Flight – arrived on the fight to the death scene led by Reginald Hoidge. A red-nosed Albatros joined in to assist the besieged Fokker Triplane. As Rhys-Davids attacked the Fokker the Albatros engaged him from astern. Maybery forced it to disengage and make a run from the uneven fight. The Triplane was now alone. Repeatedly Voss evaded the attacks of the British fighter, throwing his aircraft about the sky in a breath-taking display. Eventually, he made a flat turn, enabling Rhys-Davids to get onto his tail. Bowman believed the German was momentarily distracted, intent on attacking himself, miscalculating Rhys-Davids' ability to get onto his tail so easily. With his propeller 'boss almost on the rudder' Rhys-Davids opened fire. The Fokker dived, level and straight for the first time, heading towards the German lines. Rhys-Davids remained behind for a brief distance and then turned away. Incredibly, as Rhys-Davids made his turn, Voss turned with the Englishman and brought his machine back into the flight path of Rhys-Davids' SE.5. Rhys-Davids emptied an entire drum of ammunition into the Triplane, then broke off to avoid a collision. Climbing, Rhys-Davids saw the German machine, its engine stopped, heading west. Rhys-Davids made several more attacks, with the Fokker going down in a shallow right-hand turn. McCudden saw the machine crash:

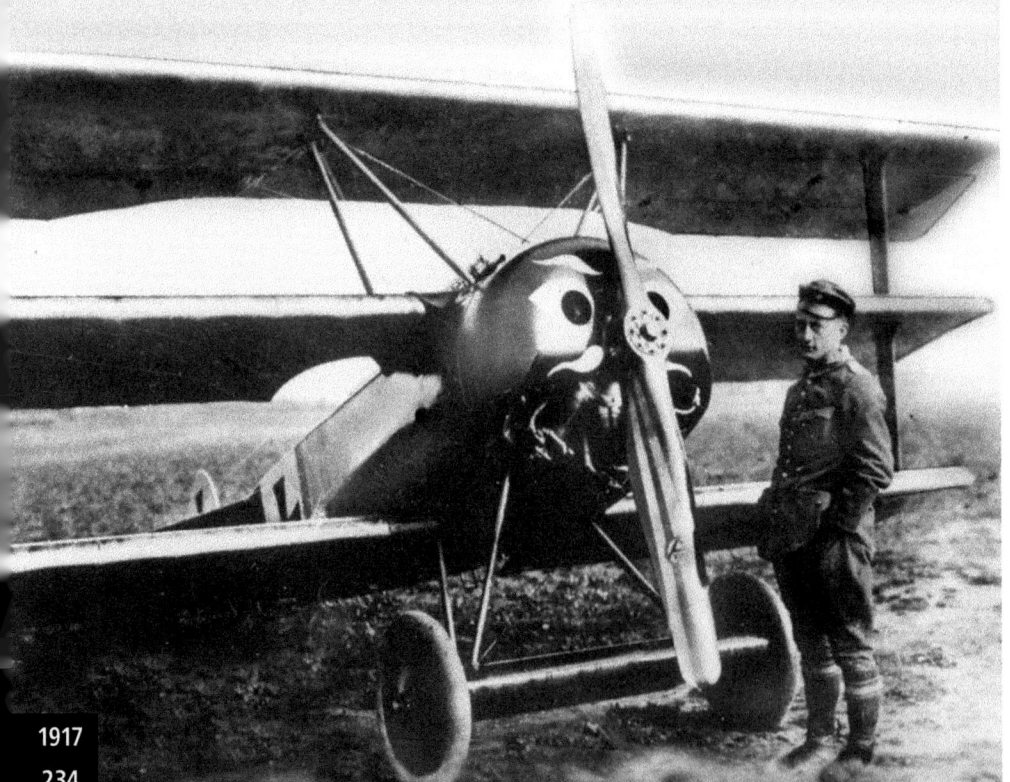

He was very low... still being engaged by Rhys-Davids. I noticed the Triplane's movements were very erratic, I saw him go into a steep dive and then saw the Triplane hit the ground and disappear into a thousand fragments.

As long as I live I shall never forget my admiration for that German pilot, who single-handed fought seven of us for ten minutes and also put some bullets through all our machines. His flying was wonderful, his courage magnificent, and in my opinion he was the bravest German airman whom it has been my privilege to see fight.

On 27 October 1917, Rhys-Davids was shot down by Karl Gallwitz and killed.

17GW583 German ace Werner Voss, commander of *Jasta 10*, of Richthofen's Circus, beside his Fokker Triplane.

17GW551 René Paul Fonck ended the First World War as the top Allied fighter ace, of the Great War – the Allied 'Ace of Aces'. He received confirmation for 75 kills (72 solo and three shared) out of 142 claims. Taking into account his probable claims, Fonck's final tally of kills could be closer to a hundred or above.

On 17 March 1917 Fonck made his second kill in conjunction with his observer by downing an Albatros. At the age of twenty-three, on 15 April 1917, during 'Bloody April', Fonck received a coveted invitation to join the élite *Escadrille des Cigognes*. The leading French ace at the time was Georges Guynemer, who flew in one of its squadrons (*escadrilles*), *N3*, and had just scored his 36th kill. Fonck continued to improve as a fighter pilot and became known for his clinical professionalism, a killer who applied mathematical principles to engagements with the enemy. His engineering knowledge regarding the capabilities of the aircraft he flew was unsurpassed among his fellow pilots. Fonck took few chances, patiently stalking his intended victims from higher altitudes where he would use accurate deflection shooting directly at the German pilots at close range. He expended minimum ammunition on each victim, perhaps a single burst of less than five rounds from his Vickers machine gun. His preferred method of aerial combat was rarely to engage in dogfights, but rather to conduct surgically merciless executions. He was also reputed to be able to spot enemy aircraft at a distance before most fellow aviators picked up their presence. By the end of 1917 Fonck had raised his tally to nineteen kills and had been commissioned, receiving the award of the *Légion d'honneur*.

During the final year of the war he claimed 56 kills; this 1918 list, in its own right, would have made him France's leading ace. Unlike many French aces, his score contained only three shared victories, nor had he shot down any observation balloons. Incredibly, only a single enemy bullet had ever struck his aircraft. Despite his amazing skill and success, Fonck never captured the heart of the French public as Guynemer had. He remained distant, arrogant, ever boastful. His fellow pilots certainly respected his skills, but even one of his few friends, Marcel Haegelen, considered him a braggart and shameless self-promoter.

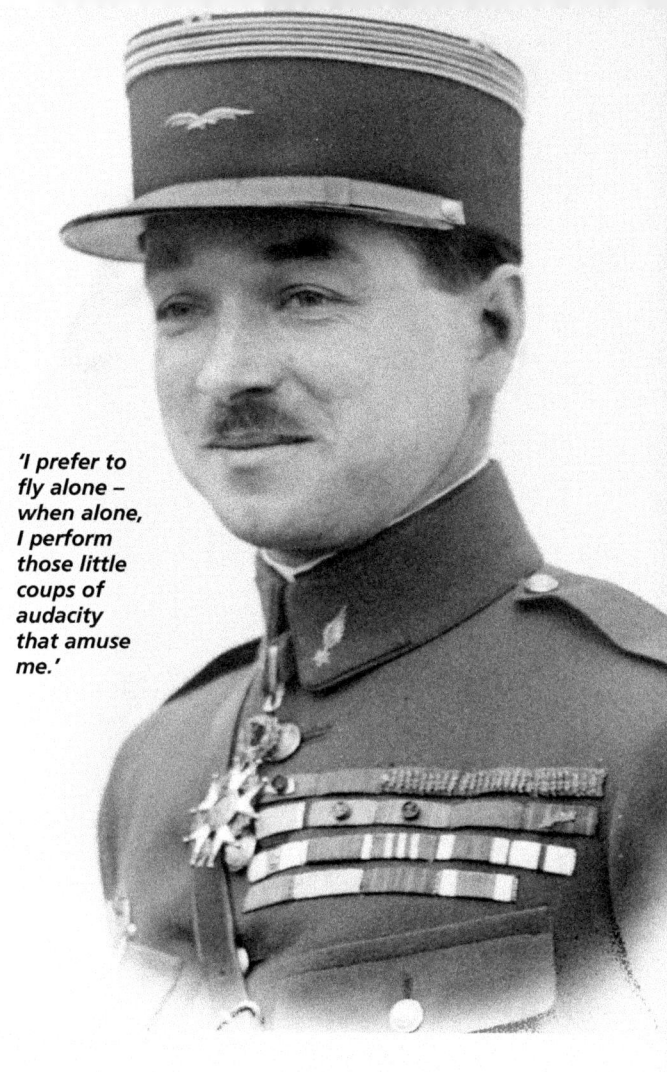

'I prefer to fly alone – when alone, I perform those little coups of audacity that amuse me.'

17GW553 René Paul Fonck standing beside his Spad XIII. He was perhaps the most clinically efficient and murderous fighter ace of all time.

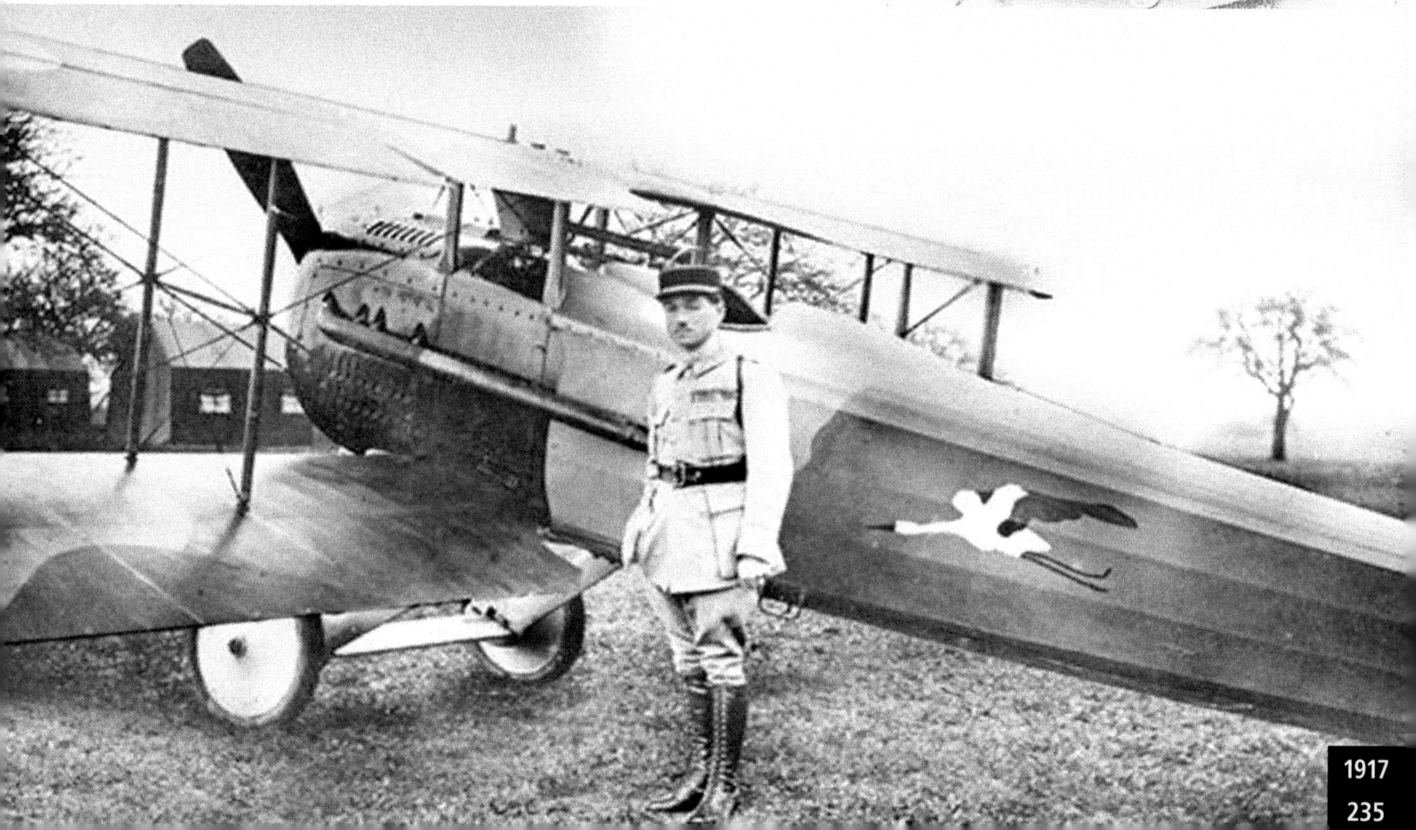

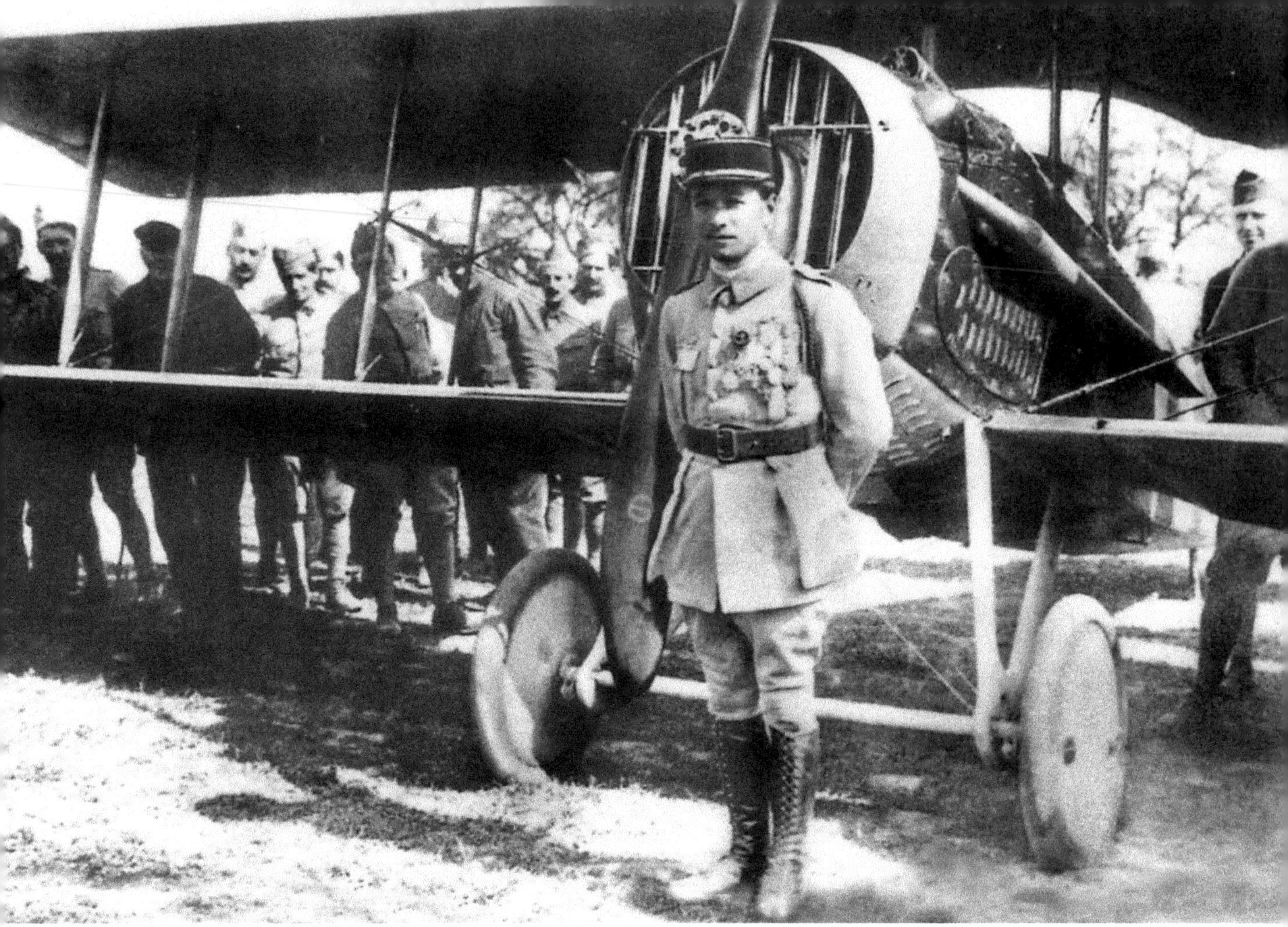

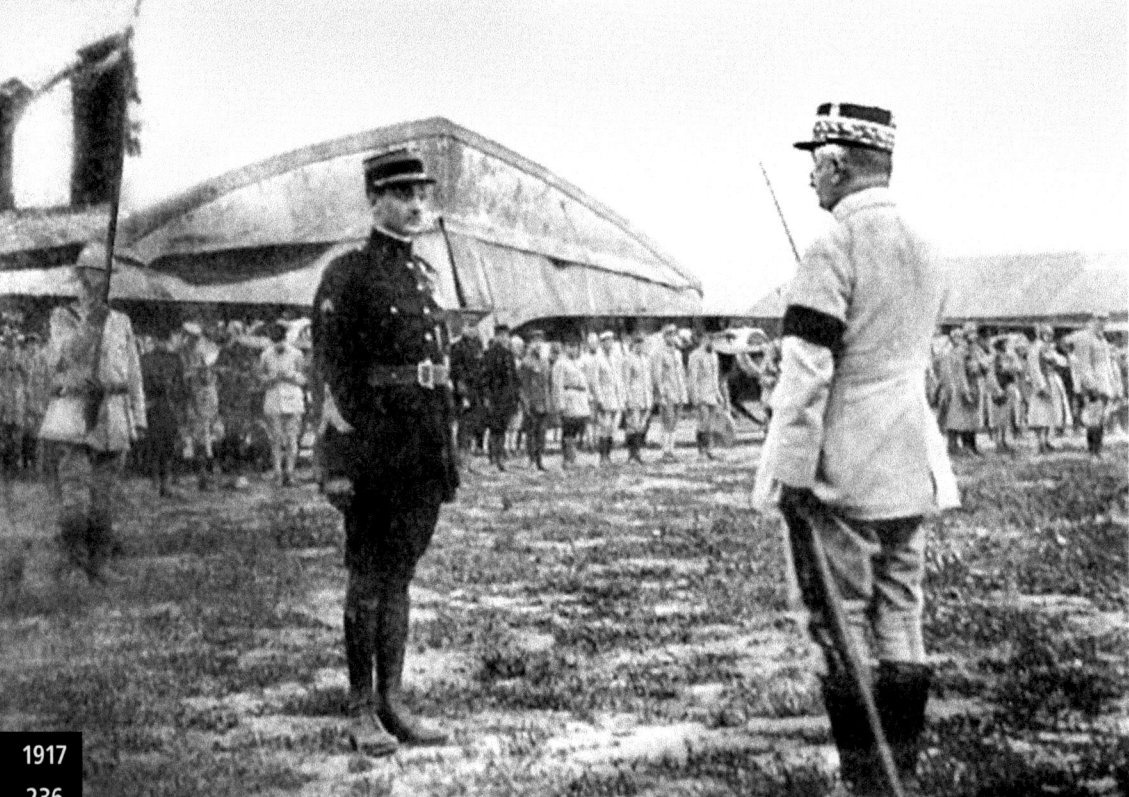

17GW592 René Paul Fonck in front his Spad XIII. He was never taken to the heart of his countrymen in the way his fellow fighter ace, Georges Guynemer, was. Despite his ability as a killer of his country's enemies, even his fellow pilots struggled to cope with his overbearing conceit.

17GW594 At Crugny airfield in the Marne, in July 1917, General Franchet d'Esperey presents the Legion of Honour to Georges Guynemer.

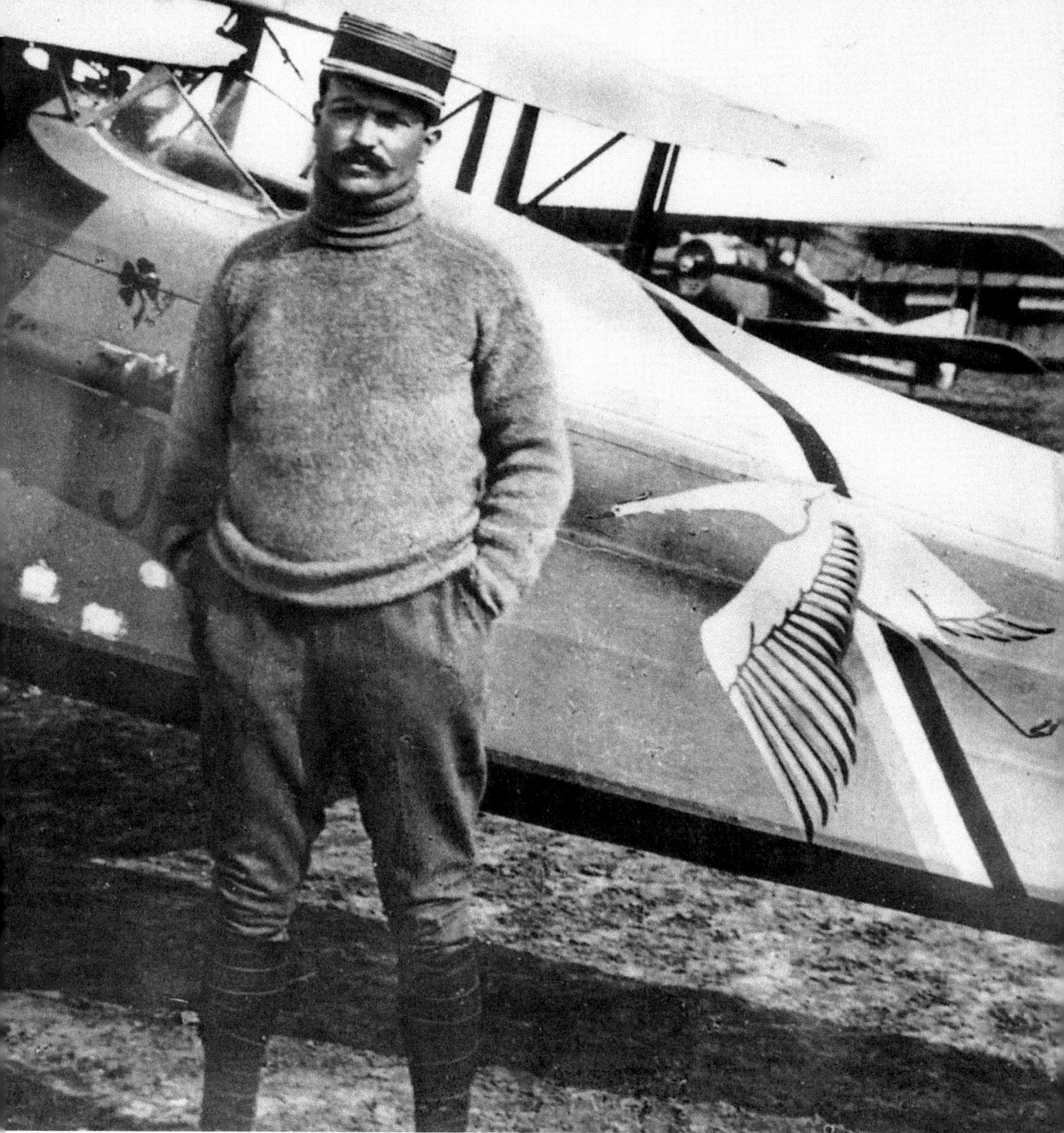

17GW593 Capitaine Felix Brocard, commanding officer of the famous French *Les Cigognes* (The Storks) group. Pilots placed images of storks in different phases of flying on their planes.

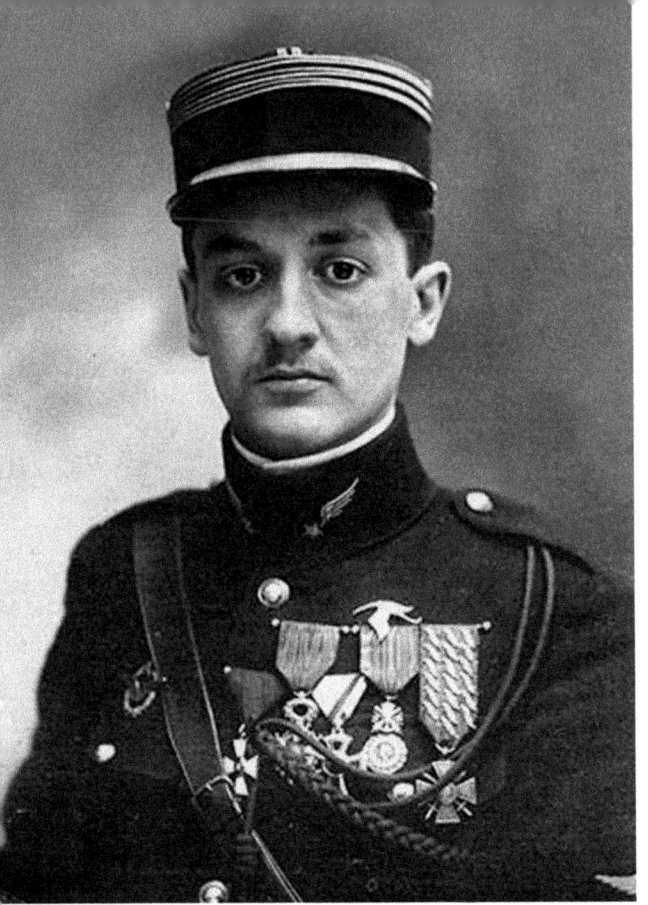

On 19 July, 1915, Georges Guynemer shot down his first enemy aircraft, a German Aviatik. After being re-equipped with Nieuport aircraft, Guynemer established himself as one of France's premier fighter pilots. He became an ace by his fifth kill in February 1916. His greatest month was May 1917, when he downed seven German aircraft.

Guynemer failed to return from a combat mission on 11 September 1917. On the 25th a report was released by the French War Department:

Guynemer sighted five machines of the Albatros type D-3. Without hesitation, he bore down on them. At that moment enemy patrolling machines, soaring at a great height, appeared suddenly and fell upon Guynemer. There were forty enemy machines in the air at this time, including Baron von Richthofen and his circus division of machines, painted in diagonal blue and white stripes. Toward Guynemer's right some Belgian machines hove in sight, but it was too late. Guynemer must have been hit. His machine dropped gently toward the earth, and I lost track of it. All that I can say is that the machine was not on fire.

An American Red Cross report provided these details:

Information received by the Red Cross says Guynemer was shot through the head north of Poelcapelle, on the Ypres front. His body was identified by a photograph on his pilot's license found in his pocket. The burial took place at Brussels in the presence of a guard of honor, composed of the 5th Prussian Division. Such is the story told by a Belgian, who has just escaped from the Germans. The burial was about to take place at Poelcapelle, when the bombardment preceding the British attack at Ypres started. The burying party hastily withdrew, taking the body with them. The German General chanced to be an aviation enthusiast with a great admiration for Captain Guynemer's achievements. At his direction the body was taken to Brussels in a special funeral car. Thither the captain was carried by non-commissioned officers and was covered with floral tributes from German aviators. The Prussian Guards stood at salute upon its arrival and during the burial, which was given all possible military honors. The French Government has been invited to place in the Pantheon, where many great Frenchmen are buried, an inscription to perpetuate the memory of Captain Guynemer as 'a symbol of the aspirations and enthusiasm of the Army'. A resolution to this effect has been introduced in the Chamber of Deputies by Deputy Lasies.

17GW554 Georges Marie Ludovic Jules Guynemer. He scored 54 kills.

17GW557, 17GW556. Guynemer air borne and standing by his machine, called 'Vieux Charles'. His Spad bears a red, white and blue riband marking around the fuselage.

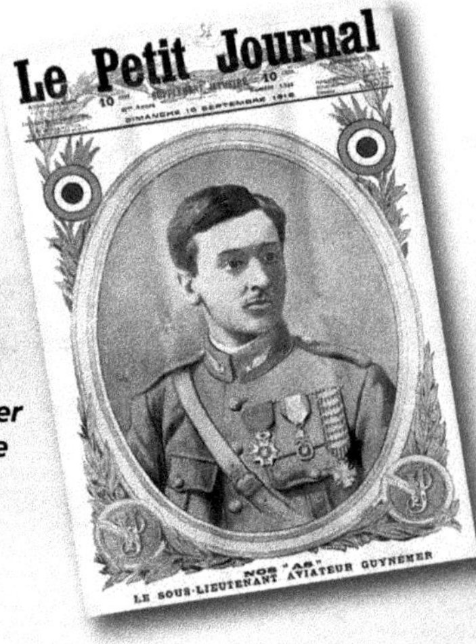

Popular fighter pilot and hero Georges Guynemer on the cover of Le Petit Journal in 1916.

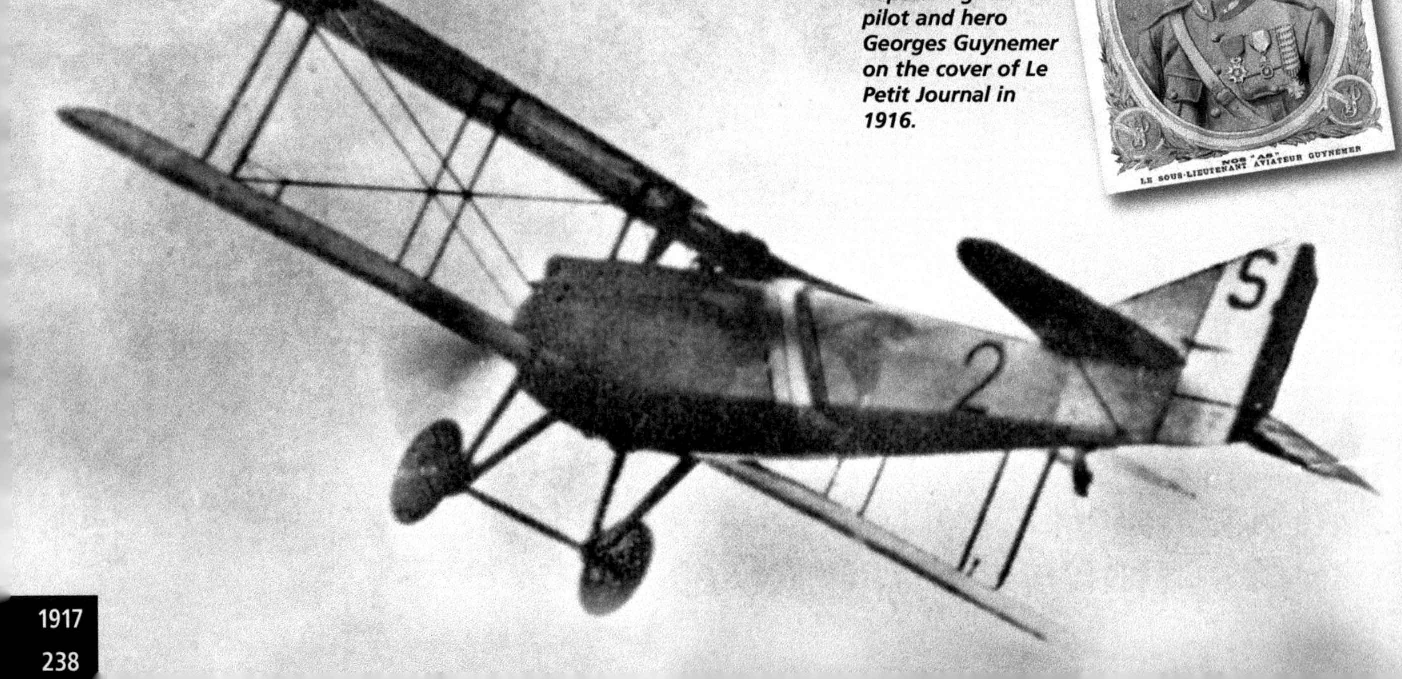

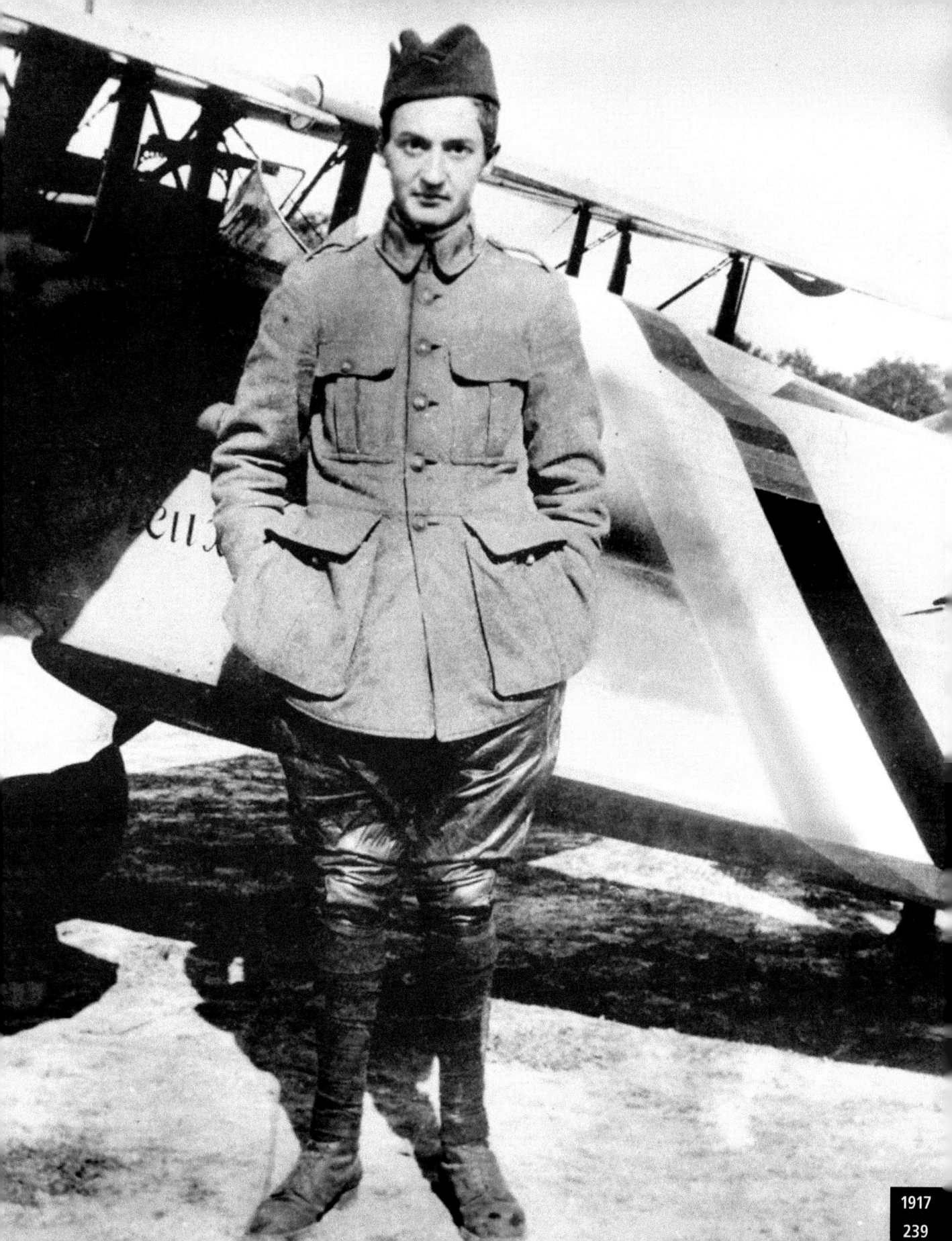

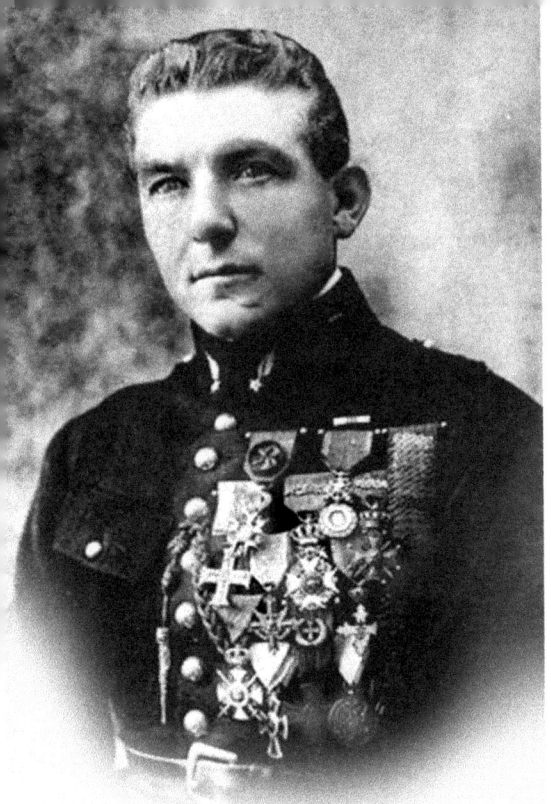

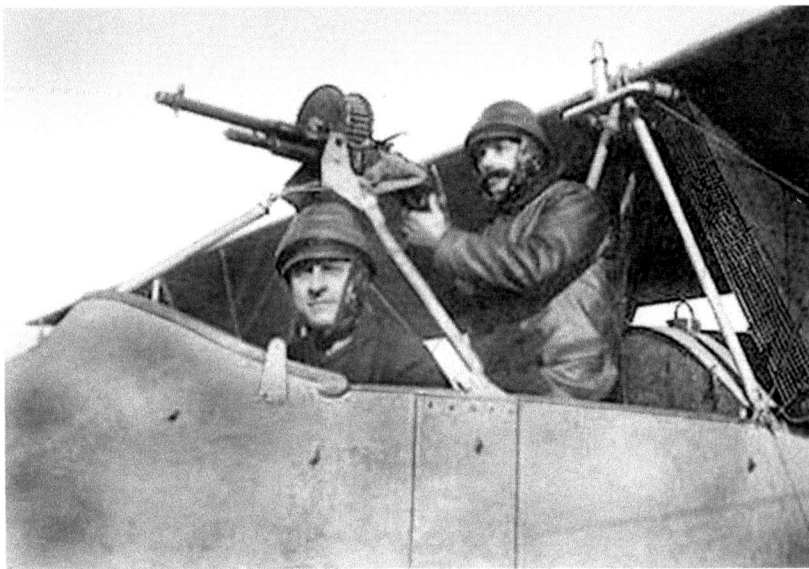

17GW567 Charles Nungesser became a wartime legend, an undisciplined warrior who gained decorations in spite of his superiors' failed efforts to tame him. How he achieved his very first victory on 31 July 1915 was typical of the man: Nungesser and his mechanic, Roger Pochon, were on standby. Despite Nungesser being ordered to non-flying duties, the two climbed into a Voisin 3LAS and took off. In an encounter with five Albatros two-seaters, the French duo shot one down near Nancy. Returning to their airfield, Nungesser was placed under house arrest for eight days for insubordination. He was then awarded the Croix de Guerre and forwarded for training in Nieuport fighters.

17GW561 The Nieuport Ni 17 of Charles Nungesser, bearing the 'The Knight of Death' insignia with its coffin, skull and cross bones and candles. By August 1917, he had pushed his score to thirty when he downed his second Gotha bomber. Despite many wounds and injuries during 1917, he finished the war with forty-five victories. His exploits against the Germans were widely publicized in France. His flamboyant personality, good looks and appetite for danger, beautiful women, wine and fast cars made him the embodiment of the stereotypical flying ace.

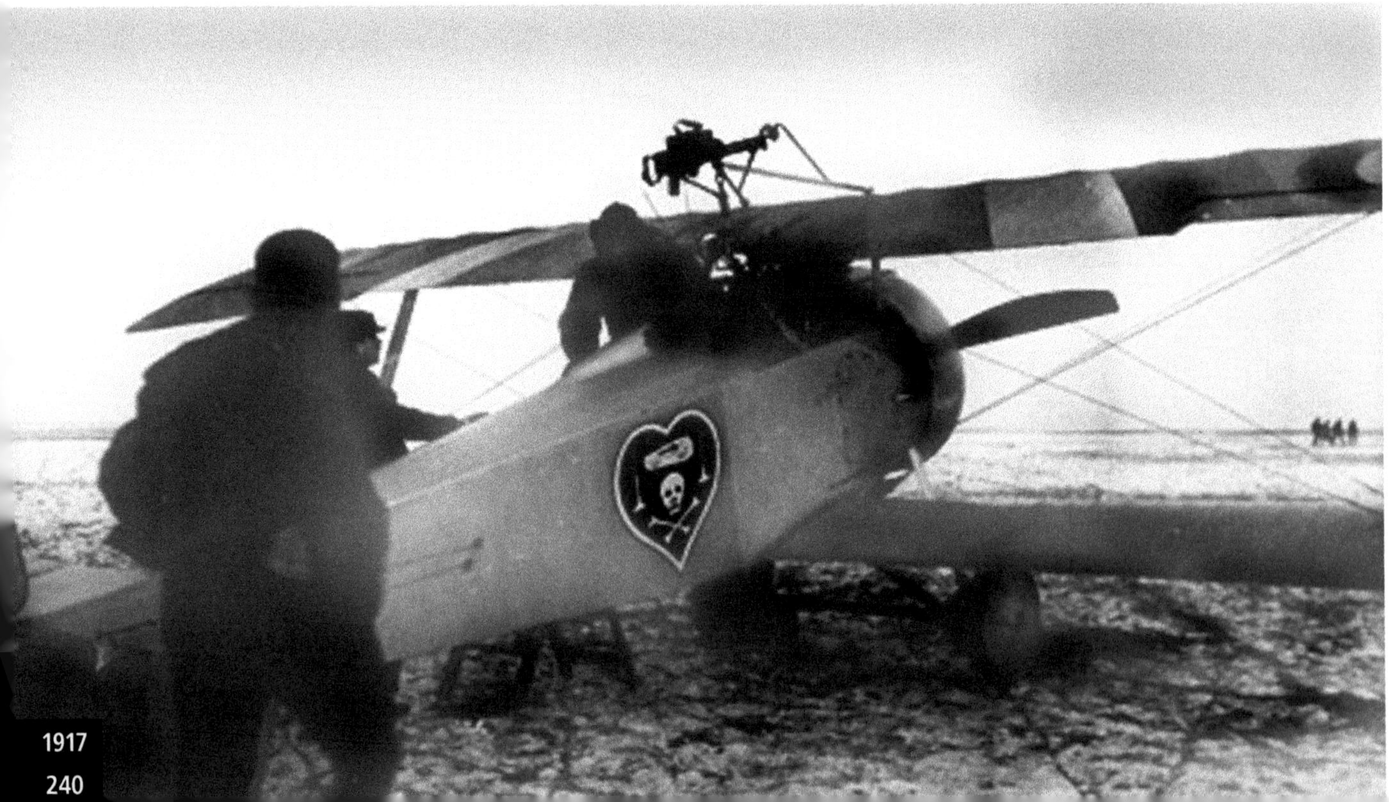

17GW560 Charles Eugène Jules Marie Nungesser, third on the list of French aces, scored 45 kills.

When attached to the famous Lafayette Escadrille, composed of American volunteers, during a period of convalescence, he called at the airfield, borrowed a plane, took off and shot down another German. By the end of 1916 he had claimed twenty-one kills

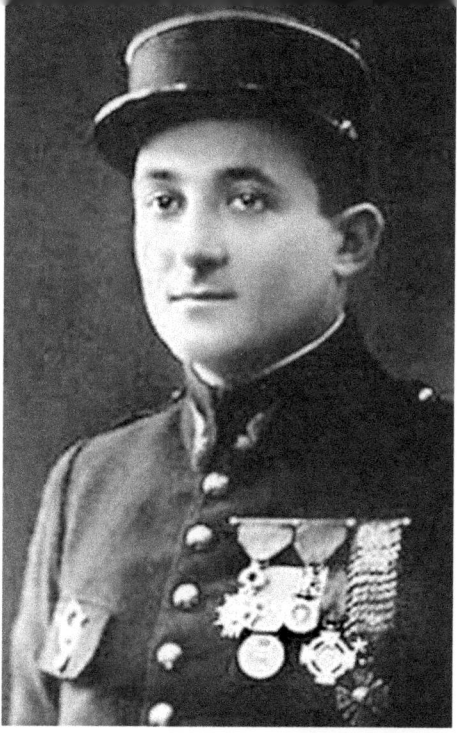

17GW568 Georges Félix Madon was ranked the fourth French air ace of the Great War. He achieved his first official kill in September 1916. After Madon had accumulated a dozen air successes, in early July 1917 he was wounded. The following February he was assigned to command Spa 38, by now with twenty-five victories to his credit. In one month alone, June 1918, he succeeded in adding a further eight to his tally. His final score reached 41 kills.

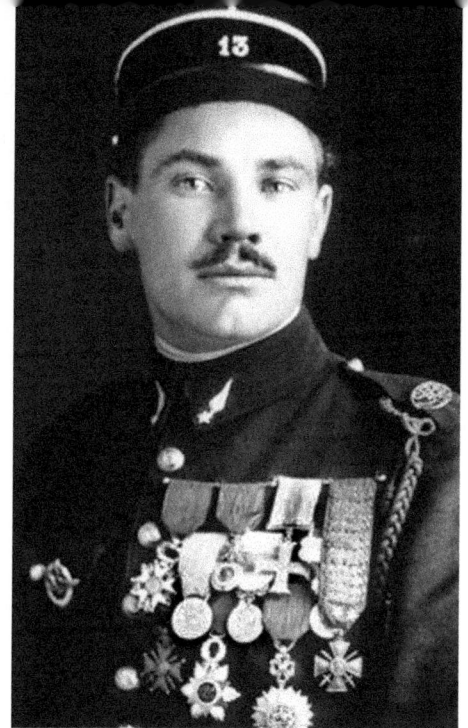

17GW570 Michel Joseph Callixte Marie Coiffard. He was notable for his success as a balloon buster, shooting down enemy observation balloons, which were always heavily defended by anti-aircraft machine guns, artillery and fighter planes. While downing his 34th victim (a Fokker D.VII) he was critically wounded in the thigh and chest. He flew twelve kilometres back to friendly territory despite his wounds but died three hours later. His final wartime score reached 34 kills.

17GW569 Maurice Jean-Paul Boyau, 35 kills. He stands next to his SPAD VII, coded '9', which is equipped for carrying and shooting rockets. He scored his first ten victories between March and September 1917, including six balloons. In the spring of 1918 Boyau pioneered the use of air-to-air rockets. Rocket tubes were secured to the inner set of struts of his Spad XIII. He made his mark with repeated successes in the summer of 1918, scoring four victories in June, nine in July, and three in August. He destroyed his last four balloons in three days of September. However, defending German fighters pounced and he was shot down and killed with German ace Georg von Hantelmann receiving the credit. He captained the French Rugby XV in 1914.

(*Leutnant* Georg von Hantelmann was credited with 25 kills during the First World War. These victories included three opposing aces shot down during the same week in September 1918: David Putnam, Maurice Boyau and Joseph Wehner.)

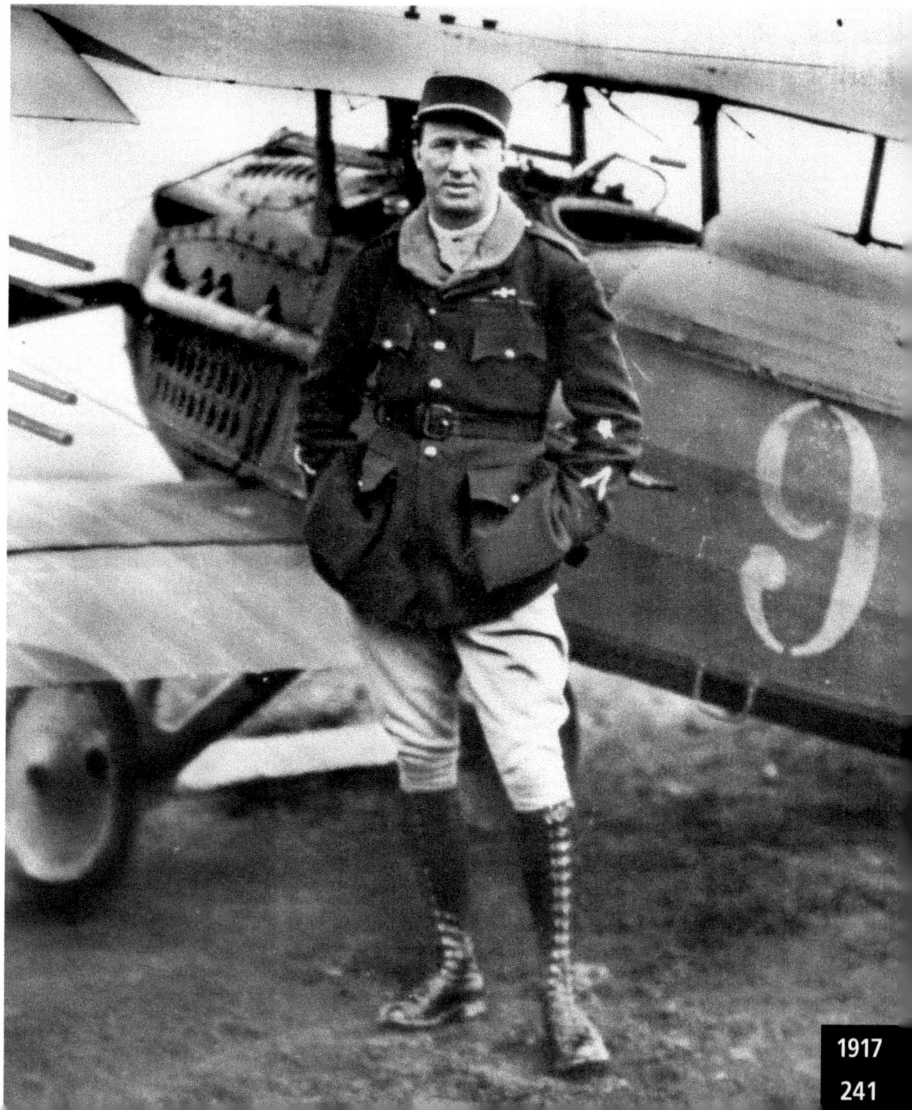

17GW571 Nieuport Type 14 aircraft were fitted with Le Prieur rockets fitted in racks and fired electronically.

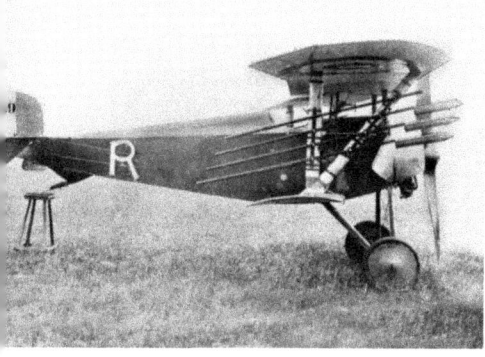

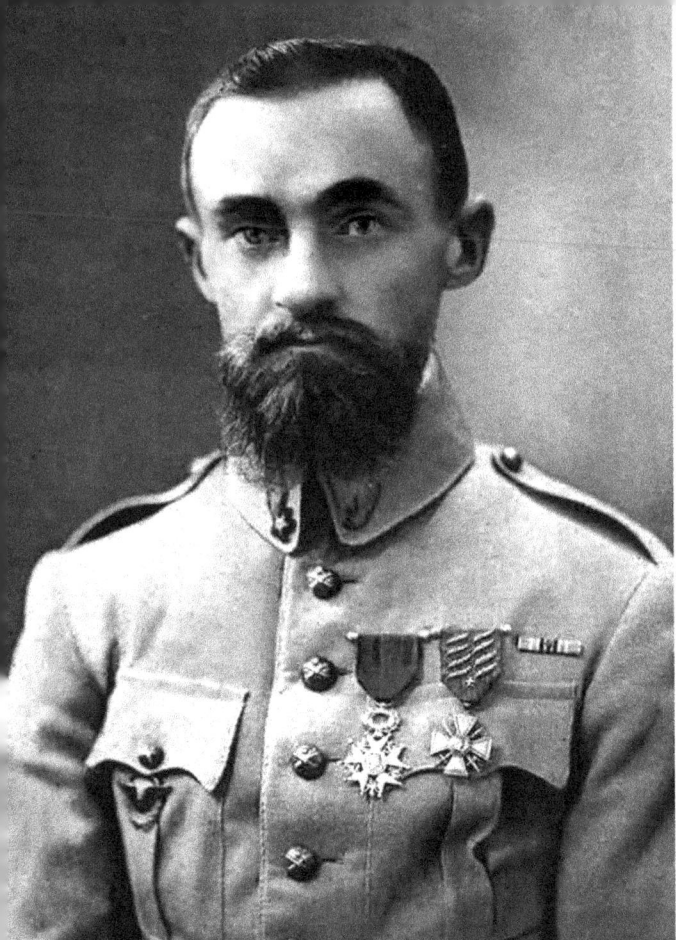

17GW572 Jean-Pierre Léon Bourjade, 28 kills, pre war studied for the priesthood.

When war errupted in 1914, Instead of continuing studying for the priesthood in Switzerland, returned to France to join the army, where he served as an artilleryman for over two years. He transferred to aviation in 1917, receiving his Military Pilot's Brevet on 17 June. He joined *Escadrille N152*; he was to become its highest-scoring pilot. Originally he flew a Nieuport with his own personal touch – a *Sacré-Coeur* (Sacred Heart) banner streaming from the back of his seat. He opened his list of victories on 27 March 1918, after his squadron re-equipped with the Spad XIII, to shoot down a German observation balloon. With one exception all of his air victories were to be over balloons. He scored another victory in April and two in May. He became an ace on 25 June with the first of his four scores for the month. His seventh, on 29 June 1918, was over a Fokker D VII, his only victory not involving a balloon. Bourjade ended the war with a victory list of 27 balloons and one aircraft shot down, with a second airplane as unconfirmed. It was a total that left him second only to Willy Coppens of Belgium as a balloon destroyer. Post war he returned to his vocation as a priest and missionary. He died in Papua New Guinea in 1924.

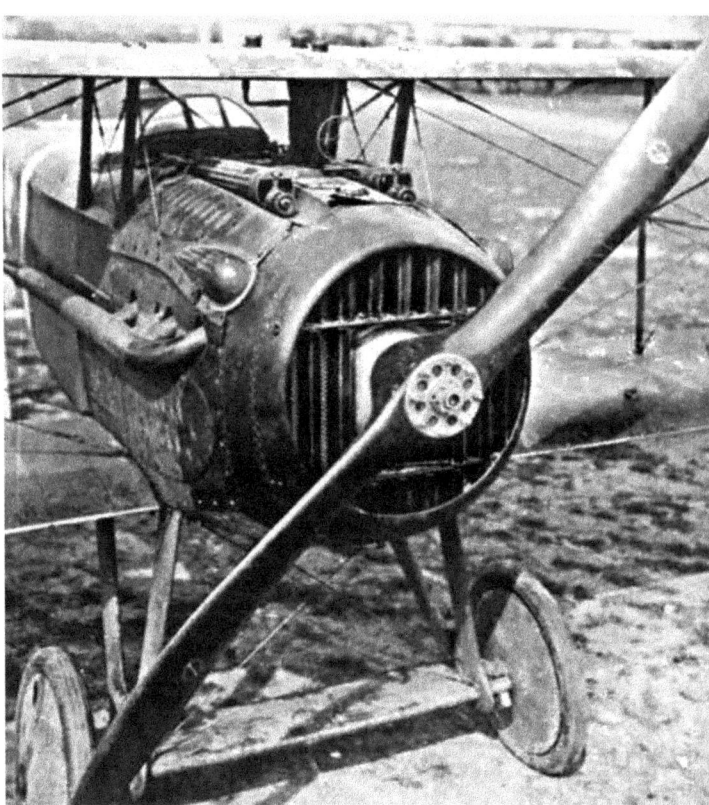

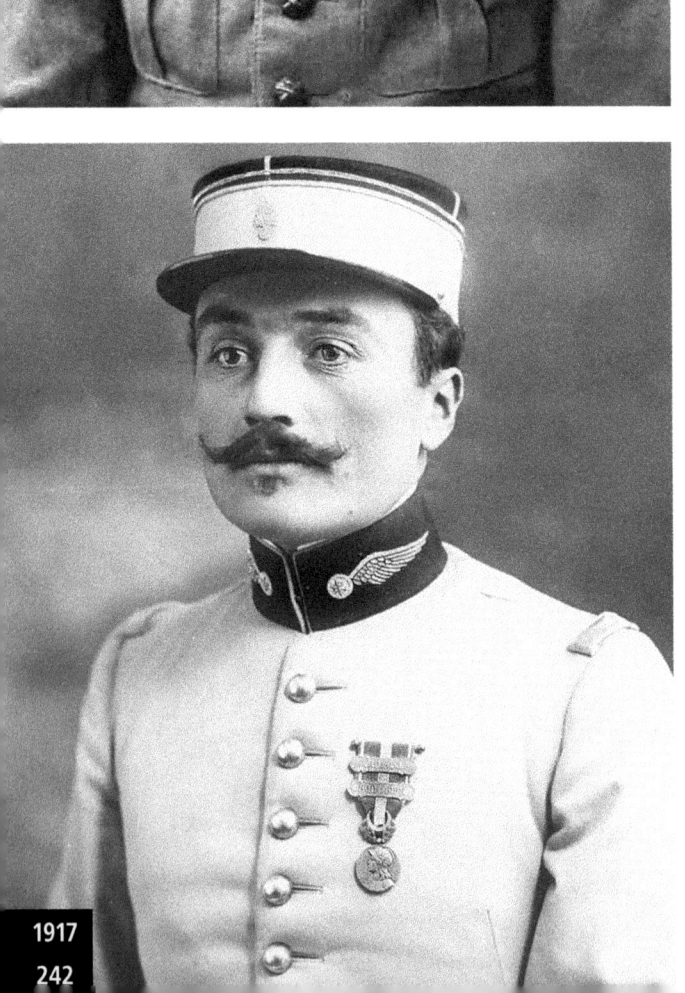

17GW573 Armand Pinsard, 27 kills.

In October 1914 he took part in a bombing raid that attempted to kill the German Kaiser. He was commissioned in November 1914 because of this bombing raid. As the fighting got underway he also was involved in the use of an aircraft to place an espionage agent behind enemy lines. He was captured by the Germans in February 1915 when his machine was forced down. Over a year later he tunneled out of his PoW camp and escaped into neutral Switzerland and was repatriated. The reward for his daring escape was retraining as a fighter pilot and a posting to France's foremost fighter squadron, *Les Cigognes*. In July 1916, he was flying a Nieuport with Squadron N26. On 7 August, in a pioneering close air support role, he made no fewer than six firing passes on German troops attempting to counter-attack a French unit. Then he and his three wingmen went on to strafe a train loaded with German troops. He was made a *Chevalier of the Légion d'honneur* for this action. He opened his list of kills in air combat in November 1916. In August 1917 he was entrusted with the first Spad VII fighter to see combat. He painted it black and entitled it *Revanche IV* (Revenge IV). Pinsard ended the war as a much-decorated captain.

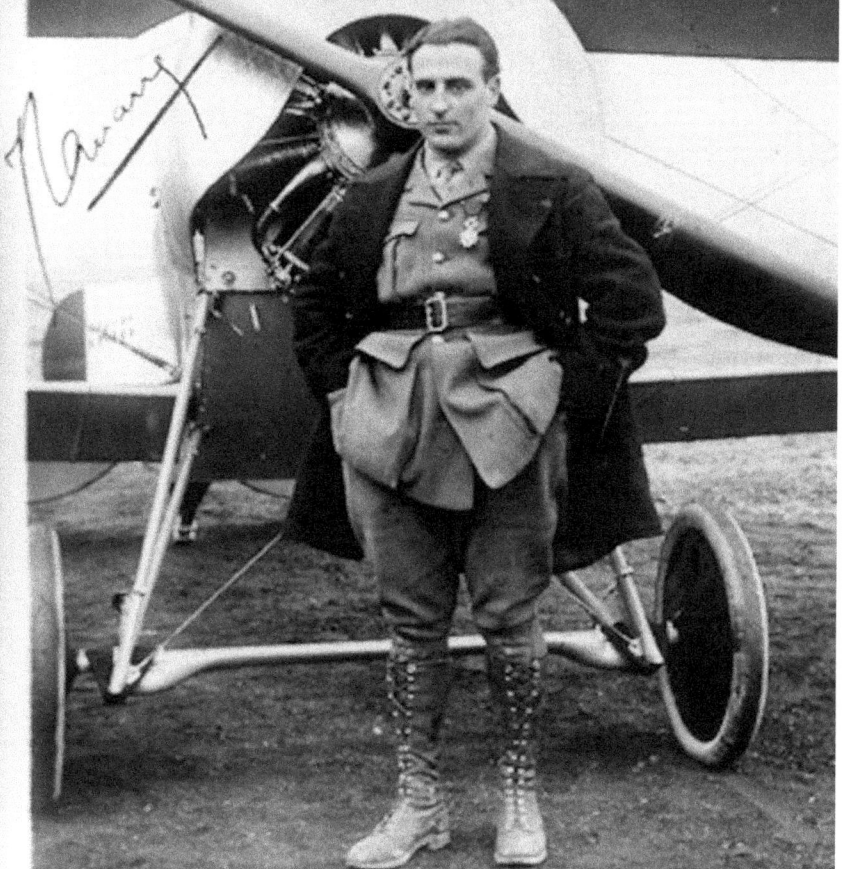

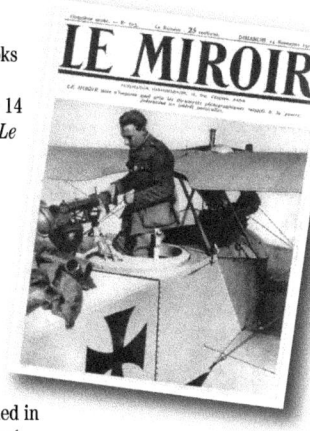

Jean Navarre looks over a captured German plane – 14 November 1915 *Le Miroir* journal.

France early recognized the morale value of her top-scoring fighter pilots. Any pilot having scored five confirmed kills was deemed to be an ace and was mentioned in an official communiqué.

When Navarre received a new Nieuport 11 fighter plane in 1916, he painted it all red to challenge and intimidate the enemy in the skies over Verdun, well before his German counterpart would gain notoriety as the Red Baron. Navarre began his victory run by scoring one of the first 'doubles' of the war, downing a Fokker E.III and a German two-seater on 26 February 1916, and becoming one of the first flying aces in history. Navarre tallied half a dozen more wins during the next three months and on May 19, 1916 he shot down an Aviatik C over Chattancourt, France, becoming the first Allied ace credited with ten kills. On 17 June 1916, Navarre teamed with Georges Pelletier d'Oisy for Navarre's twelfth win. In the process, Jean Navarre was shot down and sustained severe head injuries from which he never fully recovered. He would return to duty in 1918, though he would not again fly in combat.

17GW577 Jean Marie Dominique Navarre, one of the pioneer flying aces, he was credited with twelve confirmed aerial victories and fifteen unconfirmed. He was dubbed the first official French ace.

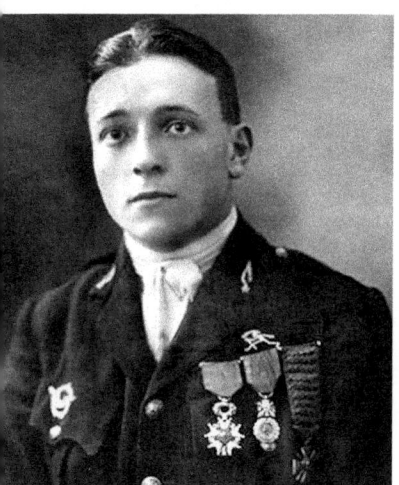

17GW578 Pierre Marinovitch, youngest French ace at twenty. Credited with 22 kills.

At the age of seventeen Marinovitch enlisted in the *27e Régiment de Dragoons* on 12 February 1916. In July, he transferred to aviation. Eventually he was assigned to *Escadrille No. 94*, 'The Reapers', who had the Grim Reaper as their insignia. In January 1918, he was awarded the *Médaille militaire* in recognition of his third aerial victory. He claimed his first four kills flying Nieuport 24s. The French press began referring to him as 'The Youngest Ace'.

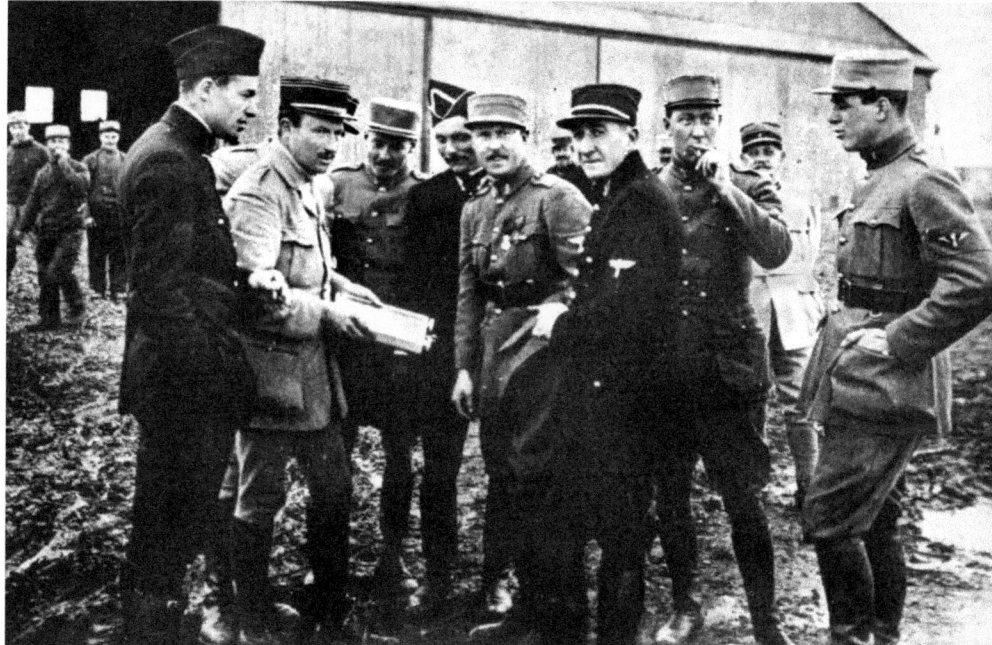

17GW587 The *Lafayette Escadrille* was an escadrille of the *Aéronautique Militaire* composed largely of American volunteer pilots flying fighters. It was named in honor of the Marquis de Lafayette, hero of the American and French revolutions. Founder members of the *Lafayette Escadrille* are seen here at Luxeuil-les-Bains: Kiffin Rockwell, Captain Georges Thénault, Norman Prince, Lieutenant Alfred de Laage de Meux, Elliot Cowdin, Bert Hall (in a black engineer's uniform), James McConnell and Victor Chapman. Thénault is holding a rolling map frame for use in an aircraft.

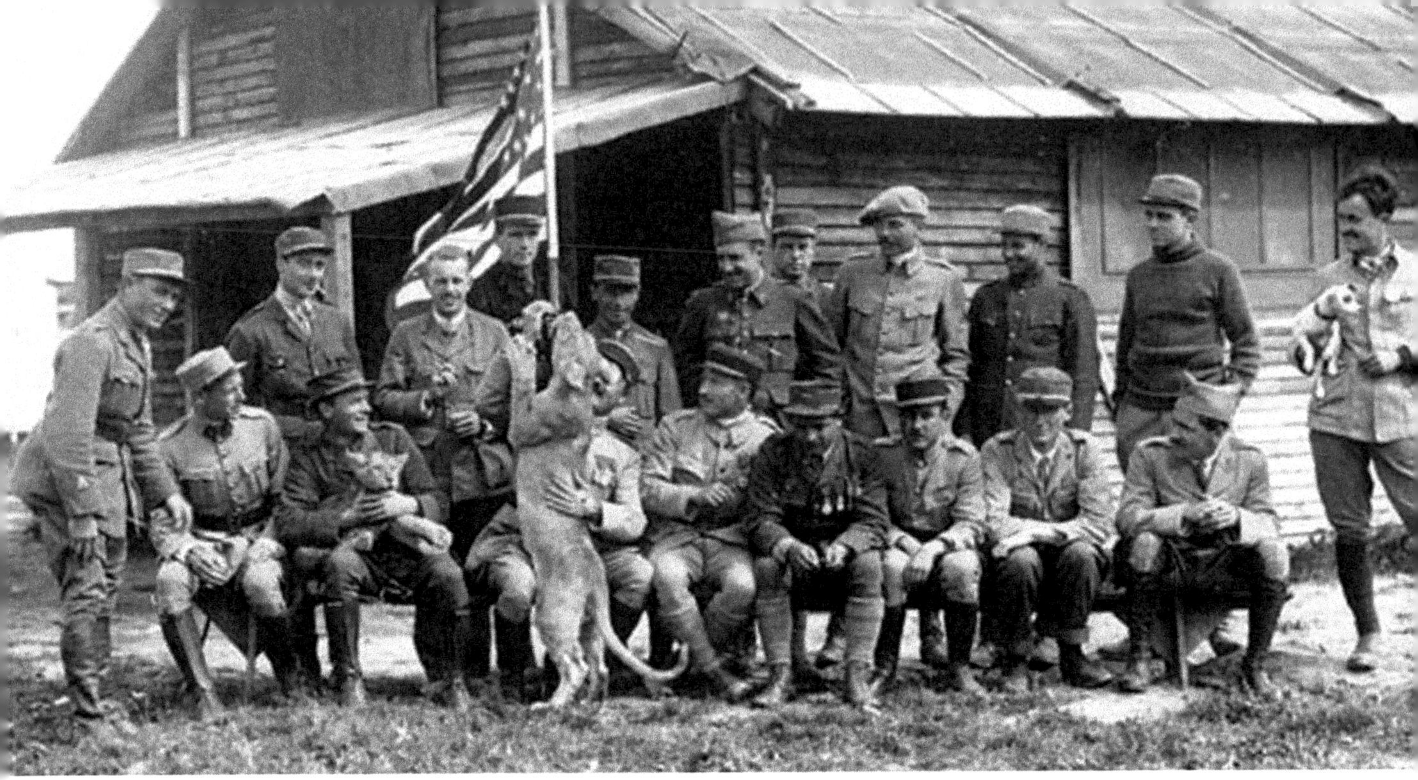

17GW590 American volunteer pilots of Flight 124 N of the *Lafayette Escadrille* at the airfield at Chaudun in July 1917. Standing from left to right: Warrant Officer Robert Soubiran; Sergent Andrew Courtney Campbell; Lieutenant Edwin Parsons; Sergent Ray Bridgeman; Sergent William Dugan; Sergent Douglas MacDonagle; Adjudant Walter Lowell; Sergent Harold Willis; Sergent Henry S Jones; Sergent David Peterson; Lieutenant Louis Verdier Fauvety; Sitting: Adjudant Dudley Hill; Adjudant Didier Masson (with Soda); Lieutenant William Thaw (with Whiskey); Captain Georges Thénault; Raoul; Lieutenant Raoul Lufbery; Warrant Officer Charles Johnson; Sergent Stephen Bigelow; Sergent Y. Kiffin Rockwell.

17GW588 Cachy airfield in October 1917, a Nieuport 17 with Lieutenant Lufbery in the cockpit. Adjudant Didier Masson holds the lion cub mascot, Whiskey. Note the markings on the aircraft: the Indian head, which had just been adopted by the squadron and three horizontal, red stripes.

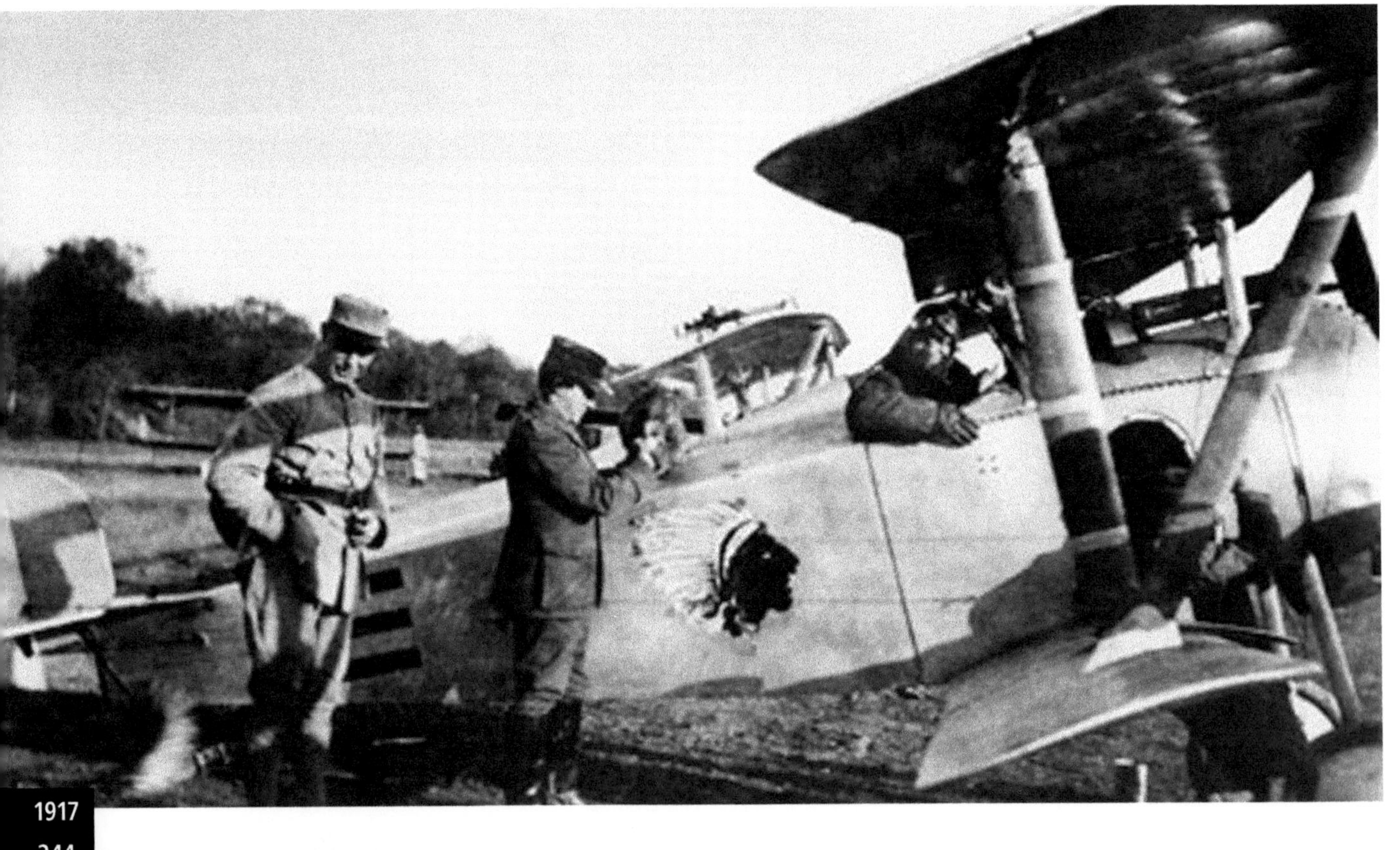

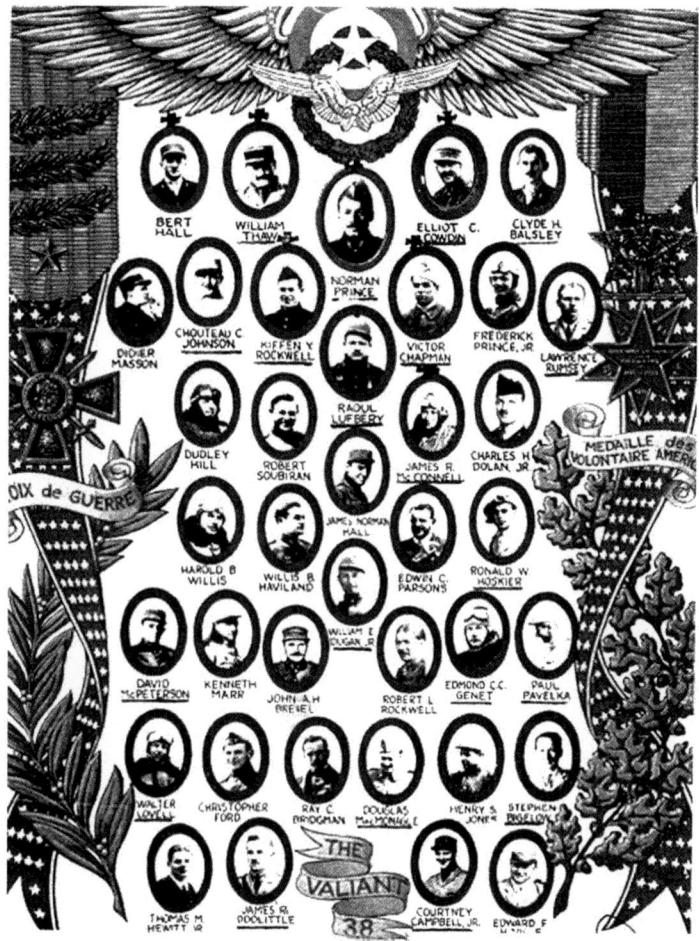

A commemoration certificate showing the 'Valiant 38' pilots of the *La Fayette* squadron 124 N / SPA 124.

17GW596 Frank Luke Jr was the second highest scorer among the American pilots, with 21 kills.

Frank Luke was an insubordinate and bitter man. He had teamed up with fellow flyer, Joseph Fritz Wehner, who was unjustly suspected of having German sympathies and of being anti-American. Wehner died fighting the Germans – shot down by a Fokker. Frank Luke took the loss of his friend deeply. When he again teamed up with another flyer, Ivan Roberts, that duo ended with Roberts being shot down and killed. Depressed, Luke twice took off without permission and his CO finally grounded him. Furious, Luke jumped into his Spad and headed for the front. The order was given for him to be arrested on landing. Flying over the American balloon headquarters at Souilly, he dropped a note which read: *Watch three Hun balloons on the Meuse,... Luke*. These were heavily defended targets and after sending the first one down in flames he was seriously wounded at his second target at Briere Farm. Undaunted, Luke carried on to his third balloon and sent it down in flames. Not content with this success he strafed German troops in the village of Murvaux. However, badly wounded he had to land and he was immediately surrounded by German soldiers demanding his surrender, but Luke was not quite finished and blazed away at them with his revolver. The return fire finally killed him. For three months he was listed as 'missing in action'.

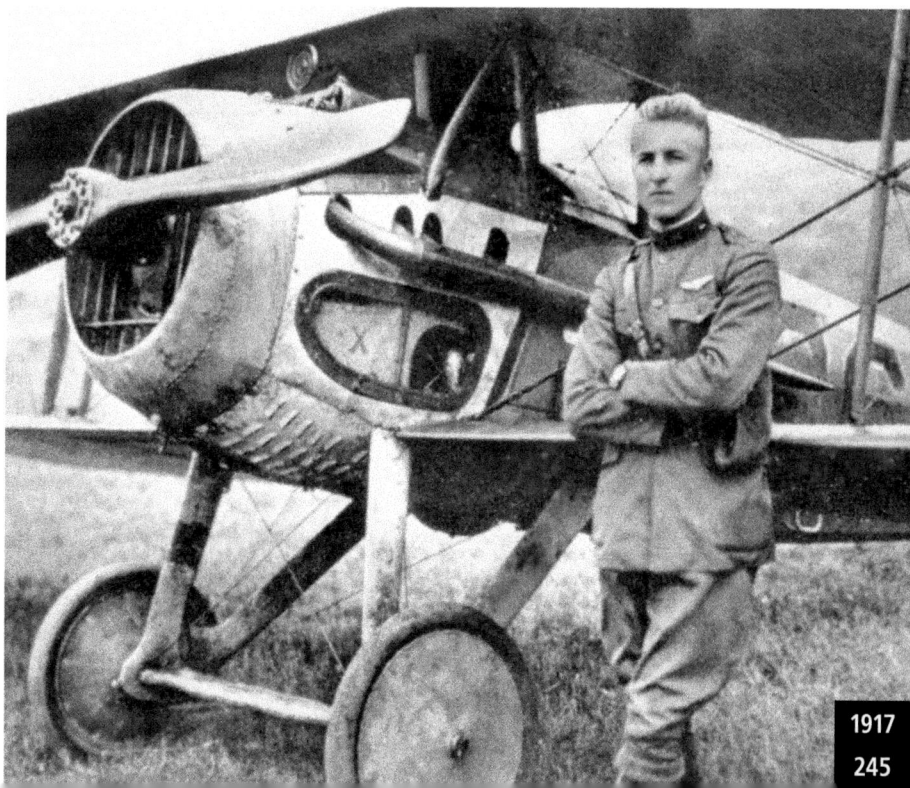

1917
245

17GW575 Edward Vernon Rickenbacker in 1917. When the United States declared war on Germany Rickenbacker enlisted in the United States Army and was soon training in France with some of the first American troops. He arrived in France on June 26 1917, as a sergeant first class. On April 29 1918, he shot down his first plane. On May 28, he claimed his fifth to become an ace. Rickenbacker was awarded the French Croix de Guerre that month for his five kills. He ended the war as the leading American ace, with 26 kills.

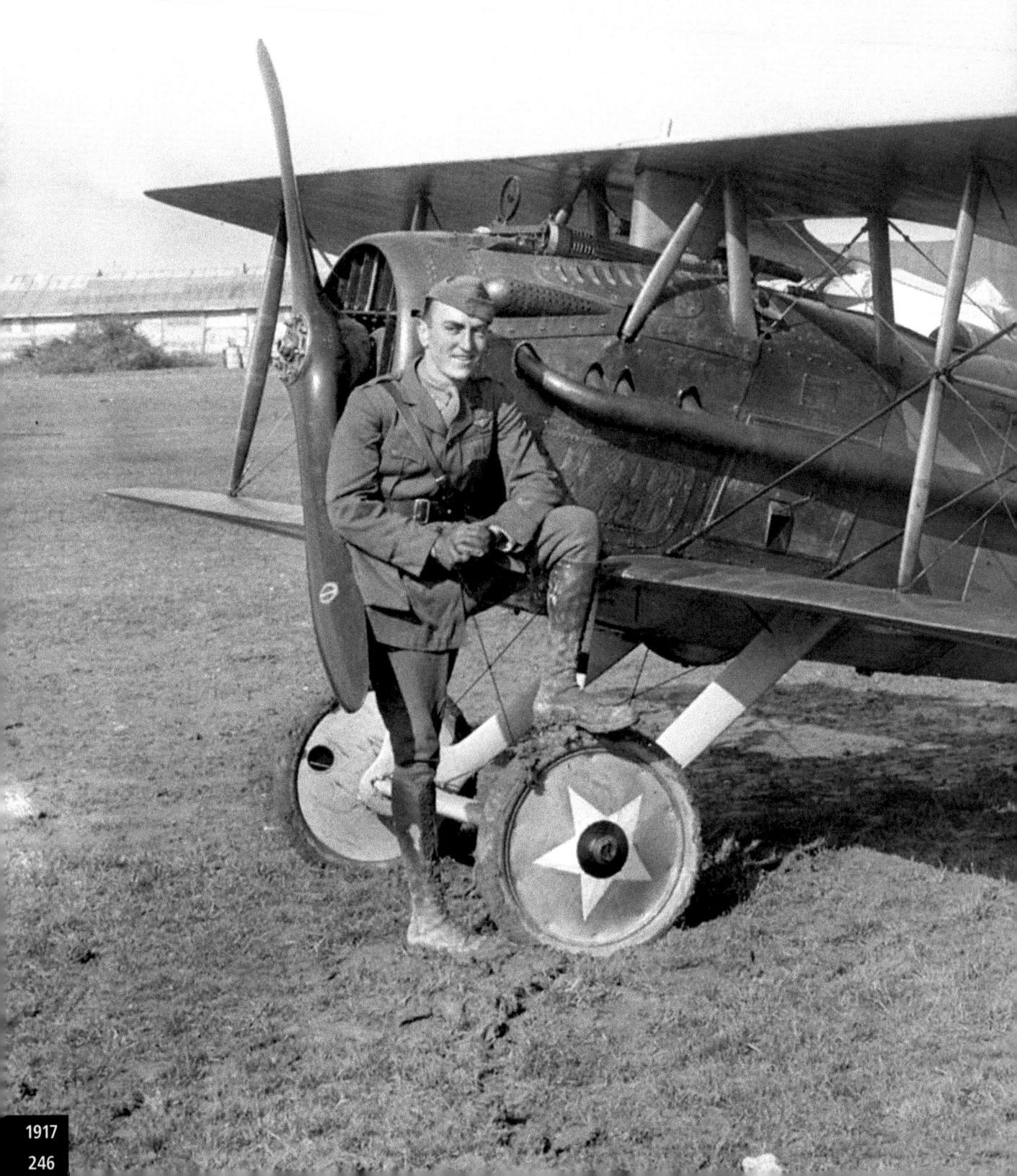

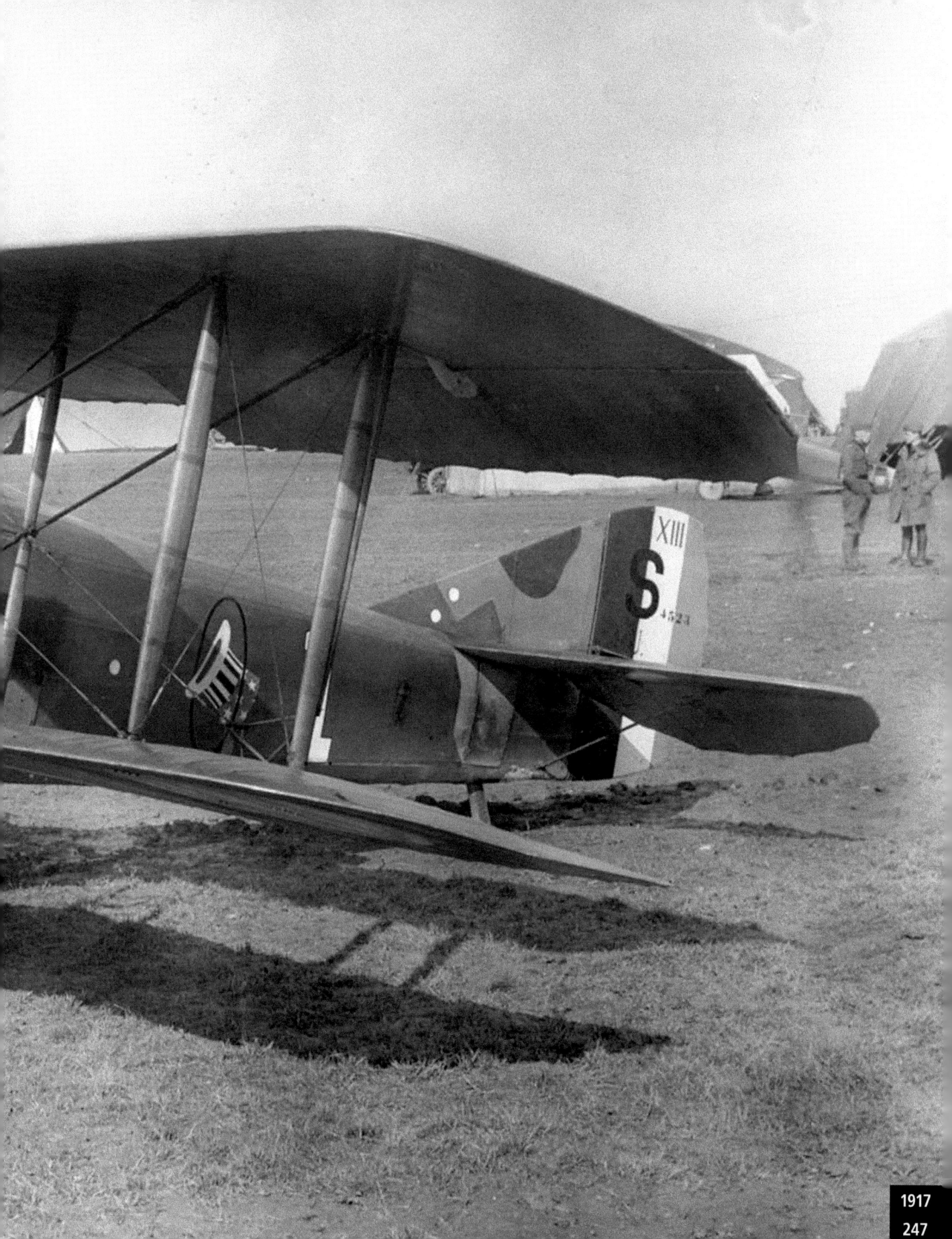

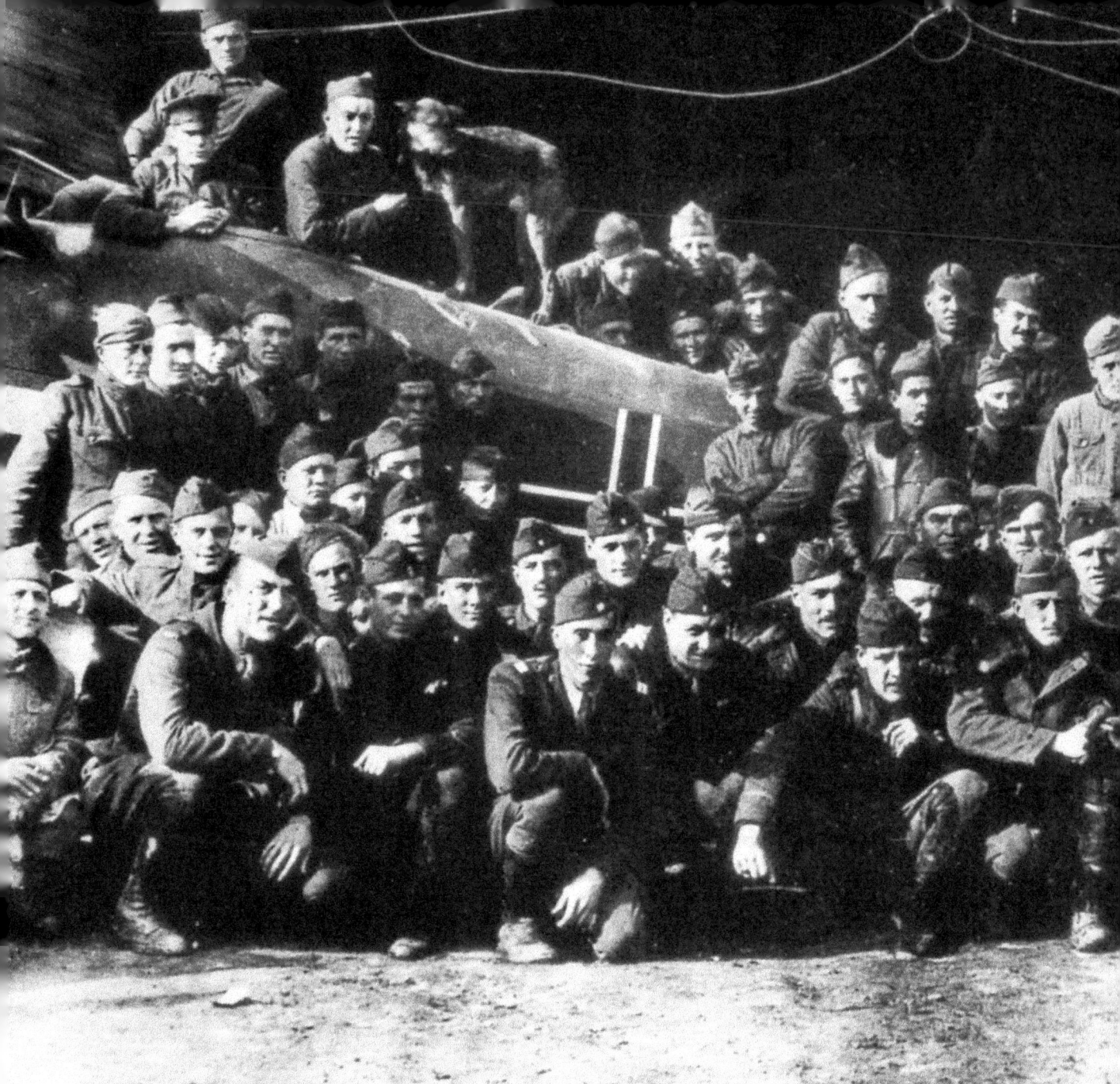

17GW595 American ace 1st Lieutenant Rickenbacker forced a German Hannover C two seater down in October 1918. With the Great War having just weeks to run, pilots of the 94th Aero Squadron, American Force, gather in front of the German machine for a squadron picture shoot. Rickenbacker is kneeling in the front row, second from the left.

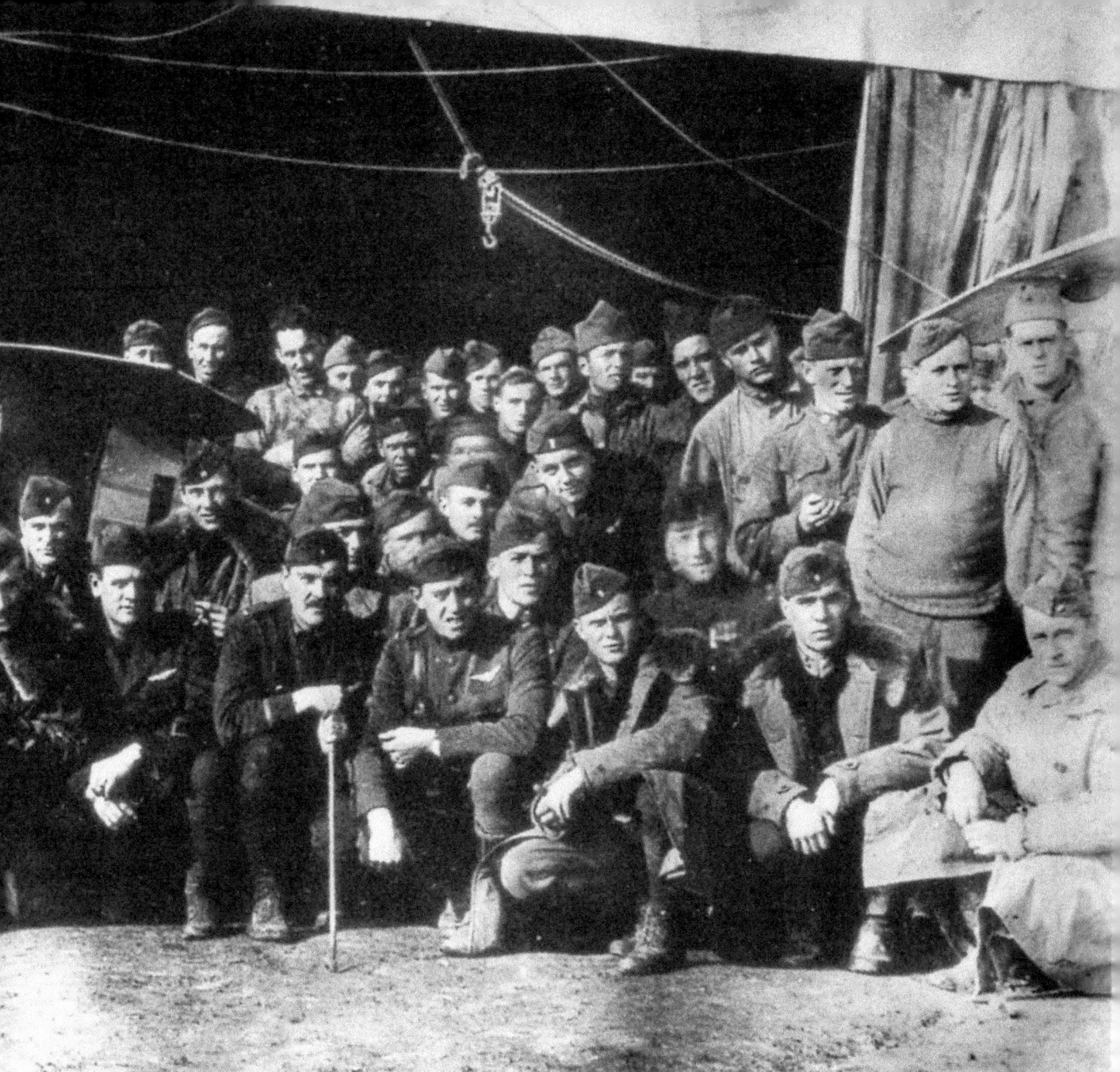

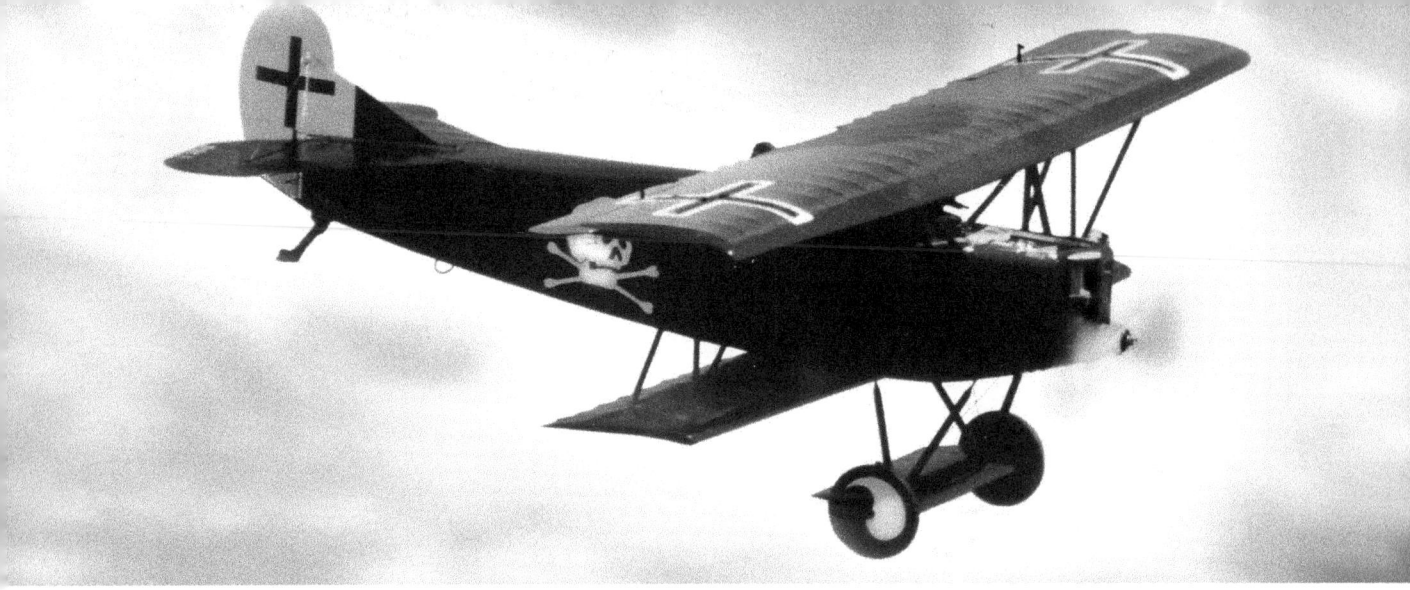

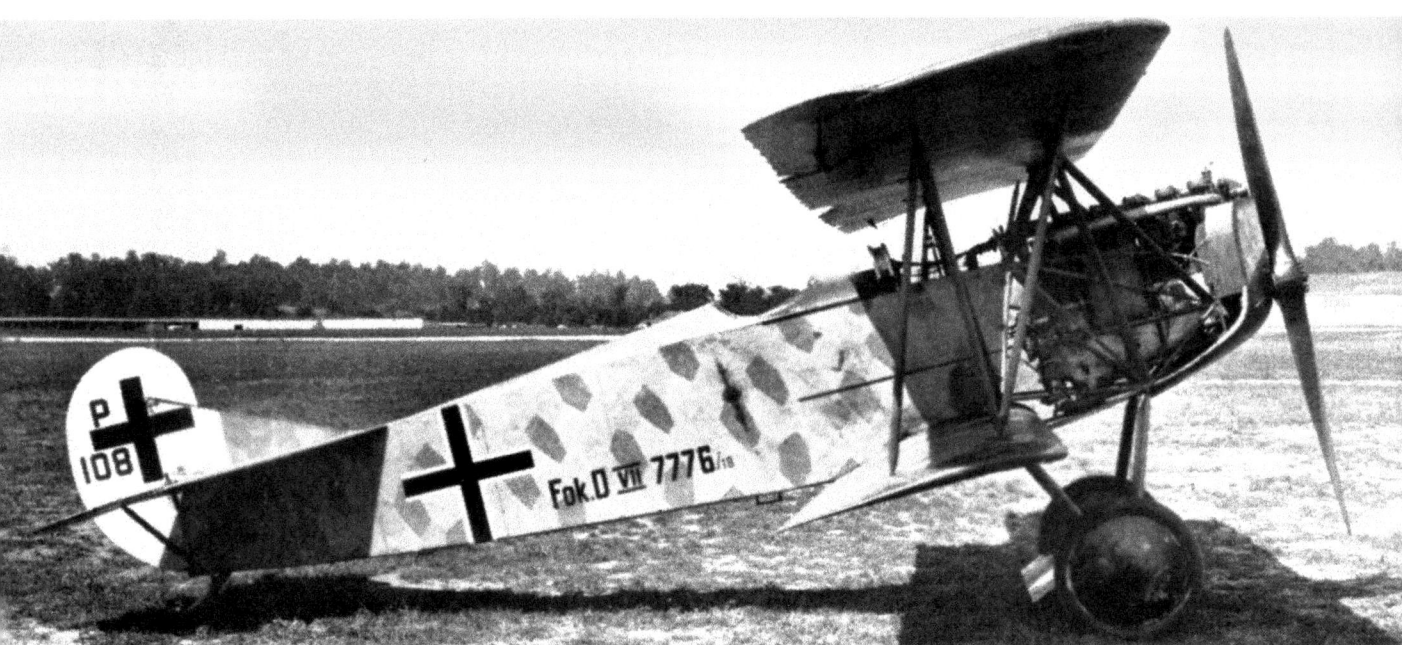

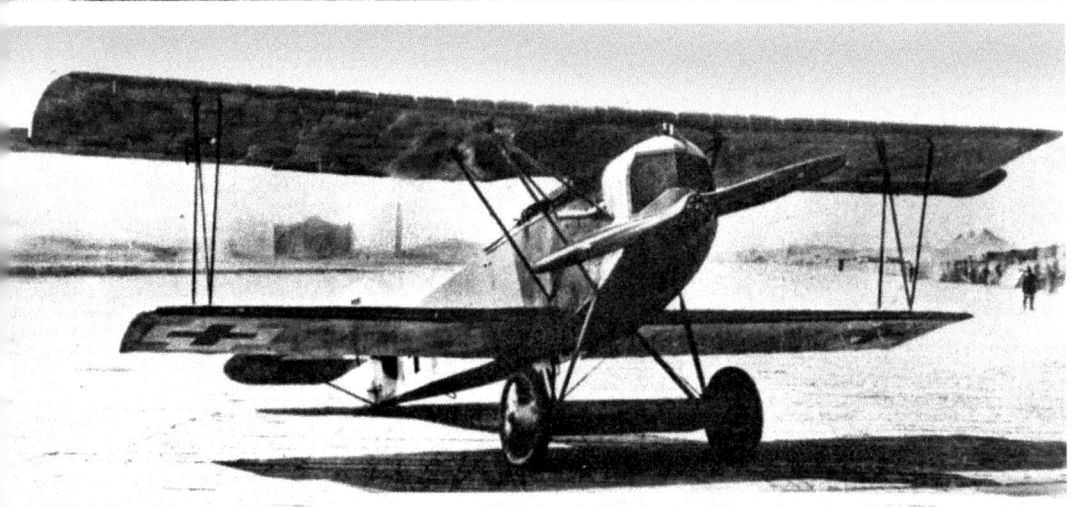

17GW332, 17GW597, 17GW598. Fokker DVII with 170 hp Mercedes engine. The machine, marked with the American USAS number P.108 on the rudder, was taken to the United States for study and evaluation. This design by Fokker represented the peak of fighter design achievemen during the final seven months of the war.

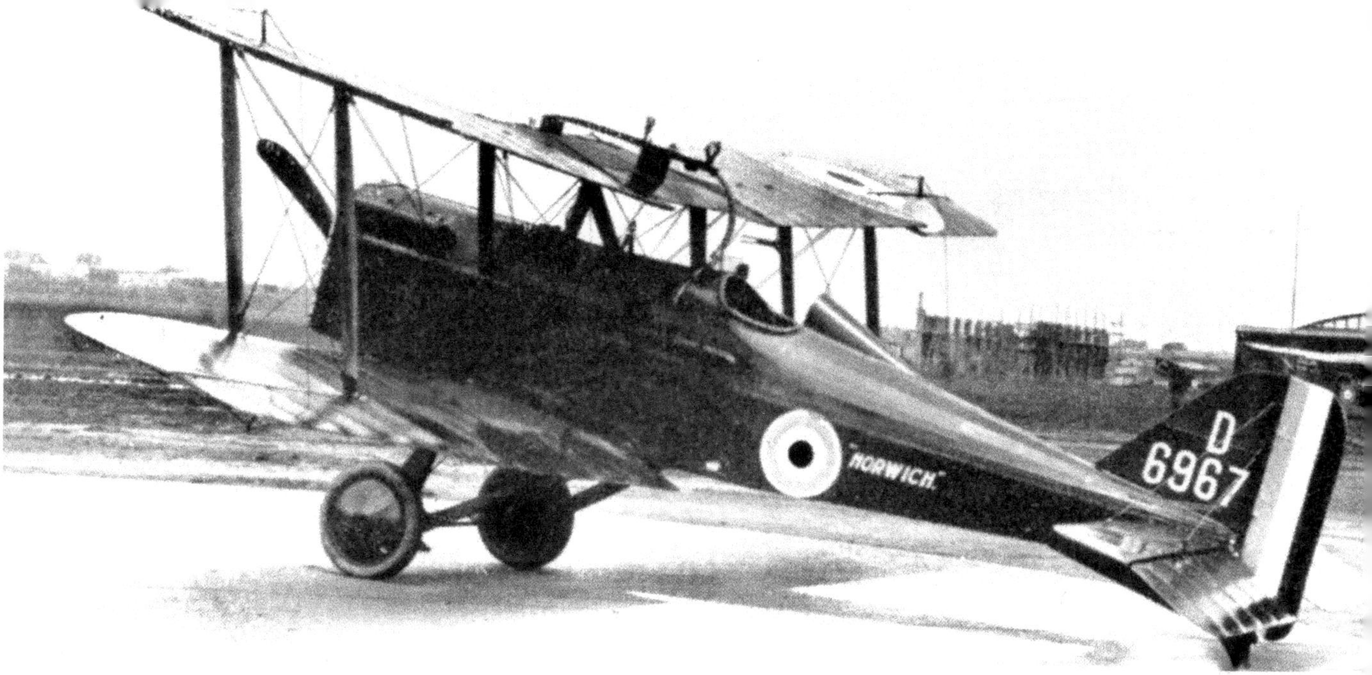

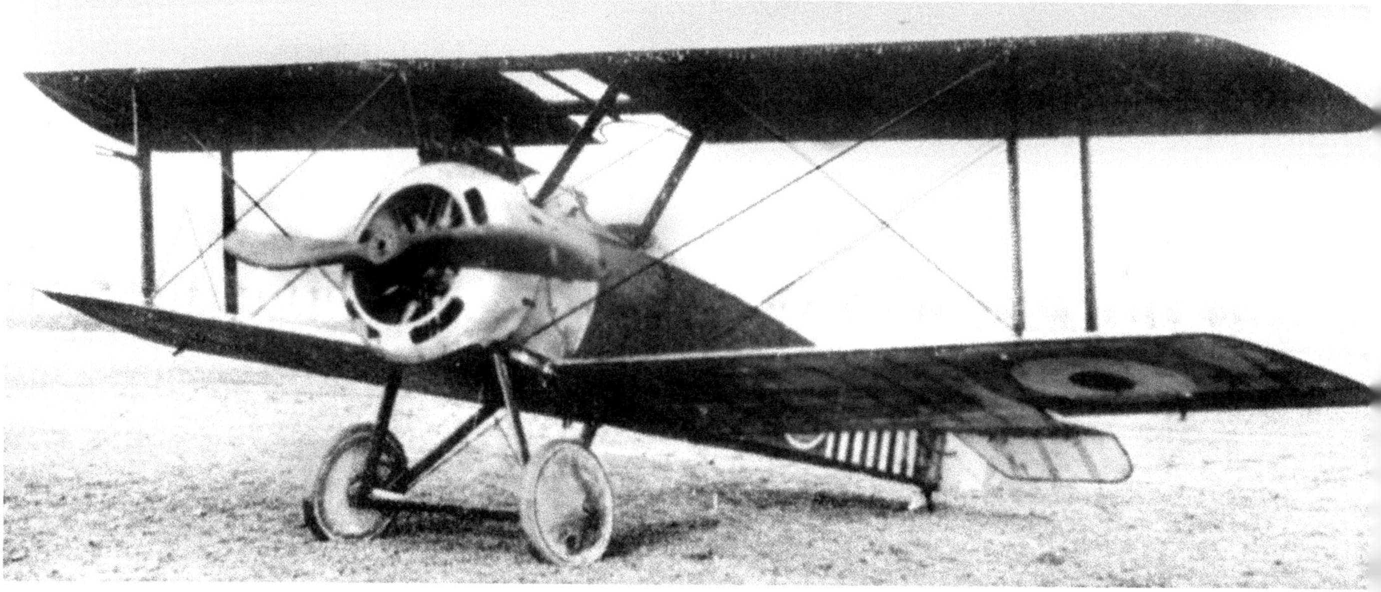

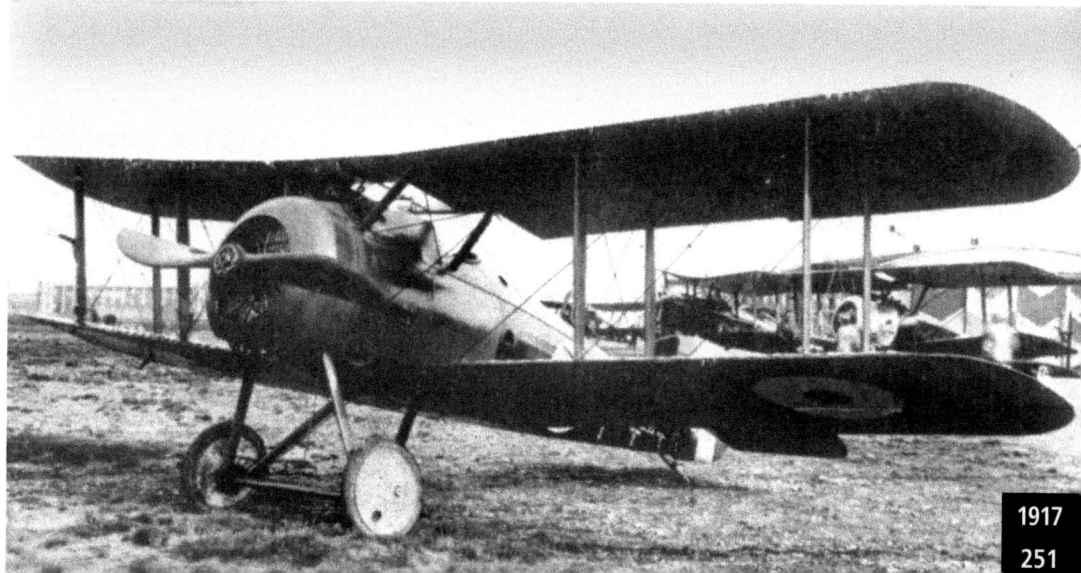

17GW599, 17GW600, 17GW601. Three British fighter aircraft developments by the end of the war, the SE.5, the Sopwith Camel; and the Sopwith Snipe.

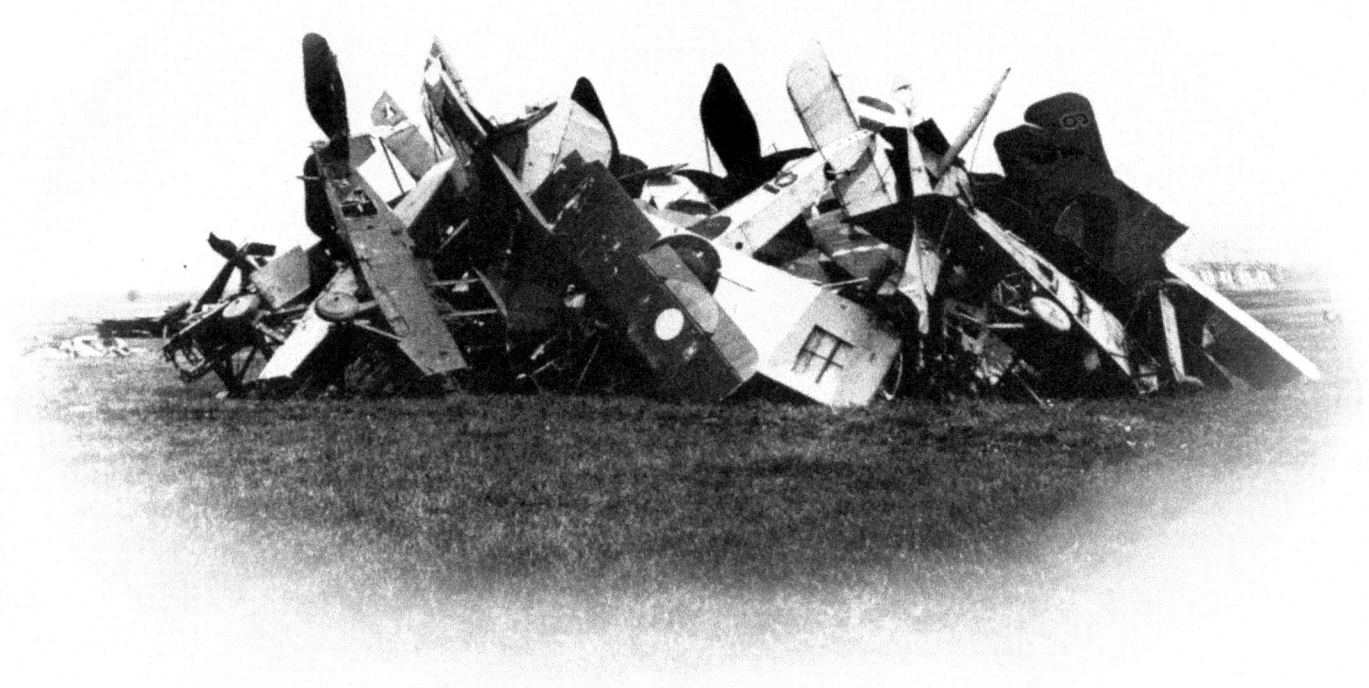

17GW467 Allied aircraft junked after the war.

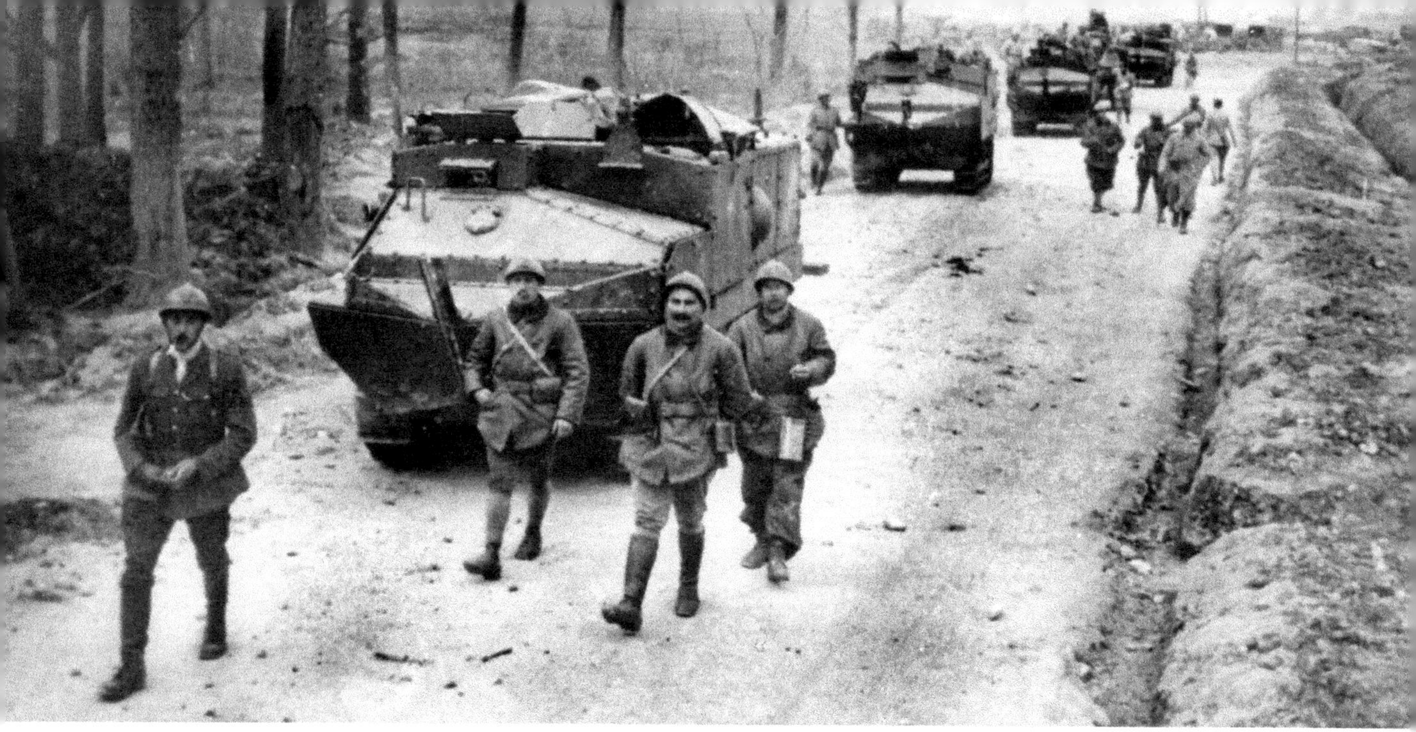

Chapter Four: The Nivelle Failure – French Army Revolt

17GW663 A battery of four Schneider tanks on its way to the Aisne. Four batteries made up a squadron of sixteen tractor machines.

17GW604 German machine gunners watching the French lines from a position on the Chemin des Dames.

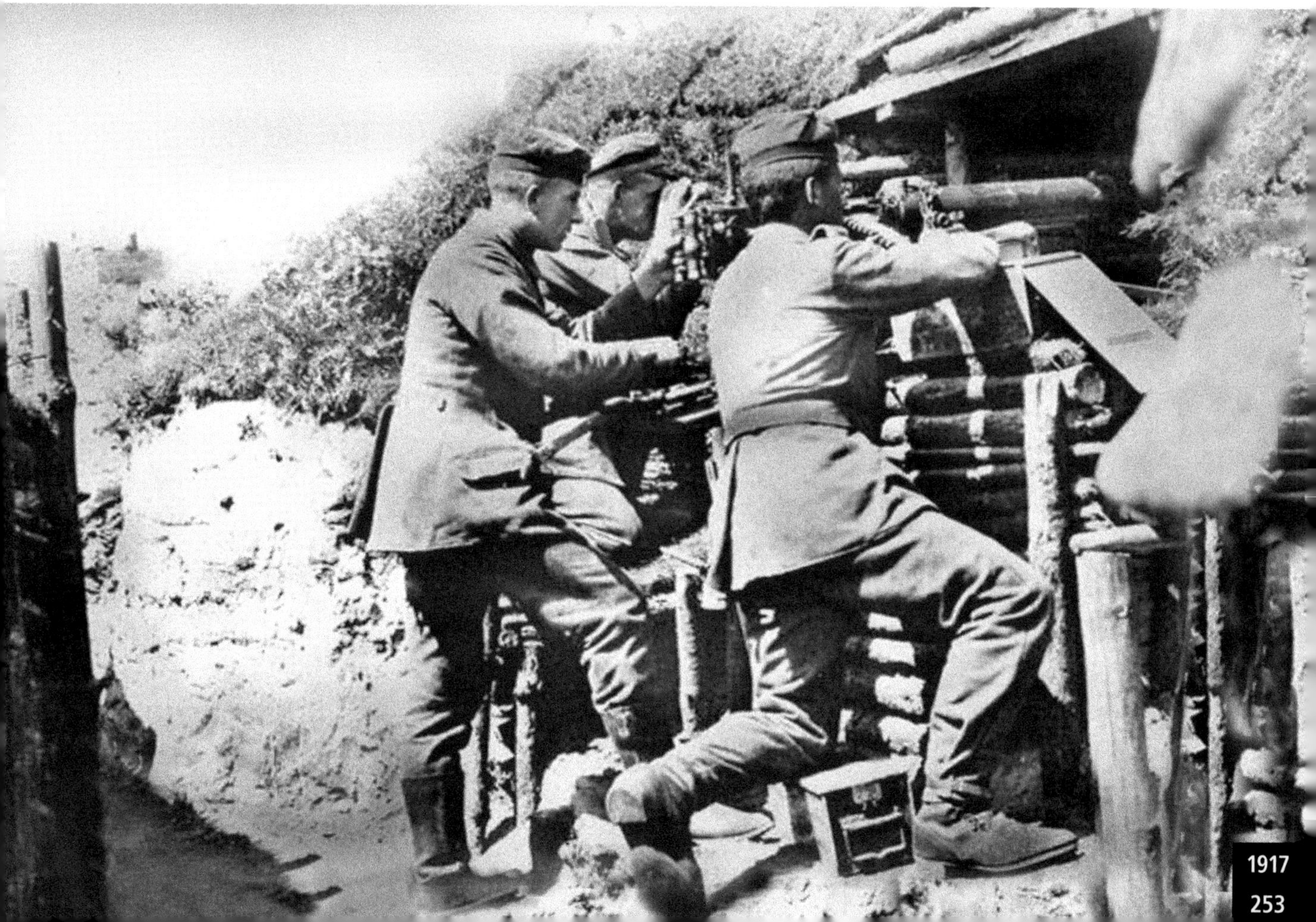

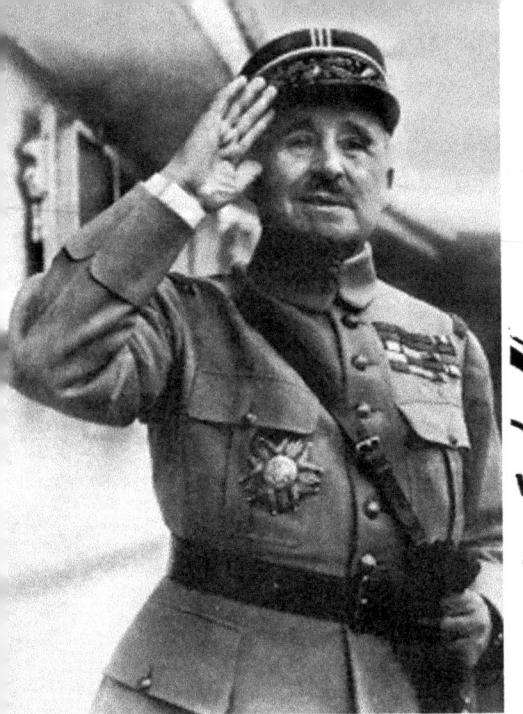

General Robert Nivelle

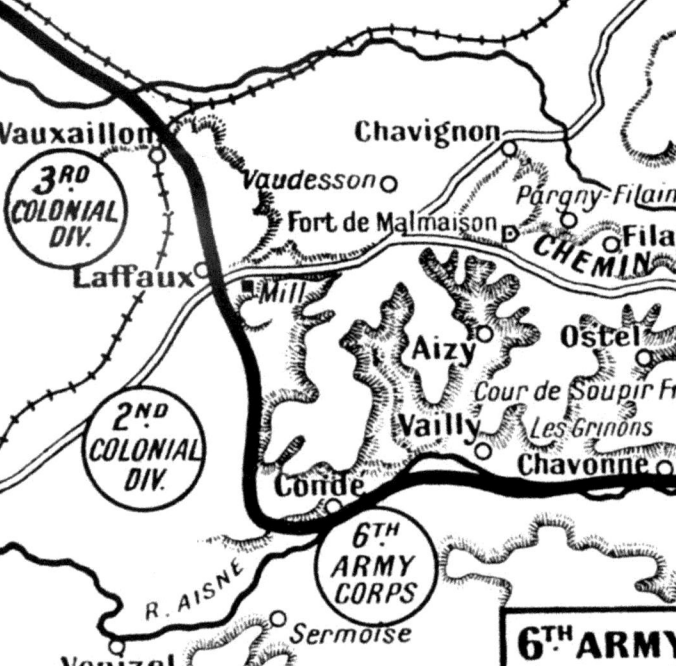

'We have the formula…Victory is certain'

The objective of the French attack on the Aisne was first to capture the prominent fifty miles long ridge of the Chemin des Dames Ridge, which had been quarried for stone for centuries. The area was a warren of caves and tunnels that were used as shelters from the French bombardments. Then they were to attack northwards to capture the city of Laon. Once they met up with the British advancing from the Arras front, the Germans would be pursued towards Belgium and the German frontier.

Nivelle's grand offensive began on 16 April, a week after the British attacked at Arras.

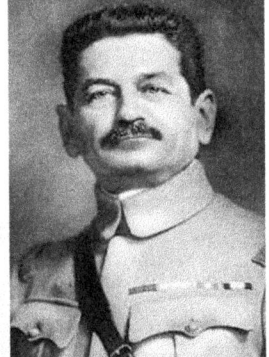

'Quoi qu'on fasse, on perd beaucoup de monde' (Whatever you do, you lose a lot of men).

General Charles Mangin

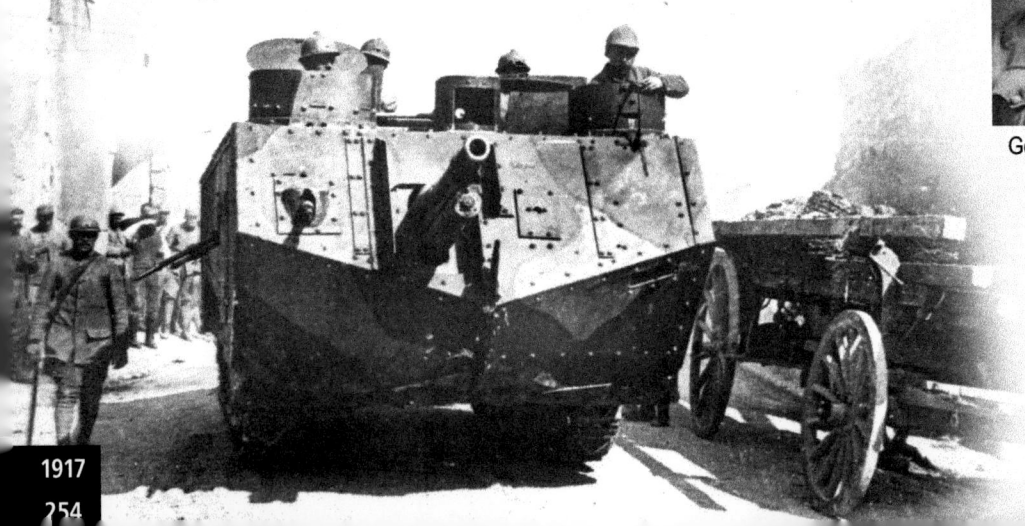

17GW690 A Saint-Chamond tank; sixteen of this type went into action for the first time at Laffaux Mill, 5 May 1917. The long bodies, with a lot of the vehicle extending forward of the short caterpillar tracks, made them liable to ditching in the trenches and cratered ground of the Chemin der Dames.

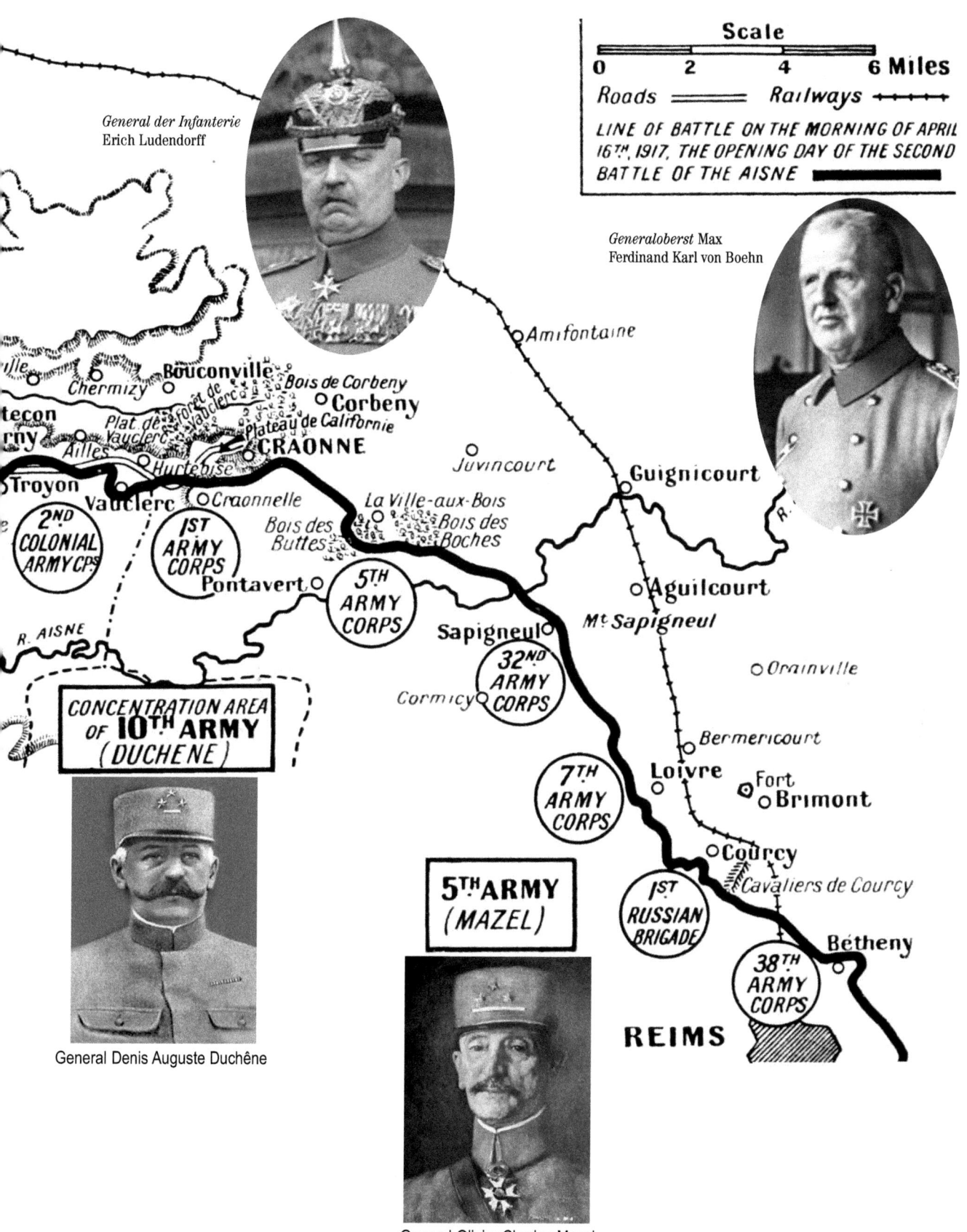

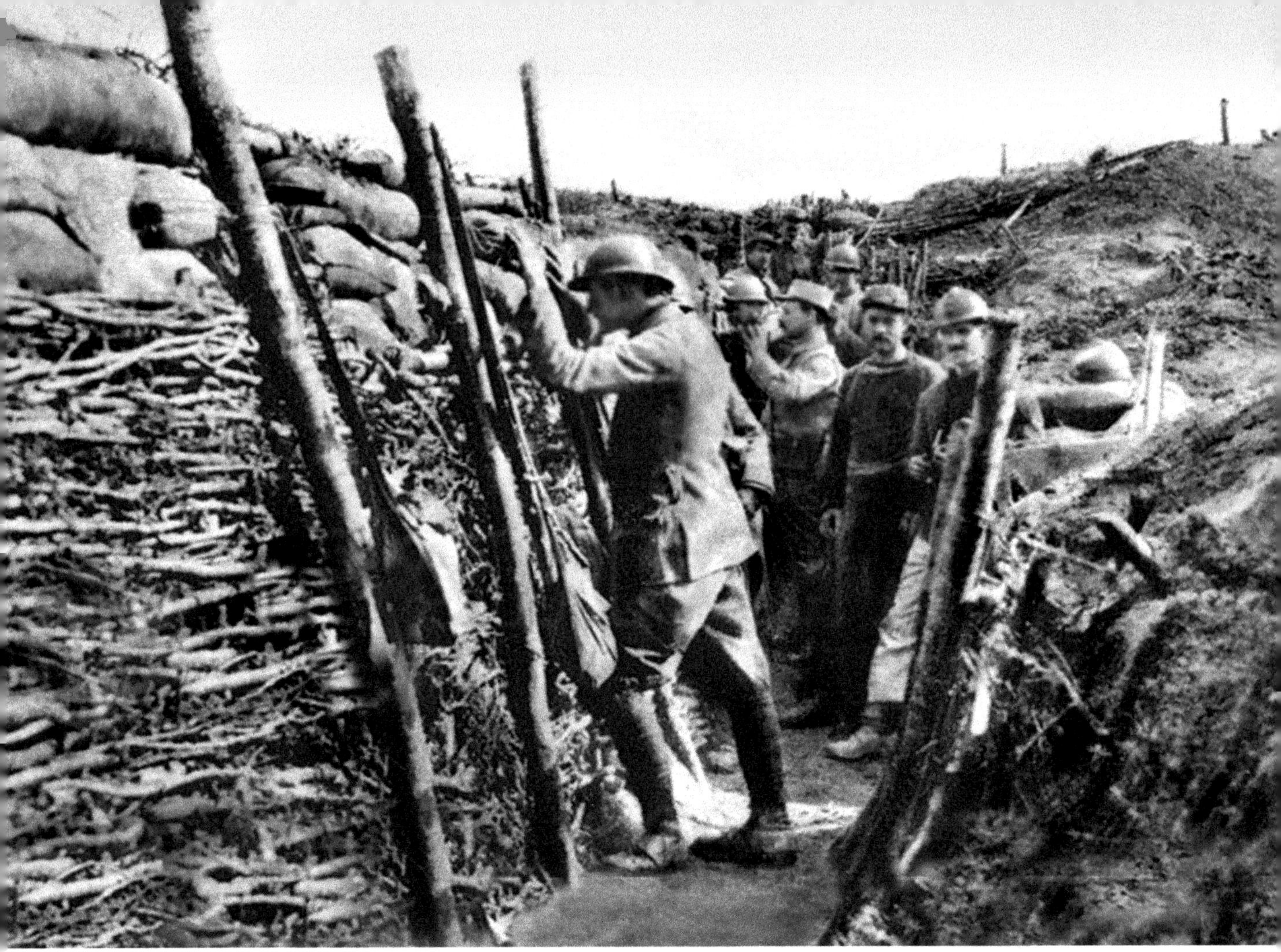

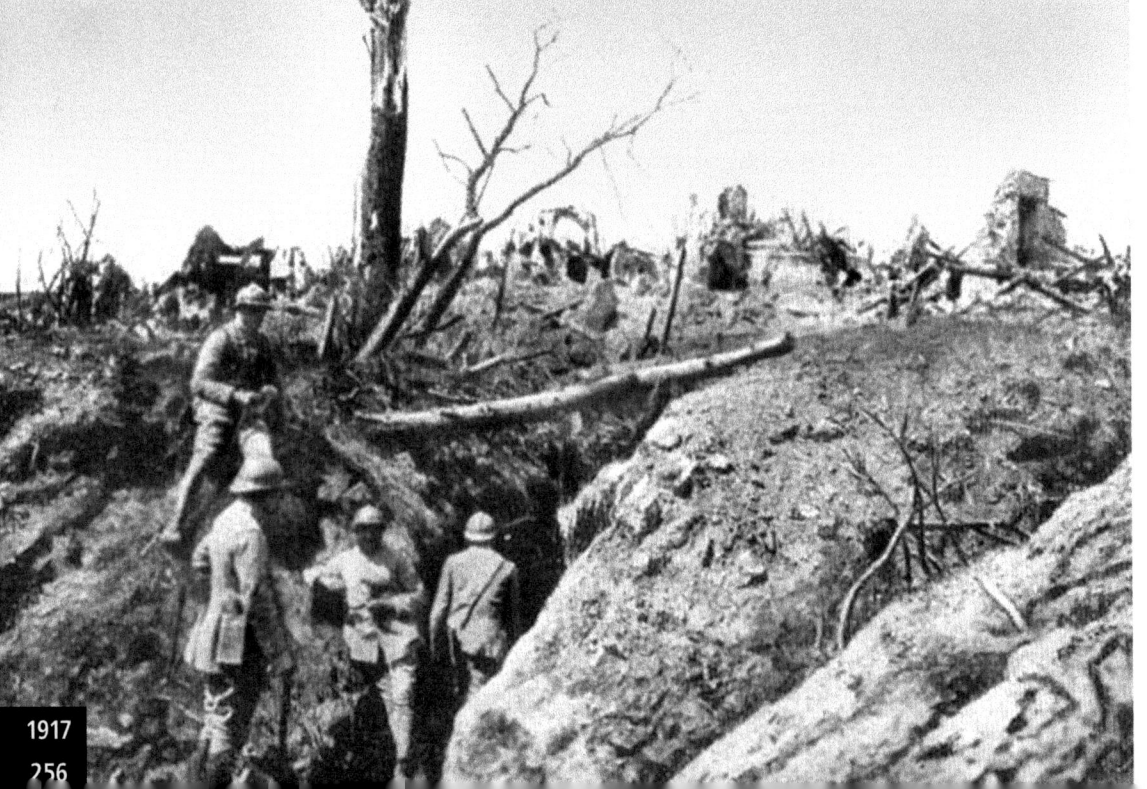

17GW612, 17GW613. Upwards of a million French infantry and supporting artillery gathered between Soissons in the west and Reims in the east. Seen here, in the centre of the line, men of the 1st Army Corps have the village of Craonne and the plateau of Californie as their immediate objectives. At 6 am on 16 April they would attack the German positions.

17GW616 A soldier of the Prussian Guard prepares for the coming attack at Chemin des Dames. The date, time and place were common knowledge both to French civilians in Paris and the German High Command.

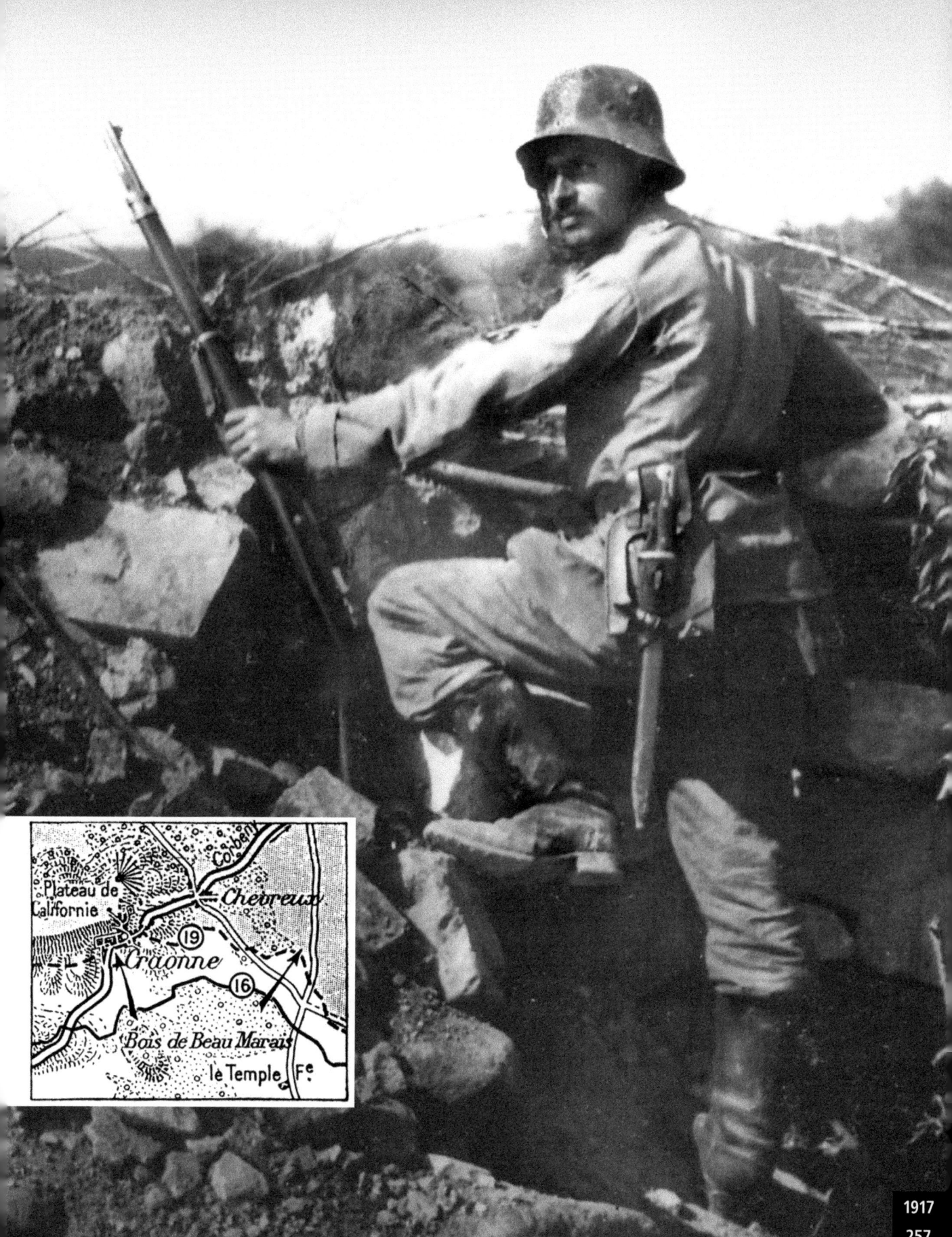

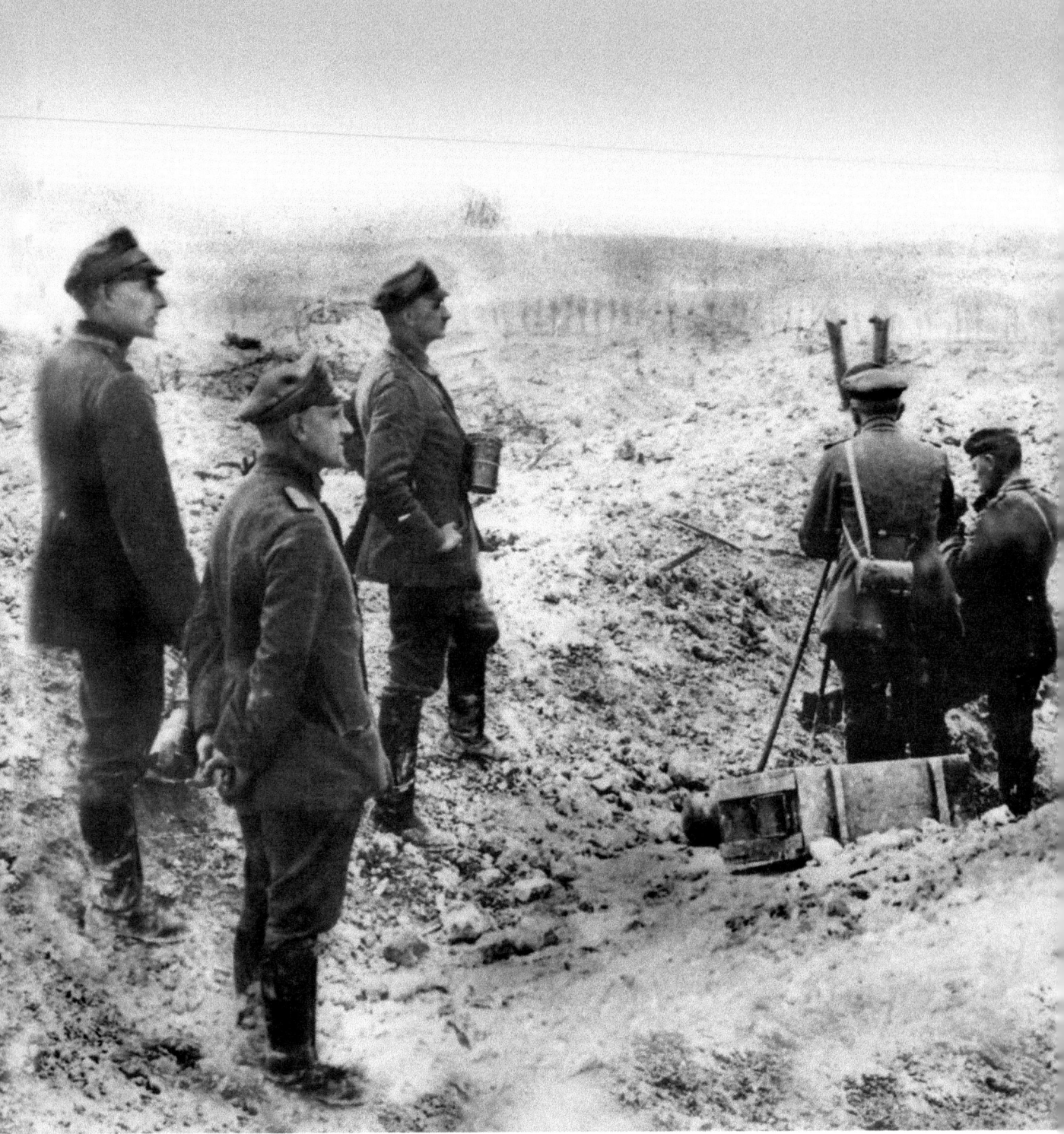

17GW617 German artillery officers ranging on French batteries preparing for the well advertised Nivelle Offensive. The position of the German heavy guns and *Beobachtungstand* (observation posts – OPs) on the high ground gave the defenders an enormous advantage.

17GW618 A very large calibre gun – probably 300 mm – being loaded from a shell carriage by six men.

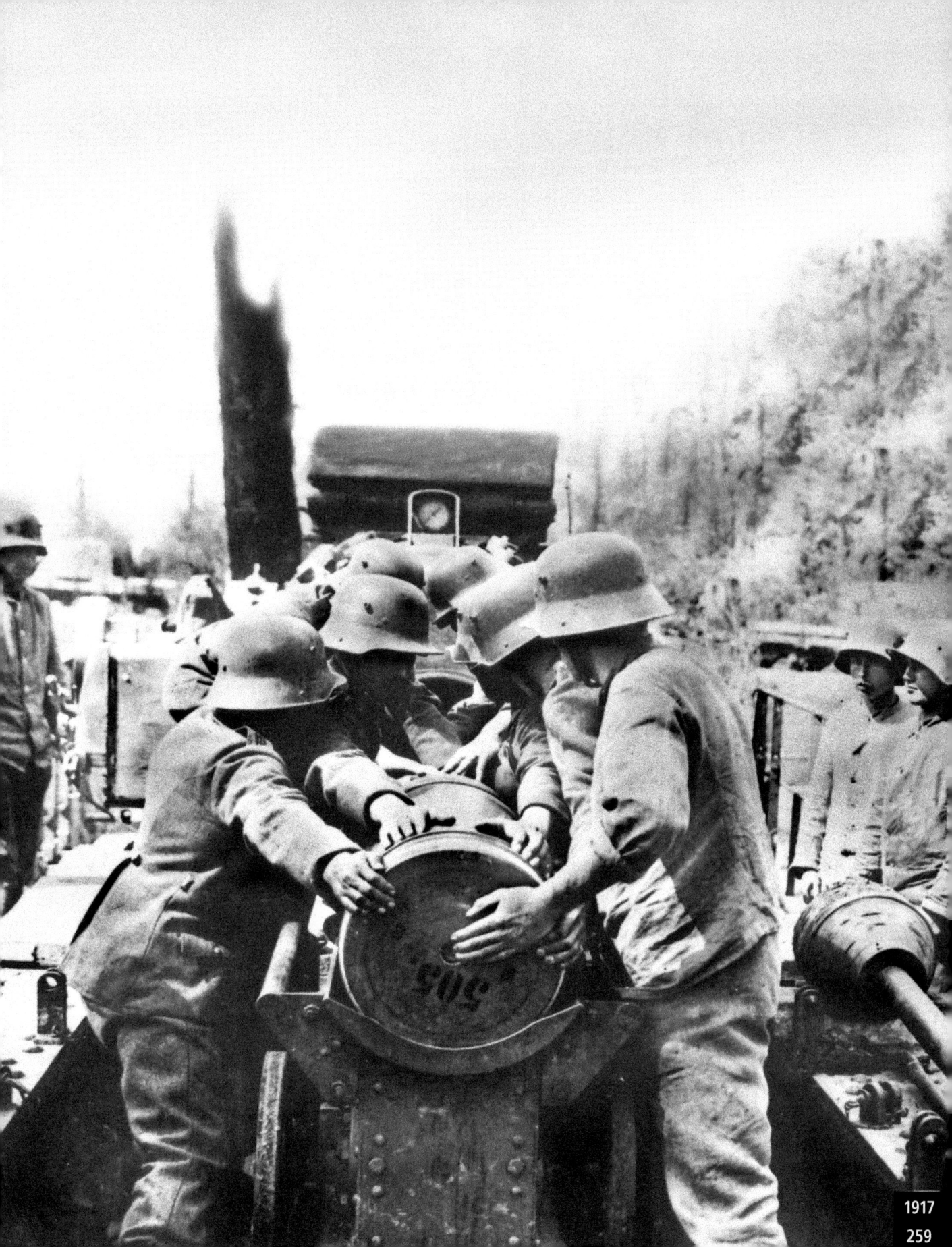

17GW619 French infantry awaiting the order to go.

Once out of the trenches, the attacking infantry were to advance 'in four bounds', covering 100 meters in three minutes: despite carrying thirty kilos of equipment; despite covering ground that had been smashed up by eight days' bombardment; under constant fire from German machine guns and a deluge of shells of all calibres.

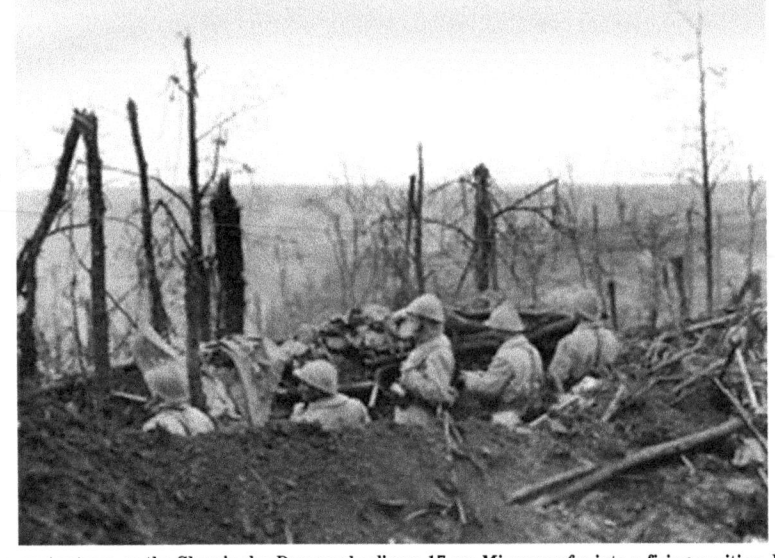
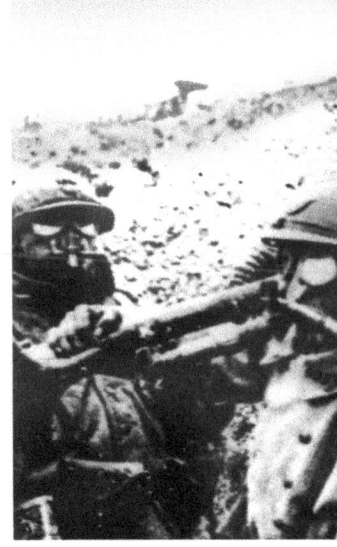

17GW625, 17GW626. German mortar team on the Chemin des Dames wheeling a 17 cm *Minenwerfer* into a firing position. It was capable of firing both high explosives and gas shells.

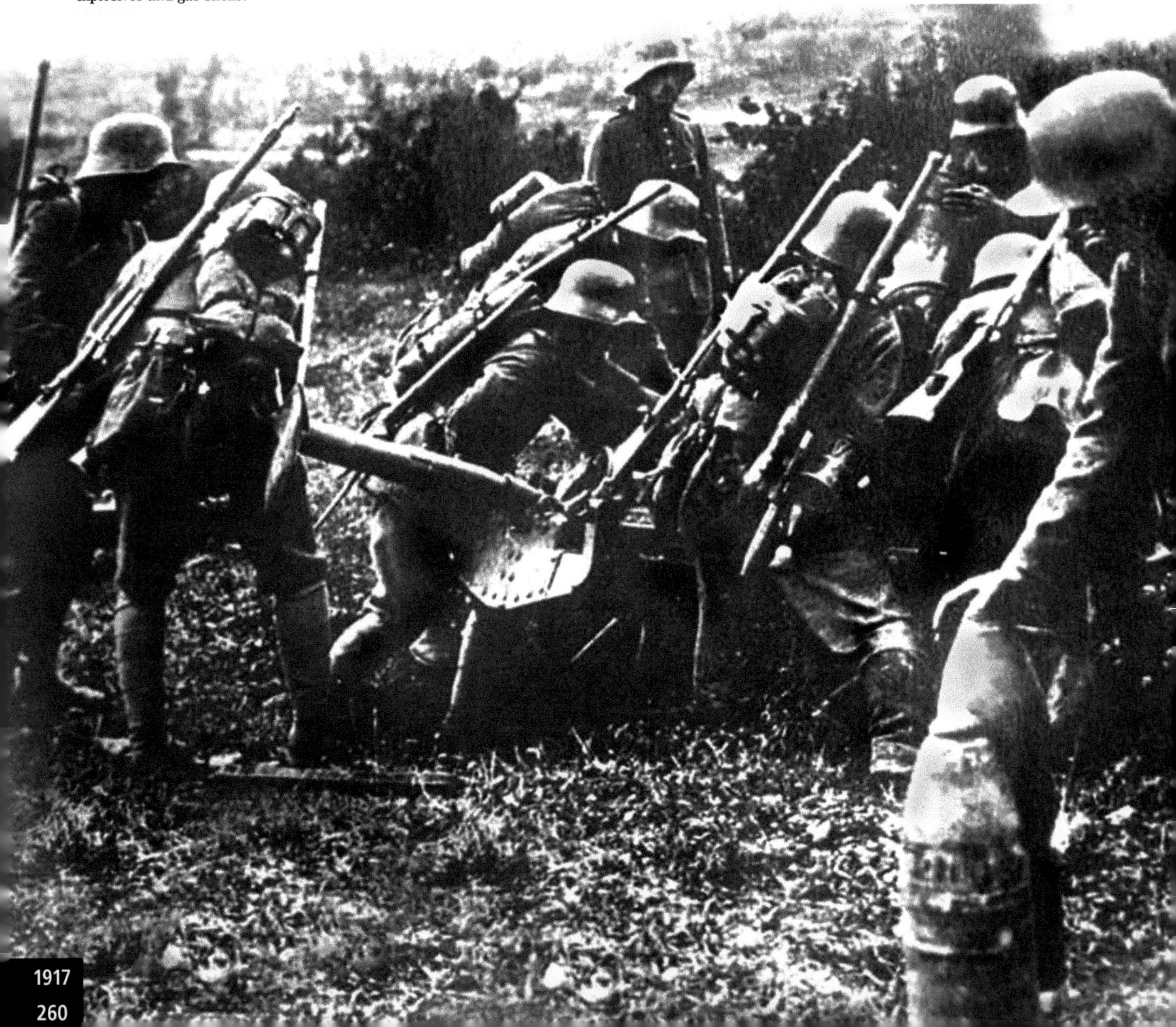

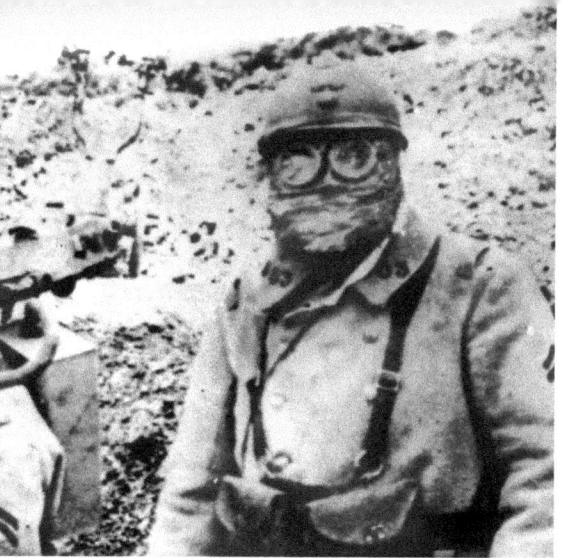
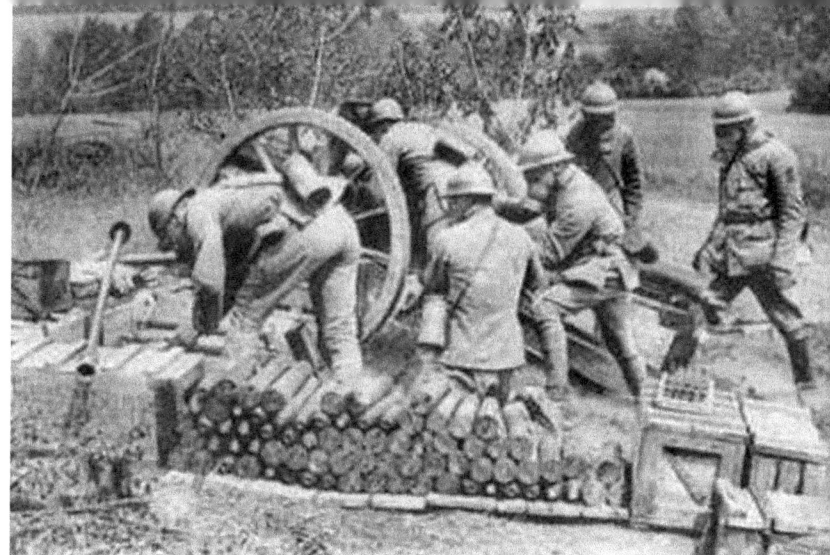

17GW621, 17GW620. A French machine gun crew forced to wear gas masks and a 75 mm gun crew working their gun in gas masks. This was a deliberate ploy by the Germans to shell French positions with gas to impede the operations of those giving covering fire during the Nivelle Offensive.

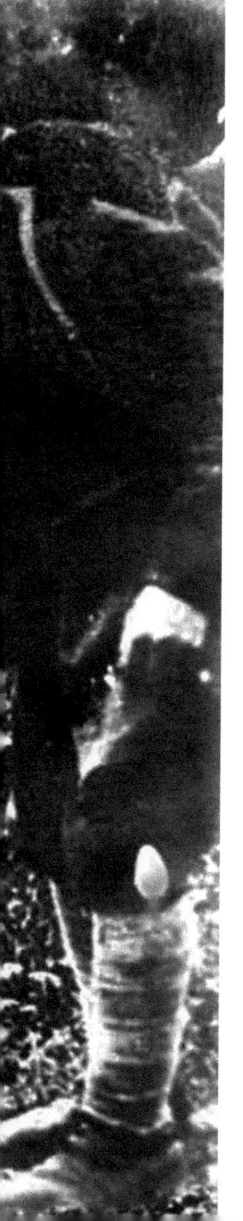

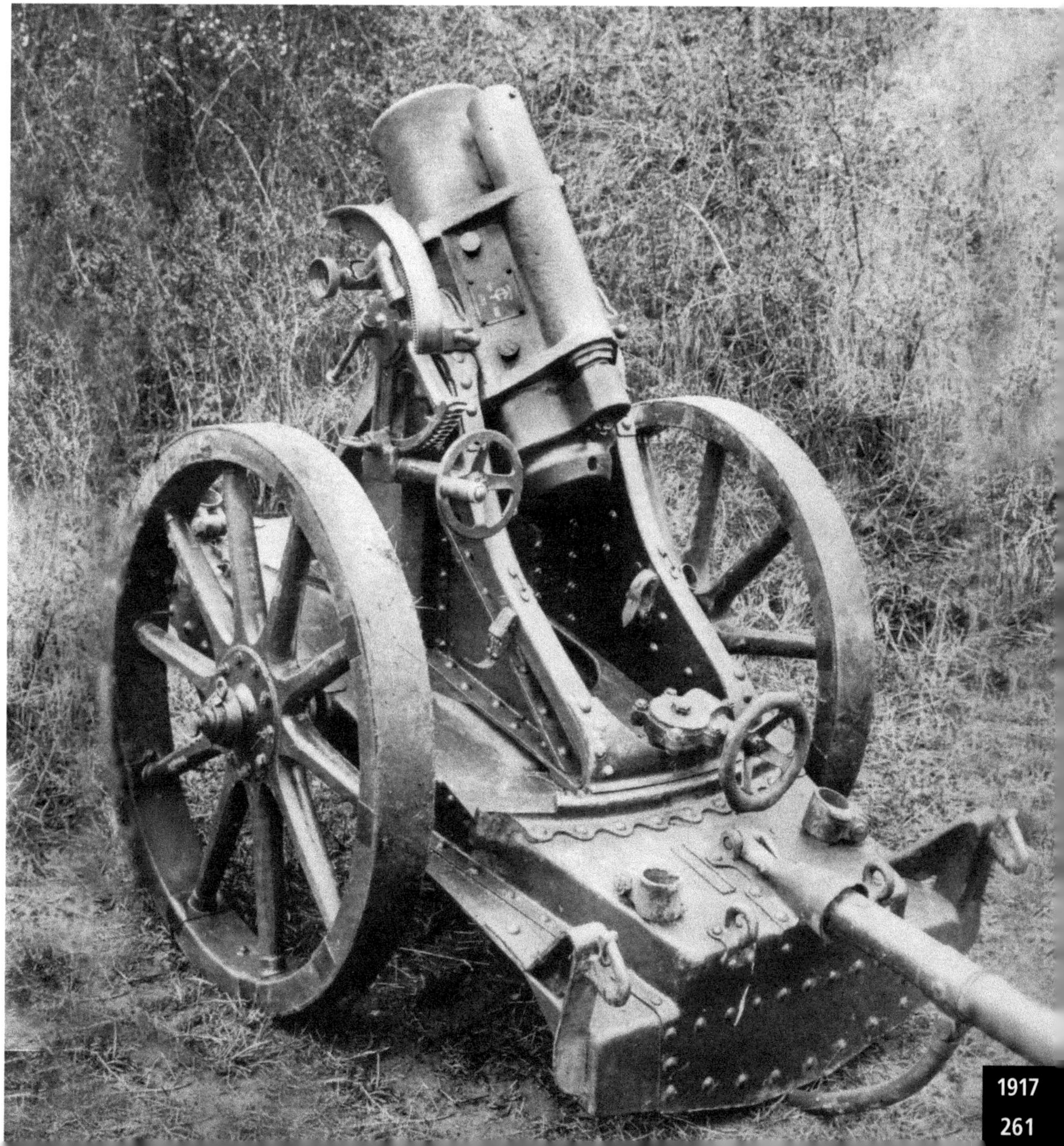

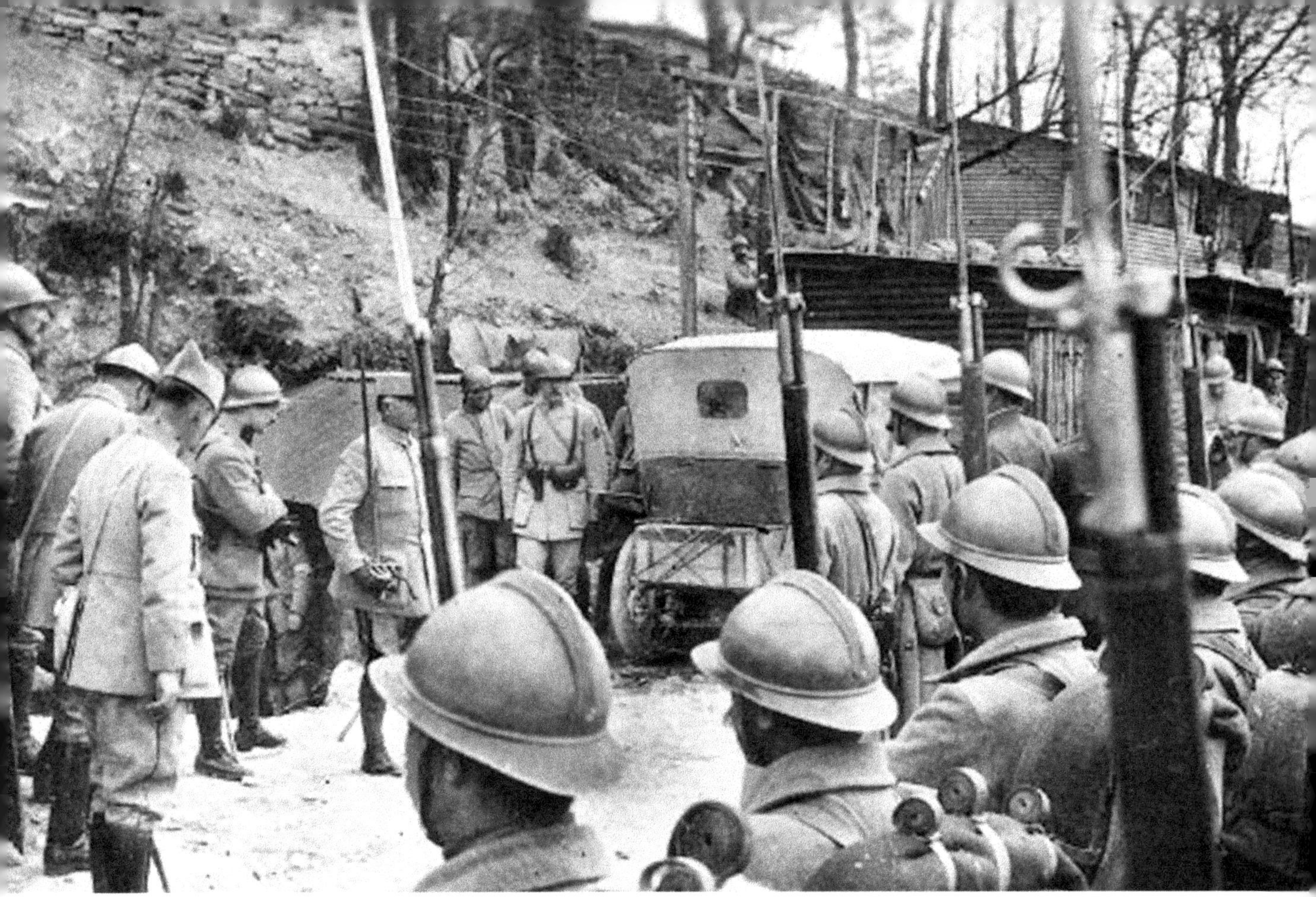

17GW633 A bogged down obsolescent artillery piece. Many of these older weapons were replaced by the Schneider 155 mm gun by April 1917. All kinds of artillery pieces were pressed into service for the Nivelle attack.

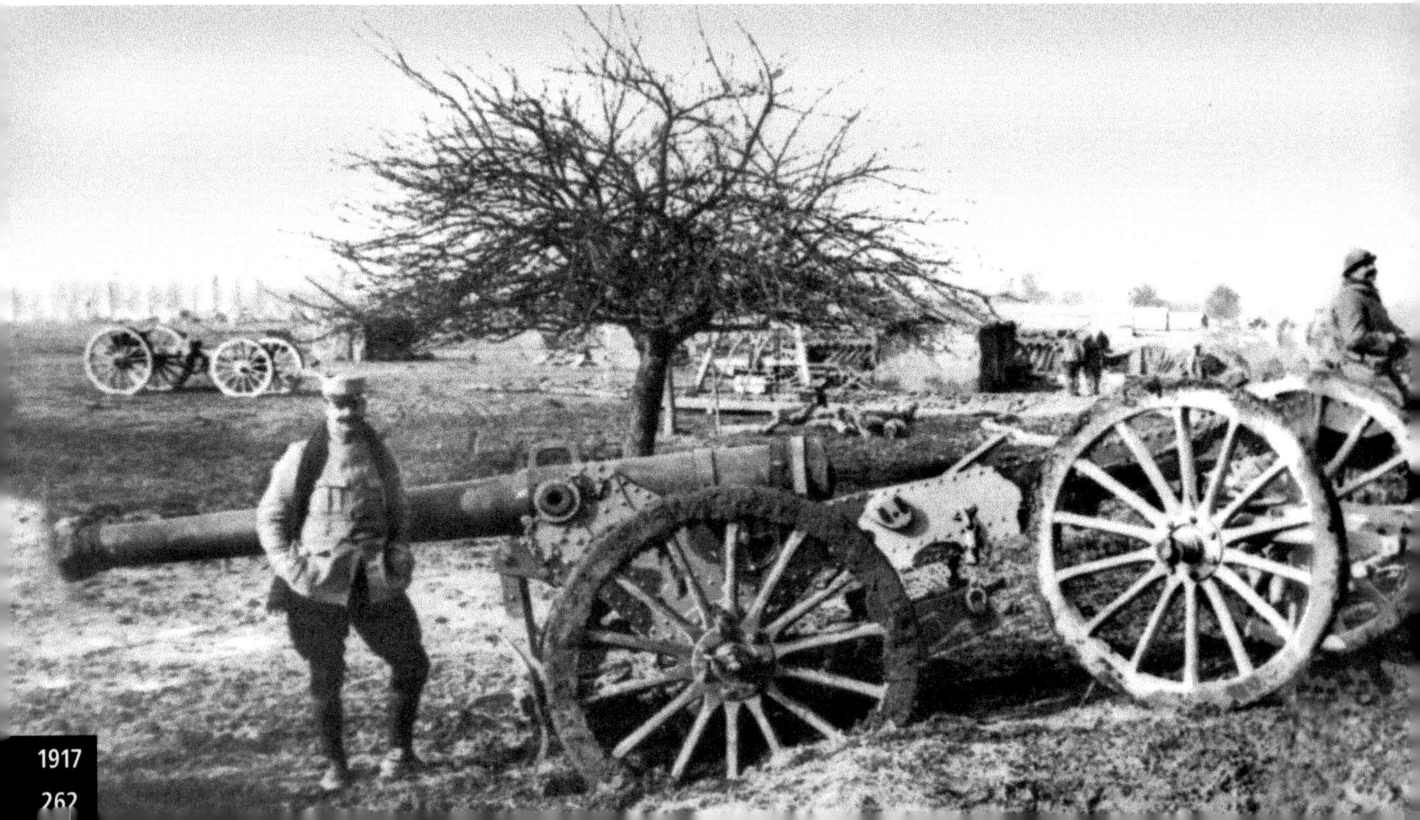

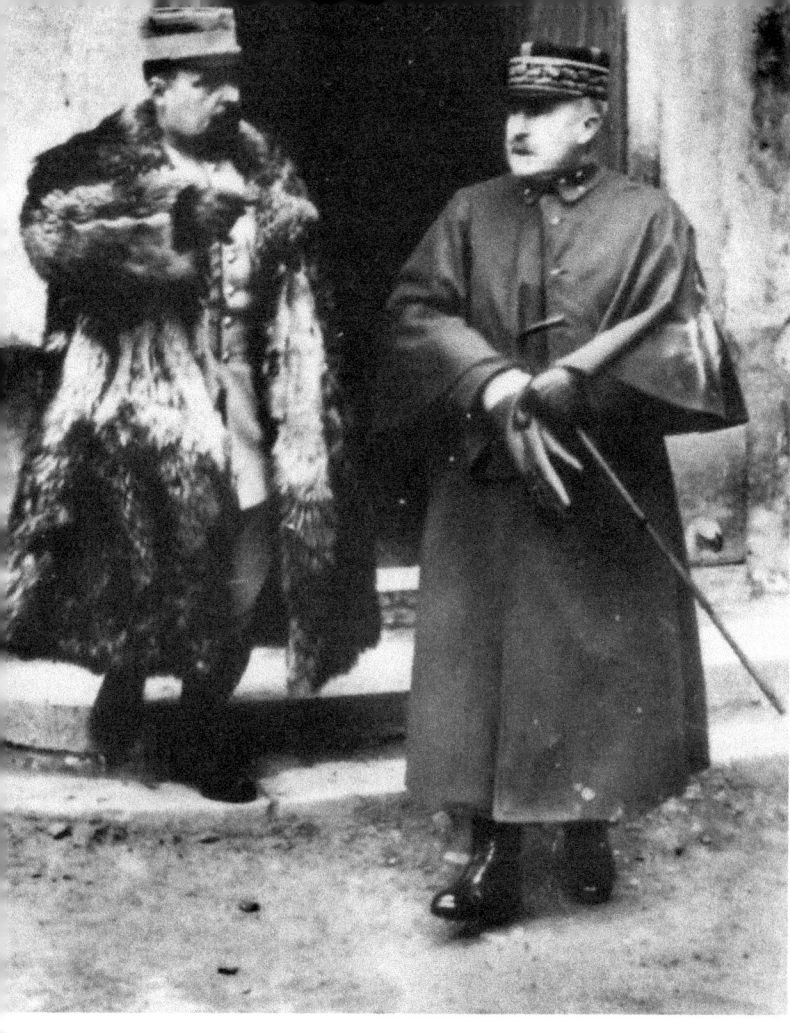

17GW627, 17GW628. General Nivelle arrives at Laffaux close to the German occupied lines on the Chemin des Dames; he is in discussion with General Mangin. The commander of Sixth Army was as optimistic as Nivelle and set the pace for his infantry's advance at an unrealistic hundred metres a minute. Nivelle knew this to be over confident but directed:

> *'I insist on the violence, brutality and swiftness of our offensive and most particularly on its first stage, breaking up the front, with immediate targets of capturing the enemy positions and the whole area of its artillery.*

To his critics, the Commander-in-Chief declared that if the assault failed to break through the front he would not persist with the offensive and would call it off after 48 hours.

17GW630 The day before the attack all commanding officers received a yellow envelope containing the message that the attack was the following morning, 16 April 1917, at 0600 hours. Thousands of men (some 1,200,000) were informed and many proceeded to write their last letters to their loved ones.

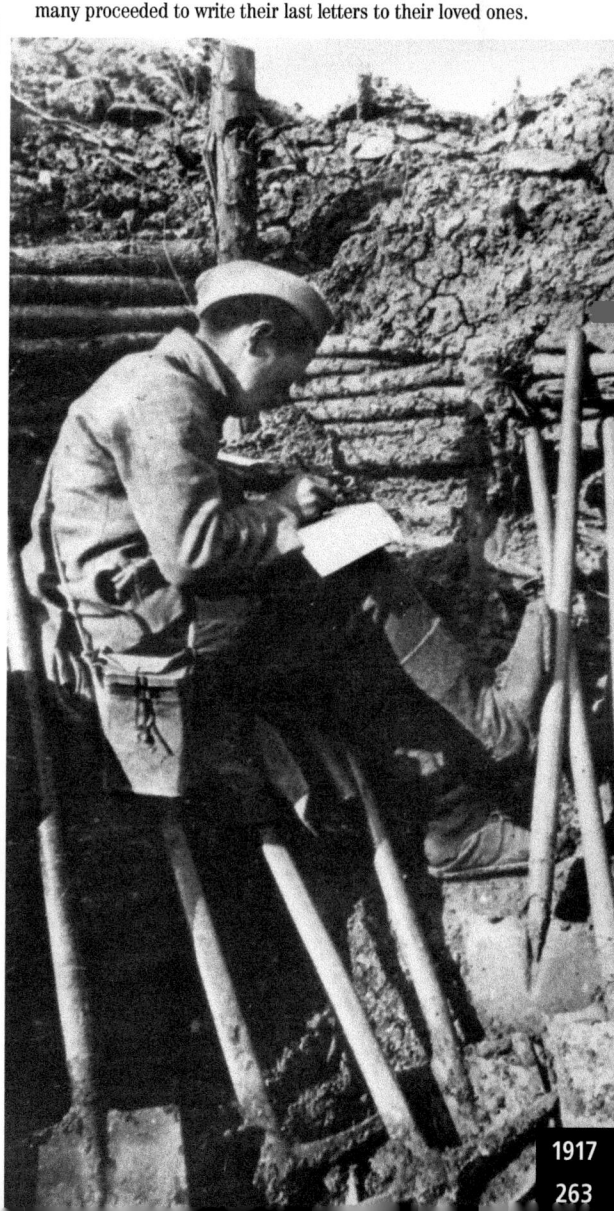

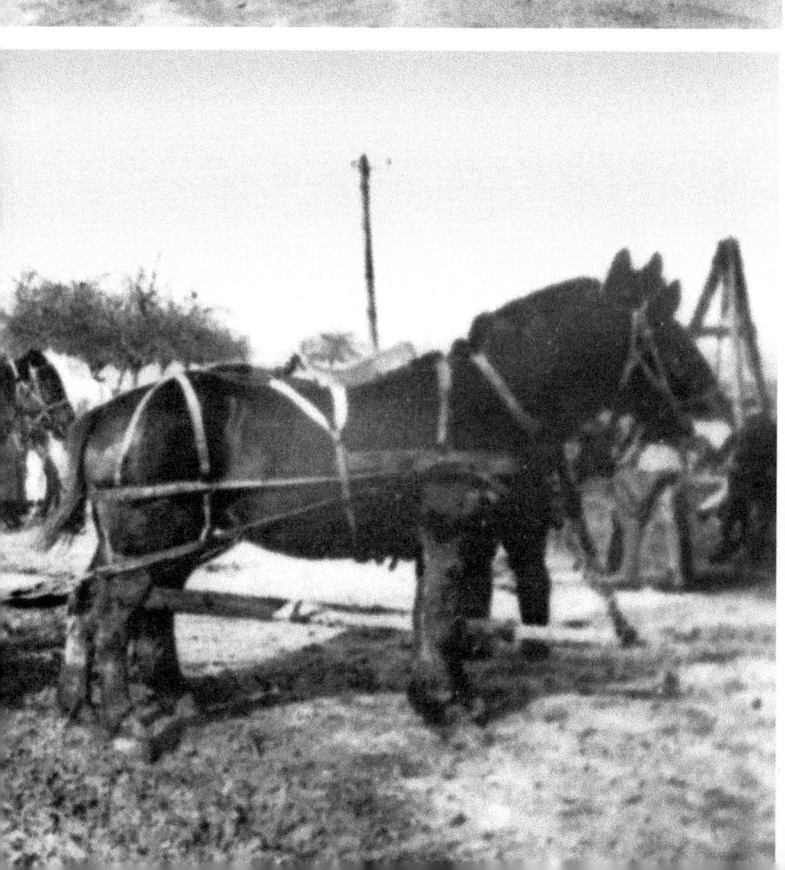

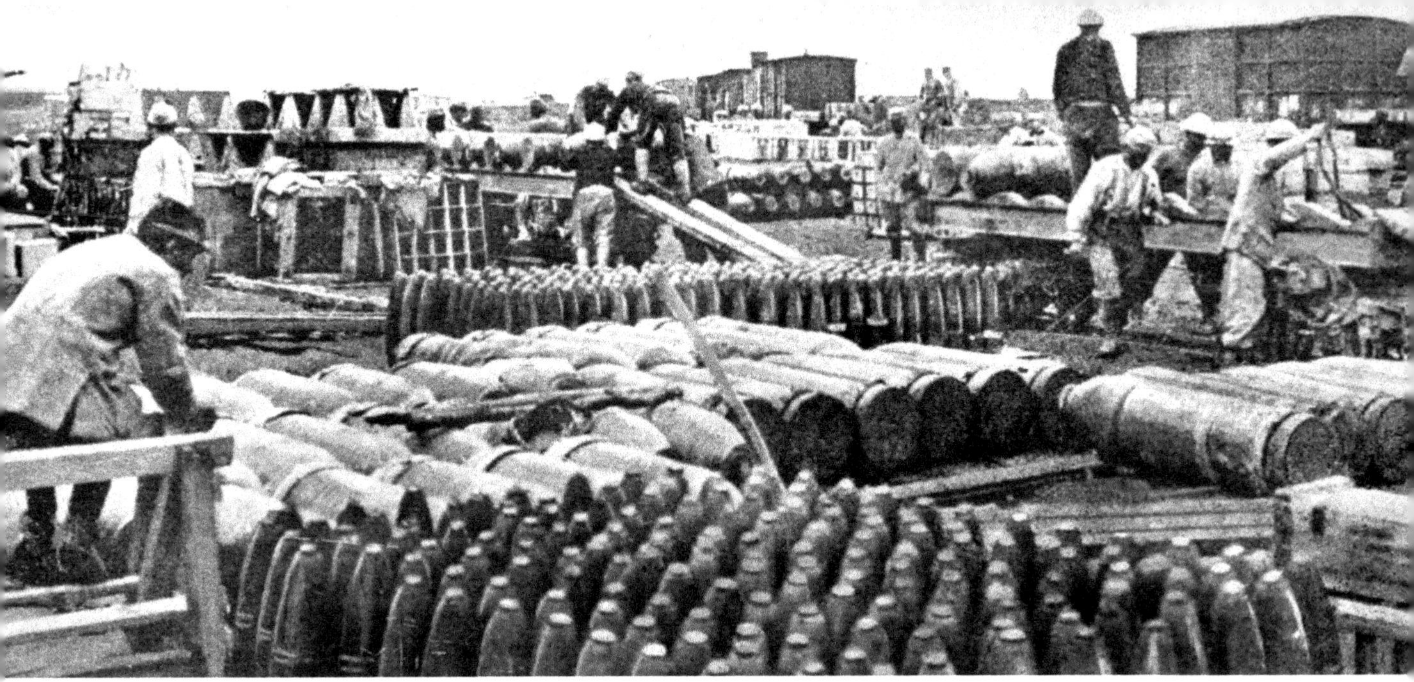

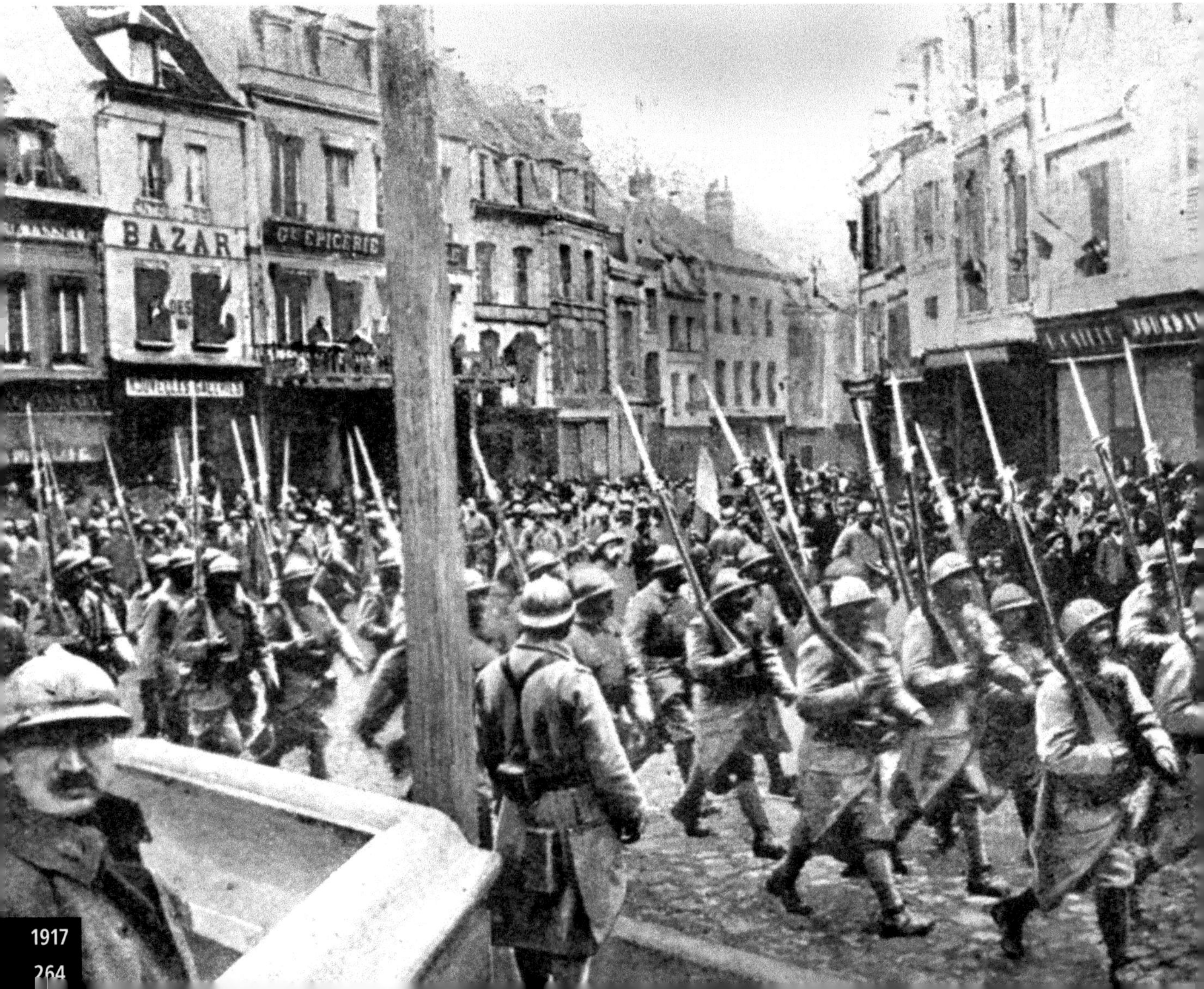

1917

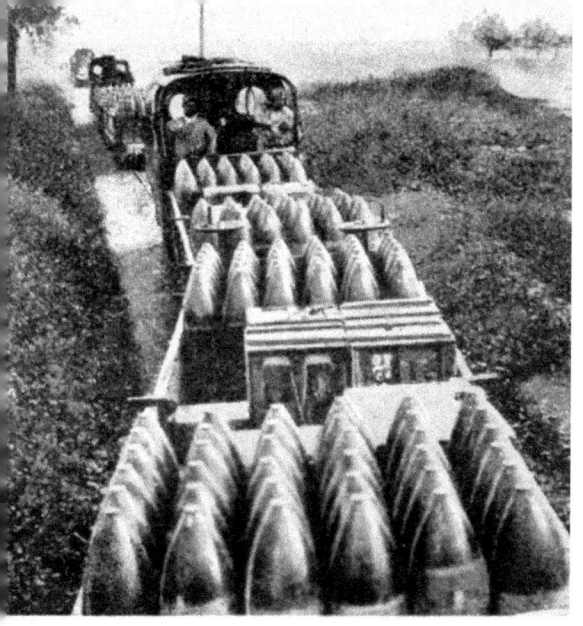
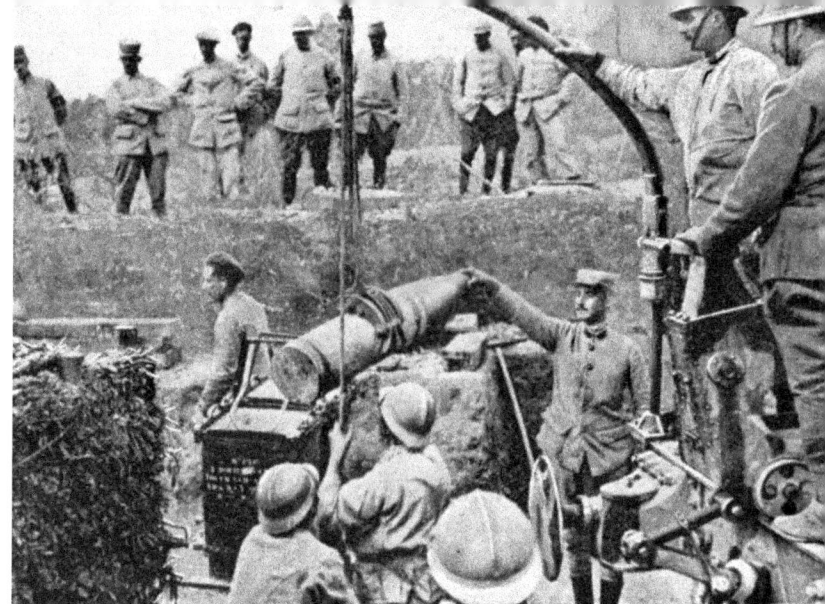

17GW634, 17GW636, 17GW637, 17GW638. At a French ammunition dump shells are being loaded on to wagons. The shells are then taken by rail to the guns. Individual shells are winched into camouflaged shelters close to the guns. A French railway gun firing at the German positions on the Chemin des Dames.

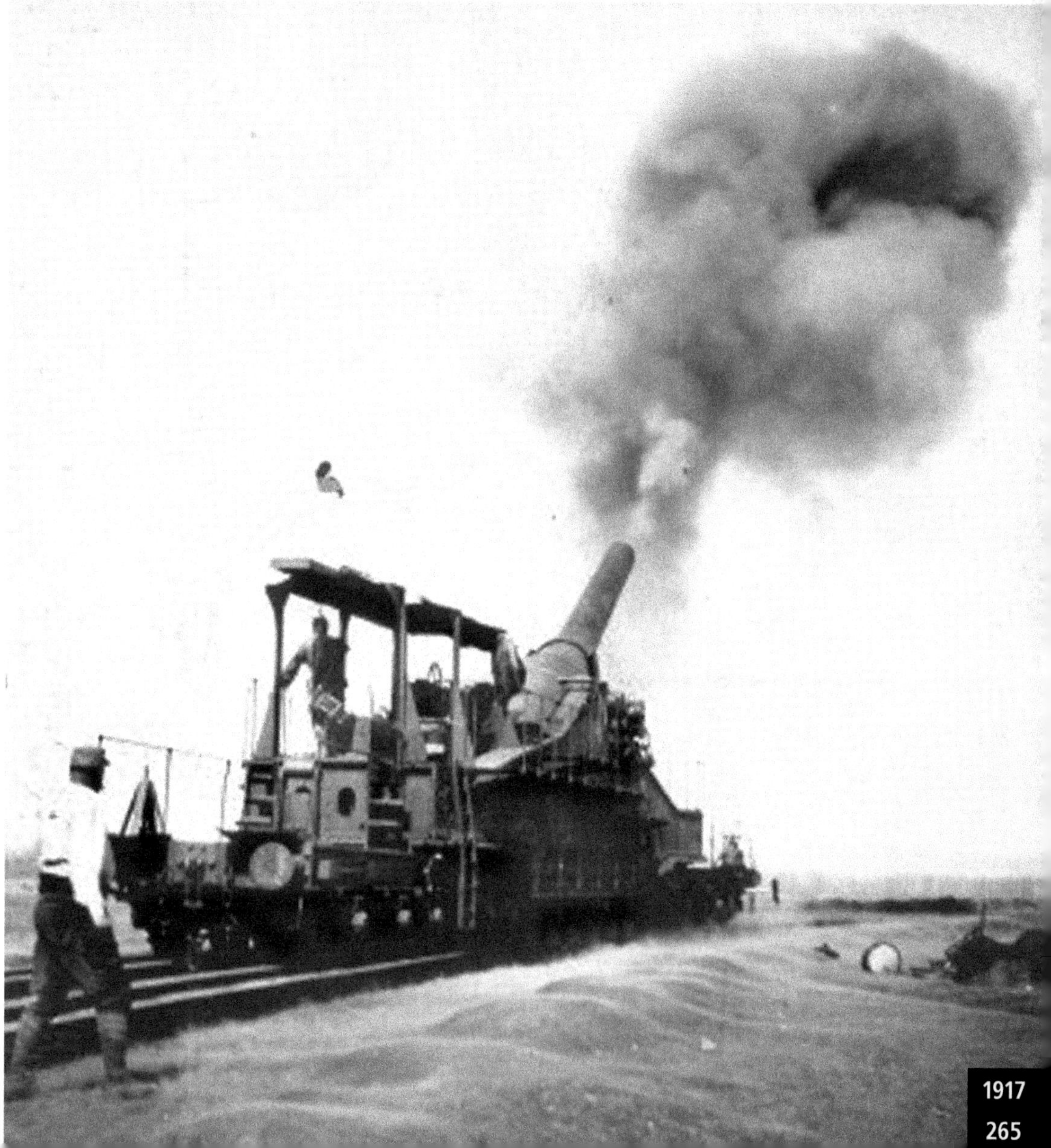

17GW635 French infantry, accompanying General Nivelle, marching through the town of Noyon in March 1917.

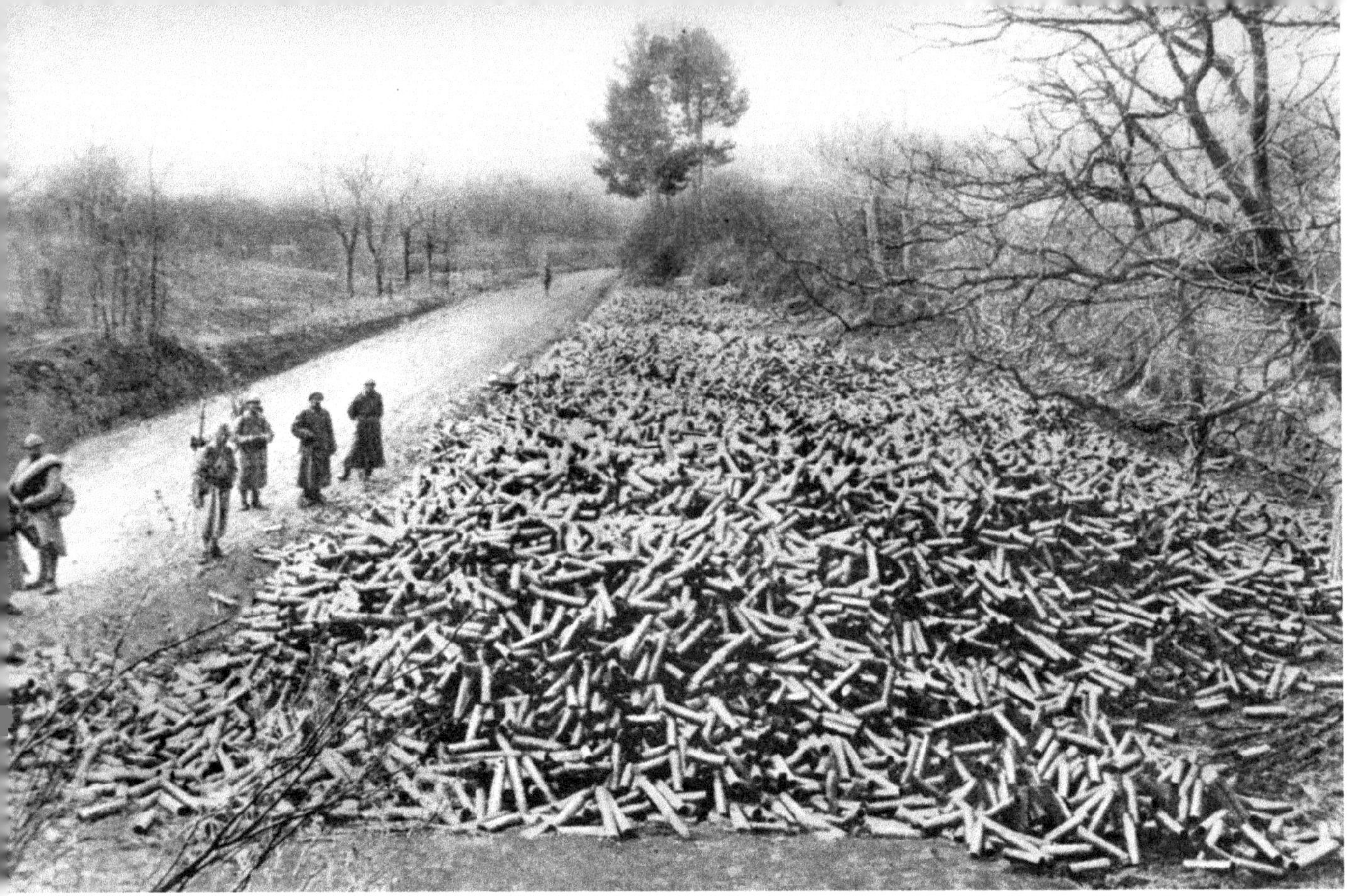

17GW641 These 75 mm shell cases give some idea of the amount a battery, consisting of four guns, could fire at the German positions at Courcy – April 1917.

17GW639 Beautifully composed photograph of a French farmer and his wife welcoming a mounted patrol – the farmer bows and the officer throws up a salute. Confidence in the outcome of the offensive and the morale of the Poilu and civilian population was high.

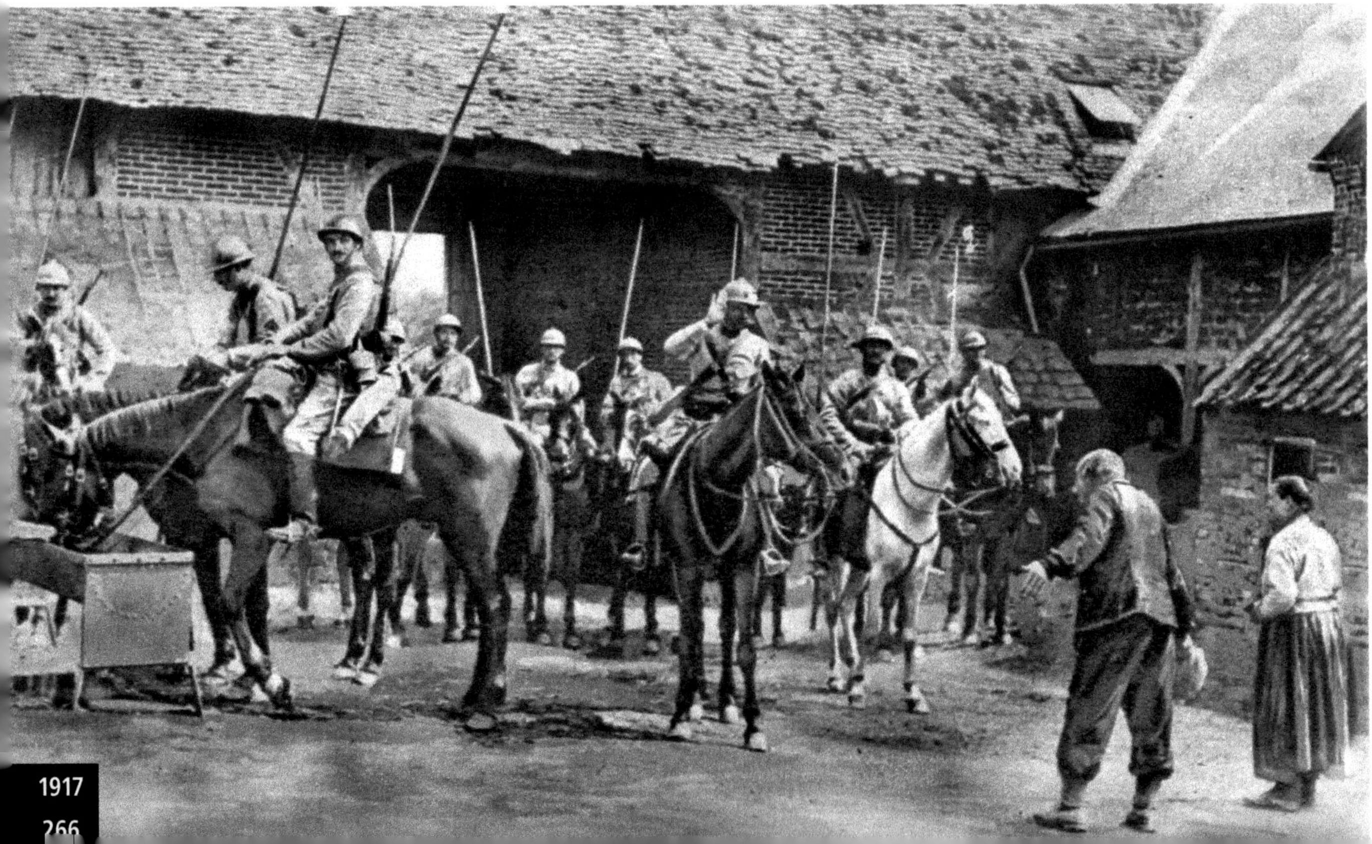

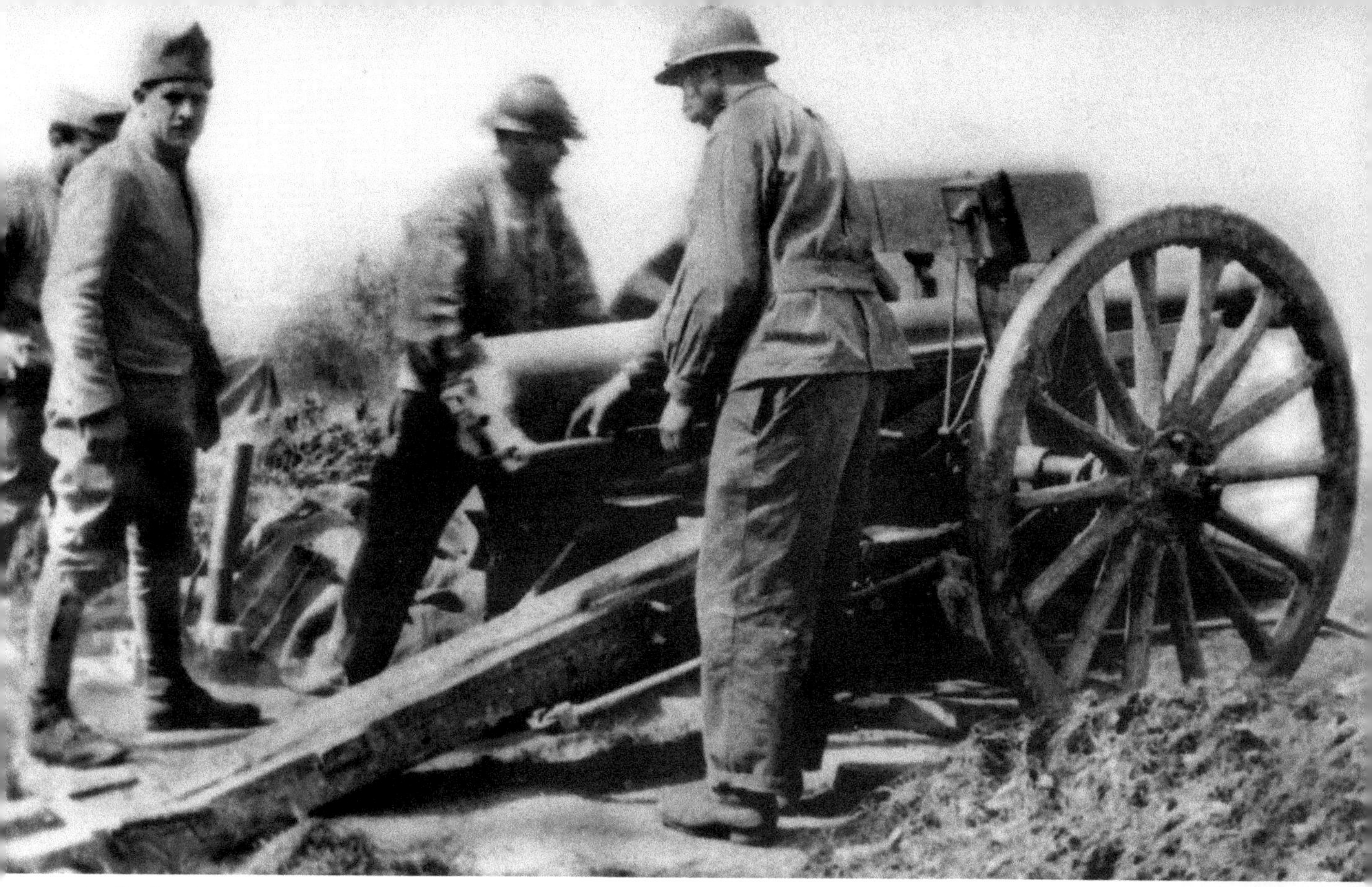

17GW642 The French '75' (75 mm) was the first field gun to include a hydro-pneumatic recoil mechanism, which kept the gun's trail and wheels perfectly still during firing. Since it did not need to be re-laid after each firing, the crew could reload and fire again as soon as the barrel returned to its resting position. It could fire fifteen rounds per minute for a distance of five miles. An experienced gun crew could almost double that rate of fire.

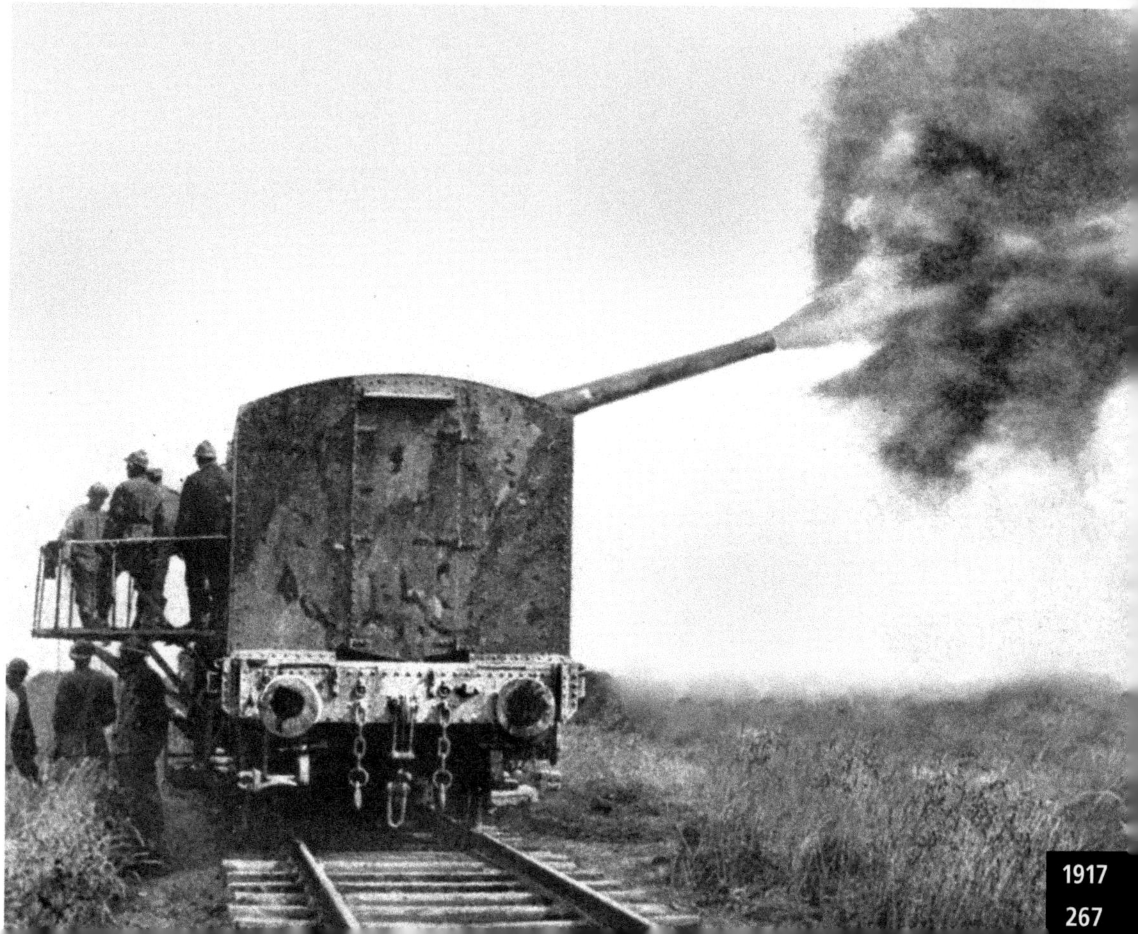

17GW643 A French heavy gun, mounted on a railway carriage, keeping up the preliminary bombardment.

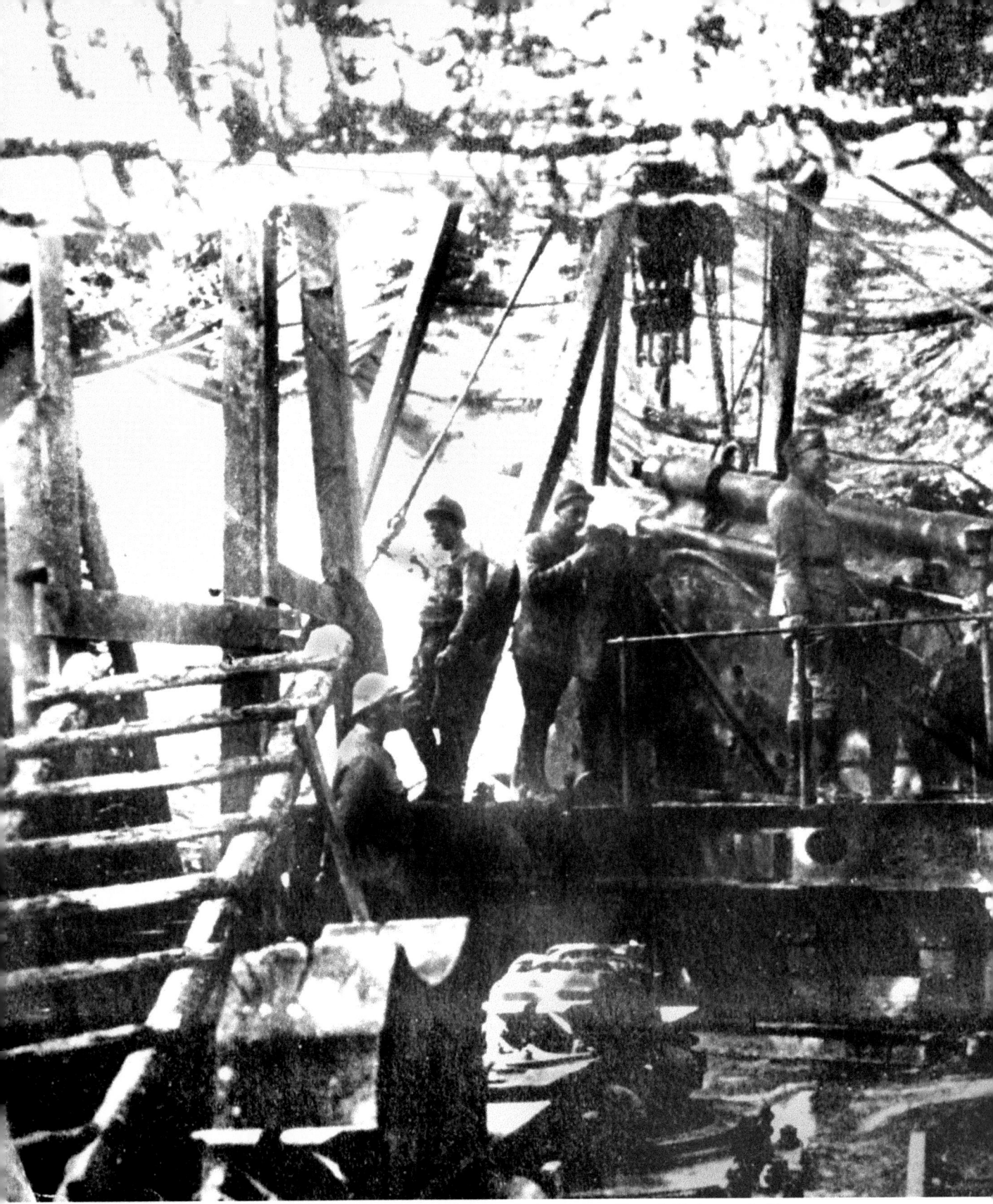
17GW662 A camouflaged French heavy artillery piece, mounted on railways tracks, in action near Vienne le Chateau, on the Marne.

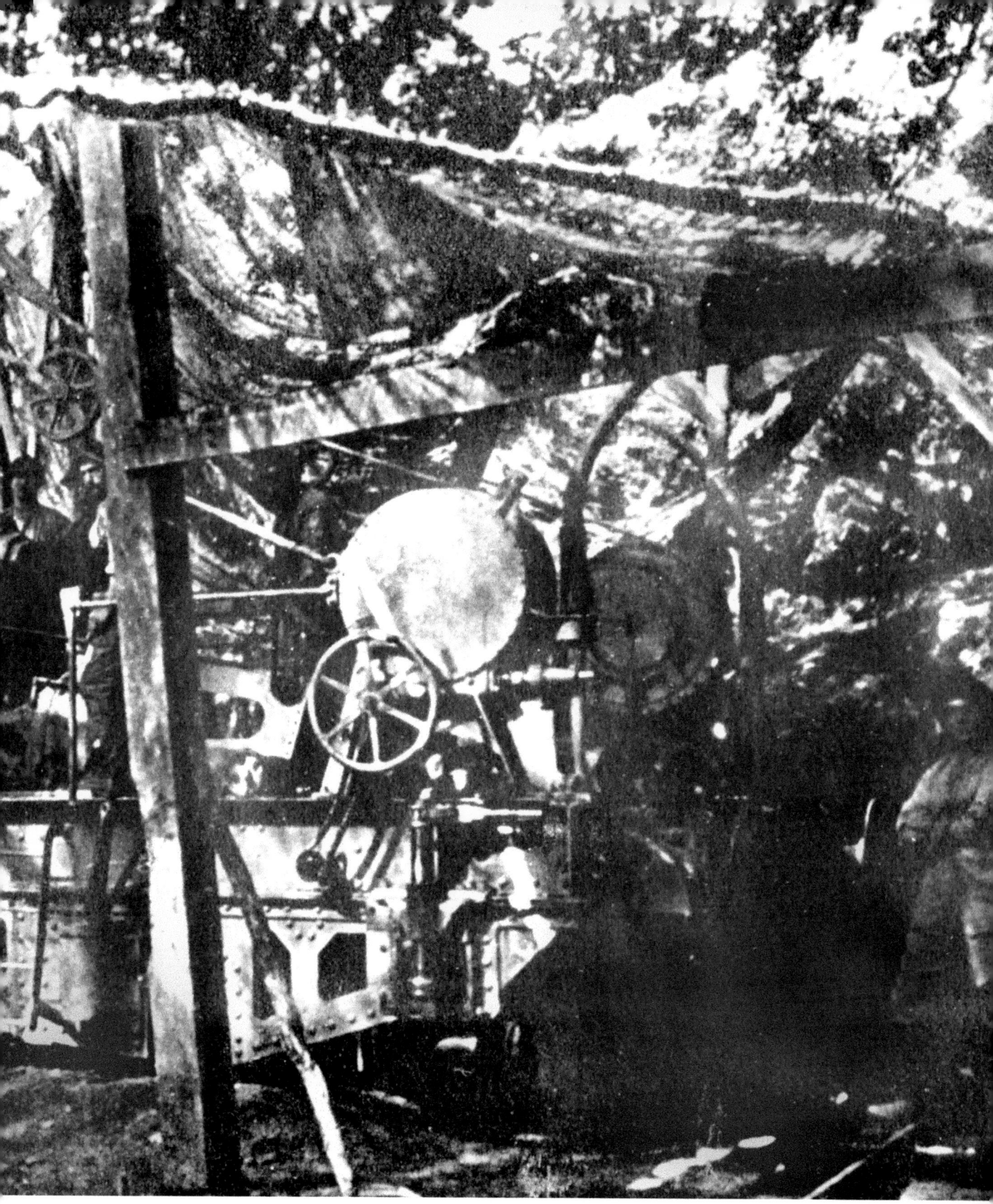

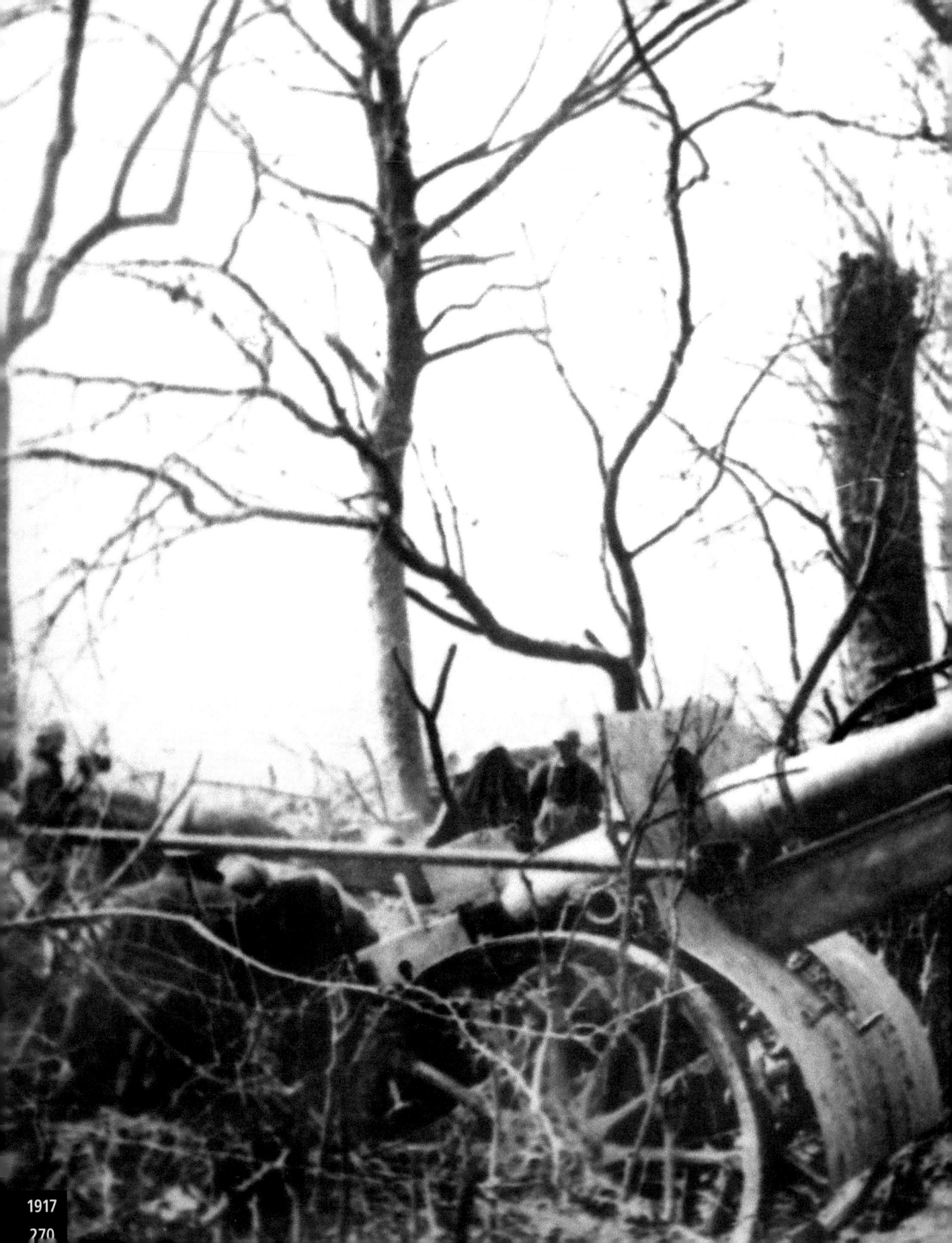

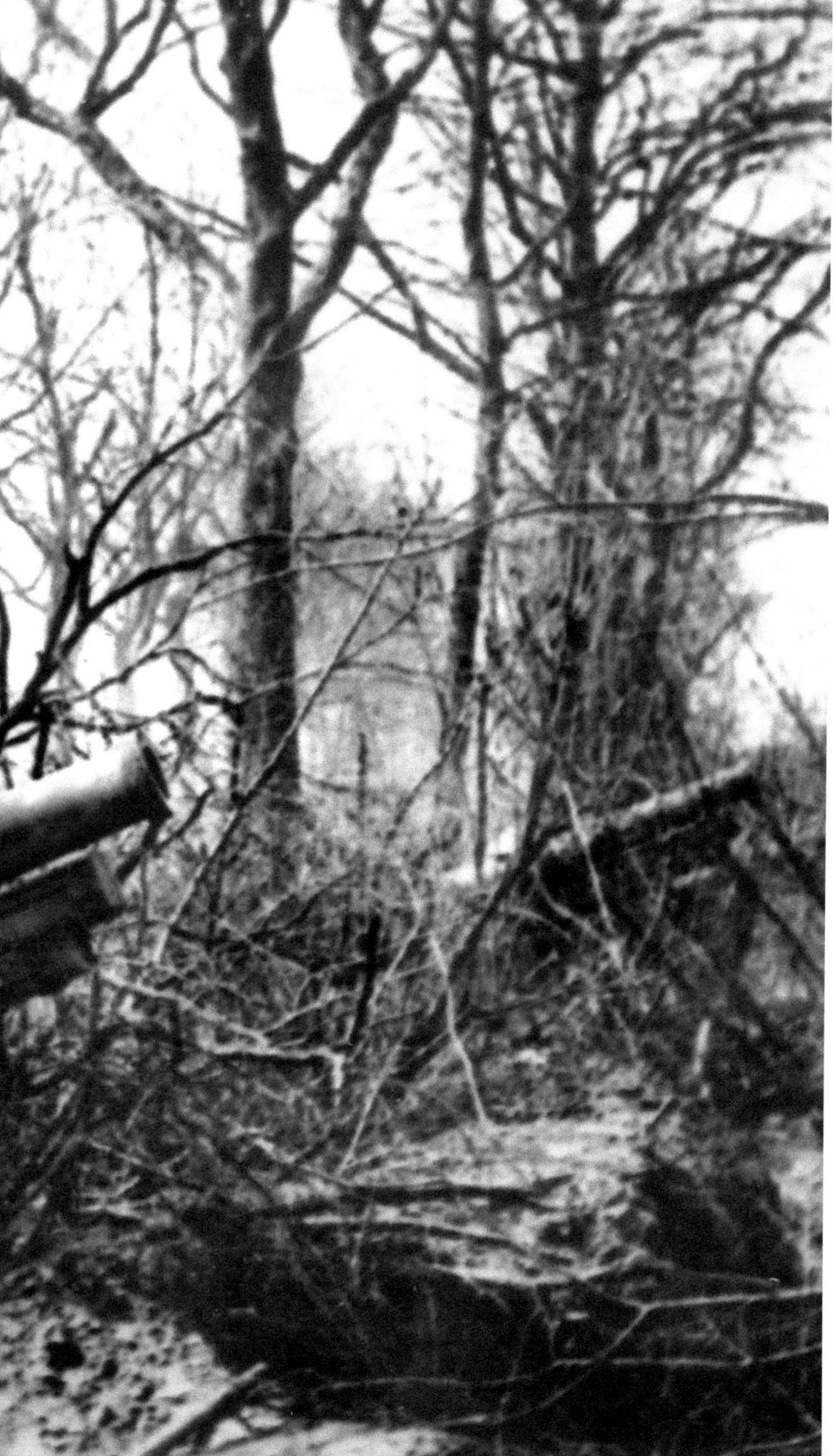

17GW645 A battery of 155 mm Sneider howitzers near Cormicy. German counter battery fire was very accurate on the French VI Corps front and by the end of the French preliminary bombardment twenty-seven of this type had been hit and wrecked.

17GW644 One of the 155 mm Sneider howitzers – named 'Nenette' by its crew, who call a halt in their toil for a gun crew photograph. The artillery bombardment started on 2 April and carried on until 11 April.

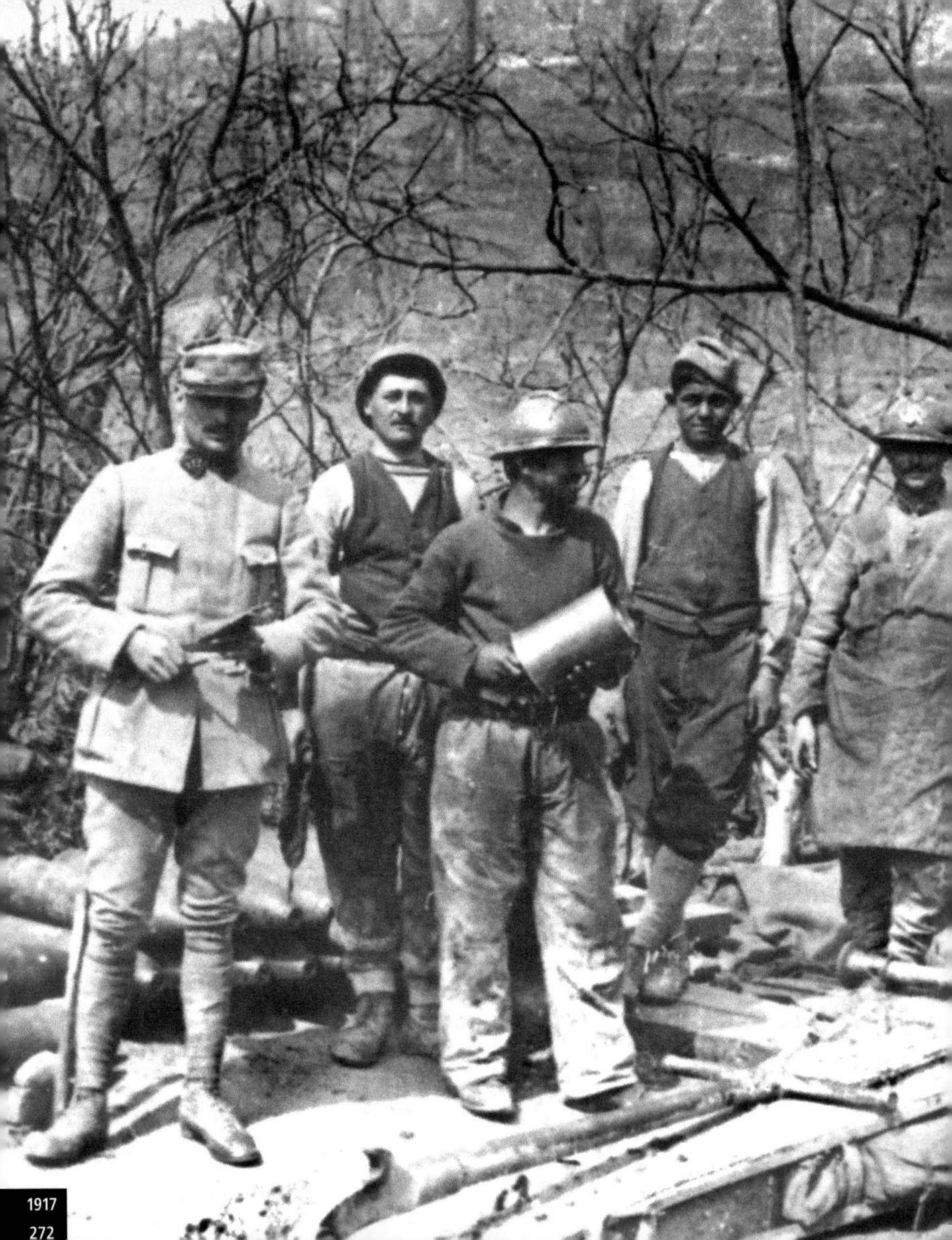

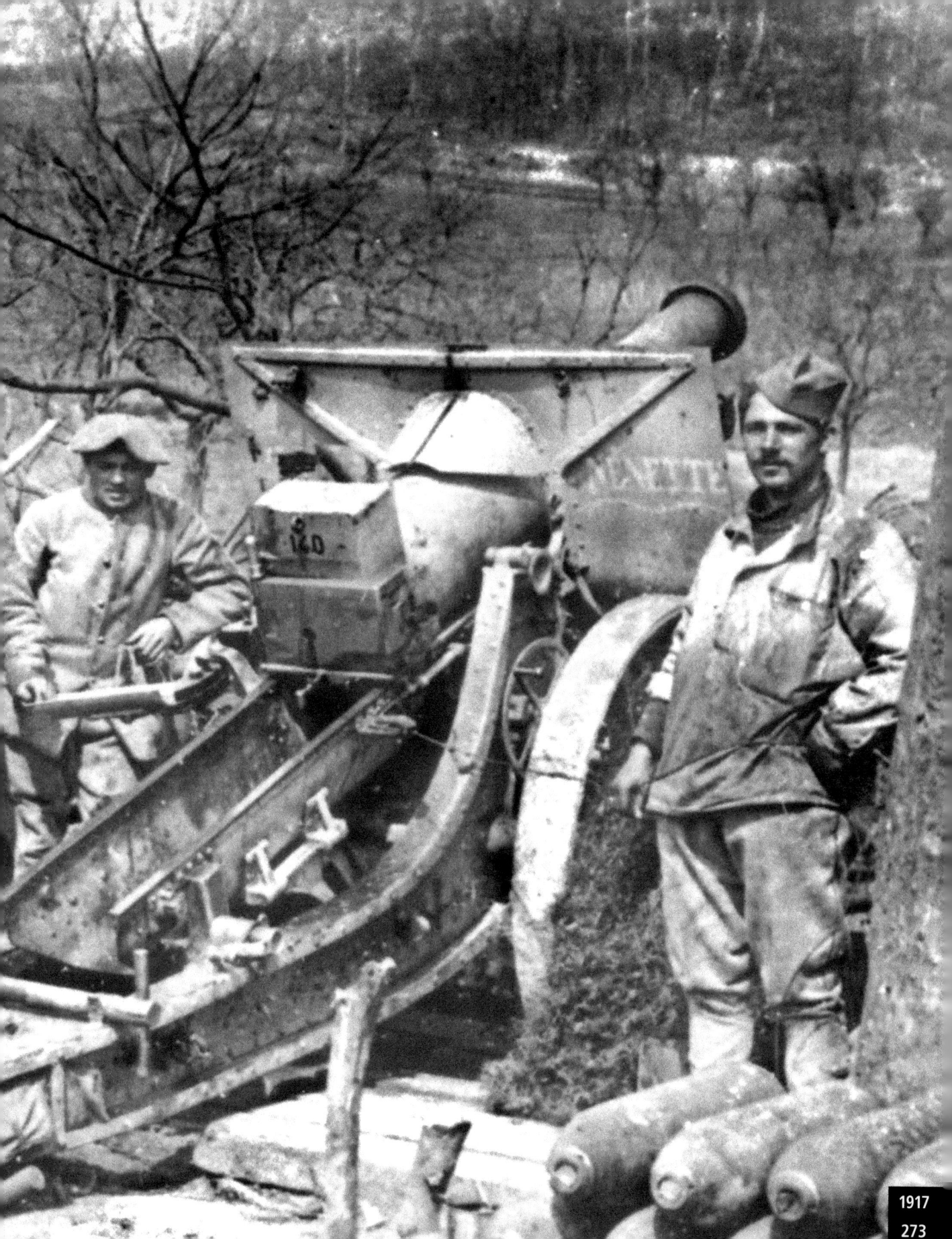

17GW647 A 155 mm Sneider howitzer at Loivre. This type of gun could fire a shell thirteen miles. A total of 5,360 guns guns of all calibres were spread behind the line to support the Nivelle attack on the Chemin des Dames.

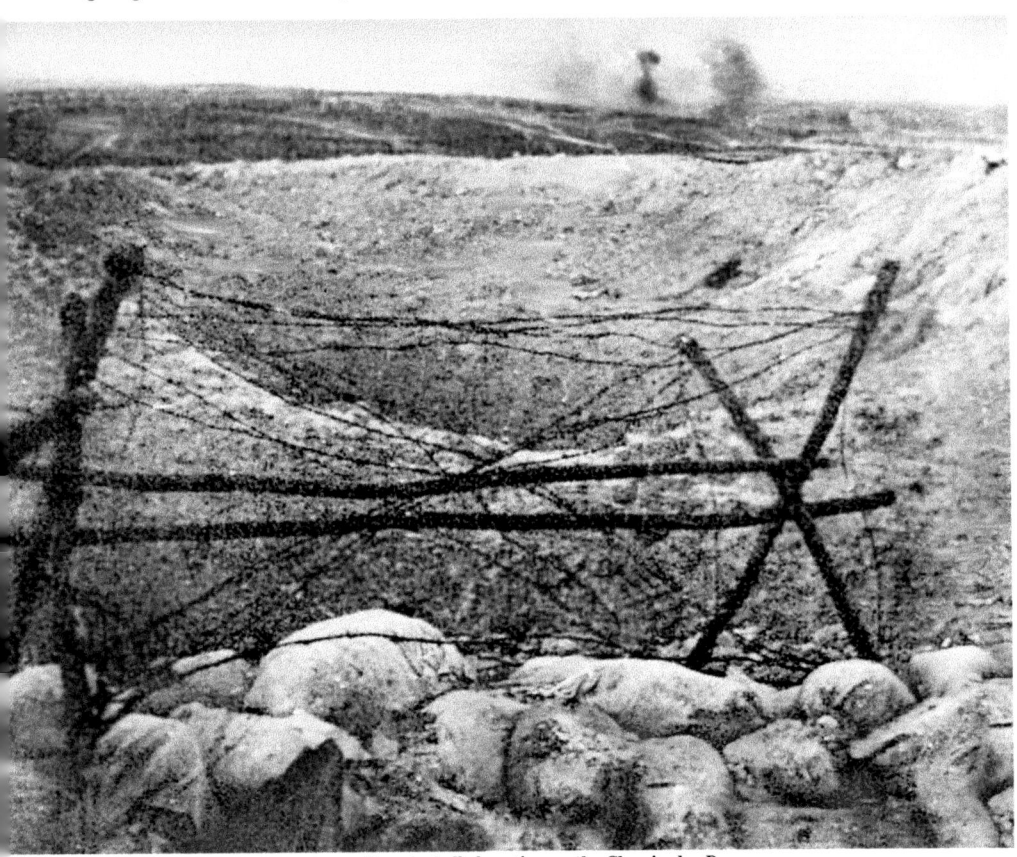

THE LANCASTRIA TRADEGY 17GW649 French shells bursting on the Chemin des Dames.

17GW648 German reinforcements coming from the road which gave its name to the battle – Chemin des Dames.

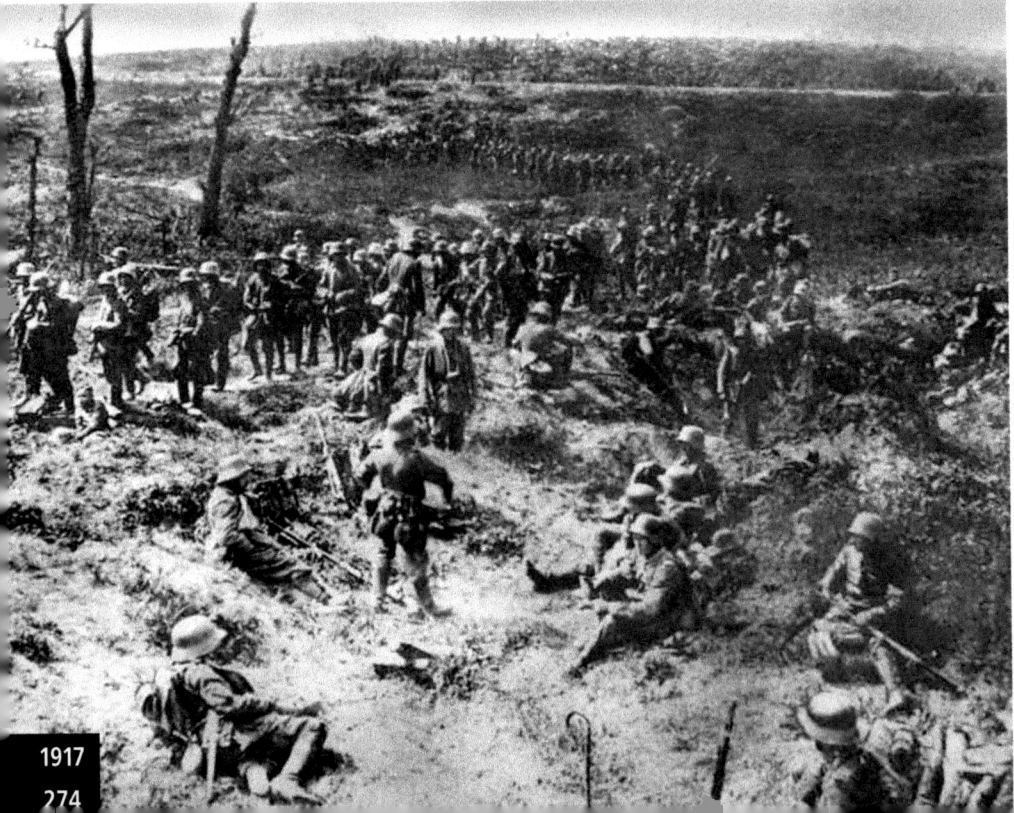

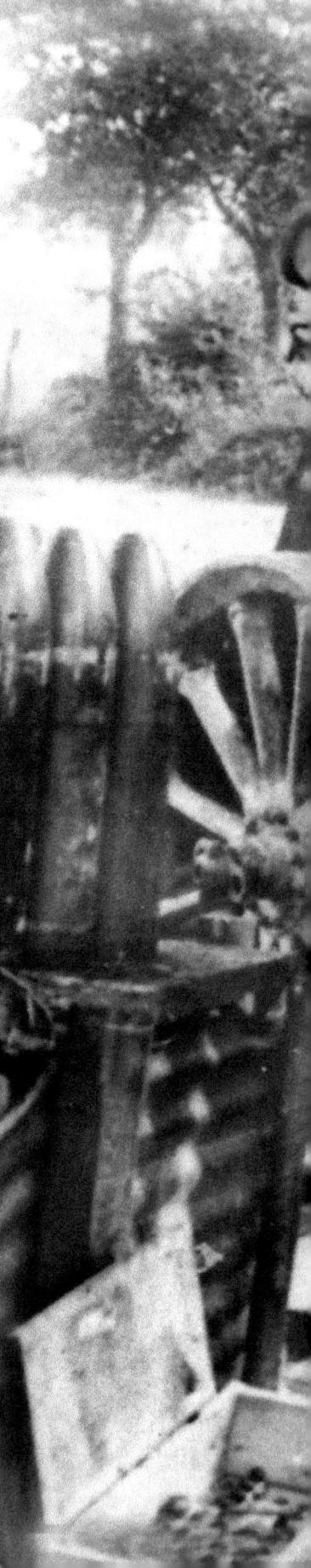

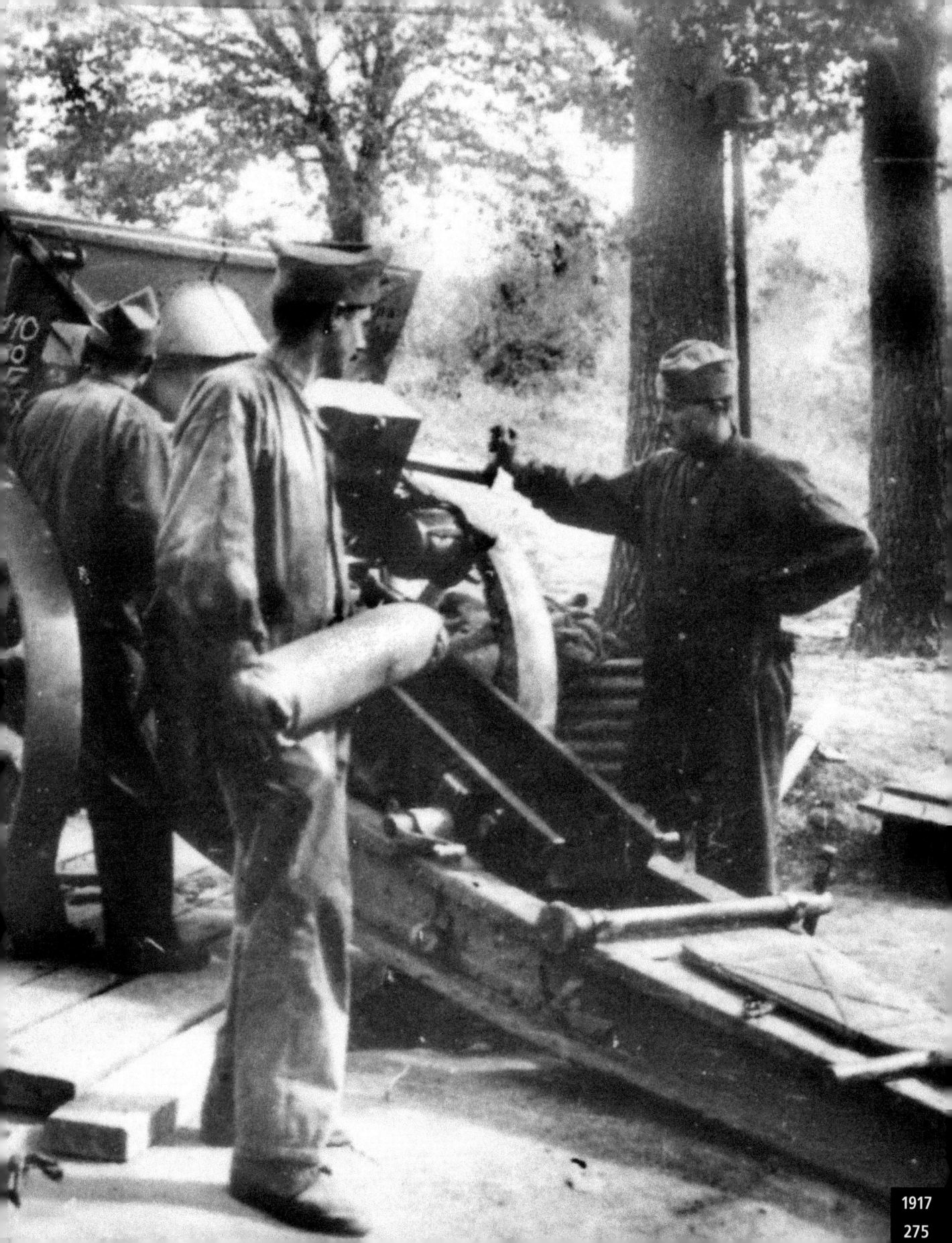

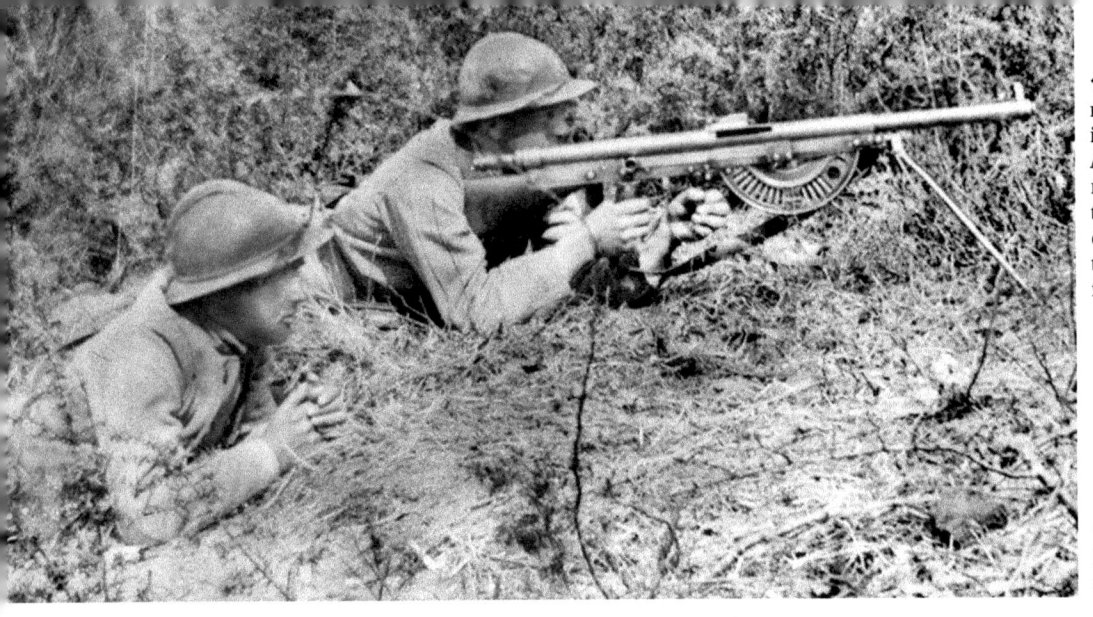

17GW650 The Chauchat light machine gun was the standard infantry support of the French Army. It earned a shaky reputation for jamming. The twenty-round magazine, with its open sides, allowed dirt and mud to interfere with the ammunition feed into the breech.

17GW651 A 155 mm gun battery bombarding the German positions at Cormicy.

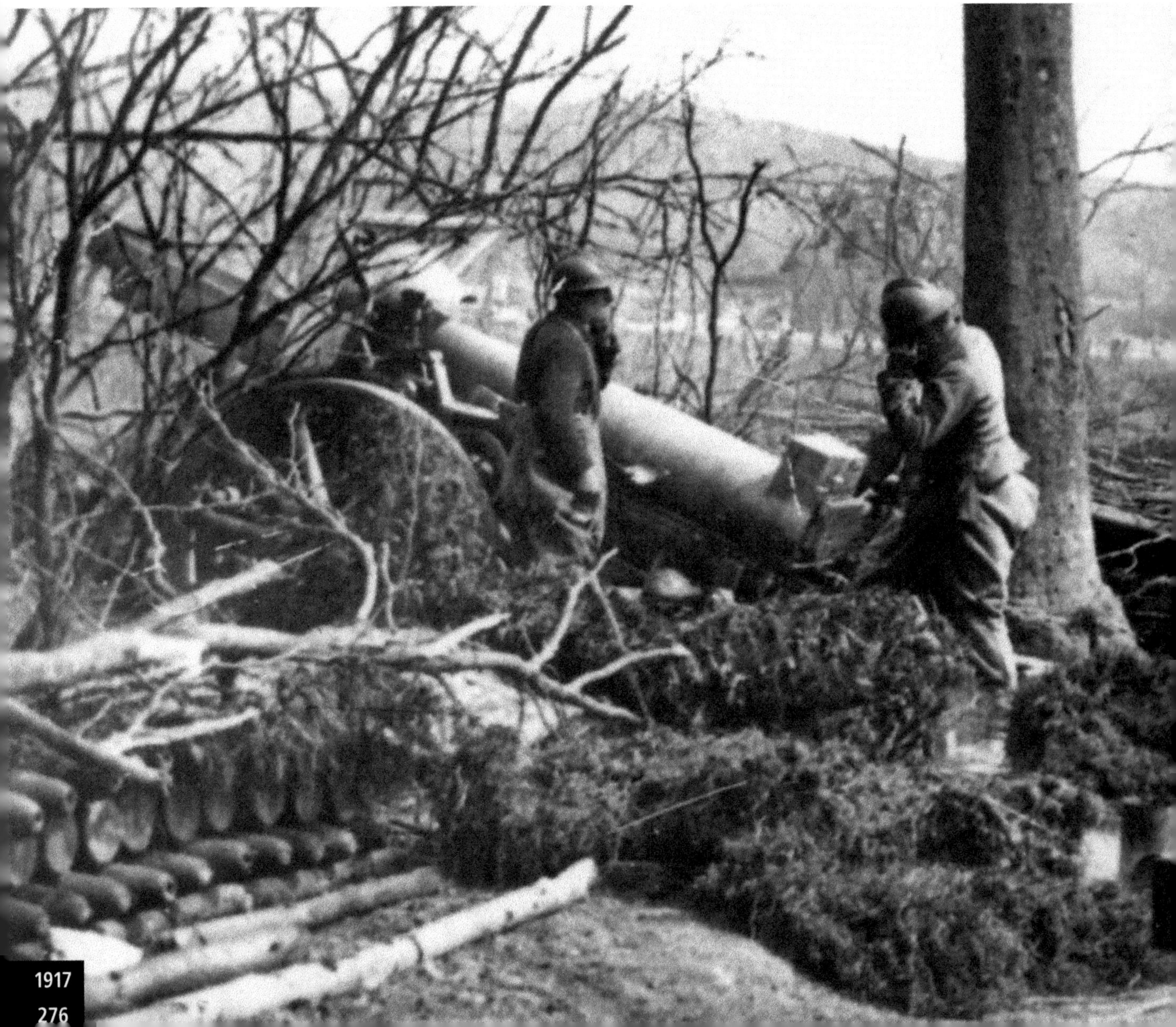

17GW654, 17GW660. A French sniper with a telescopic sighted Lebel rifle in the area of Tracy le Val.

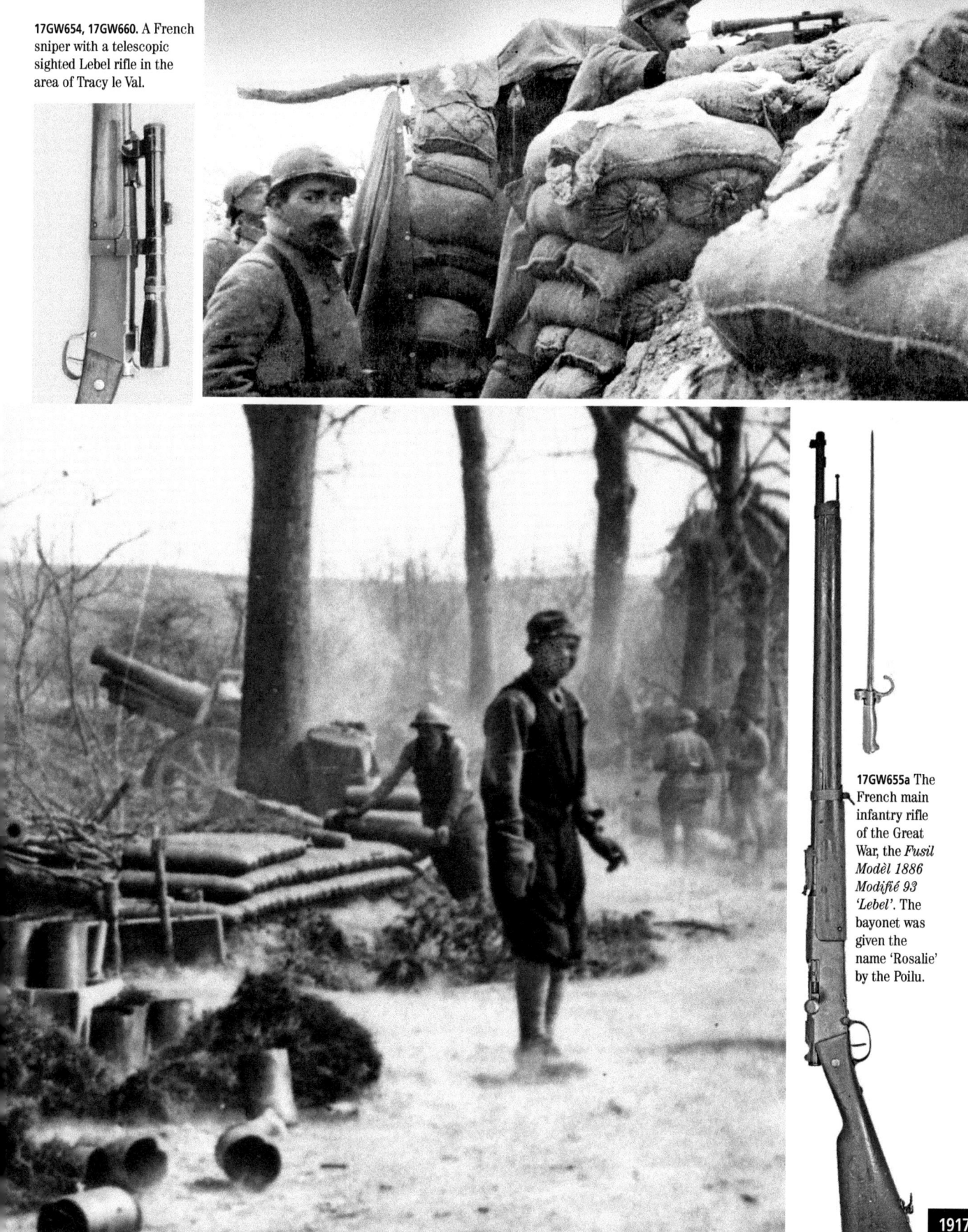

17GW655a The French main infantry rifle of the Great War, the *Fusil Modèl 1886 Modifié 93 'Lebel'*. The bayonet was given the name 'Rosalie' by the Poilu.

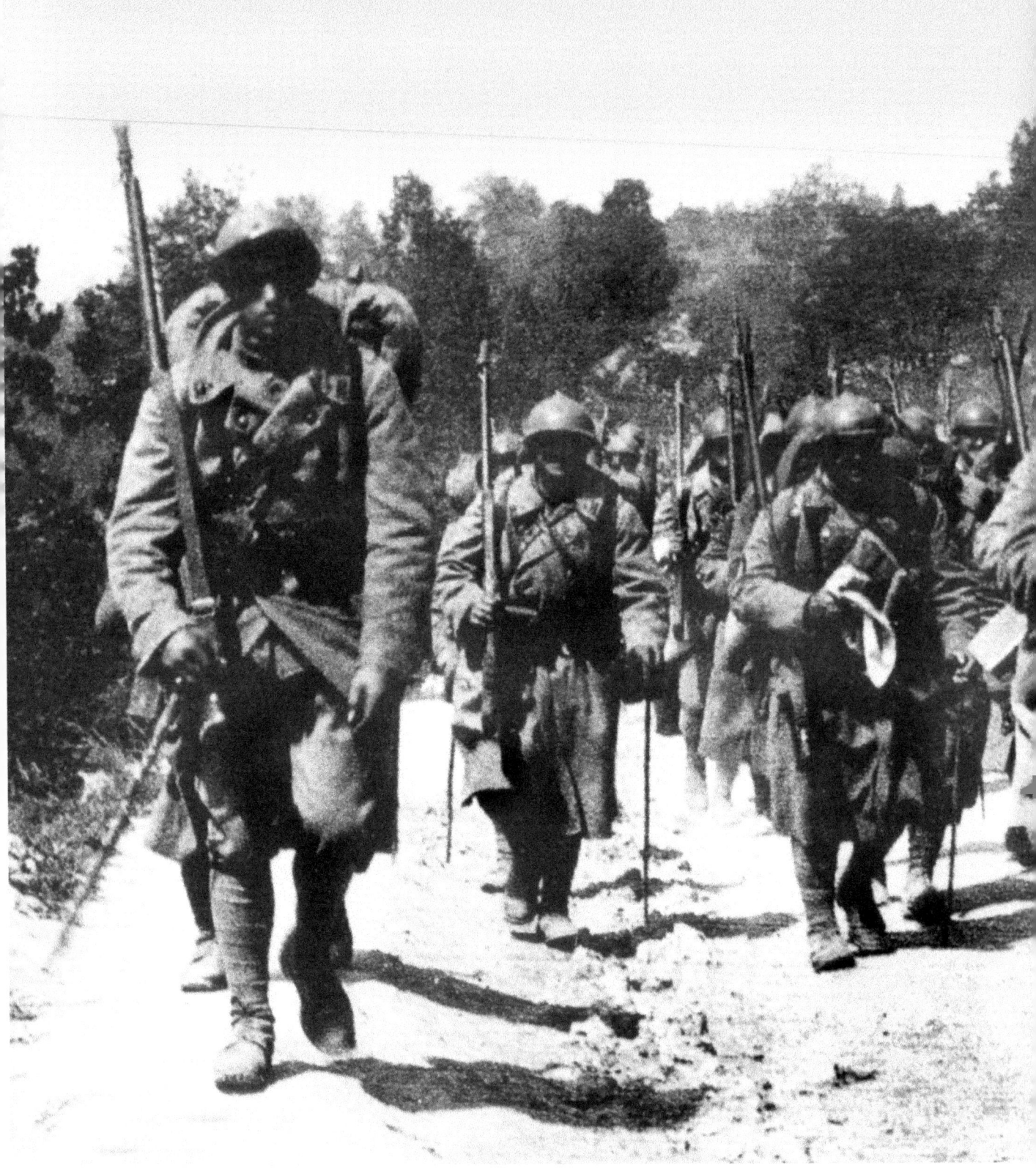
17GW603 A Company of French infantry reinforcements move up to take assault positions on the Chemin des Dames front.

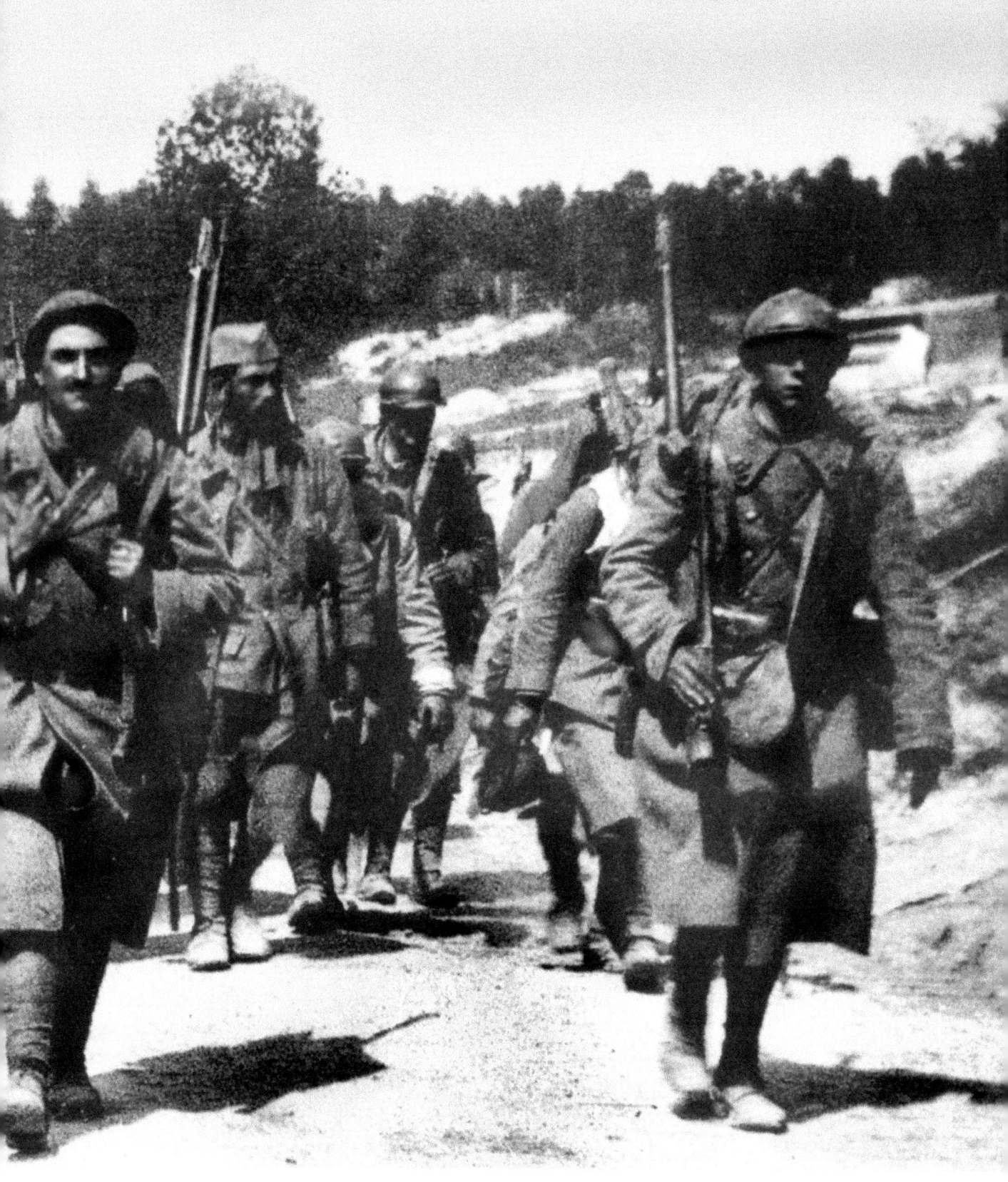

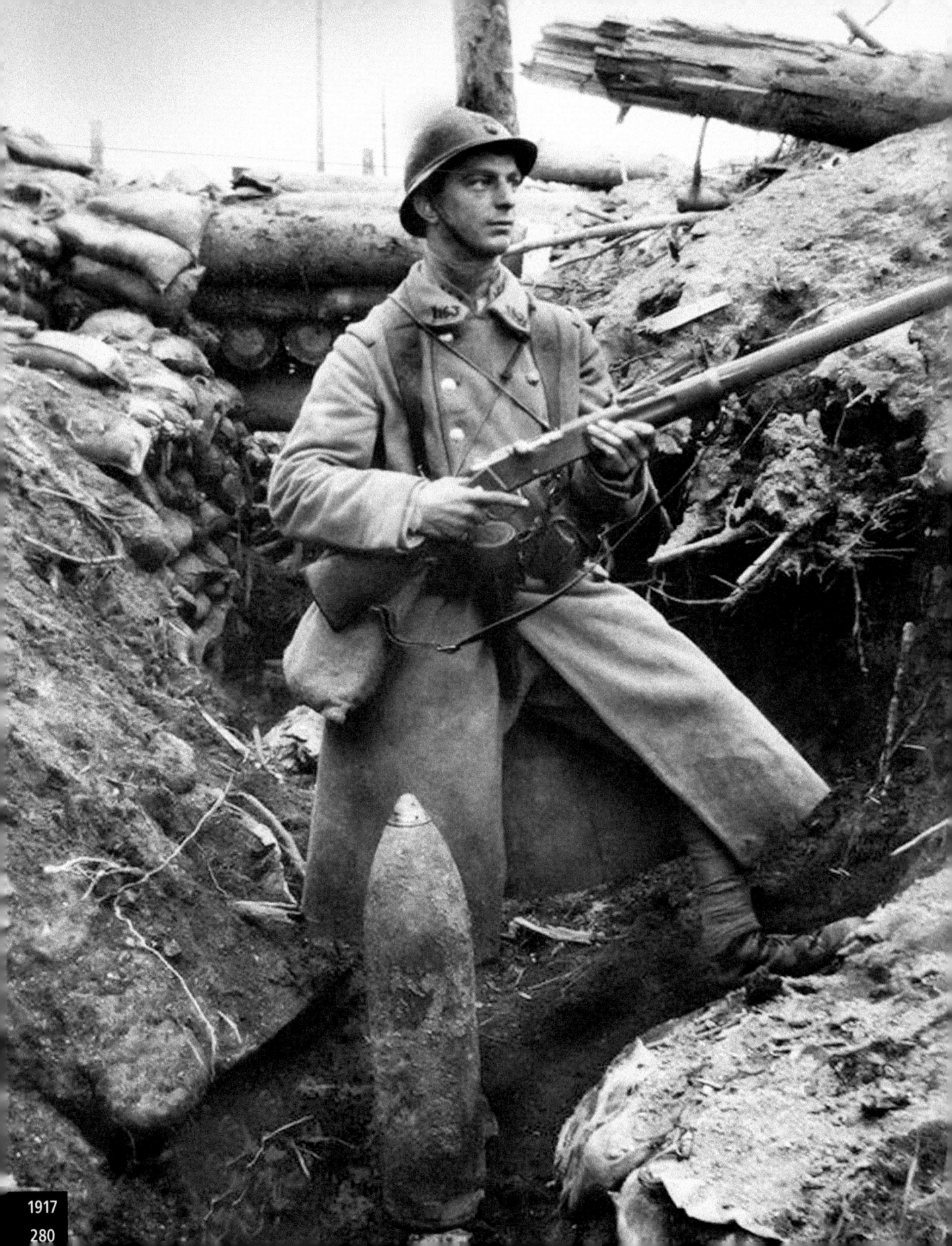

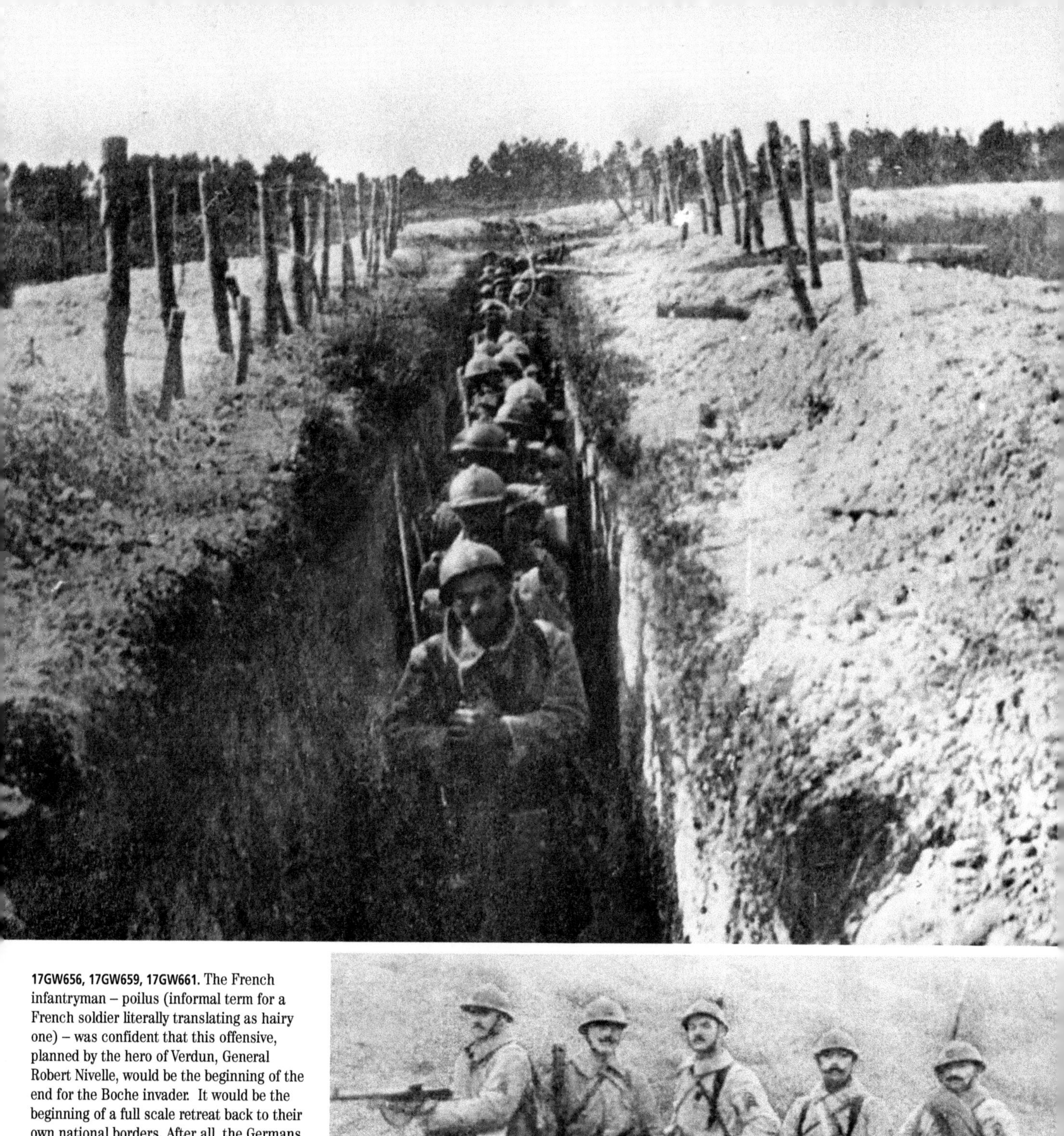

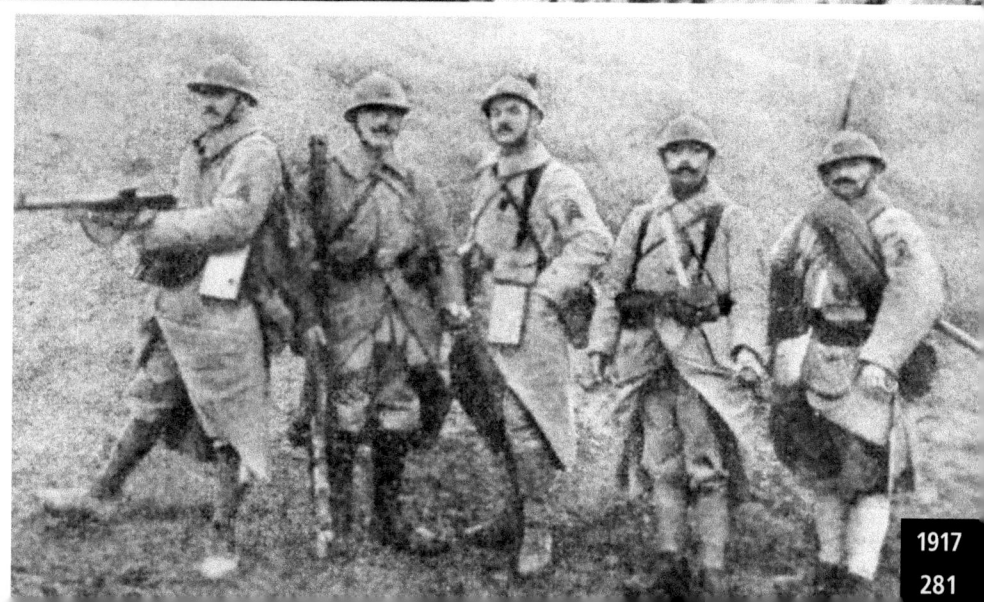

17GW656, 17GW659, 17GW661. The French infantryman – poilus (informal term for a French soldier literally translating as hairy one) – was confident that this offensive, planned by the hero of Verdun, General Robert Nivelle, would be the beginning of the end for the Boche invader. It would be the beginning of a full scale retreat back to their own national borders. After all, the Germans had just given up large ares of French territory in a massive withdrawal. The date and place of the attack, 16 April, on the Chemin des Dames front, was common knowledge throughout France. Nor was it a secret to the Germans. They had come into possession of detailled plans.

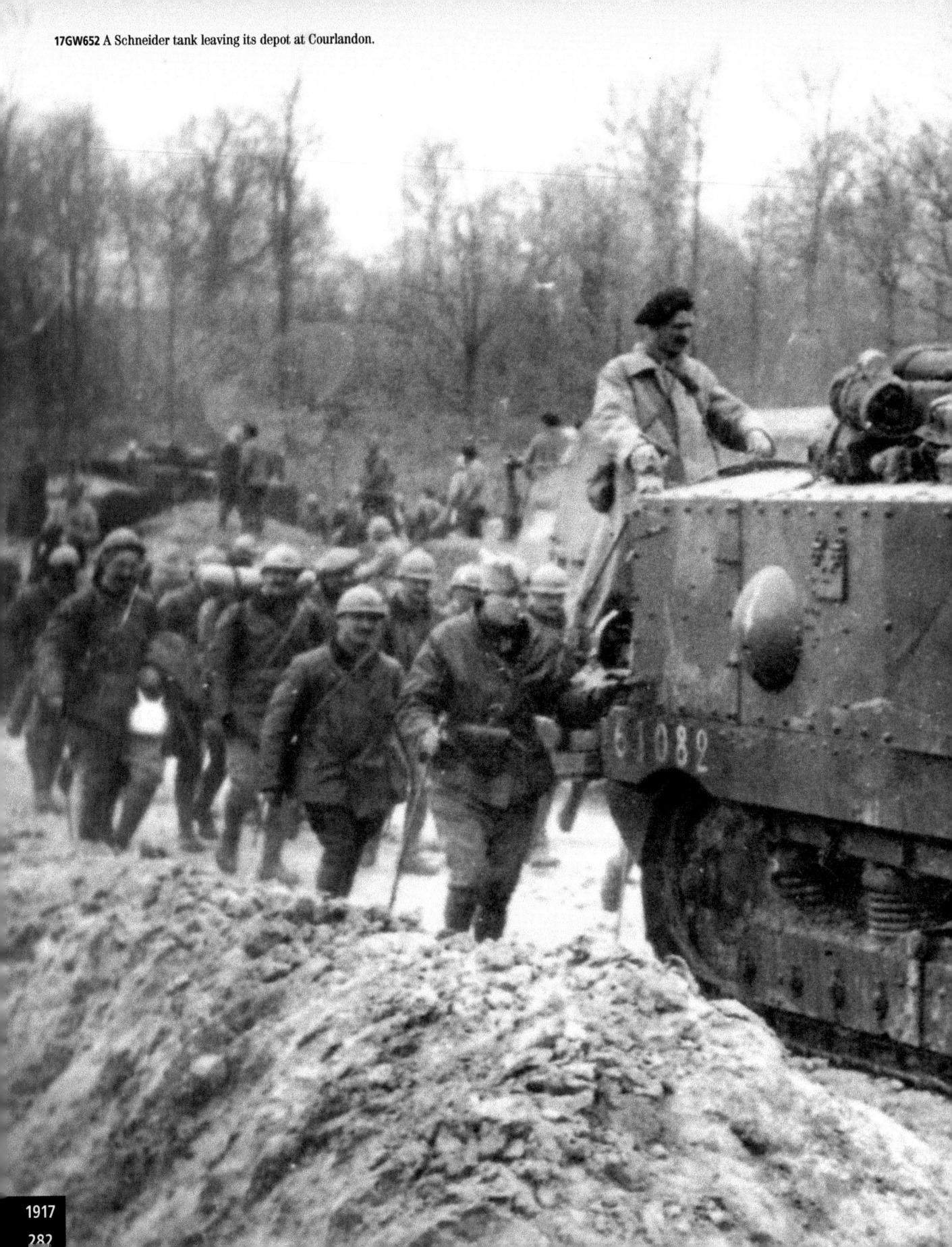
17GW652 A Schneider tank leaving its depot at Courlandon.

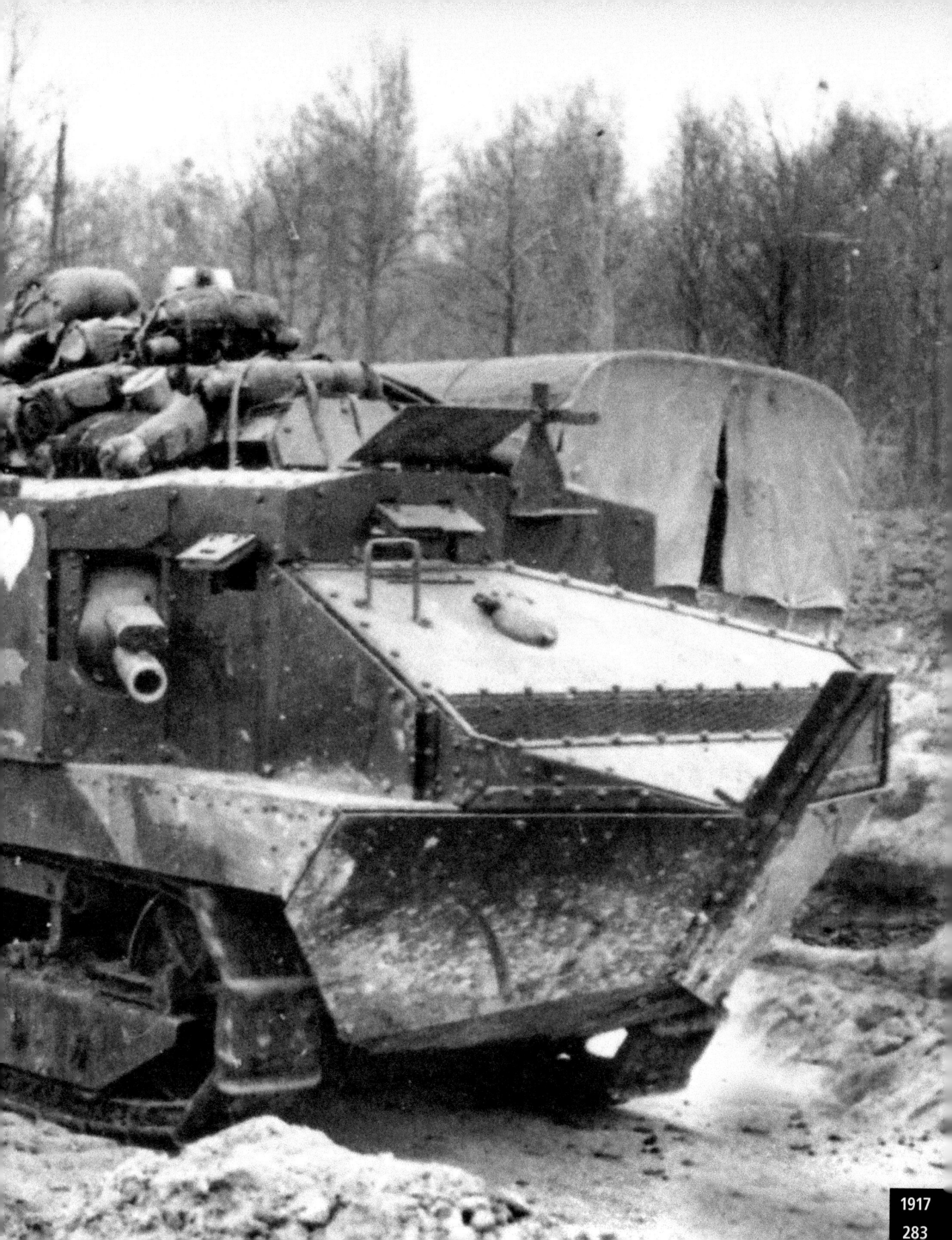

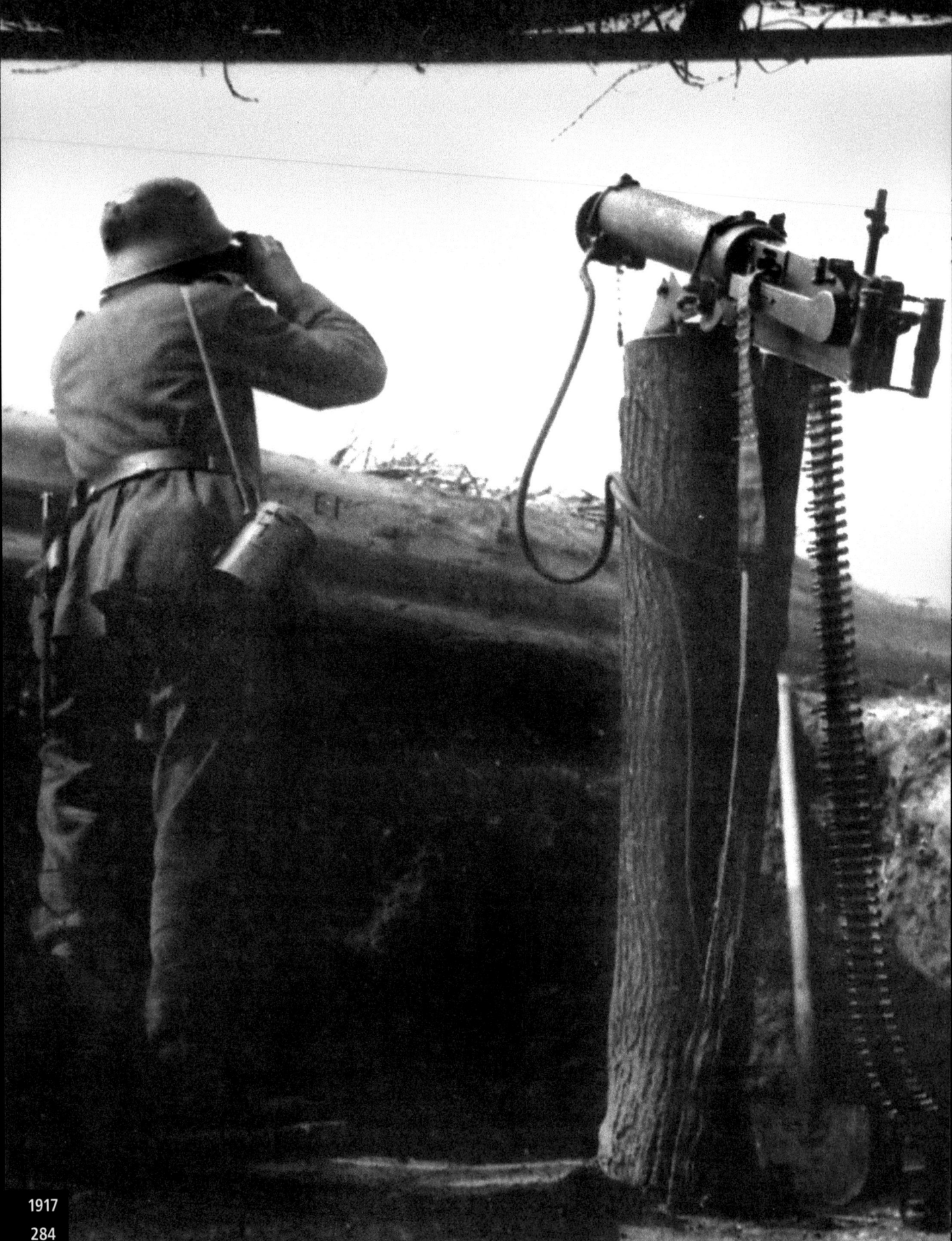

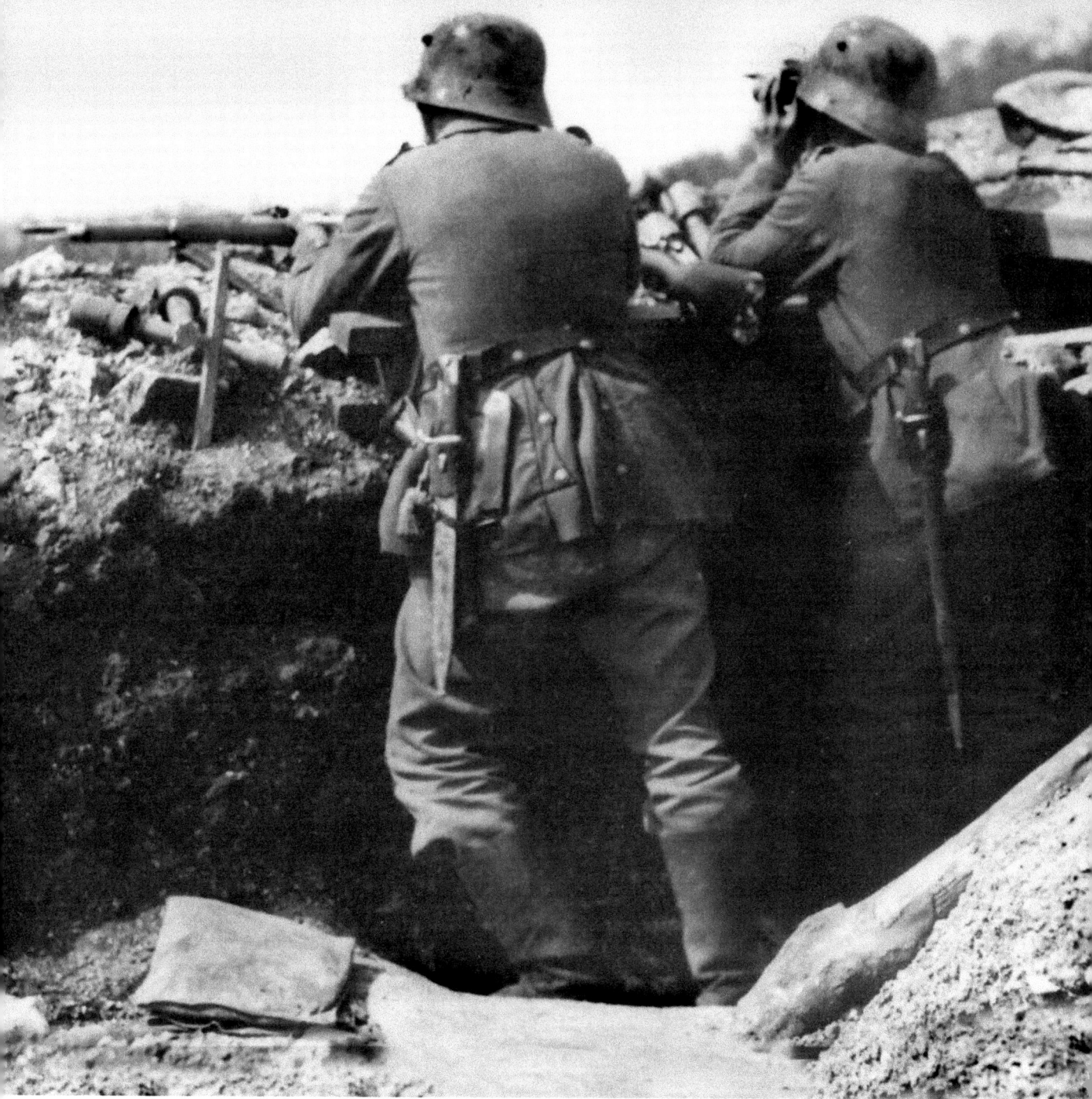

17GW666, 17GW665. The Germans were alert and ready for the French attack at dawn, 16 April, 1917. Since March, Ludendorff had allocated reinforcements for the threatened front of no less than seventeen new divisions, three Corps headquarters and put an entire Army headquarters on stand by. The number of guns of all sizes was massively increased during the lead up to the French attack on their positions. Concrete bunkers had been constructed from which fire could be poured across No Man's Land and the front line trenches. In the picture opposite, a MG 08 machine gun has been mounted on a tree trunk in an anti aircraft role.

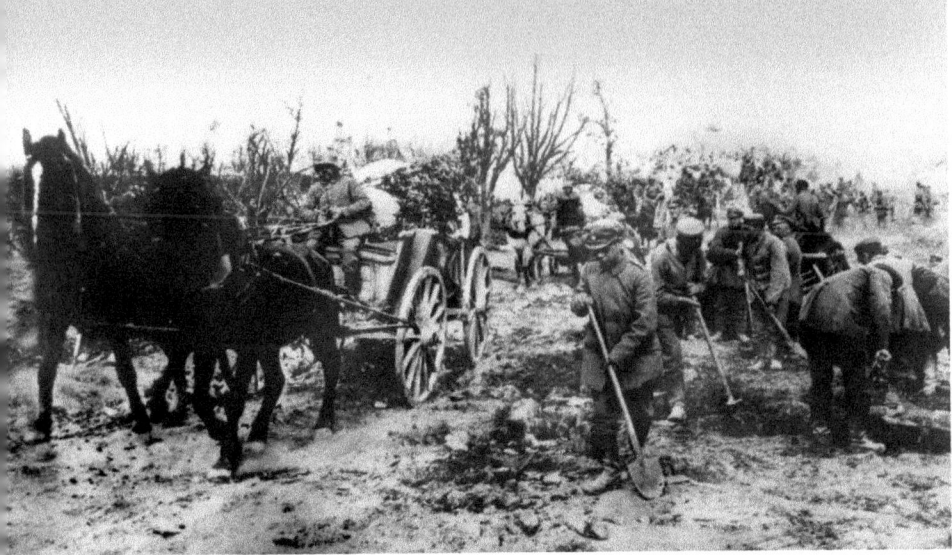
17GW667 The weather was very bad in the first week of April 1917, with heavy rain that made the roads on both sides of the lines into nigh impassable stretches of mud. German engineers widening a road.

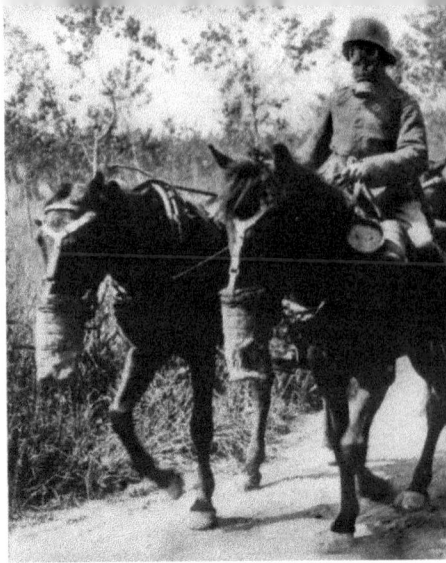
17GW668 An artillery column with both men and horses wearing gas masks.

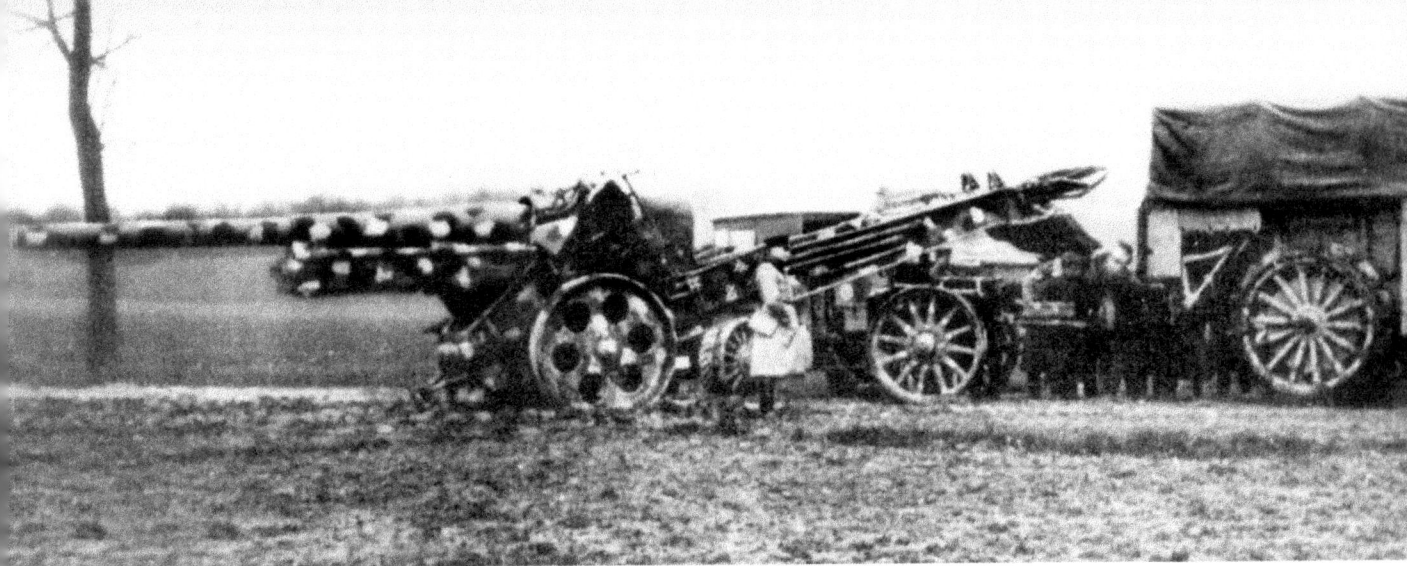

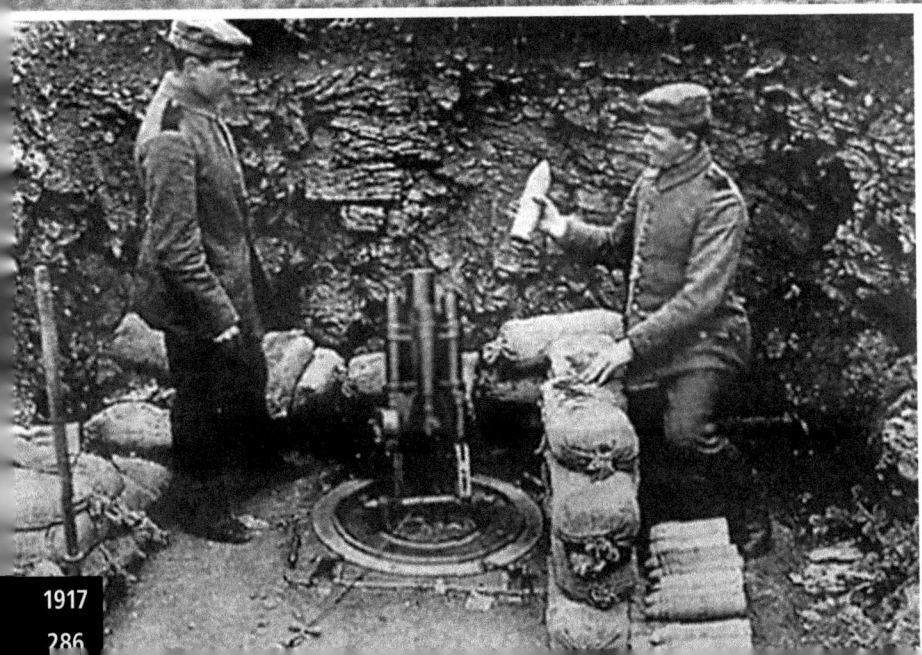

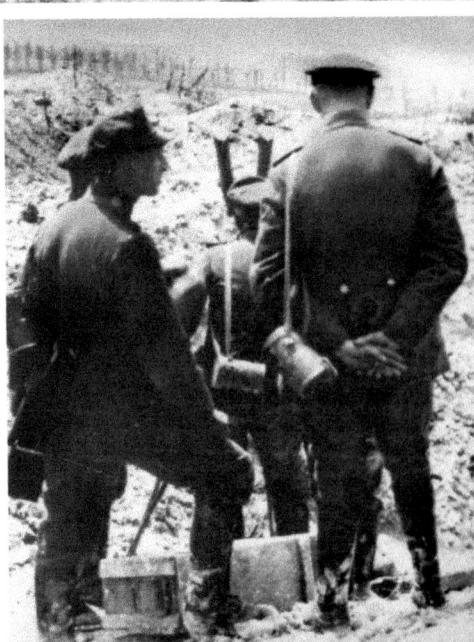

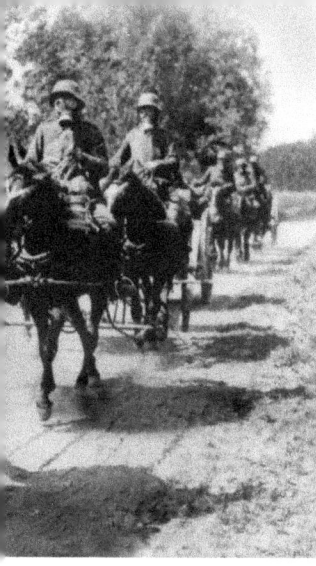

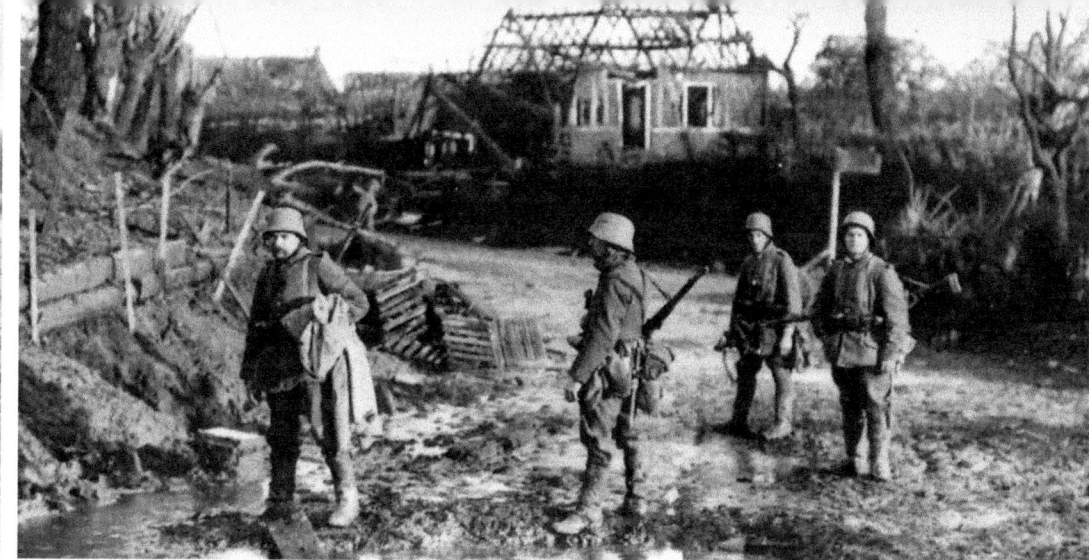

17GW669 The rear areas were given a pounding for four days with high explosives and gas shells.

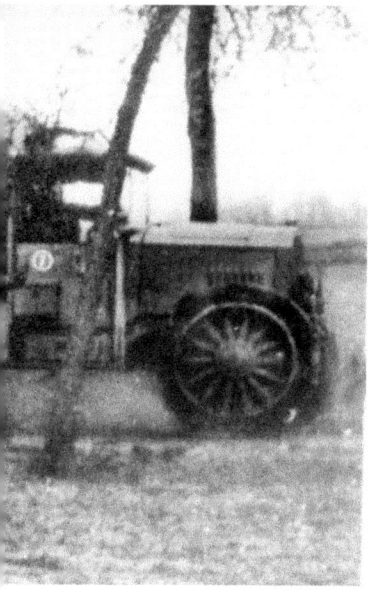

17GW670 A German 170 mm gun, still bearing the lozenge-shaped, newly painted, dazzle pattern camouflage, put on at the factory. The towing vehicle is fitted with tractor-style wheels for gripping the mud.

17GW623 A young replacement receives a quick course on being in a mortar team.

17GW671 German artillery officers ranging on French artillery batteries and likely areas for troop concentrations preparing for the Nivelle Offensive.

17GW672 Sappers of a Pioneer Battalion: equipped and ready to counter attack should the French break in to their lines.

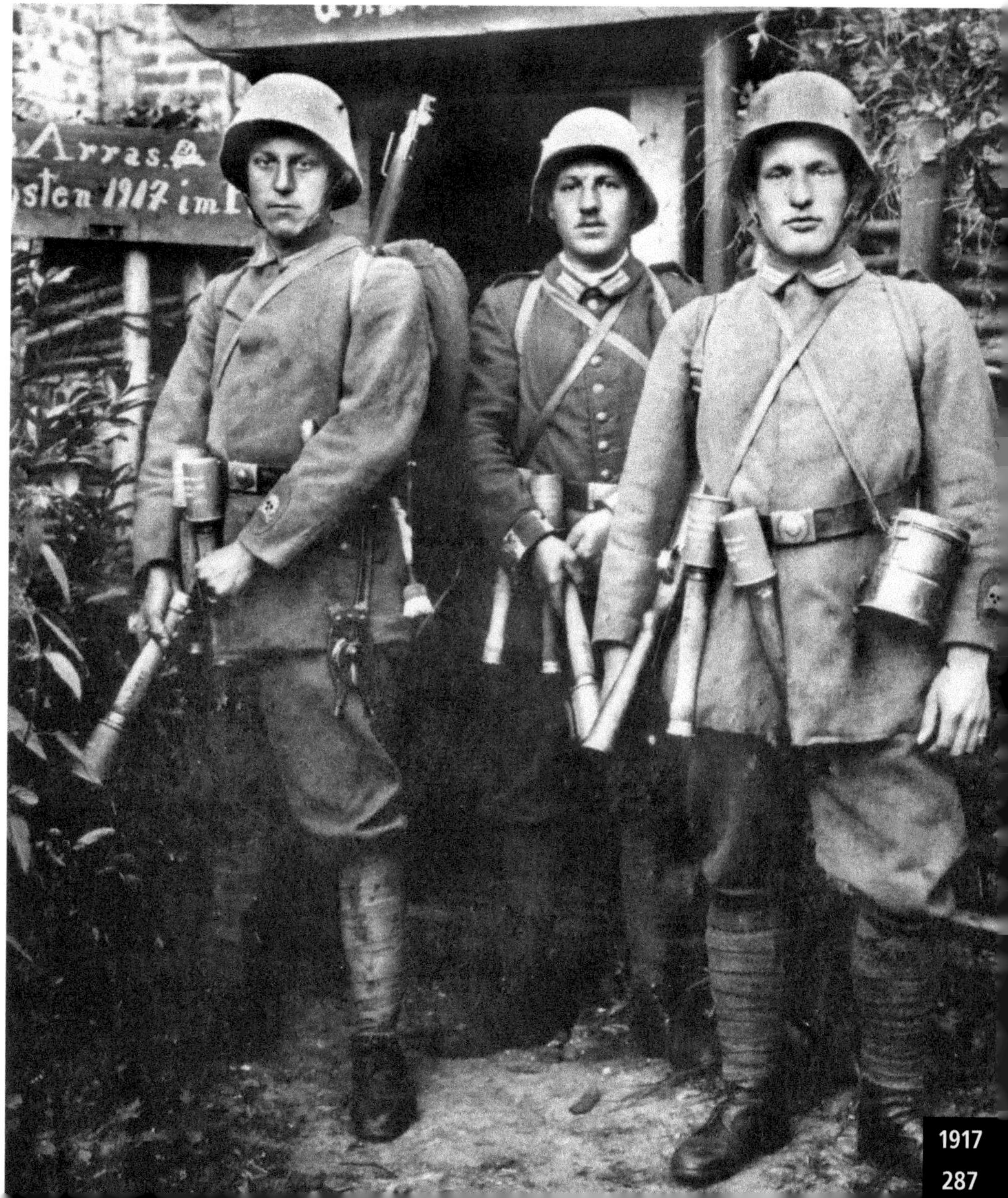

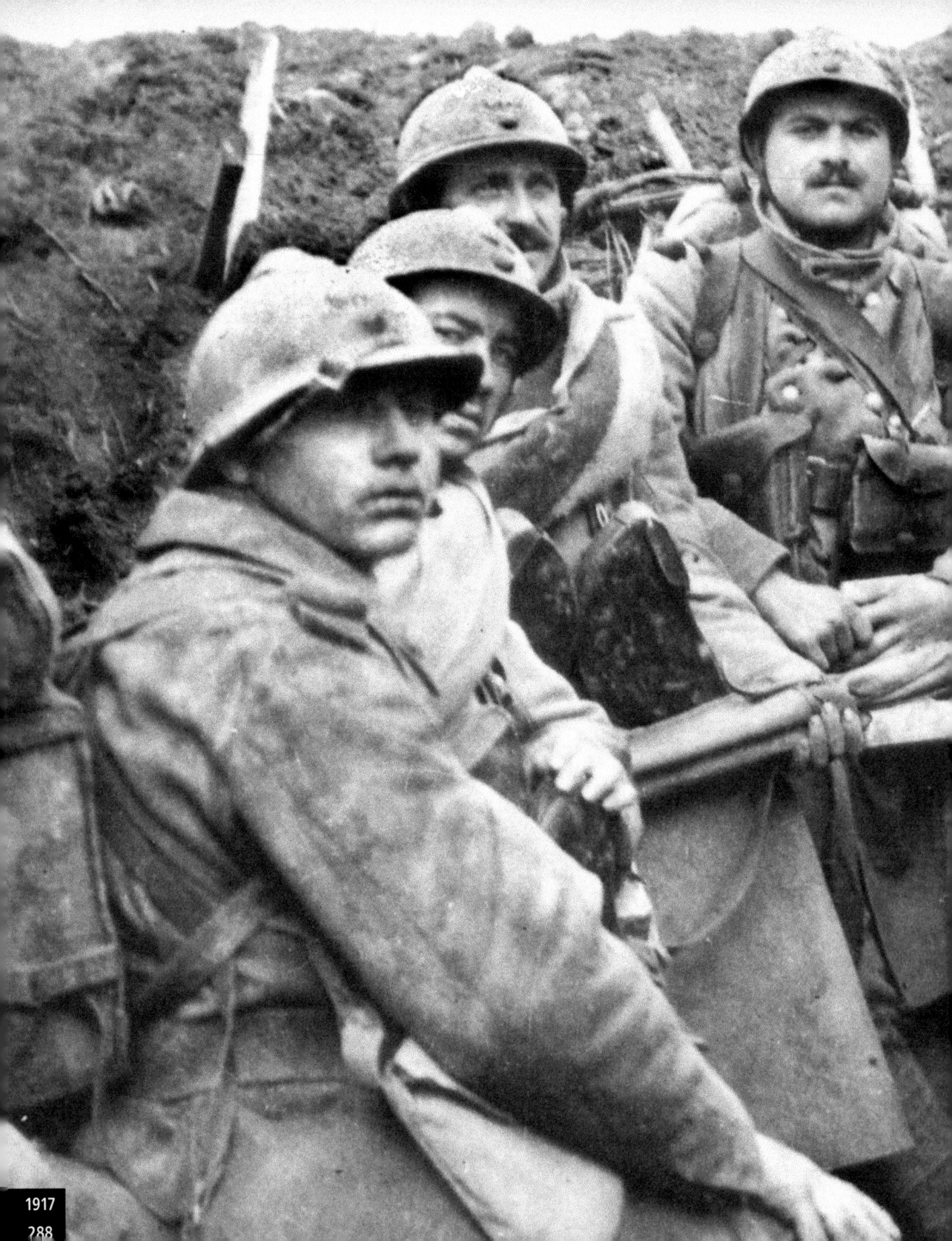

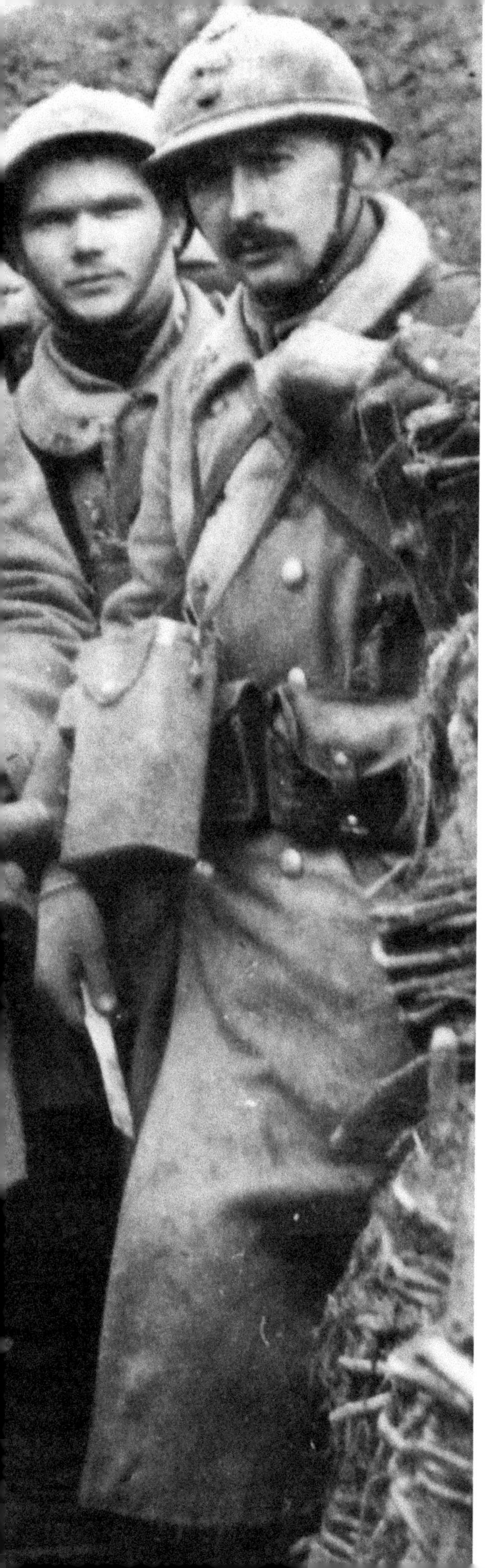

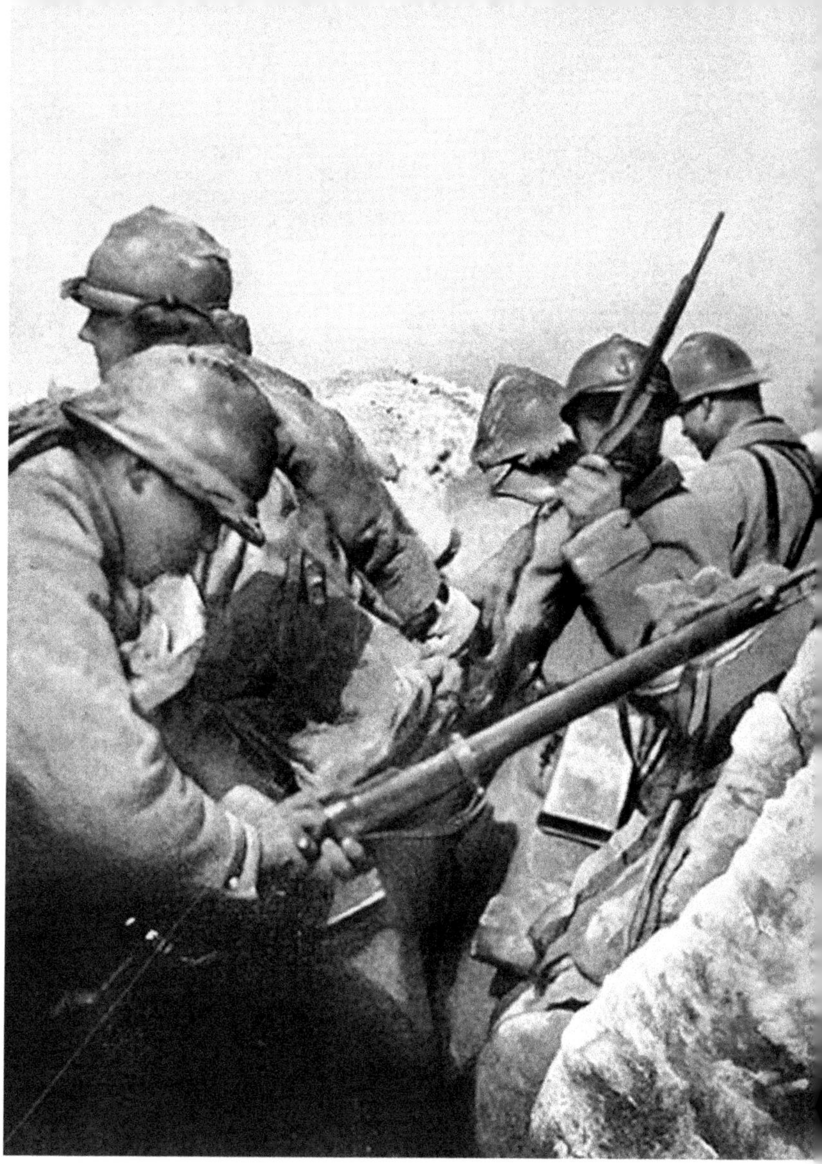

17GW674, 17GW675. Morning of the 16 April, 0600 hours: poilus ready for the big attack on the Chemin des Dames. Each man carried a load to sustain him in the captured trenches: two water bottles; a haversack for food (including a loaf of bread); haversack for personal belongings; three hand grenades and two rifle grenades; 120 rounds of ammunition; Lebel rifle and bayonet; gas mask; entrenching spade; blanket. The terrain was hilly and heavily pitted with shell holes. But the Germans were ready for them.

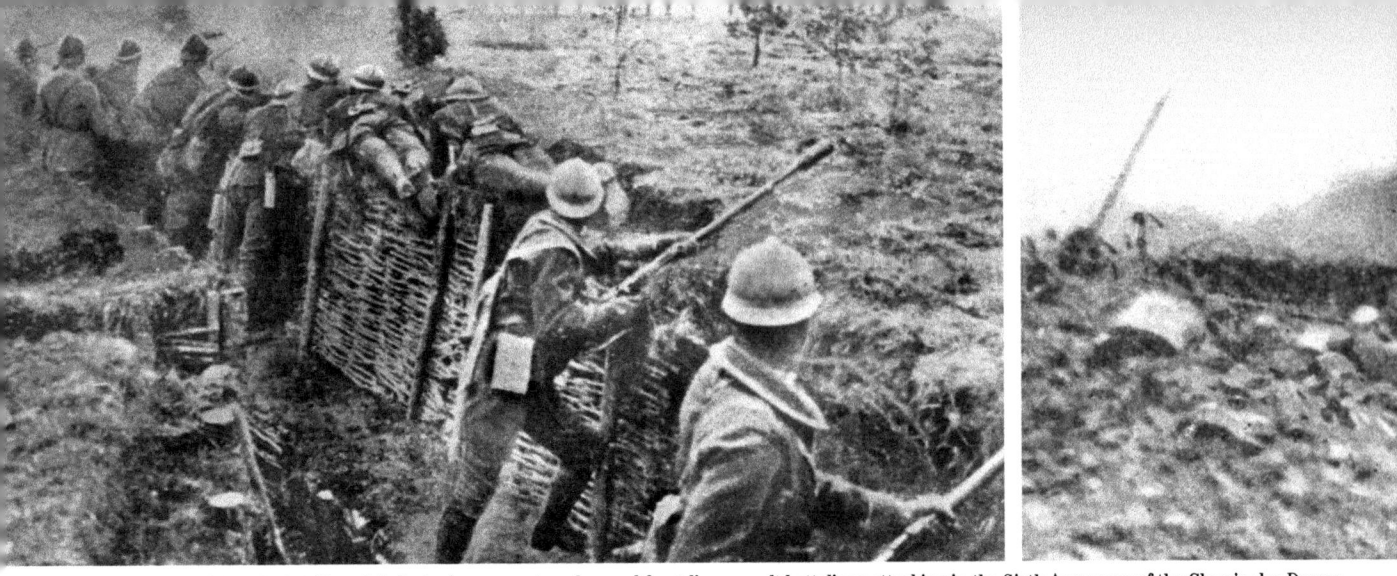

17GW640, 17GW676, 17GW611. French infantry in reserve trenches and front line assault battalions attacking in the Sixth Army area of the Chemin des Dames.

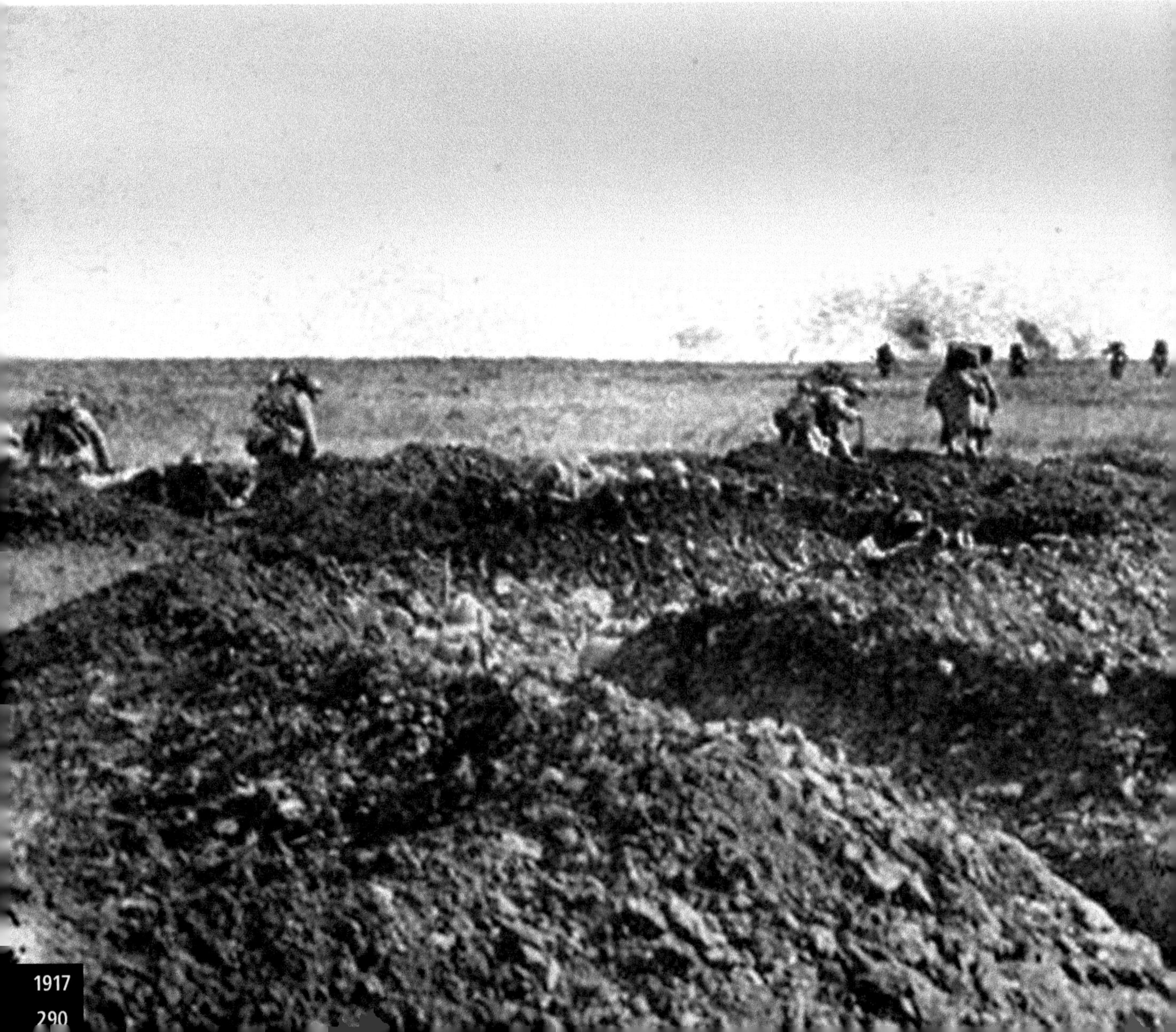

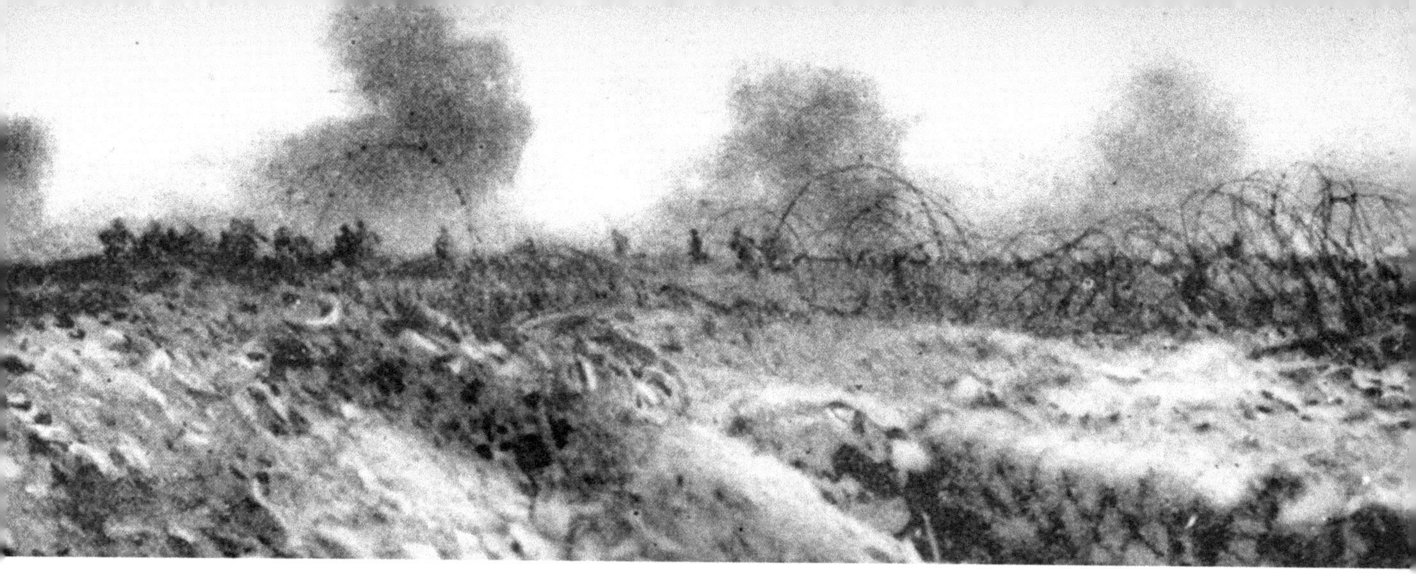

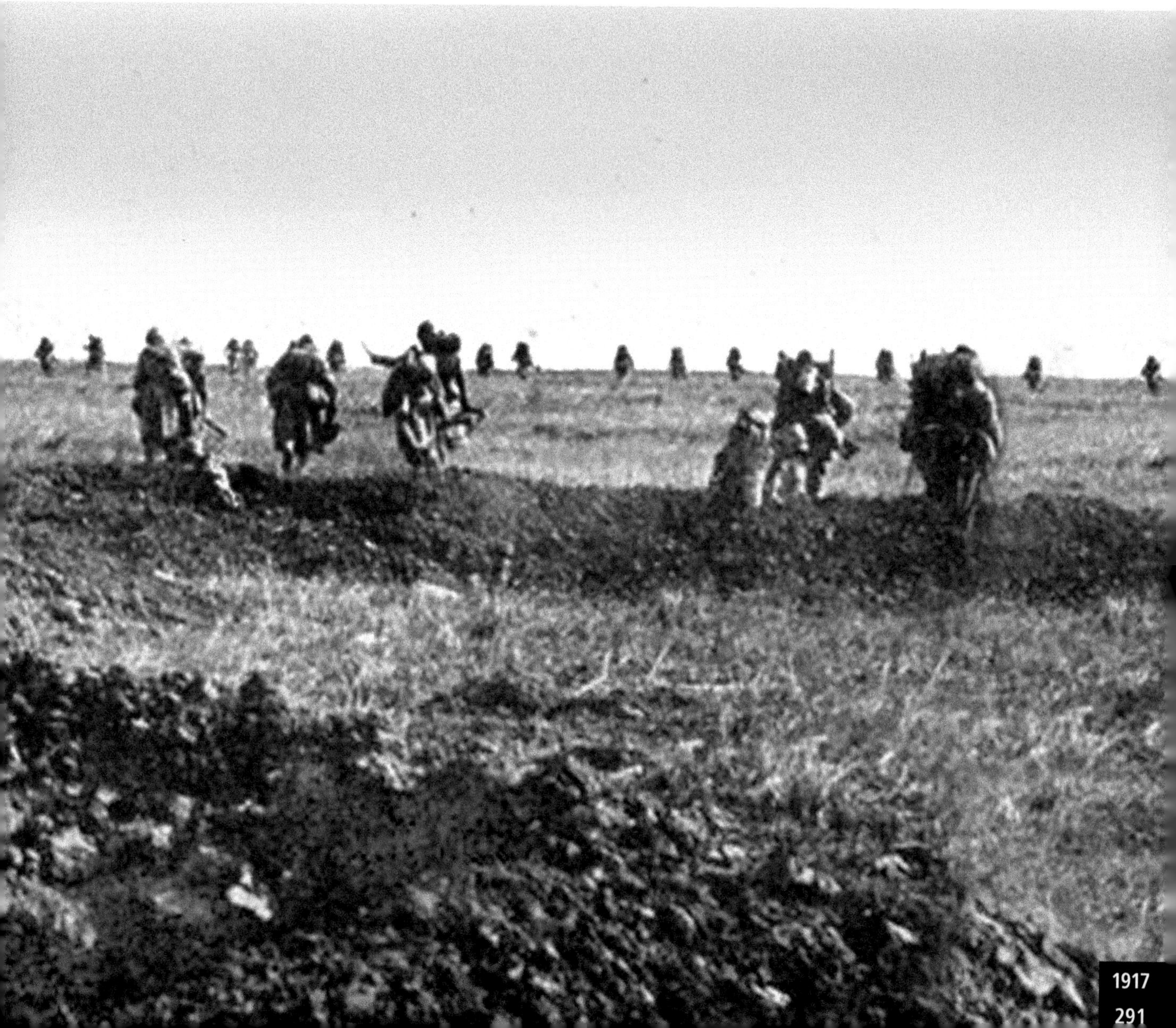

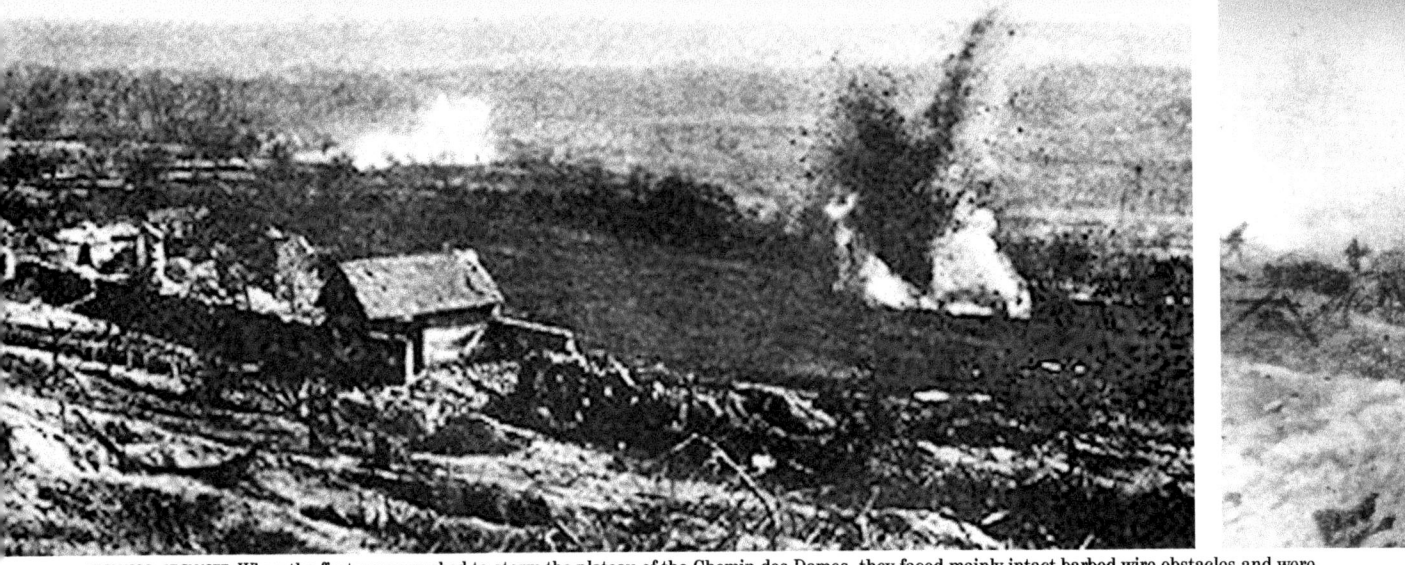

17GW629, 17GW677. When the first waves rushed to storm the plateau of the Chemin des Dames, they faced mainly intact barbed wire obstacles and were caught in cross fire from machine guns zeroed-in on the few gaps that had been created by the preliminary bombardment.

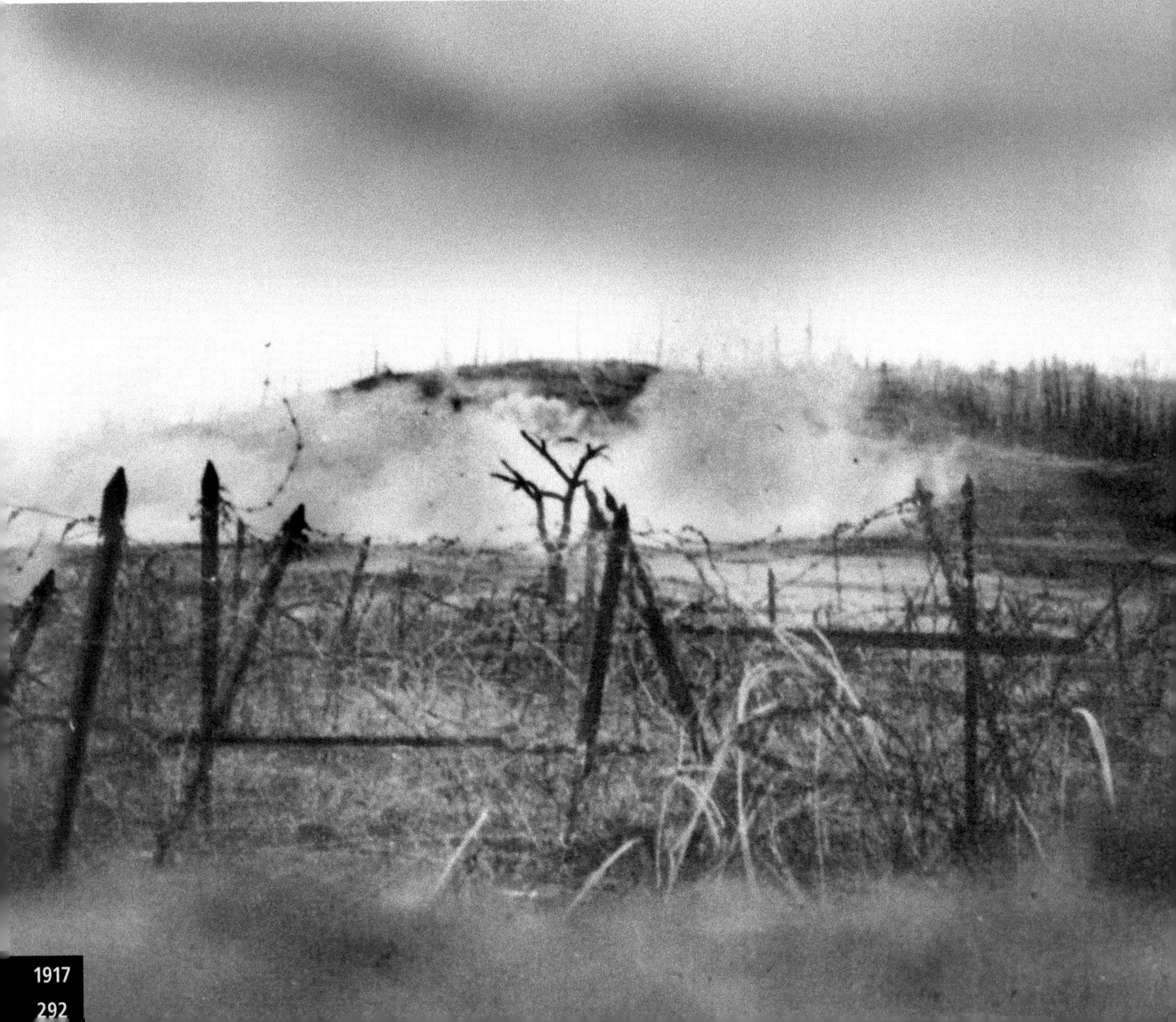

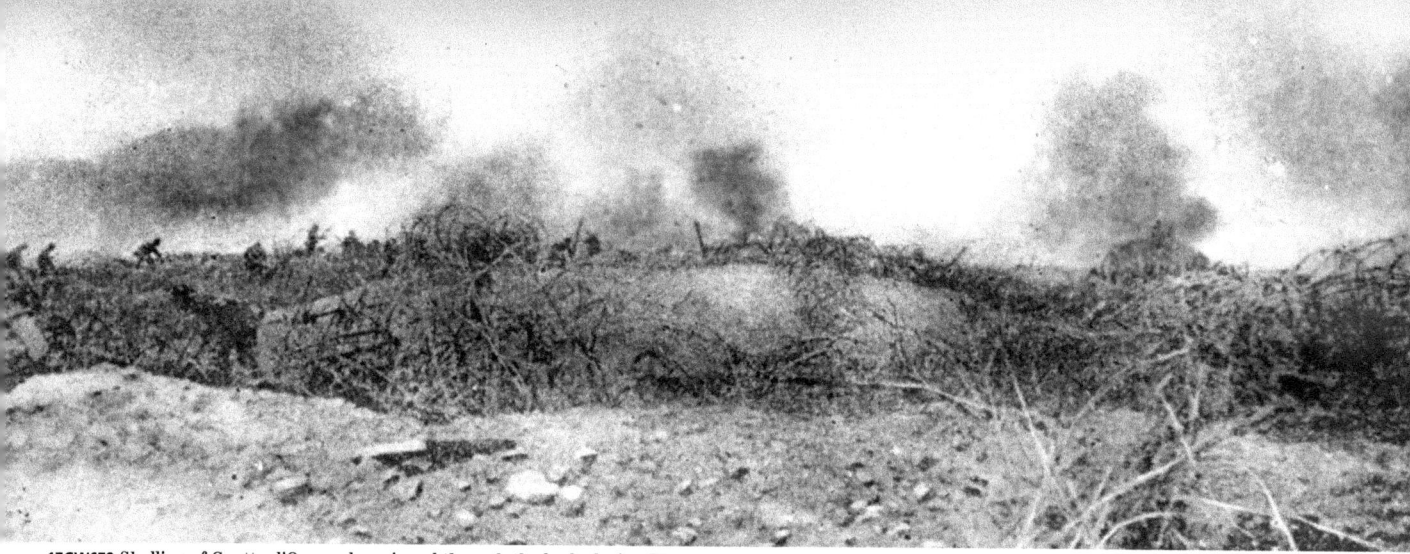

17GW678 Shelling of Goutte d'Or wood as viewed through the barbed wire. The attack here, as elsewhere, had faltered.
17GW679 Men of a battalion that had taken the first two German lines sheltering from the heavy bombardment that had stopped them from moving forward.

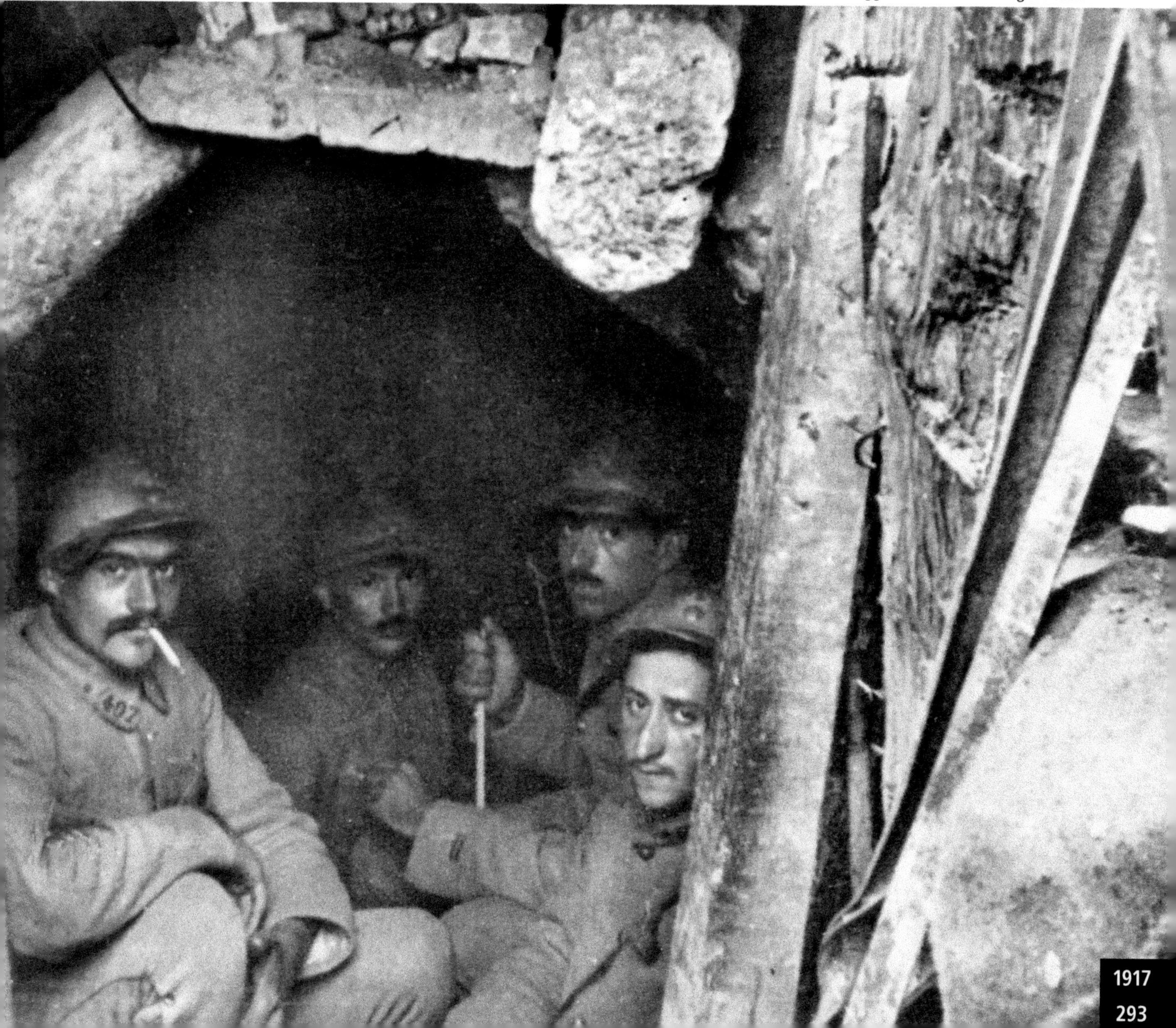

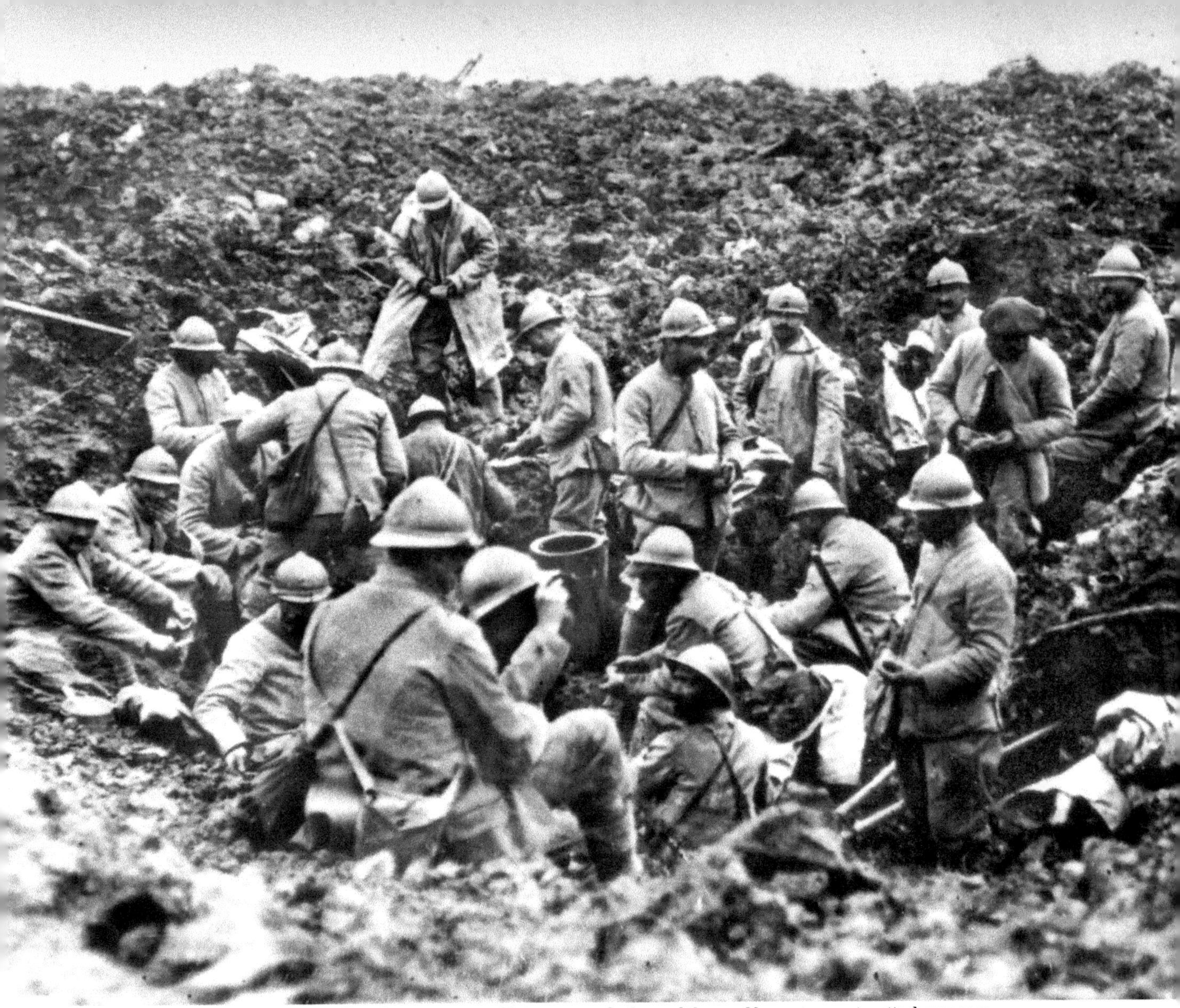

17GW680 Captured German positions – French troops were unable to progress further and they could expect a counter attack very soon.
17GW683 A French bugler killed during the attack at Moulin Laffaux.

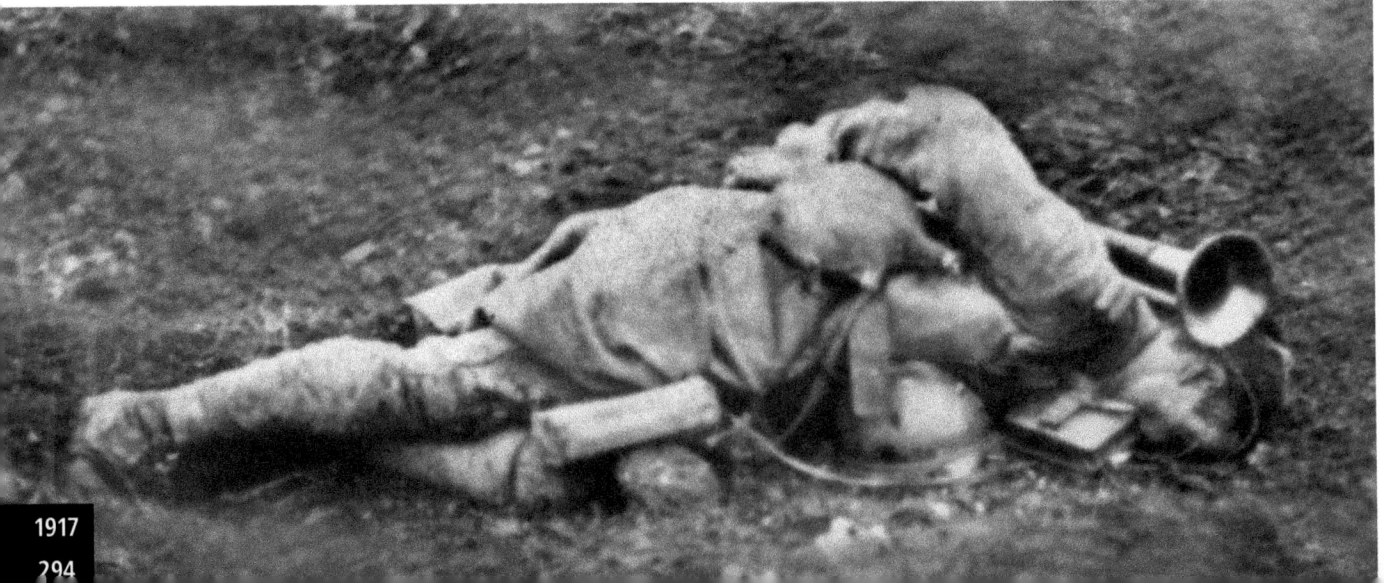

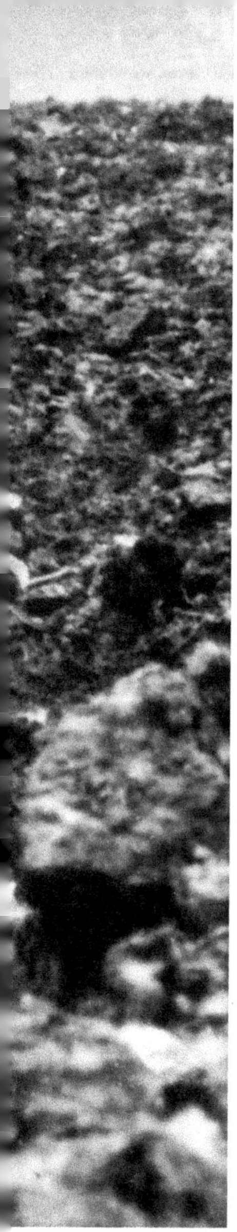

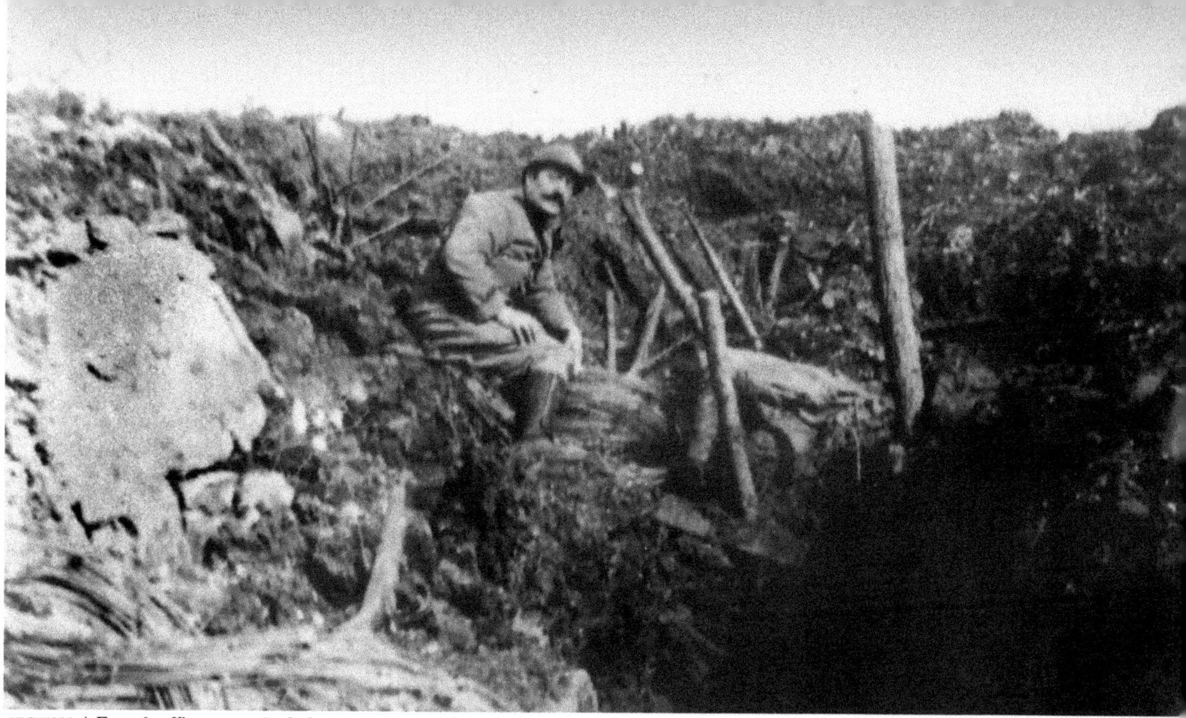

17GW682 A French officer crouched above a captured German dugout.

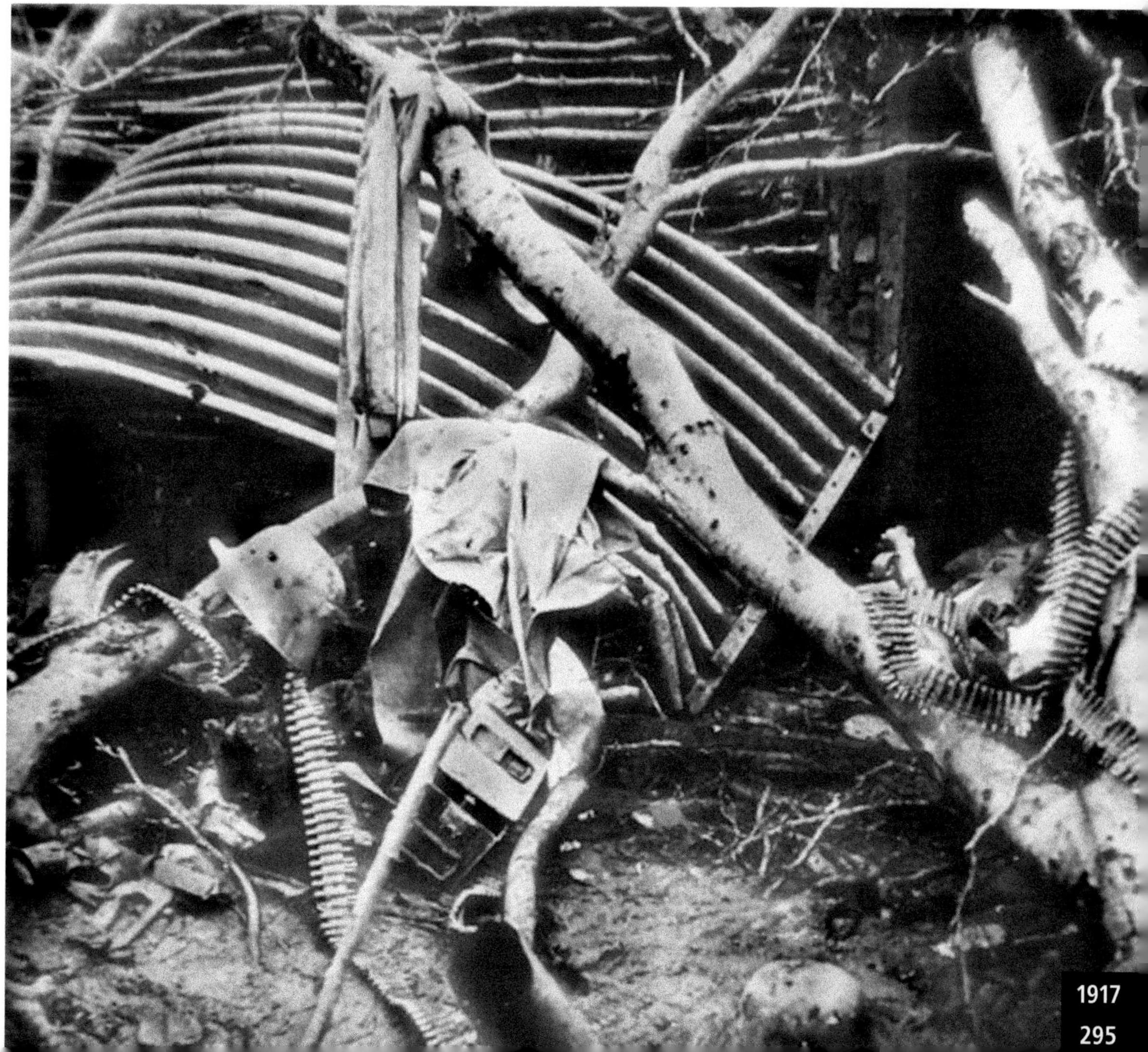

17GW681 A captured German machine gun post – the original negative reads: 'Chemin des Dames – cadavres Allemands' (dead bodies of Germans). There are no dead Germans evident in this frame, just belts of ammunition and items of equipment.

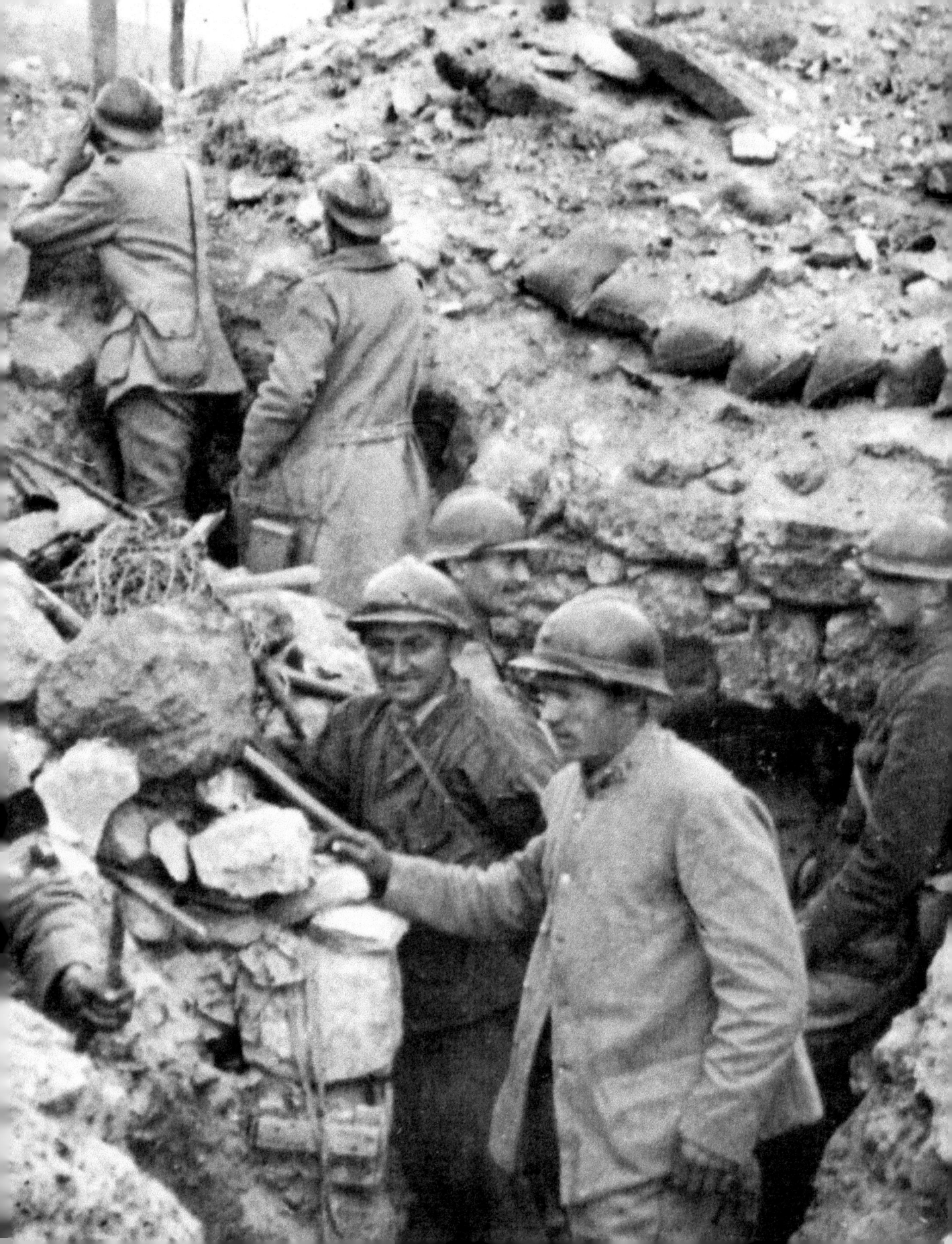

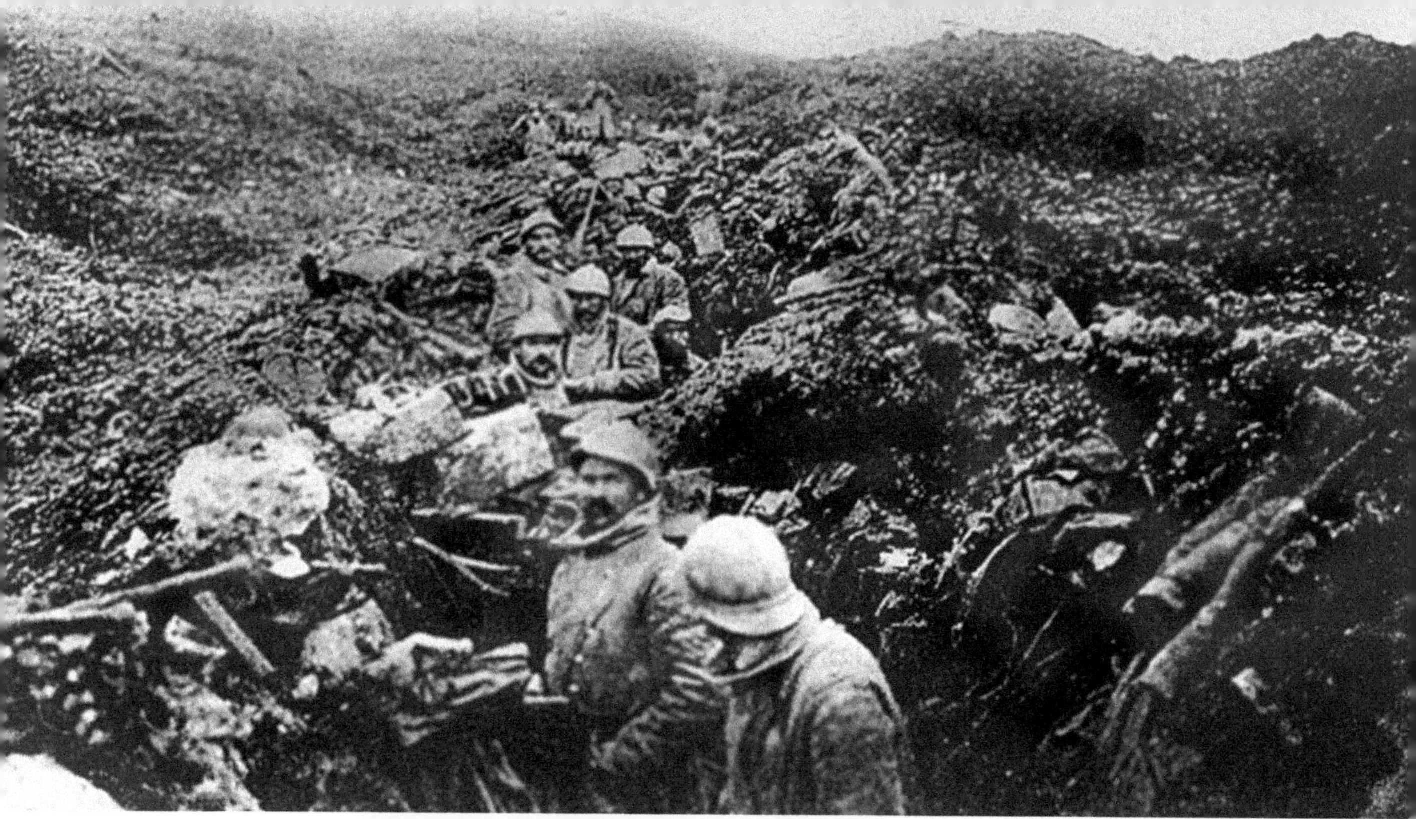

17GW689, 17GW687, 17GW622. French infantry occupy captured German positions in the Sixth Army area of Chemin des Dames.

On the XX Corps front the attack made some initial progress and reached as far as the sucrerie at Cerny; Moroccan infantry reached the edge of Paradise Wood and into the German second line, where they were stopped by fierce resistance and counter attacks.

Two hours into the attack, General Mangin realised that the anticipated breakthrough had not happened. He issued further orders to the artillery: *Try to catch up on delay; carry on with the barrage according to the scheduled plan: remember, centres of resistance are being outflanked.*

Facing the German positions at Goutte d'Or Wood the barbed wire was unbroken in spite of the preparatory bombardment. The attackers were unable to go forward and a request was made for further artillery fire to be called down on that sector. General Mangin was furious – it was already four hours into the attack. He issued the order: *Unit Hellot must continue its advance. If the wire is not destroyed have the infantry cut it themselves – we must gain ground.*

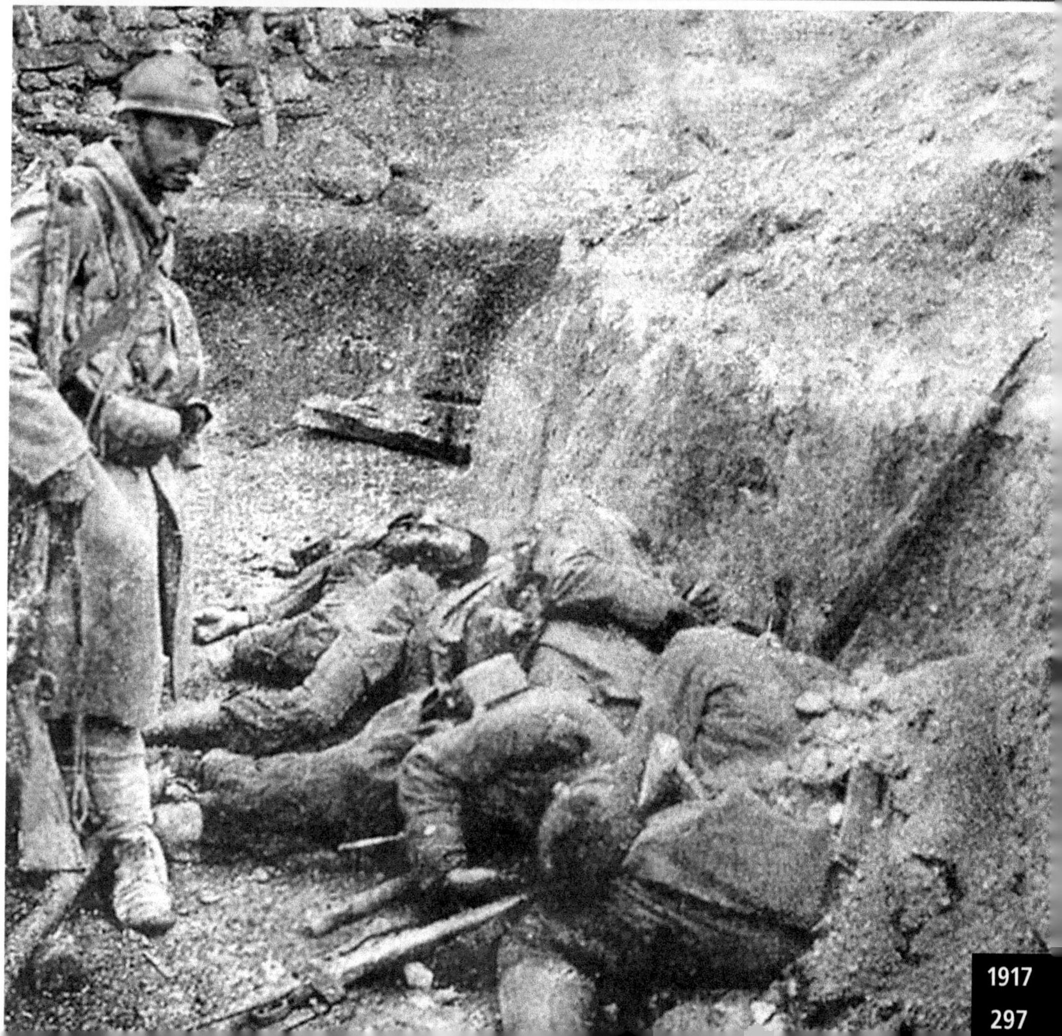

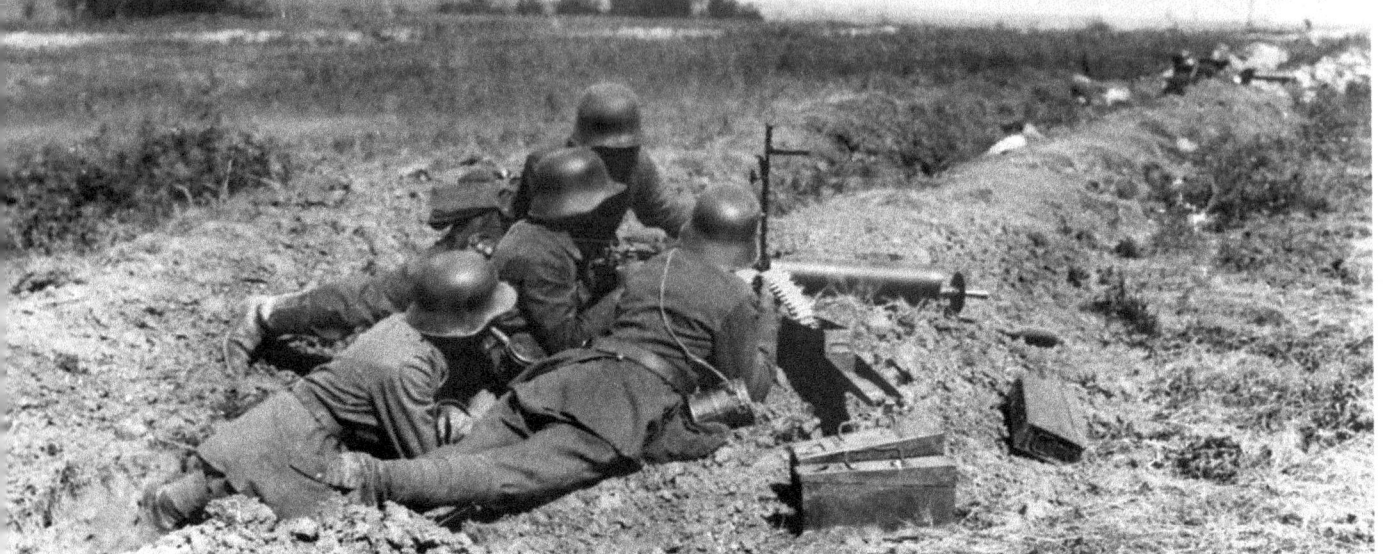

17GW691 The combination of uncut barbed wire and German machine guns, which dominated the battlefields along most of the Chemin des Dames, halted the infantry and made further progress impossible.

17GW694 Philippe Henri Joseph d'Anselme

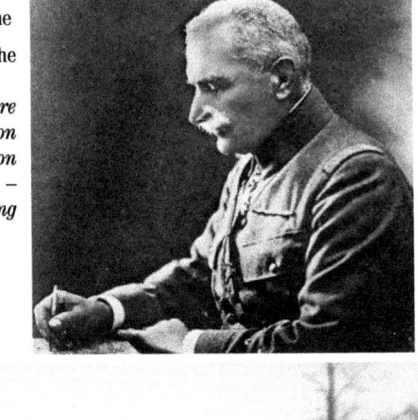

French General Henri d'Anselme, who commanded the 36th Infantry Division, wrote about the fighting for the village of Chavonne:

A fierce hand to hand fight took place in the village. In just one cellar an officer and seventeen men were wiped out. However, during a determined counter attack, Major Bruneau, who constantly led his battalion from the front, disappeared – either killed or captured. The officer who took over was himself wounded upon reaching the churchyard. Our assault waves were stopped. Now Chavonne no longer provides cover – everything has been destroyed and the German machine guns sited at les Grinons are constantly sweeping the village with fire, making it impossible to hold.

17GW693 Two Renault armoured cars in the village of Chavonne, where fierce fighting took place on 30 April 1917. A German counter attack retook most of the ruins during that day. The French held on to some of the houses and Mount Sapin. Armoured cars were very limited in their usefulness in these conditions.

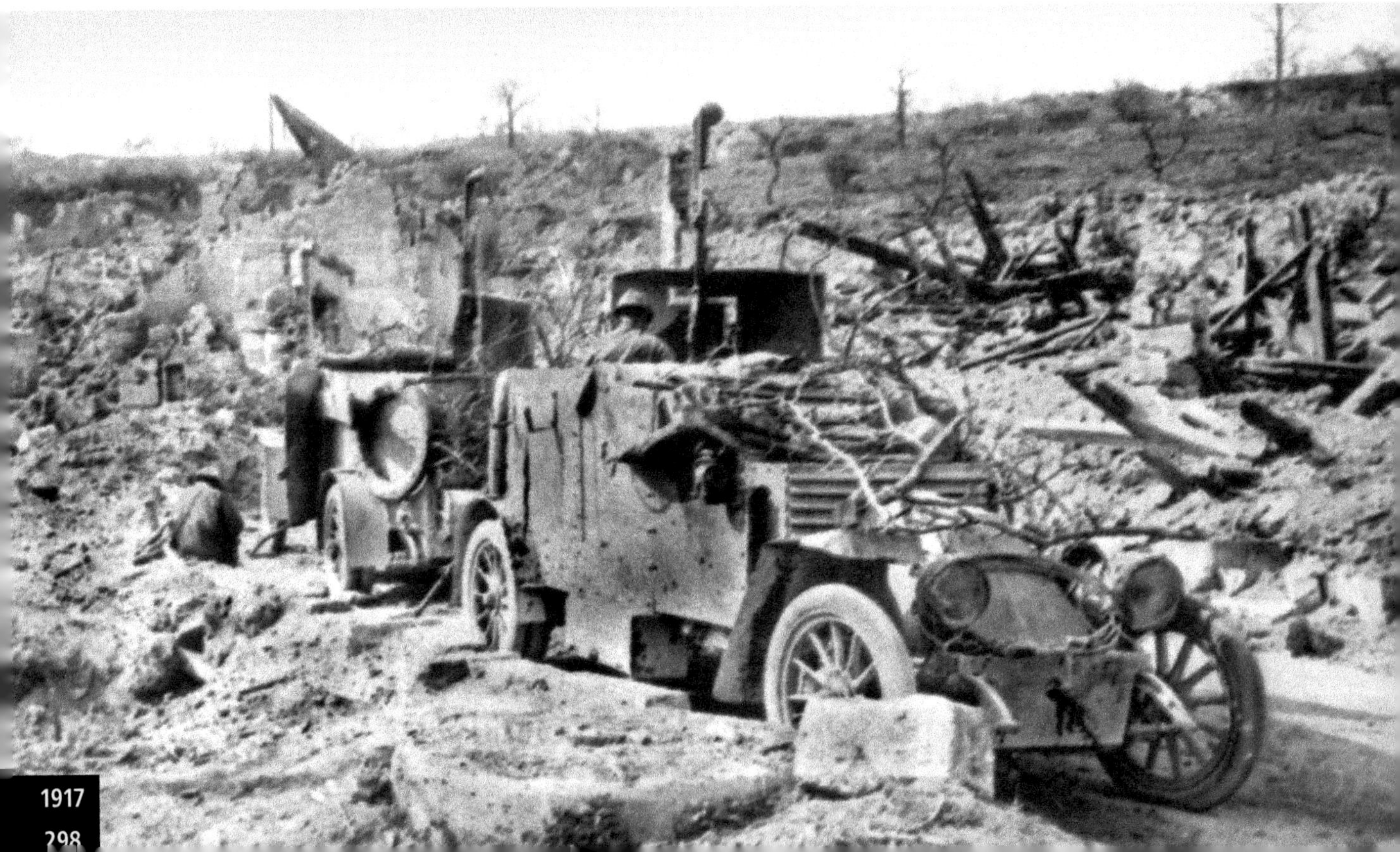

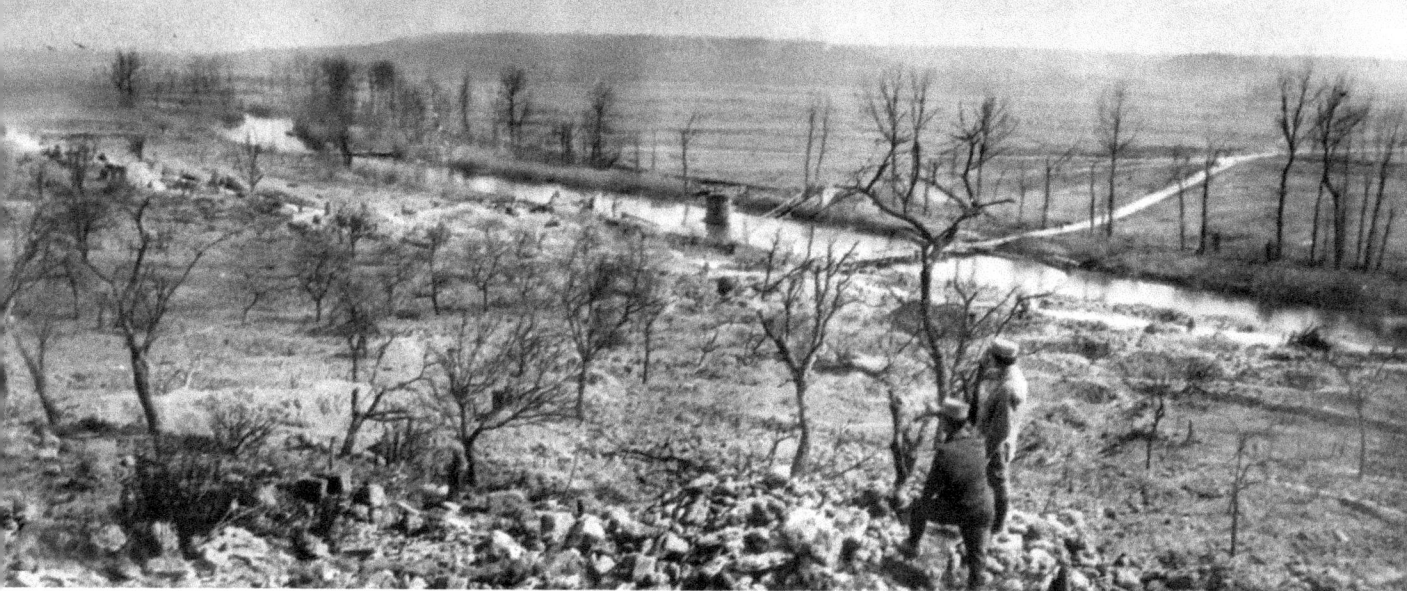

17GW692 Two French officers look along the valley and line of the Aisne river at Chavonne, 30 April 1917. The high ground was still in German hands despite the casualties suffered by the poilus. Note the centre pillar of the destroyed bridge in the water and the two pontoon bridges crossing the river.

17GW695 A blinded Sengalese soldier is assisted to an aid post following fighting in front of the mill at Laffaux.

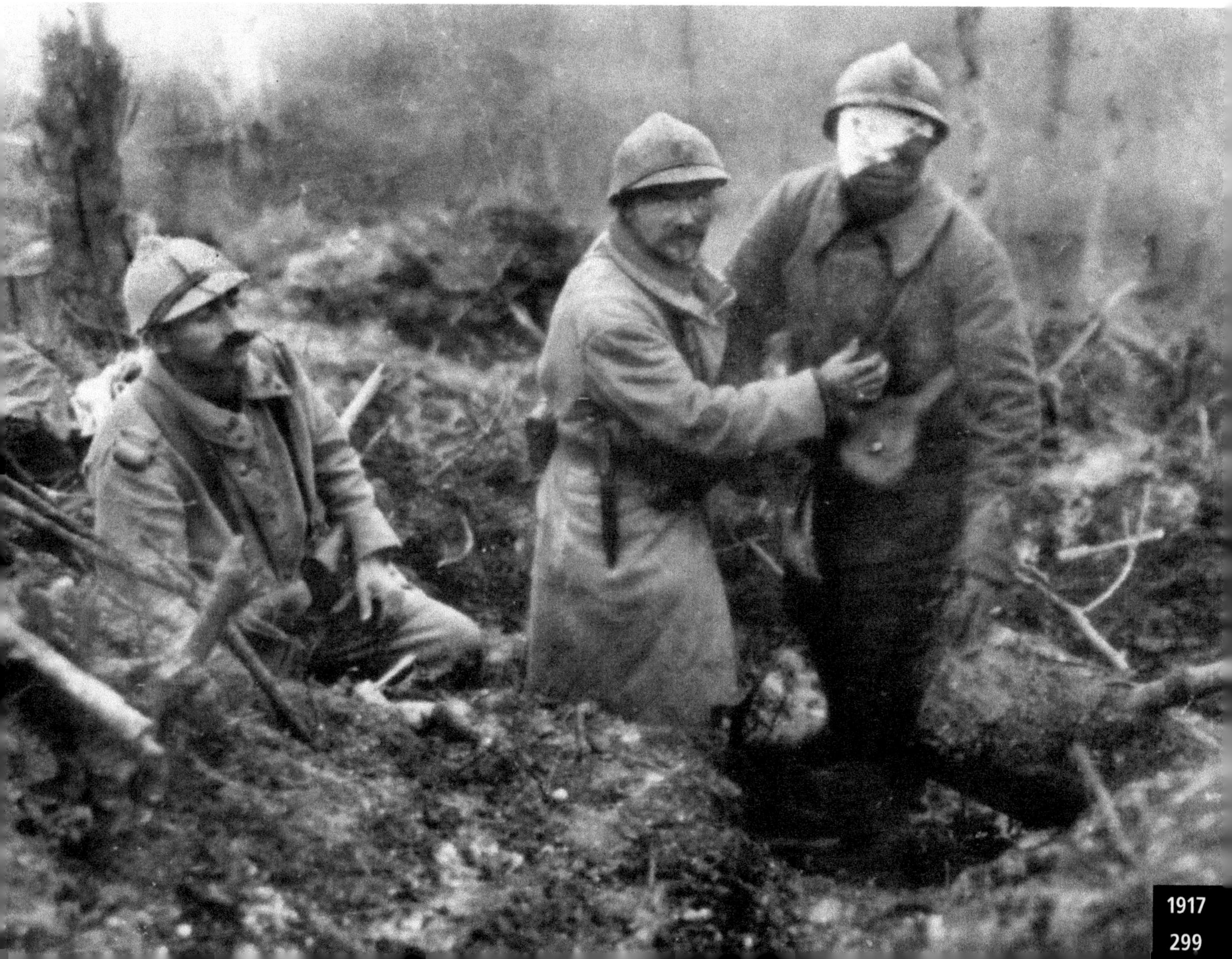

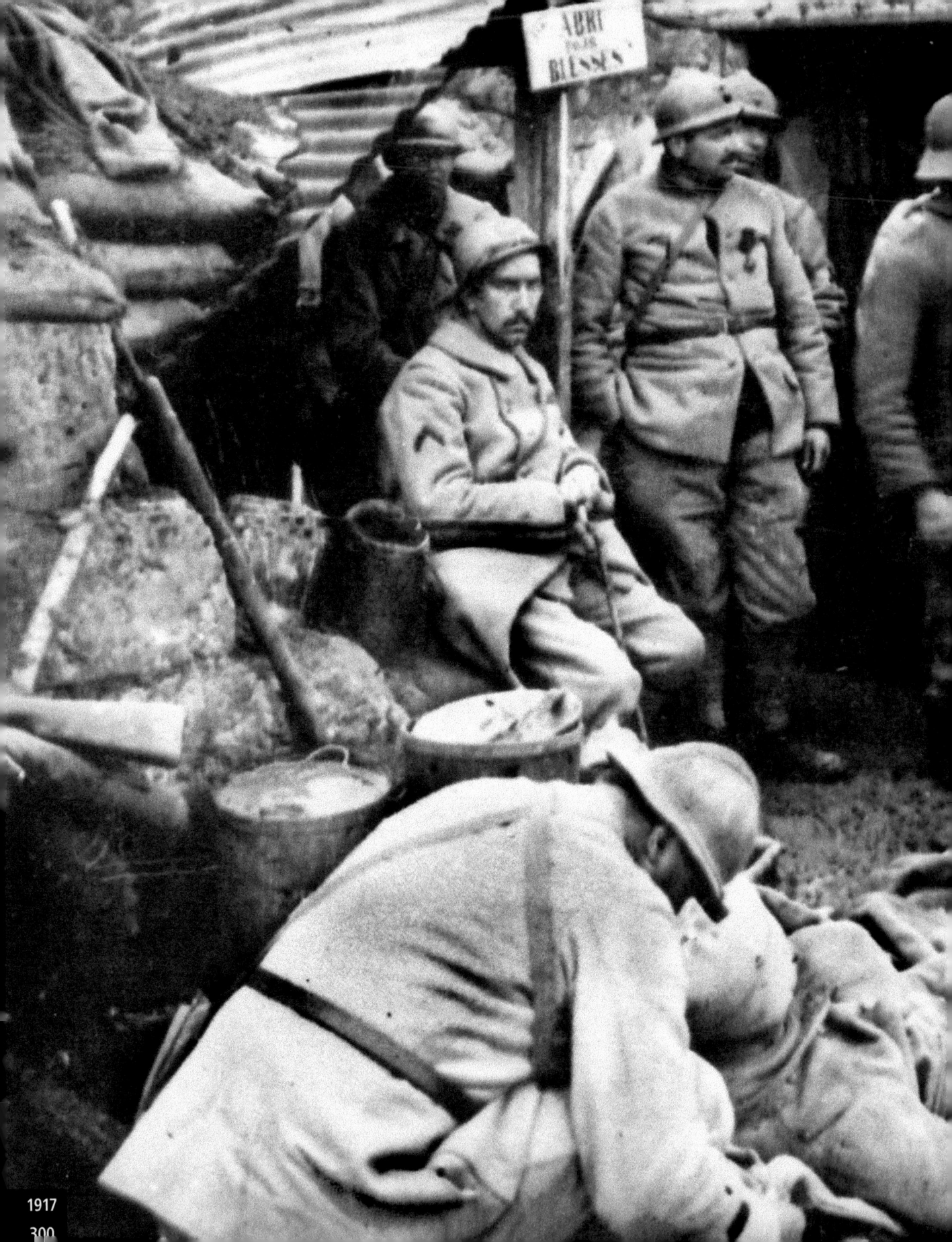

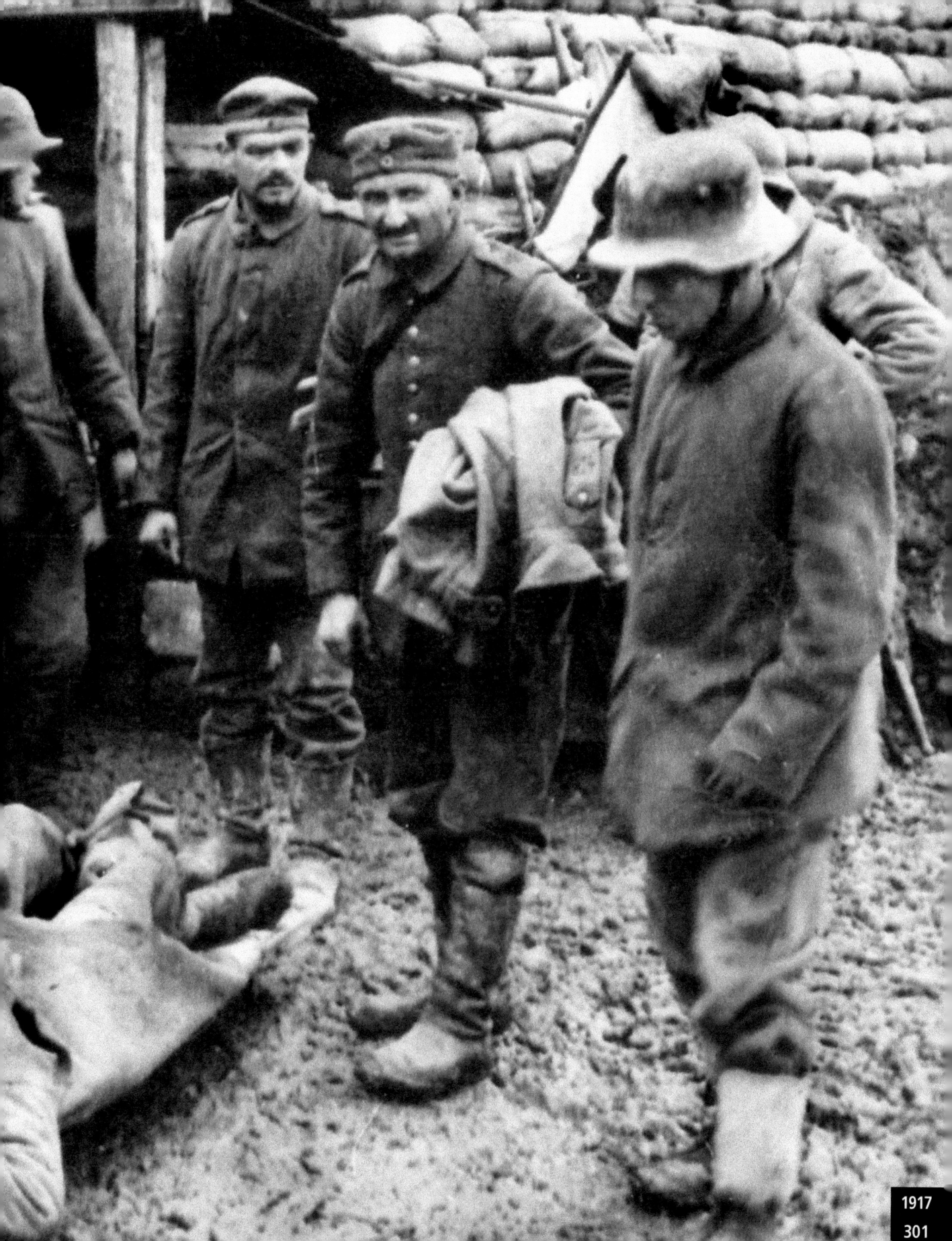

17GW698 A dressing station near Soupir. German prisoners were used to carry the wounded.

17GW696 German prisoners taken in the Vauxaillon sector.
17GW697 German officers captured in front of Craonne.

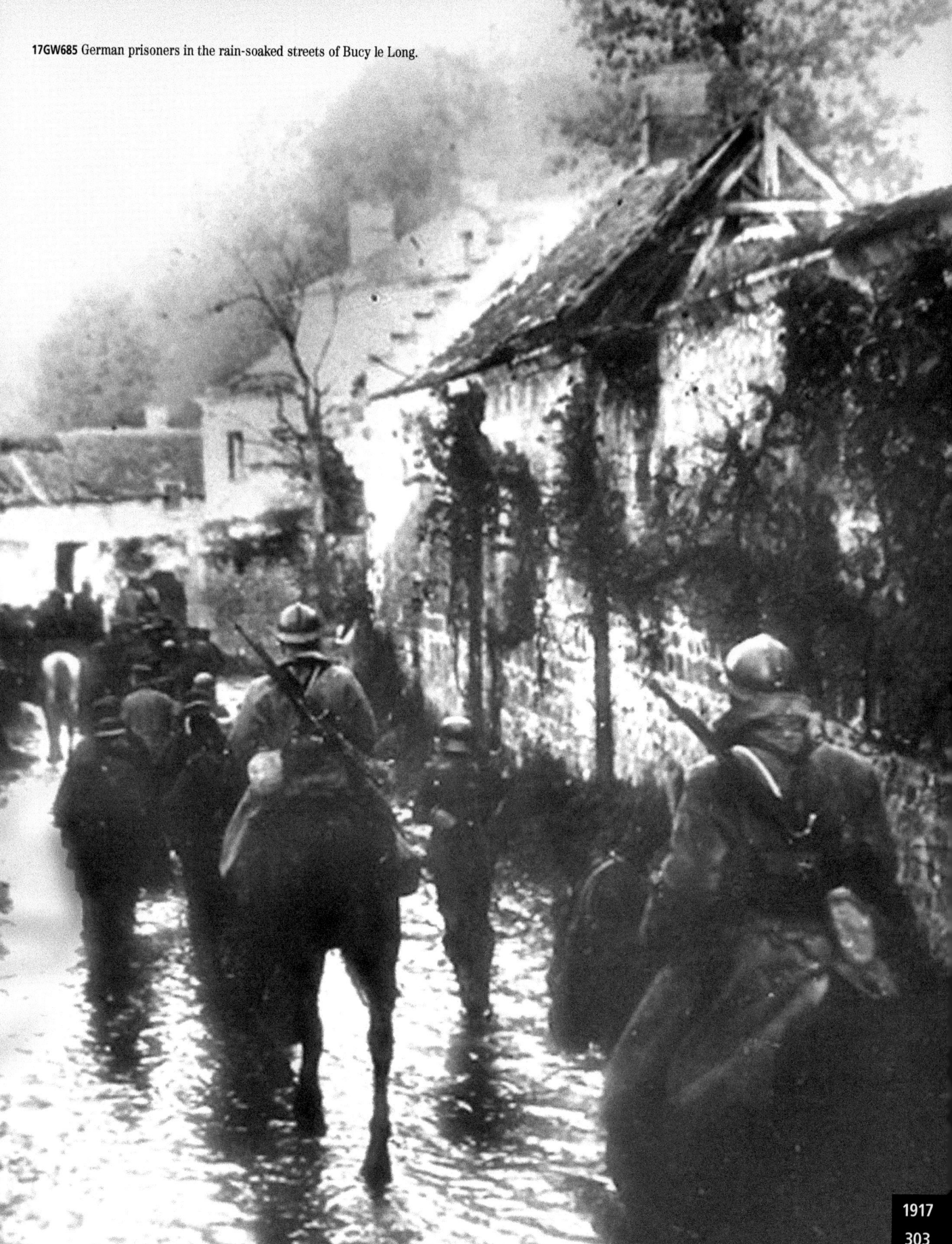
17GW685 German prisoners in the rain-soaked streets of Bucy le Long.

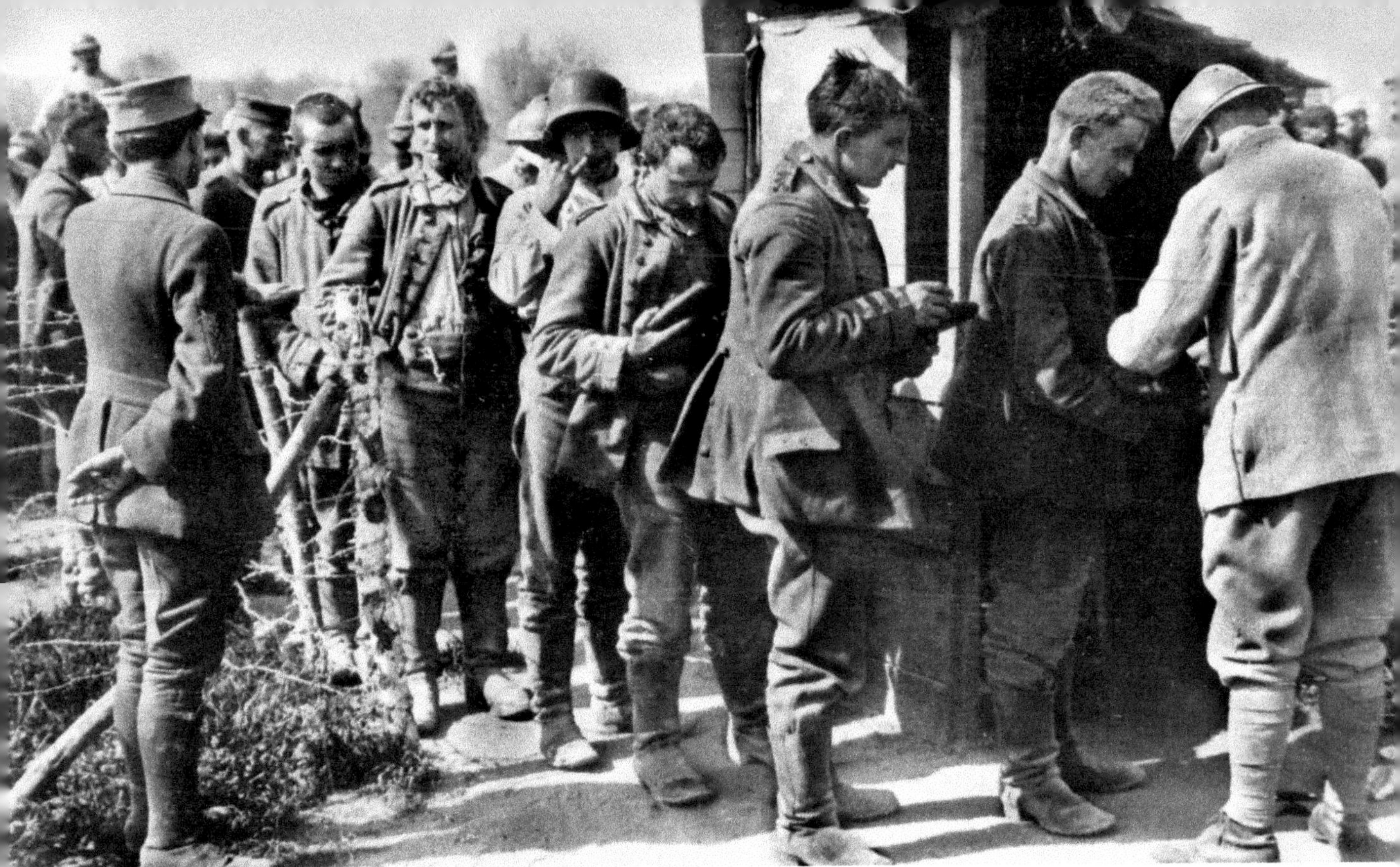

17GW699 German prisoners captured in front of Craonne in line for their *Soldbuch*, paybooks, to be examined. In four days in April, beginning on the 16th, 11,000 prisoners were taken, along with 40 artillery pieces of various calibres and 200 machine guns.

17GW700 On 19 April the order was given to move a battery of artillery up to Cour-Soupir. For much of the climb a team of eighteen horses per gun was used to cope with the incline. Here a 155 mm gun is being hauled up the last stretch by hand.

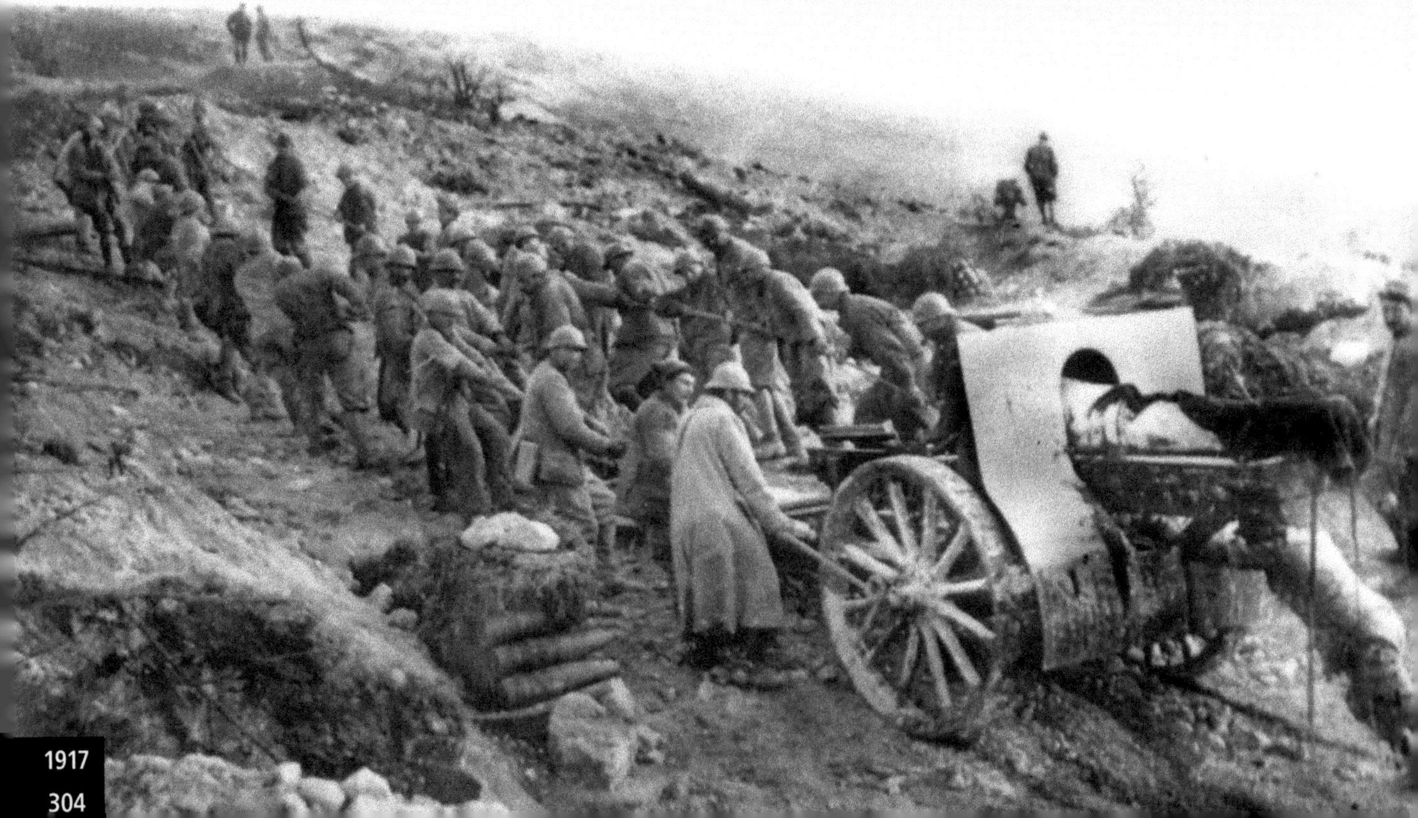

The Schneider CA-1 – Total production: 400

Dimensions:	(L x W x H) 6.32m x 2.30m x 2.05m
Weight:	13.6 tons
Crew:	6
Engine:	Schneider 4 cyl petrol, 60 hp)
Speed	8 km/h (5 mph)
Range on/off road:	80/30 km (50/19 miles)
Armament:	2x Hotchkiss 8 mm MGs 1x Schneider 75 mm) blockhaus gun
Armour:	11 mm + 5.5 mm spaced

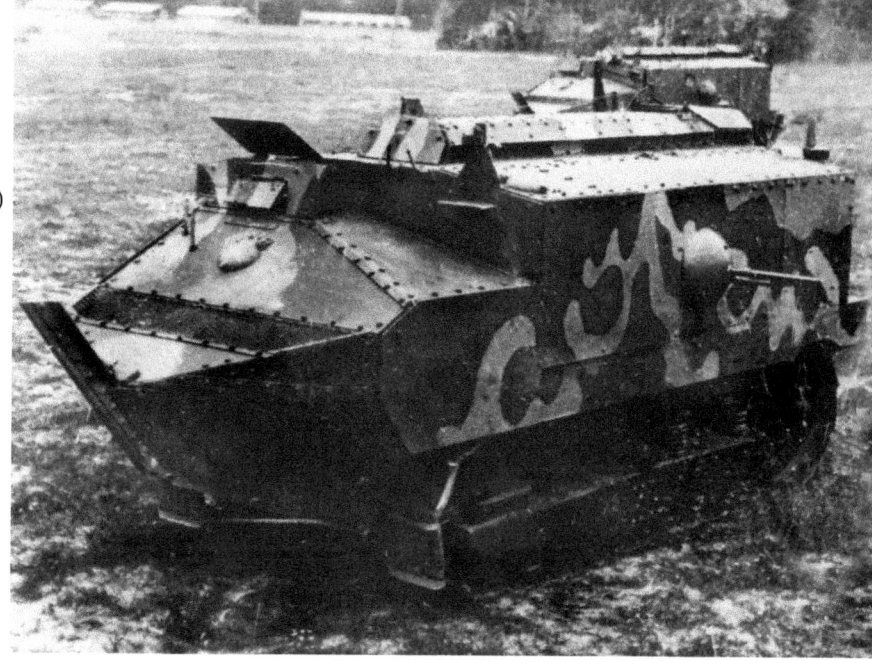

The new weapon was used by the French for the first time at Berry-au-Bac (part of the Chemin des Dames offensive). The number available at the time was 132 tanks. The weapon's debut was a disaster.

Many of the crews found the terrain was too much for their tracks and their forward, boat-shaped, prow tended to ditch the machine in any wide trench or solid obstacle. The engine lacked power and many broke down at the outset. Others advanced in broad daylight and the Germans brought down a devastating artillery barrage. Field guns at very short range fired on flat trajectories against tanks that were designed to protect against machine gun and infantry fire. The Germans quickly learned to target the exposed forward petrol reserve tank and many burst into flames, earning the nickname of *'Mobil Krematorien'* (mobile crematoria).

A total of fifty-seven CA-1s were lost on the debut day: forty-four broke down at the start; the remainder managed to reach their objectives, breaking through German first and second lines. However, poor coordination meant that the infantry failed to support them and retreated. Out of the 132 committed to the battle only fifty-six survived.

17GW703, 17GW702. Tanks in training prior to leaving Courlandon to take part in the Nivelle Offensive on the Chemin des Dames.

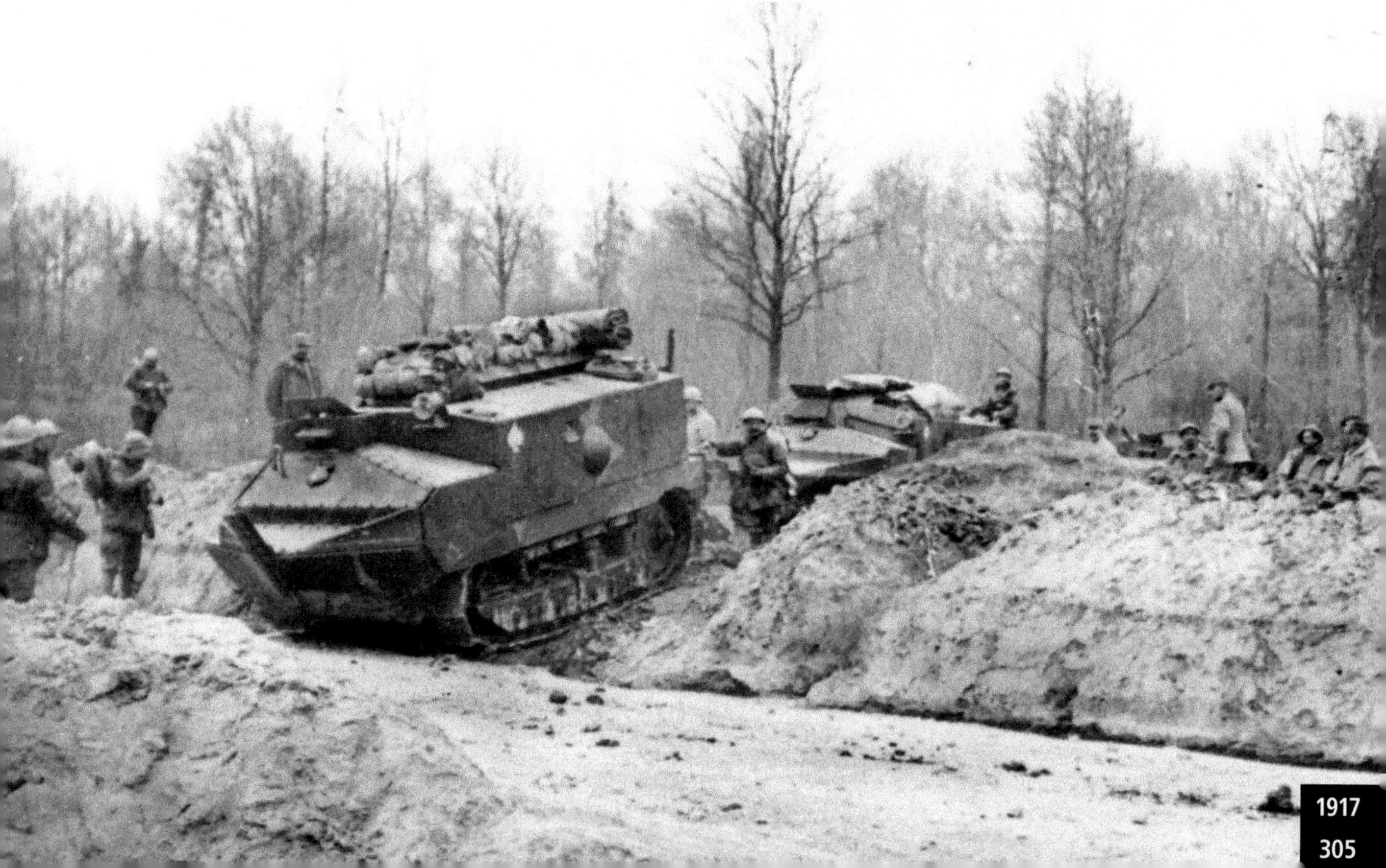

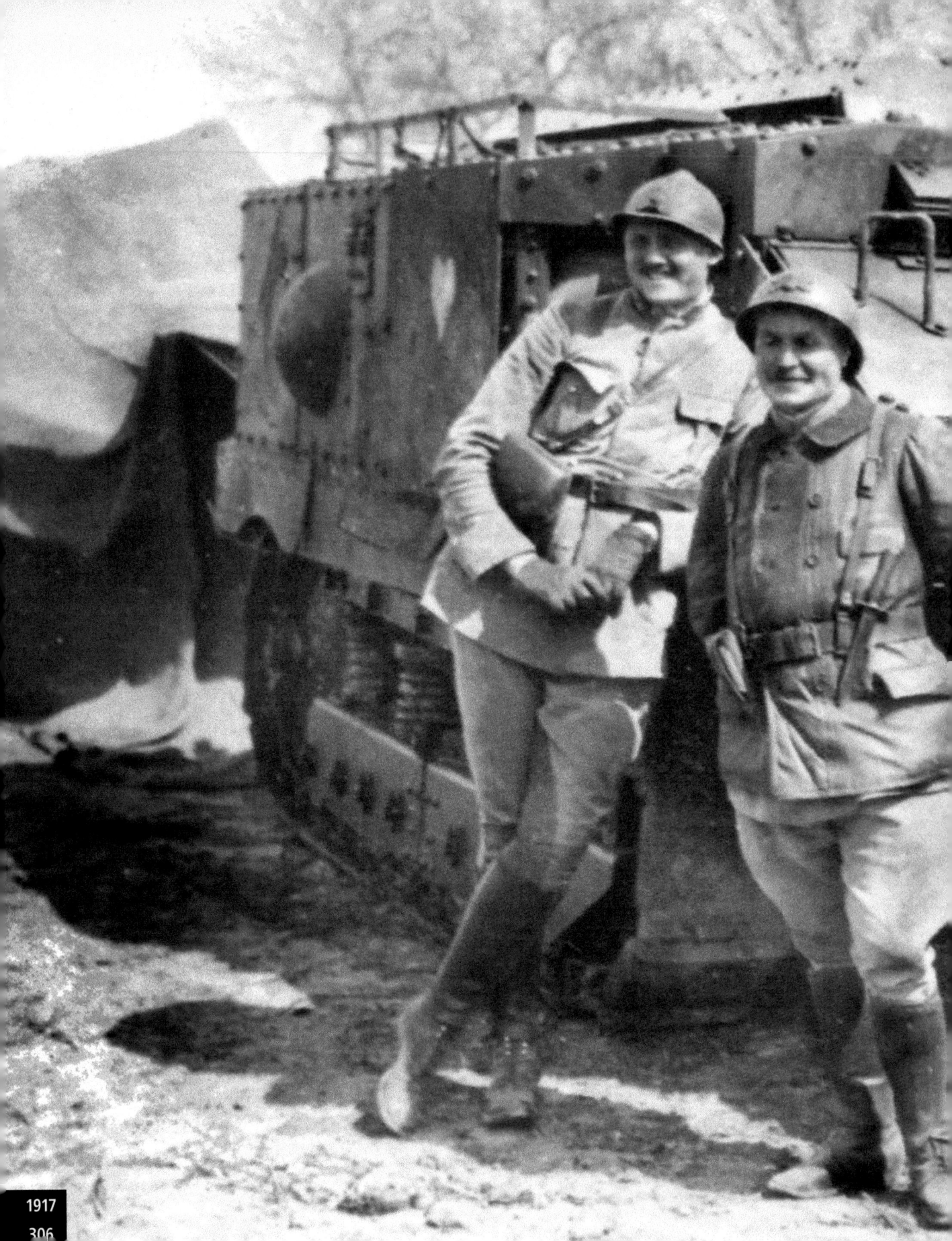

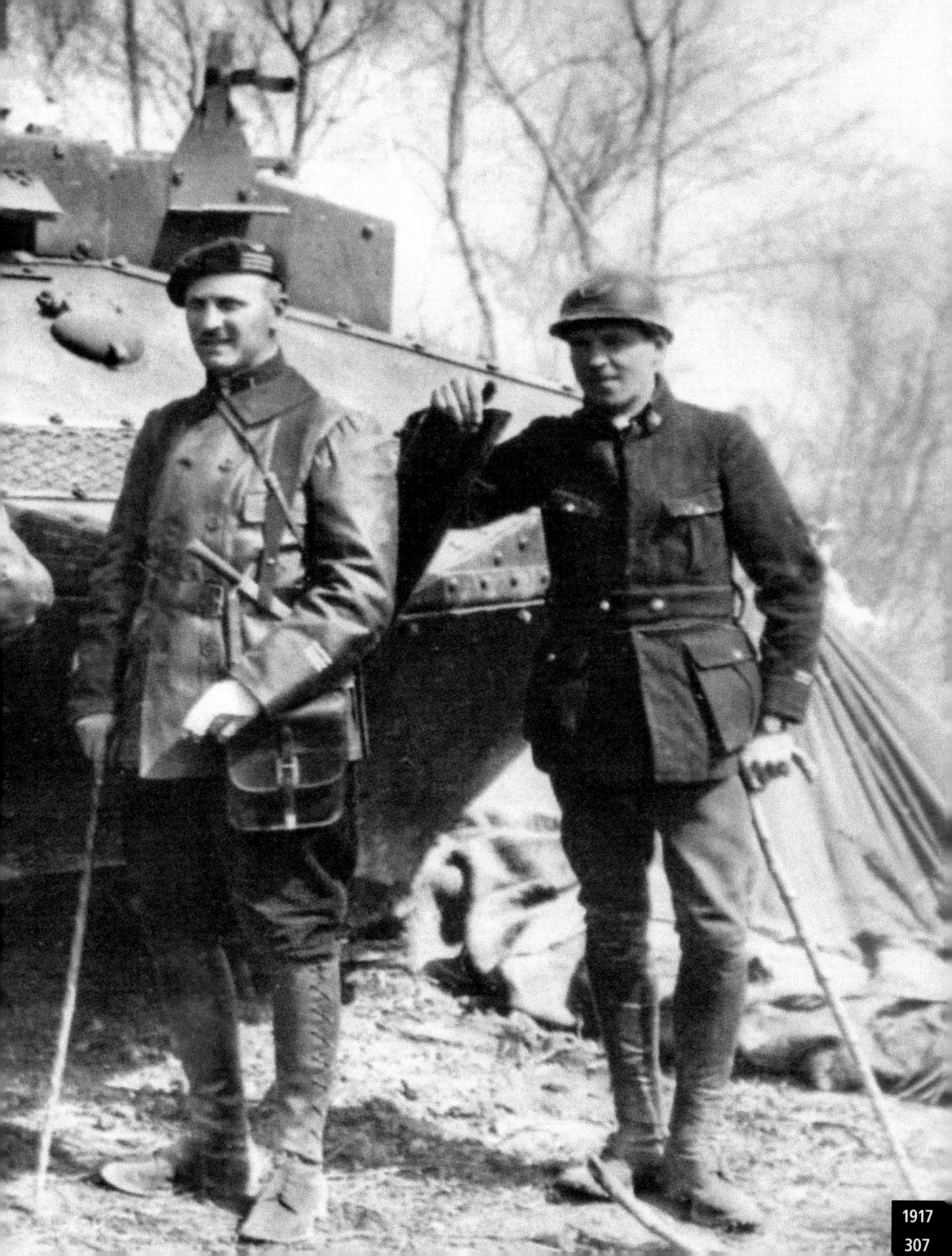

17GW705 Four of the six-man tank crew pose in front of their *char* (tank) before leaving for the area designated for their employment in the attack. This picture gives a good comparison of relative size, man to machine; room inside the Schneider CA-1 was very cramped; note the height of one of the crew – he appears to be over six feet tall.

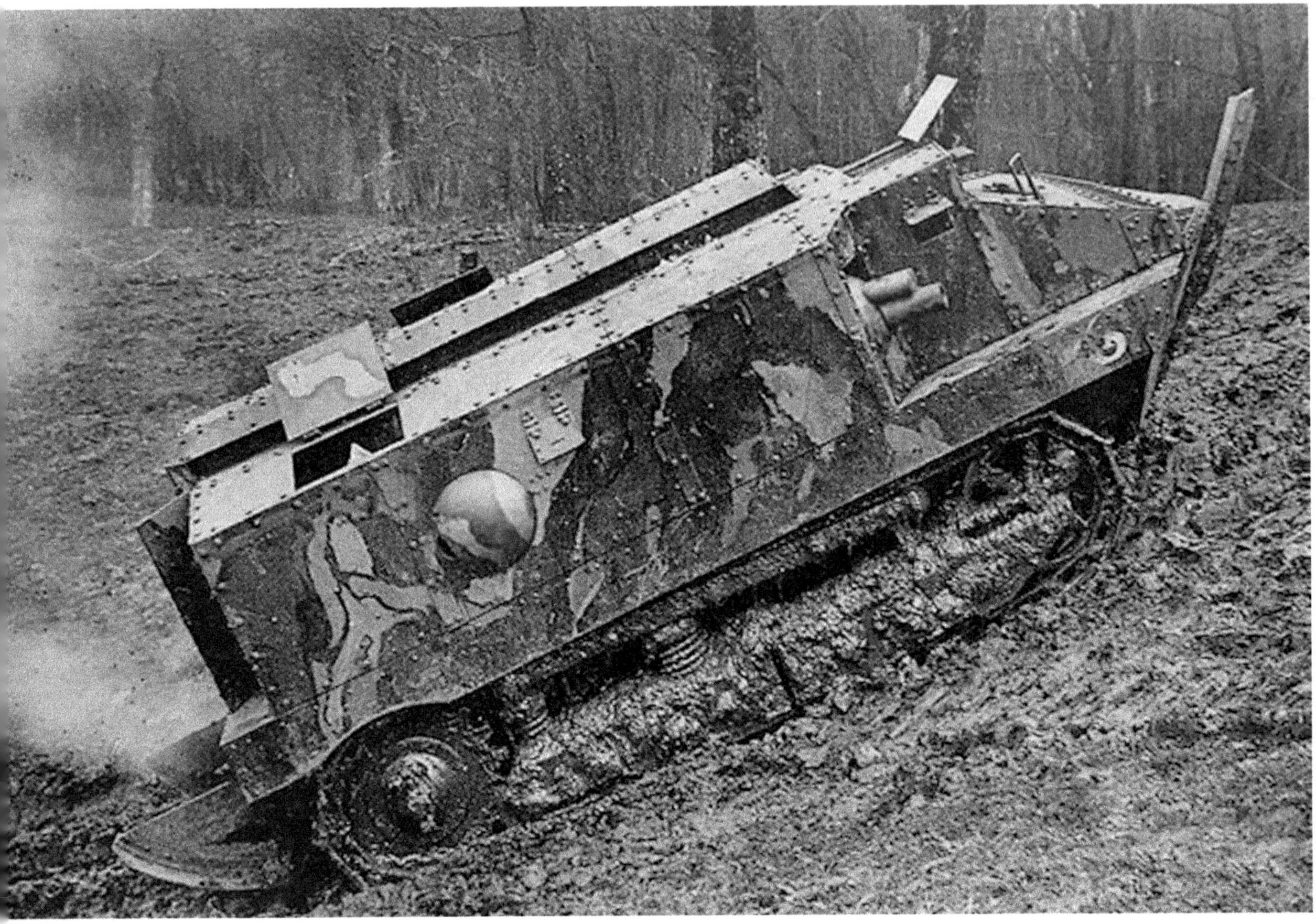

17GW706, 17GW707. A Schneider C-1 making easy going of muddy ground; crossing trenches would prove to be not so easy. The main armament was a 75 mm petard trench mortar that had been adapted to fire from a fixed position by adding a recoil compensator and gun shield. The one depicted has been unbolted and recovered from a burnt-out tank by the Germans.

One captain's report to the commander of the Fifth Army is typical of what occured:
I respectfully inform you that the tank attack of 16 April has only passed a short distance beyond the German second line, between Miette and Mauchamps farm. Many tanks of my squadron and that of Captain Pardon have been set on fire by shelling. Concerning other squadrons, I saw many tanks burning. Major Bassut is among the dead and Captain de Forsanz is missing. I will be withdrawing my remaining tanks to our starting position at Pontavert to await your further orders. I will do my best to recover those tanks that have broken down through mechanical failure.

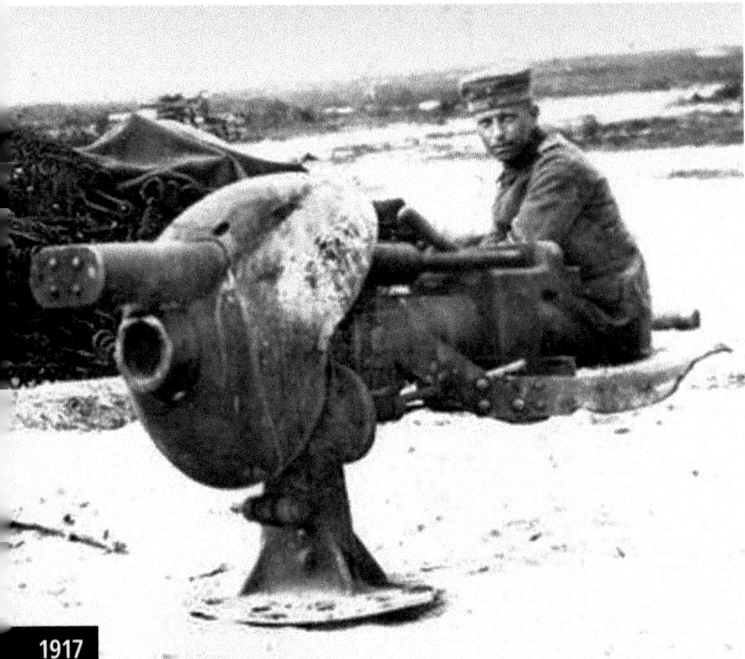

17GW701, 17GW704. A Schneider C-1 that became immobilized as it's driver attempted to negotiate across a particularly wide part of a German trench. Another tank has been hit by a shell and has burnt out. A battle-weary German soldier lies beside it for his photograph to be taken.

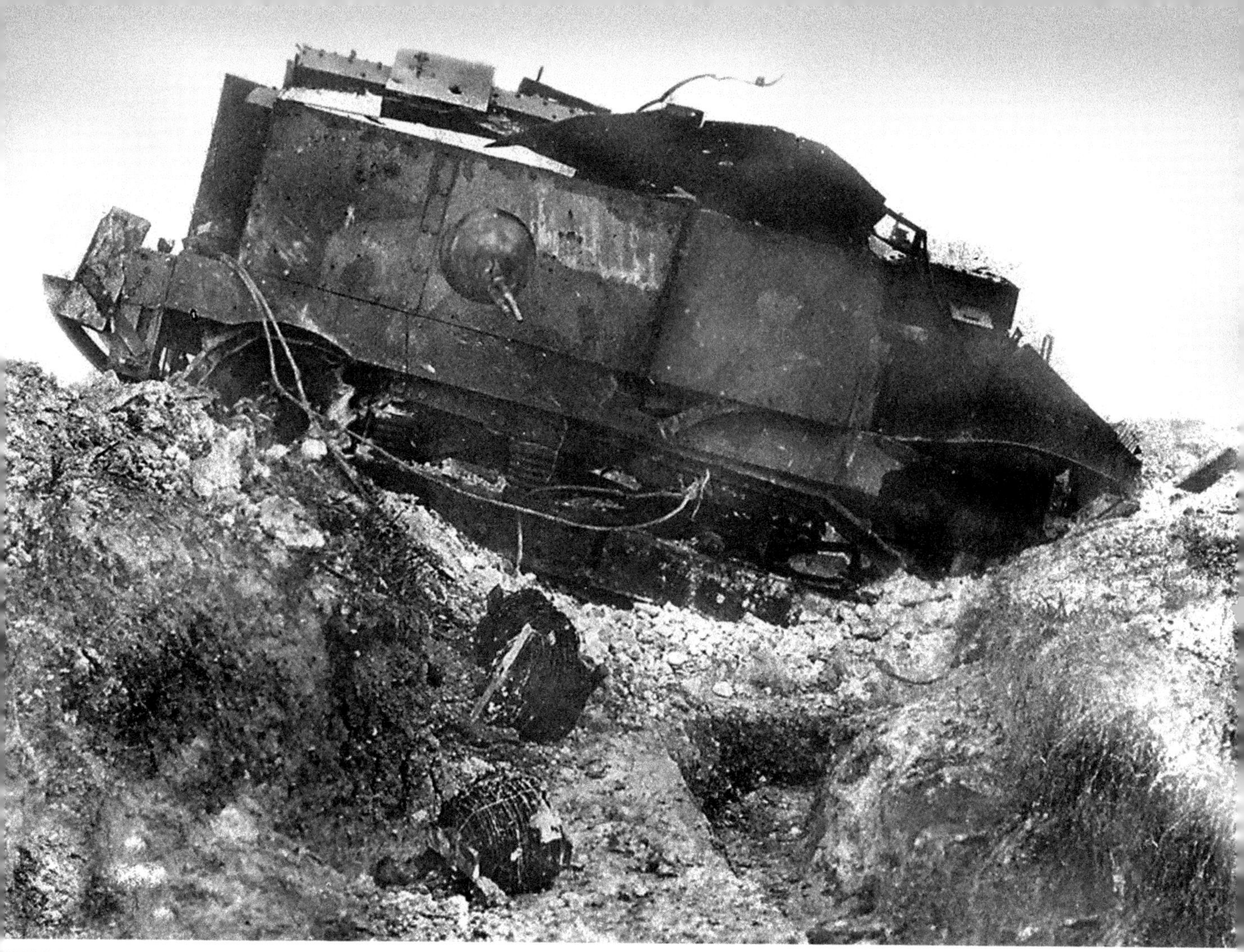

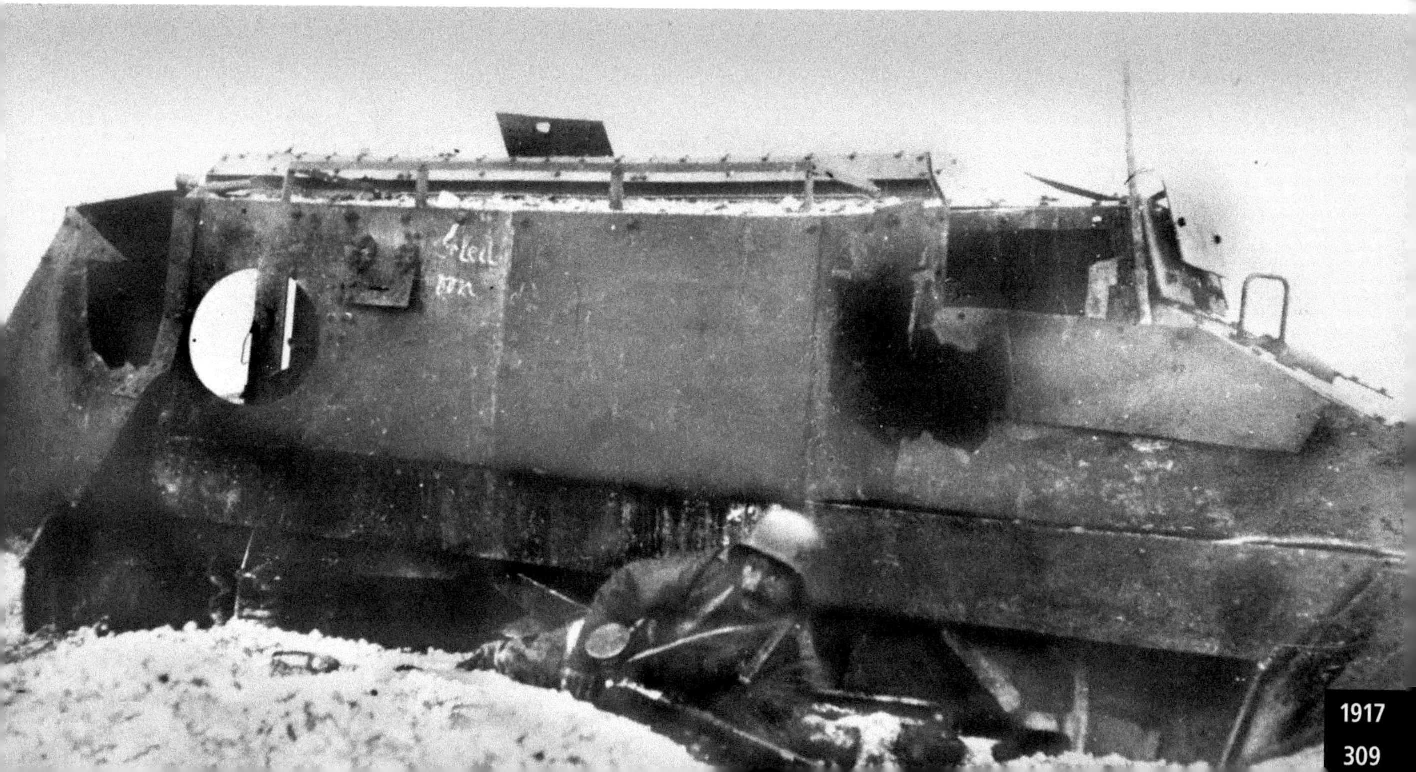

1917
309

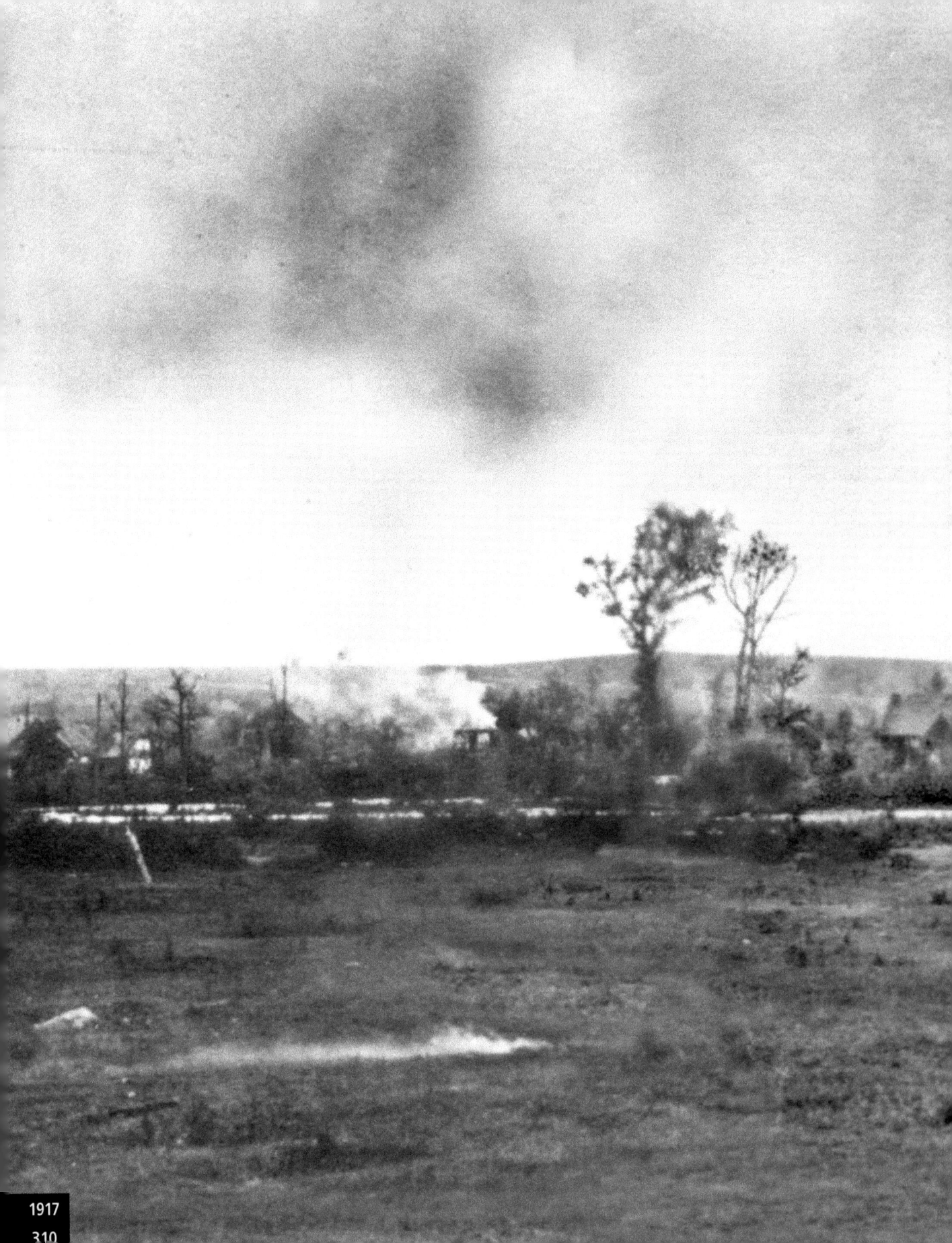

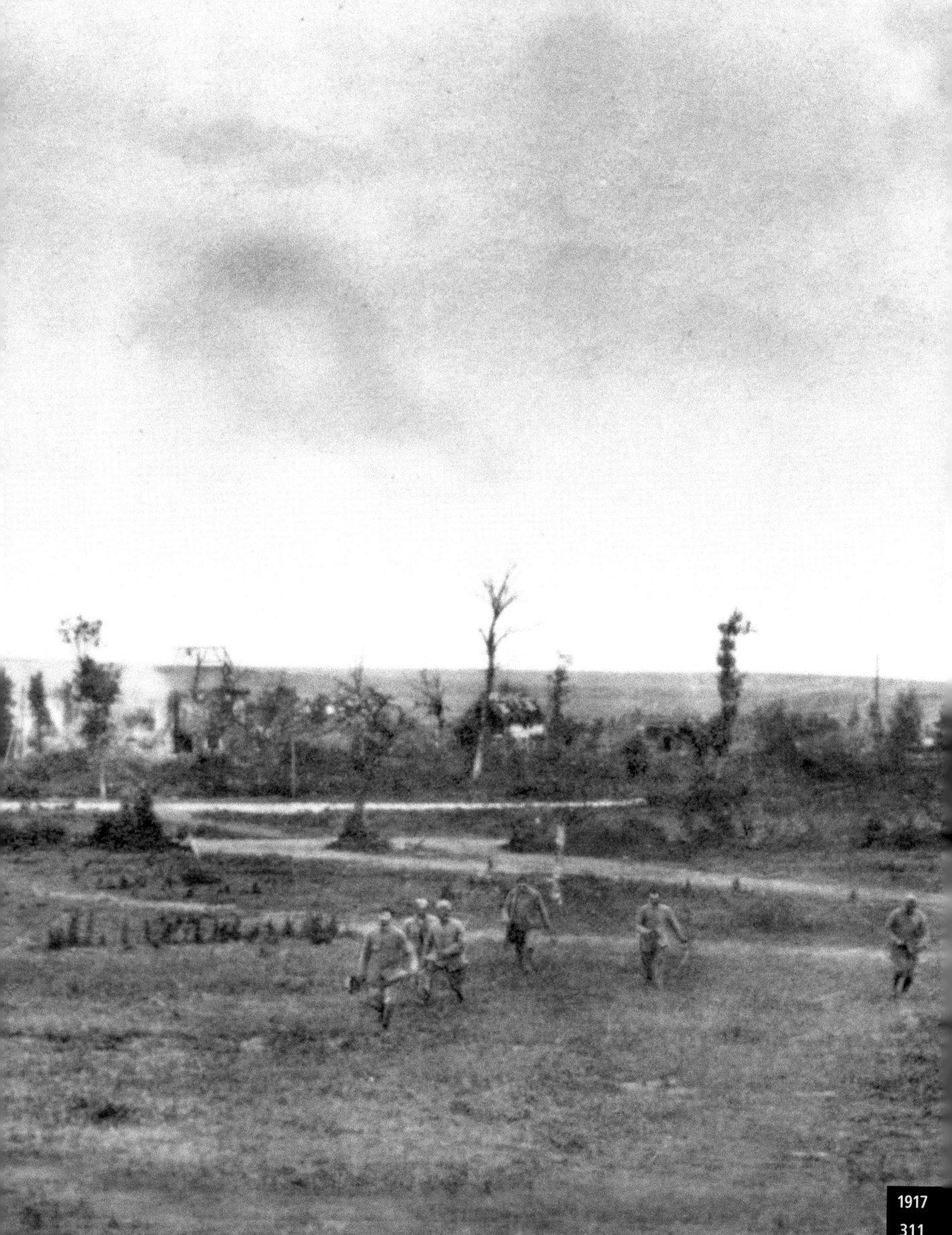

17GW653 French soldiers, having abandoned their rifles and equipment, flee from a burning village and German counter attack.

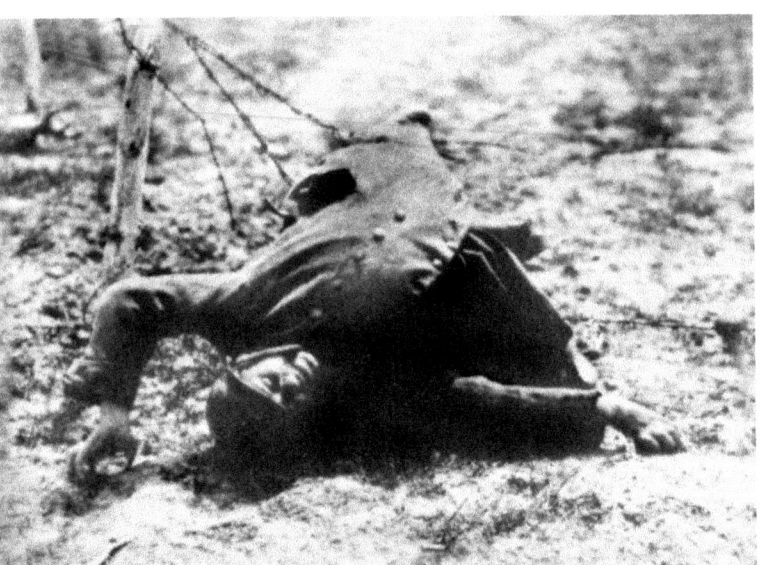

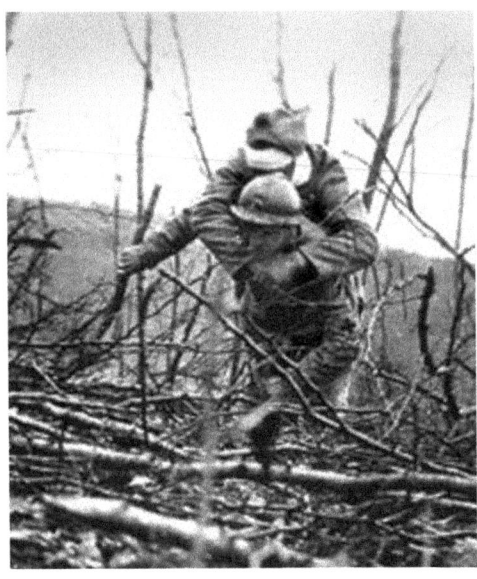

17GW646 Hanging on the wire – just one of many thousands of dead Poilu.

17GW658 Moving a wounded man over ground where stretchering was not possible.

17GW657 Mud-caked rifles being cleared from the battlefield.

17GW688 Walking wounded; the morale of the French soldier was now at its lowest.

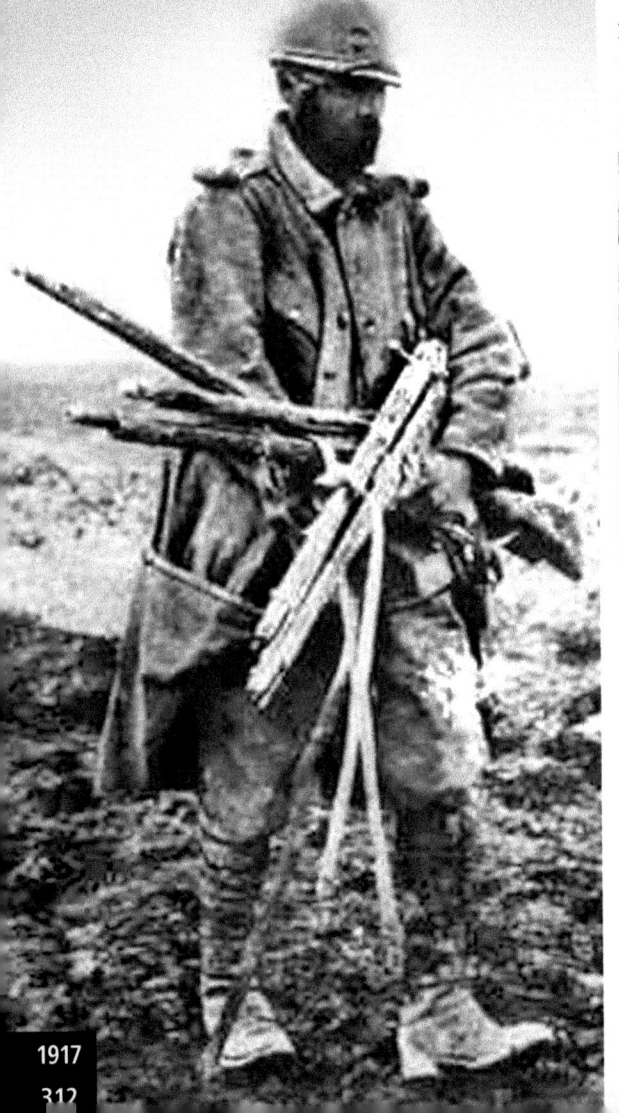

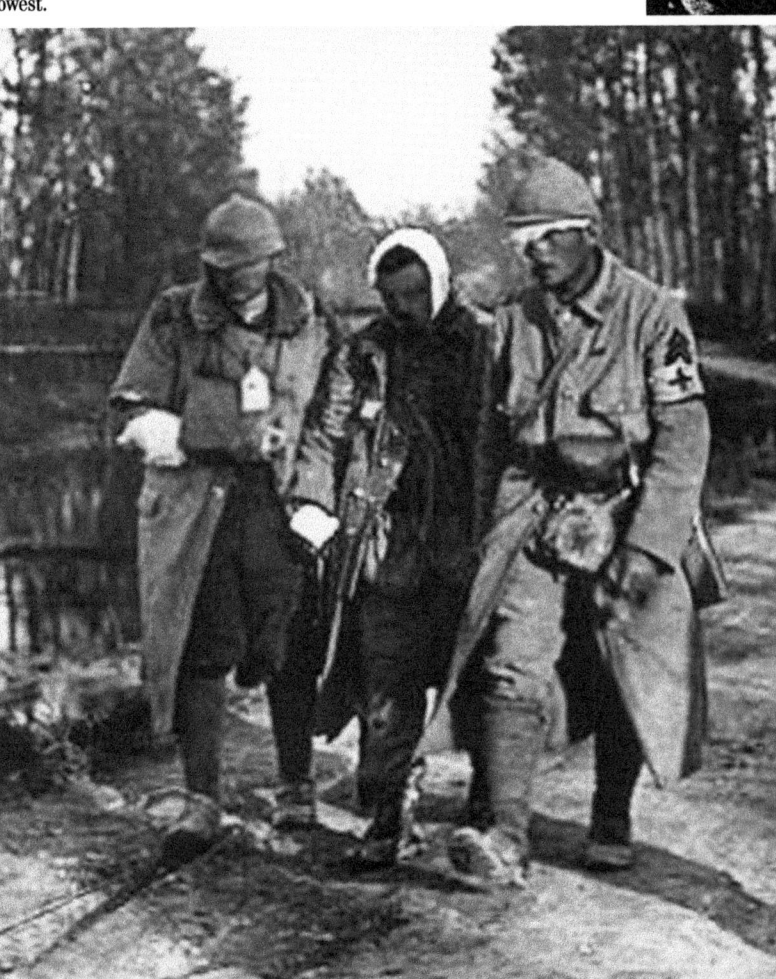

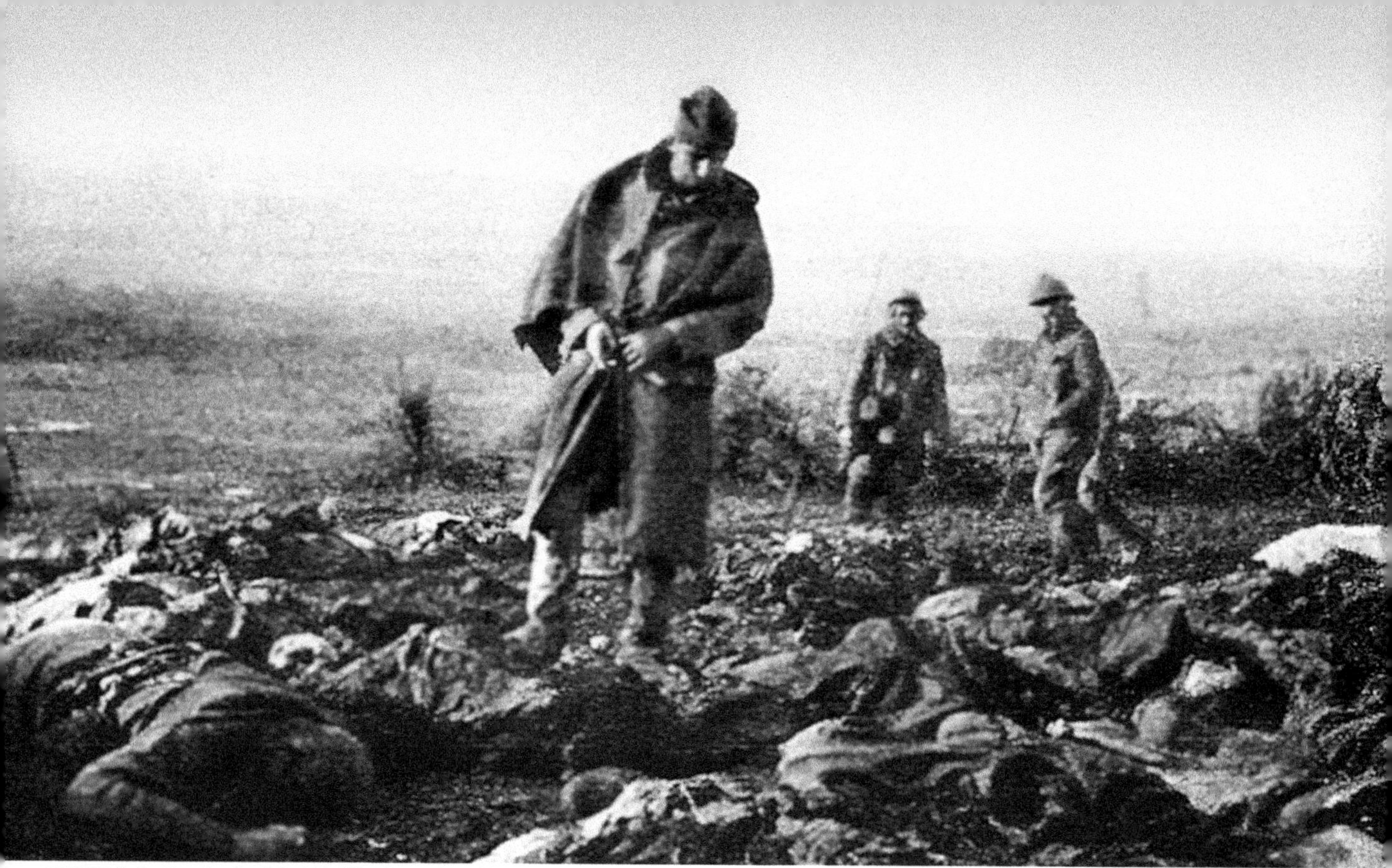

17GW686 Collecting the dead for identification and burial.

17GW686 The final count, when the offensive was over, was 271,000 French casualties.

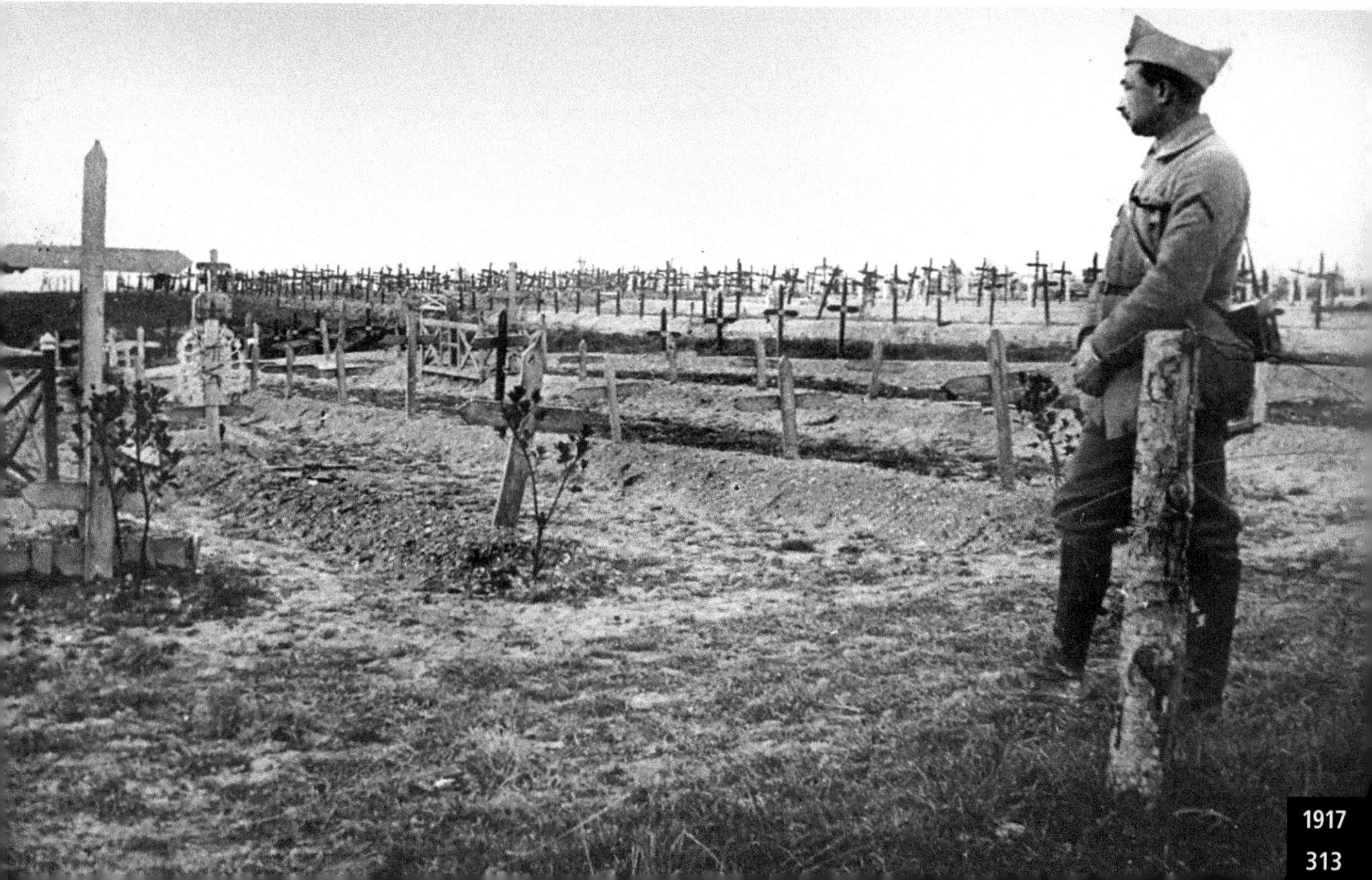

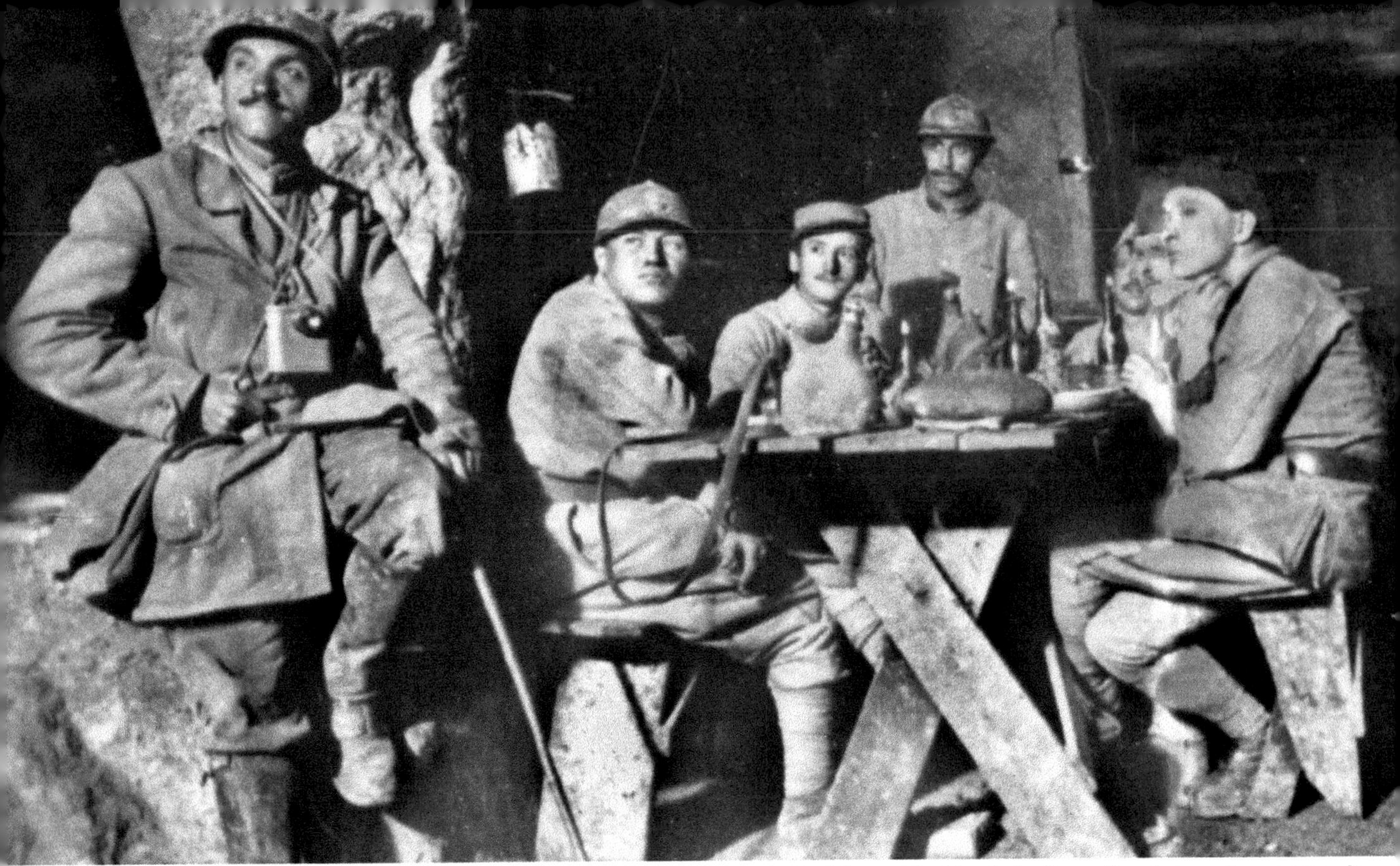

17GW712, 17GW710, 17GW709, 17GW711. Caves and stone quarries were a major feature in the fighting at the Chemin des Dames. French graves in a caverne – la Caverne du Dragon (the Dragon's Lair) at Creute Farm. Following their capture from the Germans, the caverns provided secure shelter for the poilu. The Nivelle Offensive, which included attacks before St Quentin and the Champagne, as well as along the Chemin des Dames, failed, not so much a great military failure, but that it came nowhere near Nivelle's promises. In the fighting between 16 – 25 April, the French suffered some 118,000 casualties, of whom 20,000 were killed, 5,000 died of wounds and another 5,000 were taken prisoner. The German casualties were fewer, but also quite high. The offensive dragged on until mid May despite mutiny in some formations and collective disobedience in others. By June 1917 it was estimated that up to 50 per cent of French divisions had engaged in some form of disobedience. Despite the fact that the Germans had some idea of the situation, the army was in no state to take any great advantage from it. The French Army recovered its poise remarkably quickly and was able to engage in limited, carefully prepared, attacks by the autumn and played a substantial part in the defeat of Germany in the retreat of 1918.

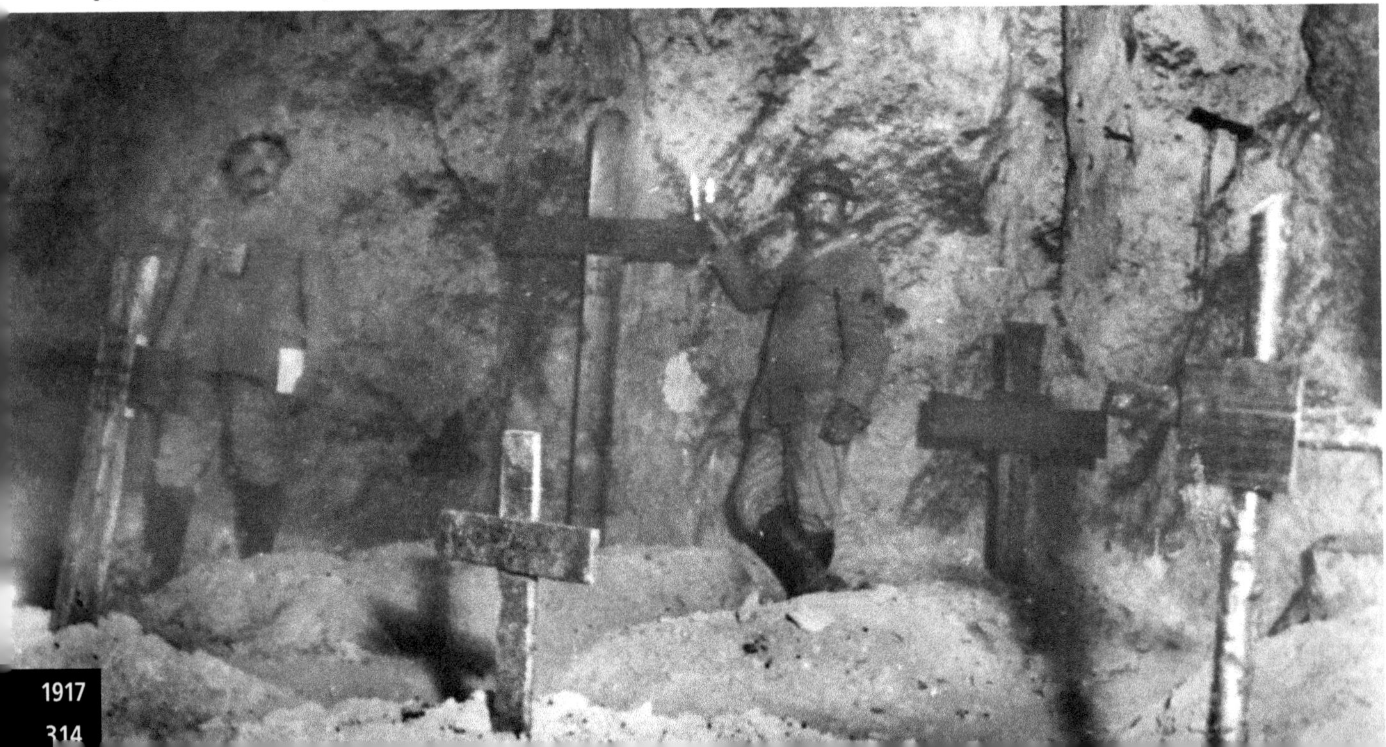

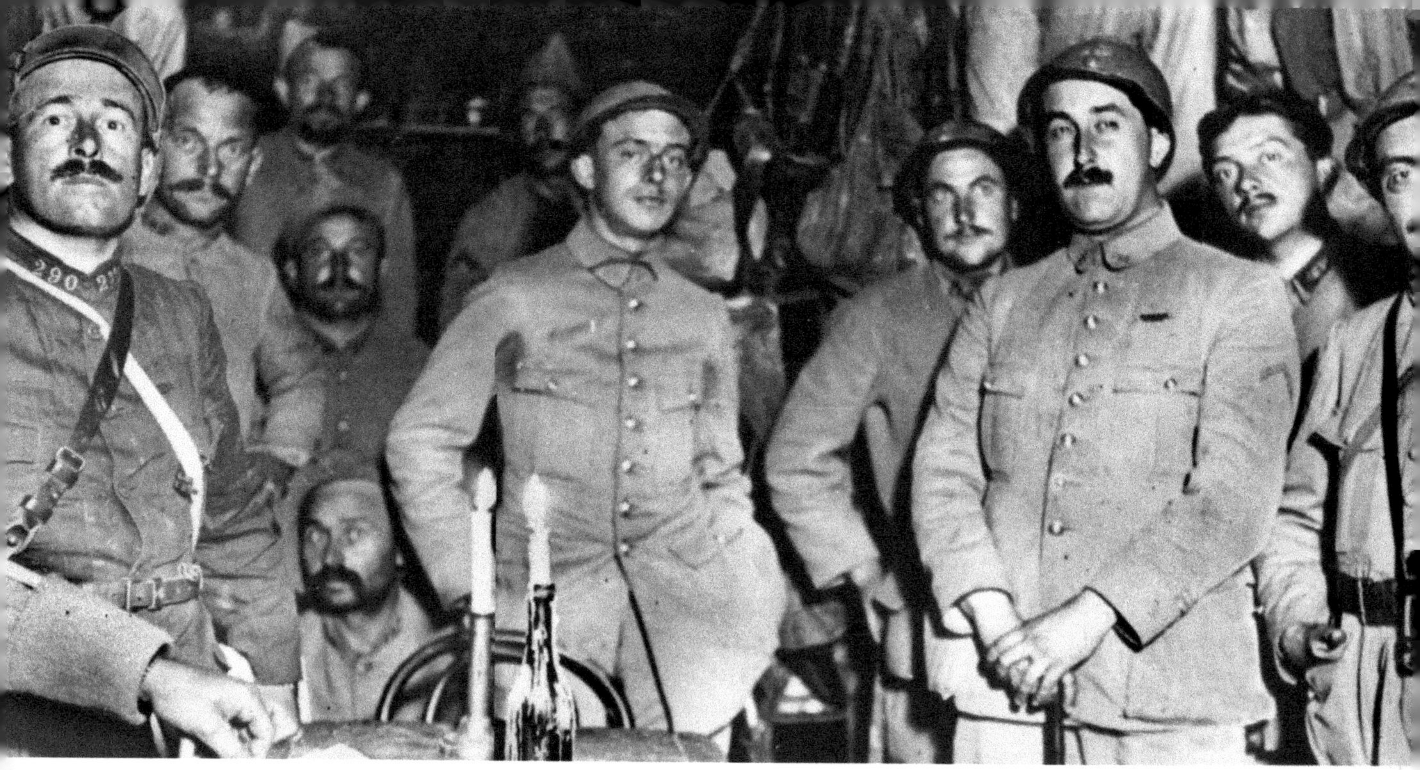

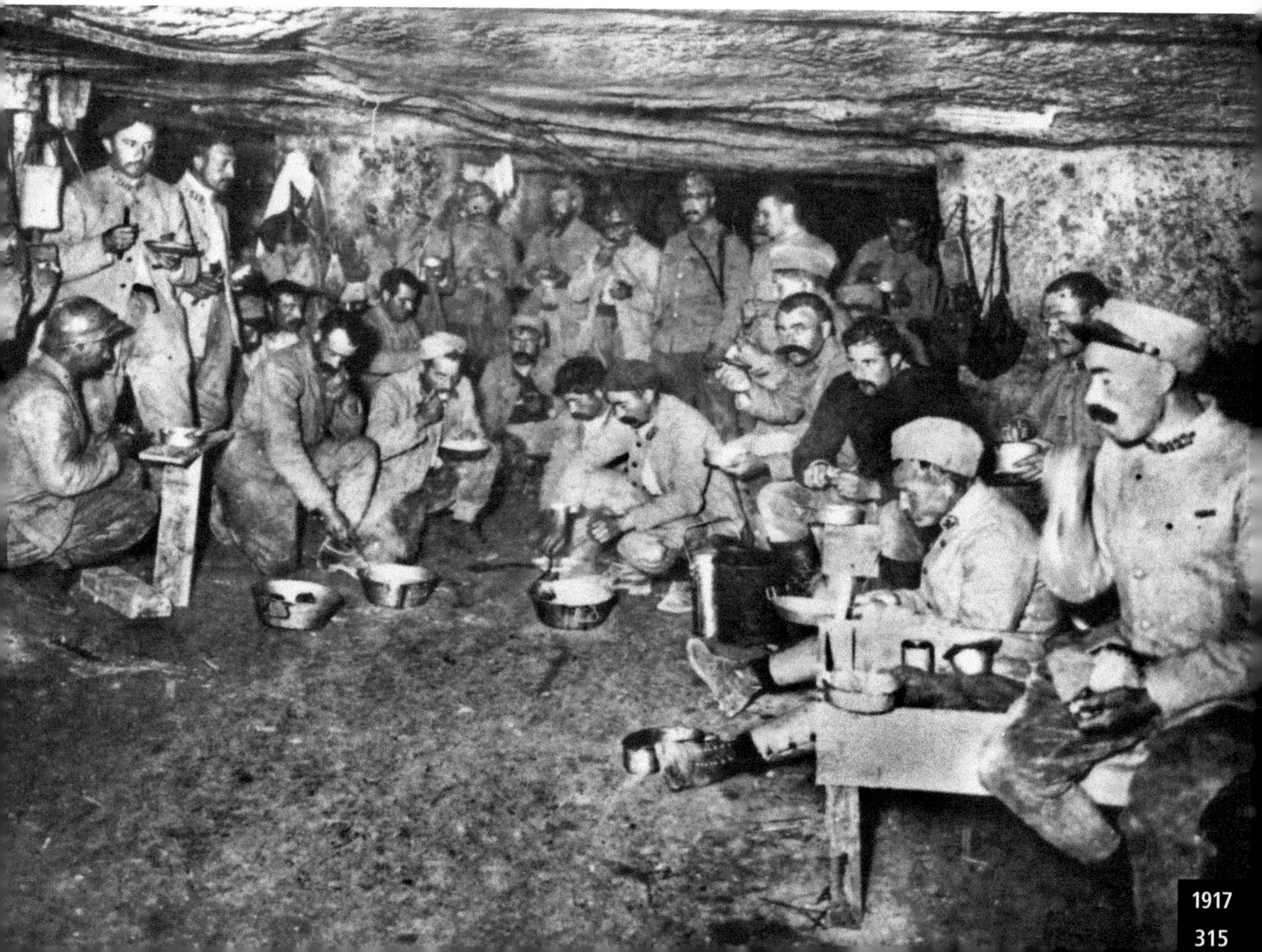

1917

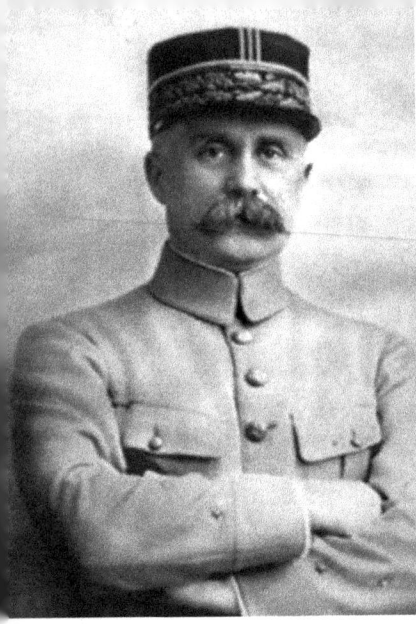

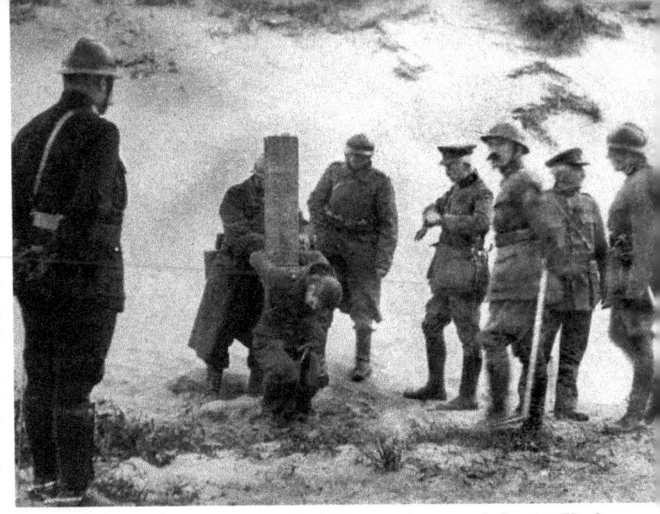

General Pétain, who had opposed the disastrous offensive, was called in to take over from Nivelle and to reestablish order. This he did without harsh collective punishments. By skilful intervention and diplomacy, General Pétain was able to regain the confidence of the poilu and the situation was stabilized. The threat of the complete disintegration of the French army was thus averted. A total of 629 men were sentenced to death, but only twenty-eight, those who had fired weapons at their superiors, were executed. Strikingly – and over time – the French army was restored to a formidable fighting force.

17GW716 The execution of one of the mutineers who had taken up arms against his superiors, carried out at Verdun.

17GW714 General Philippe Pétain.

17GW713 In a dugout at La Ferme des Hurtubise. The bearded soldier holding a stick is the chaplain.

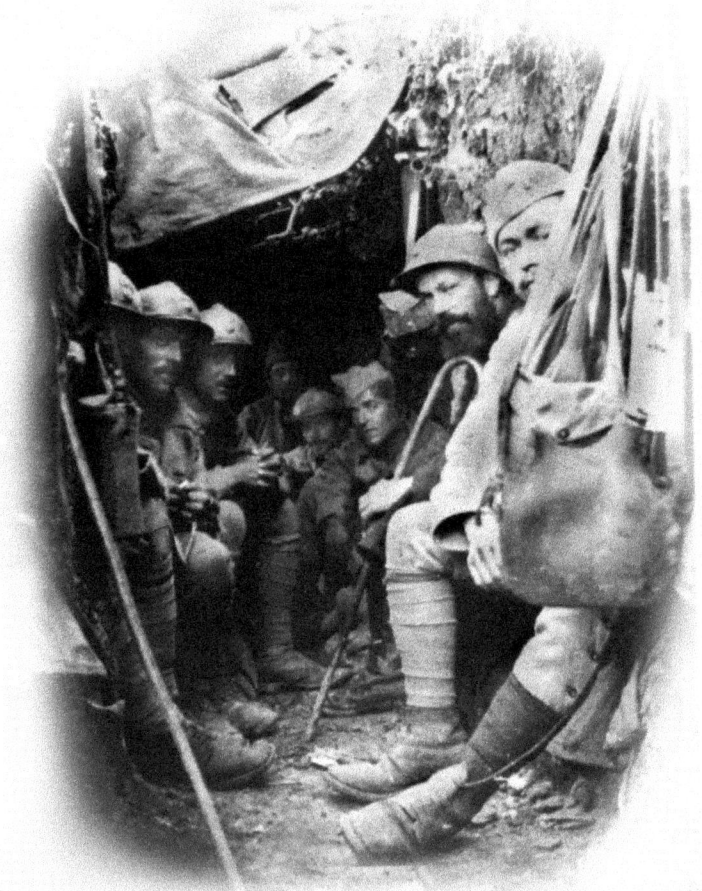

Oh mon Dieu, où étiez-Vous?

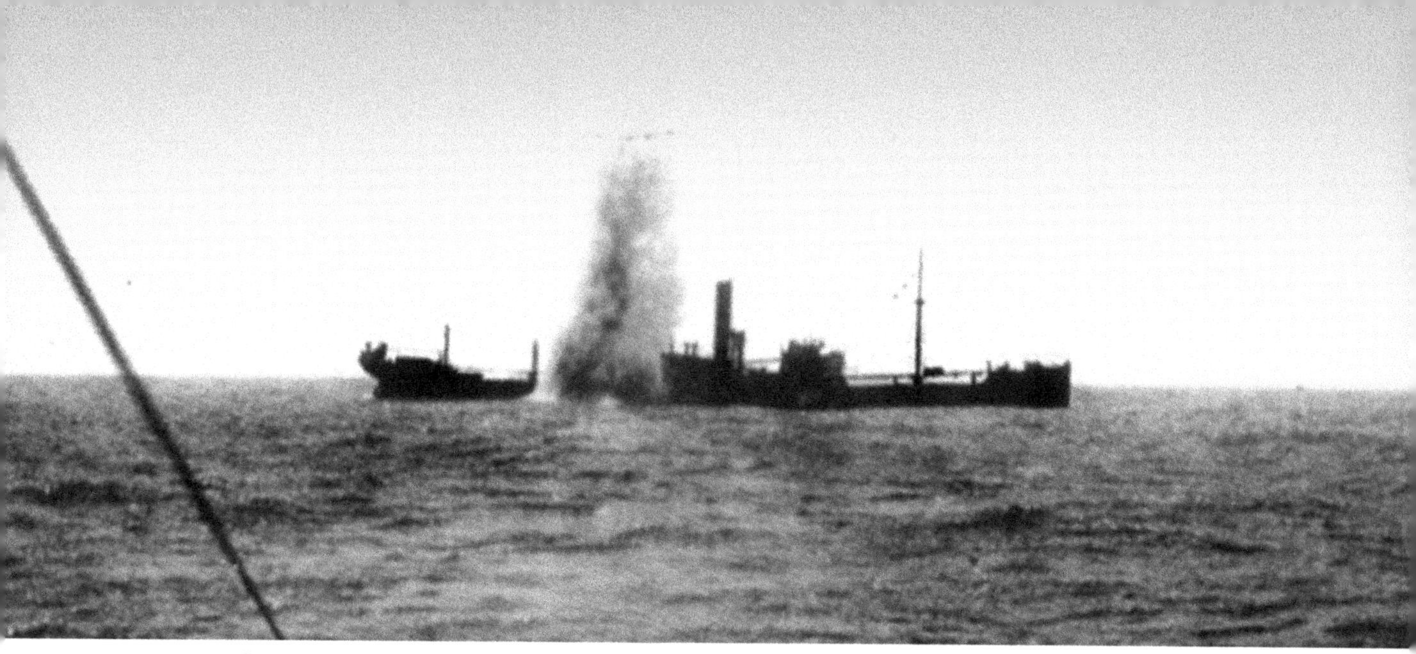

Chapter Five: Unrestricted Submarine Warfare

17GW729 The British cargo ship, SS *Maplewood*, in the process of being sunk by shell fire from the German submarine *U-35*.

17GW726 The larger *U-35* comes alongside a smaller submarine of the UB type. The figure in British military uniform is a captured British officer.

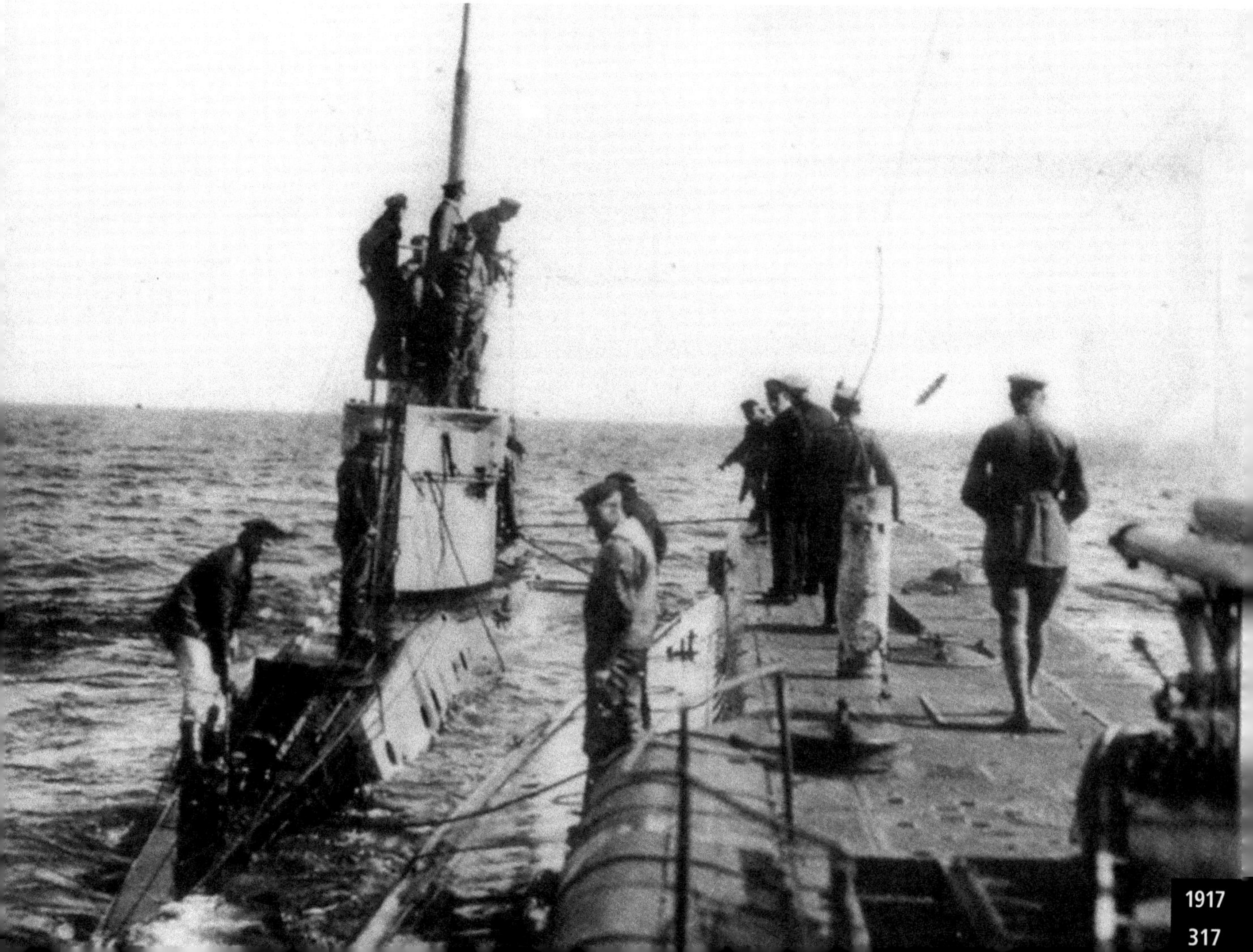

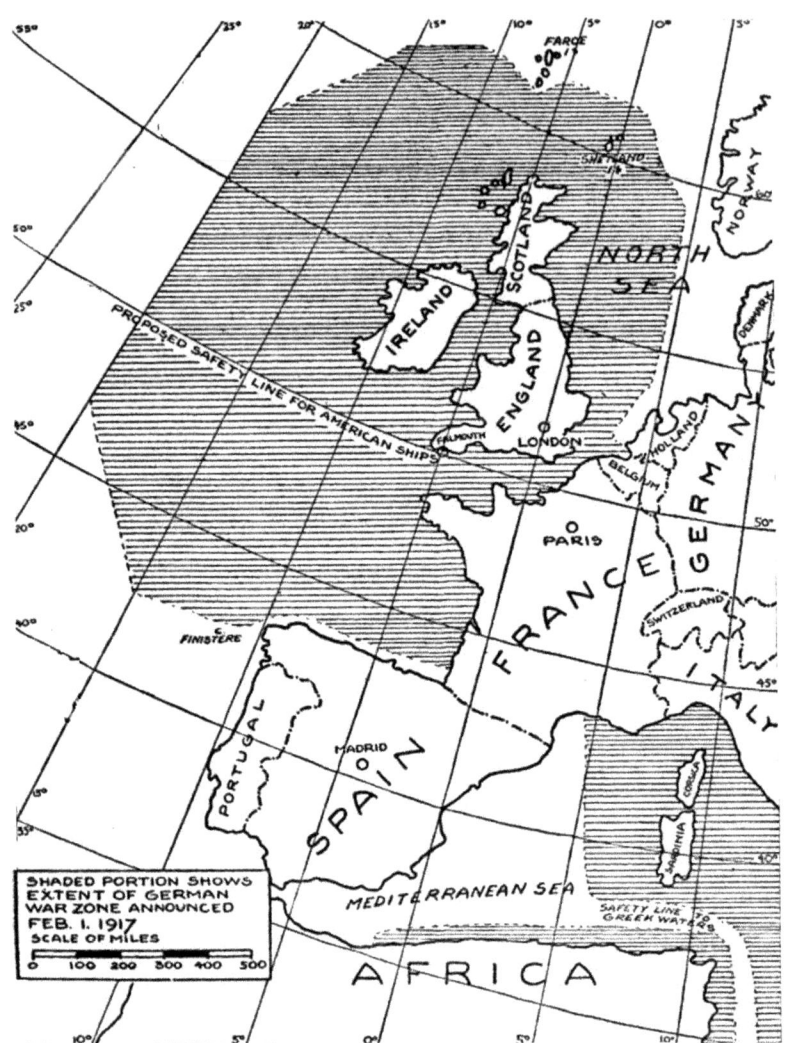

NEW GERMAN SUBMARINE WAR ZONE OF FEBRUARY 1, 1917

17GW730 Theobald Friedrich Alfred von Bethmann Hollweg.

On 9 January, 1917, the German Chancellor, Bethmann Hollweg, announced Germany's intention to resume unrestricted submarine warfare. In February 1915 Germany had declared a war zone around Britain, within which merchant ships were to be sunk without warning. This 'unrestricted submarine warfare' angered neutral countries, especially the United States; seven months later, following the loss of American lives aboard torpedoed liners *Lusitania* and *Arabic*, the tactic was abandoned. Hollweg feared that it would provoke America into declaring war on the Central Powers. However, by 1917 the war was not going well for Germany on the Western Front and at home the British blockade of Germany, was causing severe food shortges. The resumption of unrestricted submarine warfare in 1917 almost succeeded in bringing Britain to its knees. Between February and April 1917 U-boats sank more than 500 merchant ships. In the second half of April an average of thirteen ships were sunk each day. It was hoped that resumption of an intensified execution of the tactic might just keep America out of the war – should the results be spectacular and shocking enough.

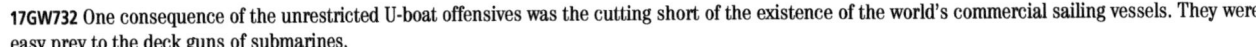

17GW732 One consequence of the unrestricted U-boat offensives was the cutting short of the existence of the world's commercial sailing vessels. They were easy prey to the deck guns of submarines.

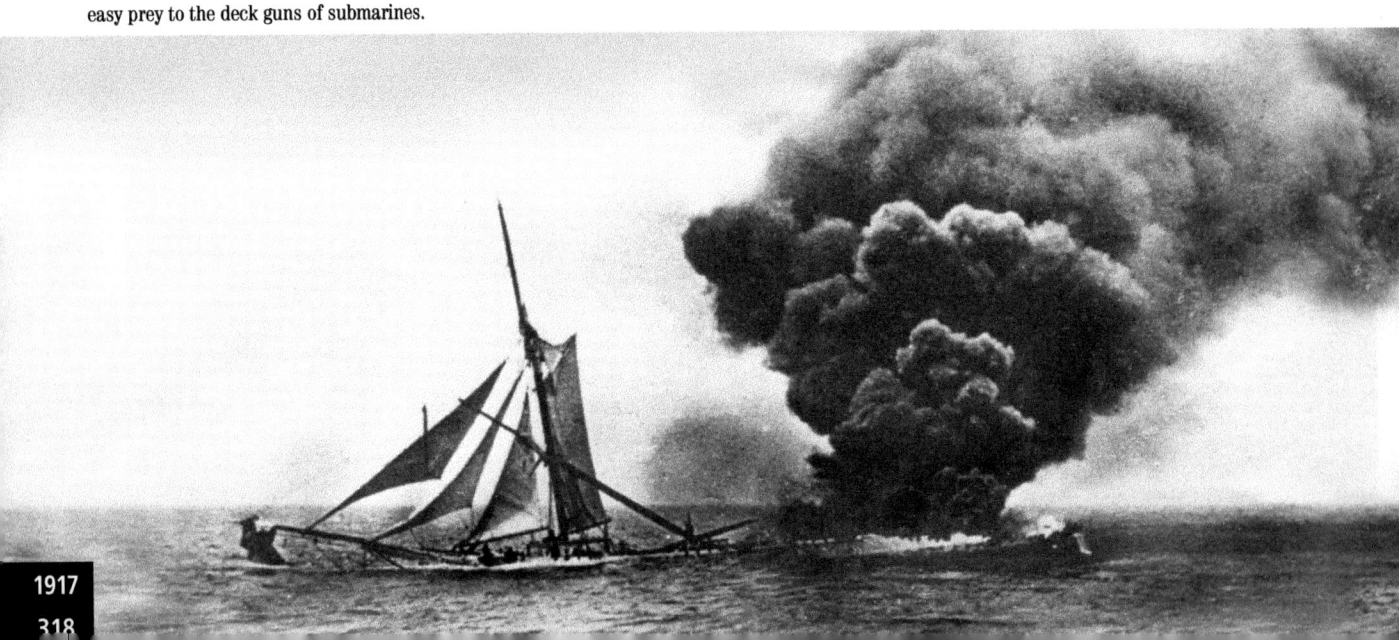

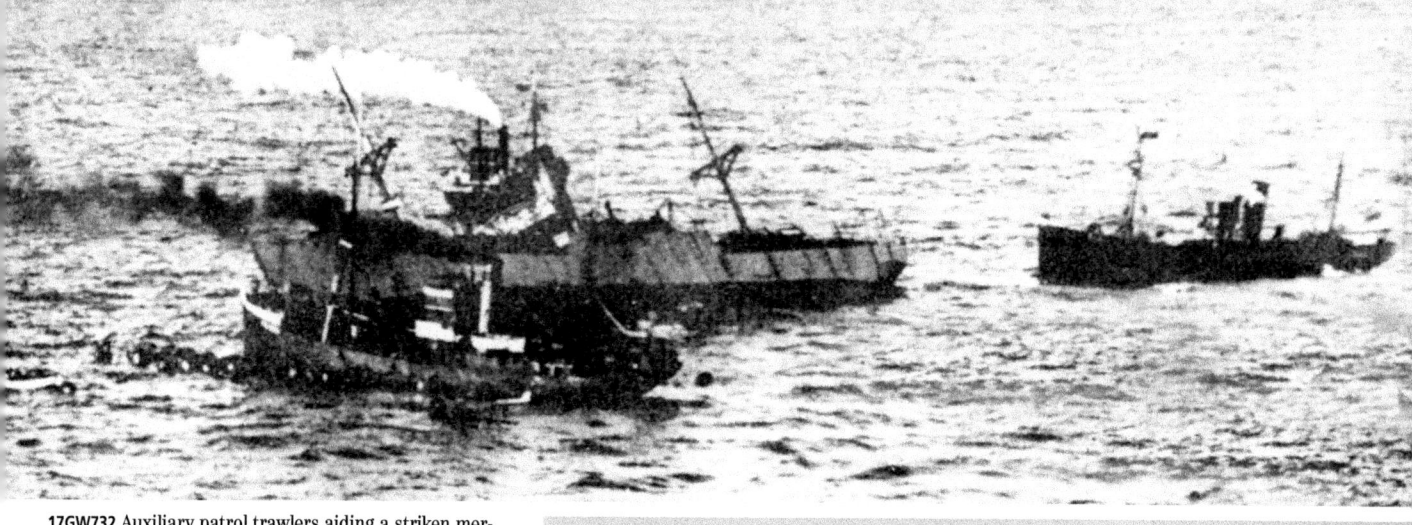

17GW732 Auxiliary patrol trawlers aiding a striken merchantman. Note the barrels floating in the water; some ships carried empty barrels to aid bouyancy in the event of a torpedo attack causing damage to the hull. They were also a help to men in the water.

17GW736 The sinking of American steamer, *Illinois*: she is stopped in the water and the crew have been ordered to take to the lifeboats by *Oberleutnant* Reinhold Saltzwedel, captain of *U-21*. She was sunk by shell fire, 18 March 1917, in the English Channel, twenty miles north of Alderney; there were no casualties. Clearly identifying herself as a neutral did not save the *Illinois*.

17GW735 A U-boat surfaces and the crew prepares to sink a victim with the 88 mm deck gun – much cheaper and more effective than a torpedo.

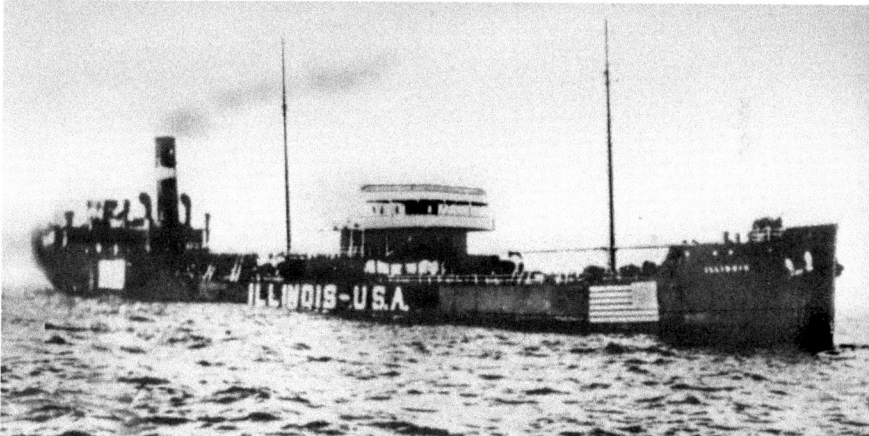

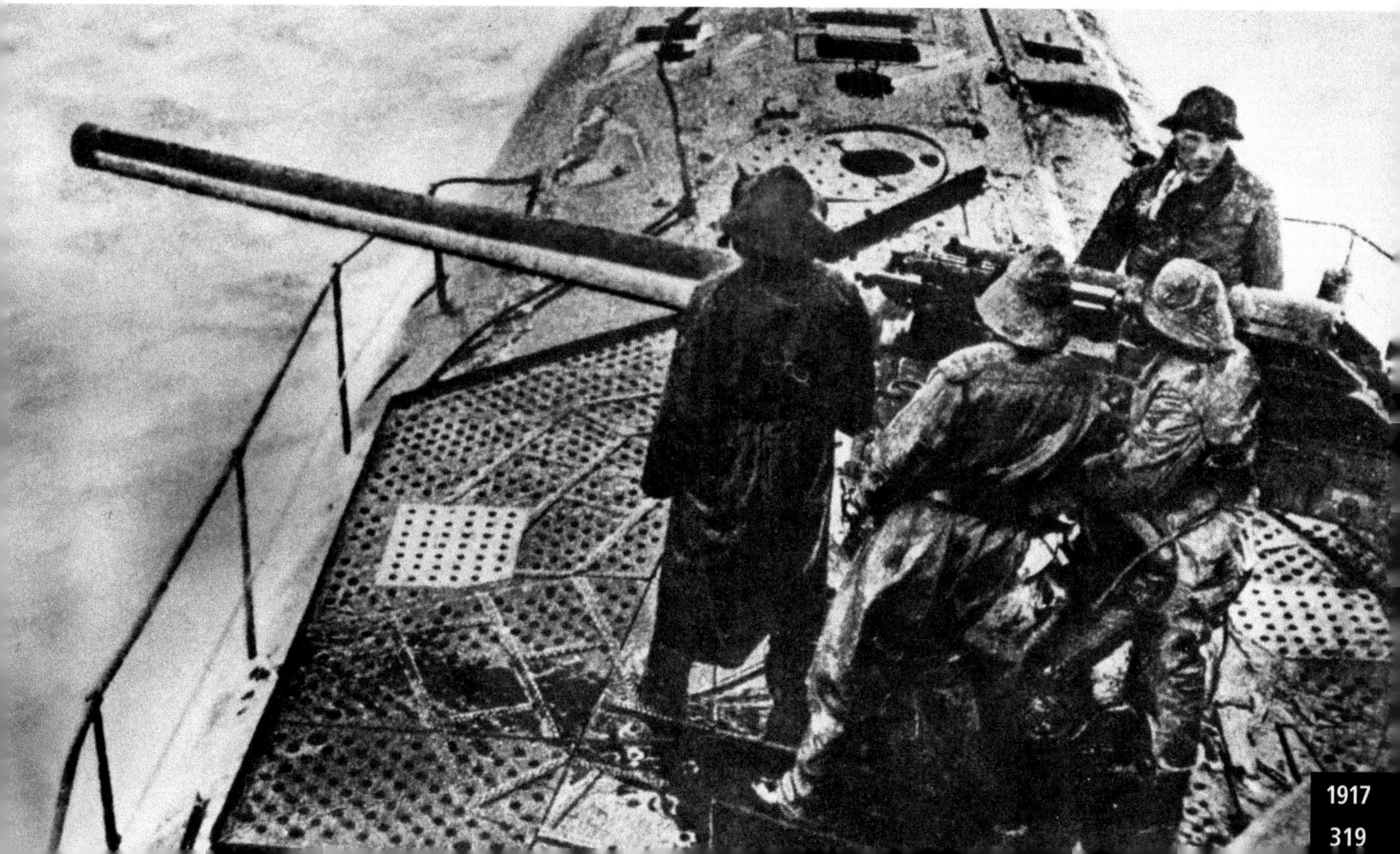

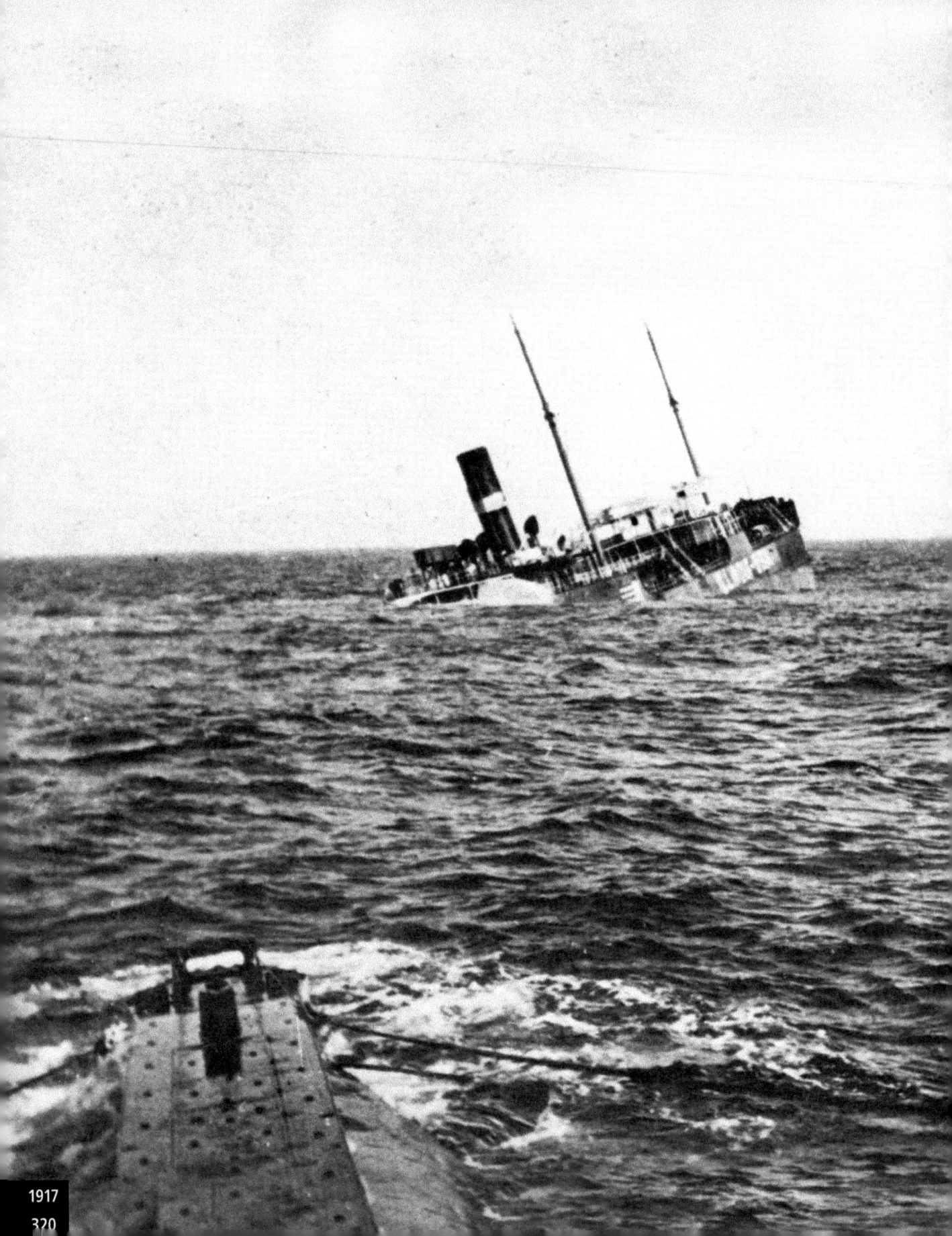

17GW738 The end of the American merchant ship *Illinois*, sunk by *Oberleutnant* Reinhold Saltzwedel, captain of *U-21*. She was sunk by shell fire, 18 March 1917, in the English Channel.

17GW737 Merchant seamen, adrift in a lifeboat and raft; hands are raised, perhaps in response to the camera.

17GW728 German officers on the conning tower of a German submarine. By the end of the war 178 had been sunk, 38 to Allied action.

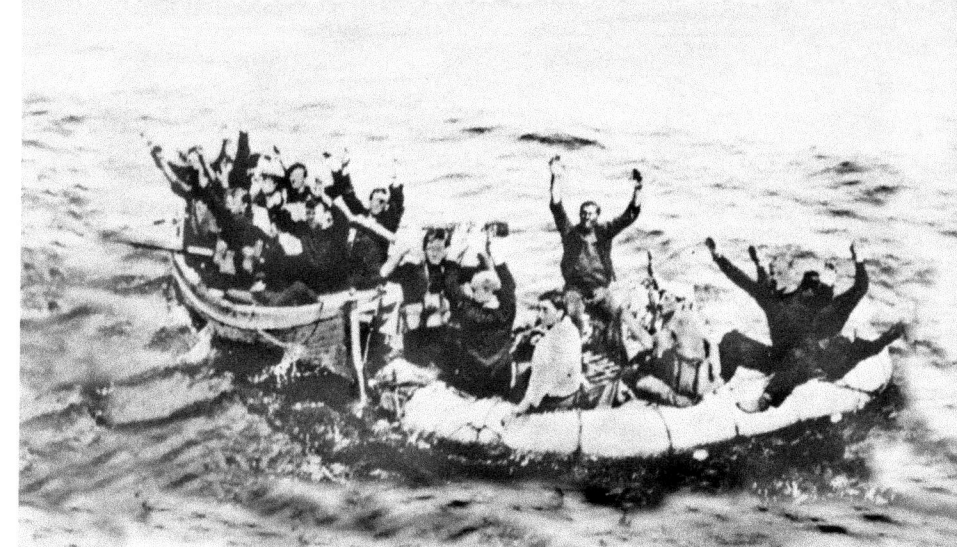

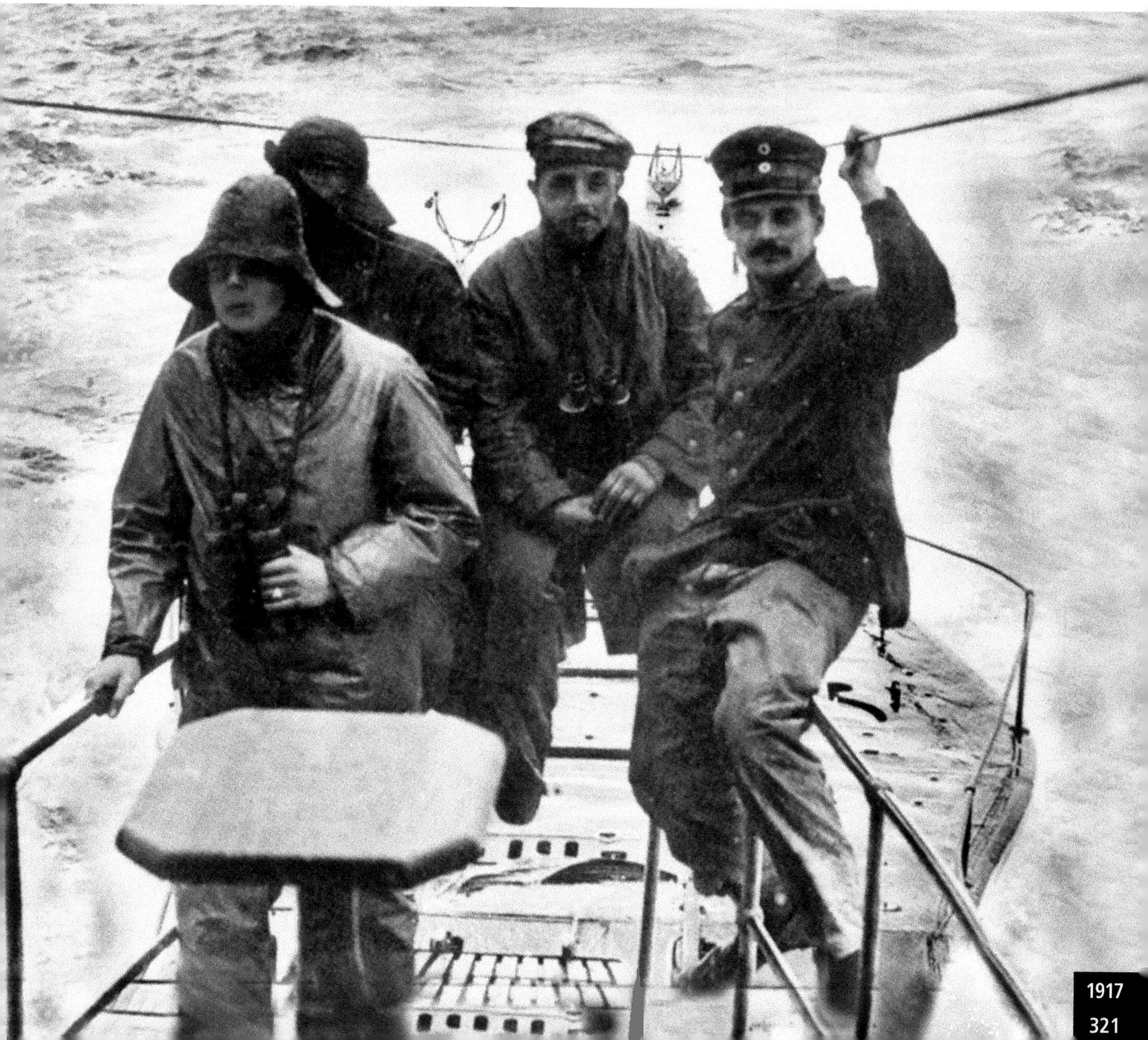

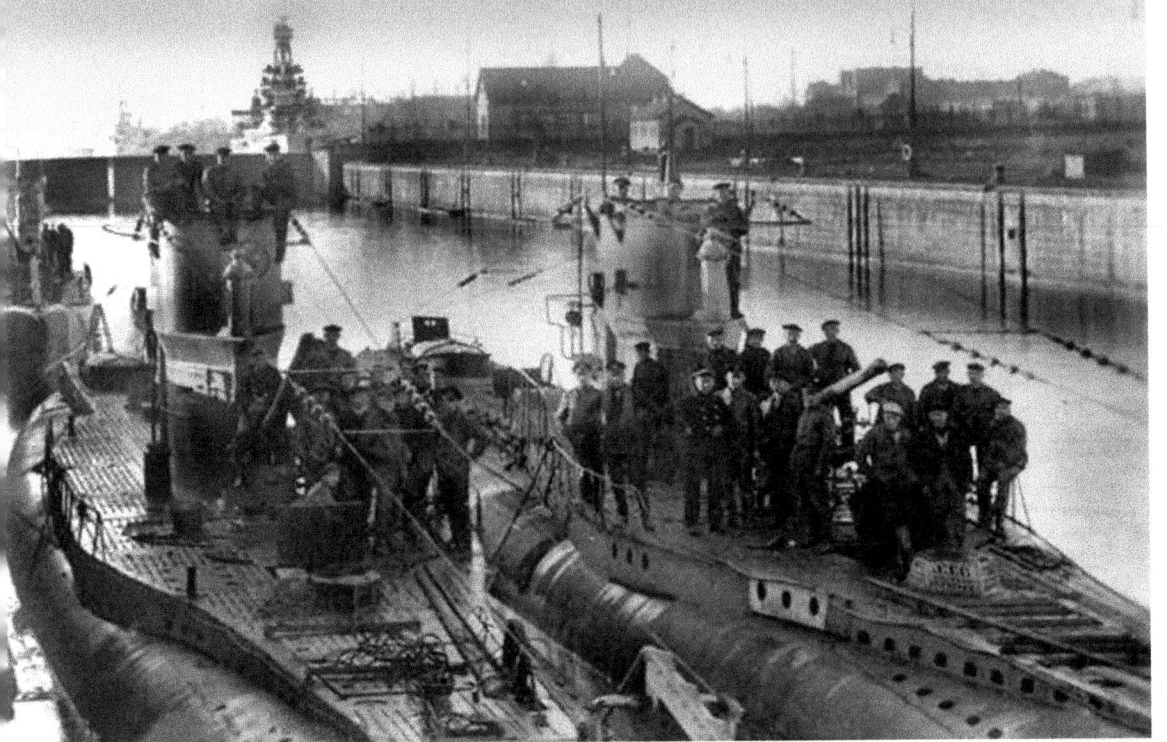 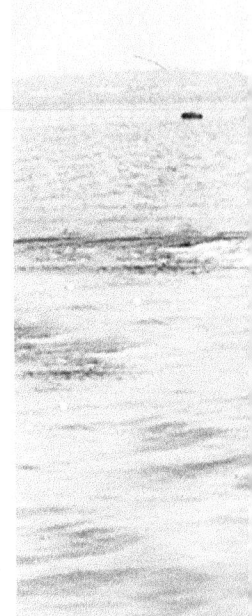

17GW749, 17GW750. German submarines at the Mediterranean naval base of Cattaro, about to set out on patrol.

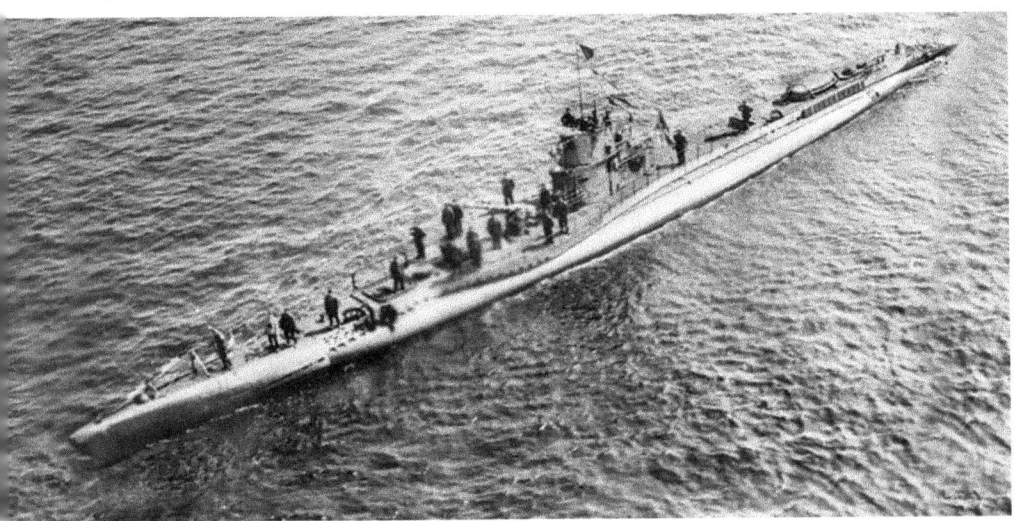

17GW744 A German submarine engaged in sinking ships by gun fire after first ordering the crew to their lifeboats.

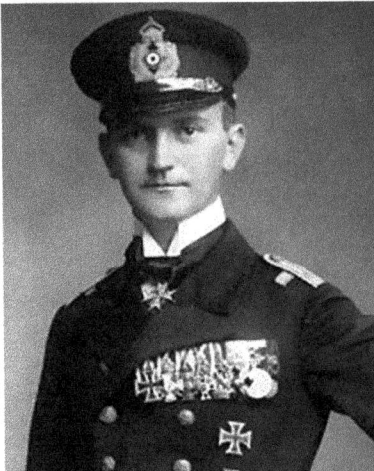

17GW748 Heino von Heimburg was in command of *UB-14* on 6 July 1915 when it torpedoed and sank the Italian armoured cruiser *Amalfi*. Later, in August, Heimburg and *UB-14* sank the Australian troopship *Southland* bound for Gallipoli. On 5 November Heimburg with *UB-14* torpedoed and sank the British submarine *E20* and, after taking command of *UC-22*, he also torpedoed and sank the French submarine *Ariane* on 19 June 1917. On 11 August, 1917 he was awarded the Pour le Mérite.

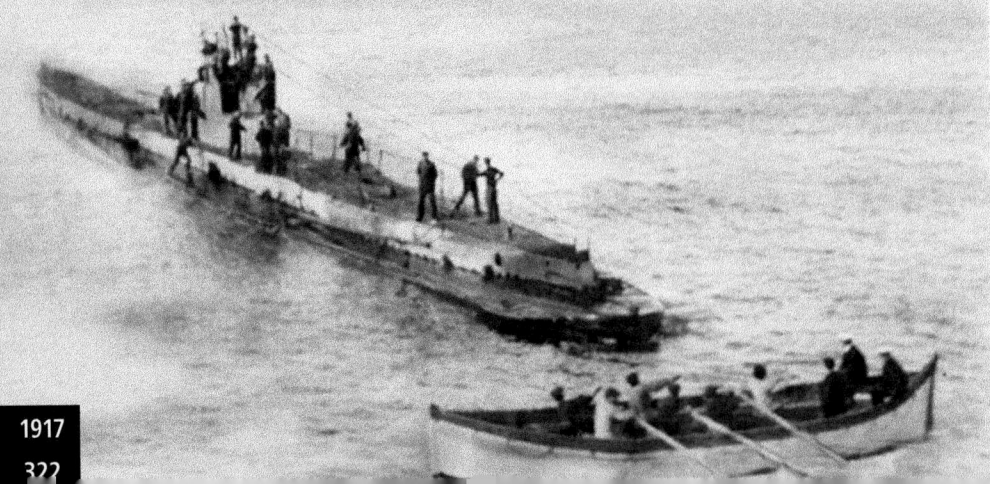

17GW739 Officers and crew of submarine *U-35* watch the approach of *U-42* at a pre-arranged rendezvous in the Mediterranean, May 1917. The U-35 was the most successful U-boat in the history of submarine warefare, sinking a total of 224 ships. See also 17GW760 for another photograph in this series (page 337).

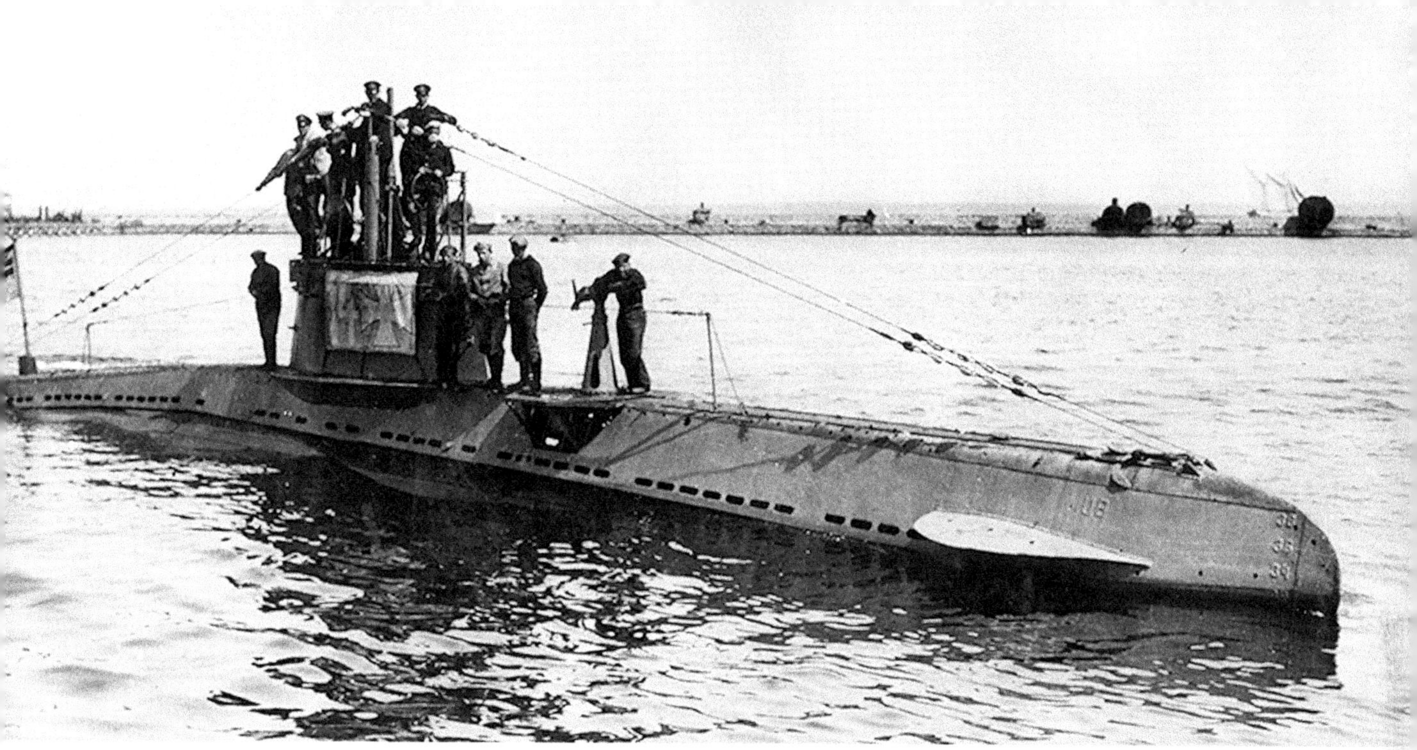

17GW742 German submarine *UB-14* coming into dock. During her first patrol in the Adriatic, she torpedoed and sank the Italian armored cruiser *Amalfi*. While sailing to Constantinople she attacked two British troopships, sinking *Royal Edward* with heavy loss of life, and seriously damaging the *Southland*. All three of her initial victims were among the largest ships attacked by U-boats during the war.

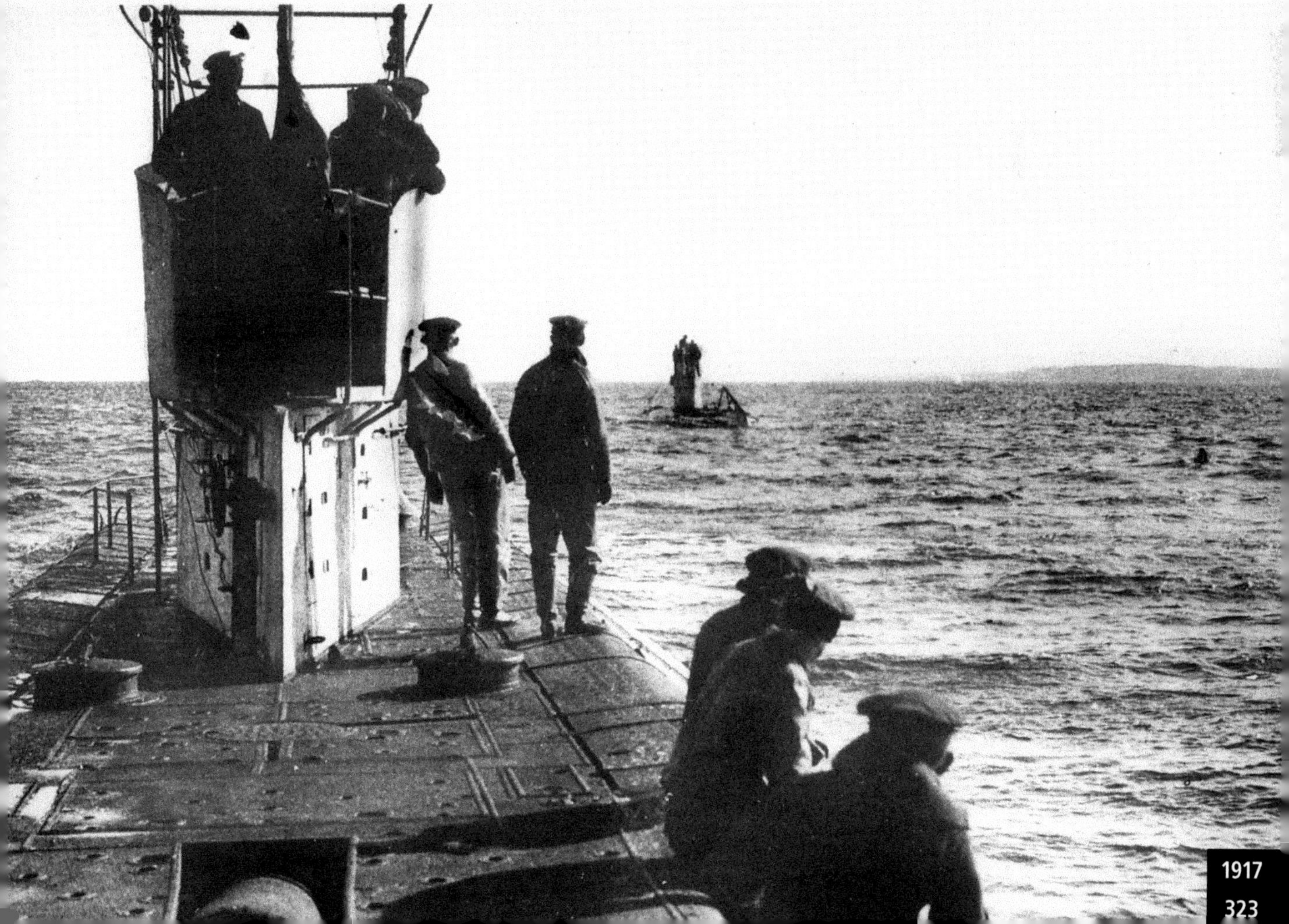

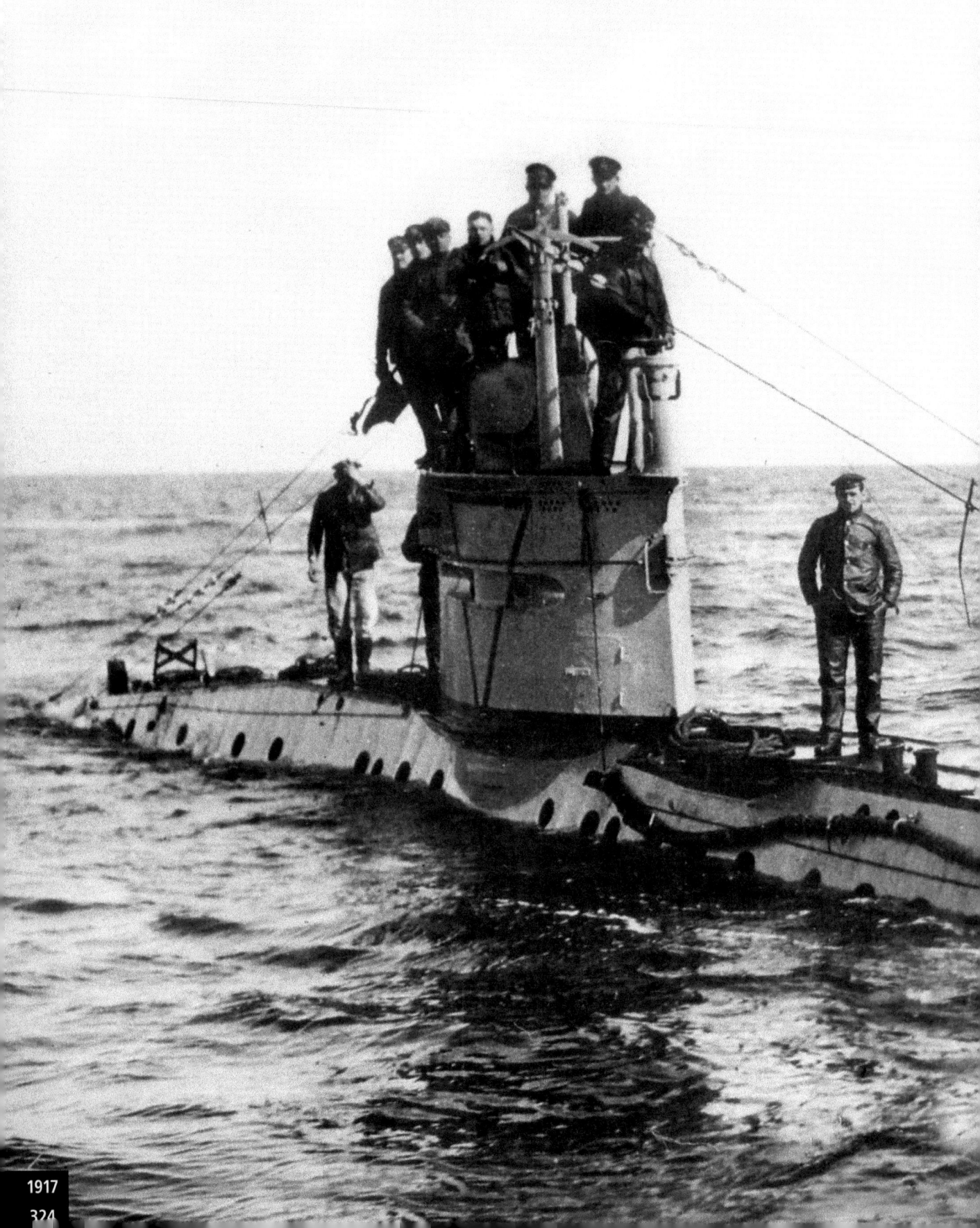

17GW725 The officers and crew crowding the conning tower and deck of this coastal U-boat gives some idea of the crowded conditions below endured by the German fourteen-man crew serving on this class of submarine.

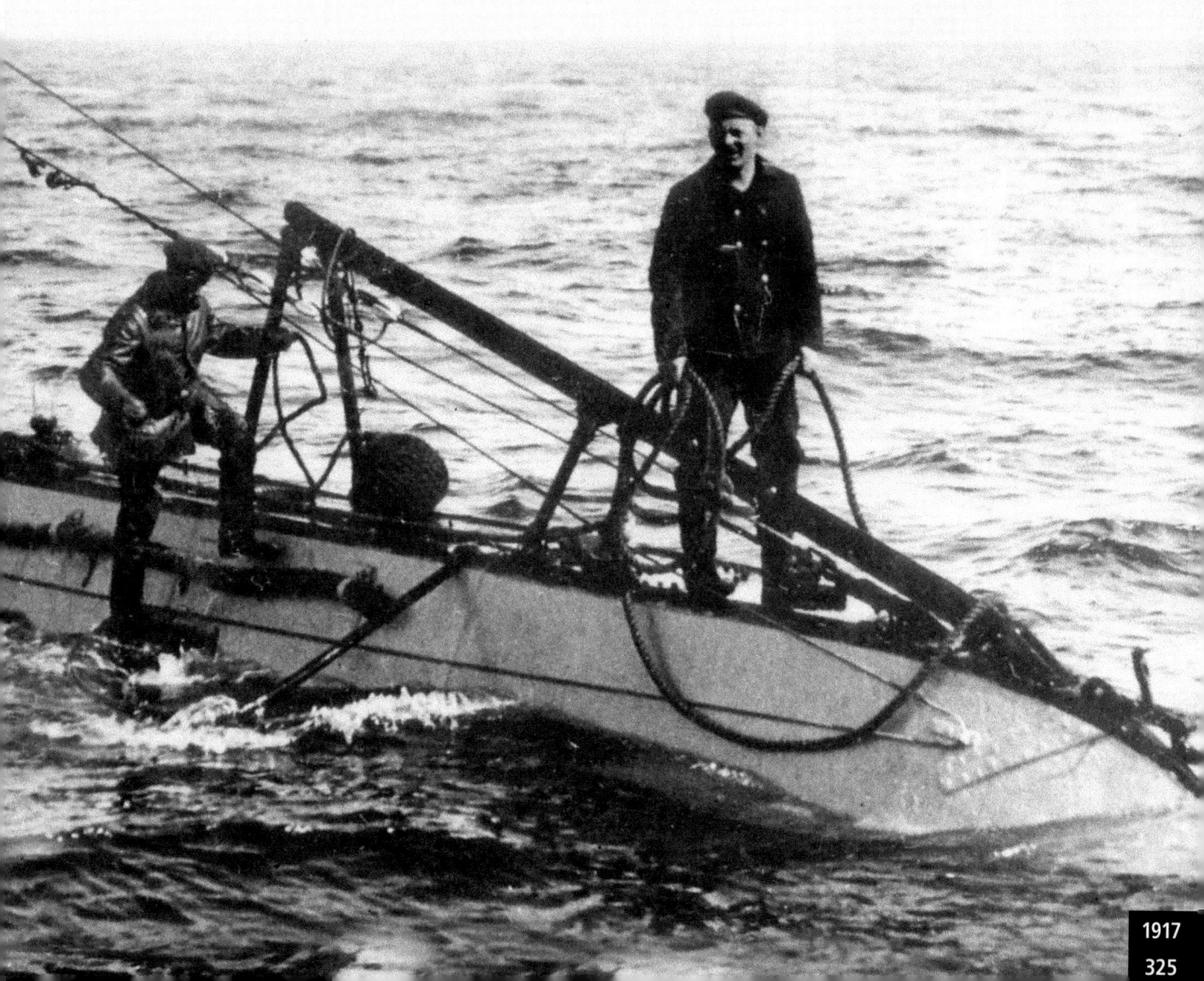

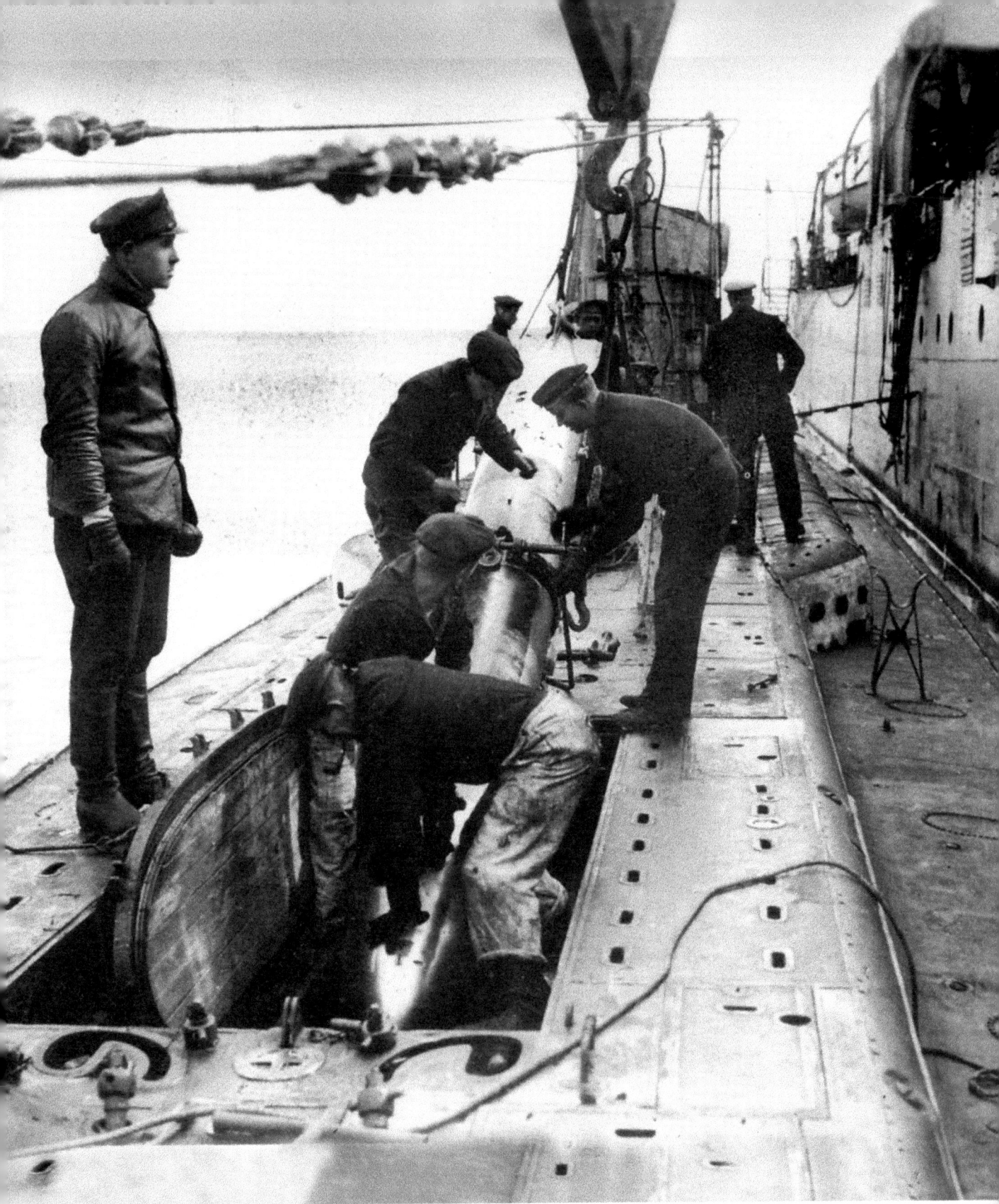

17GW741 Loading a torpedo at sea from a supply vessel.
17GW740 A torpedo being loaded into one of the two torpedo firing tubes.

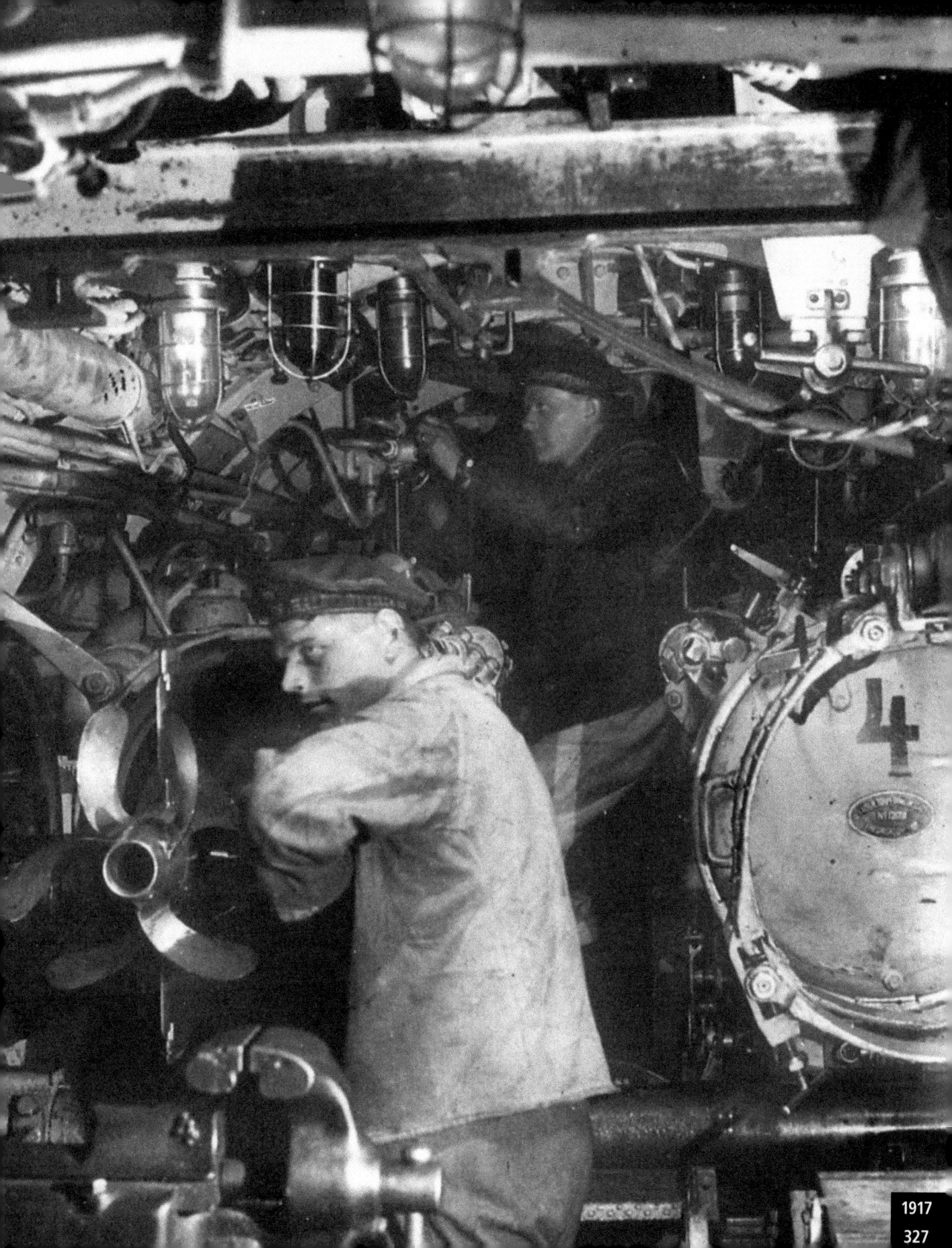

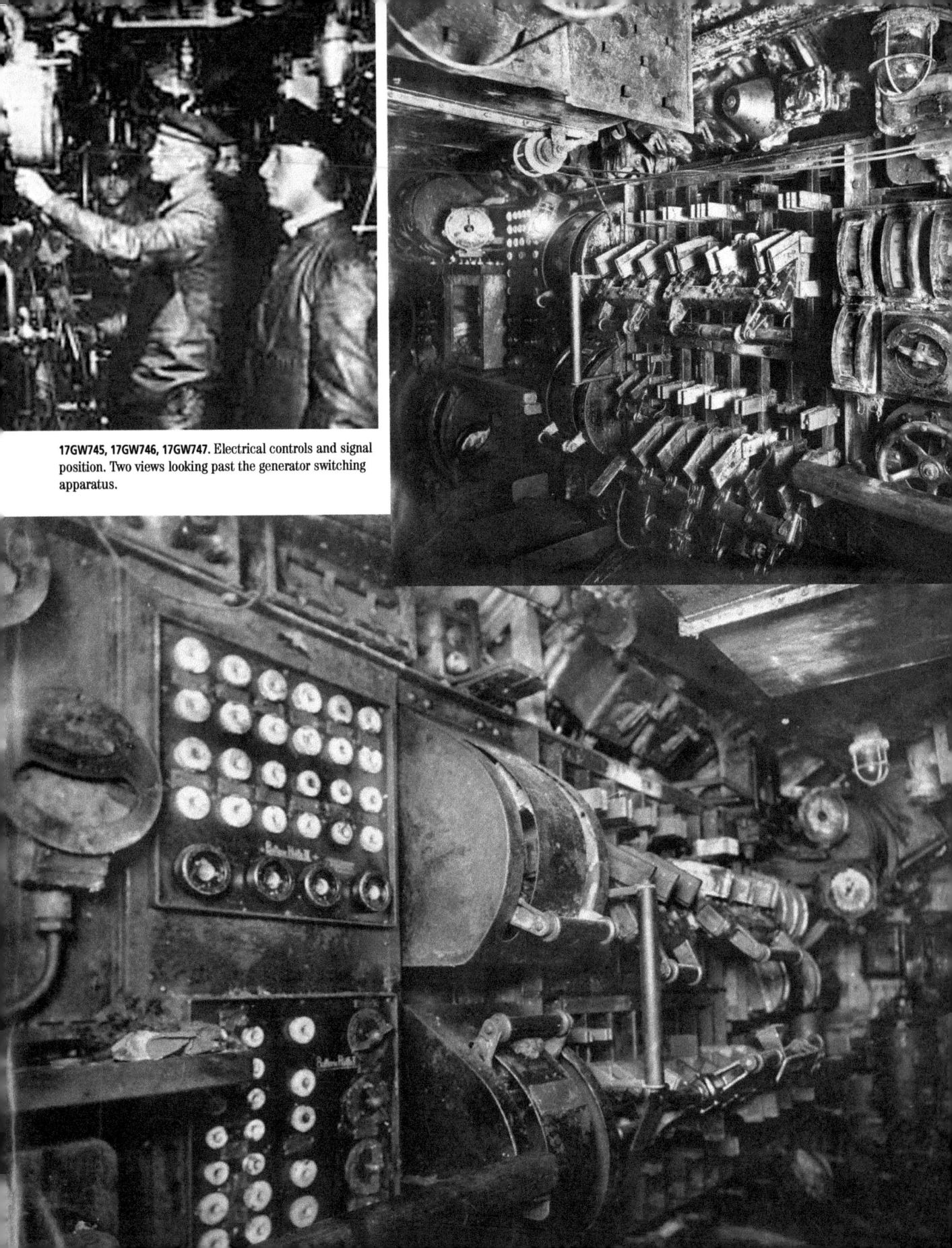

17GW745, 17GW746, 17GW747. Electrical controls and signal position. Two views looking past the generator switching apparatus.

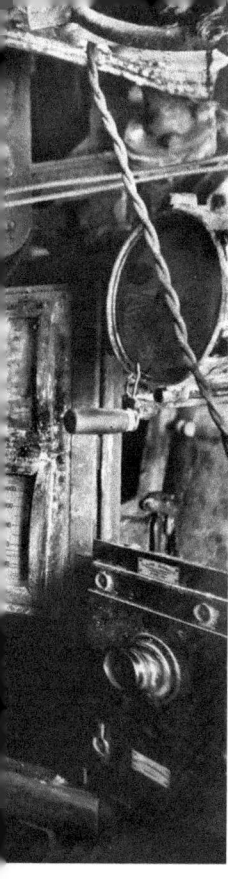

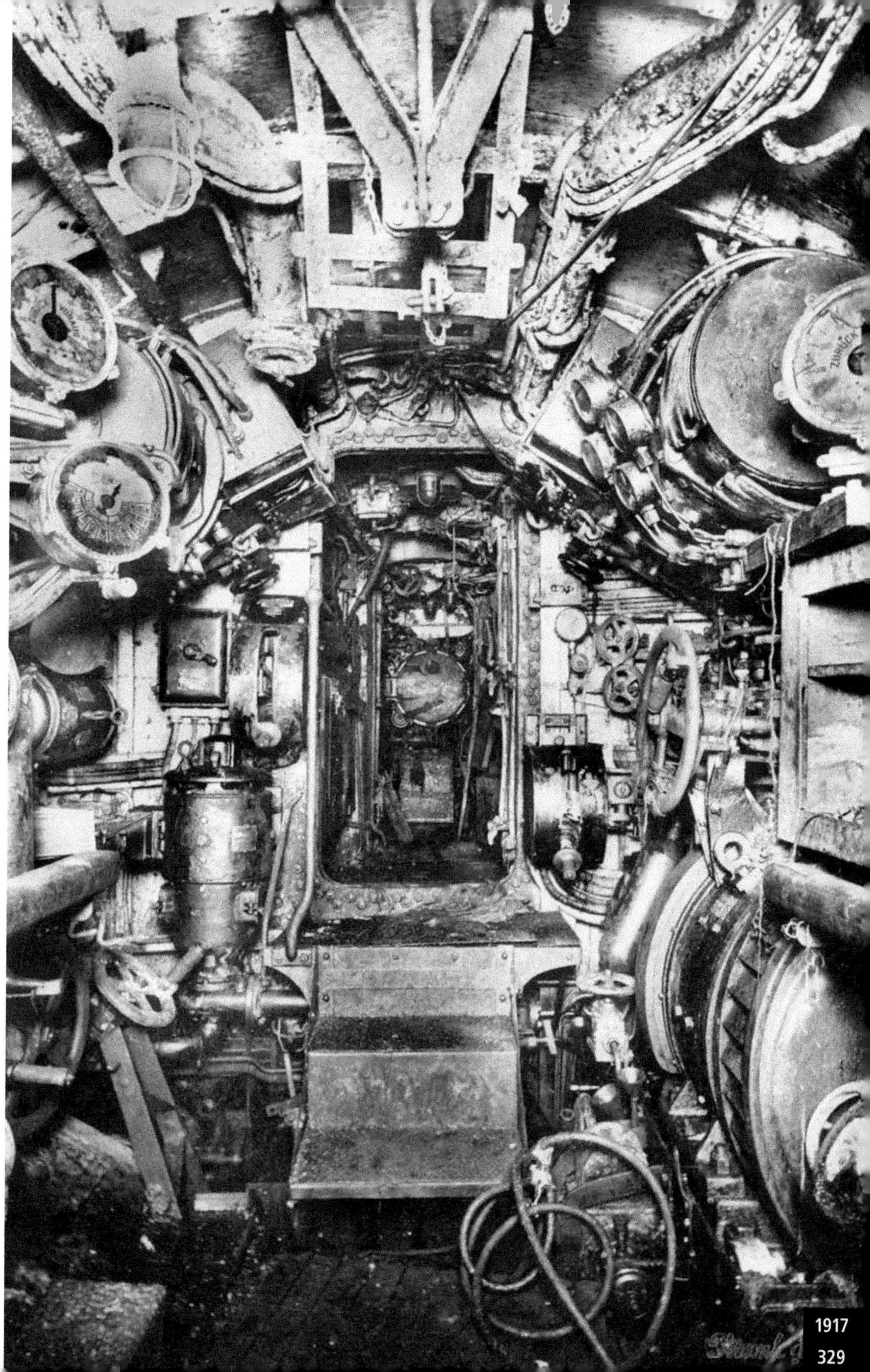

17GW751 Main control room, looking through the engine room towards the torpedo compartment.

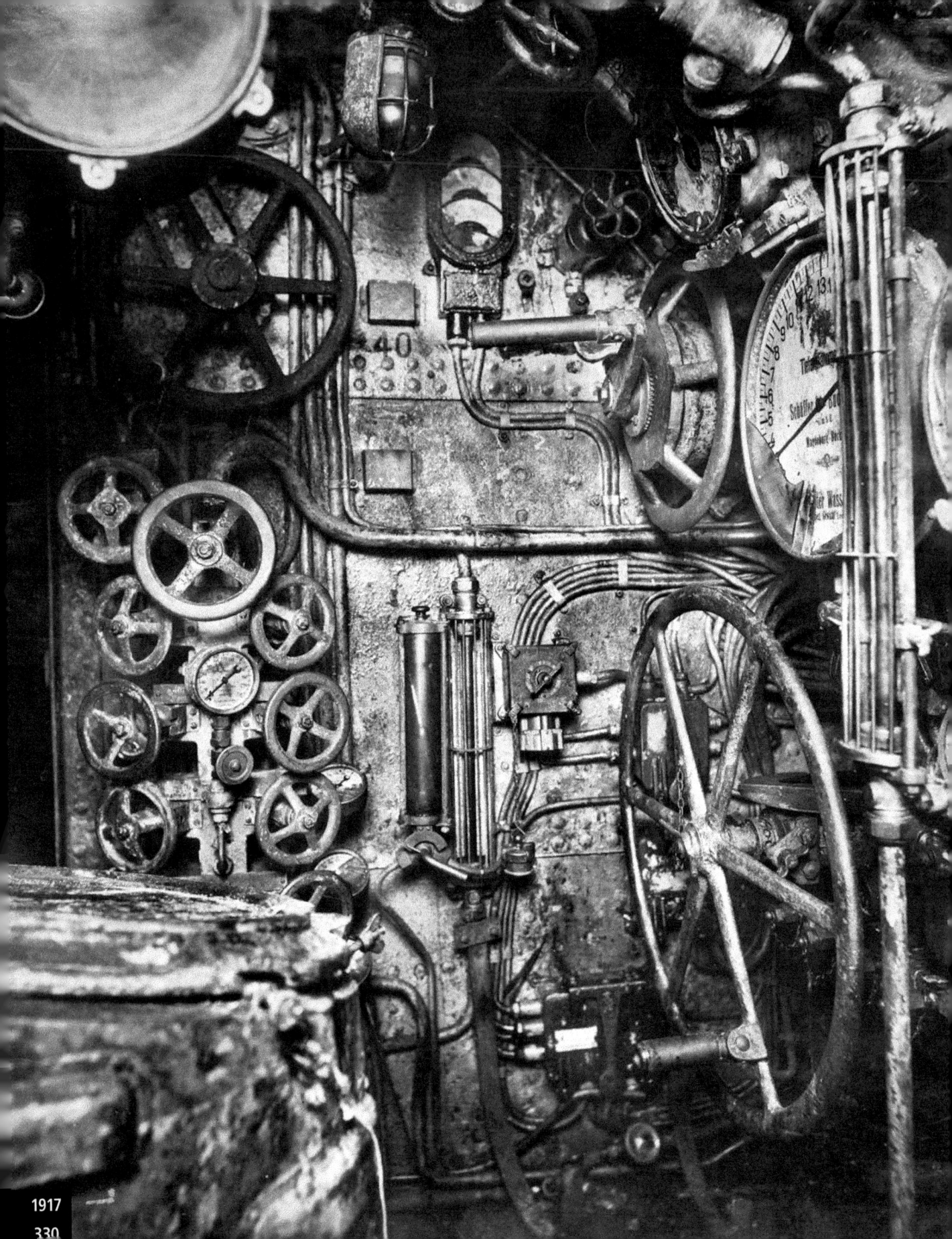

17GW752 Hydroplane control gear alongside the depth and fuel tank gauges.

17GW753 inspection hatch leading to the periscope. Visible are the hand control wheels for managing pressure along with valve gauges.

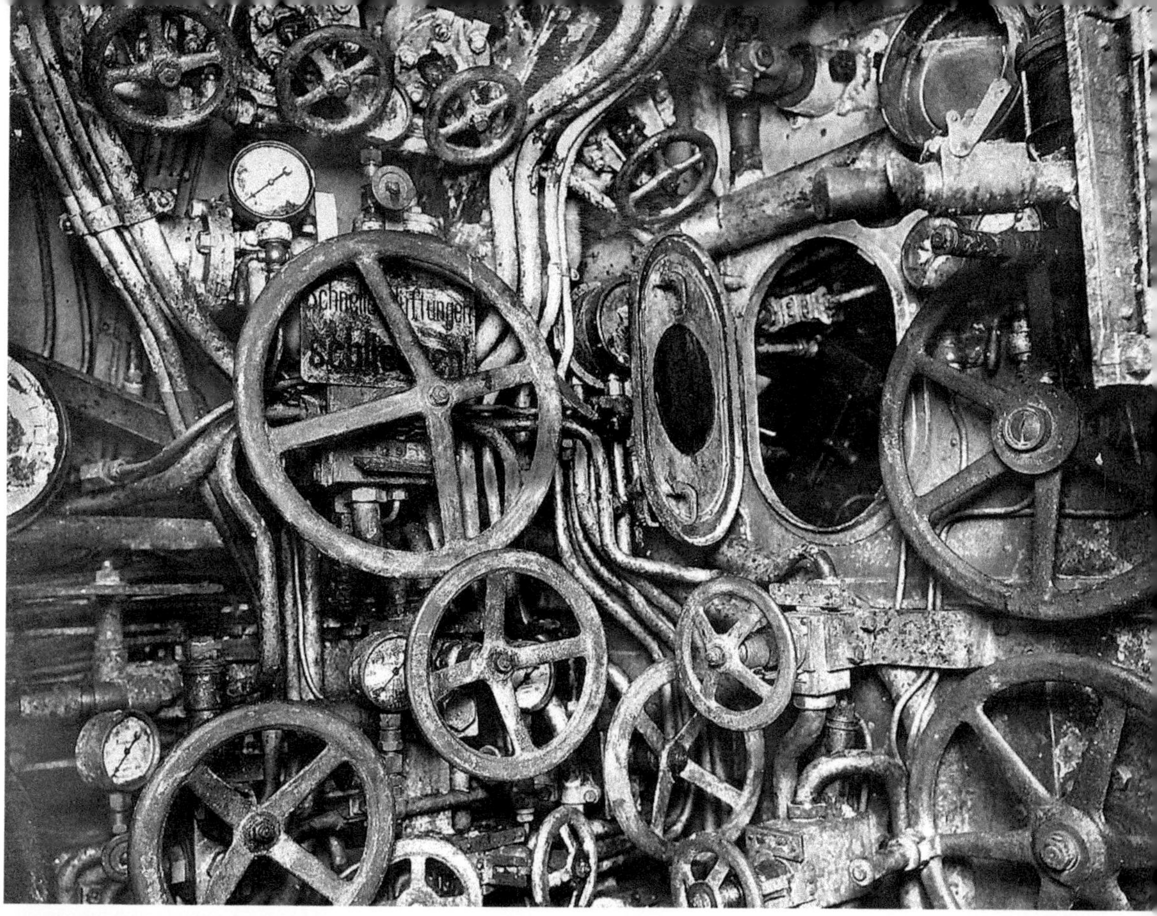

17GW754 Control wheels for managing air pressure; also the engine telegraph.

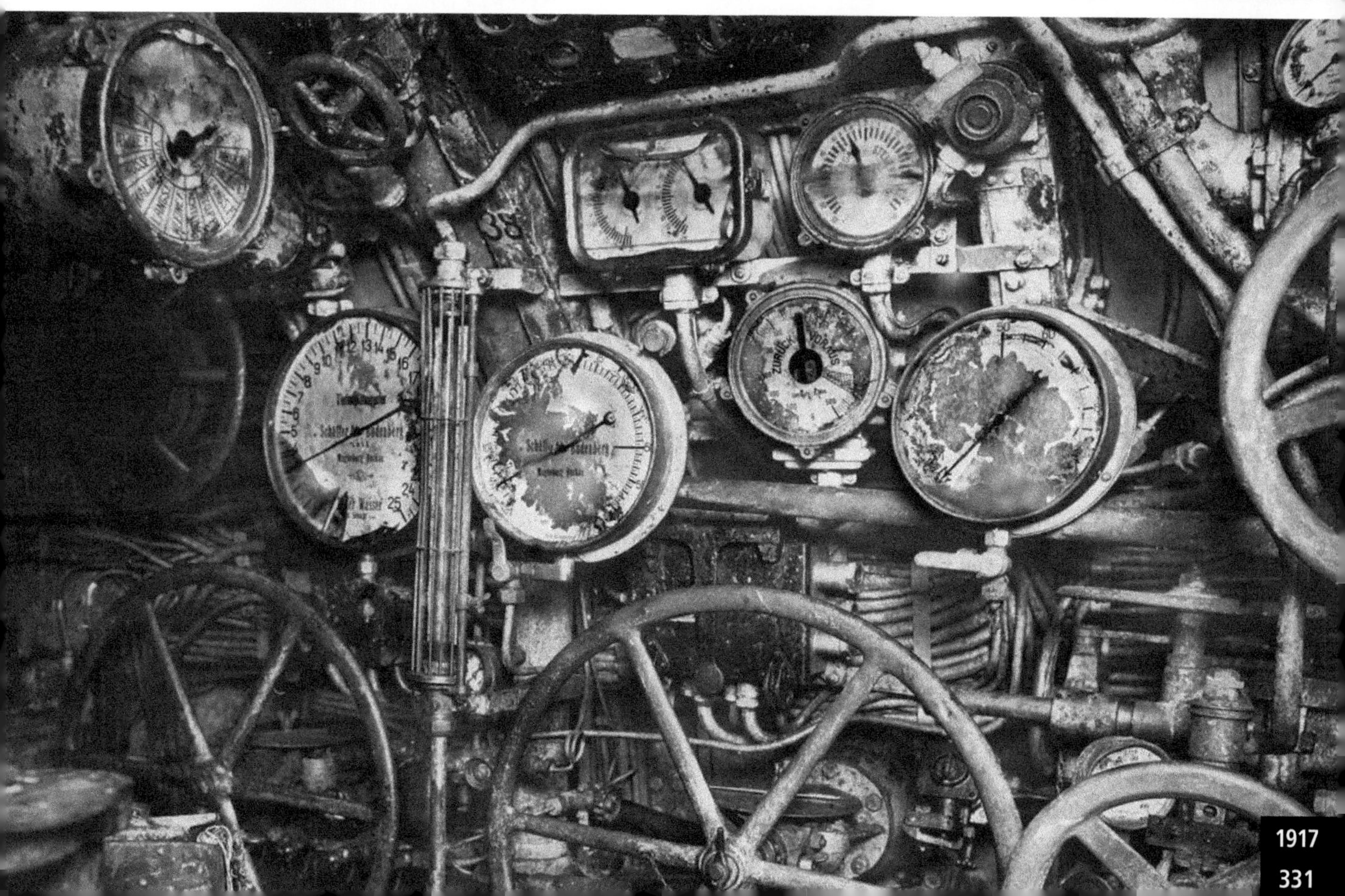

Most successful U-boat commanders of the Great War: officers that sank over 100,000 tons

	Commander	Successes
1. Kptlt.	Lothar von Arnauld de la Perière	195 ships sunk or captured (455,869 tons) / 8 ships damaged (34,312 tons)
2. Kptlt.	Walter Forstmann	149 ships sunk or captured (391,607 tons) / 7 ships damaged (30,552 tons)
3. Kptlt.	Max Valentiner	144 ships sunk or captured (299,482 tons) / 6 ships damaged (33,151 tons)
4. Kptlt.	Otto Steinbrinck	206 ships sunk or captured (244,797 tons) / 13 ships damaged (69,524 tons)
5. Kptlt.	Hans Rose	82 ships sunk or captured (221,942 tons) / 9 ships damaged (45,606 tons)
6. Kptlt.	Gustav Sieß	56 ships sunk or captured (188,295 tons) / 10 ships damaged (36,363 tons)
7. Kptlt.	Walther Schwieger	49 ships sunk or captured (185,212 tons) / 4 ships damaged (3,488 tons)
8. Kptlt.	Wolfgang Steinbauer	51 ships sunk or captured (183,871 tons) / 12 ships damaged (60,480 tons)
9. Kptlt.	Claus Rücker	80 ships sunk or captured (174,655 tons) / 3 ships damaged (9,951 tons)
10. Oblt.	Reinhold Saltzwedel	111 ships sunk or captured (172,824 tons) / 10 ships damaged (17,131 tons)
11. KrvKpt.	Waldemar Kophamel	56 ships sunk or captured (157,771 tons) / 6 ships damaged (10,176 tons)
12. Kptlt.	Hans von Mellenthin	57 ships sunk or captured (154,662 tons) / 7 ships damaged (31,556 tons)
13. Kptlt.	Otto Wünsche	77 ships sunk or captured (153,630 tons) / 6 ships damaged (25,317 tons)
14. Kptlt.	Kurt Hartwig	44 ships sunk or captured (153,082 tons) / 6 ships damaged (27,902 tons)
15. Oblt.	Johannes Lohs	77 ships sunk or captured (150,665 tons) / 16 ships damaged (89,369 tons)
16. Kptlt.	Robert Moraht	46 ships sunk or captured (147,869 tons) / 3 ships damaged (9,420 tons)
17. Kptlt.	Konrad Gansser	57 ships sunk or captured (143,667 tons) / 3 ships damaged (10,771 tons)
18. Kptlt.	Rudolf Schneider	45 ships sunk or captured (140,802 tons) / 5 ships damaged (21,956 tons)
19. KrvKpt.	Otto Schultze	54 ships sunk or captured (137,817 tons) / 9 ships damaged (31,293 tons)
20. Kptlt.	Erwin Waßner	90 ships sunk or captured (136,073 tons) / 5 ships damaged (15,297 tons)
21. Kptlt.	Ernst Hashagen	55 ships sunk or captured (135,302 tons) / 5 ships damaged (16,483 tons)
22. Kptlt.	Leo Hillebrand	52 ships sunk or captured (132,255 tons) / 1 ship damaged (7,378 tons)
23. Kptlt.	Wilhelm Werner	63 ships sunk or captured (130,499 tons) / 7 ships damaged (26,161 tons)
24. Kptlt.	Alfred von Glasenapp	51 ships sunk or captured (122,443 tons) / 6 ships damaged (47,429 tons)
25. Kptlt.	Heinrich Jeß	44 ships sunk or captured (121,088 tons) / 3 ships damaged (16,220 tons)
26. Kptlt.	Wilhelm Marschall	44 ships sunk or captured (120,460 tons) / 1 ship damaged (765 tons)
27. Kptlt.	Otto Hersing	40 ships sunk or captured (113,580 tons) / 2 ships damaged (8,918 tons)
28. Kptlt.	Matthias Graf von Schmettow	78 ships sunk or captured (111,628 tons) / 8 ships damaged (31,271 tons)
29. Kptlt.	Carl-Siegfried Ritter von Georg	75 ships sunk or captured (111,221 tons) / 8 ships damaged (19,869 tons)
30. Kptlt.	Raimund Weisbach	36 ships sunk or captured (107,763 tons) / 2 ships damaged (3,481 tons)
31. Oblt.	Herbert Pustkuchen	84 ships sunk or captured (107,520 tons) / 13 ships damaged (43,543 tons)
32. Kptlt.	Karl Neumann	69 ships sunk or captured (104,868 tons) / 3 ships damaged (8,249 tons)
33. Oblt.	Otto Launburg	39 ships sunk or captured (104,144 tons) / 8 ships damaged (38,144 tons)
34. Kptlt.	Kurt Ramien	57 ships sunk or captured (103,455 tons) / 6 ships damaged (26,509 tons)
35. Kptlt.	Hans Walther	42 ships sunk or captured (103,262 tons) / 4 ships damaged (13,451 tons)
36. Kptlt.	Ernst Wilhelms	31 ships sunk or captured (102,875 tons) / 1 ship damaged (1,648 tons)
37. Kptlt.	Ralph Wenninger	98 ships sunk or captured (102,638 tons) / 7 ships damaged (27,849 tons)

Thirty-seven commanders between them sank 2,684 ships, a total tonnage of 5,929,593 tons.

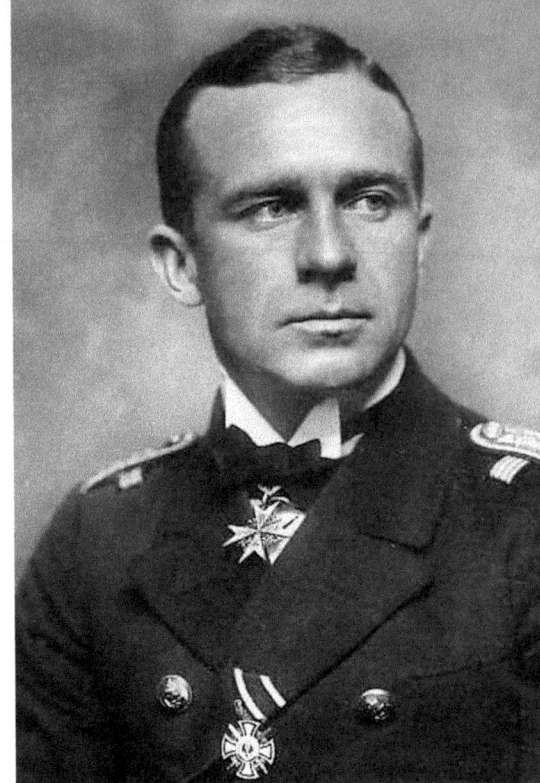

17GW721 *Kapitänleutnant* Lothar von Arnauld de la Perière, commander *U-35*. **195 ships sunk or captured; 455,869 tons**

Lothar von Arnauld de la Perière made fourteen voyages with *U-35*, during which time he sank 189 merchant vessels and two gunboats, amounting to a total of 446,708 gross register tonnage (GRT). One of his kills was the French troop carrier SS *Gallia*, which sank with great loss of life. He transferred to the *U-139* in May 1918 and sank a further five ships with a combined tonnage of 7,008 GRT. His record total of sunken tonnage and number of sunken ships is unsurpassed.

17GW722 The British cargo ship SS *Maplewood* in the process of being sunk by shell fire from German submarine SM *U-35* off Sardinia, 4 July, 1917.

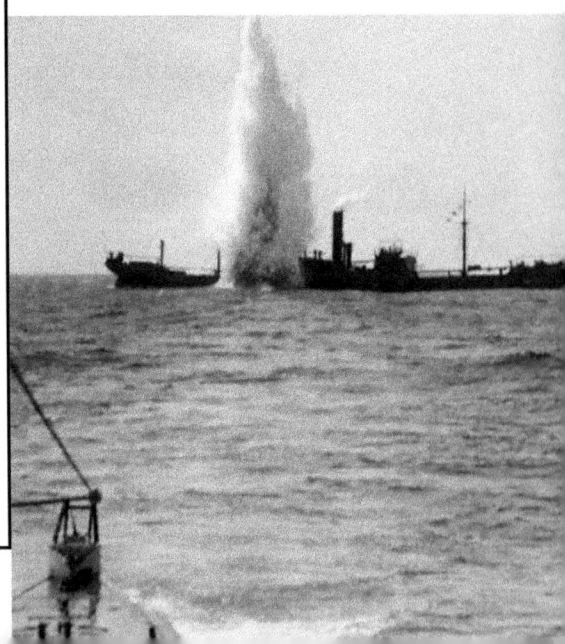

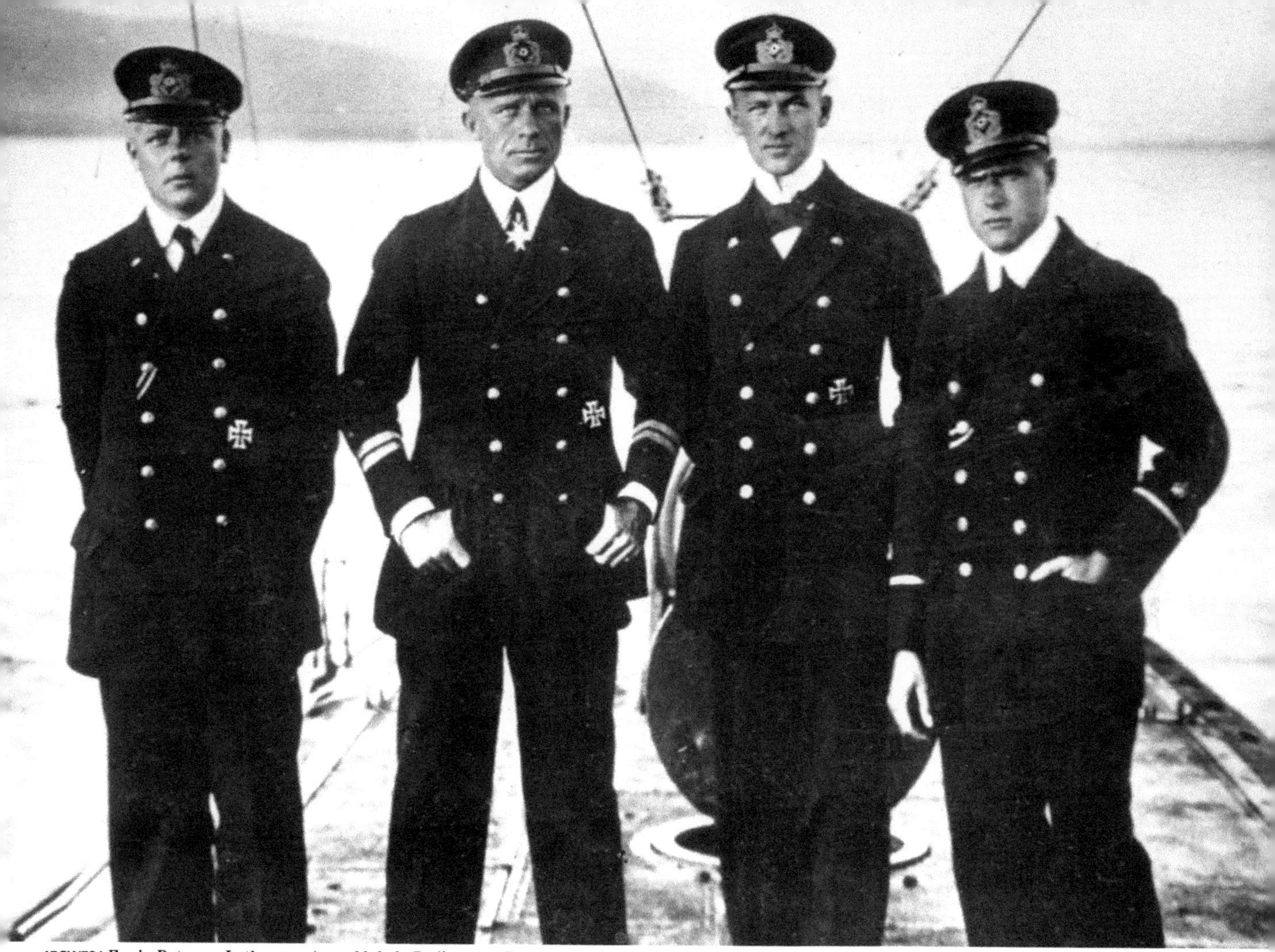

17GW721 Erwin Deterra, Lothar von Arnauld de la Perière, von Preussen and an unidentified officer of U-boat *U-35* at Cattaro.

On 3 October 1916 the *Gallia* left Toulon unescorted, destined for Thessaloniki in Greece. Aboard were 1,650 French soldiers, 350 Serbian soldiers, and 350 crew. It had a cargo of artillery pieces and ammunition. The next day, between Sardinia and Tunisia, she was hit by one torpedo from the German submarine *U-35*. Ammunition aboard *Gallia* exploded and the ship sank in fifteen minutes. Panic broke out on board, lifeboats capsized, and hundreds of soldiers jumped overboard. The ship's radio was disabled by the explosions before a distress signal could be sent. The exact number of casualties will never be known, but estimates vary between 600 and 1,800.

17GW723 SS *Gallia* before being converted from a passenger liner to a troopship.

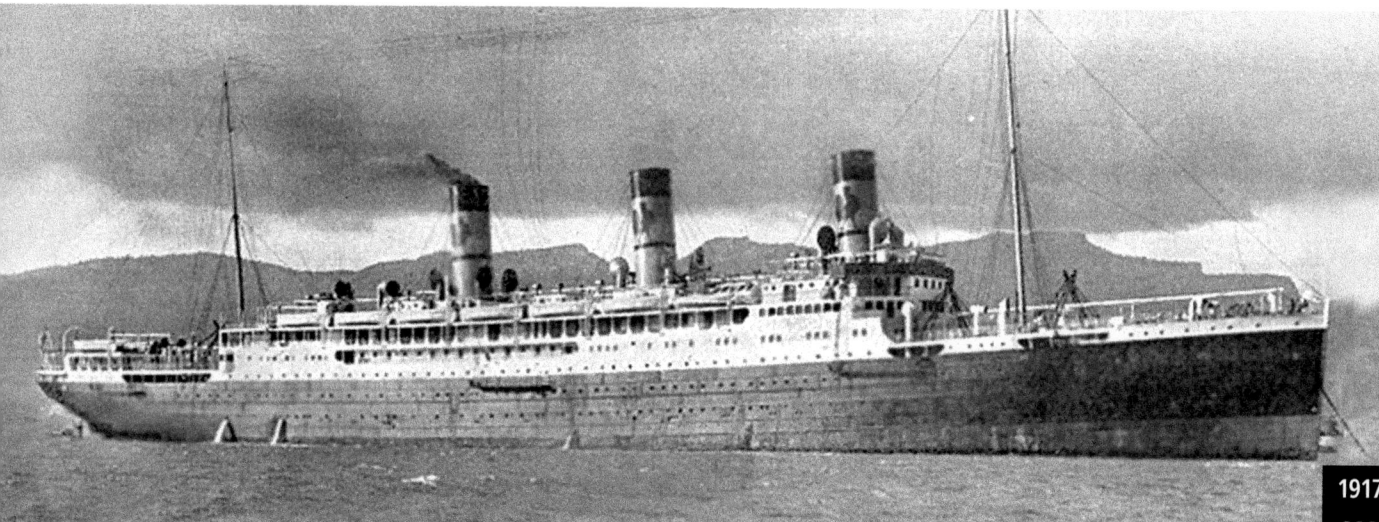

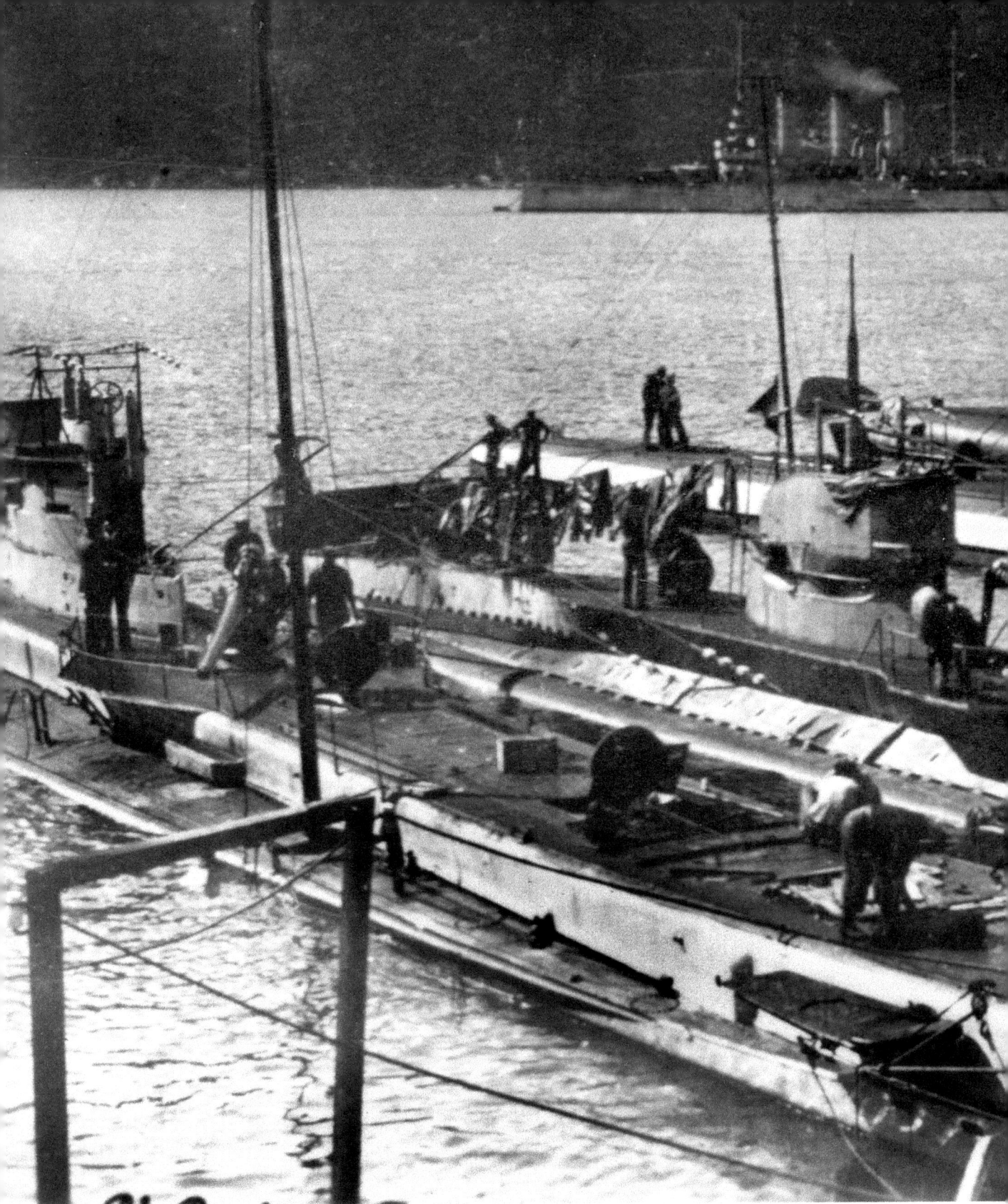

17GW756 U-boats: *U-35, U-27, U-62, unidentified*, of the German Mediterranean U-boat Division, assisting the Austro-Hungarian Navy (*kaiserliche und königliche Kriegsmarine*) at the port of Cattaro, in the Adriatic.

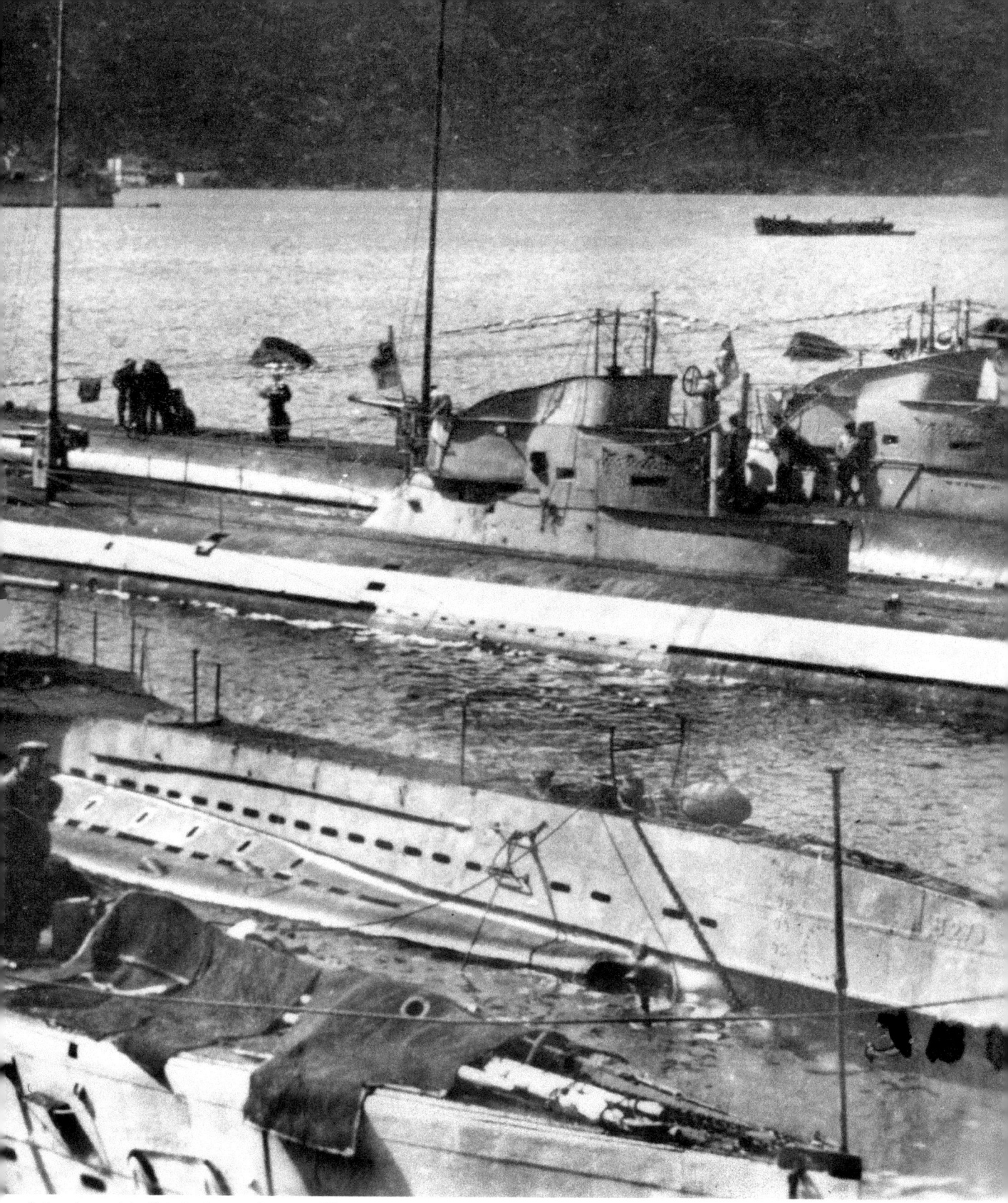

Cattaro (present-day Kotor), a town on the coast of Montenegro, was one of three main bases of the Austro-Hungarian Navy and home port to the Austrian Fifth Fleet. This consisted of pre-dreadnought battleships and light cruisers. The area was the site of some of the fiercest battles between local Montenegrin Slavs and Austria-Hungary.

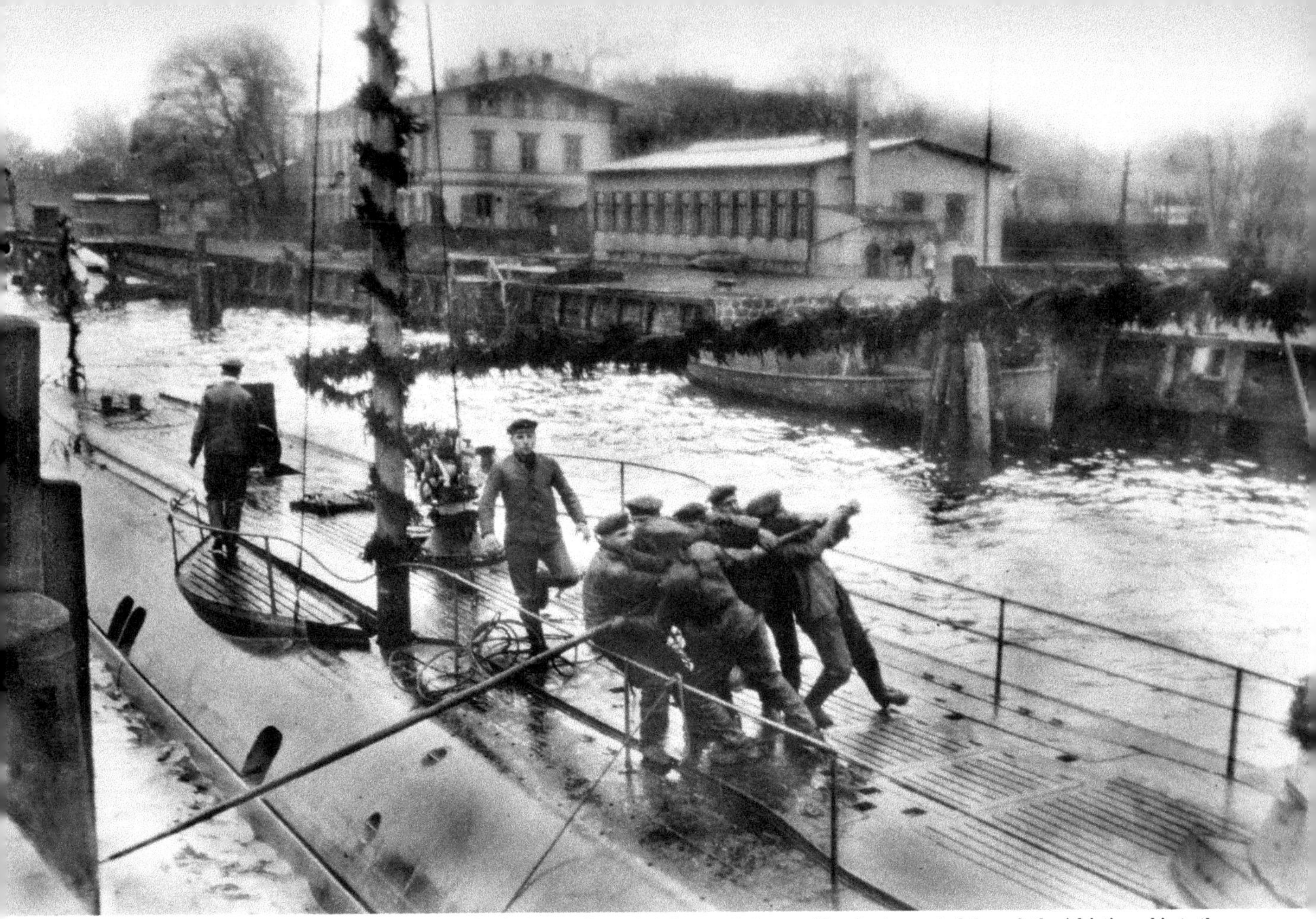

17GW757 Crew of the *U-35* fending-off as the submarine is about to leave their base at Cattaro and head out on patrol through the Adriatic and in to the Mediterranean. The boat appears to be still adorned with festive trimmings for some occasion; one source indicates the date to be April, May time 1917.

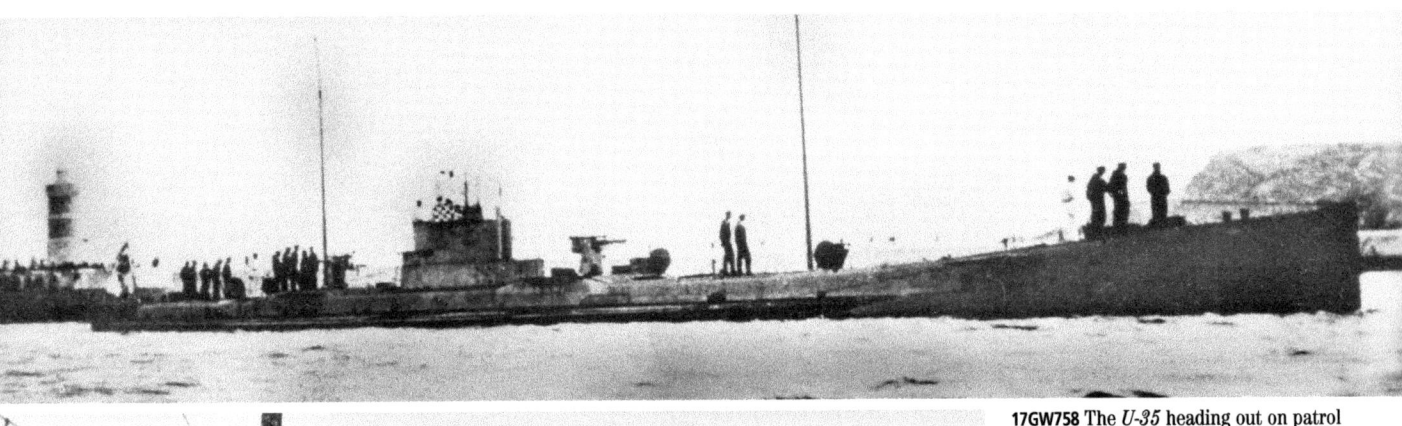

17GW758 The *U-35* heading out on patrol from Cattaro into the Adriatic.

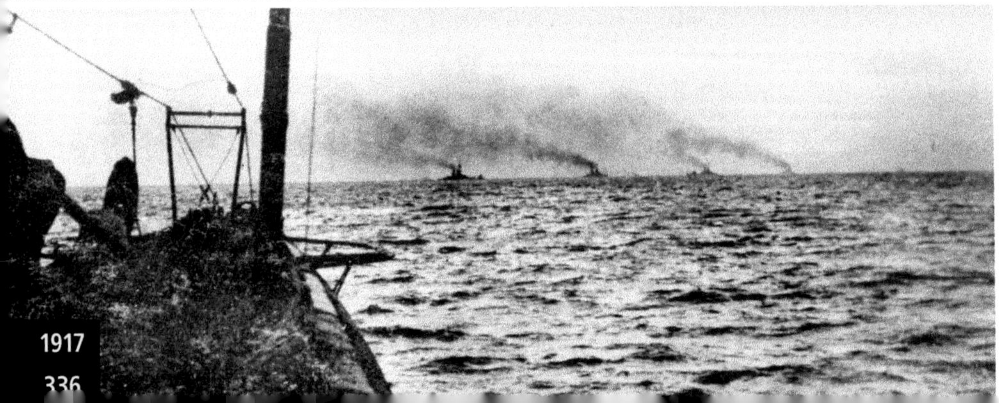

17GW759 The *U-35* heading towards the Austro-Hungarian *Kaiserliche und Königliche Kriegsmarine* battle fleet of pre Dreadnaught cruisers. The decorations seem to have been stripped from the rigging and are lying along the deck. It would seem likely that they would be either stored away or discarded before drawing much closer to the cruisers.

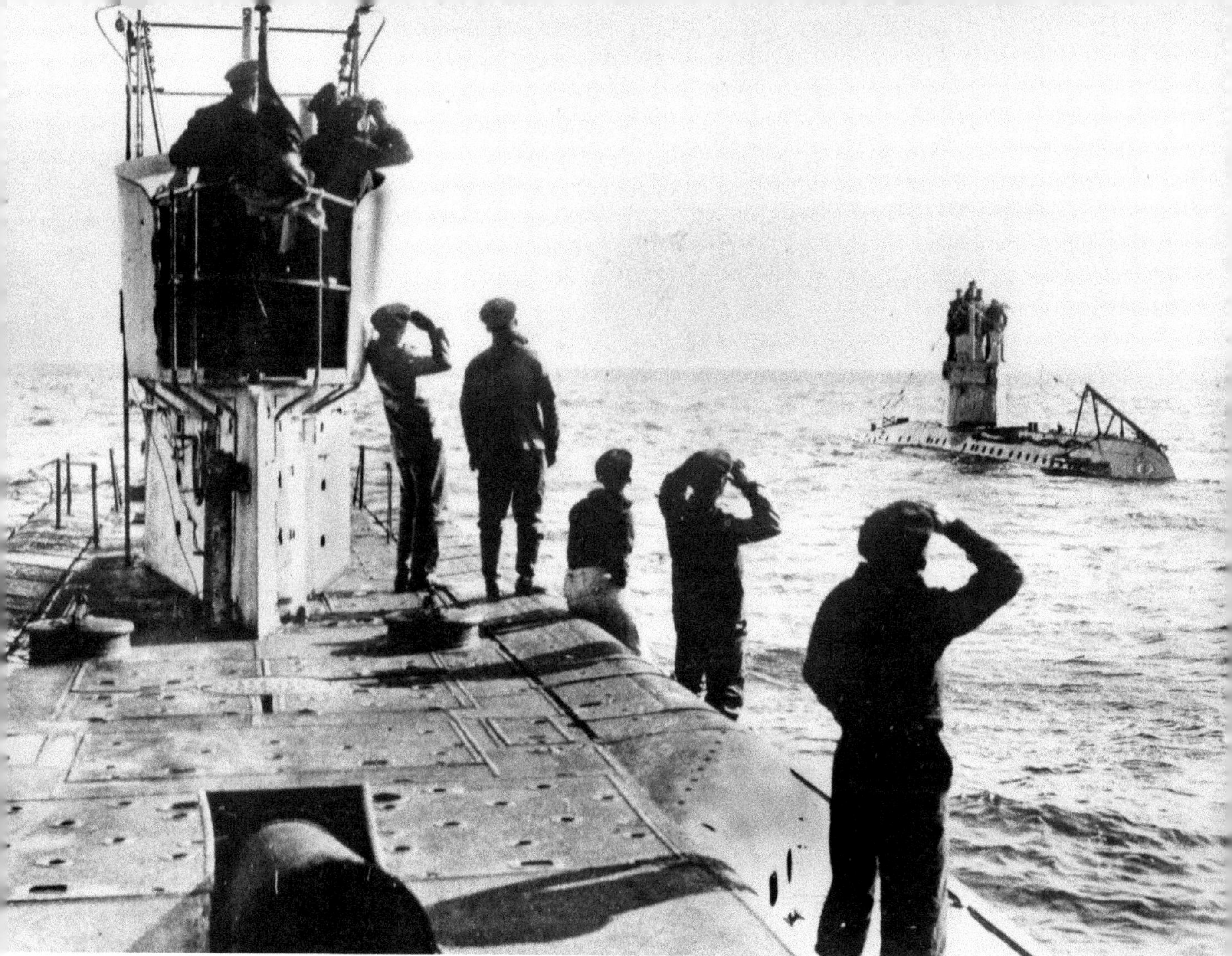

17GW760, 17GW761. Officers and crew of submarine *U-35* watch the approach of *U-42* at a pre-arranged rendezvous in the Mediterranean, May 1917. See also **17GW739** (page 323) for another photograph in this series.

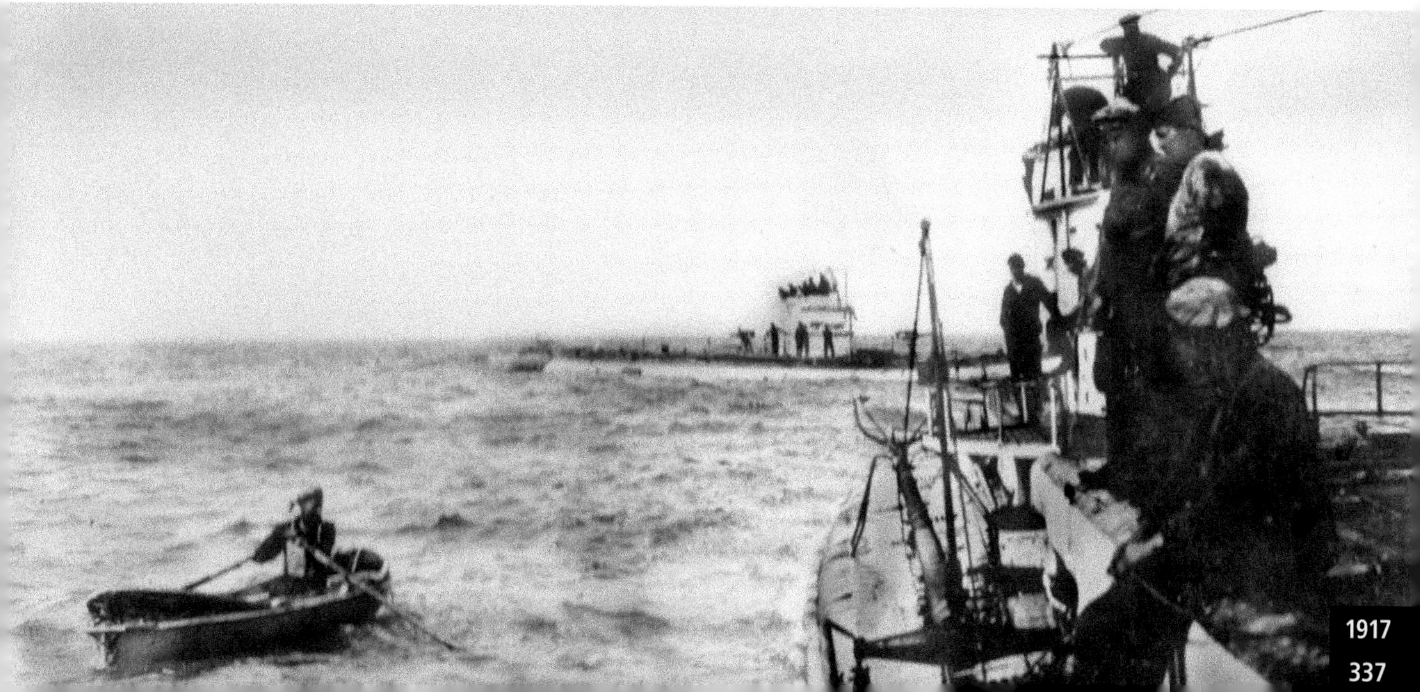

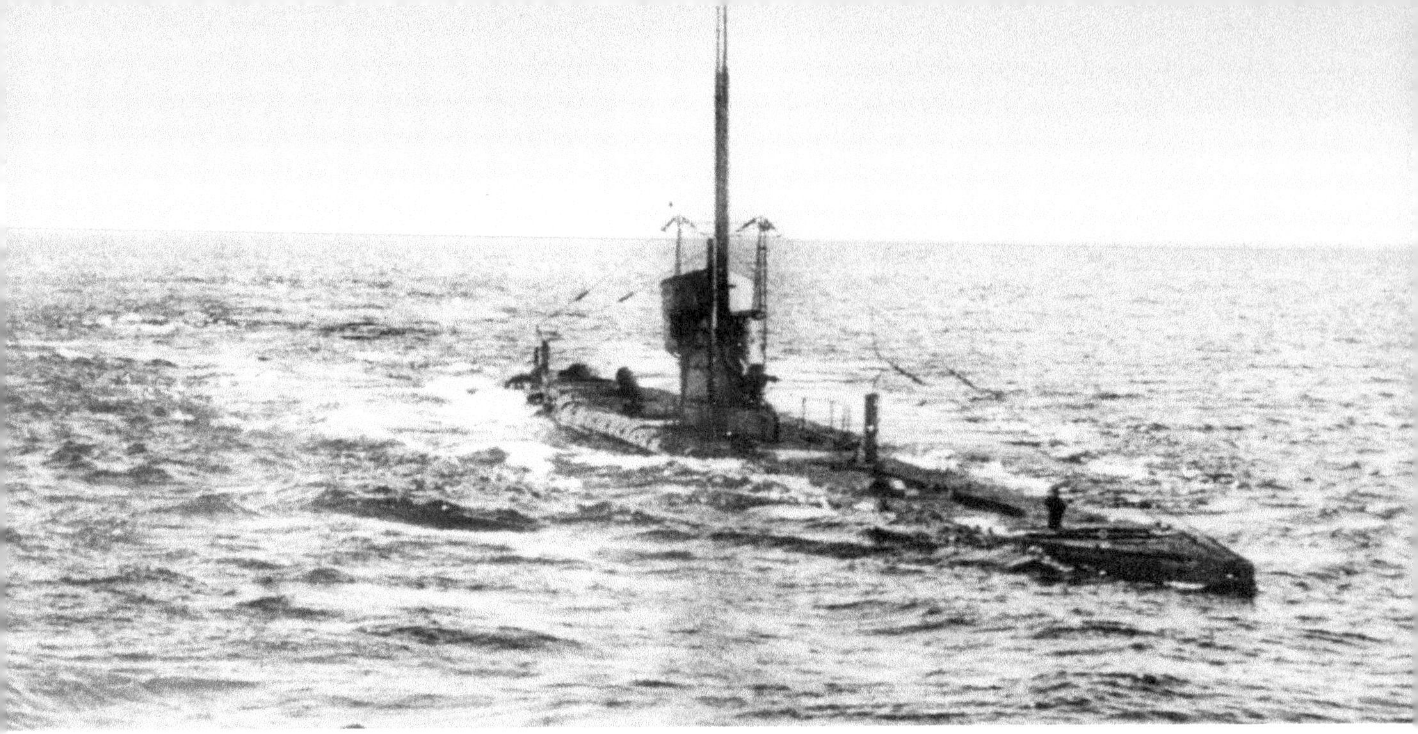

17GW762, 17GW763, 17GW764, 17GW765. The *U-35* at her deadly work in the Mediterranean: surfacing and stopping a steamer; the crew is ordered into the life boats and the captain taken prisoner aboard the submarine. Either a bombing party board the vessel and place explosive charges or the 88 mm deck gun is used to place shells below the ship's waterline. The U-boat crew are assisting a victim's crew: their lifeboat must have capsized in the launching and men cling to the overturned boat; the German sailors would help right the boat and leave the crew to be picked up. Vessels belonging to neutral countries had their ship's papers checked for cargo type and destination; should it turn out to be strategic materials bound for a port of the éntente nations, France, Britain, Italy, then she was sunk. American merchantmen were usually sunk, although still neutral in the first three months of 1917. This unrestricted submarine warfare caused the United States to break off diplomatic relations with the Central Powers. On 2 April the United States declared war on Germany.

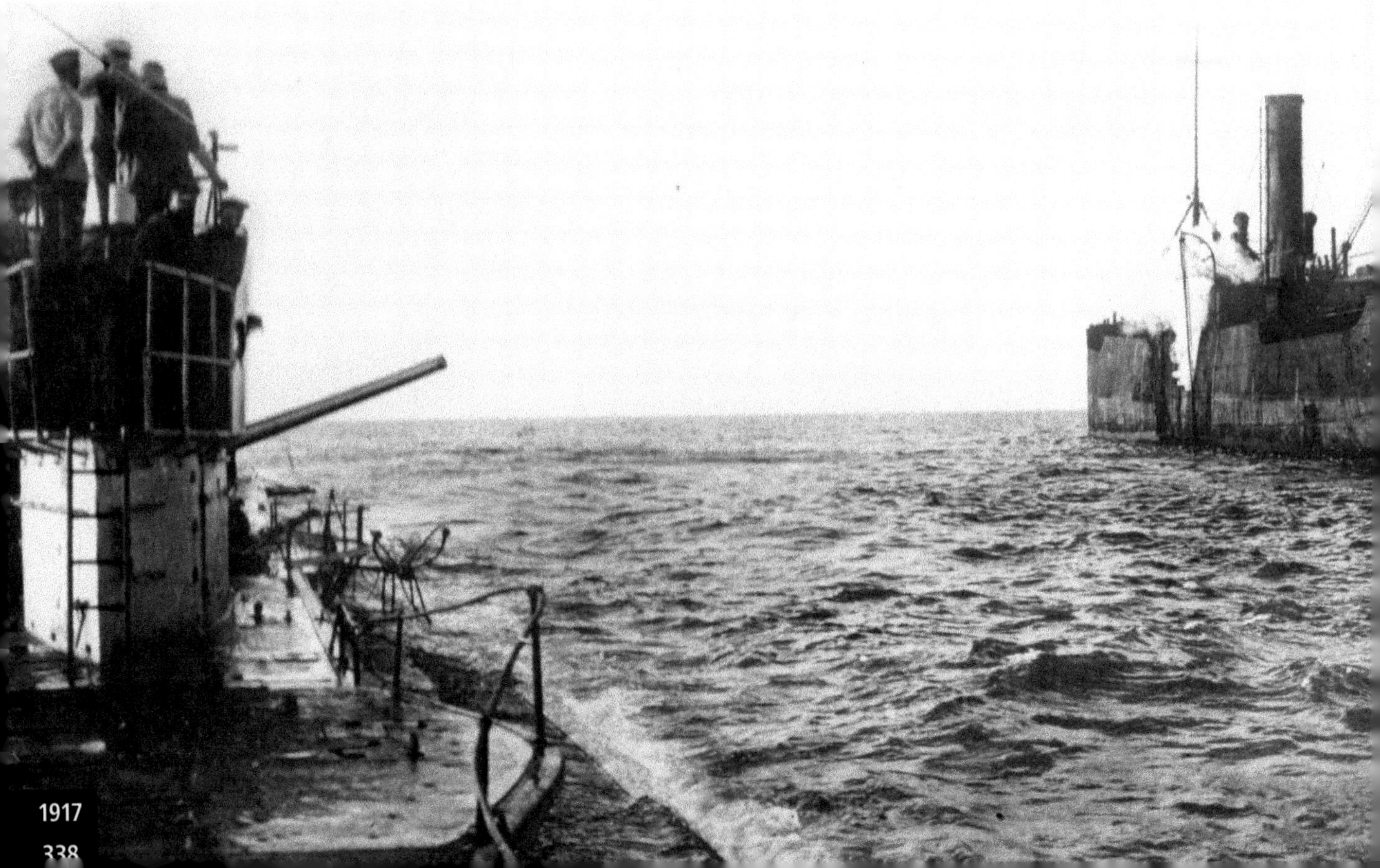

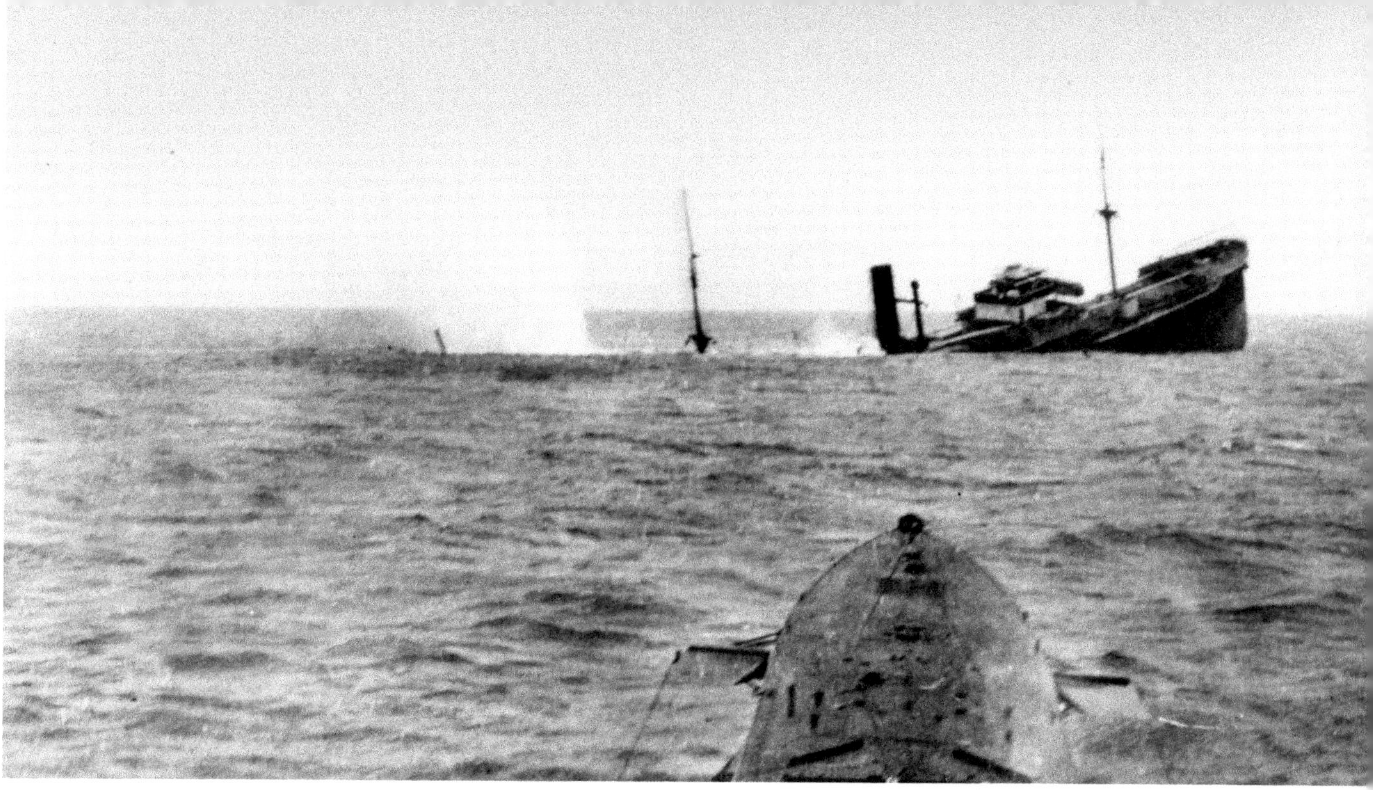

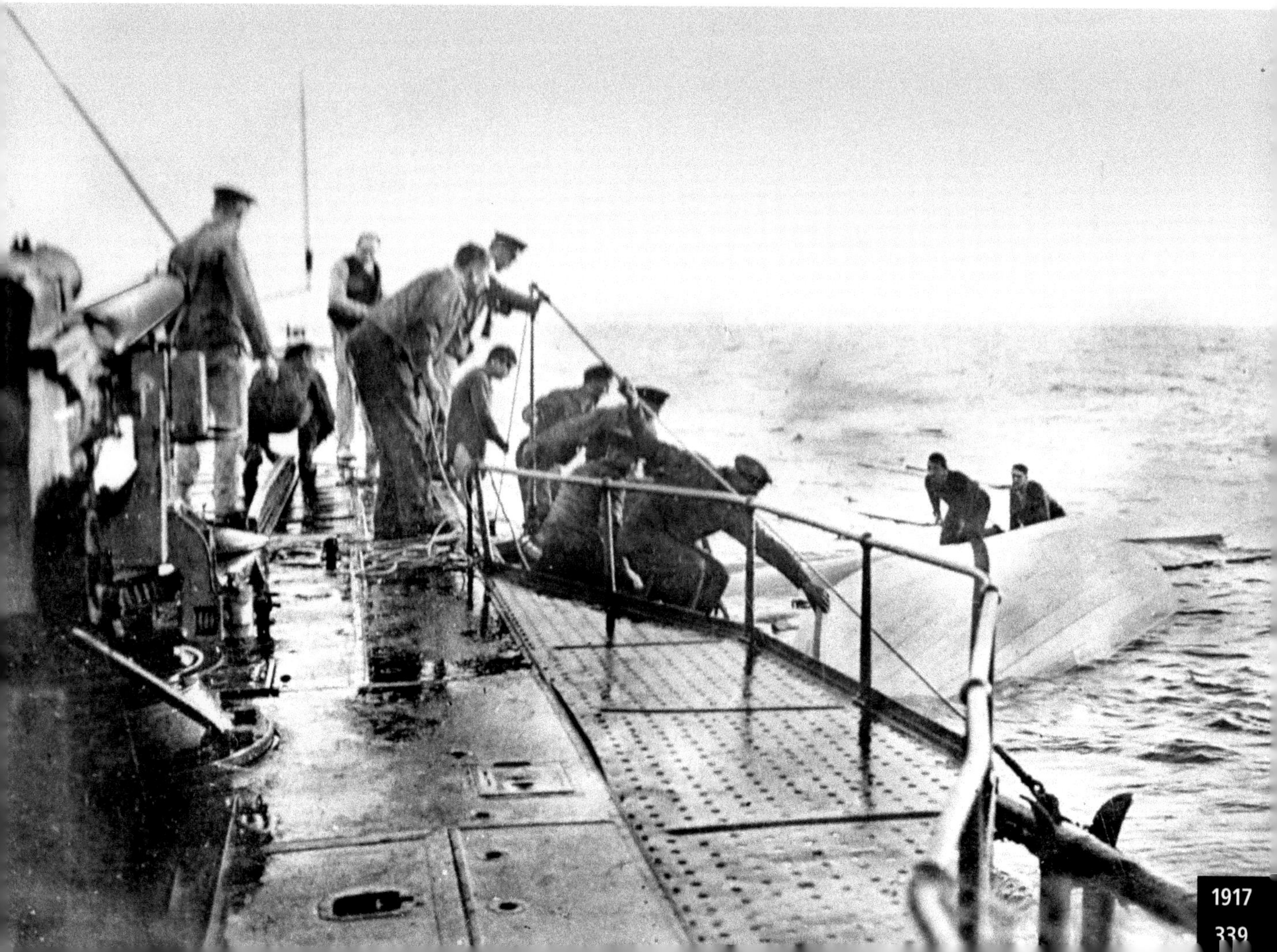

1917

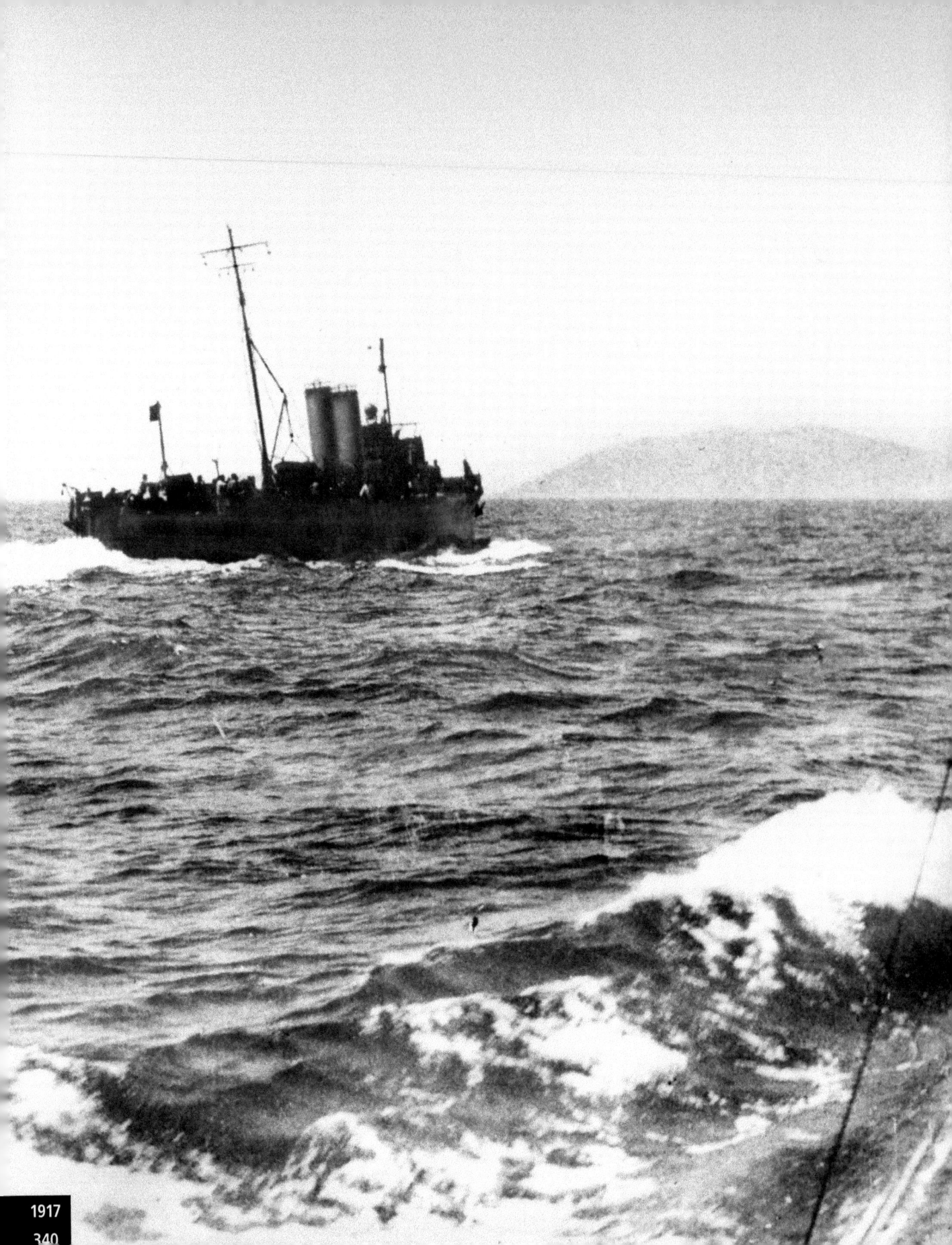

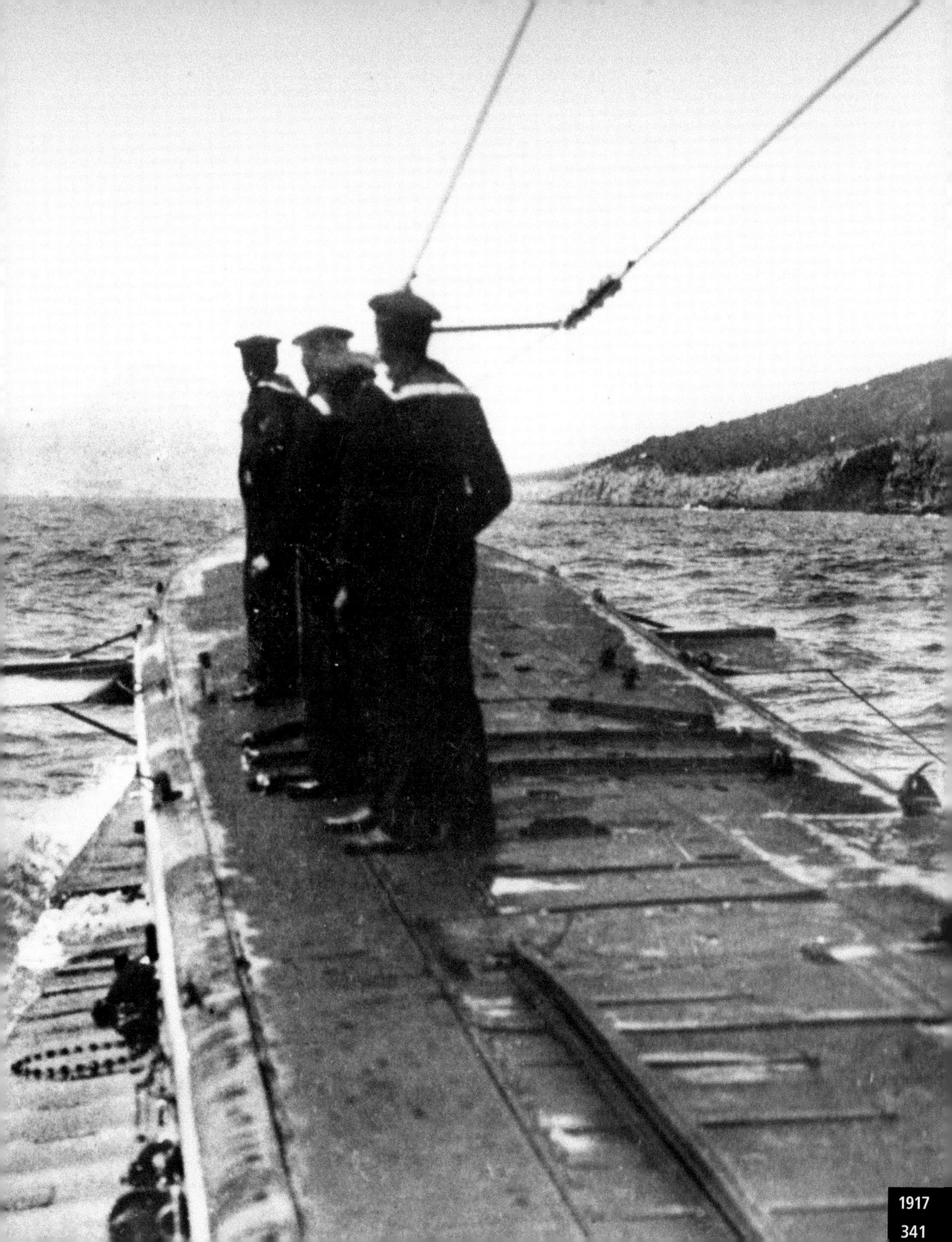

17GW766, 17GW7667. Officers and crew of submarine *U-35* in their dress uniforms proudly take up positions on the conning tower and deck, fore and aft, as they speed towards the anchorage at Cattaro. Each pennant flying from the periscope indicates a ship sunk during the highly successful patrol. The commander, *Kapitänleutnant* Lothar von Arnauld de la Perière, is in pride of place, standing above the others as the shore draws closer.

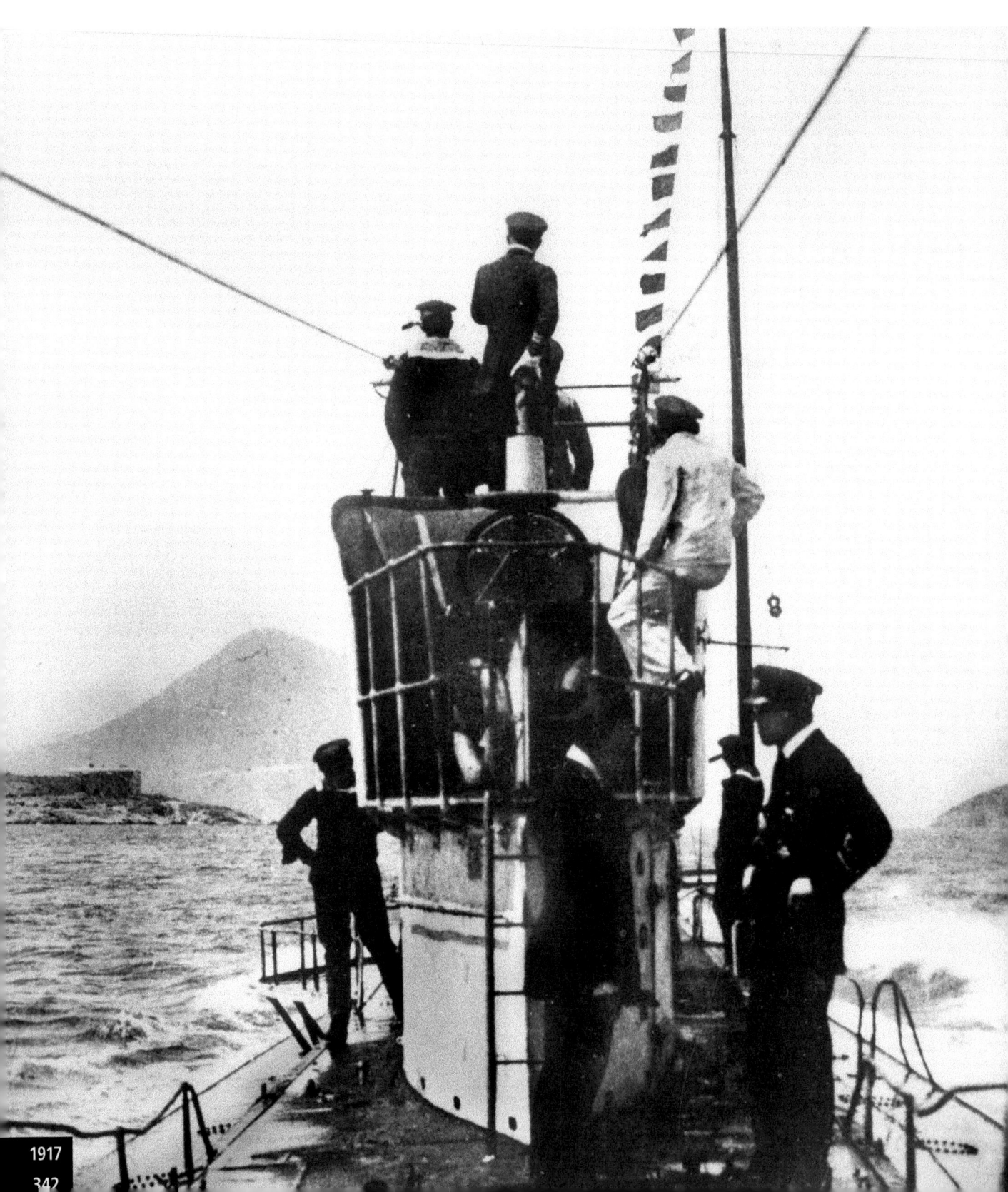

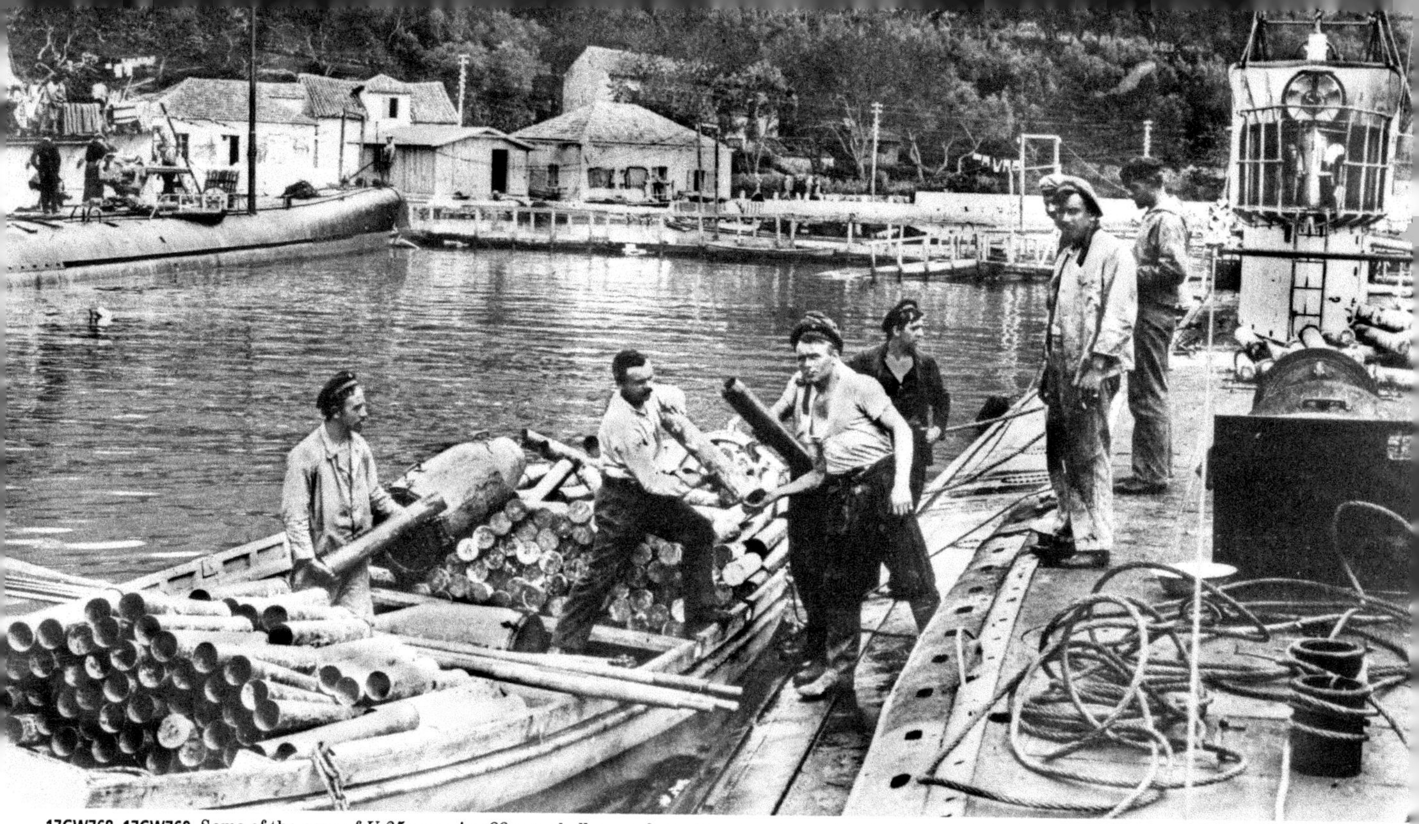

17GW768, 17GW769. Some of the crew of *U-35* removing 88 mm shell cases from the submarine berthed at Cattaro. With the onset of warmer weather the commander, Lothar von Arnauld de la Perière, has given permission for bathing from the deck of *U-35*. A shower of fresh water has been set up. Note the lookouts.

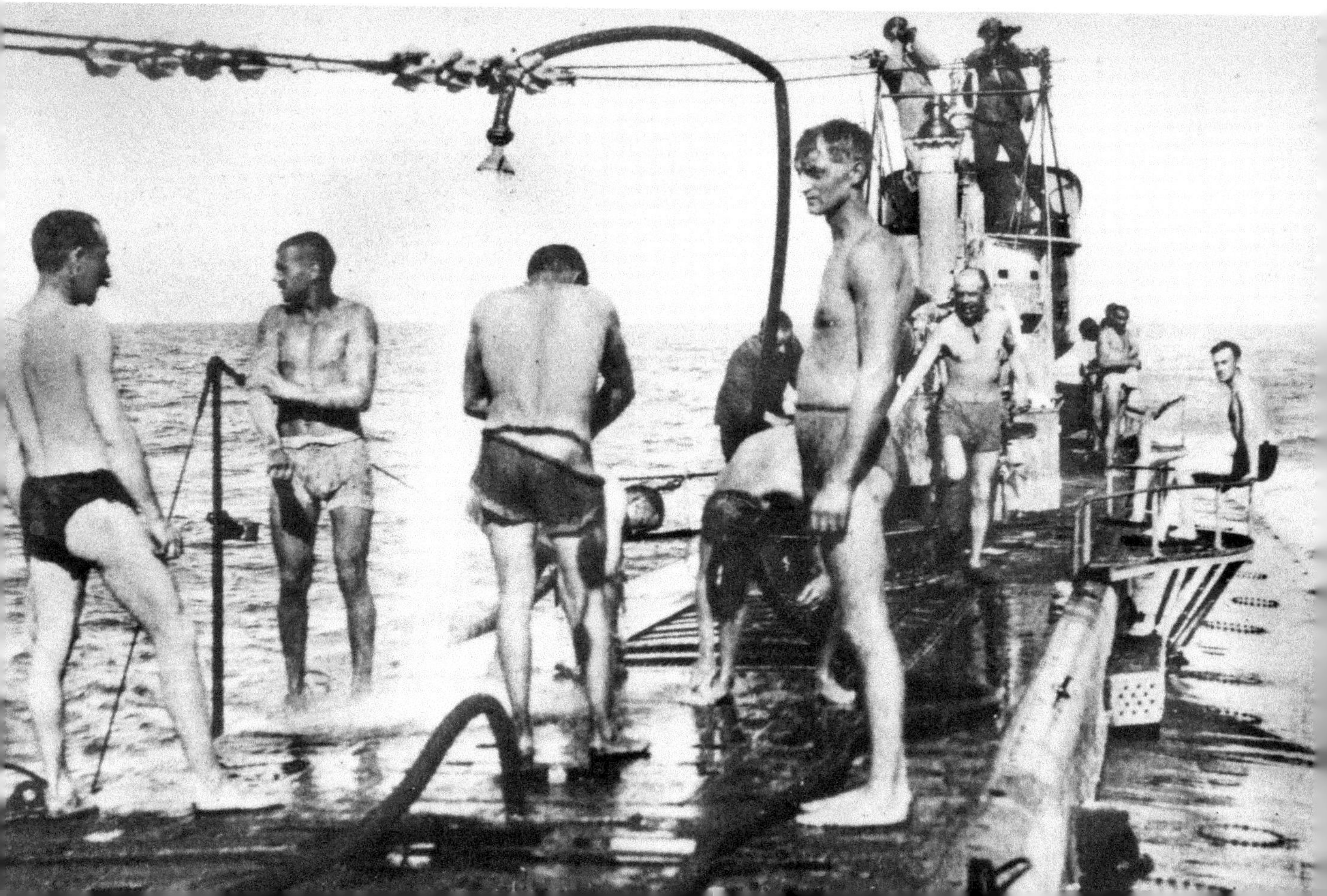

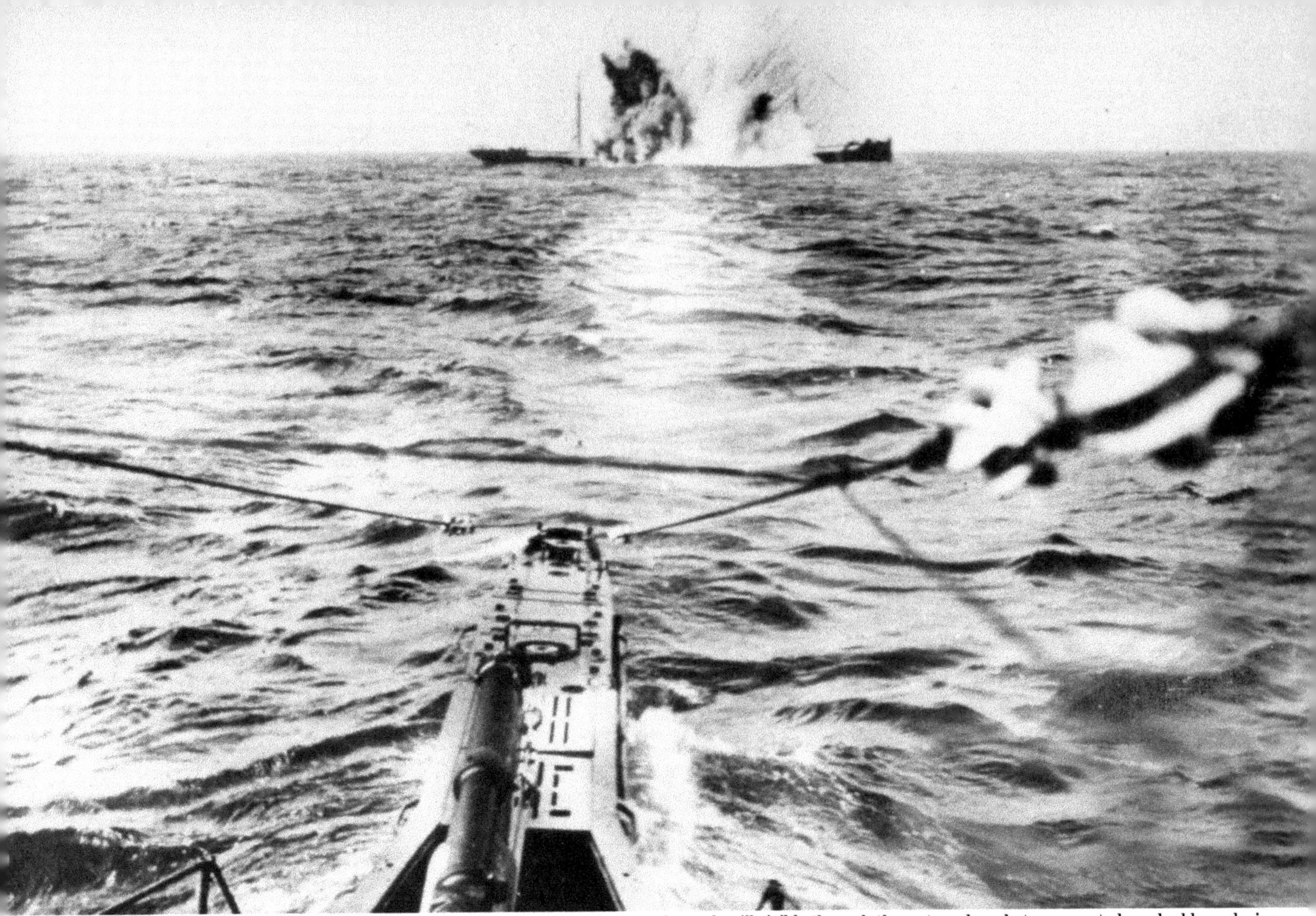

17GW784 The *U-35* scores a torpedo strike on a merchantman. Note the torpedo track still visible through the water; also what appears to be a double explosion, suggesting the ship was carrying munitions.

17GW758 The officers and men of *U-35* pose for a portrait for the record and for them to send home.

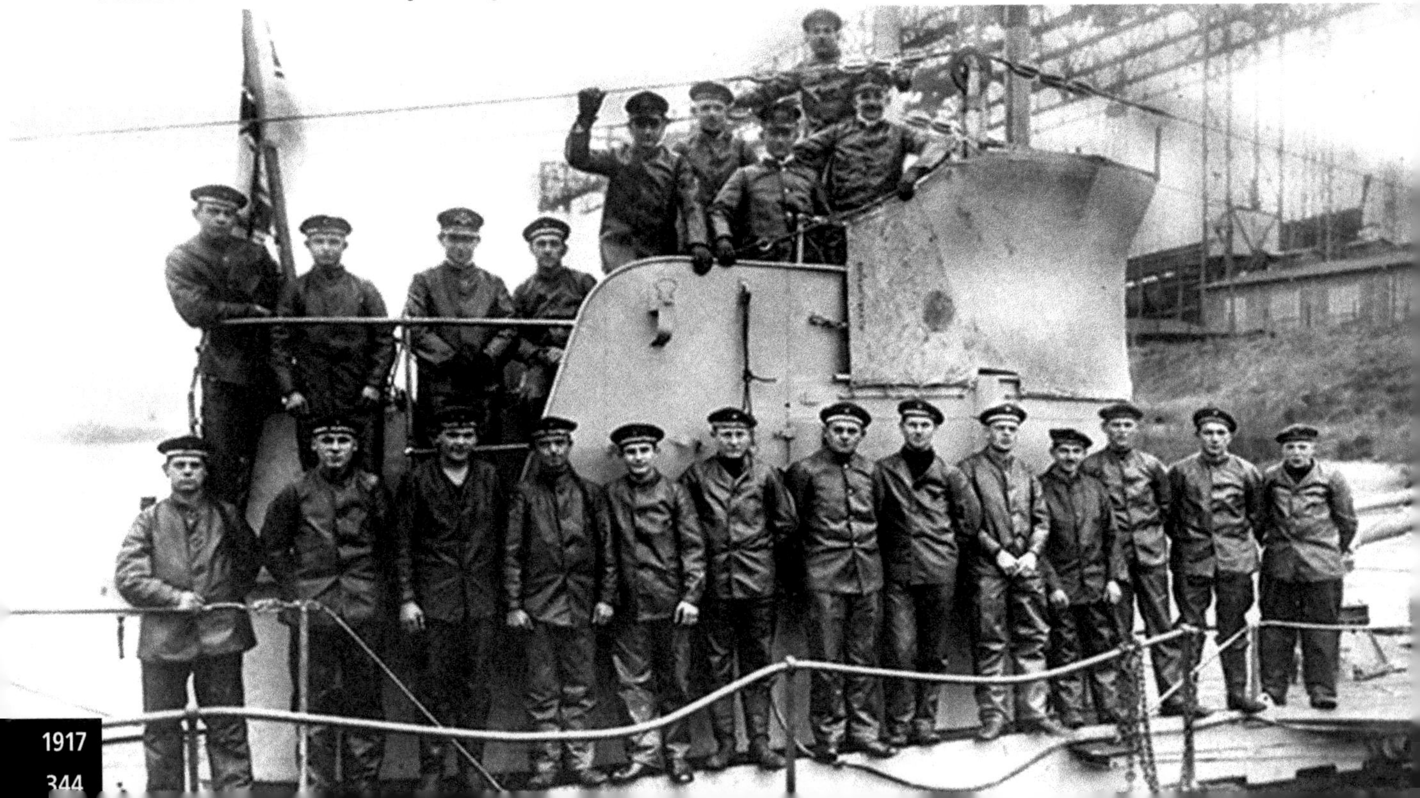

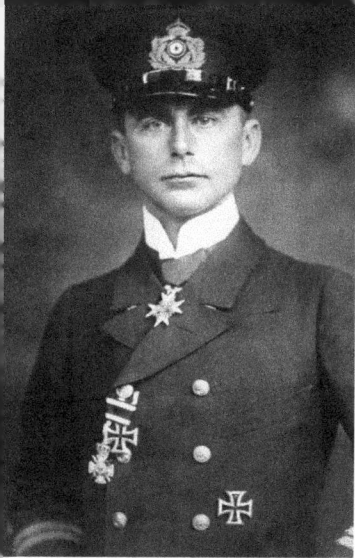
17GW771 Walther Forstmann
U-12; U-39
149 sunk or captured;
391,607 tons.

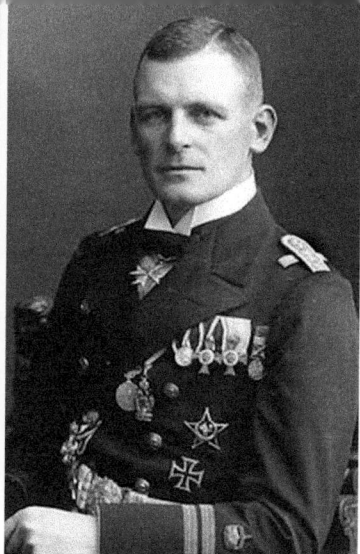
17GW772 Max Valentiner
U-3; U-38; U-157
144 sunk or captured;
299,482 tons.

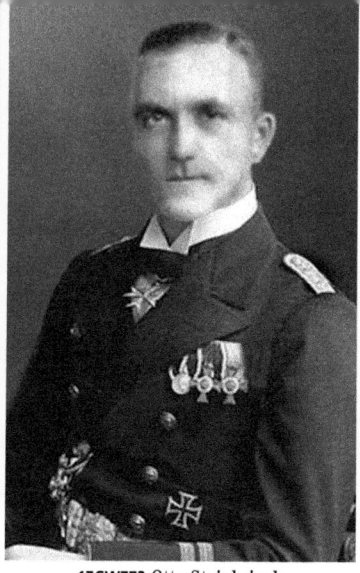
17GW773 Otto Steinbrinck
U-6; UB-10; UB-18; UC-65; UB-57
206 sunk or captured;
244,797 tons.

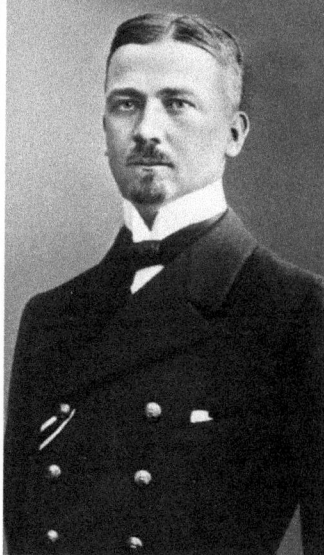
17GW774 Hans Rose
U-53
82 sunk or captured;
221,942 tons.

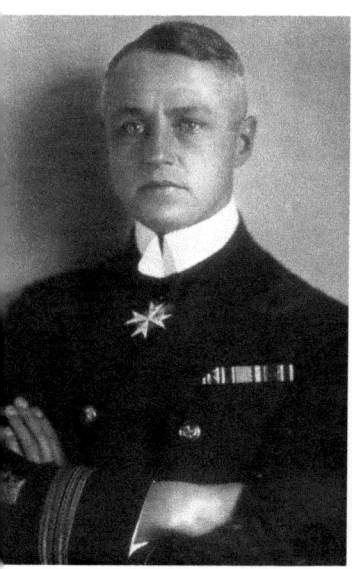
17GW775 Gustav Siess
U-73; U-33; U-65
56 sunk or captured;
188,295 tons.

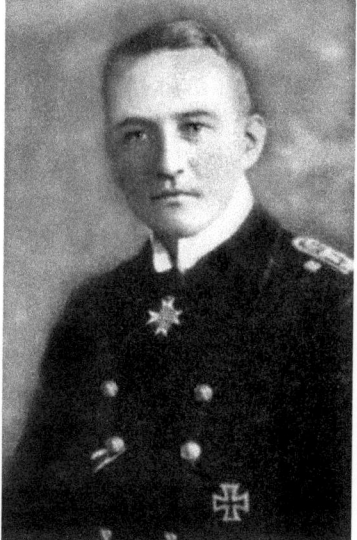
17GW776 Walther Schwieger
U-14; U-20; U-88
49 sunk or captured;
185,212 tons. Sank the *Lusitania*

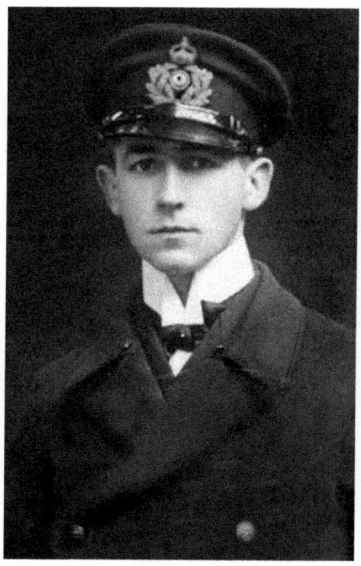
17GW777 Wolfgang Steinbauer
UB-47; UB-48
51 sunk or captured;
183,871 tons.

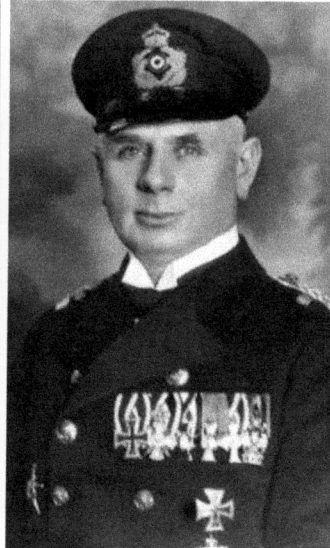
17GW778 Claus Rücker
U-34, U-103
80 sunk or captured;
174,655 tons.

17GW785 The German UB Flotilla at Zeebrugge. **UB** were coastal attack boats; **UC** were coastal minelayers; **UE** ocean minelayers.

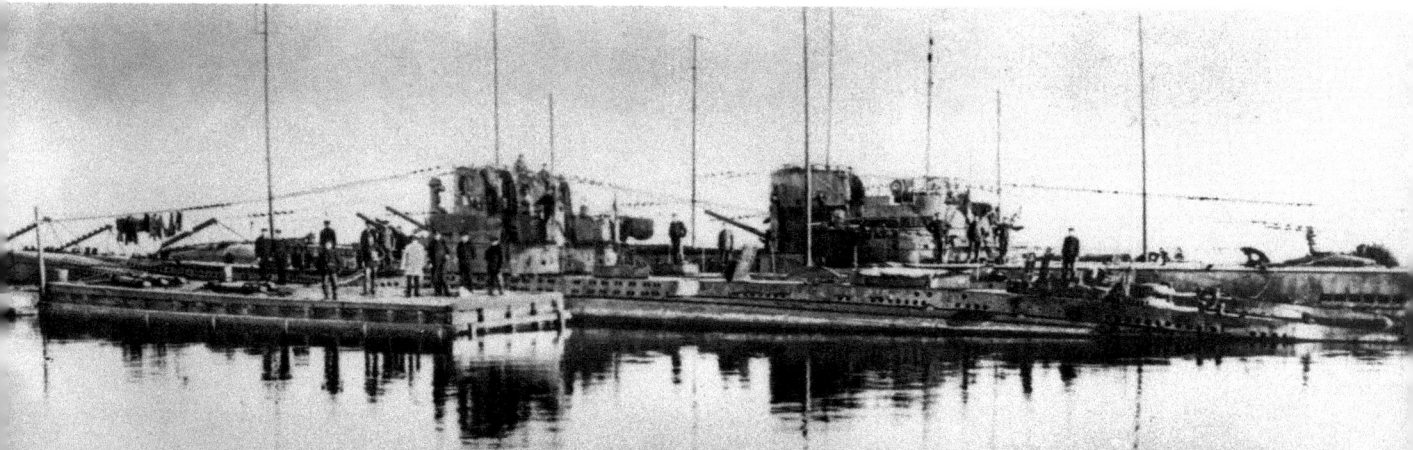

17GW780 The *Deutschland* was a blockade-breaking German merchant submarine. She is seen here entering the harbour at Heligoland in 1917.

She was one of seven submarines designed to carry cargo between the United States and Germany in 1916, doing so through the naval blockade mainly enforced by Great Britain's Royal Navy. The blockade had led to problems for German companies in acquiring raw materials. The *Deutschland* was constructed with a wide beam to provide space for cargo. The cargo capacity was 700 tons (230 tons of rubber could be stored in the free-flooding spaces between the inner and outer hulls). Obviously this was a small cargo capacity compared to surface ships.

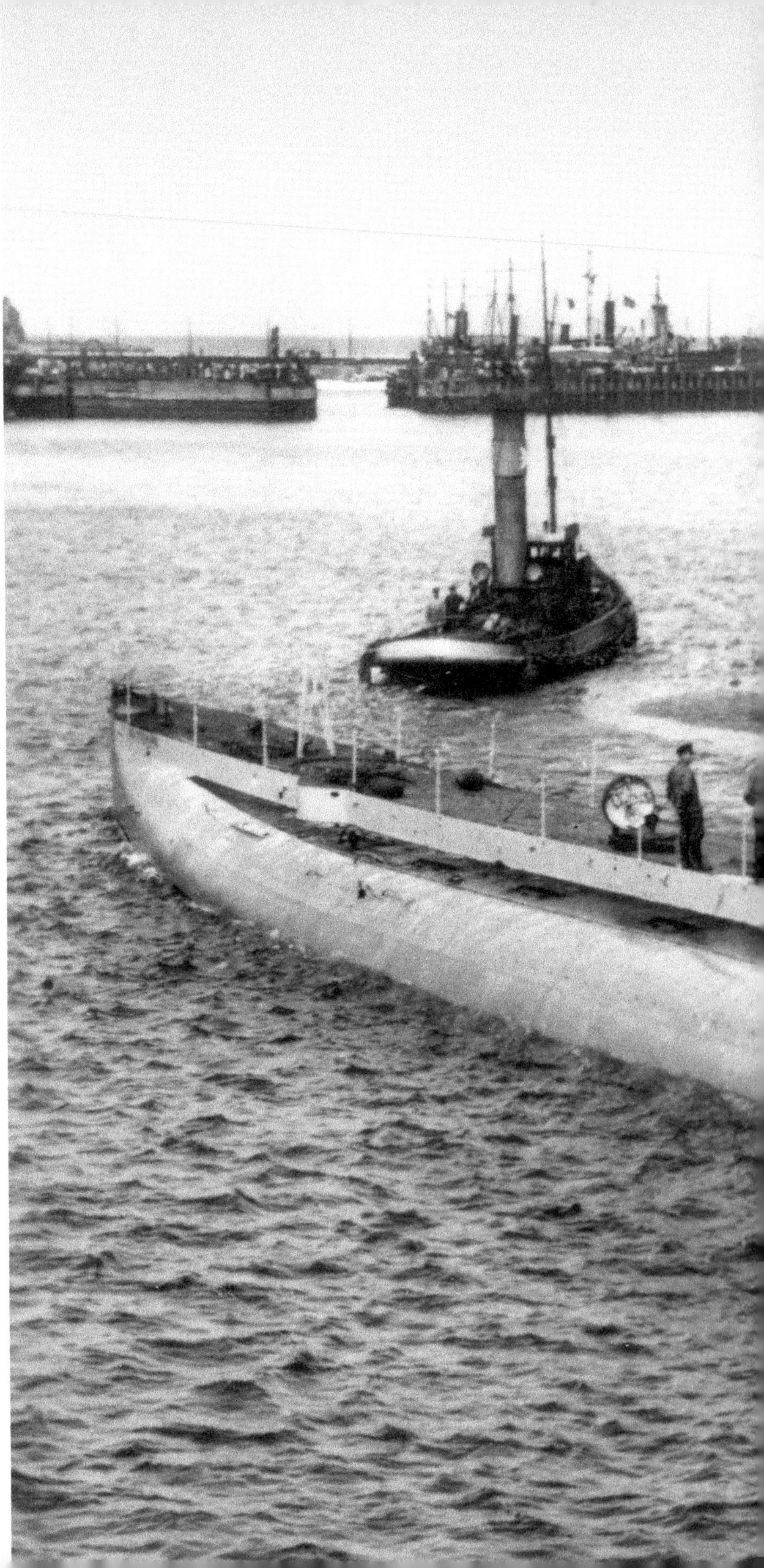

17GW781 Paul König, commander of the *Deutschland* when it was a commercial submarine. *Deutschland* was taken over by the German Imperial Navy on 19 February 1917 and converted into *U-155*, part of the *U-Kreuzer* Flotilla.

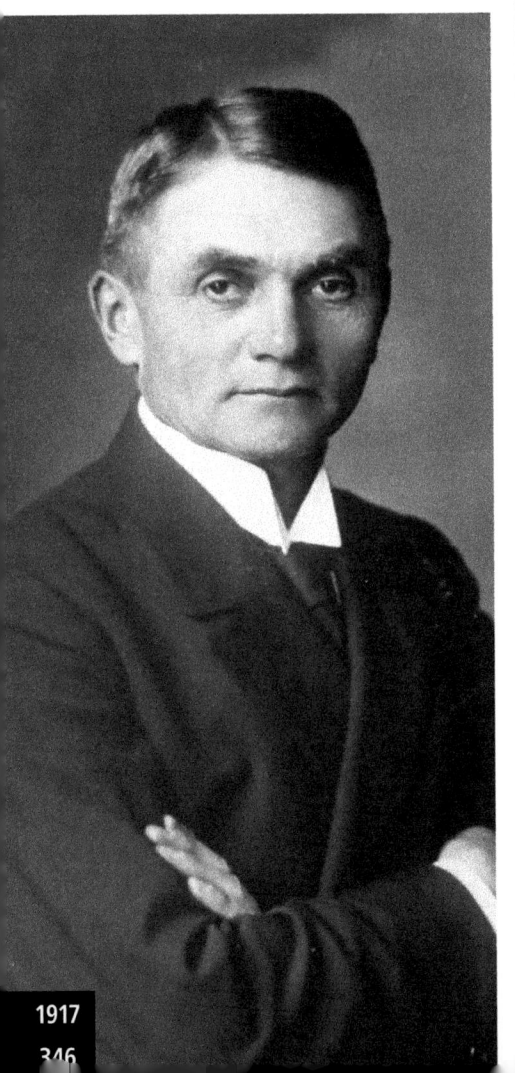

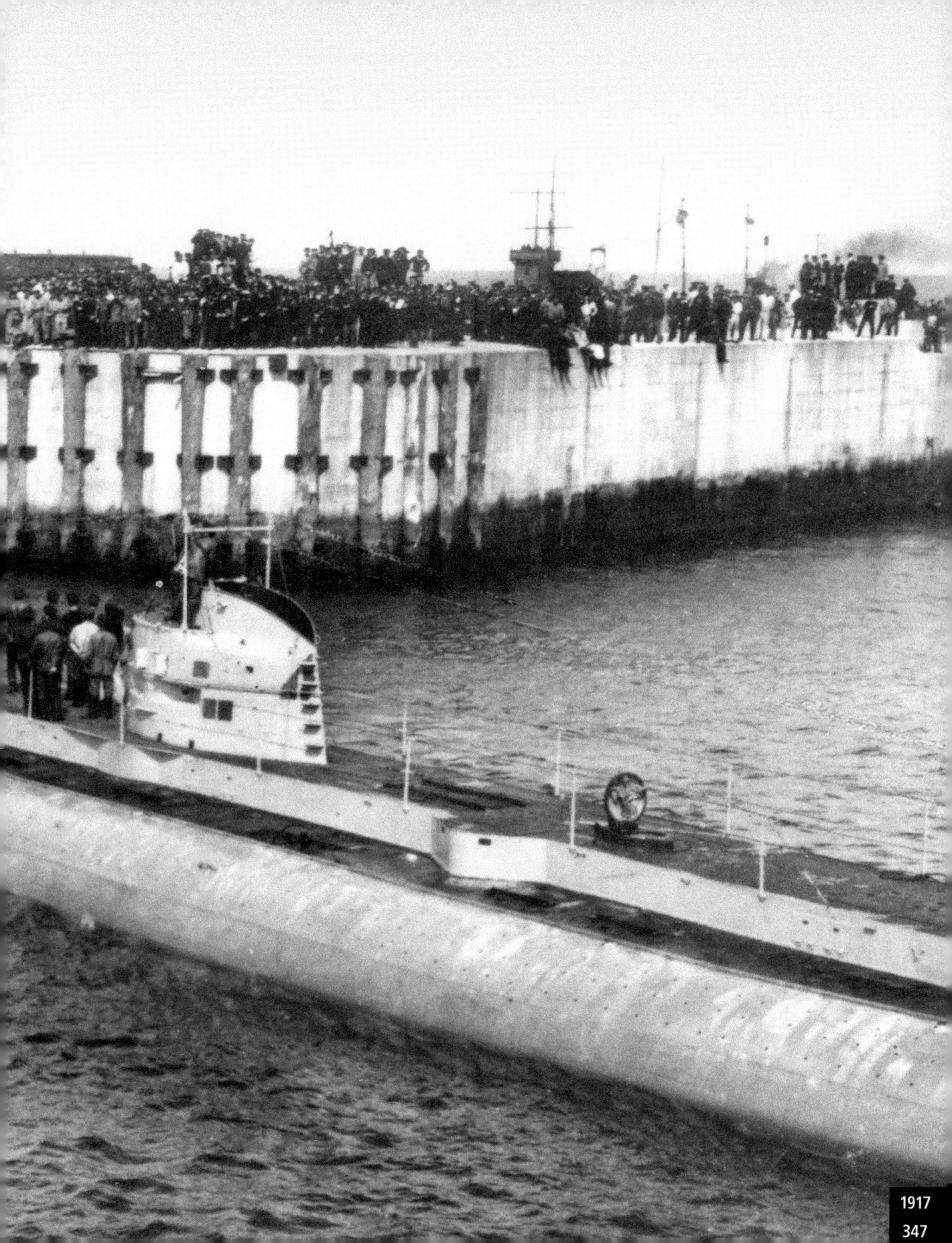

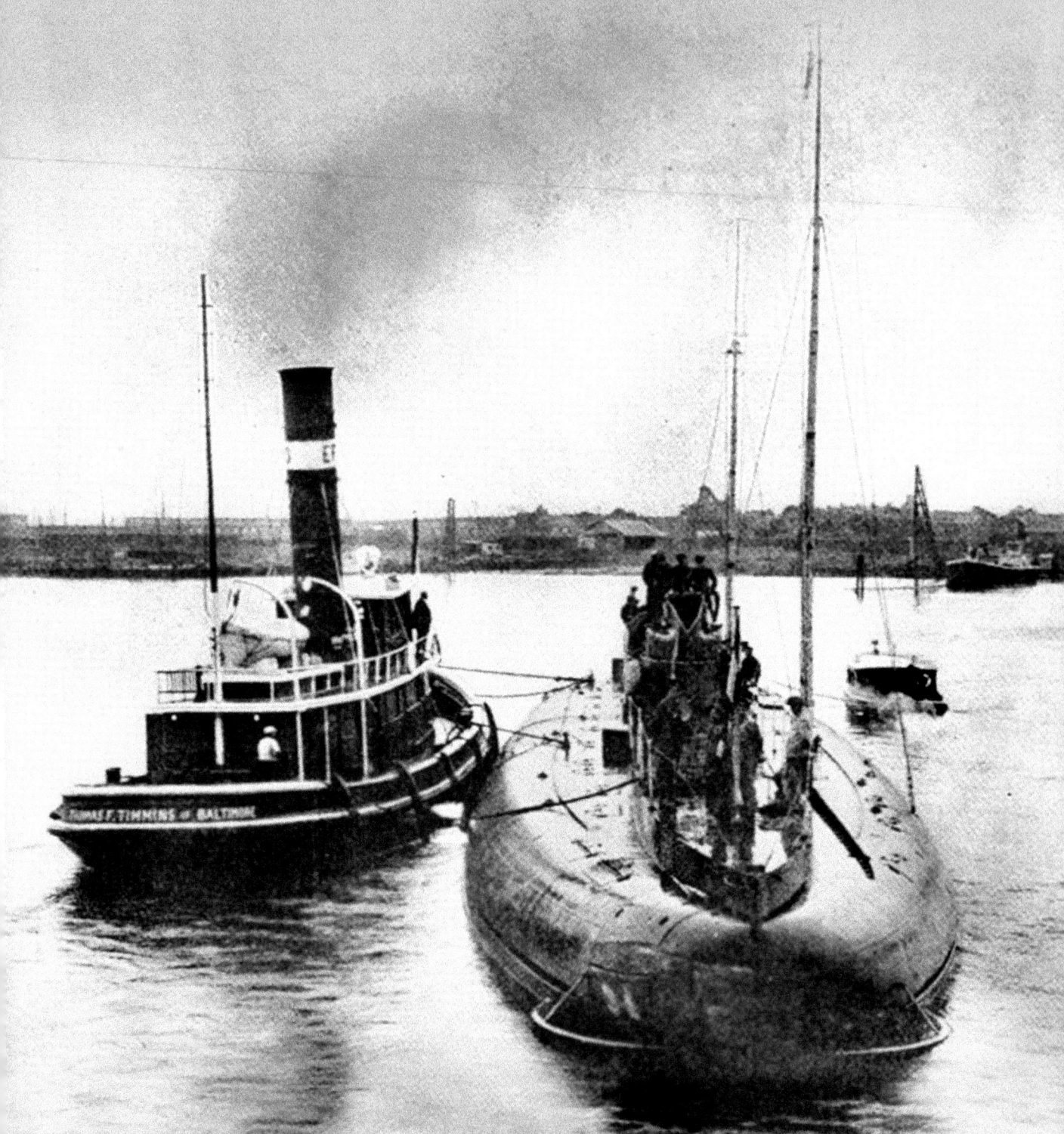

17GW783 The *Deutschland* arriving at Baltimore, July 1916, after her voyage across the Atlantic to the United States. She was commanded by Paul König, formerly of the North German Lloyd company. She carried 750 tons of cargo, including 125 tons of highly sought-after chemical dyes. In total her cargo was worth $1.5 million. During their stay in the US, the German crew were welcomed as celebrities for their astonishing journey. She left Baltimore for Bremerhaven in August, arriving on 24 August with a cargo of 341 tons of nickel, 93 tons of tin, and 348 tons of crude rubber. Her return cargo was valued at $17.5 million; she had traveled 9,720 miles.

Another trip to American voyage was planned for January 1917, but it was concelled as German-US relations had worsened following the sinking of shipping bound for the United Kingdom, often just outside US territorial waters.

17GW779 Paul König and his celebrated crew on the deck of the *Deutschland* in Baltimore; note the bouquet of flowers.

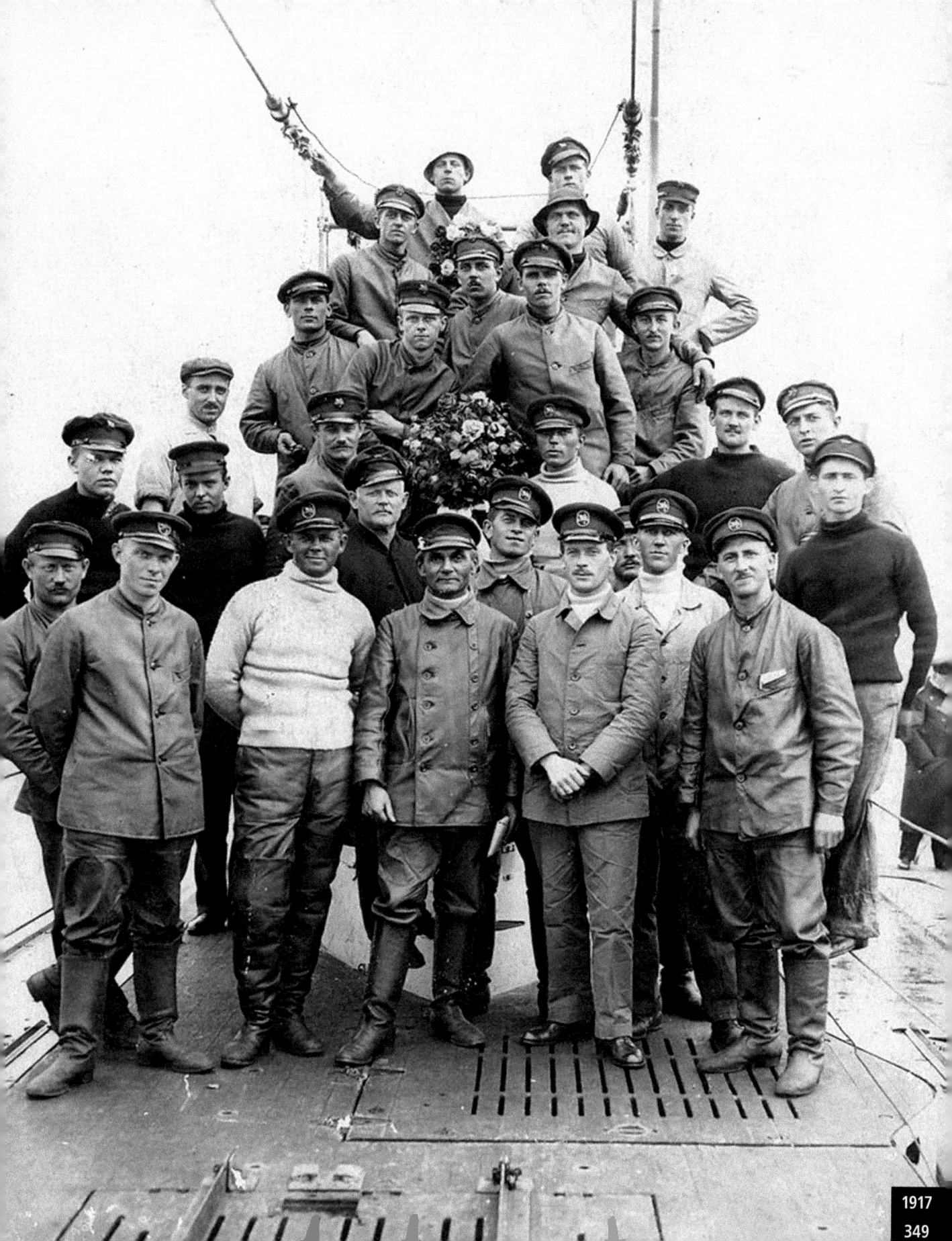

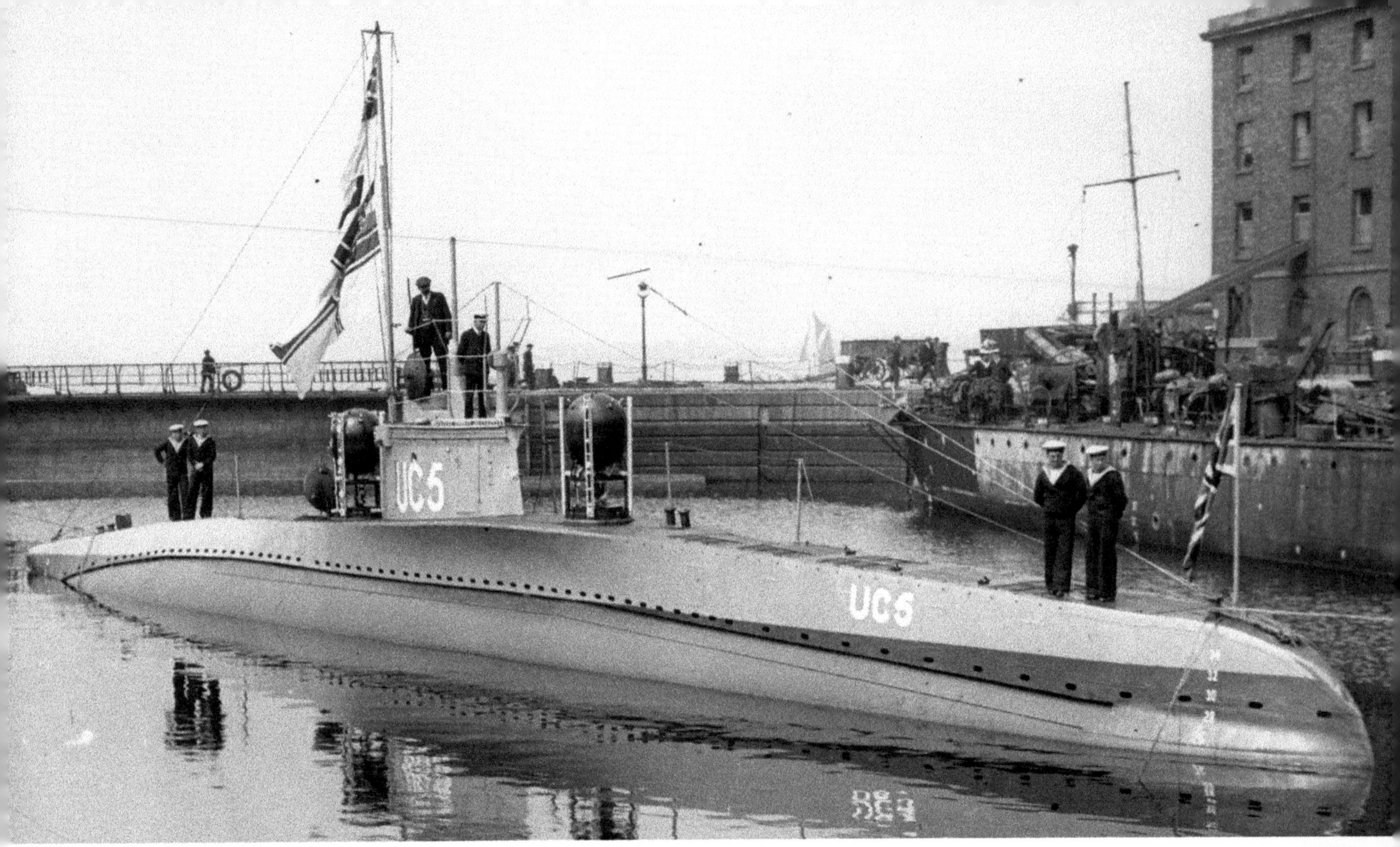

17GW787, 17GW788, 17GW789. The German minelaying submarine *UC-5*, launched in 1915, commanded by *Oberleutenant* Herbert Pustkuchen and his successor Ulrich Mohrbutter, sank thirty ships and damaged seven more before running aground on sandbanks off the Suffolk coast in April 1916. It was captured and towed to Harwich. The submarine was put on public display on the Thames, at Temple Pier, and became a tourist attraction. With the United States entering the war in 1917, the *UC-5* was taken to America and displayed in Central Park to help raise Liberty Bonds.

'I only wish we had a thousand of them!'

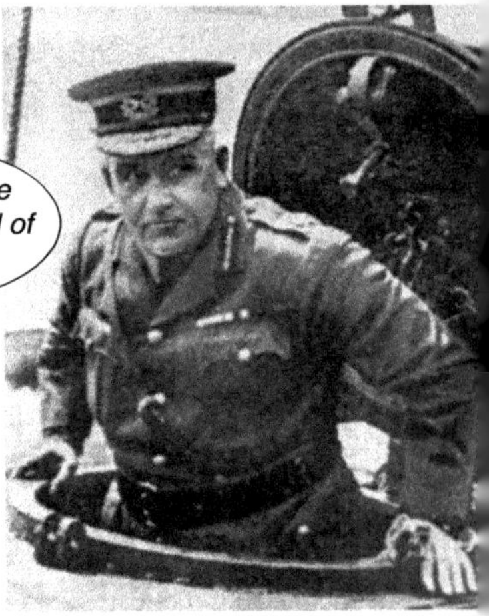

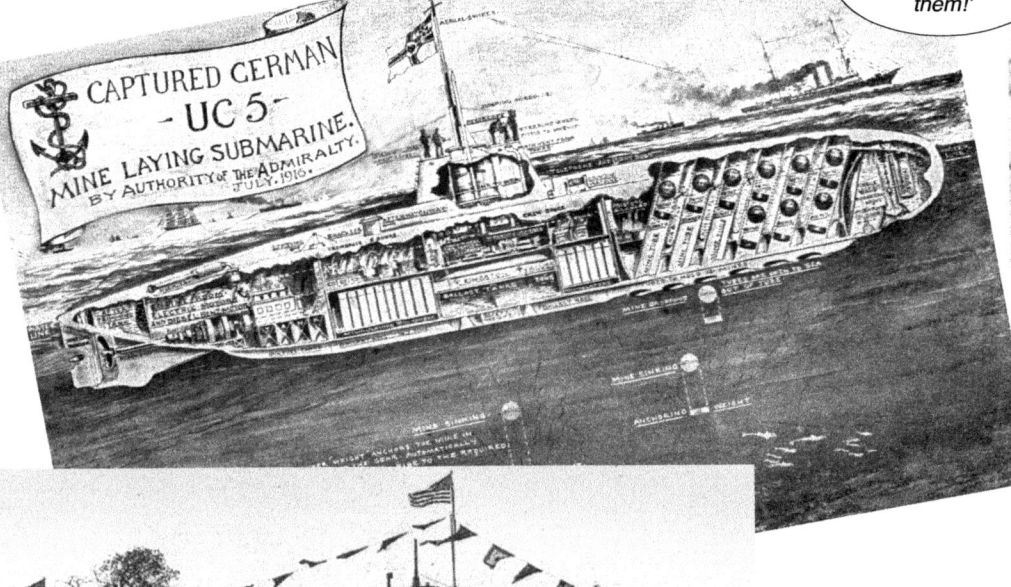

17GW790 Major General Samuel Hughes, the Canadian Minister for Militia and Defence, at Temple Pier, London, having completed an inspection of *UC-5*. (*Daily Mirror* 2 August 1916). Hughes was enthusiastic about the use of captured enemy submarines to promote the good work of the Royal Navy. Refering to the people invited to visit *UC-5*, he commented, *'I believe that whenever and wherever practicable the public should be given such first-hand opportunities as this for appreciating the wonderful work of Britain's silent sentinels on the seas'*.

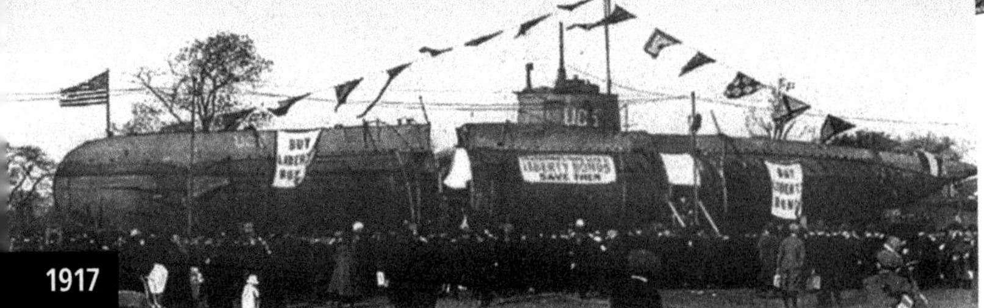

17GW791 The following year submarine *UC-5* was moved to the United States and displayed in Central Park as an advert for Liberty Bonds.

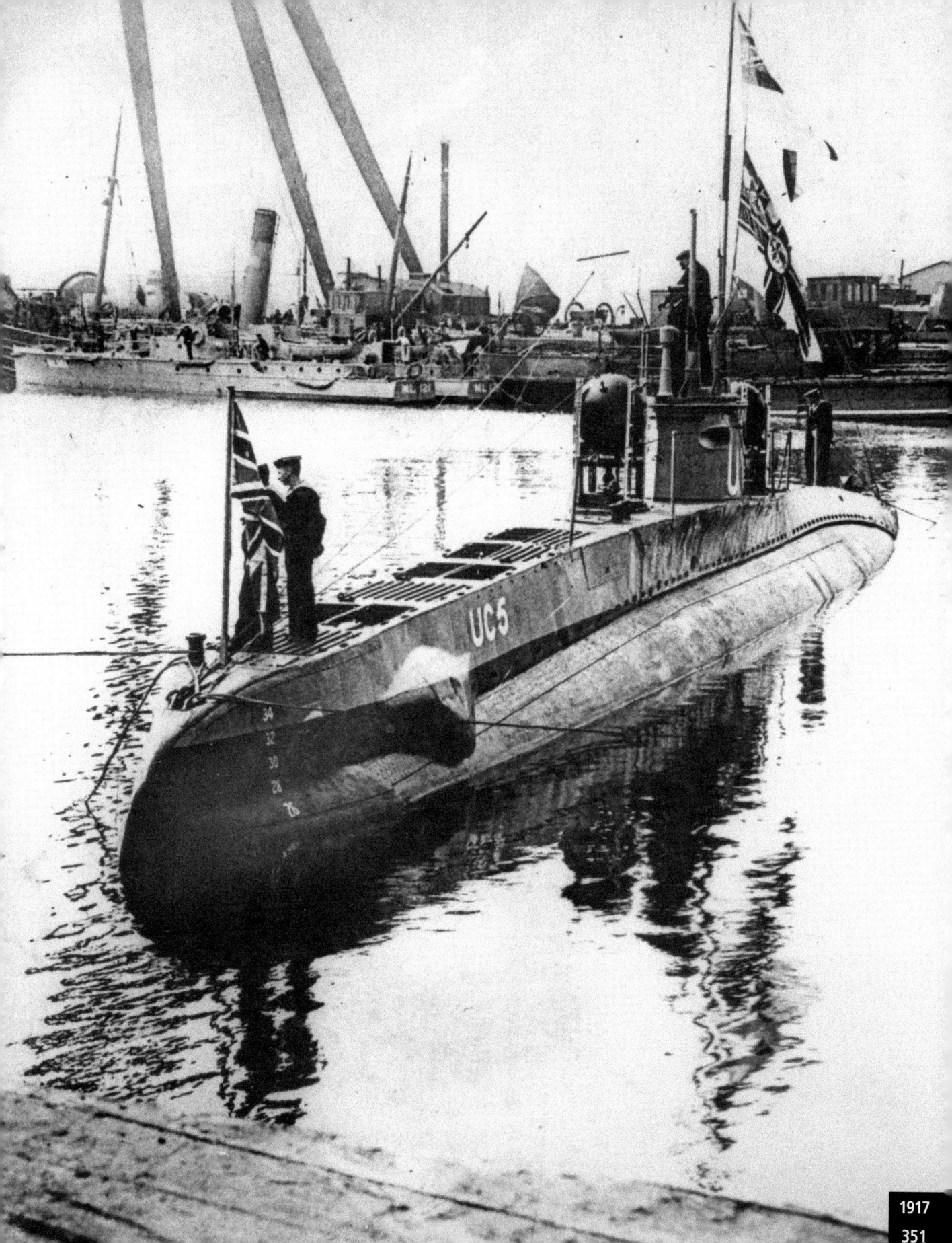

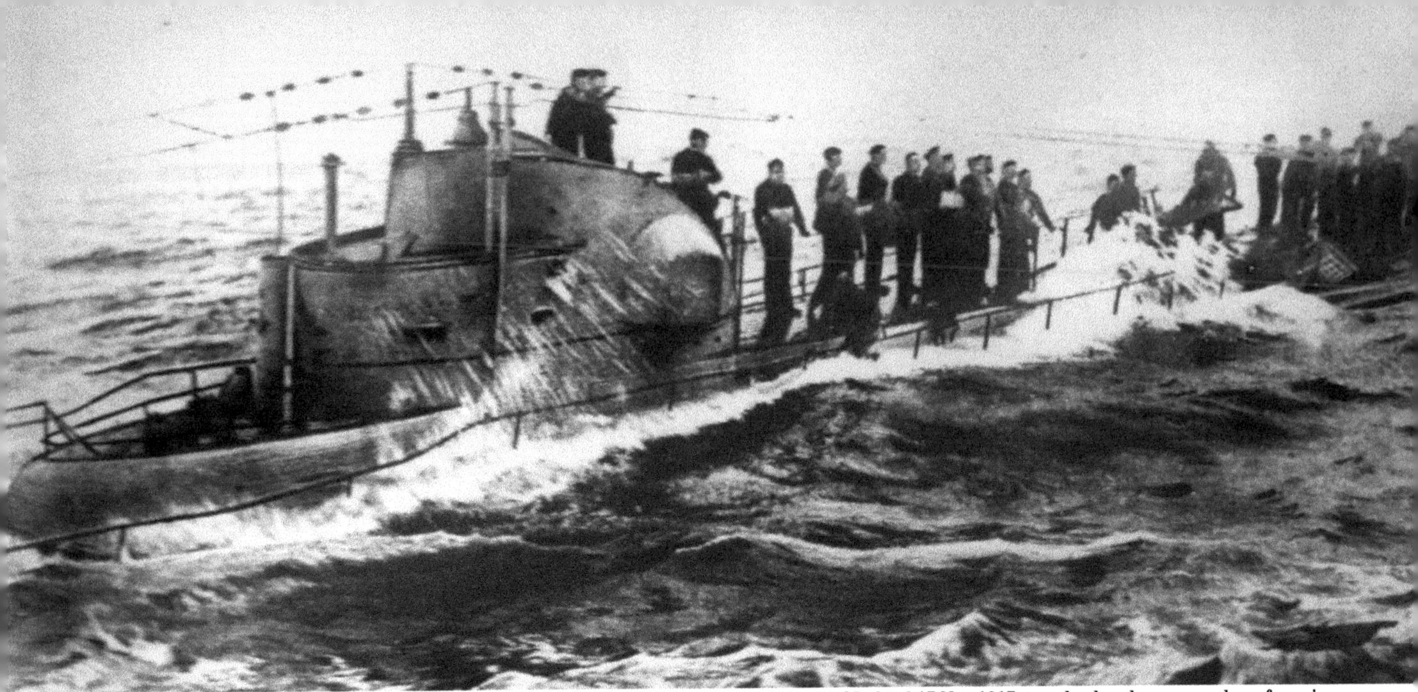

17GW792 Submarine *U-58* was depth charged by destroyer USS *Fanning* off the south coast of Ireland, 17 Nov 1917; two dead, unknown number of survivors.

17GW793 The *U-56* was sunk by gunfire from the Russian destroyer *Grozovoi* off Khorne Island, Norway (near Vardö), 3 November 1916.

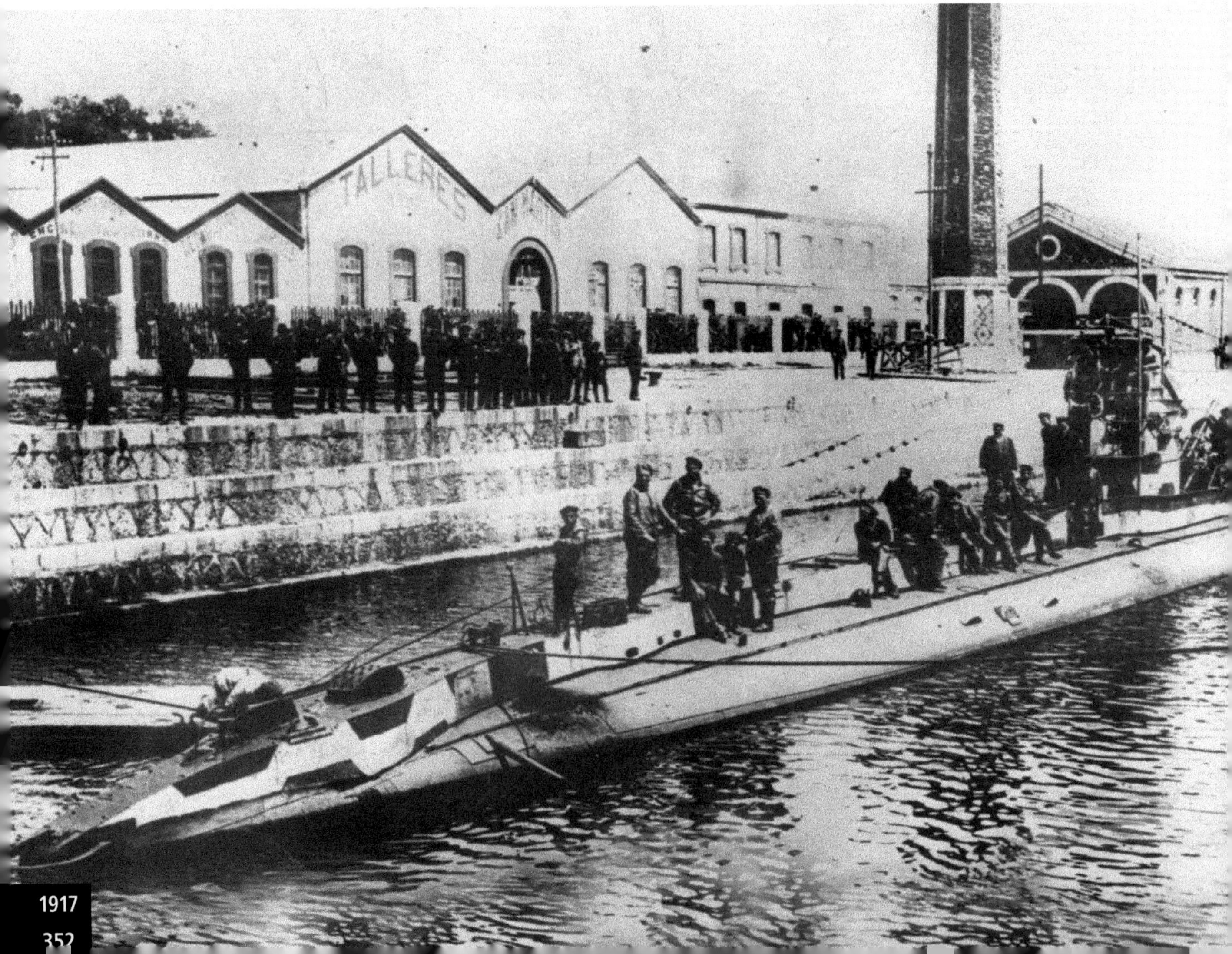

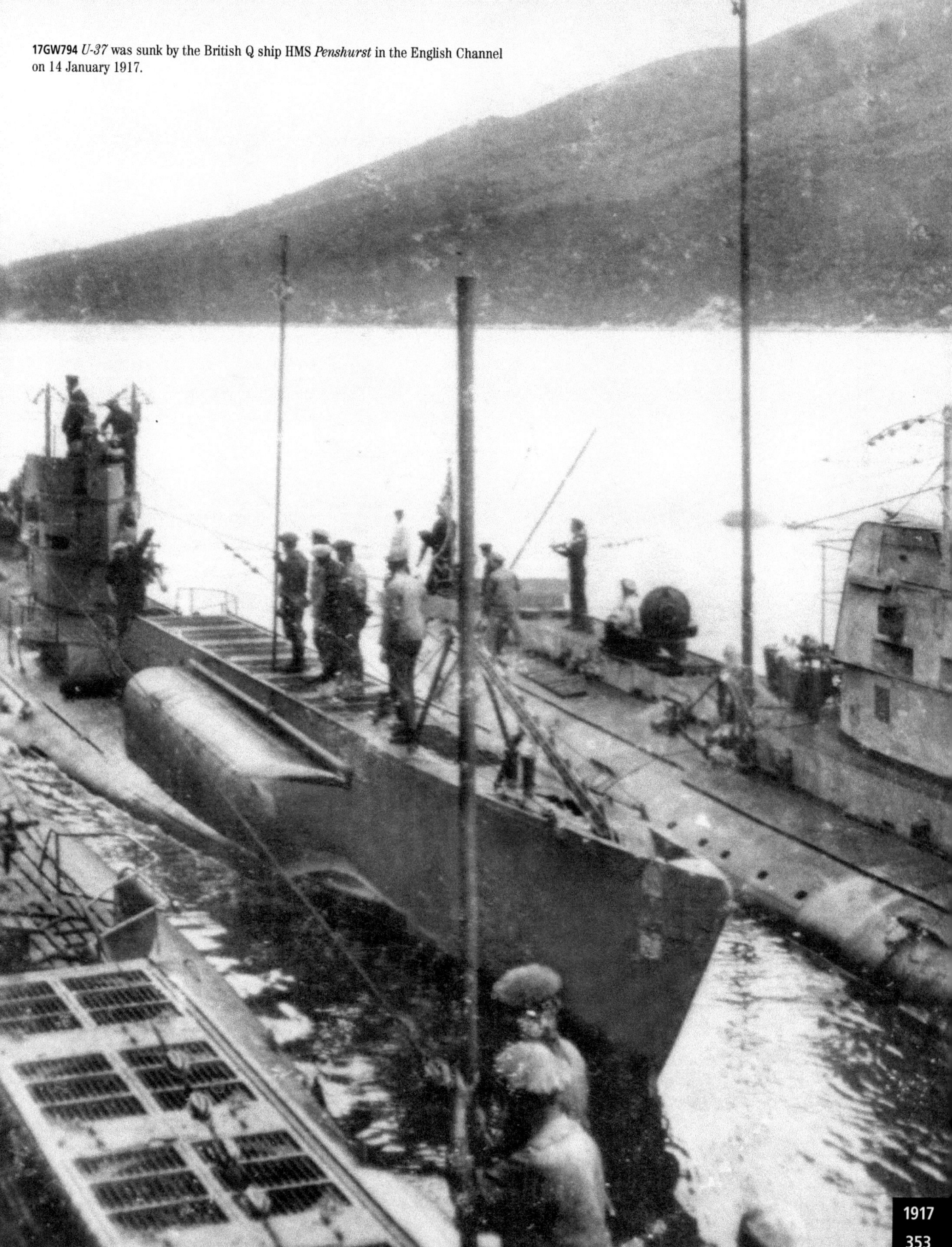

17GW794 *U-37* was sunk by the British Q ship HMS *Penshurst* in the English Channel on 14 January 1917.

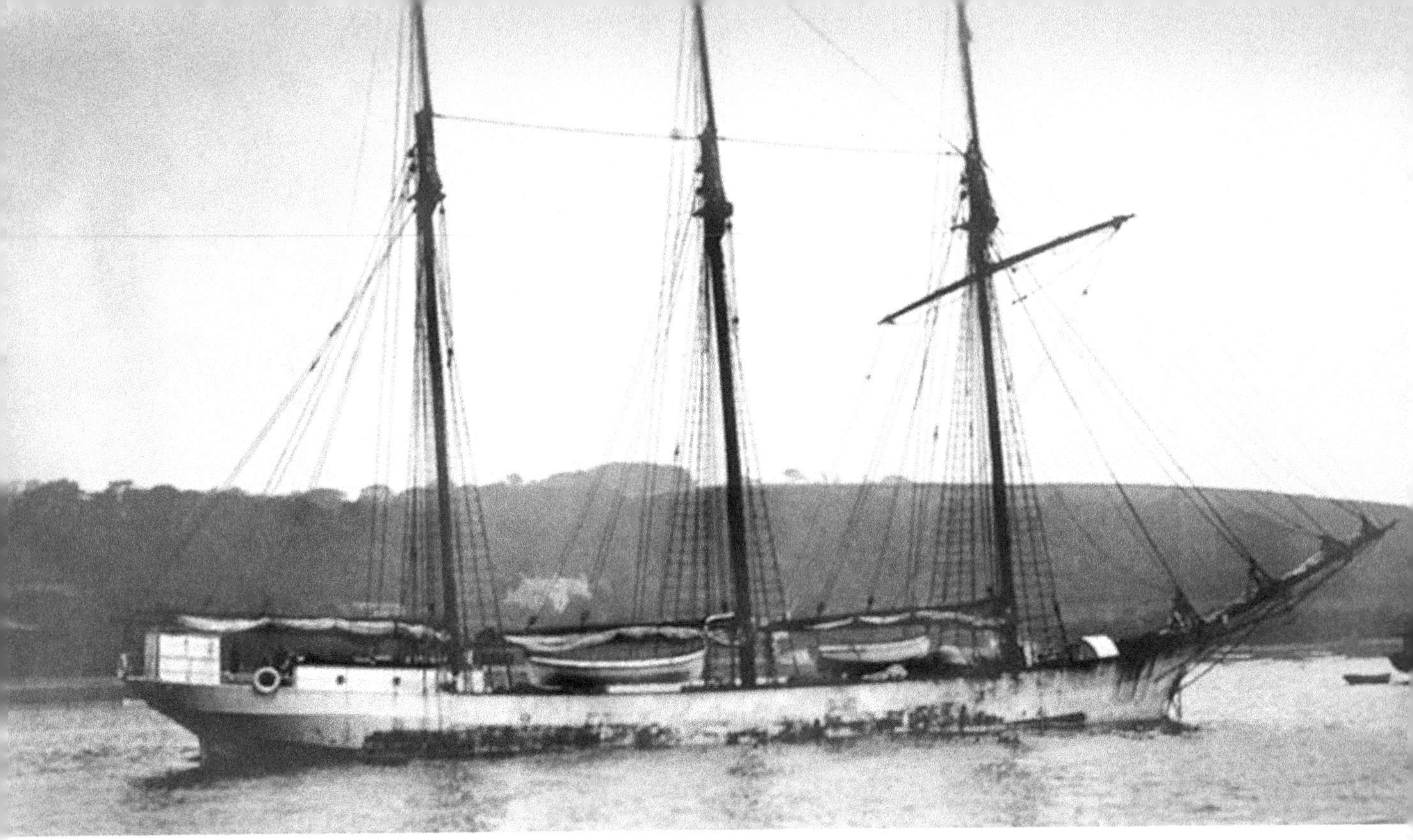

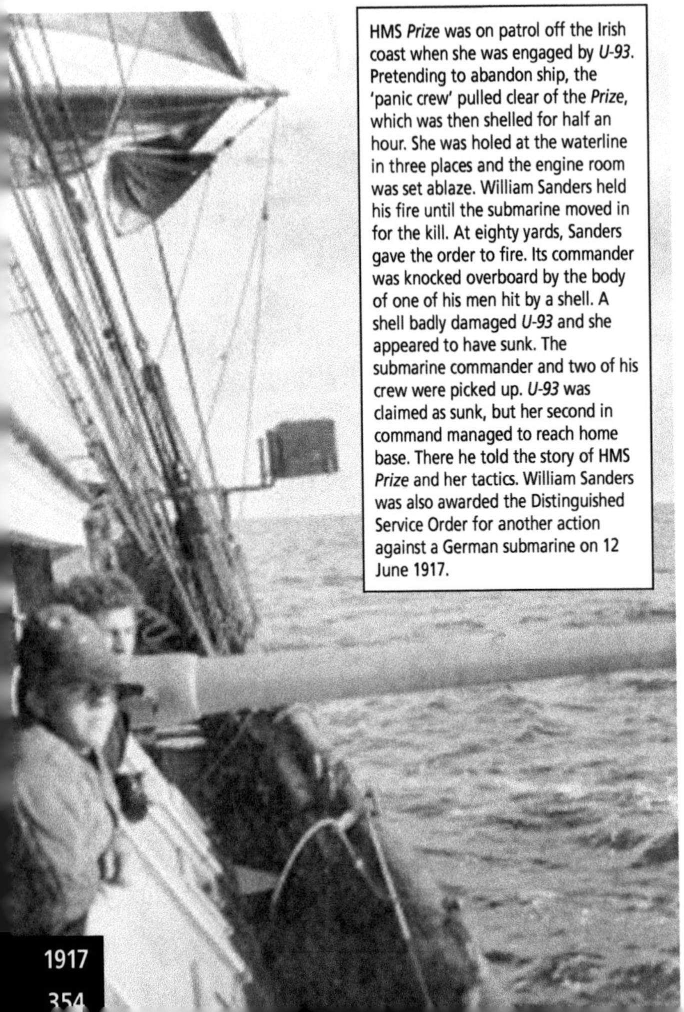

HMS *Prize* was on patrol off the Irish coast when she was engaged by *U-93*. Pretending to abandon ship, the 'panic crew' pulled clear of the *Prize*, which was then shelled for half an hour. She was holed at the waterline in three places and the engine room was set ablaze. William Sanders held his fire until the submarine moved in for the kill. At eighty yards, Sanders gave the order to fire. Its commander was knocked overboard by the body of one of his men hit by a shell. A shell badly damaged *U-93* and she appeared to have sunk. The submarine commander and two of his crew were picked up. *U-93* was claimed as sunk, but her second in command managed to reach home base. There he told the story of HMS *Prize* and her tactics. William Sanders was also awarded the Distinguished Service Order for another action against a German submarine on 12 June 1917.

17GW800, 17GW801, 17GW799. Captured German ship *Else*, which became HMS *Prize*, a Q-Ship with two concealed guns to take on the unwary submarine attackers. The *Prize* is seen with two of the crew by the gun, immediately following the fight with *U-93*. Captain of HMS *Prize*, Lieutenant Commander William Sanders, a New Zealander, was quietly awarded the Victoria Cross for this action (it was a secret service). The method of operation for Q-Ships was to give the illusion of an innocent merchantman; as the submarine approached to check it out they would see a flag flying indicating, maybe, a Dutch vessel. As it would be in waters deemed to be trading with Britain an attack was announced by the submarine crew; immediately the impression was given that the crew were abandoning the ship – a special detail called a 'panic crew' would take to the lifeboats. As the submarine began firing its deck gun to sink the 'victim', whilst moving closer, the concealed guns would be unmasked and the White Ensign run up. Outgunned, the German sailors would be in serious trouble. That is what happened when HMS *Prize* lured *U-93* into range. The men remaining on board Q-Ships to man the guns had to endure accurate shell-fire from close range, requiring discipline and courage of the highest order and were all volunteers.

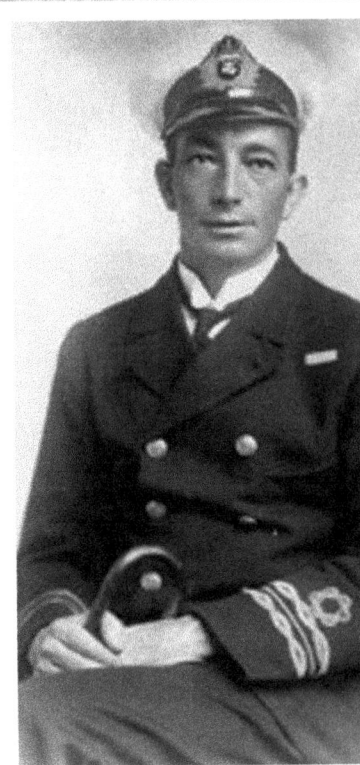

HMS *Prize* was sunk on 13 August 1917, by *U-48* with loss of all hands.

Surprisingly, out of the two hundred and two U-boats sunk during the Great War, only ten were the result of action with a Q-Ship, the last being in June 1917, when HMS *Pargust* sank *UC-29*.

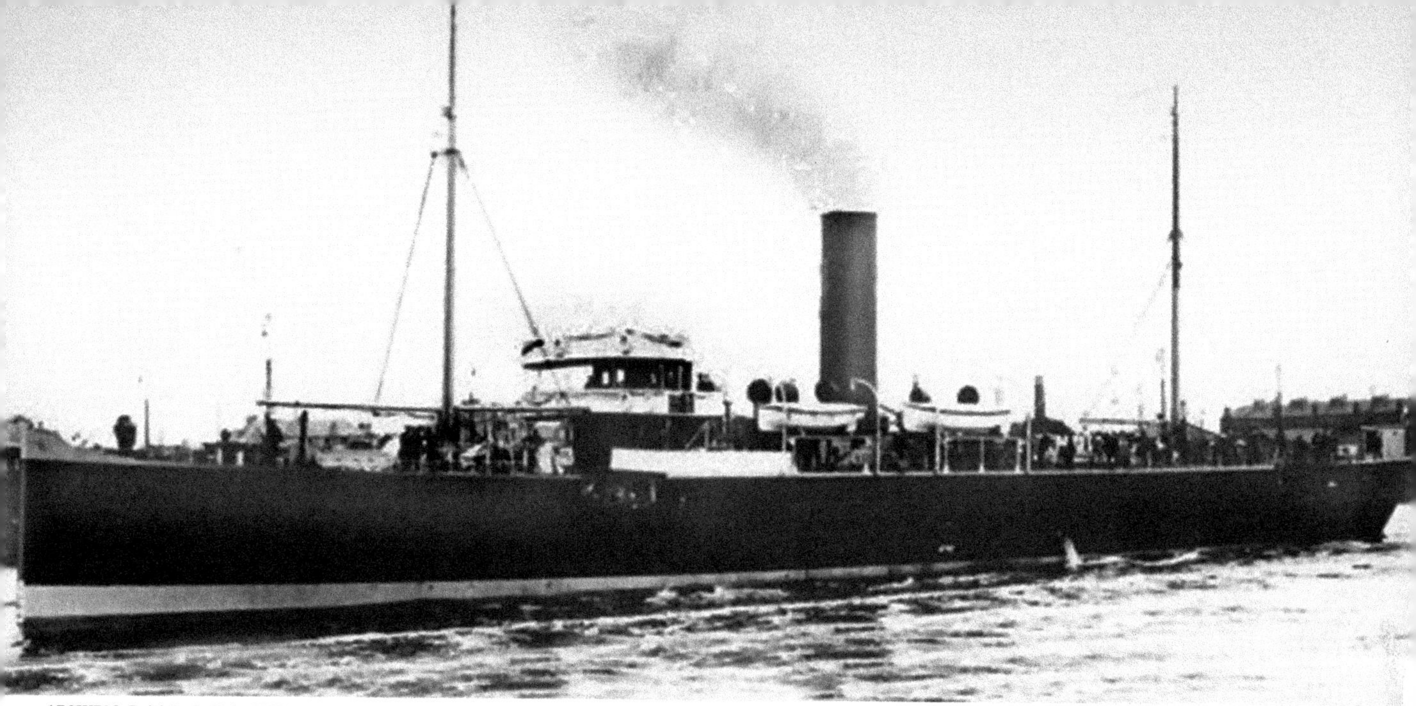

17GW798 British Q-Ship HMS *Tamarisk,* one of the mystery vessels; these were heavily armed merchant ships with concealed weaponry, designed to lure submarines into making surface attacks. This gave the crews the opportunity to open fire and sink them. The Germans called them *falleschiffe* 'trap ships'. About half of the Q-Ships were sailing vessels and the bulk of the others were colliers.

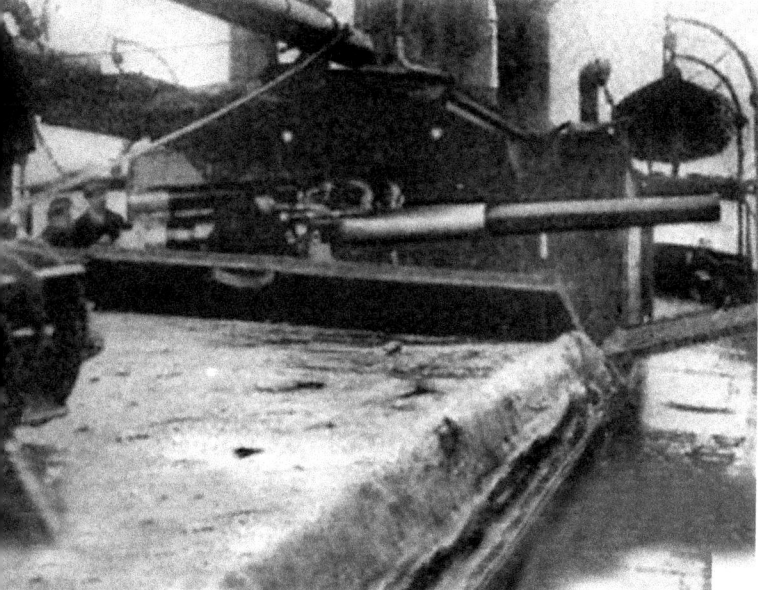

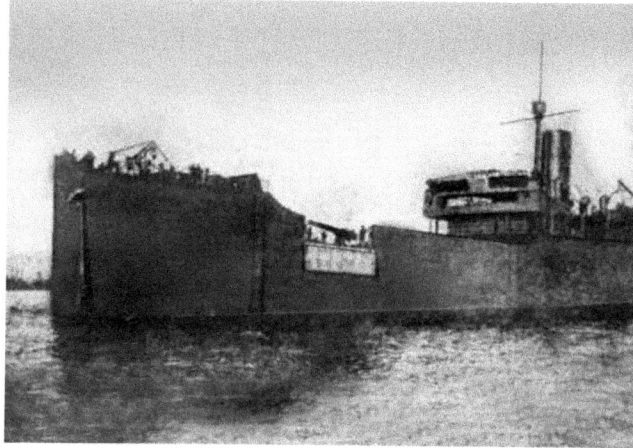

17GW797 A Q-Ship clearly showing her forward deck gun, the panel having being dropped. In the period 1915 to 1917 the number of these vessels entering service increased to a peak of forty-nine in 1917, with the last being commissioned in mid-1918, a total of about one hundred.

17GW804 HMS *Polyanthus* was a dazzle painted sloop of the *Aubretuia* class fitted out as a Q-Ship. The paint pattern was a ploy used by the Royal Navy to confuse the spotting and sighting-up of German submarine commanders. It was claimed by captured U-boat crews that it did not appear to worry their officers. More than one German submarine commander inquired what it was for. Their evidence was considered suspect. Experiments with dazzle painting were made in Germany after its introduction by the Allies, which suggests that it had at least some effect.

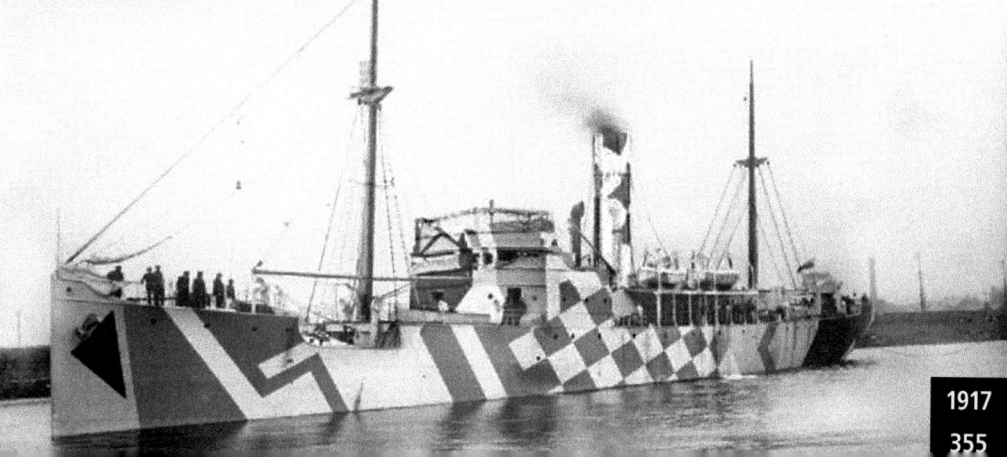

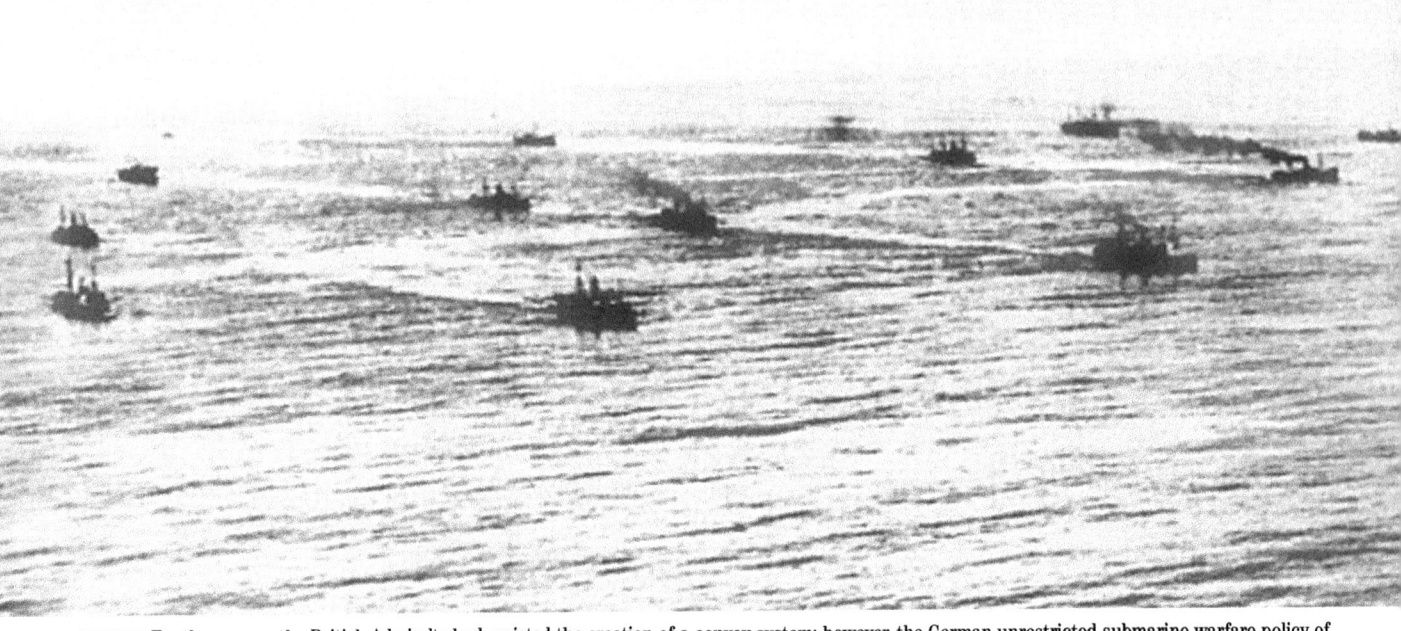

17GW803 For three years the British Admiralty had resisted the creation of a convoy system; however, the German unrestricted submarine warfare policy of targeting neutral shipping resulted in the month of May 1917 Britain suffering an unsustainable peak in sinkings – 373 ships amounting to 873,754 tons. The Germans were aiming to bring Great Britain to the negotiating table as a result. On 24 May 1917 Britain introduced its convoy system. It marked the beginning of a sharp decline in the scale of German submarine damage and, along with it, the death of hopes to starve Britain into submission.

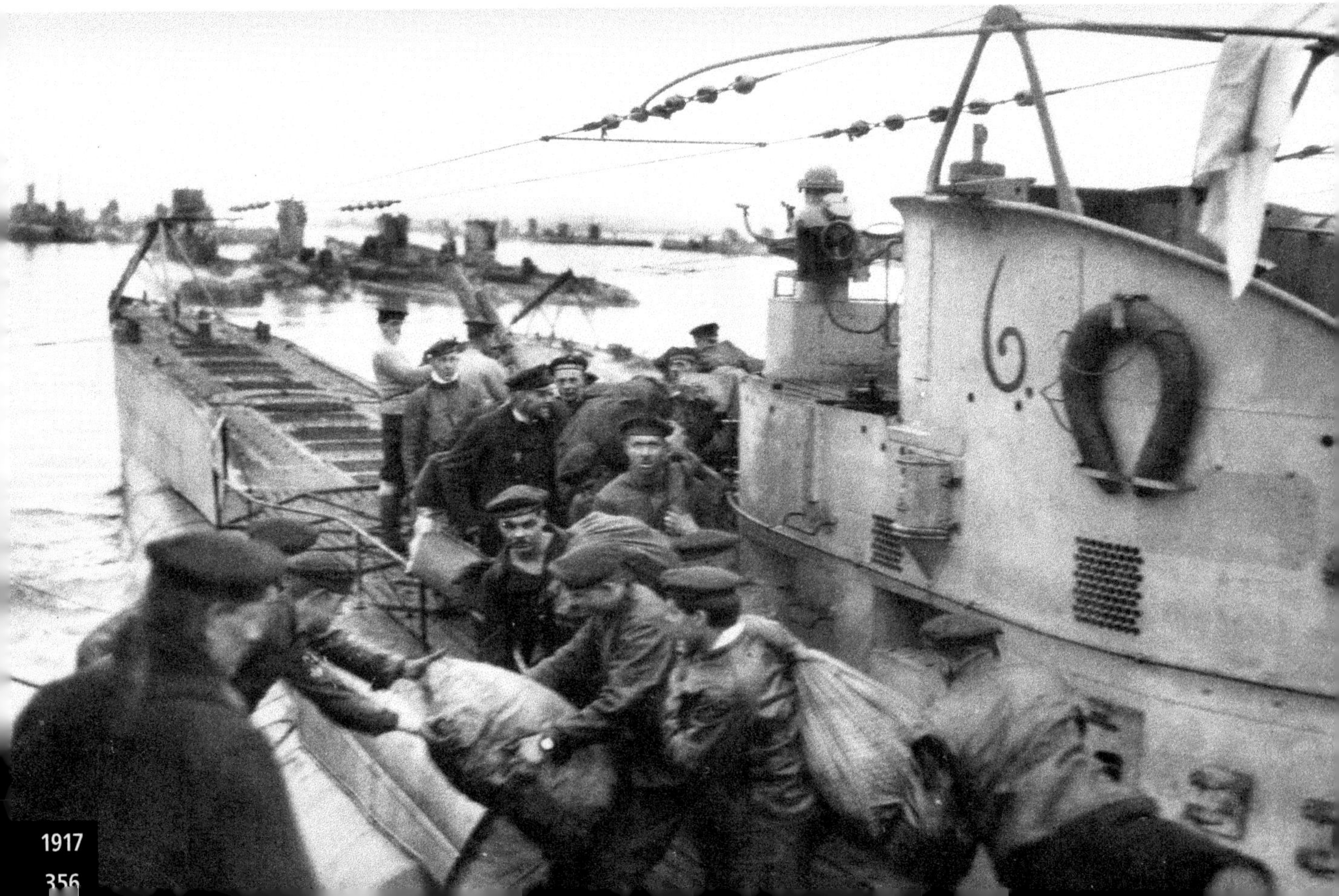

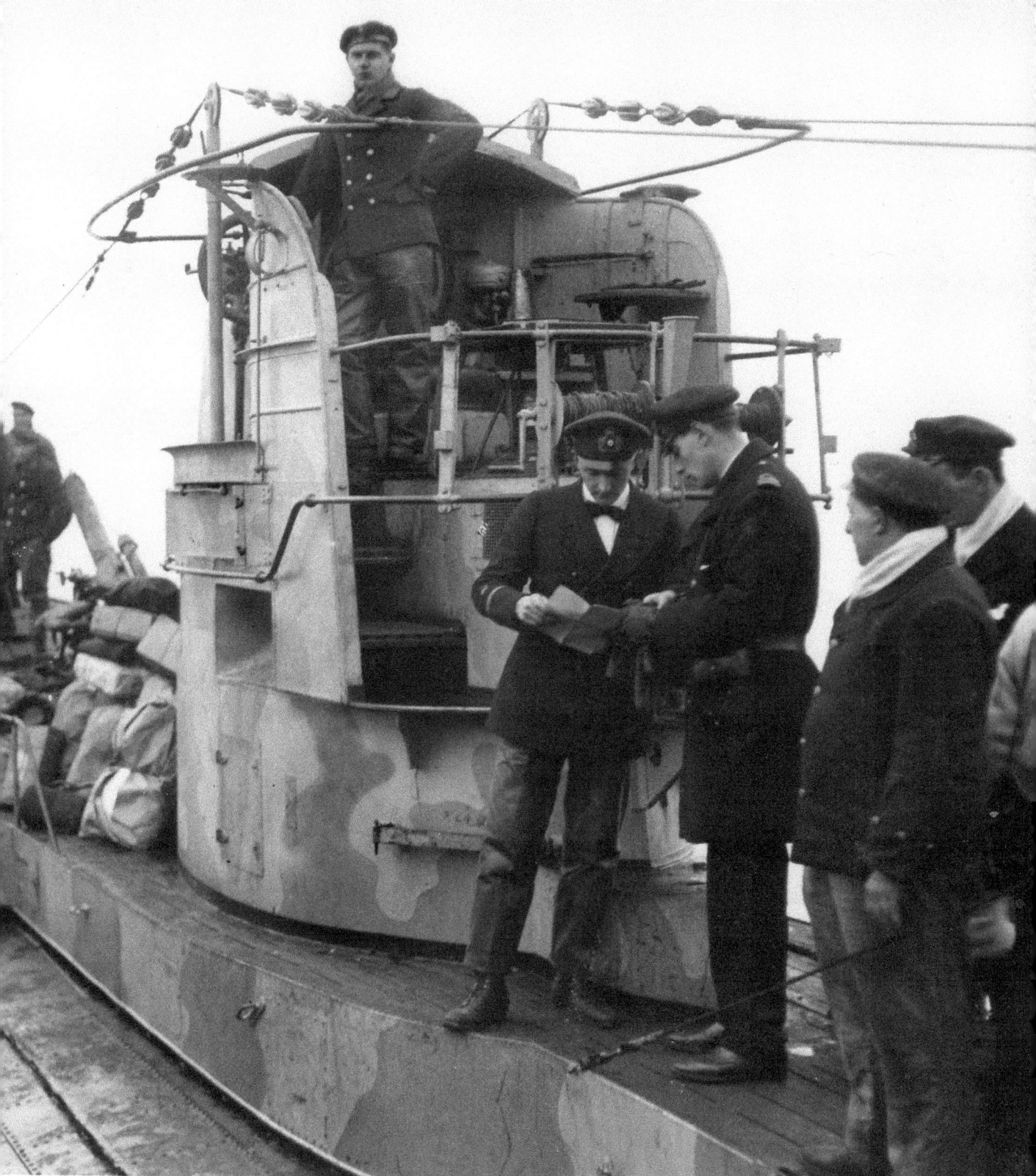

17GW805, 17GW806. German submarines surrendering in November 1918. A German officer, dressed for the historic occasion, hands over papers for *U-48* to a British officer at Harwich. Note the German sailor in the conning adopting a defiant stance. Unlike their sailor comrades of the German High Seas Fleet who had mutinied, refusing to sail out in one final attack on the Royal Navy Grand Fleet at the beginning of that month, the submariners had fought to the bitter end.

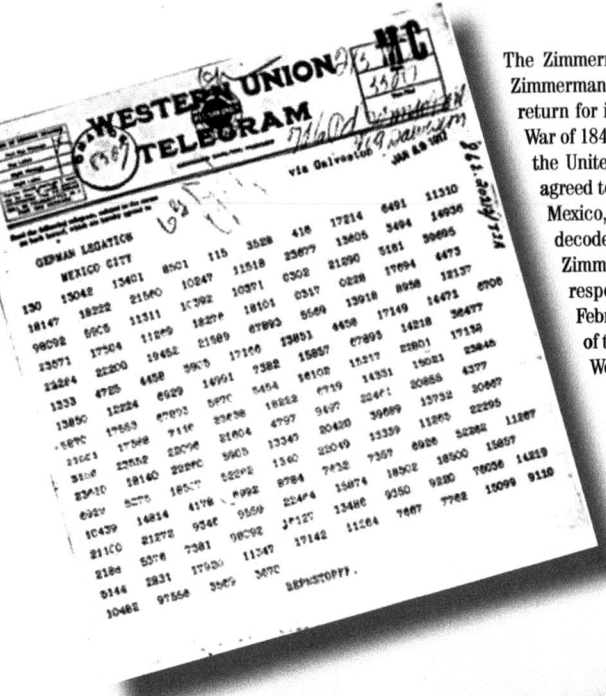

The Zimmerman note of 19 January, 1917, was a message from German Foreign Minister, Arthur Zimmermann, to the Ambassador of Mexico. In the note Germany proposed an alliance with Mexico. In return for its assistance, Mexico would regain all land lost to the United States during the Mexican War of 1846-1848. The Mexican War had lasted for two years. Under the Treaty of Guadalupe Hidalgo, the United States acquired Texas, New Mexico, Arizona, Utah, Nevada, and California. If Mexico agreed to form an alliance with the Central Powers, it would become a danger to the United States. Mexico, however, did not form an alliance with Germany. The telegram was intercepted and decoded. Wilson received the note on 24 February, 1917. The publication of the contents of the Zimmerman note on 1 March, 1917 roused the nation's support for America to enter the war. In response to the Germans recommencing their unrestricted submarine warfare campaign, 3 February, President Wilson had severed diplomatic relations with Germany and, on the heels of the Zimmermann telegram, on 6 April, 1917, the United States Congress approved President Woodrow Wilson's declaration of war. Some have claimed that the telegram was a fake.

We intend to begin on the first of February unrestricted submarine warfare STOP We shall endeavour in spite of this to keep the United States of America neutral STOP In the event of this not succeeding, we make Mexico a proposal of alliance on the following basis make war together, make peace together, generous financial support and an understanding on our part that Mexico is to reconquer lost territory in Texas, New Mexico, and Arizona STOP The settlement in detail is left to you STOP You will inform the President [of Mexico] of the above most secretly as soon as the outbreak of war with the United States of America is certain and add the suggestion that he should, on his own initiative, invite Japan to immediate adherence and at the same time mediate between Japan and ourselves STOP Please call the President's attention to the fact that the ruthless employment of our submarines now offers the prospect of compelling England in a few months to make peace STOP

Signed ZIMMERMANN

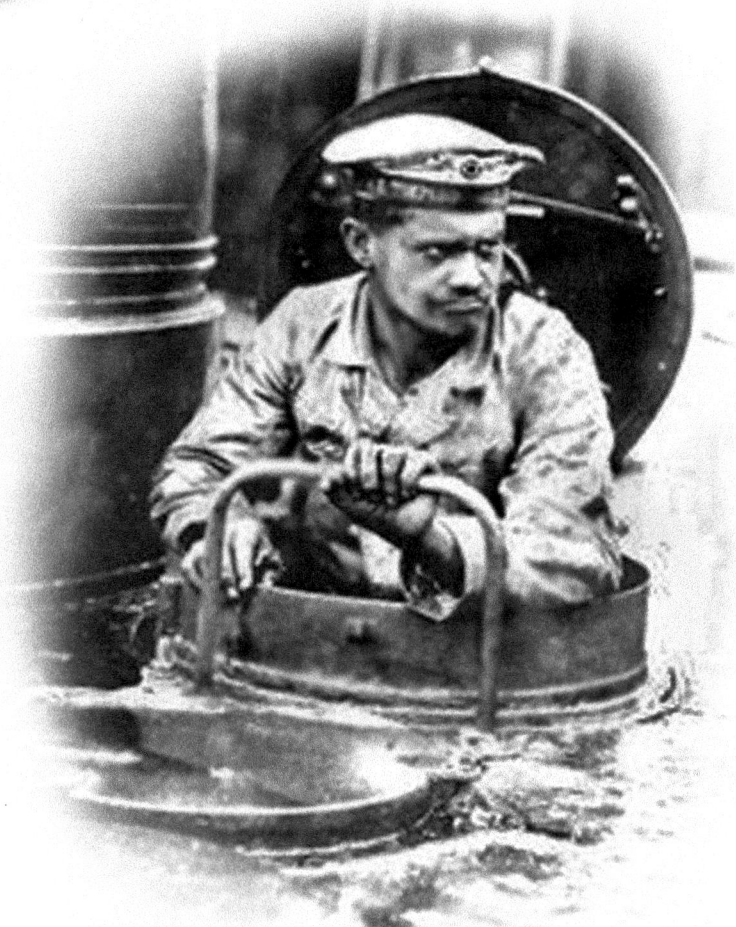

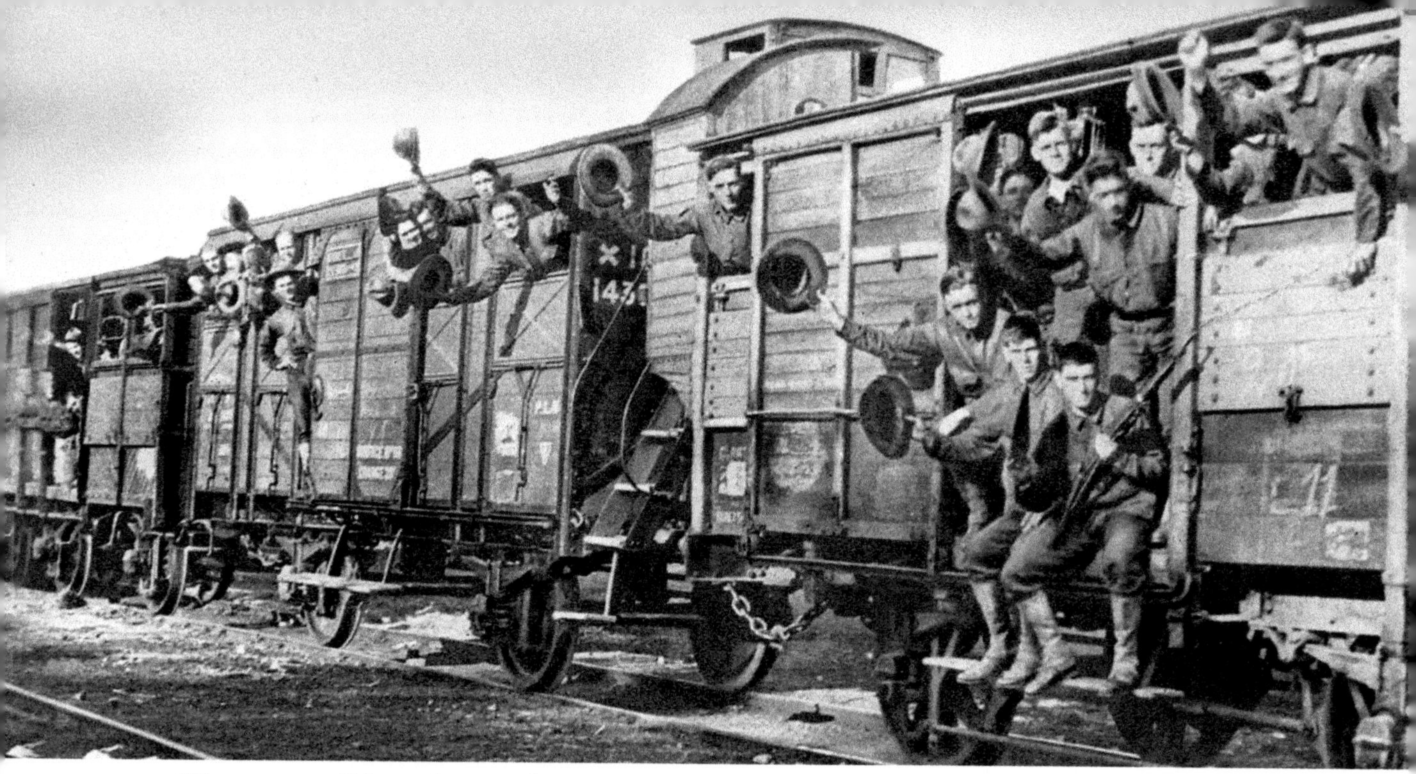

Chapter Six: America Joins the Fray – Russia Leaves

17GW811 Fifth US Marines en route to a training area in France, June 1917. Their first ride in French railway wagons bearing the sign: 40 men or 8 horses.

17GW812 Vladimir Lenin, leader of the Bolsheviks, speaking at a meeting in Sverdlov Square in Moscow, 1917.

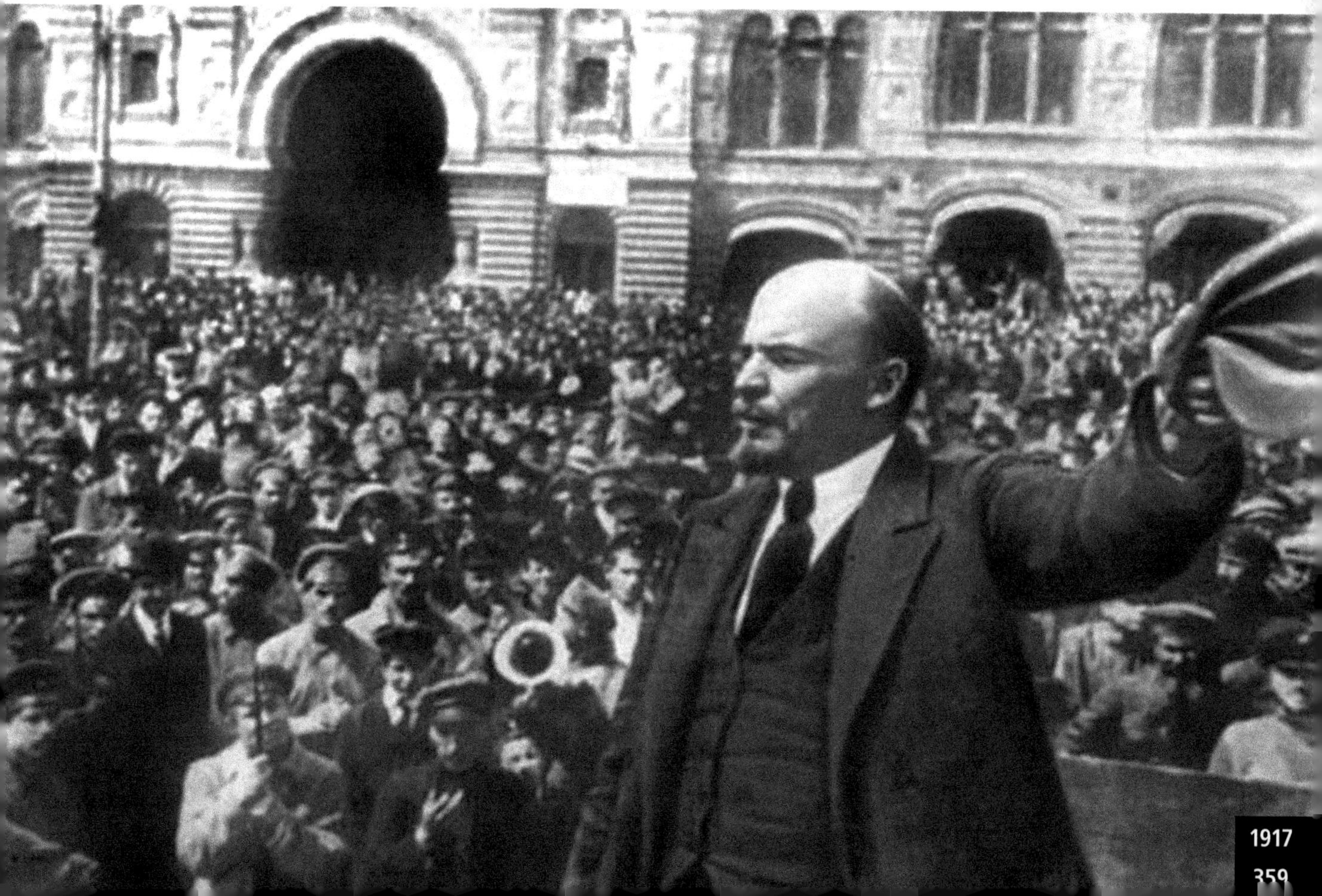

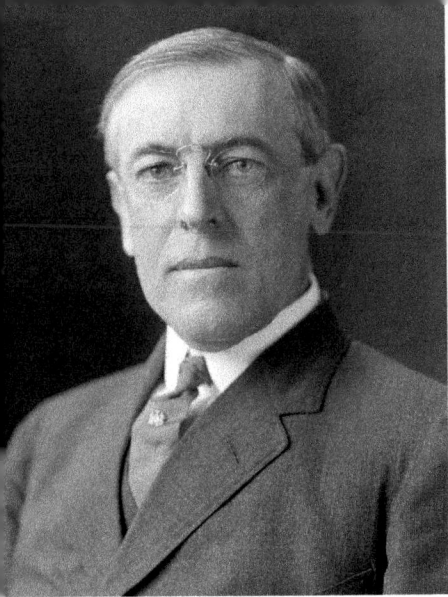

17GW810, 17GW813. Thomas Woodrow Wilson, the 28th President of the United States, on 2 April, 1917, appeared before Congress and read his message recommending that a state of war be declared to exist between the United States and Imperial Germany. The war resolution was passed by the Senate 4 April and by the House, 6 April. It was signed by the President and became effective the same day.
The Americans were in.

17GW814 The Proclaimation of the state of war between America and Germany, signed by the President and the Secretary of State.

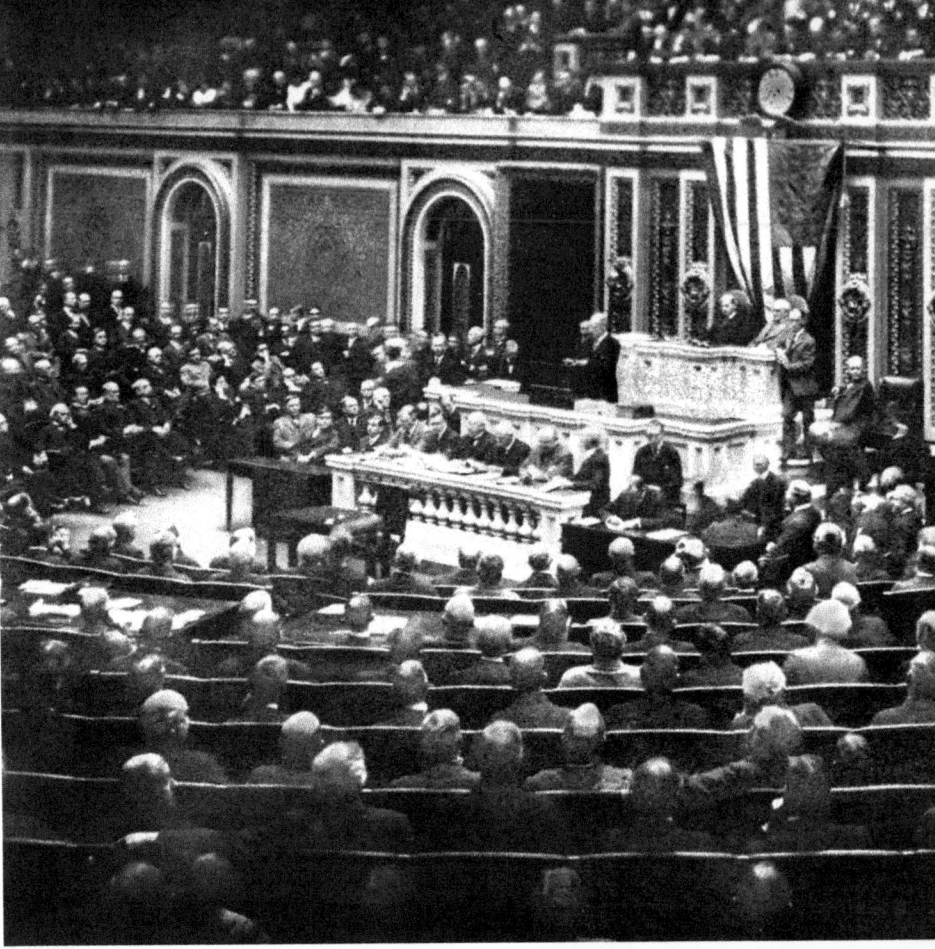

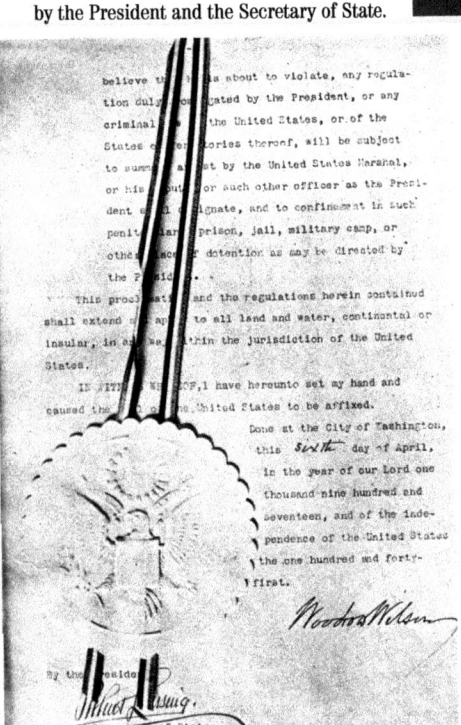

17GW815 The Secretary of State, Robert Lansing.

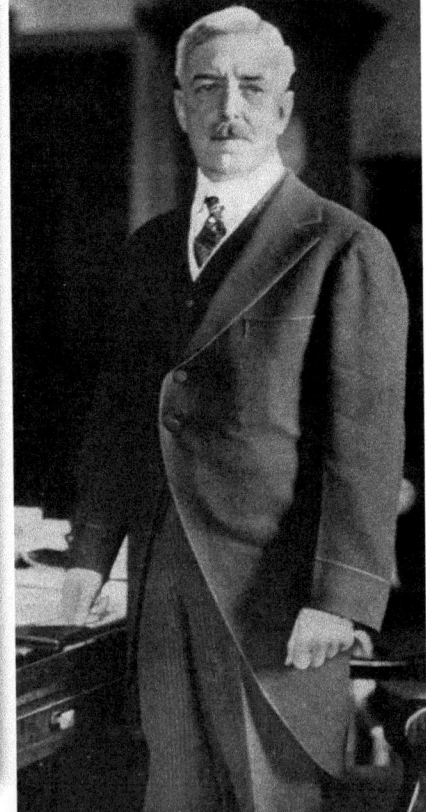

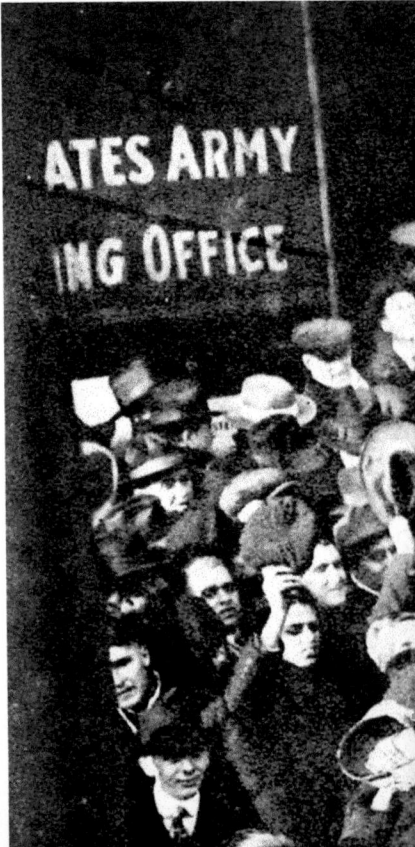

1917
360

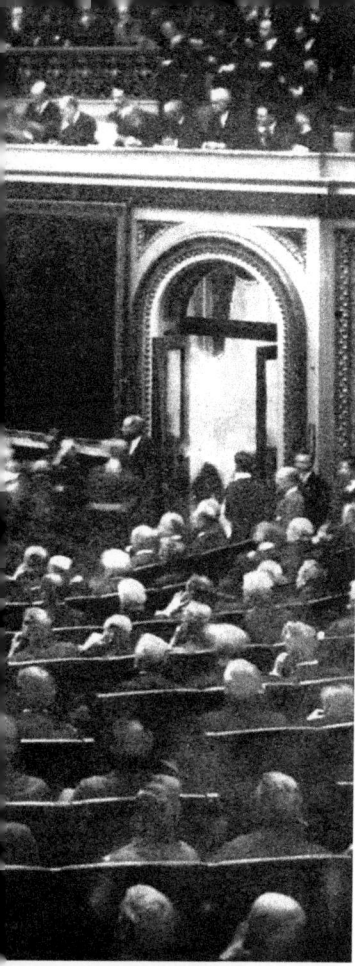
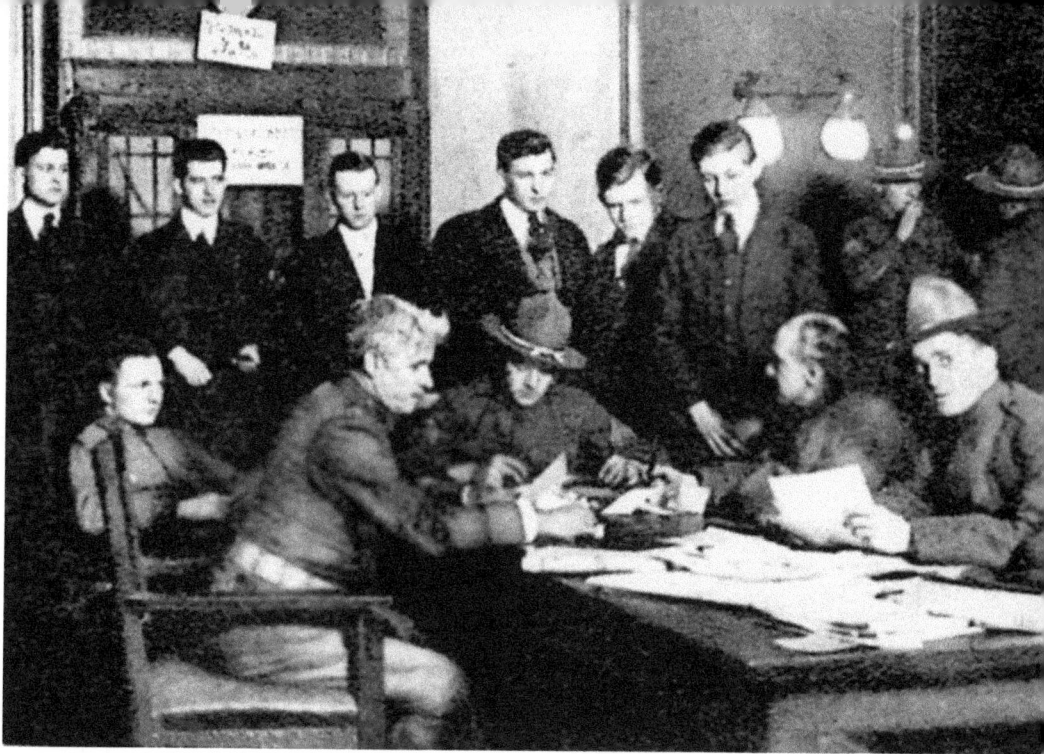

It is a fearful thing to lead this great, peaceful country into war, into the most terrible and disastrous of all wars, civilization itself seeming to be in the balance. But the right is more precious than peace... the day has come when America is privileged to spend her blood and her might for the principles that gave her birth and happiness amid the peace which she has treasured. God helping her, She can do no other.
President Wilson to Congress

17GW817, 17GW816
Headquarters of the National Guard, New York City, when the call went out for the first volunteers.

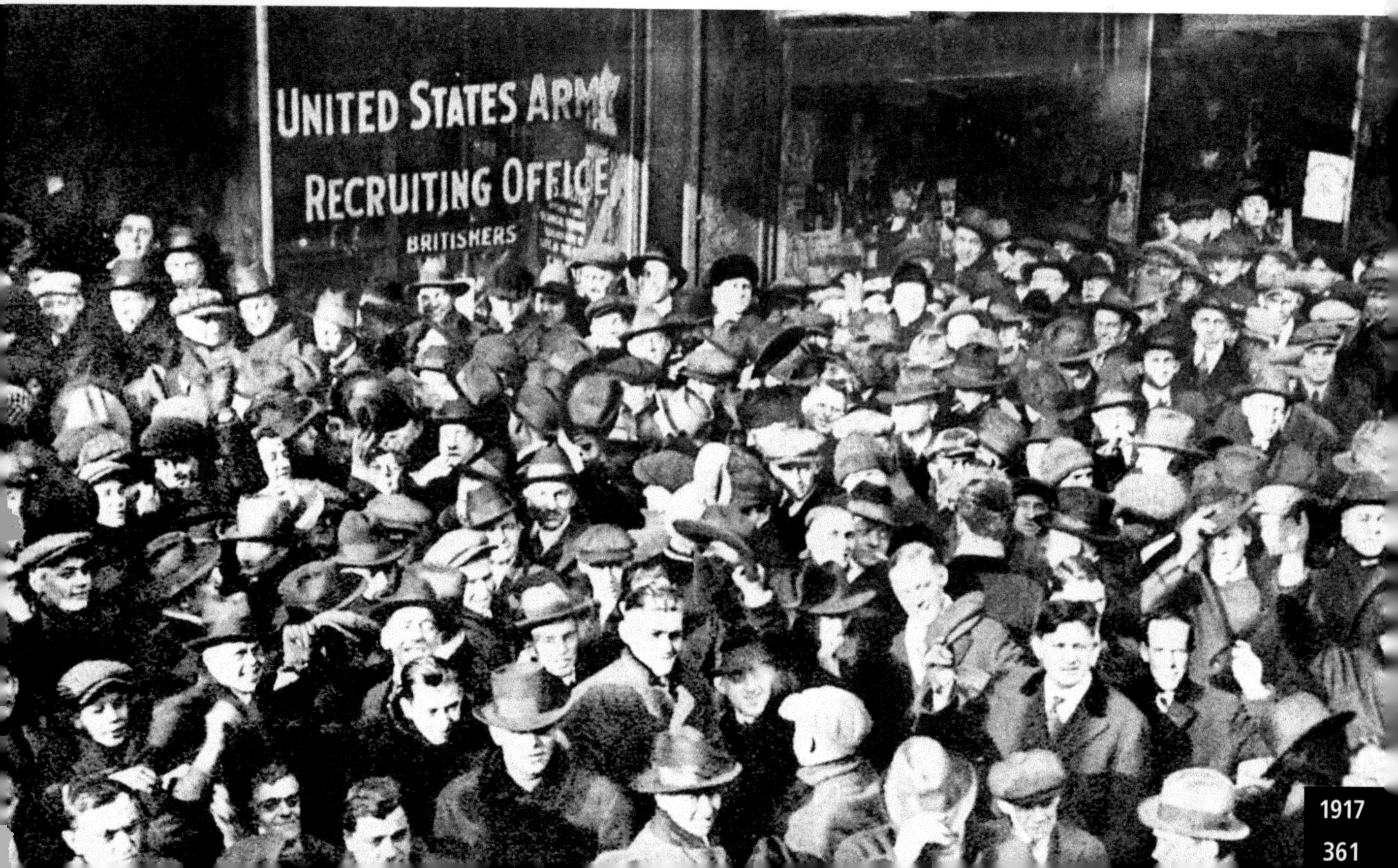

1917

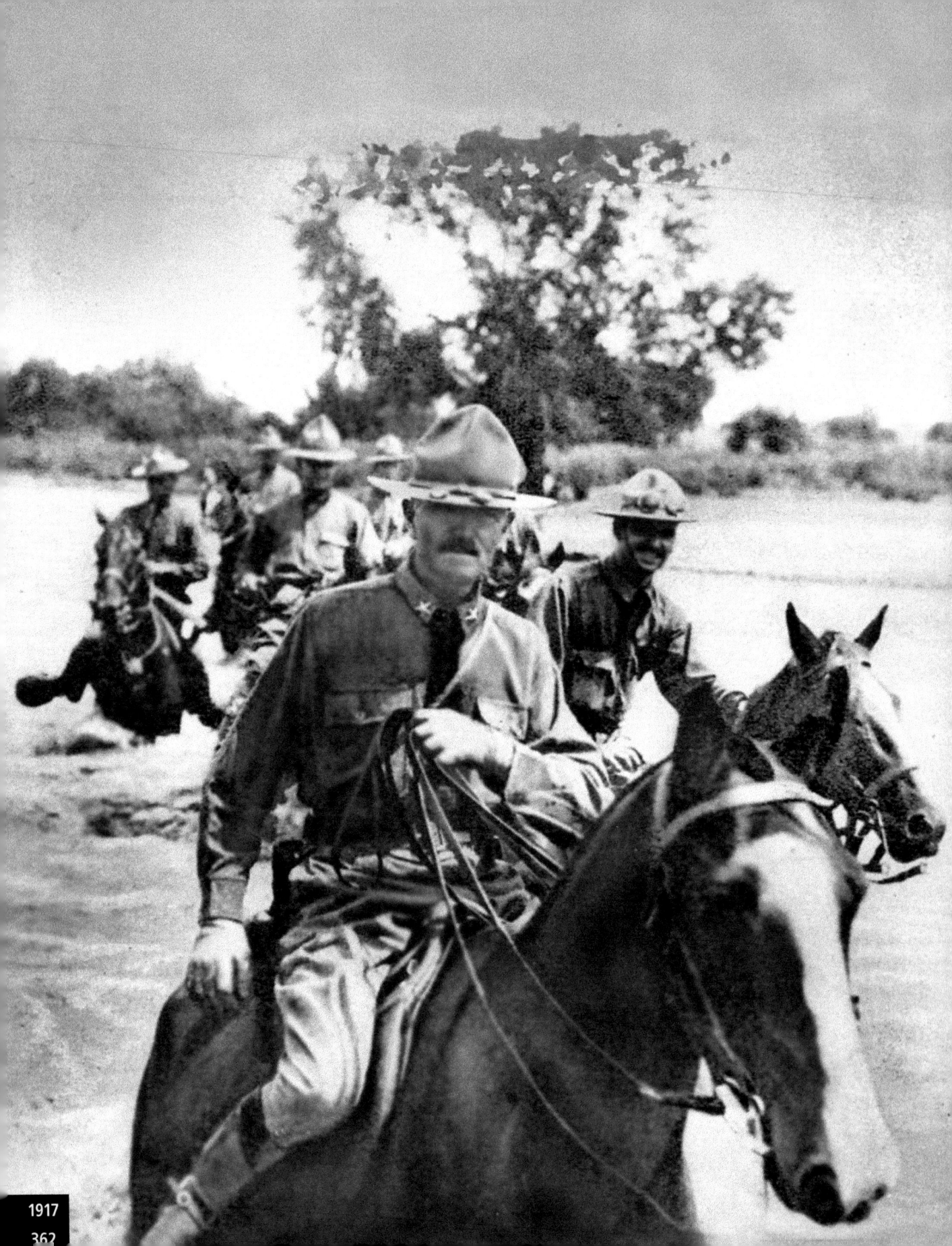

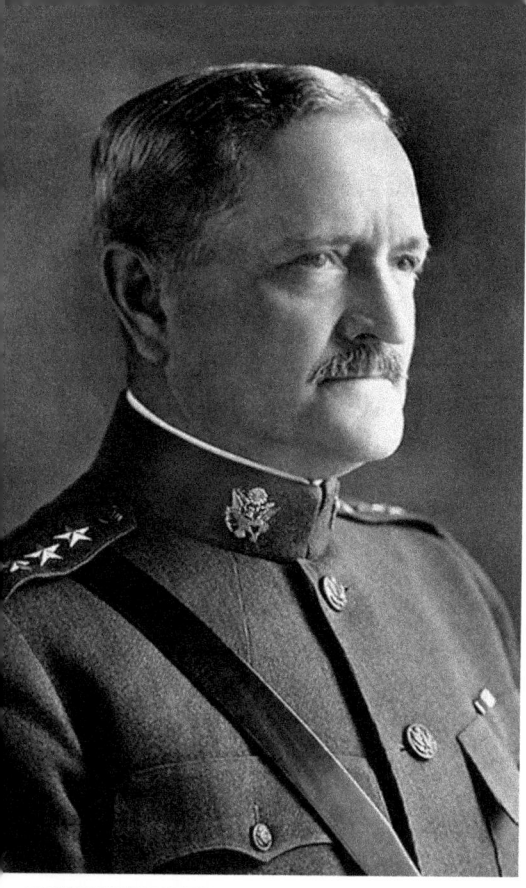
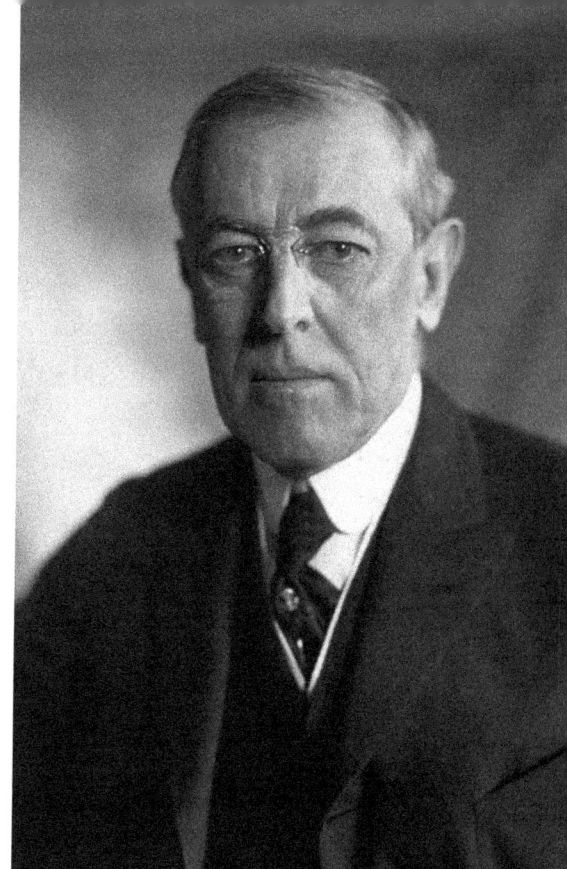

17GW834, 17GW835. President Wilson named John Joseph 'Black Jack' Pershing as commander in chief of the new American Expeditionary Force. Pershing was promoted to full general and was made responsible for the organization, training and supply of a combined professional and draft army, as well as the National Guard. The force under his charge grew from 27,000 to two armies numbering over two million men. He rejected British and French demands that American forces be integrated with their armies, and insisted that the AEF would operate as a single command under him. However, some American divisions did fight under British command and Pershing permitted all-black units to be integrated with the French Army.

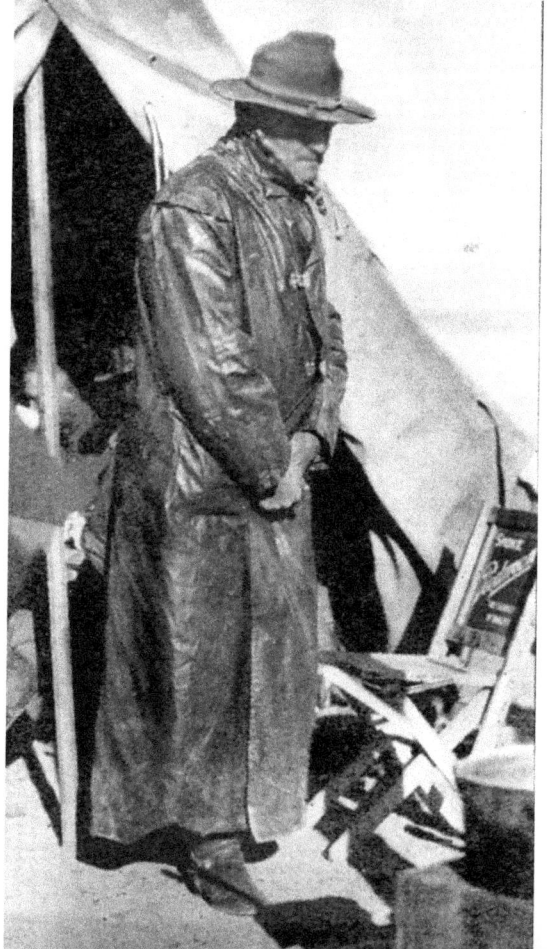
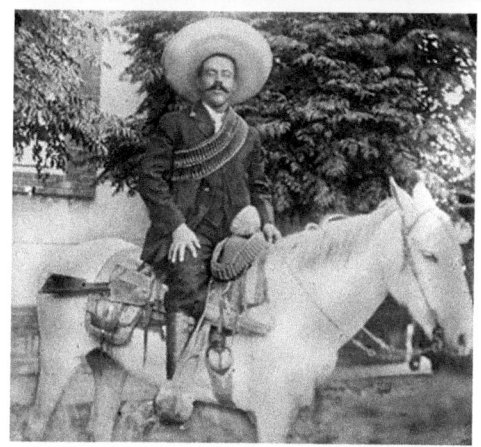
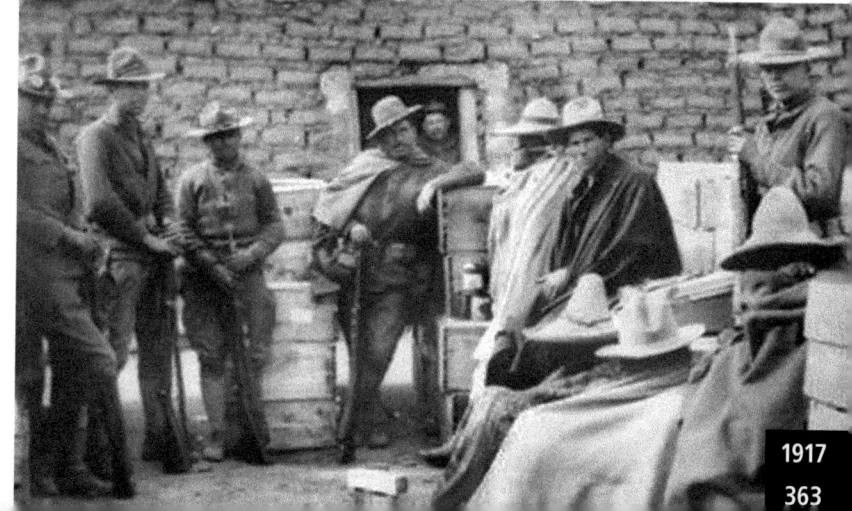

17GW833, 17GW836, 17GW837, 17GW838. General Pershing on campaign in Mexico, leading the hunt for the revolutionary leader Pancho Villa. The elusive bandit and some of his men captured men under guard by Pershing's soldiers.

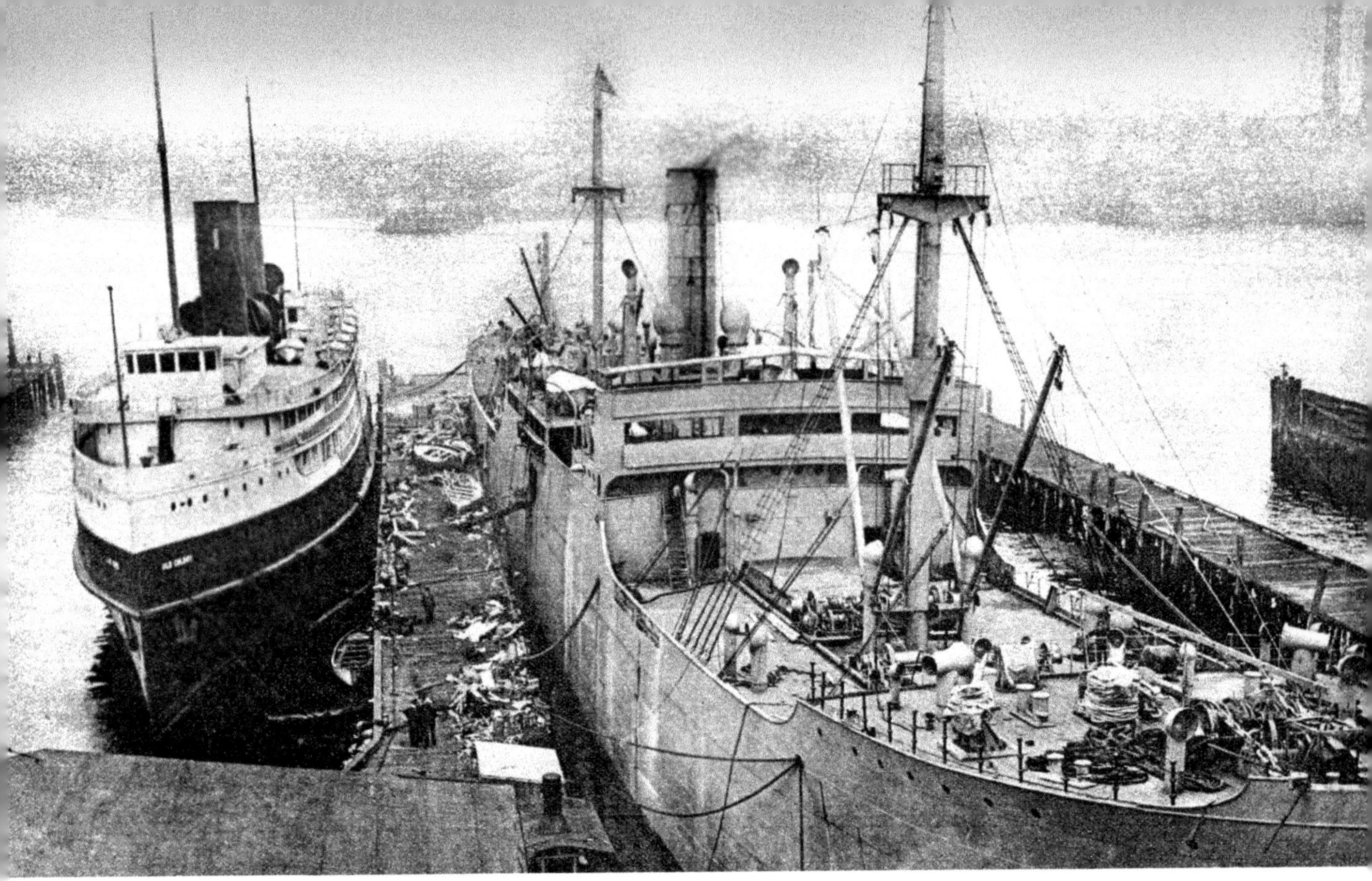

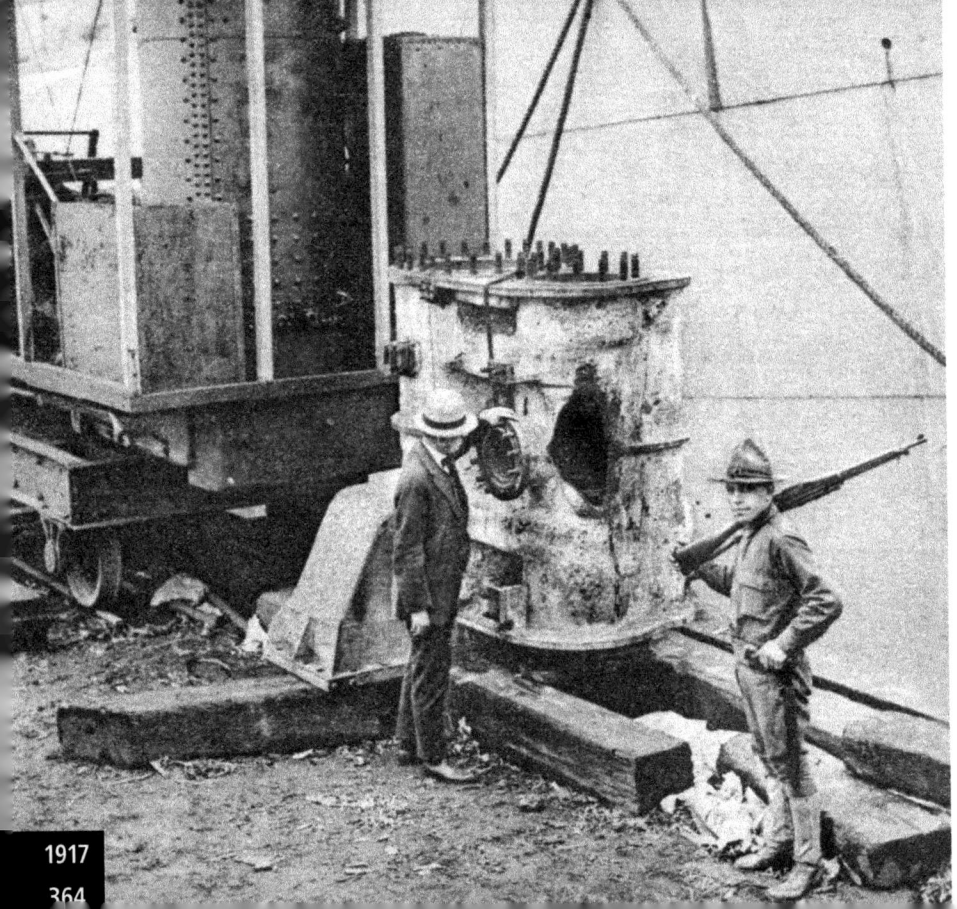

17GW818, 17GW819. The 5,621 ton German steamer *Ockenfels*, having been seized on the orders of the United States Government, is being prepared to take its place in the American mercantile marine. Items of equipment have been damaged by the ship's crew and are being removed for repair or replacement.

The first act in recognition of a state of war between the United States and Germany was the seizure of all German ships that had taken refuge in American ports during the first three years of the Great War. Preparations for seizure were in hand and at the declaration of war Federal troops took possession of the ninety-one German merchant ships in American waters. The total in value, estimated at the time, was approximately ten million dollars. The seizures were mostly without incident and the crews were interned. In anticipation of the action the German crews had carried out acts of sabotage and damaged much of the machinery on board. One of the exceptions to the deliberate damage inflicted was on the 54,000 ton *Vaterland*, where her equipment was left intact.

17GW821 The rudiments of rifle handling is being carried out under the instructors – 'Present arms!' – with the the M1903 Springfield, used primarily during the first half of the 20th century. It was officially adopted as a United States military bolt-action rifle on June 19, 1903, and saw service in the Great War.

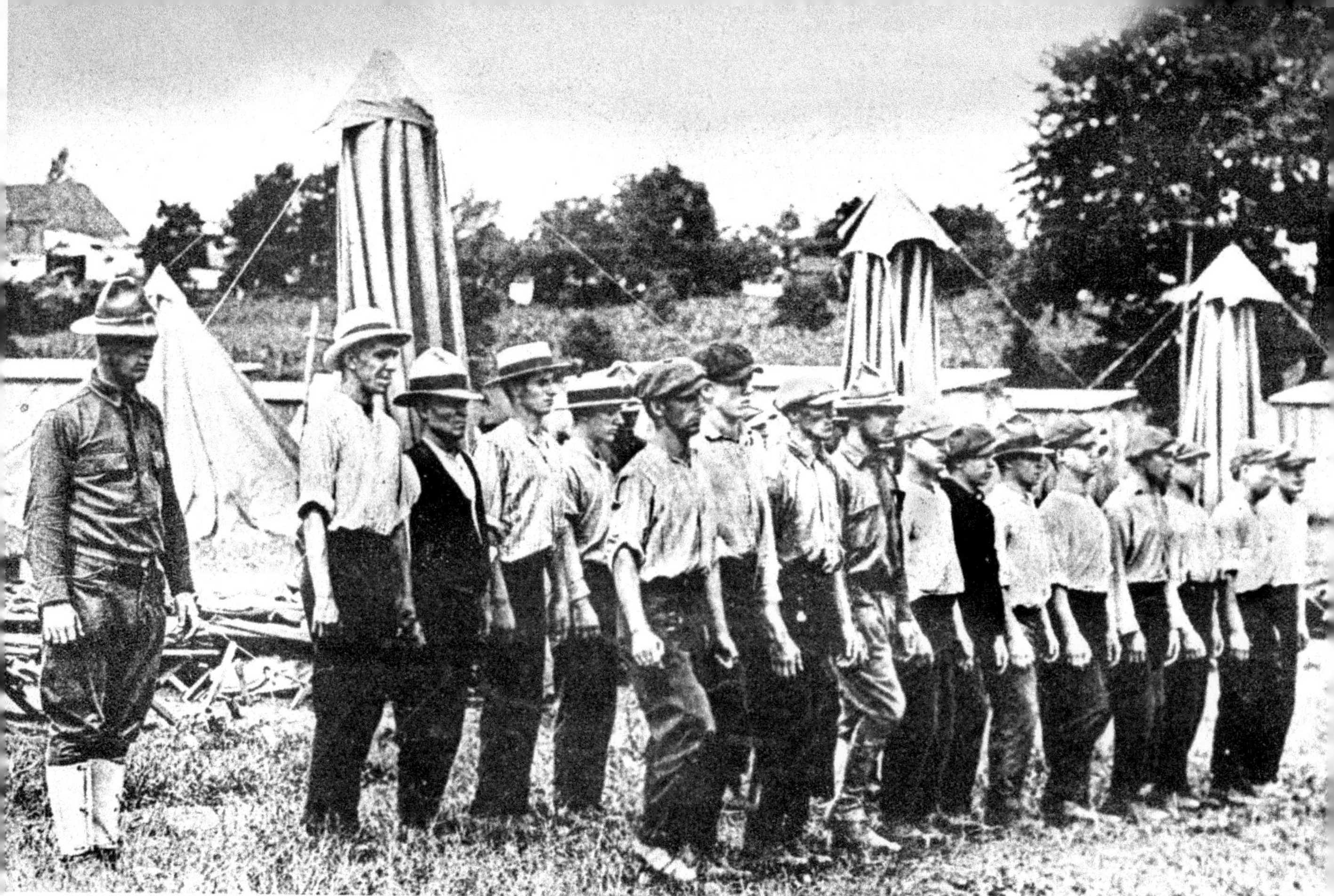

17GW820 New recruits, having just arrived at the Gettysburg military camp, begin their training immediately by first learning to march on the spot – in time.

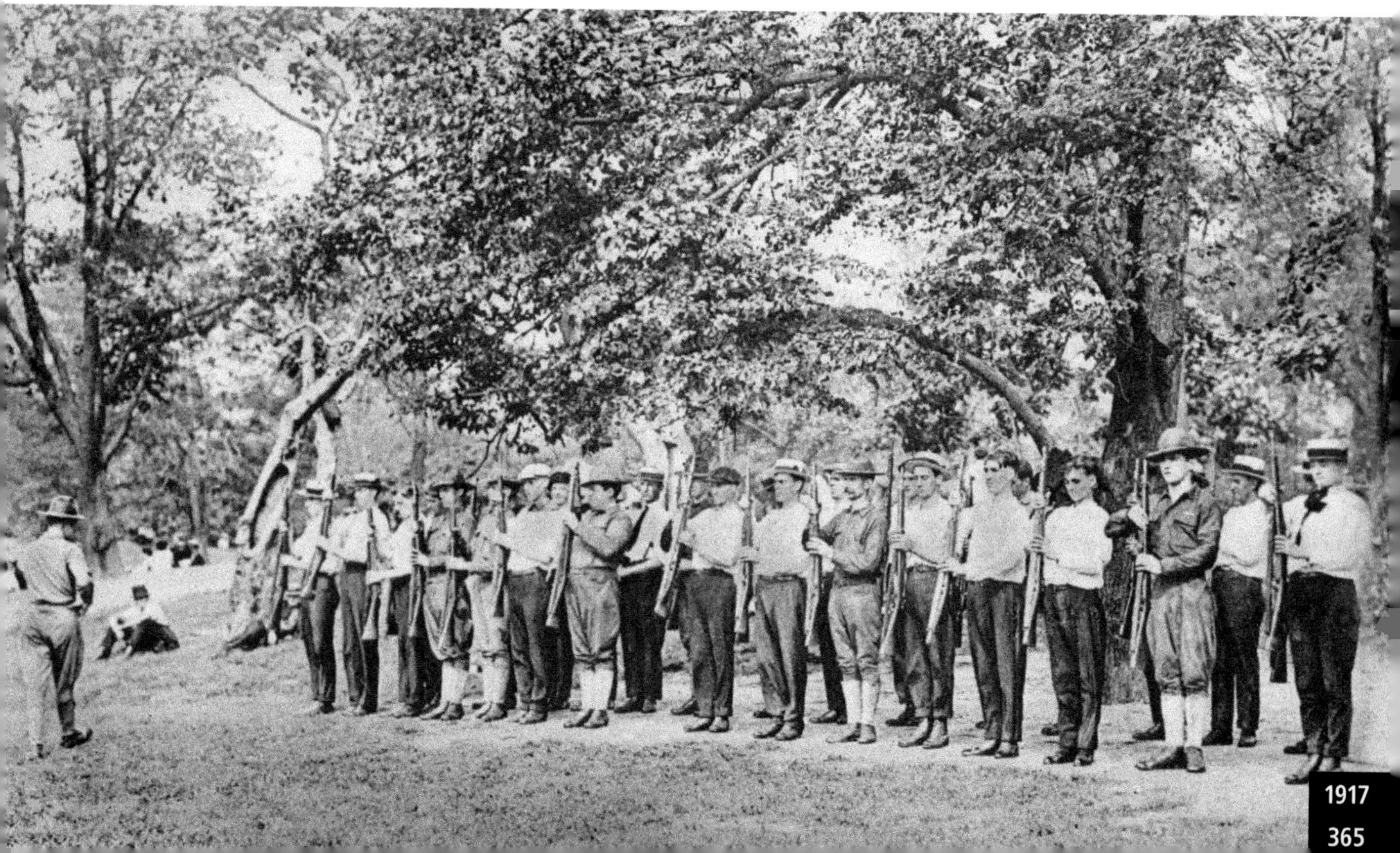

1917
365

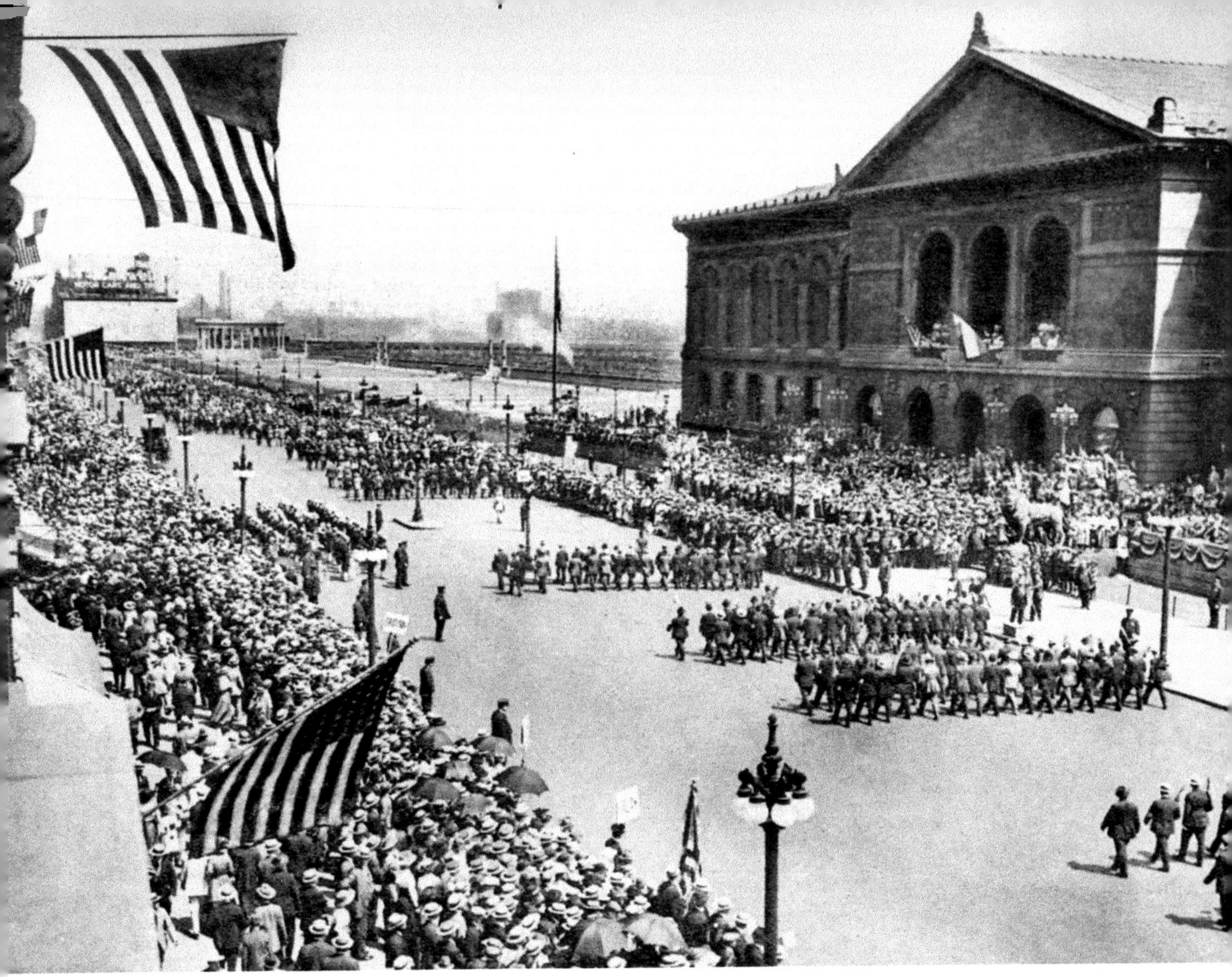

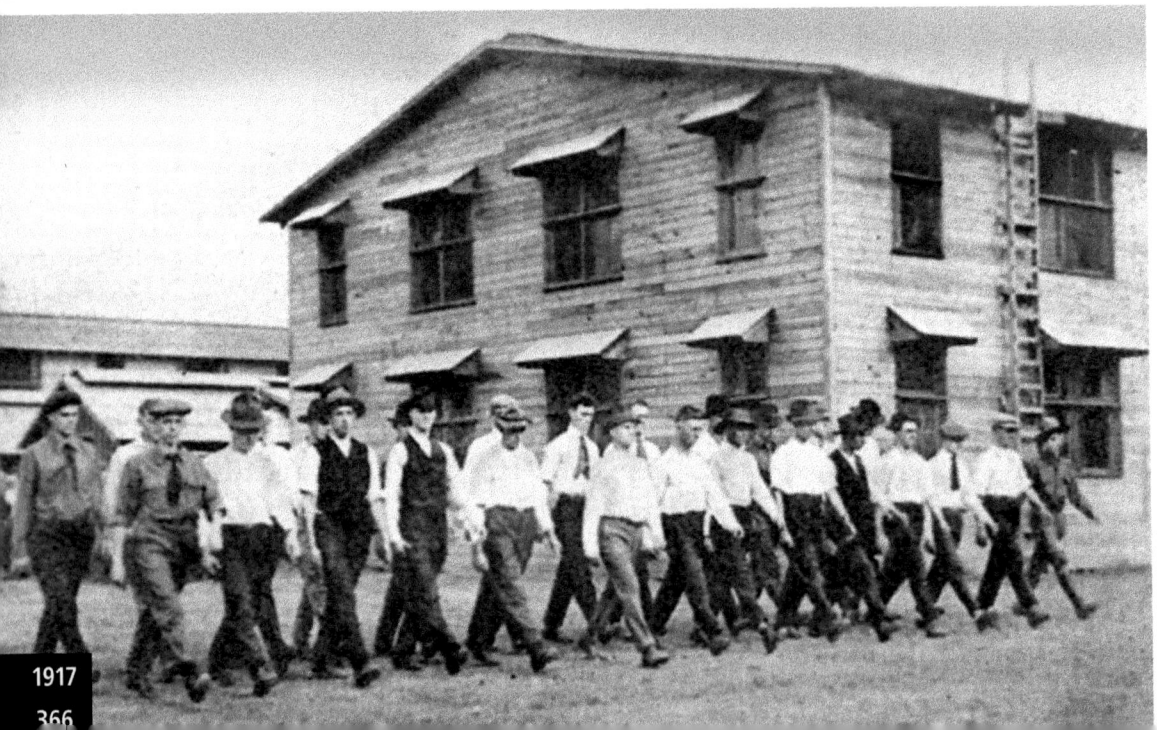

17GW866 Chicago. Thousands turn out to cheer these drafted men as they parade along Michigan Avenue. The original caption reads: 'This helped them to feel that the nation was behind their sacrifice'.

17GW867 There was a woeful lack of uniforms to cope with the army's sudden increase. These men in Cincinnati drill in their civilian clothes.

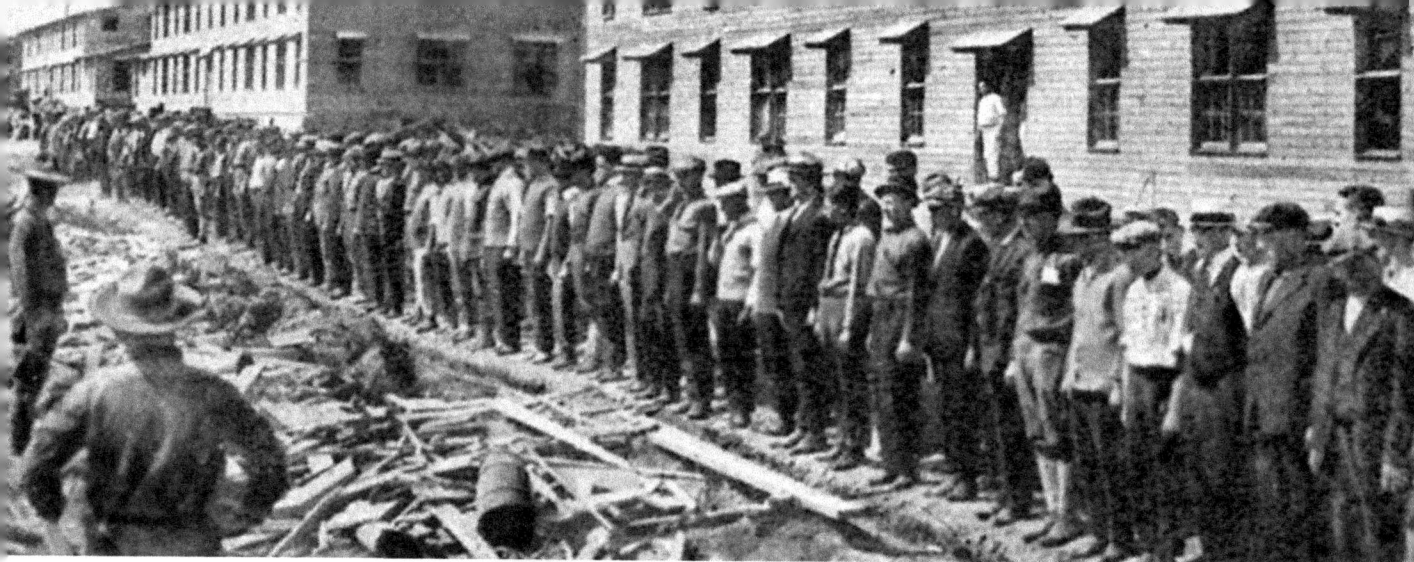

17GW868 Camps were still being completed when the drafted men arrived in large numbers. Evidence of building can be seen all around as these men, still in civilian clothes, parade in front of their barracks.

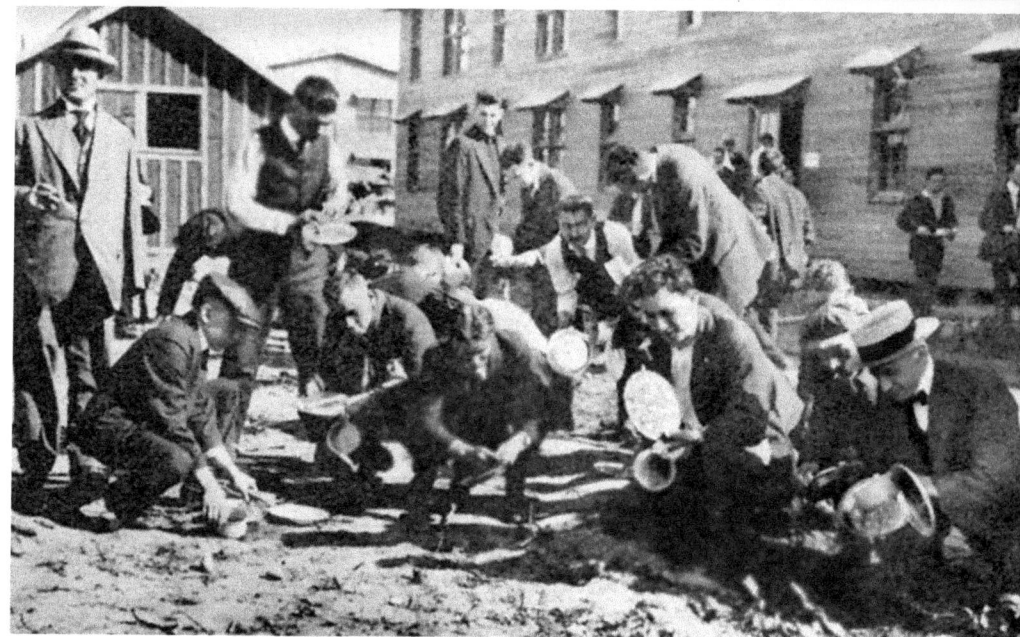

17GW869 Draft 'rookies; from New York, after their first army meal in camp, are introduced to the novelty of cleaning their mess tins in building sand. Water was still to be piped in; the cleaning method would serve to train them for the rigours of trench life awaiting them in France.

17GW870 Drafted men at a camp in Texas, in uniforms for the first time. The barracks behind them have still to have the windows glazed.

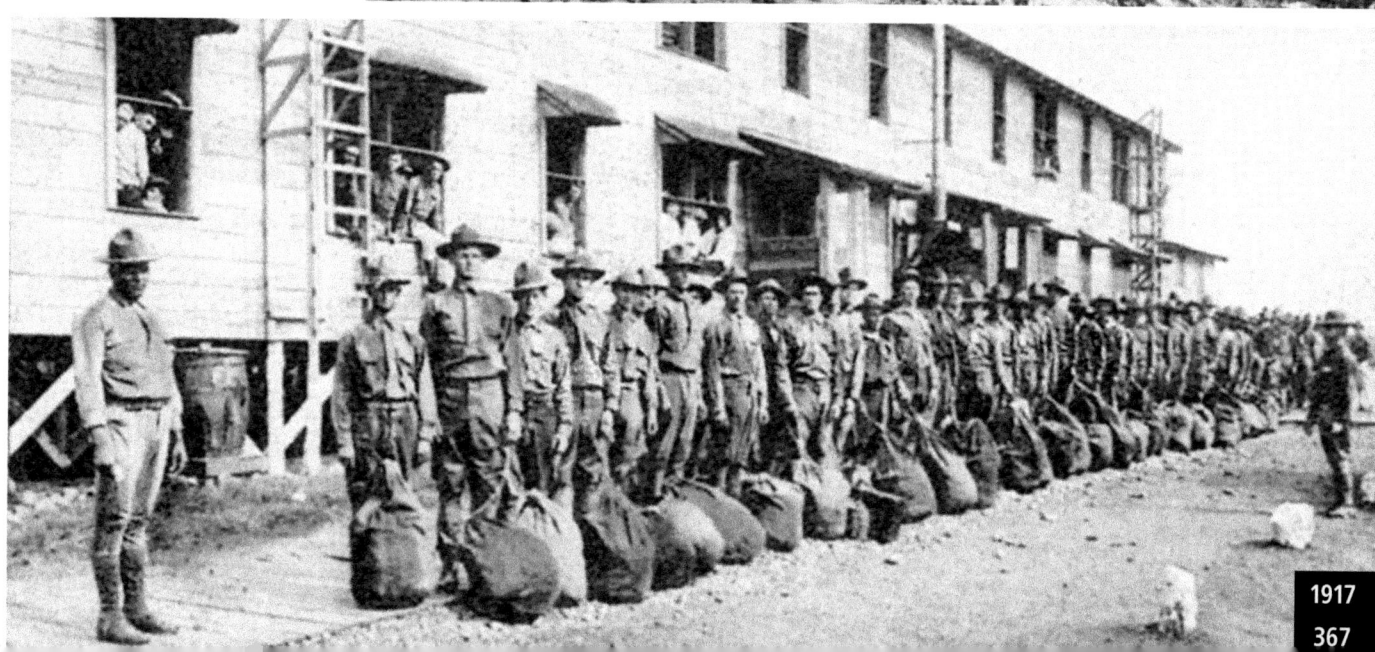

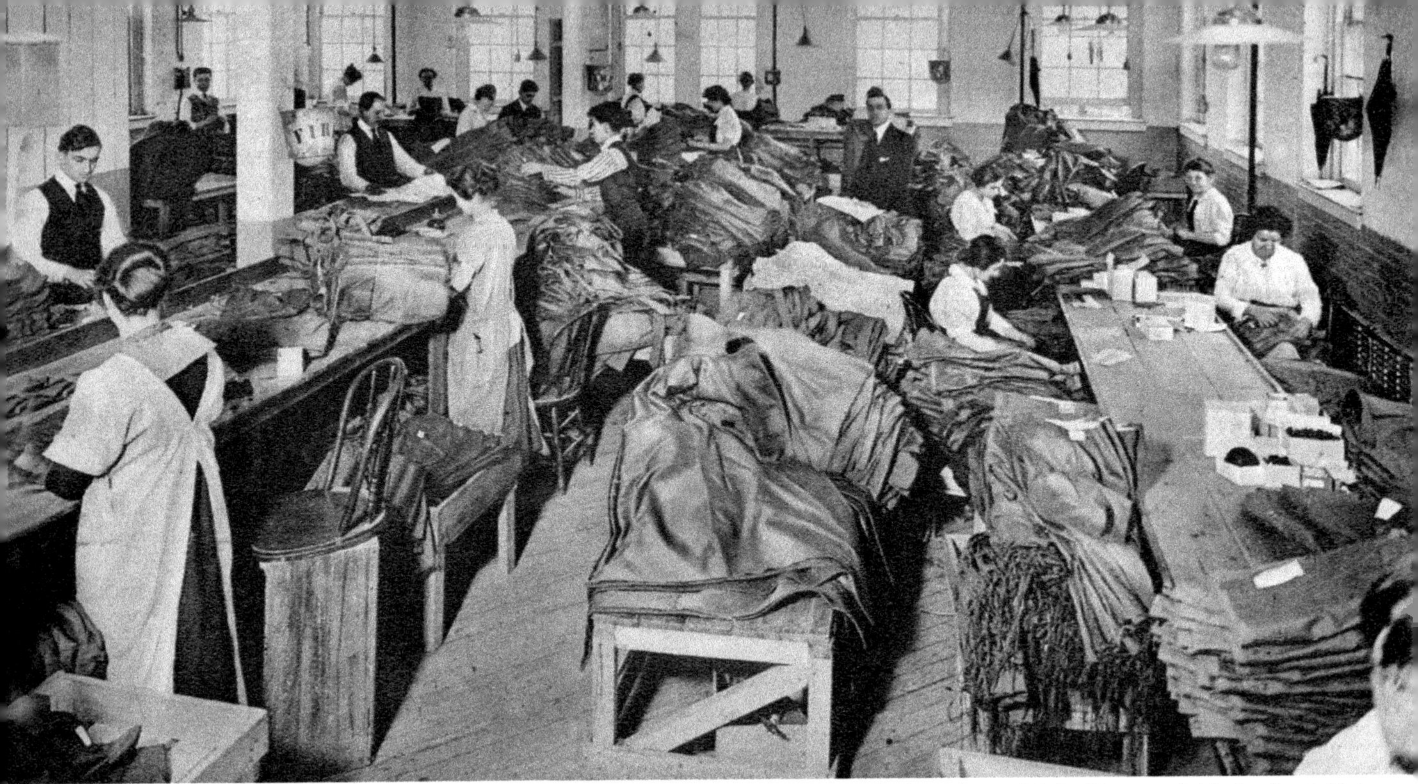

17GW872, 17GW871. One and a half million uniforms were required for the army. The final process is where the completed uniforms are finished and sorted into sizes and where a Government Inspector makes an examination before passing them for packing. Electric bladed machines are cutting through three hundred thicknesses of material at one time.

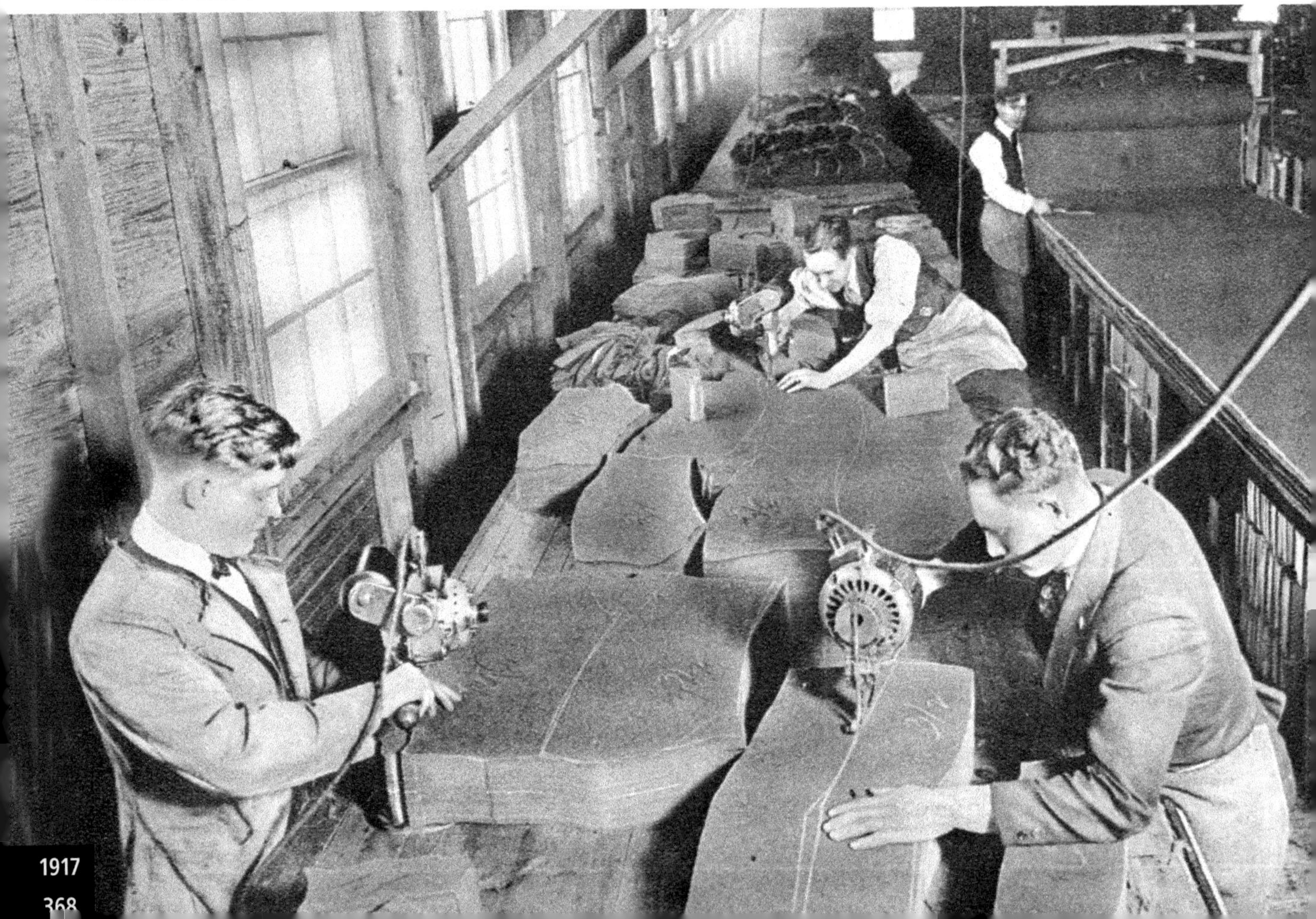

1917

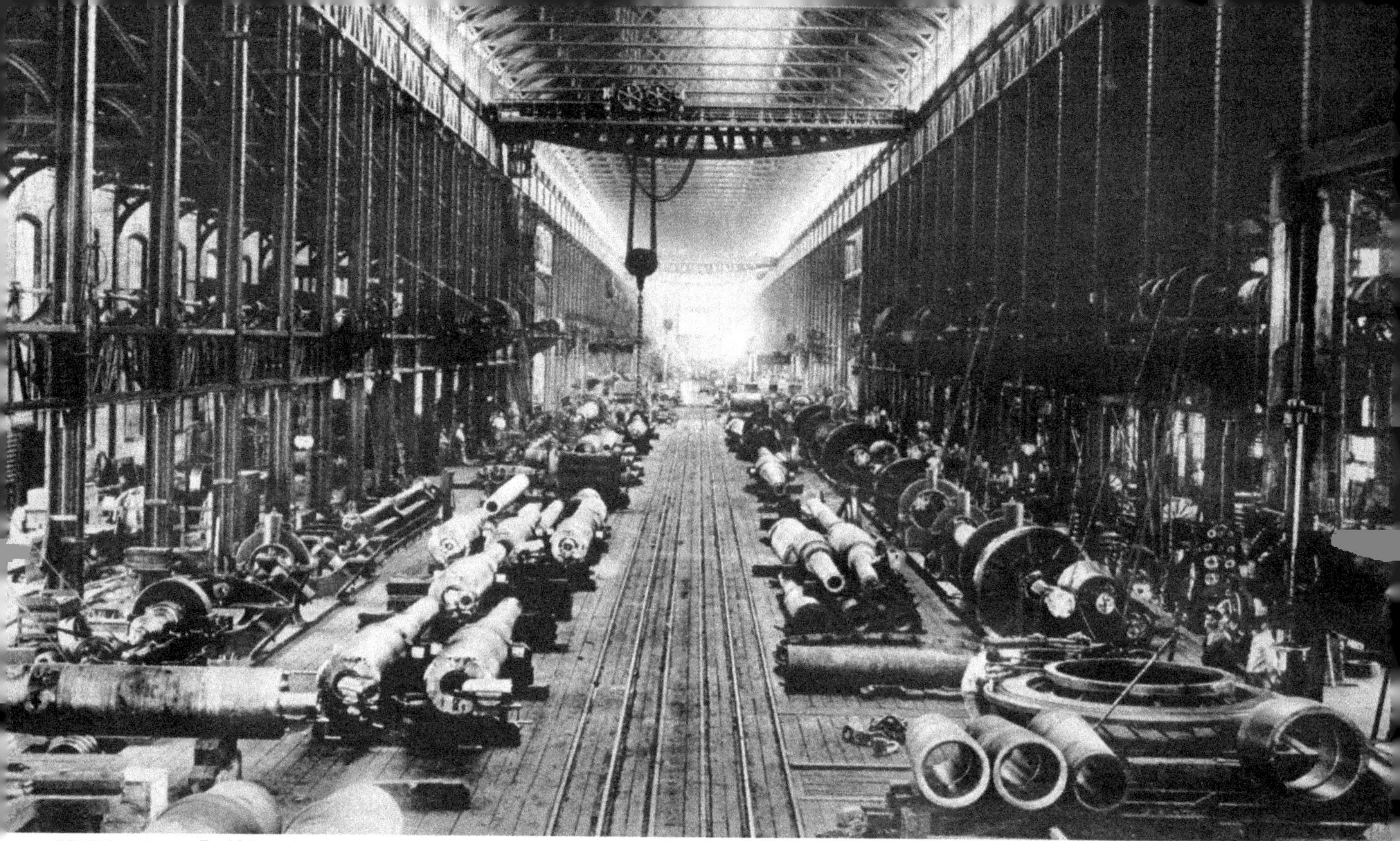

17GW873, 17GW875. Bethlehem Steel Corporation's naval gun manufacturing plant at Bethlehem, Pennsylvania. Barrels, cradles and turret rings for 6 inch, 10 inch and 15 inch guns nearing completion.

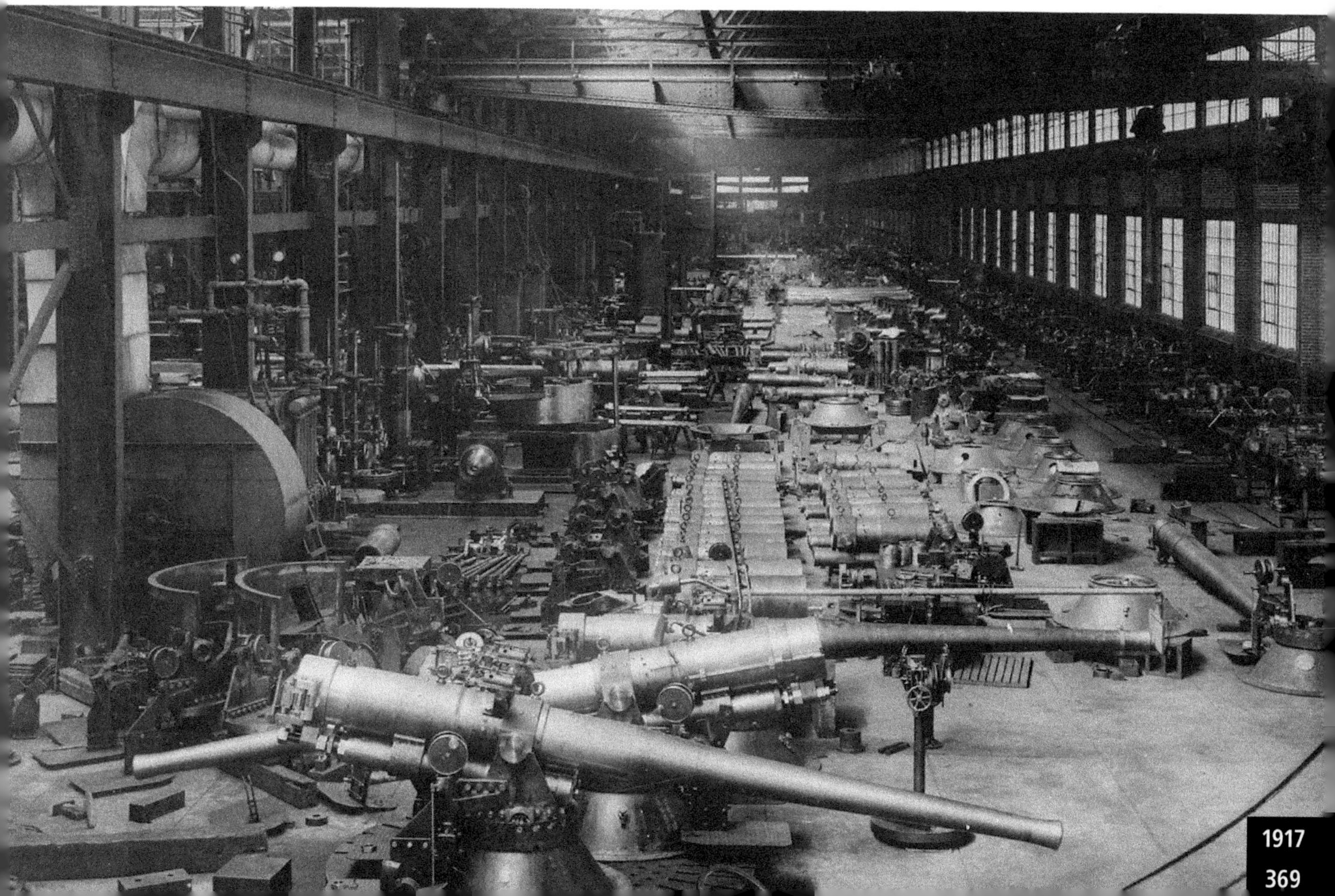

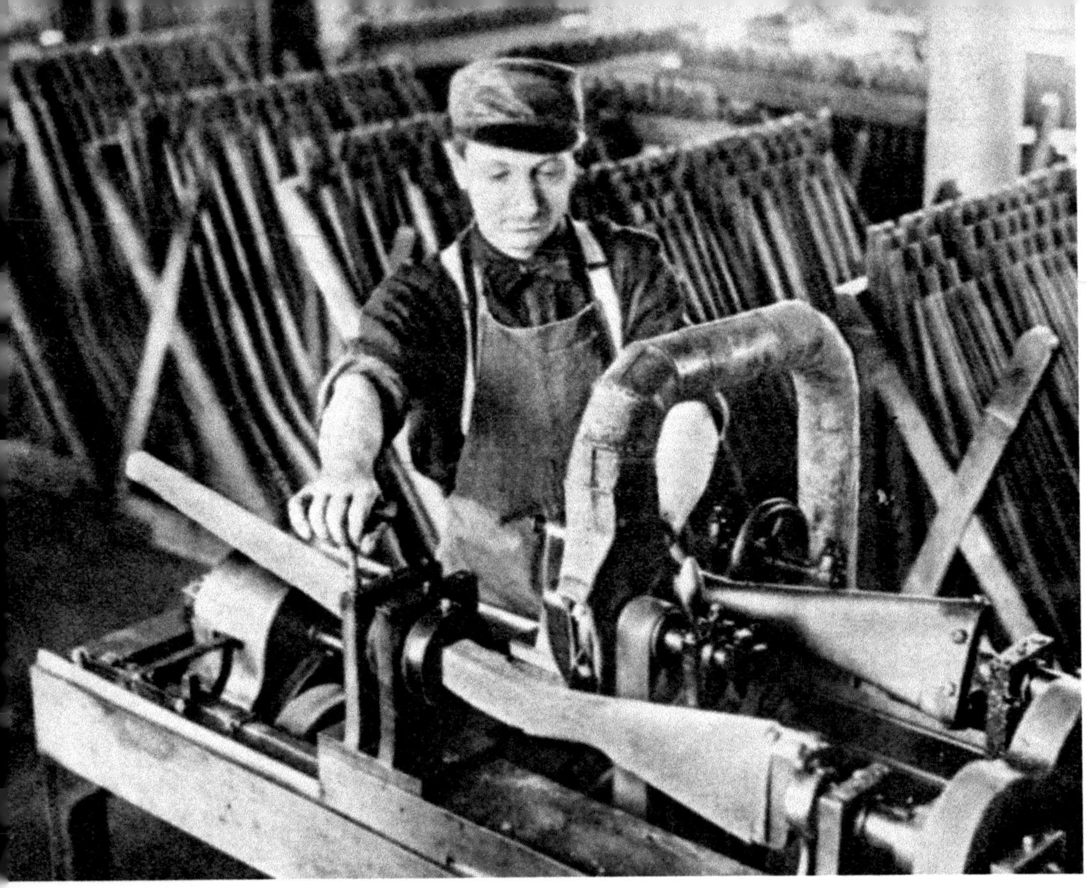

17GW823, 17GW822, 17GW825, 17GW824, 17GW826, 17GW827. With the declaration of war the Government armoury at Springfield, Massachusetts, increased its production of the famous M1903 Springfield Rifle: turning rifle stocks; a general view of the armoury where rifles are being assembled; marrying of bayonets to a particular rifle; the finished product; test firing weapons; illustrations from the manual.

The M1903 became commonly known among its users as the 'ought-three' in reference to the year of first production. The War Department had carefully studied several examples of the Spanish Mauser Model 93 rifle captured during the Spanish–American War and copied it. Despite Springfield Armory's use of slight design alterations, the 1903 was, in fact, a Mauser design; and after that company brought suit, the United States Government was ordered to pay $250,000 in royalties to Mauser Werke.

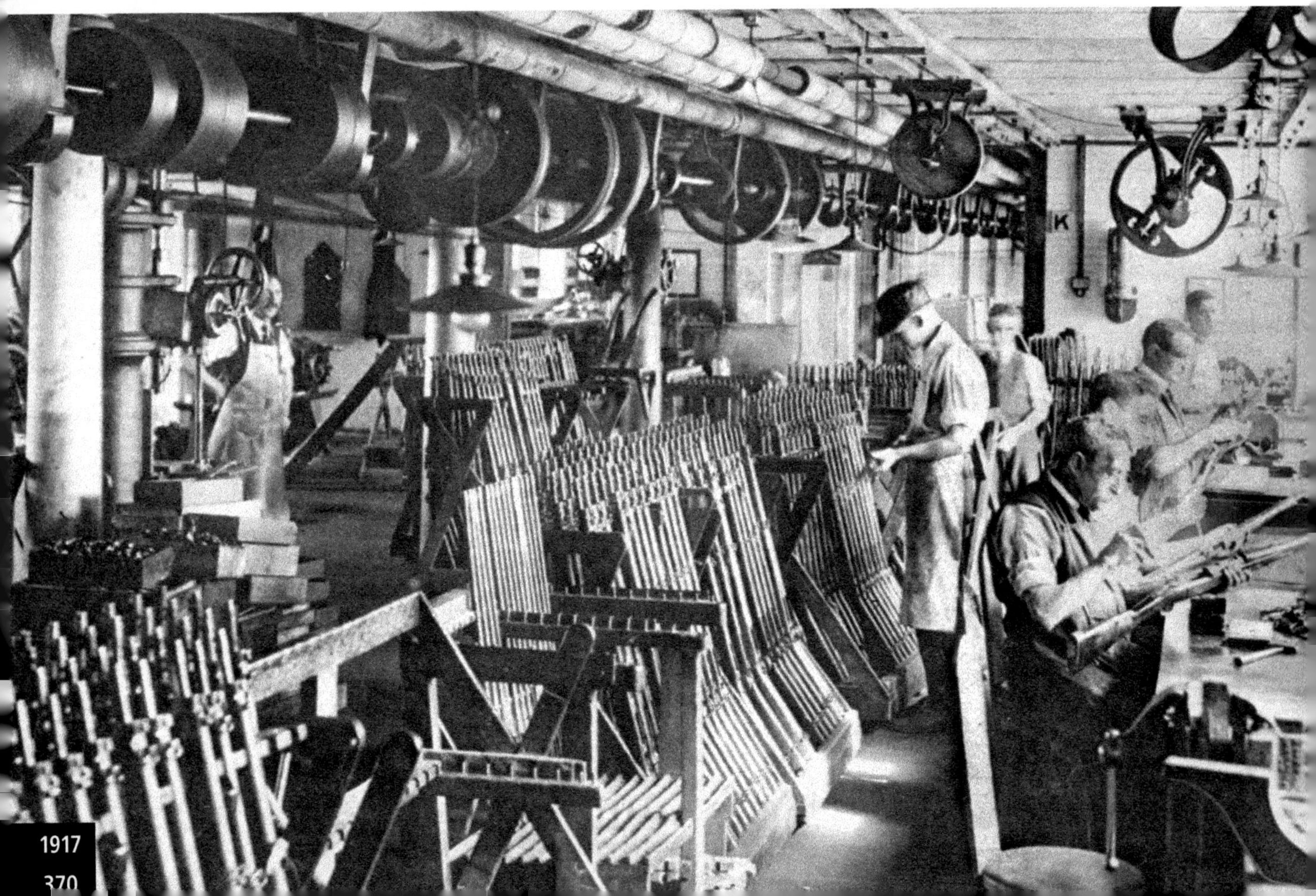

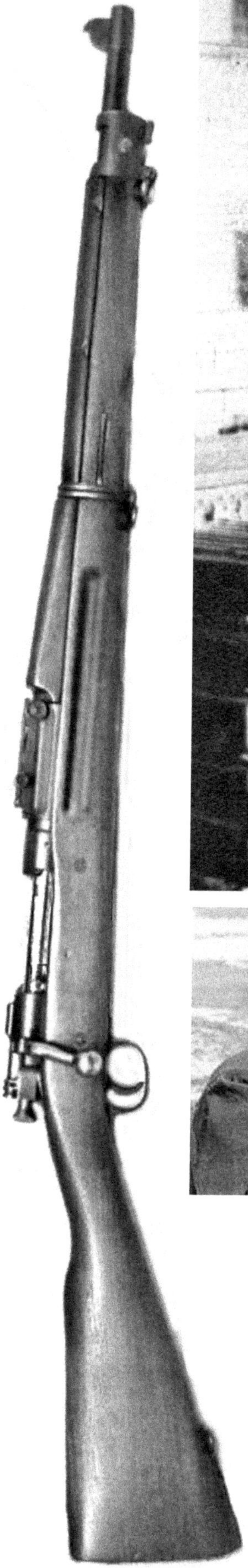

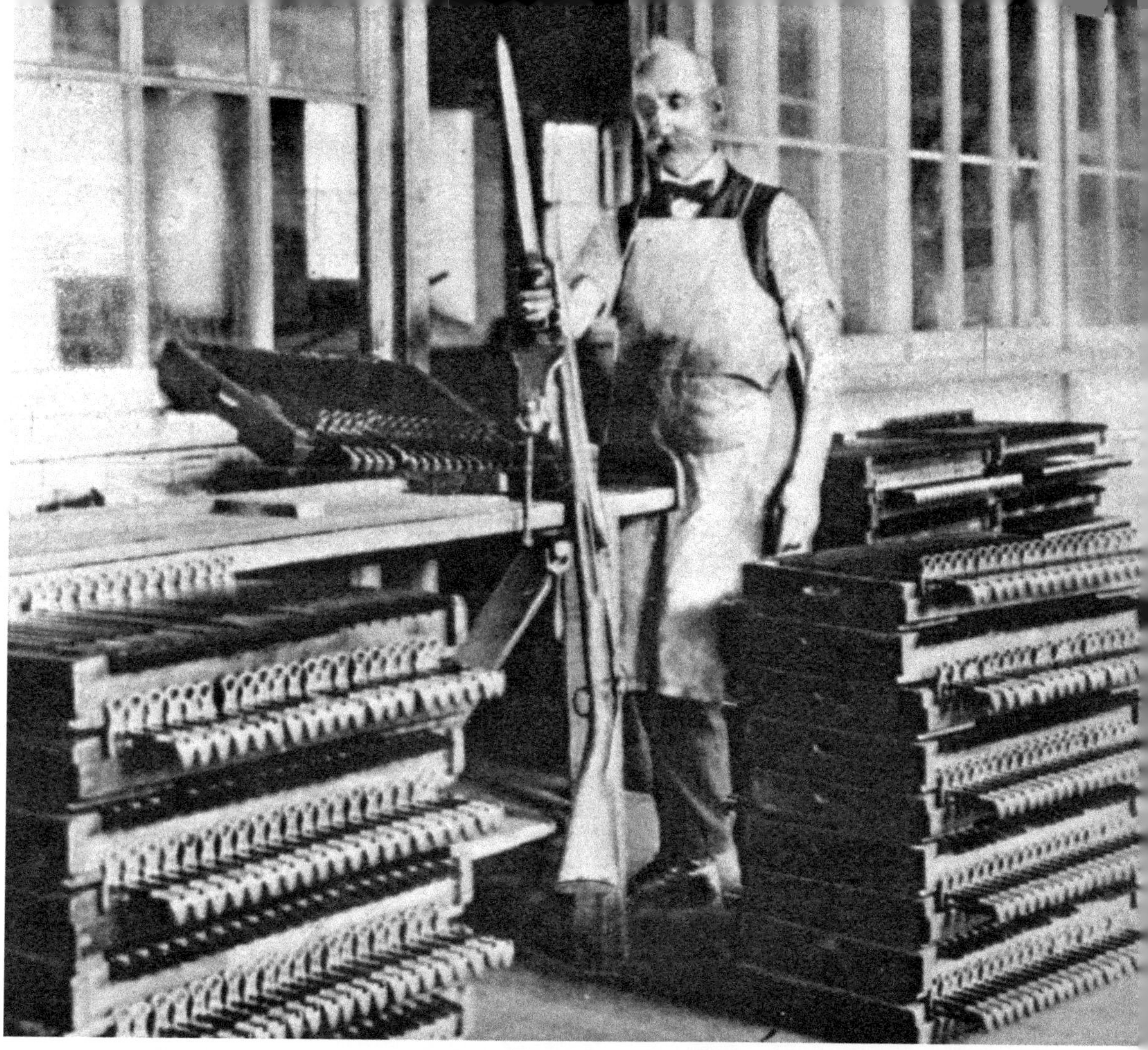

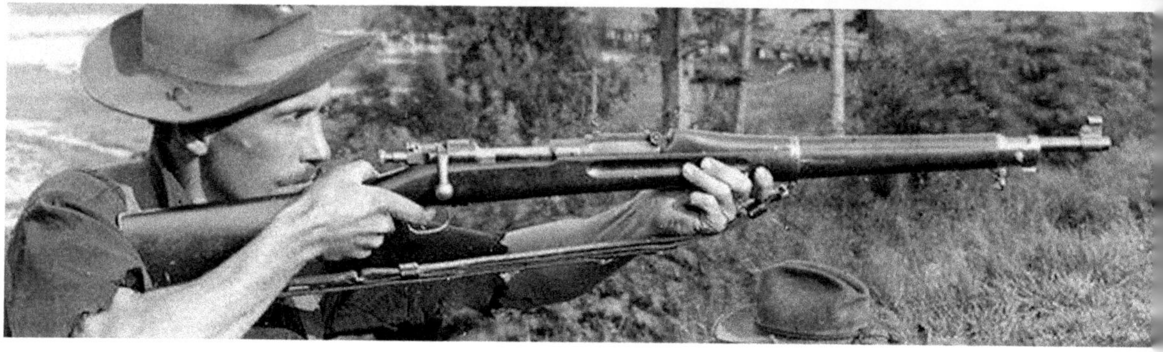

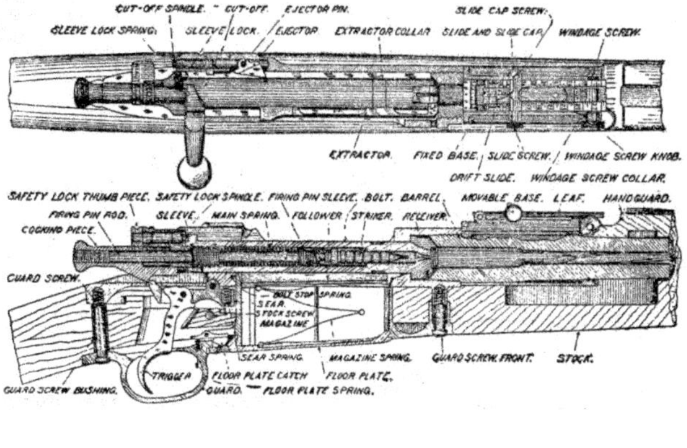

1917

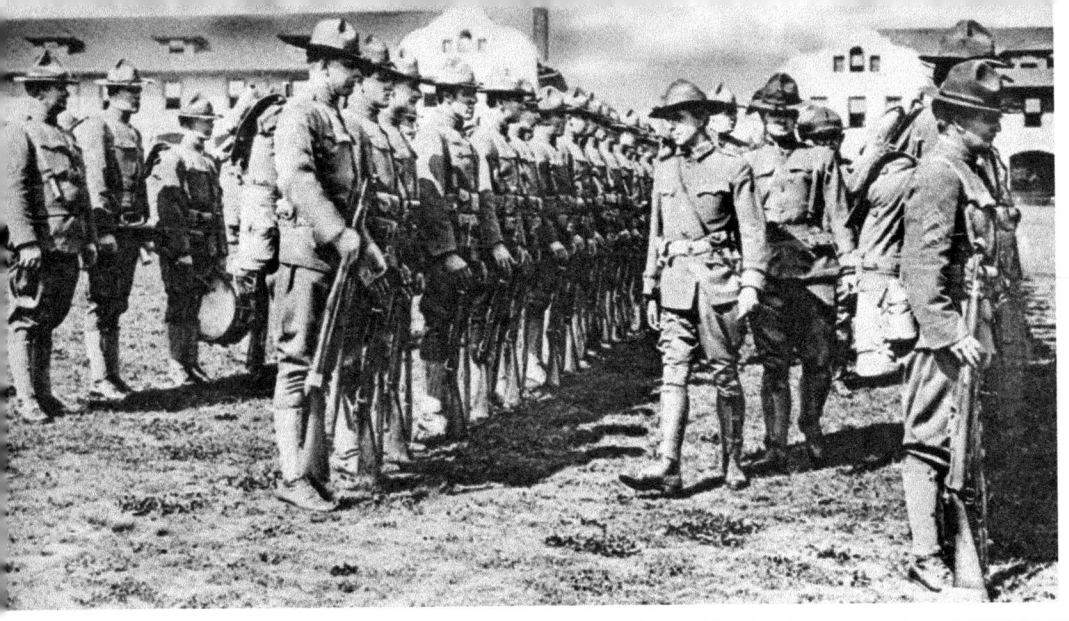

17GW829 Men ready for France wearing full field equipment except steel helmets and gas masks.

17GW828 Bayonet practice at Plattsburg city, New York State.

17GW830 Recruits towards the end of their training are being taught how to set the sights on the Springfield rifle.

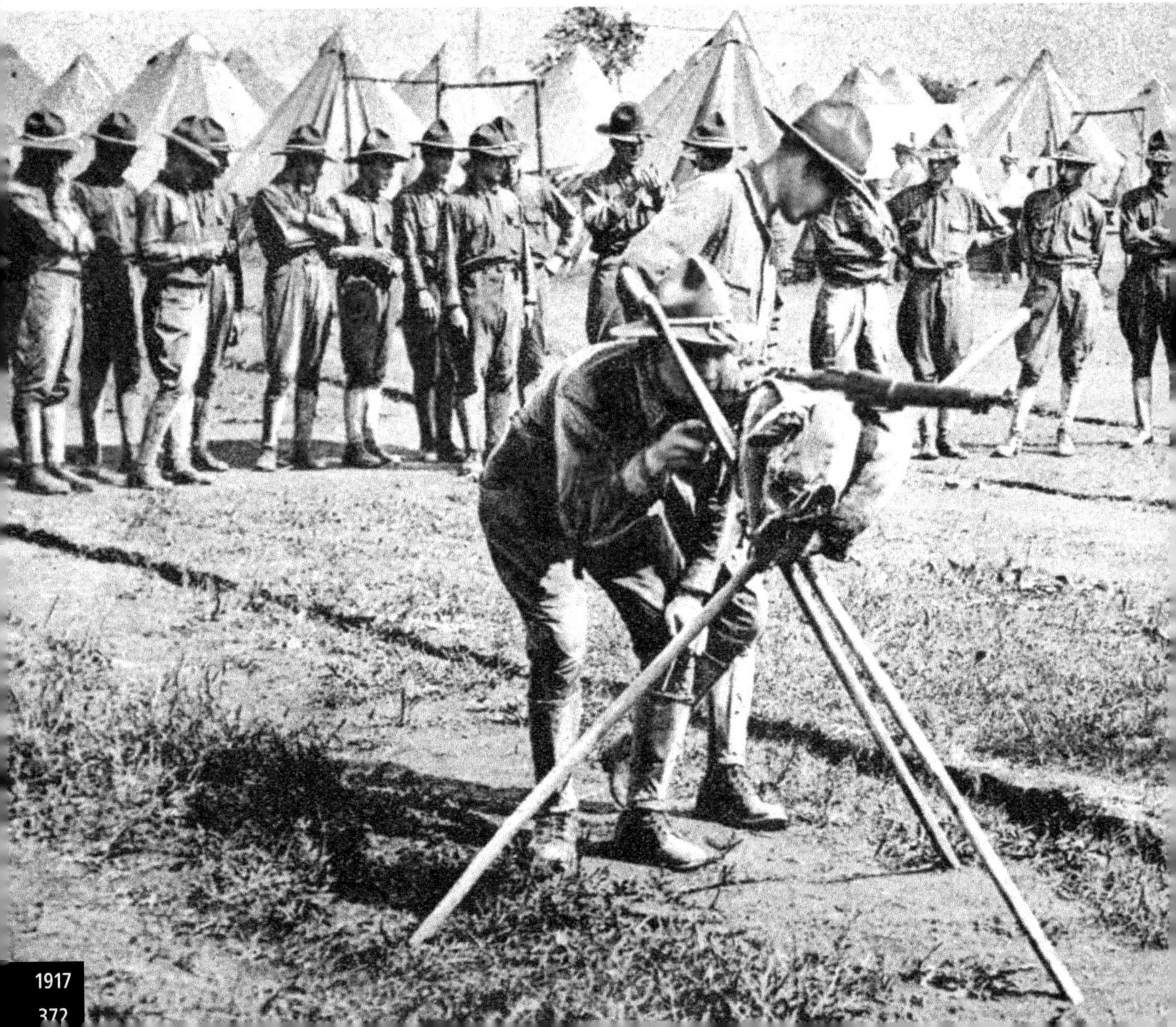

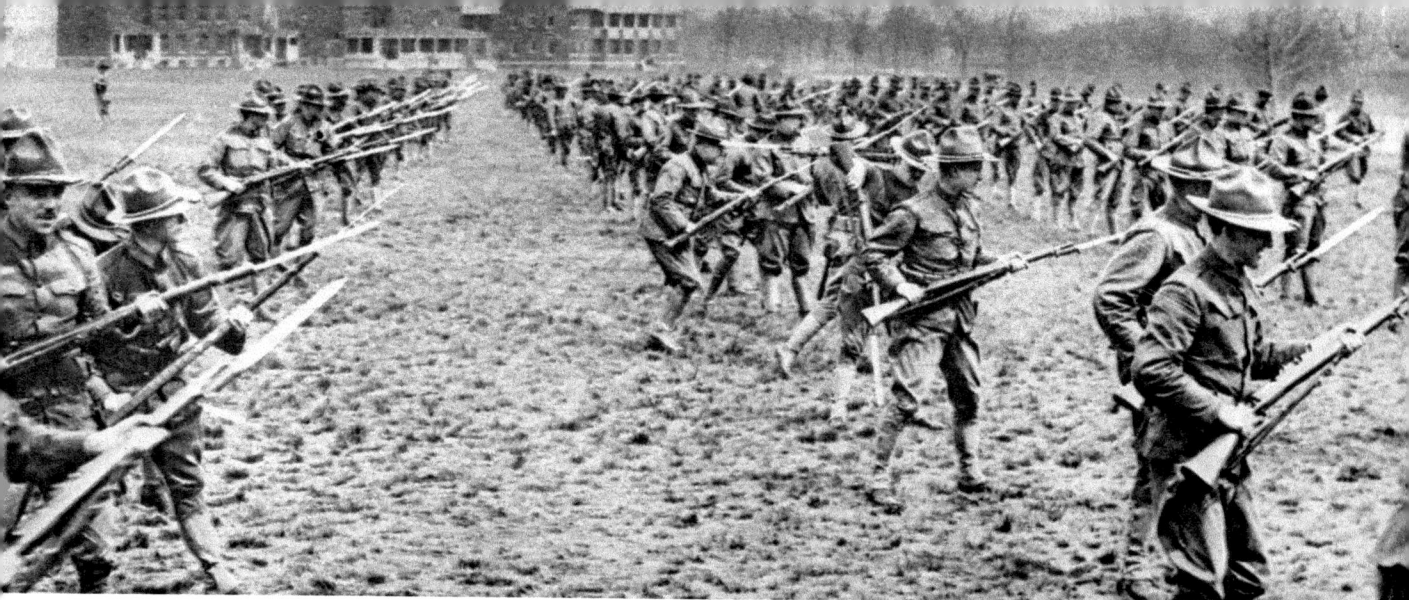

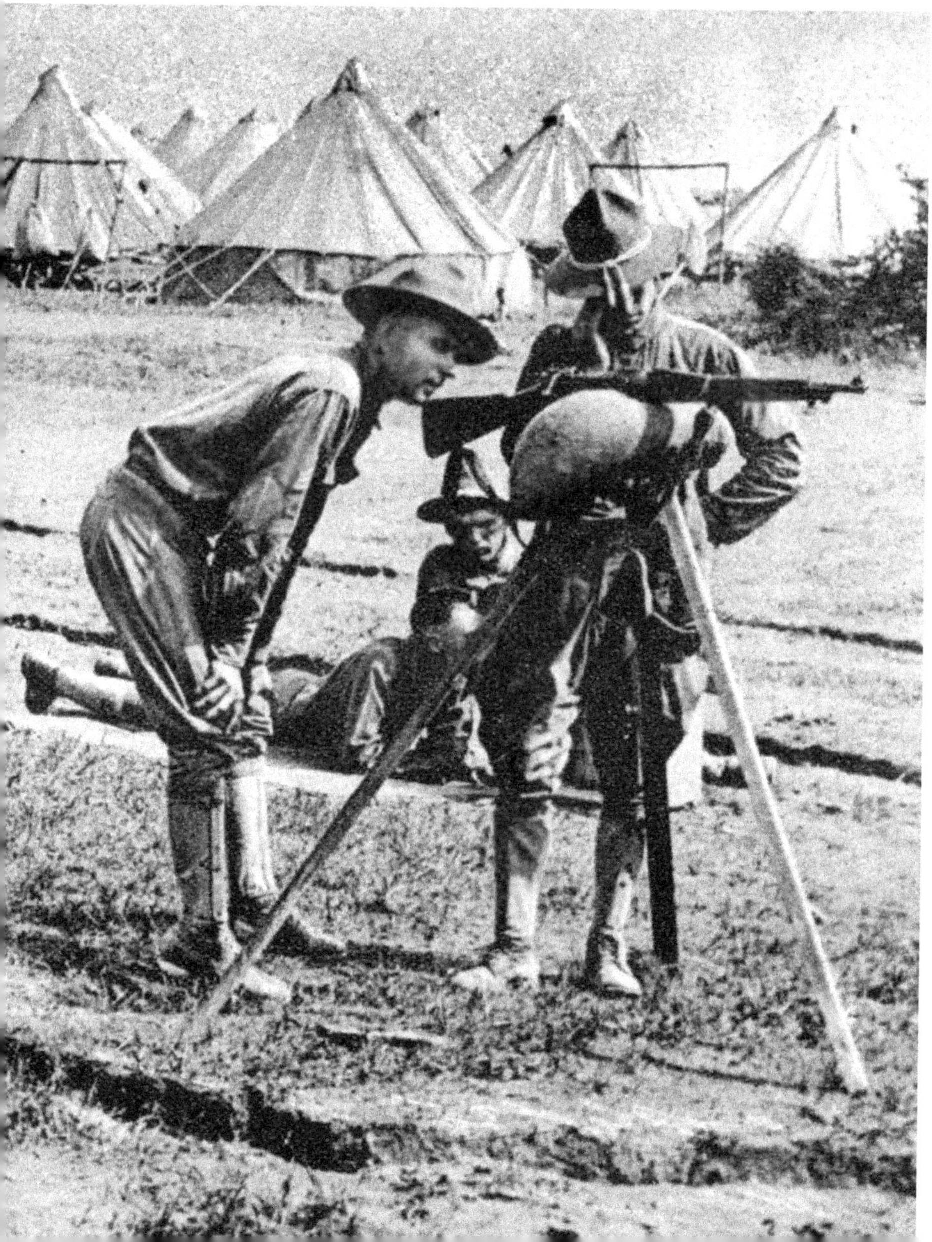

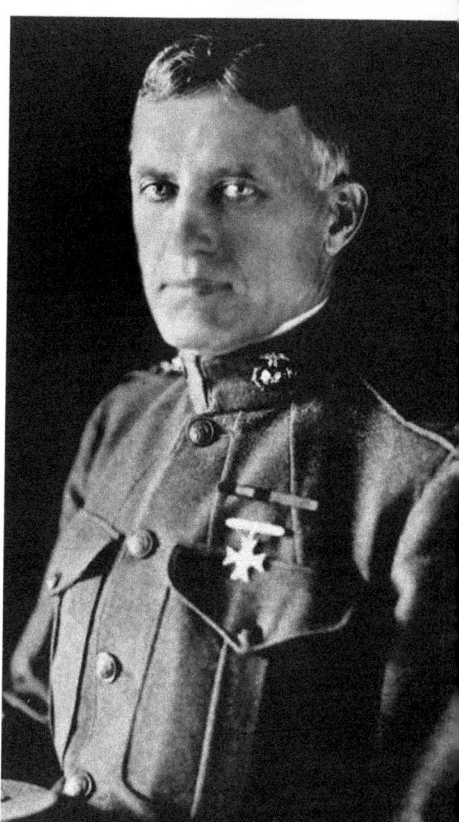

17GW832 Colonel Charles A. Doyen, commanded the 5th Regiment of Marines (a US regiment was equivelent to a British brigade). The formation was activated on 8 June 1917 in Philadelphia and immediately deployed to France.

17GW831 Soldiers learning the most necessary words and phrases in the French language – requesting bread and issuing a challenge. Likely the doughboys would have their own list of French language phrases they were intending to use.

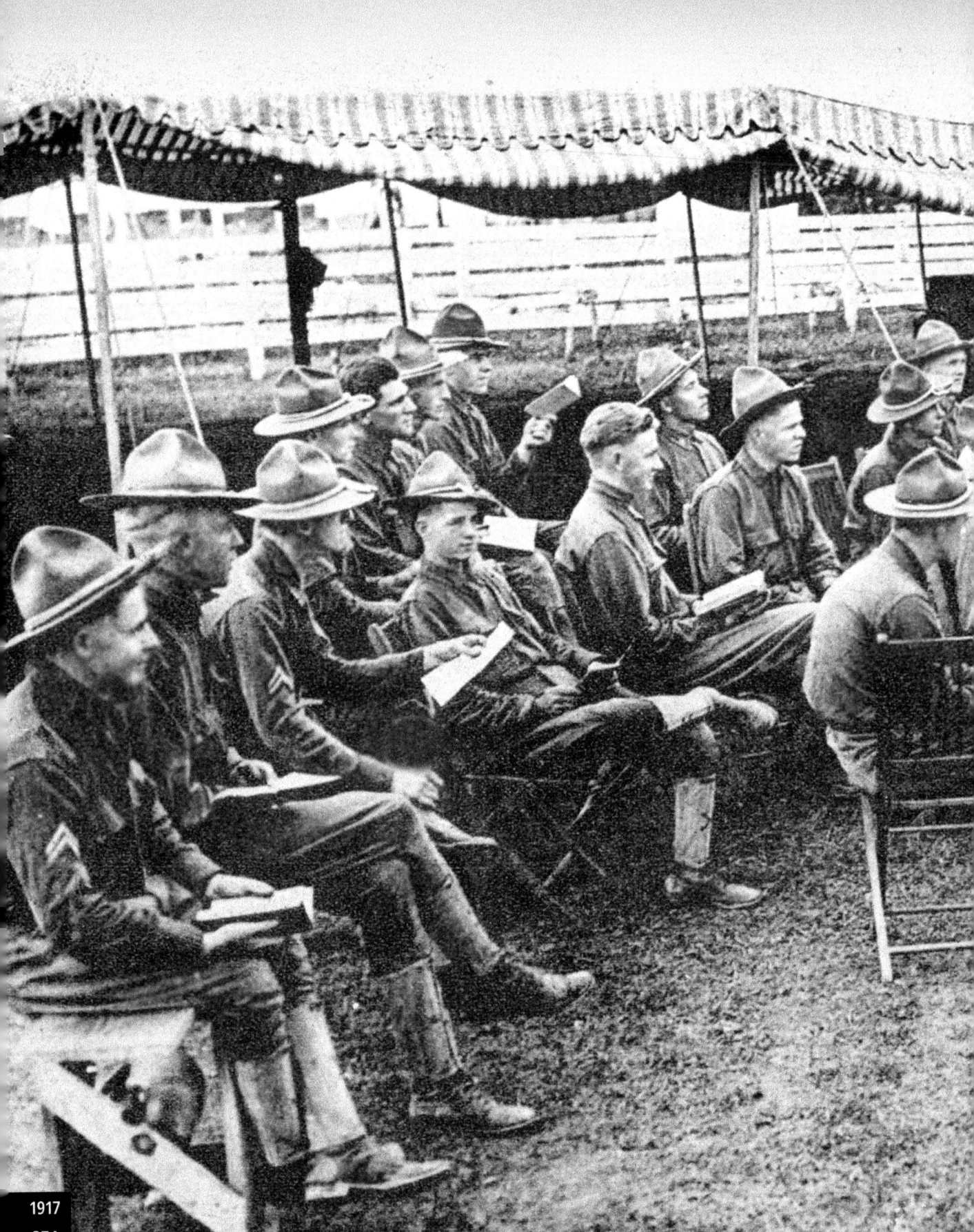

Donnez moi du pain
(Give me some bread)
1. Qui va la? (Who goes there?)
2. Qui vive? (Who goes there?)
  (1) Challenge for civilians
  (2)   "   " soldiers
Ans: "America" (name of unit)

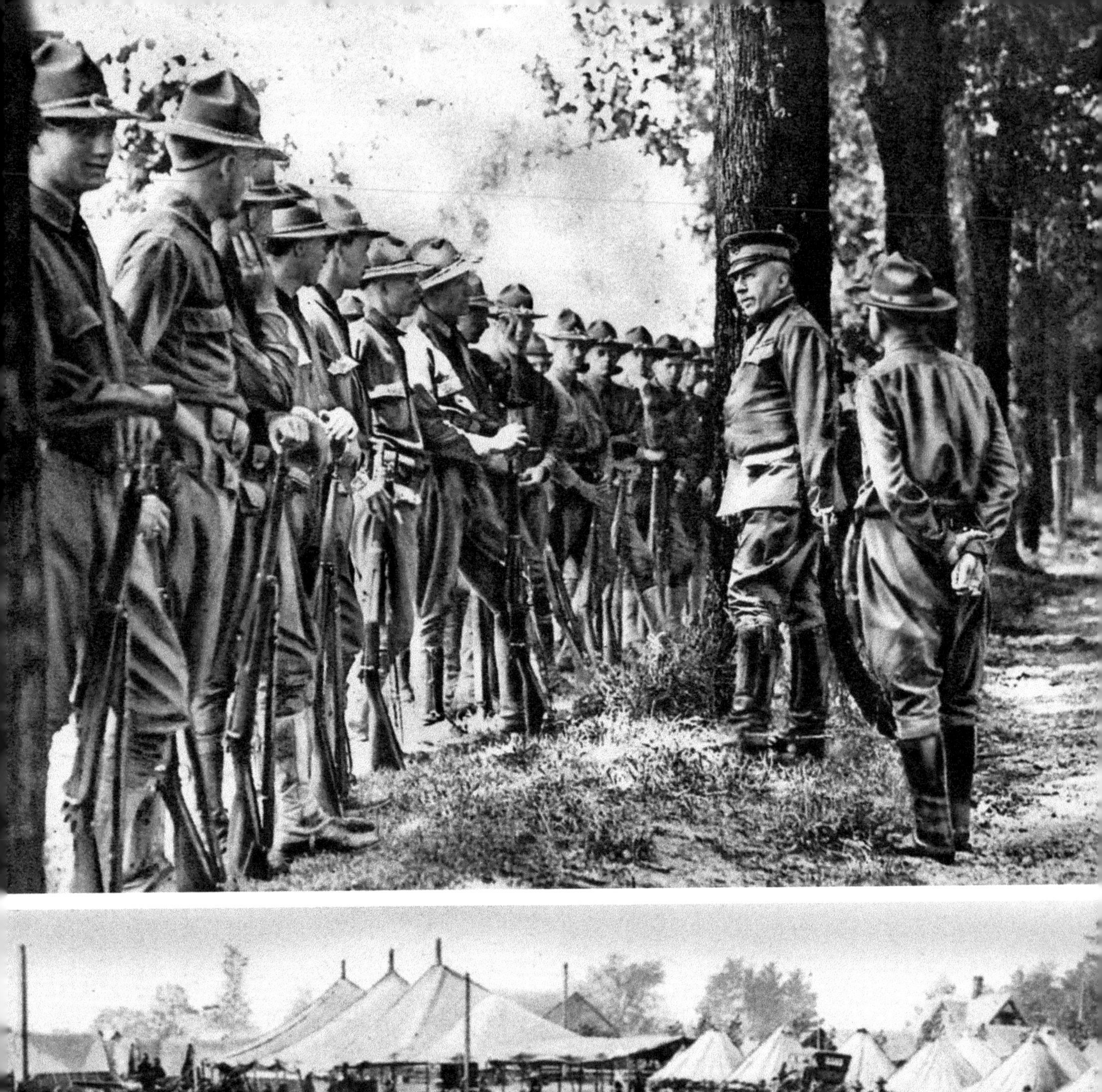

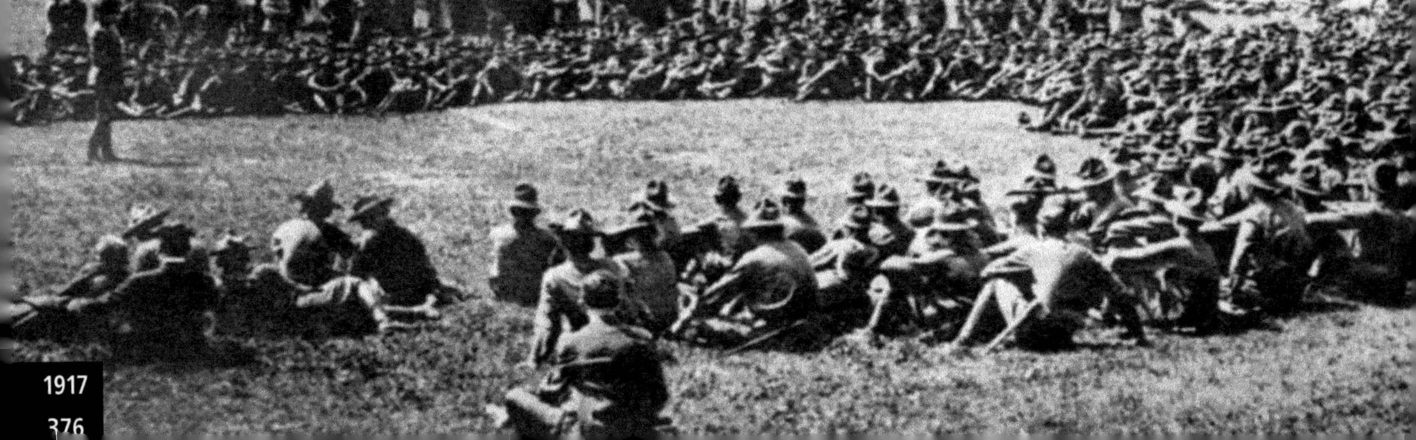

1917

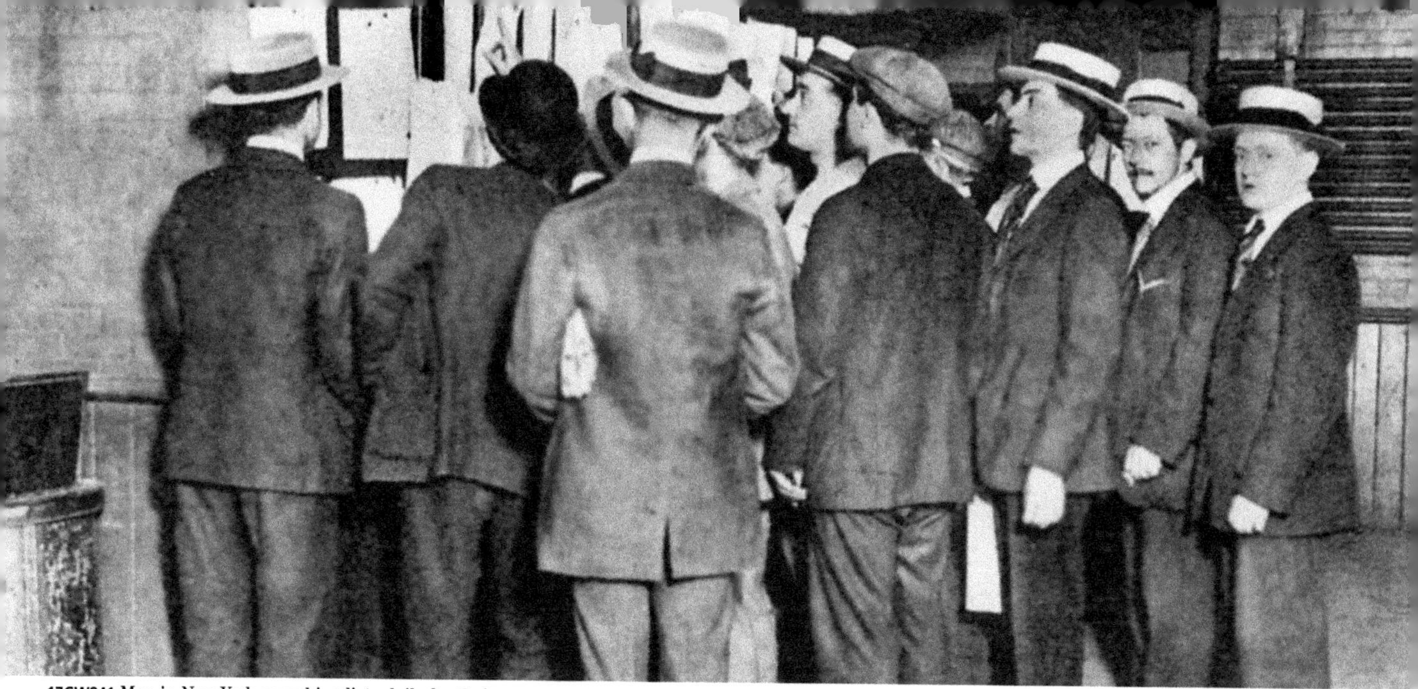

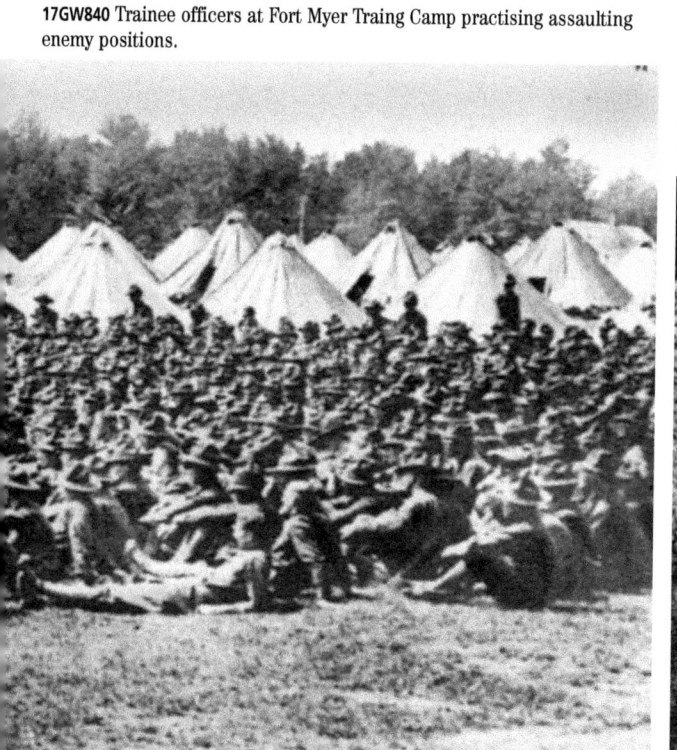

17GW841 Men in New York searching lists daily for their names in the America's biggest lottery. Blind folded, the Secretary of State picked out a number of names from the 4,577 selected draft districts. As the numbers were drawn lists were posted throughout the country.

17GW839 Trainee officers being addressed by Major General Wood at Fort McPherson, First Officer's Training Camp, Plattsburg. Officer cadets at an open air lecture. Making an officer took three months training.

17GW843, 17GW844. Major Theodore Roosevelt III, directing a group of officer candidates to the officers' mess at Plattsburg Camp. Major Roosevelt went to France with the First Division; he was wounded, decorated and returned home a lieutenant colonel. He was posthumously awarded the Medal of Honor in the Second World War, having died of a heart attack in Normandy.

17GW840 Trainee officers at Fort Myer Traing Camp practising assaulting enemy positions.

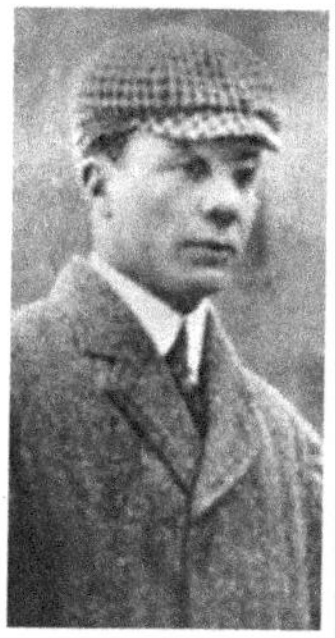

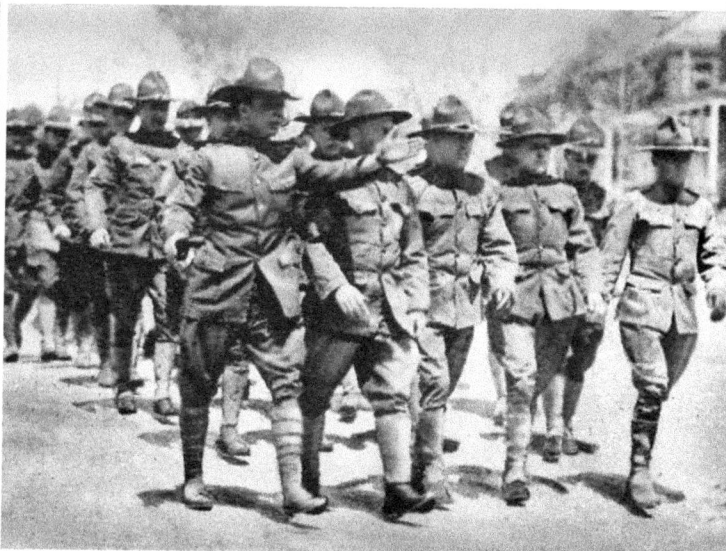

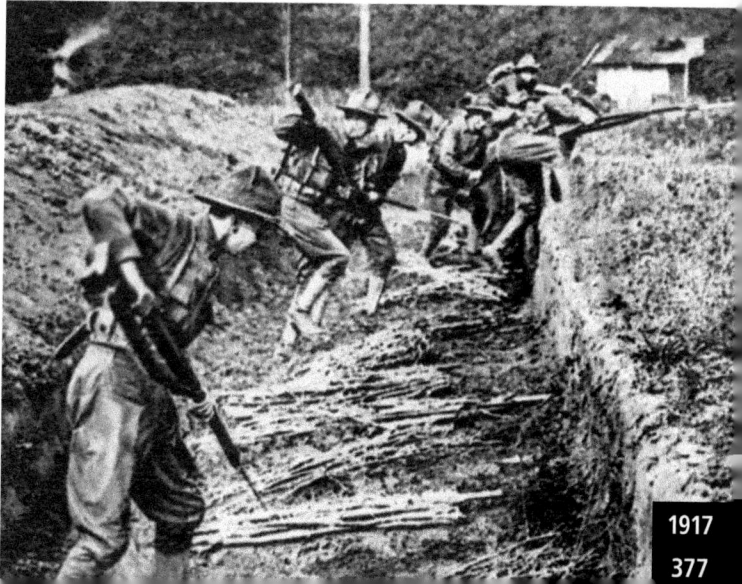

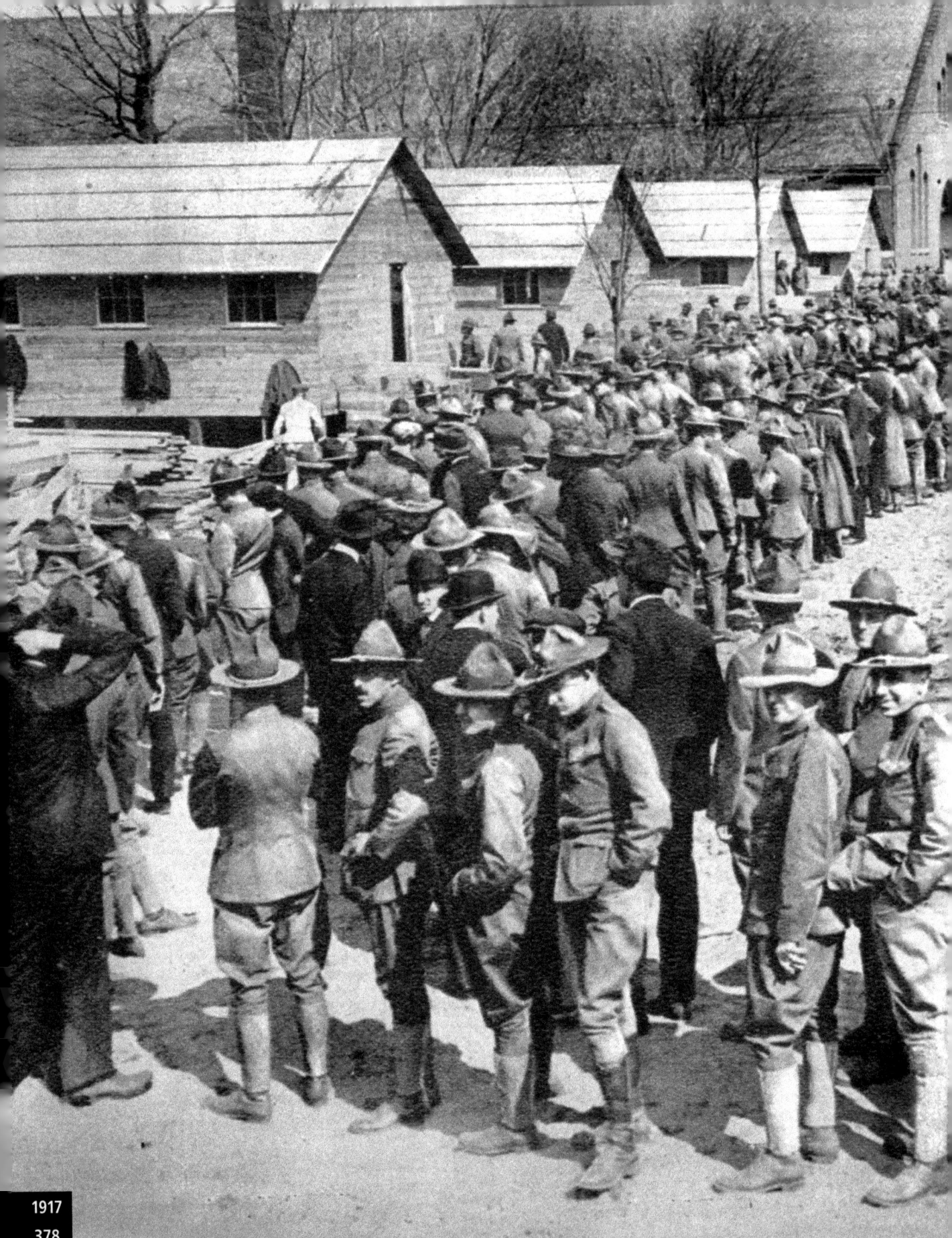

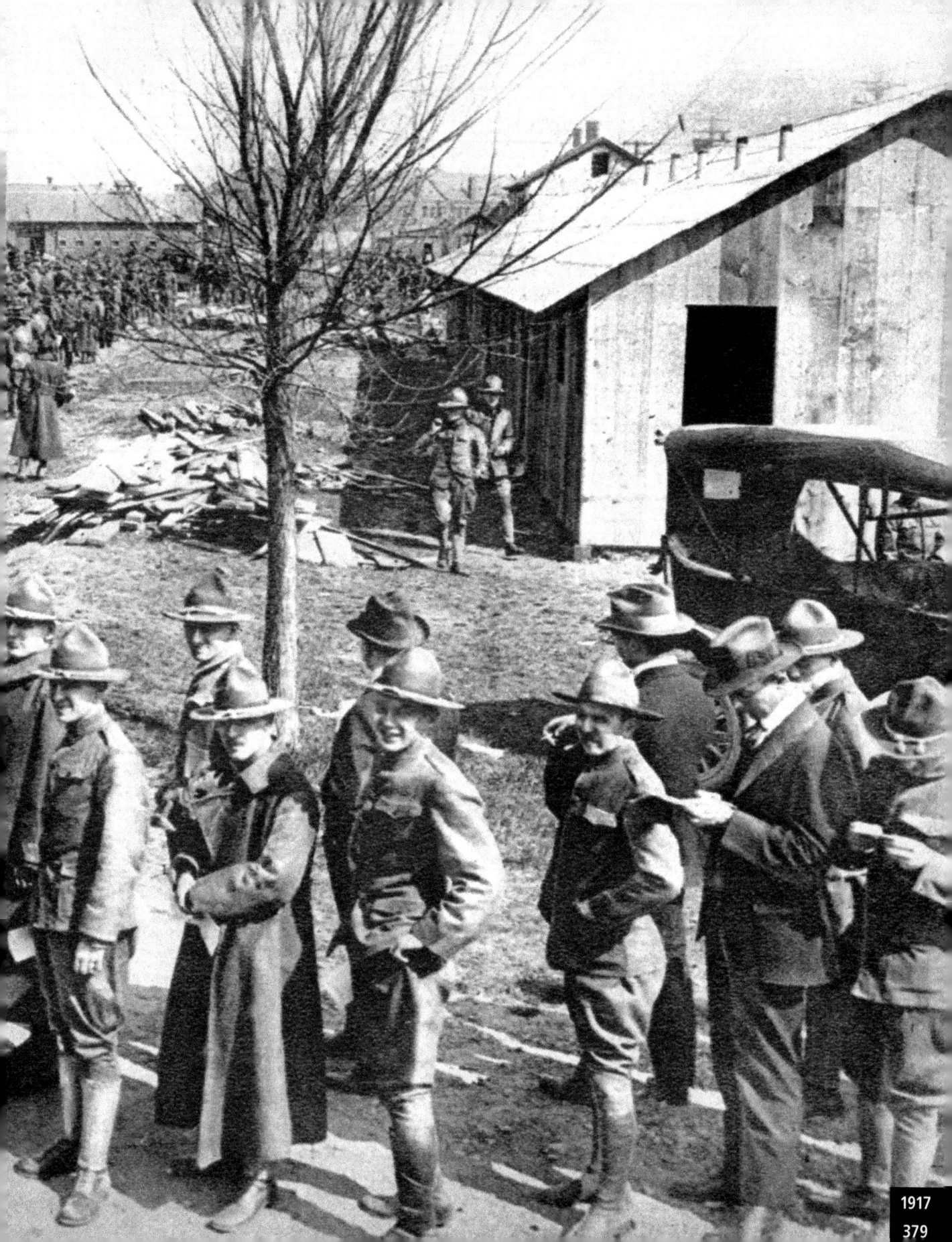

17GW846, 17GW845 More arrivals at the First Officer's Training Camp, Plattsburg. men queuing for their equipment to be issued; some have not yet been fitted with their uniforms. An overall view of the officers' training camp shows construction of huts is still underway.

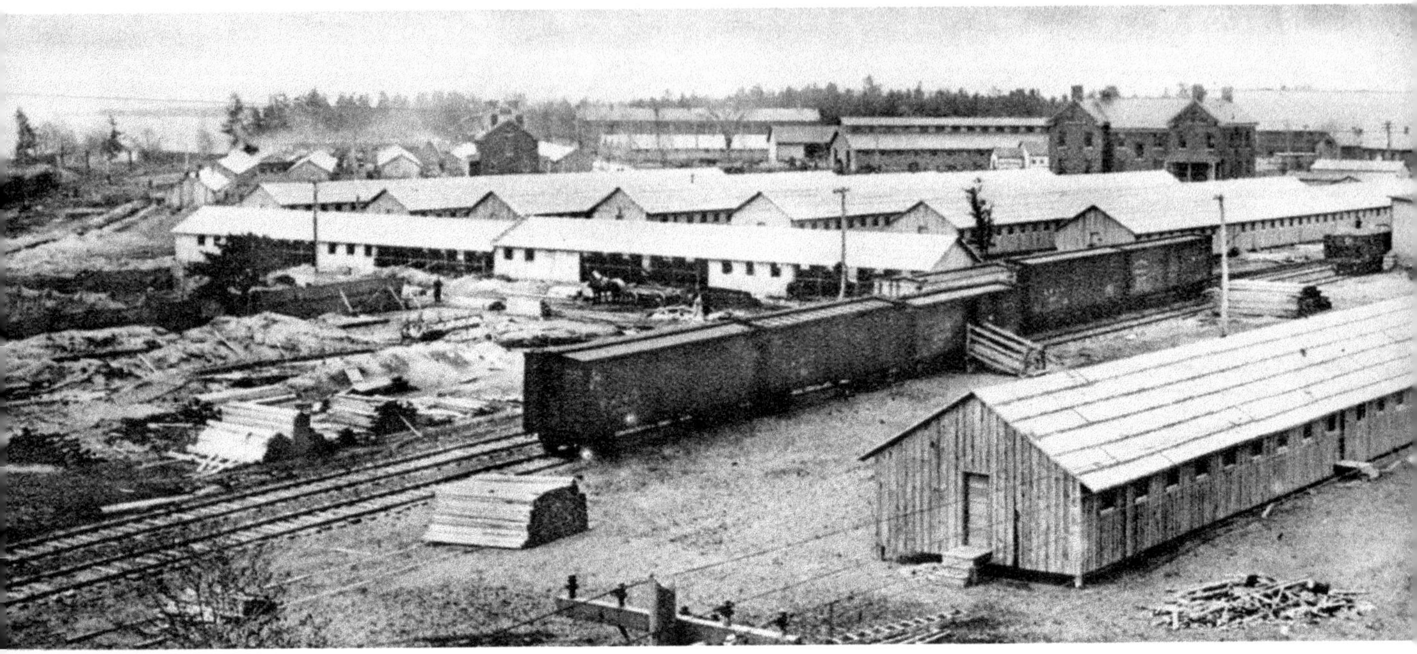

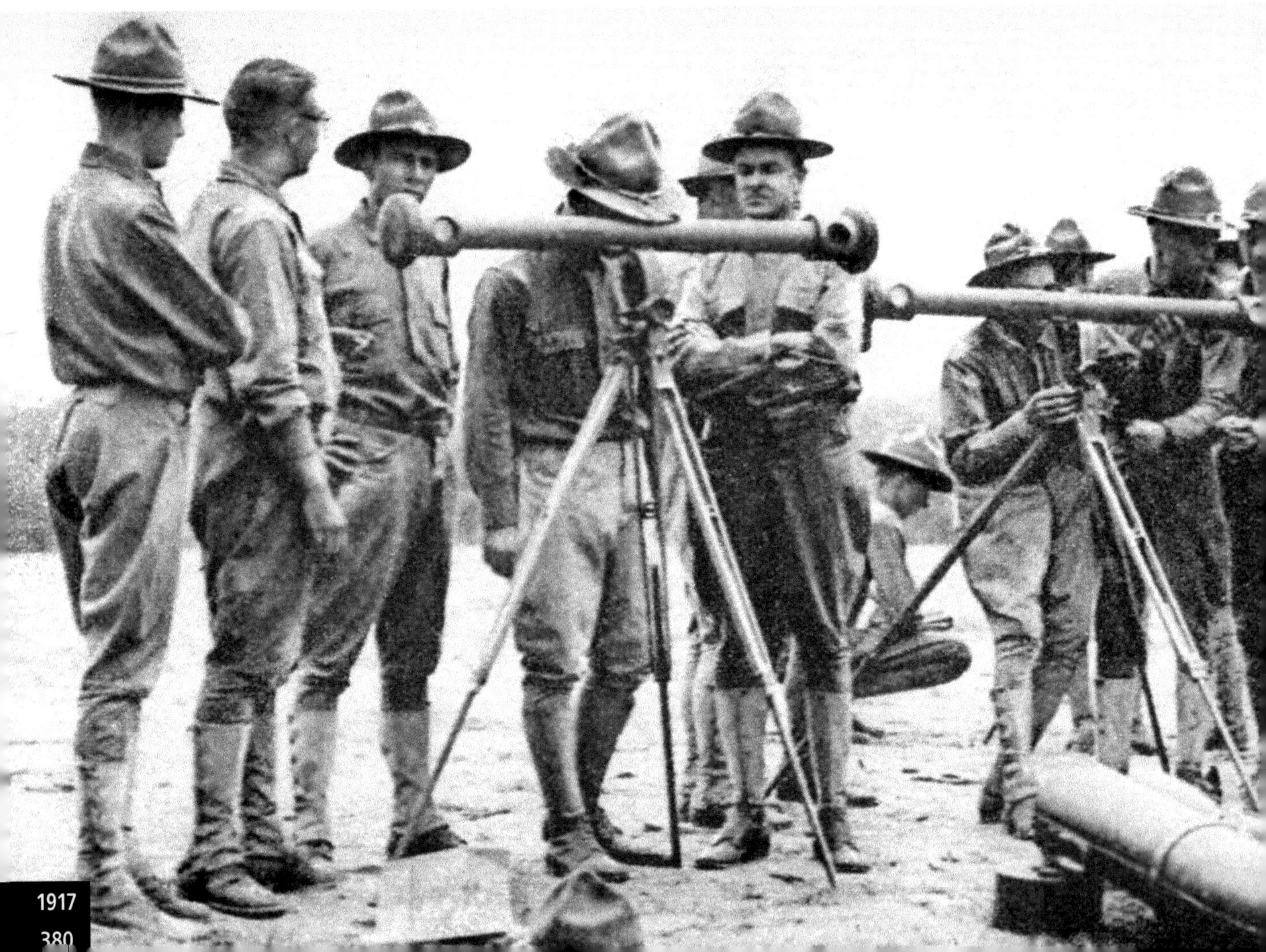

17GW849 A 4.7 inch howitzer. These pieces would be left behind in the United States as the guns would be supplied in europe by France and Britain. This saved shipping space on the Atlantic crossing.

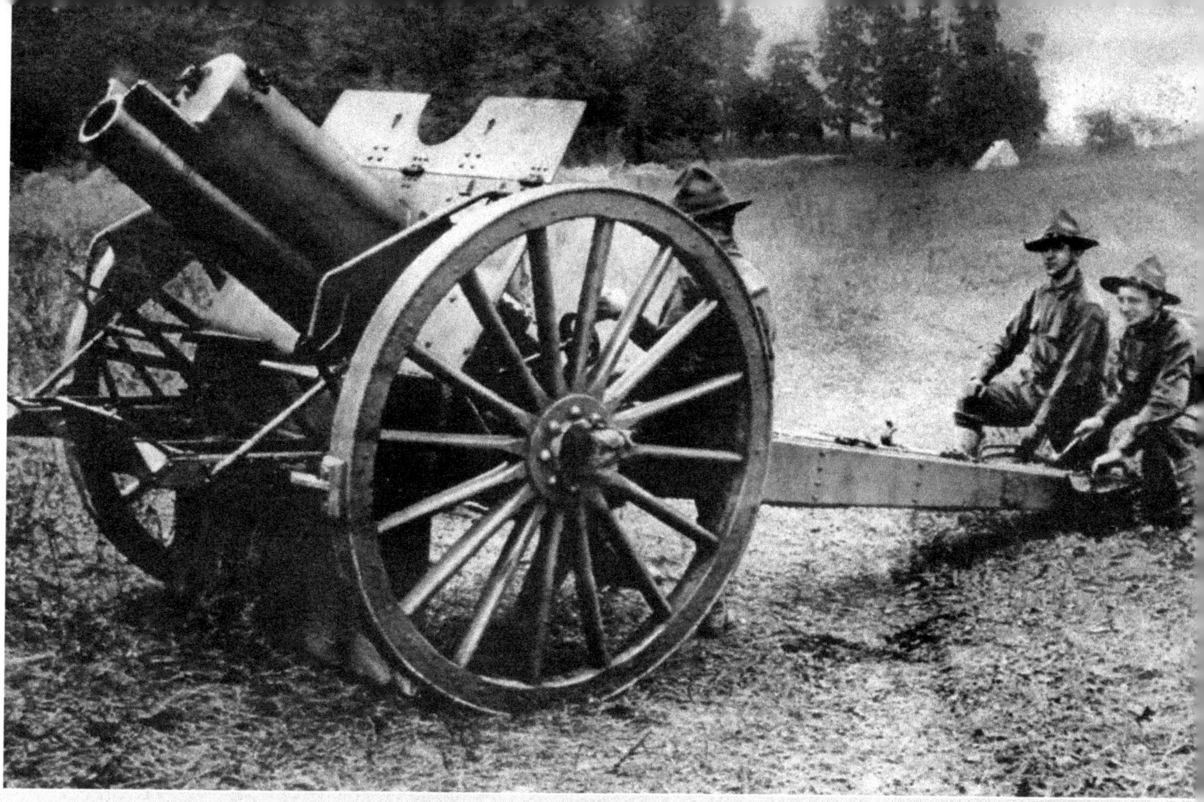

17GW847 Officers at Fort McPherson Training Camp, Georgia using artillery range finders during qualification sessions.

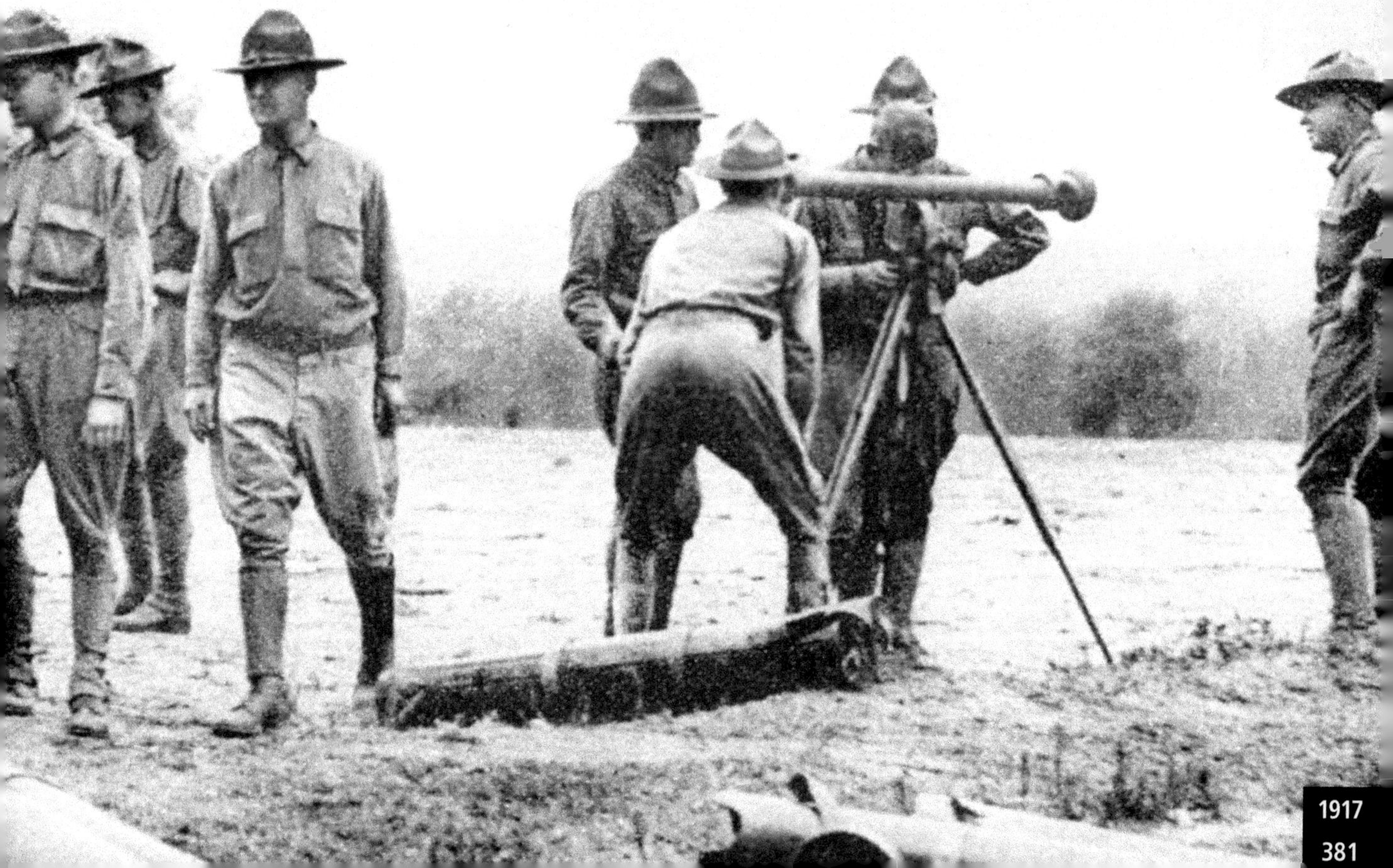

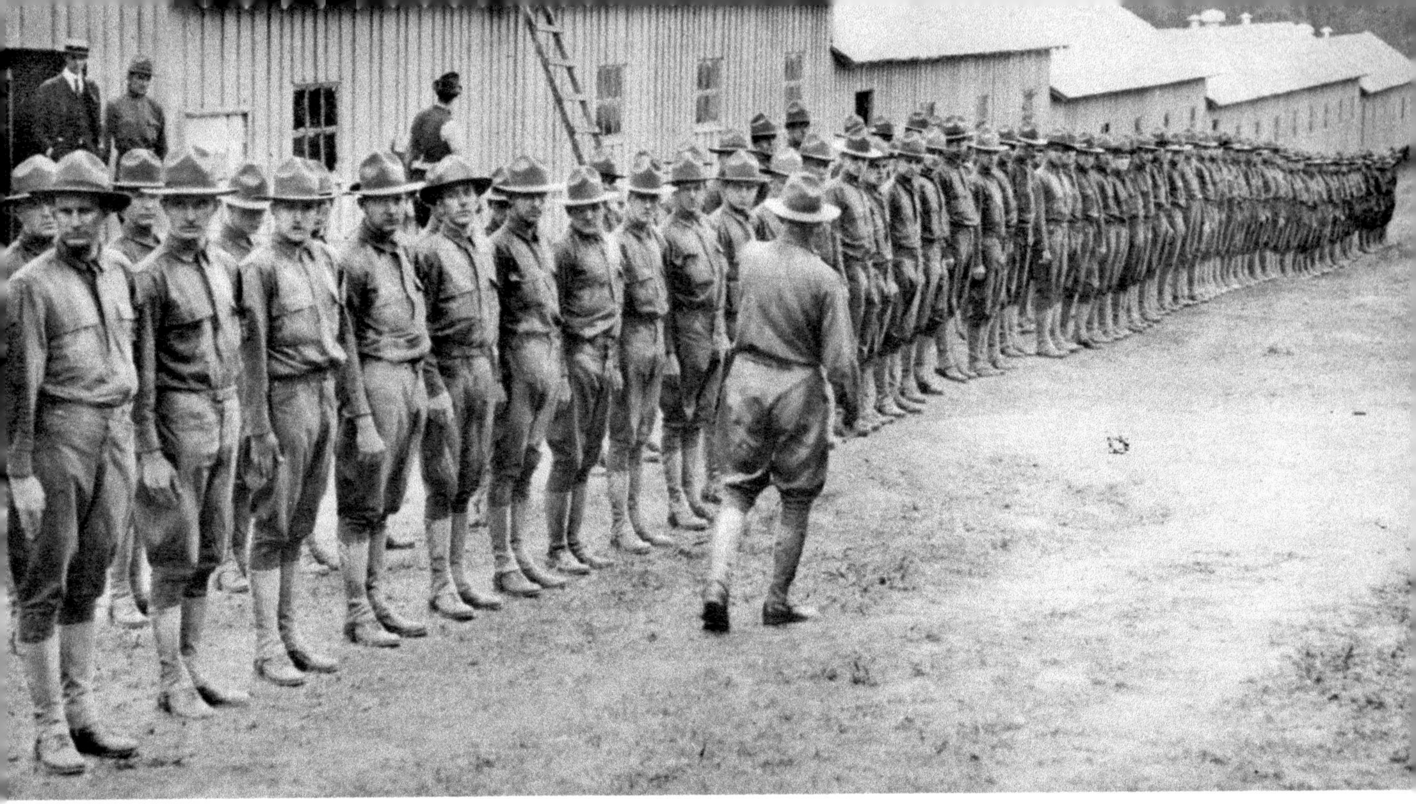

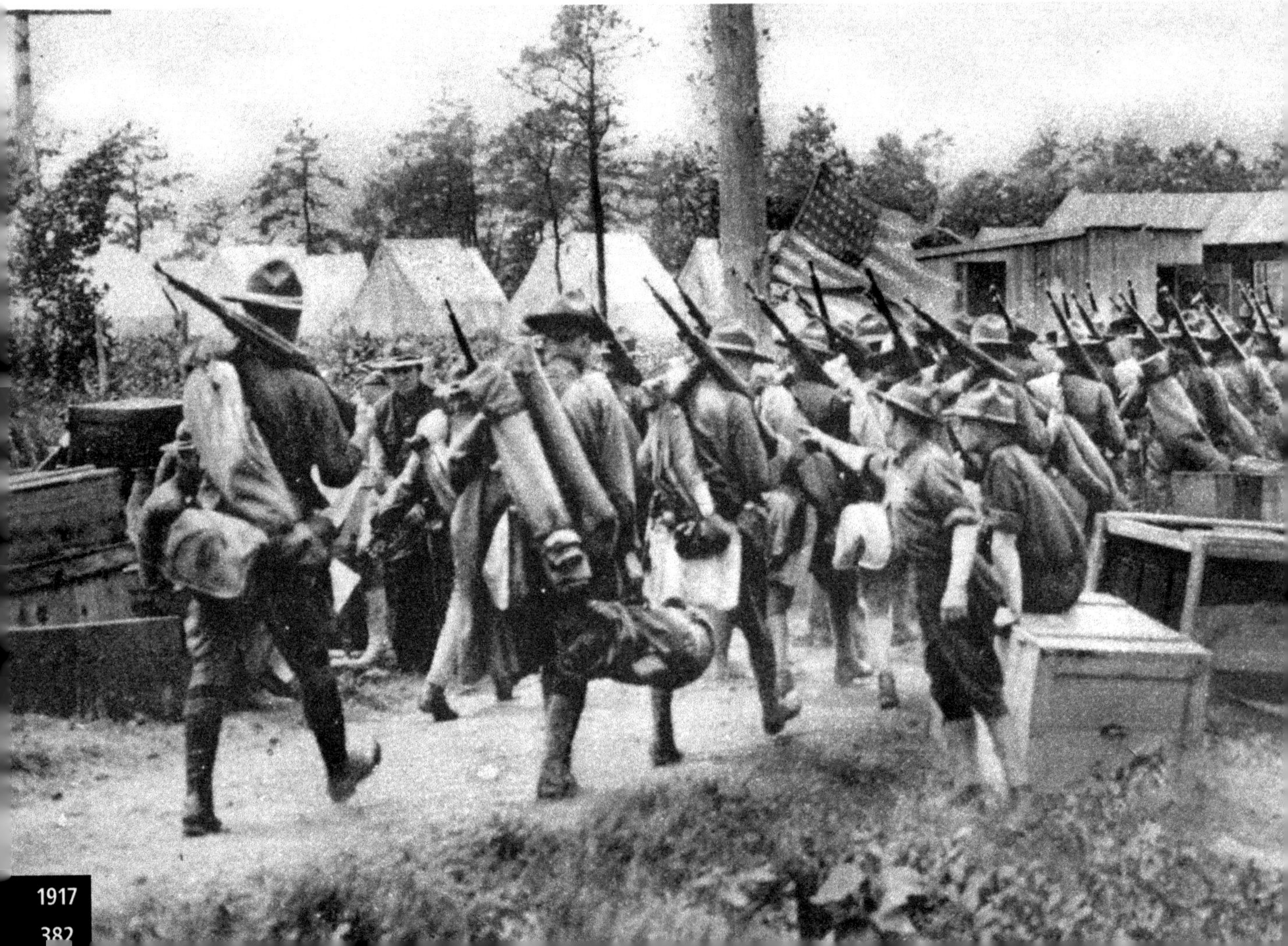

1917

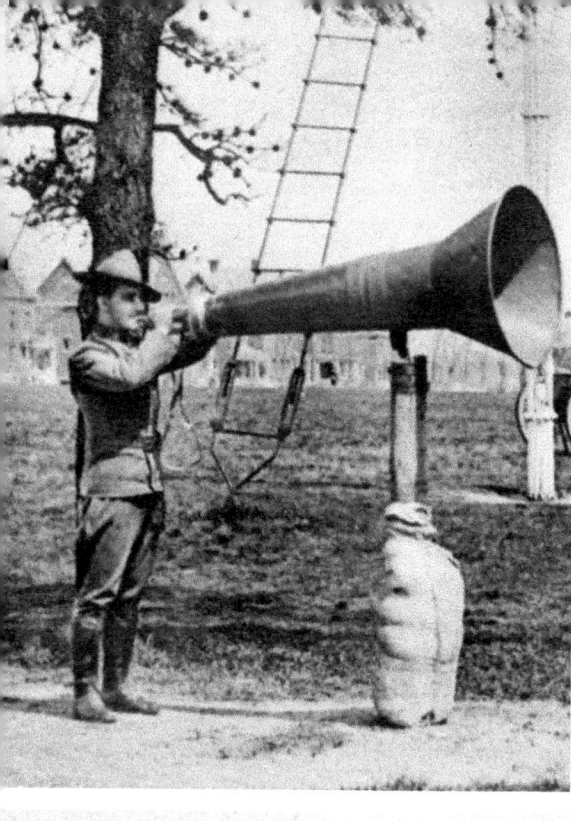

17GW850 More officers in the making lined up at Fort McPherson, East Point, southwest of Atlanta, Georgia.

17GW851 Getting the trainee officers out of their beds at 5.30 am, Plattsburg. The bugler has the aid of a megaphone to enhance his bugle sounding Reveille.

17GW848 The 5th Maryland Guards arriving at Yaphank Camp, Long Island, New York, where one of sixteen cantonments to train the new draft army was being constructed.

17GW852 Trainee officers at Fort Sheridan, Illinois, engaged in sighting drill among huts under construction.

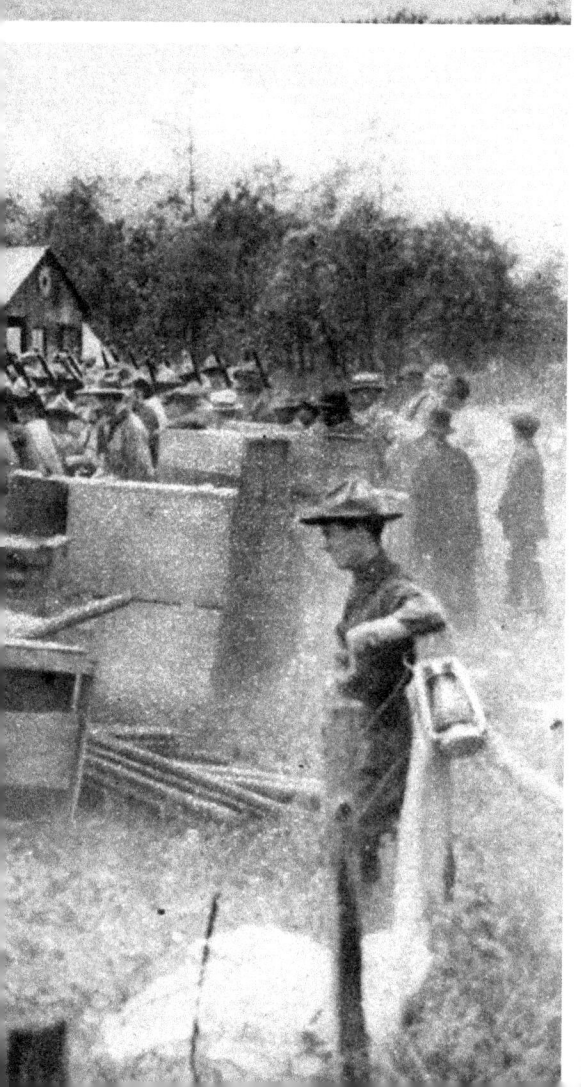

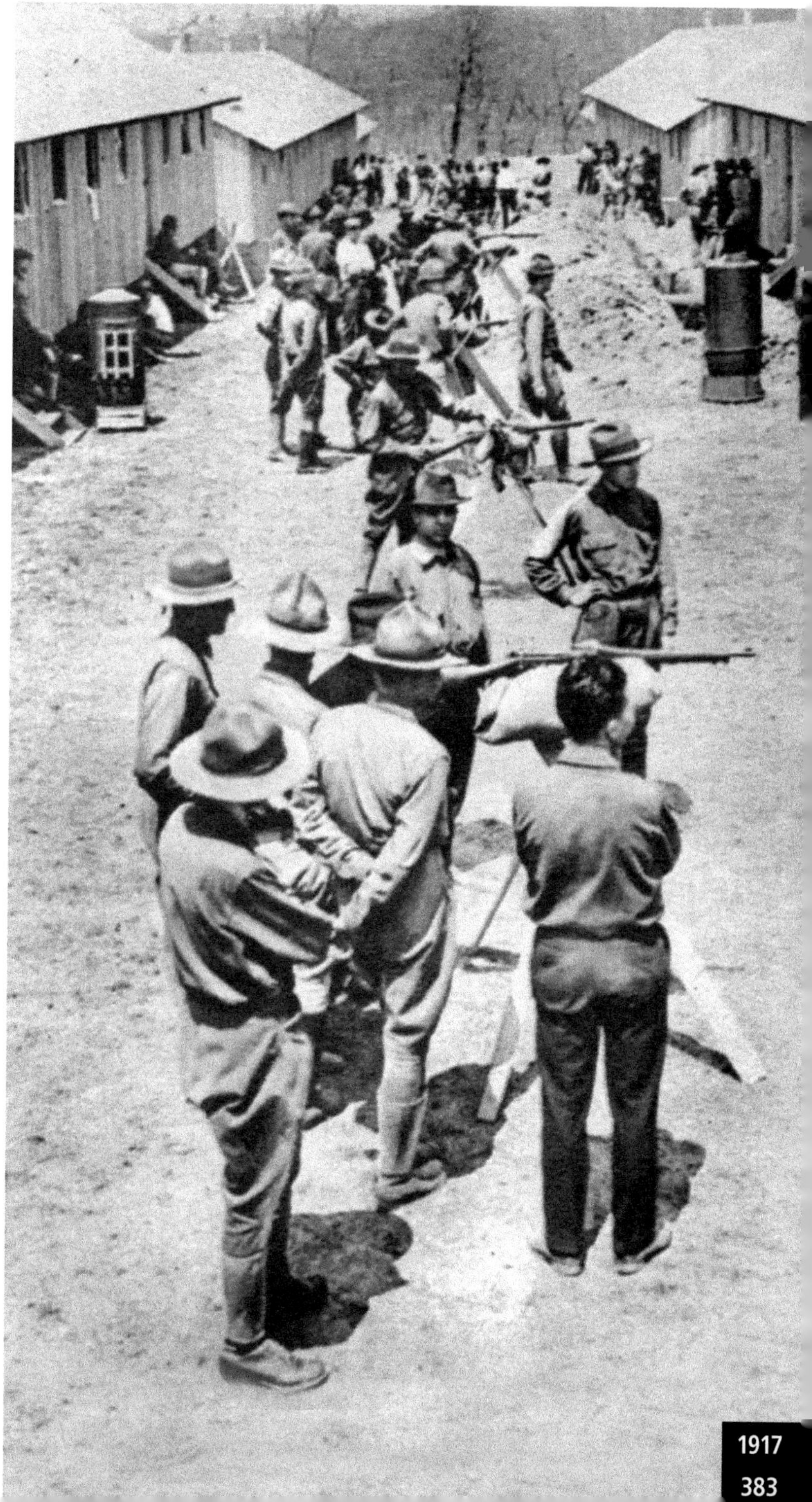

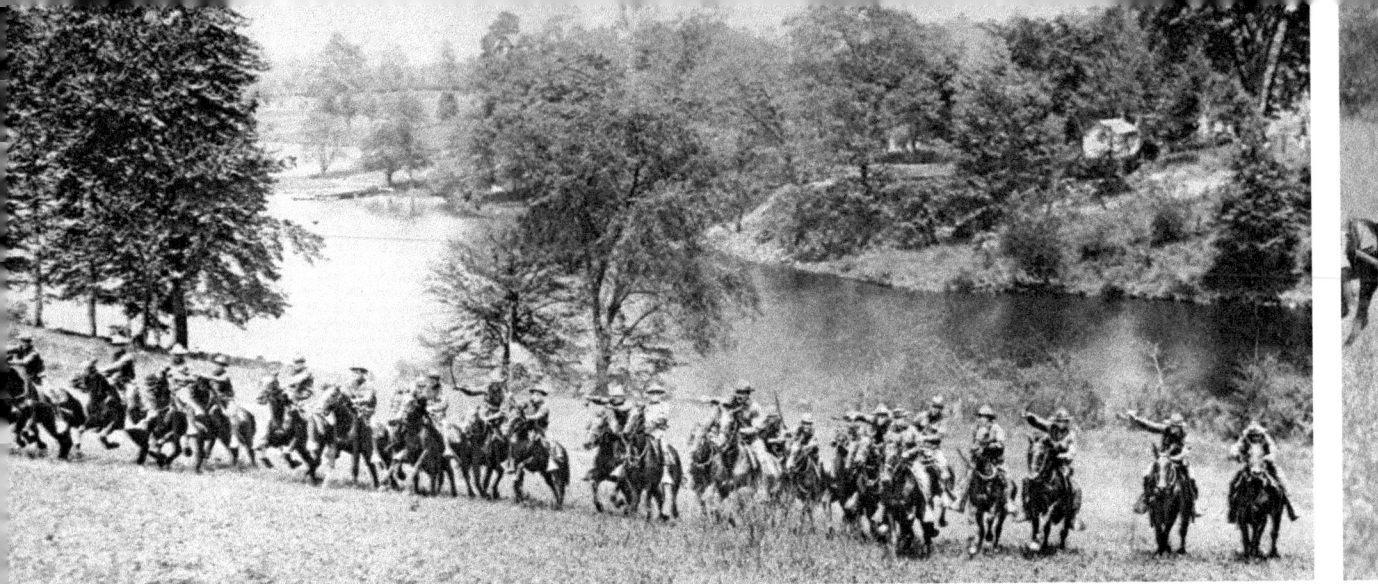

17GW855, 17GW853. F Troop First Cavalry, New York National Guard, reliving the past on Staten Island, New York. Opportunities to charge the enemy in modern twentieth century conflict would be rare – and highly risky against machine guns and massed artillery fire.

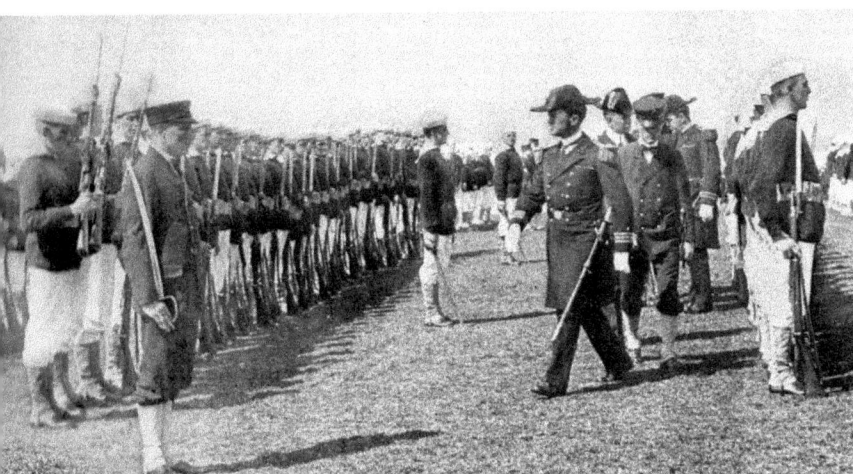

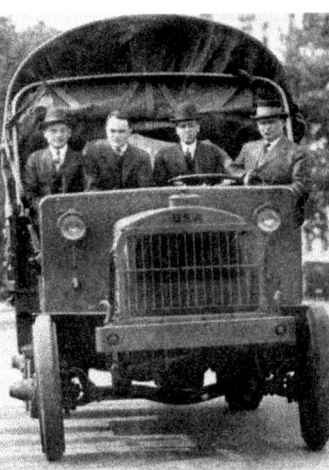

17GW858 Captain's inspection of new recruits at the Naval Training Station, Newport, Rhode Island. From here men were assigned to war ships.

17GW859 The Secretary of State for War, N. D. Baker, is trying out one of the new Liberty Trucks on the streets of Washington.

17GW854 Men of the American Signal Corps with semaphore flags supposedly signalling, for the cameraman, 'We want to go to France'. This form of signalling had been discontinued by the British Army in Flanders since 1915.

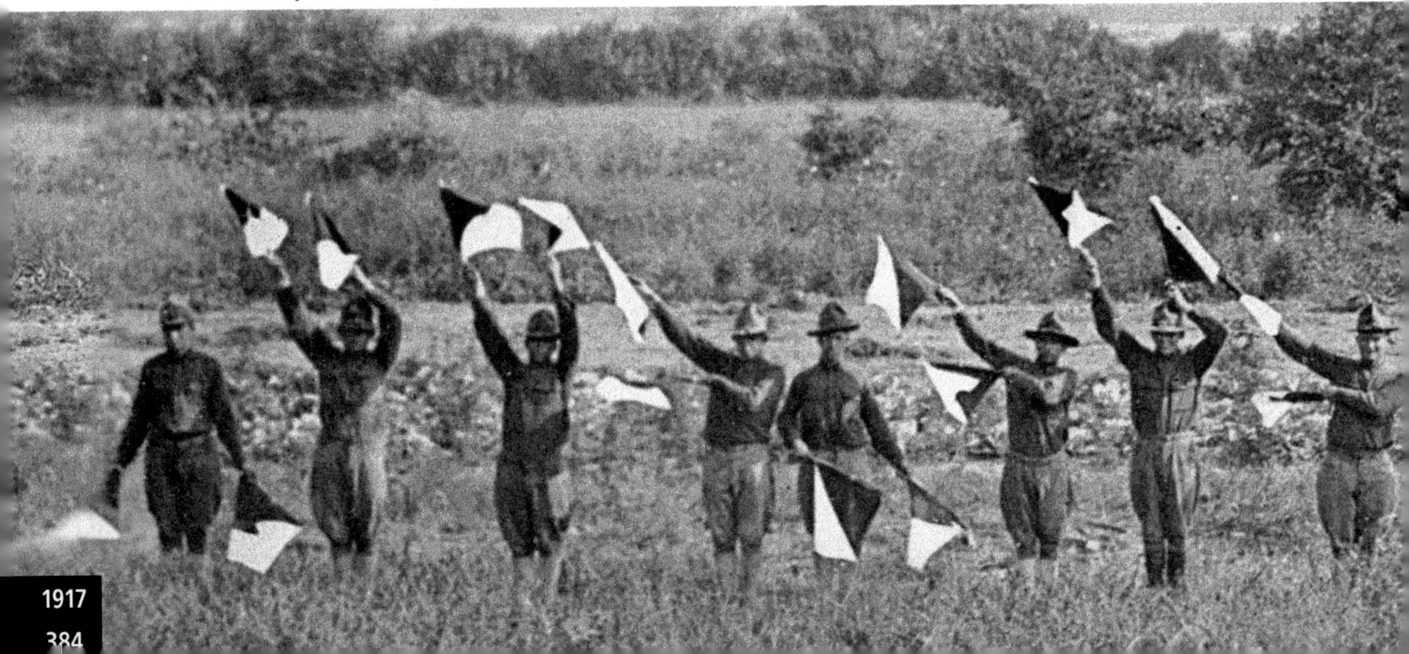

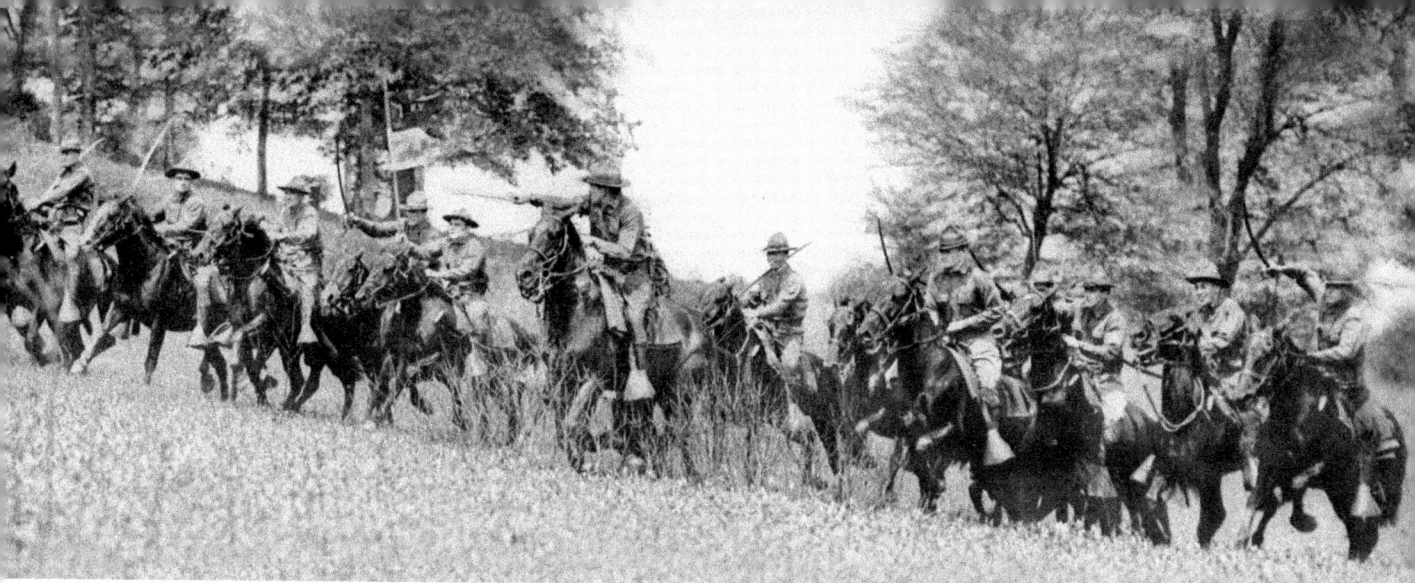

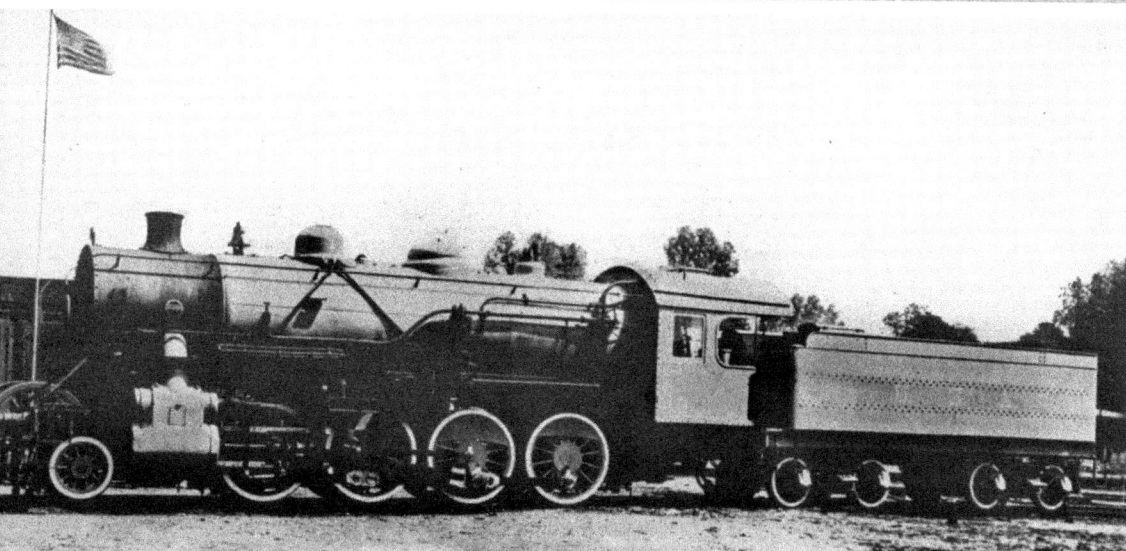

17GW857 An American locomotive for war service in France. Railway engines were turned out by factories for service in europe; as were standard gauge freight cars.

17GW856 Field telephones being set up on the firing range at Camp Devens, Massachusetts, Spring 1917.

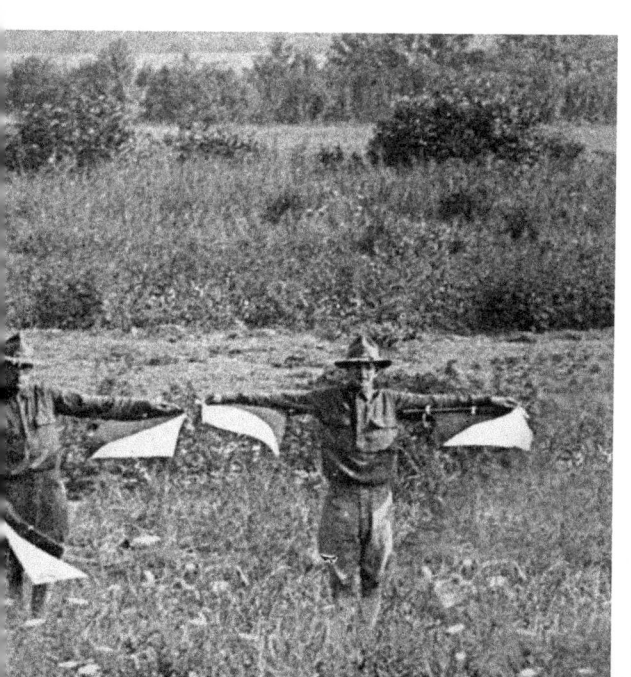

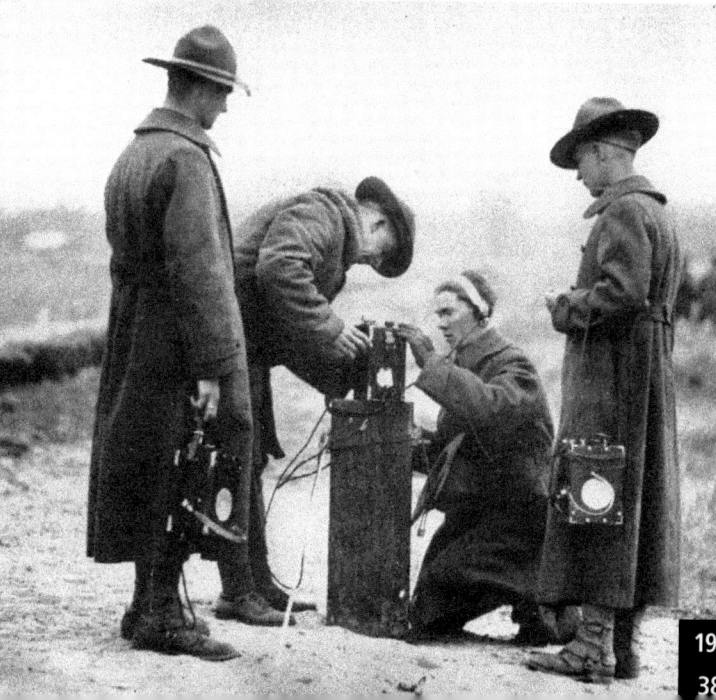

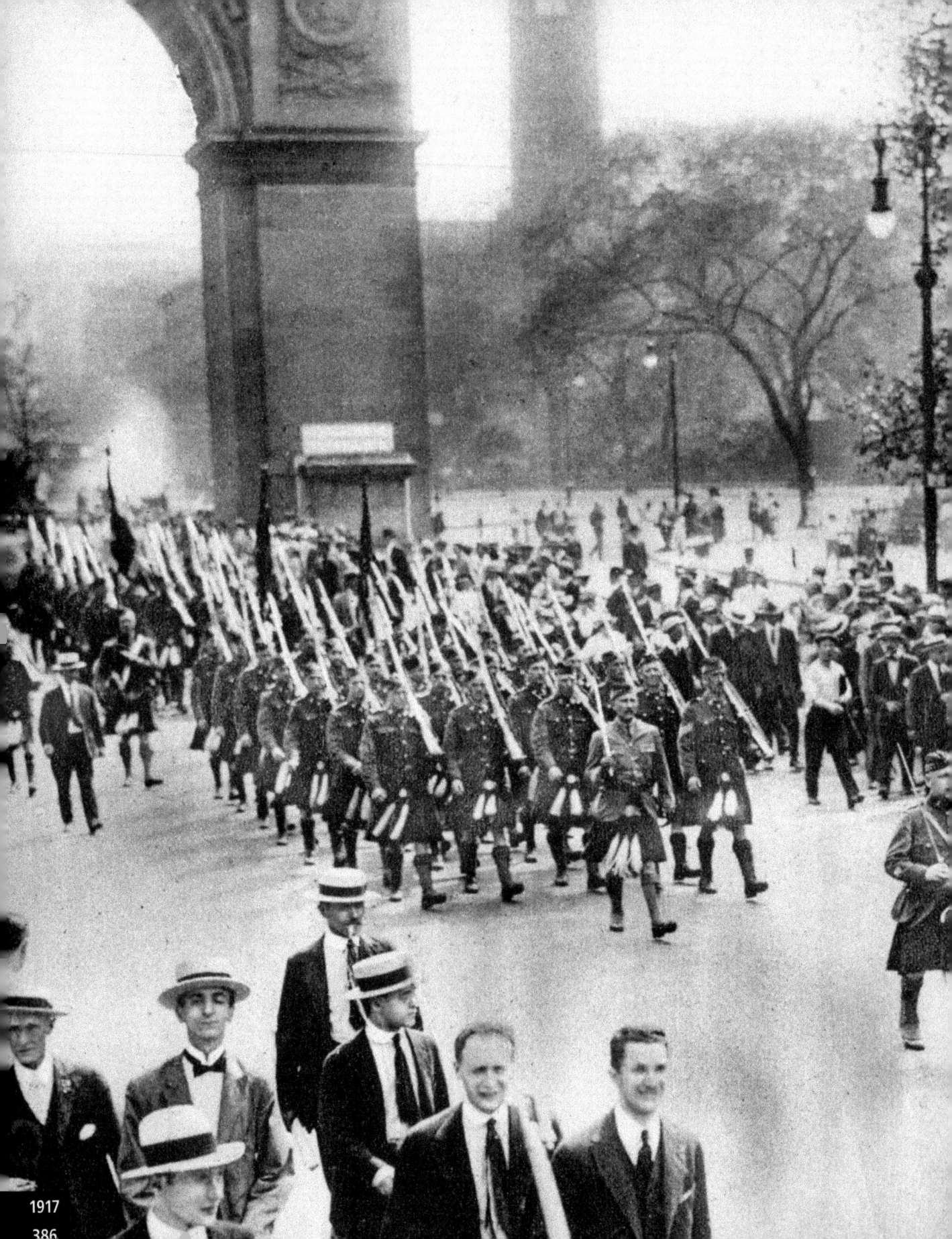

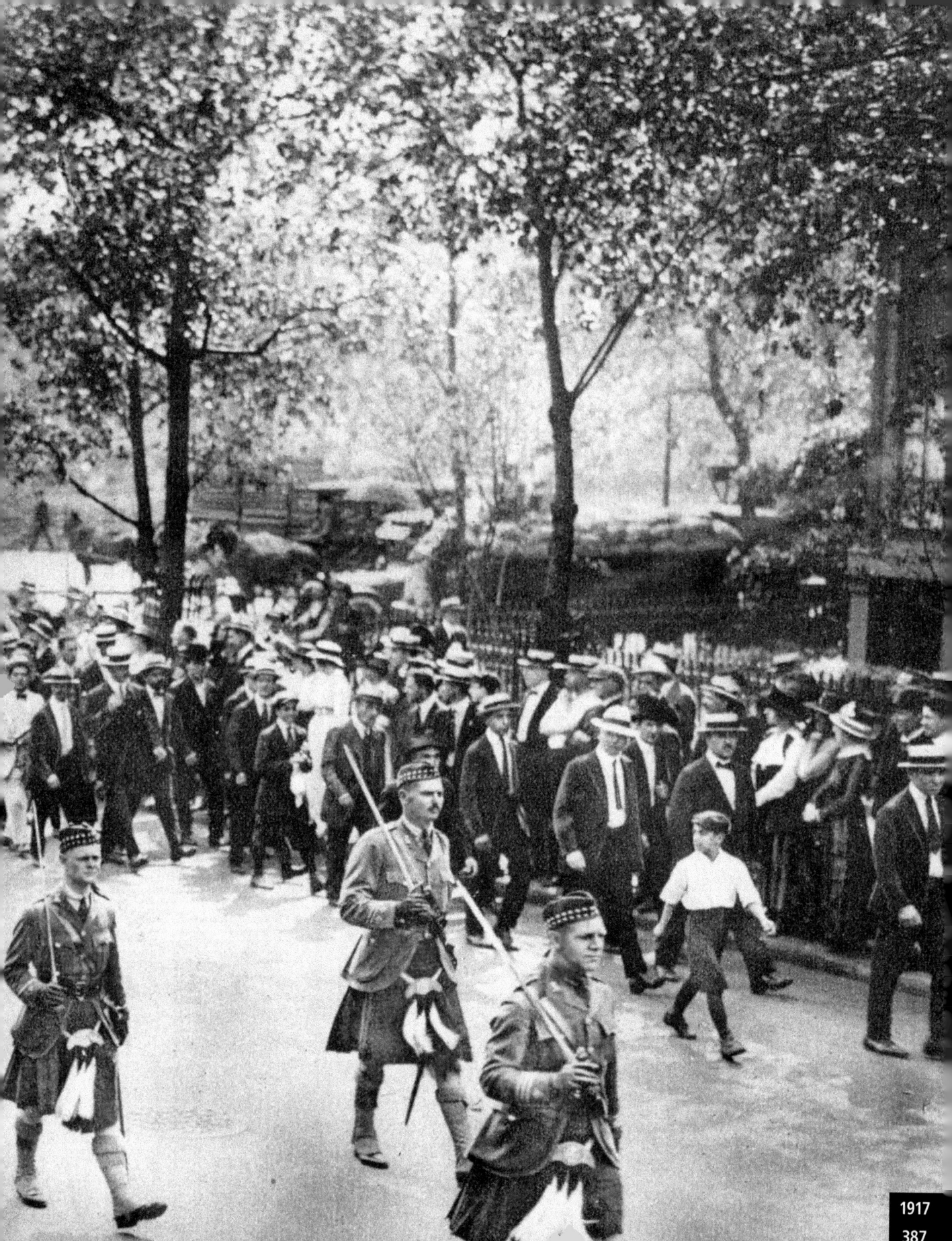

17GW860 Two hundred kilted Canadian Highlanders, accompanied by a band of pipers, marching through the streets of New York, 16 July 1917, in support of a 'British Recruiting Week' that had been organized to encourage British nationals living in the United States to join the colours.

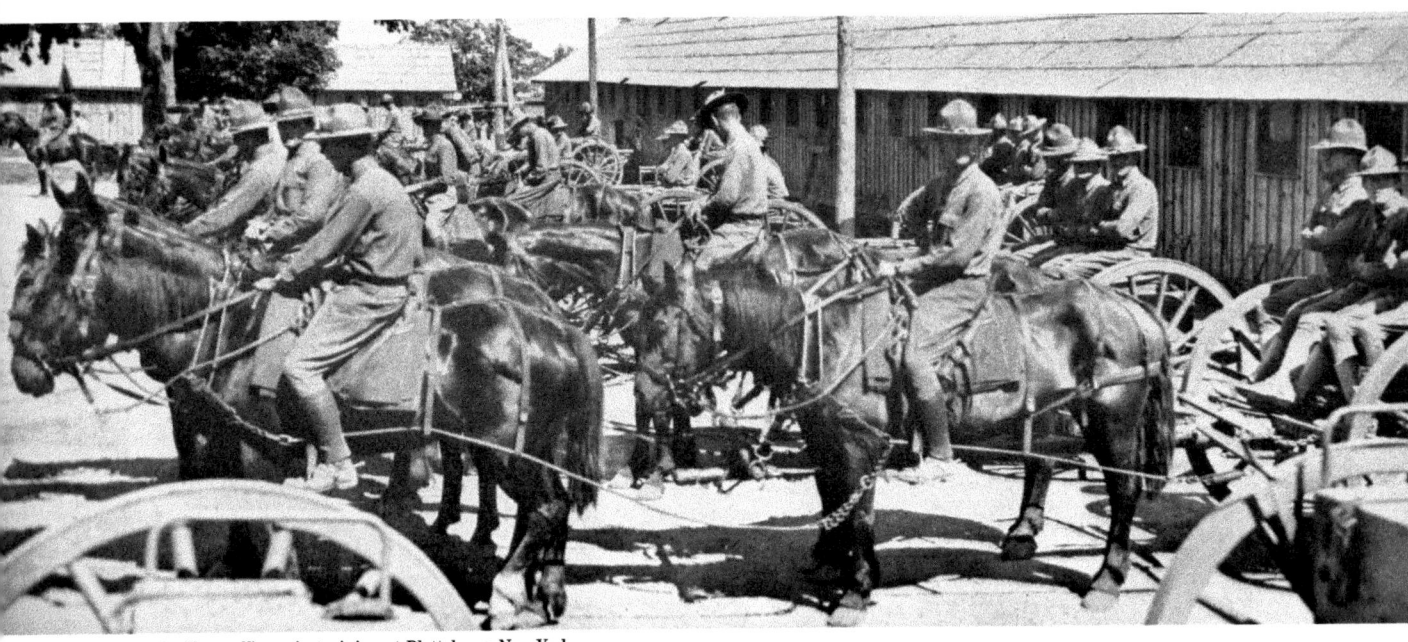

17GW874 Artillery officers in training at Plattsburg, New York.

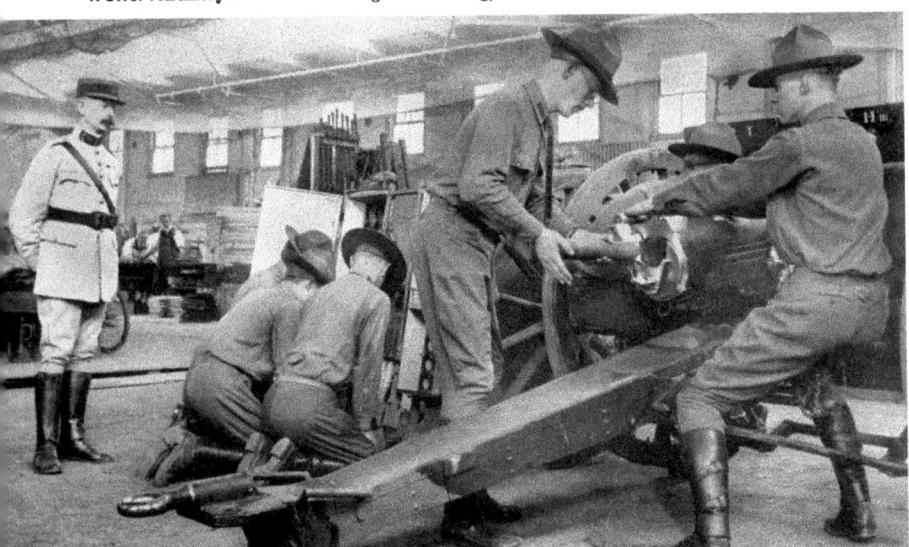

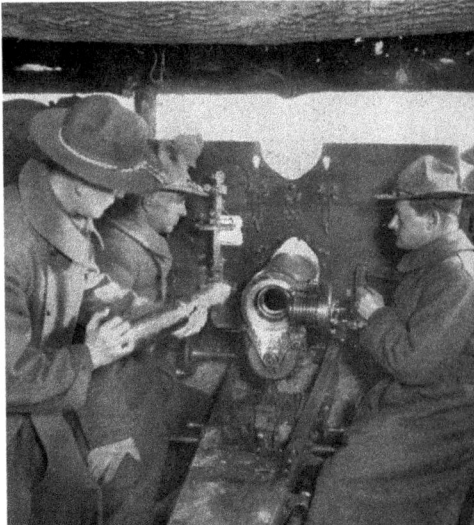

17GW878, 17GW879 Training on the French 75 gun with instruction from a French artillery officer at Yale. In position and firing 'live' rounds on the artillery range at the Officers' Training Camp at Fort Sheridan.

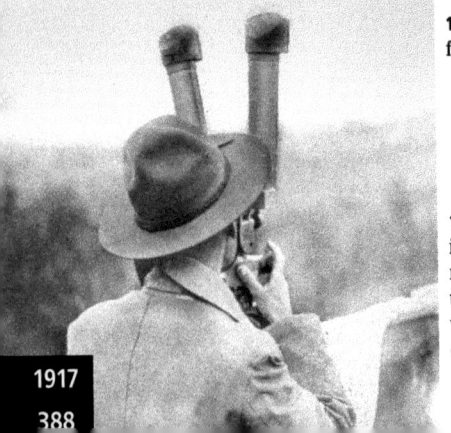

17GW883 Using a range finder for the 75s.

17GW880 Artillery spotters in an outpost – a two-man team, one locates the target and the other writes down the co-ordinates.

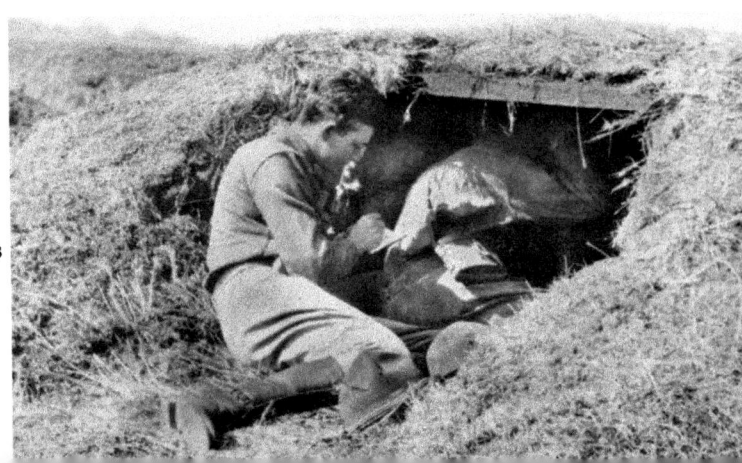

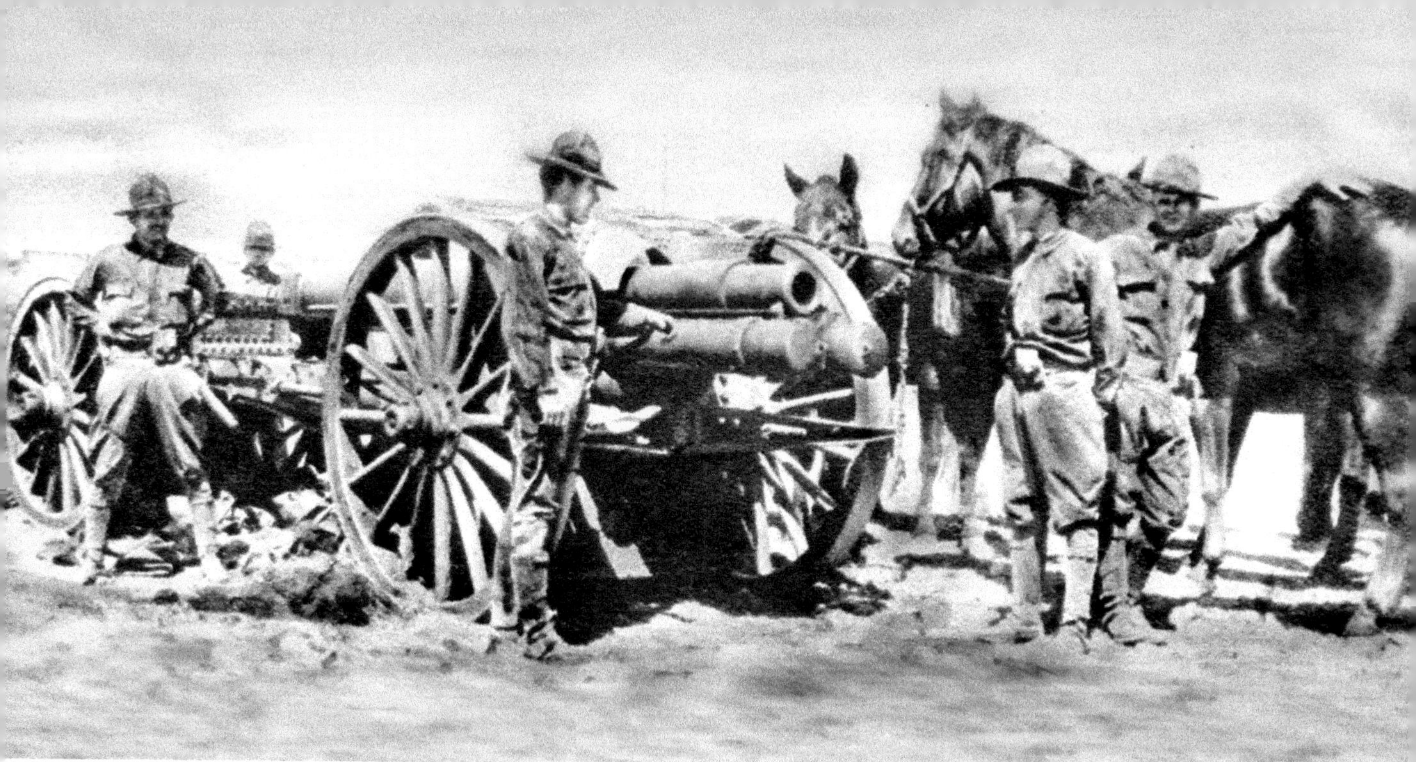

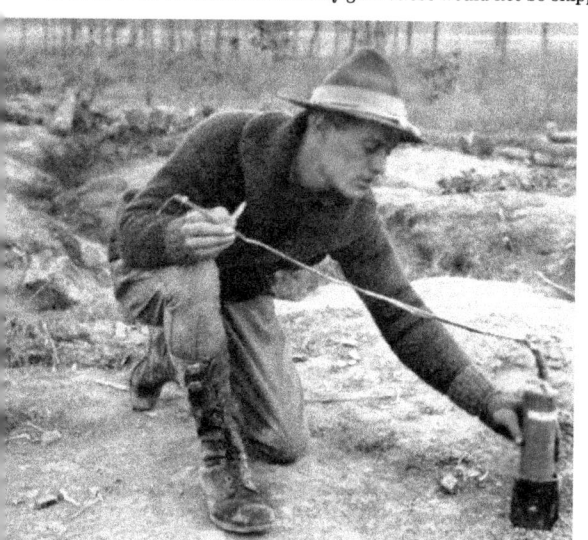

17GW877 A 4.7 inch medium artillery gun. These would not be shipped to France; artillery pieces were supplied by France and Britain.

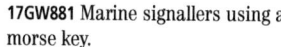

17GW882 Igniting an artillery warning flare at Fort Sheridan.

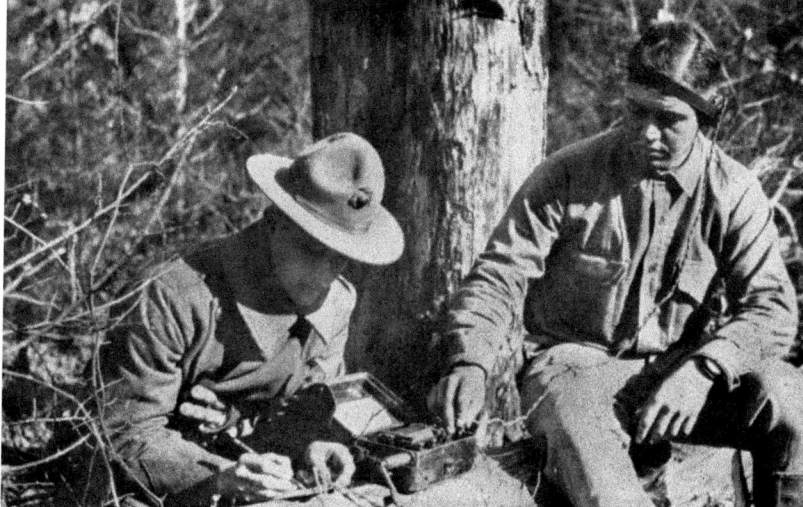

17GW881 Marine signallers using a morse key.

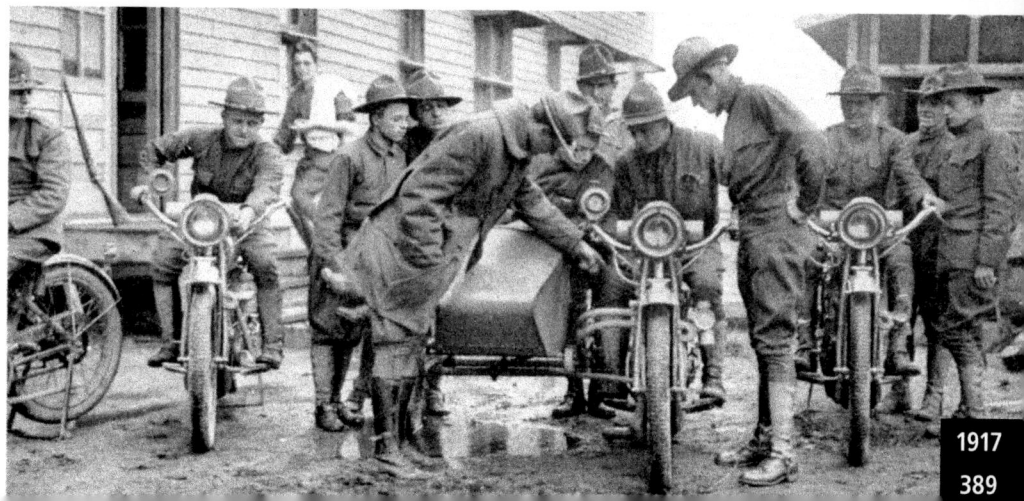

17GW884 Despatch riders at Camp Upton, Long Island, New York.

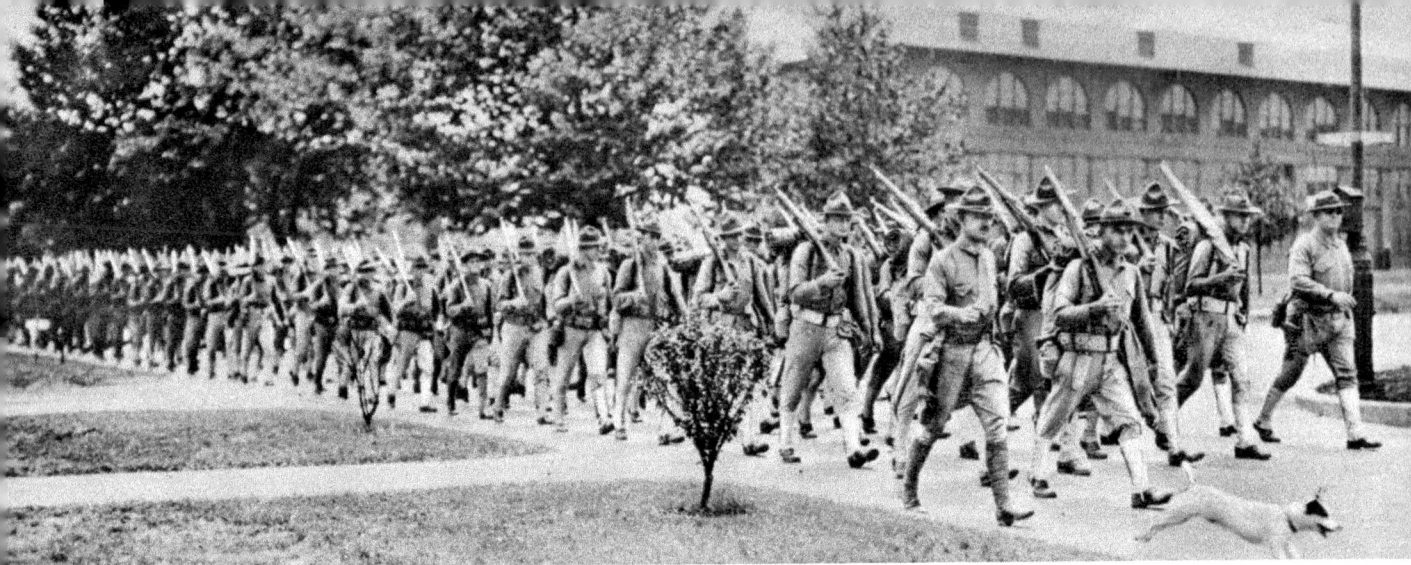

17GW886 United States Marines marching to their final parade before embarking on transports to France.

17GW887 Troops moving up to the ferry boats on Alpine Landing, New Jersey. The ferries will take them to the transport vessel at Hoboken.

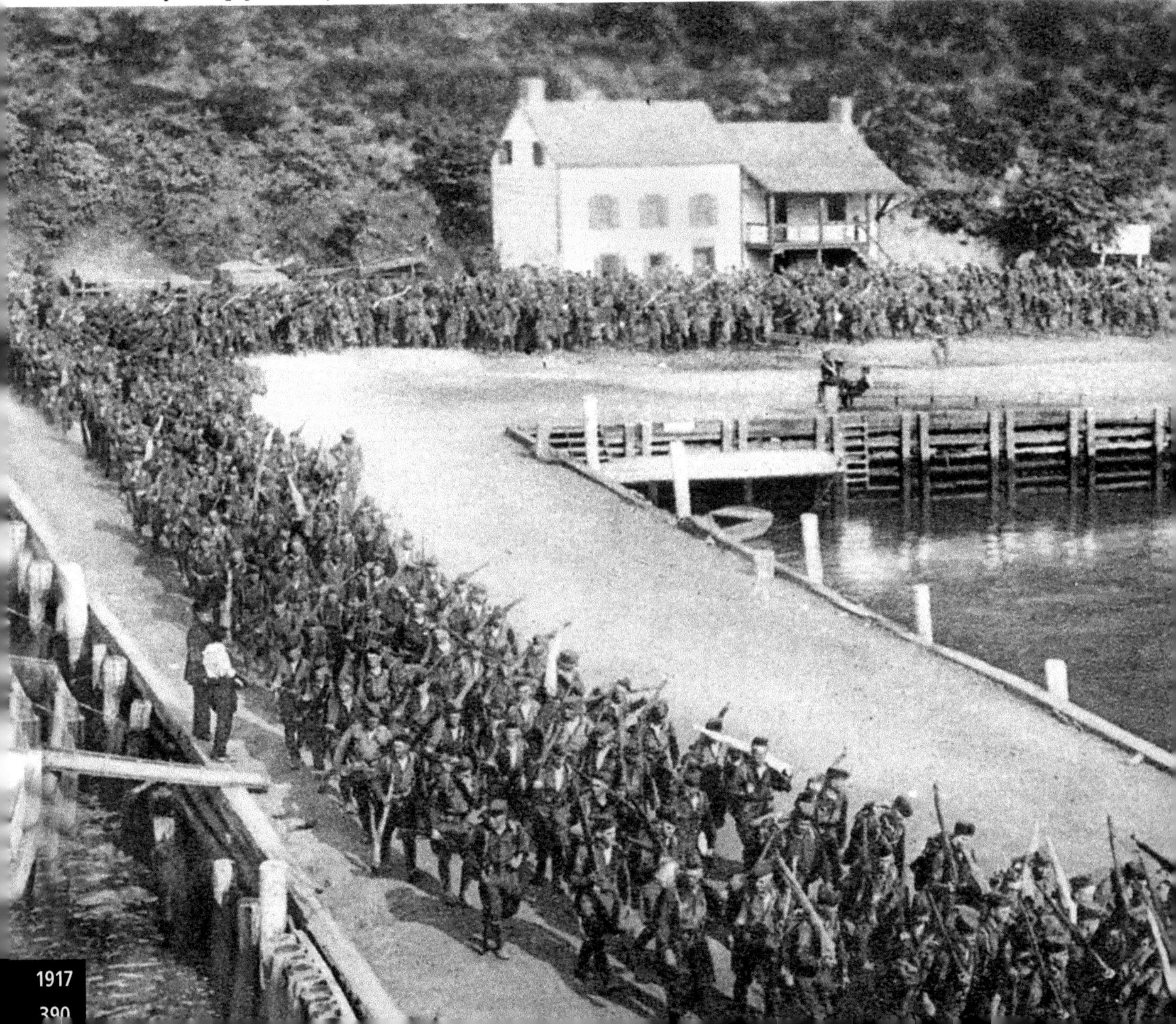

17GW885 All manner of military and general stores being loaded onto transports for the cross-Atlantic voyage.

17GW888 'The Yanks are coming': soldiers boarding the transport *Leviathan* (which could hold 12,000 men) at the port of Hoboken. In the nineteen months of American involvement more than two million men were transported to europe.

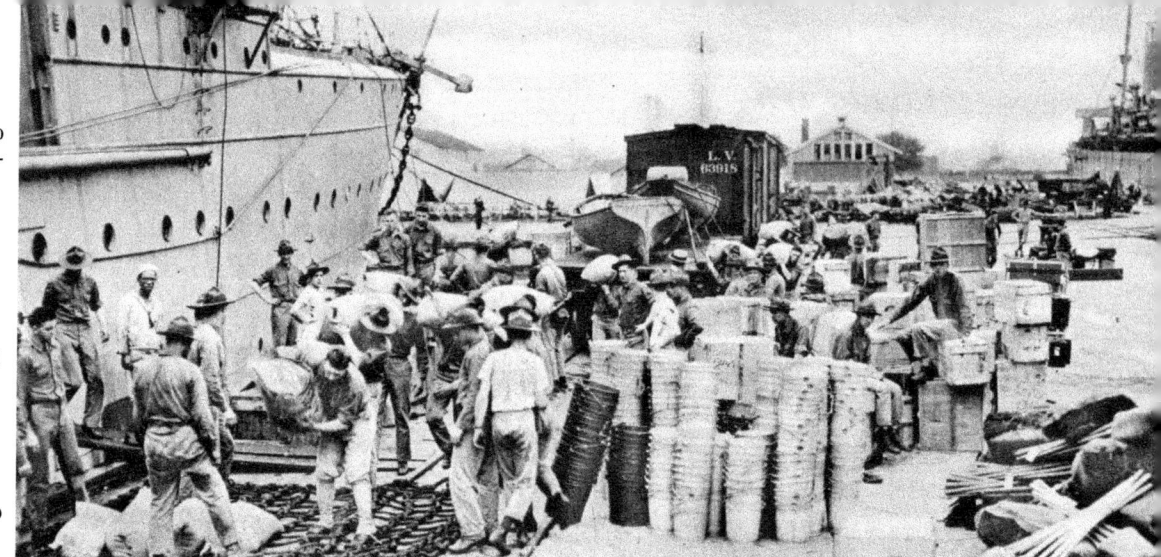

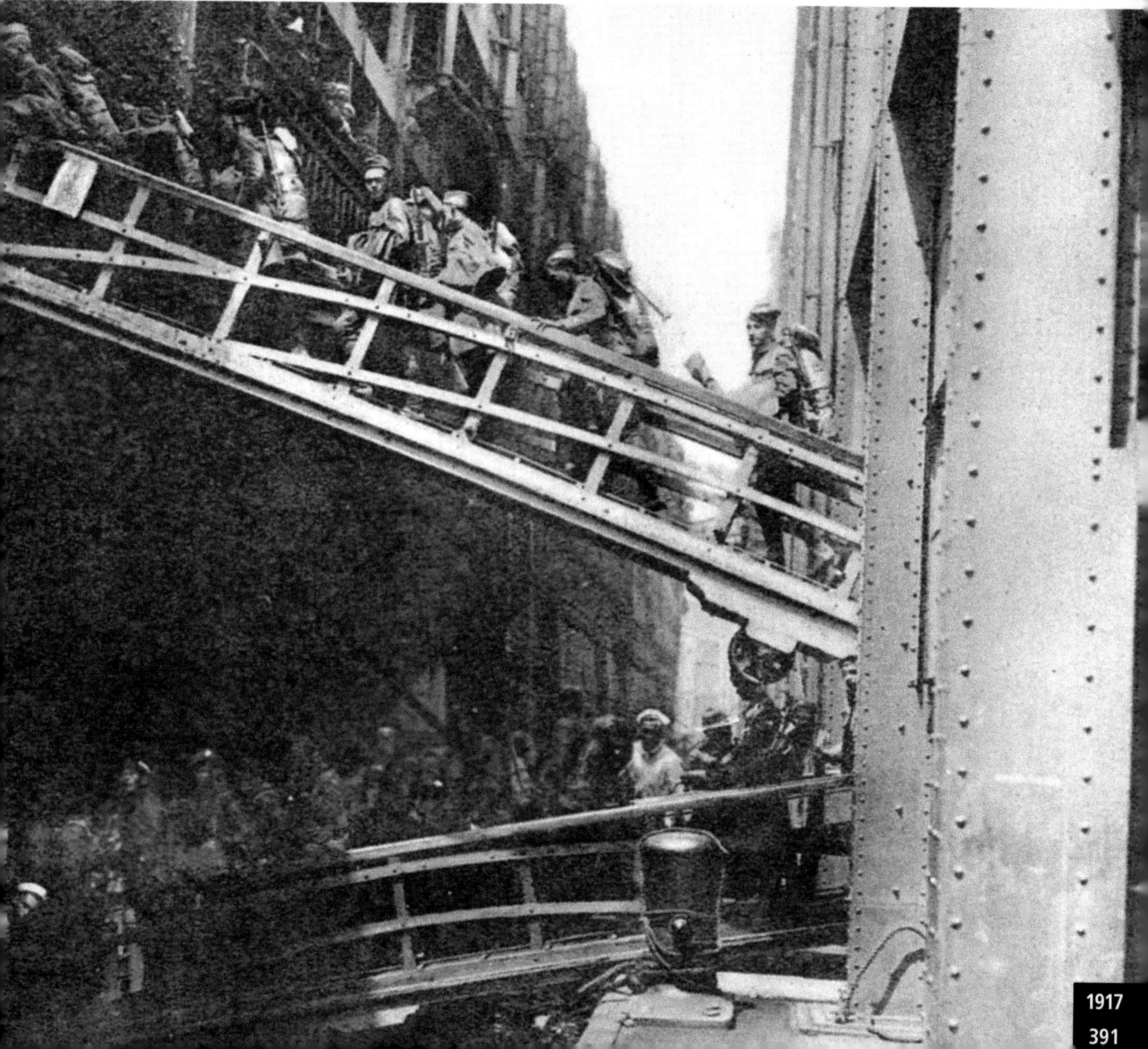

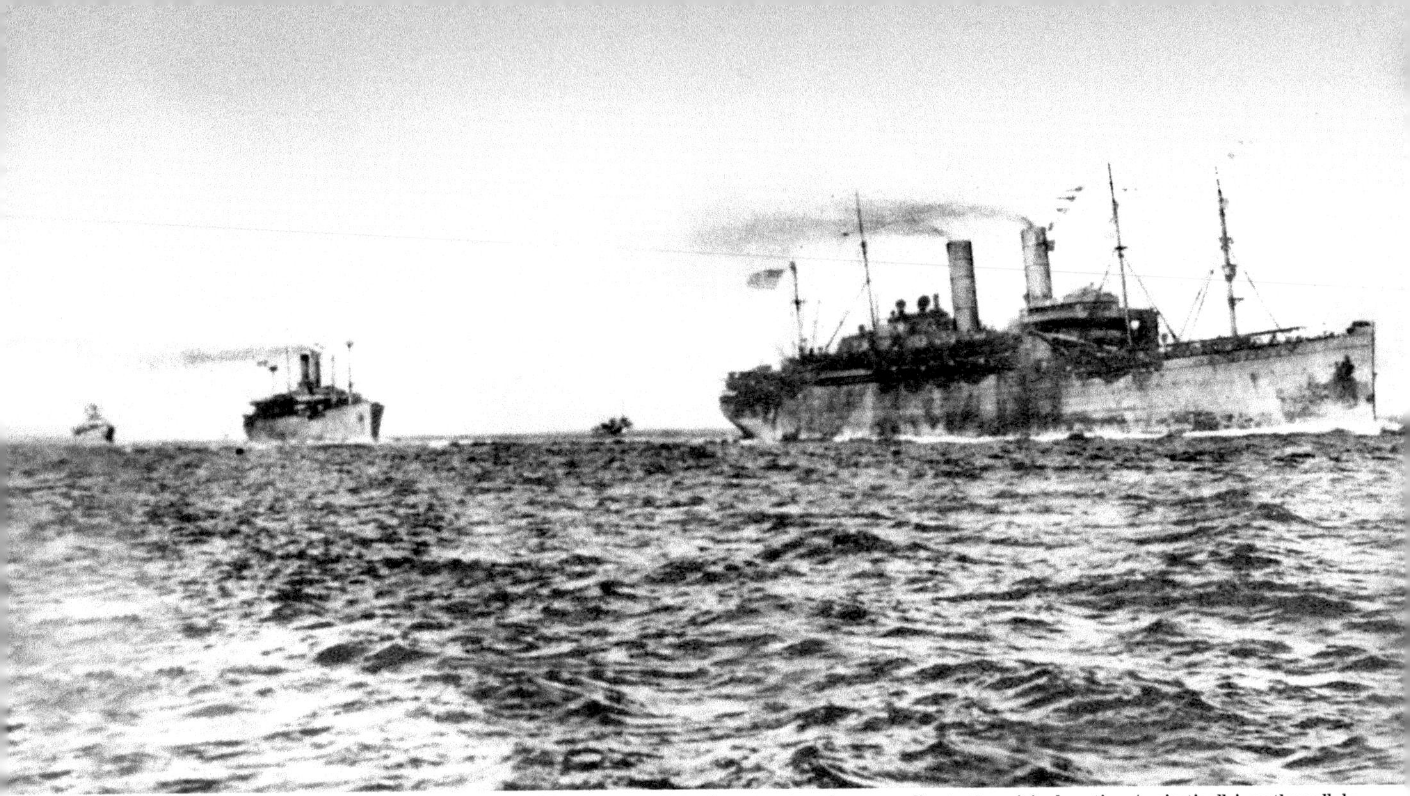

17GW889 In this line of troop transports are the *George Washington* and the *America* steaming, according to the original caption, 'majestically', as they all do.

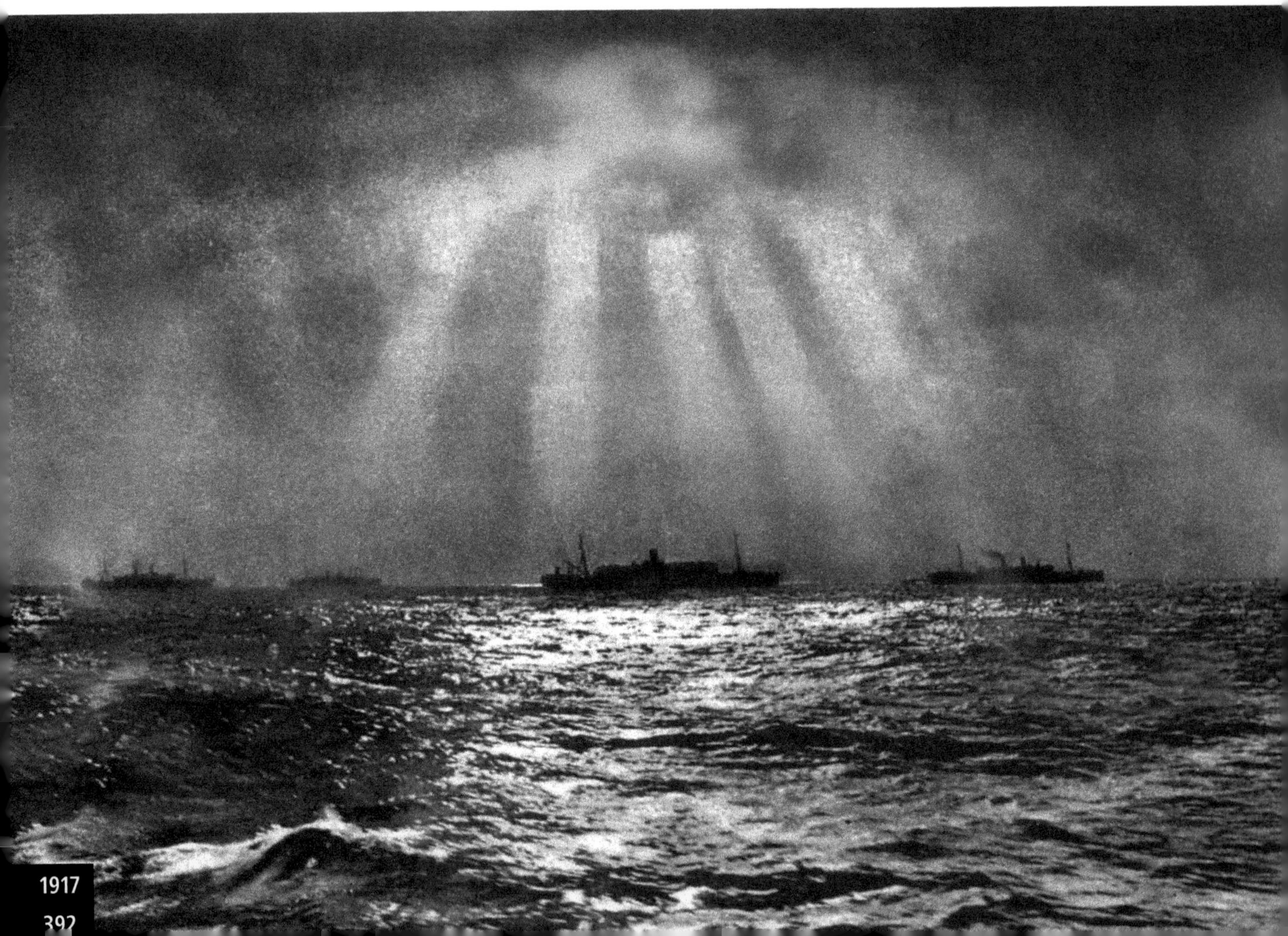

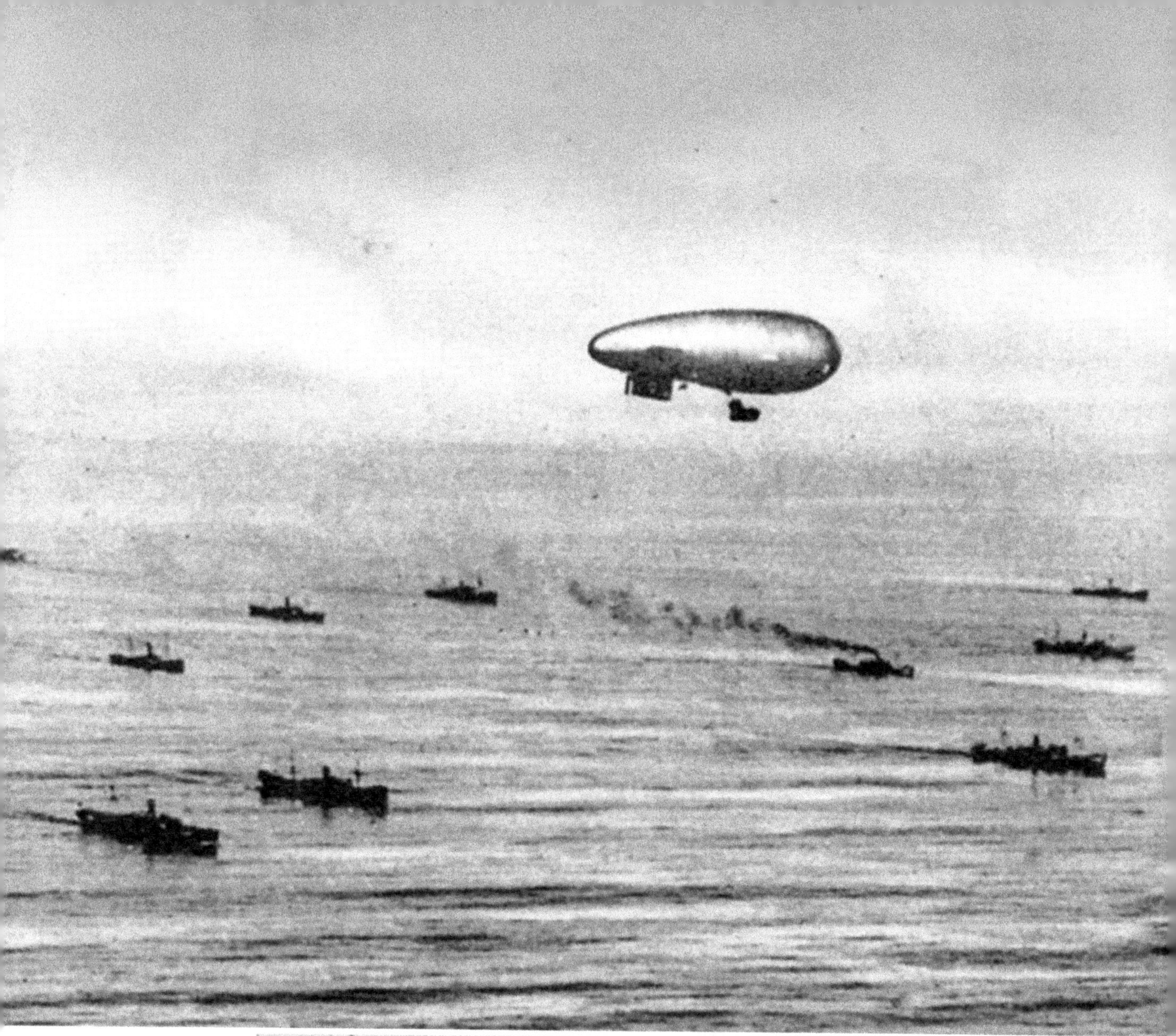

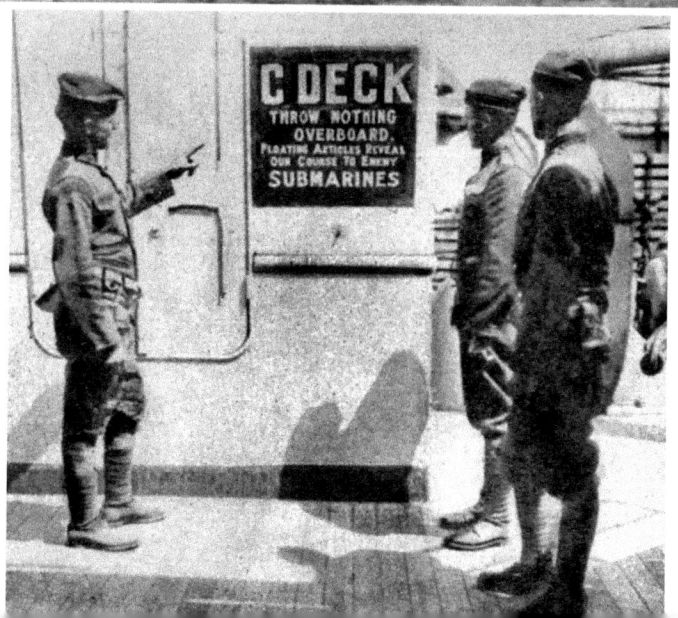
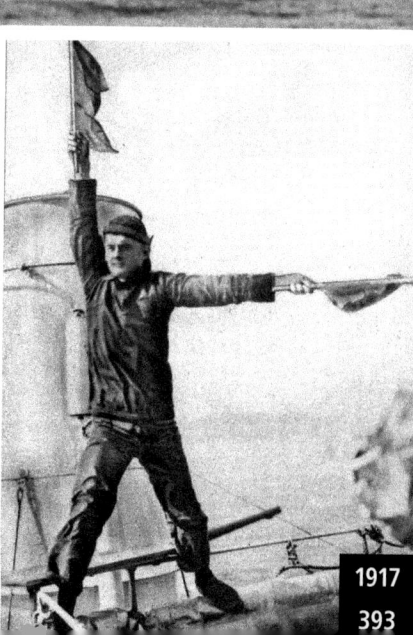

17GW893 An Atlantic convoy under escort and with a dirigible on the lookout for any tell-tale wash from a German submarine's periscope.

17GW890 A dramatic moon-lit scene of an American convoy in mid-Atlantic.

17GW894 Attention is being drawn to the danger of German submarines.

17GW891 Signalling by flags from one of the escorting destroyers. As some danger been spotted?

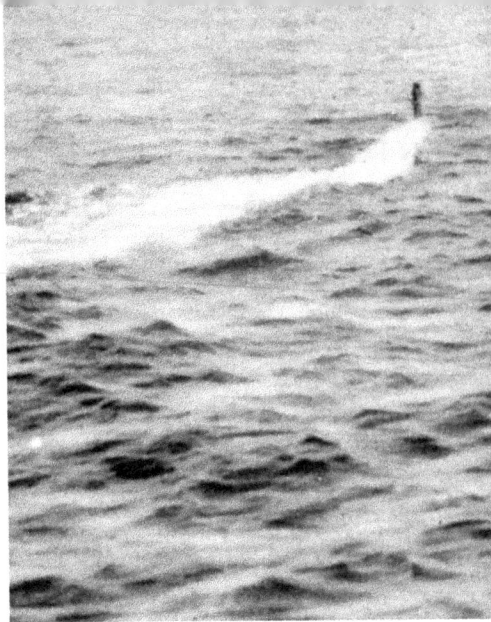
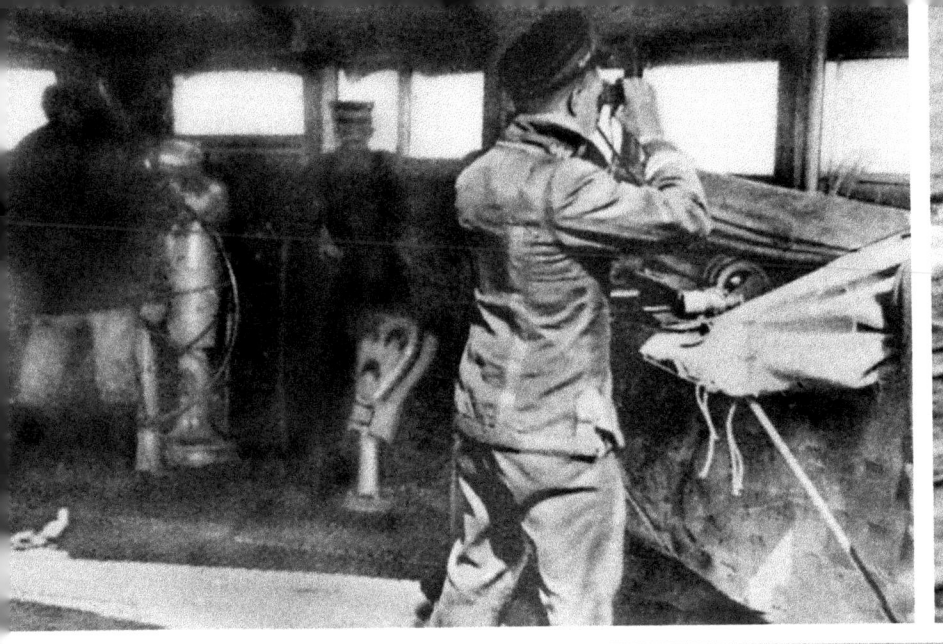

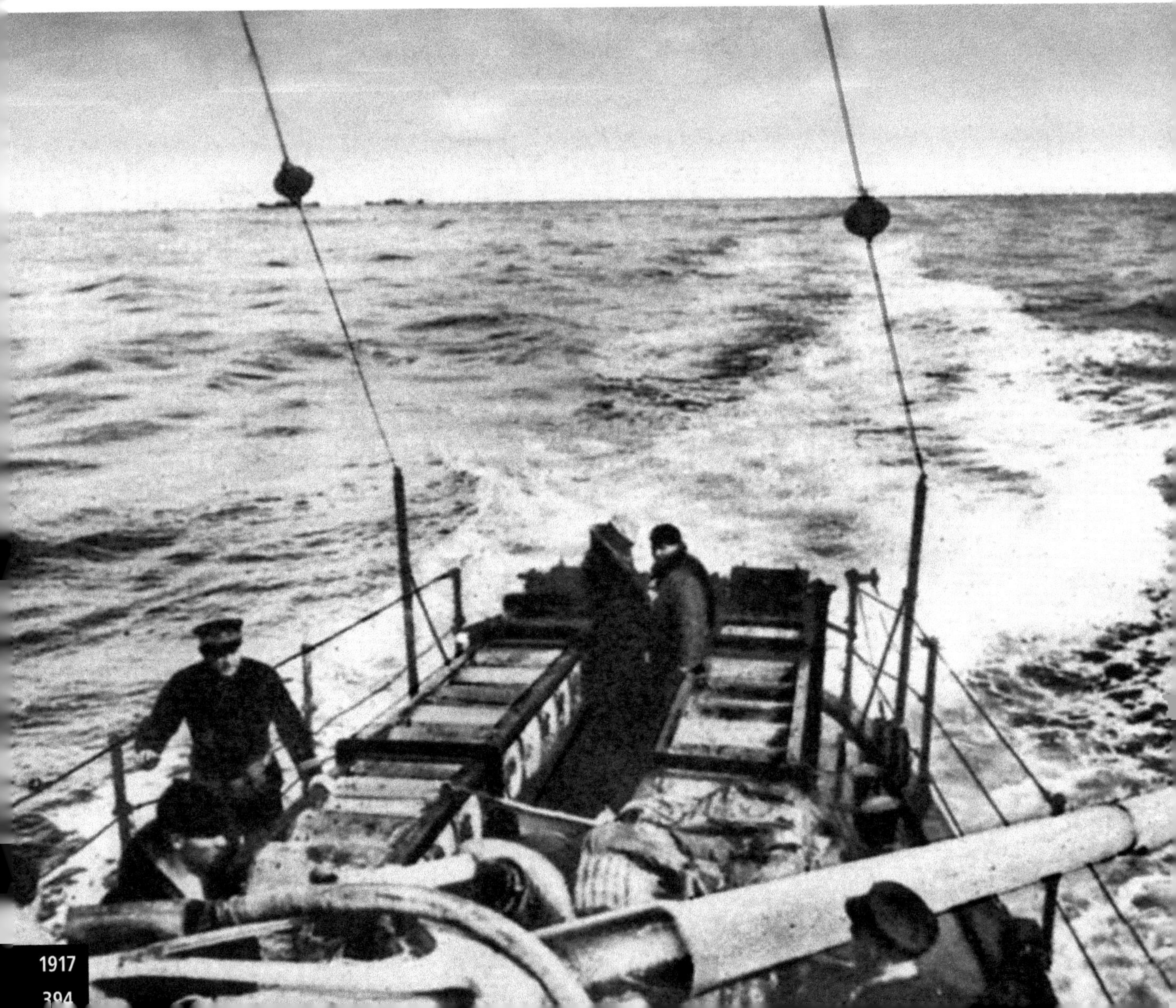

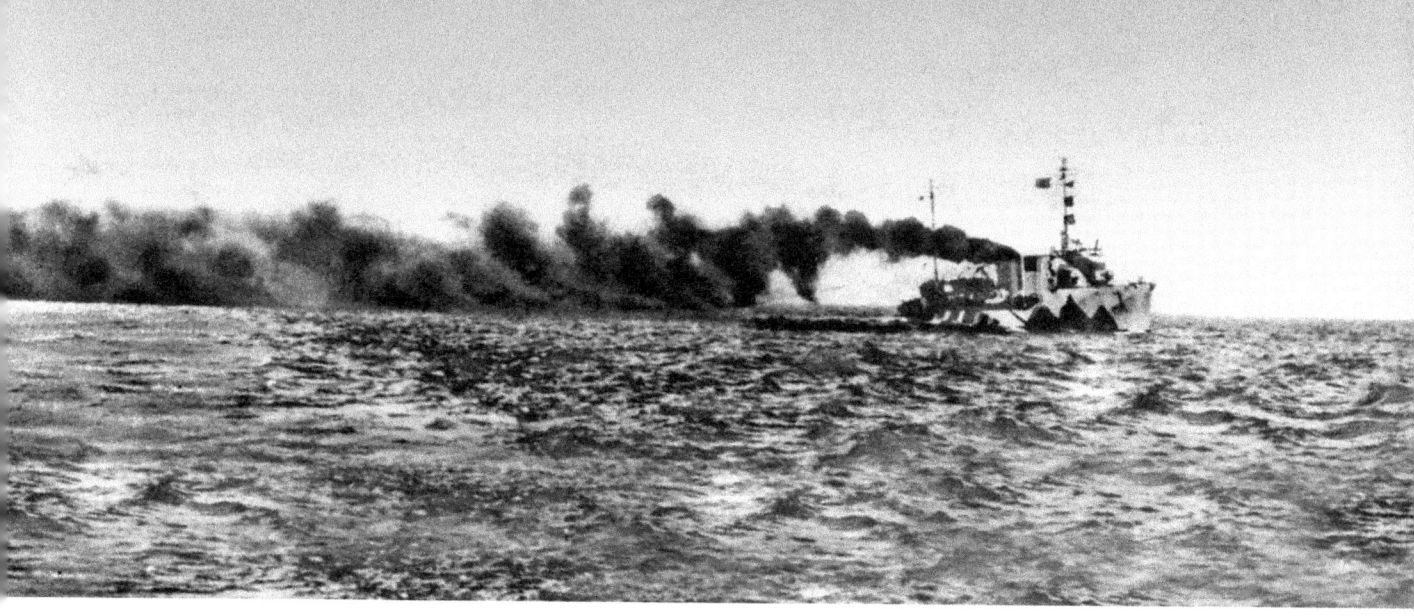

17GW895, 17GW896, 17GW892, 17GW897, 17GW898, 17GW899. Scanning the sea from the bridge of an escorting destroyers. A submarine periscope; the destroyer USS *Henderson* zig-zagging and laying down a smokescreen between the sighting and the convoy; on board USS Whipple viewing the depth charges being rolled in a pattern from the aft deck and with with the ship at 'full ahead'; a depth charge exploding at a previously set depth. Success! a German submarine is blown to the surface.

Owing to the vigilance of the US Navy, not one east-bound American transport vessel was lost to German submarine activity.

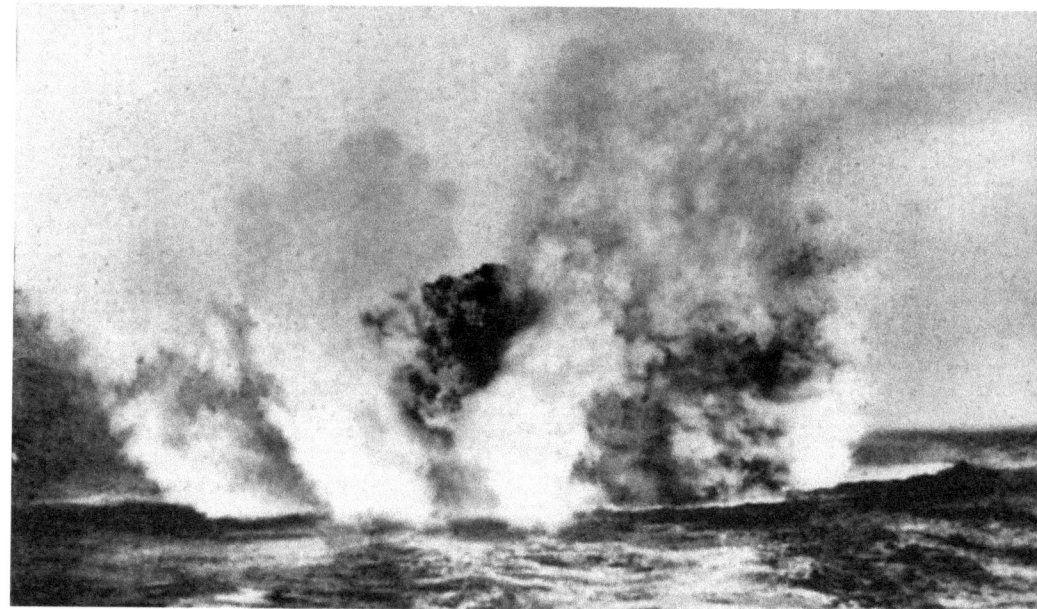

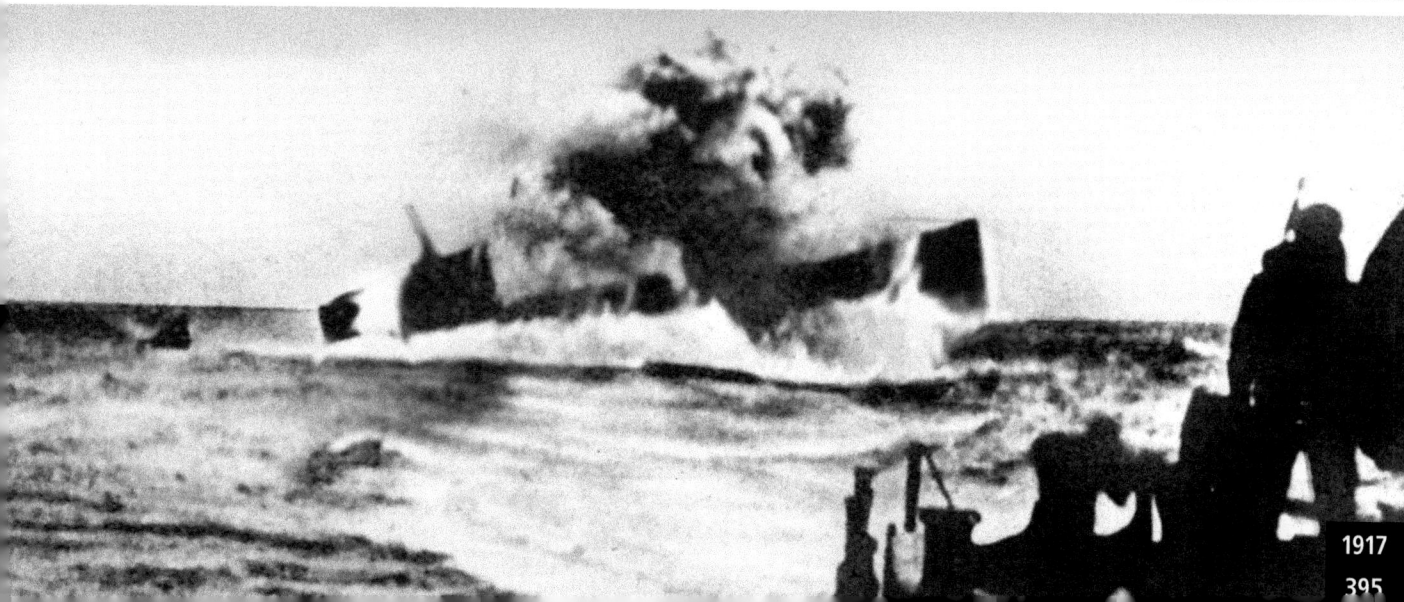

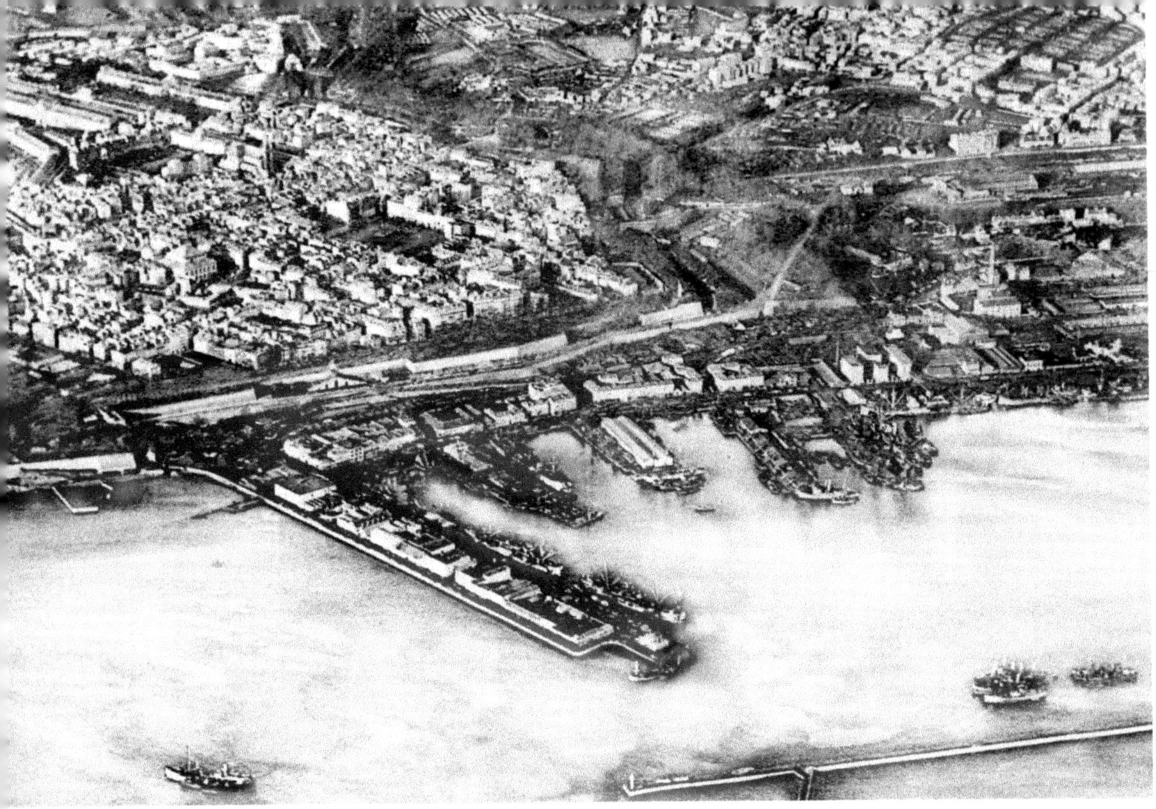

17GW863 The French west coast seaport of Brest. Here upwards of 80,000 American soldiers first set foot on european soil.

17GW862 The first American troop transport to arrive in France. Alongside are two destroyers that acted as escorts. Twice German submarine attacks were made on the convoy, but each time the submarines were beaten off.

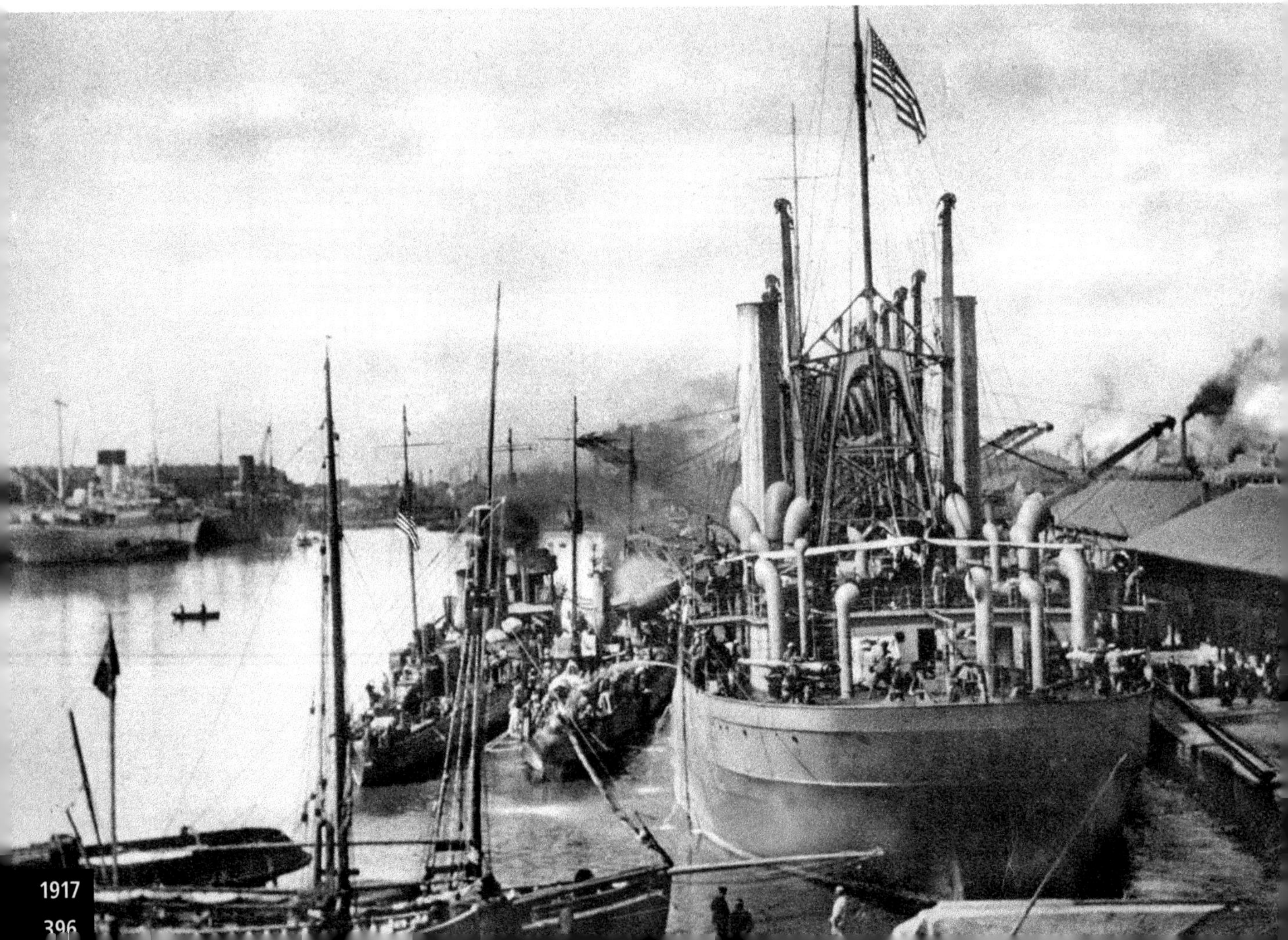

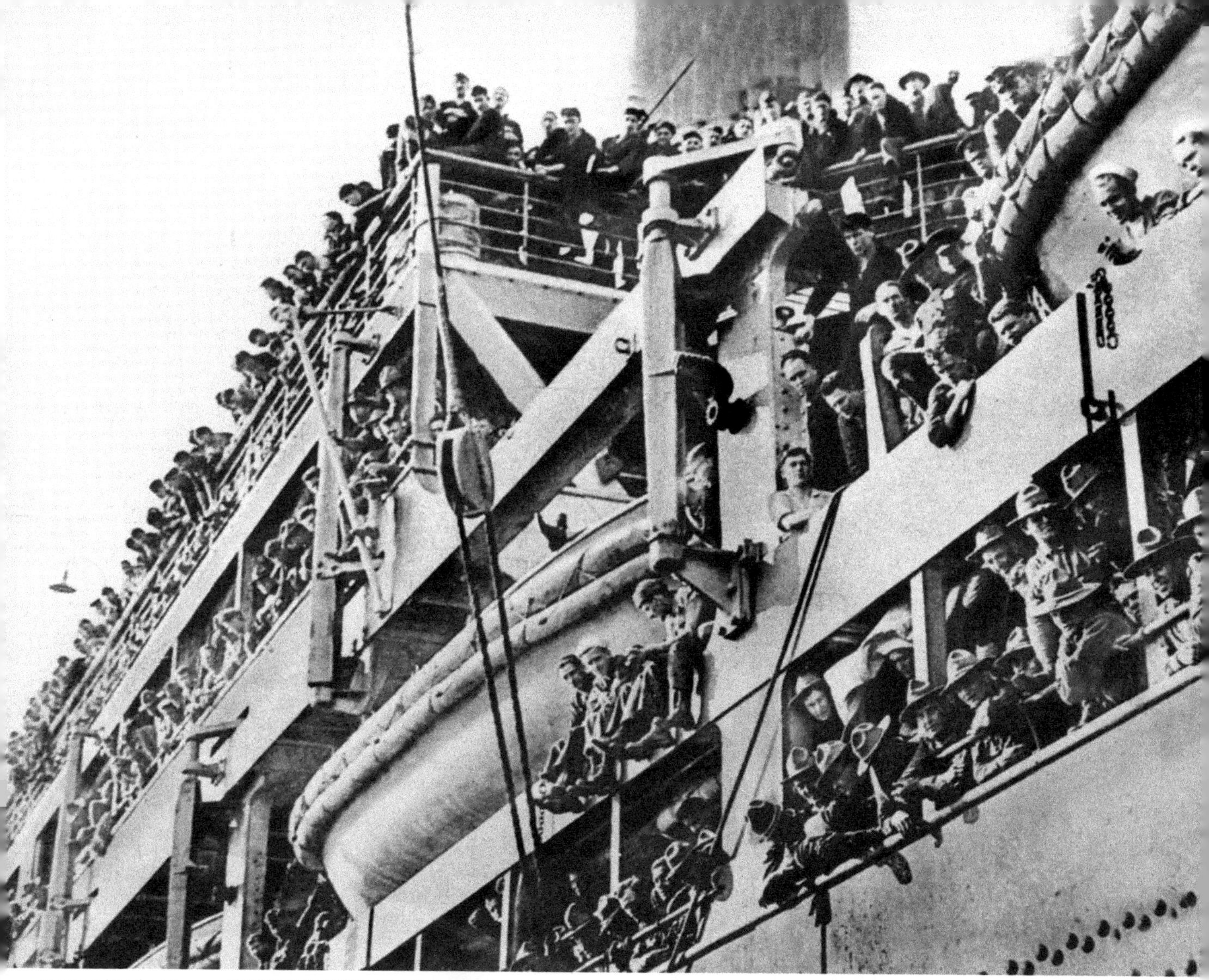

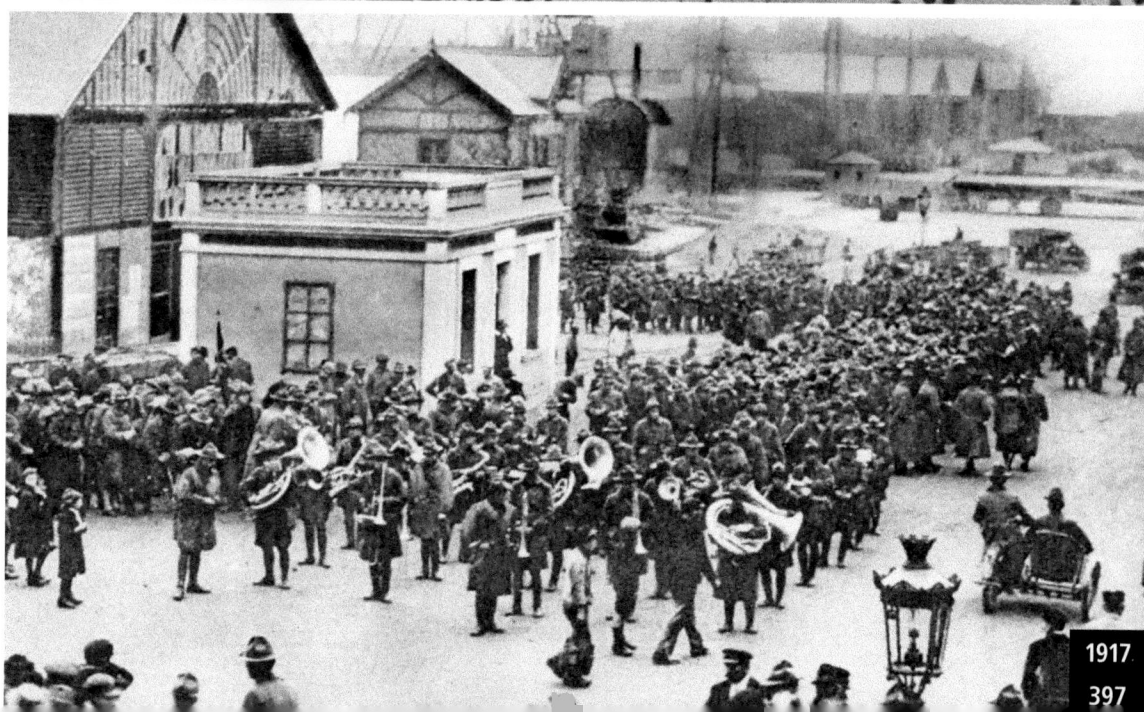

17GW864 American troops arriving at Brest on the *Leviathan*, which had arrived carrying 12,000 soldiers, 4,000 sailors and 200 Red Cross nurses.

17GW865 French civilians gathered to welcome the arrival of the US Rainbow Division at St Nazaire, 1 November 1917. The Division was made up of National Guardsmen from twenty-seven states and Washington DC. Other contingents landed at Brest and Liverpool throughout November to 7 December.

1917
397

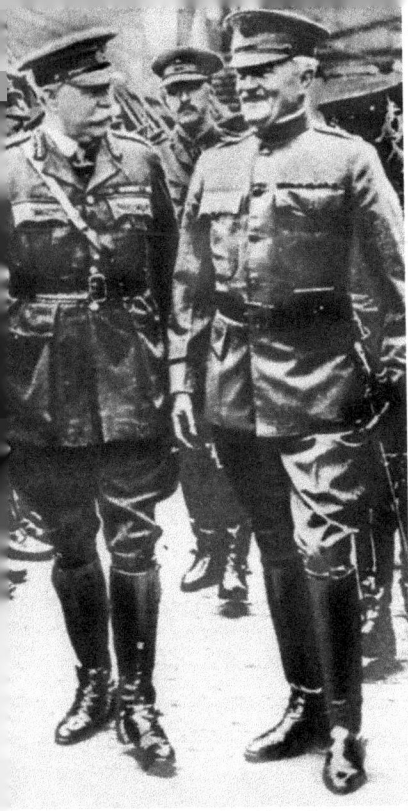
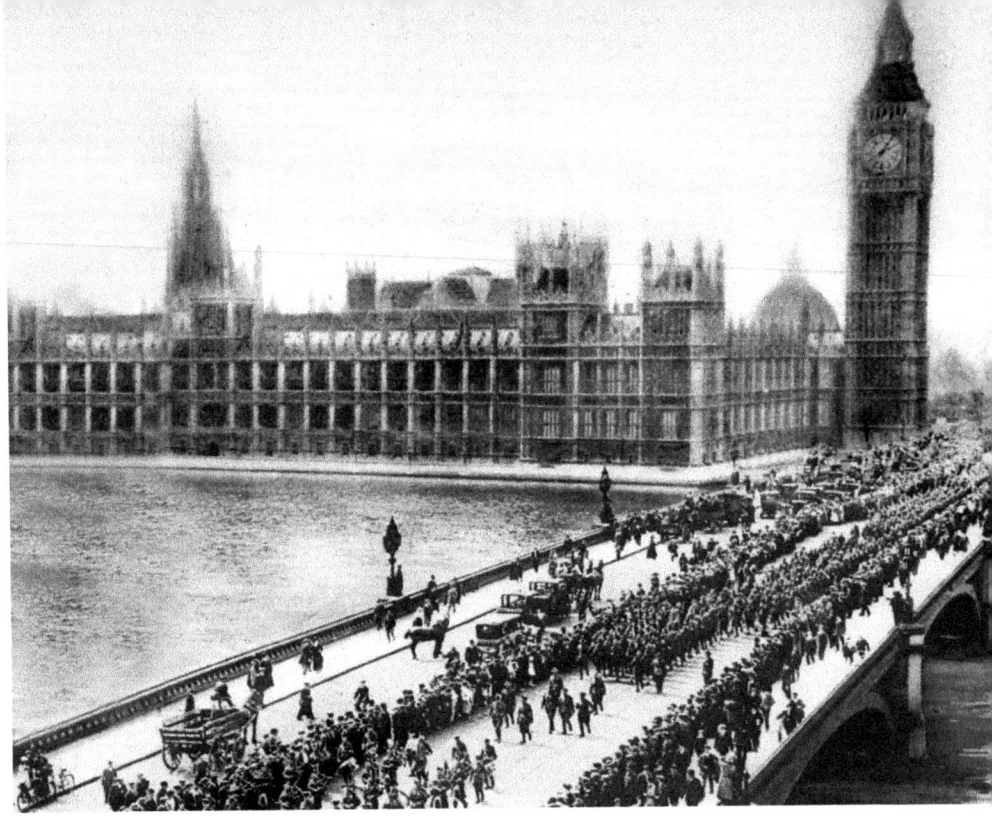

17GW901 General Pershing, Commander-in-Chief of the American Expeditionary Force, landed at Liverpool, 8 June, 1917. The following day he was welcomed by King George V.

17GW900 The first armed force of a foreign power to march in England's capital since William the Conqueror: 13th Engineers (Chicago) crossing Westmister Bridge, 15 August, 1917; also present were the 11th Engineers (New York) and the 15th Engineers (Pittsburg).

17GW902 General Pershing arrives at Boulogne, 13 June 1917.

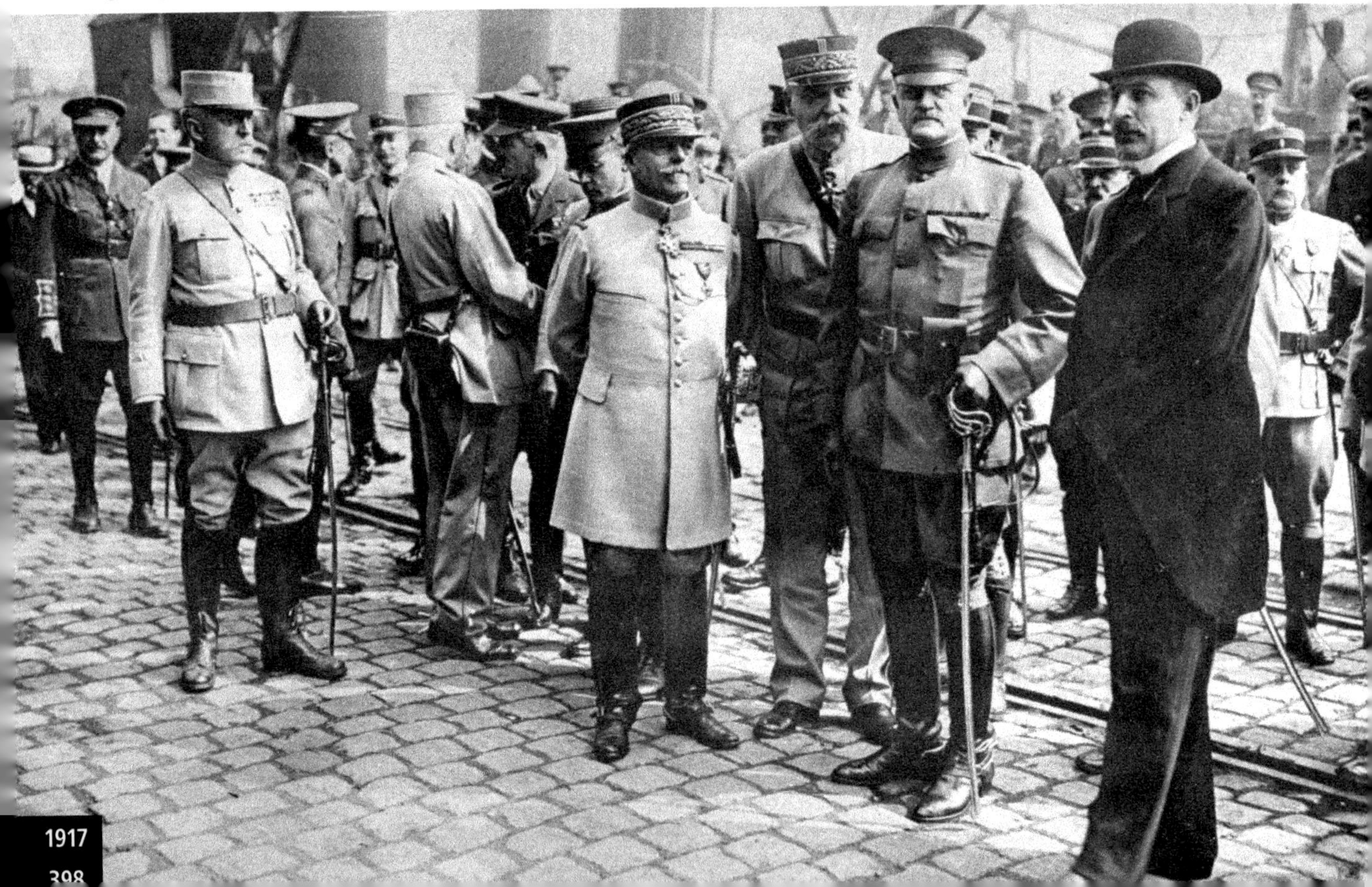

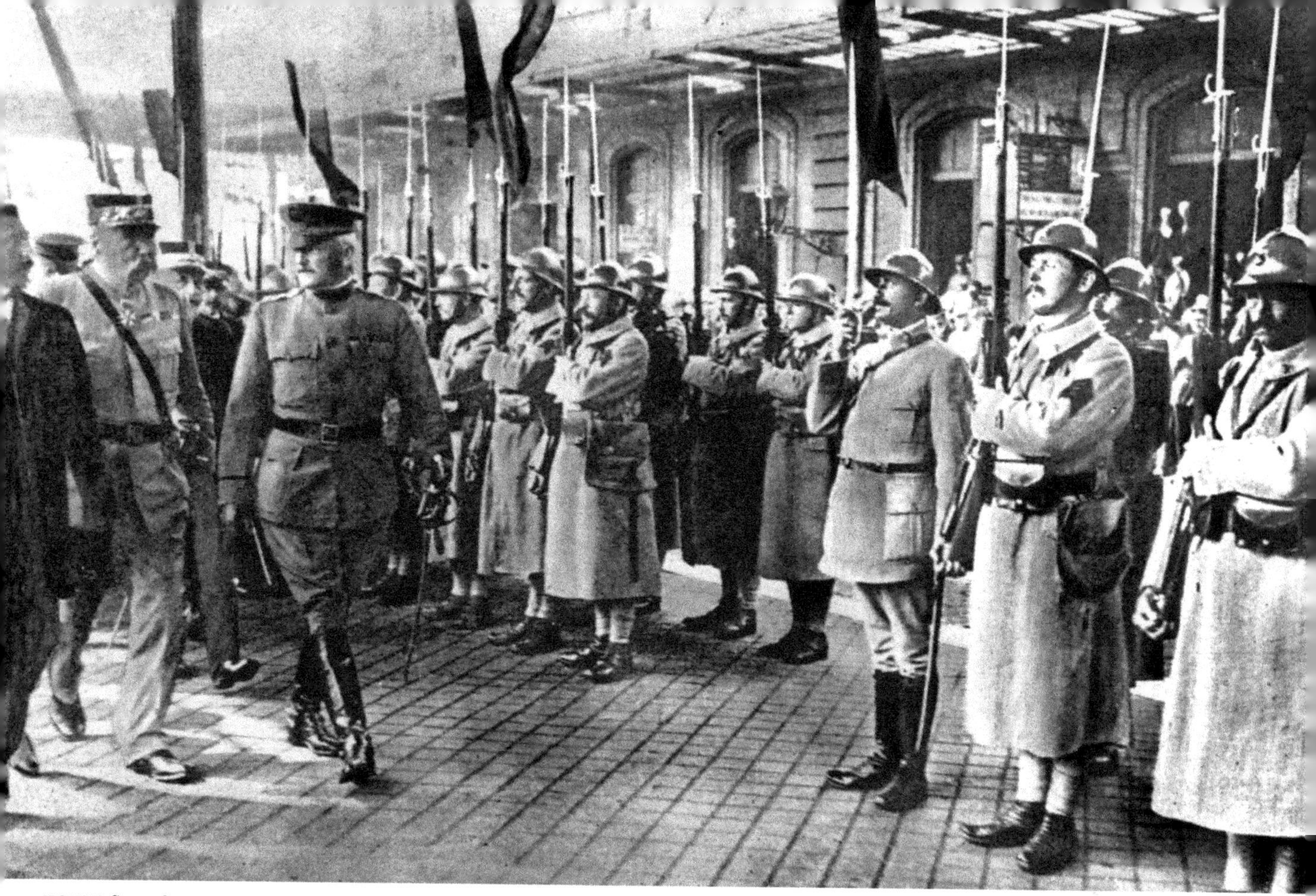

17GW903 General Pershing at Boulogne, railway station, 13 June 1917, inspects a guard of honour before boarding a train for Paris.

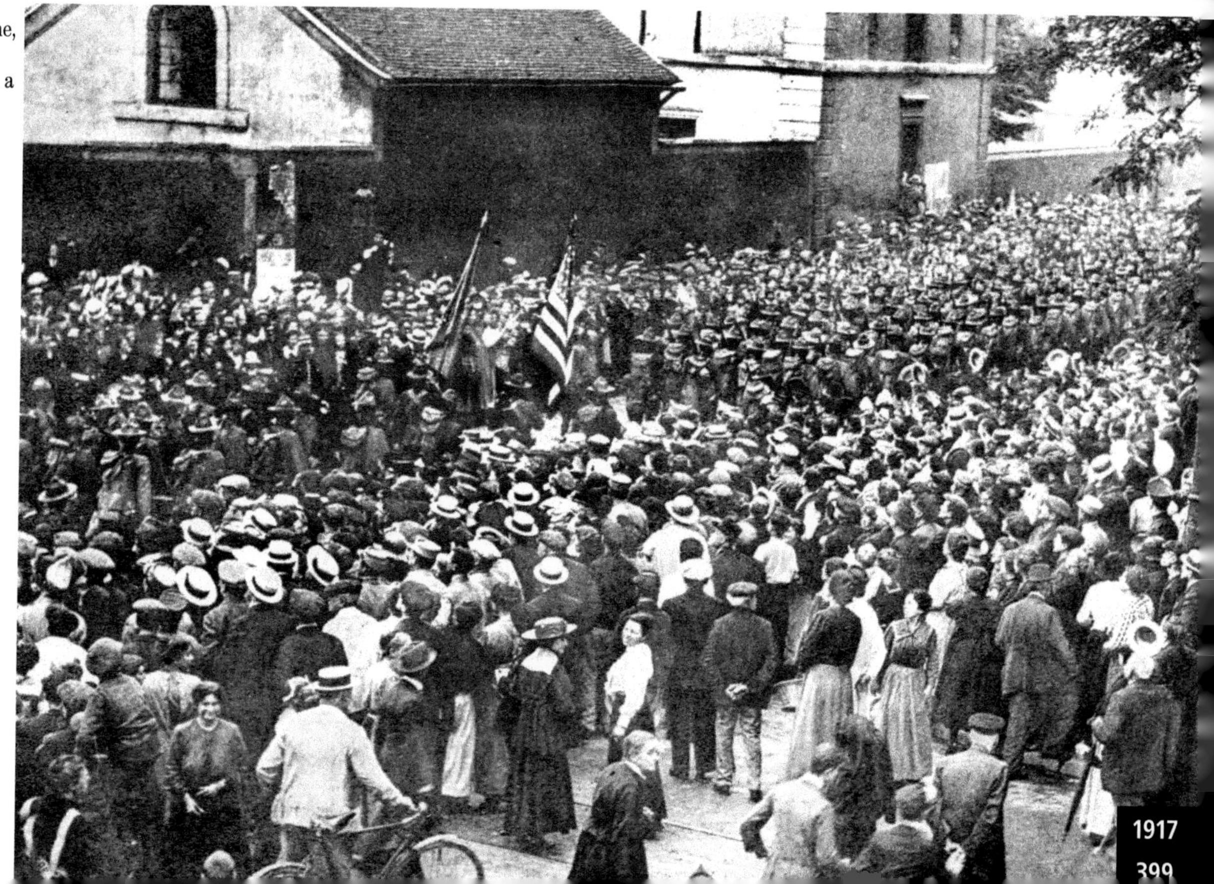

17GW904 A Paris crowd show their delight at the arrival of the American troops.

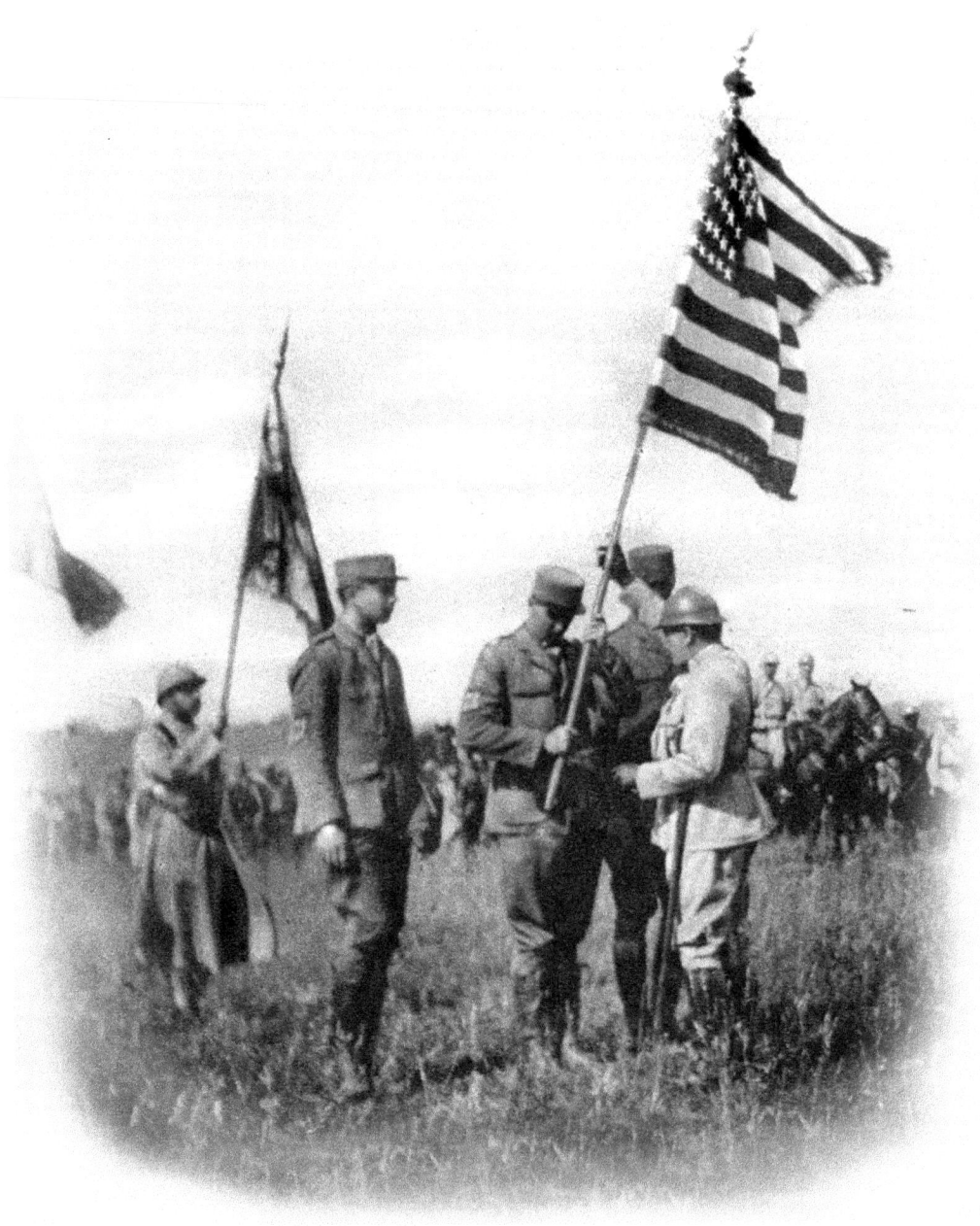

17GW861 The first United States national flag sent officially to the French front being saluted in a special ceremony. This particular flag was presented by the US War Department to the president of Stanford Junior University, California, who in turn gave it to French army commander General Mangin. The general had his troops march past in salute. A team from the California university formed part of the American Ambulance attached to General Mangin's army.

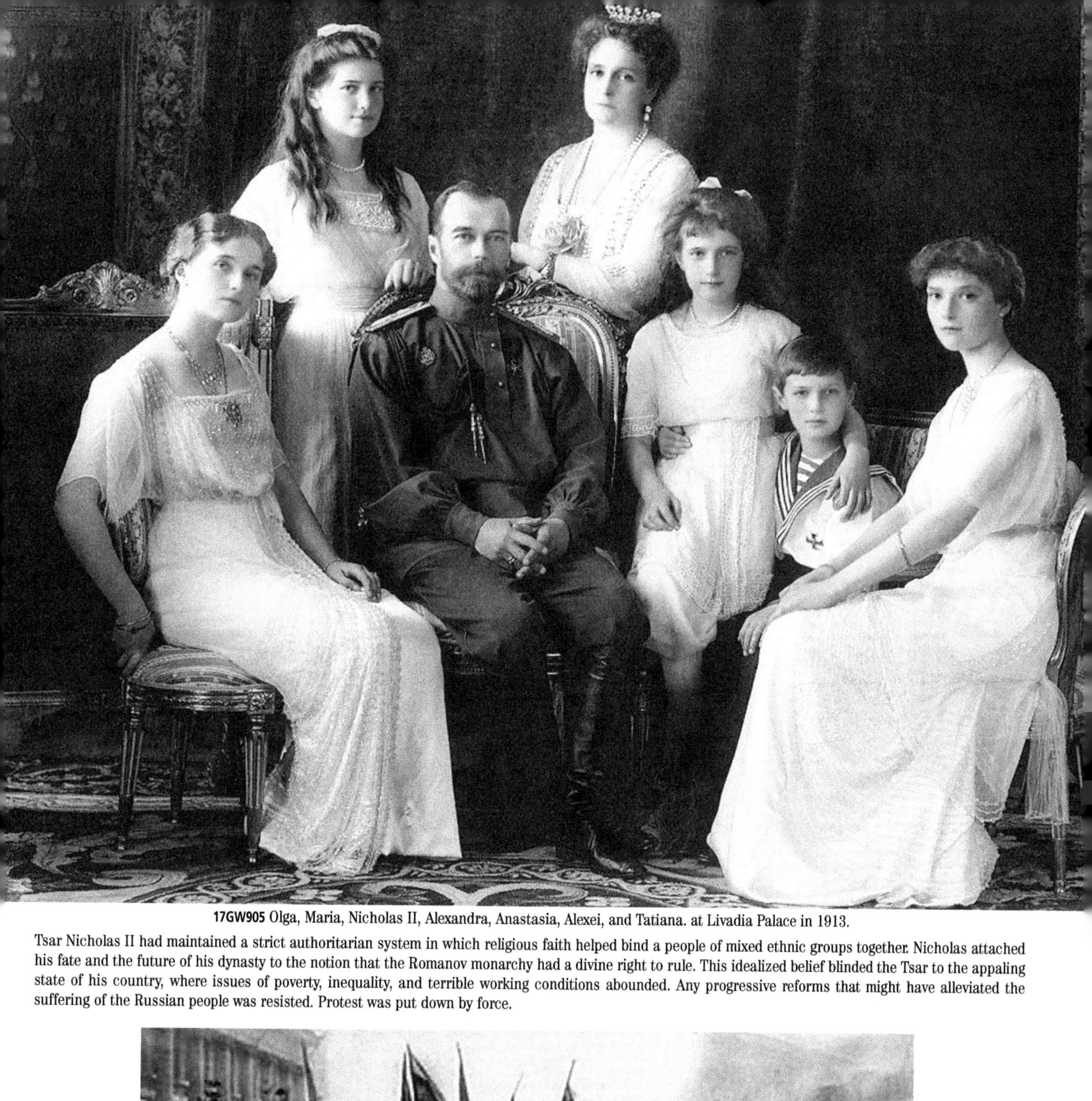

17GW905 Olga, Maria, Nicholas II, Alexandra, Anastasia, Alexei, and Tatiana. at Livadia Palace in 1913.

Tsar Nicholas II had maintained a strict authoritarian system in which religious faith helped bind a people of mixed ethnic groups together. Nicholas attached his fate and the future of his dynasty to the notion that the Romanov monarchy had a divine right to rule. This idealized belief blinded the Tsar to the appaling state of his country, where issues of poverty, inequality, and terrible working conditions abounded. Any progressive reforms that might have alleviated the suffering of the Russian people was resisted. Protest was put down by force.

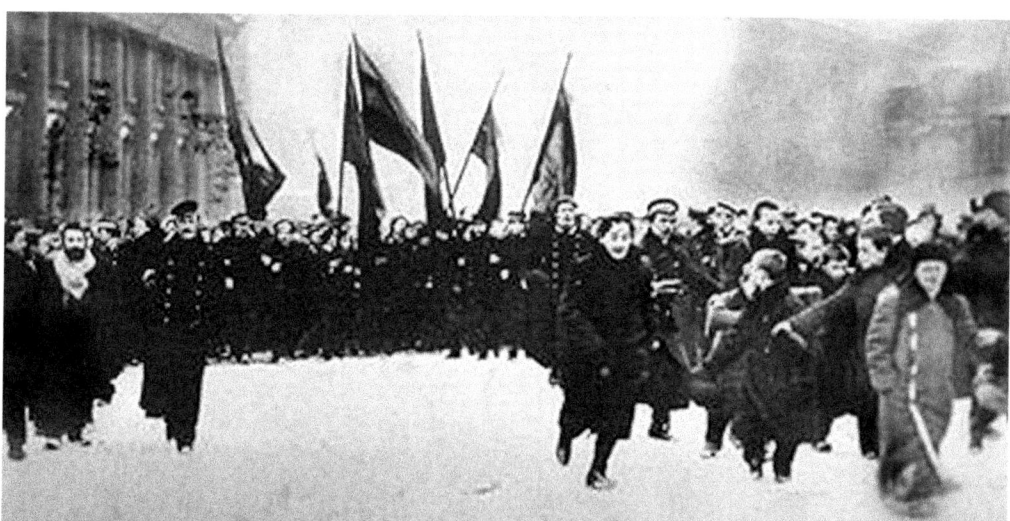

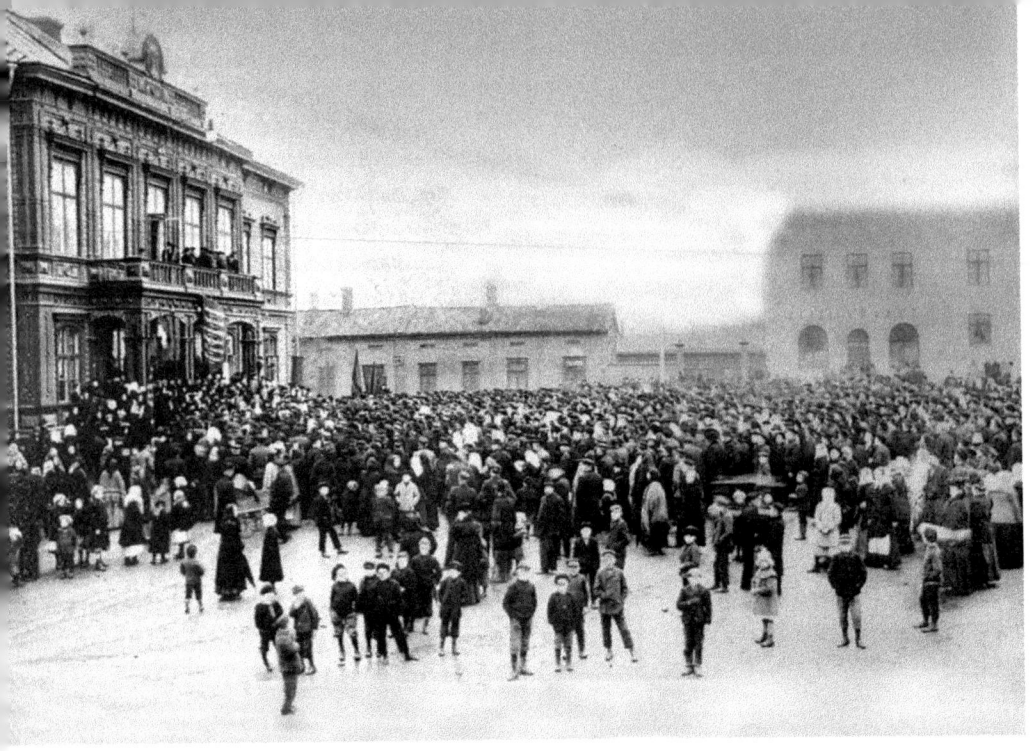

Russian people were used to working an eleven hour day, with ten on Saturdays. When there was a decrease in wages in 1904 the workers finally banded together in the Assembly of Russian Workers. 150,000 people signed a petition for an eight hour working day; higher pay (including equal pay for women); improved working conditions; medical care; and freedom of speech and press. On 22 January, 1905, they marched peacefully to the Winter Palace in St. Petersburg to present the petition to Tsar Nicholas II and appealed for change. They were met by the police and the Cossacks, resulting in the massacre of 1,200 and casualties of 3,000. These numbers also included civilians who were caught in the crossfire when the protesters fled to nearby houses for shelter from the attack. This assault on the people became known as 'Bloody Sunday' and ignited the Russian Revolution of 1905.

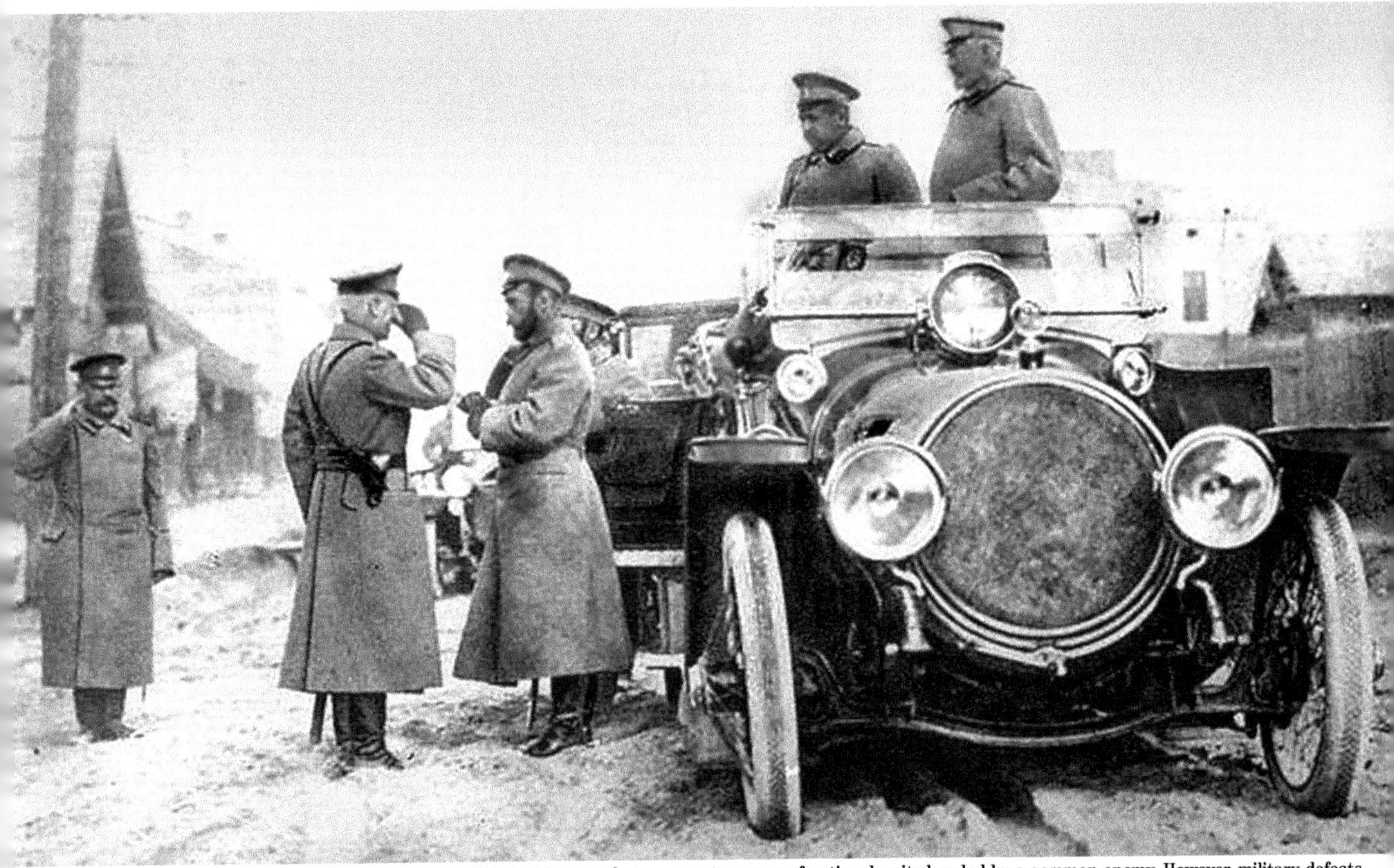

One of the Tsar's rationales for risking war in 1914 had been to foster a greater sense of national unity bonded by a common enemy. However, military defeats and horrifying slaughter of Russian troops undermined both the monarchy and society to the point of collapse. In the opening moves in 1914, at the Battle of Tannenberg, over 30,000 Russian troops were killed or wounded and 90,000 captured. In 1915 Nicholas took direct command of the Russian army, leaving his wife, Alexandra, overseeing the government. Corruption and incompetence in the Imperial government began to show, with the monk Grigori Rasputin suspected of influencing the Tsarist regime to its detriment. By the end of October 1916, Russia had lost upwards of five million men, killed, missing or captured.

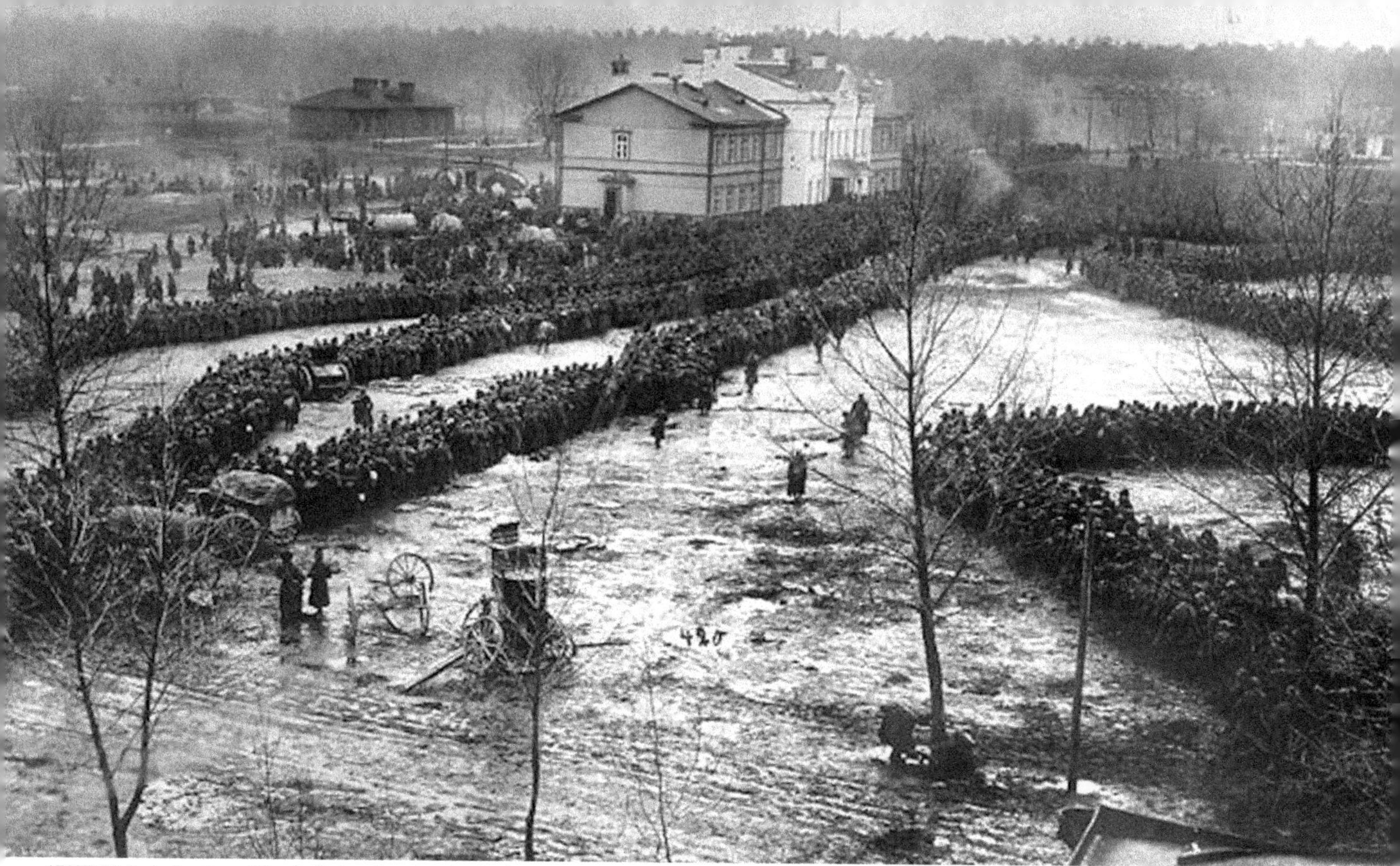

17GW909 An indication of the declining situation developing throughout the Tzar's huge army -- 15,000 Russian prisoners in German hands at Augustow, a city in north-eastern Poland, where in 1914 the Russians had experienced some success when they counterattacked the German army in the lead-up to the Battle of the Vistula River.

17GW912 Photograph taken of the Imperial Russian family and bodyguard shortly before the Revolution: Anastasia; Olga; The Tsar; Alexei; Tatiana; Marie.

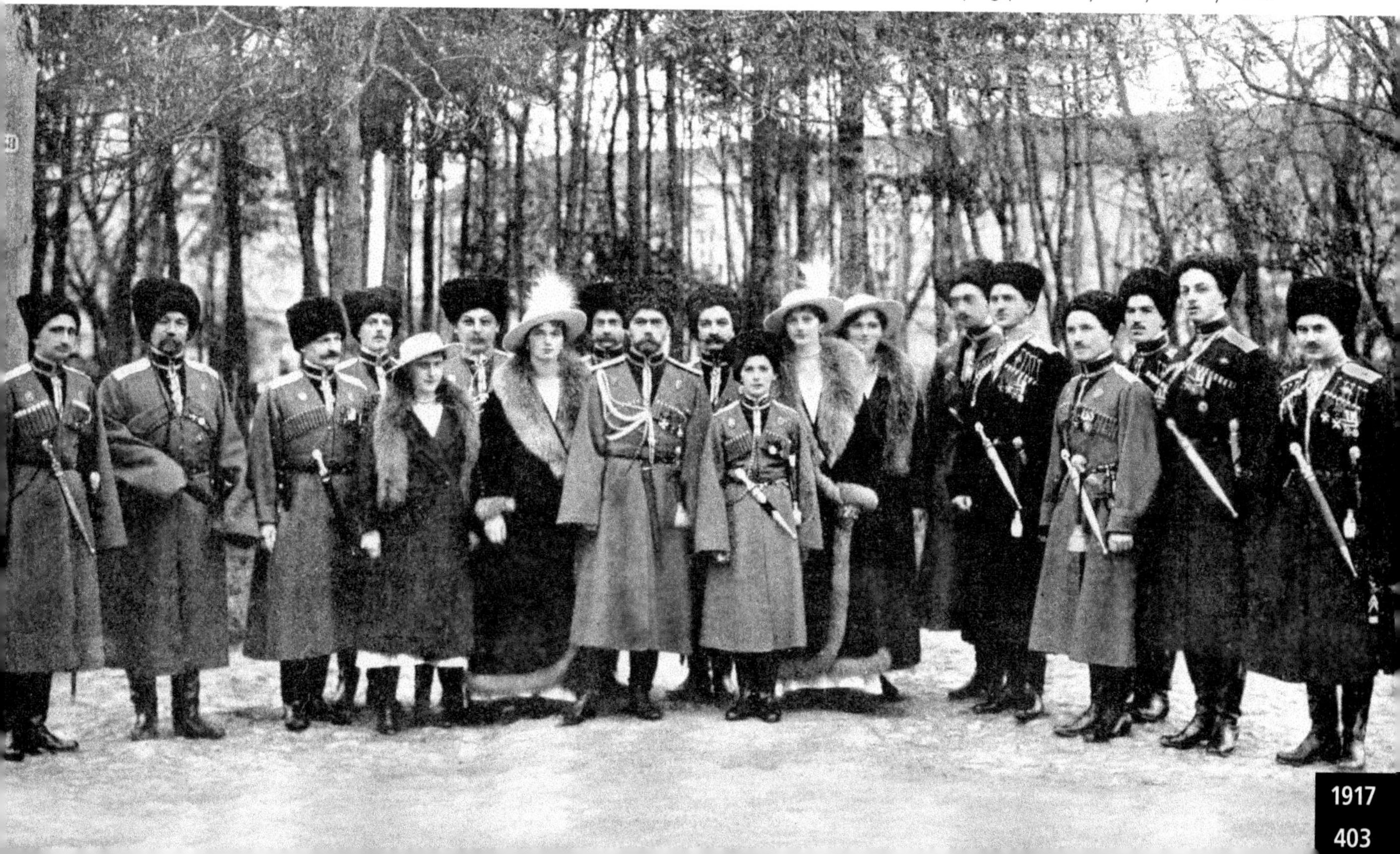

In February and March a series of strikes, involving hundreds of thousands of workers, broke out, centred on the capital Petrograd. The Tsar ordered the army to suppress the rioting by force; however, troops mutinied and some shot their officers rather than confront the protesters with guns (many of the workers were women). Symbols of the Tsarist regime were torn down around the city and governmental authority collapsed. When the Tsar travelled to the capital, Petrograd (Saint Petersburg), by train, the army commanders and his ministers suggested he abdicate the throne. He was placed under house arrest, along with his family, at the Alexander Palace at Tsarskoye Selo. His guards took pleasure in addressing him as 'Nicholas Romanov'.

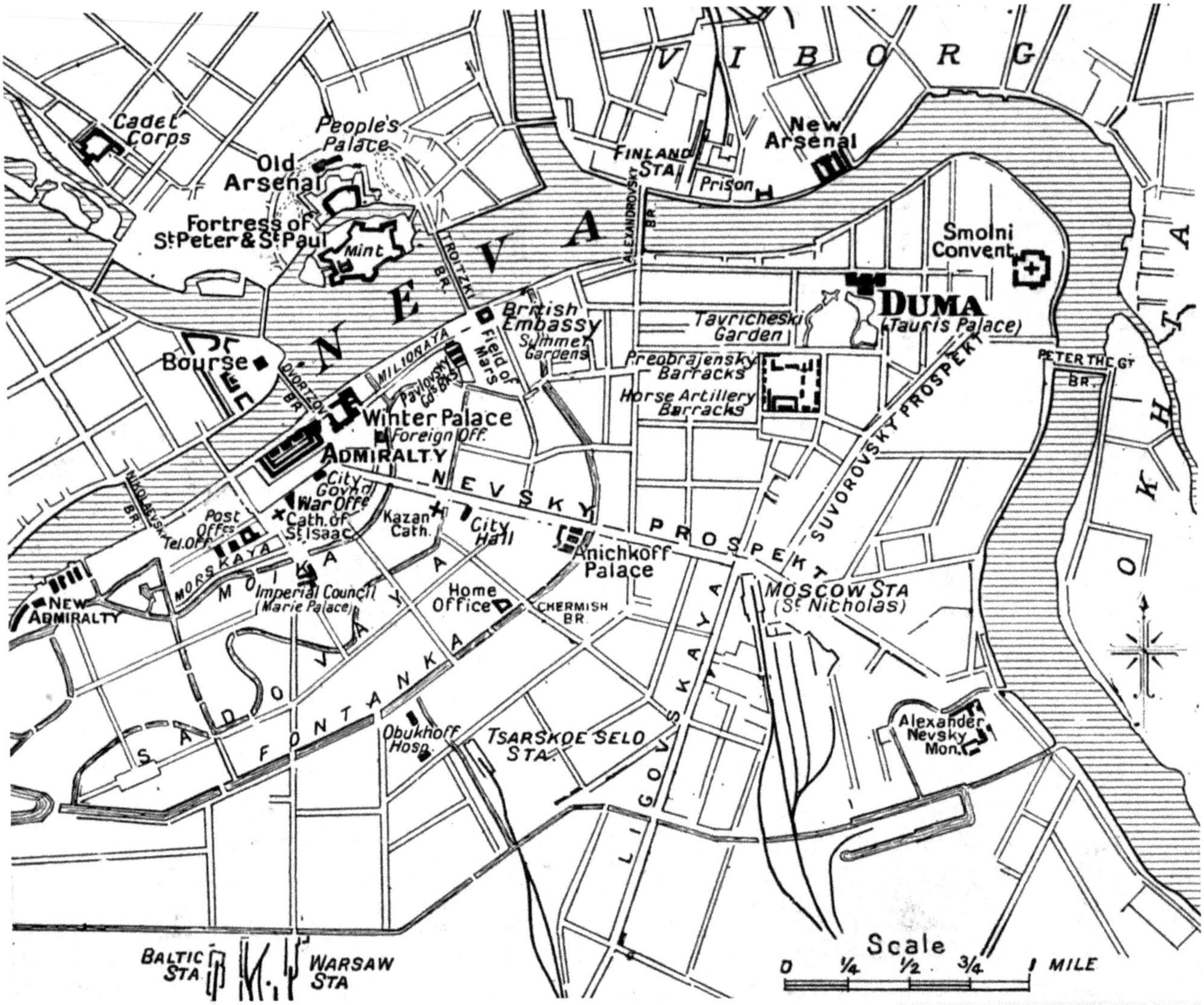

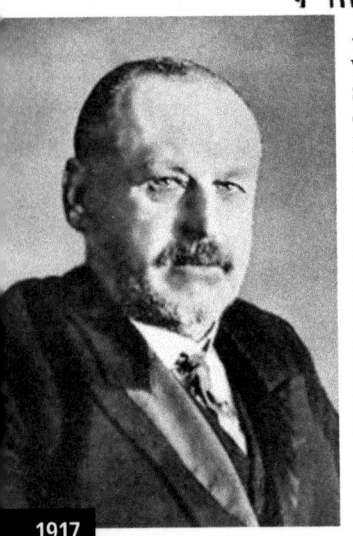

17GW939 Mikhail Vladimirovich Rodzianko, State Councillor and Chamberlain of the Imperial family; Chairman of the State Duma; one of the leaders of the February Revolution of 1917, during which he headed the Provisional Committee of the State Duma. He was a key figure in the events that led to the abdication of Nicholas II of Russia on 15 March 1917.

Telegram from Mikhail Rodzianko to Tsar Nicholas, 12 March 1917:
The situation is getting worse. Measures must be taken quickly. The last hour has sounded, when the fate of the country and the dynasty will be decided.

Telegram to Tsar Nicholas on the same day from the elected members of the Council of Empire:
The maintenance of the old Government in office is tantamount to the complete overthrow of law and order, involving defeat on the battlefield, the end of the dynasty, and the greatest misfortunes for Russia.
We consider that the only way of salvation lies in a complete and final rupture with the past, the immediate convocation of Parliament and the summoning of a person enjoying the confidence of the nation.

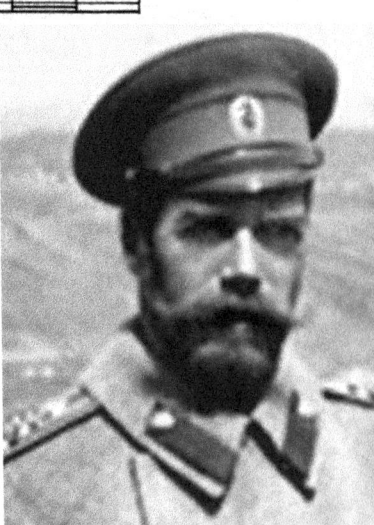

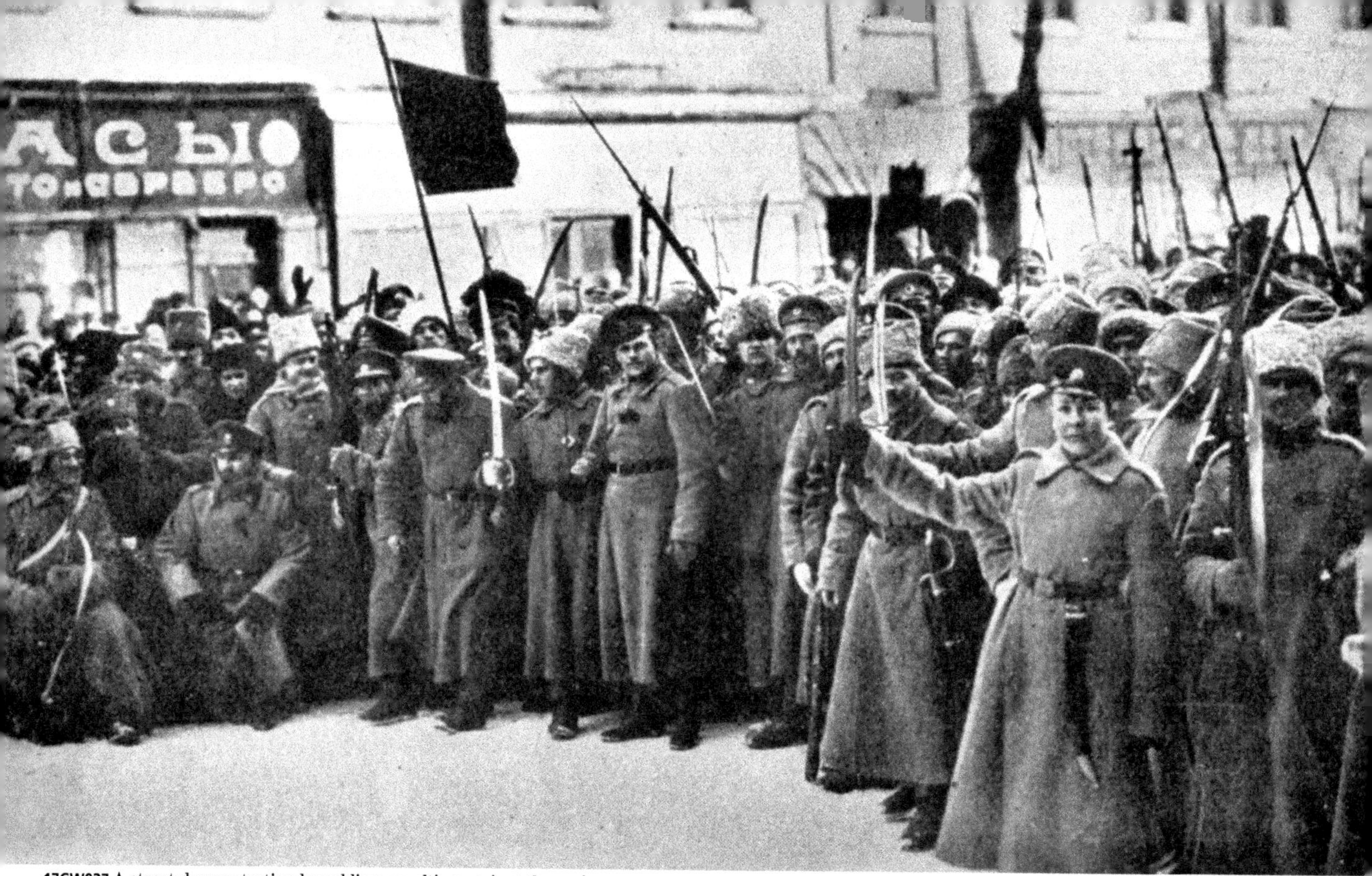

17GW937 A street demonstration by soldiers revolting against the regime.

17GW947 A barricade with artillery pieces on the Liteiny Prospect, the main street through Petrograd. The enemy were the police and military units loyal to the Tsar and his government.

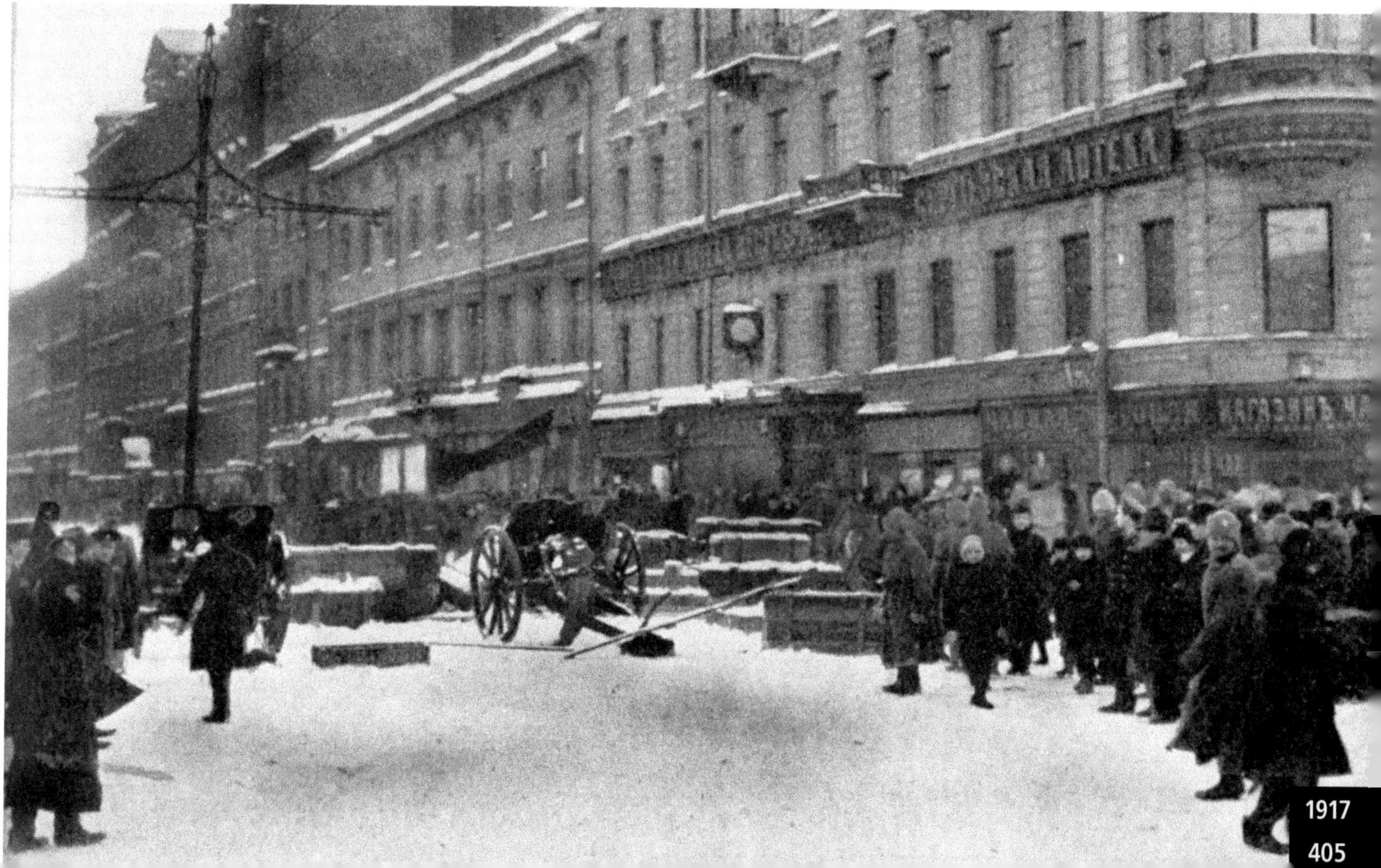

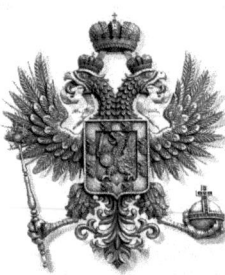

The double-headed eagle was a main element of the coat of arms of the Russian Empire from the 13th century. It was associated with Tsarist rule.

17GW935 One of the last sittings of the Duma (Parliament) under the old regime. The situation on the streets of the capital, Petrograd, were being described as dangerous.

17GW934 The Duma, with workers and soldiers packed in to hear details of a new government; addressed by Rodzianko.

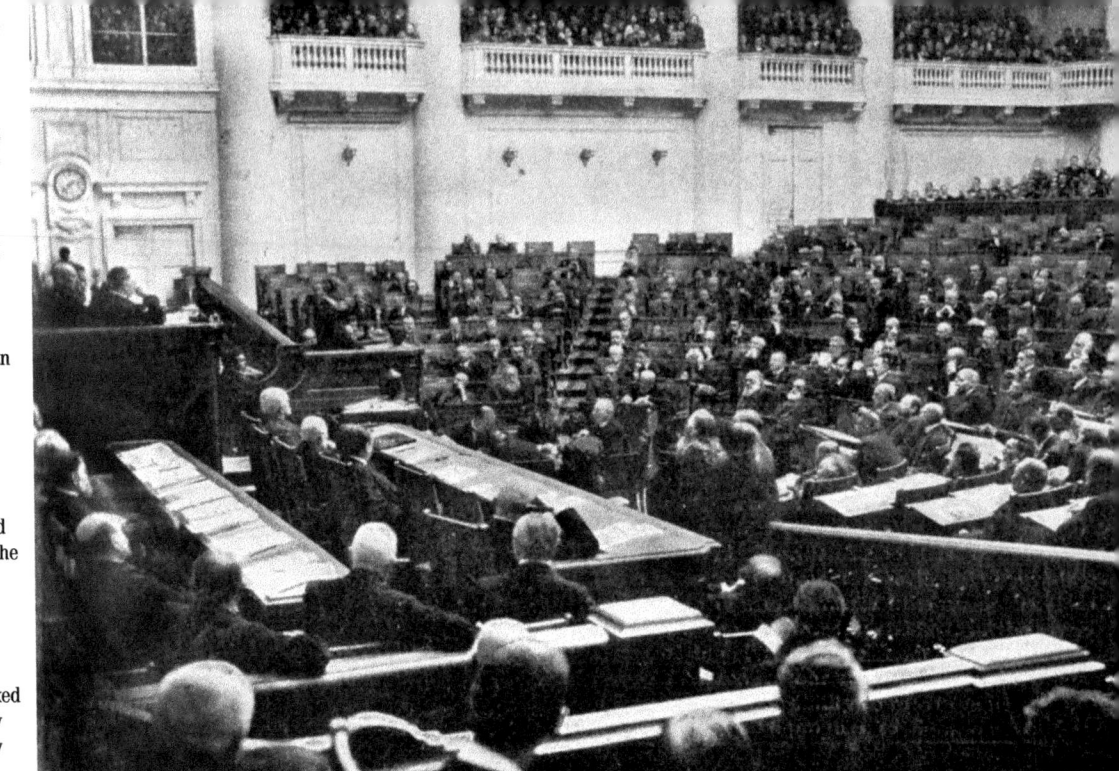

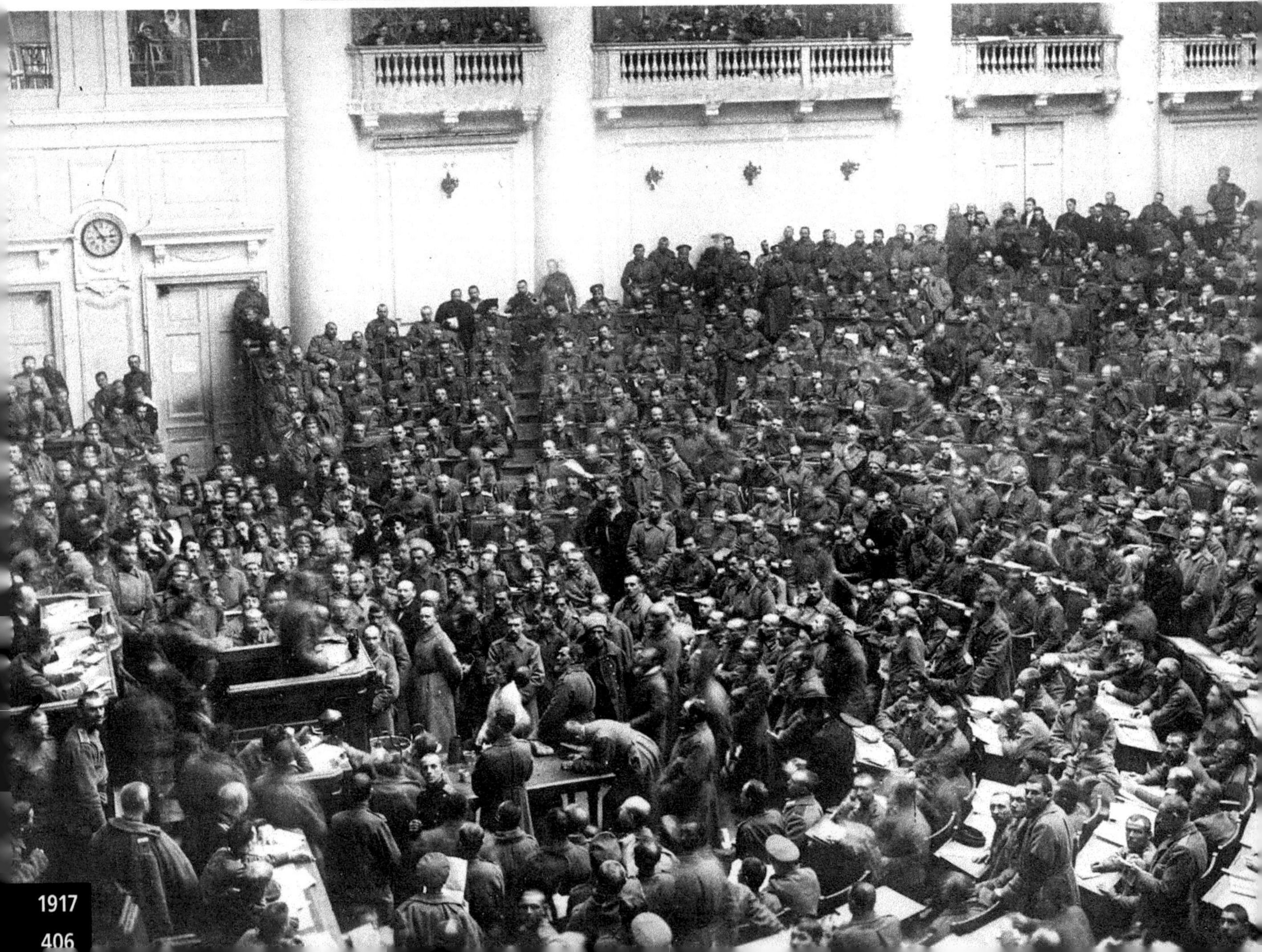

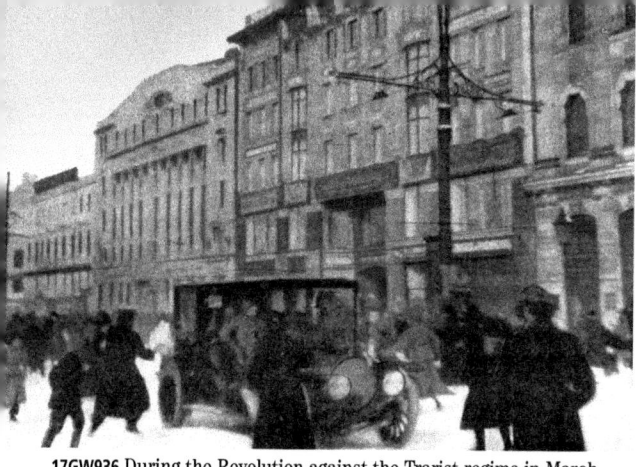
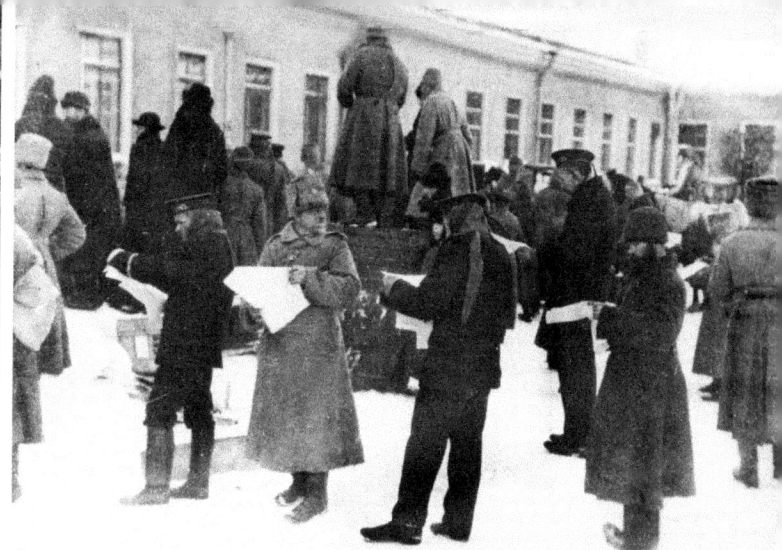

17GW936 During the Revolution against the Tsarist regime in March 1917 – shots fired into the street.

17GW946 Bulletin sheets dispensing the latest news being distributed in the Nevsky Prospect thoroughfare during the revolution.

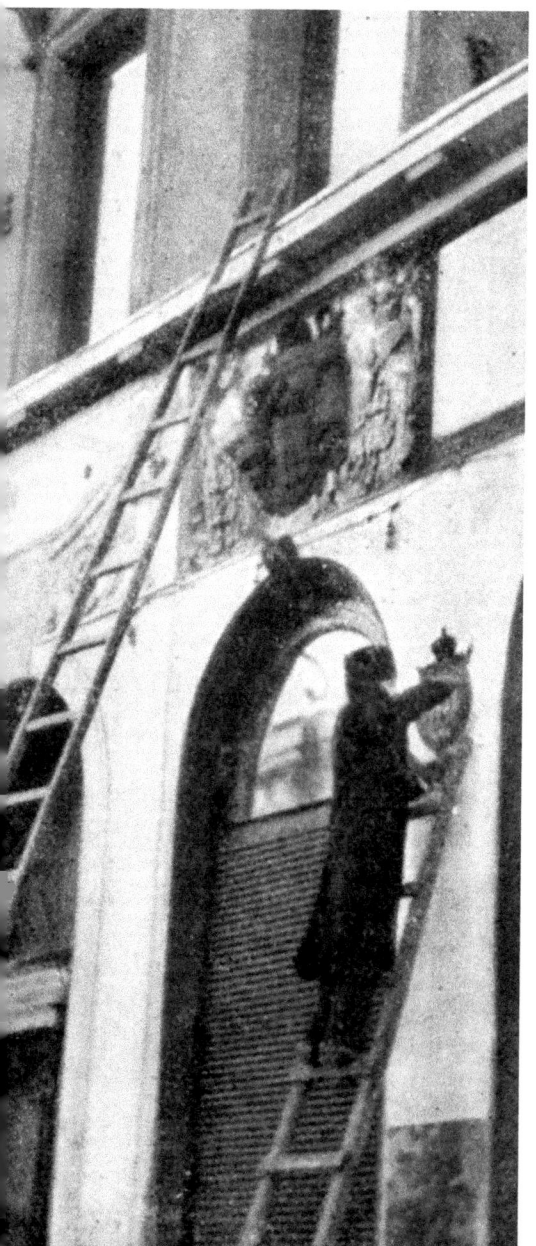
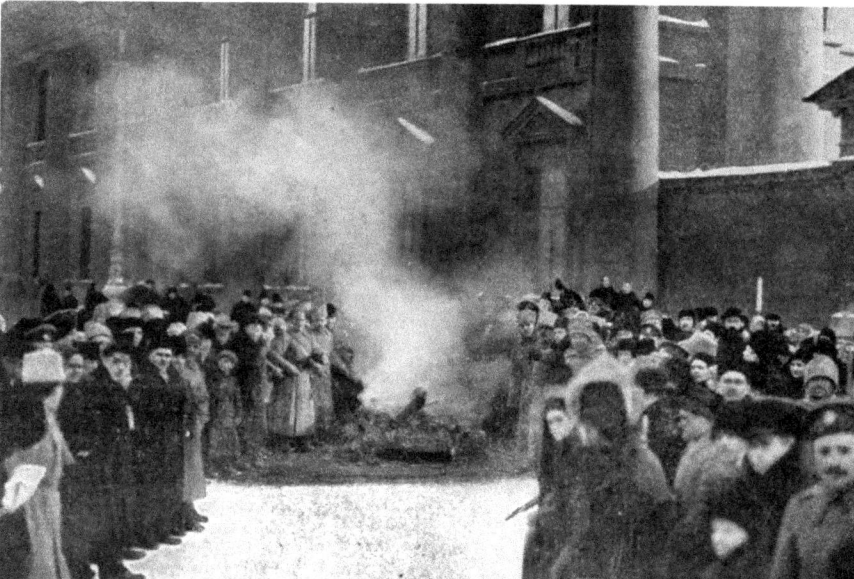

17GW948. 17GW949. Imperial insignia on public buildings were removed and destroyed.

17GW950 Restoring public order on the streets of Petrograd.

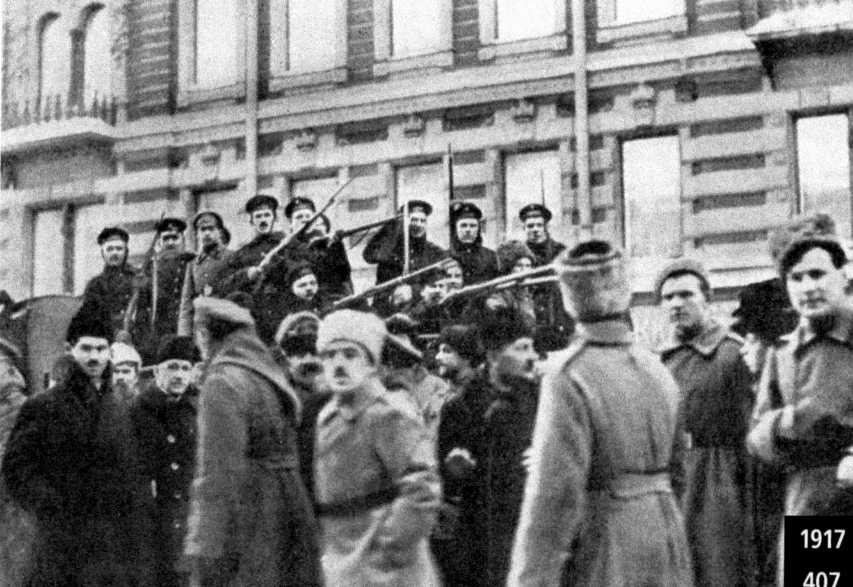

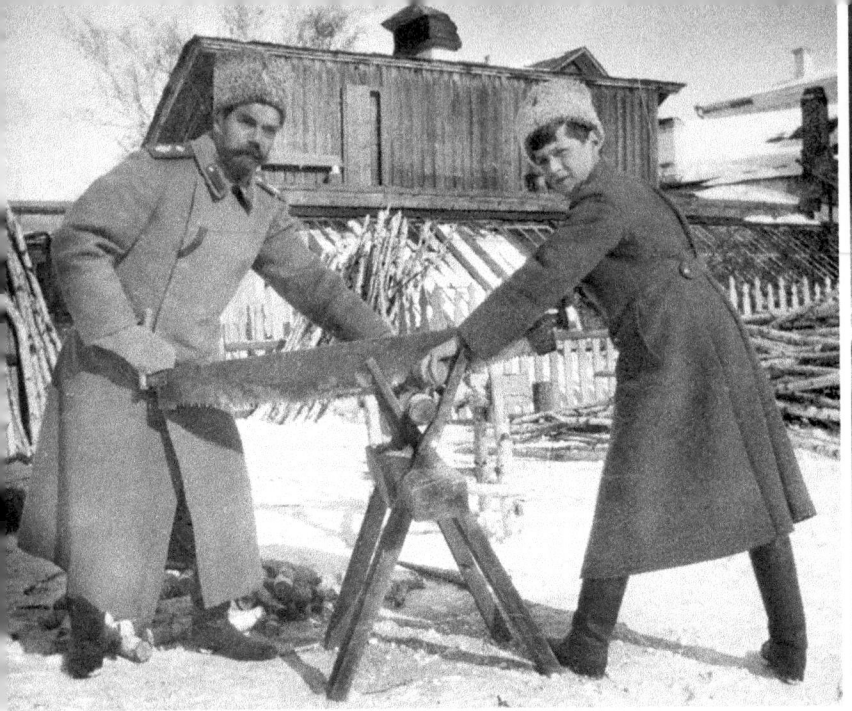
17GW940 The Tsar Nicholas II and his son Alexei in captivity in Tobolsk in 1917.

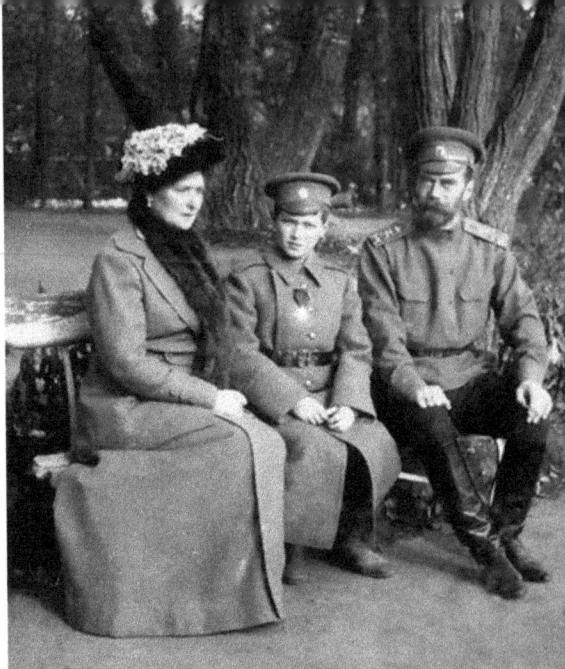
17GW941 Empress Alexandra Feodorovna, Tsarevich Alexei Nikolayevich and Emperor Nicholas II at Tsarskoye Selo.

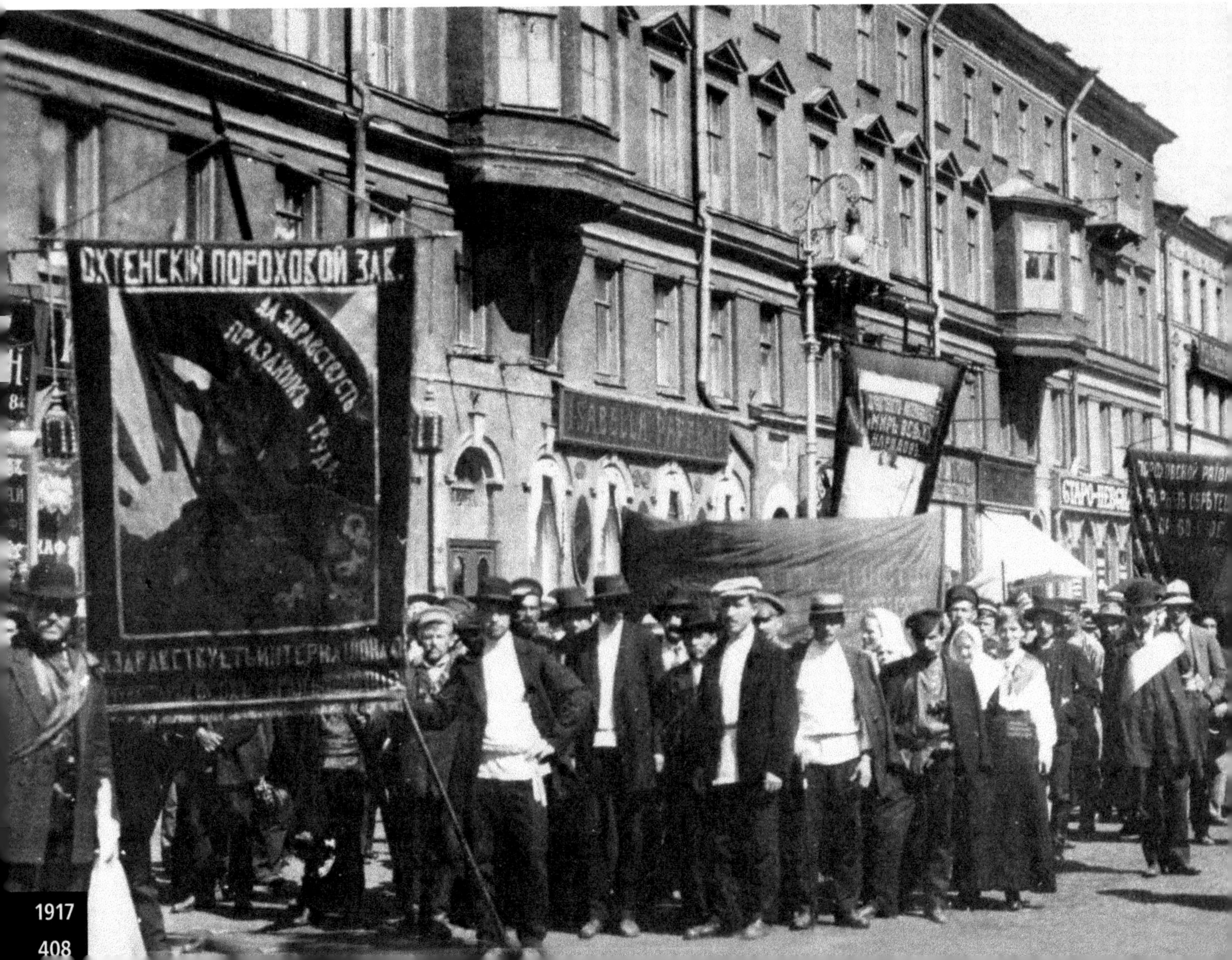

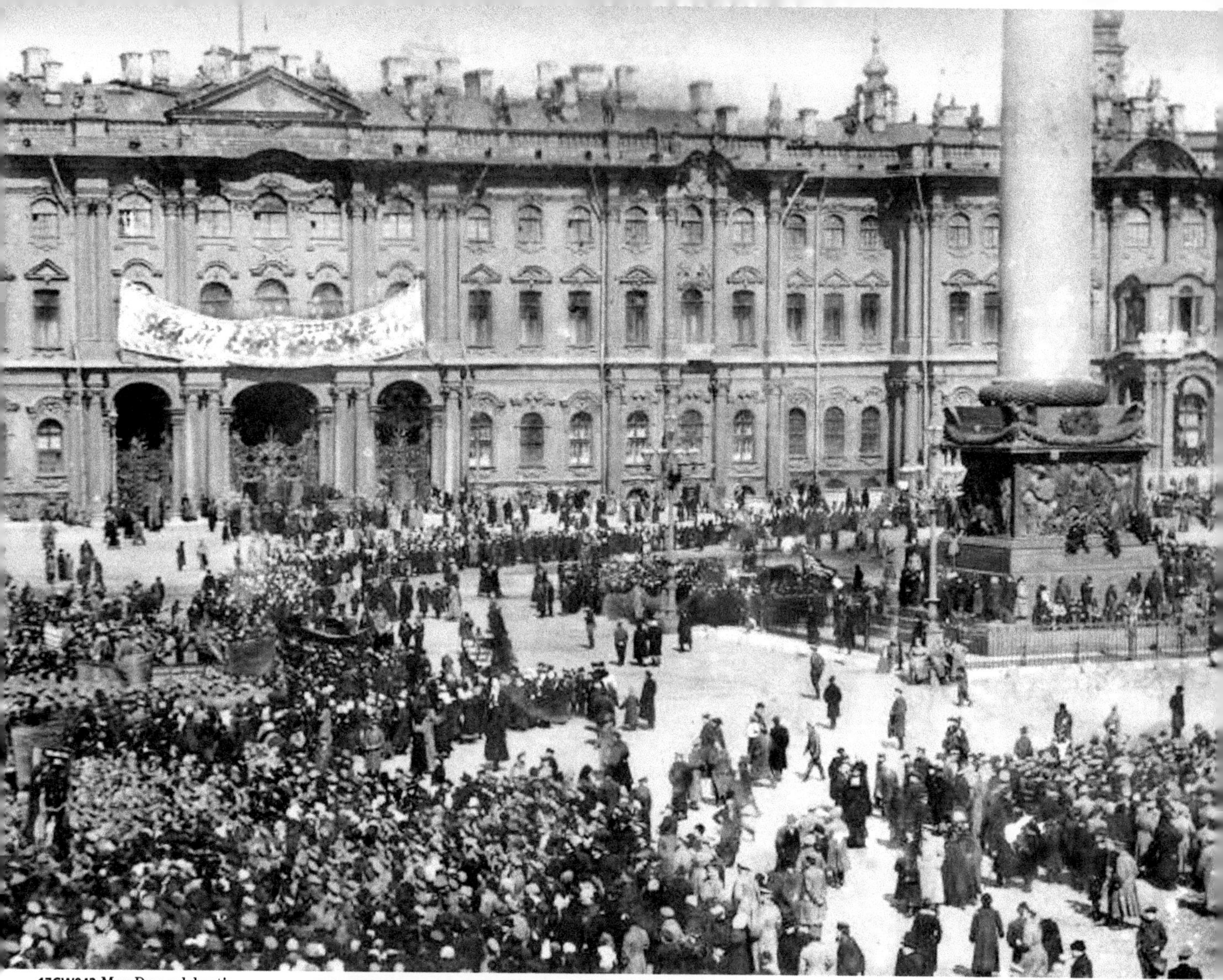

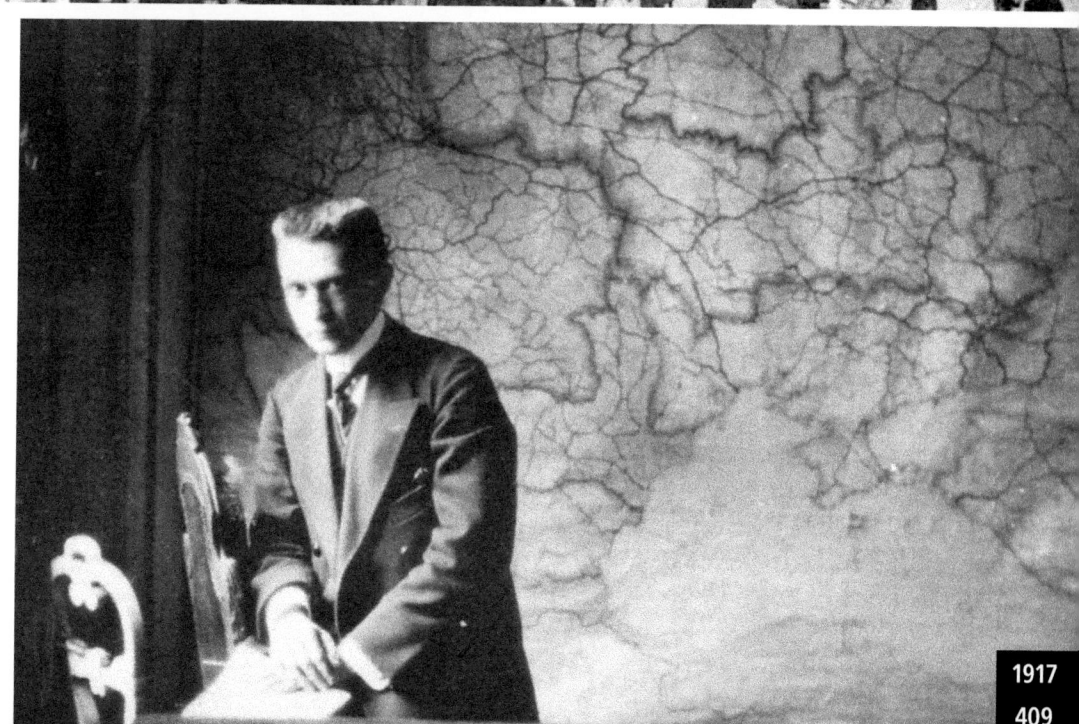

17GW943 May Day celebrations, 1917, crowds gathered at the Winter Palace. The banner on the front of the palace reads: 'Our International'.

17GW944 On the streets of Petrograd in June 1917 during the months of the Provisional Government, which had been founded following the overthrow of the Tsar. The Bolsheviks made it known that they would make peace.

17GW945 Russian Minister of War, Alexander Kerensky, was determined to continue the war against the Central Powers and began planning an offensive.

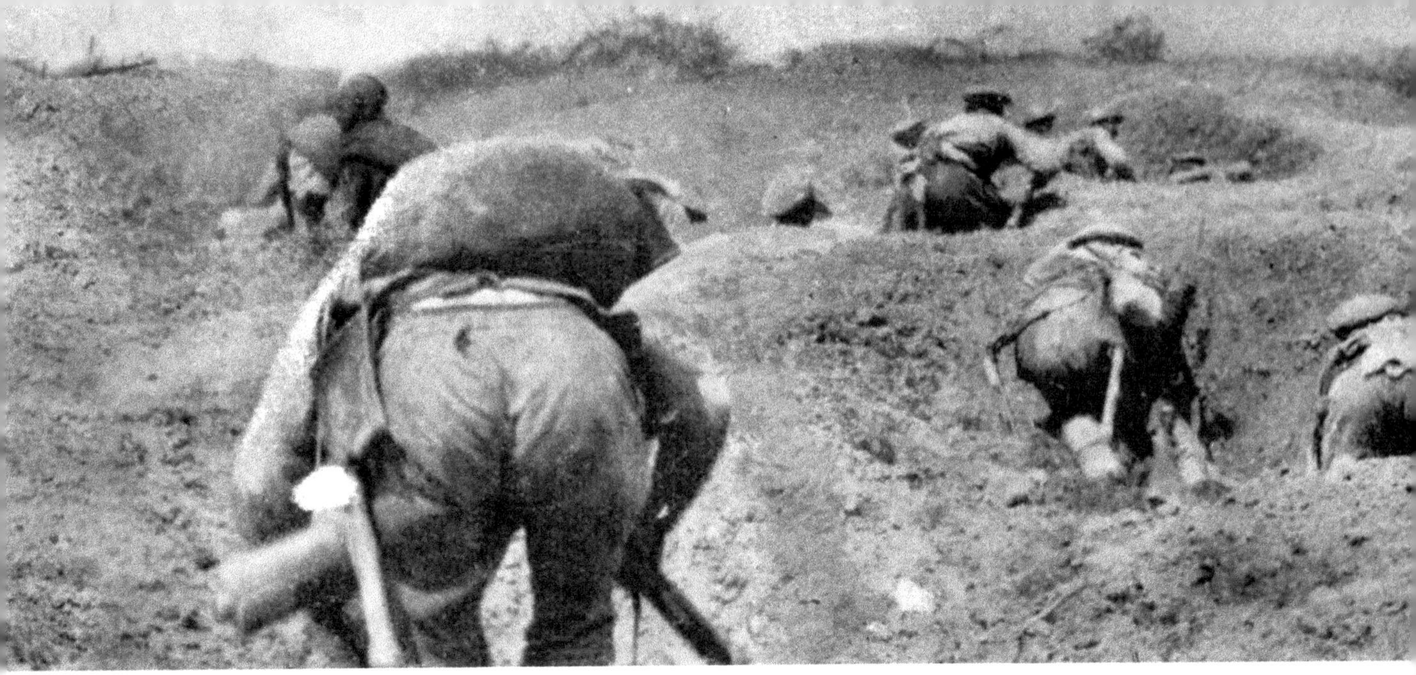

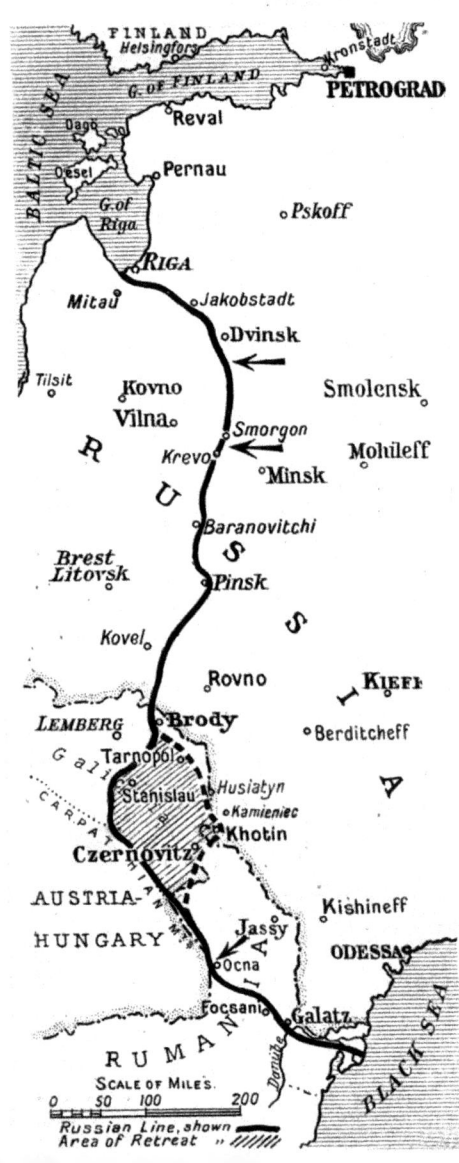

1917
410

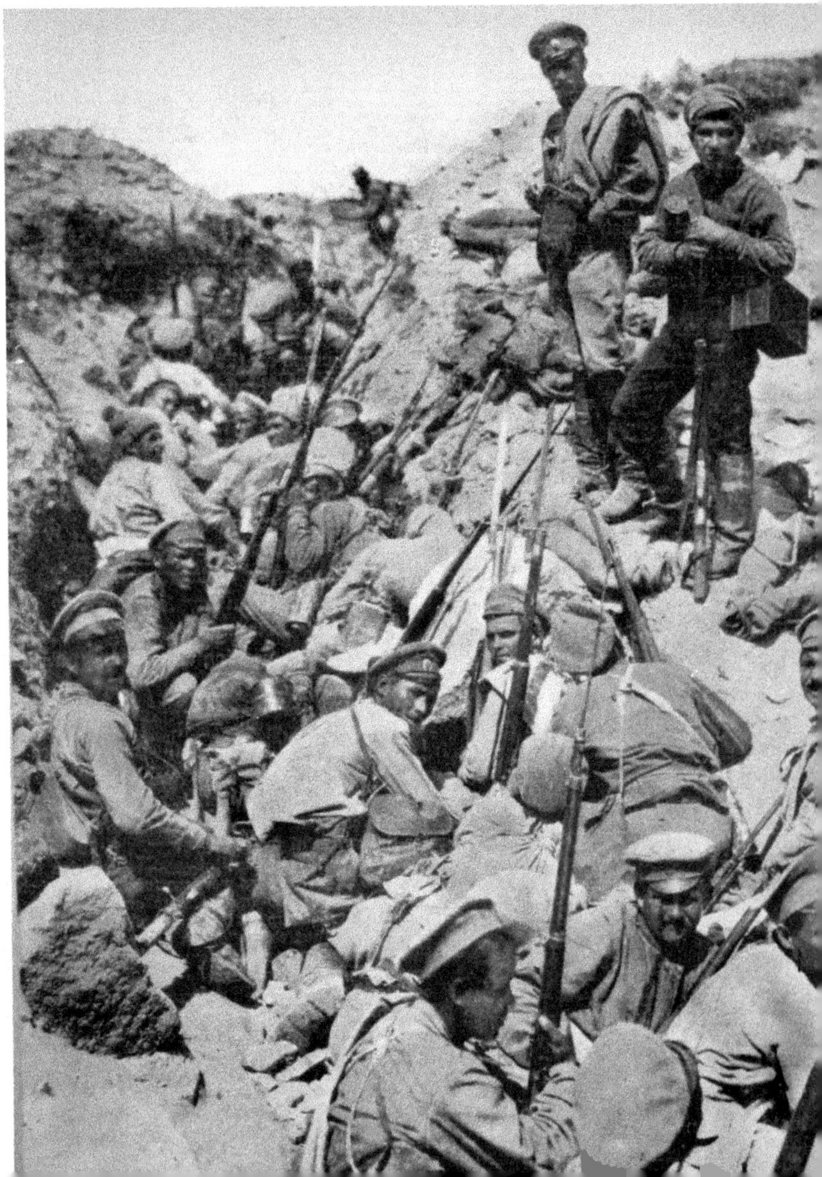

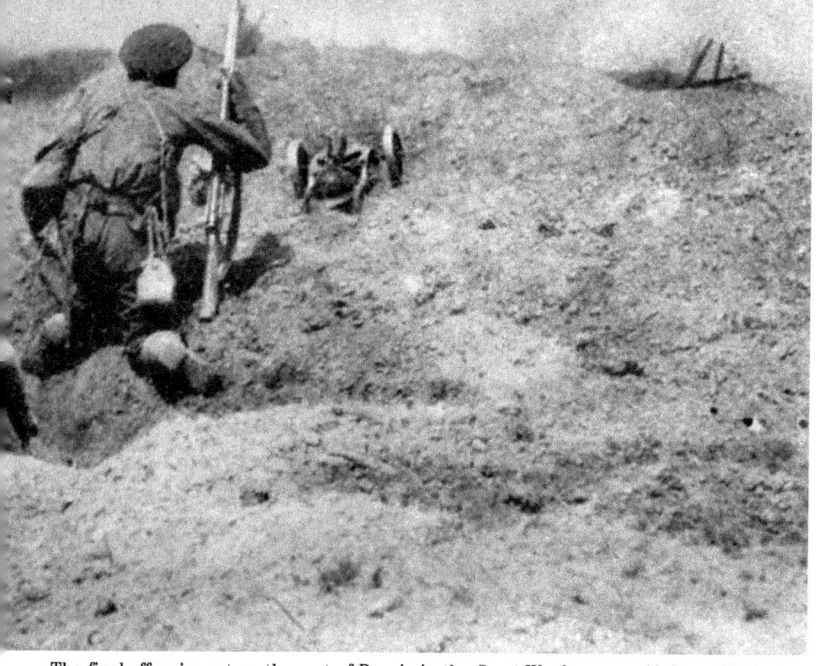
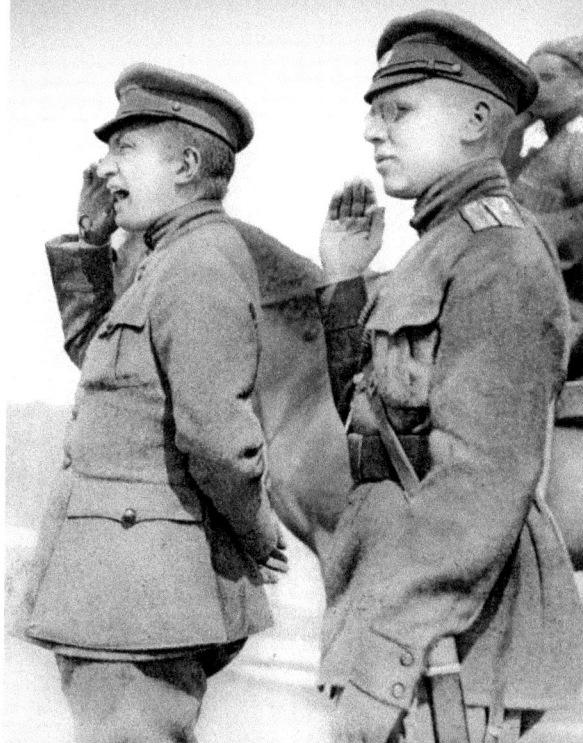

The final offensive act on the part of Russia in the Great War began on 18 June, 1917, when Kerensky ordered Russian forces to begin an offensive against the Austro-Hungarians in Galicia. The attack was a failure, resulting in 400,000 Russian casualties. Lenin announced that the Bolsheviks had seized power and urged the nation to prepare for a Soviet government.

17GW913 Map of the Kerensky attack against the Austrians. The black line shows the furthest Russian gains, south west of Lemberg. The arrows in the north indicate abortive attempts on 20 July; as does the arrow at Ocna. The dotted line and shaded area shows the 100 mile retreat by the Russians which followed.

17GW915 Siberian infantry attacking over shell cratered ground in July 1917.

17GW914 The second wave of Siberian infantry waiting for the order to advance. The attack was successful in capturing Dzike-Lany, a fortified summit south west of Brzenzany.

17GW911 Kerensky, Minister of War of the Russian Provisional Government, addressing the troops before the offensive.

17GW916, 17GW917. Russians retreating after the failure of the Kerensky offensive, July 1917. Lenin coined the phrase: 'They are voting with their feet!'

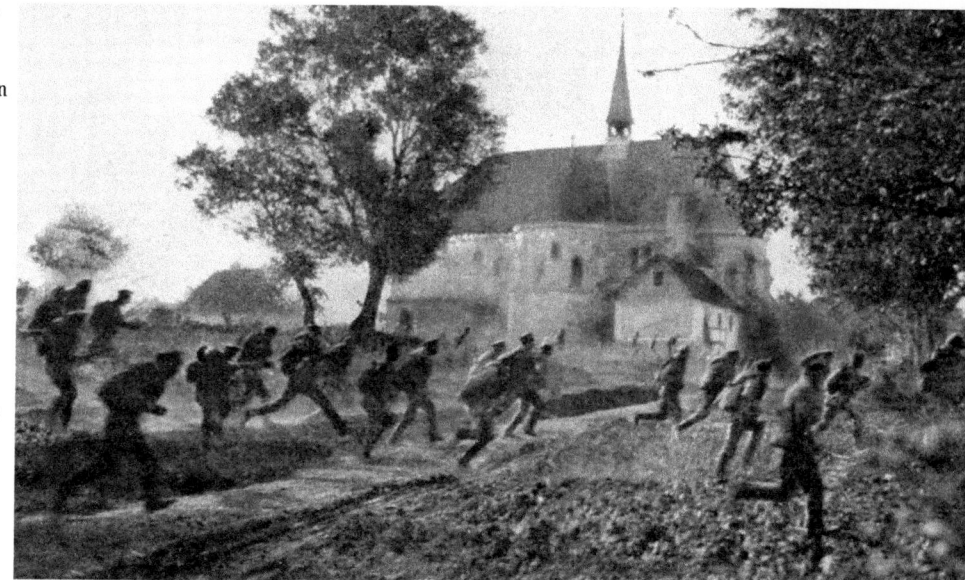
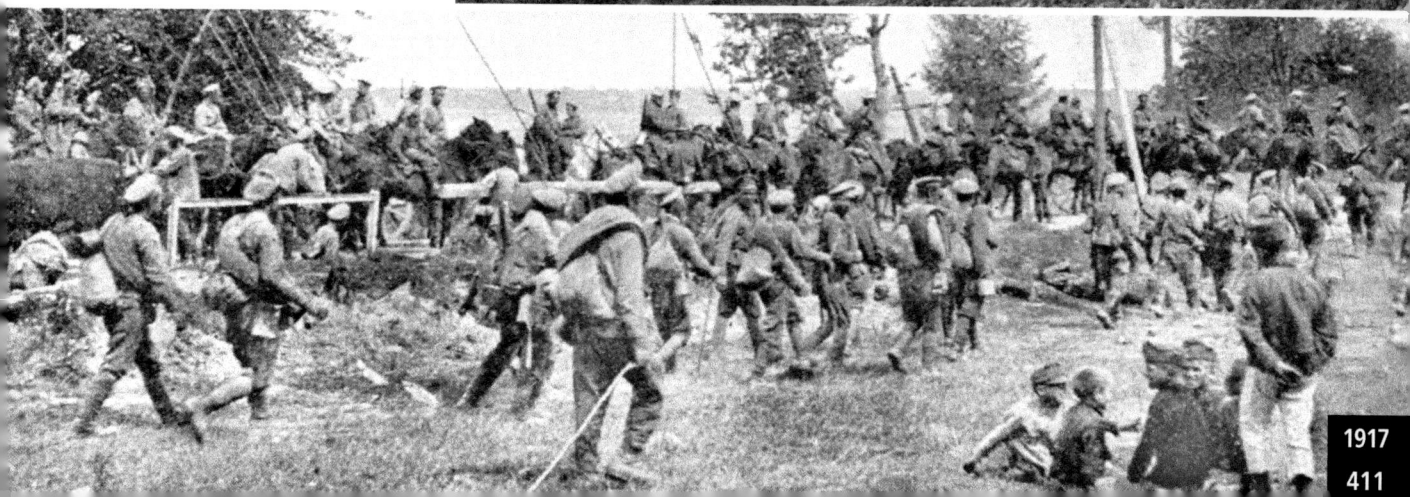

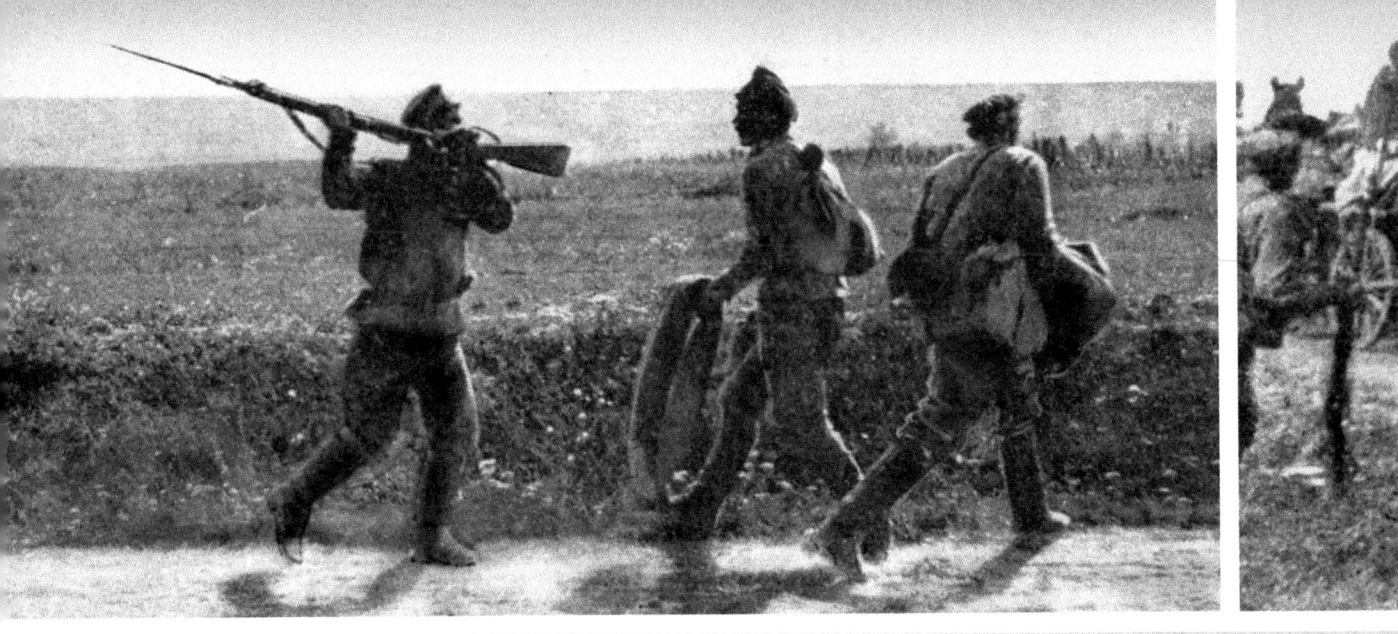

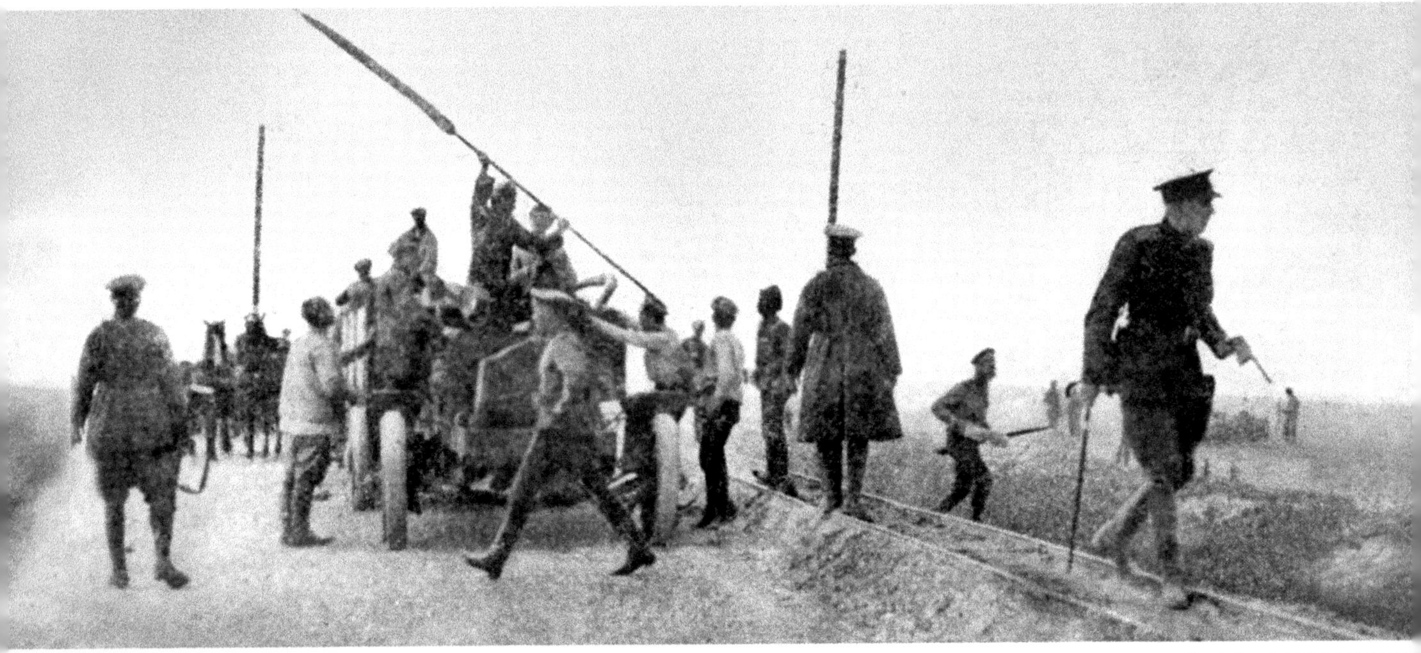

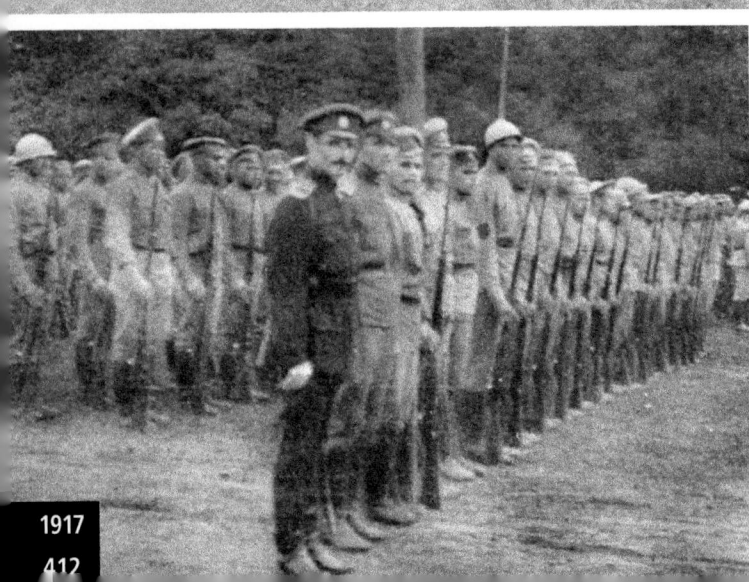

17GW922 Survivors of the 2nd Orenburg Storming Battalion, which had been thrown into the line, despite having only just arrived and when the Russian armies were in full retreat. The battalion comprised volunteers from the Urals and it had fought hard for three days without food, losing half their number killed. Here we see them drawn out to refit and take in replacements. However, none of the reserves at the front would join them.

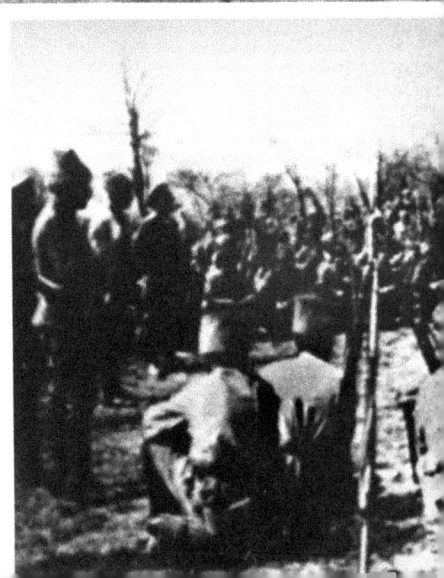

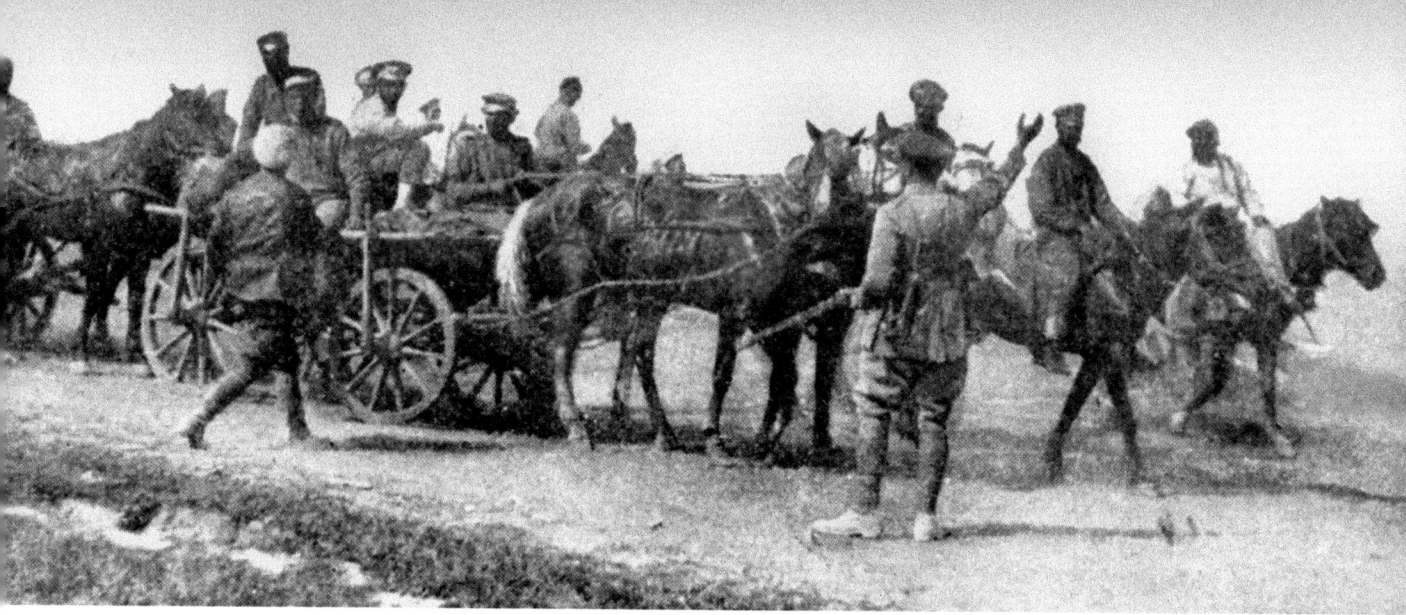

17GW918 A soldier loyal to the Russian Provisional Government attempting to stop deserters after the defeat of the Kerensky offensive, July 1917.

17GW920, 17GW921. British officers, acting as advisors to the Russian army, halting fleeing Russian soliders. Note the officer with the Mauser pistol.

17GW919 Deserters moving in haste, in some cases one hundred miles away from the Austrians and Germans.

17GW923 A Russian officer informing his men of the reinstitution of the death penalty on the orders of the Commander-in-Chief of the Provisional Government's armed forces, General Lavr Kornilov:
I consider the voluntary retreat of units from their positions as equivalent to treason and treachery. Therefore, I catagorically require that all commanders in such cases should, without hesitation, turn the fire of machine guns and arttillery against the traitors. I take all responsibility for the victims on myself.

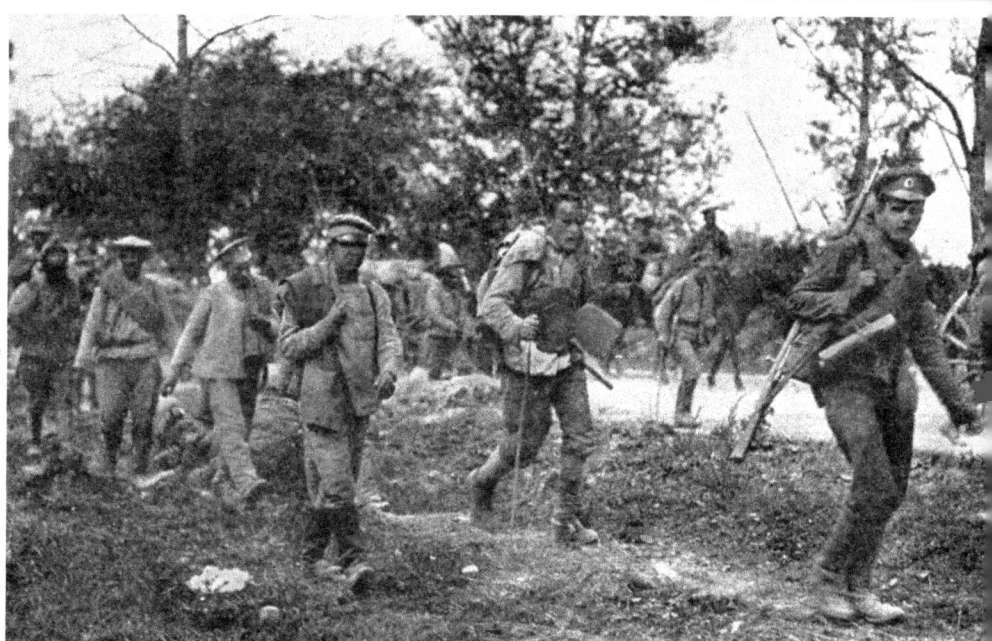

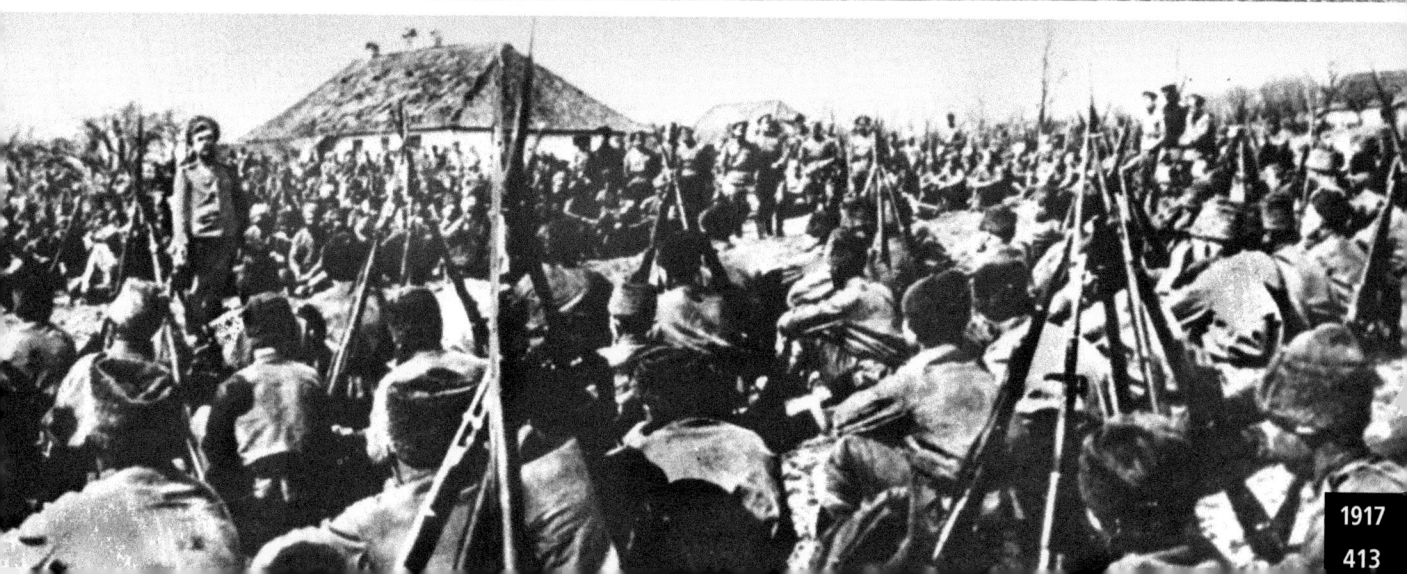

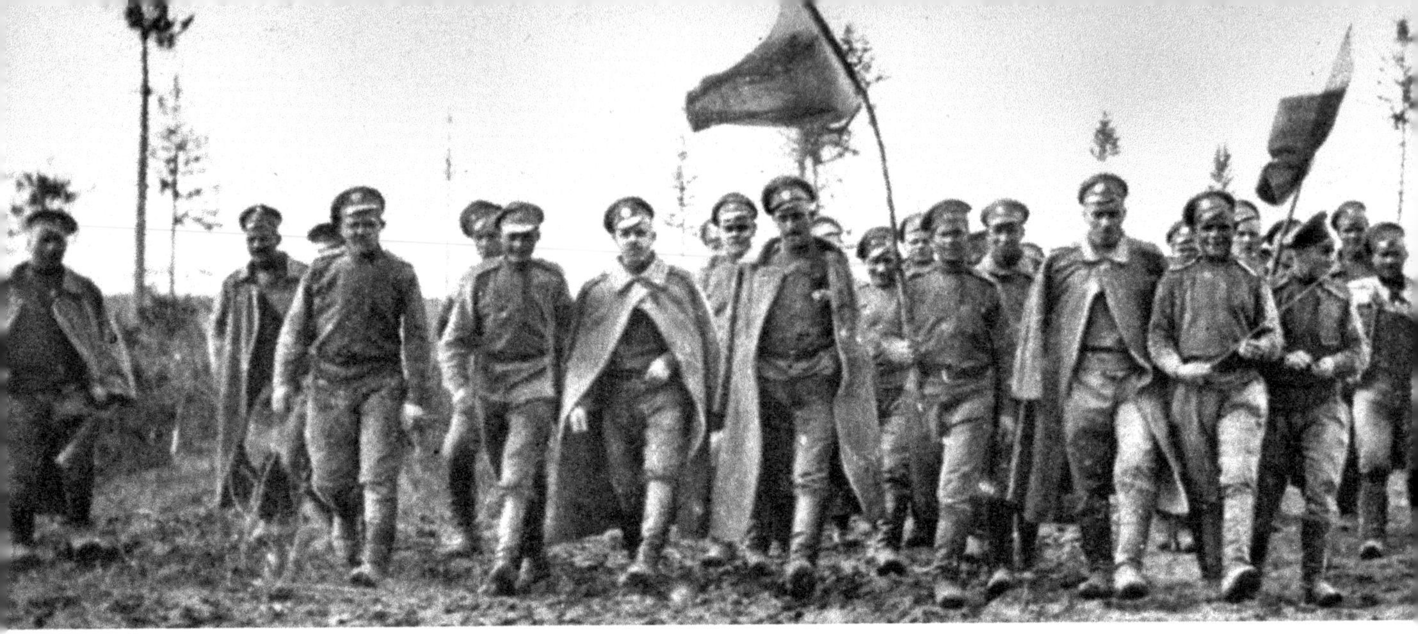

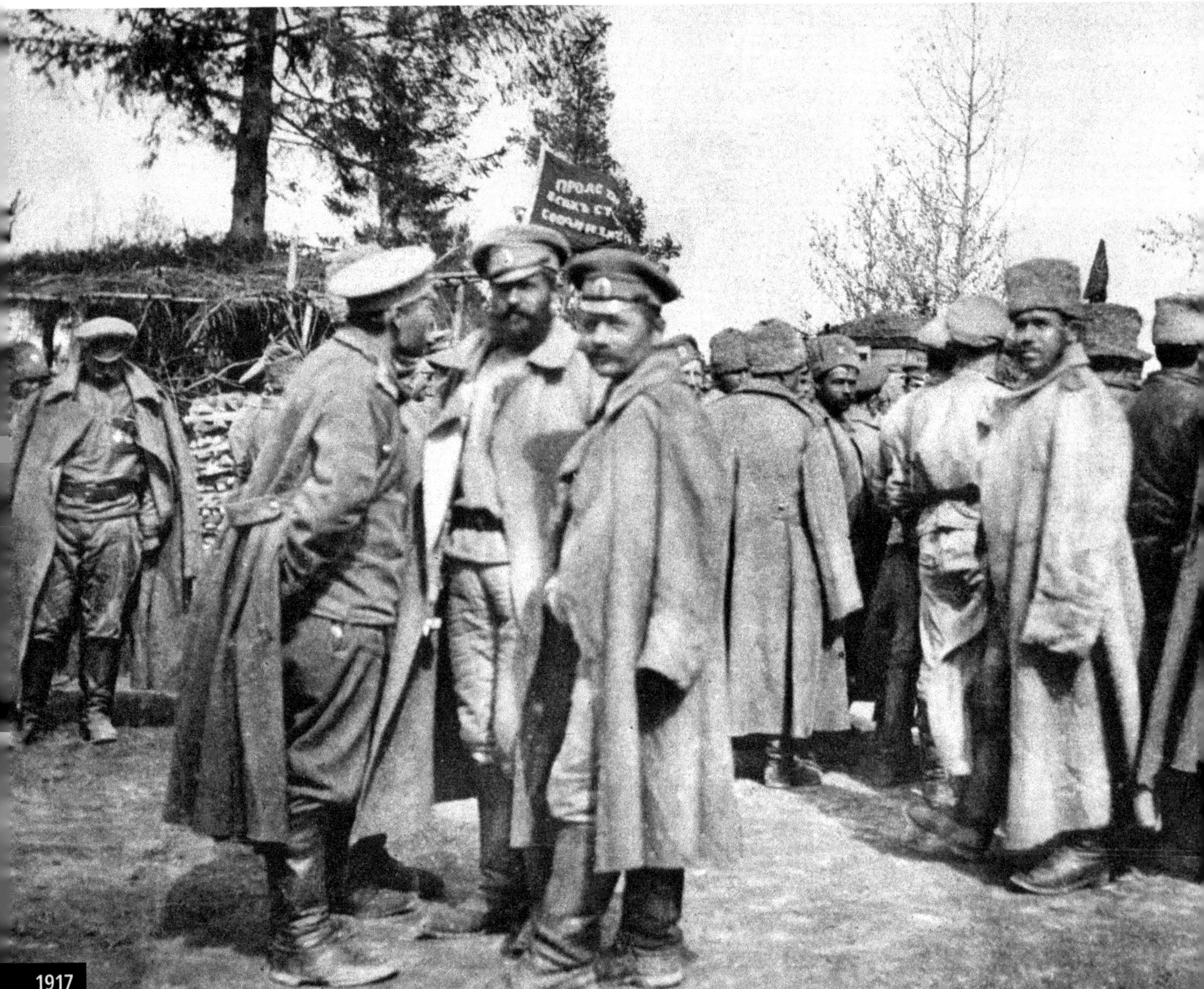

1917

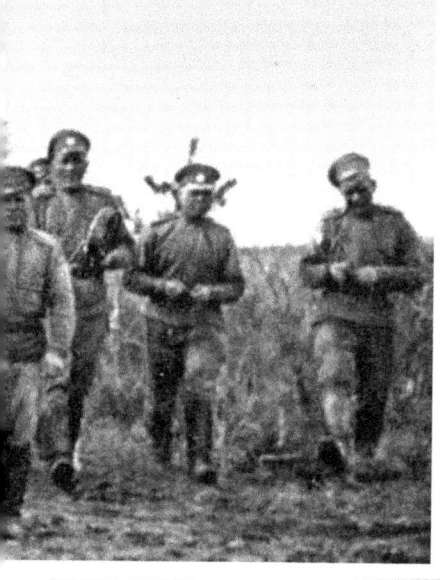
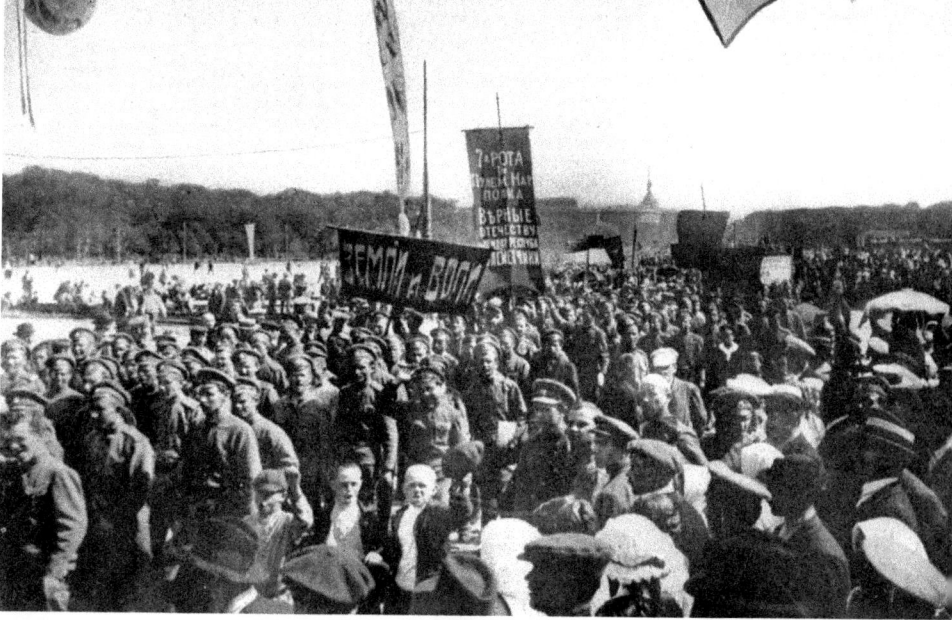

17GW925, 17GW926. Russians soldiers enjoying a new freedom – going from camp to camp with red flags, showing support for the Bolsheviks.

17GW928 General Lavr Georgievich Kornilov.

17GW929 Bolshevik troops stand on a street corner in Petrograd reading leaflets criticising the Kerensky coalition government. They wanted a negotiated peace

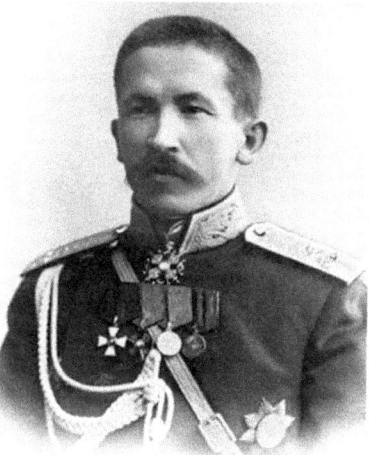
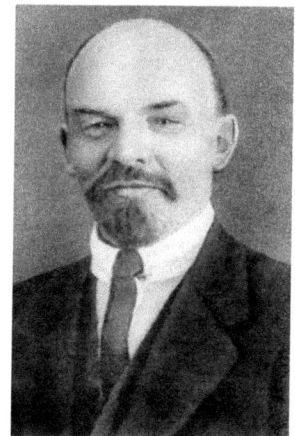

17GW927 A Bolshevik demonstration against the Kerensky led Provisional Government. General Kornilov attempted to lead a coup but was thwarted. In October Kerensky formed a coalition government, but within weeks the Bolsheviki seized control.

17GW933 Vladimir Lenin played a leading role in the October Revolution that overthrew Kerensky's government.

17GW930 Alexaner Kerensky, the socialist leader who became Minister of War on 17 May 1917, and went on to become Premier of Russia for a few short months. His policy to continue fighting the war ensured the downfall of both him and his government.

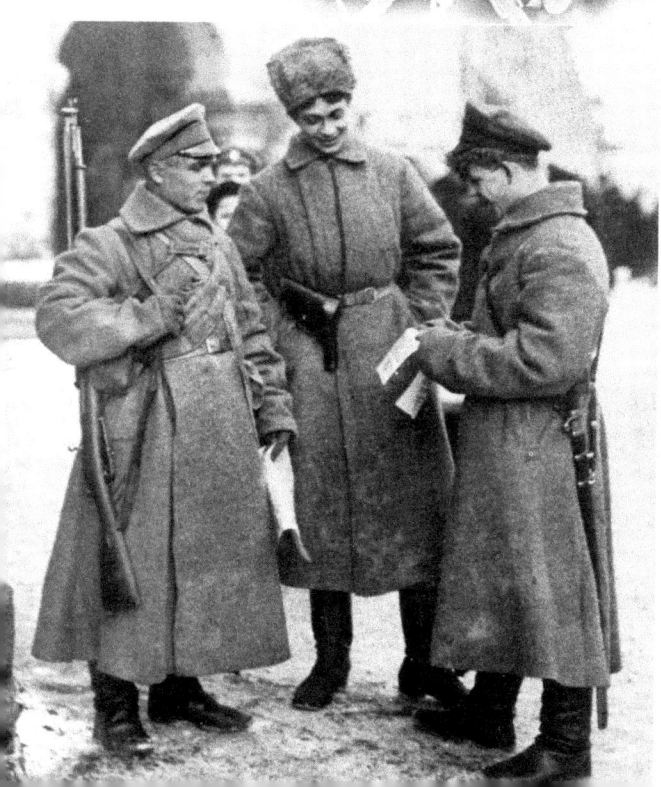
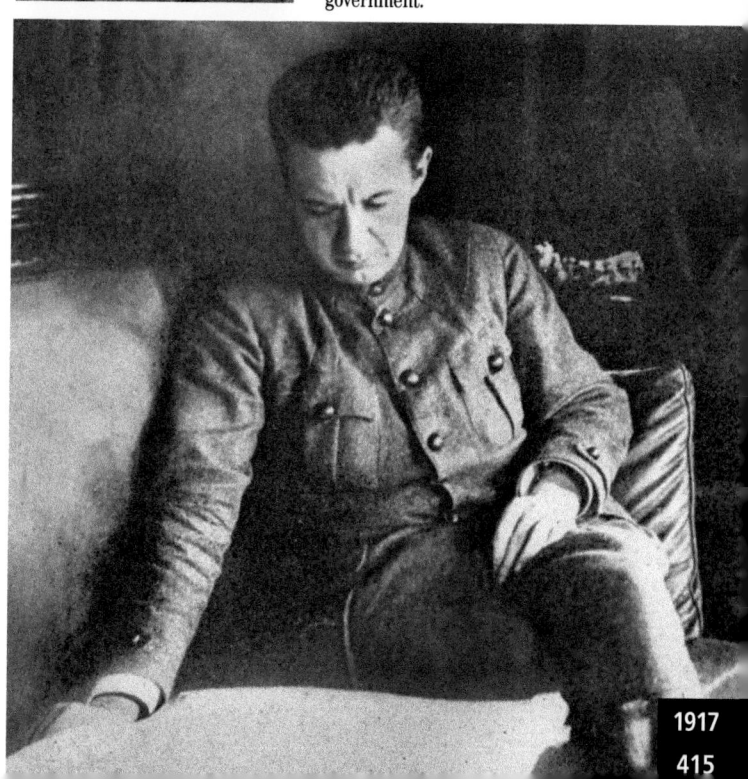

1917

In October Lenin issued the Decree on Peace, urging an immediate ceasefire and a treaty with the Central Powers. On 19 November a Bolshevik delegation began peace negotiations with German officers at Brest-Litovsk, Poland. An armistice was declared: **The Russians were out.**

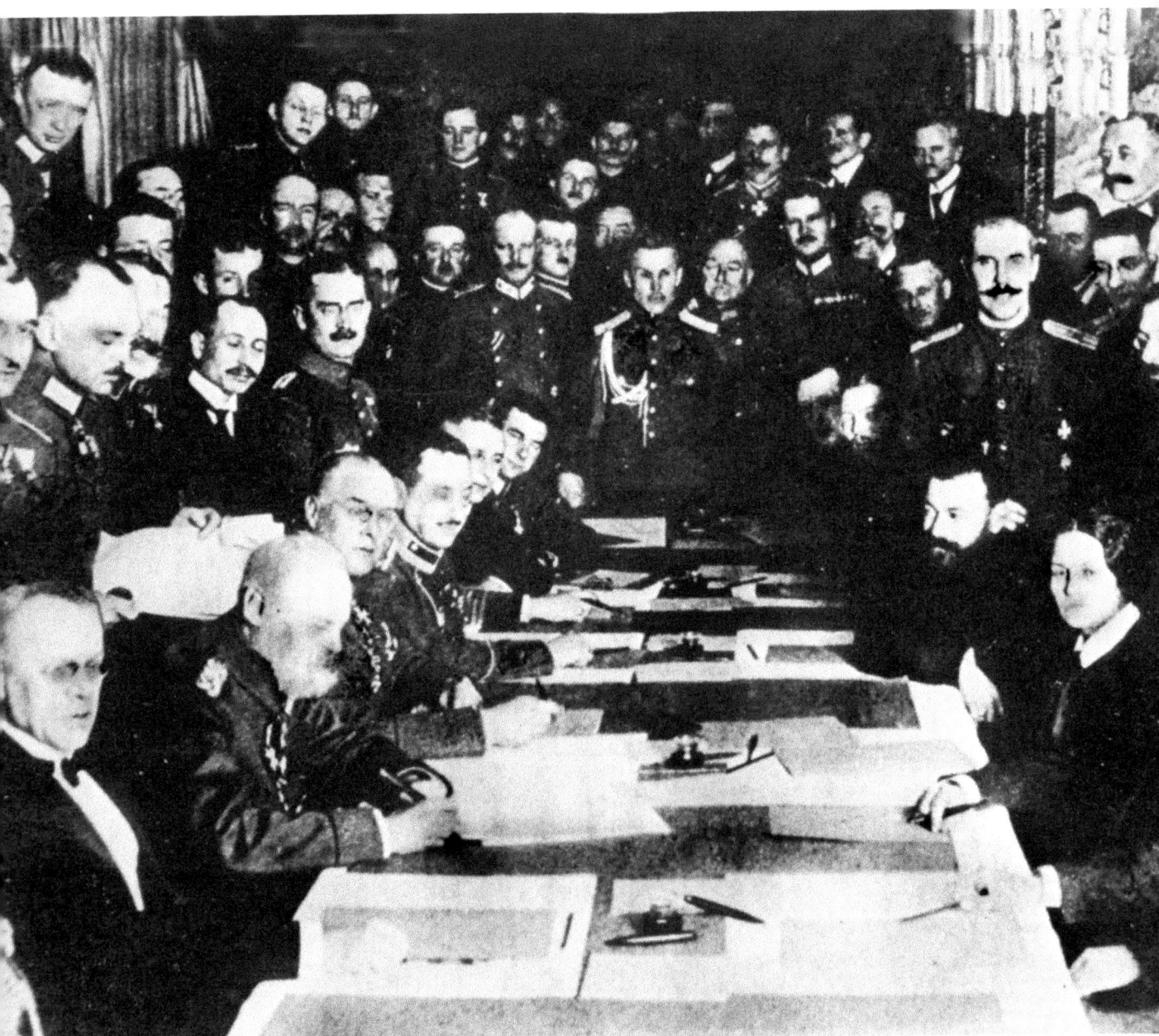

17GW911 Locked in conference at Brest-Litovsk, Germans on the left and Russians on the right; sat on the Russian side is a woman interpreter translating the German terms to her countrymen.

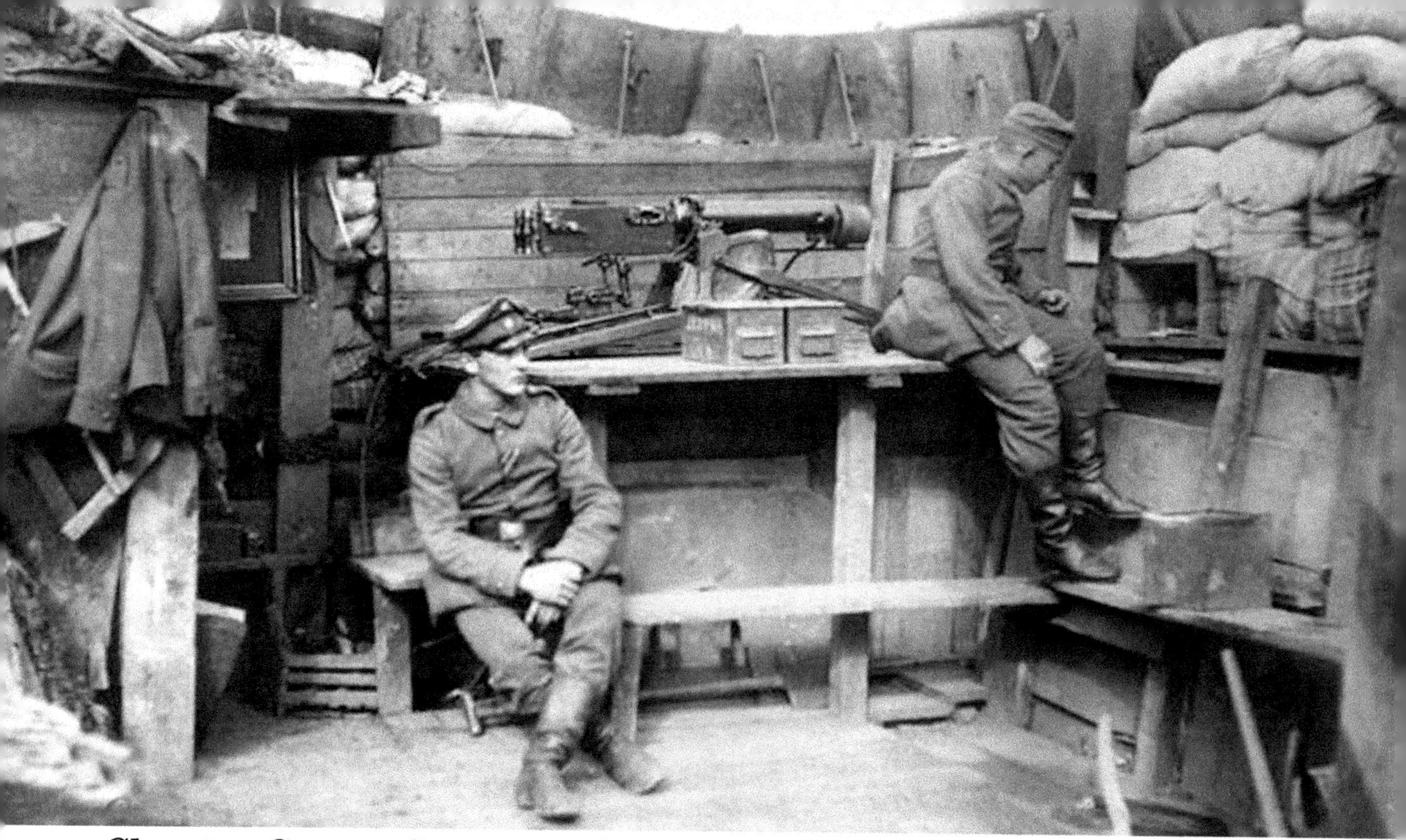

Chapter Seven: Capture of The Wytschaete–Messines Ridge

17GW961 A well constructed German machine gun position adding an impression of permanency to their occupation of Belgian and French territory.

17GW953 New Zealanders watching the tanks advancing towards Messines Ridge in Belgium during the attack of 7 June 1917.

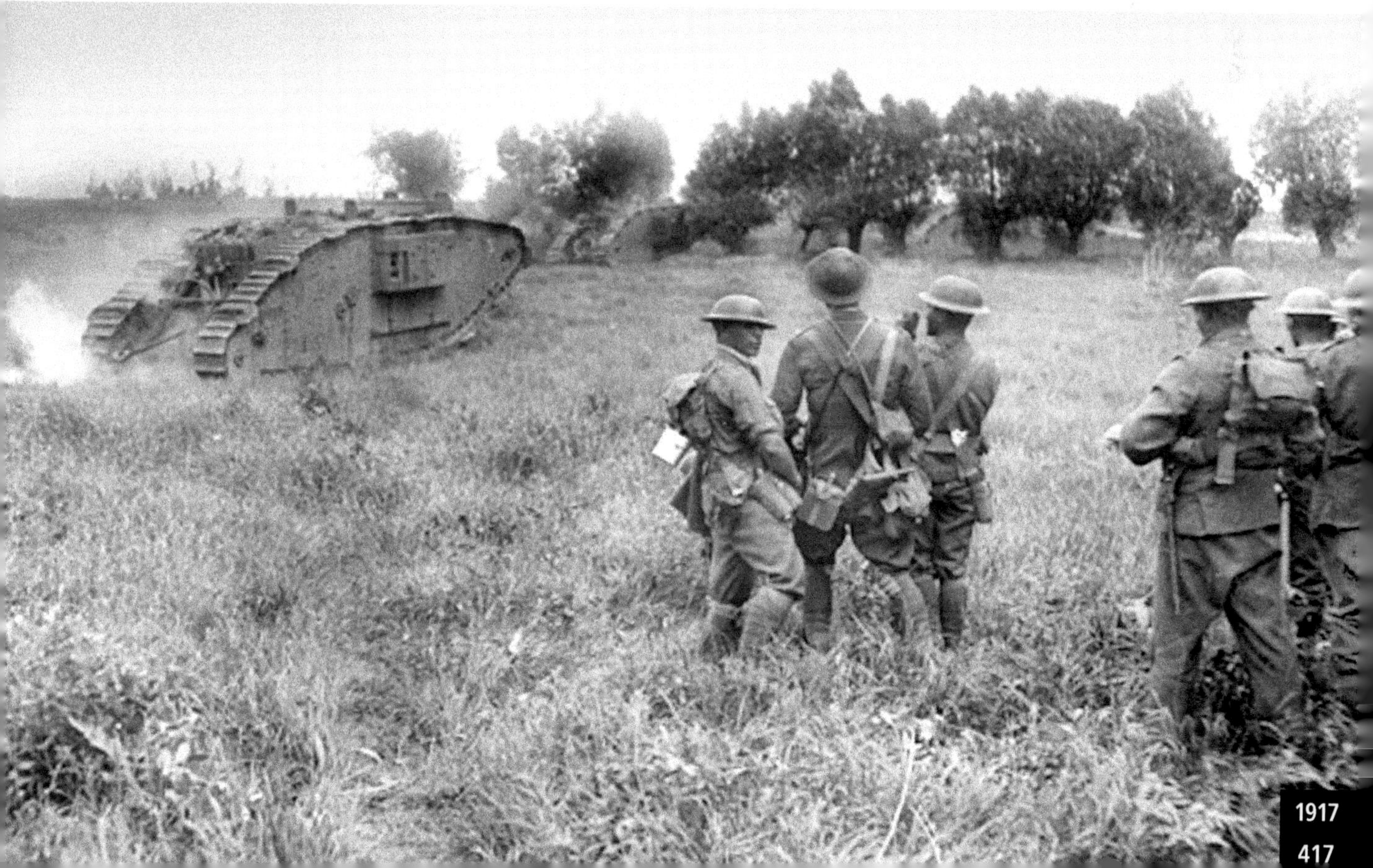

Field Marshal Sir Douglas Haig decided that the main British effort for 1917 would take place in the Ypres Salient. He planned to drive east from Ypres towards Passchendaele and on to the coast, thereby securing his vital supply routes from Britain and threatening German submarine pens.

To the south of Ypres a stretch of high ground runs southwest from the Gheluvelt plateau through Mount Sorrel, Hill 60 and St Eloi; before turning southwards to run through the village of Wytschaete and on to the village of Messines before sloping in the direction of Ploegsteert Wood. The Germans had taken this high ground during the First Battle of Ypres in 1914 and had dominated the surrounding countryside ever since. It gave them an important advantage over the British – they could see north across the Ypres Salient and observe troop and supply traffic in the rear areas. It was vital that the Germans were ejected from this ridge if General Haig's grand offensive to secure the North Sea coast was to take place.

Field Marshal Sir Douglas Haig gave the task of removing the Germans from the high ground, known as Messines Ridge, to General Sir Herbert Plumer, commander of the British Second Army.

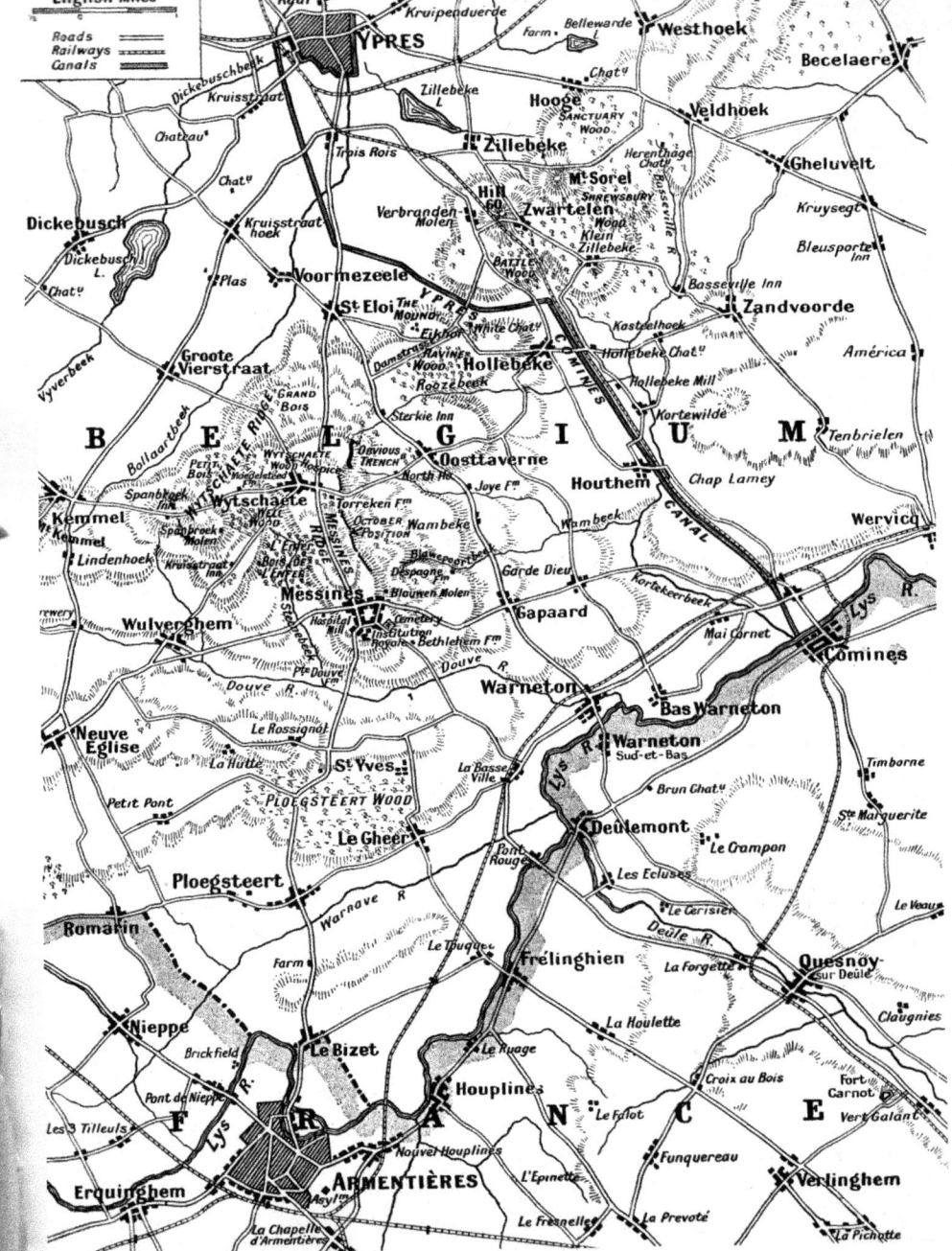

General Plumer used three of the five corps available to Second Army in the assault. Militarily, it was a brilliantly planned and executed attack that resulted in the successful capture of the Wytschaete-Messines ridge just as Haig had ordered as a preliminary move in a greater assault.

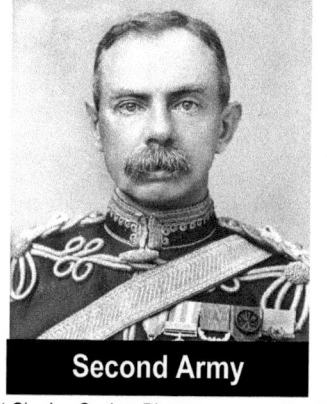

Second Army

This all-important, strategically motivated, attack, took place 7 June 1917, opening with the exploding of nineteen enormous and long-prepared underground mines, immediately followed by one of the heaviest artillery bombardments of the war. Tanks and aircraft were also employed.

General Herbert Charles Onslow Plumer, commanding Second Army.

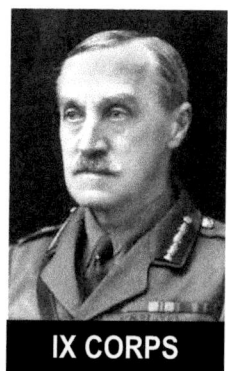

IX CORPS

Lieutenant General Sir Alexander Hamilton-Gordon

11th (Northern) Division
16th (Irish) Division
19th (Western) Division
36th (Ulster) Division

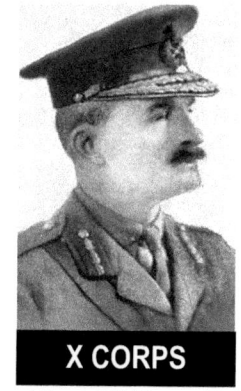

X CORPS

Lieutenant General Sir Thomas Morland

23rd Division
24th Division
41st Division
47th (2nd London) Division

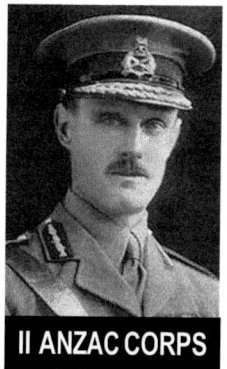

II ANZAC CORPS

Lieutenant General Sir Alexander Godley

25th Division
3rd Australian Division
4th Australian Division
New Zealand Division

17GW981 An example of the thoroughness employed in the planning for the Wytschaete – Messines Ridge battle: the features of the terrain were laid out to scale on the ground for officers, NCOs and other ranks to study their objectives.

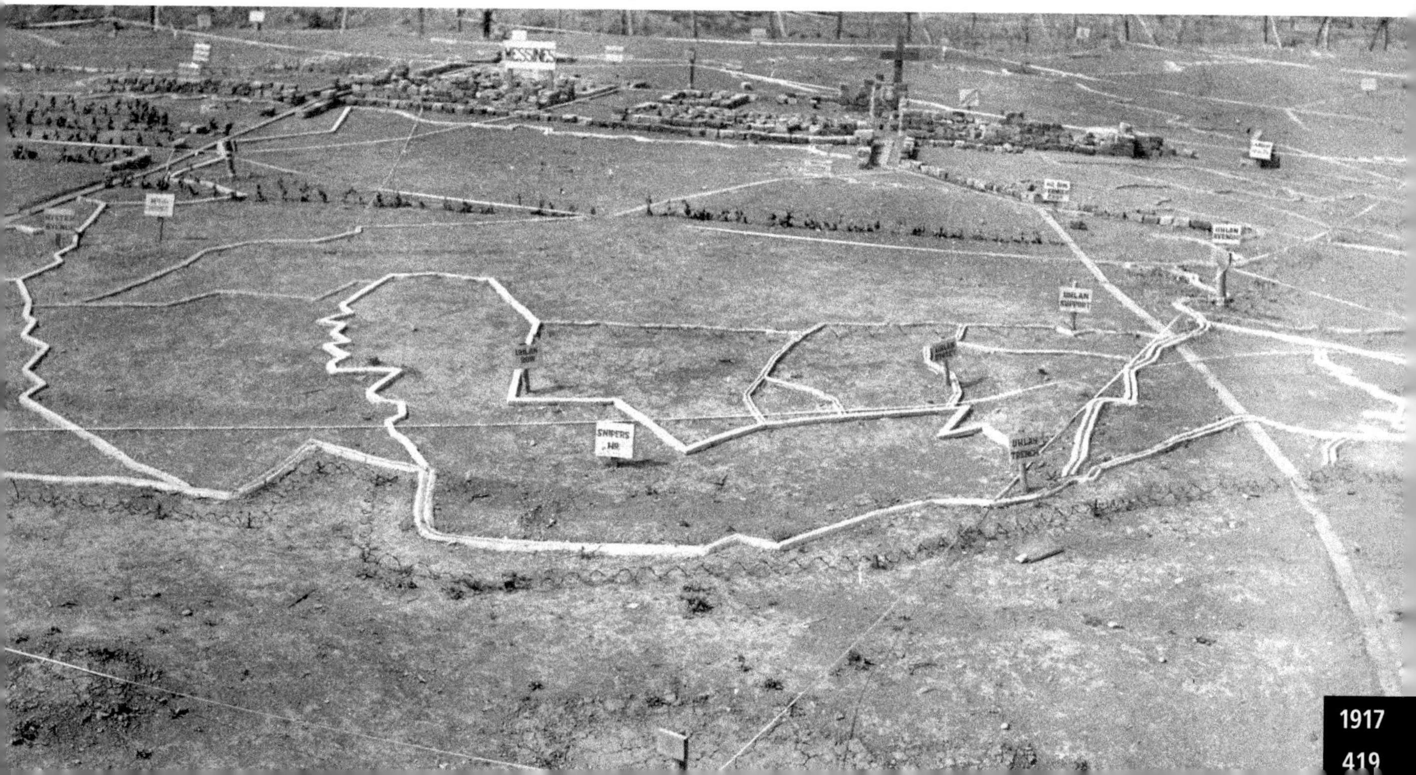

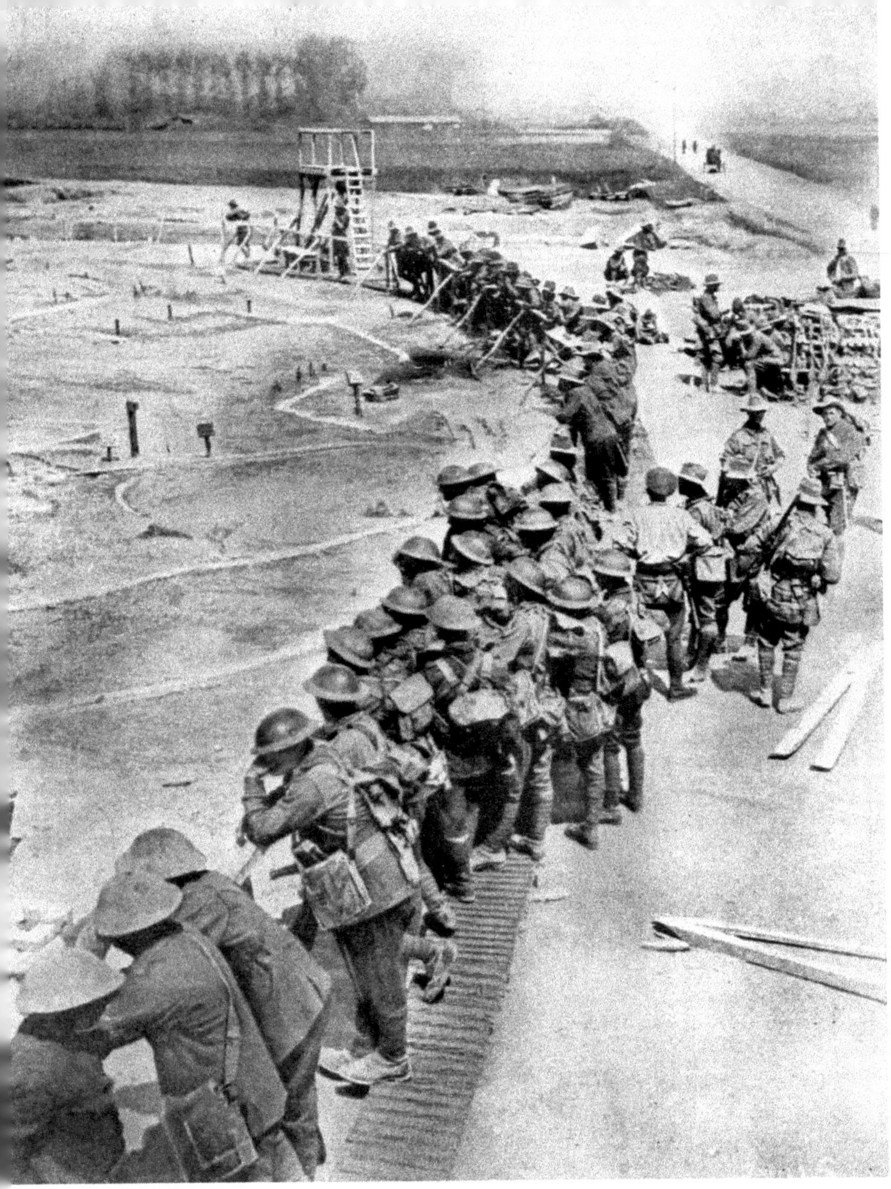

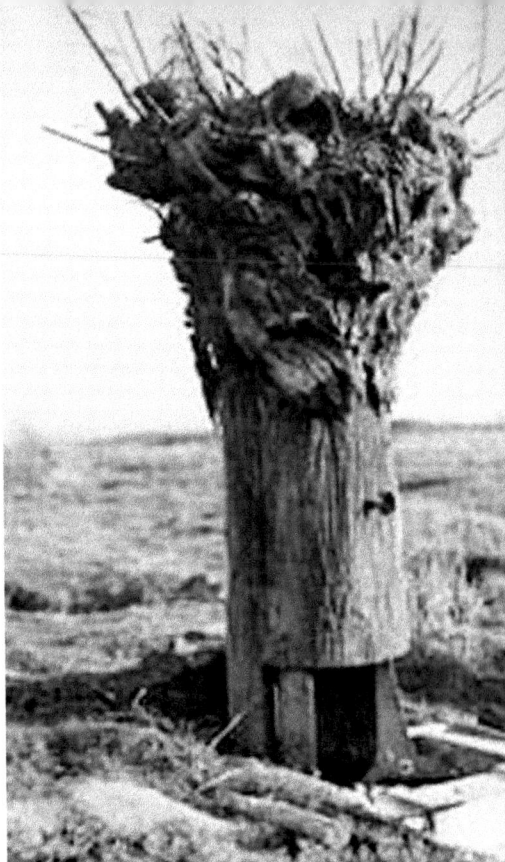

17GW968 A dummy tree used as an observation post on Hill 63 by Australian troops during the Battle of Messines on 7 June 1917.

17GW984 On 6 June, Australians of 30 Brigade study the diorama laid out to give the attackers an awareness of the over-all layout of the German defences. At this point, like the Germans, most were unaware of the secret tunnelling activity taking place under their feet.

17GW985 Messines Ridge seen from the Australian positions before the attack. The ruins of Messines village can be seen on the skyline.

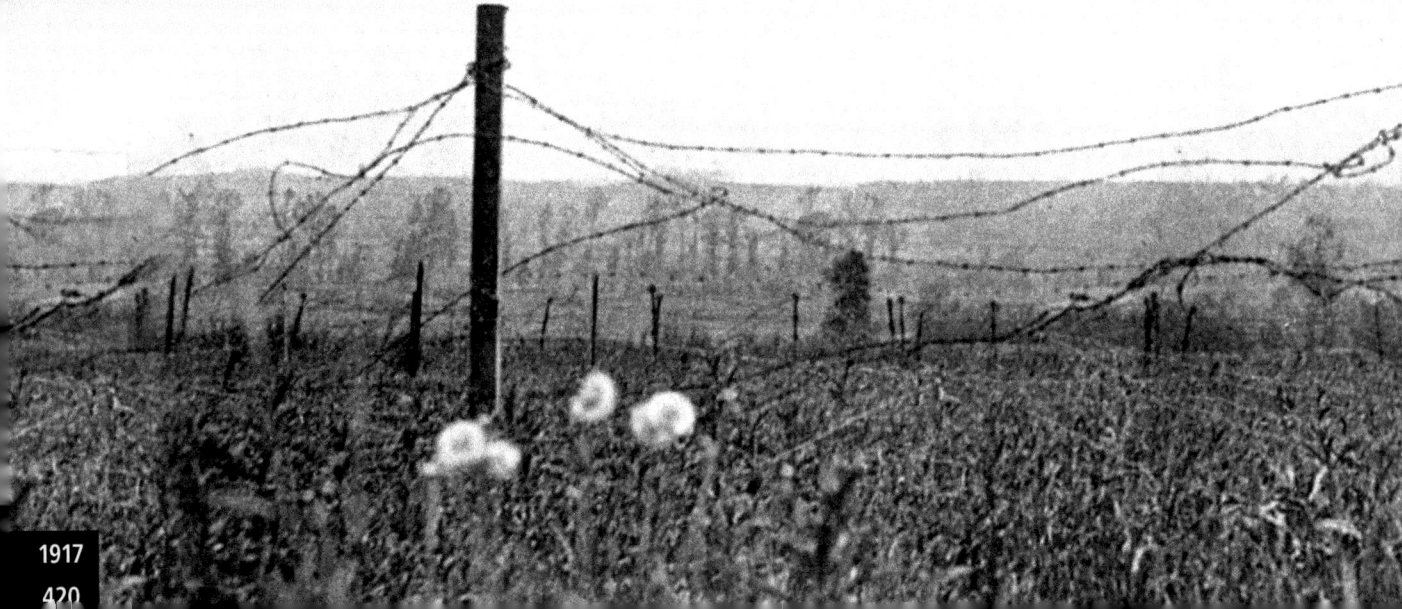

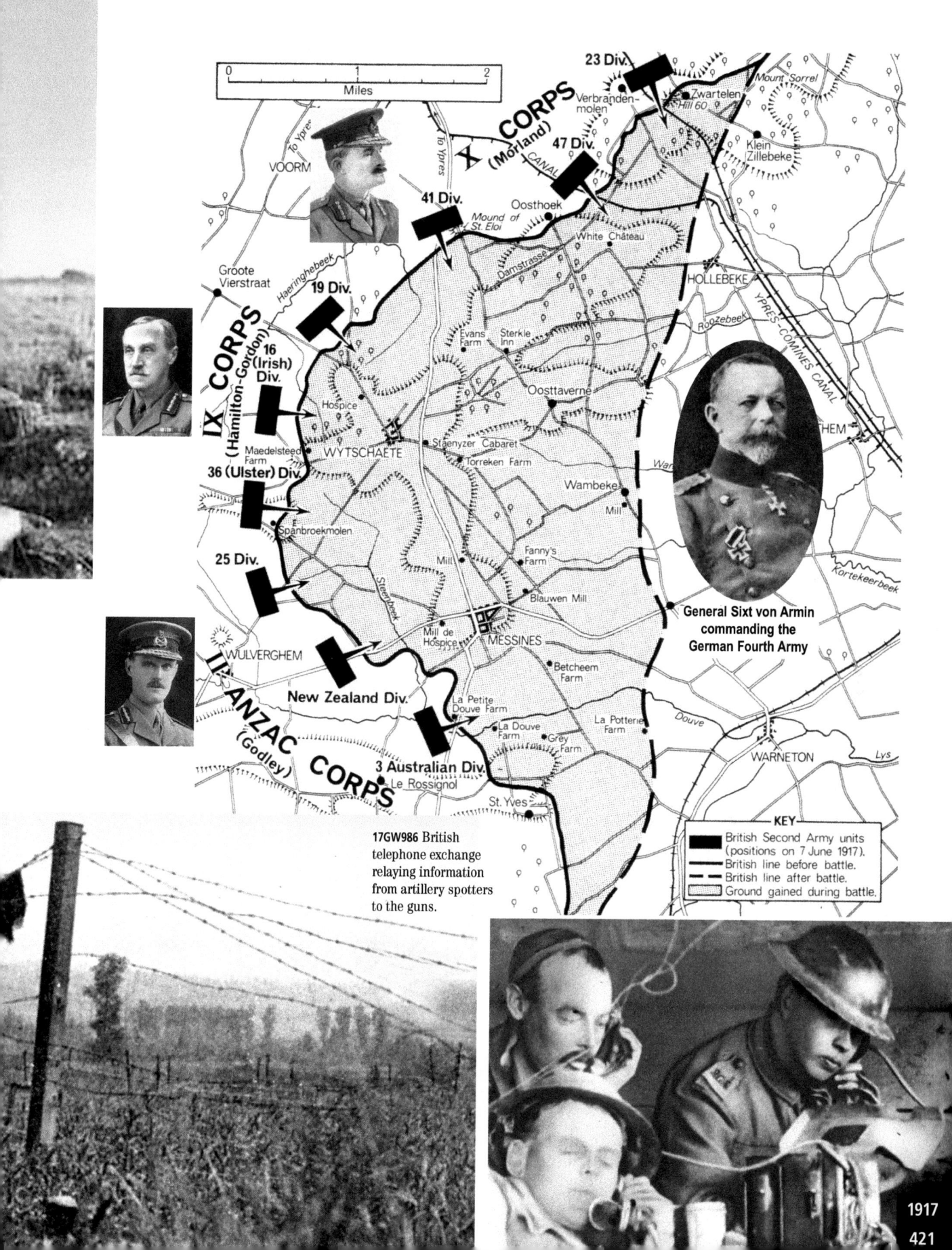

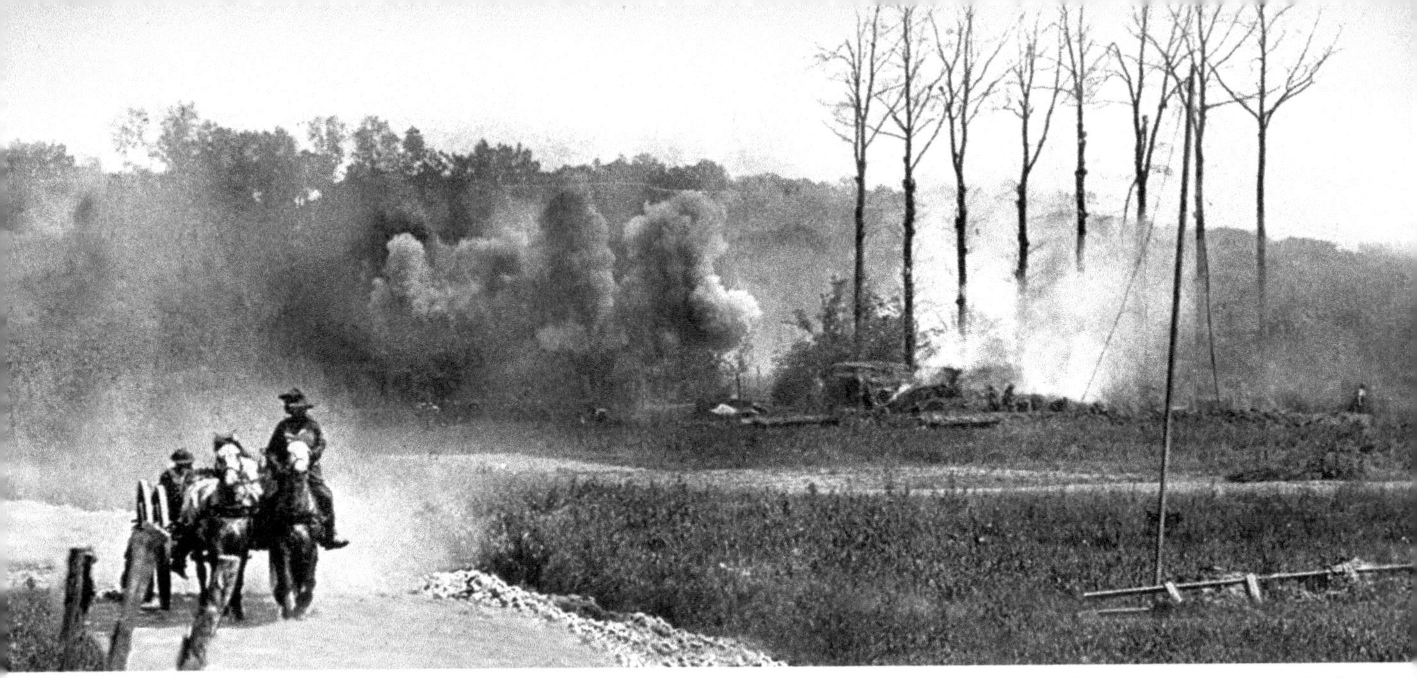

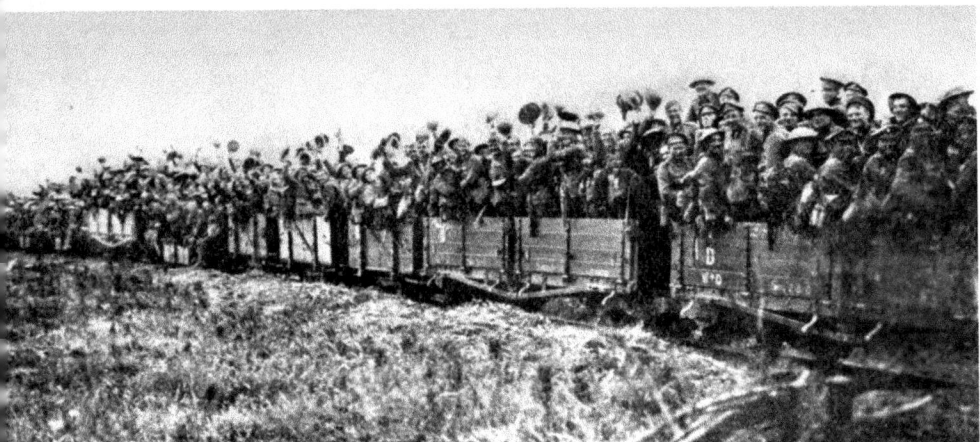

17GW988 Shells exploding in the vicinity of an Australian field battery behind Hill 63 as German guns seek to locate them. Camouflage netting over the guns and ammunition is in flames and men can be seen fighting the fires. A waggon is being driven away from the danger zone.

17GW990 Infantry arriving for the coming assault on Messines Ridge.

17GW991 British Infantry in trenches before the high ground of Messines Ridge.

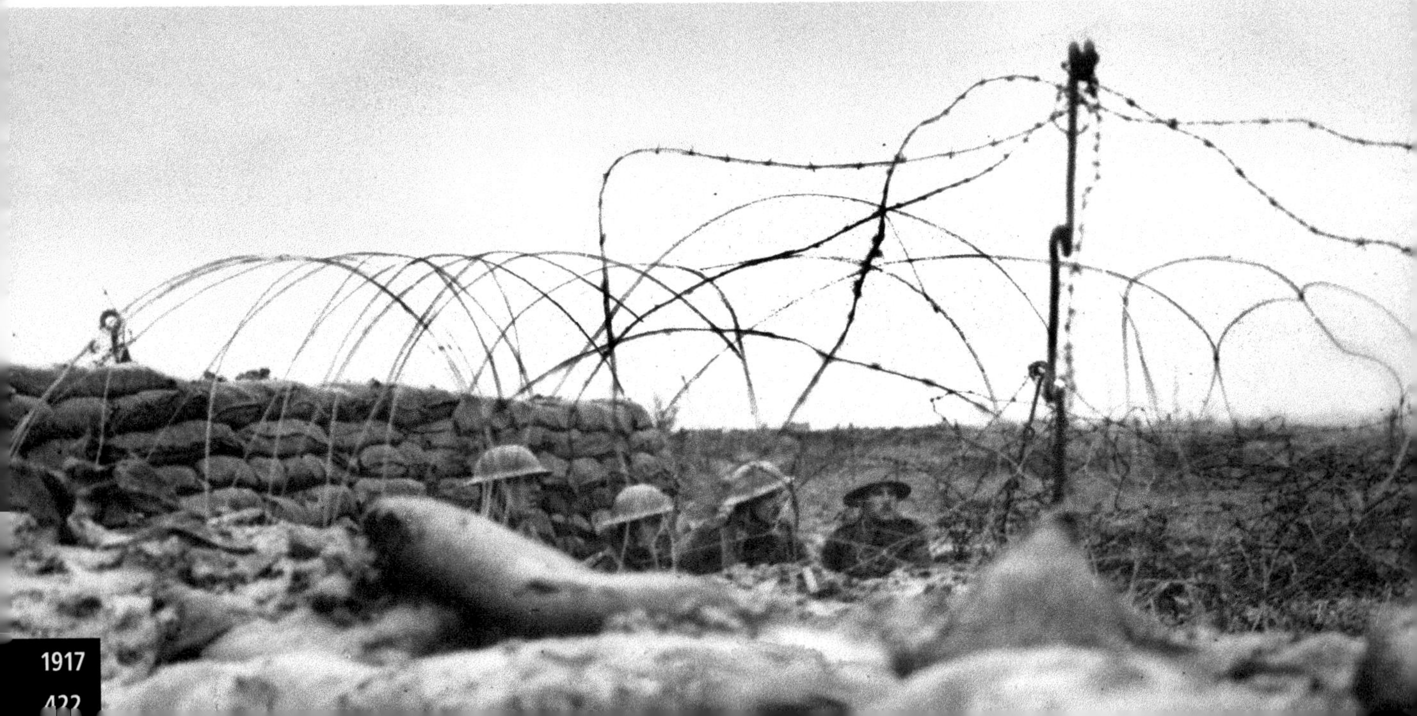

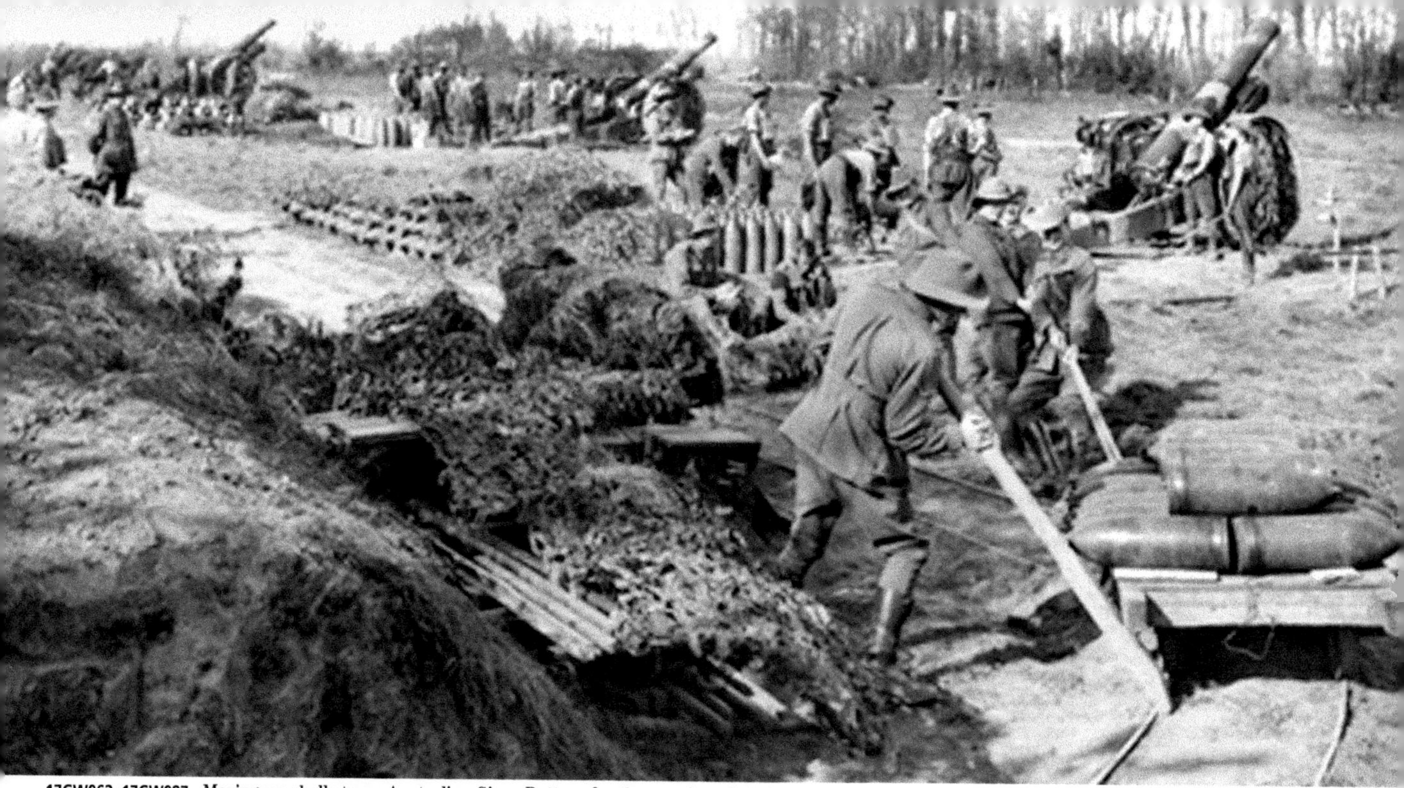

17GW962, 17GW987. Moving up shells to an Australian Siege Battery for the opening of the barrage at the Battle of Messines, June 1917.

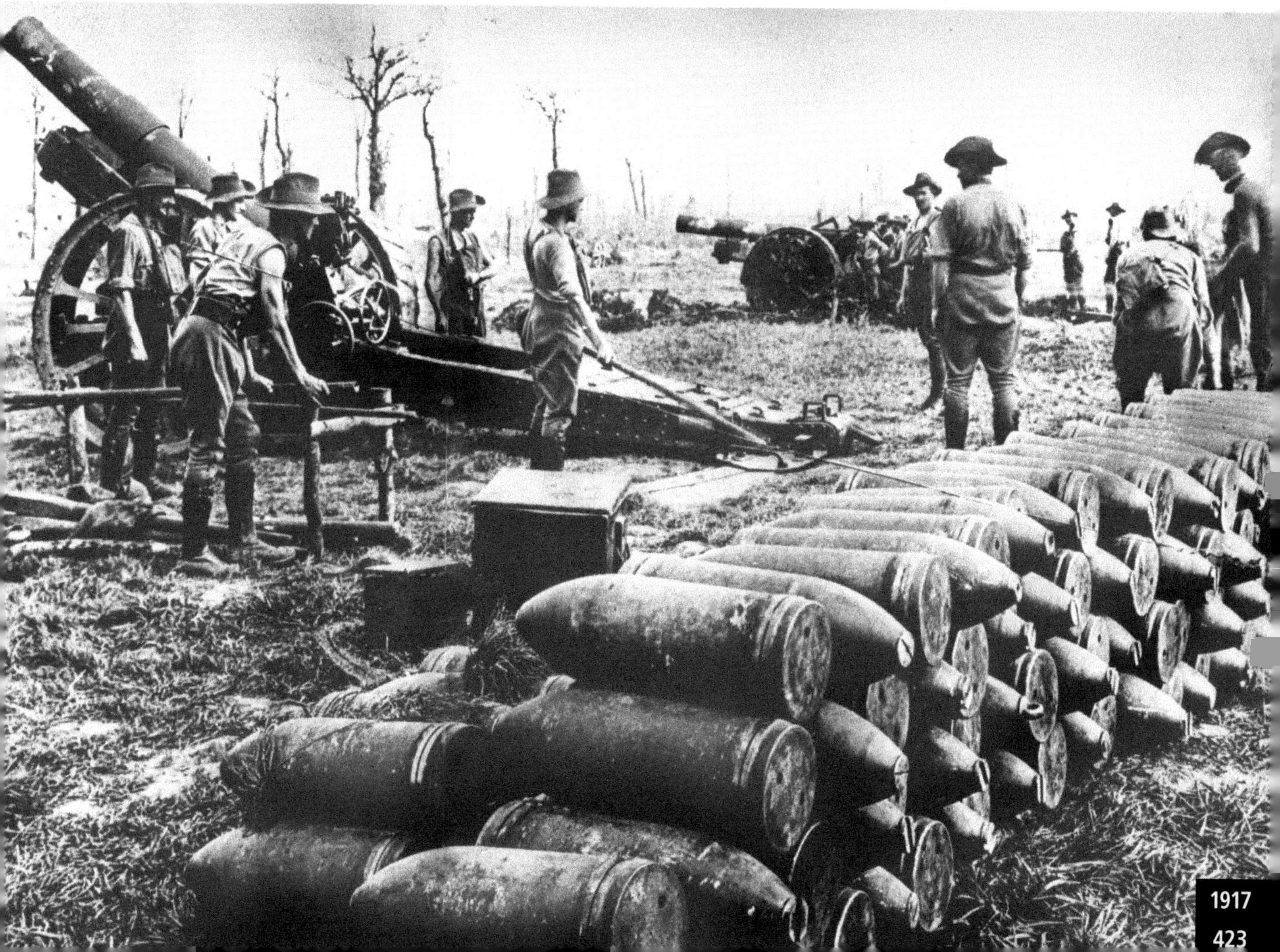

The line of mines under Messines Ridge were charged with ammonal and gun cotton. They were positioned as follows: two mines were dug under Hill 60 on the northern flank; one mine at St Eloi; three at Hollandscheschur Farm; two at Petit Bois; single mines at Maedelstede Farm, Peckham House and Spanbroekmolen; four at Kruisstraat; one at Ontario Farm and two each at Trenches 127 and 122 on the southern flank. A group of four mines was placed under the German strongpoint 'Birdcage' at Le Pelerin, near Ploegsteert Wood. The mines were completed and charged by September 1916.

17GW992, 17GW993, 17GW951, 17GW995 17GW974. Entering the shaft leading to the mine tunnels; the tunneler is wearing a breathing apparatus used in coal mine rescue operations in Britain. Canaries were also used in the workings to give warning of dangerous gases. The men below are working beneath Hill 63.

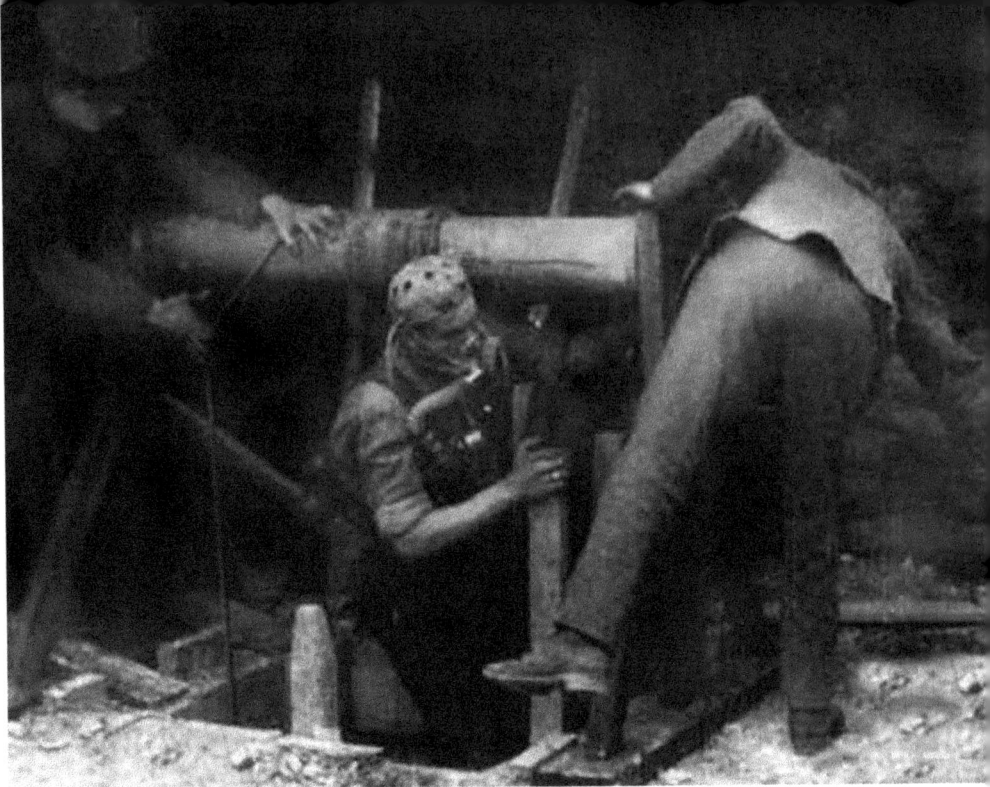

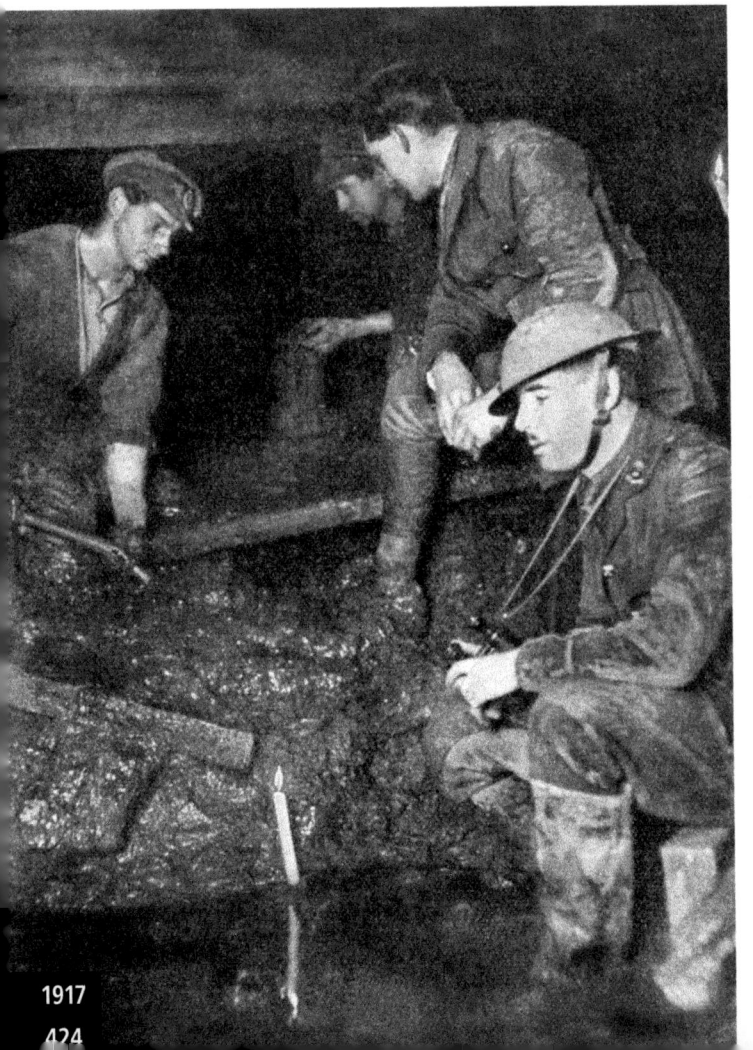

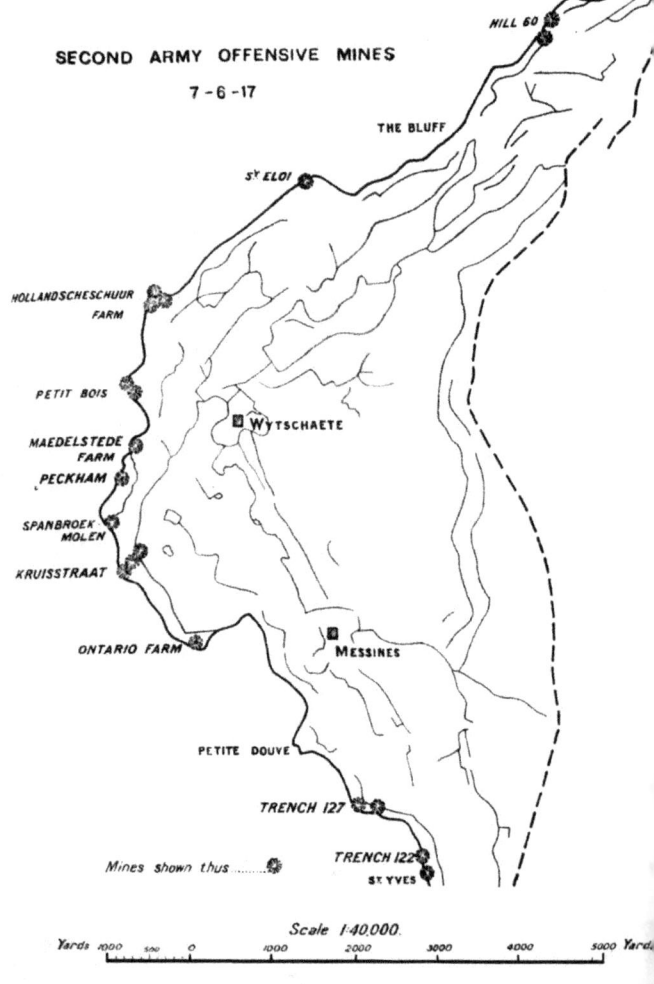

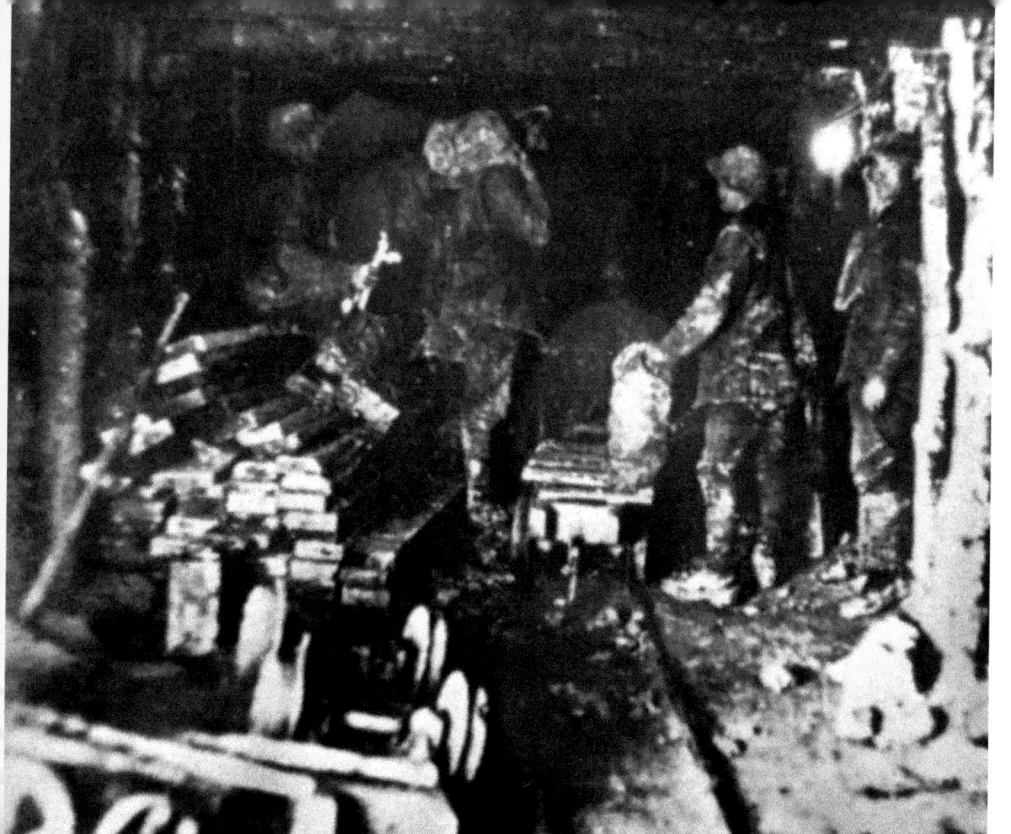

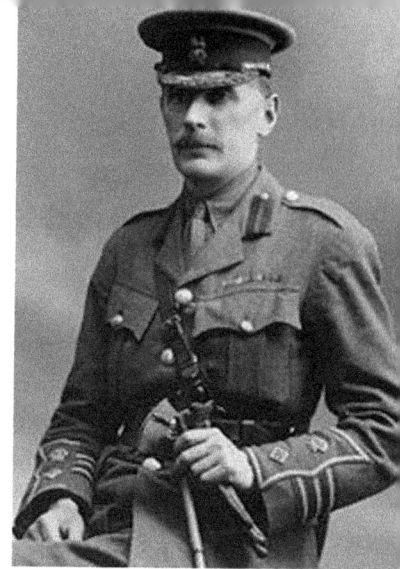

17GW994 General Sir Charles Harington, Chief of Staff to General Herbert Plumer. In a press interview he told reporters: 'Gentlemen, we may not make history tomorrow, but we shall certainly change the geography'.
The mining operations carried out at Messines marked the zenith of mine warfare.

'The ground under our feet literally rocked. It writhed again as the spreading wave of shock from the annihilated Messines Ridge broke upon us and passed on.'
Aubrey Wade, Royal Artillery

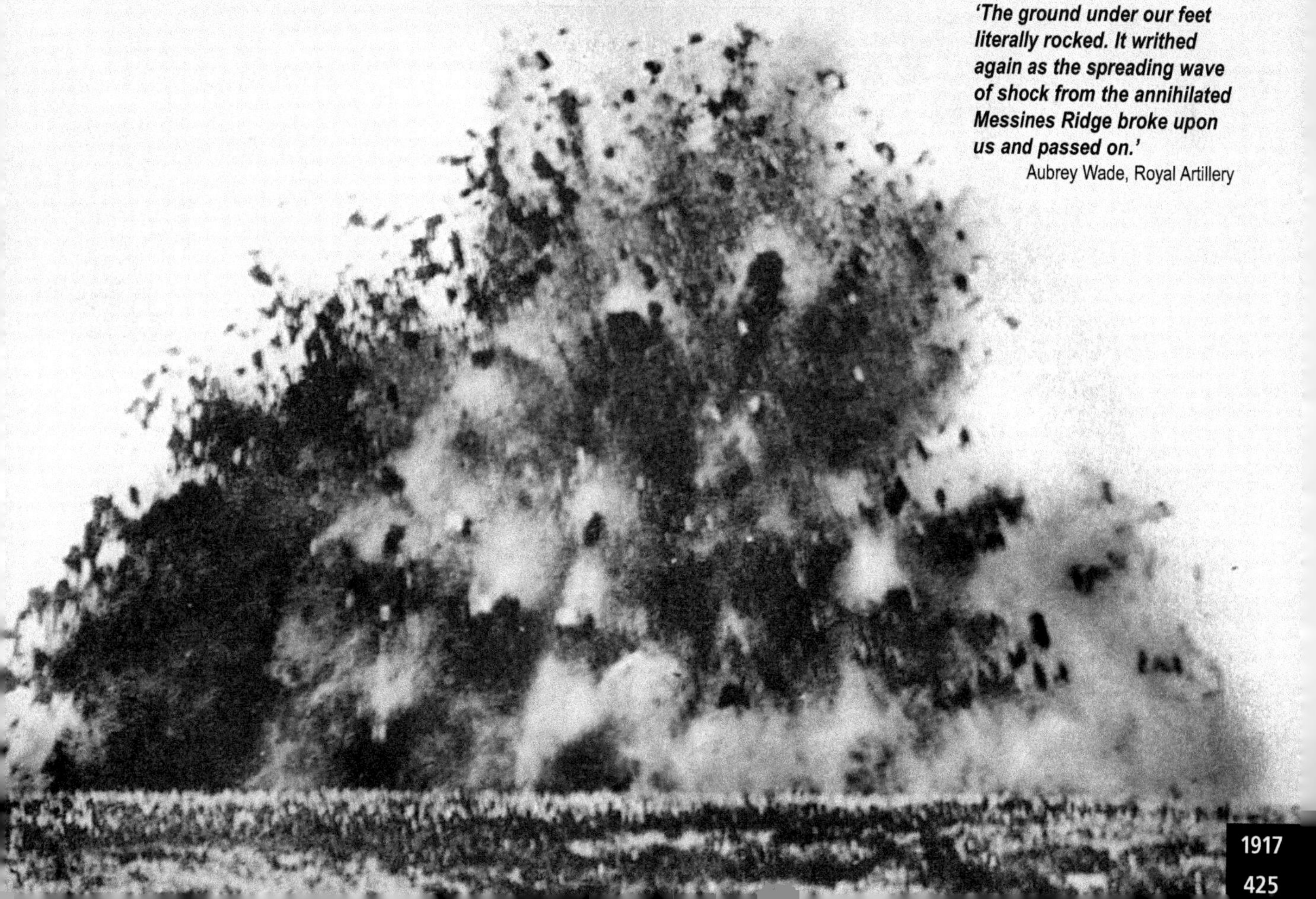

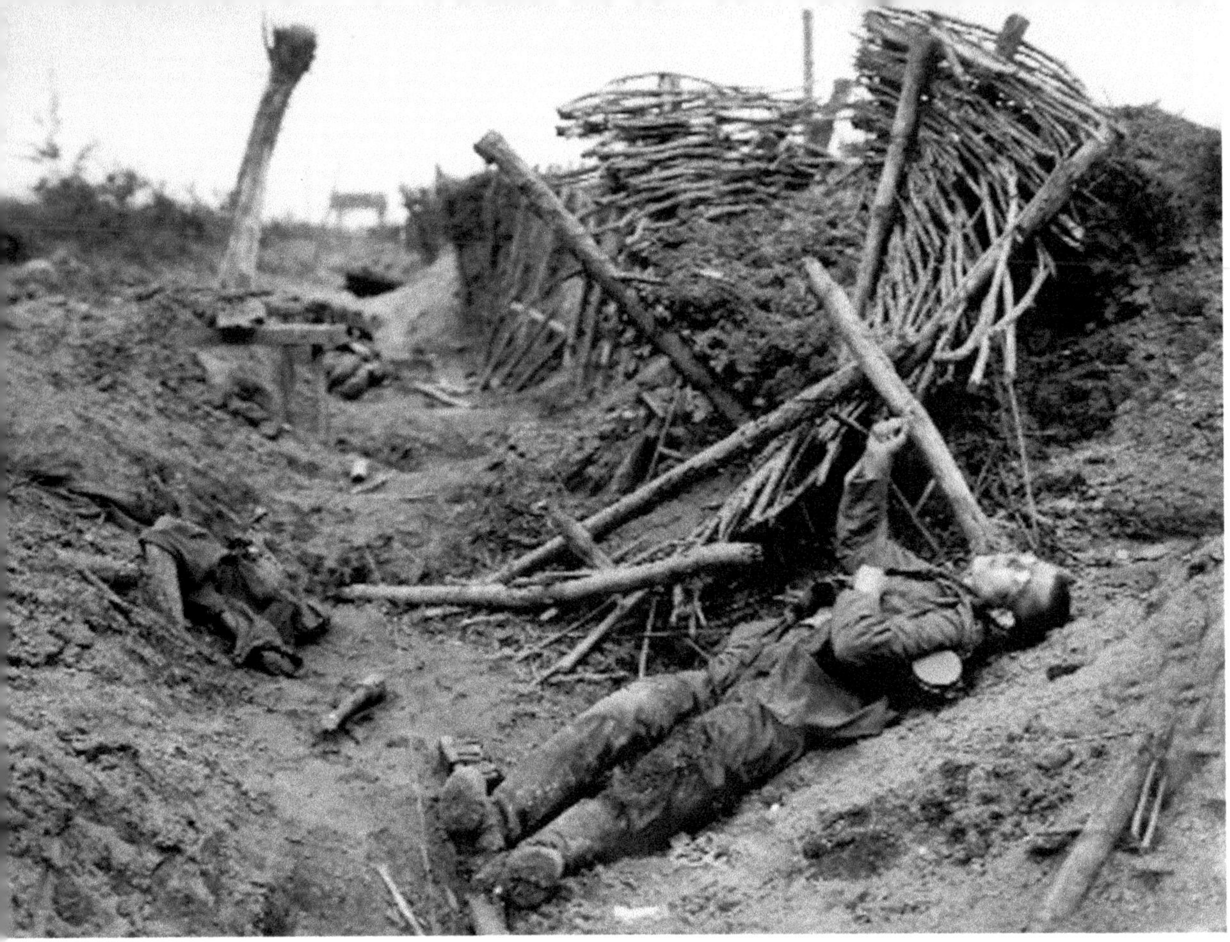

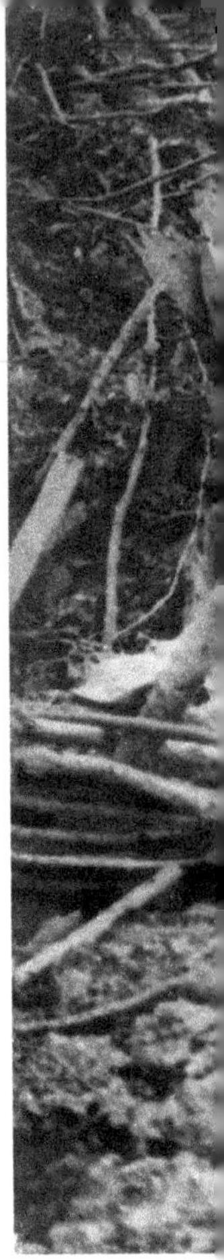

17GW957, 17GW972. When the mines were fired simultaneously at 03.10 on 7 June hundreds of German soldiers were killed.

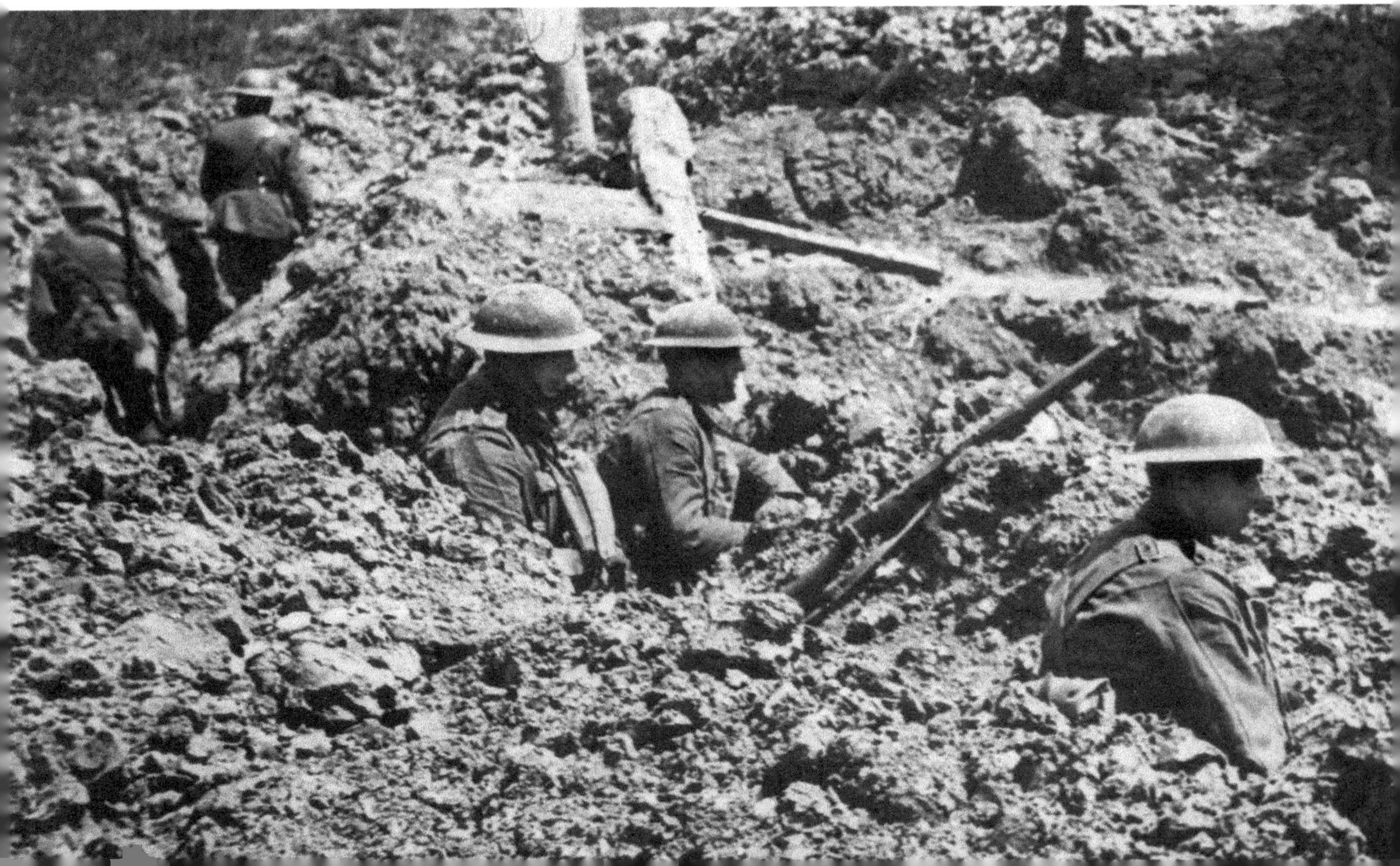

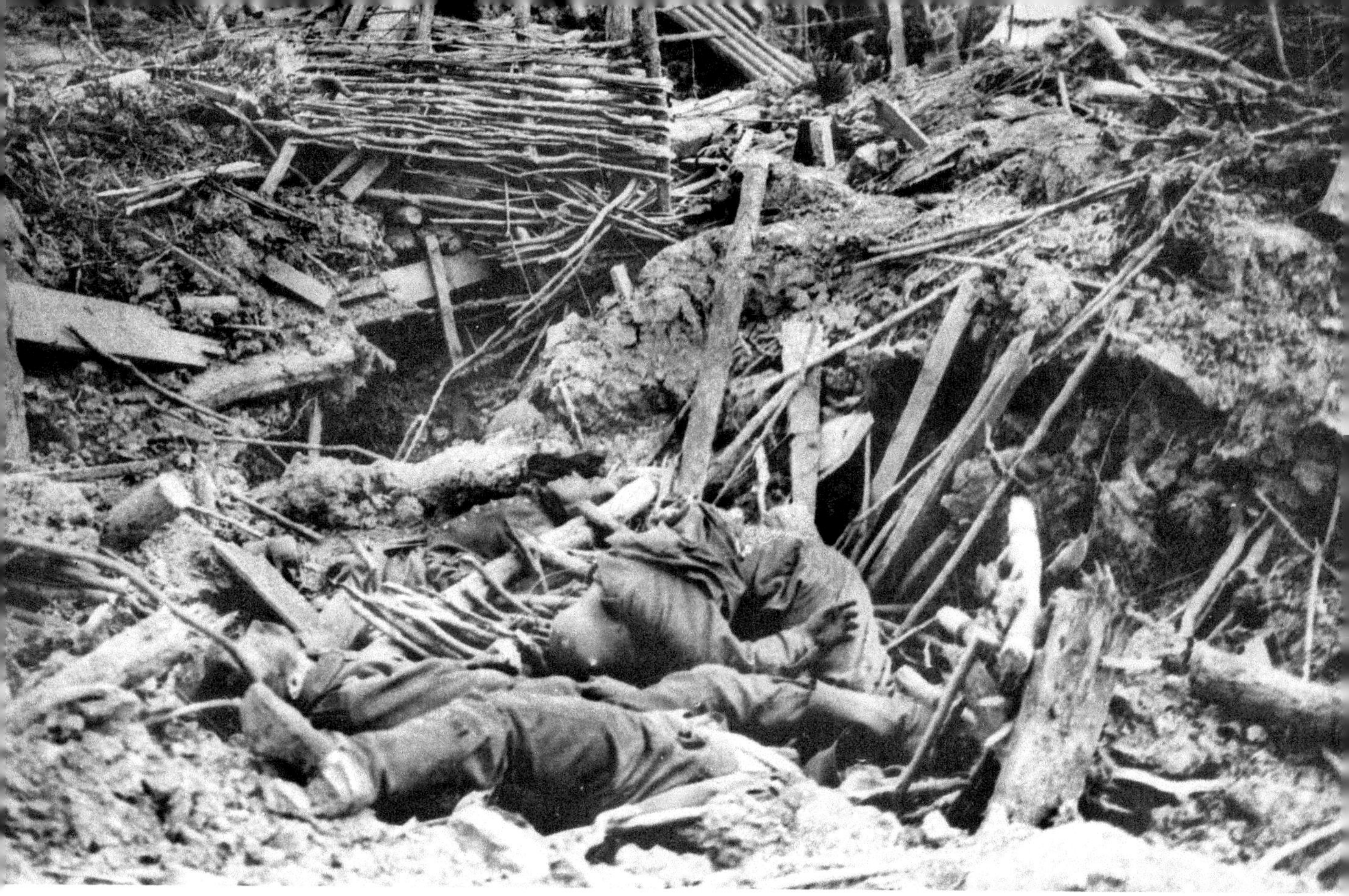

17GW997 British soldiers occupying former German positions after the explosions and advance.

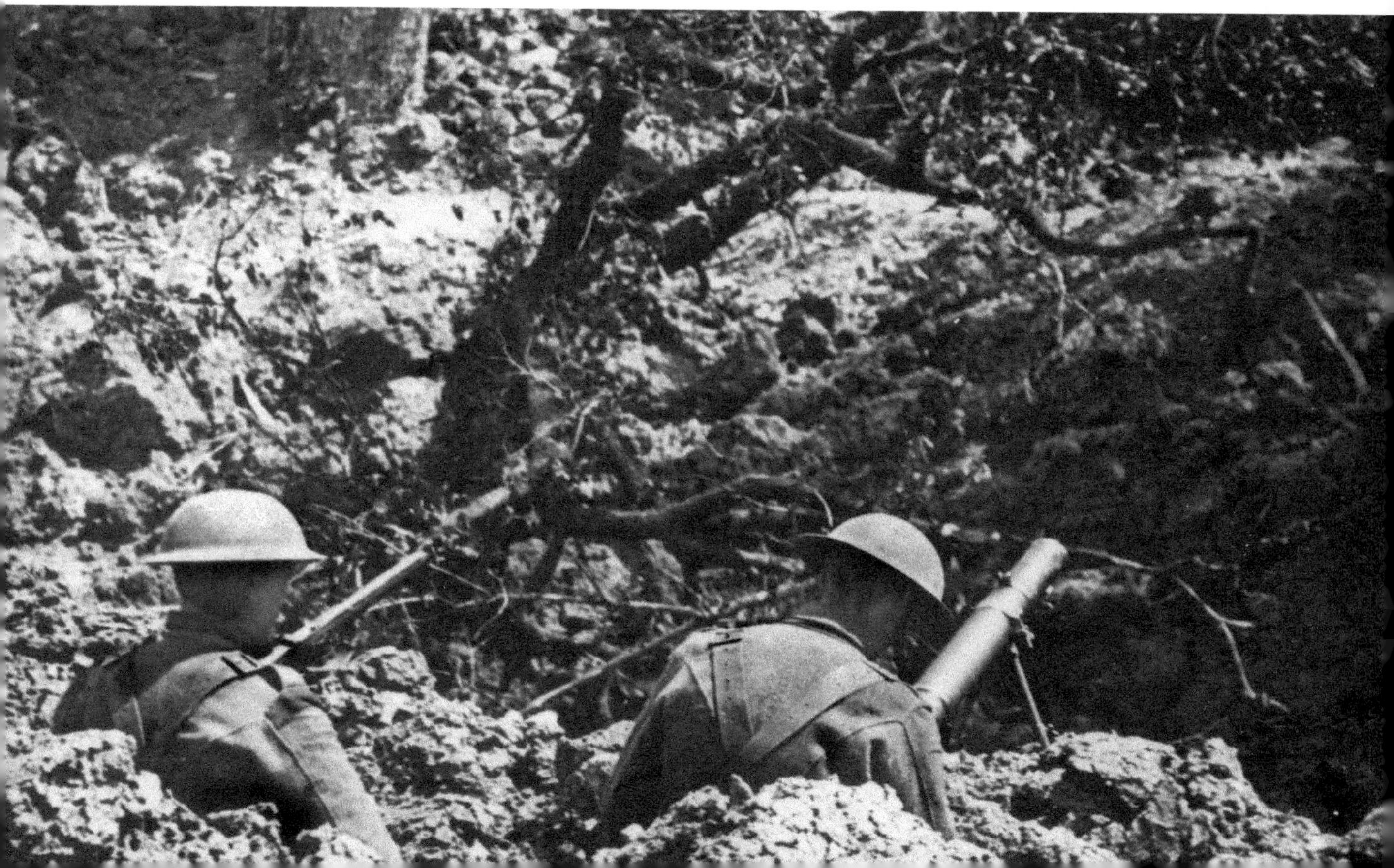

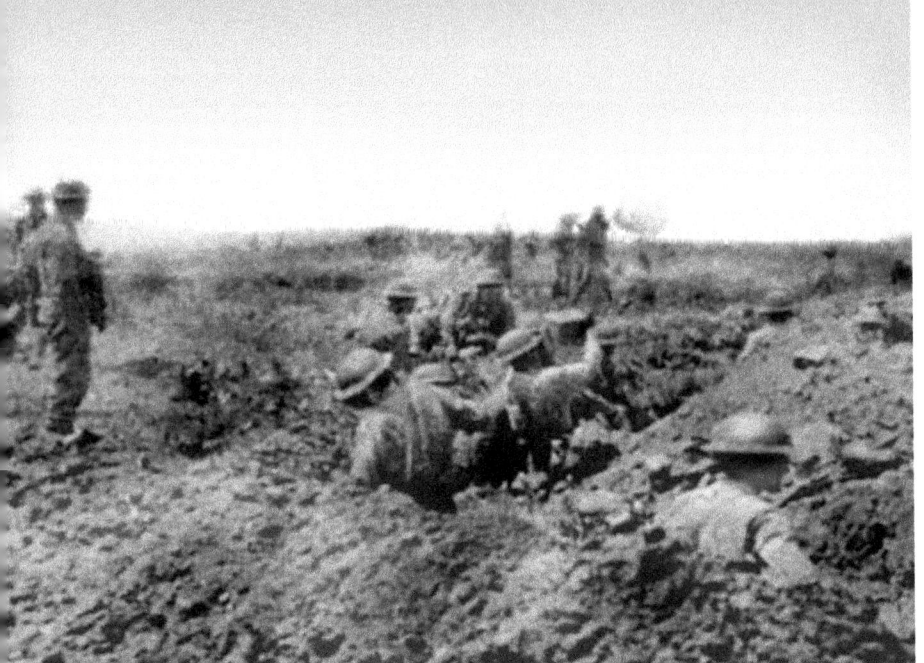
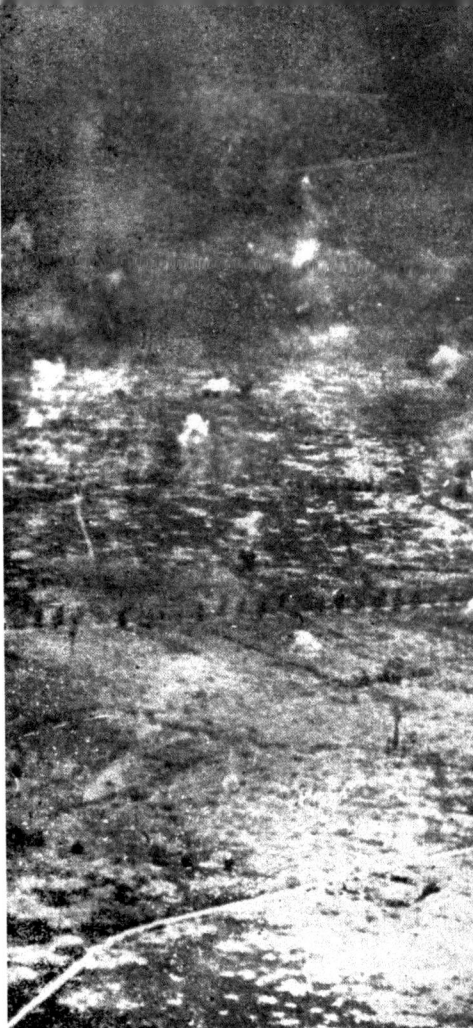

17GW998 The British barrage at around 15.00 hrs. This was against the Oosttaverne Line, at a section of the line called 'Huns' Walk'. This barrage preceded the second pase of the battle, which involved attacks by the 3rd and 4th Australian Divisions.

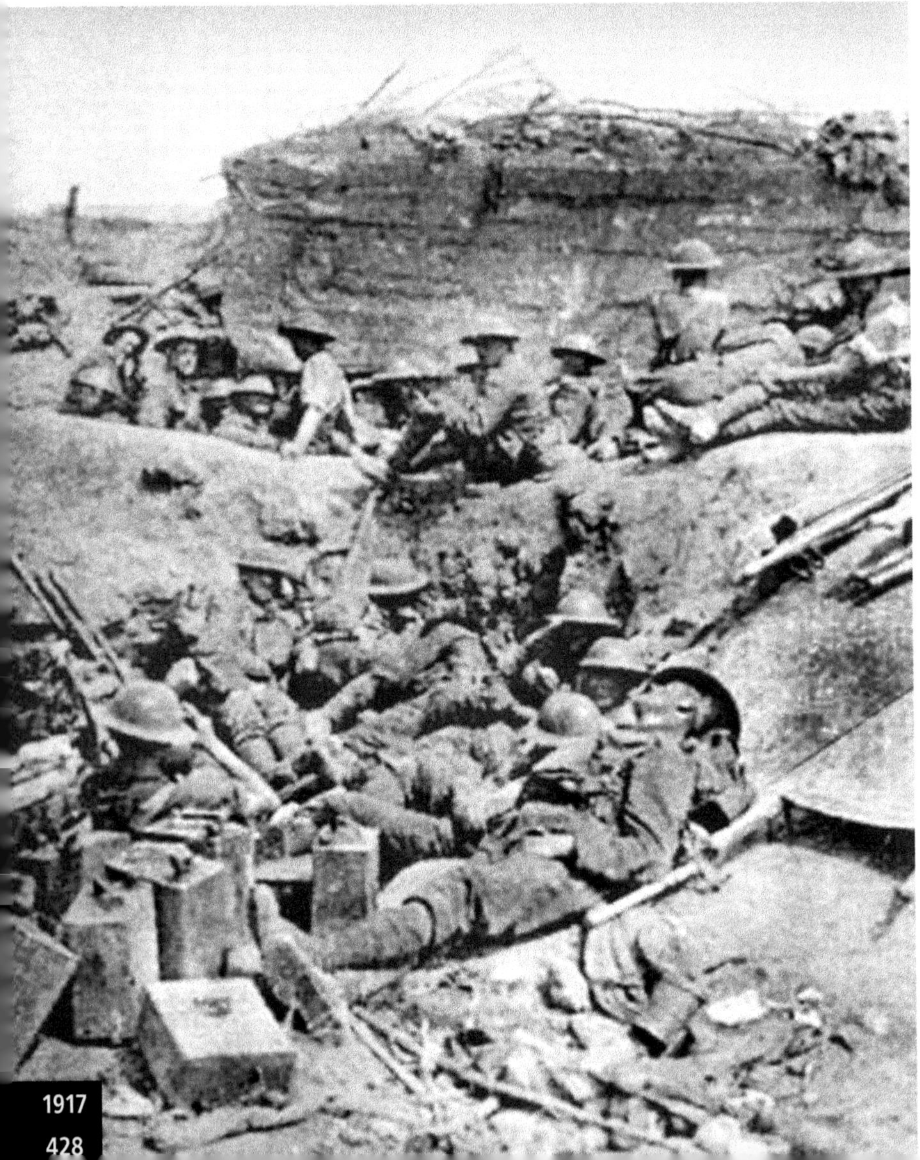

17GW963, 17GW964. Men of the 3rd Battalion, Worcestershire Regiment, after taking their objective on Messines Ridge. Battalion Headquarters was established in the ruins of Hell Farm.

17GW1002 Some members of a pioneer battalion helping to consolidate the captured high ground near Messines by digging a communication trench. The advance at the deepest point was about two miles and the crest of Messines Ridge, in the centre, was taken early on the first day, 7 June 1917.

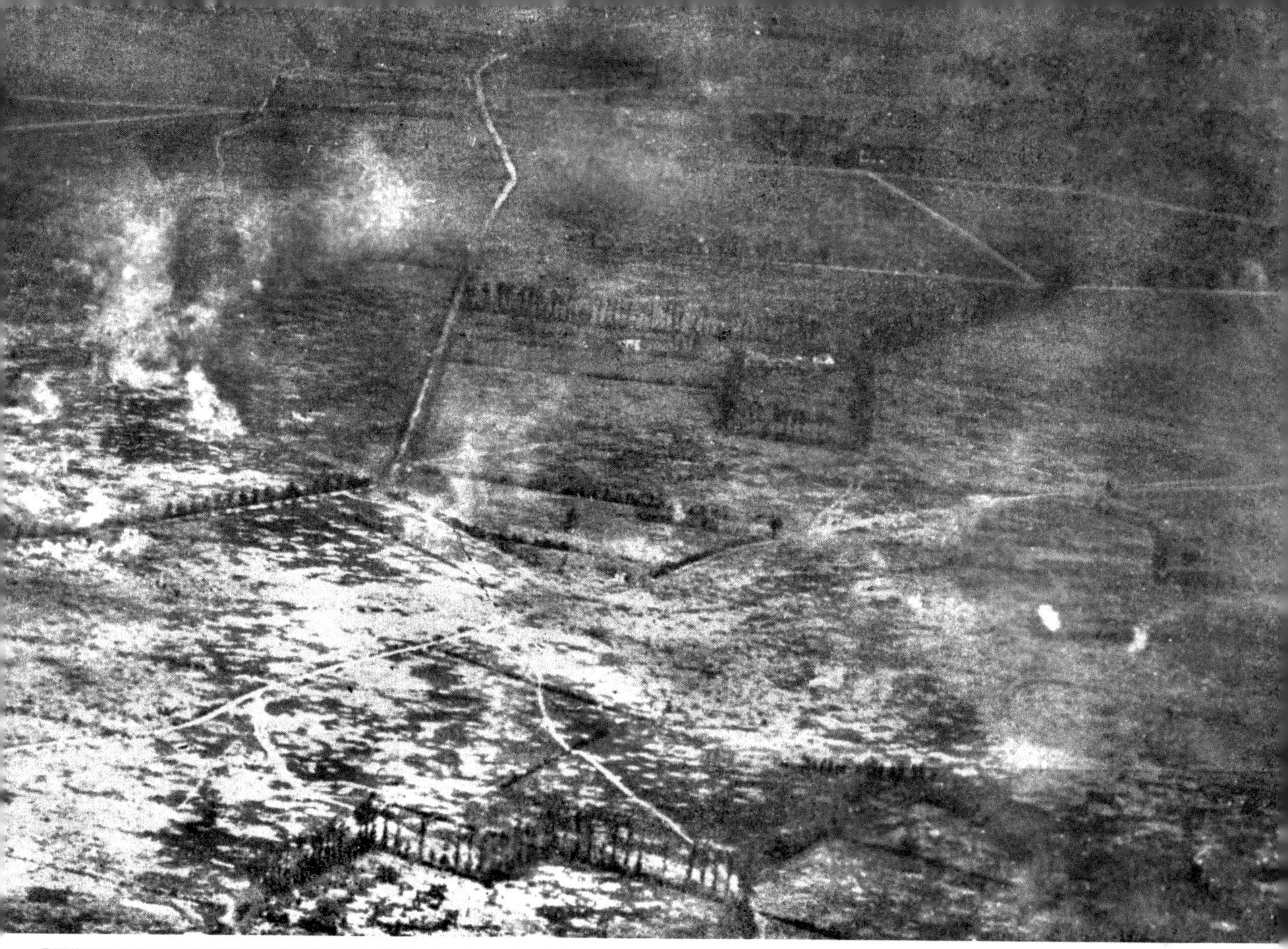

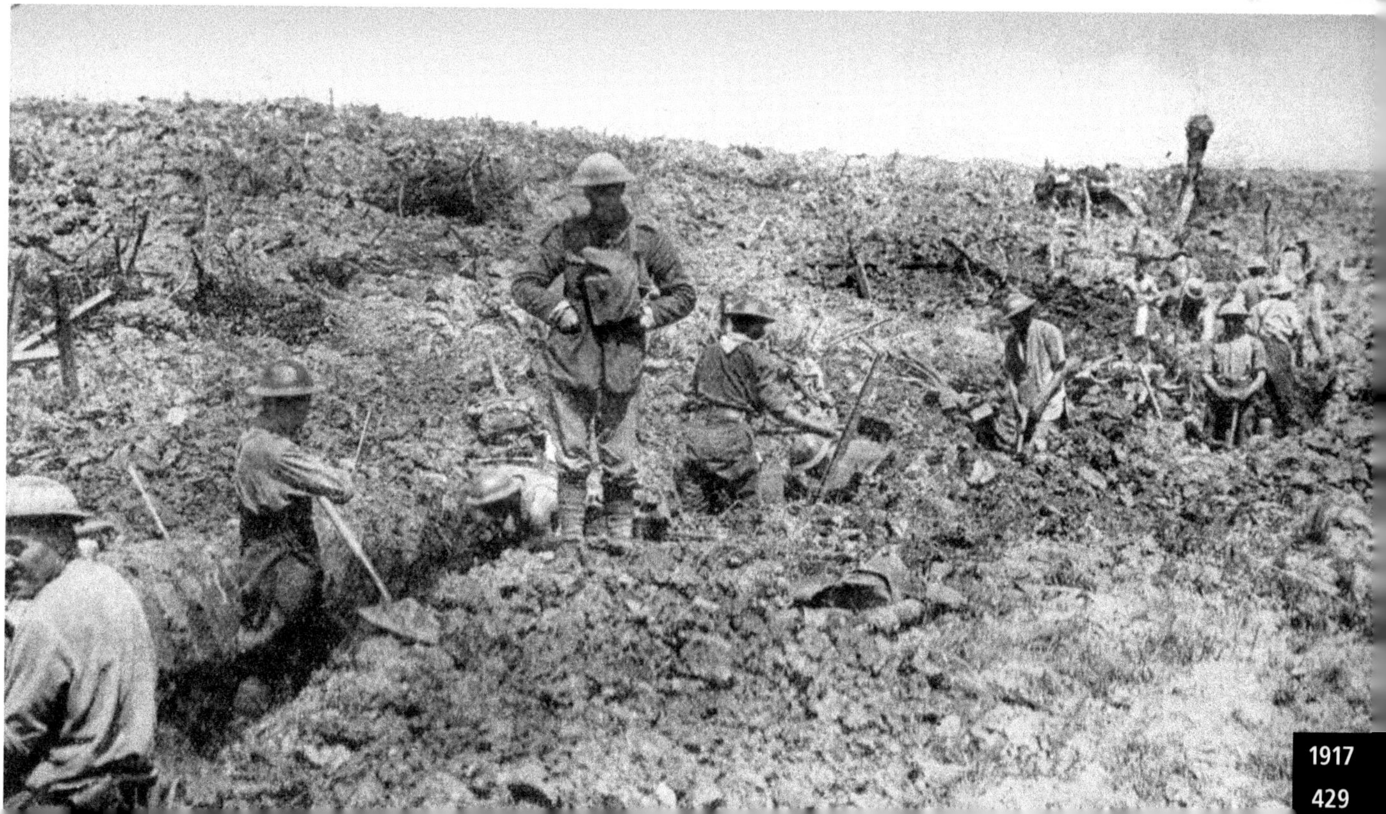

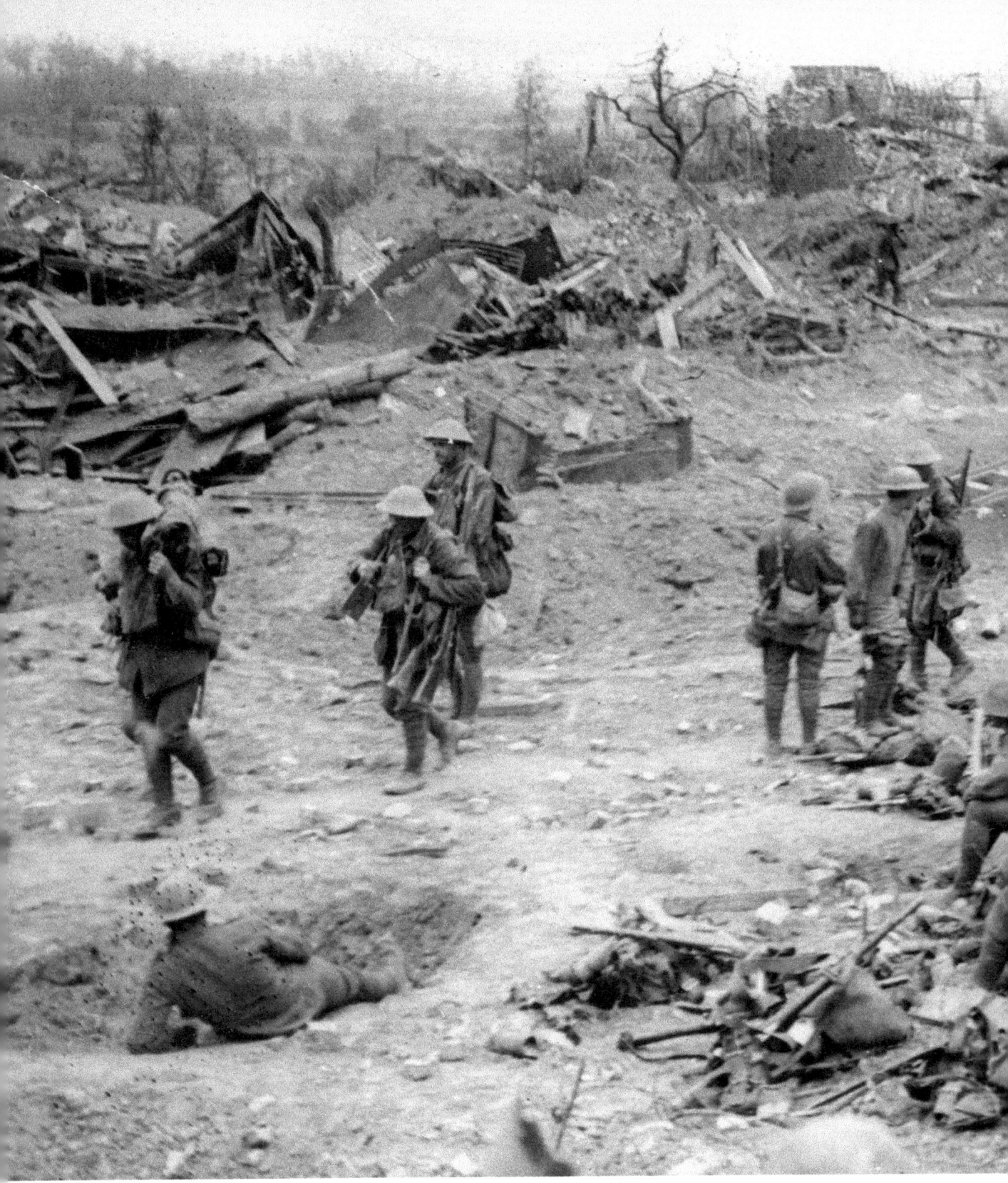
17GW996 The village of Wytschaete captured by the 16th (Irish) Division and 36th (Ulster) Division.

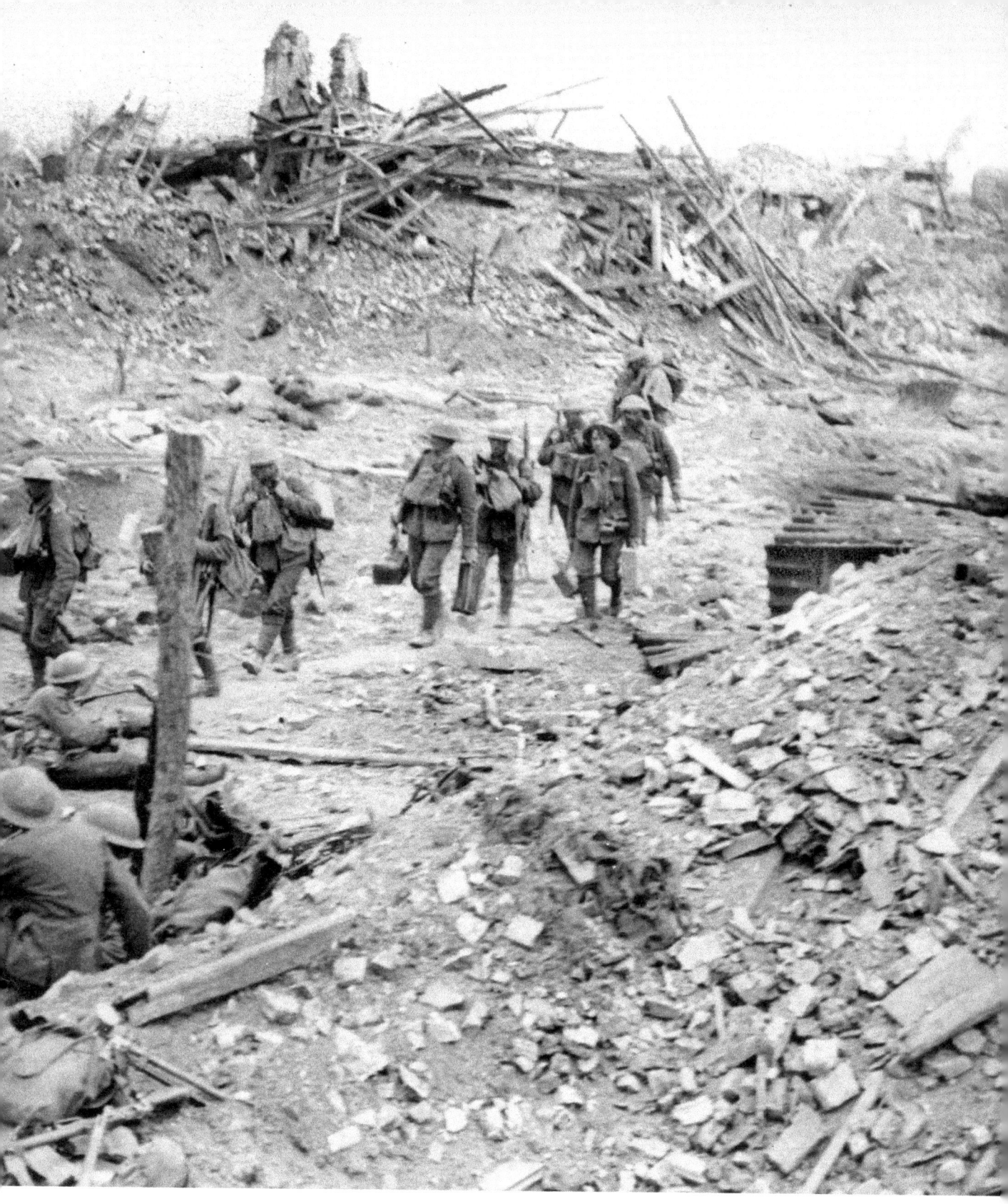

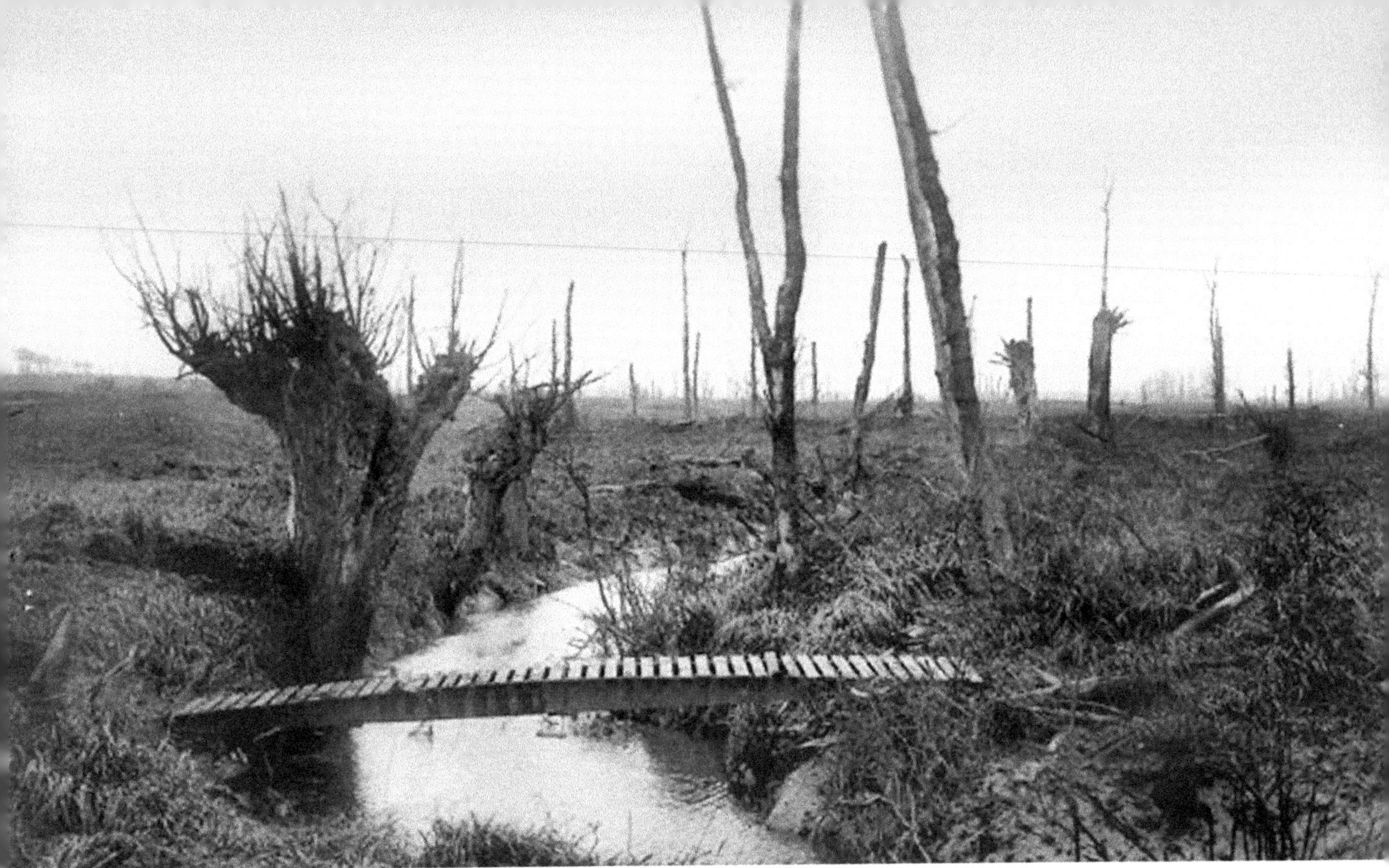

17GW970 A bridge placed over the Douve River by the 40th Battalion (Tasmania) AIF immediately after their attack on 7 June 1917.

17GW954 Australian soldiers in demolished German trenches at Messines.

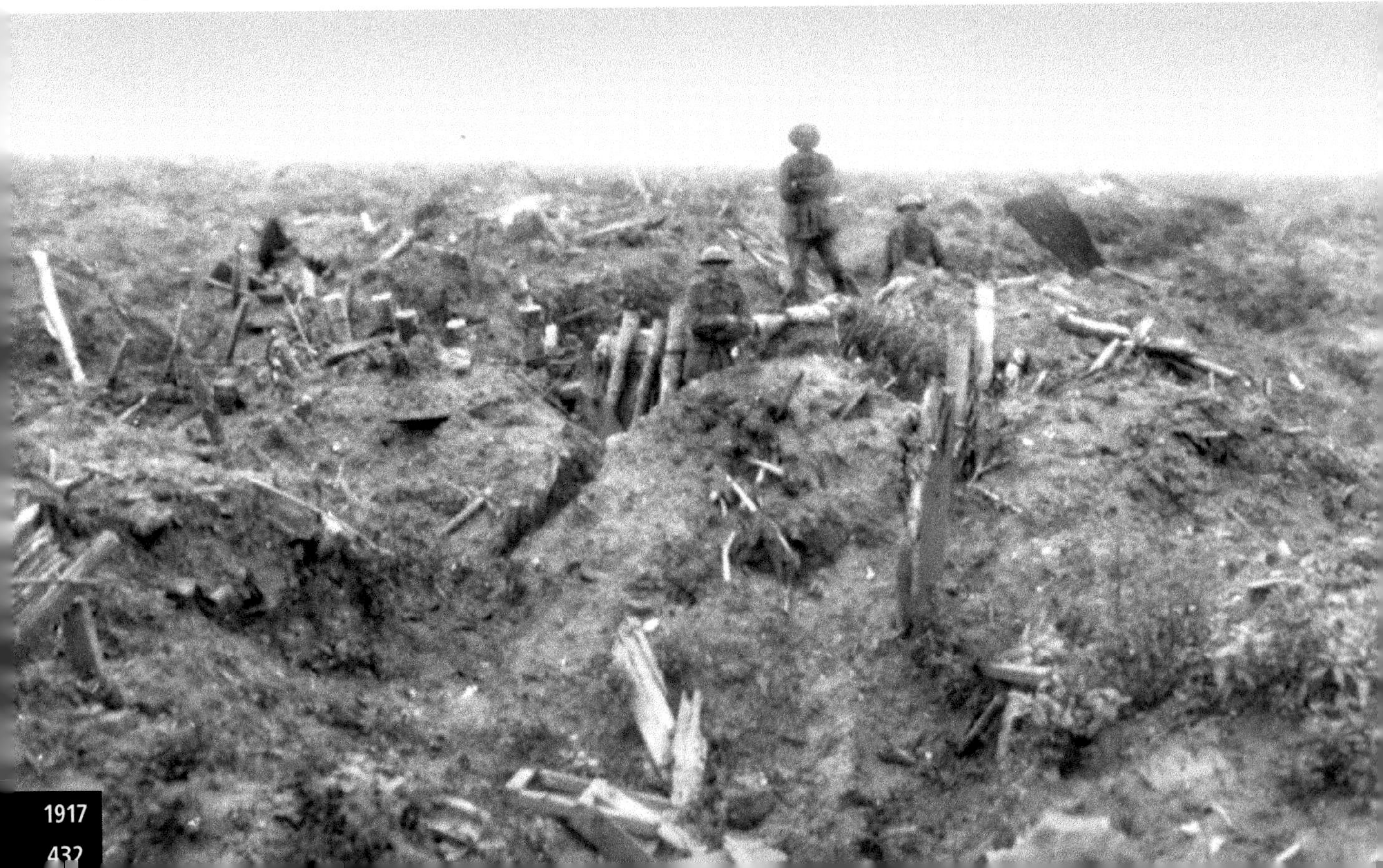

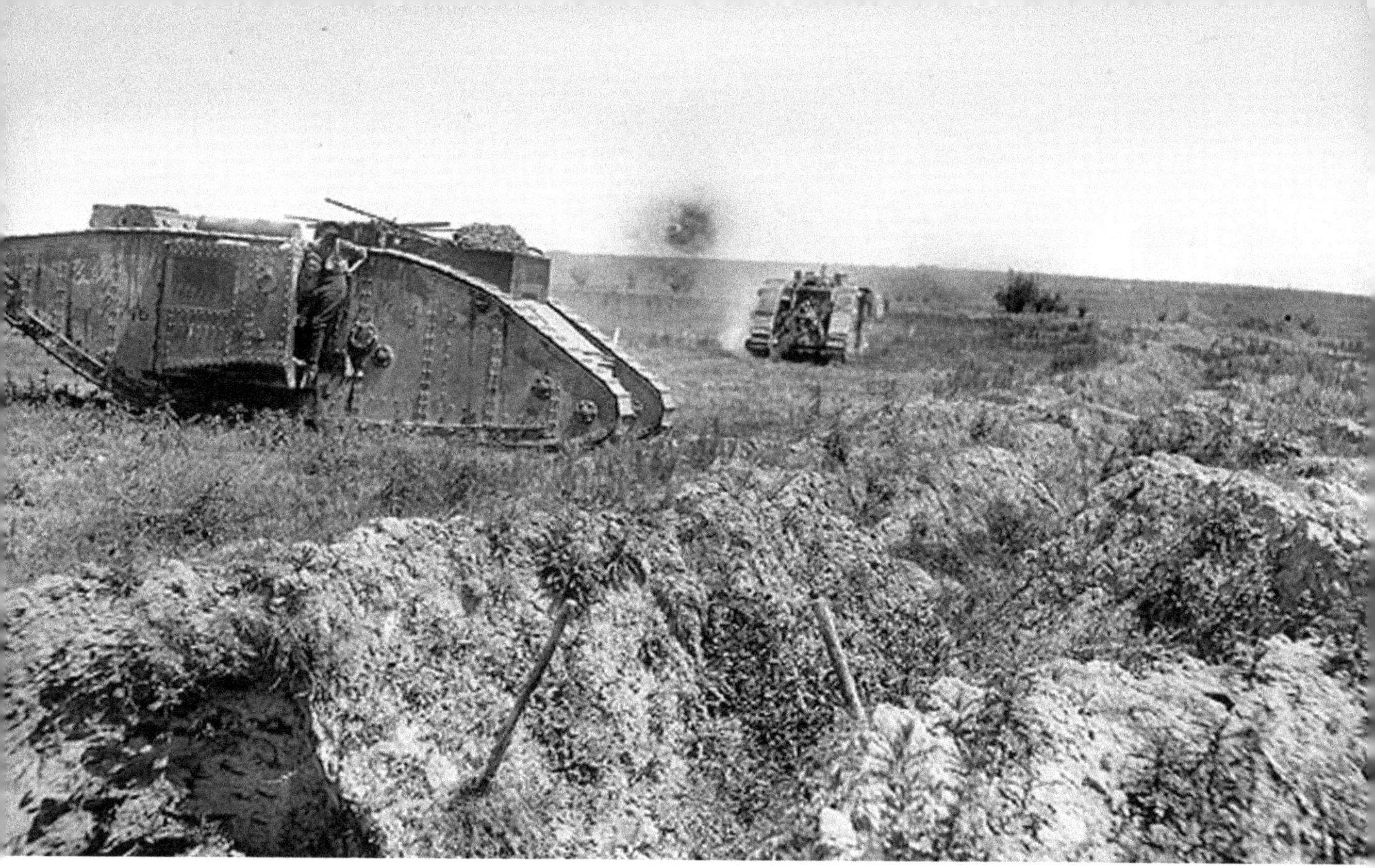

17GW969, 17GW1000. Tanks moving into action during the second phase of the Battle of Messines, 7 June, 1917.

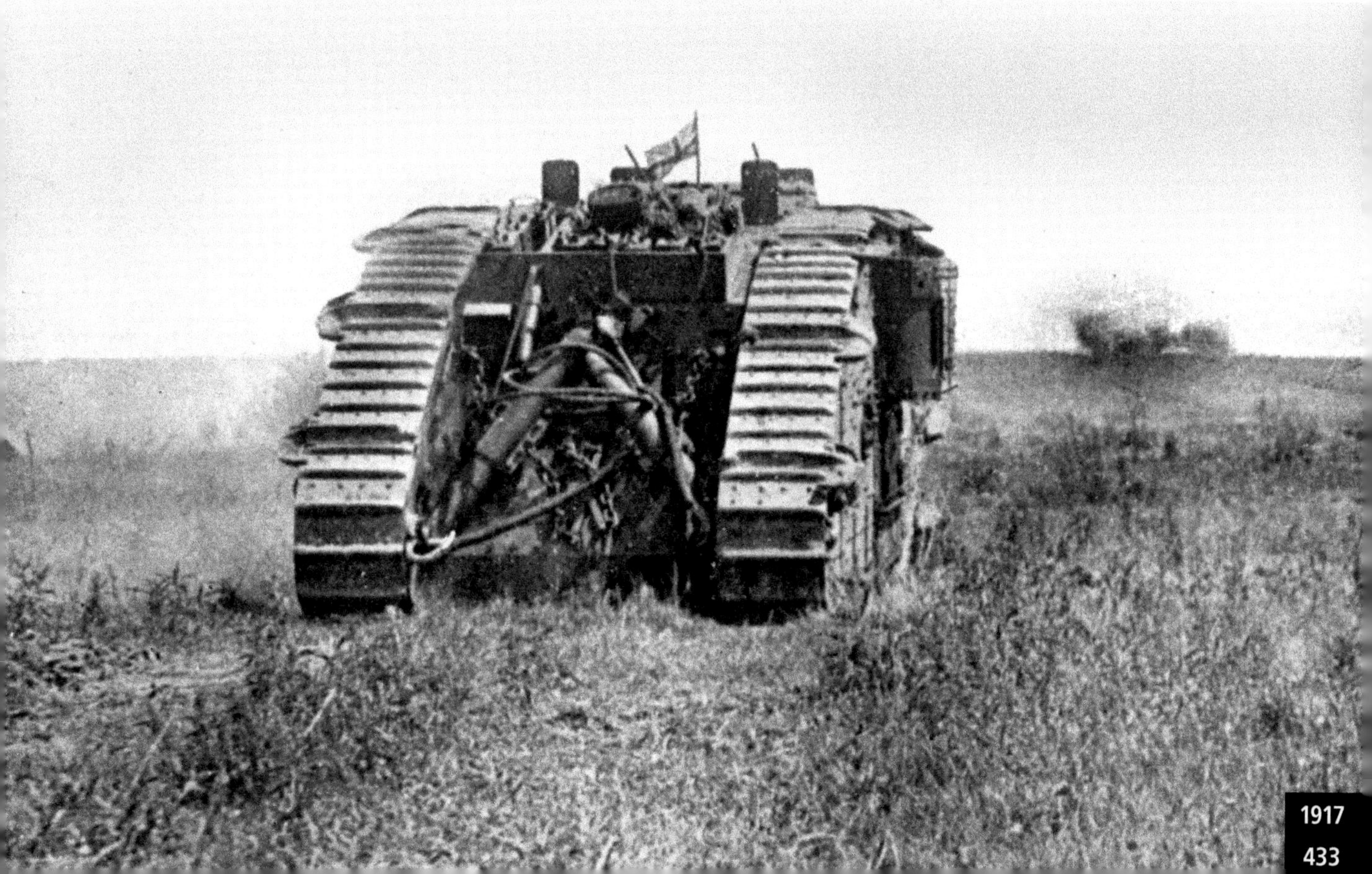

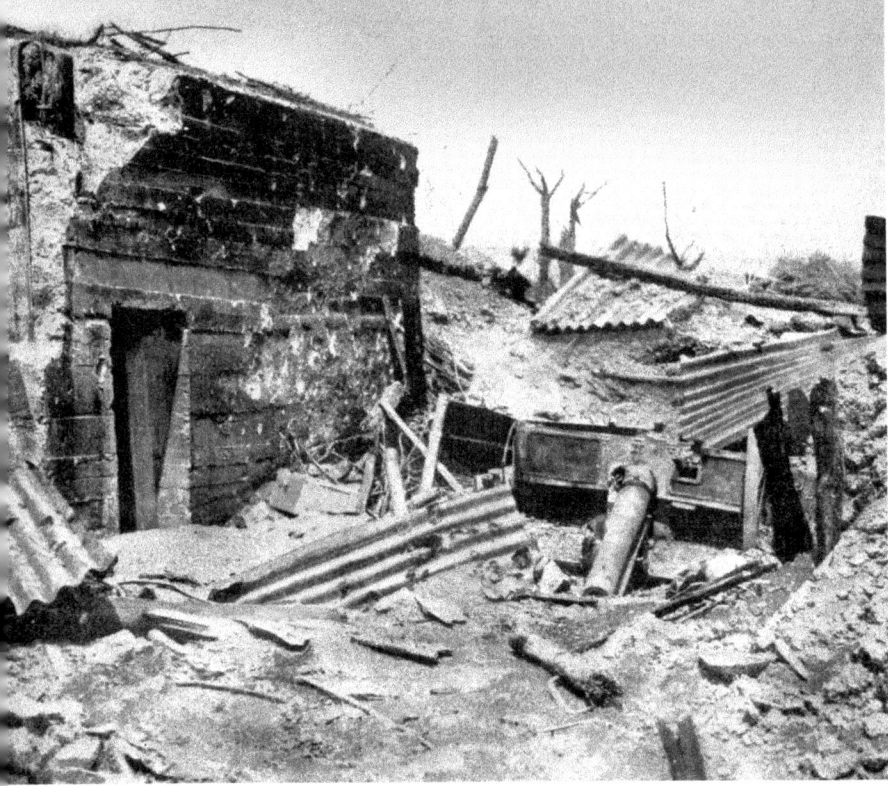

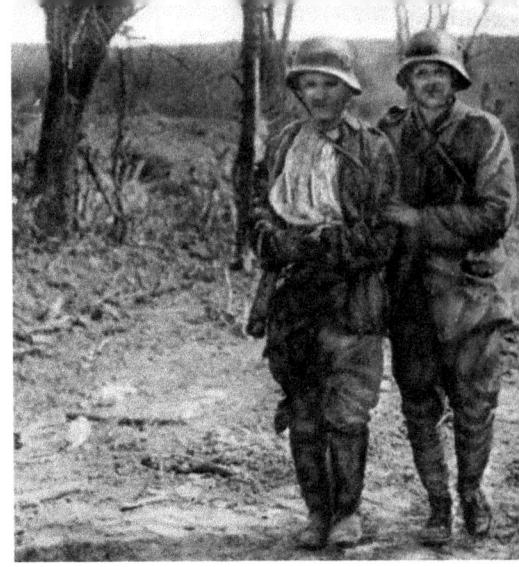

17GW1003 A German 77 mm field gun wrecked by the British creeping barrage laid across the high ground between the villages of Wytschaete and Messines. However, the concrete shelter for the gunners remains intact.

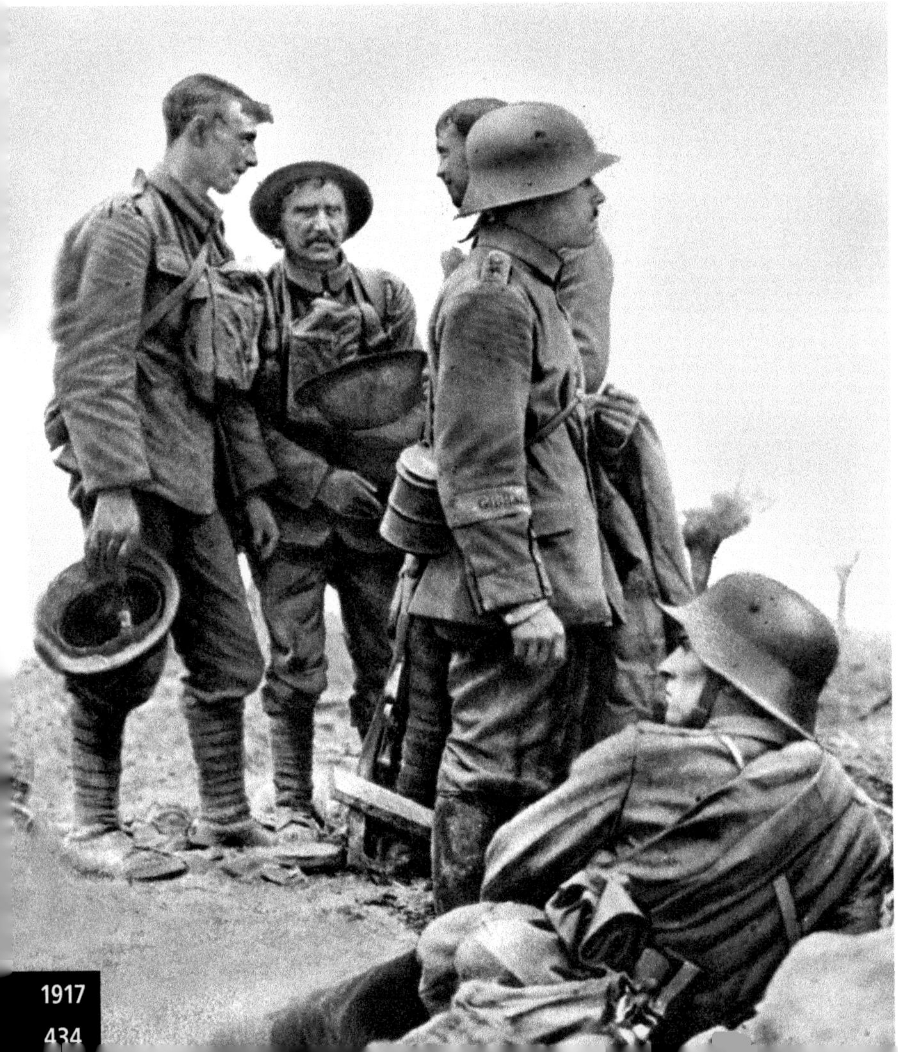

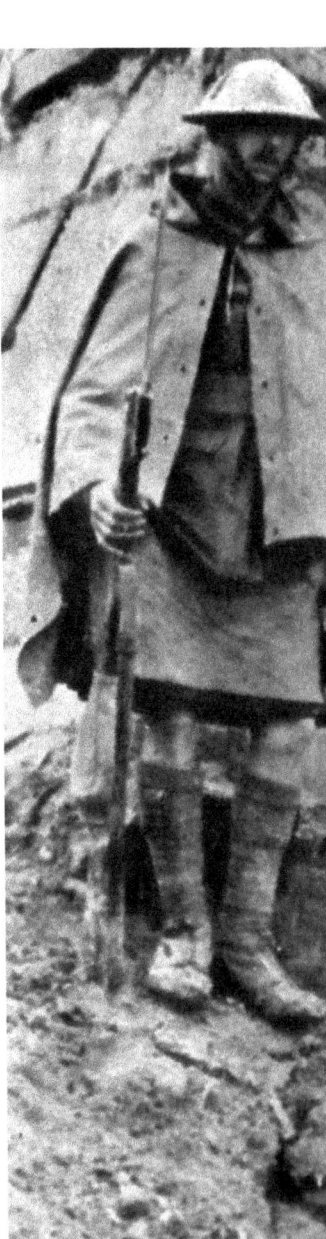

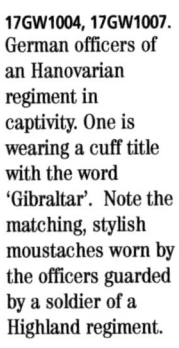

17GW1004, 17GW1007. German officers of an Hanovarian regiment in captivity. One is wearing a cuff title with the word 'Gibraltar'. Note the matching, stylish moustaches worn by the officers guarded by a soldier of a Highland regiment.

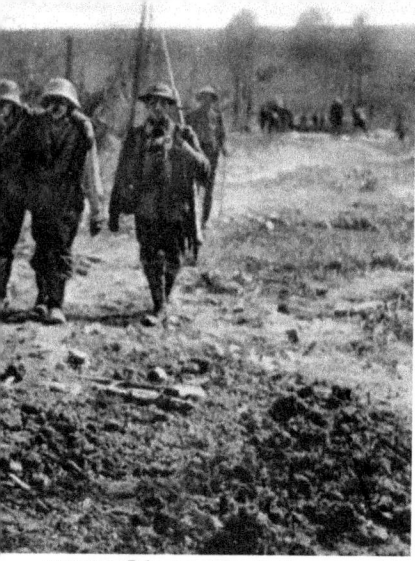
17GW1006 Prisoners taken in the successful assault, with the ridge in the background.

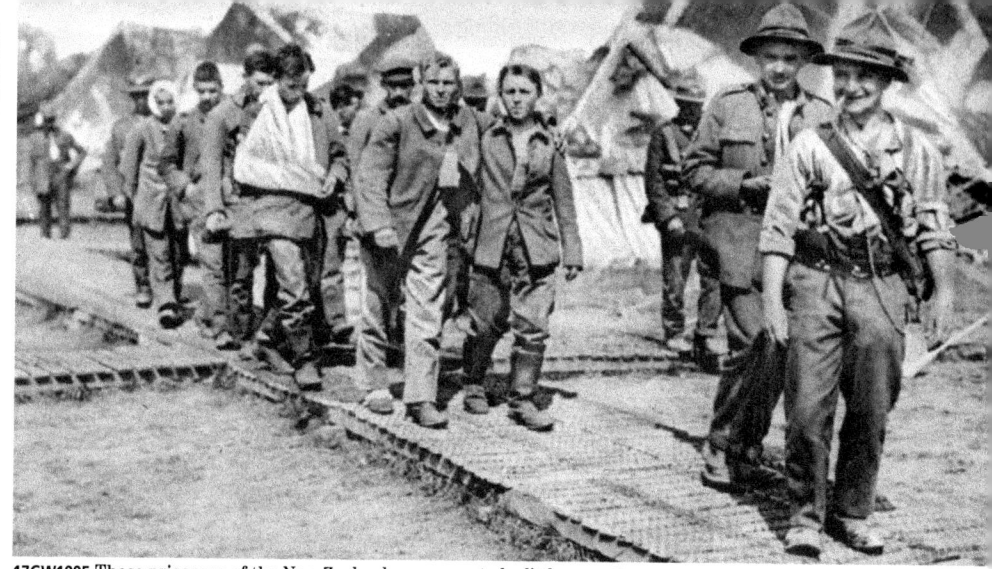
17GW1005 These prisoners of the New Zealanders appear to be little more than teenagers.

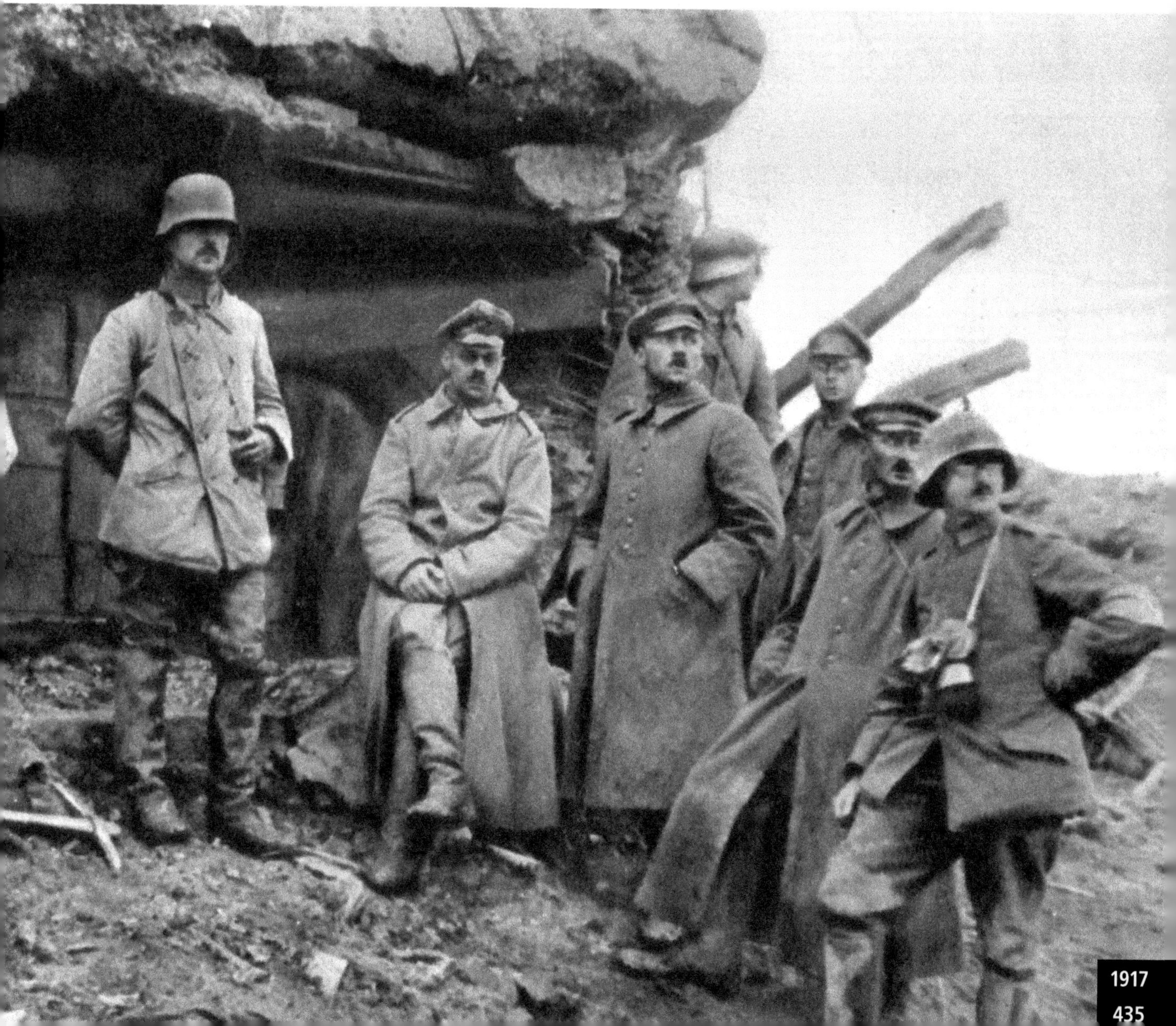

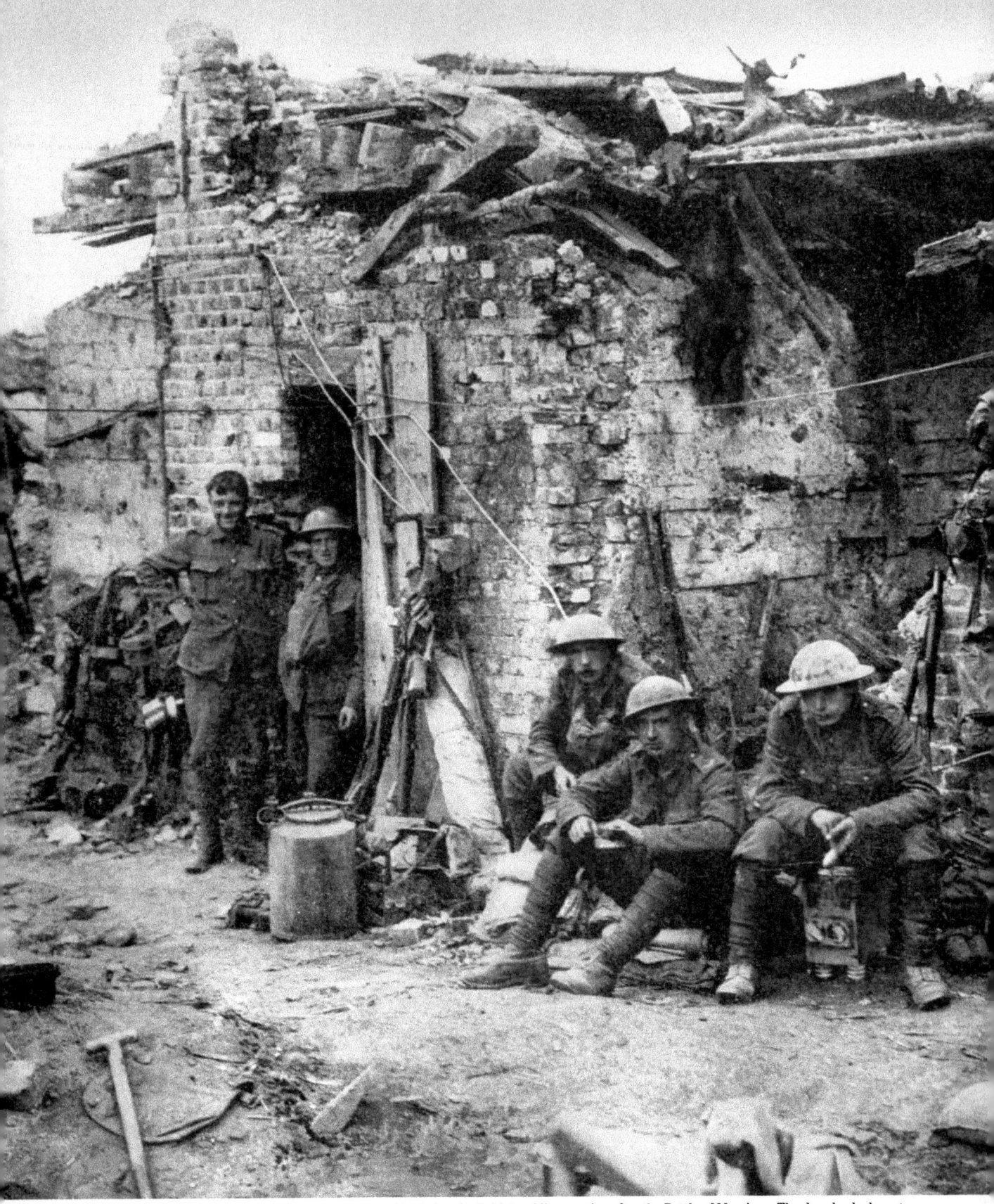

17GW1008 The smashed buildings of a farm house provide shelter for British soldiers resting after the Battle of Messines. The door leads down to underground shelters dug by the Germans.

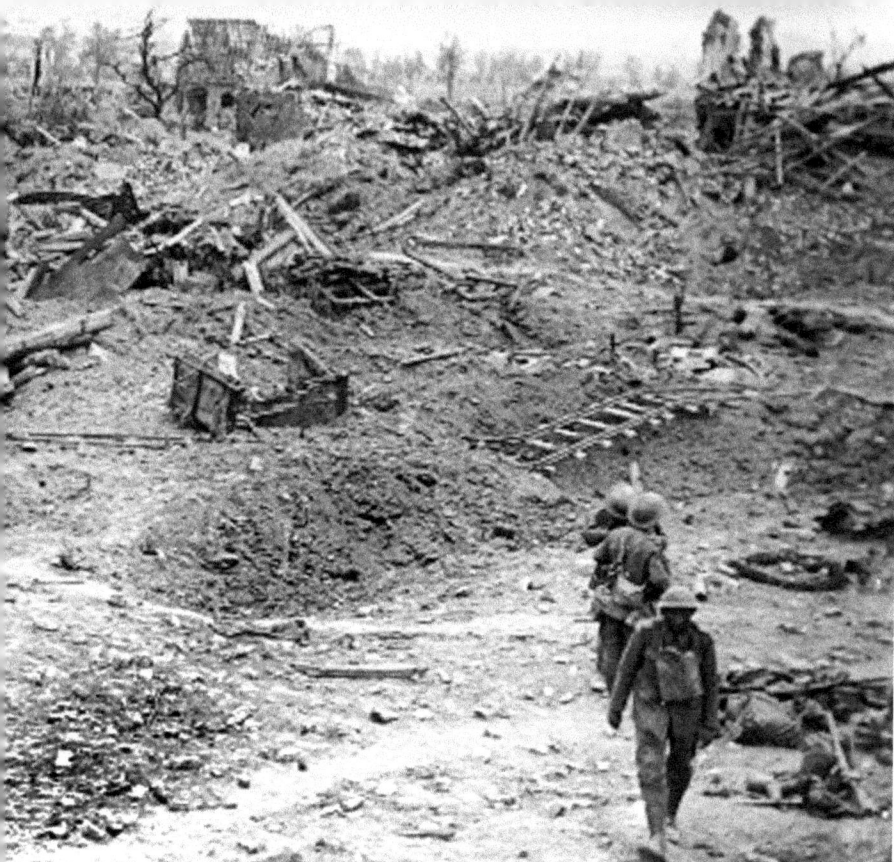

17GW958 Men of the 16th (Irish) Division in the ruined village of Wytschaete after its capture.

17GW1001 Soldiers of the Royal Garrison Artillery at a forward observation post; one of them is operating a Fullerphone, a telegraph system using Morse code.

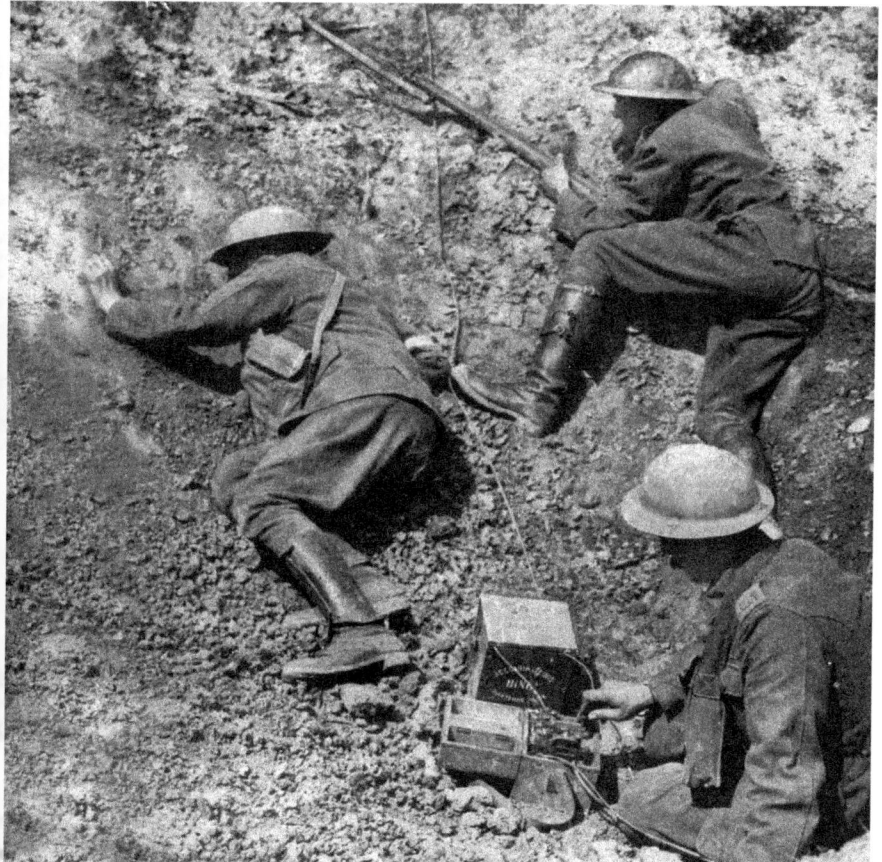

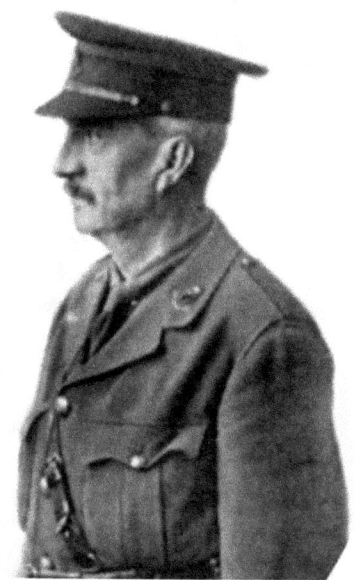

Major William Hoey Kearney Redmond.

Willie Redmond MP was a politician with strong Irish Nationalist views. On the day of the Battle of Messines he was serving with his unit, the 6th Battalion Royal Irish Regiment (the Derry National Volunteers), 16th (Irish) Division (Roman Catholic); also in IX Corps was the 36th (Ulster) Division (Protestant). In other circumstances the two parties would be estranged; however, in the Great War they were united against a common enemy. On this occasion elements of both divisions were moving up along Kemmel Road and into the attack on the high ground. Suddenly the fifty-six year old Major Redmond was cut down and wounded. An Ulsterman, stretcher bearer John Meeke, 11th Battalion Royal Inniskilling Fusiliers (Donegal & Fermanagh), was searching the battlefield for the wounded when he saw Major Redmond fall. Using shell holes as cover, he braved the heavy machine gun fire and reached Redmond. As he finished dressing the major's wound, Meeke was wounded on his left side. Major Redmond saw the young man bleeding profusely and ordered him to retreat to safety. Meeke refused and was hit again. He stayed with Redmond until they were both eventually rescued by a patrol of the 36th (Ulster) Division. Major Redmond was carried to the safety of a Field Dressing Station where he died several hours later. He was originally buried in the grounds of a convent in Locre, Belgium. Today his grave stands isolated and outside the boundary wall of the nearby CWGC cemetery.

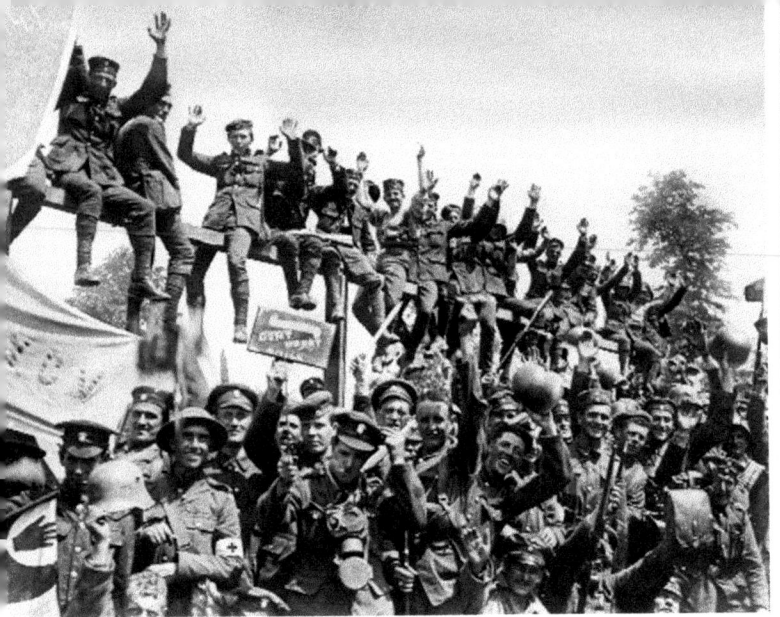
17GW959 Men from the Royal Inniskilling Fusiliers and Royal Irish Rifles celebrating their victory at Wijtschate, June 1917.

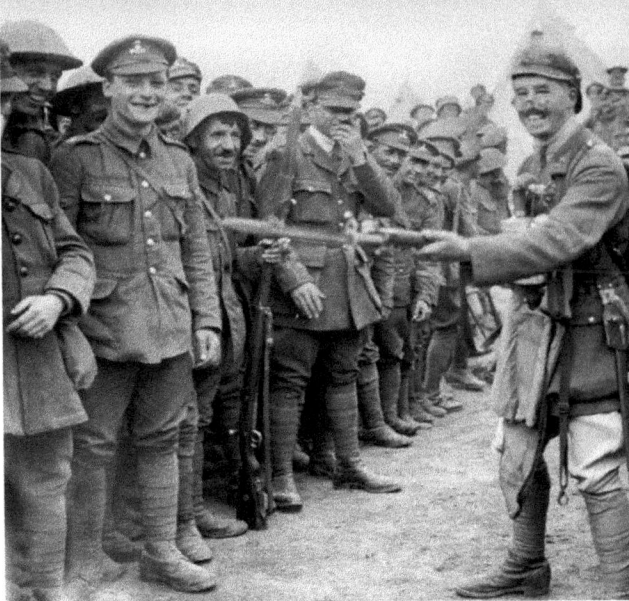
17GW956 The Royal Dublin Fusiliers celebrating their victory at Wijtschate, June 1917.

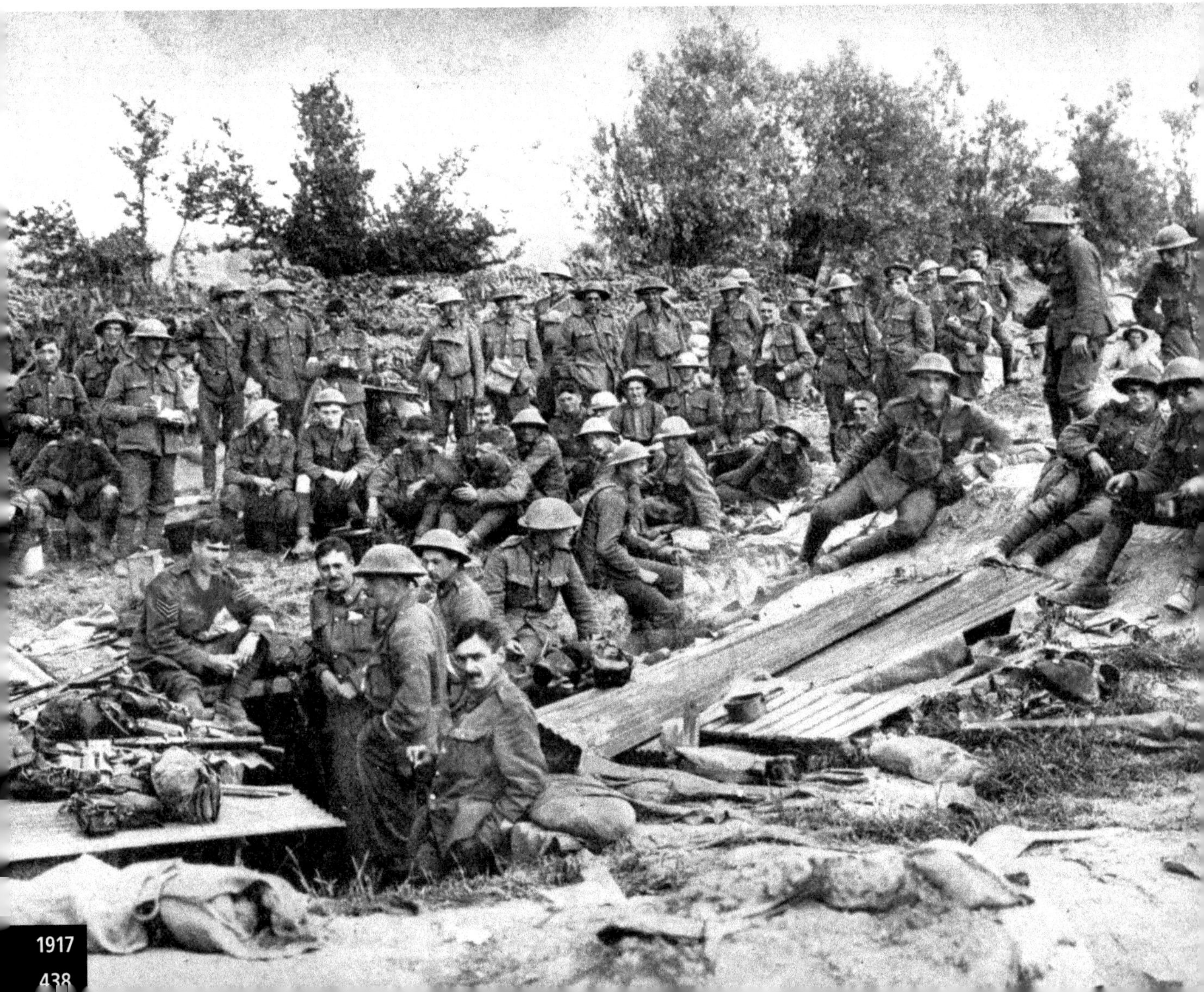

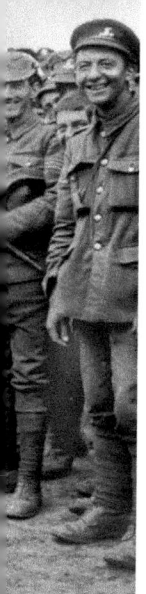

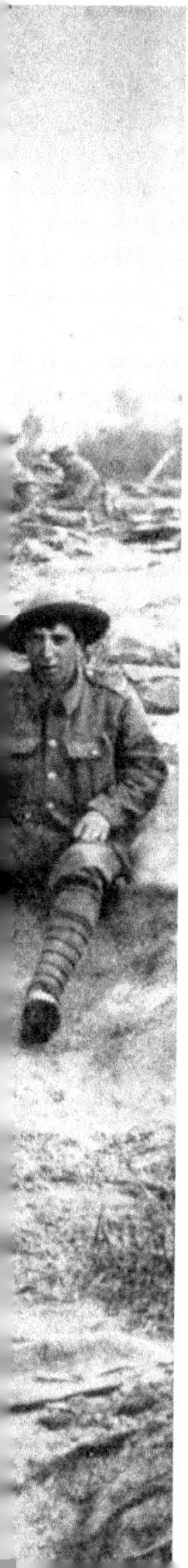

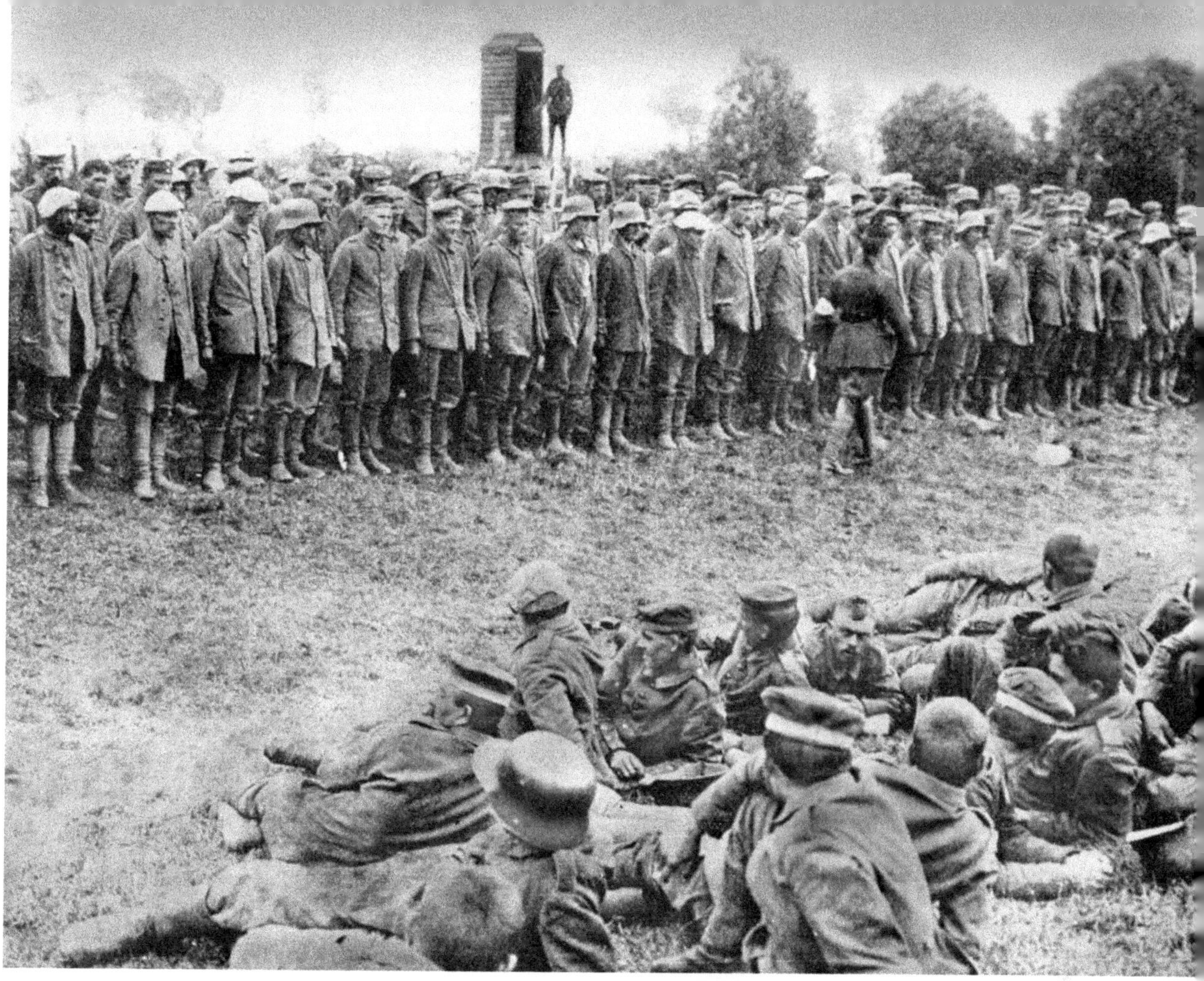

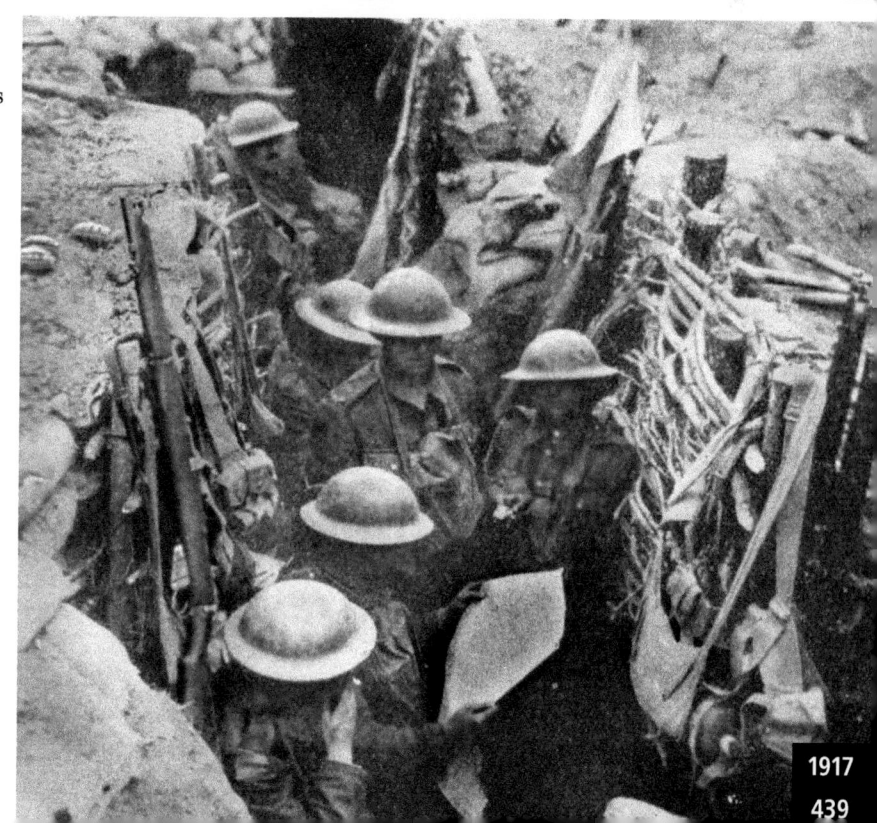

17GW1010 Some of the 7,000 prisoners who fell into British hands during the fighting at Messines and Wijtschate, June 1917. Some of them are being paraded as their comrades look on. Raised above the compound is a sentry standing besides his box.

17GW1009 Men of the 12th Battalion East Surrey Regiment, resting up four days after they had successfully stormed the high ground north of Wijtschate.

17GW1011 A British communications trench north of Ploegsteert Wood, filled with troops waiting to go forward to relieve those in the front line.

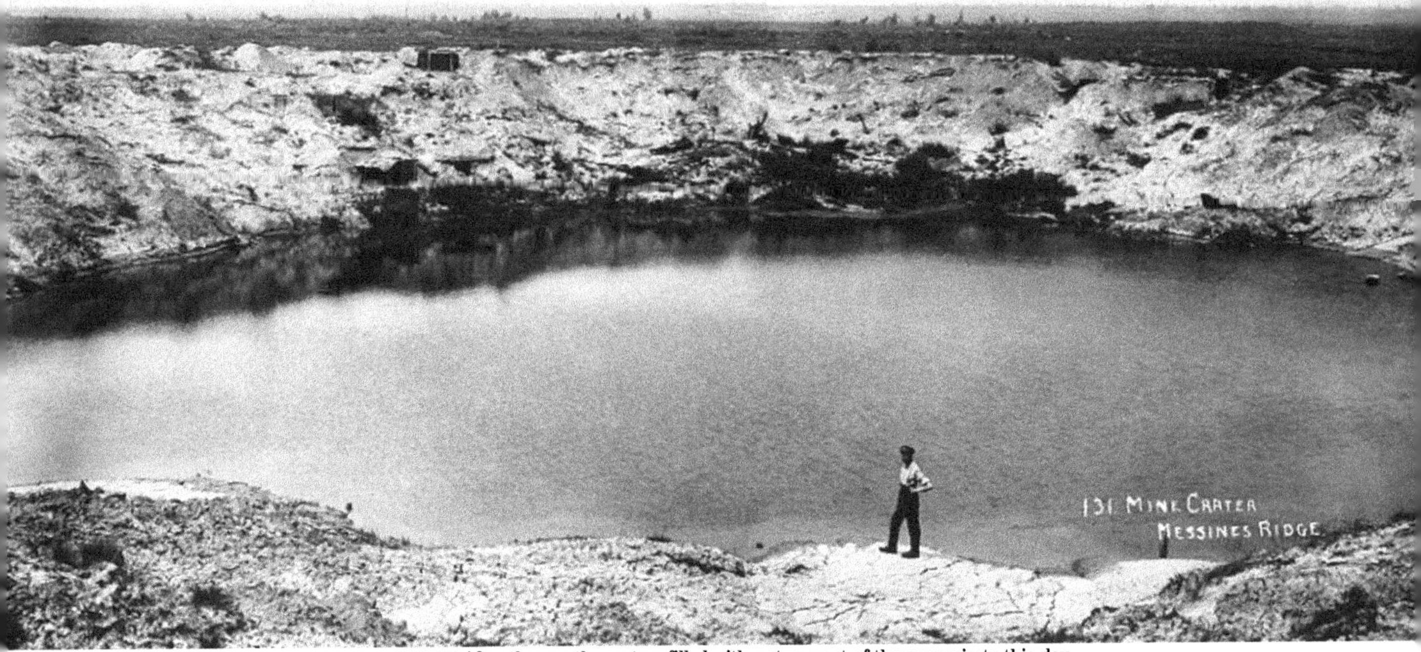

17GW952 After the war the craters filled with water; most of them remain to this day.

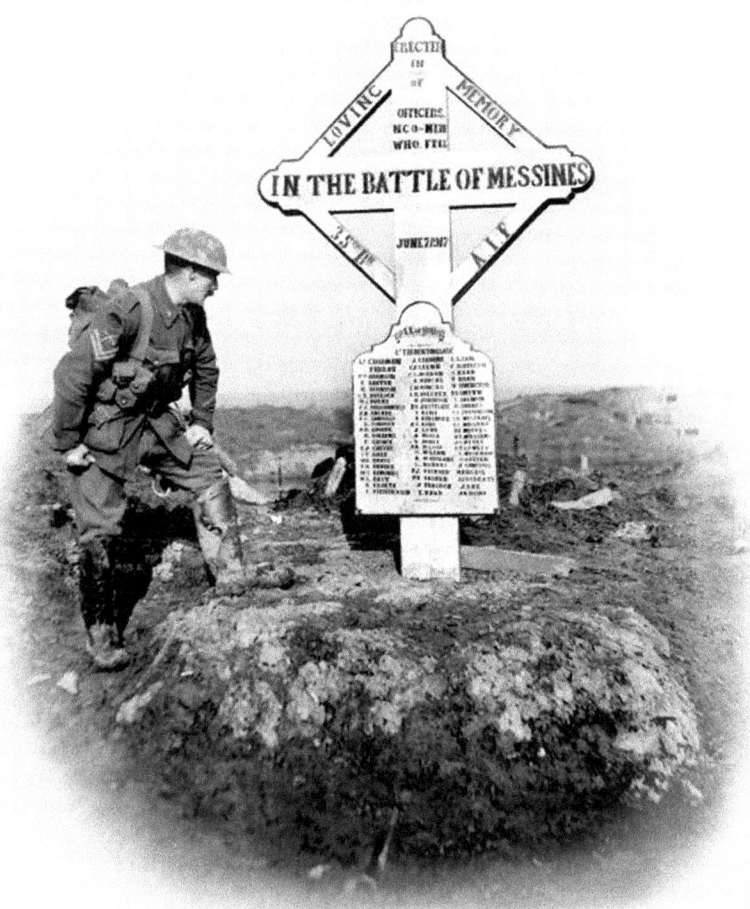

17GW966 The memorial erected in memory of their comrades of the 35th Battalion (New South Wales) AIF, who died in the Battle of Messines, 7 June 1917.

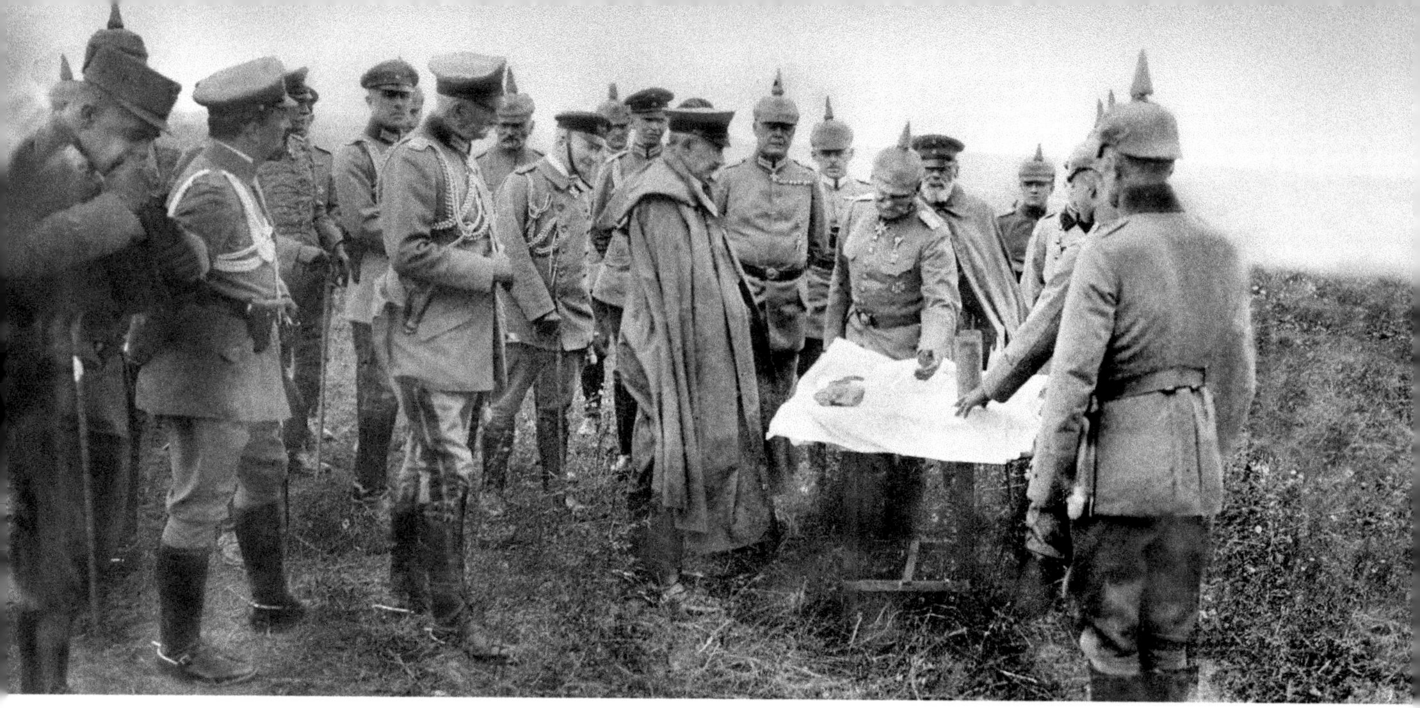

Chapter Eight: Third Battle of Ypres – Passchendaele

17GW1017 The Kaiser and his staff officers assessing the situation on the Western Front following the recent Allied gains.

17GW1012 Men of the 10th Field Artillery Brigade, Australian 4th Division passing through Chateau Wood in the Ypres Salient, October 1917.

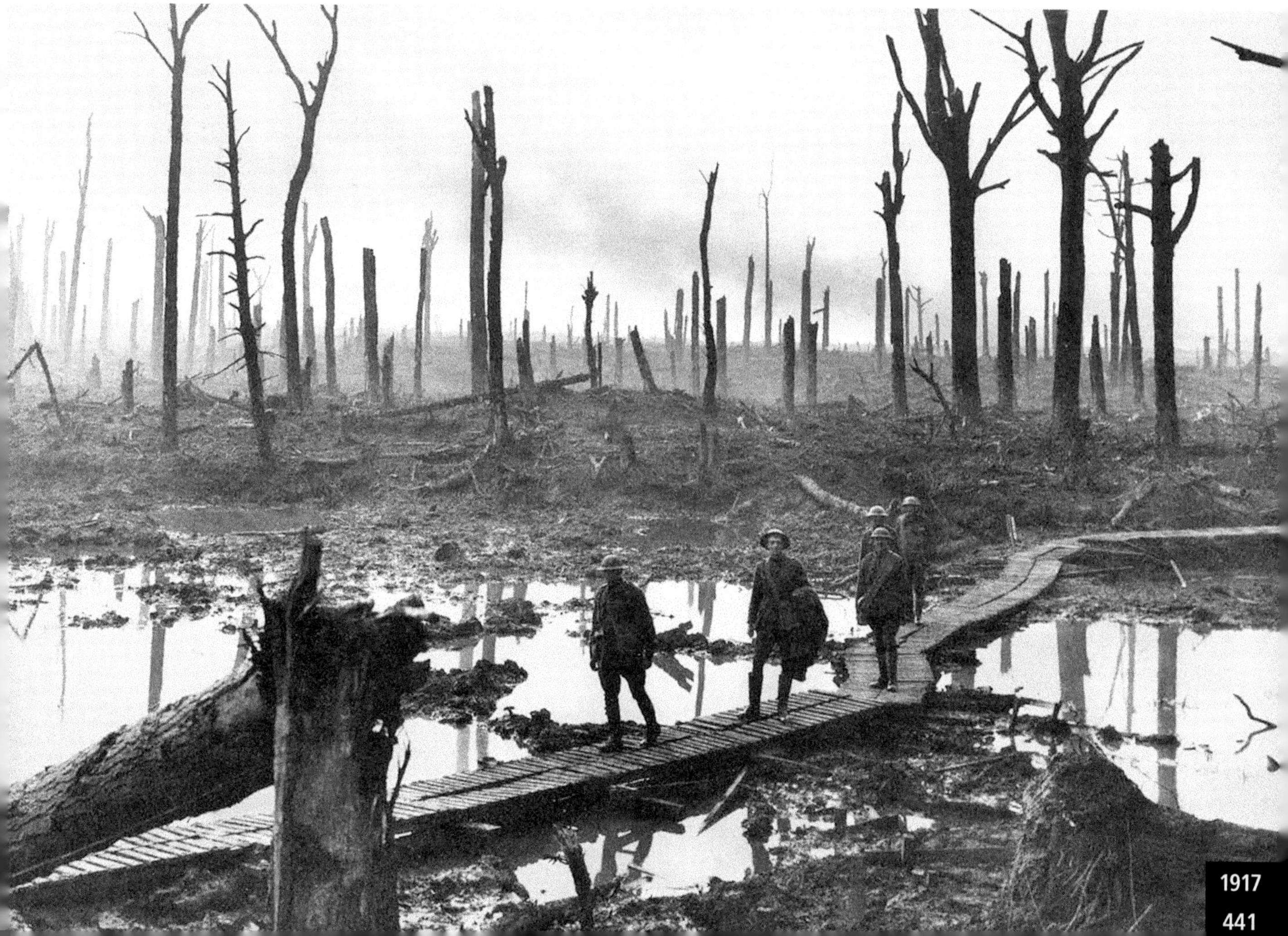

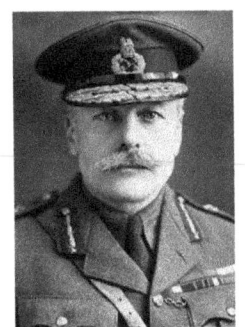

Field Marshall Douglas Haig

The Third Battle of Ypres or Passchendaele refers to the fighting that took place at Ypres, 31 July – 10 November 1917. It was an attempt by Field Marshal Haig to reach the Belgian coast to put out of action the German submarine bases. He and his staff were encouraged by the success of the attack on Messines Ridge and hoped for a breakthrough. However, the Germans knew an attack was coming and the initial bombardment, fired by 3,000 guns over two weeks, served as a final warning. The infantry advance on the left flank succeeded in taking early objectives, but elsewhere the attack failed. After a few days the heaviest summer rain in thirty years fell turning the ground into a massive swamp.

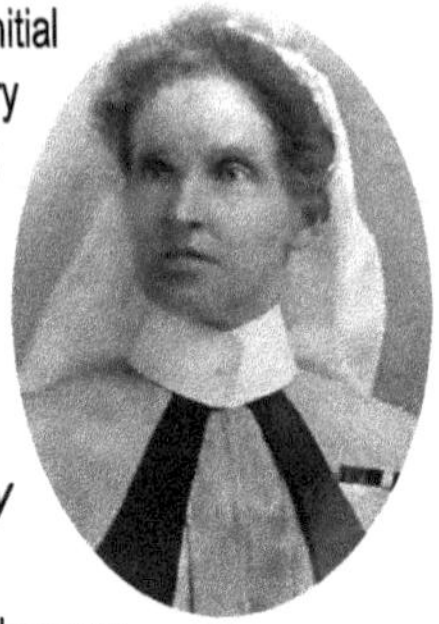

Kate Luard, a nurse coping with the flow of abdominal, chest and femur wounds, wrote in her diary: *Can God be on our side, everyone is asking – when His (alleged!) Department always intervenes in favour of the enemy at all our best moments?*

Mud aggravated the terrible wounds and deaths mounted. Weapons became clogged and movement, especially of tanks, became very difficult. On 16 August the attack was resumed, to little effect. It was stalemate until an improvement in the weather prompted another attack on 20 September. The **Battle of Menin Road Ridge**, along with the **Battle of Polygon Wood** on 26 September and the **Battle of Broodseinde** on 4 October finally managed to establish British possession of the ridge east of Ypres. The eventual capture of **Passchendaele village** by British and Canadian forces on 6 November gave Haig the excuse to claim success and halt the offensive. In just over three months, casualties amounted to 325,000 Allied and 260,000 Germans. The Ypres Salient was expanded and high ground had been taken.

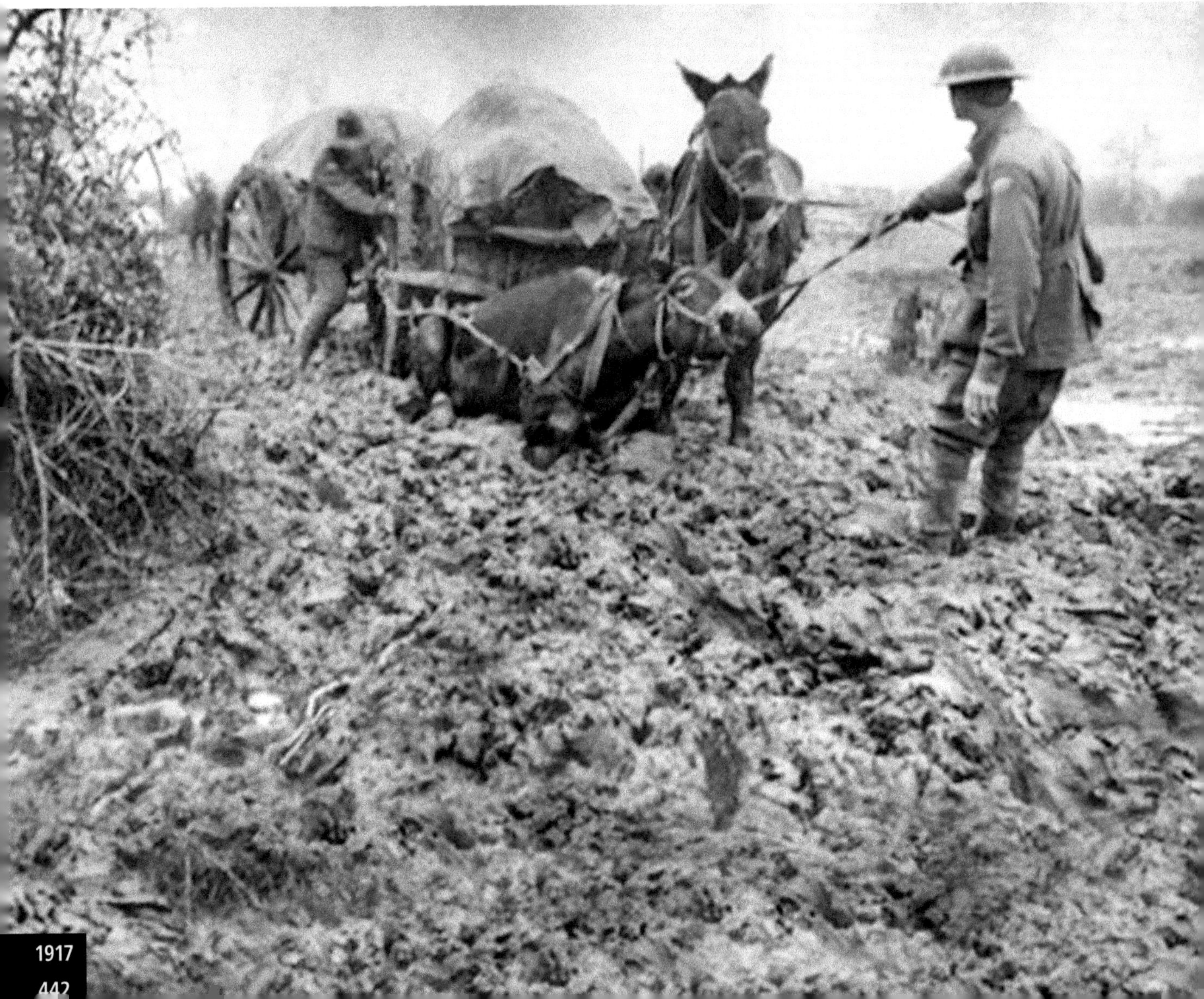

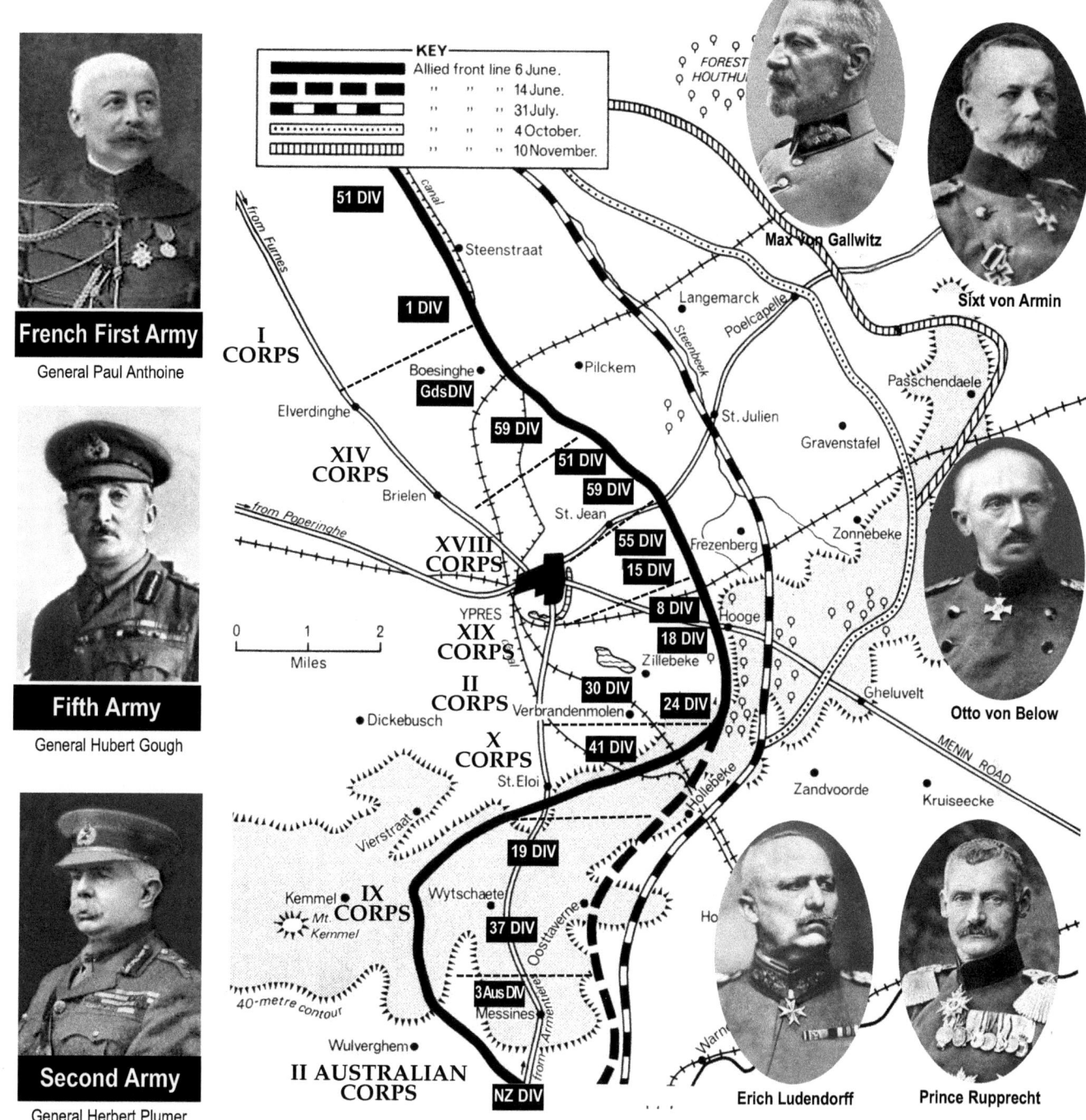

The Battle of Menin Road, which took place from 20–25 September was the third British set piece attack of the Third Battle of Ypres; with a ratio of 3 to 1 in artillery pieces over the Germans the attacking infantry captured most of their objectives.

The Battle of Polygon Wood, 26 September – 3 October, in the area from the Menin Road to Polygon Wood and then north to the area beyond St. Julien. The Australians advanced a kilometre, largely clearing Polygon Wood by taking two lines of German trenches. General Plumer successfully employed new infantry tactics, known as 'bite and hold' where infantry made a limited gain, then dug in; a second wave passed through, captured ground and consolidated.

The Battle of Broodseinde was fought on 4 October largely over an area known as the Gheluvelt plateau, and proved to be the most successful Allied attack of the Third Ypres. the British devastated the German defence, which prompted alarm among the German commanders and caused a loss of morale in the German Fourth Army.

The Battle of Passchendaele on 12 October, was a further attempt to gain ground around Passchendaele village. Heavy rain and mud again made movement difficult. Allied troops were exhausted and morale had fallen. After a modest British advance, German counter-attacks recovered most of the ground lost opposite Passchendaele. There were 13,000 Allied casualties, including 2,735 New Zealanders, 845 of whom had been killed or lay wounded and stranded in the mud of no man's land. Haig ended major operations on 10 November 1917.

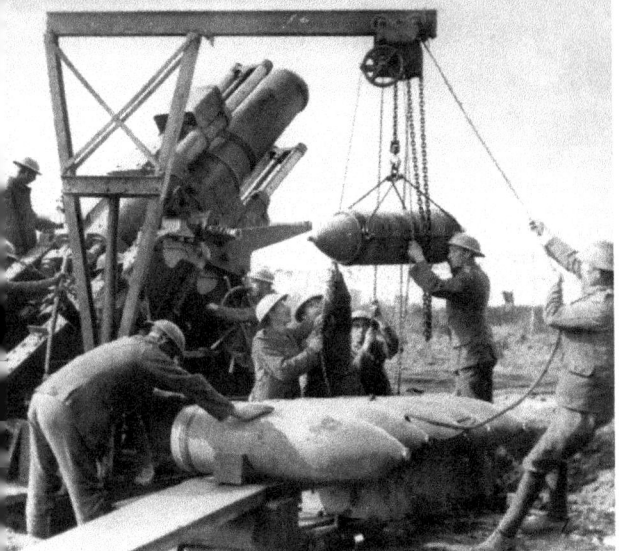

17GW1023 Loading a 15-inch howitzer.

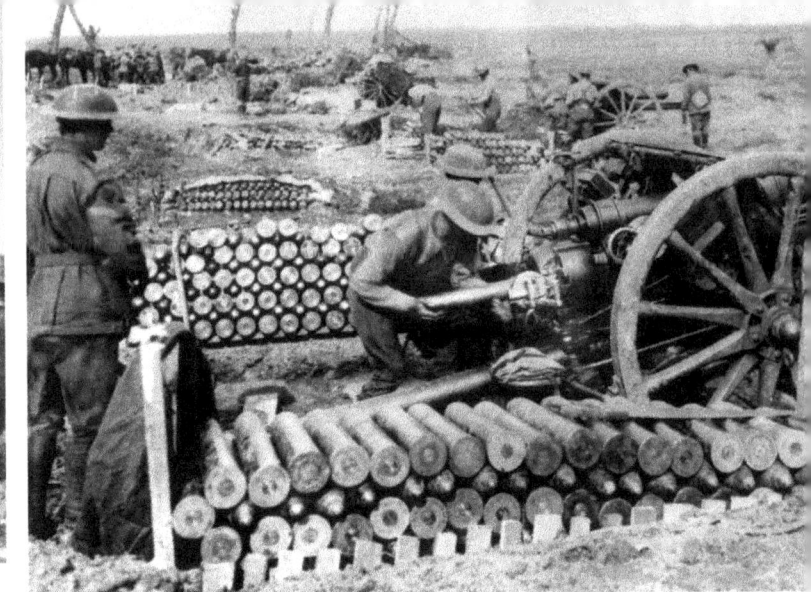

17GW1024 With the Australians – a battery of 18 pounders in action.

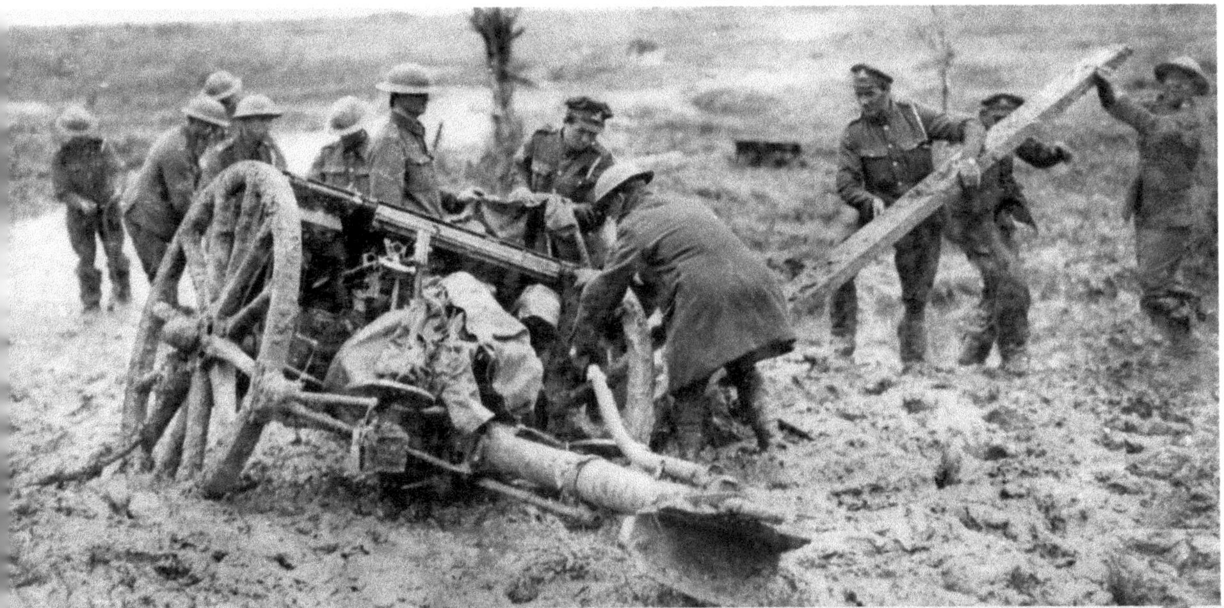

17GW1027 The fighting for Pilckem Ridge took place in terrible conditions – this 18-pounder has sunk up to its axle in the August rains.

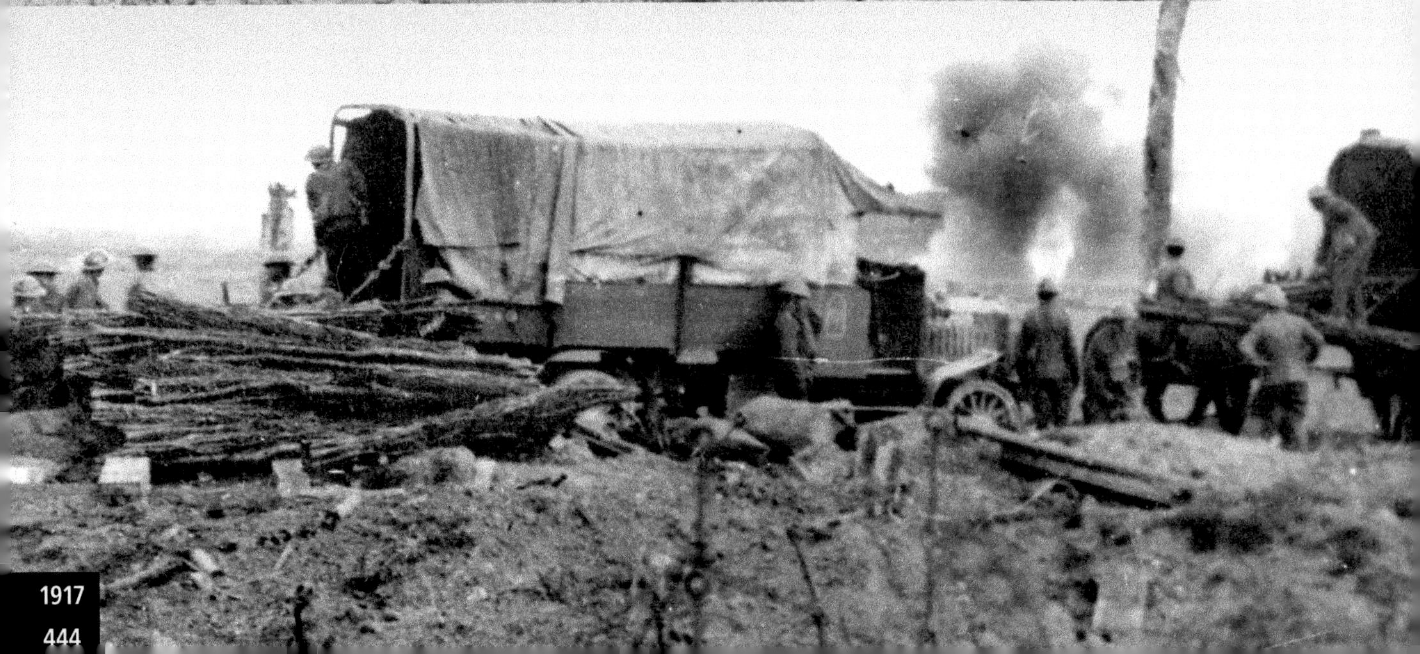

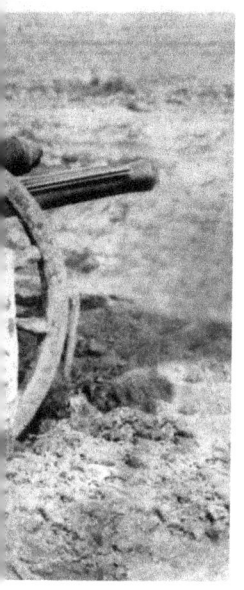
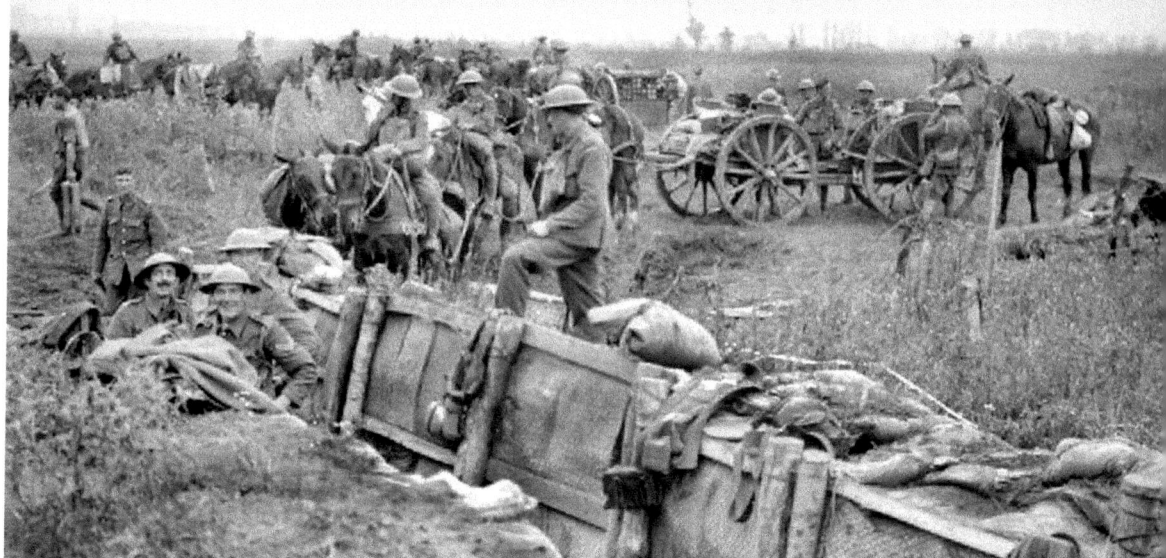

17GW1023 During the Battle of Pilckem Ridge. A British 18 pounder RFA gun battery takes up new positions close to a communication trench near the Belgian village of Boesinghe, 31 July 1917.

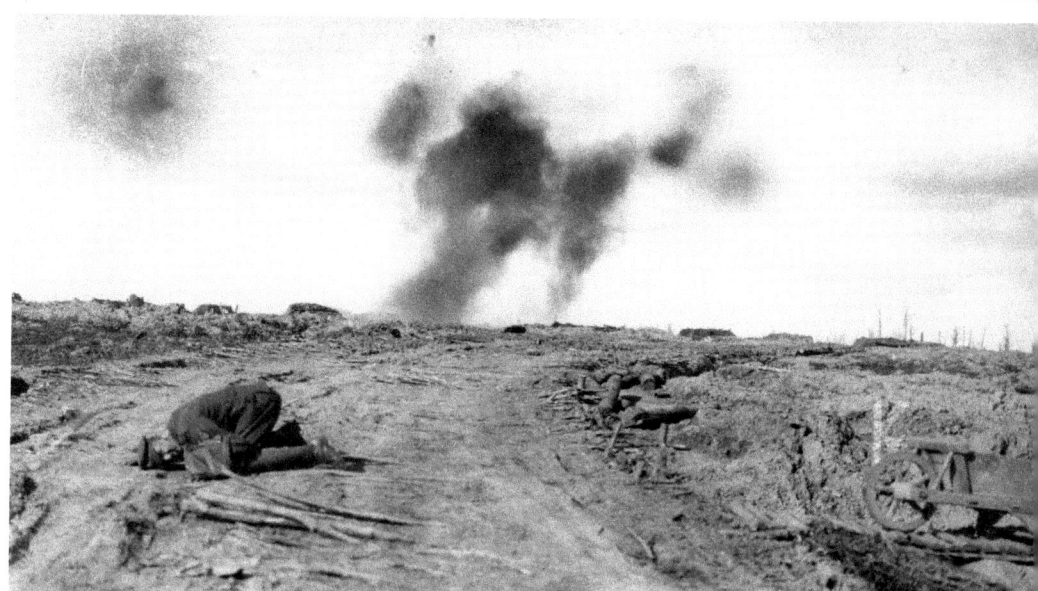

17GW1028 German shells exploding on Pilckem Ridge 18 August 1917; a sergeant takes cover and the cameraman, apparently, does not.

17GW1029 During the Battle of Passchendaele. A German artillery battery seeks to drop shells on this road and supply convoy.

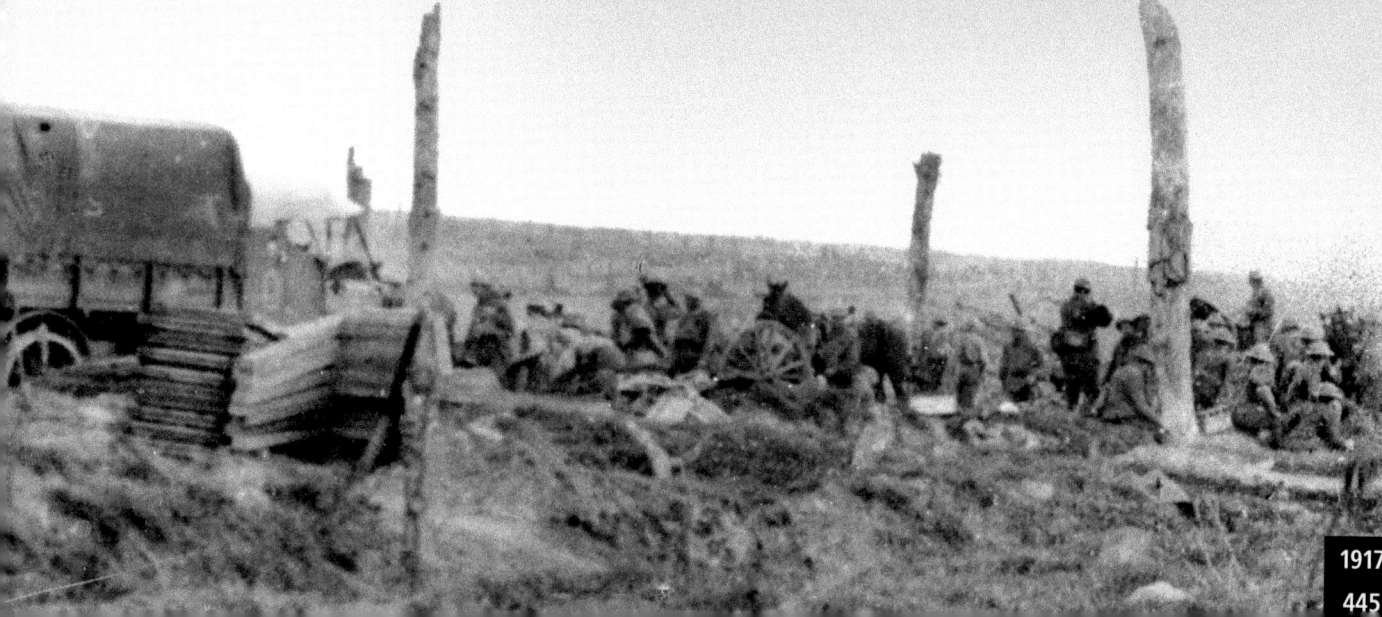

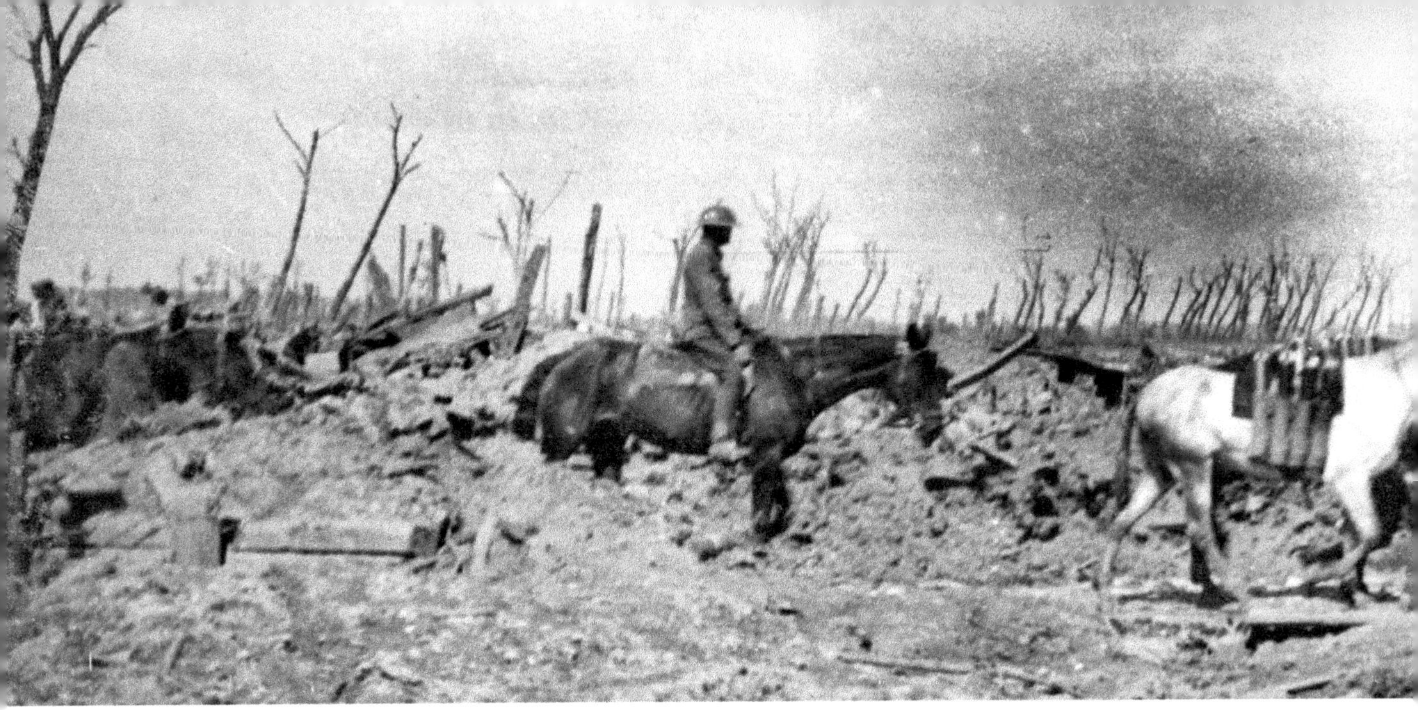

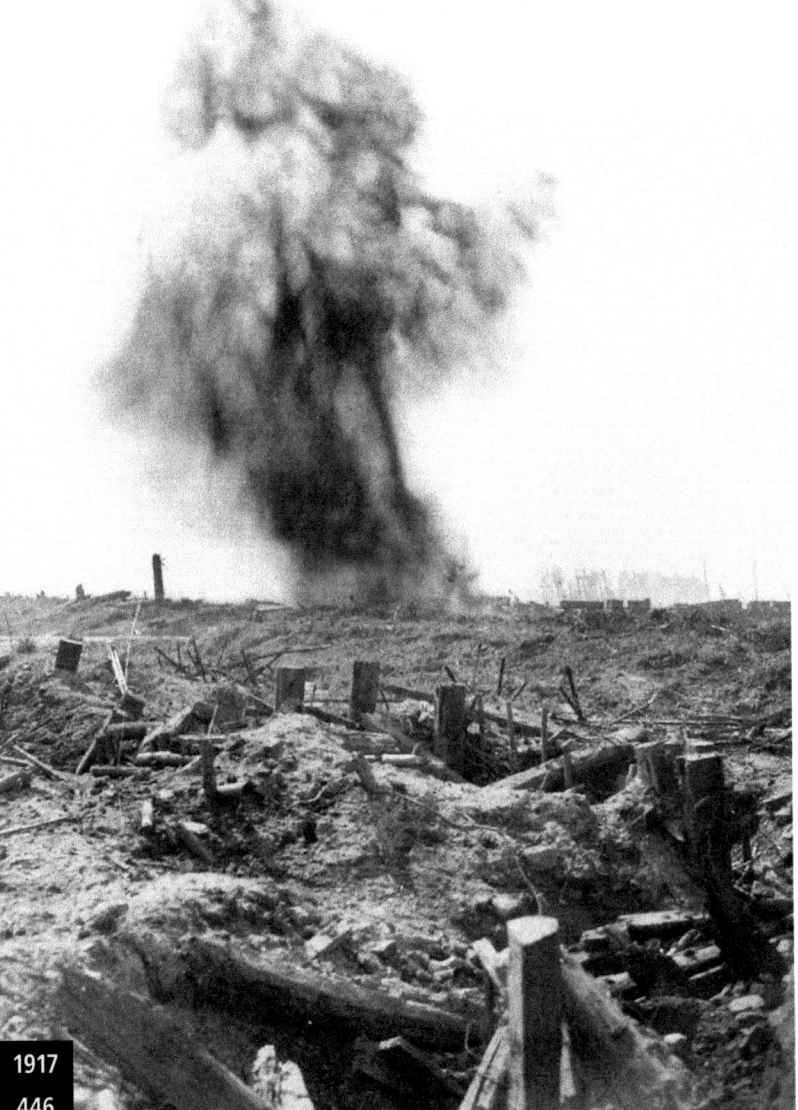

17GW1030 Mules carrying artillery shells to the guns on Pilckem Ridge.

17GW1031 German shells falling around the ruins of Boesinghe Station during the Battle of Langemarck, August 1917. The outline of train wagons can be seen in the distance.

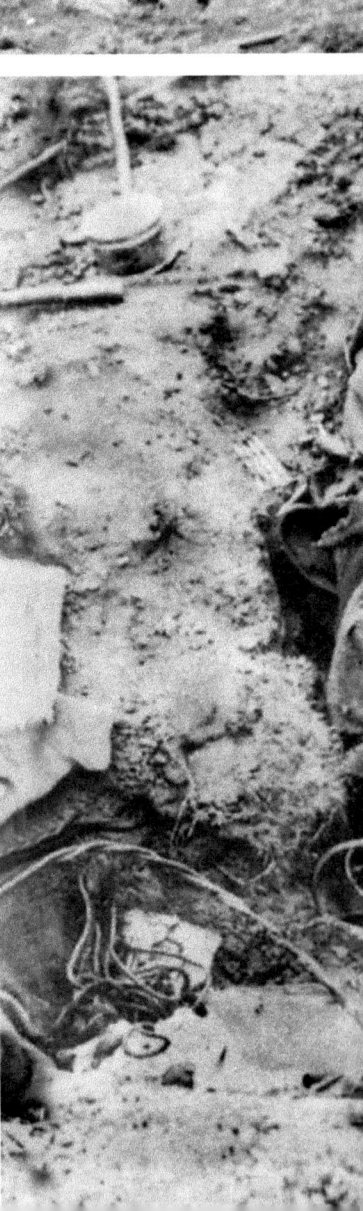

17GW1032 German dead, victims of the bombardment that preceded the Allied attack largely to the east of the Ypres Salient, 31 July 1917.

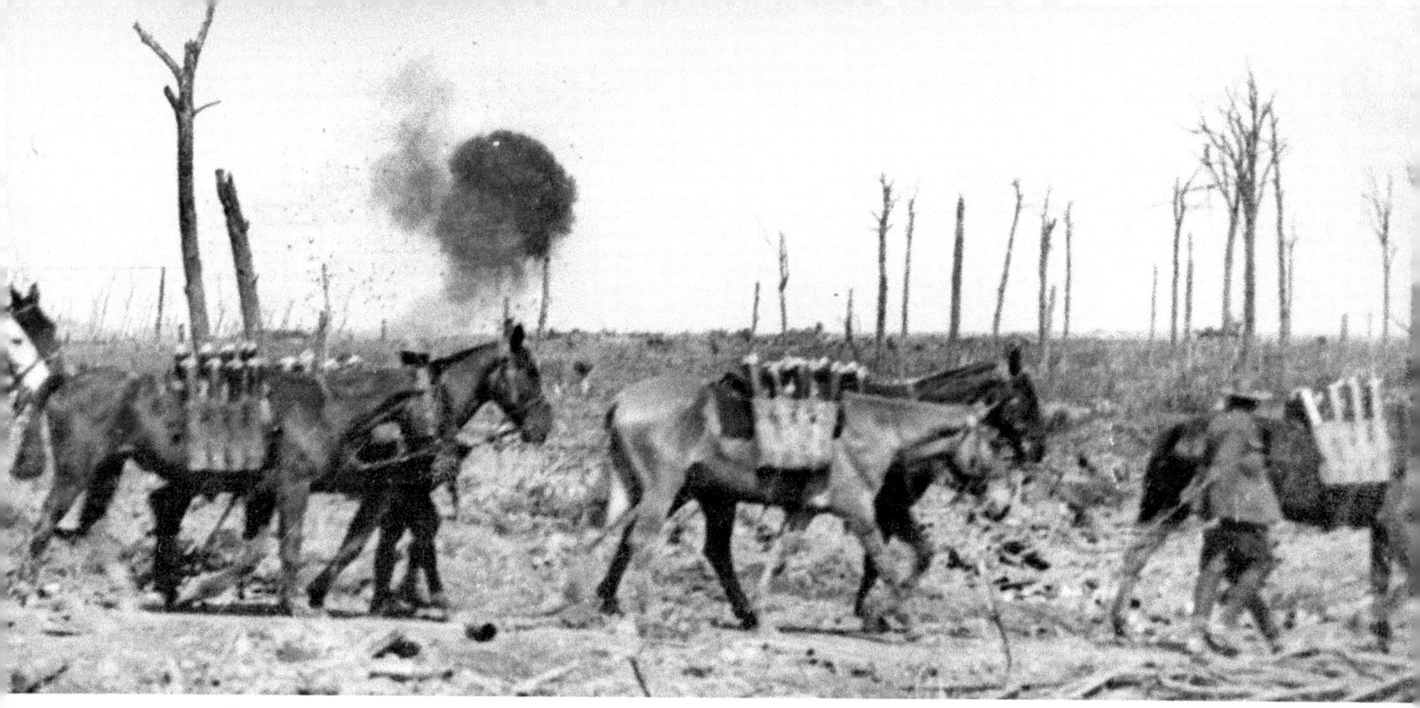

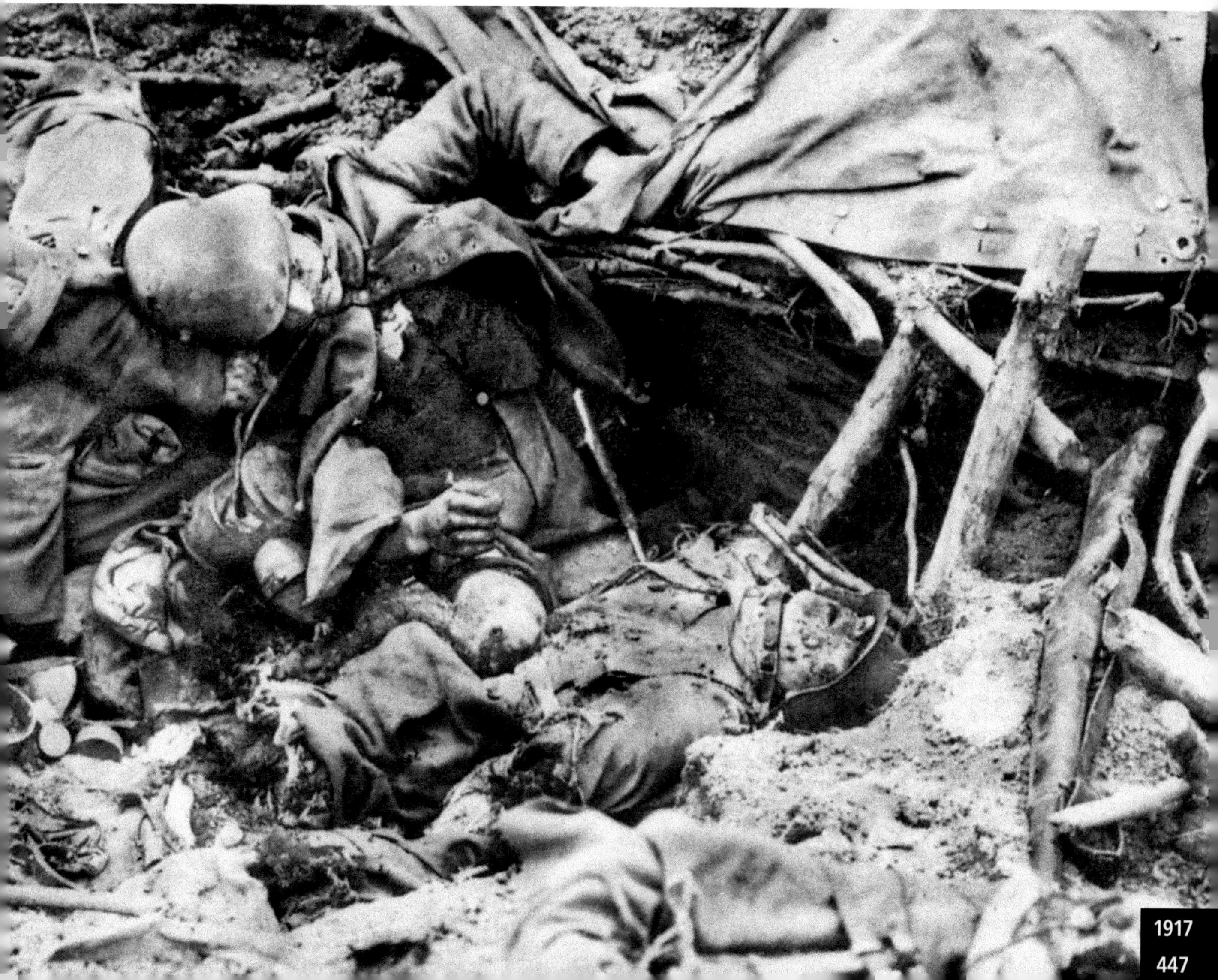

1917
447

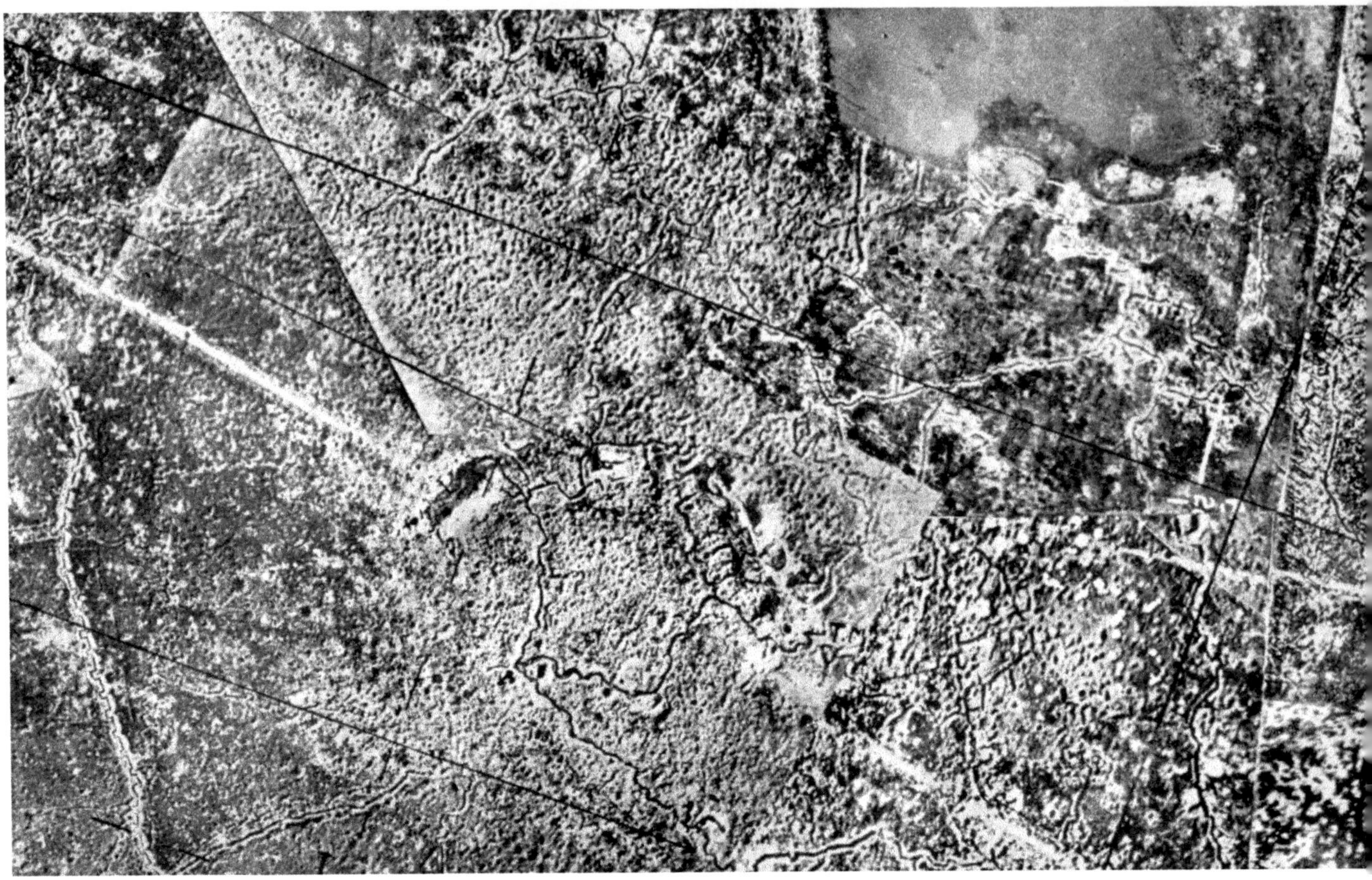

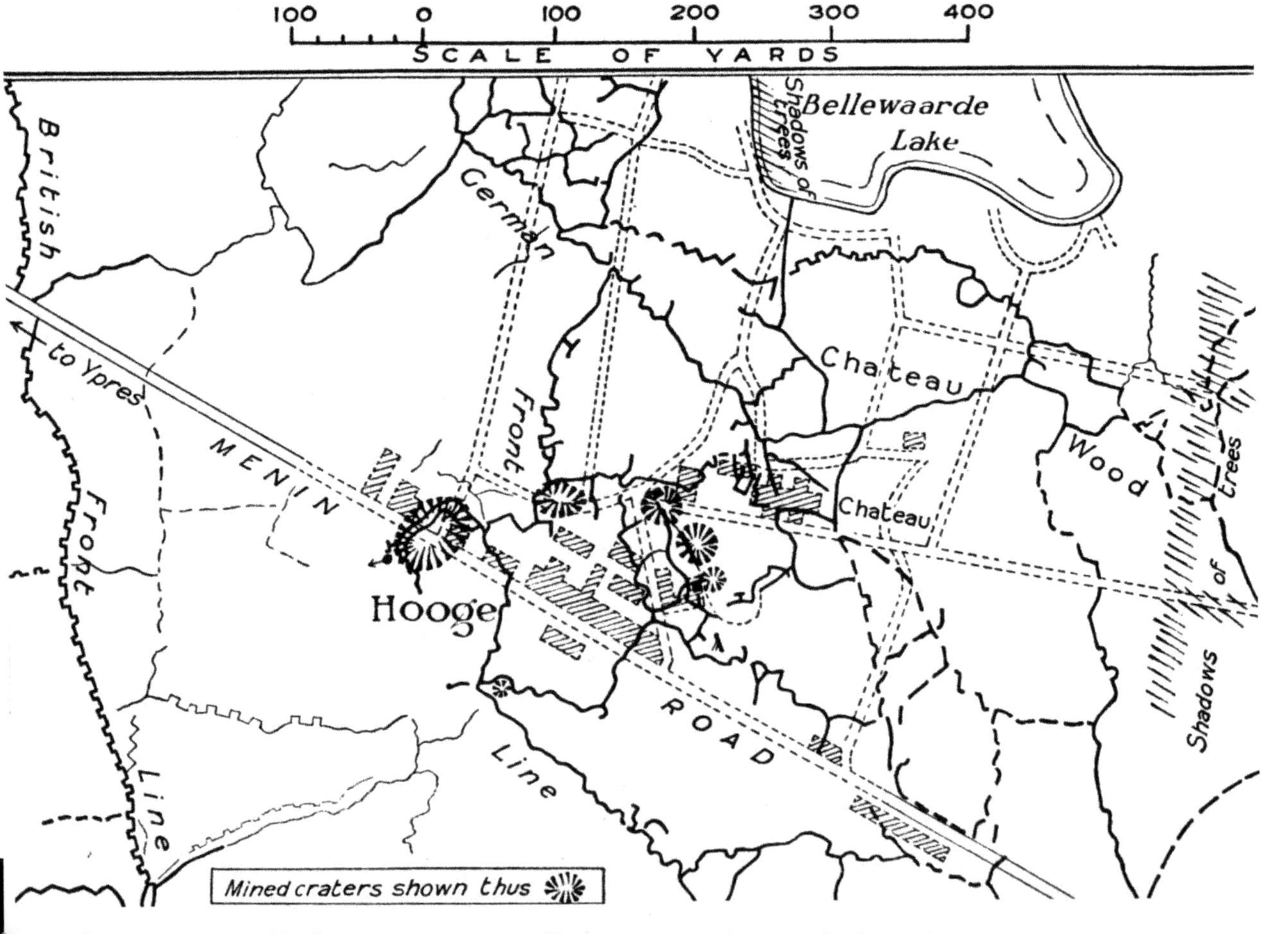

100 0 100 200 300 400
SCALE OF YARDS

Bellewaarde Lake

British Front Line

to Ypres

MENIN

German Front

Chateau

Chateau Wood

Shadows of trees

Hooge

ROAD

Mined craters shown thus

17GW1043, 17GW1044. The part of the line from which the Third Battle of Ypres started. Aerial photograph and key; the photograph was taken in June 1917. In the centre, Hooge village and the Menin road are already obliterated by mine and shell craters. Hooge had, at an earlier stage, been in possession of the British, who were driven from it. Former British trenches can be seen in No Man's Land. Bellewaarde Lake was formerly the ornamental water in the grounds of Hooge Chateau. The lines drawn on the photograph were made at the time for staff purposes.

17GW1045 Staff of 3 Brigade (Brigadier General Bennett) in a mined deep underground dugout built by the 1st Australian Tunnelling Company specifically for the Third Ypres operation. Water had to be pumped out continuously; the steel helmets hanging from the ceiling were placed to catch the leaks.

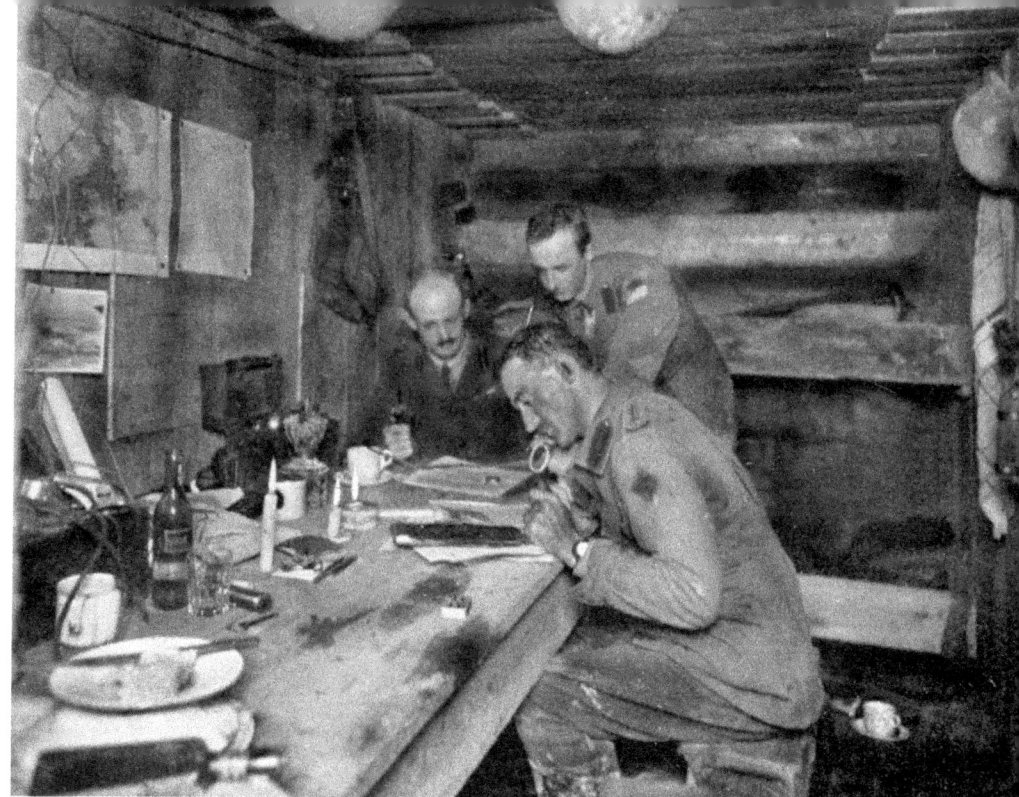

17GW1046 A German shell bursting over Glencorse Wood during the Battle of the Menin Road.

17GW1047 One of the German reinforced concrete shelters on the Westhoek Ridge. Such constructions were often built inside the walls of village houses and farm buildings, which served to camouflage their existence. It was from here that elements of the 2nd Australian Division attacked.

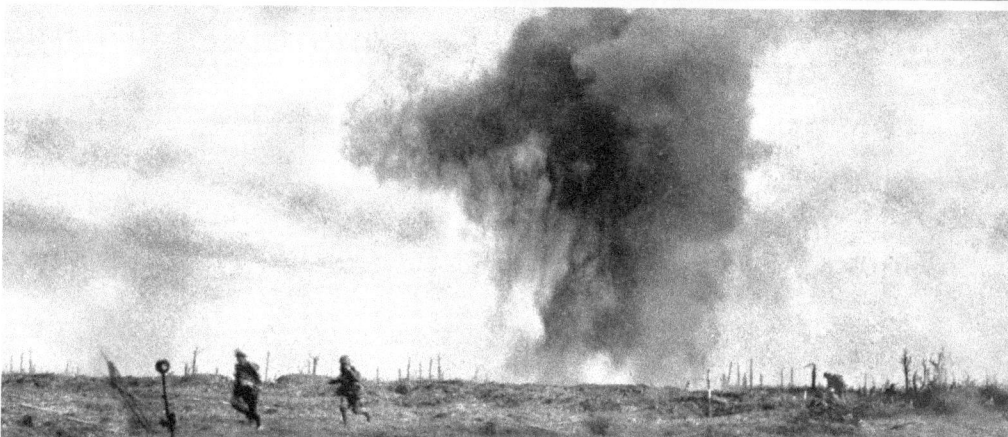

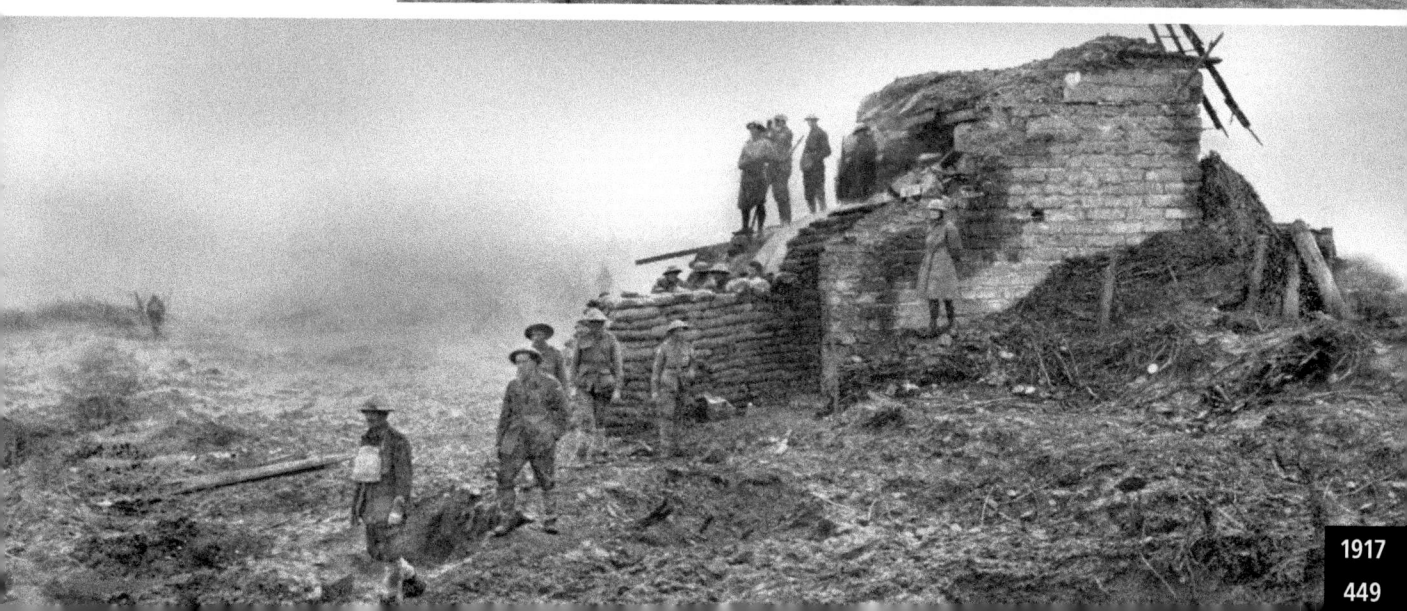

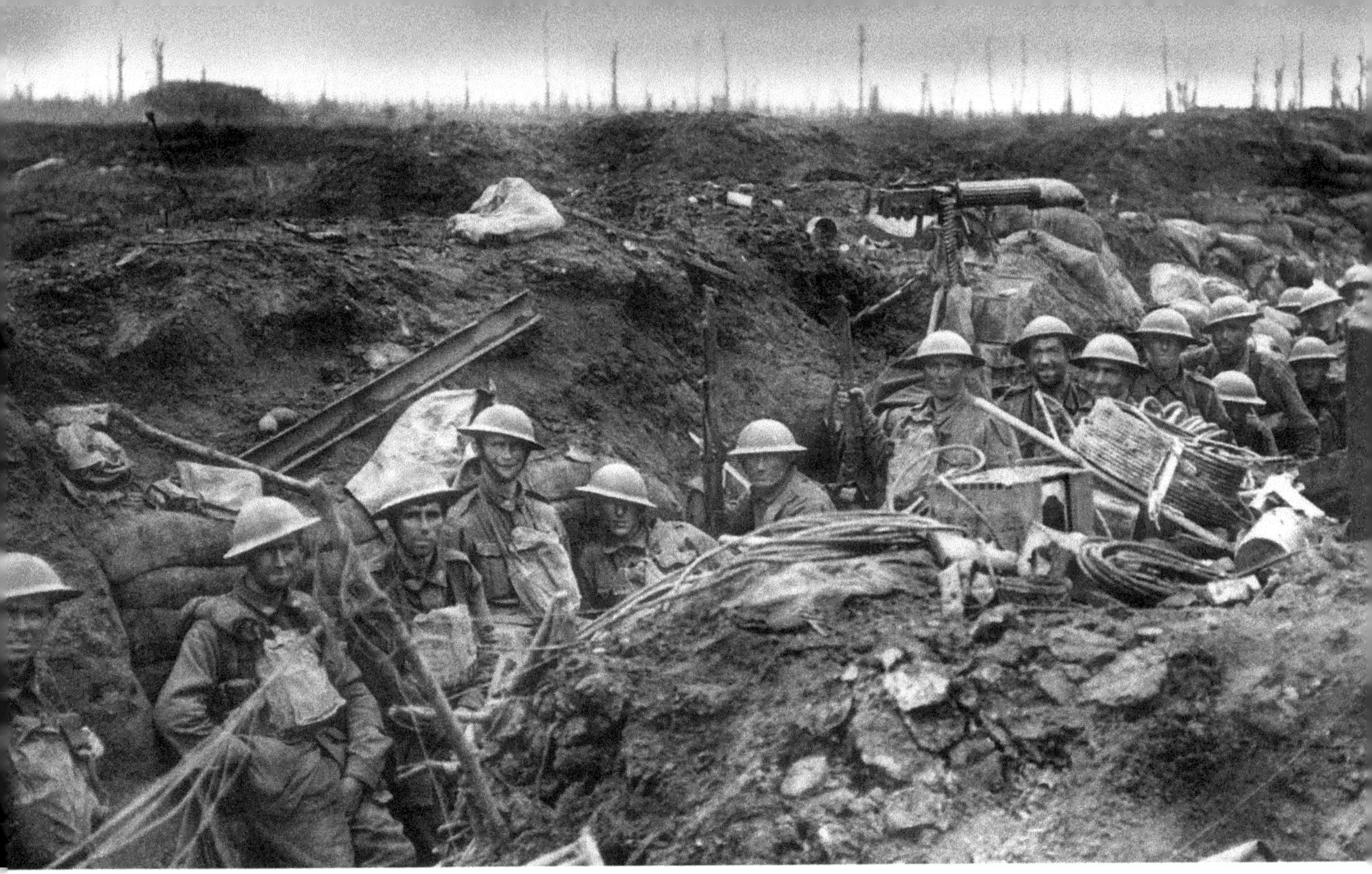

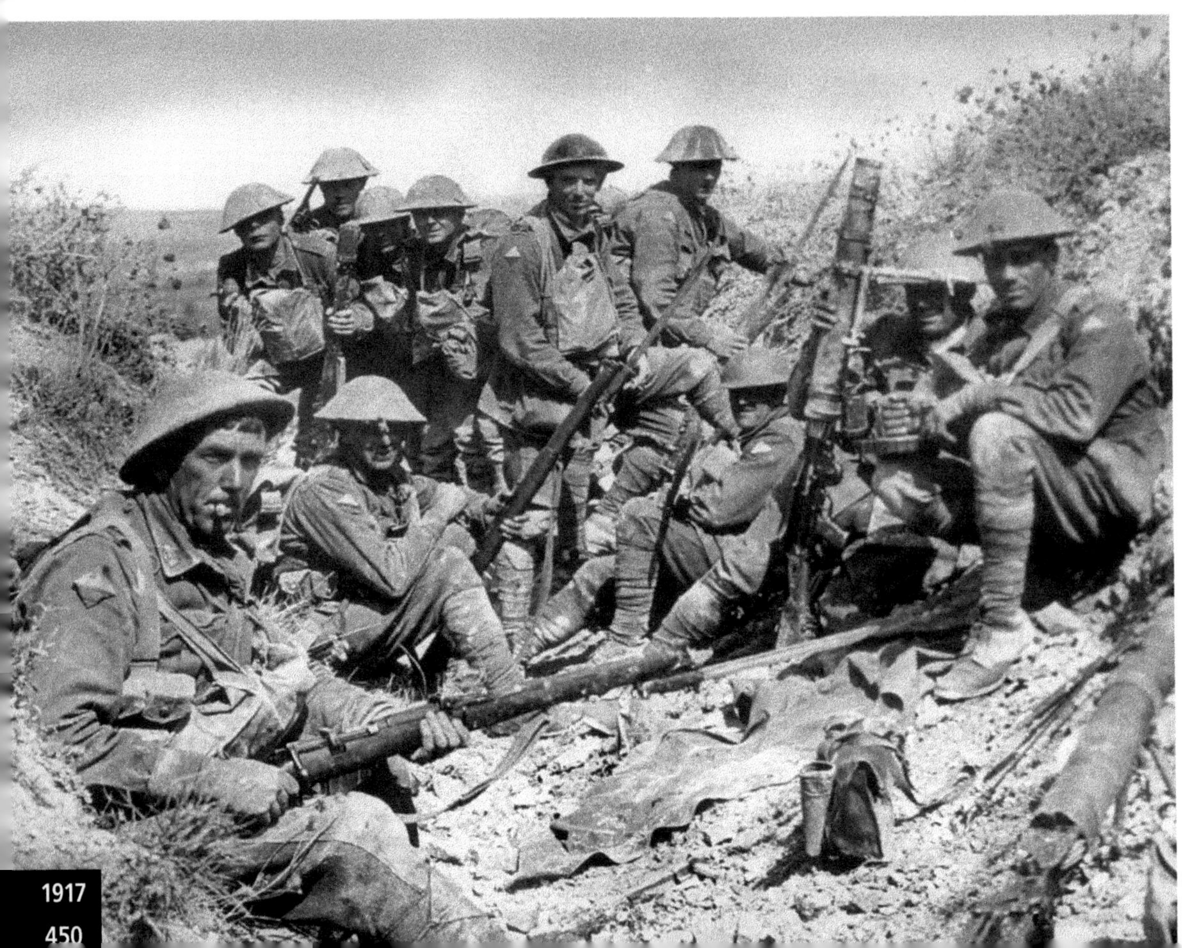

17GW1041 Battle of Menin Road: the starting point. Part of the line at 'Clapham Junction', from where the 1st Australian Division attacked Glencourse Wood. A few hours later and men of 3rd Battalion are garrisoning the jumping off trenches.

17GW1037 Germans awaiting an attack.

17GW1038 German dead after some close quarter fighting.

17GW1042 Battle of Menin Road, the edge of Polygon Wood after the battle. Lewis gun teams of 7 Brigade in a group of unconnected trenches, which was the new way of figthing.

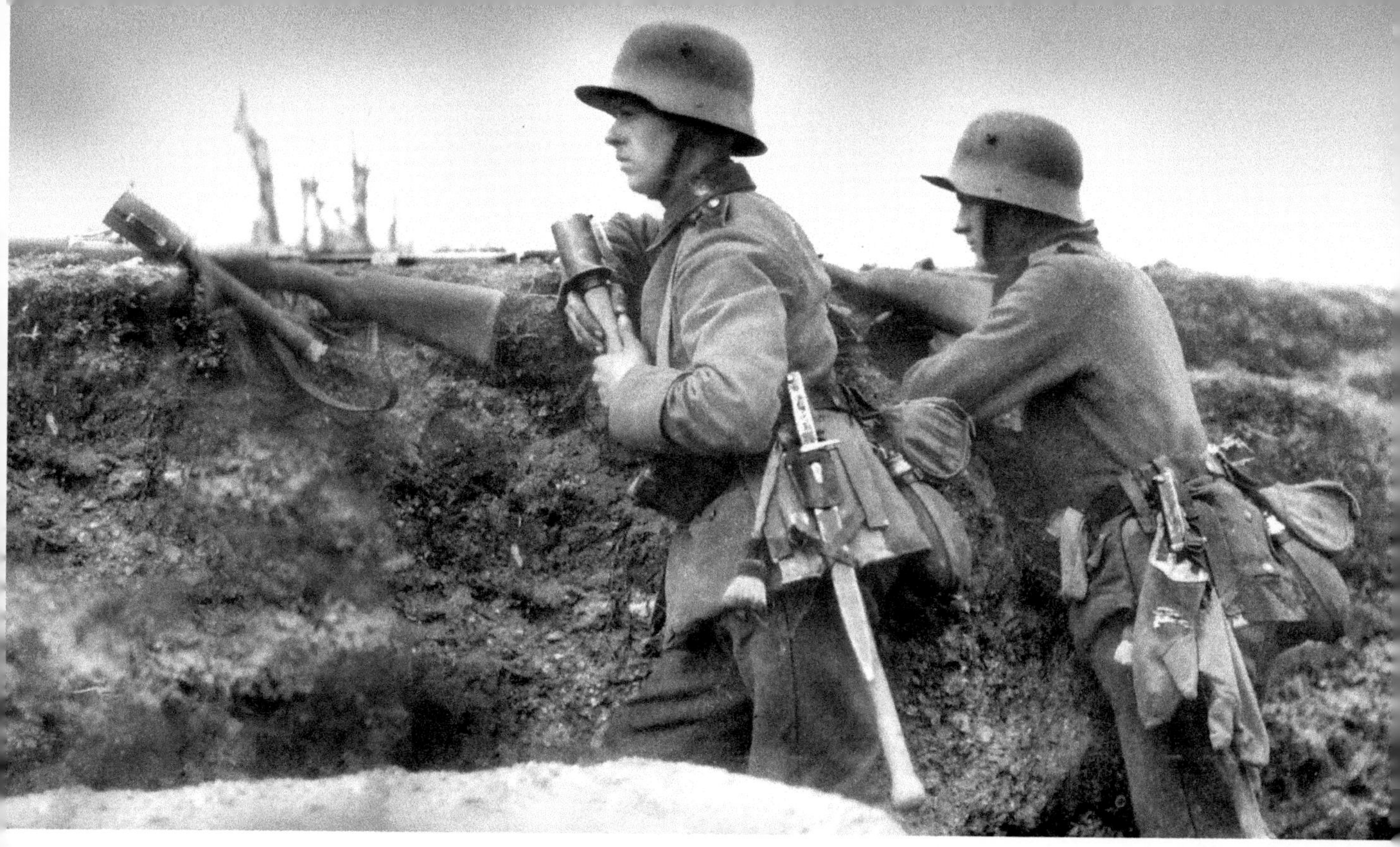

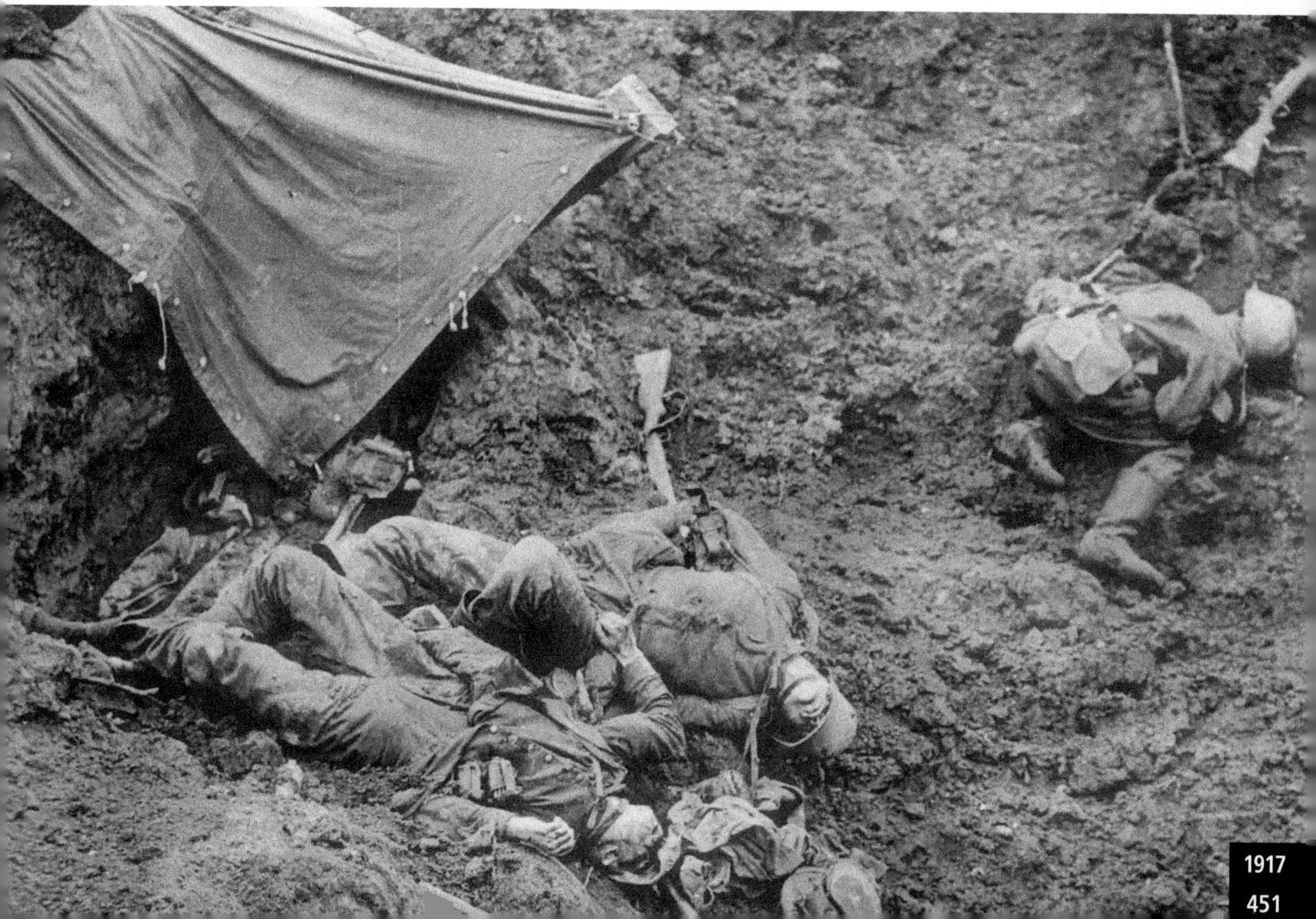

1917

451

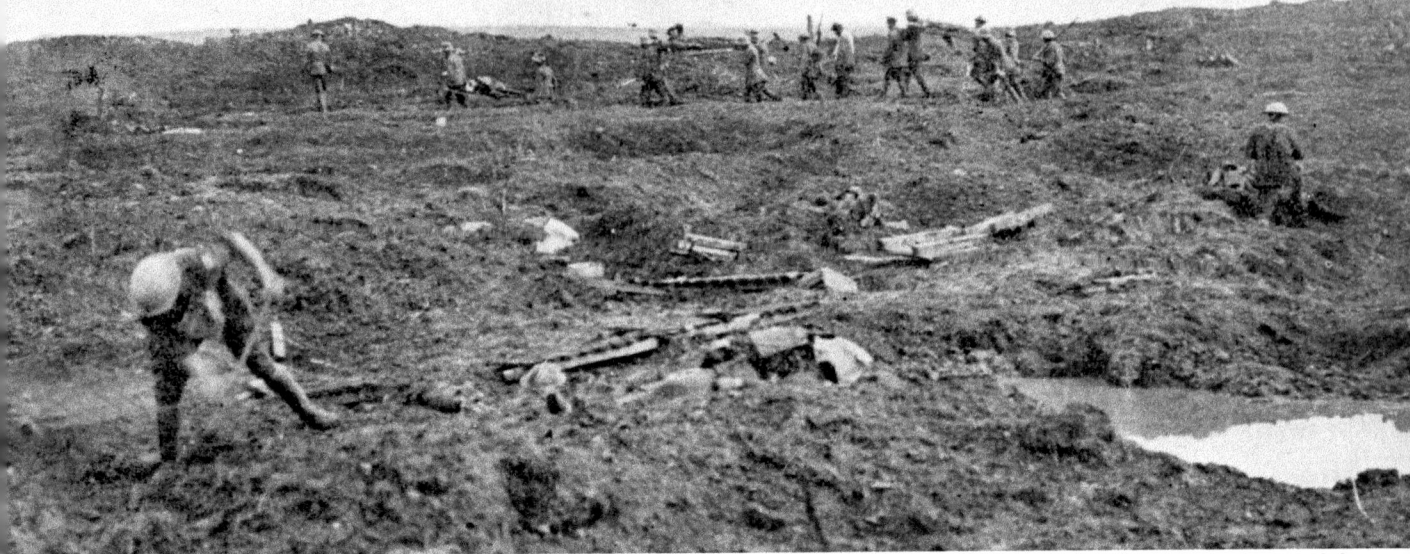
17GW1048 Signallers laying a telephone line through the remains of Iverness Copse, which has just been captured. Prisoners can be seen carrying wounded.
17GW1051 The Menin Road near 'Clapham Junction': a German shell has just burst among troops of 1st Australian Division, causing many casualties.

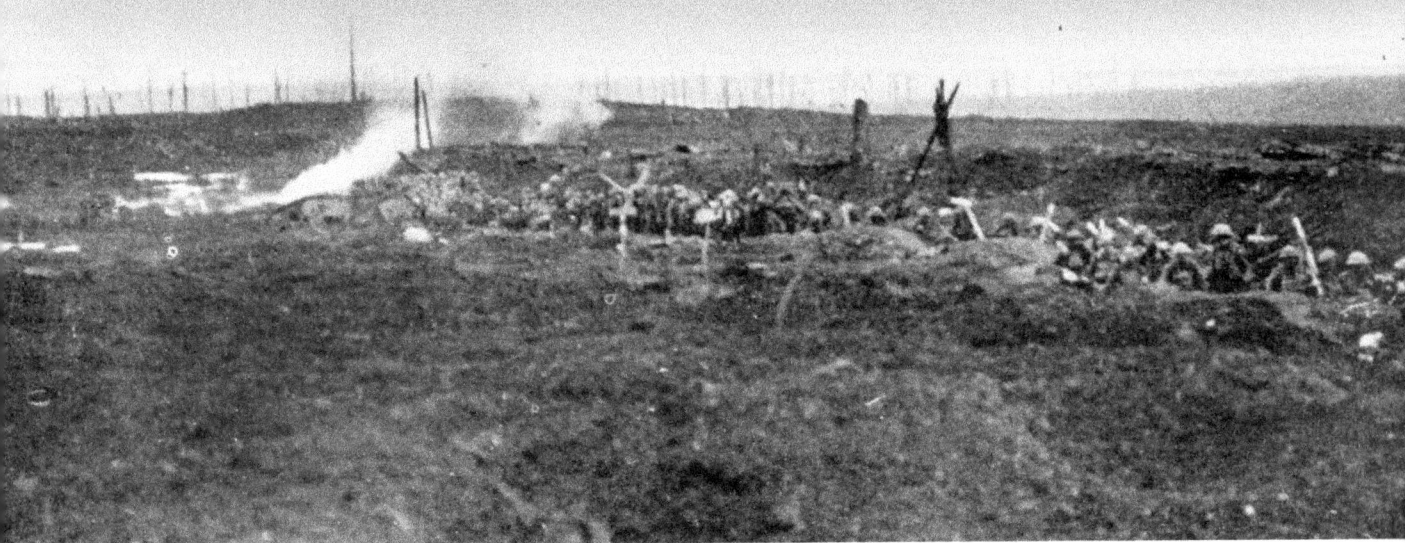
17GW1052 Battle of the Menin Road at Nonne Bosschen: German pillboxes captured by troops of the 1st Australian Division, 20 September 1917.

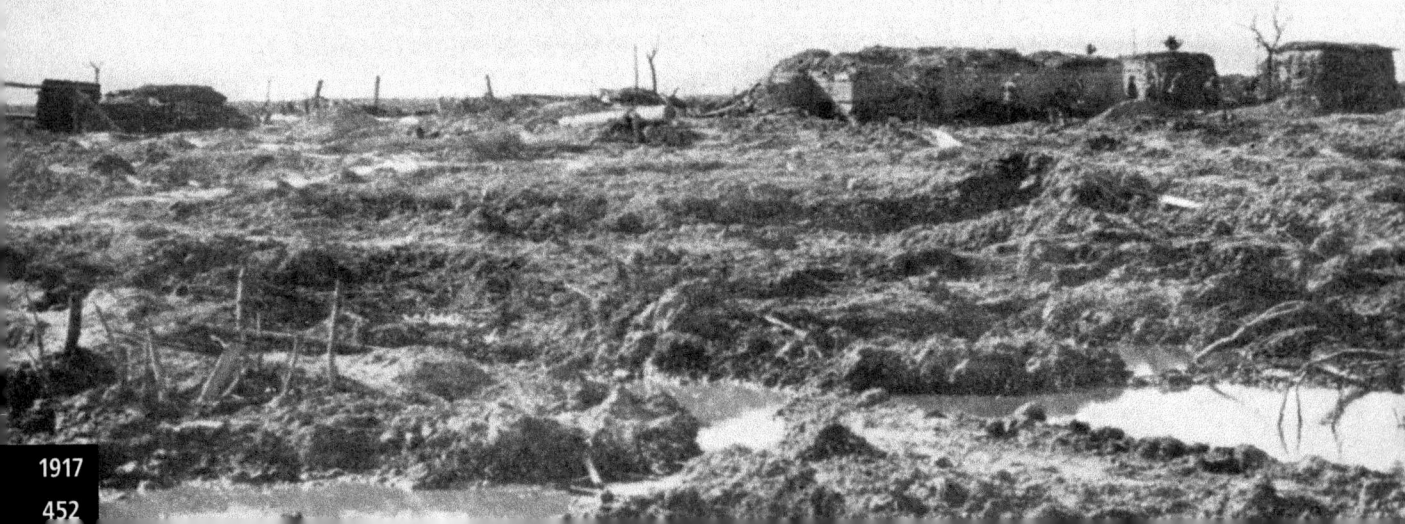

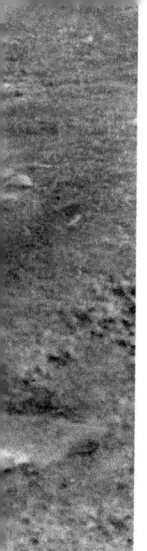
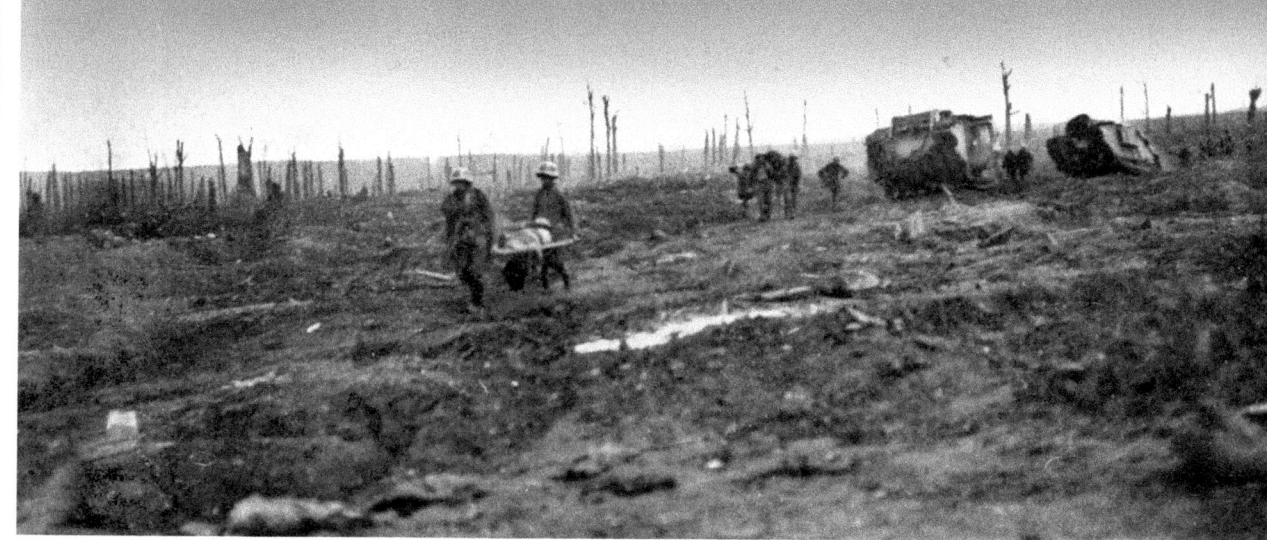

17GW1049 Disabled British tanks near the Menin Road, close to 'Jackdaw Switch'. German prisoners are stretchering wounded to the rear.

17GW1053 A German shelter near the Hannebeek (stream) with fatalities caused by the 2nd Australian Division in the advance towards Zonnebeke. The view is looking back towards Westhoek in the distance, from where the advance began.

17GW1050 The former German concrete shelter and high ground known as 'Stirling Castle'. The dead scattered about are Australians and German prisners killed when the German artillery laid down retaliatory fire. It was from this point that the attack on Glencorse Wood started.

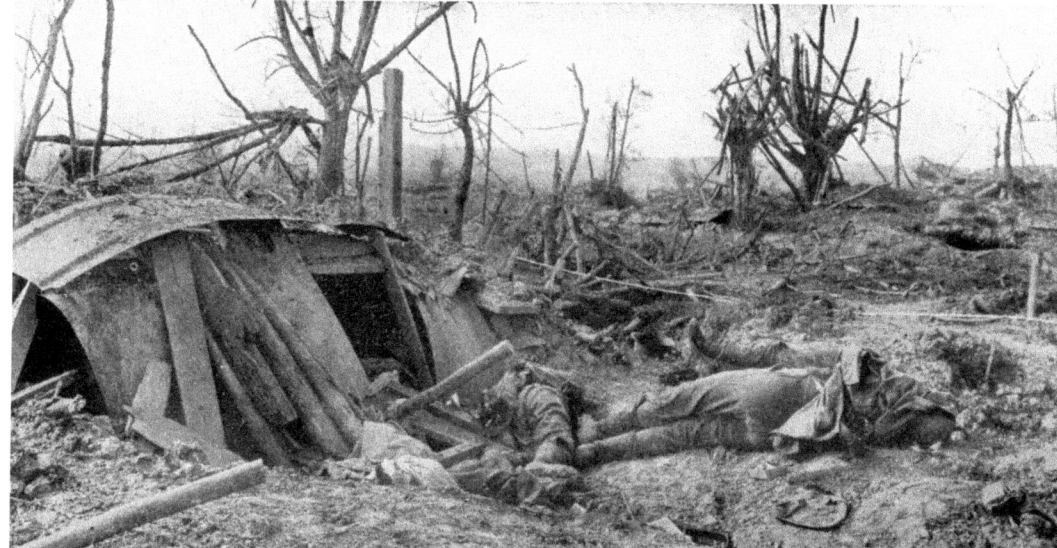
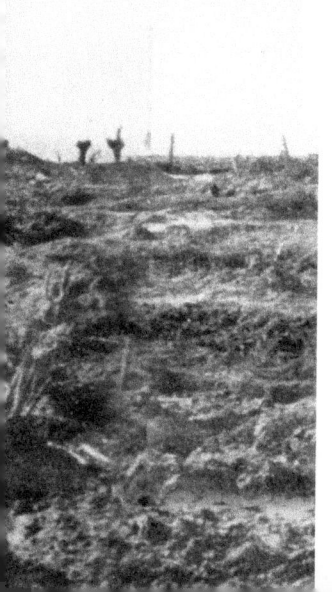
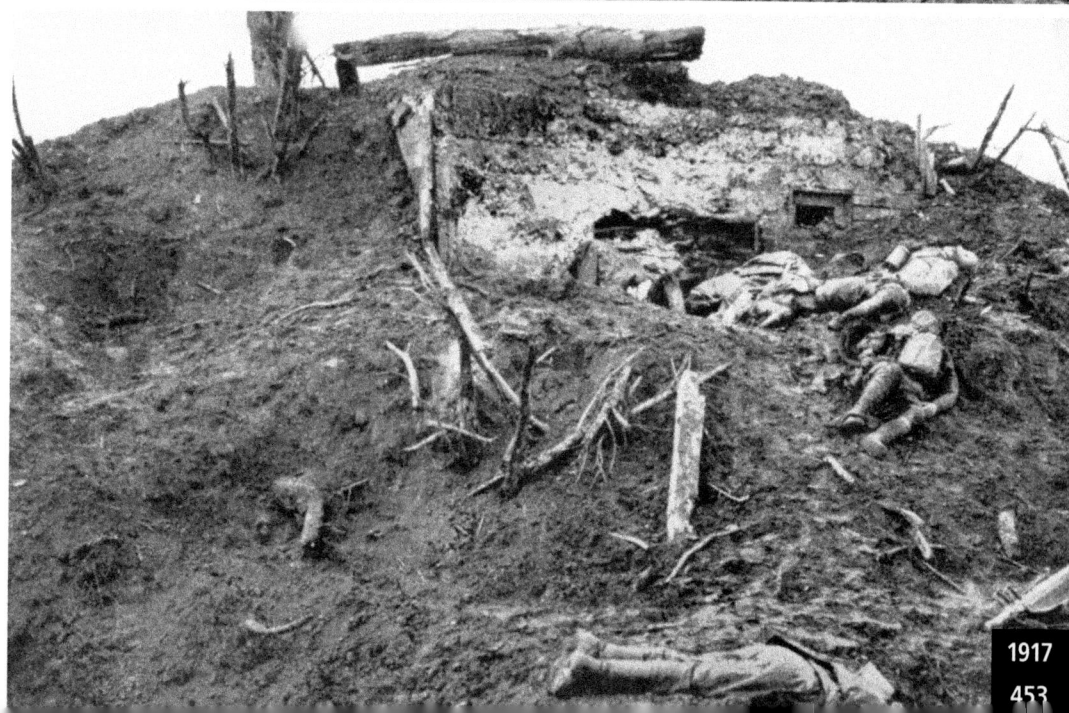

1917

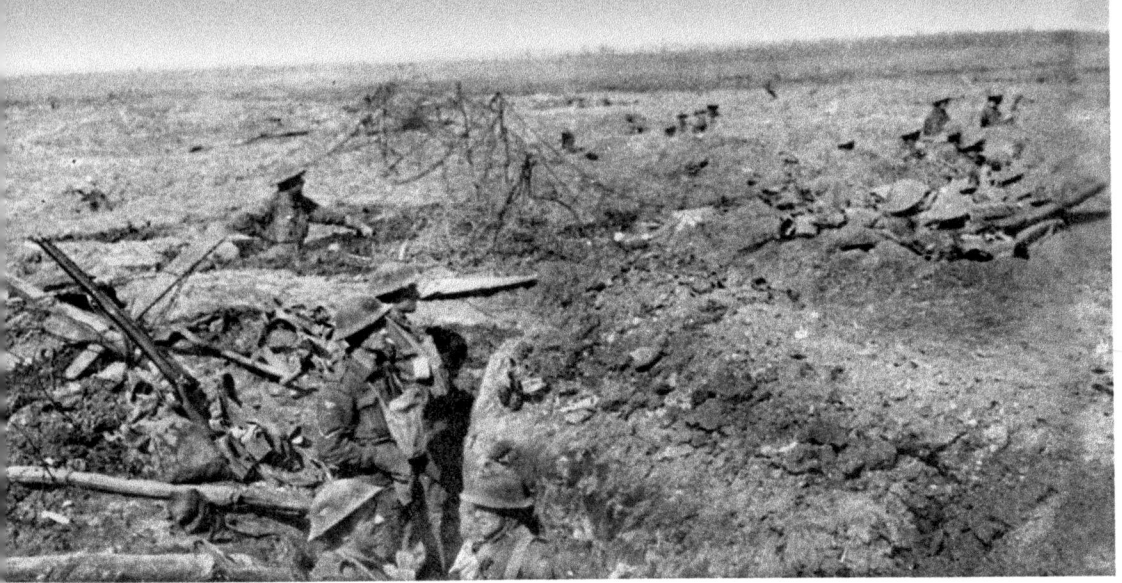

17GW1055 The line on the edge of Polygon Wood after the Battle of the Menin Road.

17GW1054 Wounded Australians returning down the Menin Road towards Ypres, near 'Birr Cross Road', 20 September. At this point the more seriously wounded cases were deposited by stretcher bearers to be picked up by motor ambulances. Some of the men on the stretchers appear to be stretcher beareres taking a break from their arduous labours.

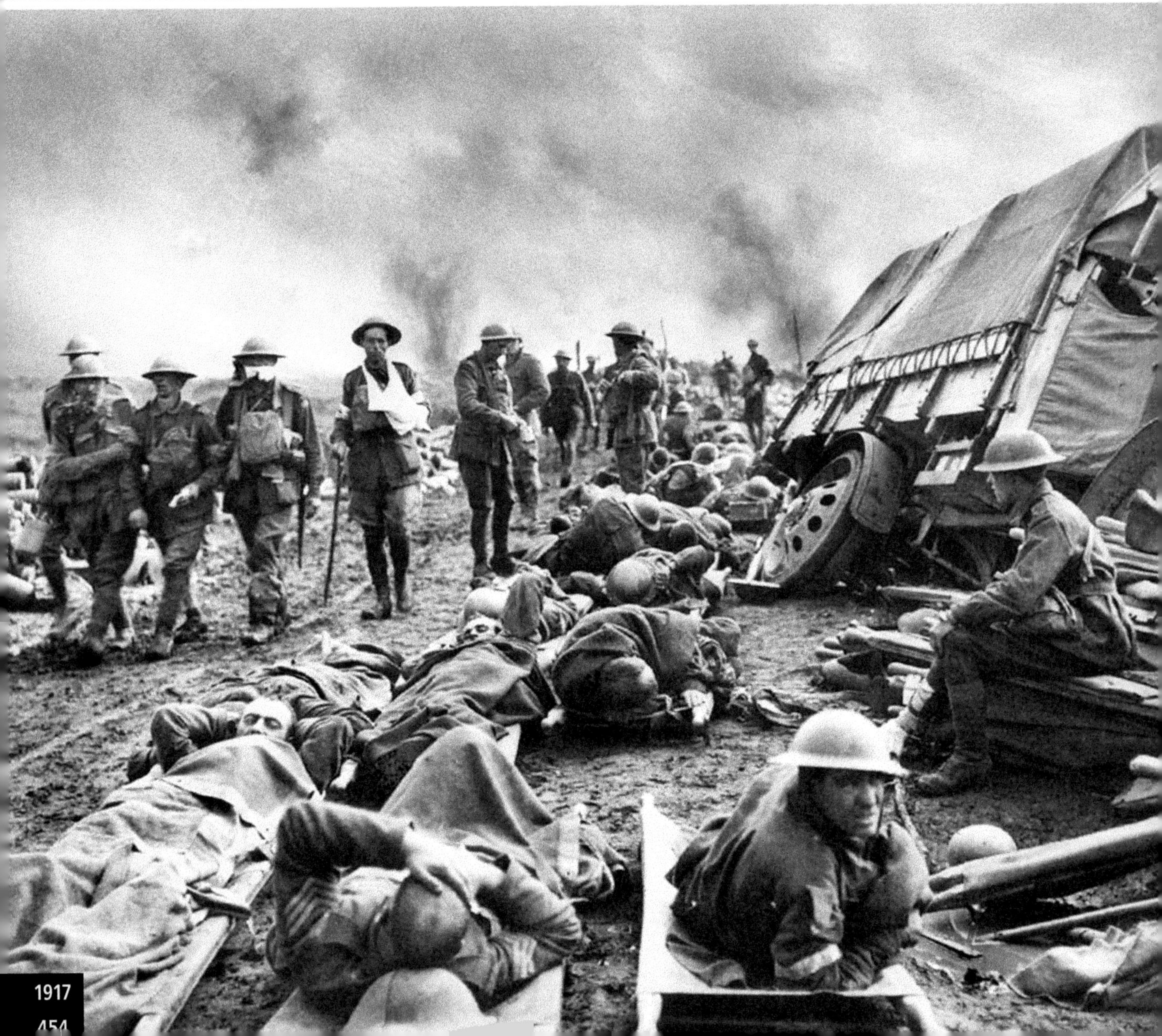

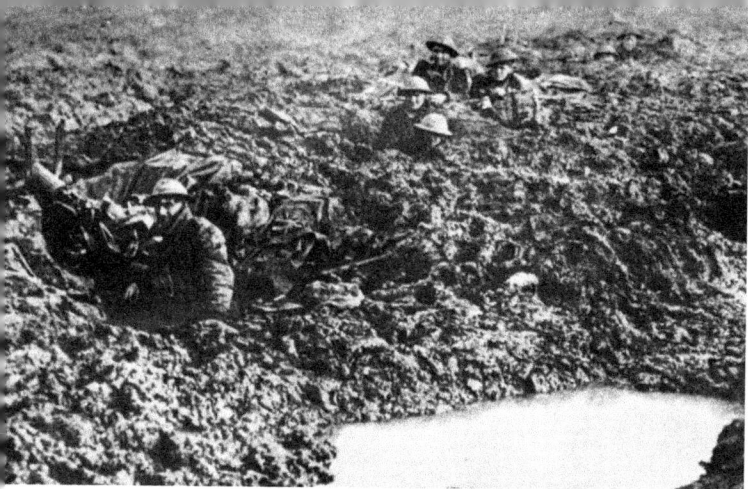

17GW1074 Personnel of the 16th Canadian Machine Gun Company Company holding the line in shell holes during the Battle of Passchendaele.

17GW1057, 17GW1058, 17GW1059. Knee deep mud stretching for miles made moving the wounded to safety a major task and involving many hands.

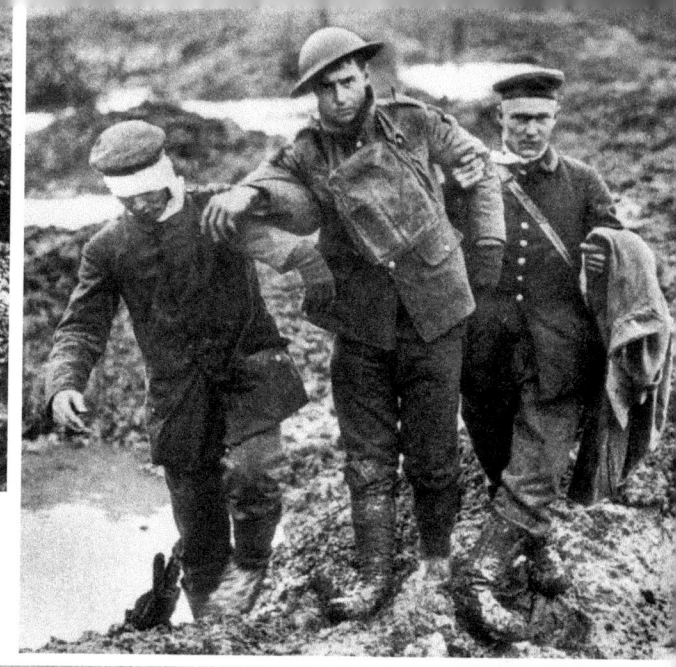

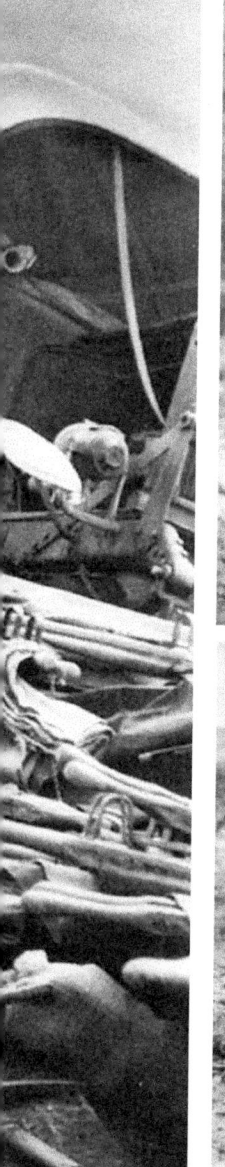

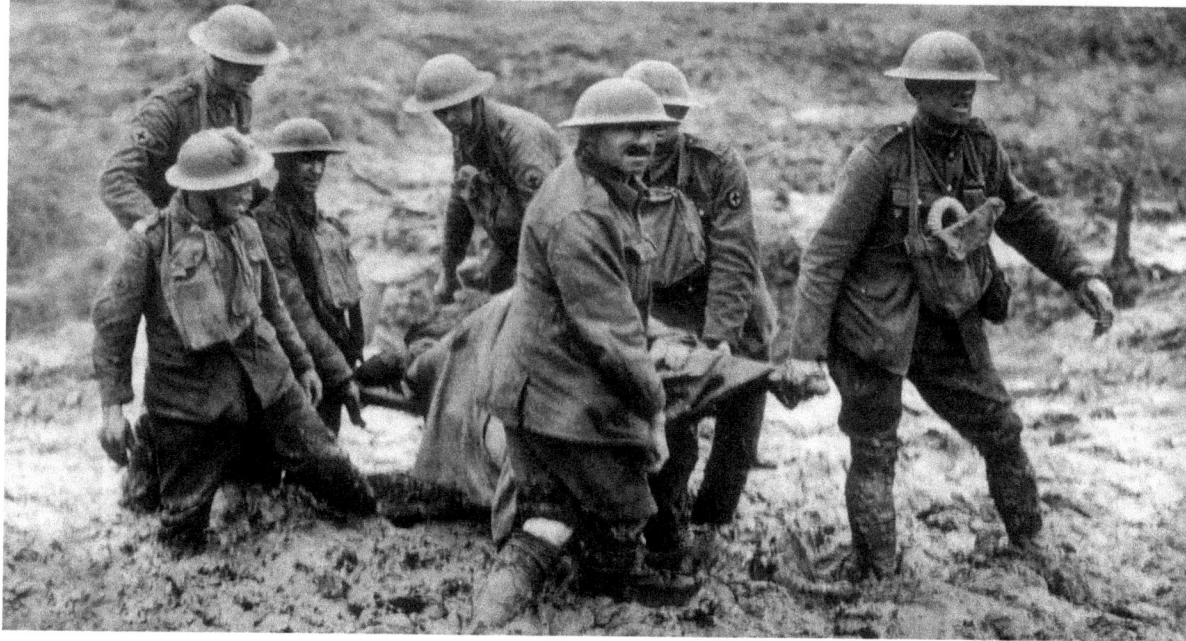

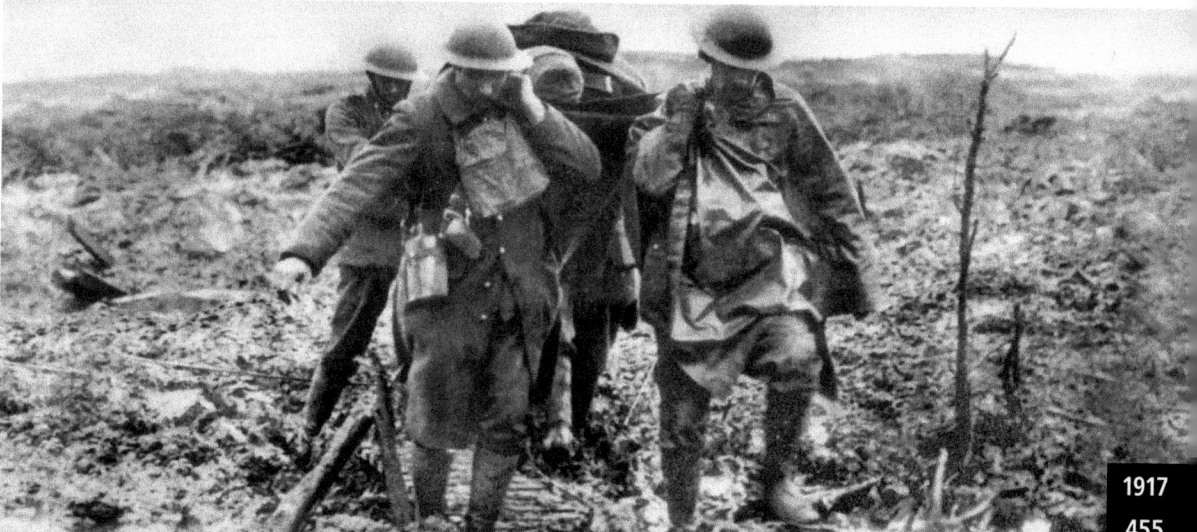

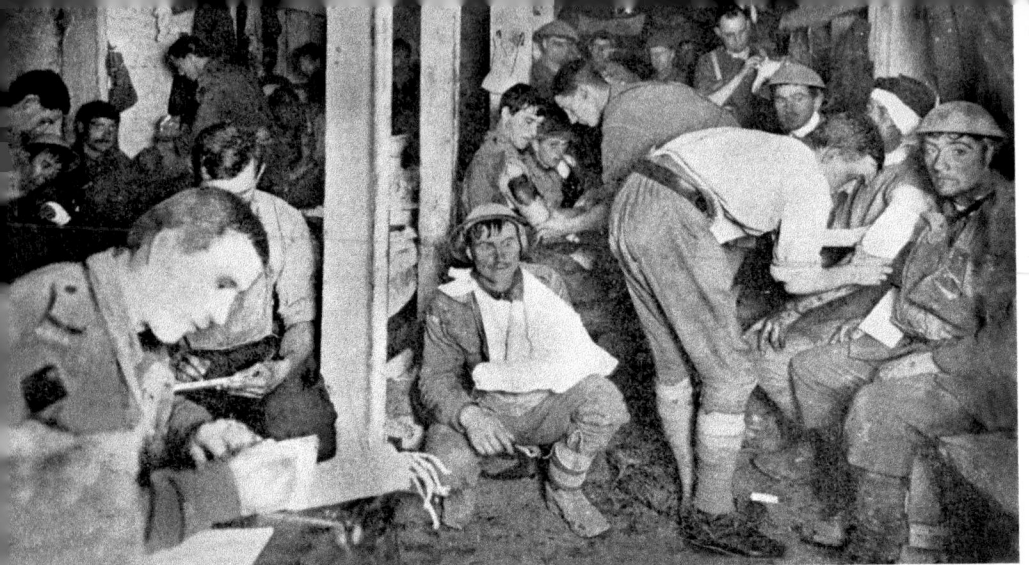
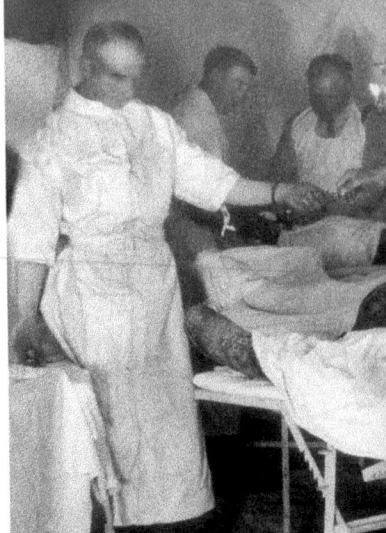

17GW1060, 17GW1062, 17GW1061.
Wounded men crammed into an Advance Dressing Station of the 2nd Australian Division on the Menin road, 20 September. Some of the men being attended to appear taumatised by their experiences.
An operation being carried out at the Third Field Hospital, Ypres.
A Casualty Clearing Station, where nurses were part of the staff and operations were performed.

17GW1063, 17GW1064.
Infantrymen of the Royal Gloucestershire Regiment breaking stones for road making near Zillebeke, 5 October 1917. Men of a pioneer battalion constructing a new road across the mud-soaked ground.

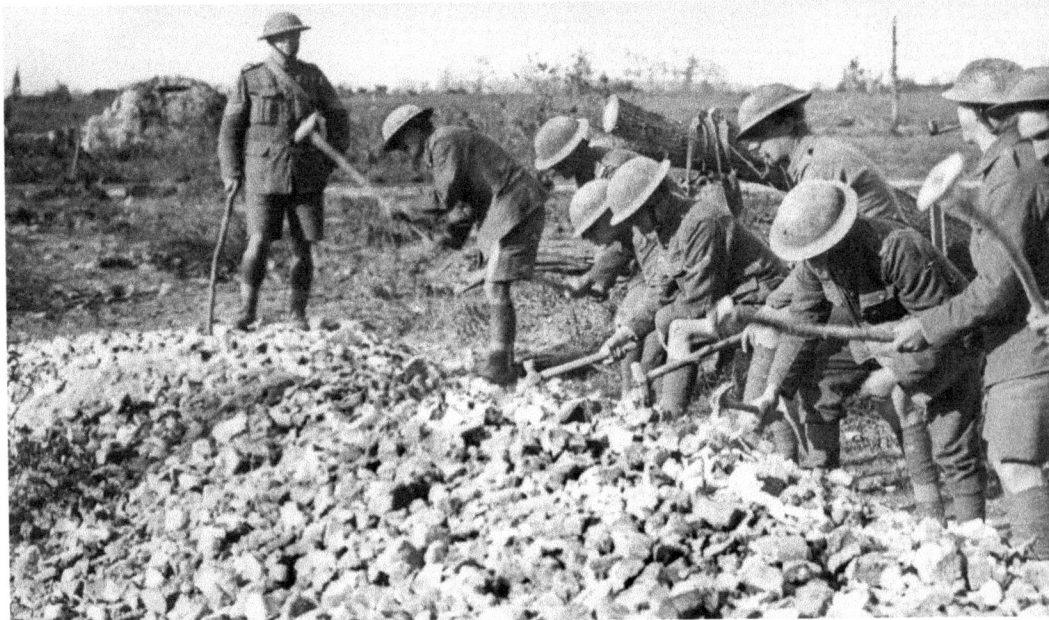

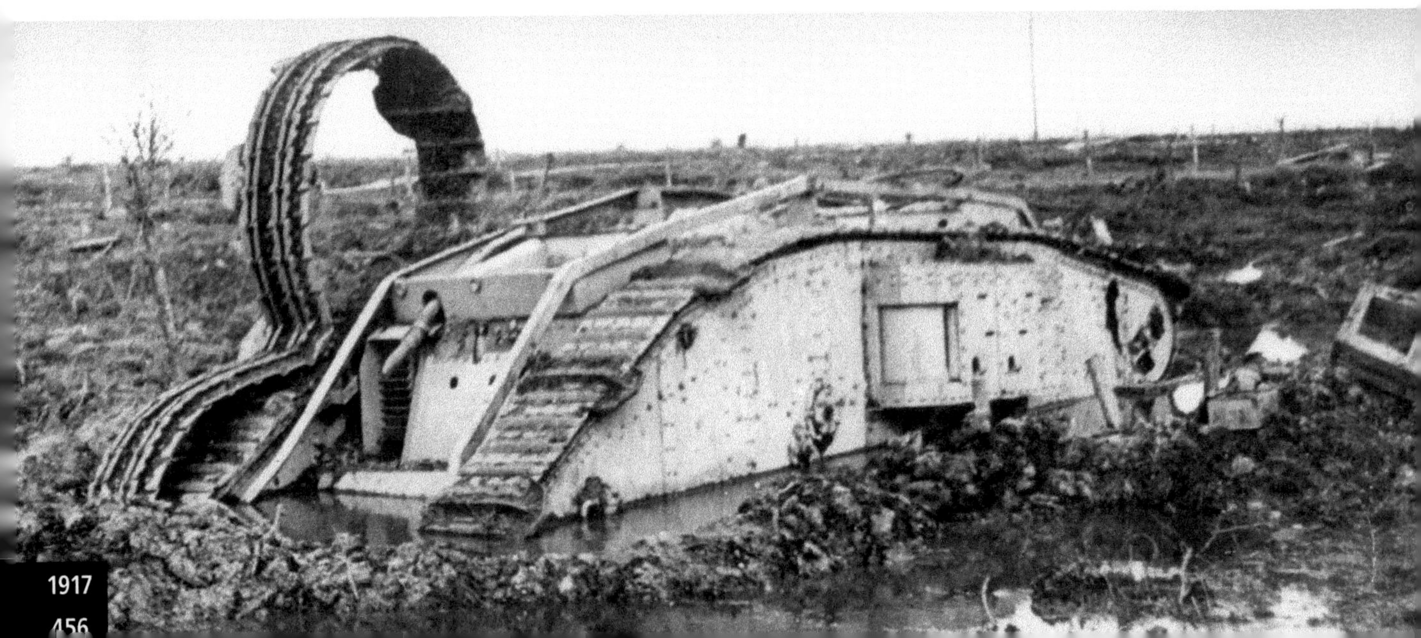

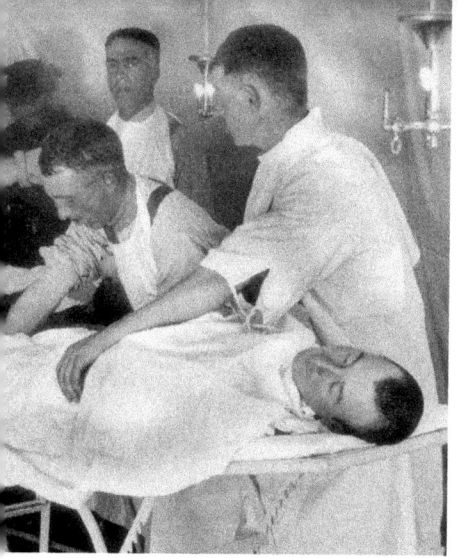
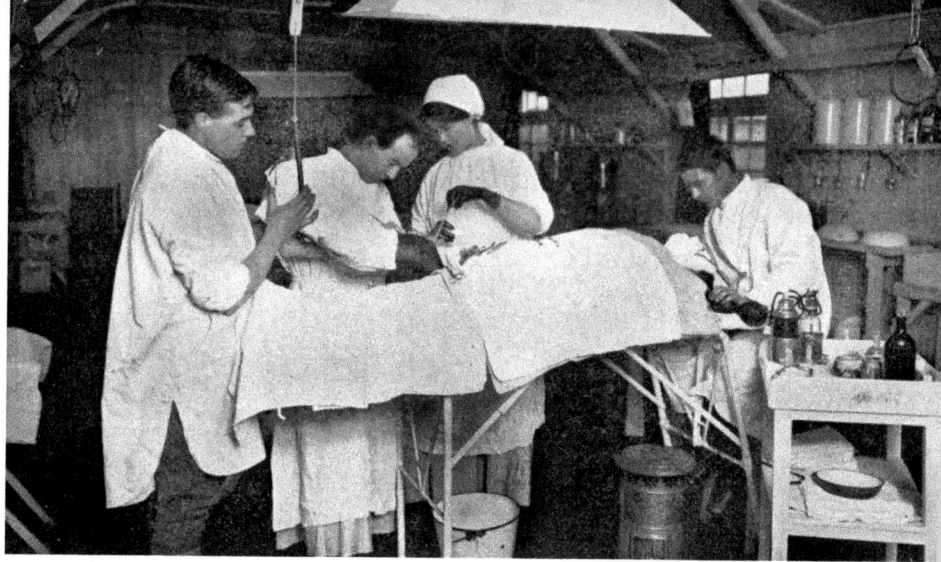
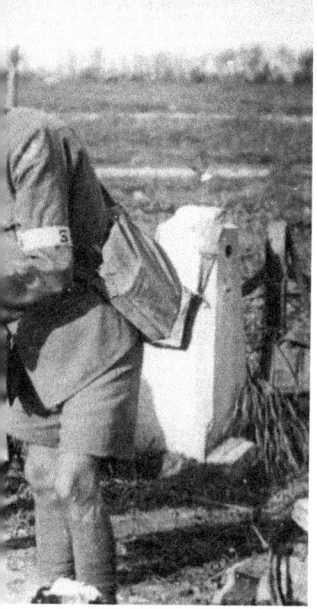
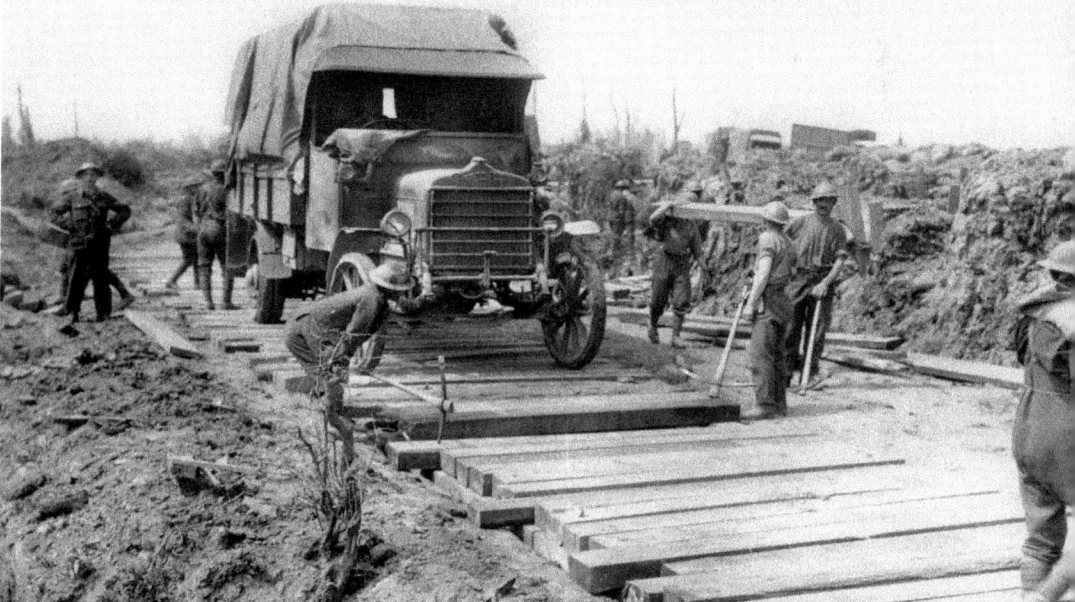

17GW1065 A partially submerged tank near St Julien, in the Ypres Salient, 12 October 1917.

17GW1066 Passchendaele village and church, on the ridge north of Broodseinde, the objective of the preliminary advance and main attack planned for 9th and 12 October respectively. The road runs northwards along the summit of the ridge from Broodseinde. In these attacks the 66th British and 3rd Australian Divisions respectively spproached the outskirts of the village on this road but were forced to fall back.

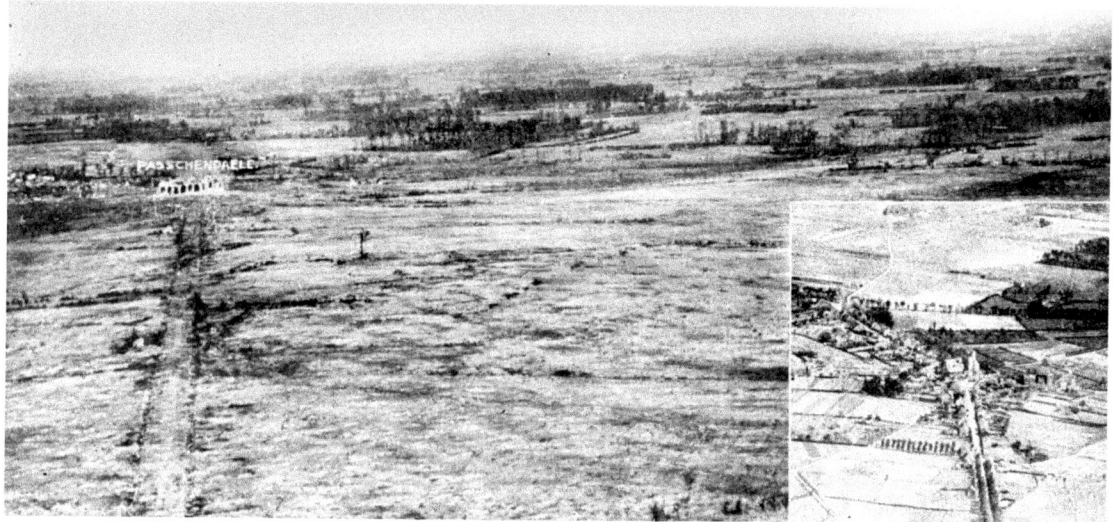

Inset: German aerial photograph taken in 1915.

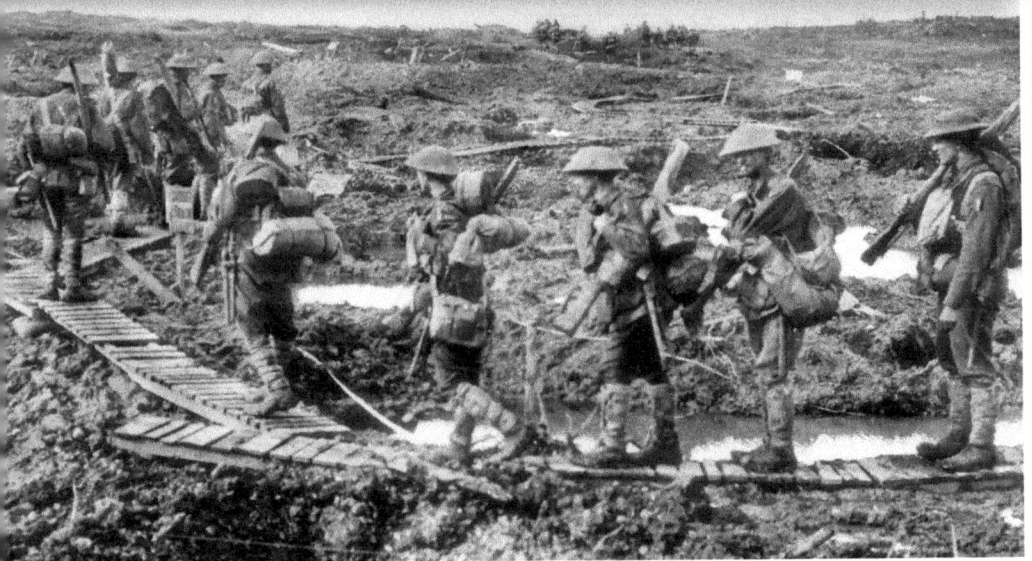
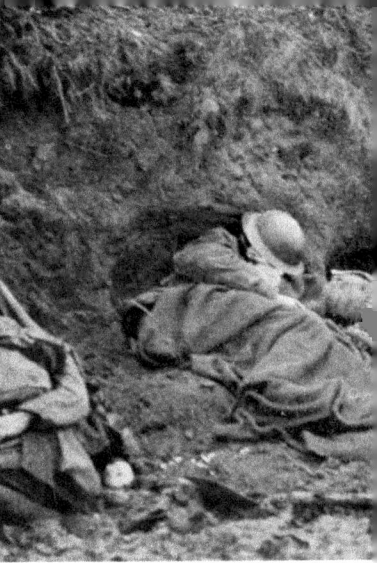

17GW1067 A battalion of the 5th Australian Division moving up near Albania Wood, along a duckboard path known as 'Jabber Track' towards the final part of the I Anzac Corps' participation in the Third Battle of Ypres. Second Army's offensive in the last weeks was virtually confined to the Canadian Corps, which had relieved the II Anzac Corps in the attack on Passchendaele, the Australians undertaking supporting actions on the Canadian flank. Note the men have tied sandbags around their legs as extra protection against the mud.

17GW1068 Dead and wounded in the railway cutting at Broodseinde during the battle, 12 October.

17GW1069 Wounded Australians collected around this captured German blockhouse near the site of Zonnebeke railway station

17GW1070, 17GW1071. Former defenders of the blockhouses killed in the fight to capture them.

17GW1039 German prisoners burying their dead.

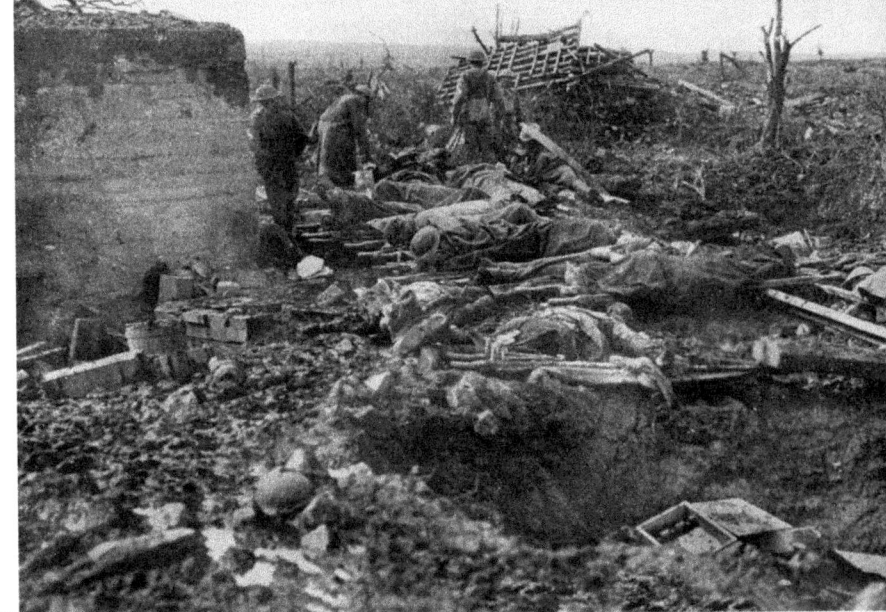

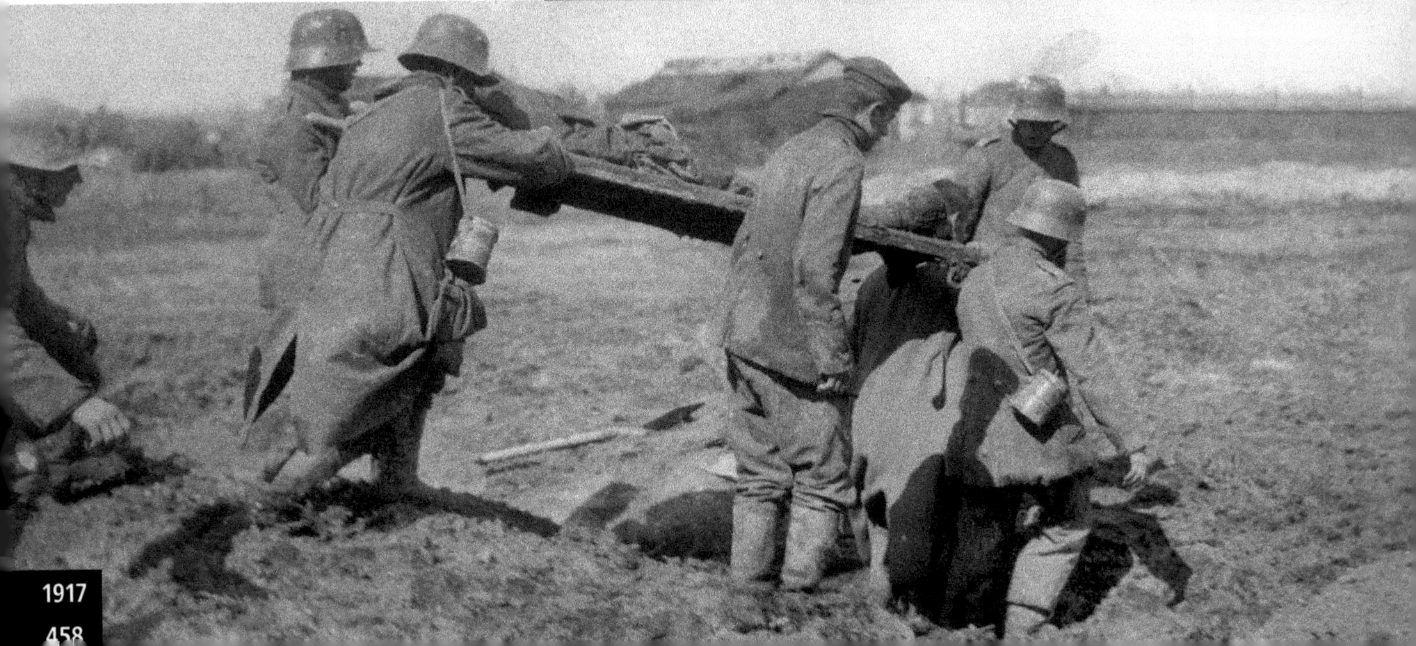

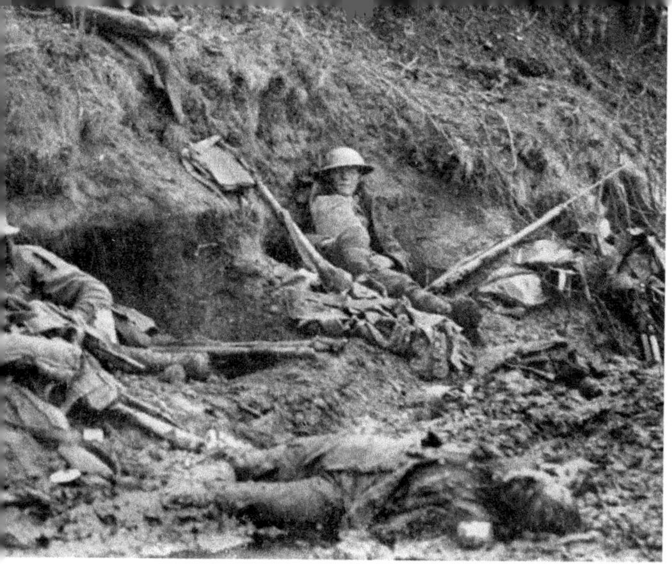

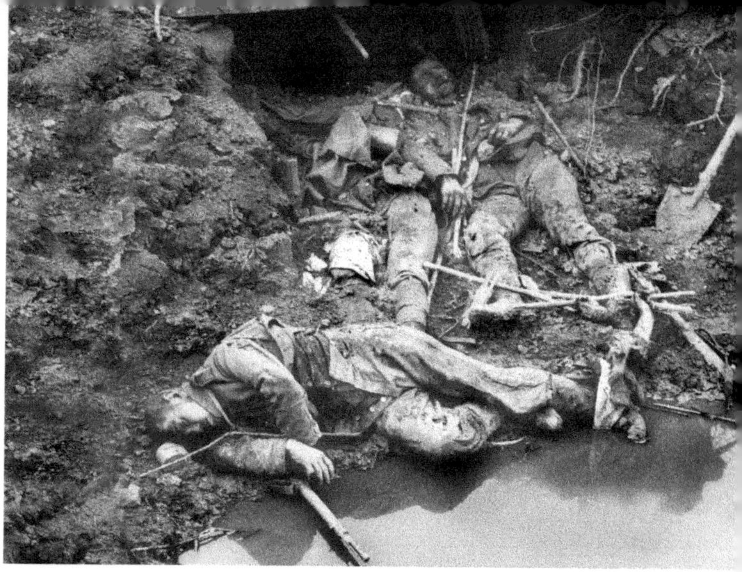

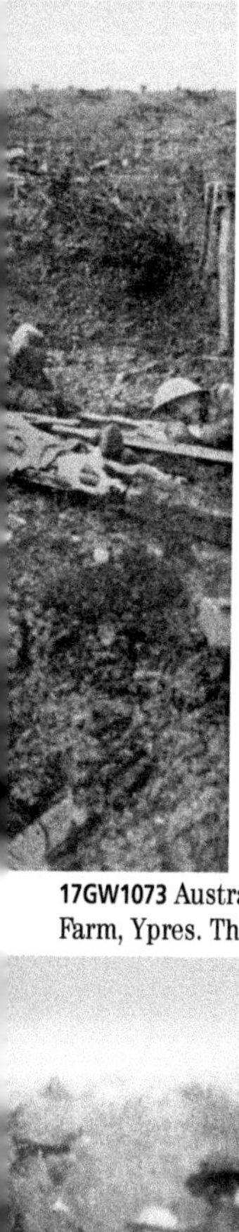

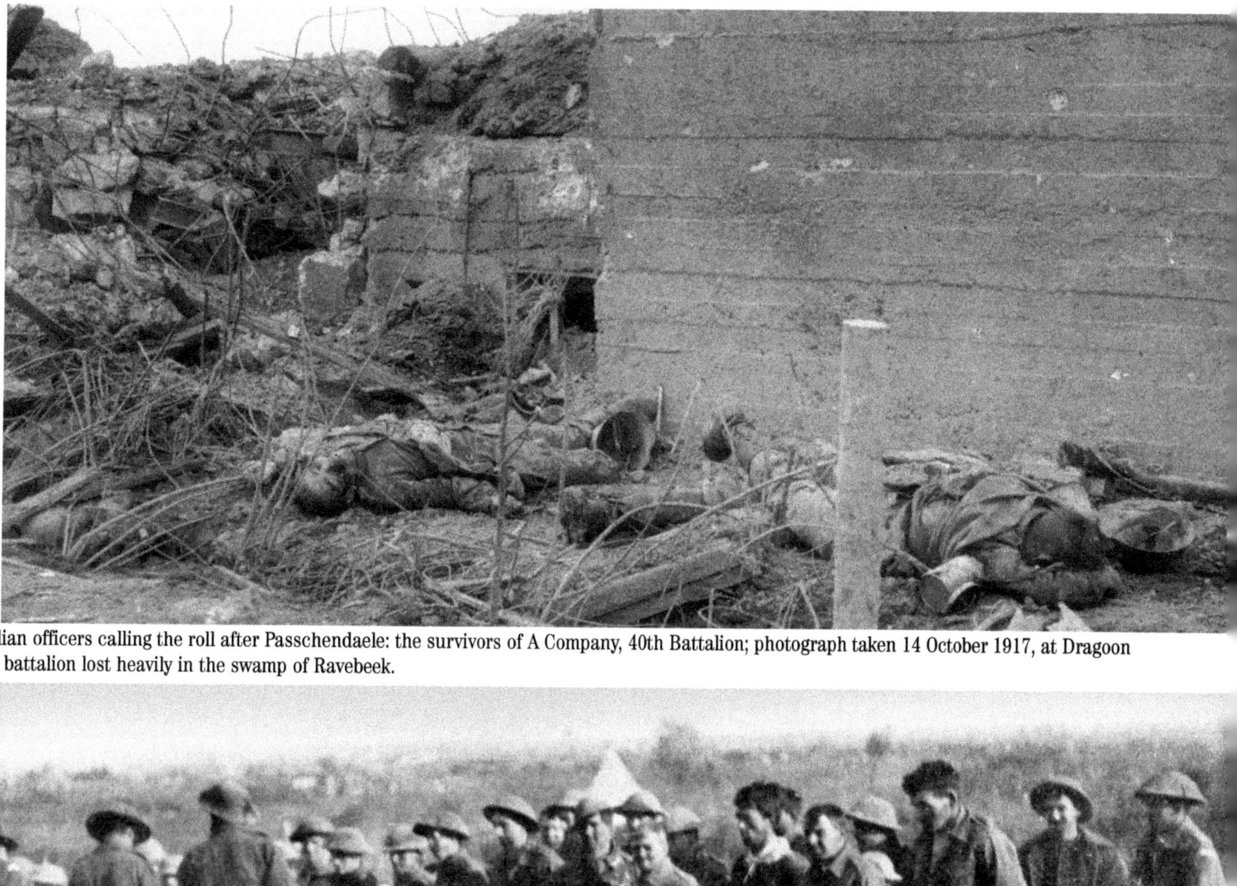

17GW1073 Australian officers calling the roll after Passchendaele: the survivors of A Company, 40th Battalion; photograph taken 14 October 1917, at Dragoon Farm, Ypres. The battalion lost heavily in the swamp of Ravebeek.

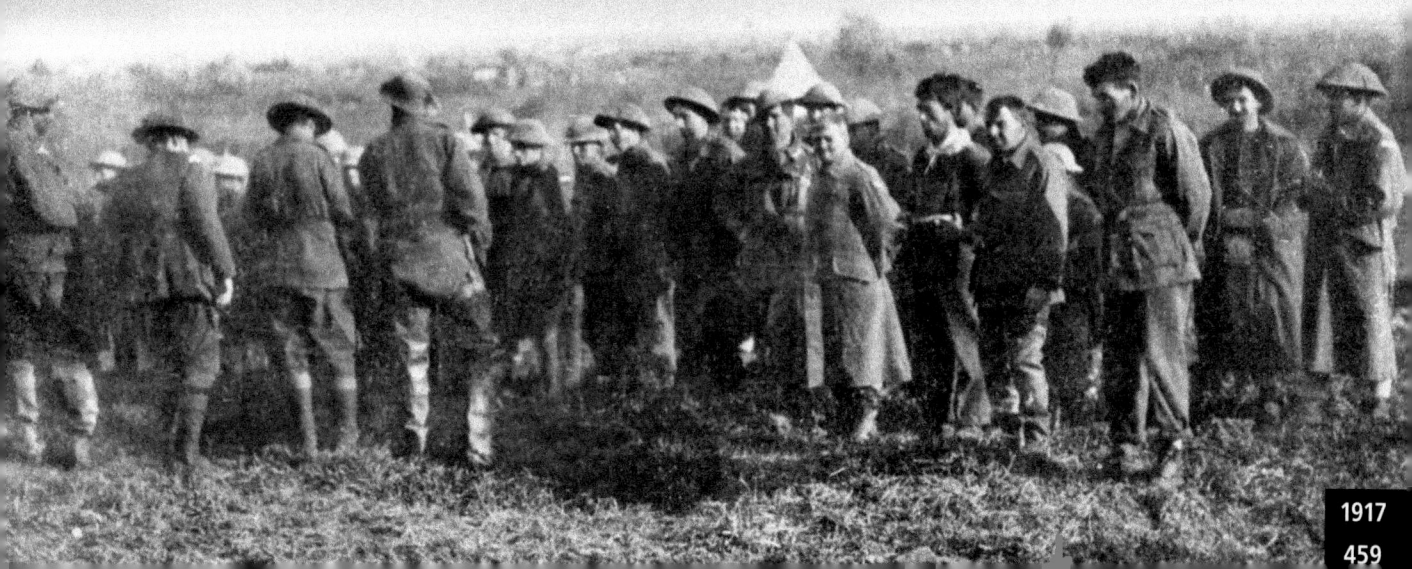

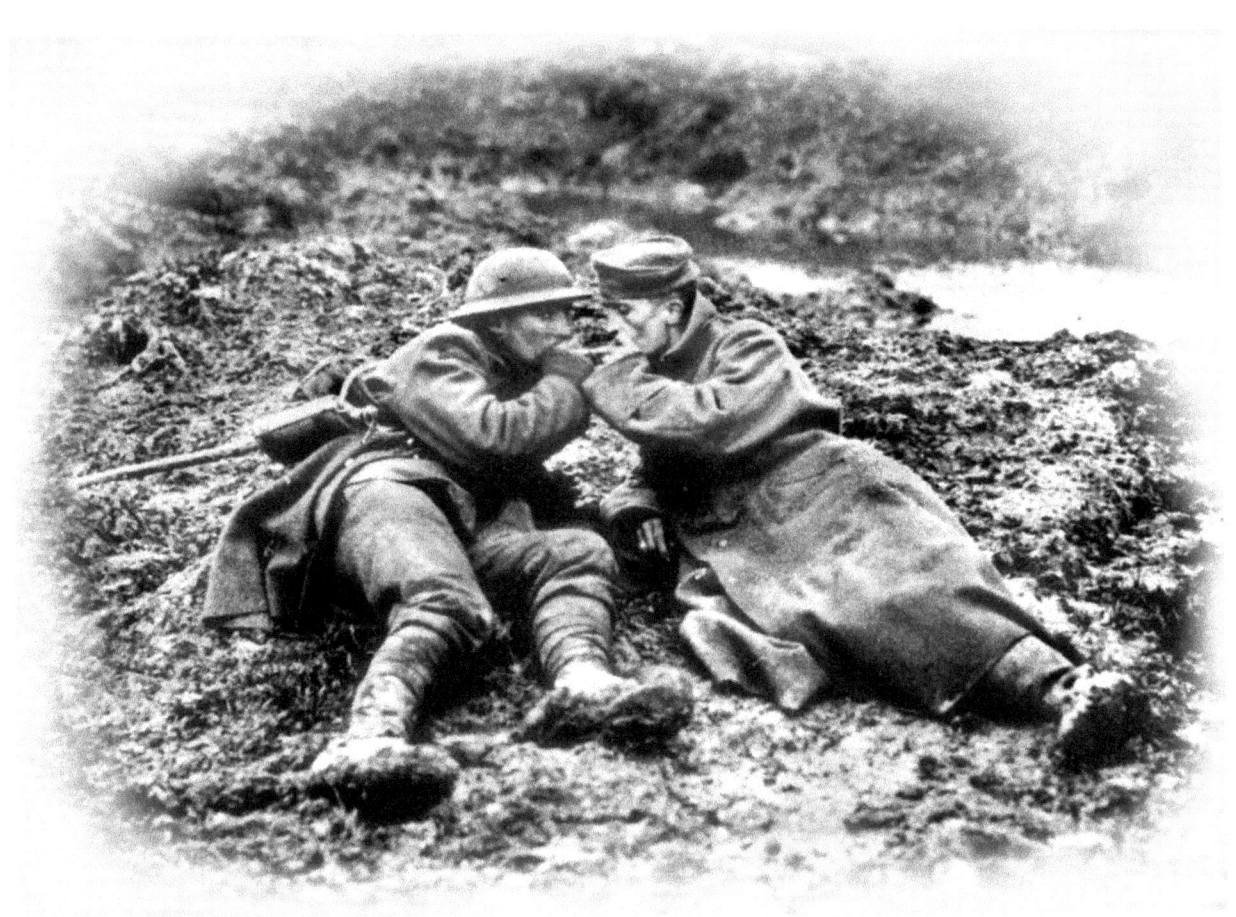

Canadian soldier lighting a German prisoner's cigarette,
Passchendaele, November.
Haig halted major operations on 10 November 1917.

Information used in this chapter was based on the following titles in the **Battleground Europe** series of guide books:
Sanctuary Wood & Hooge by Nigel Cave
Walking the Salient by Paul Reed
Hill 60 by Nigel Cave
Polygon Wood by Nigel Cave
Passchendaele by Nigel Cave
St Julien by Graham Keech
Boesinghe by Stephen McGreal

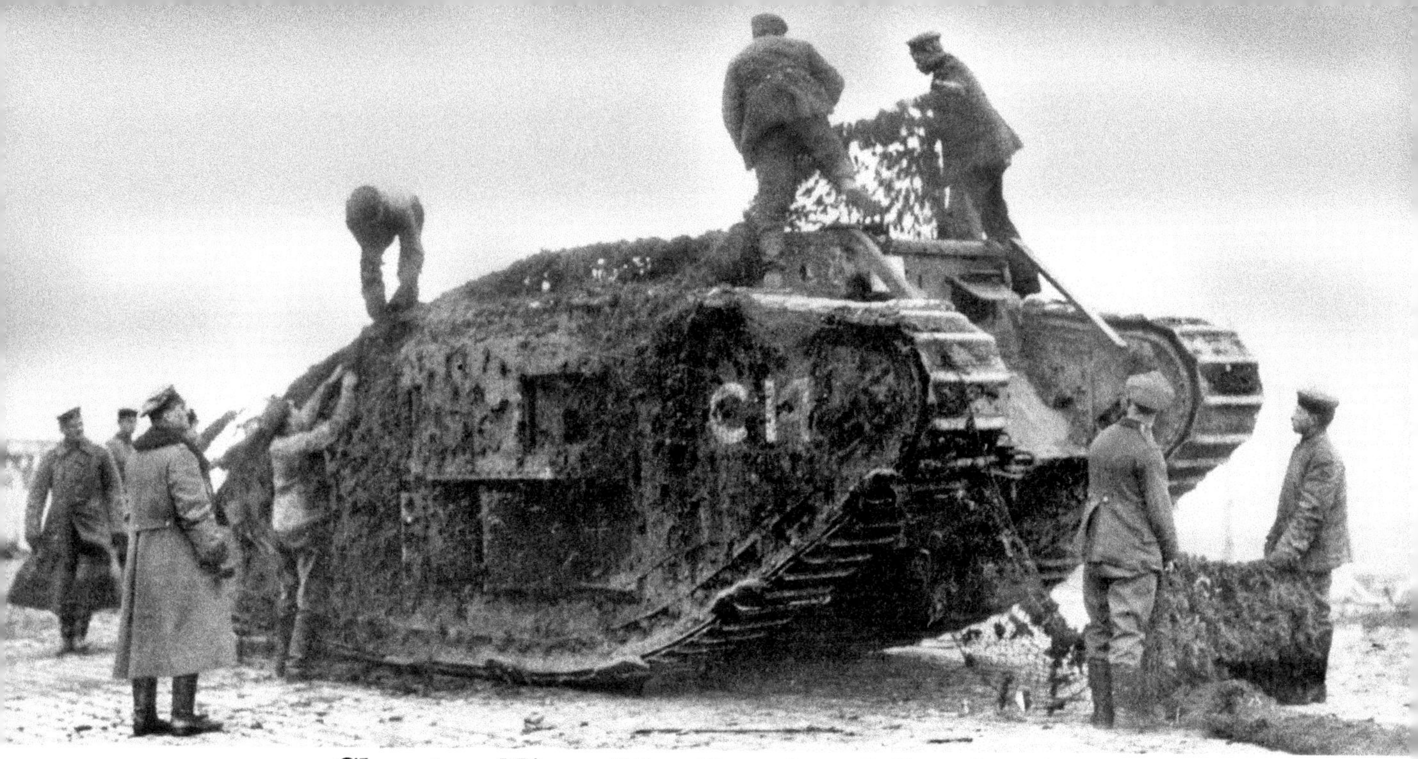

Chapter Nine: The Battle of Cambrai

17GW1075 A captured British tank being covered with camouflage netting to hide its location from Allied aircraft.

17GW1026 Men of a Scottish regiment 'embusing' to be driven to another part of the line.

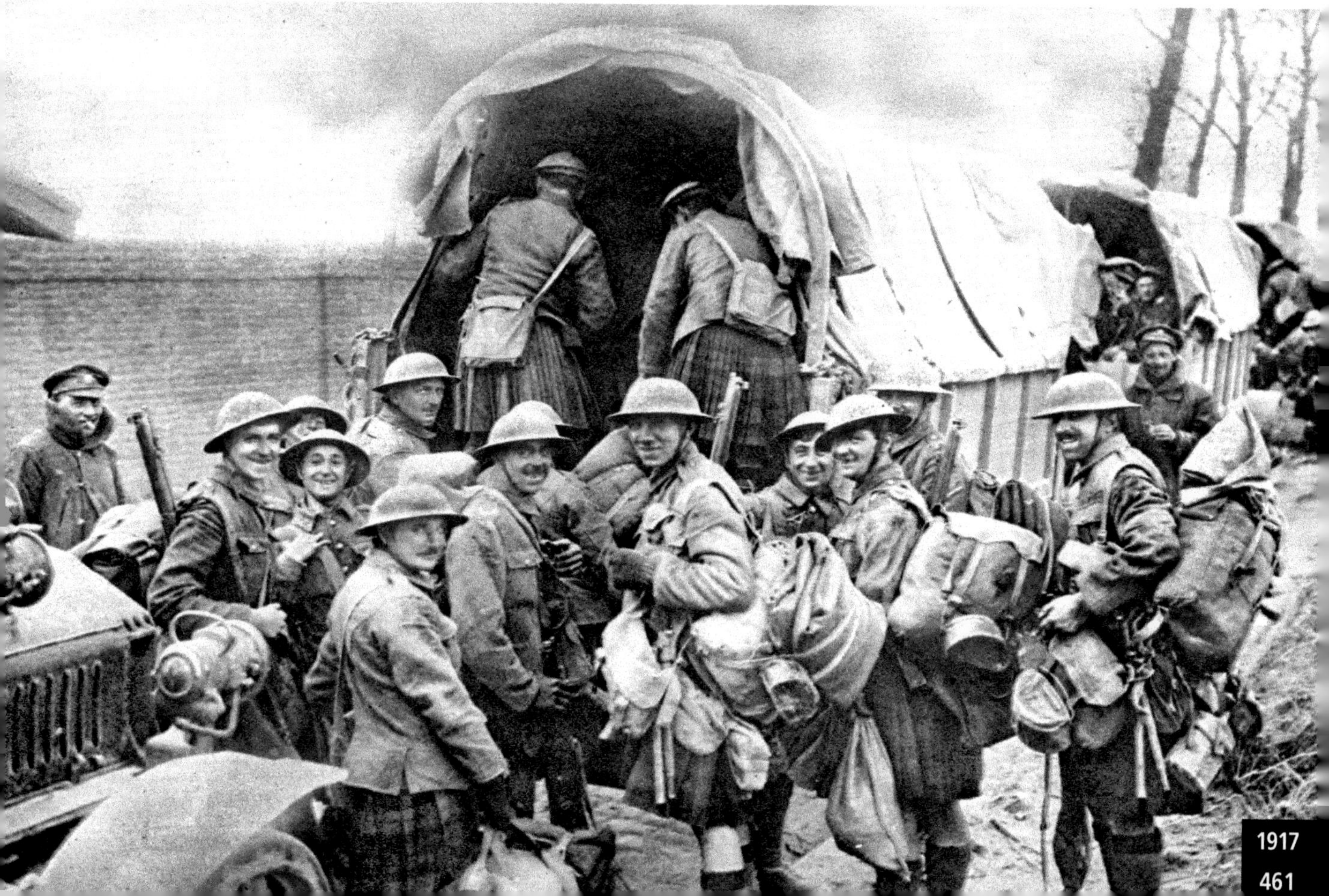

The Battle of Cambrai, 20 November – 7 December 1917, was originally intended to be a massive raid using a concentrated mass of tanks. New artillery techniques would be implemented. Initially it proved to be very successful, with large gains. However, ten days later a German counter-attack regained much of the ground.

General Georg von der Marwitz

The plan: A deep attack on a 5.6 mile front that would be 'widened as soon as possible'. Once the key German Masnières-Beaurevoir line had been breached by III Corps, the cavalry would pass through to isolate Cambrai from the rear and cut the supply network to the German forces fighting in Belgium and northern France.

General Sir Julian Byng

17GW1078 The British attack showing the ground gained in nine days.

17GW1079 The German counter attack 30 November that took much of it back again.

17GW1081 Plateau Railhead with flat cars loaded with tanks with fascines to aid crossing the deep German trenches. Spearheading the attack were 476 tanks.

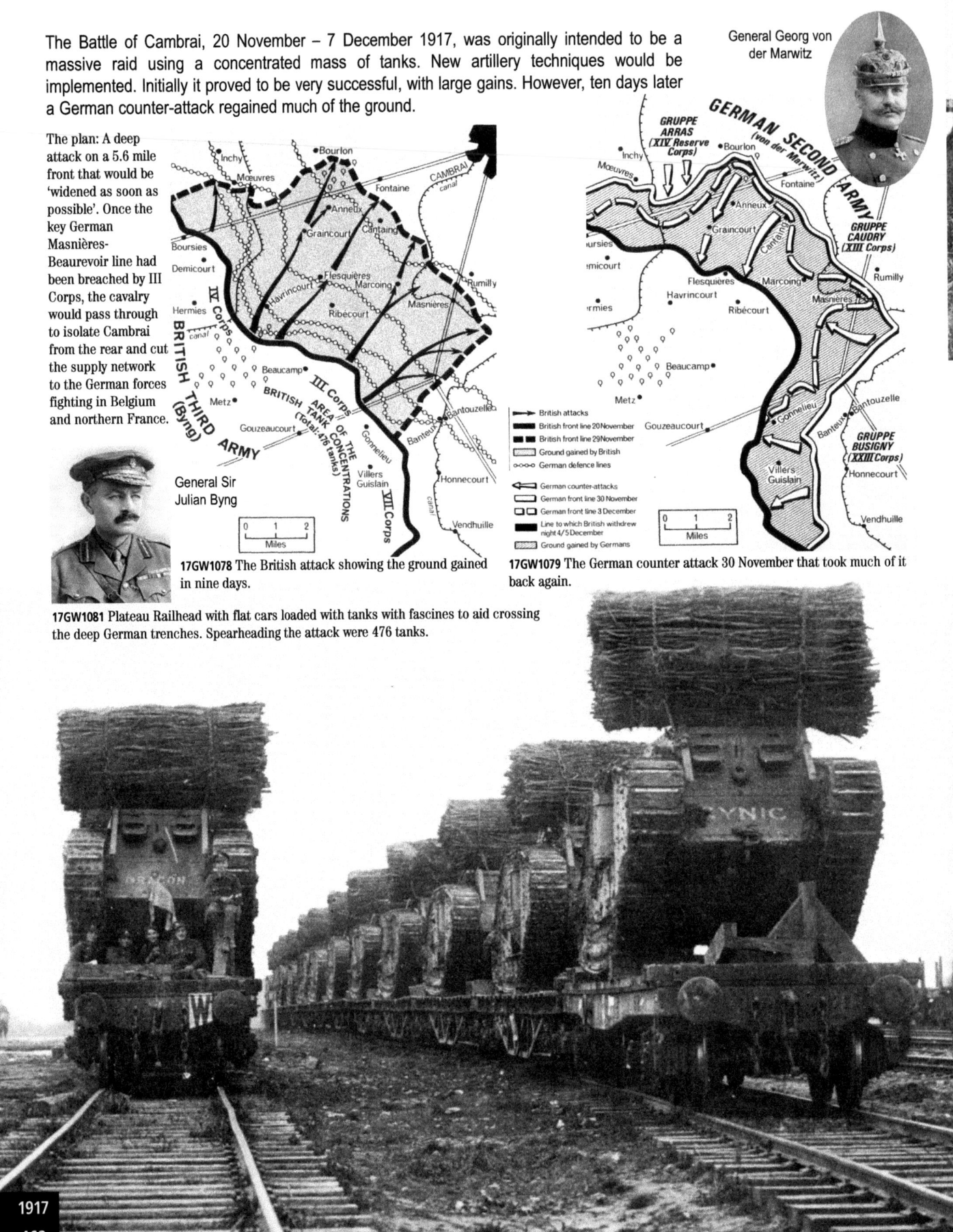

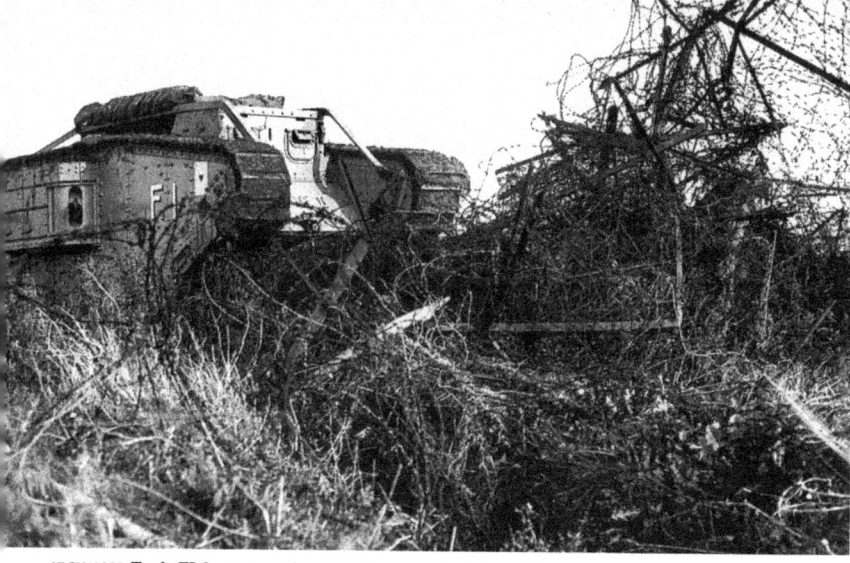
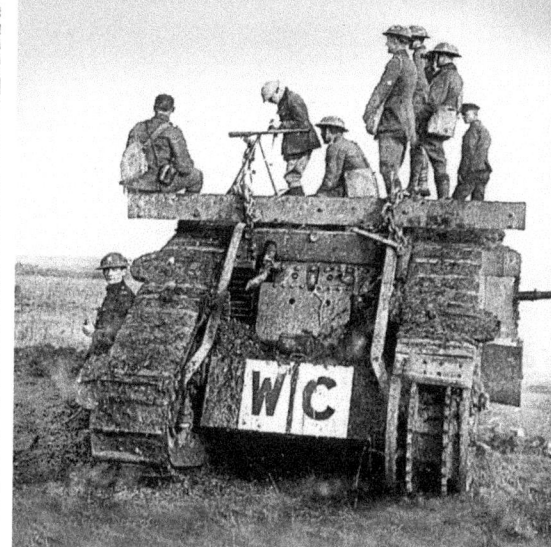

17GW1082 Tank *FI* demonstrating how to flatten barbed wire at Wailly, 21 October 1917.

17GW1083 A tank, having shed a track, now being used as an observation post. The large letters 'WC' indicate that the tank was used specifically as a wire cutter.

17GW1084 A tank of G Battalion passing a captured German battery of 77 mm field guns on the Graincourt side of Flesquières Ridge.

17GW1085 Uncompleted German defences at Flesquières. The reinforcing rods awaiting the pouring of concrete gives some indication of the size of the shelters being constructed by the Germans along the Hindenburg Line.

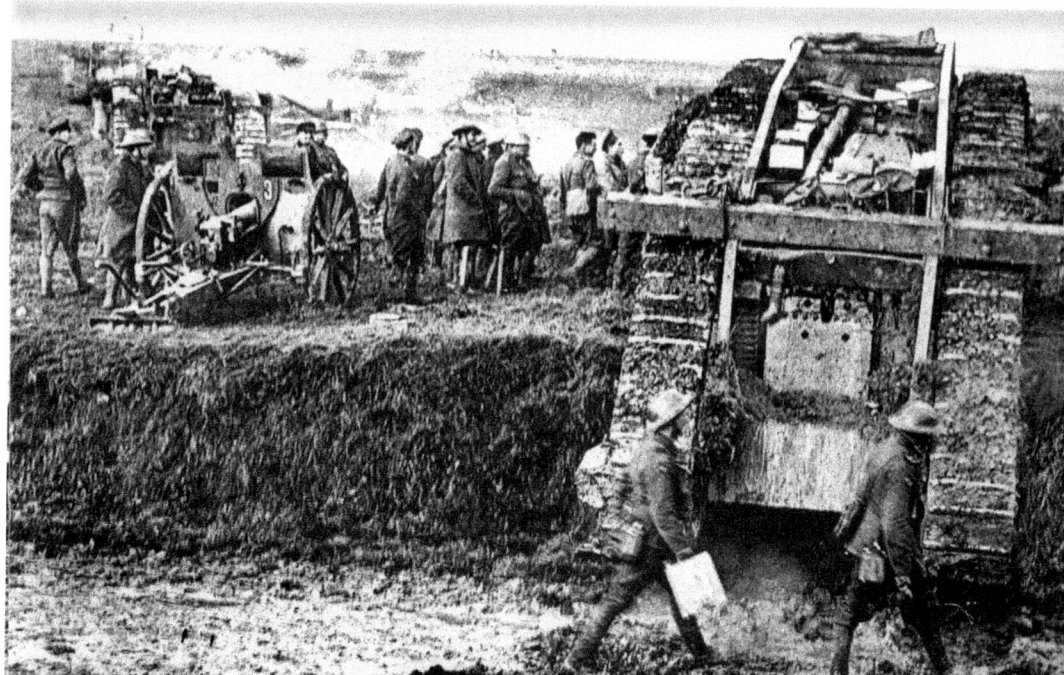
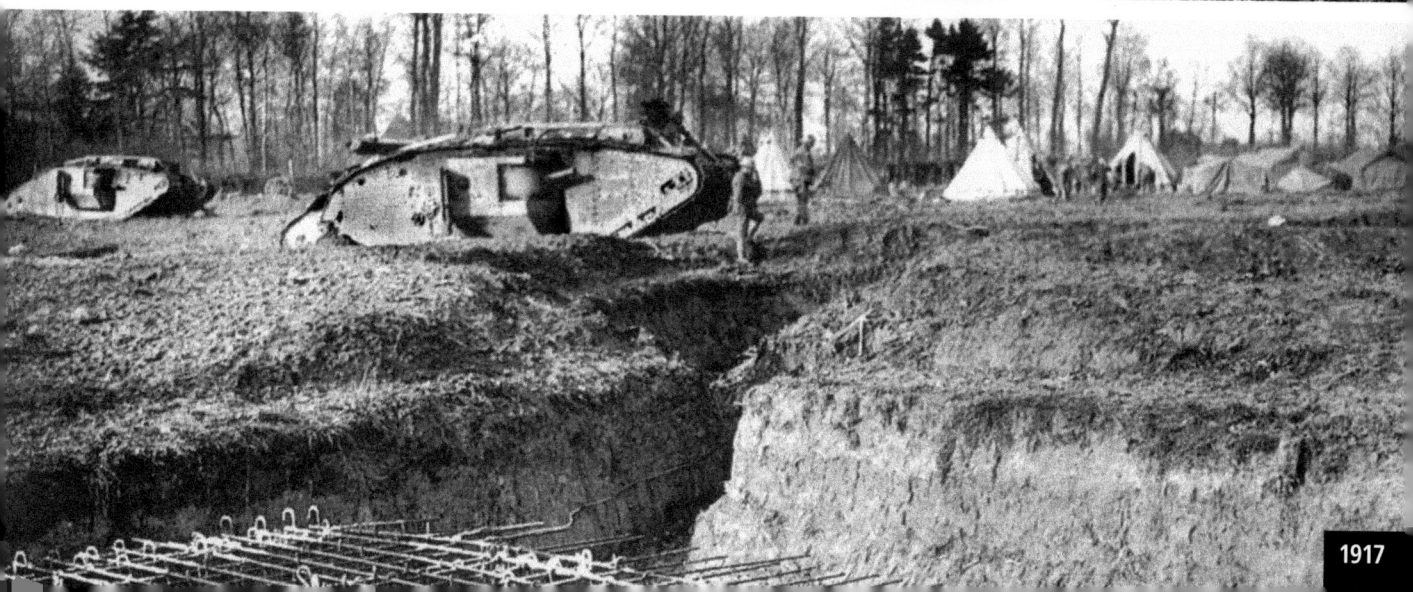

1917

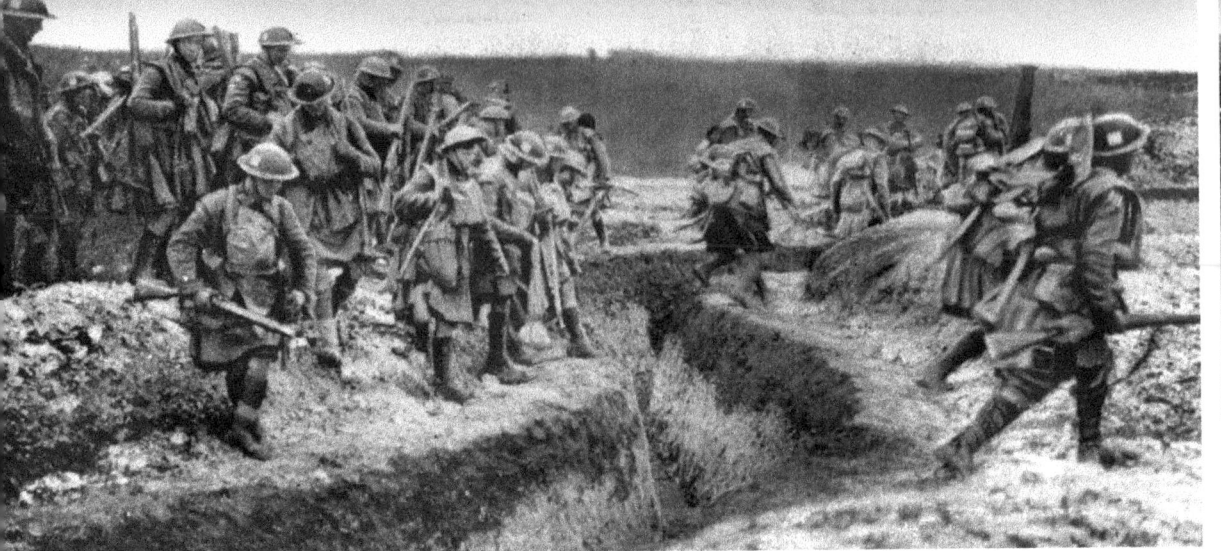
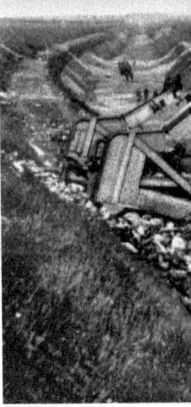
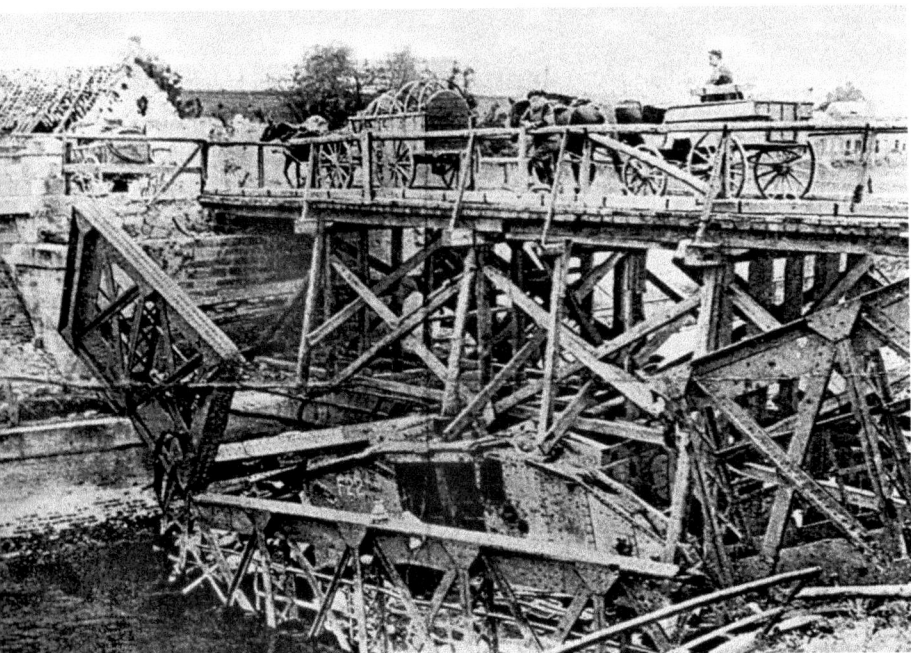
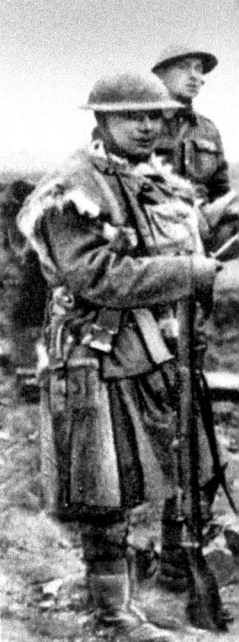

17GW1086 Highlanders of a Territorial battalion of the 51st Division crossing a German trench at Flesquières; they took 500 prisoners in a five mile advance.

17GW1089 The bridge over the Canal du Nord at Masnières brought down by the weight of *Flying Fox*, a tank under the command of Lieutenant Edmunson.

17GW1092, 17GW1093. Motorcycle combinations at Ribécourt allowing the cavalry through, 22 November. Lancers filling up the road at Trescault.

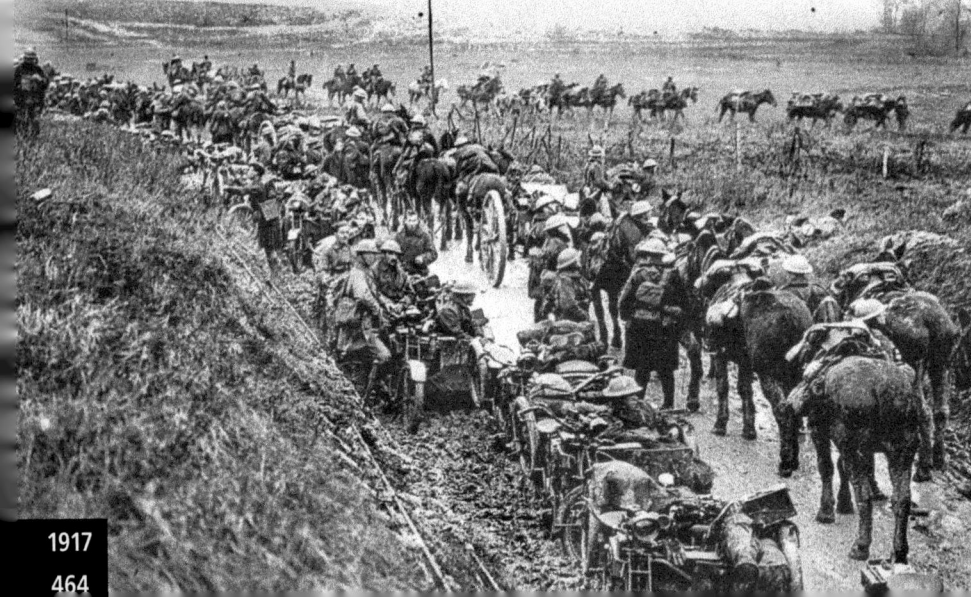
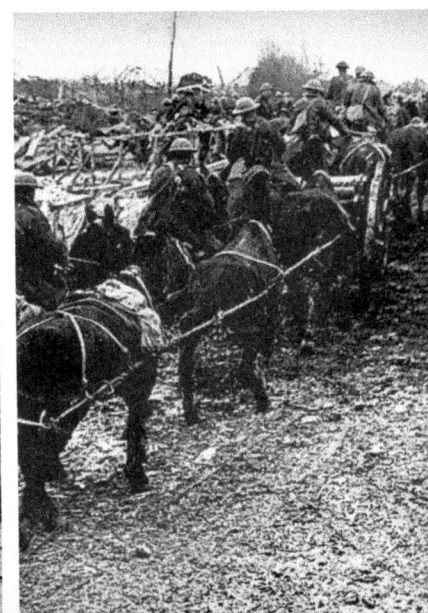

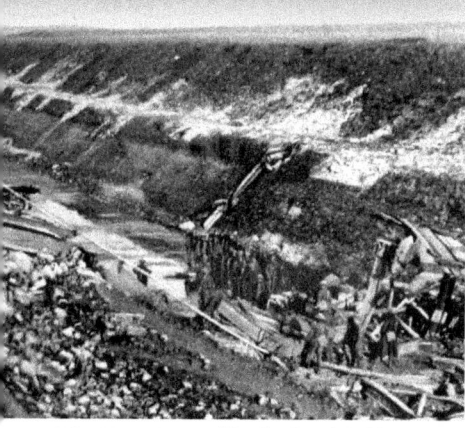
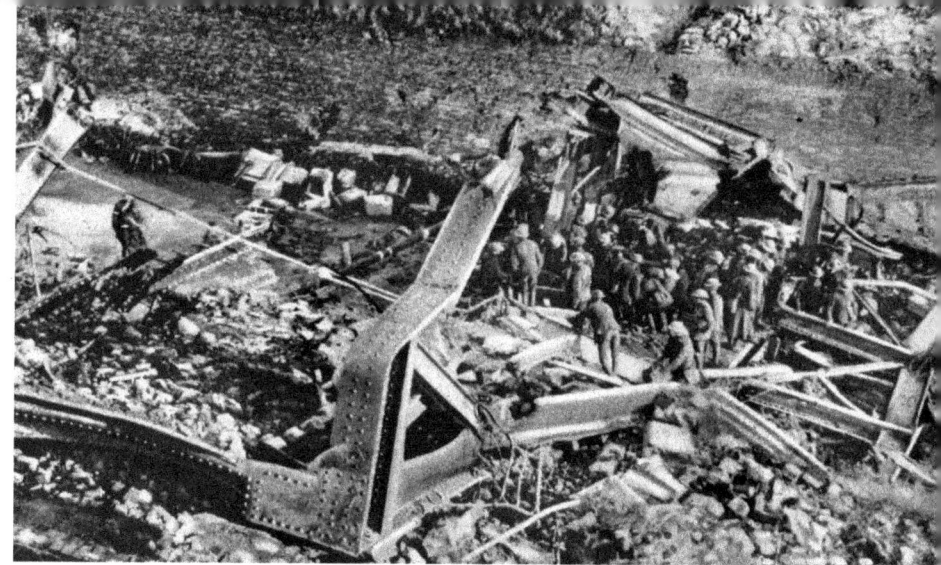

17GW1087, 17GW1088. The dry Canal du Nord proved a serious obstacle to the advance; Royal Engineers clearing the remains of a bridge blown up by the Germans.

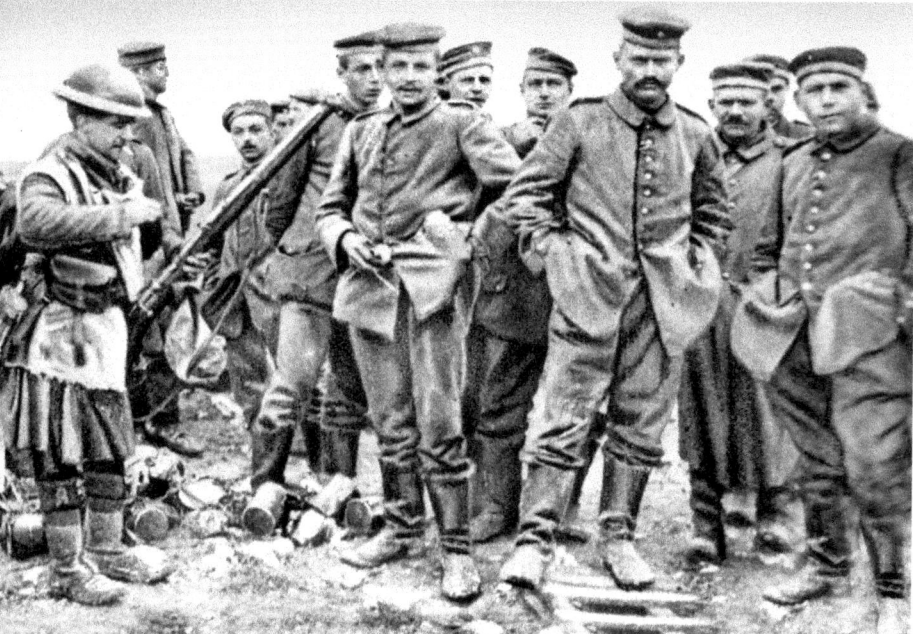

The British official press release:
Ulster battalions moved northwards up the west bank of the Canal du Nord – English, Scottish, Irish and Welsh battalions secured crossings of the canal at Mesnières and captured Marcoing and Neuf Wood. The West Riding troops made remarkable progress east of the Canal du Nord, storming the village of Graincourt and Anneux and, with the Ulster troops operating west of the canal, carried the whole of the German line northwards to the Bapaume-Cambrai Road.

17GW1091 Sending messages from a tank by pigeon.

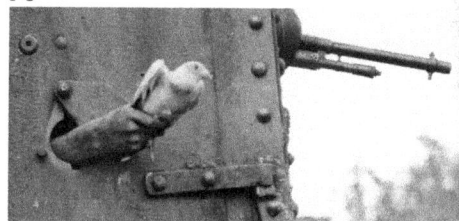

17GW10890, 17GW1094. Highlanders of a Territorial battalion with prisoners taken at Flesquières.

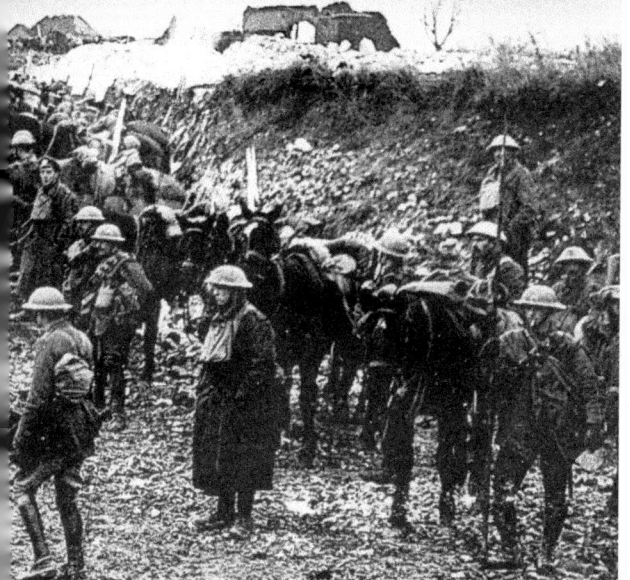
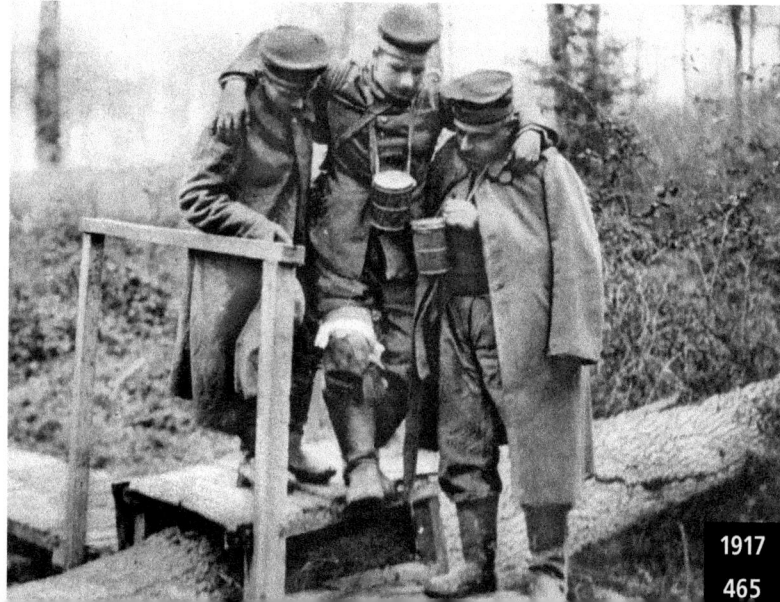

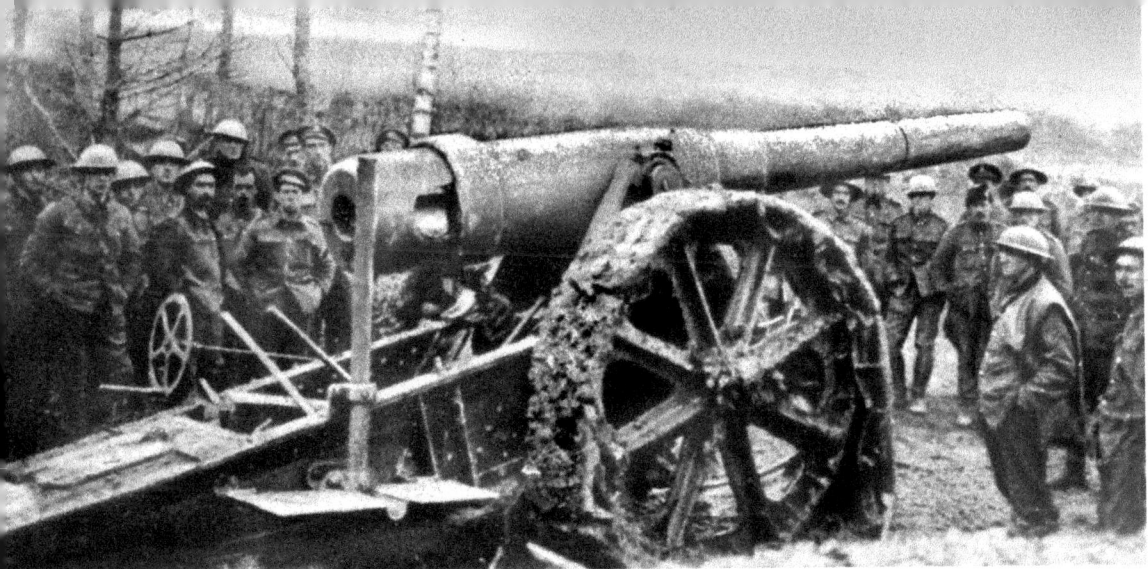

17GW10895, 17GW1096. A type of gun nicknamed 'Whistling Percy' by the British soldiers because of the sound of its shells in flight. The German had no time to remove it this. The 5.9-inch naval gun is easily towed away by a British tank. The German line had been forced back 10,000 metres. A German counter offensive recaptured most of the ground.

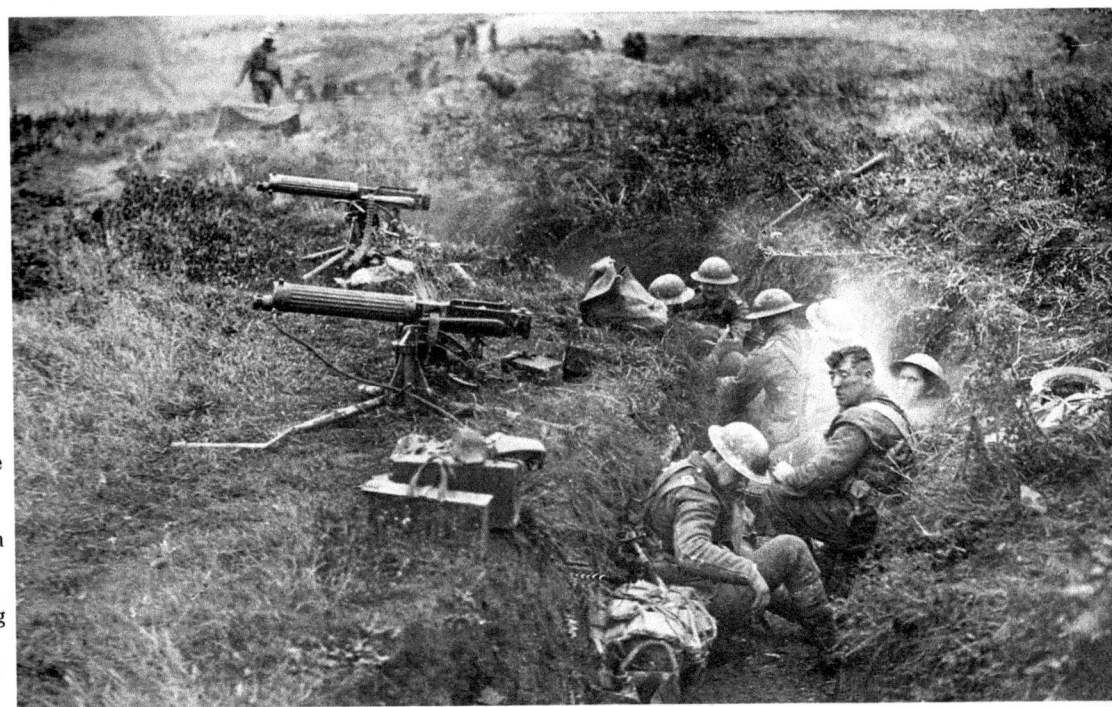

17GW1097 Men of the 11th Battalion, Leicestershire Regiment, 6th Division's pioneer battalion, resting in the German Second Line at Ribécourt, 20 November 1917.

17GW1099 A squad (*Schützengruppe*); by 1917 this had become the smallest combat unit in the German army and was trained to advance in depth while providing mutual covering support. In the forthcoming spring offensive the fighting technique would be used to the full.

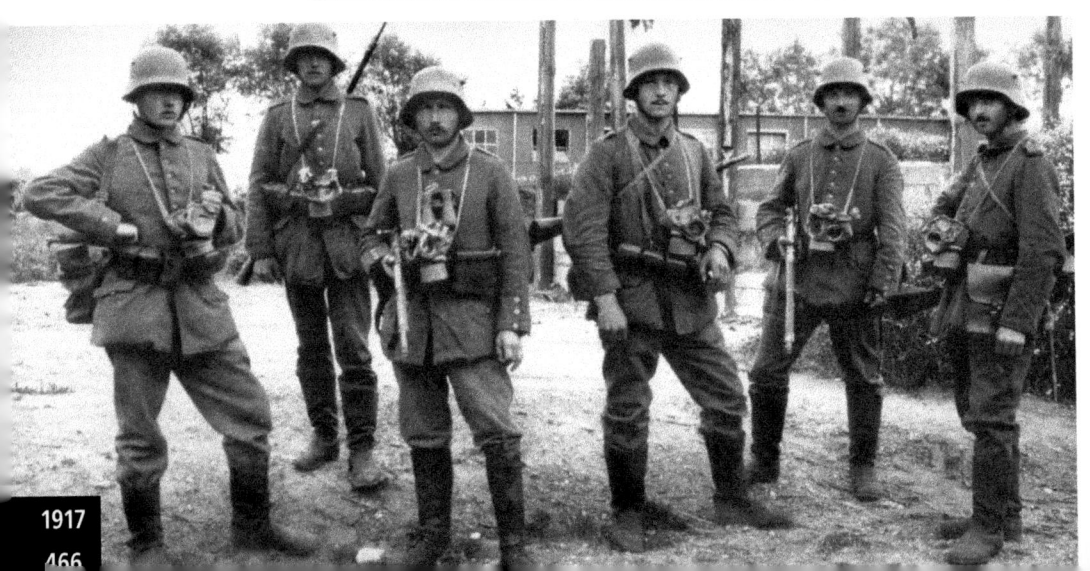
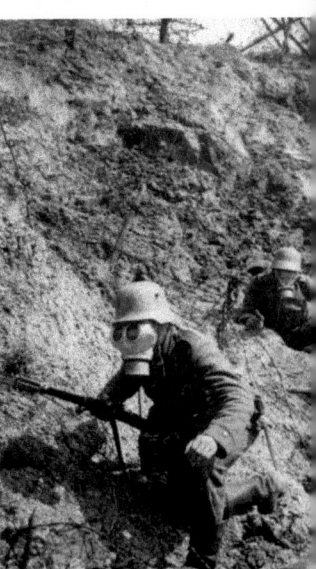

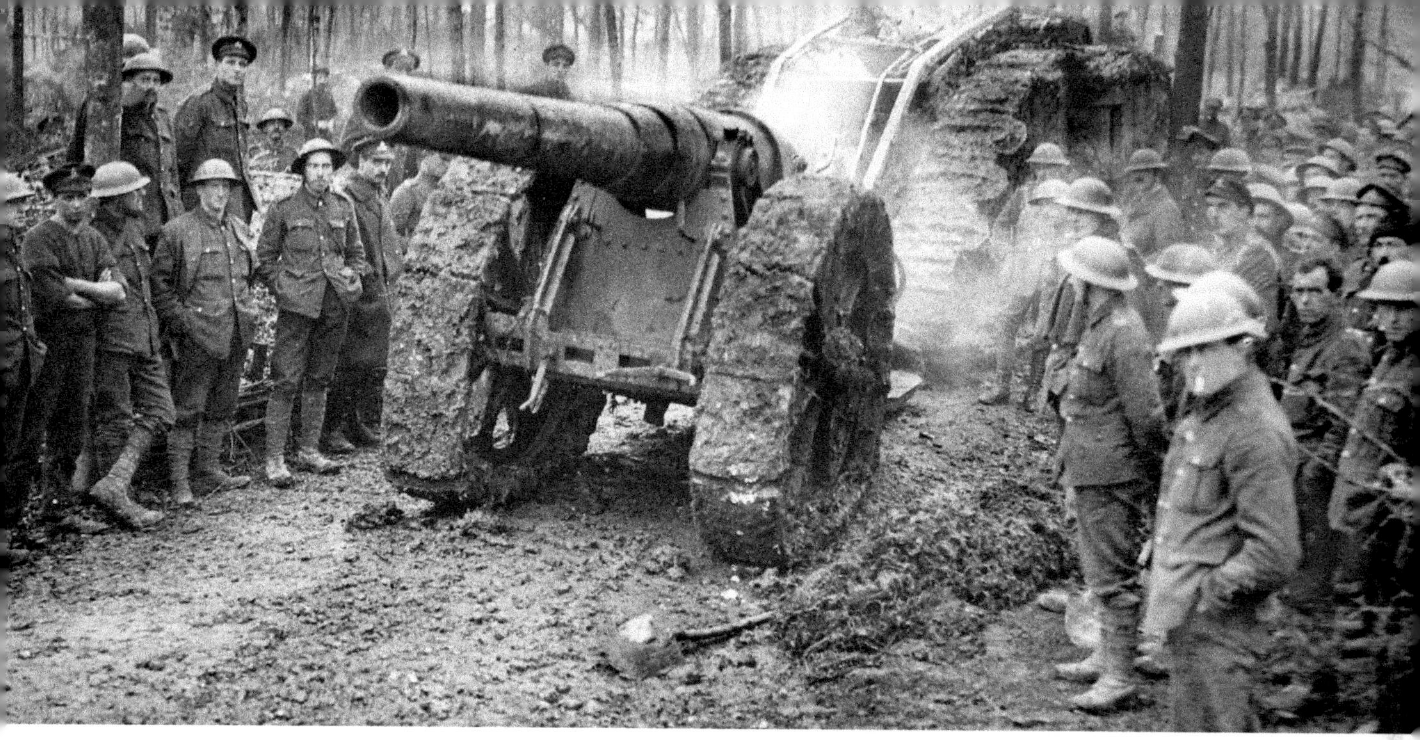

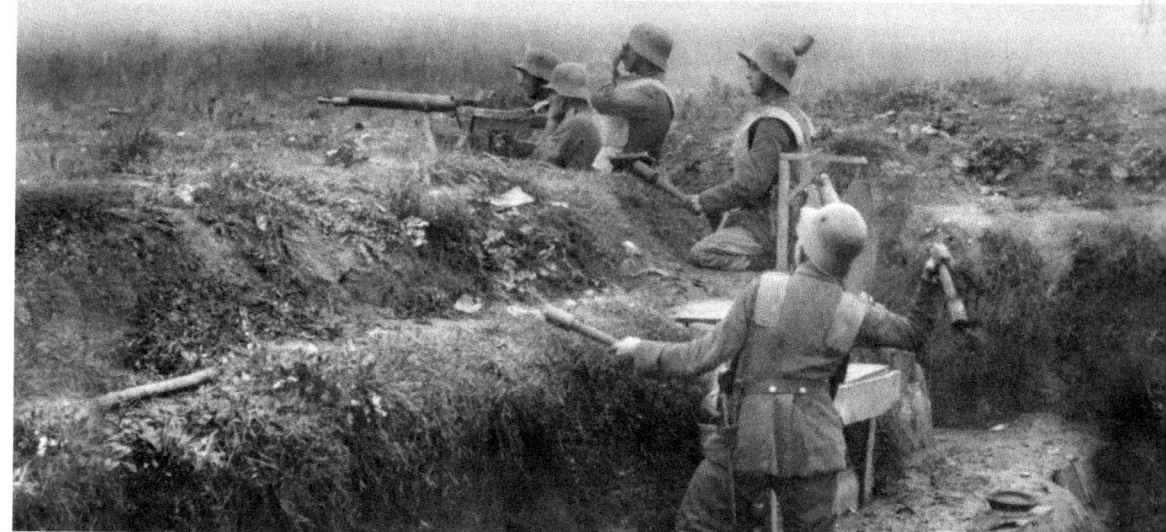

17GW1102 A German machine gun crew in trenches at Cambrai, November 1917.

17GW1101 A German squad await orders to advance and drive the Tommies back.

17GW1076 General Georg von der Marwitz, commander of the German Second Army (on the Kaiser's left); the commander in chief visiting the Front at Cambrai, December 1917. A snowfall heralds another bitter winter.

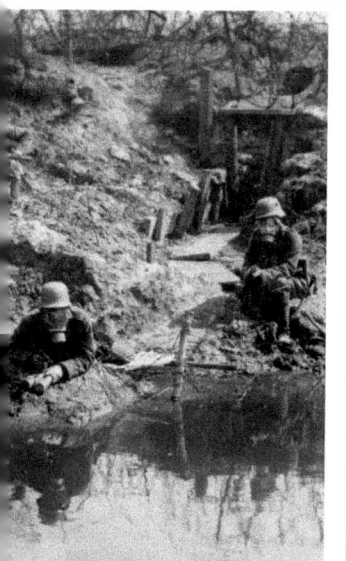

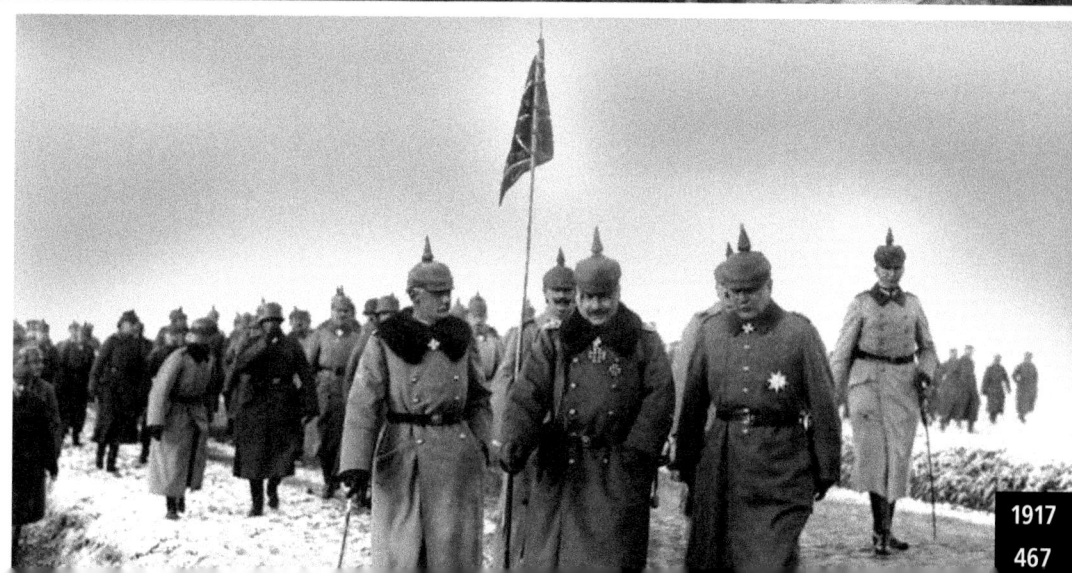

At the end of the Battle of Cambrai, the Third Army reported losses of dead, wounded and missing of 44,207 between 20 November and 8 December. Of these, some 6,000 were taken prisoner in the enemy major counter attack that commenced on 30 November. Enemy casualties were estimated by the British Official History at approximately 45,000.

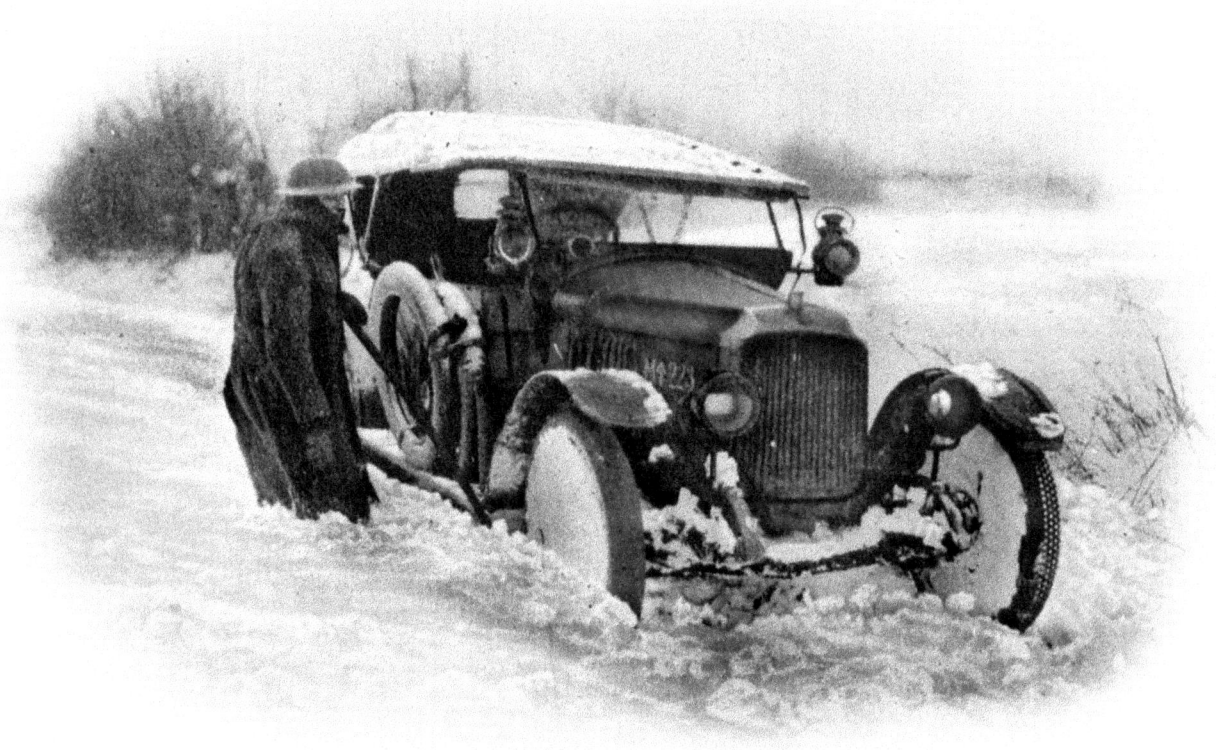

17GW1098 The British Army HQ in France announced: *'Snow has fallen along the whole front'*. The war had entered its fourth severe winter.

Information used in this chapter was based on the following titles in the **Battleground Europe** series of guide books:
Hindenburg Line – Cambrai Right Hook by Jack Horsfall & Nigel Cave
Hindenburg Line – Cambrai Flesquières by Jack Horsfall & Nigel Cave
Hindenburg Line – Bourlon Wood by Jack Horsfall & Nigel Cave

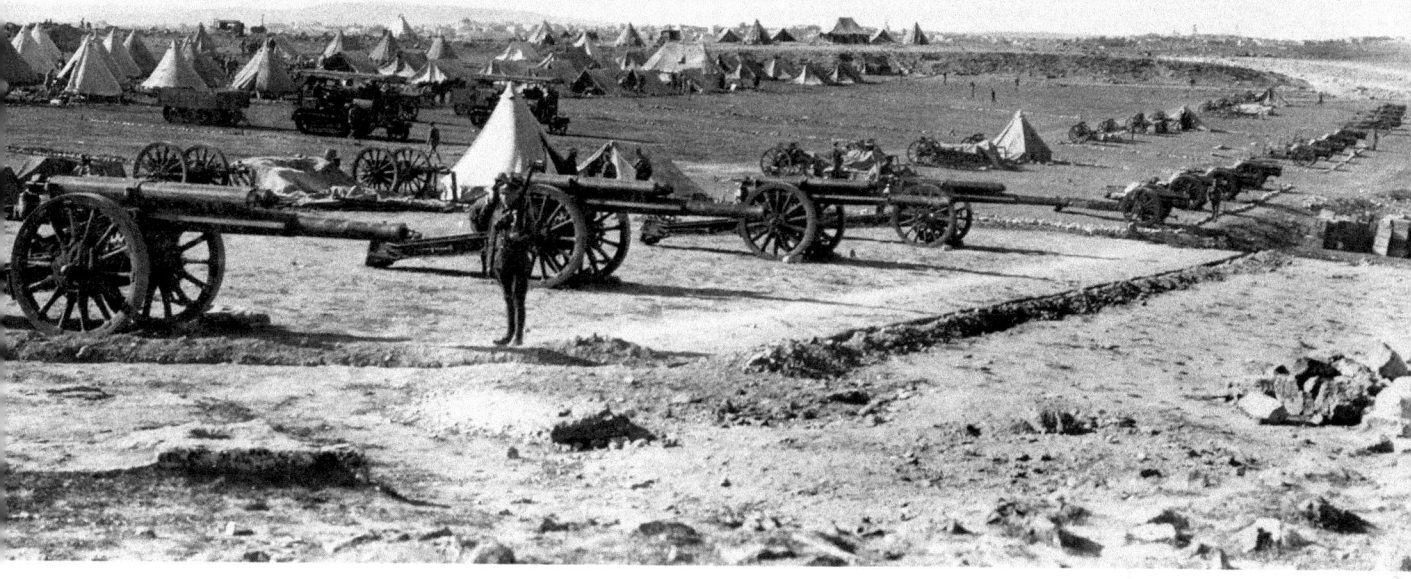

Chapter Ten: Highlight of 1917 – the Capture of Jerusalem

17GW1103 The camp of the 94th Heavy Battery on Mt Scopus after they helped in the capture of Jerusalem.

17GW1104 Ottoman light artillery positioned for the defence of Jerusalem, November 1917.

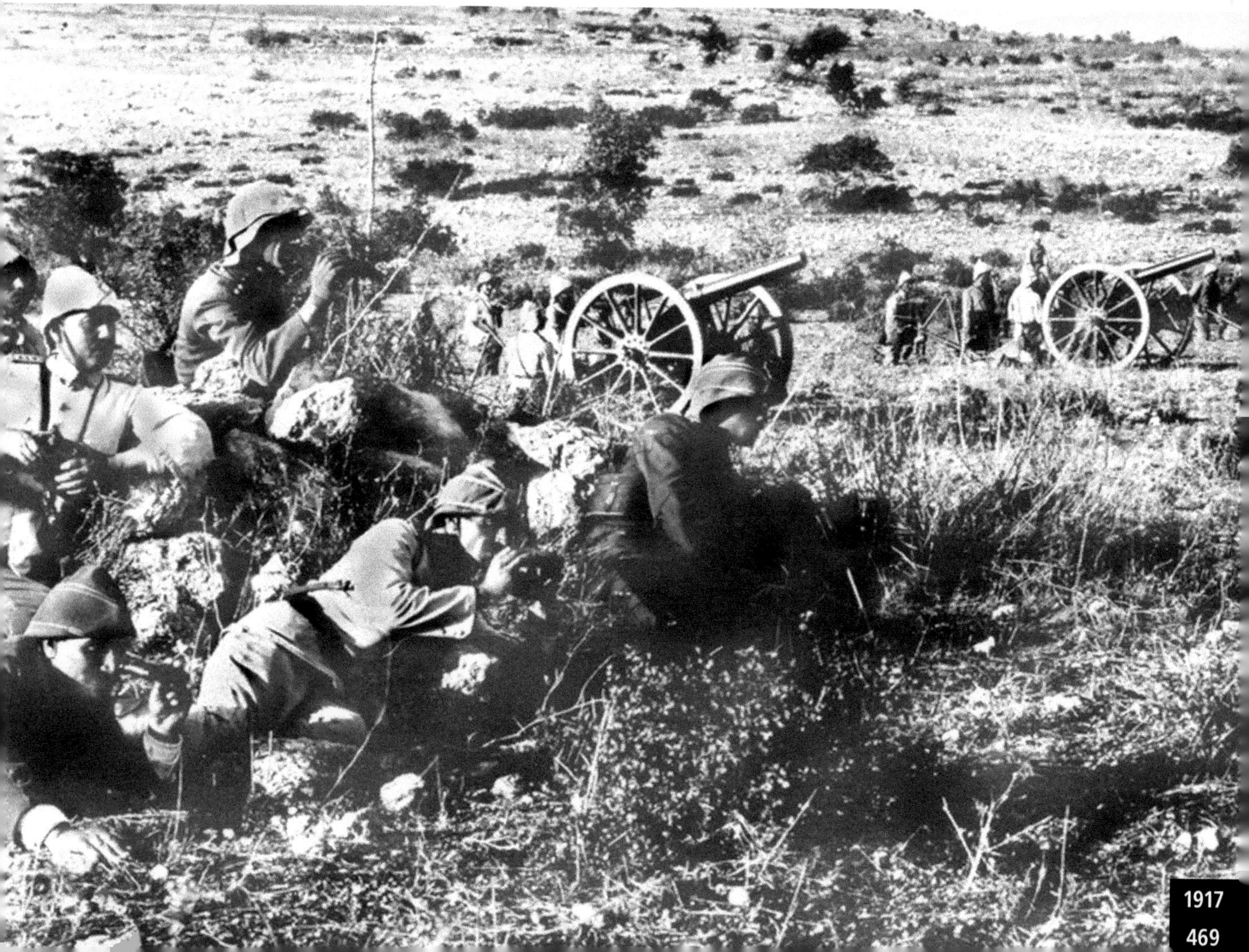

Fighting for the city of Jerusalem, regarded as holy by three great religions, developed from 17 November and continued after its surrender, on 9 December, until the 30th. The series of battles in the weeks after Jerusalem's fall was fought successfully by British XX Corps, XXI Corps and the Desert Mounted Corps, against strong opposition from the Turkish Yildirim Army Group's Seventh Army in the Judean Hills and its Eighth Army north of Jaffa. The loss of Jaffa and Jerusalem, together with the loss of fifty miles of territory during the Egyptian Expeditionary Force's (EEF) advance from Gaza, constituted a grave setback for the Ottoman Empire.

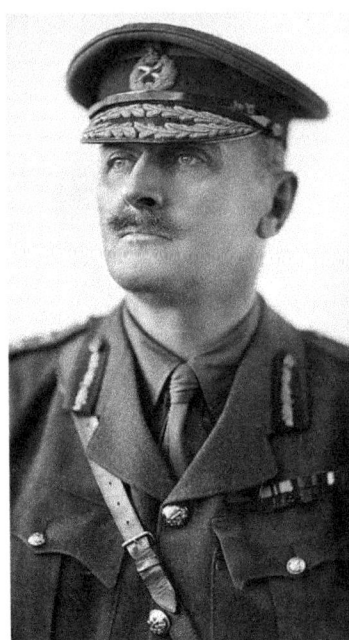

17GW1109 General Sir Edmund Allenby, commanding the British Empire's Egyptian Expeditionary Force.

17GW1114 The 4th Battalion, Sussex Regiment, marching through Bethlehem, just five miles from Jerusalem, 9 December 1917. They were part of the 53rd (Welsh) Division.

17GW1115 The Australian 4th Light Horse Regiment approaching the Judean Hills during the fighting around Jerusalem.

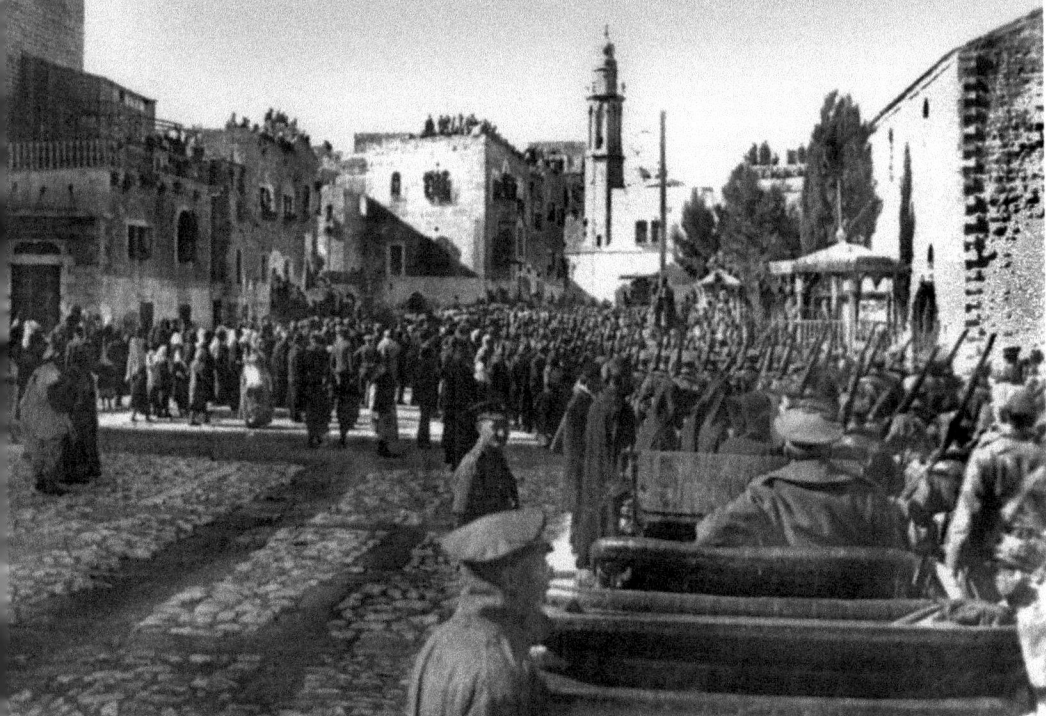

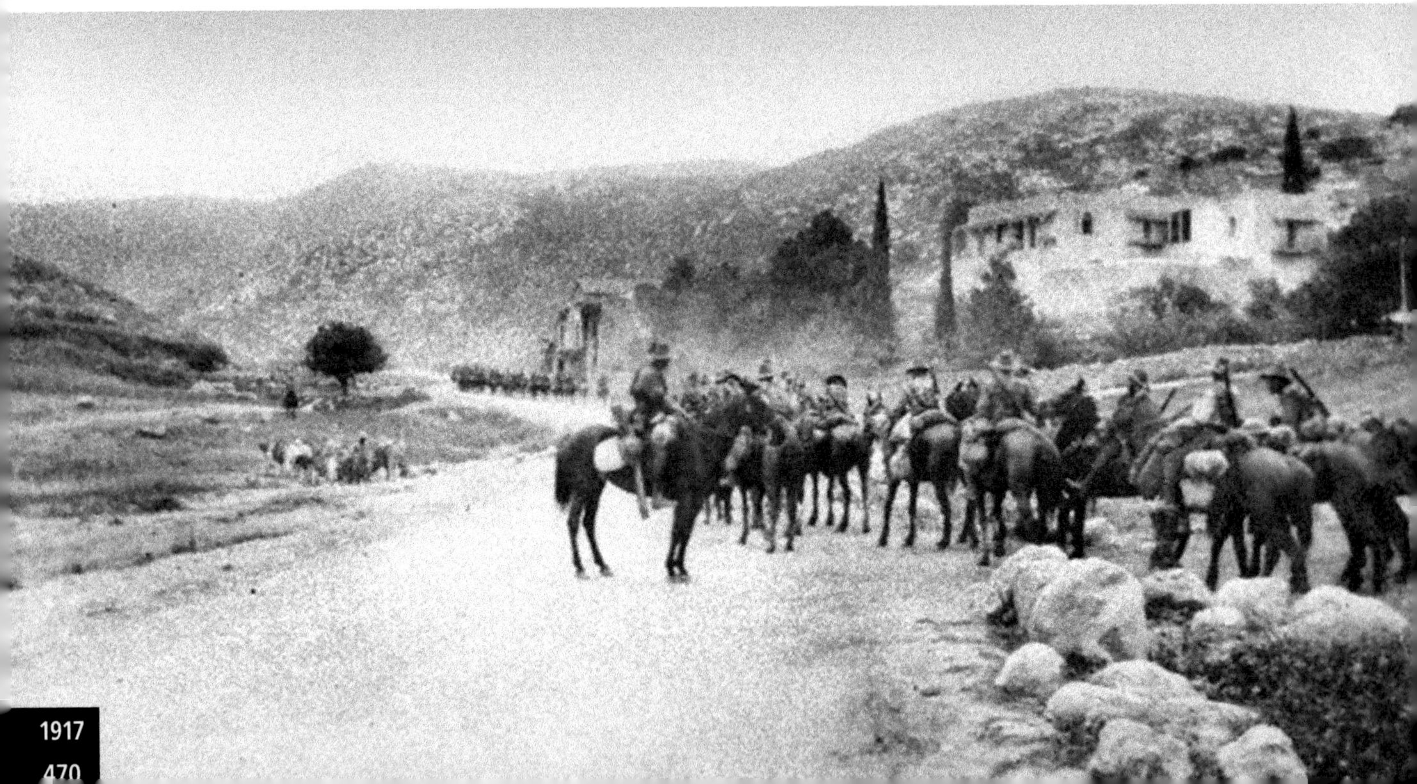

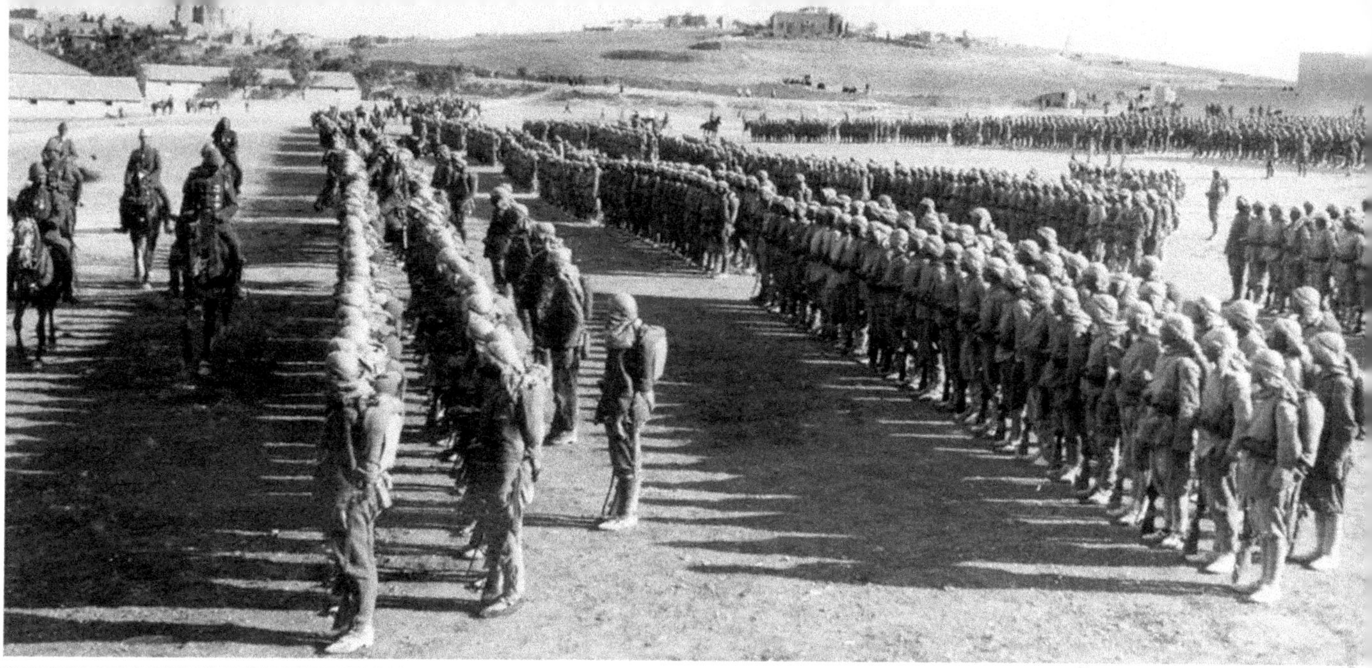

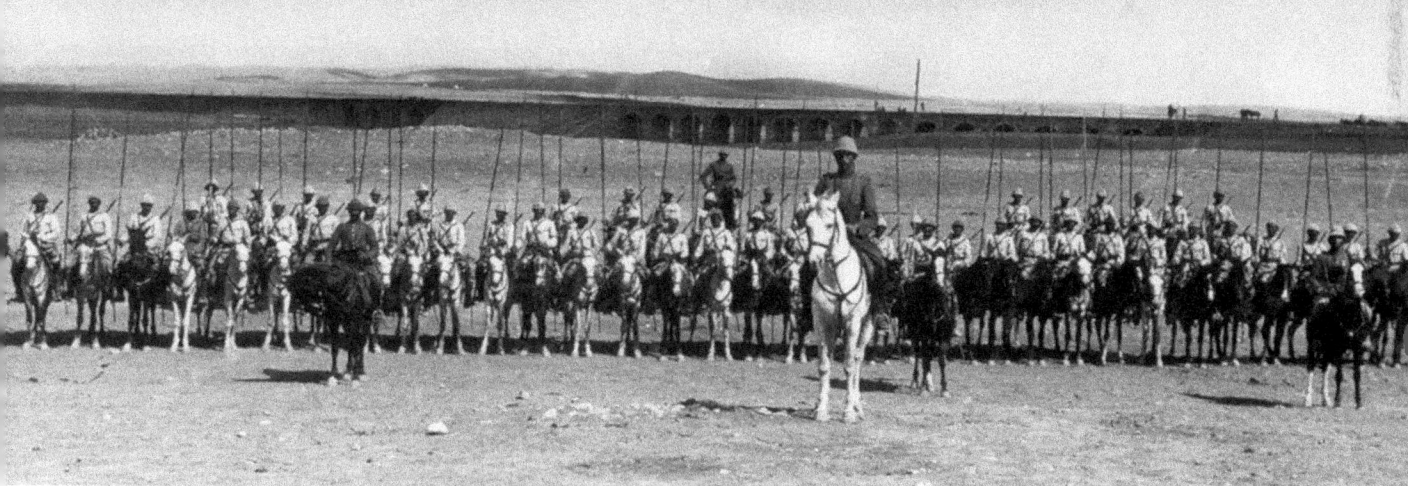

17GW1110, 17GW1118. Ottoman forces being inspected before the fighting for the Holy City of Jerusalem.

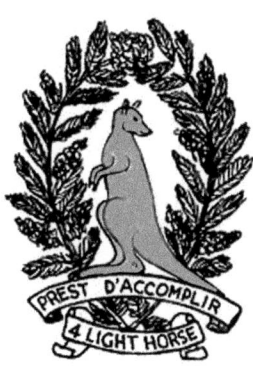

17GW1115 Australian cavalry during the campaign.

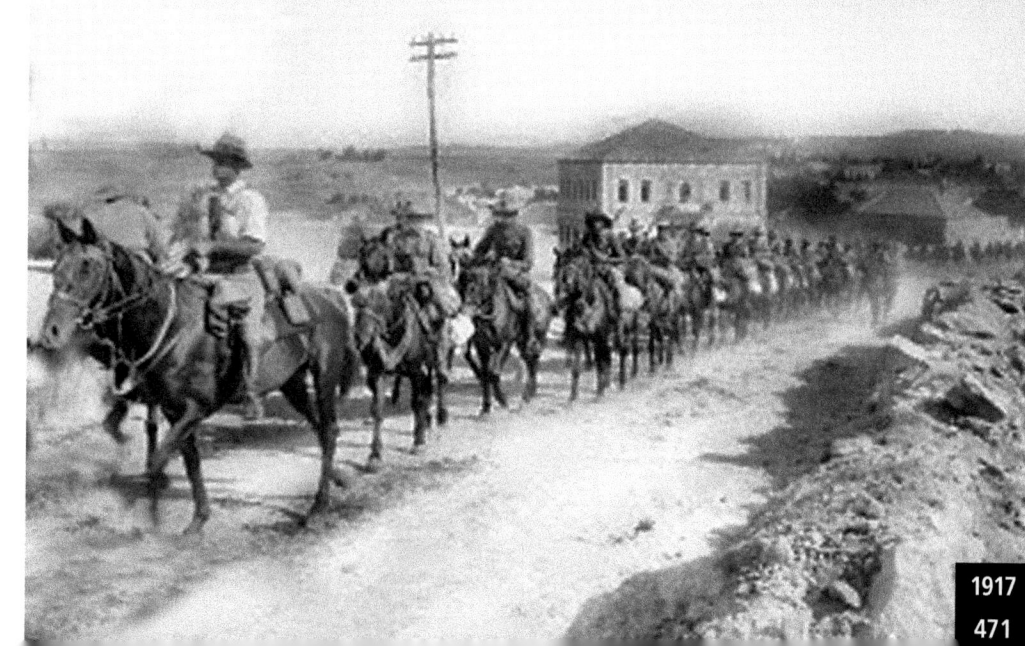

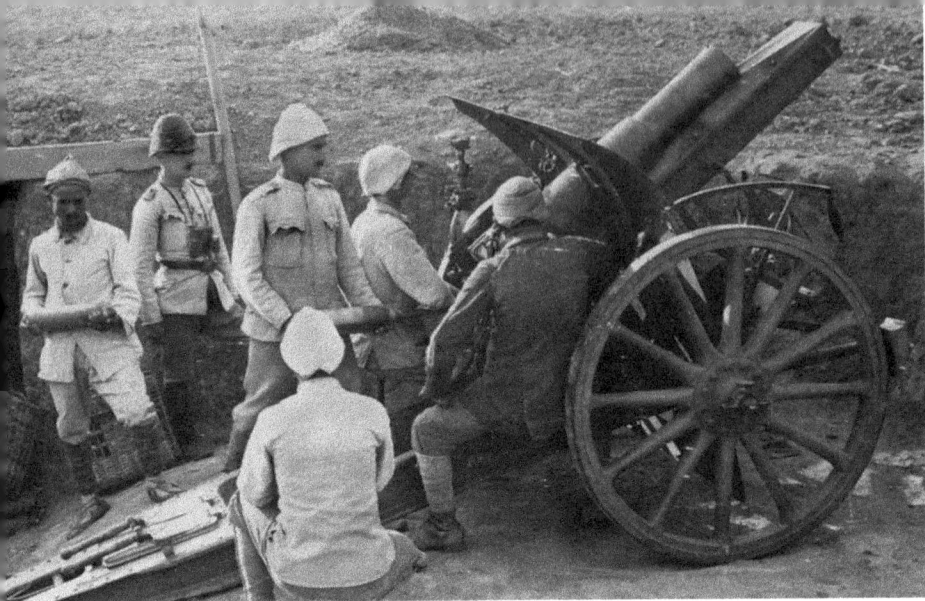
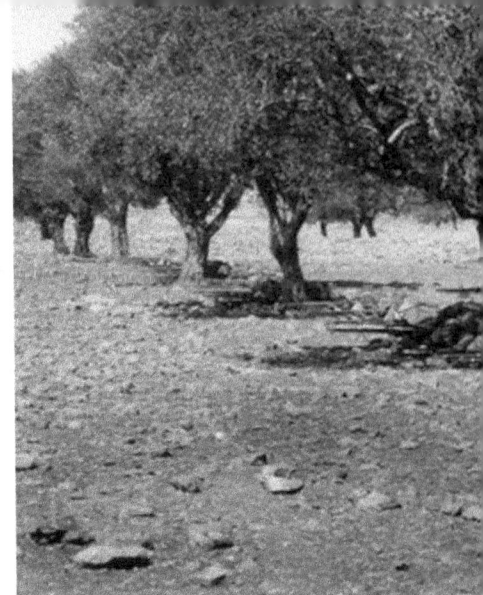
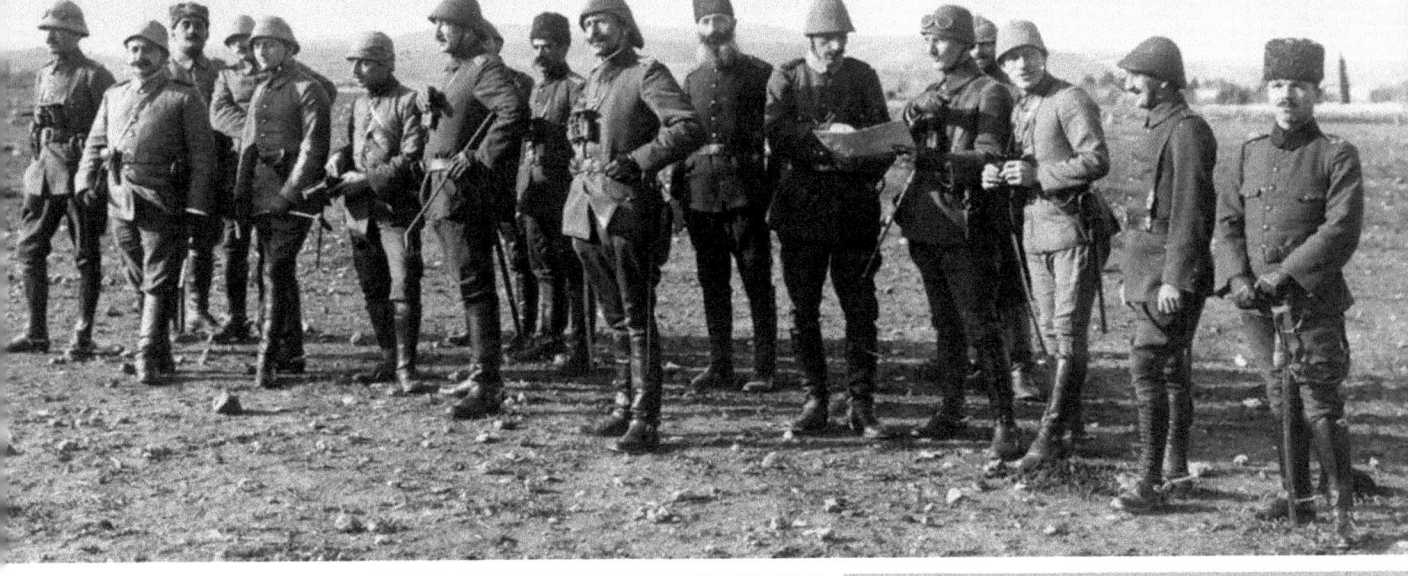
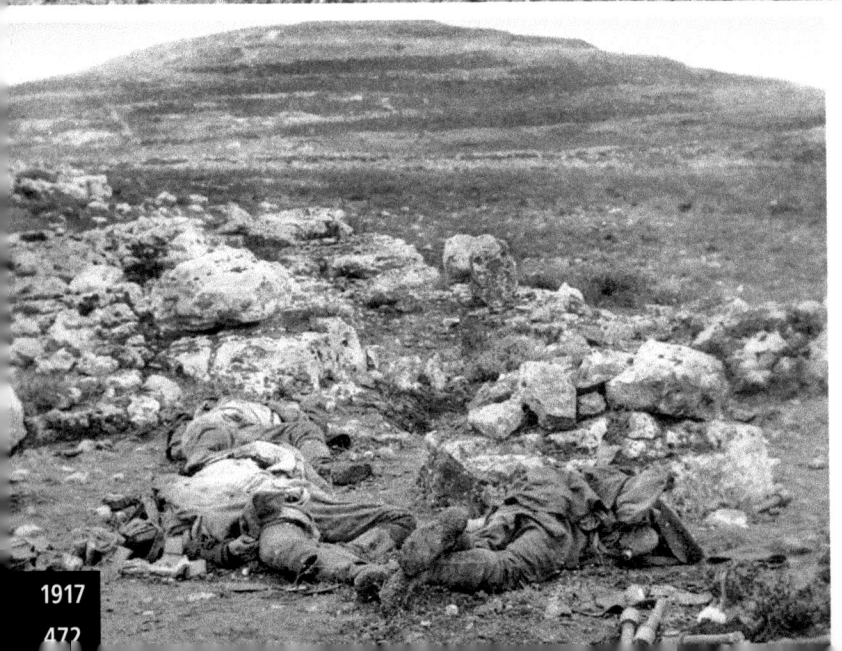
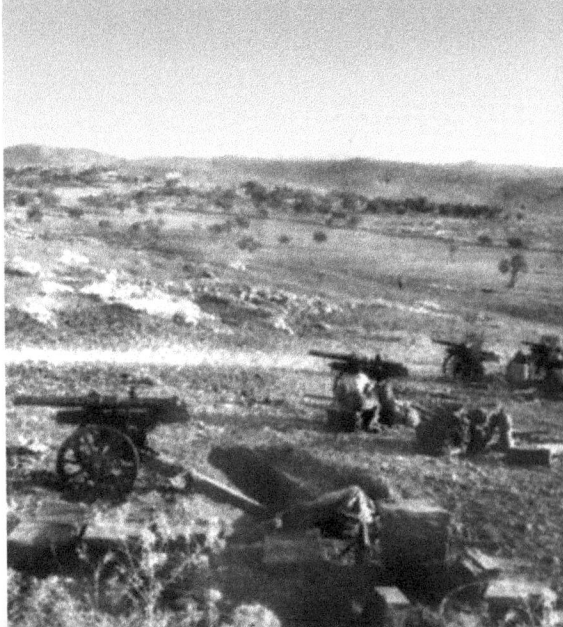

1917

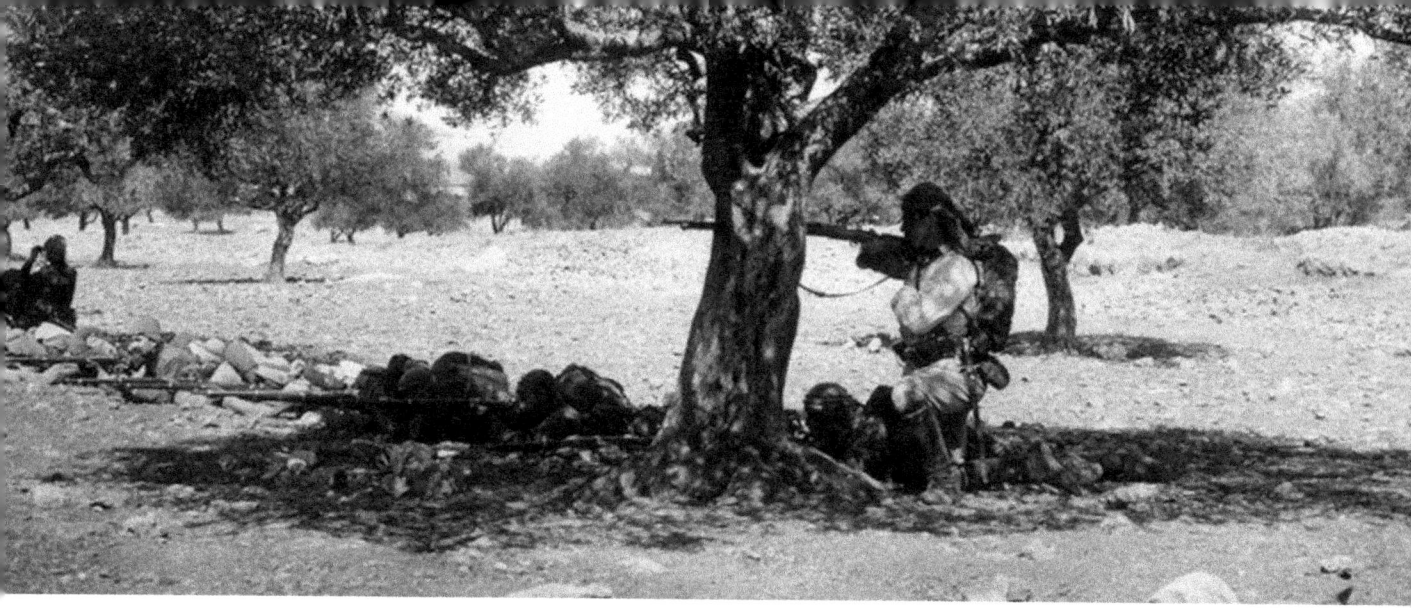

17GW1112, 17GW1111, 17GW1113.
Ottoman artillery team at Hareira in 1917, manning a 10.5 cm *Feldhaubitze* 98/09 (field howitzer).
Turkish infantry in a shallow trench defensive position before their withdrawal from Jerusalem.
Ottoman officers, infantry, cavalry and artillery commanders.

17GW1116 Dead Ottoman soldiers at Tel el Ful in 1917; note the German model stick grenades.

17GW1116 British mountain gun battery in action near Beit Ur el Tahta during the fighting for Jerusalem.

17GW11107 The mayor of Jerusalem, attempted to deliver the Ottoman Governor's letter surrendering the city to Sergeants James Sedgewick and Frederick Hurcomb of 2/19th Battalion, London Regiment, outside Jerusalem's walls, 9 December 1917. The two sergeants, who were scouting ahead of Allenby's main force, refused to take the letter. It was eventually accepted by a British brigadier general.

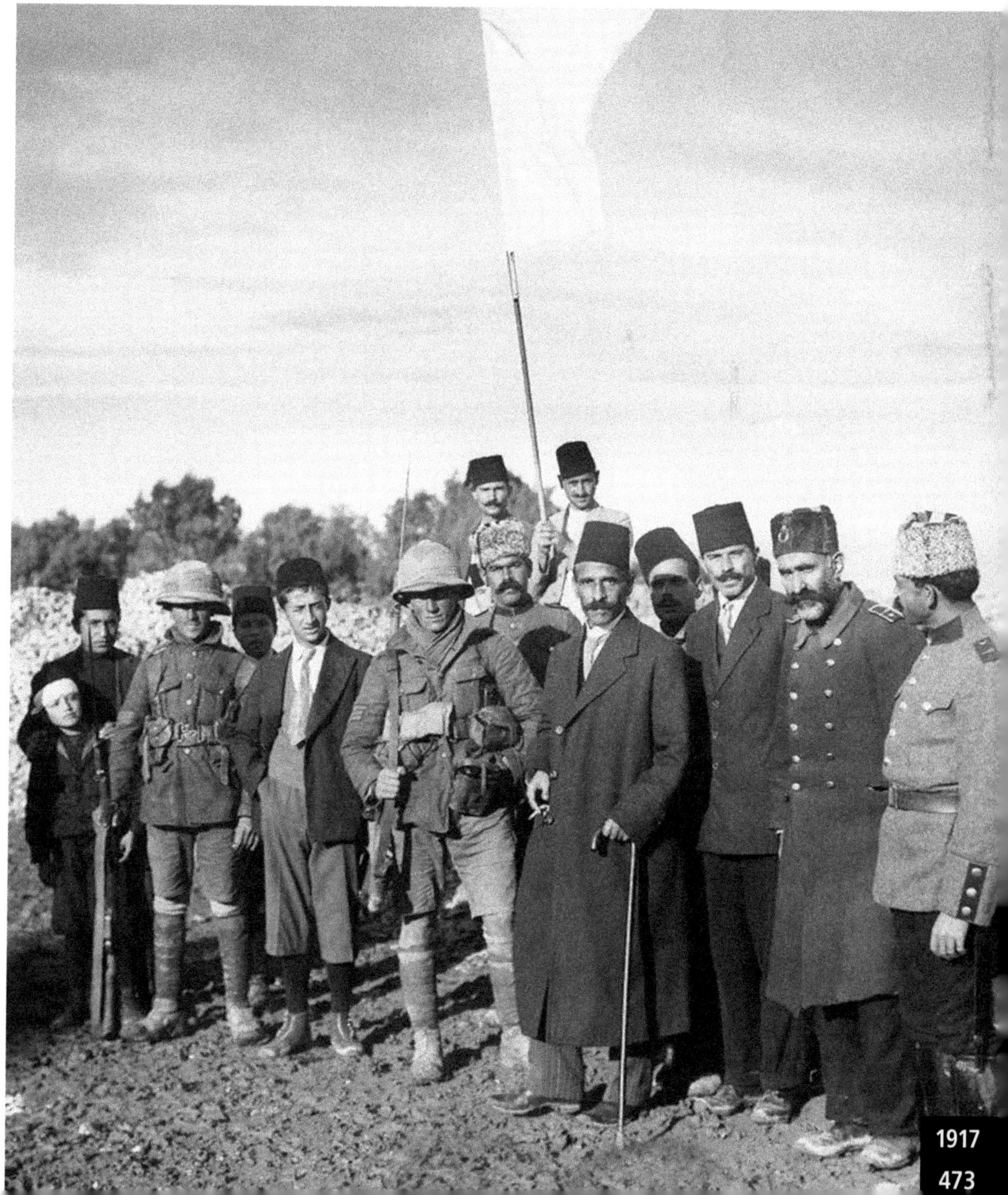

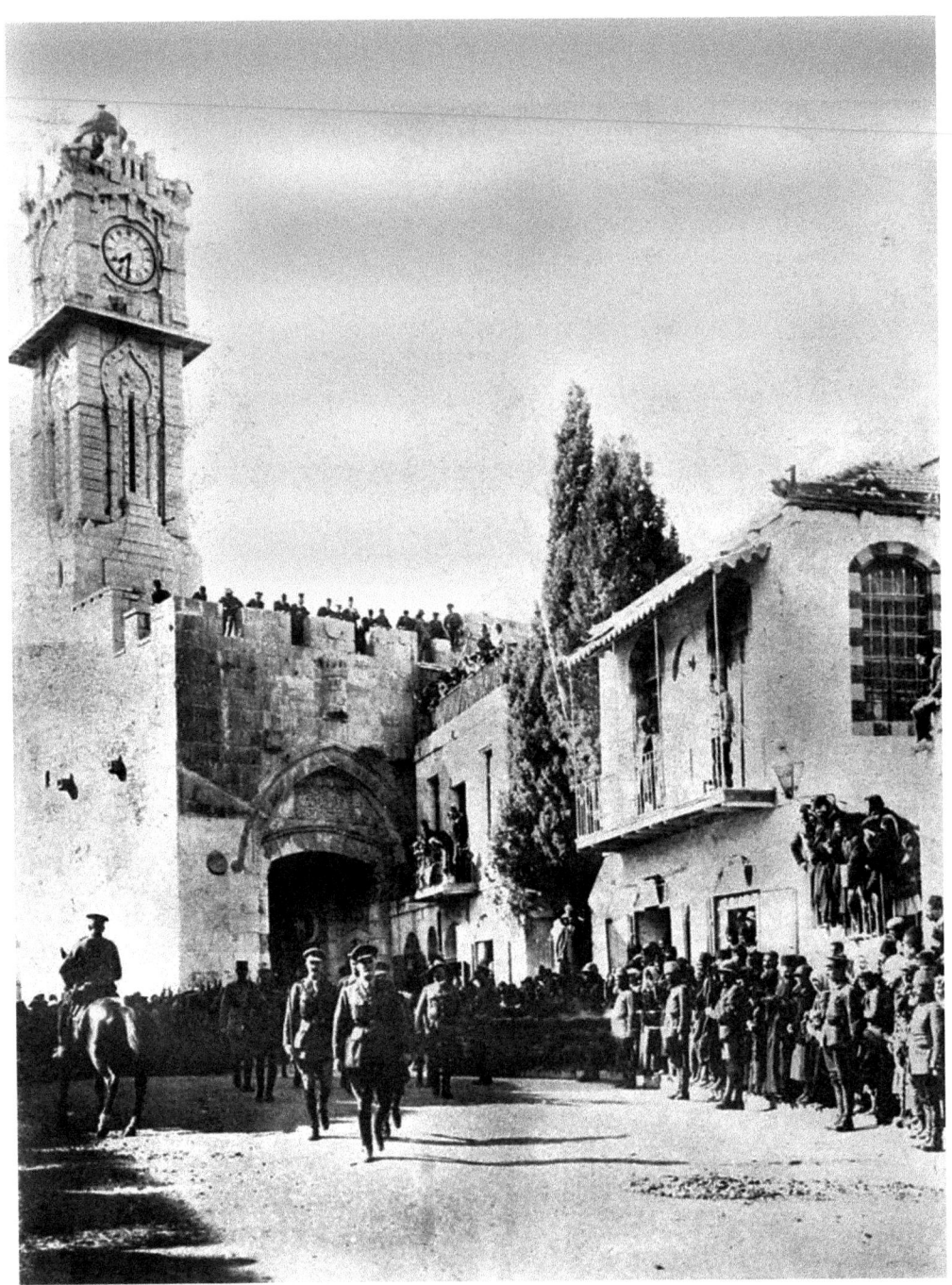

17GW1108 General Allenby enters Jerusalem on foot, 11 December 1917

The Prime Minister of Great Britain, David Lloyd George, described the capture of Jerusalem as 'a Christmas present for the British people'. The capture of the holy city was a great morale boost for the British Empire, whose arms had, along with its Allies, endured a year of military disappointments.

The Great War Illustrated in Focus
by Jon Wilkinson

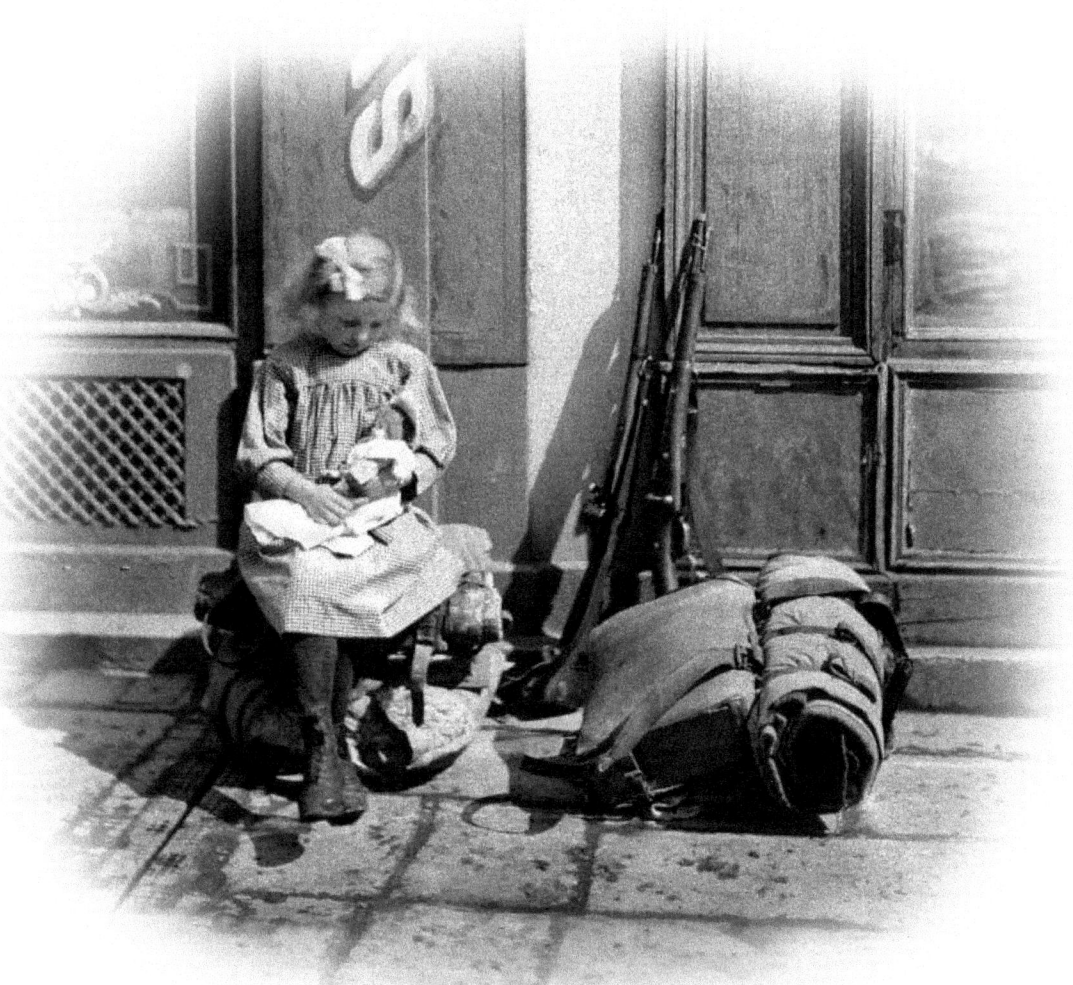

La petite fille avec sa poupée – Reims 1917

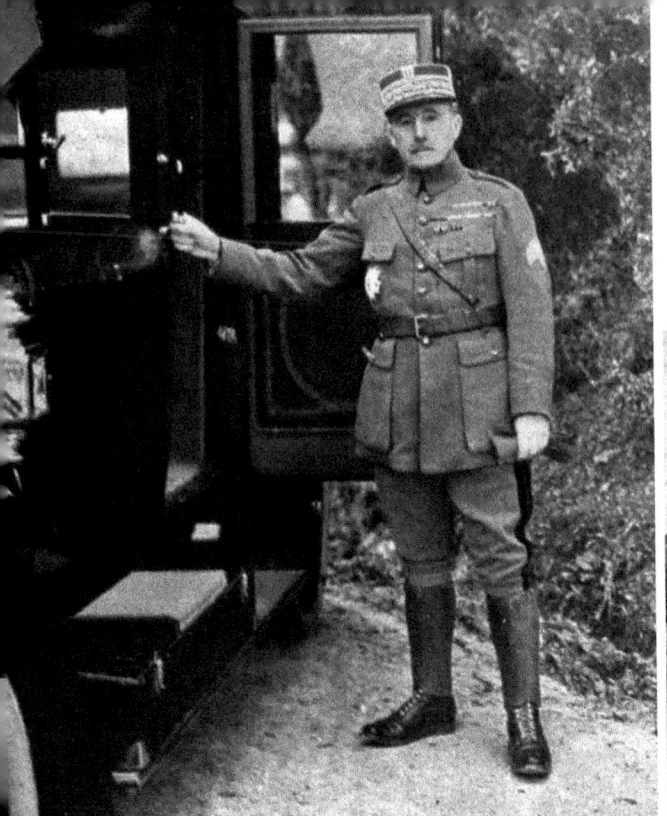

17co02 General Robert Georges Nivelle promised a great victory but instead failed spectacularly and shook the French army into multiple acts of disobedience.

17co03, 17co04, 17co05. The French Cyclone, a 370 mm railway gun (former naval ordnance) being manned and operated by the 320th Artillery Regiment and targeting the German occupied town of Noyon, 5 September 1917. Their large size and limited mobility made railway guns vulnerable to air attack.

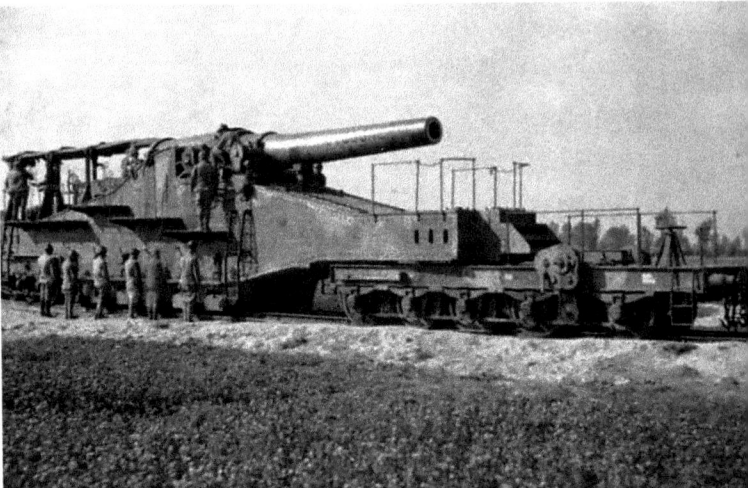

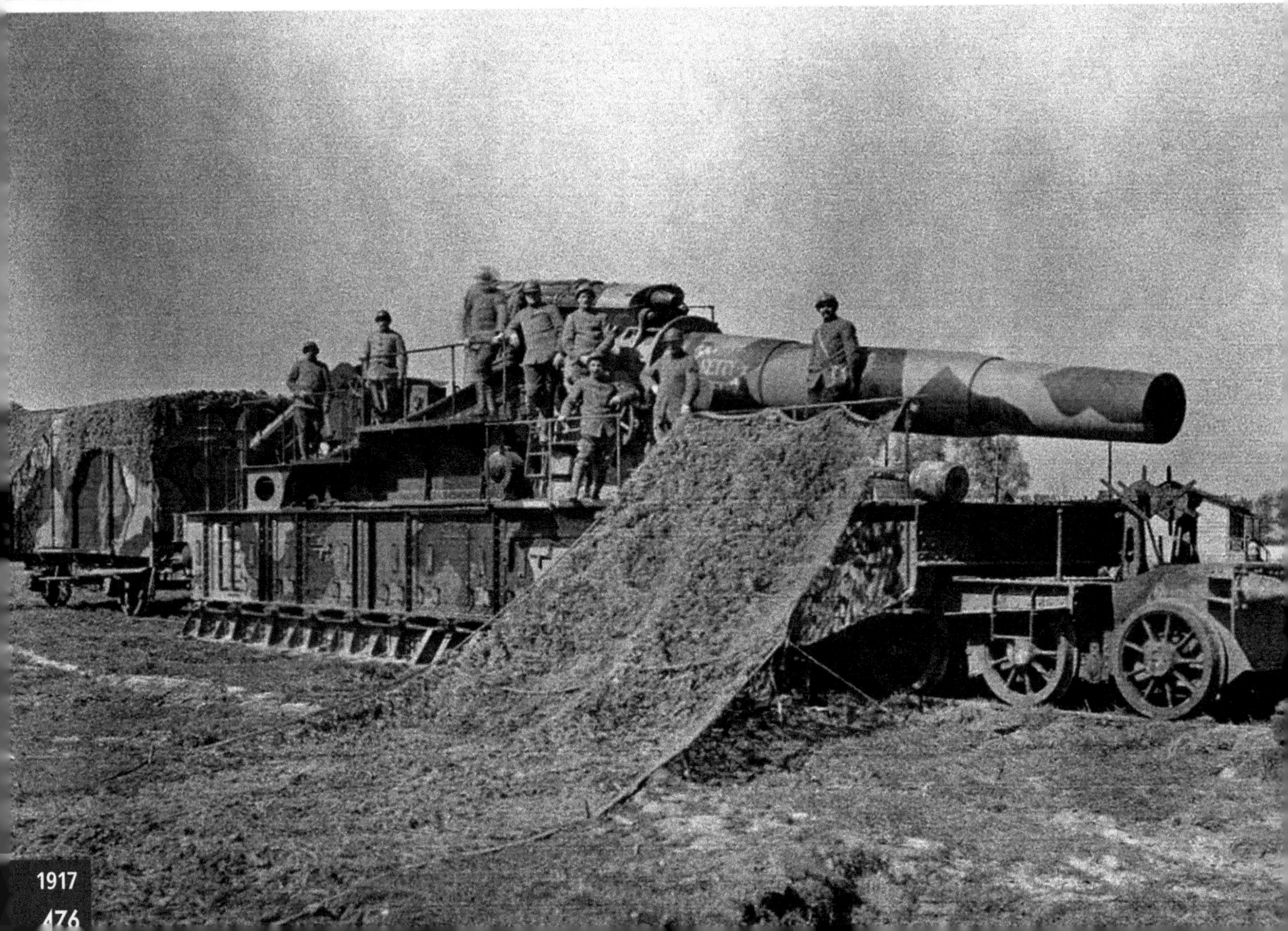

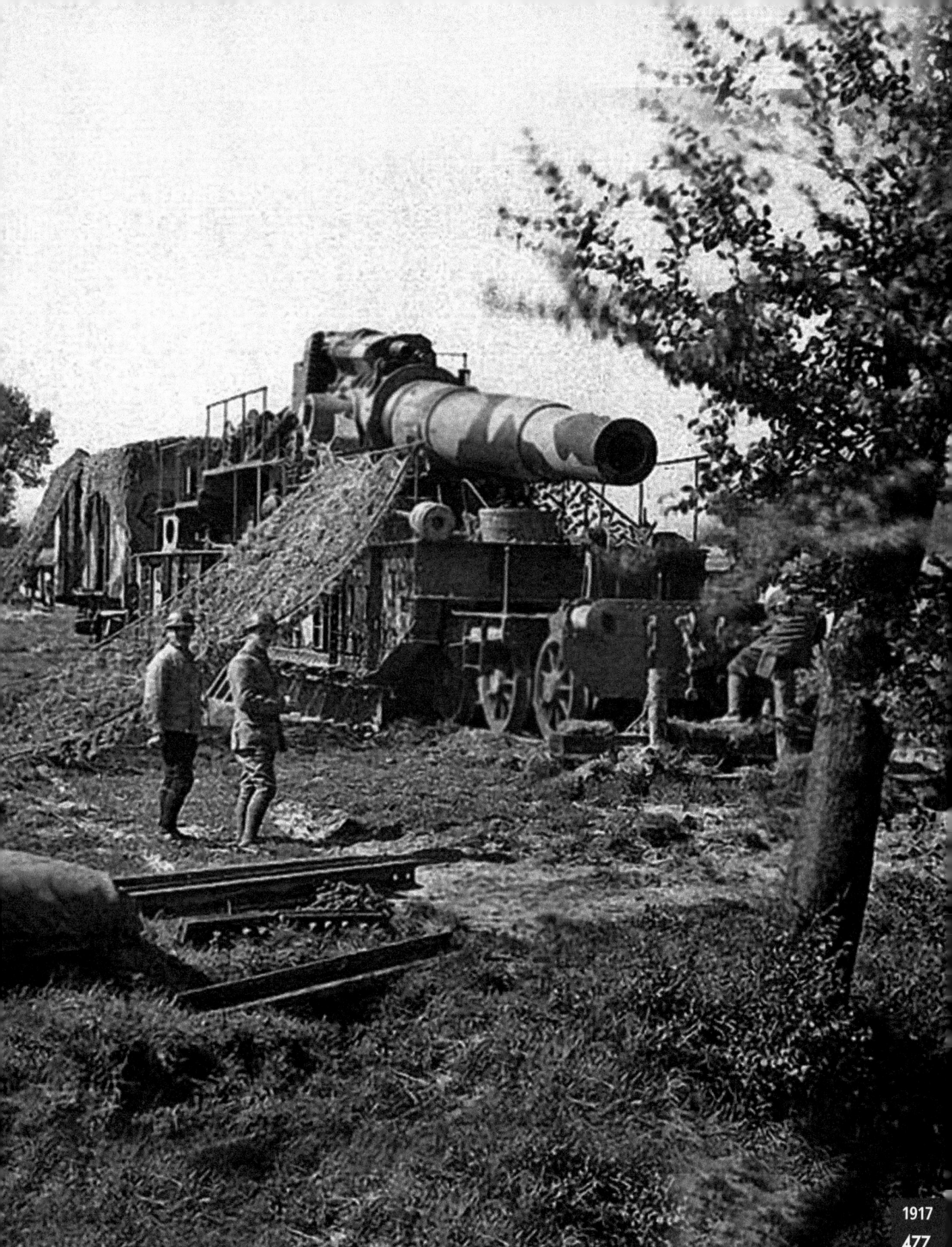

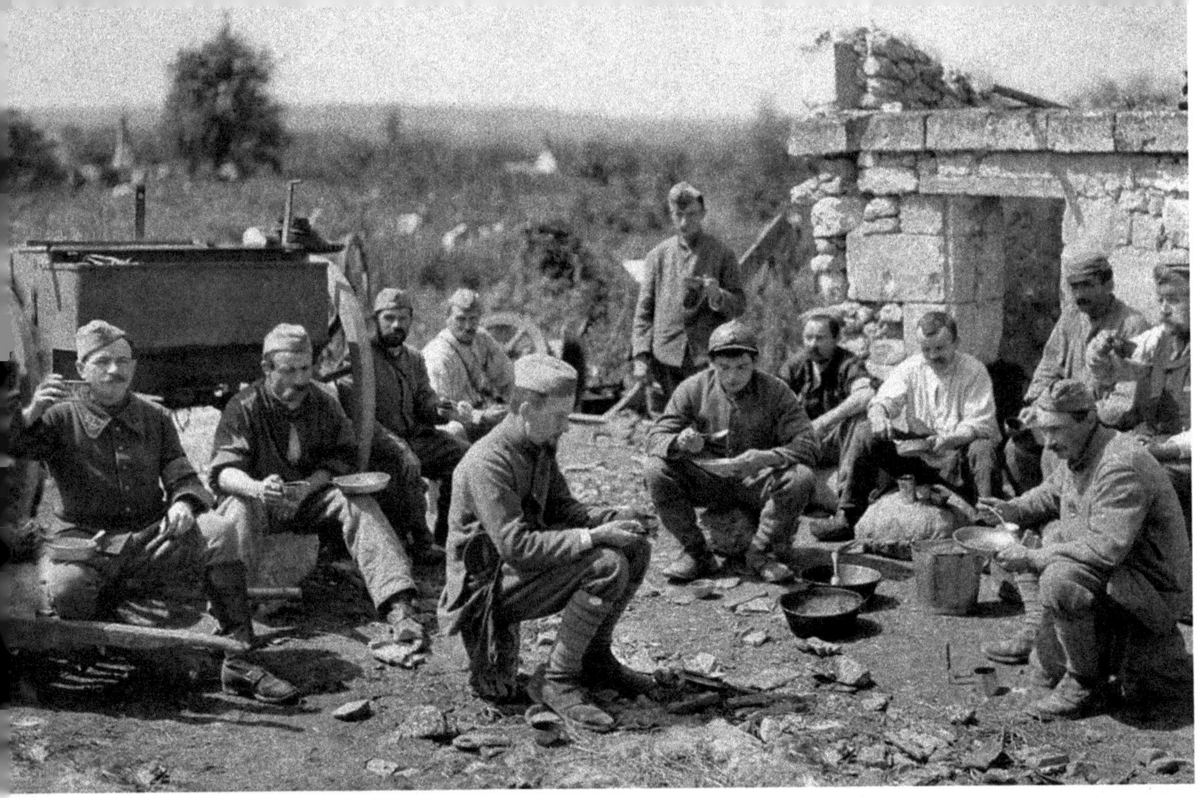

17co07 French soldiers of the 375th Infantry Regiment enjoying a mid-day meal prior to the Nivelle offensive The initial objective of the French attack on the Aisne was to capture the prominent fifty miles long ridge of the Chemin des Dames.

17co08 Confidence in the success of the Nivelle offensive was high among French troops as can be seen in this group at the Chemin des Dames.

17co06 Ruins of the city of Reims, with the Cathedral Notre-Dame de Reims framed by the arch.

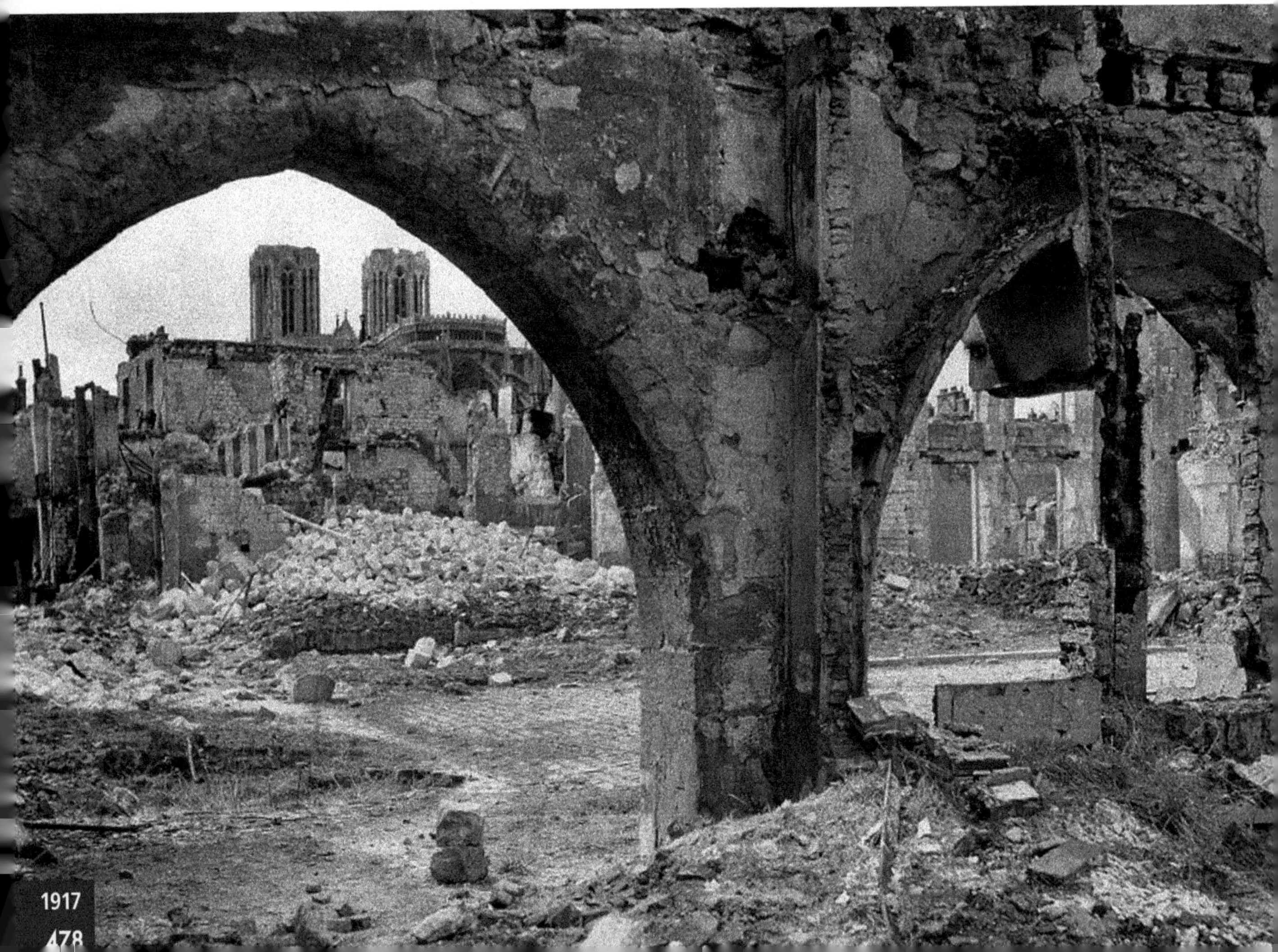

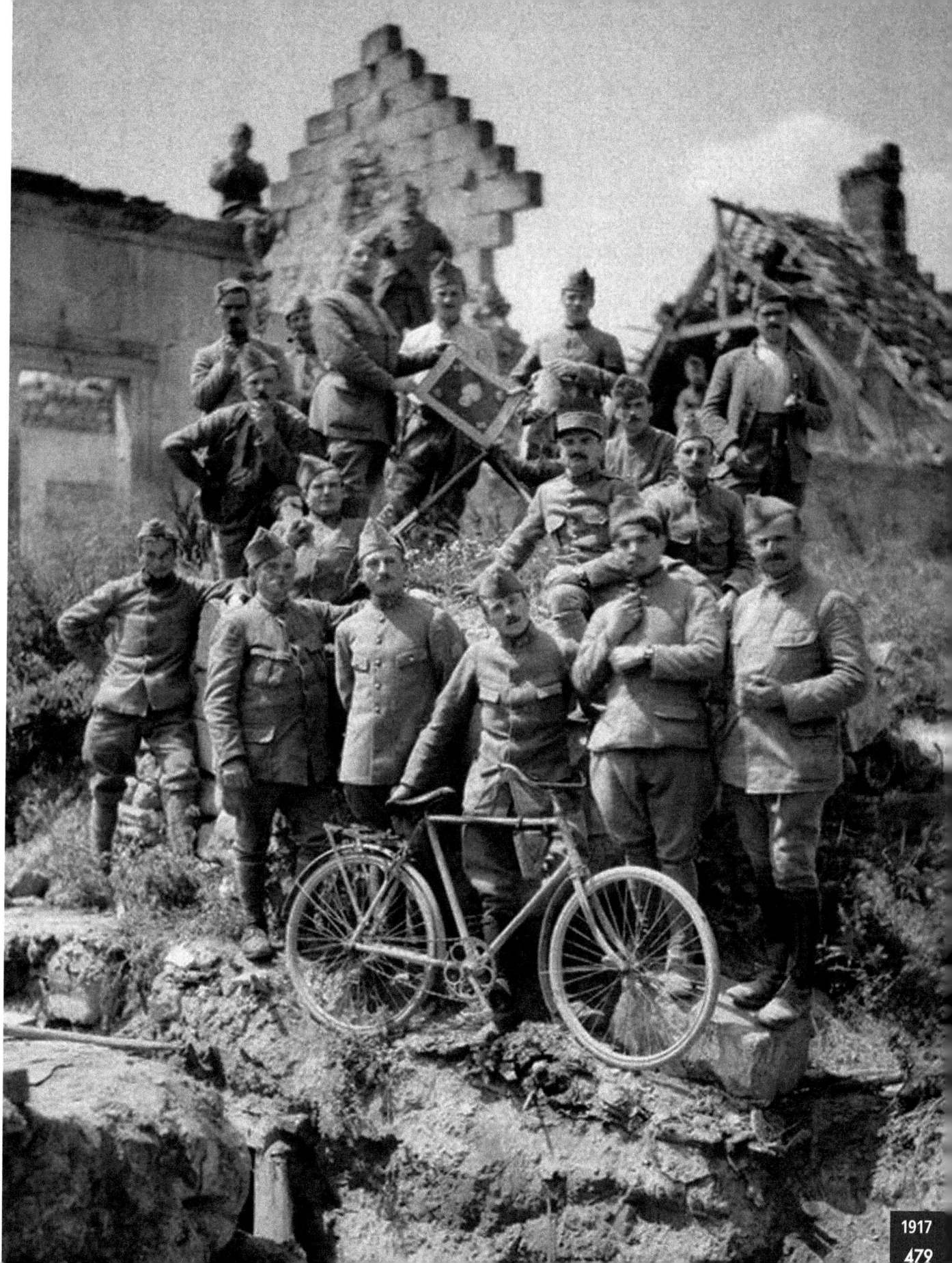

17co10, 17co09. French soldiers at Bucy le Long during the Battle of the Aisne. They are using the St. Étienne Mle 1907 heavy machine gun. The muddy conditions of trench warfare caused this mechanically complex gun to jam frequently. It was difficult to maintain by front-line soldiers and, beginning in 1917, was gradually withdrawn and replaced by the more reliable Hotchkiss 1914 model machine gun.

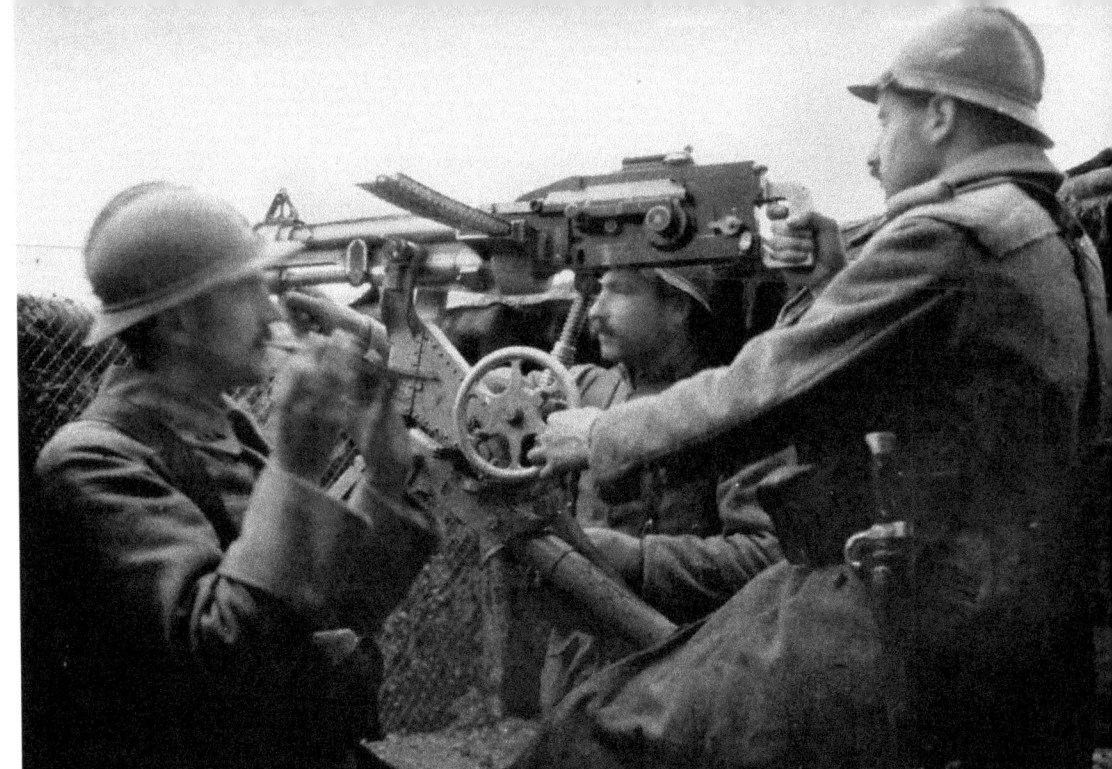

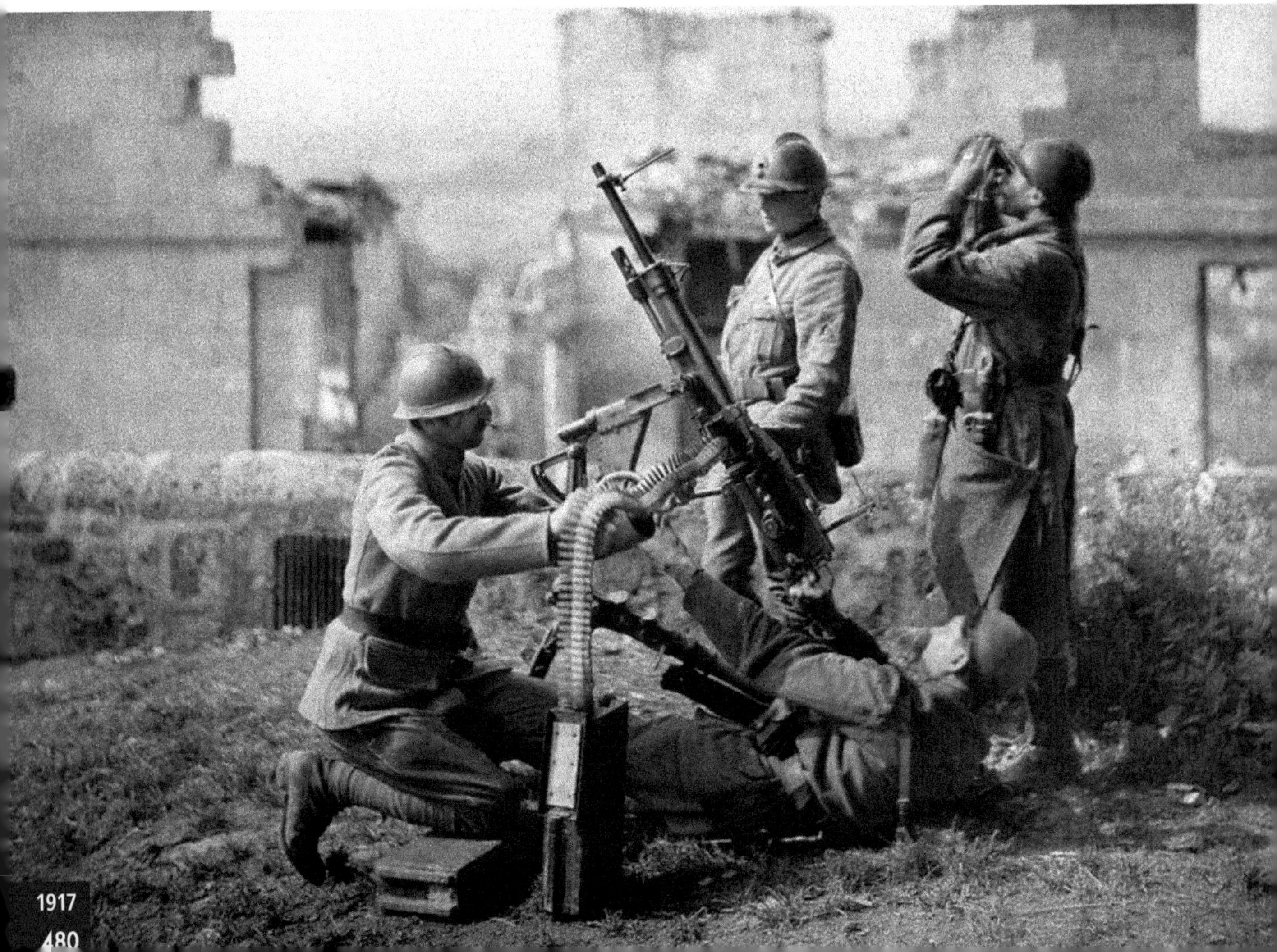

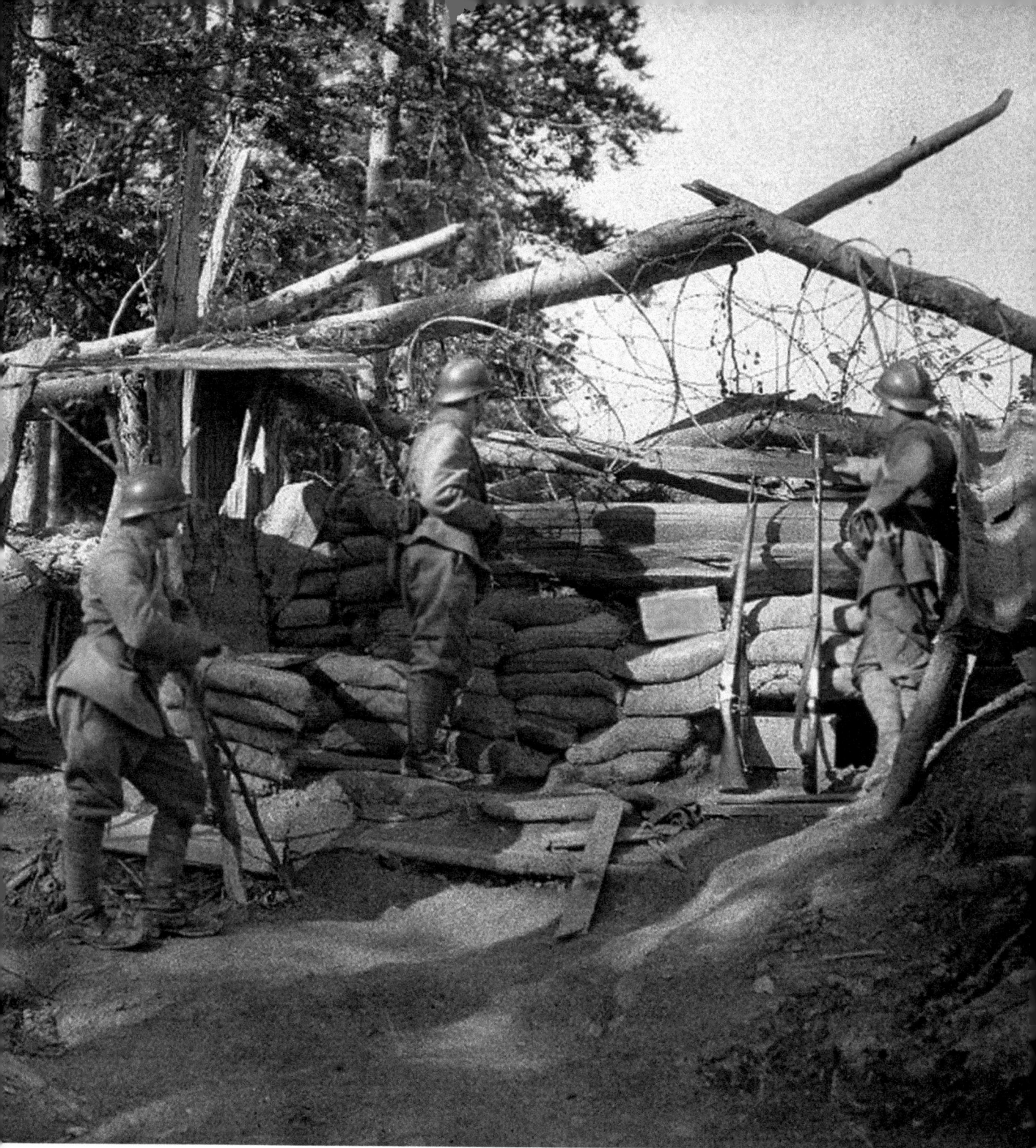
A summer 1917 photograph of a trench barricade close to the German positions at Hirtzbach, a village in Alsace, a region which had historically been the focus of Franco-German rivalry.

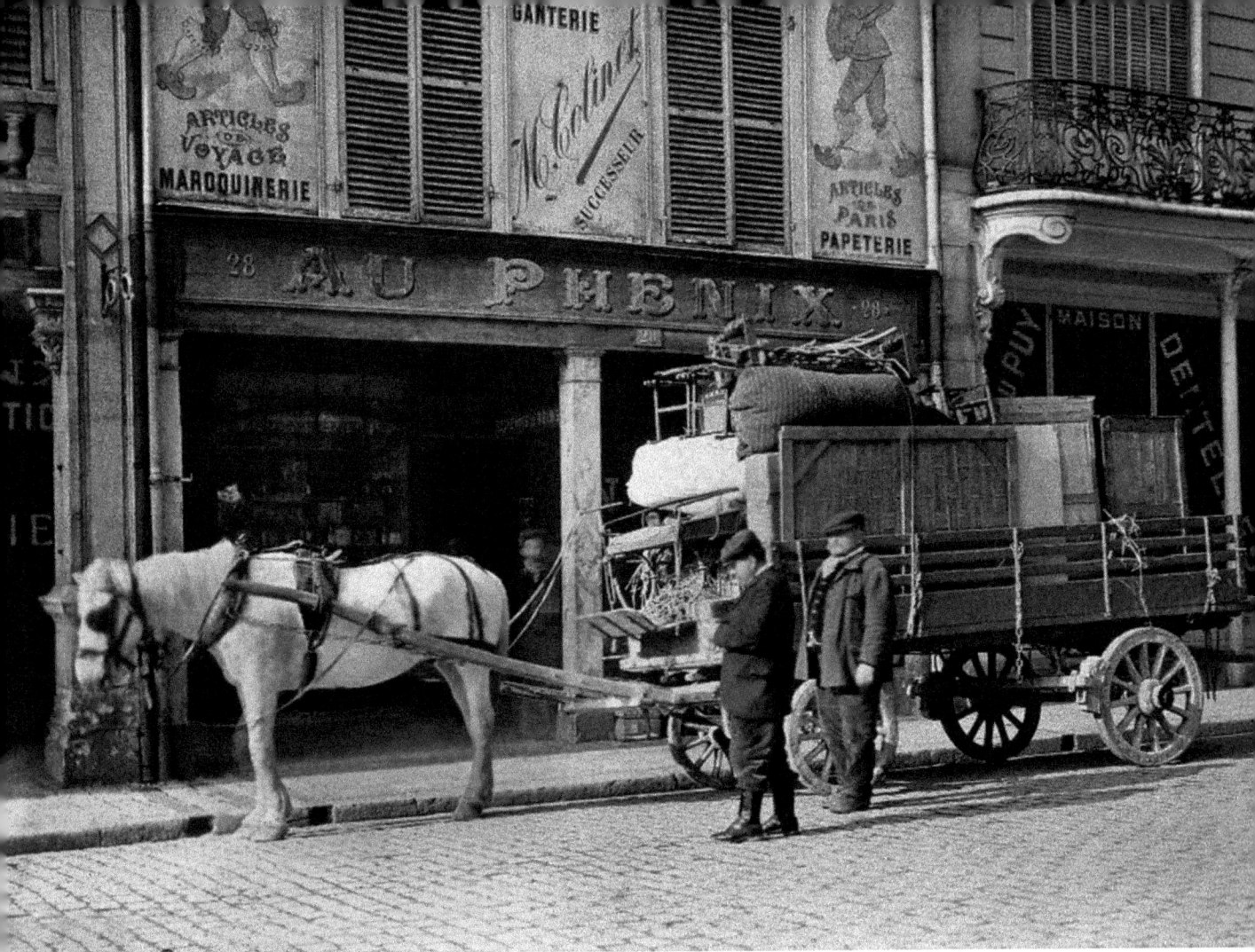

17co12 Many civilian residents (here a shop owner) of Reims packed up and left the city knowing that a large French offensive was about to take place. They also knew the initial objective, the Chemin des Dames Ridge, some fifteen miles north west of the City; many even knew the date to within a day or two. So did the Germans. Utterly inadequate security, which extended as high as Nivelle and his staff, can only have helped produce the dramatic failure of the offensive – despite the use of tanks – against an alert and well prepared enemy.

17co13 Canadian troops at Vimy Ridge.
Easter Monday, 9 April 1917, was chosen by the British to launch the Arras offensive, which, was a huge diversionary attack carried out in the days leading up to the French Nivelle offensive.

The attack on Vimy Ridge, spearheaded by a much reinforced Canadian Corps, was the northernmost sector of the Battle of Arras.

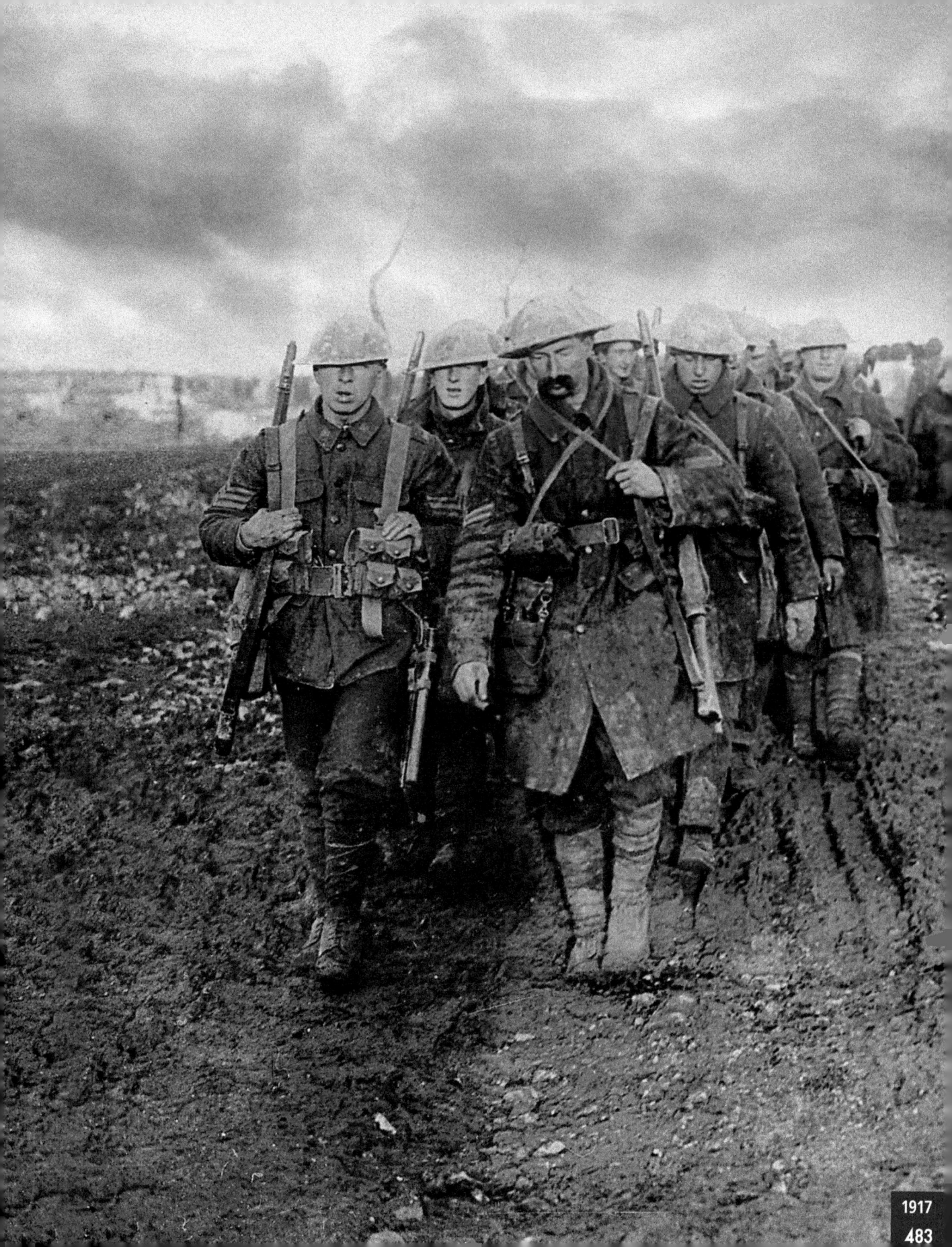

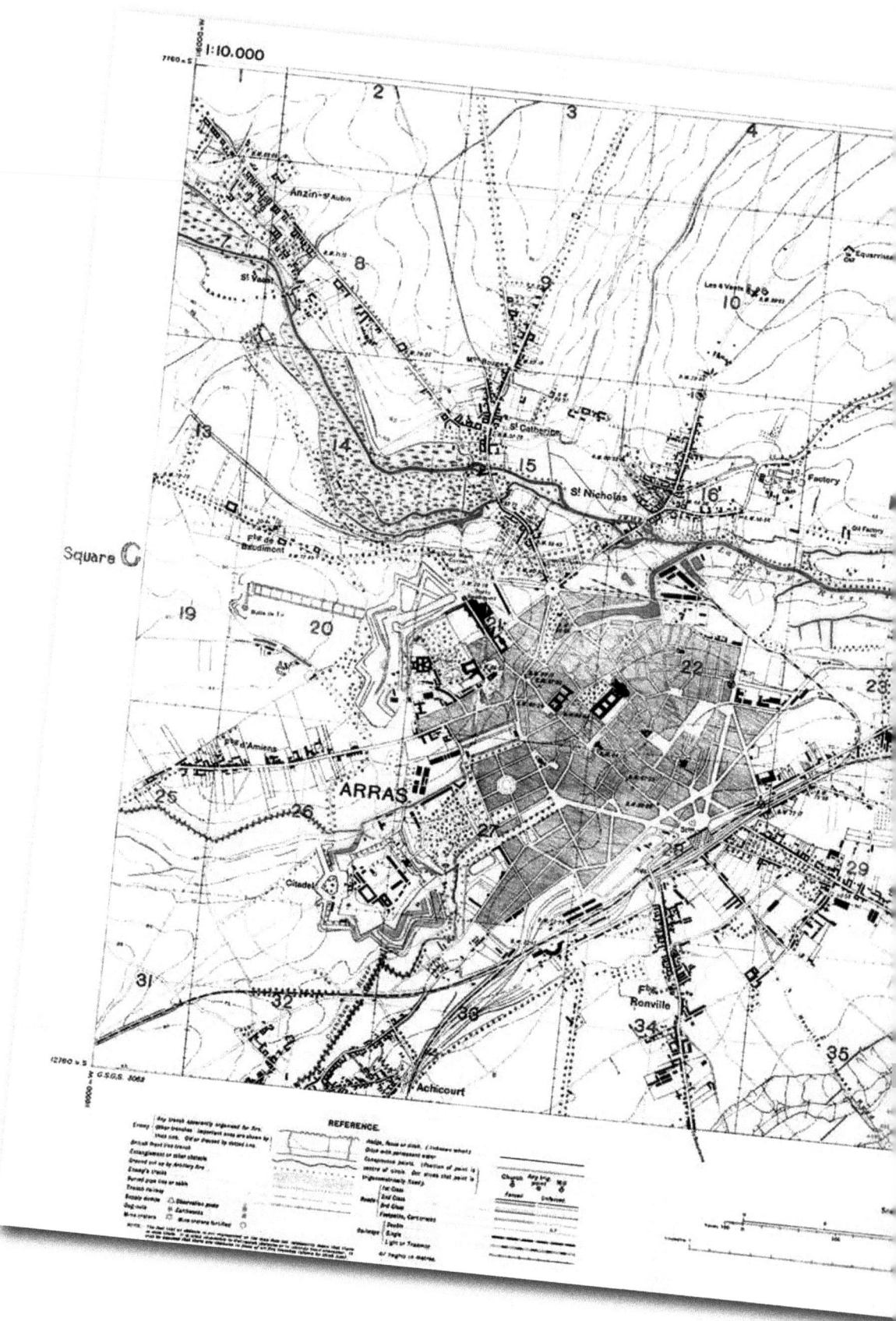

A trench map of Arras and its immediate surrounds: Allied trenches are marked in blue and the German defences in red.

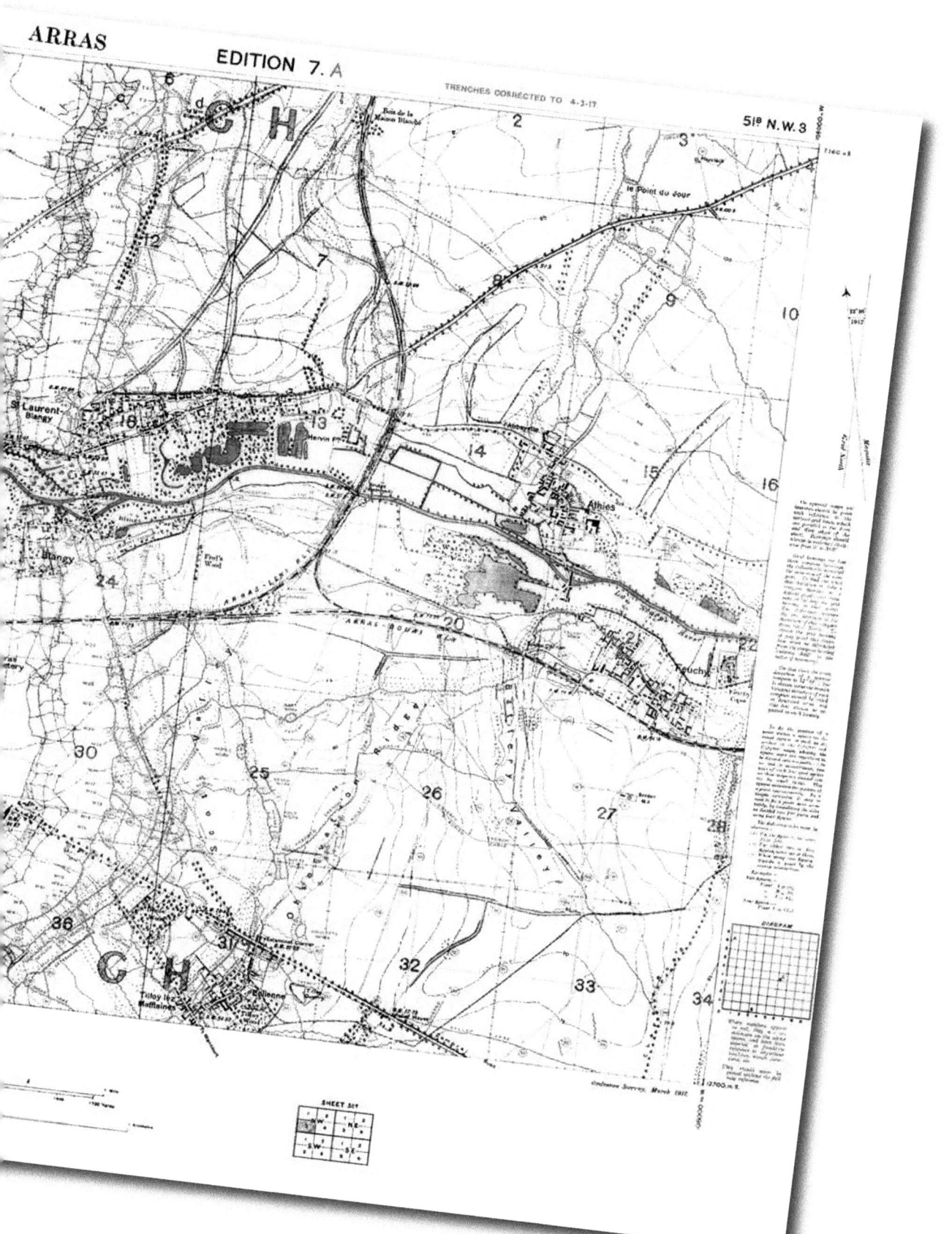

17co14 A Vimy Ridge Barrage map. The Allied trenches are on the right and German lines of defence are on the left. The forty plus lines represent the planned raising of the range of the guns in timed increments to support the attacking Canadian infantry. The fire plan was well executed and largely succeeded in its objective of minimizing an effective German defence.

The Canadian assault on Vimy Ridge was supported by over 1,000 guns of various calibres. The Canadians and supporting British infantry took the ridge in four days, suffering 10,000 casualties.

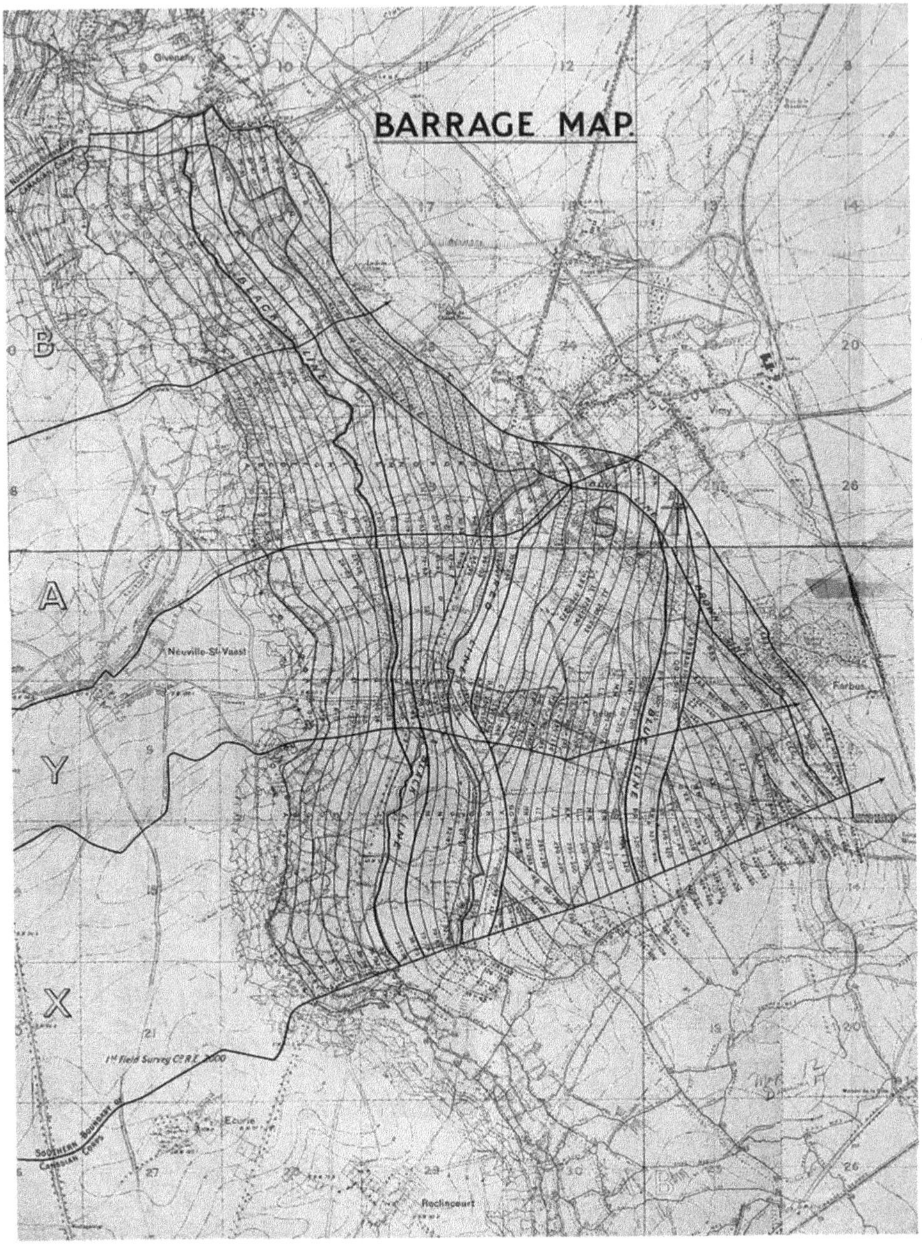

17co15 A battery of 18-pounder field guns being hauled into firing position in increasing muddy conditions as the Arras battlefield succumbed to heavy rain.

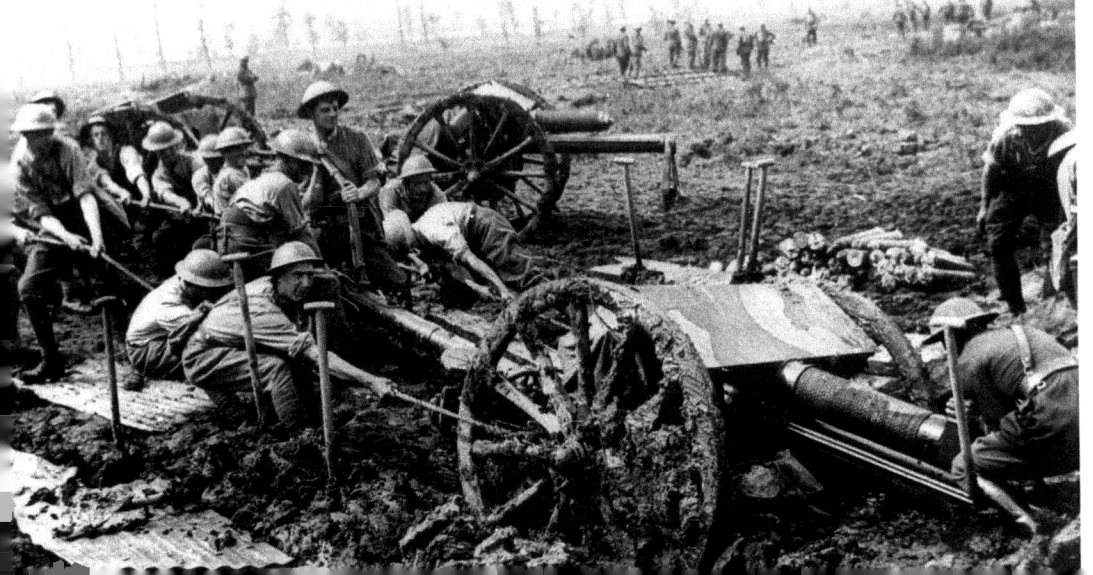

17co16 Royal Engineers fixing scaling ladders in front line trenches, 8 April 1917, the day before the planned infantry assault.

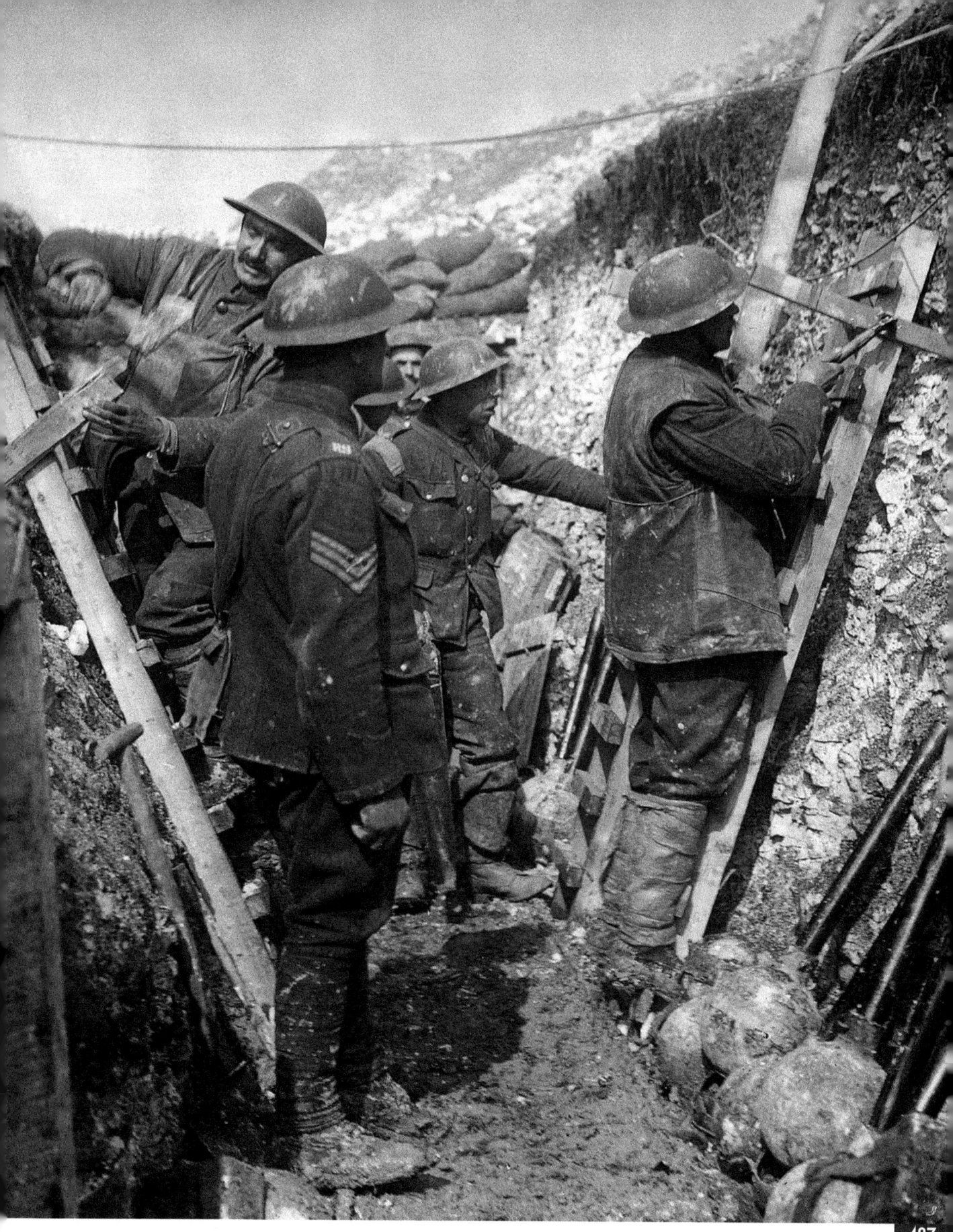

Fighter aces

The term 'Ace' referred to a pilot who achieved five confirmed 'kills' or victories. Along with aircraft development flying aces began to appear, men who, in the main, conducted themselves in a chivalrous manner and were likened to the knights of old. However, in aerial combat they were often extremely ruthless.

In March 1917, with the arrival at the Front of the 'Red Baron', Manfred von Richthofen, with his experienced and better equipped *Jagdstaffel – Jasta 11* (Richthofen's Flying Circus), losses of Allied pilots increased. April 1917 was to become known in the RFC as 'Bloody April'.

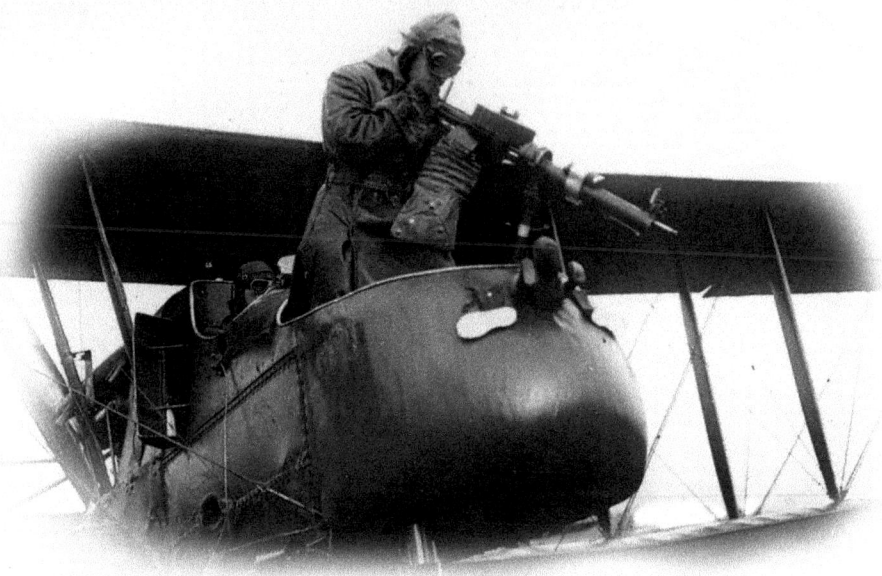

17GW365 Max Immelmann scored 15 kills before he fell in June 1916. He was the first German flying ace. A pioneer in fighter tactics, he originated an aerial combat manoeuvre that was associated with his name.

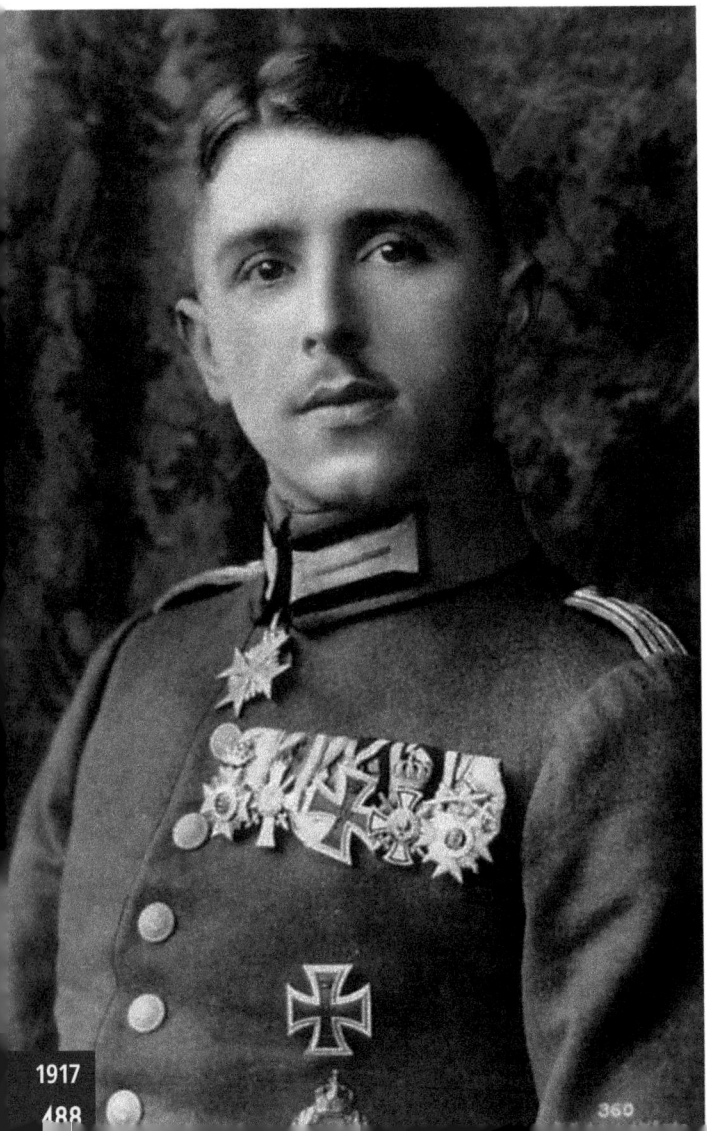

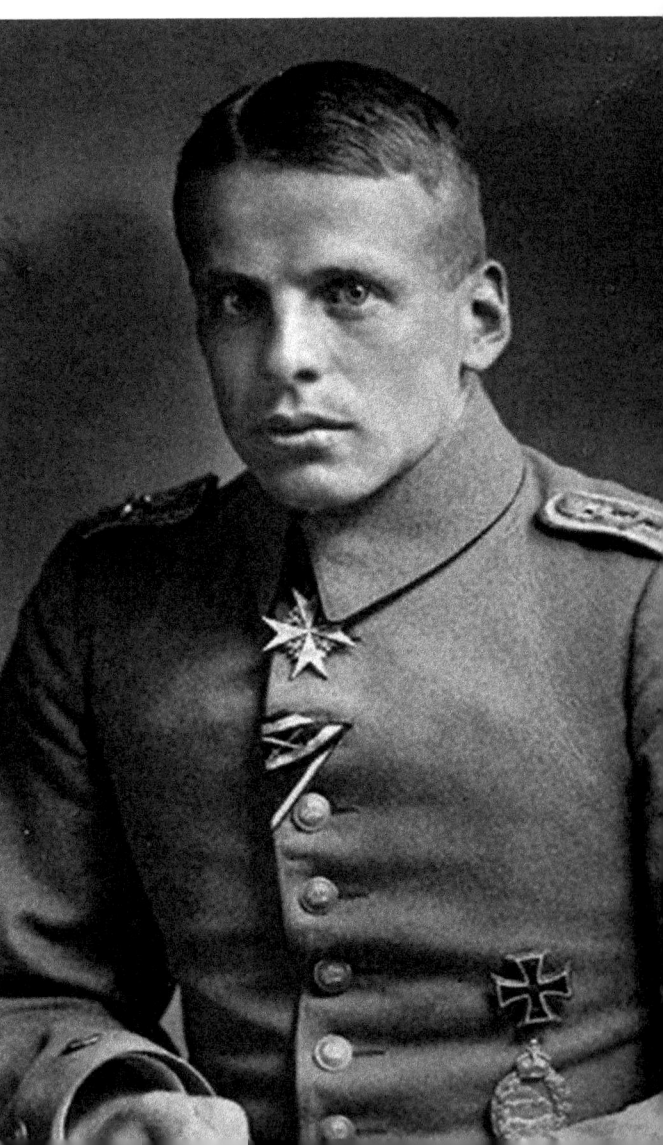

17co18 Oswald Boelke scored 40 kills. Died October 1916.

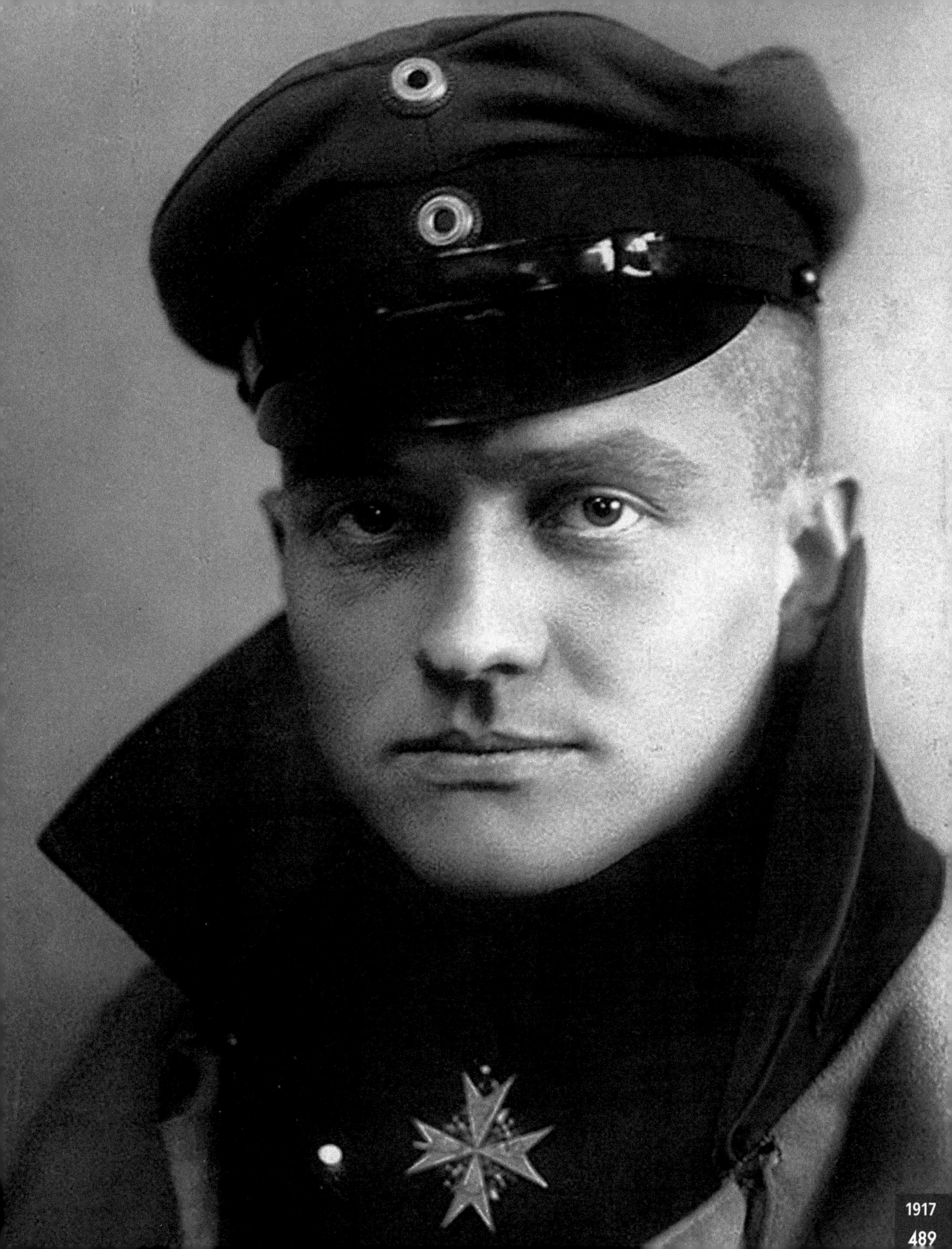

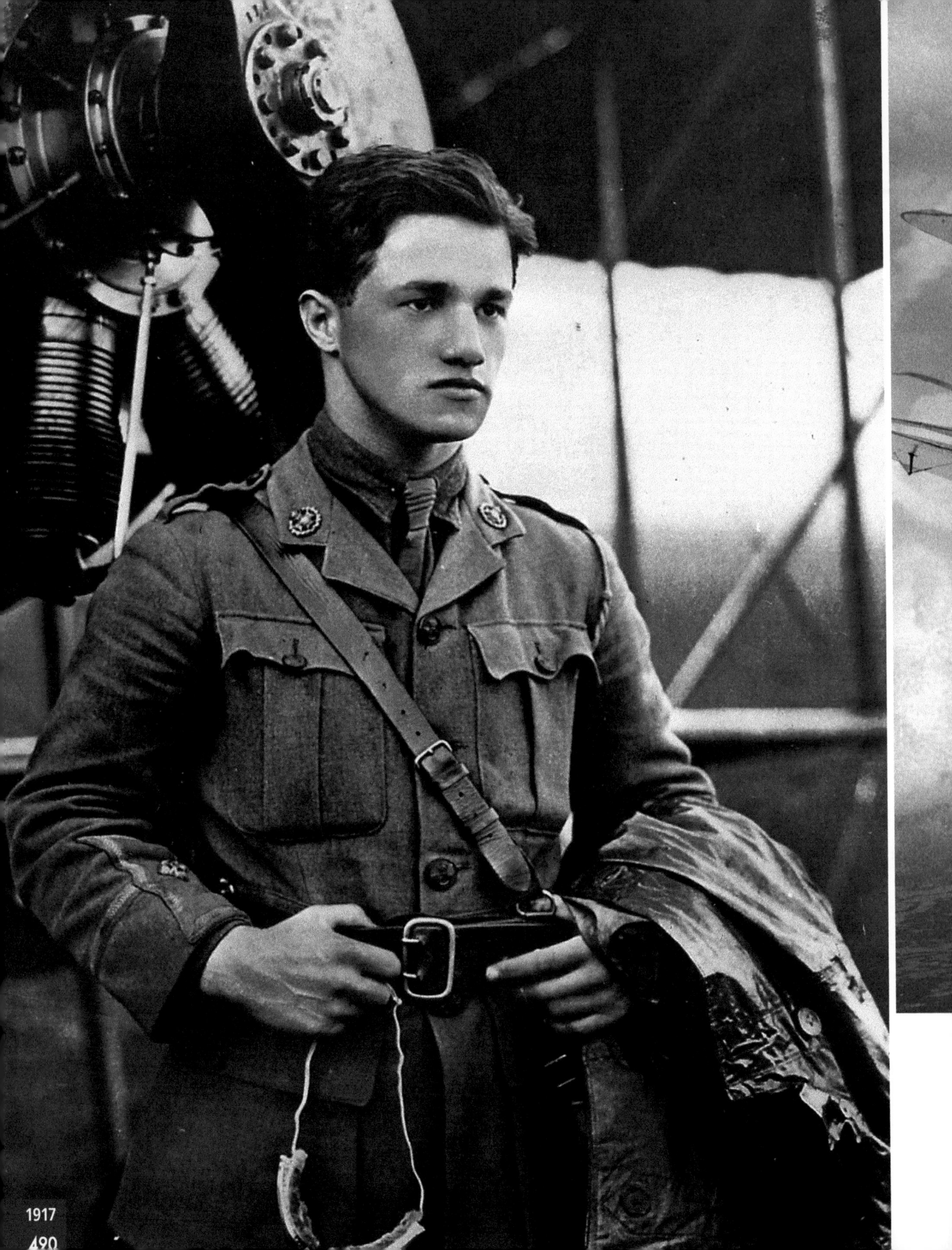

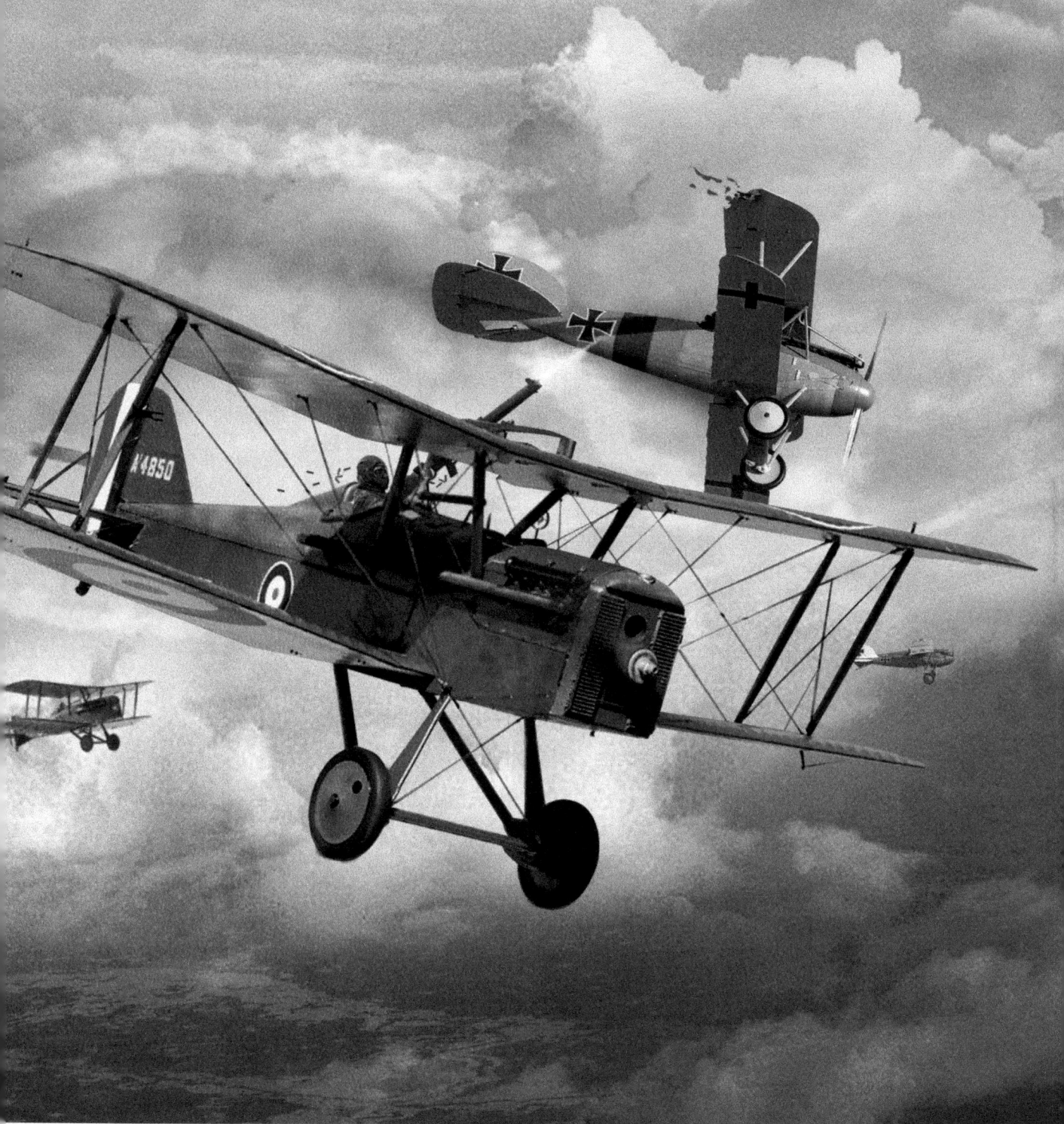

17co21 Albert Ball, VC, DSO and Two Bars, MC.
17co22 Ball's final action is depicted here, with Ball firing at the Albatros flown by Lothar von Richtofen, the Red Baron's brother. At the time of his death, on 7 May 1917, he was the United Kingdom's leading flying ace, with 44 kills. He remained its fourth highest scorer, behind Edward Mannock, James McCudden, and George McElroy. He was awarded the Victoria Cross posthumously for his 'most conspicuous and consistent bravery in action from 25 April to 6 May 1917'.

On the evening of 7 May 1917, near Douai, eleven fighters from No. 56 Squadron, led by Ball in an S.E.5, encountered German fighters from *Jasta 11*. A running dogfight in deteriorating visibility took place. Ball was last seen by fellow pilots pursuing the Albatros D.III of the Red Baron's younger brother, Lothar von Richtofen, who eventually landed near Annœullin with a punctured fuel tank. Ball was observed flying into a thundercloud. A German pilot officer on the ground, Lieutenant Hailer, saw Ball's plane dropping inverted from beneath the cloud with a stopped engine. The Germans reported that there was no battle damage evident on the crashed machine. Neither were bullet wounds found on Ball's body, he had been killed by the impact when the plane hit the ground.

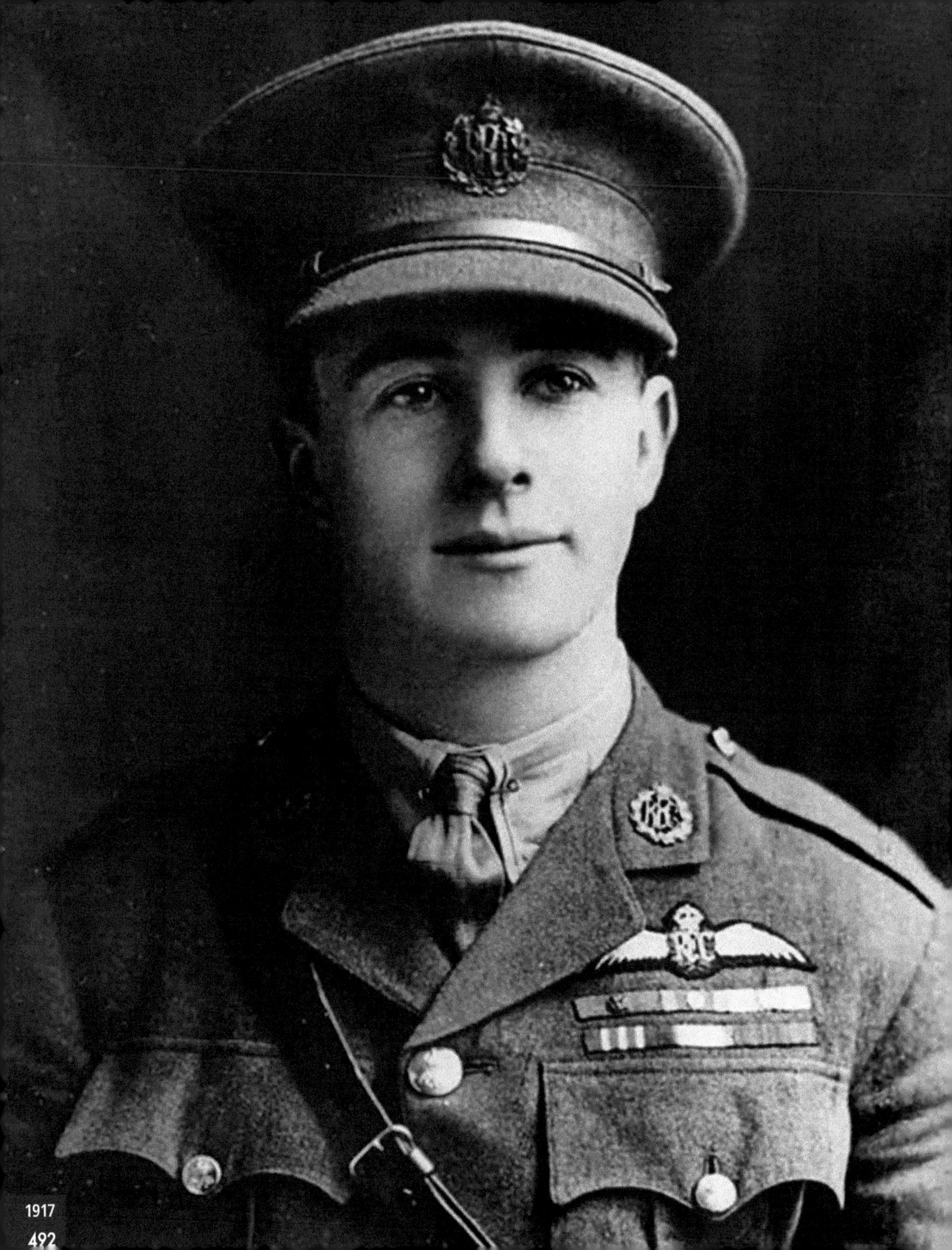

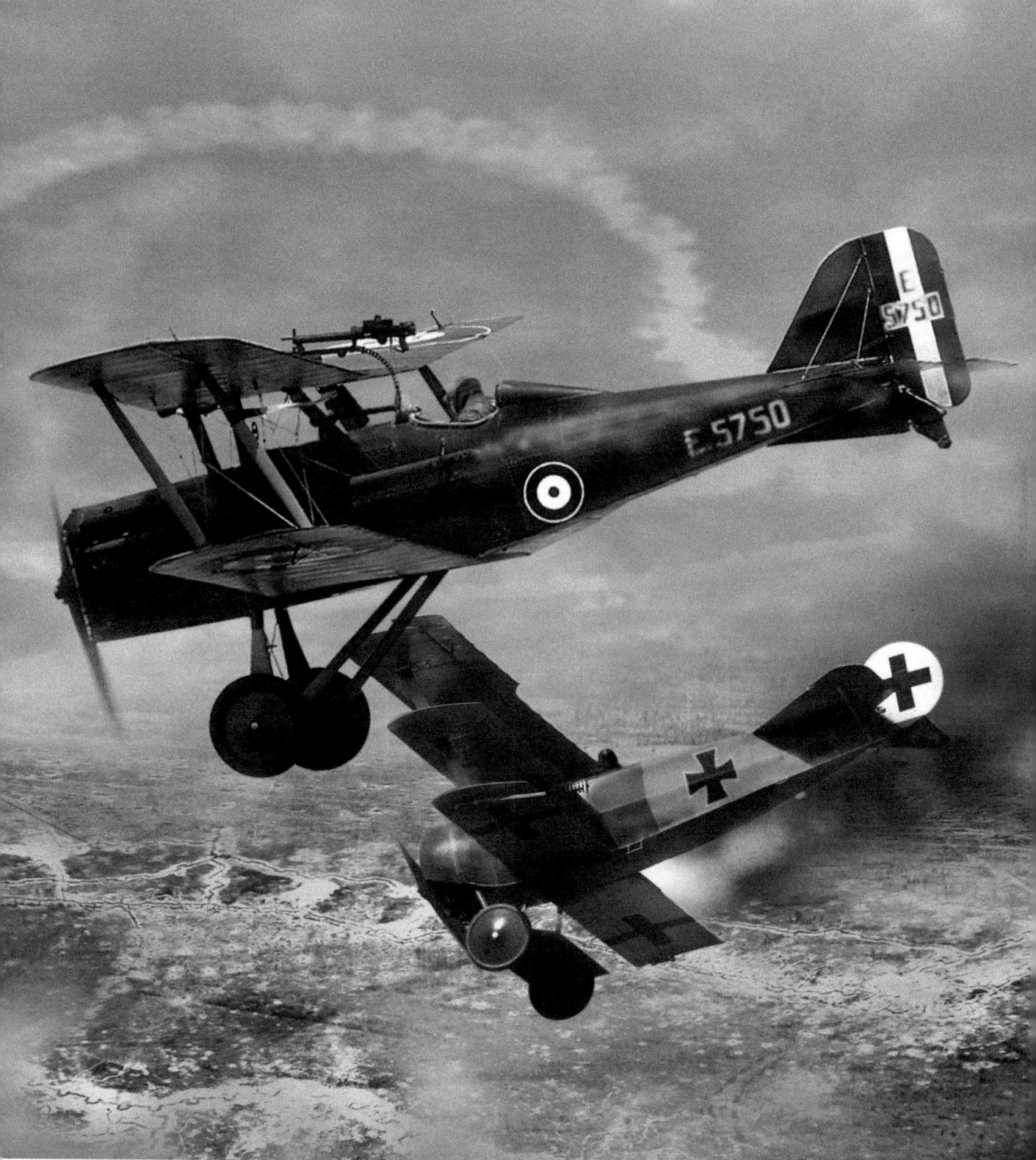

17co23 James Thomas Byford McCudden, VC, DSO and Bar, MC and Bar, MM, CdeG. Credited with 57 kills.

He was seventh on the list of the war's most successful aces. The majority of his successes were achieved with 56 Squadron RFC, while flying the SE5a. McCudden at one stage achieved nine kills in only six days. On 2 April 1918 he was awarded the Victoria Cross. The citation in the *London Gazette* reads: *For most conspicuous bravery, exceptional perseverance, keenness, and very high devotion to duty*. During a routine flight from England to France, 9 July 1918, Major McCudden VC was killed in a flying accident.

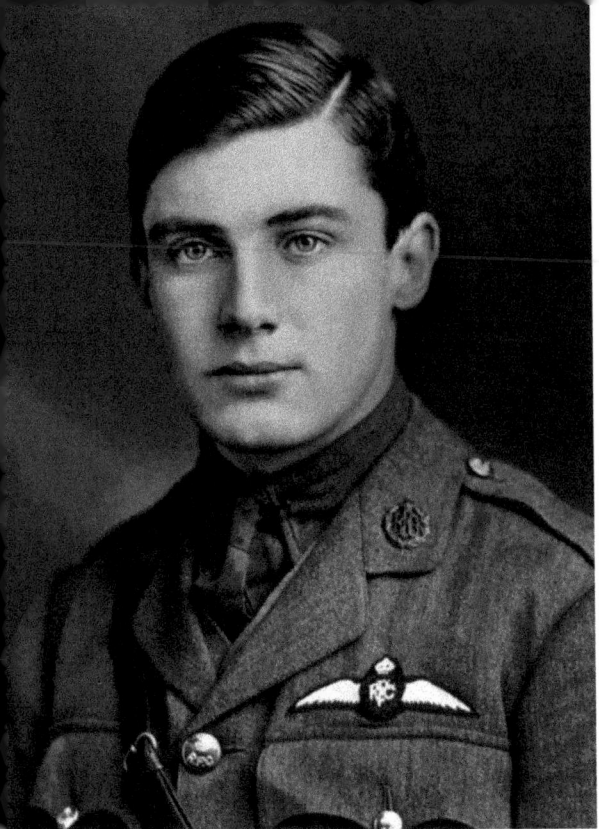

17GW584 Arthur Percival Foley Rhys-Davids was an ace of No. 56 Squadron RFC and had 23 kills. In September 1917 he was involved in a dogfight with German ace Werner Voss, commander of *Jasta 10*, part of Richthofen's Circus, who shot him down, killing him.

It is often considered to be the most famous air action of the war.

'If only I could have brought him down alive!'
Rhys-Davids

As long as I live I shall never forget my admiration for that German pilot, who single-handed fought seven of us for ten minutes and also put some bullets through all our machines. His flying was wonderful, his courage magnificent, and in my opinion he was the bravest German airman whom it has been my privilege to see fight.

McCudden

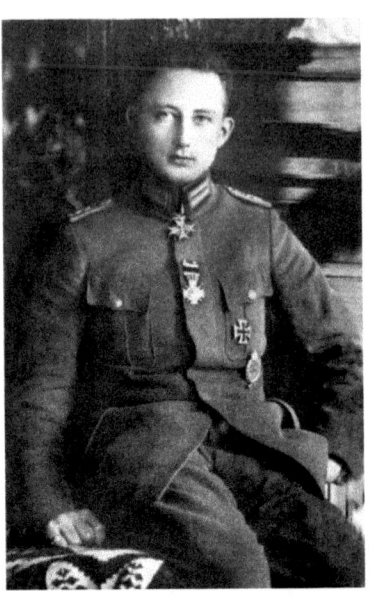

17co27 Probably the most famous aerial engagement of the war – the moment when Werner Voss dives away, his engine stopped, is depicted.

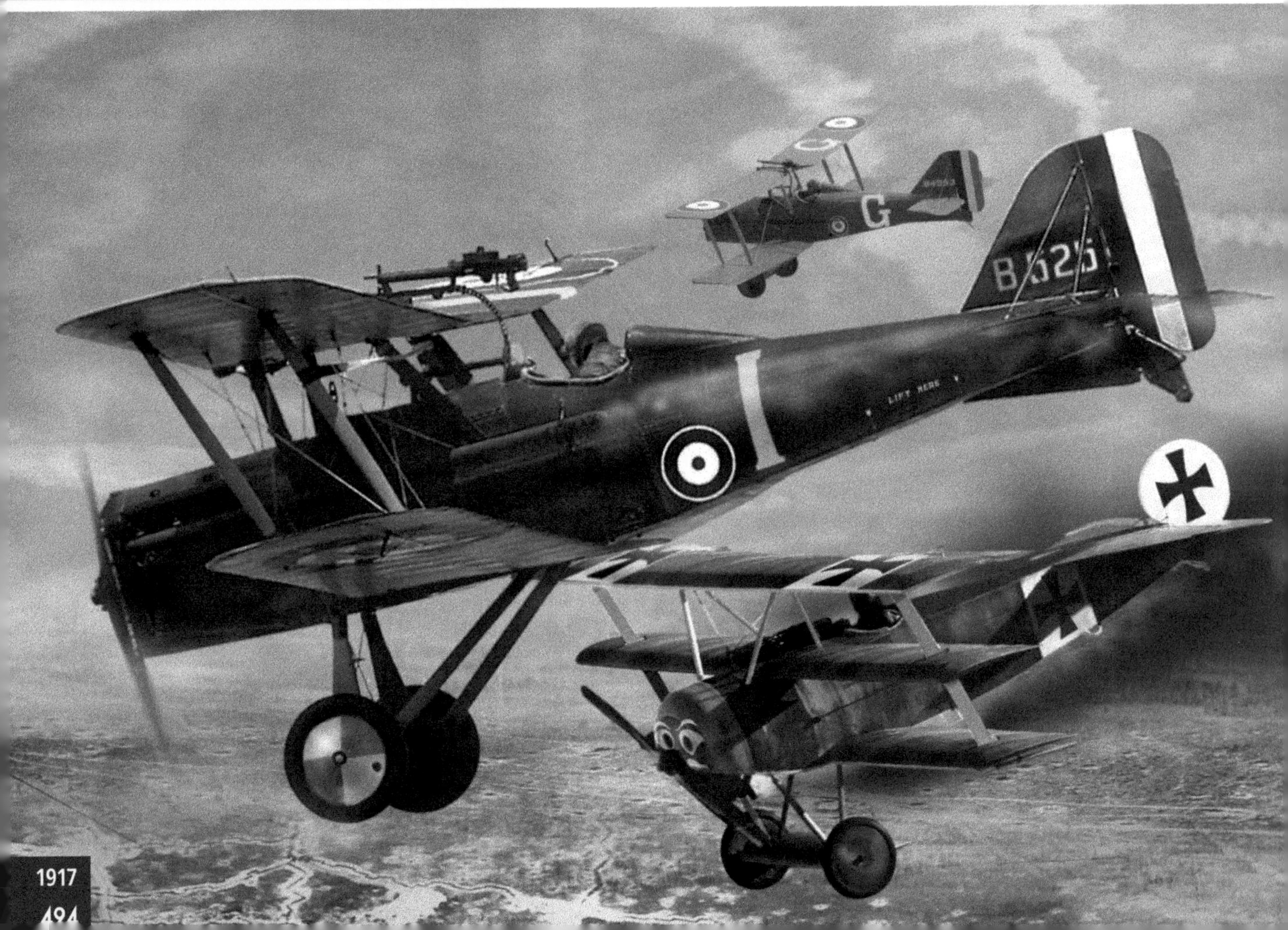

The mysterious killer of Huns, Captain X

The Royal Flying Corps, unlike the Germans, which promoted their air heroes, had a policy of keeping their pilots' identities firmly under wraps, believing it to be more useful to promote a squadron's team effort rather than any individual's glory. The effect was that while photos and stories of the Red Baron appeared in newspapers worldwide, in Britain the leading kills scorer, Major 'Mick' Mannock, or the mysterious 'Captain X', as the press referred to him, was virtually unknown until the policy gradually changed.

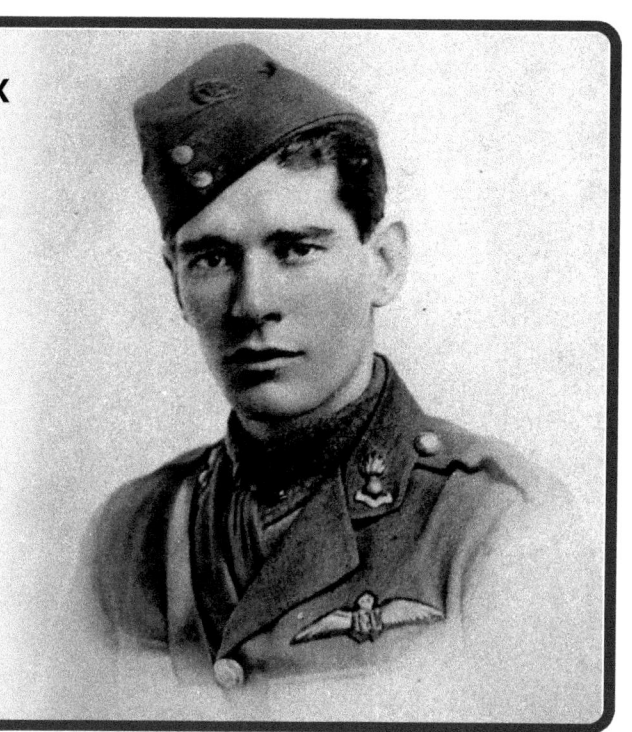

17GW503 Edward Corringham Mick Mannock VC, DSO and 2 Bars, MC and Bar.
Mannock was the highest scoring British ace, with 73 kills. He was driven by hatred for the 'Hun' and when officers of his squadron proposed a toast to the memory of 'a chivalrous foe' – the Red Baron – he walked out of the mess, muttering 'I hope he roasted all the way down'.

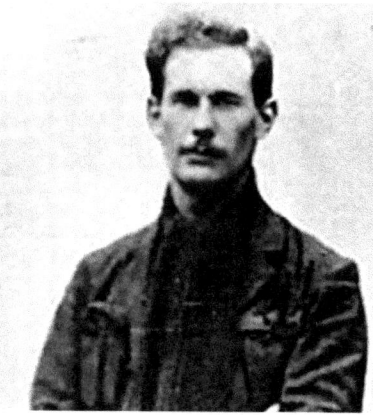

17co28 Final action of Duncan William Grinnell-Milne, eleven days before the war ended. He had escaped from a prisoner of war camp to fight again.

Following his first kill, in 1915 Grinnell-Milne was shot down and spent two years in a PoW camp in Germany. He escaped from captivity and made his way back to England. Grinnell-Milne returned to aerial combat with No. 56 Squadron RAF, flying the SE.5a. On 5 October 1918 he destroyed a balloon south-west of Busigny. On 21 October he destroyed a Fokker D.VII north of Bousies. Over Mormal Wood on 29 October he forced down two more D.VIIs. Then on 3 November 1918 he destroyed his fifth and final aircraft, another D.VII, north-east of Valenciennes.
Duncan William Grinnell-Milne MC, DFC* was credited with six confirmed aerial victories.

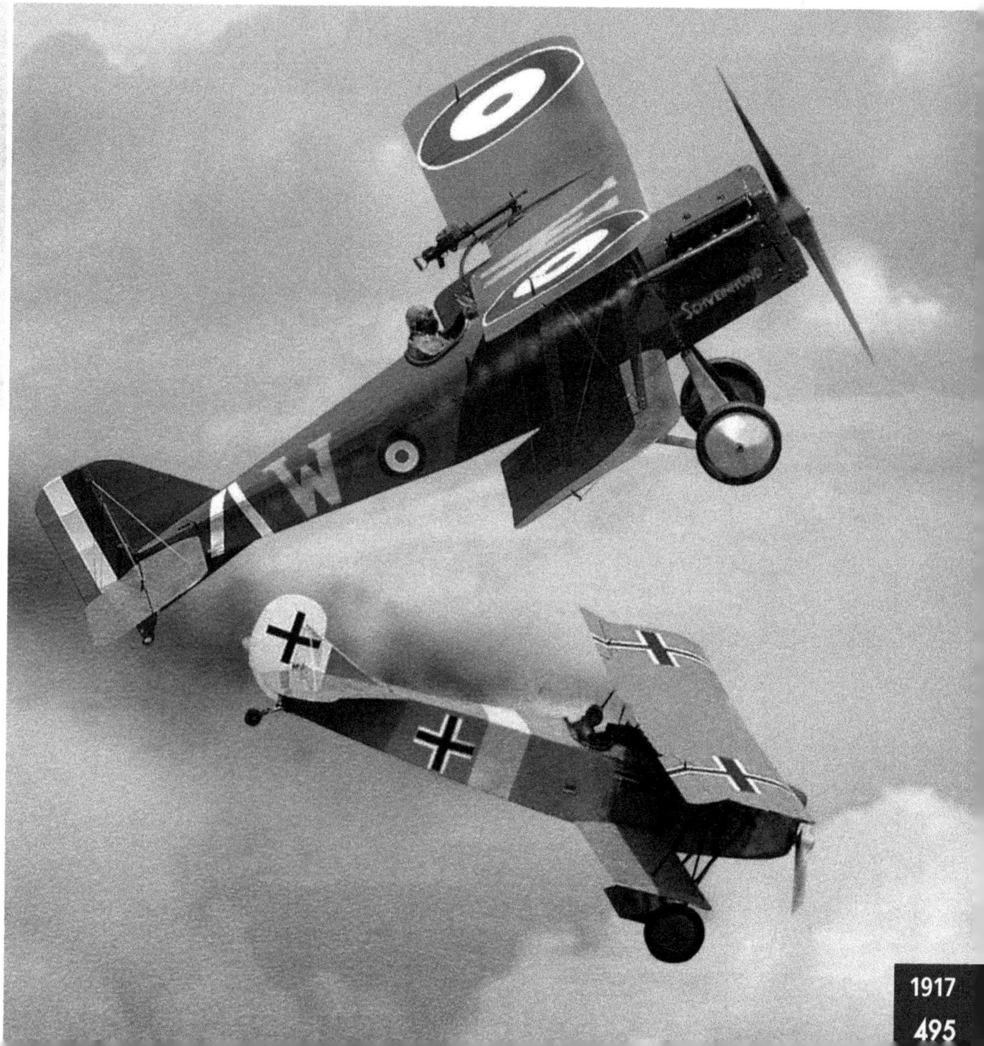

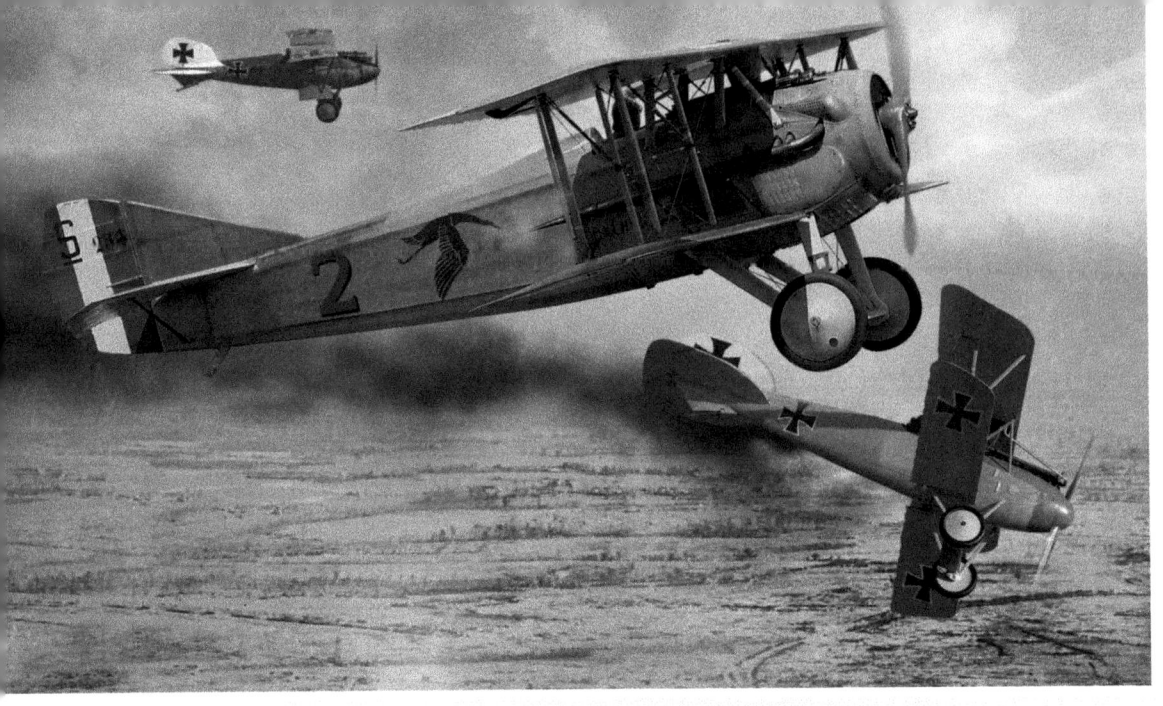

17co30 French ace and popular hero Georges Marie Ludovic Jules Guynemer scored 54 victories. He failed to return from a combat mission on 11 September 1917. He is depicted here flying his Spad 7 and bringing down an Albatros.

17co32 British infantry taking precautions against a German gas attack during the Third Battle of Ypres.

17co31 A Sopwith Camel after a heavy forced landing behind the British lines.

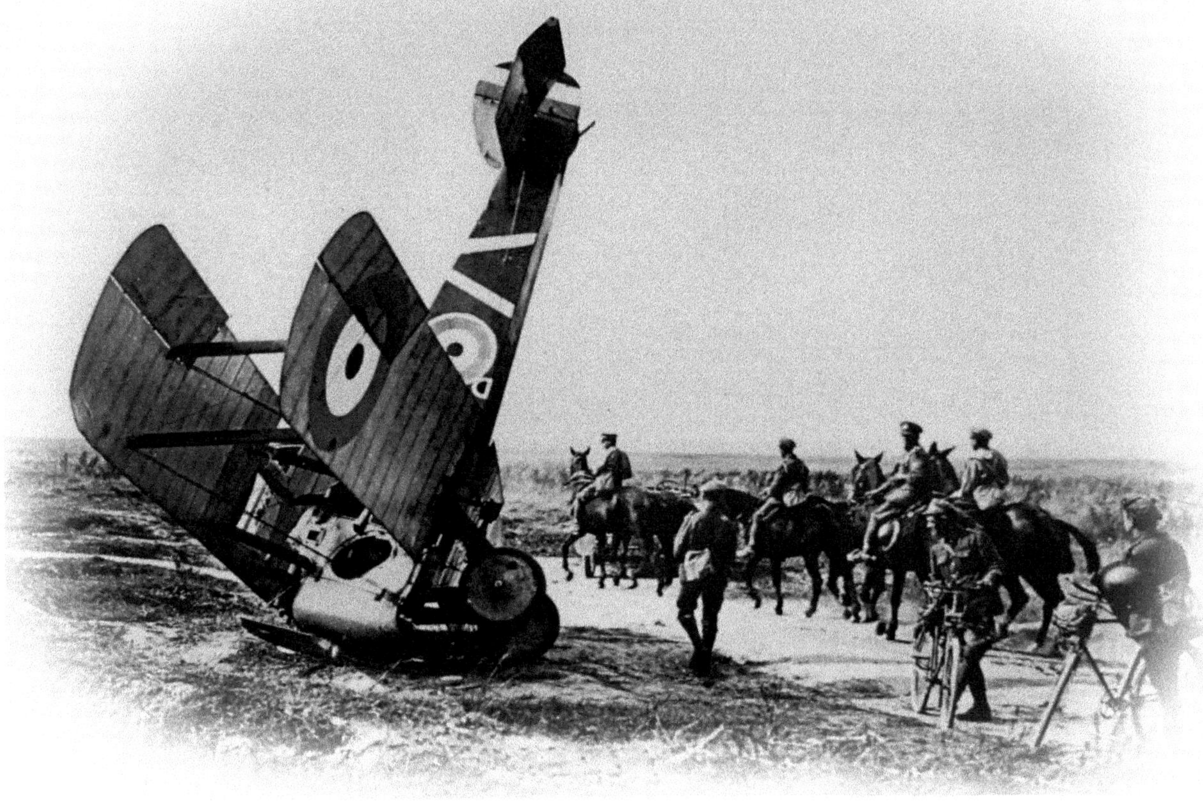

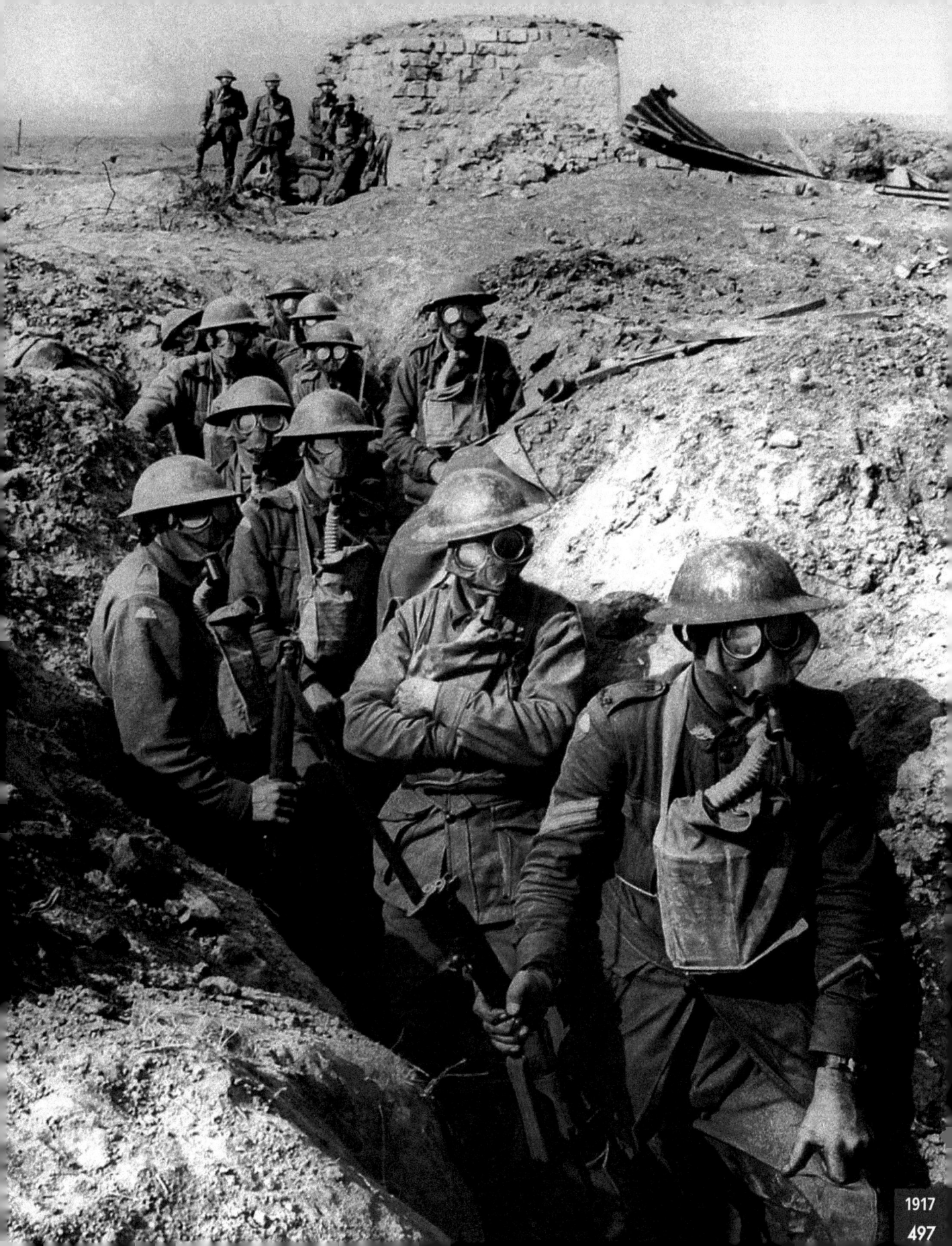

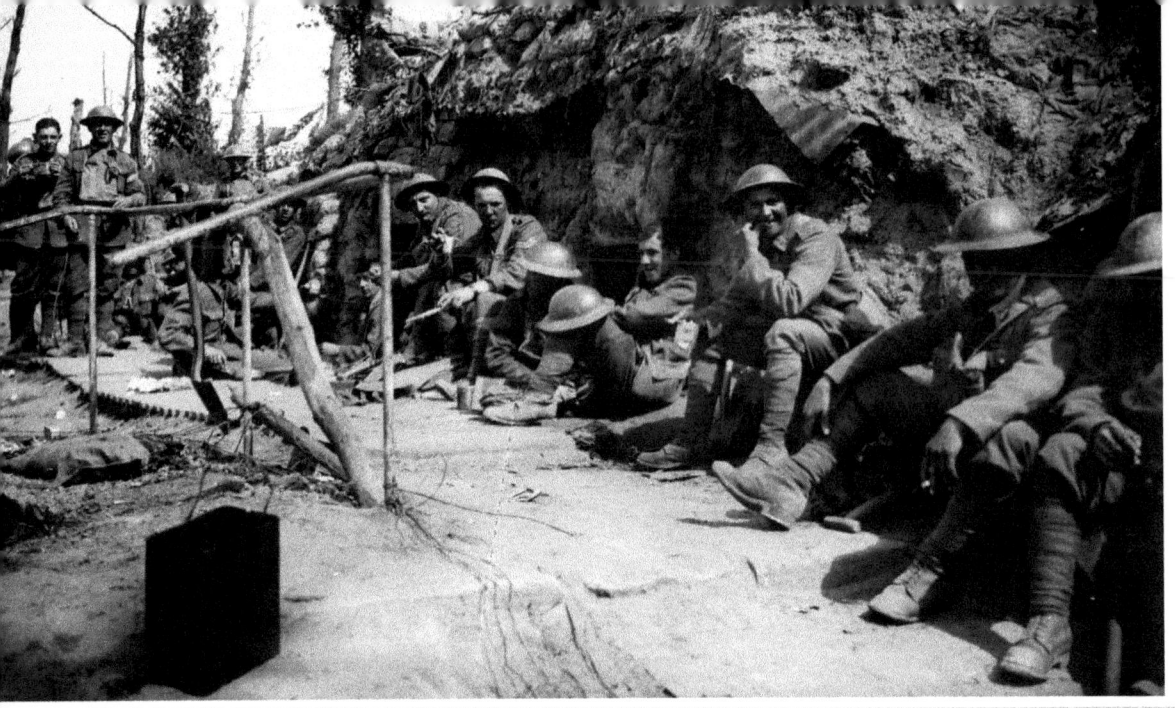

17co48 Men of the Leicestershire Regiment resting on their way up to Polygon Wood to relieve the Australians.

17co49 To operate effectively, artillery pieces require a firm, level base; conditions brought about by heavy August rains made this difficult in the fighting in the Ypres Salient, in the autumn of 1917.

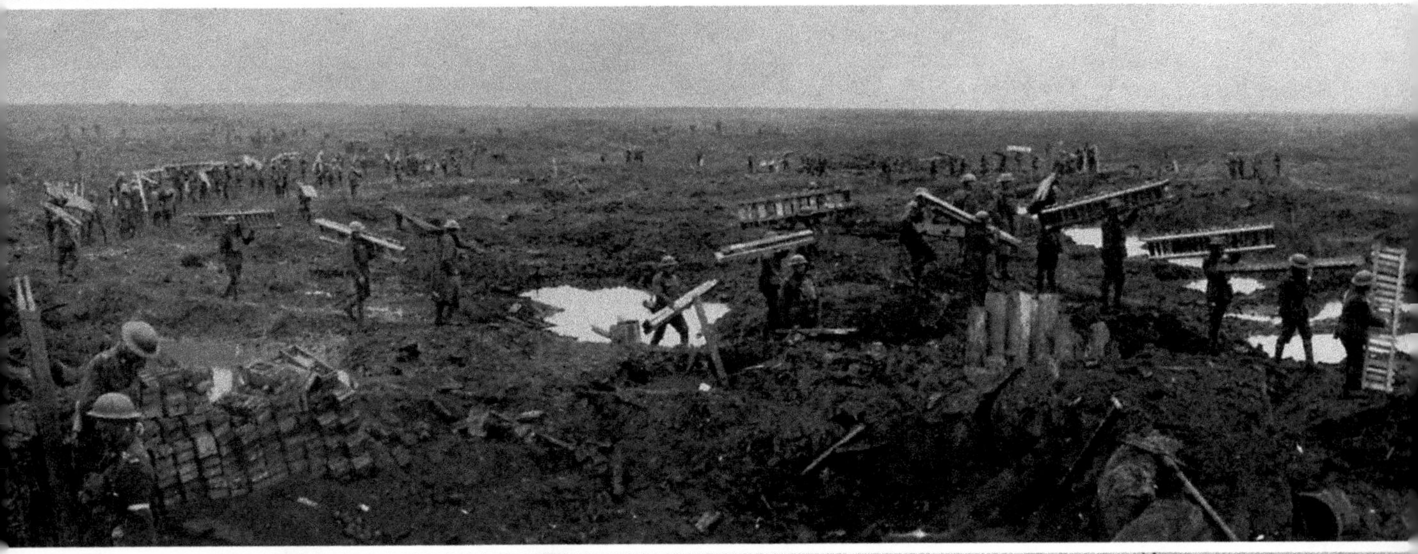

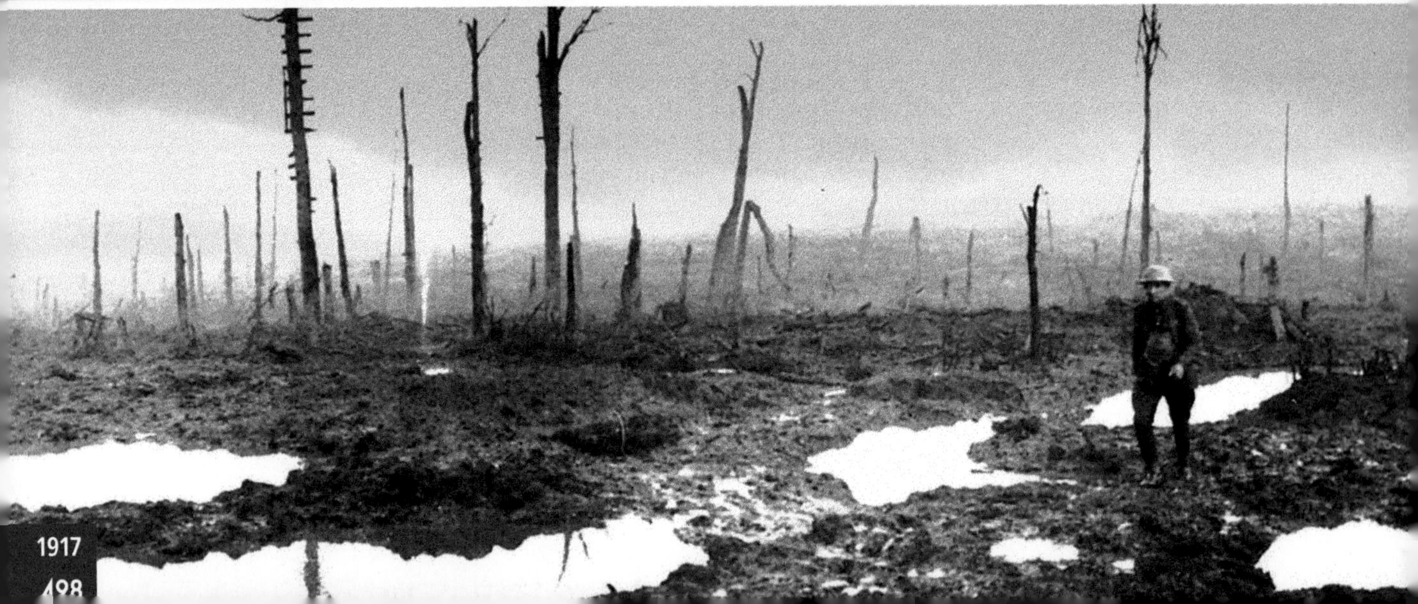

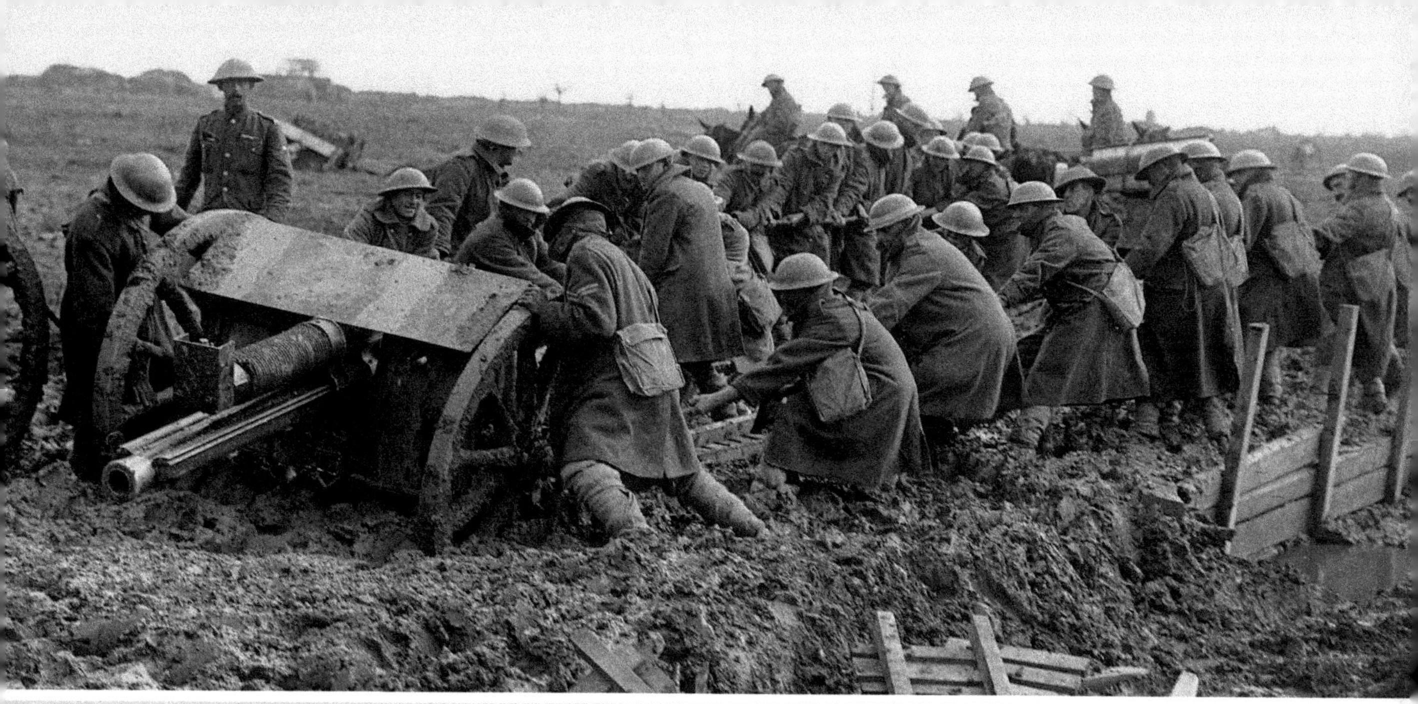

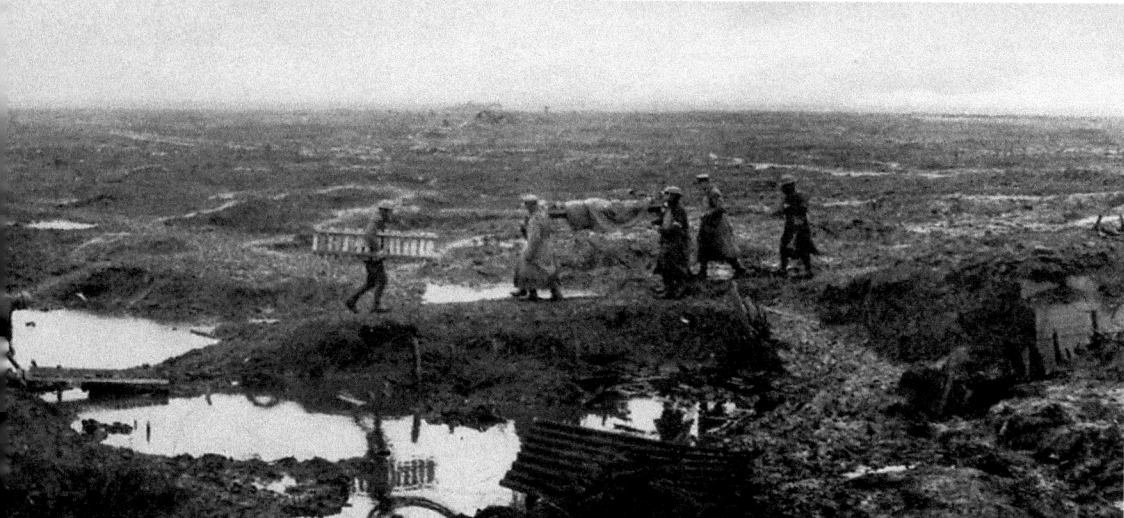

17co50, 17co51. The Passchendaele landscape.

It is claimed that Haig's Chief of Staff, Lieutenant General Sir Lancelot Kiggell, when visiting the battlefield near the end of the offensive broke down and said:

'Good God, did we really send men to fight in that?'

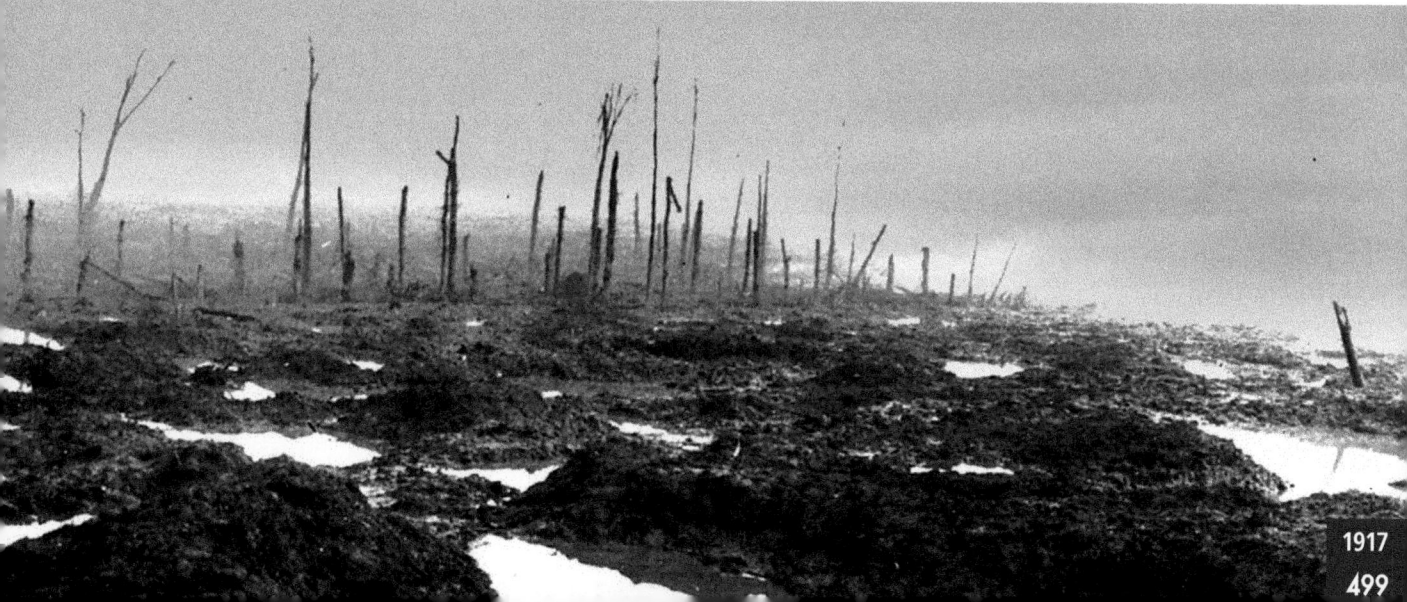

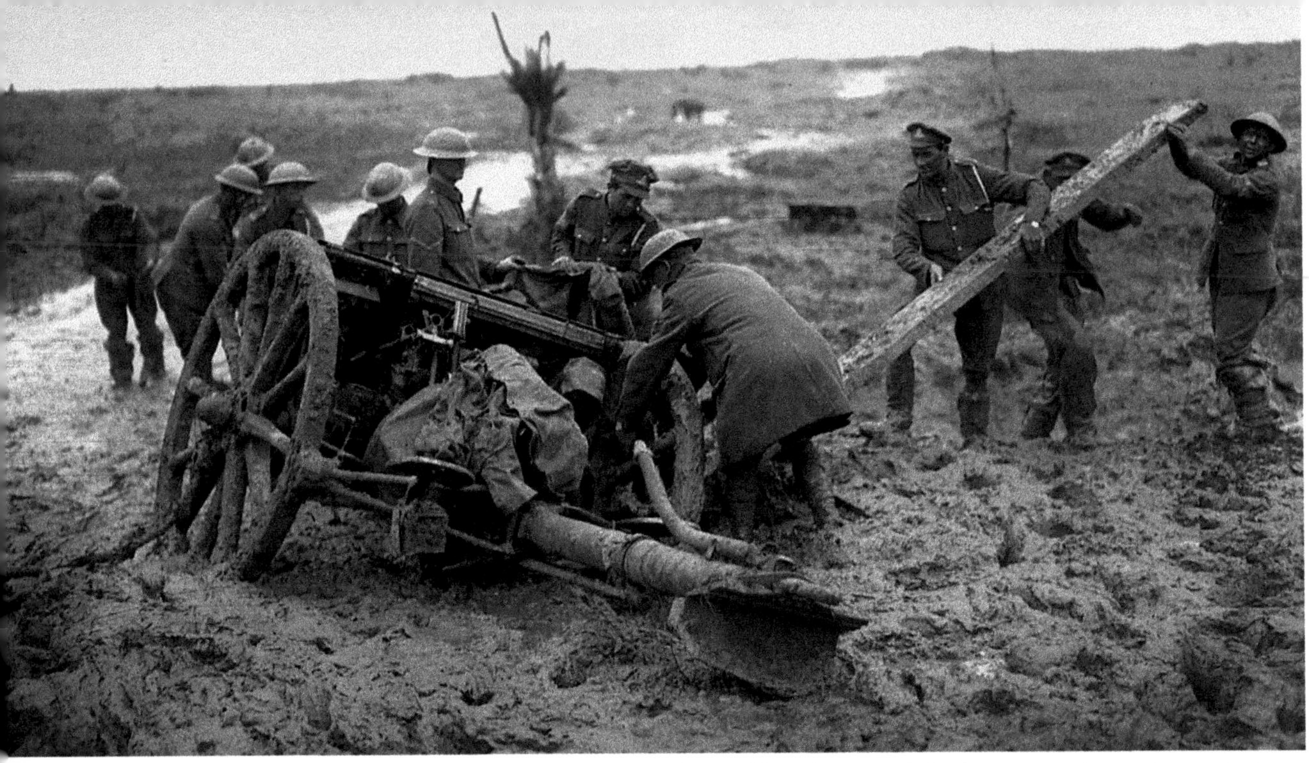

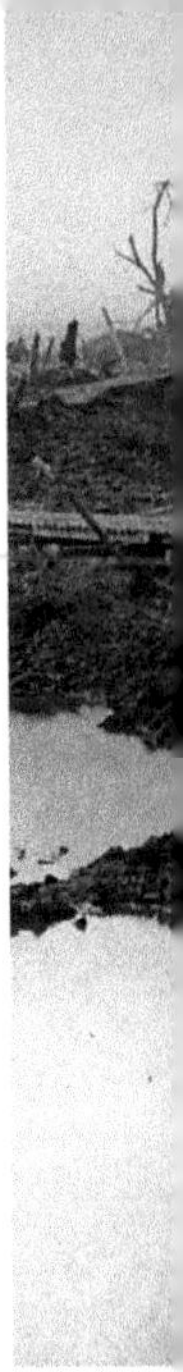

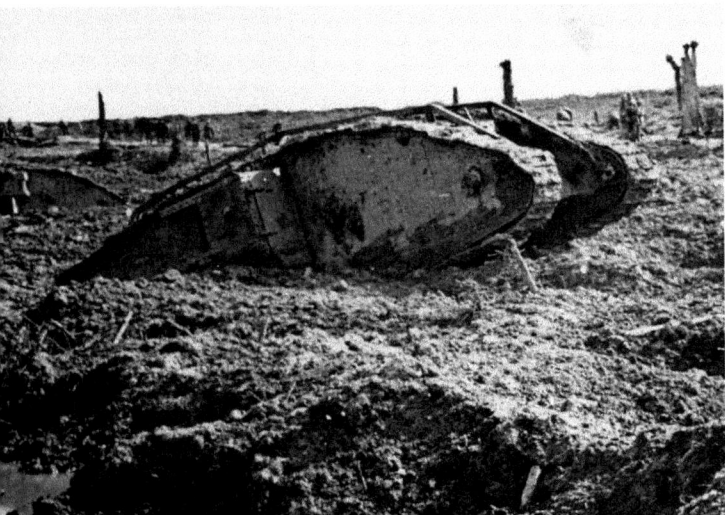

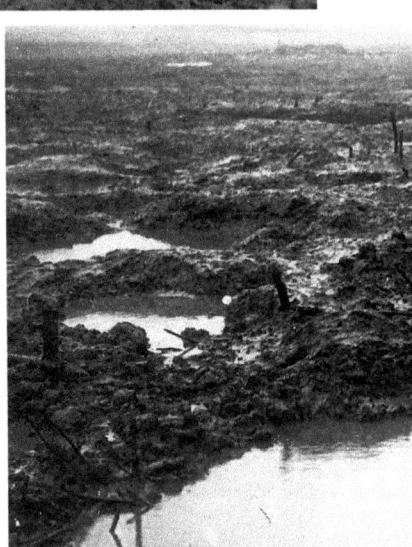

17co40 To leave roads, tracks or corduroy road was to invite disaster in the tortured terrain. Here an 18 pounder has come off the track and promptly sunk up to its axle.

17co42 Men resting during their task of taking up more duckboards.

17co36, 17co37, 17co38, 17co39. Wet weather – which commenced almost immediately the offensive was launched, produced impossible conditions for tanks to operate. They soon became bogged down and thus easy targets for German guns.

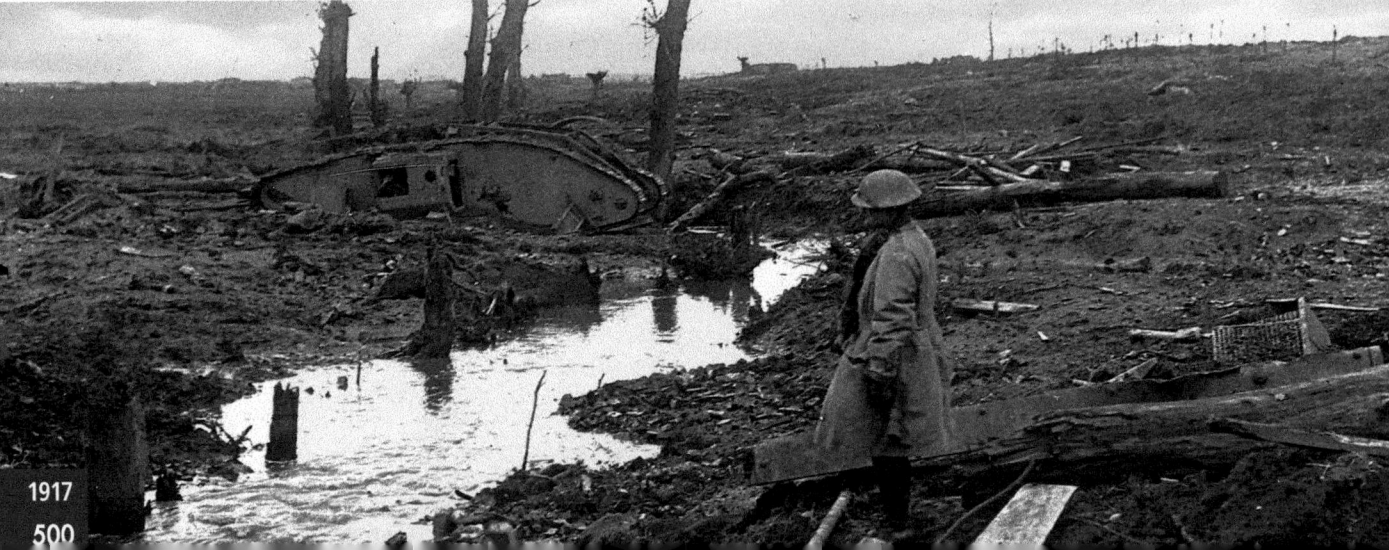

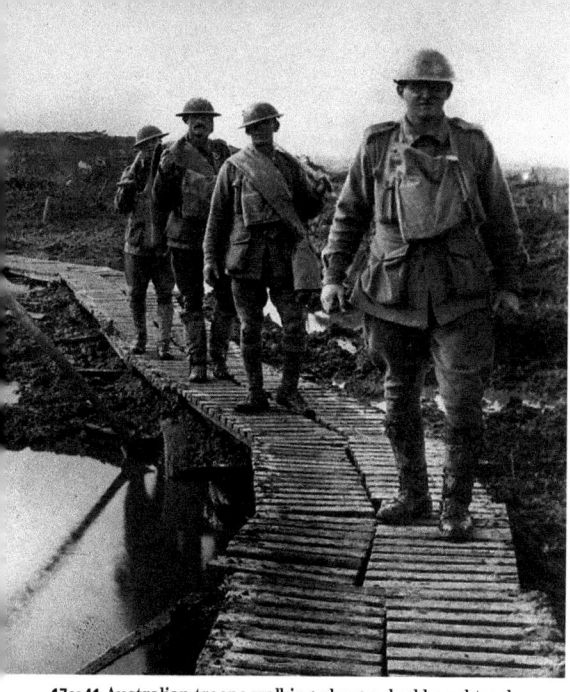

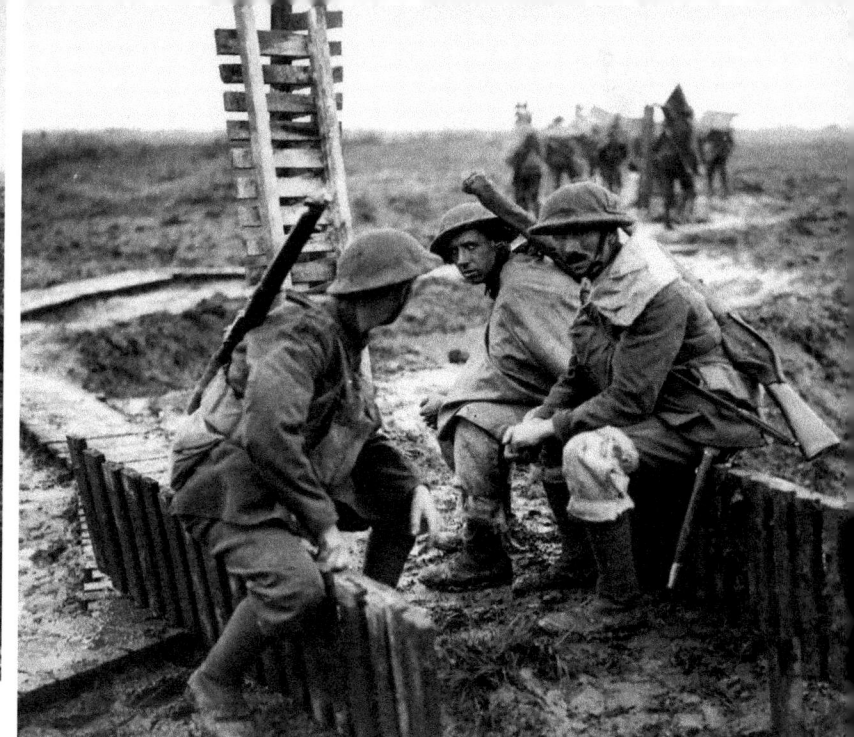

17co41 Australian troops walking along a duckboard track near Zonnebeke in the Ypres sector, October 1917.

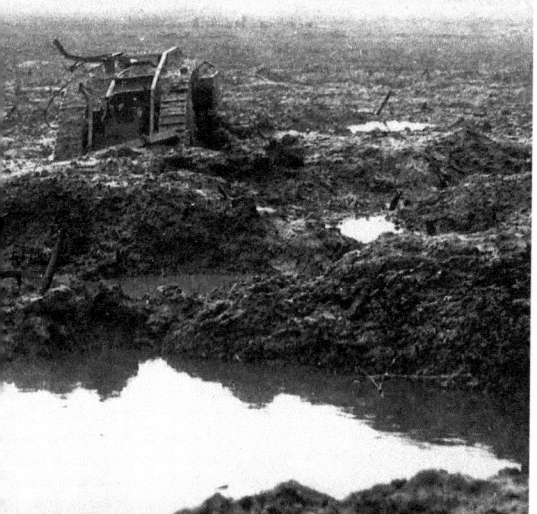

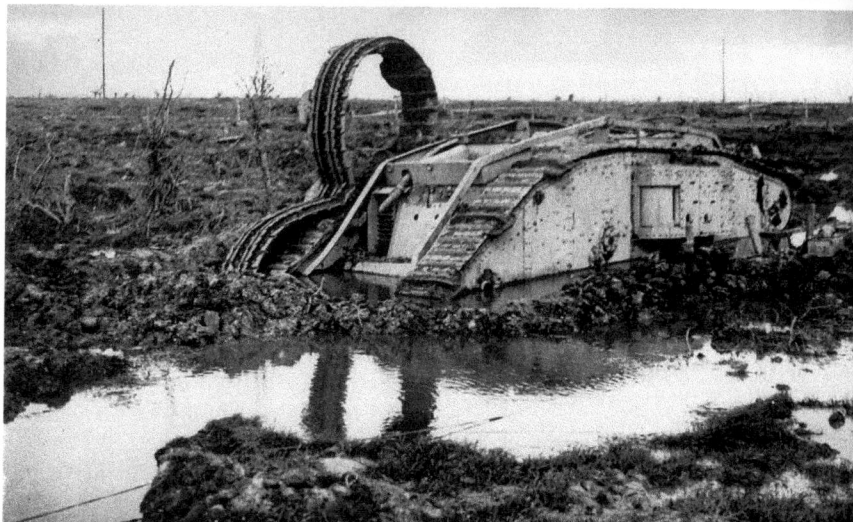

17co31 Tanks caught and wrecked by German artillery fire in Bourlon Wood during the Battle of Cambrai.

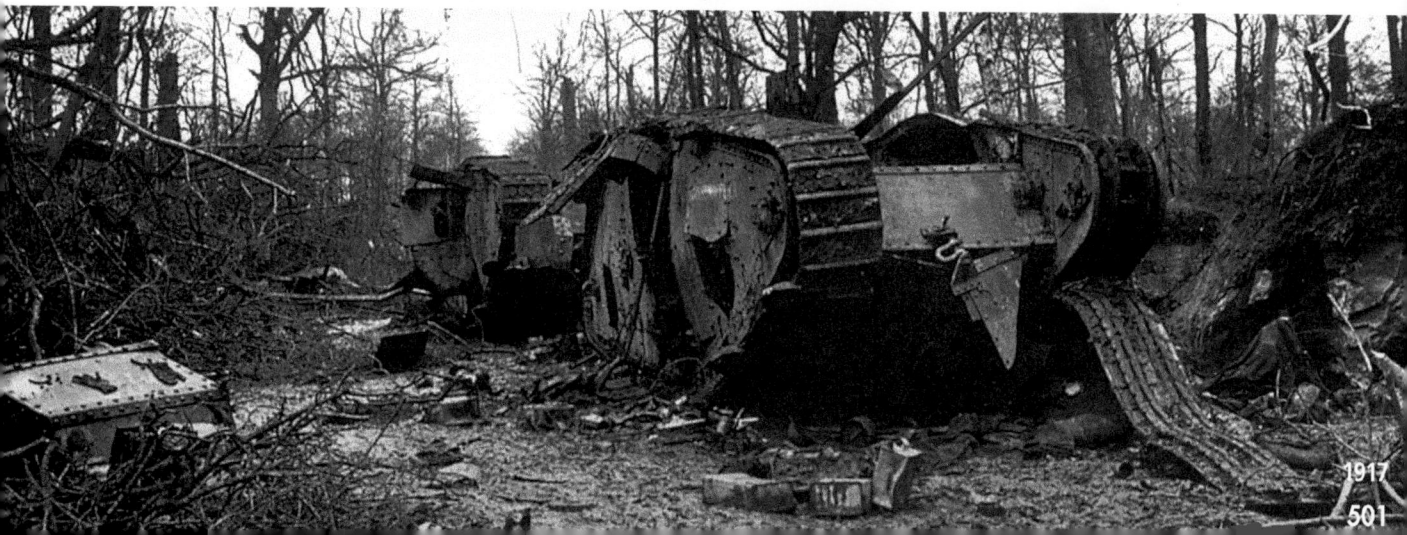

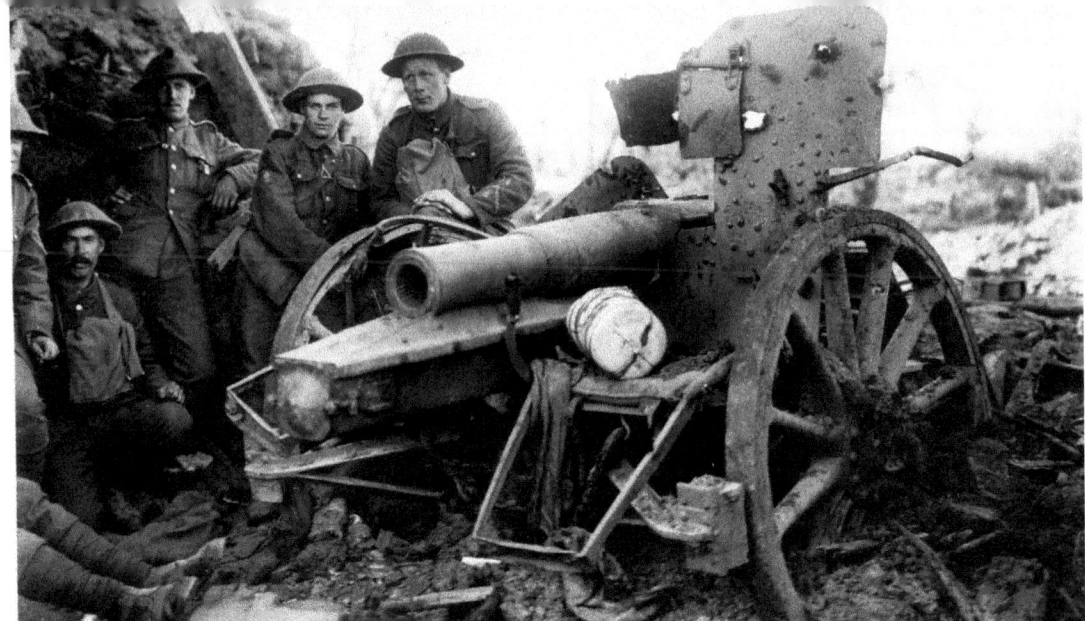

17co47 Several British troops, members of of the Royal Garrison Artillery, grouped beside a German 5.9 inch gun captured at Langemarck. The artillery position received a direct hit from a shell during an action that took place on 23 August, 1917.

17co46 British soldiers pause to look at the mangled corpse of a German soldier during the fighting near Passchendaele.

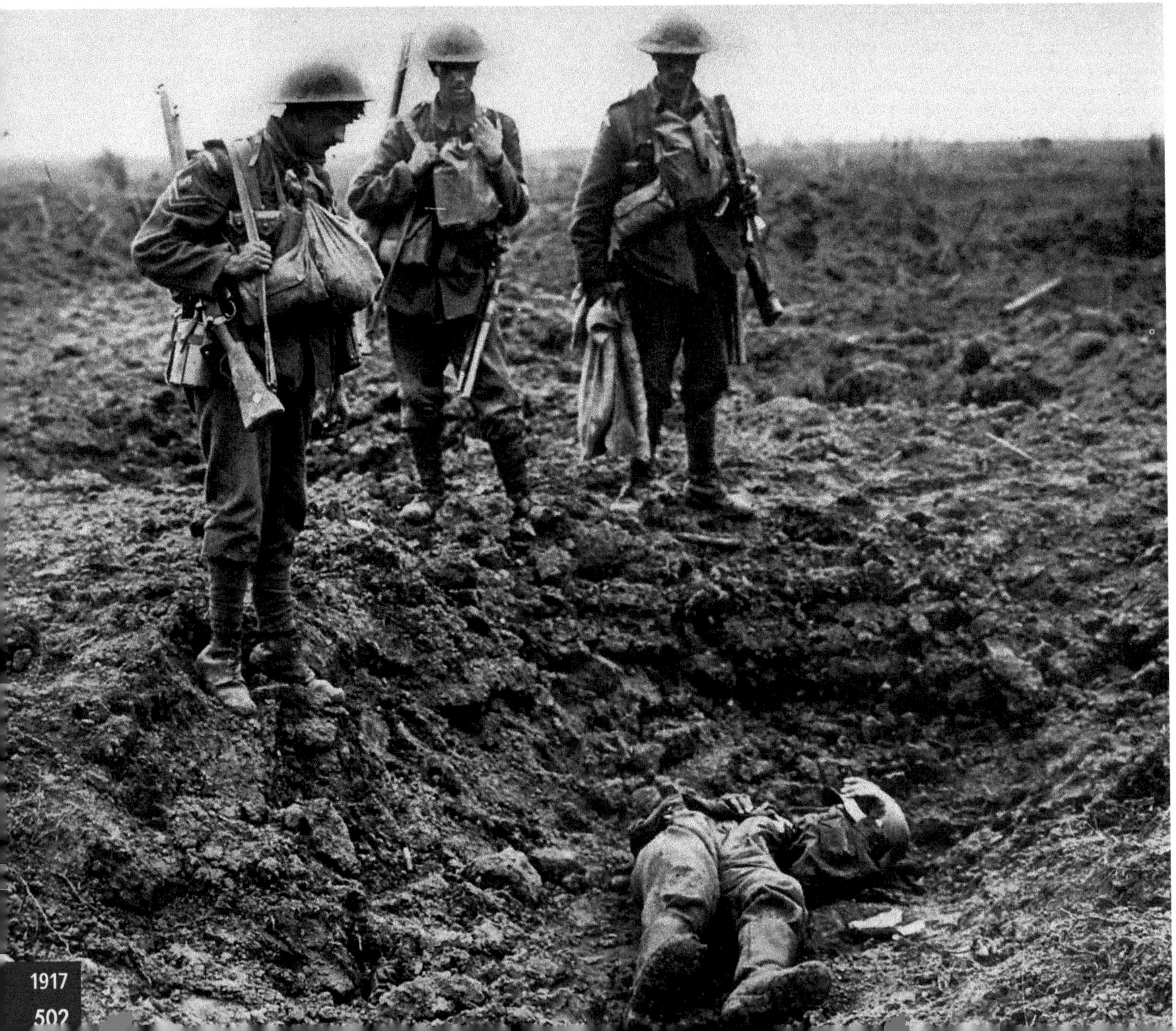

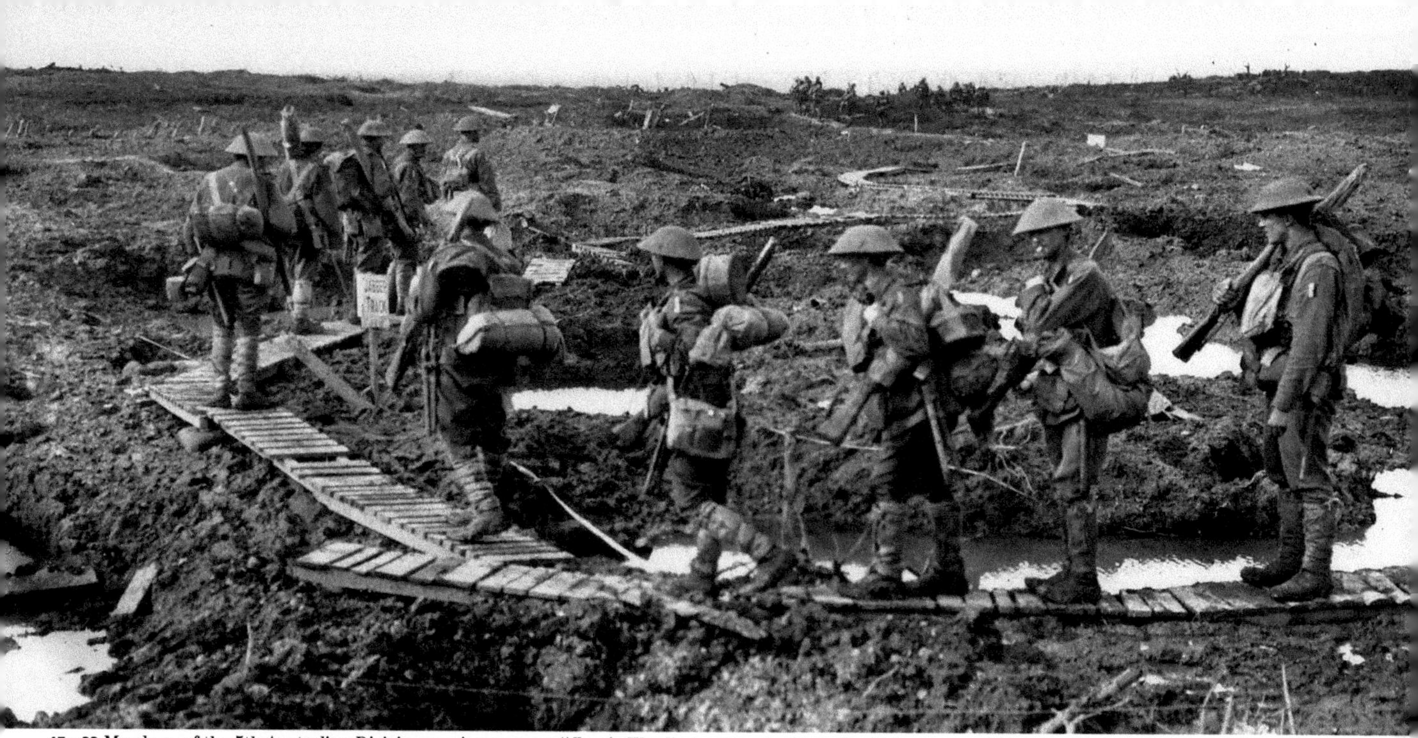

17co33 Members of the 5th Australian Division moving up near 'Albania Wood' along the duckboard path known as 'Jabber Track', towards the end of the I Anzac Corps' participation in the Third Battle of Ypres.

17co34 Men of a machine gun company and a pioneer battalion (the 11th Leicesters) having a brew-up in a ditch at Ribécourt, near Cambrai, after the village had been captured by the 9th Norfolks.

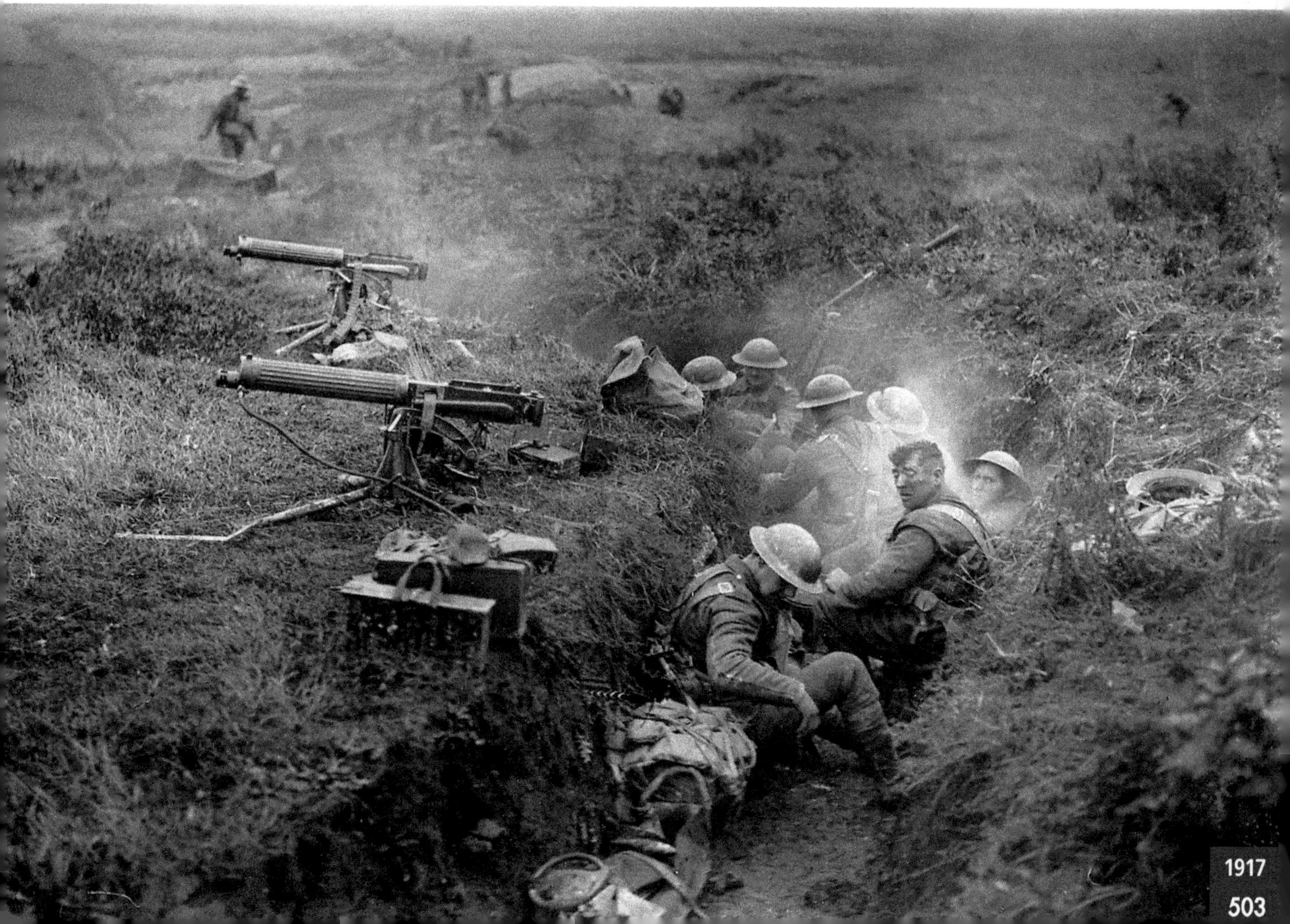

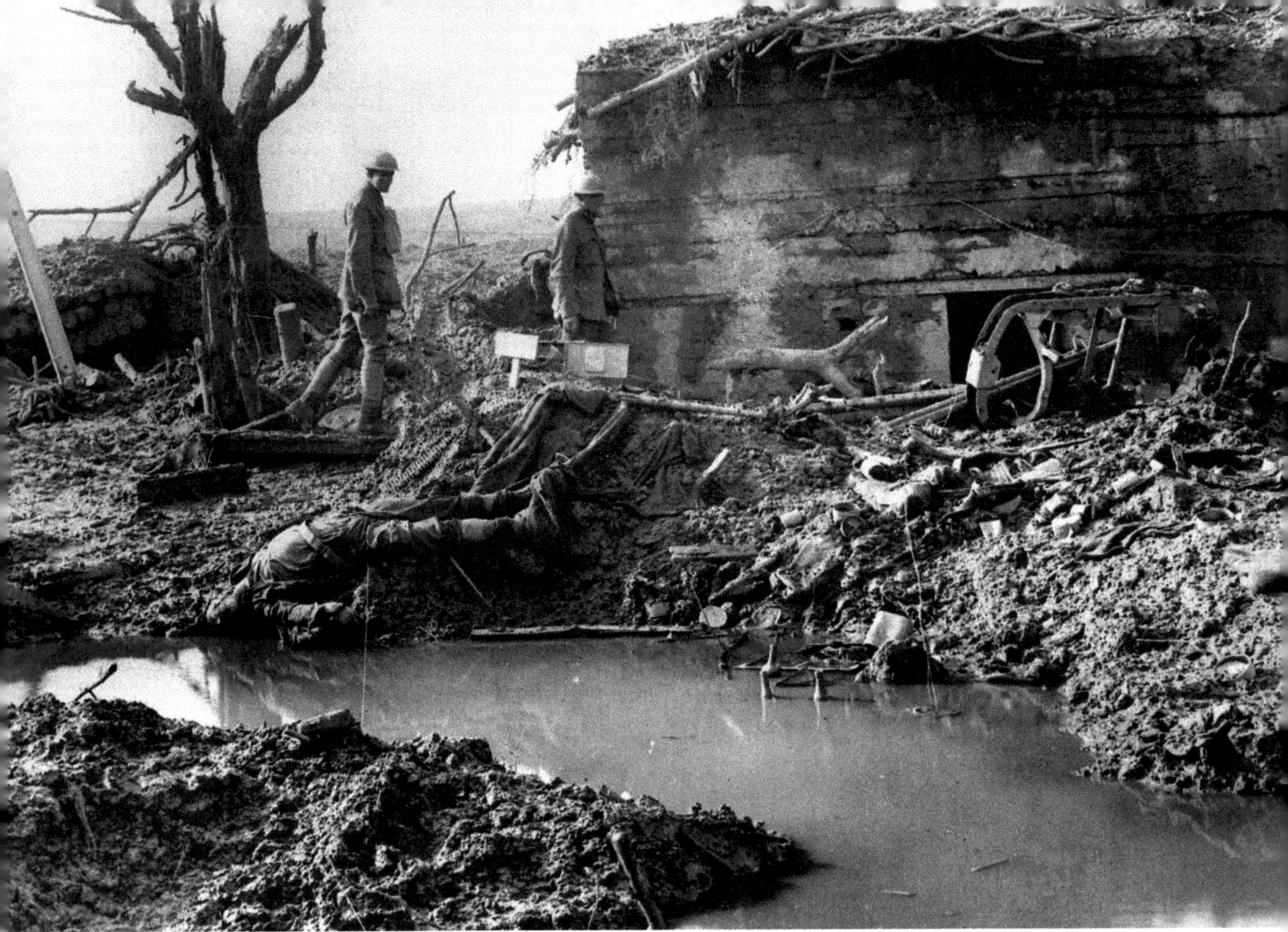

17co45 Battle of the Menin Road: German pillboxes at Nonne Bosschen captured by troops of the 1st Australian Division, 20 September 1917.

17co43 British stretcher bearers, Pilckem Ridge, east of Boesinghe, August, 1917; floundering through mud, they struggle to bring a wounded man to the rear.

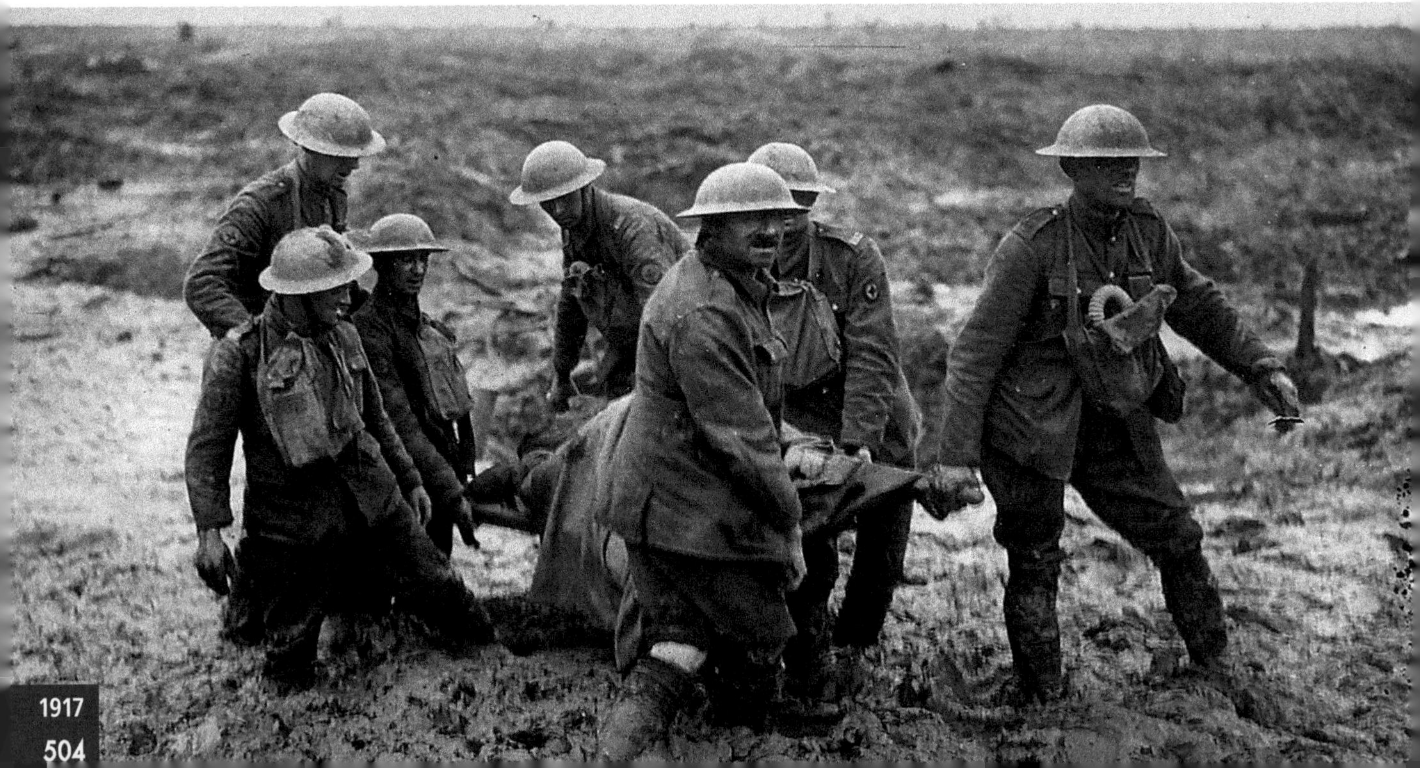

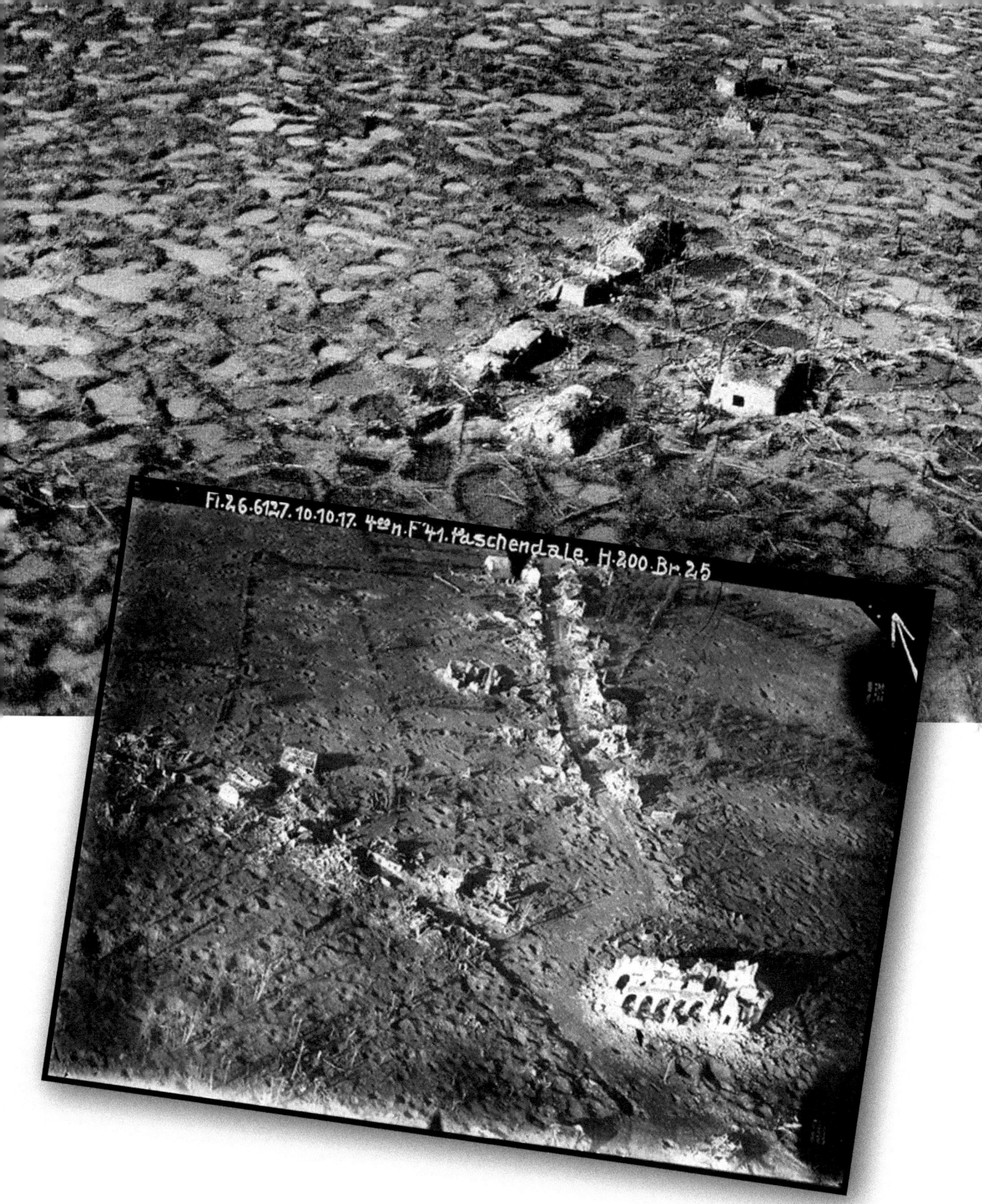

17co44 The village of Passchendaele taken from the air by a German aircraft, 10 October 1917, towards the end of the fighting. Haig halted the offensive on 10 November shortly after the village fell to the Canadians.

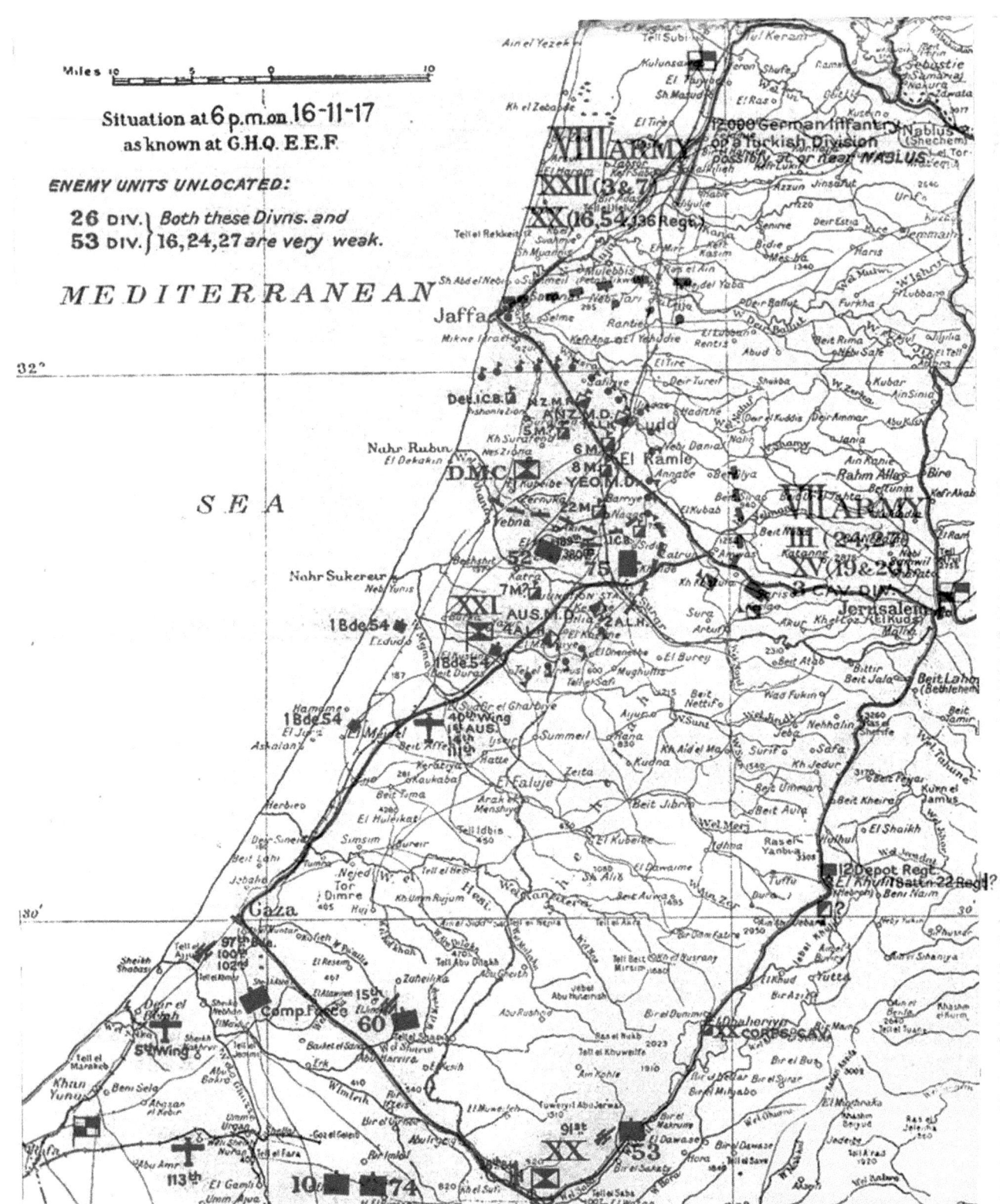

17co53 Fighting for the city of Jerusalem, regarded as holy by three great religions, developed from 17 November and continued after its surrender (on 9 December) until the 30th. The series of battles in the weeks after Jerusalem's fall was fought successfully by British XX Corps, XXI Corps and the Desert Mounted Corps. The map shows the situation as it was understood by the British generals the day before the action began.

Index

Achiet, 220
A Company 40th Battalion, 459
Advanced Dressing Station, 81, 121
Aéronautique Militaire, 243
94th Aero Squadron, 247–8
Airco DH.2, 200–1
Airco DH.5, 221
Aircraft V of No.85 Squadron, 224
Air war, 177–252
Aisne, 253–4, 299
Albatros, 184, 190, 208, 210, 213, 220, 225, 234–5
    C.I, 177, 220
    D.II, 220
    DIII, 186, 189–90, 207
    DVa, 190
    DVIII, 208
    type D-3, 238
Albert-Bapaume road, 11
Alexander, Marcus, 226
Alexandra, 401, 403
Alexei, 401, 403
'All-Black Flight', 226
Allenby, Gen Edmund, 87, 470, 473–4
Allmenroeder, Karl, 207
Alpine Landing, New Jersey, 390
Amalf (Italian armored cruiser), 323
American Expeditionary Force (AEF), 363
American Red Cross, 238
American Signal Corps, 384
American soldiers, 396–7, 399
Anastasia, 401, 403
Andrews, Capt, 220
Annay, 199
Annoeullin Cemetery, 231
Anthoine, Gen Paul, 443
Ariane (French submarine), 322
Arras, 36, 41–4, 46–50, 52–4, 57, 85, 87, 89, 92–6, 98, 104, 106, 109, 113, 121, 124, 138, 145, 147–8, 164, 174, 176, 189, 196, 204, 225, 230, 254
    British attack at, 36
    British supply convoy entering, 44
    pack mules in, 48
    prisoners taken at, 85
    Rolls Royce armoured cars in, 47
    Scottish regiment pipe band, 41
    soldiers forming working party in, 44
Arras-Cambrai road, 56, 125, 169
Arras cave, 89
Arras-Vimy sector, 50
Artillery, 54, 73, 104, 158, 162, 241, 256, 263, 297, 304
Artillery batteries, 133, 287
Artillery gun, 389
Artillery warning flare, 389
Assembly of Russian Workers, 402
Athies, 18, 104
Augustow, 403
Australian cavalry, 471
Australian Division, 11, 147, 149, 419, 428, 449–50, 452–3, 456–8
2nd Australian Division, 11, 30, 32
5th Australian Division, battalion of, 457
Australian Flying Corps (AFC), 222
Australian gunners, 152
Australian infantry, 152–3, 159
4th Australian Infantry Division, 174
22nd Australian Machine Gun Company, 166
Australian 2nd Division, 147, 449, 453, 456
Australian prisoners, 173
Australian 3rd Division, 457
Australian Siege Battery, 423
Australian soldiers, 32, 162–4, 432
Australian 8th Battalion, 169
Australian 48th Battalion, 174
Australian 4th Division, 147, 149, 154, 218
Australian 4th Light Horse Regiment, 470
1st Australian Tunnelling Company, 449
Austrian Fifth Fleet, 335
Austro-Hungarian Air Service, 186
Austro-Hungarian Navy, 334–5
Auxi-le-Chateau, 227
Aviatik, 238
AWFKS, 221

Ball, Capt Albert, 186, 231
Baltimore, 348
Bapaume, 11, 14, 29–32, 220
Bapaume road, 29
Barbed wire obstacles, 148, 292–3, 297–8, 463
Barker, William George 'Billy, 229
15th Battalion, (48th Highlanders of Canada), 59
35th Battalion (New South Wales), 440
40th Battalion (Tasmania) AIF, 432
30th Battalion, Australian corporal of, 38
12th Battalion East Surrey Regiment, 439
12th Battalion, London Regiment, 113
10th Battalion Royal Fusiliers, 56
6th Battalion Royal West Kents, 131
12th Battalion The King's (Liverpool) Regiment, 146
3rd Battalion, Worcestershire Regiment, 428
91st Battery, Royal Garrison Artillery, 93
Baudimont Gate, 44, 48
Bäumer, Paul, 187
Bayonet, 372
BE.2, 198
BE.12, 221
Beattie, Kim, 59
Beauchamp-Proctor, Andrew Frederick Weatherby, 228
BE.2c, 181, 221
BE.2d, 221
Belgian air force, 181
Belgium, 183
Bellewaarde Lake, 449
Bennett, 449
Bertangles, 220, 223
Berthold, Rudolf, 187
Bethlehem, 369
Bethlehem Steel Corporation, 369
Bigelow, Sgt Stephen, 244
Bird, Lt Algernon F., 211
Bishop, William Avery 'Billy, 225, 228
Black Death, 226
Black Flight, 226
Black Maria, 226
Black Prince, 226
Black Roger, 226
Black Sheep, 226
Blangy, 43
Blériot, Louis Charles Joseph, 180–1
Blériot monoplane, 181
Blériot XI-2 series, 180
'Bloody Sunday', 402
Blue Max *see Pour le Mérite*

Boelke, Oswald, 186
Boiry-Notre-Dame, 121
Bois du Sart, 135
Bolle, Karl, 188
Bolsheviks, 409, 415
Bongartz, Heinrich, 188
Booby traps, 30–1
Bosschen, Nonne, 452
Boulogne, 398–9
Bourjade, Jean-Pierre Léon, 242
Bowman, Geoffrey Hilton, 234
Boyau, Maurice Jean-Paul, 241
Brauneck, Otto, 207
Breguet 14A2 biplane, 185, 200
Bremerhaven, 348
Brest-Litovsk, 416
Bridgeman, Ray, 244
Briere Farm, 245
8 Brigade, 29
12 Brigade, Australian 4th Division, 154
5 Brigade band, 33
Briquet, Raoul, 32
Bristol Boxkite, 179
Bristol F2A, 198, 221
Bristol F2B, 212, 221
Britain, 224, 318, 338, 350, 354, 356, 381, 389, 418, 424
British Army, 178, 468
British artillery, 66, 71, 103, 133, 147
British 151 Brigade, 11
British cavalry, 46, 123, 130
British communication trench, 104, 106, 439
66th British Divisions, 457
British Expeditionary Force (BEF), 104, 176, 179
British infantry, 43, 146, 422
British 62nd Division, 147
British 60-pounder gun, 94
'British Recruiting Week', 388
British RE.8 two-seater, 191
British Royal Artillery naval guns, 53
British Second Army, 418
British 7th Division, 147
British Tommies, 20
British XX Corps, 470
Brocard, Felix, 237
Broodseinde, 442–3, 457–8
Brown, A Roy, 218–19
Brown Line, 121, 123
Bruneau, 298
Büchner, Franz, 187
Buckler, Julius, 188
Bucy le Long, 303
Bullecourt, 147–8, 157, 161–2, 164, 166, 169

Burstall, H.R., 52
Butte de Warlencourt, 11–12
Byng, Julian, 52

Cachy airfield, 244
Cambrai, 121, 461–2, 467–8
Cambrai Road, 87
Campbell, Andrew Courtney, 244
Camp Devens, Massachusetts, 385
Canadian Corps, 43
  field artillery, 56
  plan for attack on Vimy Ridge, 52
2nd Canadian Division, 58
20th Canadian Field Battery, 56
Canadian Highlanders, 388
Canadian infantry, 71, 86
16th Canadian Machine Gun Company, 455
Canadian reinforcements, 64
Canal du Nord, 465
Cappy, 214
Casualty Clearing Stations, 81, 456
Cattaro, 334–5, 342
Cavalry, 104, 121, 124, 131, 136, 138, 140, 462, 464, 473
1st Cavalry Division, 121
3rd Cavalry Division, 124
Champagne, 10
Chapman, Victor, 243
Chauchat light machine gun, 276
Chaudun, 244
Chavonne, 298–9
Chemin des Dames, 36, 50, 253–4, 256, 260, 263, 265, 273–4, 278, 281, 289–90, 292, 295, 298, 305, 314
Chemin des Dames Ridge, 50
Chicago, 366
Cincinnati drill, 366
City of London Regiment, 89
Coiffard, Michel Joseph Callixte Marie, 241
Collishaw, William, 228
Communication trench, 428–9, 439
Constantin, Esser, 207
Copse, Iverness, 452
Cormicy, 276
Cossacks, 402
Courlandon, 282, 305
Cour-Soupir, 304
Courtrai, 204, 209
Cowdin, Elliot, 243
Craonne, 302, 304
Croisilles, 87
Cross-Atlantic voyage, 391
Crugny airfield, 236
Currie, Arthur, 52

'Cuthbert' mine crater, 54
Cyclist Corps, 35

d'Anselme, Philippe Henri Joseph, 298
Daylight Signalling Lamps, 138
de Lafayette, Marquis, 243
de Meux, Alfred de Laage, 243
Desert Mounted Corps, 470
Despatch riders, 389
Deutschland, 346–50
DFW C.V, 230
5th (British) Division, 52
16th (Irish) Division, 430, 437
36th (Ulster) Division, 430
56th (London) Division, 113
Dogfight, 192, 208, 220, 229, 234–5
Döre, Gustav, 188
Dorsetshire Regiment, 142
Douai, 119, 121
Douglas, William Sholto, 228
Doyen, Charles A., 373
3rd Dragoon Guards, 124
Dressing station, 302
Duchêne, Denis Auguste, 255
Dugan, William, 244
Duma, 406

E20 (British submarine), 322
Easter Monday, 42
East Surrey Regiment, 141
Écourt-St Quentin, 204
Egyptian Expeditionary Force (EEF), 470
Eindecker Focker EIII, 183, 186
6ème Escadrille, 198
11th Engineers (New York), 398
13th Engineers (Chicago), 398
15th Engineers (Pittsburg), 398
Erwin Deterra, 333
Escadrille Br.127, 200
Escadrille des Cigognes, 235
Escadrille, Lafayette, 240
Escadrille MF5, 179
Escadrille N152, 242
Escadrille No. 94, 243
Essex Yeomanry, 124

Falkenhausen, *Generaloberst* Freiherr von, 52
Fampoux, 87, 136
Fanning, USS (destroyer), 352
Farbus, 119
Farbus Wood, 87
Farman, Henri, 180
Farman HF20, 180–1
Fauvety, Louis Verdier, 244

FE.8, 199, 221
FE.2b, 193, 208, 221
FE.2d, 221
Feodorovna, Alexandra, 408
Fergusson, Lt Gen, 87
Ferry boats, 390
Festner, Sebastian, 189, 207
Feuchy, 106, 136, 140, 145
10th Field Artillery Brigade, 441
Field Dressing Station, 125
Field telephones, 385
Filescamps Farm, 225
First Army, 43, 56, 73, 94
First Officer's Training Camp, 379
Flanders, 209, 384
Flesquières, 463–5
Fliegerabteilung (A), 204, 229
'Flying Circus', 215
Flying Fox (tank), 464
Flying school, 178
Fokker, Anton Herman Gerard, 182
Fokker Dr.I Triplane, 212
Fokker D.V biplanes, 210
Fokker D.VII, 241–2, 250
Fokker E.III, 243
Fokker Eindecker, 182
Fokker Triplane, 210, 216, 222, 234
Fonck, René Paul, 235–6
Forstmann, Walter, 332, 345
Fort McPherson, East Point, 383
Fort Sheridan, 383, 388–9
France, 180
Franchet d'Esperey, 236
French '75', 267
French Army, 36, 50, 276, 314, 316, 363
French artillery, 50
French Caudron G.3, 200
French First Army, 443
French Nieuport 23, 200
French VI Corps, 271
French west coast seaport of Brest, 396–7
F Troop First Cavalry, 384
Fullard, Philip Fletcher, 230

Gallia, SS, 333–4
Gallwitz, Karl, 234
Gansser, Konrad, 332
Garnett, William P, 196
Garros, Roland Georges, 183
Gas masks, 261, 289
Gas shells, 287
Gavrelle, 138, 142, 145, 196
Gendarme, 230
George, David Lloyd, 36, 474

George V, King, 398
George Washington (troop transport), 392
Gerlich, 213
German aircraft, 183, 208, 220, 226, 229–30, 238
German barbed wire, 159–60
German High Seas Fleet, 357
German Imperial Navy, 346
German machine gunners, 112
German machine guns, 73, 85
German 77 mm field gun, 75
German prisoners, 78–80, 82–3, 85, 113–14, 141, 176, 302–4, 453, 458–60
  carrying comrade, 85
German Second and Third lines, 96
German Second Army, 467
German shells, 48, 158
German Sixth Army, 52
German submarines, 317, 319, 321–2, 332, 354, 356–7, 393, 395–6, 442
German trenches, 20, 147, 162, 308, 432, 443, 462, 464
German UB Flotilla, 345
Germany, 358
Geschwader, 209–10
Geschwader 1, 210
Gettysburg military camp, 365
Gilmour, John Inglis, 232
Godley, Alexander, 419
Gontermann, Heinrich, 185, 188
Gontrode, 213
Goodfellow, Lieutenant, 229
Göring, Herman, 215
Gotha bombers, 230, 240
Gough, Hubert, 147, 443
Goutte d'Or wood, 293
Grand Place, Arras, 44, 48
Grozovoi (Russian destroyer), 352
Guynemer, Georges Marie Ludovic Jules, 235–6, 238

Haegelen, Marcel, 235
Haig, Douglas, 418–19, 442
Halberstadt two-seater, 232
Haldane, Lt Gen, 87
Hall, Bert, 243
Hamersley, Harold A., 234
Hamilton-Gordon, Alexander, 419
Hannebeek, 453
Hannover C, 231, 247–8
Hannover CIII, 228
Hannover CL.III, 231
Hanovarian regiment, 434
'Happy Valley,' 137

Hareira, 473
Harington, Charles, 425
Hartwig, Kurt, 332
Hashagen, Ernst, 332
Hawker, Lanoe George, 220
94th Heavy Battery, 469
Heligoland, 346
Hemingway, Ernest, 229
Hendecourt-lès-Cagnicourt, 147
Henderson, USS, 395
Hersing, Otto, 332
Hill, Dudley, 244
Hillebrand, Leo, 332
Hindenburg Line, 9–11, 13–15, 32, 39, 50, 104, 147–8, 150, 154, 157, 164, 169, 174, 176, 468
  preparing defences of, 15
  troops manning, 15
Hindenburg Line defence system, 169
Hintsch, Hans, 207
Hoboken, 391
Hollweg, Theobald Friedrich Alfred von Bethmann, 318
Hooge, 449
Horne, Henry Sinclair, 43
Hotchkiss machine, 182
Howitzer, 56, 75, 77, 92–4, 96, 137–8, 148, 381, 444
Hughes, Samuel, 350
'Huns' Walk,' 428
Hurcomb, Frederick, 473
10th Hussars, 124

Illinois (American steamer), 319–21
Immelmann, Max, 186
Imperial German Army Air Service, 182
Imperial Germany, 360
Imperial Russian family, 403
17. Infantrie Division, 141
Infantrie Regiment 76, 141
111 Infantry Brigades, 124
112 Infantry Brigades, 124
Iron Duke (tank), 91

Jabber Track, 458
'Jackdaw Switch,' 453
Jacobs, Josef, 187
Jaffa, 470
Jasta 10, 210
Jasta 11, 189, 191, 204, 206, 208, 214
  Albatros DIII fighters, 189
  pilots, 207
  victims, 196–7
Jerusalem, capture of, 469–74
Jeß, Heinrich, 332

JG 1, 213–14
Joffre, 50
Johnson, Charles, 244
Jones, Henry S, 244
Jones, James Ira Thomas 'Taffy', 232

Kaiser, 209, 242, 441
Kaiser Truppenschau, 204
Kampfgeschwader 3 bomber, 213
Kerensky, Alexander, 409, 411, 415
King's Royal Rifle Corps, 140
Kitchener, Lord, 179
Kleine, Rudolf, 213
Koekelare, 198
König, Paul, 346, 348–50
Könnecke, Otto, 188
Kophamel, Waldemar, 332
Kornilov, Lavr Georgievich, 413, 415
Krefft, Esser, 207

Lafayette Escadrille, 243–4
La Fayette squadron 124 N / SPA 124, 245
La Ferme des Hurtubise, 316
Langemarck, 446
Lansing, Robert, 360
Large-calibre shells, 50
Launburg, Otto, 332
Le Barque, 11
Lebel rifle, 277, 289
Leicestershire Regiment, 466
Lenin, Vladimir, 359, 411, 415–16
Le Sars, 11–12, 29
    memorial in German cemetery at, 13
    narrow gauge trench railway line near, 12
Les Cigognes, 237, 242
Le Verguier, reserve lines at, 9
Leviathan, 391, 397
Lewis, David Greswolde, 220
Lewis gun, 182–3, 208
LFG Roland CII, 186
Liberty Bonds, 350
Lipsett, Louis, 52
Little, Robert Alexander, 230
Liverpool, 397
Loerzer, Bruno, 187
Loewenhard, Erich, 187
Lohs, Johannes, 332
Lowell, Walter, 244
Luard, Kate, 442
Ludendorff, Erich Friedrich Wilhelm, 40, 255, 285
Lufbery, Raoul, 244
Luftstreitkräfte, 204, 224
Luke, Frank Jr, 245

Lusitania (tank), 92
Lusitania, RMS, 318

MacDonagle, Douglas, 244
24th Machine Gun Company, 218
Machine guns, 11, 62, 73, 106, 109, 112, 124, 154–5, 160, 183–4, 191, 219–20, 222, 233, 285, 292, 304–5, 384, 413, 437, 467
MacLaren, Donald Roderick, 228
Madon, Georges Félix, 241
Mairie (town hall), 31–2
Mangin, Charles, 254, 263, 297
Mannock, Edward Corringham Mick, 224, 231
Maplewood, SS, 317, 332
Maria, 401, 403
Marinovitch, Pierre, 243
Marne, 269
Marschall, Wilhelm, 332
Mart, F J, 222
Martinsyde G100, 221, 232
5th Maryland Guards, 383
Maschinengewehr, 164
Maschinengewehr 08 (MG 08), 109
Masson, Didier, 244
Maurice Farman built machines, 179
Mauser Werke, 370
Maxim machine guns, 73
Maybery, Richard, 234
May Day celebrations, 409
May, Wilfrid R, 218–19, 222
Mazel, Olivier Charles, 255
McConnell, James, 243
McCudden, James Thomas Byford, 227, 231, 234
McElroy, George Edward H, 231
McPherson Training Camp, 381
Medieaval subterranean quarries, 89
Mellersh, 218
Menckhoff, Carl, 187
Menin Road Ridge, 442–3, 449–50, 452–4, 456
Méricourt, 211
Messines Ridge, 95, 417–18, 420, 422
Mexico, 358
Michaelis, Herr Georg, 213
Michigan Avenue, 366
Minenwerfer, 260
Mine tunnels, 424
Mine warfare, 425–7
Mohrbutter, Ulrich, 350
Monchy, 133–5
Monchy-le-Preux, 56, 103, 124–5, 130, 133, 146
Moraht, Robert, 332
Morane-Saulnier, 183
Moritz (dog), 206, 216–17

Morland, Thomas, 419
Moroccan infantry, 297
Moulin Laffaux, 294
Müller, Max, 188
Mulroney, N., 222
Murvaux, 245
Muspratt, Keith, 234

Nash, Gerry, 226
National Guard, 363
National Guardsmen, 397
Naval gun manufacturing plant, 369
Naval guns, 54
Naval Training Station, 384
Navarre, Jean Marie Dominique, 243
Neumann, Karl, 332
New York National Guard, 384
New Zealanders, prisoners of, 435
New Zealand tunnelers, 89
Nicholas II, Tsar, 401–4
    abdication of, 404
    in captivity in Tobolsk, 408
    rationales for risking war, 402
'Nicholas Romanov', 404
Nieuports, 196, 221, 225, 230, 238, 242–4
Nieuport Type 14 aircraft, 241
Nikolayevich, Tsarevich Alexei, 408
Nivelle, Robert, 10, 36, 50, 176, 254, 263, 265, 316
No.1 Naval Squadron, 226
No.10 Naval Squadron, 226
Noreuil, 166
Northamptonshire Yeomanry, 136
Nova Scotia Rifles, 62
Noyon, 265
Nungesser, Charles Eugène Jules Marie, 240

Observation balloons, 233
Ockenfels (German steamer), 364
Officer's Training Camp, 388
Olga, 401, 403
Oppy, 138
Oppy Wood, 142–3
Orange Hill, 103
2nd Orenburg Storming Battalion, 412
Osterkamp, Theo, 188
Otersdorf, Fräulein Kätie, 209
Ottoman forces, 471, 473
Ottoman light artillery, 469

Parabellum MG14, 184
Parados, 20
Pargust, HMS, 354
Parsons, Edwin, 244

Passchendaele, 42, 220, 418, 441–5, 455, 457–60
Pasteur, Arras, 49
Penshurst, HMS, 353
Perière, Lothar von Arnauld de la, 332–3, 342–3
Periscope, 395
Péronne, 9–10
   havoc in, 24–8
   mischief carried out at, 15
Pershing, John Joseph 'Black Jack', 363, 398–9
Pétain, Philippe, 316
Peterson, David, 244
Petite Place (Place des Héros), Arras, 46, 48
Petrograd, 409
Pfalz Scout, 232
Pilckem Ridge, 444–6
Pinsard, Armand, 242
Pioneer Battalion, 287
2nd Pioneer Battalion, Australian troops of, 29
Place Faidherbe, 33
Plattsburg, New York, 388
Plumer, Herbert Charles Onslow, 418–19, 425, 443
Pochon, Roger, 240
Poilus, 266, 277, 281, 289, 299, 314, 316
Polyanthus, HMS, 355
Polygon Wood, 442, 454
Popkin, Cedric Bassett, 218
Portuguese Expeditionary Corps, 116
Poulainville, 219, 222
18-Pounders, 56–7, 96, 152–3
Pour le Mérite, 192
Prince, Norman, 243
Prisoners, 62, 79, 85, 113, 173–4, 204, 304, 314, 435, 439, 452, 464–5, 468
Prize, HMS, 354
5th Prussian Division, 238
Prussian Guards, 238, 256
Puisieux, 18–19
Pustkuchen, Herbert, 332, 350

Q-Ships, 353–5

RAF Kite Balloon Section, 229
Ramien, Kurt, 332
Raoul, 244
Rasputin, Grigori, 402
Raymond Collishaw, 226
RE.8, 221, 229
Red Baron, 177, 189, 193, 198, 206–14, 216, 218–22, 224, 243
Redmond, William Hoey Kearney, 437
27e Régiment de Dragoons, 243

5th Regiment of Marines, 373
Reid, Ellis, 226
Reims, 256
Reinhard, Wilhelm, 215
Renault armoured cars, 298
Revenge IV, 242
Rheims exhibition, 180
Rhys-Davids, Arthur Percival Foley, 234
Ribécourt, 464
RichthofenGeschwader, 214
Rickenbacker, Edward Vernon, 246–8
Ridgway, George, 219
Riencourt-lès-Cagnicourt, 169
Roberts, Ivan, 245
Rockwell, Y. Kiffin, 243–4
Rodzianko, Mikhail Vladimirovich, 404, 406
Rolls Royce, troops of, 47
Romanov monarchy, 401
Roosevelt, Theodore III, 377
Rose, Hans, 332, 345
Royal Aircraft Factory, 181
Royal Canadian Air Force, 228
Royal Corps of Signals, 138
Royal Dublin Fusiliers, 438
Royal Engineers, 98
Royal Engineers Signal Service, 138
Royal Field Artillery, 29th Division, 145
Royal Flying Corps (RFC), 179, 181–2, 185–6, 189, 192, 195, 200, 204, 208, 211–12, 224–7, 229, 232
10th Royal Fusiliers, 145
Royal Garrison Artillery, 116, 437
Royal Gloucestershire Regiment, 456
Royal Grenadiers, 220
Royal Horse Guards, 124
Royal Inniskilling Fusiliers, 438
Royal Irish Rifles, 438
Royal Naval Air Service (RNAS), 225, 230
Rubble, 20, 22
Rücker, Claus, 332, 345
Rumey, Fritz, 187
Russia, 359, 402, 404, 411

Sachsenberg, Gotthard, 188
Saint-Chamond tank, 254
Saint-Quentin, 50
Saint Sauveur tunnel, 89
Saltzwedel, Reinhold, 319, 321, 332
Sanders, William, 354
Sappers, 102
Scaling ladders, 98, 102
Scarpe, 87, 109, 123, 136, 140
   artillery column on banks of, 104
Scarpe River, 87, 98

Schaefer, Karl Emil, 189, 207
Schneider C-1, 308
Schneider CA-1, 305–9
Schneider 155 mm gun, 262
Schneider, Rudolf, 332
Schneider tanks, 253, 282
Schultze, Otto, 332
Schwieger, Walther, 332, 345
SE.5, 251
SE.5a, 192–3, 221, 224, 227–8
Sedgewick, James, 473
Sharman, J E, 226
Shells, 265–6, 274, 422–3, 445–6, 449
Siberian infantry, 411
Siegfried Line, 10, 15
Siess, Gustav, 332, 345
Smout, Ted, 219
Sneider howitzers, 271, 273
Sniper, 277
Snow, Lt Gen, 87
The Snows of Kilimanjaro, 229
Soissons, 256
Somme, 10, 11, 18, 42, 213, 218
Sopwith Camels, 218–21, 228, 230, 251
Sopwith Pups, 204, 221, 227, 230
Sopwith Snipe, 229, 251
Sopwith Strutter, 184, 221
Sopwith Tabloid, 180
Sopwith, Thomas Octave Murdoch, 180
Sopwith Triplanes, 208, 226
Soubiran, Robert, 244
Soupir, 302
Southland (Australian troopship), 322
Spa 38, 241
Spad, 221, 235–6, 238, 241–2, 245
Spad 87, 221
Spad VII, 241
Spad XIII, 235–236
Spandau IMG 08, 222
Spanish Mauser Model 93 rifle, 370
Springfield Rifle (M1903), 370
1 Squadron RFC, 230
3 Squadron AFC, 222
3 Squadron RNAS, 230
8 Squadron RNAS, 230
11 Squadron, 231
20 Squadron, FE.2b of, 208
46 Squadron RFC, 211, 228
56 Squadron, 231, 234
60 Squadron RFC, 196
66 Squadron, 226
74 Squadron, 232
84 Squadron, 228
85 Squadron, 225

203 Squadron, 230
208 Squadron, 229
209 Squadron, 218–19
Staten Island, New York, 384
Steinbauer, Wolfgang, 332, 345
Steinbrinck, Otto, 332, 345
'Stirling Castle,' 453
St Nazaire, 397
St Nicholas's hospital, 209
Sturmtruppen, 41
Sussex Regiment, 470
Sverdlov Square, 359

Tailliandier, Albert, 32
Tamarisk, HMS, 355
Tatiana, 401, 403
Taube, 182
Thaw, William, 244
Thélus, 58, 73, 77
Thénault, Georges, 243–4
Third Army, 73, 87, 96, 98
    tanks, 92
Thomas, Alan, 131
Thuy, Emil, 188
Tilloy-lès-Mofflaines, 121
Tobolsk, 408
Tornado, 53
Tracy le Val, 277
Treaty of Guadalupe, 358
Trenchard, Hugh Montague, 179
Triplanes, 212–13, 216, 218, 220, 226, 230, 234
Truppenverbandplatz, 164
Turkish Yildirim Army Group, 470

U-21, 319, 321
U-27, 334
U-35, 317, 322, 332–4, 336–43
    officers and men of, 344
    torpedo strike, 344
U-37, 353
U-42, 322, 337
U-48, 354, 357
U-56, 352
U-58, 352
U-62, 334
U-93, 354
UB-14, 322–3
U-boat, 322–5
    commanders of the Great War, 332
    conning tower and deck of, 325
    electrical controls and signal position, 327–8
    hand control wheels, 331

hydroplane control gear, 330
inspection hatch, 331
main control room, 329
offensives, 318–19
torpedo loading, 326
UC-5 (submarine), 350–1
UC-22 (submarine), 322
US Marines, 359
US Rainbow Division, 397

Valentiner, Max, 332, 345
Vaterland, 254
Vauxaillon sector, 302
Vaux-sur-Somme, 219
Veltjens, Josef, 188
Verdun, 10, 36, 316
Verschoyle Cronyn, 234
Vickers machine gun, 74, 174, 176, 235
VI Corps, 87, 136
    British troops of, 43
Vienne le Chateau, 268
'Vieux Charles,' 238
VII Corps, 87
'Villa Barbara,' 125
Villa, Pancho, 363
Villers-Bretonneux, 220
Vimy Ridge, 43, 53, 66, 71, 82, 85–6, 109, 175
    plan for attack on, 52
Vitry-en-Artois, 138
Voisin 3LAS, 240
von Boehn, Ferdinand Karl, 255
von der Marwitz , Georg, 462, 467
von Georg, Carl-Siegfried Ritter, 332
von Glasenapp, Alfred, 332
von Hantelmann, Georg, 241
von Heimburg, Heino, 322
von Hoeppner, General, 213
von Lossberg, Karl, 210
von Mellenthin, Hans, 332
von Moser, Otto, 147
von Richthofen, Lothar, 187, 189, 206–7, 210, 212
von Richthofen, Manfred Albrecht Freiherr, 177, 189–90, 198, 204, 206–11, 216, 218–22, 224, 238, 243
    see also Red Baron
von Schleich, Eduard Ritter, 187
von Schmettow, Matthias Graf, 332
Voss, Werner, 187, 210, 234

Wade, Aubrey, 425
Wagnonlieu, 56
Walfisch (Whale), 186

Walther, Hans, 332
Wancourt, 142
War, N. D. Baker, 384
Waßner, Erwin, 332
Watson, David, 52
Waverns Military Cemetery, 227
Wehner, Joseph Fritz, 245
Weisbach, Raimund, 332
Wenninger, Ralph, 332
Werner, Wilhelm, 332
Wervicq, 208
Westhoek Ridge, 449
Whealey, 226
'Whistling Percy', 466
Wijtschate, 438, 439
Wilhelm, Erich Friedrich, 10
Wilhelms, Ernst, 332
Willis, Harold, 244
Wilson, Thomas Woodrow, 10, 358, 360, 363
Witcomb, O G, 222
'*Woche des Leidens*', 73
Wolf, Immelmann, 193
Wolf, Karl, 193, 199
Wolff, Kurt, 188–9, 207
Wood, General, 377
Wright biplane, 178
Wright, Orville, 178
Wright, Wilbur, 178
Wünsche, Otto, 332
Wytschaete, 430, 434
Wytschaete-Messines ridge, 419

XIV Reserve Corps, 147
XVII and VI Corps, 98
XVII Corps, 87, 92, 136
XX Corps, 297
XXI Corps, 470

York and Lancaster Regiment, 142, 145
Ypres, Third Battle of, 449, 458
Ypres salient, 418, 441–2, 446
Ypres sector, 228

Zeebrugge, 345
Zimmermann, Arthur, 358
Zonnebeke, 453